The Boston Gazette

The
BOSTON GAZETTE
1774

Introduction by
Francis G. Walett

THE IMPRINT SOCIETY

Barre, Massachusetts : 1972

Copyright © 1972 Imprint Society, Inc.
All rights reserved
Library of Congress Catalog Card Number 79-175099
International Standard Book Number 87636-022-3
Printed in the United States of America

INTRODUCTION

Numerous history textbooks, scholarly monographs, biographies, and popular accounts make readily available many facts about the momentous events and great figures of the Revolutionary War. All sorts of historical works have dealt with the controversy between England and the American colonies and the importance of this struggle for the future of the nation. British colonial policies in the period 1760 to 1776 and the opposition of the colonists to such measures as the Sugar Act, the Stamp Act, the Townshend Acts, the Tea Act, and the Intolerable Acts have been studied in depth. Also, the situation in the individual colonies and the interrelationships of the colonies have been examined in great detail. It is less common to find descriptions and analyses of the social and economic conditions in the colonial scene at this time. These conditions, which closely affected the lives of all—great men and common folk alike—have to be studied in private letters, diaries, account books, town and church records, inventories, wills and contemporary newspapers. Many of these original sources are available only in manuscript form in research libraries or in scattered local depositories.

Colonial newspapers are an indispensable source of information about both the great events and the commonplace happenings of those days, but their use is not easy. While extensive files (usually incomplete) of original papers and some microprint copies are available in widely separated libraries, access to them is usually limited to professional researchers, and modern printings of Revolutionary papers are fragmentary. The purpose of this facsimile printing of the *Boston Gazette* for 1774 is to make part of a representative Patriot newspaper available in a more general way and to recapture some impressions of life in the era of the American Revolution. Readers will find it not only an extremely important source of detail about the period but also very interesting and even entertaining reading.

The American colonial world was rather small and slow moving, a world unknown and virtually incomprehensible to the average person in the twentieth century. In our age of technological marvels, with almost instantaneous news about events the world over, and with an enormous amount of information about most subjects available to all, nothing today seems very remote. It is difficult for the person accustomed to daily newspapers, radio, television, and communication satellites to comprehend the provincialism of the age of the American Revolution when news travelled very slowly and the pace of life was not nearly so frantic as now. Most of the colonists, particularly in the interior, lived out their lives without knowing more about the outside world than could be gained from newspapers, occasional letters, word of mouth, and infrequent trips to neighboring towns.

Localism was the order of the day in colonial American society two centuries ago. This was due in large part to the difficulty, danger, and slowness of travel and communication. It was, for example, still about a day's journey on horseback from Boston, the capital of Massachusetts, to Worcester, a country village some forty-five miles to the west. To go from Boston to a distant place like New York City was a major undertaking. Overland travel on rough or muddy roads was painfully slow and often precarious: horse-drawn coaches were most uncomfortable and overturns in deep ruts or ditches were fairly common; and dangerous river-crossings (particularly on the Connecticut) were not infrequently accompanied by accidents. A somewhat easier way to journey from Boston to New York was to go overland to Narragansett and then by ship through Long Island Sound, but coaches and vessels did not operate on regular schedules and there were dangers in this kind of travel, too. It is small wonder that most colonists had a limited outlook on affairs.

People living in the principal seacoast towns

were better off with reference to news and information than their neighbors in the interior. Ships brought letters and dispatches from England, Europe, and other colonies; news came by word of mouth, too. The major seaports were also in most cases the capitals of colonies. Thus, they were both the largest business and commercial centers of their area and the places where important governmental and political events took place. Taking advantage of business opportunities, printers usually published their newspapers in these coastal towns. For those who lived in the interior, getting the news was a different matter. Much information was carried by travellers (couriers were sent when important news had to be circulated), and people going from one town to another brought letters and news with them. Public postal service—at least outside of the major towns—was unknown, and the sending of letters (or mail as we call it) was in large part a private matter. Colonial newspapers were sent to subscribers throughout each province, to be read eagerly and handed about. The development of the American colonies in the eighteenth century and the approach of the Revolution gave the increasing number of newspapers an opportunity to play a larger role in almost every aspect of life and to cultivate a growing awareness of the problems people faced both as citizens of individual colonies and as subjects of England.

From 1704, when America's first successful newspaper was started, until the outbreak of the Revolutionary War the population of the English colonies on the mainland of North America rose from about 300,000 to nearly 3,000,000. This rapidly growing population, with its expanding business and political activity, needed and could support an increasing number of newspapers. By 1750 there were twelve weekly papers being published on a regular basis; a decade later the number had risen to twenty-one. As the quarrel with the mother country intensified during and after the French and Indian War, many more newspapers were founded. In the fifteen years between 1760 and 1775, the number of colonial papers more than doubled, and jumped from twenty-one to forty-nine. Only incomplete and inaccurate information about newspaper circulation is available because of fragmentary records and the hopeful exaggerations of publishers who were eager to obtain more subscribers, increase their business, and gain wider influence. It is certain, however, that the circulation of colonial newspapers (the *Boston Gazette* among them) rose sharply in the period just before Lexington and Concord. Of great importance, too, is the fact that bundles of papers were sent from one colony to another. On the eve of the Revolution, the effect of the growth of the number and circulation of American newspapers was very great. With reference to the struggle between Great Britain and the colonies, it is difficult to conceive any amount of united action by the Americans without the colonial press and particularly the newspapers of the time.

BOSTON HAS BEEN CALLED "the cradle of American journalism," for it was there in 1704 that the first regular weekly paper in the English colonies was begun. This thriving commercial center, the largest colonial town and the busiest port in America, was the hub of the New England Puritan world of 100,000 people. The possibility of business success as well as the real need for a news journal induced John Campbell to begin publication of the *Boston News-Letter*, April 24, 1704. This small weekly paper (roughly the size of today's tabloids) was printed on both sides of a single sheet. The *News-Letter*, which was increased somewhat later to four pages (one large sheet of paper folded in the middle), was typical in format of colonial newspapers down to the Revolution. Occasionally, when a heavy volume of news or advertisements required it, a "Supplement," "Postscript," or "Extraordinary" was printed. Official documents, governmental proceedings, foreign news that was several months old, customs reports, notices of ship arrivals and sailings, bits of local news, and very interesting business advertisements were the kinds of items that the *Boston News-Letter* and other early American papers printed. Publishers freely copied dispatches from foreign newspapers and magazines and from other American publications later on. Little more than this type of material was carried by colonial newspapers until the eve of the Revolution, when they printed many articles relating to the controversy with the mother country and much propaganda.

On December 21, 1719, William Brooker began publication of the *Boston Gazette*, America's second oldest newspaper, a distinction that it earned by appearing one day earlier than Andrew Bradford's *American Weekly Mercury* at Philadelphia. For about six months the *Gazette* was printed by James Franklin, the older brother of Benjamin. Boston's new paper followed the same style as the *News-Letter* and contained many of the same kinds of material. The publisher was, however, much interested in promoting the business and trade of the community, and for a time printed a market report of "Prices Currant" of various commodities. As Brooker put it: "To make this paper the more acceptable to the Trading Part of this town and other parts of America, every other week will be published an account of the Prices of All merchandise, how they govern at this place, in the nature of a Price Currant." In early reports the *Gazette* gave quotations of the prices of both imported and domestic items, including such things as Holland duck, woolens, German duck, linens, Madeira wines, copper, brass, pewter, butter, cheese, beef, "mackeral," bear and other skins, and Indian corn. The pictorial masthead of the *Boston Gazette* (itself an innovation) made reference to the purposes of the paper, the encouragement of trade and the distribution of news. On one side of the name of the newspaper was the figure of a postboy delivering the news and on the other side was the picture of a sailing ship. From time to time, these symbols were changed but they always indicated something of social, economic, or political significance.

After a succession of changes of publishers and printers (and some variations in title) the *Boston Gazette* passed into the hands of Benjamin Edes and John Gill in April, 1755. These partners, acting as both publishers and printers, continued the newspaper until the time of the battles of Lexington and Concord, twenty years later. Under Edes and Gill the paper bore the name of the *Boston Gazette or Country Journal*, and during this time it became the tool of Samuel Adams and other Whigs, who strongly denounced British policies which, they felt, were subverting American constitutional rights and liberties. Royal governors and other prerogatived officials were angrily attacked in the *Gazette*, too. One modern author has declared: "The *Gazette* was unquestionably the most vigorous organ of propaganda in the colonies and was utilized to inflame the minds of the colonists against the crown."

Benjamin Edes was born in Charlestown in 1732. Of his youth and education little is known except that he learned the printing trade, probably as an apprentice to some local printer. His future partner, John Gill, also a native of Charlestown, was apprenticed to the Boston printer Samuel Kneeland, one of whose daughters he later married. In any event, Edes and Gill were operating their own print shop "near the East End of the Town-House, in King-Street" by 1754. In March of the next year the partners proposed to publish a weekly newspaper, *The Country Journal*, but were delayed in this venture because subscriptions were slow in coming in. Edes and Gill declared: "Our principal Intention is to make our Paper free in the strictest sense—free to any Gentlemen who will favour us with their Speculations upon any Art, Science, or Political Subject, provided they are wrote with Decency and Spirit." At about this time Samuel Kneeland, publisher of the *Boston Gazette*, announced his intention of discontinuing the newspaper on April 30, 1755. Edes and Gill bought the paper, and Kneeland, who was busy with other matters, stopped publication April 1. The first issue of the *Boston Gazette or Country Journal* printed by the new owners was that of April 7, 1755.

Despite their intention of publishing a "free" paper and keeping it open to all viewpoints, the turn of events and the publishers' own inclinations caused them to turn more and more toward the Patriot side in the colonists' quarrel with the mother country. Isaiah Thomas, the fiery Patriot and printer of the *Massachusetts Spy* (another Whig newspaper begun in Boston in 1770), called Benjamin Edes "a warm and firm patriot" and John Gill "an honest Whig." The latter, according to Thomas, was sound in principle "but did not possess the political energy of his partner." That Edes was a zealous Whig is evidenced in many ways. He wrote some anti-British pieces himself and his editorial work is seen throughout the *Boston Gazette*. More important, he opened the pages of his paper to article after article attacking British policies by Samuel Adams, John Adams, Joseph Warren, James Otis, and others. The Patriots gathered frequently at the Queen Street office of Edes to plan articles for the *Gazette*. In September, 1769, John Adams wrote in his diary that he "supped with Mr. Otis, in company with Mr. Adams, Mr. William Davis, and Mr. John Gill. The evening spent in preparing for the next day's newspaper—a curious employment, cooking up paragraphs, articles, occurrences, etc., working the political engine!" Governor Francis Bernard and his friends complained bitterly but in vain about the torrent of abuse, lies, and distortions that came from the *Gazette's* "sink of meanness and defamation." A disgusted Loyalist told of a Negro, who, having heard Benjamin Edes say that there was no late news, remarked, "Well, if you've nothing new, Massa Edes, I s'pose you print the same damn old lie over again."

Edes was also one of the "Loyall Nine" of Boston, who directed riots, demonstrations, and other activities of the Sons of Liberty. Throughout the controversy between the colonists and England he was completely aware of the meetings and other events planned by the Sons of Liberty. Preparations for the famous Boston Tea Party and the disguising of Sam Adams's "Mohawks" took place, in part at least, in the home of Benjamin Edes. And such was the zeal of Edes, he may have been involved in the Tea Party itself! A letter addressed to His Majesty's troops in Boston in 1774 listed the names of the Sons of Liberty who should be put to the sword "the instant rebellion happens," and concluded "Don't forget those trumpeters of sedition, the printers, Edes and Gill, and Thomas."

The dedication of the *Boston Gazette* and its publishers to the Patriot cause can also be seen in the masthead device that was adopted. In January, 1770, Paul Revere noted in his daybook that he had charged Edes and Gill six shillings for engraving a lead plate to be used in the newspaper. This was the design for the masthead of the paper, which the publishers continued to use for a number of years and which can be seen in the facsimiles reproduced in this work. The symbolism of this engraving by Revere is interesting and important: the figure of Minerva, seated on the left, holds with the left hand a spear on which is placed the cap of liberty; and the right hand is opening the door of a cage (resting on a pedestal) to liberate a bird which appears to be flying toward a tree standing at some distance from a city. Paul Revere did other work for Edes and Gill in 1770, for his engraved cut of the five victims of the Boston Massacre appeared in the March 12 and 19 issues of the *Gazette*.

※

IT WAS THE ENACTMENT by Parliament in 1765 of the Stamp Act that turned American printers and newspaper publishers unreservedly against English policy. The publishers, who were fully aware of the possibility of legal reprisals and official pressures that could hurt business or even cause failure, had normally abstained from severe criticism of British policies and had thus avoided trouble. They had complained about certain temporary measures during the French and Indian War, tighter customs regulations, the use of writs of assistance, and the Sugar Act of 1764. These complaints were very mild and cautiously worded compared to the loud outcry against the hated Stamp Act. This tax, which (if effective) would have been felt by many colonists throughout America, would have been particularly onerous to the printers. Since each newspaper, advertisement, almanac, and liquor license, most legal and business forms, and even printer's apprenticeship indentures were to bear stamps, it is not difficult to understand why newspaper publishers and printers in general angrily denounced the new measure as illegal and unconstitutional. Fearful that their business might suffer and insisting that they were upholding freedom of the press, publishers, including Edes and Gill, continued in defiance of the law to print newspapers without using stamps. Their action contributed significantly to the failure of the Stamp Act.

It is quite understandable that printers who had defied British and colonial authorities with impunity during the Stamp Act crisis were now keenly aware of the political and economic power that they could wield. Both Patriots and Tories used the newspaper press to try to shape public opinion in their favor as new controversies arose. Additional parliamentary laws like the Townshend Acts, the Tea Act, the Quebec Act, and the Intolerable Acts were condemned as unconstitutional by the Whigs; and capable and resourceful Patriot writers generally had the better of it in running newspaper feuds with their Loyalist opponents. Royal officials in America and their friends felt the sting of angry charges and accusations, and their position became increasingly difficult and dangerous. It is unmistakably clear that Patriot newspapers like the *Boston Gazette* played a large part in the undermining of British authority in the American colonies.

Sharp criticisms of governors and other royal officials in America led at times to efforts to silence the newspapers. During the Townshend Acts controversy, Joseph Warren, writing as "A True Patriot" in the *Boston Gazette,* February 29, 1768, complained of one British authority's "obstinate perseverance in the Path of Malice." Nettled by this barb, Governor Francis Bernard of Massachusetts tried in vain to get the provincial Council to support him in an action against this "libellous and seditious publication." Another enemy of the Sons of Liberty, Lieutenant Governor Thomas Hutchinson of the Bay Colony, denounced the popular conception of freedom of the press as "A Liberty of reviling and calumniating all Ranks and Degrees of Men with Impunity, all Authority with Ignominy." Samuel Adams eagerly entered this contest with an article in the *Boston Gazette*, March 14, 1768. Writing as "POPULUS" he declared:

> There is nothing so *fretting* and *vexatious*, nothing so justly TERRIBLE to tyrants, and their tools and abettors, as a FREE PRESS. The reason is obvious; namely, because it is, as it has been very justly observed, in a *spirited* answer to a *spirited* speech, '*the bulwark of the People's Liberties*'. For this reason, it is ever watched by those who are forming plans for the destruction of the people's liberties, with an envious and malignant eye.... It is not at all surprising, that *your* press is hated, and *your* paper branded with the name of 'infamous', by some men: These are the men who formed and pushed to the utmost of their power, the late *detested Stamp-Act*: These are the men, who have been forging chains and manacles; and when they could not, after the most impudent attempt, *force* them upon the people, have with intollerable insolence endeavor'd to persuade them that they had better *put them on themselves*: But *your* Press has sounded the alarm; or to use the words of a *minion,* 'rung the alarm bell'; *Your* Press has spoken to us the words of truth: It has pointed to this people, their danger and their remedy; It has set before them Liberty and Slavery; and with the most persuasive and pungent language, conjured them, in the name of GOD, and the King, and for the sake of all posterity, to choose Liberty and refuse Chains: Go on, for you have been already prosper'd.

Such ringing statements as this had the desired effect; popular indignation over British enactments increased, and supporters of English policy were regularly attacked in the press and increasingly discredited everywhere.

The Tea Act of 1773, giving preferential treatment to the East India Company in the tea trade with America, aroused another storm of protest among the colonists, and set in motion a series of events that culminated in violence and American independence. Assailing the new measure, Patriots protested again about taxation without representation, complained about the injury to independent tea dealers, and deplored the possibility of additional favors that might be given the East India or some other company. In Massachusetts, affairs came to a head in mid-December, 1773, when Governor Hutchinson insisted that tea consigned to East India agents be landed, and the Sons of Liberty prevented this by dumping the tea in Boston harbor. This rather high-handed act was defended by "An Impartial Observer" in the *Gazette* (December 20): "The body of the people determined the tea should not be landed; the determination was deliberate, was judicious, the sacrifice of their Rights, of the Union of all the Colonies would have been the effect, had they conducted [themselves] with less resolution." The year 1774 was ushered in amidst the concern of all about the possible consequences of the Tea Party. Would other Americans support Boston at this critical time, and what would Parliament do in the face of this deliberate challenge to British law?

Readers of the facsimile *Boston Gazette* will see that as the new year began, the Whig propagandists continued their assault on Governor Hutchinson and his supporters as they waited to see what kind of action the English were going to take after the destruction of the tea. A writer in the *Gazette* on January 3 condemned the Governor as "The great CAPITAL OFFENDER" and "The origin of all our public calamities." On February 21, 1774, "America Solon" continued the harangue: "So rapid have been the strides of TYRANNY for a number of years past, that the continued succession of *new* injuries make us forget the *former*; and a man must have the pen of a ready writer to record the abuses this people receive from a despotic administration, who have evidently nothing less in view than the total abolition of all American liberties." When it was reported in March that a vessel with some East India tea had arrived, the Boston Sons of Liberty expressed their determination not to let the tea be landed, and the *Gazette* reported "The SACHEMS must have a *Talk* upon this matter—Upon THEM we depend to extricate us out of this *fresh* Difficulty; and to their Decisions all the good People will say, AMEN!"

In the late spring and early summer of 1774, the *Gazette* reported the news that Parliament had decided that the time for coercion of the colonies had come: the port of Boston was to be closed and the customs officials removed to Salem until the destroyed tea was paid for; the Massachusetts government, as constituted under the charter of 1691, was to be drastically altered; and on May 13 General Thomas Gage, accompanied by British soldiers, arrived in Boston to replace Thomas Hutchinson as governor. It was clear that the English government now felt that there could be no further retreat in the face of colonial opposition to parliamentary law, and the time for coddling the American colonists had passed. The Massachusetts Sons of Liberty immediately expressed their determination to resist the new measures and their defiance of the new Governor and his redcoats. Paul Revere, the "Patriot Express," was sent off to New York and Philadelphia to spread the news and obtain help for Boston, and when he returned, the *Gazette* printed the heartening news that the other colonies regarded the cause of Massachusetts as their own. Such matters as the calling of the First Continental Congress, the approval of the Suffolk Resolves, and the adoption of the Continental Association (a comprehensive plan of economic pressure against England), can be followed in the successive issues of the *Boston Gazette* in the summer and fall. Among the public events reported in the newspaper in the last part of 1774 were numerous town meetings and their resolutions of defiance of General Gage, the establishment of an extralegal government of Massachusetts, the punishment of violators of the nonimportation agreement, the gathering of supplies of war, and increased colonial military preparations.

Although many forces contributed to the destruction of British authority in America between 1763 and 1776, the Patriot newspapers, which informed citizens of momentous events taking place and spread Whig propaganda widely, played an unusually large role in the movement toward independence. In fact, it has been said that in this movement the power of the press was equal to that of the sword. The contribution made by one ardently Patriot paper is recorded in this printing of the *Boston Gazette* for the critical year 1774.

For those interested in the social history of eighteenth-century America, newspapers are an indispensable source of information. This is not true because these small journals were full of details of everyday events, however, for in fact the publishers felt little need to print much of that kind of material. The very interesting reports of ship arrivals and sailings were carried regularly by the *Boston Gazette* and other papers mostly because of their importance to the commercial interests. The same may well be true for the notations about the tides. It took an unusual event to make local "news"—perhaps the visit to town of some important person, extraordinary weather conditions, a startling crime, a strange accident, or the death of some important person in the colony. Occasionally, the reader comes upon a sad but revealing item like the following one from the

Gazette of January 31, 1774. Jemima Lewis, the wife of a sailor, "was found dead on the floor of her apartment; an inquisition was taken upon her body, and it was fully proved to the jurors, that the preceding evening, she was intoxicated with spirituous liquor, and being destitute of the common necessaries of life, and the weather being extreme cold, was frozen and by that means came to her Death." Another time it was reported that a notorious counterfeiter, who had escaped from the Worcester jail, had been apprehended. Some readers may be amused by, or find some social significance in, the story of Daniel Wiswal and his wife, who were warned out of Charlestown first, and then Boston, for "keeping an infamous house." The unsavory Wiswal, who endangered the lives of "peaceable passengers" by getting the guard at the ferry intoxicated, and his wife, who openly entertained "notorious prostitutes," were finally chased by the constable out of Boston to Cambridge, where they disappeared from view. Glimpses of events like these indicate well enough that not all Americans were deeply concerned with the great happenings of the time.

Newspaper advertisements, which sometimes occupied half or more of an issue, are infinitely more important than the occasional local "news" tidbit that appeared in the *Gazette*. First of all, then as now, advertisers alone made possible the publication of newspapers. An early New York publisher put it succinctly: "Subscribers alone, allowing them to be quadruple to what was ever known in this city, would not support a newspaper establishment; and, in fact, it is the advertiser who provides the paper for the subscriber." Printers had other sources of revenue, but it was the advertisements that were the very lifeblood of the newspapers and kept them in business. The advertisements are, moreover, a veritable treasure trove of all kinds of information of great interest. Fascinating and endless details that can be gleaned from these sources are invaluable to the historian who endeavors to reconstruct the social and economic scene of two hundred years ago.

Merchandise offered for sale in the *Boston Gazette* (and in other newspapers) gives us an excellent opportunity to learn about the furnishings and goods used by the people of Revolutionary New England. The variety listed in auctions and other sales was virtually without limit. Merchants regularly advertised goods that had arrived from abroad, and by studying these advertisements readers can get the story of much trade that was taking place. Exotic items ranging from Lisbon lemons, Jamaica spirits, and Madeira wines to numerous spices, sugar, chocolate, and Nova Scotia oats tempted the colonists' palates. Among the vast number of household items advertised that will fascinate lovers of antiques were cloth and textiles of many kinds, London and Bristol pewter plates, basins and spoons, "Staffordshire, Nottingham and Bristol Ware," watches and clocks, firepans, brass and iron candlesticks, "Turkey carpets," and all sorts of furniture. Merchants also sold drugs, medicines, and imported surgeon's instruments. During 1774, Edes and Gill themselves had "Keyser's Famous Pills" for sale, and the *Gazette* assured readers "that this excellent Medicine is beyond any thing in all Foulness and Impurities of the Blood, having performed many astonishing Cures in Scorbutic Eruptions, Leprosies, White Swellings, Stix Joints, Gout and Rheumatic Disorders, etc."

Examples of notices in the *Gazette* which refer to important activities are the advertisement of a farm for sale in Lancaster, the auction of "the old SNUF MILL" in Milton, the meeting of the proprietors of Royalston, and the petition of the Indians of Martha's Vineyard to the House and Council regarding their claims to "Chobboquiddock." Services and business opportunities were frequently advertised in the paper: the brigantine *Betsey* offered to take on freight while waiting to sail for Philadelphia; insurance on vessels and goods was made available; George Hamlin's hackney coach was ready to carry people about Boston; a mason was seeking an apprentice to learn that trade; and a woman "with a choice young Brest of Milk" said that she "would be glad to go into a Gentleman's Family to Suckle." Grim and unpleasant, but very important, were advertisements concerning Negro slaves. On March 14, 1774, for example, someone advertised in the *Boston Gazette:* "*A likely, healthy, strong Negro Girl, about 12 years of age can be well recommended.*" Another revealing notice was that of Jonathan Reed of Wrentham, who offered a reward of $5.00 for the return of "a Man Servant," who had "bound himself to said Reed for Theft."

Educational opportunities in addition to the well known schools that had been in existence for some time were to be found in the pages of the *Gazette*. John and Eleanor Druitt, at their school on Hanover Street, offered instruction in numerous subjects, and Eleanor advertised to teach many kinds of needlework. Berry and Crane informed the public, January 24, 1774, "that they open their school this Evening, for teaching Psalmody, at the house next to Mr. Greenlaw's near Liberty Tree." Other information about the reading interests of Americans in the Revolutionary era may be found in the offer for sale of such publications as the *Poems of Phillis Wheatley* and the *Royal American Magazine*, which was begun in Boston by Isaiah Thomas in February. Musical activities in Boston may have been somewhat limited two centuries ago, but readers will see references to violins, flutes, fifes, "jews harps," spinets, and harpsichords. Rather unusual is the advertisement of a concert of vocal and instrumental music that was held in Boston on March 23, 1774.

LIFE COULD NOT always proceed "as usual" during the trying days of 1774, but life did have to continue, and whenever possible the colonists followed their daily business in the manner to which they had become accustomed. Merchants carried on trade as best they could, and shopkeepers continued to offer whatever goods they had to sell. Tradesmen, artisans, and farmers pursued their usual activities as well as conditions would permit. It was impossible to ignore the great events of the time, but everyday life had to go on. The contemporary newspapers provide better insights into the social scene of colonial America than any other single source, and the *Boston Gazette* of 1774 will give readers some impression of life as it was for the average person in those troubled days.

FRANCIS G. WALETT

THE
BOSTON GAZETTE
1774

THE
Boston-Gazette,
AND
COUNTRY JOURNAL.

Containing the freshest Advices, Foreign and Domestic.

No. 978.

MONDAY, January 3, 1774.

IMPORTED from ENGLAND, BY

JOHN WELSH,

And to be Sold at his Shop No. 6, Union-Street, BOSTON;

A general Assortment of English GOODS, suitable for all Seasons.

ALSO,

A large Assortment of Hard-Ware GOODS, Cutlery, Jewellery, Goldsmith's, Clock and Watch Articles, viz.

SUPERFINE, middling and low-priz'd broad cloths, with shalloons and trimmings to match, a fine assortment of serges, duffils, lambskins, bearskins, bath beavers knap'd and plain, cape velvet, olive velvet and velverets, fine ratteens, green, crimson and red Colchester and drapery bays, flannels, swanskin, blankets, camblets, cambleteens, dorseteen, yd. wide fig'd stuffs, crapes, brilliants, missinets, grizet, Denmark lustres, worsted damasks, sagathies, duroys, everlastings, russells, callimancoes, durants, tammies, laces, snail, ermins, muffs, drawboys, sprig'd & plain sattins, figur'd mode, allamode, persians, tiffity, sarsnets and other silks, gauzes, catgut, cap wire, cambricks, plain and flower'd lawns, muslin, diapers, diaper table cloths, Irish linnens and cotton checks of all widths, furniture checks, bag holland, bed ticks, strip'd & brown holland, Russia drab, callicoes, bengalls and penniascoes, chip hatts, silk, cotton and linnen handkerchiefs of all sorts, men's breeches pieces of all colours, men's & women's gloves & mitts, an assortment of men's and women's hose, women's English & Lynn shoes & pumps, silk knee straps, worsted ditto, sewing silk, silk twist and wax thread per lb. a large assortment of buttons, dowlass, ozenburgh, buckram, white and brown dit. coat, shoe and quality bindings, and gartering per groce, silk ferrets, ribbons, fustians, thicksetts, wilton, pins, hair ditto, needles of all sorts, threads, tapes, cruels, men's worsted caps, indigo, cotton wool, English soles, &c. &c. &c.—

Hard-Ware.

Bath stoves, tin plates, all sorts of glass, (in half and quarter boxes,) nails, tacks and brads, brass kettles, brass and bell metal skillets, warming pans, warming pan bottoms, ditto tops, frying pans, short handle ditto, English, German, blister'd and cast steel, bar lead, holster and pocket pistols, English and French flints, gun hammers, London and Bristol pewter dishes, plates, basons, cans, spoons, &c. coffee mills, sugar knippers, chafin dishes, andirons, shovel & tongs, fire pans, brass and iron candlesticks, box irons and grates, flat irons, snuffers, bellows, velvet corks, cork pullers, cork screws, men's and women's thimbles, knitting kneedles, pinking irons, a large assortment of brass handles and escutcheons, locks, hinges, &c. for desks, chest draws, book cases and clock cases, carpenters, joiners and turners tools, shoe maker's hammers, knippers, pincers, knives, awl blades and hafts, tacks, punches, lasts & stretches, cross-cut, hand and mill saw files, rasps, farrier's ditto, syckles, spoak shaves, taylor's shears large and small, sheep and glover's ditto, men's and women's stirrup irons, snaffle & curb bitts, white setts, brass nails, girth and straining webb, throat lash buckles, tin tacks & bullion, brass cocks, brass scales, a fine assortment of coat and breast buttons, horn & ivory comb, pewter, brass, leather & paper ink pots, English glue, chalk lines, window pullies and lines, house bells, gimblets, chest, till, cubbard, and box locks, stock locks, padlocks, thumb latches, brass knob locks, hinges of all sorts, flat bolts, snuff and tobacco boxes, fiddle strings, mettal, steel and pinchback shoe knee and stock buckles, common and temple spectacles, carving knives, case knives, penknives, cutteaus, scissars, common and cast steel rasors, ivory handle knives and forks in cases, curling irons, shaving boxes and brushes, hones and straps, brass dividers, iron compasses, cloak pins, nail knippers, center, dowling and pin bitts, pack and sewing thread, hunting and coach whips, farmer's iron shovels, devonshire ditto, bed castors, brass knobs and rings, steel key rings, money scales and weights, penny weights and grains separate, mops, broom brushes, painting brushes, masons brushes, lathing hammers and trowells, hearth, dust, cloth and table brushes, comb dit. teeth and flesh ditto, hard and soft, shoe and buckle ditto, wheel ditto, fish hooks, chimney hooks, mouse traps, curry combs, iron pitch ladles, four and five blade fleems, jews-harps, small brass padlocks, metal cane-heads, marking irons, marking letters, &c. &c. &c.—

Goldsmith's & Jewellery.

Anvills, hand standing and bench vices, a compleat assortment of women's plated buckles, men's shoe, knee and stock dit. paste ditto, a large assortment of brilliant and cypher earings, button, brickle ring and locket stones, ruby and white foyl, steel top silver thimbles, stick coryl, hammers, skillets, crucibles, blue pots, casting sand, ring swages, screw & drawing plates, brass stamps, beak irons, blow pipes, borax boxes, thimble stamps, cutting knippers, plyers, shears, brass and iron wire of all sizes, steel ditto, files of all sorts, freezing punches, gravers, black & white enamel, Turkey oil stones, shoe & knee chapes, emery and sand paper, corn and flour emery, per doz. pumice and rotten stone, sandover, borax, per dozen, allum, salt petre, speter sorder, glazier's diamonds, &c.——

Clock & Watch Articles.

Watches, clock dial plates, ornaments &c. all sorts of clock and watch files, musical bells, clock-gut gilt balls, brass & iron scratch brushes, clock and watch riveting hammers, clock and watch hands, watch crystals, main springs, pendants, verges, silk strings, steel chains, seals and keys, watch dial plates, clock and watch screw drivers, broaches, endle's screw keys, Turkey slips, Bohemia stones, &c. &c. &c. ALSO,

An assortment of STATIONARY, and many other Articles.

Just Published, and to be sold by

JOSEPH GREENLEAF,

At his Printing Office in Hanover-Street, Boston,

AN Abridgment of Burn's Justice of the Peace, and Parish Officer:

To which is added,

An Appendix, containing some general rules and directions, necessary to be known and observed by all Justices of the Peace.

Subscribers for said book (Stitched) are desired to send for them. Those who are to have them bound, may have them the beginning of next week.

N. B This abridgment includes all that is applicable to the practice here, and may be had for nine Shillings stitched, or eleven shillings bound. The London edition of this book cannot be had under six dollars.

Also to be sold at said office,

The following PAMPHLETS, viz.

A calm Answer to the Question, Why are you a Dissenter from the Church of England.

The cause of the dissenting ministers; by Israel Morduit.

England's Warning Piece; a sermon occasioned by the Murder of Mr. William Allen, by a party of soldiers in George's Fields.

An anniversary sermon, being a sequel to the above.

The Adulateur; a Tragedy. By a Lady.

A Dissuasion from the Slave Trade. With a number of other pamphlets, also Testaments, Psalters, spelling books, Psalm books, Primers, Writing Paper, ink-pots, and other Stationary; also blanks of various sorts, some never before printed, particularly for the use of Justices of the Peace.

L I K E W I S E,

A Dissertation on the rise, progress, views, strength, Interest and characters, of the two parties of the Whigs and Tories.

Just Published, (Price 11s. L. M. well Bound) and

TO BE SOLD

By James Foster Condy,

At his BOOK STORE in Union-Street, directly opposite the Cornfields, Boston,

AN Abridgement of Burn's Justice of the Peace, and Parish Officer: To which is added,

An APPENDIX, containing some general Rules and Directions, necessary to be known and observed by all Justices of the Peace.

Also to be sold at said Store (very reasonably) the following Books printed in America, viz.

Blackstone's Commentaries, 5 Vol. 4to.
Robertson's History of Charles 5th, 3 Vols. 8vo.
Hutchinson's History, 3 Vols. 8vo.
Palladium of Conscience, 4to.
Evans's Poems, 8vo. Vicar of Wakefield, 12mo.
Dissenting Gentleman's Answer to Mr. White's three Letters, 12mo.

P A M P H L E T S.

Poem, Entitled the Grave.
Doddridge's Family Religion.
Smith's Essay on Universal Redemption.
Recovery from Sickness — Rush on Mineral Waters.
Critical Commentaries against Bishops.
Sermons to Doctors in Divinity.
(Lord Sommers) On Nations and King's.
Death) A Poetical Essay.
Letters from Yorrick to Eliza— Sermons to Asses.
History of Bellisarius, &c. &c. &c.

At said Store may be had, the most modern and esteemed Books, in every Branch of polite Literature, Arts and Sciences, (Catalogues may be had at said Store) at such Prices as will fully satisfy the Purchaser.

TO BE LETT, a small convenient Tenement near the Market. Inquire of Edes and Gill.

THE Subscriber having compleated a very large and extensive Survey of the New Ceded Countries to the Southward, which long wanted Discovery he has attained, at a vast Expence and bodily Fatigue, and now offers to the Public.

The Navigation through the Gulph Stream, over the Bahama Bank and in the Gulph of Mexico, is more particularly laid down therein than was ever done before, or than any Map Compiler has ever had an Opportunity to do. And as every Trader from North-America, especially the Merchants who trade to Jamaica, Hispaniola, and to the two Floridas, are more particularly interested in this necessary Work, he addresses himself more immediately to them; and begs Leave to direct them to his printed Proposals, which have been put up & distributed through this Town.

He has come here to procure if possible, the Assistance of some Gentlemen (Lovers and Encouragers of American Literature) towards the Publication of this Work. He has for these eight Years past done it at his own Cost, but being now very near the Close of it, he finds the Expence to outrun his Expectation, and therefore thus throws himself on the generous Public.—New-York, Philadelphia and South-Carolina have given him Encouragement; he hopes therefore Boston will not withold her helping Hand.

A great Part of the Work is already printed, for that Reason he presumes the ordinary Thought of its falling through will not so much as be suspected, especially as our most esteemed Societies have thought it worthy of recommendation as beneficial to Mankind.

There is added to the Maps a Book of 500 Pages, in octavo, which will, no doubt, amuse the studious and learned, especially such as are Enquirers into the Wonders of the three Kingdoms of Nature, Botany more particularly; the inland Country is very minutely described, and the Maps will explain even the Land laid out on the river Missisippi; plain aad ample directions to Navigators will likewise be given, and extensive Soundings on the Coast pointed out, so as to render the Whole as desirable for the Sage in his Cabinet as for the Mariner in his Ship.

The elegance of the Map added to its large Size, of twelve Feet by seven, will likewise render it an ornamental Piece of Furniture.

In this exceeding difficult and dangerous Navigation are a great many watering Places not hitherto known, which will be described and directed to, and by which Means it is hoped many a poor distressed Crew will be saved from Ruin, even when they perhaps despair of Life.

His Stay will be short in Boston, therefore he begs the Well-wishers of American Science and Navigation to give their Names soon, in order that he may return to the compleating of the Work with redoubled Ardour.

About July, 1774, it is thought the Work will be compleated, and the Public may rest assured, that the Favours will be amply recompensed not only by this Work, but by one of much more extensive Nature, which he has now in Contemplation, he having devoted his Life to Pursuits of this Kind.

*** He may be heard of at Mess. Cox and Berry's; Mr. Knox's, Mr. Joshua Brackett's, Mr. Joseph Ingersoll's, and the Printers of this Paper. B. ROMANS.

Staffordshire, Nottingham and *Bristol*

WARE.

William Porter,

ACQUAINTS his Friends and the Public in general, That he has imported in the last Ship from Bristol—A large and general Assortment of cream-coloured, enamell'd, black, white and brown Stone, Glass and Flint Ware, too many to be enumerated in an Advertisement, which are now open for Sale at his Shop lately opened, a little to the Southward of LIBERTY-TREE, *Boston,* either by the Crate, Groce, Dozen or single Article, as cheap as can be bought at any Shop or Store in the Province.

Likewise equally as cheap—A general Assortment of Groceries and West India Goods.——Town and Country Traders are invited to call and see how extremely low they may be supply'd.

TO BE SOLD,

ABrigantine about 100 Tons, a Sloop about 92 Tons, and a Sloop about 84 Tons, built in Boston of the best white Oak. Inquire of the Printers.

A Woman with a choice young Breast of Milk, would be glad to go into a Gentleman's Family to Suckle. Inquire of Edes and Gill.

All Persons indebted to the Estate of Capt. John Hayward, late of Braintree, deceased, are desired without delay, to pay the same to David Person Hayward, or Ebenezer Hayward, of Braintree, Administrators on said Estate: And all Persons that have any Demands on said Estate, are desired to bring in their Accounts to said Administrators, in order for a speedy Settlement.

NEDHAM'S REMEMB'RANCER, N. III.

Stand back, thou *manifeſt* CONSPIRATOR.
——————Tell me what they deſerve,
That do conſpire our Death with deviliſh plots ?
——————————O conſpiracy !
Where wilt thou find a cavern dark enough,
To maſk thy monſtrous viſage ? Seek none, conſpi-
Hide it IN SMILES and AFFABILITY. [racy,
SHAKESPEARE.

GREAT pains have been taken to bring his Excellency out of the company with whom he is found, and to ſave him from ſharing the guilt of thoſe with whom he has *openly* and SECRETLY aſſociated himſelf. This is no doubt renouncing the conduct of *many* as, indefenſible to ſave *one* from his juſt portion of ignominy and reproach. But it was no doubt good policy to conſign the *minor* villains to ſhame and infamy, if this would reinſtate *their leader* in favor and influence.

But I never yet could diſcern any propriety in judging the conduct of a band of conſpirators ſeperate and apart, the one from the other, when all appear, from beginning to end, jointly conſpiring to the ſame purpoſe, adopting the ſame meaſures and acting in the cloſeſt union and concert.

If a gang of robbers combine to attack my houſe, and each agrees upon his ſeparate part ; if they unite in *the plot*, and when they come to the time of execution ;—one watches my door, another enters my houſe, a third rifles my family, and a fourth ſheds my blood ;—while the reſt ſtand without for the purpoſe of carrying on the *common plan* ;—ſurely they muſt be *all equally guilty* in the eye of reaſon and common ſenſe. And what difference is there, between thoſe, who aſſiſt in the invaſion of a *private* edifice, and they who attack the *public* building of the Commonwealth ;—between thoſe who rifle and deſtroy my houſe, and thoſe who plunder and overturn the fabrick of the ſtate ? Surely none, which makes in favor of *any one* of the aſſailants, or can exempt from a common abhorrence and puniſhment, any member of the combination.

Not one of the advocates (baſe and ſhameleſs as they have been) for *the chief conſpirator* againſt our laws and liberties hath ever ſo much as mentioned a word (to my knowledge) in defence or juſtification of the writings and conduct of Oliver, Hallowell or Paxton. Yet what was this triumvirate without their hero ? Oliver was too timid to be formidable, Hallowell too much the man of arms to be an aſſaſſin ; and Paxton too contemptible to be regarded. Hallowell would have croſſed the ocean, harmleſs & unnoticed as any other ſeaman, without *a political letter of credit* from the governor ; Paxton might have *frothed* the "open rebellion of Boſton,"* & remained as little regarded, as when he fawned or flattered, without countenance from the ſame perſonage, & a recommendation from his Excellency's brother "as a *good friend*"; § and Oliver would have trembled to liſp a "a taking off incendiaries" † had not his Excellency talked of "marks of parliamentary reſentment to the *province in general* or PARTICULAR PERSONS"—and gave his ſanction—that "IT OUGHT TO BE SO." ‡

THE PRESENT GOVERNOR, therefore, I conſider as the great CAPITAL OFFENDER :—To him I look as the origin of all our public calamities—becauſe without his aid, his ſanction, his authority and influence, our public enemies would have remained a *paltry few*, a ſpiritleſs body, a deſpicable cabal.

Thus whenever we ſcrutinize the manœuvres of the *ſub-confederates*—we ought to attend to *their connexions* and *accomplices* :—We ſhall ever find the grand mover of their miſchievous operations *lurking in the dark* ;—for in all the more *capital* movements, the *arch agent* keeps himſelf as much as poſſible diſguiſed, while, like *the maſter of puppets*, he holds the political wire, and directs all their motions—*behind the curtain*.

MARCHMONT NEDHAM.

* See his Letter to Whateley.
§ Letter 13th February 1769.
† Letter 20th January.
‡ Letter 7th May 1767.

[*To be continued.*]

CHARLES-TOWN, (*South-Carolina*) *Dec.* 6.

LAST Wedneſday evening came in over the bar, and the next Morning anchored before the town, the ſhip London, Alexander Curling maſter, from London ; with no leſs than *Two Hundred & fifty ſeven* CHESTS OF TEA on board, which were ſhipped by the Eaſt-India Company in London, and conſigned to ROGER SMITH, Eſq; and Meſſrs. LEGER and GREENWOOD, merchants here, to be by them received and diſpoſed of in this province, *after the payment* of a Duty of *three-pence ſterling* a pound, impoſed (in the year 1767) by the very ſame *act of parliament of Great-Britain*, which alſo laid the (ſince repealed) duties on *paper, paints* and *glaſs*, for the EXPRESS PURPOSE OF RAISING A REVENUE IN AMERICA WITHOUT OUR CONSENT, and which duty *on Tea* was, by the Miniſtry, expreſsly declared to be retained, not for the ſake of the revenue it might produce, but merely to eſtabliſh a *precedent*, to *confirm the power aſſumed* by the ſame parliament, in the *declaratory Act*, TO PASS LAWS BINDING UPON THE COLONIES IN ALL CASES WHATSOEVER—which, if admitted in *America*, will be acknowledging an *equal power*, to raiſe *hearth-money* on, and to *tax the coloniſts* for even the *light of heaven*—and render Repreſentatives of their choice merely *nominal*.

So great a quantity of Tea arriving at once, under ſuch circumſtances, juſtly gave an univerſal alarm : For, though the importation of a few cheſts, from time time, in the ſeveral London ſhips had been *overlooked* (not being ſuſpected) thoſe who thought it would be *criminal* tamely to give up any of *our eſſential rights* as Britiſh ſubjects, and involve *our poſterity* in a ſtate little better than ſlavery, began to look about them, and to think it high time to *contend, legally*, and to diſpute the *aſſumed* power.

In theſe circumſtances, hand bills were diſtributed on Thurſday, and advertiſements ſtuck up at all the uſual and moſt public places, inviting all the inhabitants, without exception, particularly the landholders, to aſſemble in the Great Hall over the Exchange at 3 o'clock on Friday afternoon, as well with a view to prevent any raſh or violent proceedings, as to take the ſenſe of the people ſo collected, what would be abſolutely neceſſary to be done in the preſent caſe ?

The inhabitants accordingly met on Friday—and a very worthy & honourable Gentleman, having been unanimouſly requeſted to take the chair was placed therein.

After ſome time ſpent in calm deliberation, it appeared, to be the ſenſe of the people, that the gentlemen in trade ſhould be requeſted to enter immediately into a written agreement, *not to import any more teas, that would pay duties, laid for the* UNCONSTITUTIONAL *purpoſe of raiſing a revenue upon us*, WITHOUT OUR CONSENT—which ſenſe being declared by Mr. Chairman, the form of a proper agreement was called for, approved of and ſigned, by ſeveral of the gentlemen preſent, and runs, in the following expreſs words, viz.

WE the underwritten, do hereby agree, not to import, either directly or indirectly, any Teas that will pay the preſent duty, laid by an act of the Britiſh Parliament, for the purpoſe of raiſing a revenue in America.

It was next propoſed and agreed to, that the gentlemen to whom the Eaſt-India Company's tea had been conſigned, ſhould be deſired to attend ; and that Mr. CHAIRMAN ſhould acquaint them, that *the receiving the ſaid tea ſubject to a duty which they apprehending to be* UNCONSTITUTIONALLY *laid, would be exceedingly diſagreeable to their fellow-citizens, and the body of inhabitants of this province* ; and that *therefore* it was requeſted THEY would *not accept the ſaid commiſſion*, but *return the tea*, to the proprietors thereof, in the *ſame bottom* that brought it.

Mr. SMITH, and Meſſrs LEGER and GREENWOOD, accordingly attended ; and Mr. CHAIRMAN having delivered what he had in Charge, thoſe gentlemen ſeverally ſhewed the regard they had for their country, by declining to receive the tea, as the people had requeſted—and Mr. Smith added, to his laſting honour that HE *had determined ſome Weeks before it arrived, not to have any concern in a buſineſs, which his countrymen conceived to have ſo fatal a tendency*. This was followed by repeated thanks and loud ſhouts of applauſe.

Capt. *Curling* apprehending himſelf involved in ſome Difficulties, by this determination, then deſired to be informed, how he ſhould extricate himſelf from them. He was anſwered, "*by keeping all the tea on board his Veſſel, and returning with it to England.*"

A committee was then appointed, to wait, the next day, upon ſuch gentlemen in trade, and other importers, as were not preſent, with the agreement already ſigned by ſeveral, *not to import any more teas, ſubject to the aforeſaid duty*, in order that they might add their names : And the Committee were, Capt. GADSDEN, Col. PINCKNEY, THOMAS FERGUSON, CHARLES COTESWORTH PINCKNEY, Eſq'rs and Mr. DANIEL CANNON. Then the meeting was diſſolved, after unfeigned thanks had been returned to the Chairman, &c.

On Saturday the ſaid committee diligently and faithfully performed what was requeſted of them : And we have the pleaſure to inform the public, that upwards of Fifty reſpectable names were that day ſubſcribed to the agreement. Some gentlemen were abſent, others deſired a little time to conſider of the matter ; they will both have an opportunity to ſubſcribe their names as ſoon as it is determined in whoſe hands the agreement ſhall be lodged.

In the mean time, the principal planters and landholders have tho't it proper to enter into another agreement, which is ſigned very faſt, and we are told runs in theſe words, viz.

WE the underſigned, inhabitants of this province, being now fully convinced, that we have vainly flattered ourſelves, with hopes of the repeal of an act of Parliament of Great-Britain, paſſed in the year 1767, impoſing a duty on Teas imported from thence, for the purpoſe of raiſing a revenue upon us, in America, without our conſent, DO hereby ſolemnly promiſe and agree, each for him or herſelf, that we will not either directly or indirectly import, buy or ſell, or any way encourage or countenance the importation, buying or ſelling, any Teas that will pay the aforeſaid duty : And that we will not purchaſe any goods of any perſon or perſons whatever, that ſhall hereafter import, buy or ſell any ſuch Teas : And this we do, becauſe we conceive that the payment of ſuch duties will be acknowledging a power which the Britiſh Parliament hath aſſumed, and which we deny them to have under our excellent conſtitution, "to tax us againſt our conſent."

The eſtabliſhing of *Tea Ware-Houſes* in America, by the *India* Company, 'tis ſaid, is intended to pave the way for introducing large *Factories* for other goods, at all the principal ports, and then to bring in an *Honourable Board of* EXCISE.

NEW-YORK, December 23.

By the Ship Renown, Capt. Steele, which arrived Yeſterday Morning, from Newcaſtle on Tyne, but laſt in two Days from Philadelphia, we are informed, that he ſaw a Ship lying at Anchor about ten Miles within Delaware Bay, which his Pilot told him was Capt. Ayres's Ship with Tea for that Port, from the honorable Eaſt India Company.

Captain Steele ſailed from the Downs on the 19th of November, in Company with the above Capt. Ayres, the Tea Ship for New-York, and 300 other Veſſels.

Tueſday Night an Expreſs arrived here from Boſton, who left it on Friday laſt, and brings ſundry Letters, giving and confirming Accounts of the Deſtruction of the Teas at that Place, the Thurſday preceeding.

We have inexpreſſible Satisfaction in acquainting our Readers, that it is determined, on the Arrival of the ſhip Nancy, Capt. Lockyer, with the Tea from the honorable Eaſt-India Company, the Commander will be made acquainted with the Sentiments of the Inhabitants reſpecting the ſhipping that Article, which will indubitably occaſion his Return with it in ſtatu quo, to England, and that he will be provided with every Neceſſary for his Voyage Home ; by which diſcreet Intentions, every Fatality, both to this Colony and the Honourable Company, will be moſt happily prevented, and a Succeſſion of that bleſſed Tranquility, which we enjoy under the preſent wiſe and ſerene Adminiſtration, will be ſecured.

AT a Meeting of the Inhabitants of the Town of Ipſwich, *duly warned and legally aſſembled December* 23d, 1773, *the following Reſolves paſs'd in a very full Meeting.*

1. THAT the Inhabitants of this Town have received real Pleaſure and Satisfaction from their Brethren of the Town of Boſton, and other Towns, to prevent the landing of the deteſted Tea lately arrived there, from the Eaſt-India Company, ſubject to a Duty, for the ſole Purpoſe of raiſing a Revenue, to ſupport in Idleneſs and Extravagance, a ſet of Miſcreants, whoſe vile Emiſſaries and Underſtrappers ſwarm in the Sea-Port Towns, and by their diſſolute Lives and evil Practices, threaten this Land with a Curſe more deplorable than Egyptian Darkneſs.

2. That they hold in utter Contempt and Deteſtation the Perſons appointed Conſignees of ſaid Eaſt-India Company's Tea in Boſton, who by their equivocal Anſwers to Committees from a reſpectable Body aſſembled in the Town of Boſton, and final refuſal to comply with the reaſonable Deſires of their Fellow-Citizens and Countrymen, have rendered themſelves juſtly odious to every Perſon poſſeſs'd of the leaſt Spark of Ingenuity and Virtue in America.

3. That whoever ſhall import any Tea of any kind into this Province ſo long as the Act paſſed by the Britiſh Parliament impoſing a Duty on Tea imported into America is in Force, ſhall be conſidered as an inveterate Enemy to his Country by the Inhabitants of this Town.

4. That it is the Determination of this Town, that no Tea ſhall be brought into it during the Term aforeſaid ; and if any Perſon ſhall have ſo much Effrontery and Hardineſs as to offer any Tea to Sale in this Town, in Oppoſition to the general Sentiments of the Inhabitants, he ſhall be deemed an Enemy to the Town, and treated as his ſuperlative Meanneſs and Baſeneſs deſerve.

Voted, That the Town-Clerk be directed to deliver an atteſted Copy of the foregoing Reſolves, to the Committee of Correſpondence of this Town, and that they tranſmit the ſame to the Committee of Correſpondence of the Town of Boſton.

Copy on File, Examined,
Atteſt, *John Baker*, Town-Clerk.

Meſſieurs EDES & GILL,

IT has been frequently Queſtioned whether the Governor of this Province and other Officers that receive their Commiſſions from the King, are obliged on forfeiture of their Poſts, to partake of the Sacrament of the Lord's Supper, in ſome Epiſcopal Church, once a Year or oftner ? If any of your Correſpondence will favour the Public with a ſatisfactory Anſwer, in your Paper, it will oblige many, and eſpecially your humble Servant,

A CONFORMIST.

Brandy and Geneva.

A few Casks Old Brandy, and a few Caſes Geneva to be Sold by CHARLES MILLER, at his Store in King-Street.

ALSO,

Superfine and common Philadelphia Flour,	Small Green Coffee, by large or ſmall quantities,
Barr Iron,	A few Bags excellent Cotton,
Liſbon Wine,	Philadelphia Furkin Butter.
Liſbon Lemmons,	CHEAP FOR CASH.
Jamaica Spirits, &c. &c.	

To be Sold by public Vendue, by Order of Court, by *Samuel Whitney* and *John Buttrick*, Adminiſtrators on the Eſtate of *John Homer*, late of Winchendon, deceaſed, on February 15. 1774, at One o'Clock Afternoon, at Levi Nichols's, Innholder in Winchendon aforeſaid,——THE Real Eſtate of ſaid *Homer*, conſiſting of a good Farm, containing 120 Acres, with a good Houſe and Barn, with good Mowing, Ploughing and Paſturing, with a young Orchard. The whole of ſaid Farm, or two Thirds, may be ſold, as will beſt ſuit, ſaving to the Widow the Improvement of her Thirds during her Life.

Concord, Dec. 17, 1773. *Samuel Whitney*, *John Buttrick*, } Adminiſtrators on ſaid Eſtate.

N. B. The above Farm lays upon the Great Road to No. 4, and within 80 Rods of the Meeting-Houſe.

New-York Poſt not arriv'd at X o'Clock.

Messieurs EDES & GILL,

Please to publish the following in your ORACLE OF LIBERTY.

To all Nations under HEAVEN.

Know Ye,

THAT the PEOPLE *of the* AMERICAN WORLD, *are Millions strong,—countless Legions compose their united* ARMY *of* FREEMEN*—whose intrepid Souls sparkle with* LIBERTY, *and their Hearts are steeled with Courage to effect what their Wisdom dictates to be done*—AMERICA *now stands with the Scale of* JUSTICE *in one Hand, and the Sword of* VENGEANCE *in the other, and whatever Nation or People who dares to lift a hostile Hand against her, to invade her serene Regions, or sully her Liberty, shall————————Let the Britons fear to do any more so wickedly as they have done, for the Herculean* ARM *of this* NEW WORLD *is lifted up—and Woe be to them on whom it falls! ——At the Beat of the Drum, she can call five Hundred Thousand of her* SONS *to* ARMS*—before whose blazing Shields none can stand——Therefore,* ye that are Wise, *make Peace with Her, take Shelter under Her Wings, that ye may shine by the Reflection of* Her Glory.

May the NEW YEAR *shine propitious on the* NEW WORLD*—and* VIRTUE, *and* LIBERTY, *reign here without a Foe, until rolling Years shall measure* TIME *no more.*

MARLBOROUGH.

At a legal and very full Meeting, of the Freeholders, and other Inhabitants of the Town of *Charlestown*, December 28, 1773.

The following Votes were *Unanimously* passed.

1. CONSIDERING the Advantages that will result to this Community (in every Point of Light) from the Disuse of *India Tea*; We will not by ourselves, or any from or under us, buy or sell, or suffer to be us'd in our Families, any such *Tea*, till the British Act of Parliament, imposing a Duty on the *same* shall be repealed.

2. That a Committee be chosen to collect from all the Inhabitants of this Town, all the *Tea* they may have by them; and that such Persons, as shall deliver up the *same* to said Committee, be paid by the Town the Price it cost them. And that the *Tea* so collected, be destroyed by Fire, on Friday next at Noon-Day, in the Market Place.

3. That Mess's. *Isaiah Edes, Samuel Conant, Caleb Call, Benjamin Hurd, Samuel Wait, Battry Powars* and *David Wood*, jun. be the committee for the Purposes above-mentioned.

4. That the above named Persons, be a Committee of Inspection, to see that all the aforegoing Votes be fully complyed with.

5. That if any of the Inhabitants of this Town, shall do any thing to counteract, or render ineffectual the foregoing Votes, they are not only inimical to the Liberty of AMERICA in general, but also show a daring Disrespect to this Town in particular.

6. That the Committee of Correspondence, for this Town confer with the Committee of Correspondence for the Town of *Boston*, and desire their Influence, that similar Measures may be taken in their Town.

7. That the above Proceedings of this Town, be published in the News-Papers.

A Copy,

Attest. SETH SWEETSER, Town Clerk.

B O S T O N, January 3, 1774.

The Express that went from hence the Friday Afternoon after the Destruction of the Tea, arrived at New-York the Tuesday Evening following, and returned back last Monday, performing his Journey in a shorter Time than could be expected at this Season of the Year: We learn, That when the Inhabitants of that City received the Intelligence, they were in high Spirits, and vast Numbers of People collected, one and all declaring that the Ship with the Tea on board designed for that Port, should on her Arrival, be sent back, or the Tea destroyed: That they highly extolled the Bostonians for what the Indians had done here; and immediately forwarded the Account to Philadelphia.

Our Informant left the City after the Papers were printed, which contained the foregoing Articles under the New-York Head, and adds further, that the Tea-Ship was not then arrived.—That Capt. Ayscough went to the Coffee-House that Day, and said he had dined with the Governor, and declared before a great Number of Merchants, that as soon as the Tea-Ship arrived at the Hook, he should go down and supply her with what Necessaries she might be in Want of for her Passage back, and inform the Captain of the Resolutions of the People.

On Tuesday Morning early the Bells in this Town were set to ringing on receiving the above Intelligence.

It is said the behaviour of Governor Tryon at New-York, with regard to the Tea, will redound much to his honour—whilst the conduct of a Hutchinson will be execrated to the latest period of time! (Spy.)

Whereas it was reported that one Withington, of Dorchester, had taken up and partly disposed of a Chest of the East-India Company's Tea: a Number of the Cape or Narragansett-Indians, went to the Houses of Capt. Ebenezer Withington, and his Brother Philip Withington, (both living upon the lower Road from Boston to Milton) last Friday Evening, and with their consent thoroughly searched their Houses, without offering the least offence to any one. But finding no Tea they proceeded to the House of old Ebenezer Withington, at a place called Sodom, below Dorchester Meeting House, where they found part of a half chest which had floated, and was cast up on Dorchester point. This they seized and brought to Boston Common where they committed it to the flames.

The conduct of Mess's. Paxton and Hallowell is really diverting. On every stir of the people to take their general sense respecting the invasion of their Charter Rights, away go my Lords to an armed Ship or the Castle, now wretchedly perverted from the place of our defence to an Assylum for our worst enemies; and after they have forwarded their packets to the British Ministry, declarative of the tremendous danger their important personages are in, we see them, strutting about in the same Insolence of Office they used to appear. It is said their *sublime* Highnesses the TEA CONSIGNEES have a strong yearning to imitate their example—But beware of Mistakes, Gentlemen! Remember you are Voted Public Enemies, by more than 30,000 of your fellow countrymen!

The Inhabitants of Charlestown, agreeable to a unanimous Vote of said Town the Tuesday preceeding, on Friday last voluntarily bro't *all* their TEA into the public Market Square, where it was committed to the Flames at high Noon-Day.—*An Example well worthy Imitation.!!*

The Vessel which bro't up the Goods (last Saturday) saved out of Capt. Loring's Brig, was the same Evening thoroughly searched by Indians, and no TEA found on board. Such a good Look-out being kept, *What occasion is there for* TIDE-WAITER'S, PIMPS, *or* INFORMERS?

From the NEW-HAVEN POST-BOY, *Dec.* 24.

Hartford, Dec. 21. *Quere*, Whether it would not be for the general Utility of Connecticut to warn a Meeting of the Inhabitants immediately to convene at Hartford, to adopt Measures similar to those of our sister Colonies, respecting the baneful Article, TEA.

MARRIED] Last Evening, by the Rev. Mr. Walter, Mr. *Zechariah Brigden*, Goldsmith, to Miss *Elizabeth Gillam*.

Married by the Rev. Mr. Walter, Mr. James Gammage, to Mrs Burt, Widow to the late Capt. James Burt.

DIED] On Wednesday last, in the 55th Year of his Age, Mr. Andrew Cunningham Hatter—A Gentleman well esteemed as an honest worthy Citizen.

Mrs. Hooton, Widow of the late Mr. Hooton, Oar-Maker, deceased.

Last Friday Night died here much lamented by all her Frineds and Acquaintance, Mrs. Ann Payson, aged 64, Consort of Col. Jonathan Payson. Her Funeral will be attended to-morrow at 4 o'clock, when the Relations and Friends are desired to attend.

DIED] At Palmer, of a Nervious Fever, Dec. 1st. Doctor Abner Stone, a few Days under 25 Years.

THIS DAY IS PUBLISHED,

MILLS and HICKS's BRITISH and AMERICAN

REGISTER,

And to be Sold at their Printing-Office in School-Street.

Charles Sigourney

HAS just IMPORTED in Capt. Coulson, from BRISTOL, an additional Supply of Hard Ware

G O O D S

of all Sorts, which will be Sold at his usual low Prices, at his Shop just above the Market. Also, Dutch Brushes in setts, Holland Scates, Looking Glasses, best English double refin'd Loaf Sugar, Brimstone, Copperas, &c &c.

TO BE SOLD by PUBLIC AUCTION, On WEDNESDAY the 12th Instant at Eleven o'Clock in the Forenoon.

A Quantity of West-India FISH, now lying in a Store on Gray's Wharf.

N. B. The Fish may be seen any Time before the Sale, by applying to Mr. John Brewer, Block-Maker, on said Wharf.

TO BE SOLD

By Benjamin Church,

On THURSDAY next,

At ELEVEN o'Clock in the Forenoon,

BY PUBLICK AUCTION,

A large Assortment of valuable Articles belonging to a Gentleman lately deceas'd. Consisting of

SUPERFINE middling and course Broad Cloths—Ratteens—Frizes—Half Thick—Kerseys—Shalloons—Calamancoes—Irish Linnens—Checks—Mens and Womens Hose—Velveretts—Handkerchiefs—Case Knives and Forks—Inkhorns—Penknives, &c. &c.—Sundry Articles of Household—Wearing Apparell—Watches, &c. &c. &c. Thursday next, 11 o'Clock A. M.

LIGNUMVITÆ.

A LARGE Quantity of LIGNUMVITÆ, of different sizes, uncommon straight and sound; to be sold Cheap for Cash, or Barter for any Merchandize that may offer & suit the Owner. Inquire of the Printers.

New AUCTION-ROOM, Cornhill, TO-MORROW at TEN in the MORNING, Will be Sold by PUBLIC VENDUE,

At *Greenleaf*'s Auction-Room,

A very large and valuable Assortment of Goods, Amongst which are

A variety of blue, claret and drab broad cloths ratteens, kerseys, German Serges, forest cloths, red and blue duffils, coatings, shalloons, tammies, durants, striped and plain camblets, callamancoes, duroys, green and black everlastings, manchester velvets, velverets, grizets, misenets, blue, yellow and black India taffaties, sattins, figured and plain modes, ribbons, a few lb. white thread, Irish linnens, cotton checks, strip'd gingams, flower'd and plain lawns, muslins, callicoes, chints, cotton and linnen stampt handkerchiefs, necklaces, silver watches, feather beds, one suit green harrateen curtains, &c. &c.

W. GREENLEAF, Auctioneer.

ALSO FOR PRIVATE SALE.

Lutestrings, ducapes, sattins, silk damasks, two handsome eight day clocks, one mahogany desk & book case, two large looking glasses, one new chaise and harness compleat. To Morrow Morning,

The sale will begin precisely at TEN o'Clock.

New AUCTION-ROOM, *Cornhill.*

On FRIDAY NEXT,

At TEN o'Clock in the Morning will be sold by PUBLIC VENDUE,

At *Greenleaf*'s Auction-Room,

A variety of GOODS as usual.

W. GREENLEAF, Auctioneer.

To be Sold by *Jonathan Williams*,

At Store No 8, South Side Town Dock,

Superfine and common Philadelphia Flour, Barr Iron, Cotton per Bag, Coffee, Cocoa, and Lisbon Salt, also a fine new SNOW of about 152 Tons burthen, 11 Months old, with all her Appurtenances, a she now lies in said Town Dock.

A few Crates of well assorted Earthen WARE, each Crate an Assortment for a Shop, one best of German Steel, and Brimstone, to be sold cheap for the Cash. Inquire of the Printers.

TO BE SOLD

A convenient BRICK-HOUSE, in good Repair, situate in Cold-Lane, accommodated with a retired Back Yard, and a Well of Water that never fails. Inquire of the Printers.

All Persons Indebted to the Estate of the late Mrs. Ruth Sinclair, Shopkeeper, deceas'd, are desired to pay their respective Ballances to Joseph Bradford or Joseph Bradford, junr. Administrators to the deceas'd's Estate, and all that have any Demands on the same are desired to bring in their Accounts to said Administrators.

The Shop Goods and House Furniture of the deceas'd will be sold on Friday next, at Ten o'Clock in the Forenoon, at the House of said deceas'd, near the Drawbridge, consisting of Woollens, Linnens, Silks, and a great many other Articles of Shop Goods.

A. OLIVER, Auctioneer,

At GOULD's *Auction Office*,

In Back Street,

T O-M O R R O W,

At half past NINE o'Clock in the Morning, Will be Sold by PUBLIC VENDUE,

The L I B R A R Y of the late Mr. *Robert Jenkins*, deceased, with many other valuable B O O K S received from different Hands, consisting of near 100 Volumes of the Universal, the new Universal, the London and the Gentleman's Magazines, all neatly Bound; about two Hundred loose ditto; together with a large Collection in Divinity, History, Philosophy, Mathematicks, Voyages, Travels, Commerce, Plays, Novels, Geography, Dictionaries, &c. &c &c. Also one large Glass Case suitable for a Gentleman's Library, with sundry others fit for Stores or Shops.

R. GOULD, Auctioneer.

N. B. The Books may be viewed the Day before the Sale, but no Catalogues will be Published.

On Wednesday the 5th Day of January Inst. at Ten o'Clock in the Morning, will be sold by Public Vendue, at the House of Mr. John Proctor, School-Master, deceased, in Queen-Street,

The House Furniture of said deceased, consisting of,

GEnteel mehogany desk and book case, dining and snapt tables, chest of draws, black walnut leather bottom chairs, looking glasses, beds, bedsteds and bedding, a variety of kitchen furniture, such as pewter, brass, copper, iron, bell mettle and tin ware, a good jack, genteel guns, a good horse and chaise, bridle and saddle, some silver plate, viz.—a handsome tankard, tea pots, porringers, pepper castors, large and small spoons, snuff and tobacco boxes, and wearing apparel—and a number of other articles—To be seen the day before the sale.

N. B. A number of Rheams of Writing Paper, Writing Books and Slates, a Case of Mathematical Instruments.—The Horse and Chaise to be put up between 1 and 2 o'Clock in the Afternoon.

A. OLIVER, Auctioneer.

For Private Sale,

At the NEW AUCTION ROOM, South Side of the Town House, viz.

A few Boxes of choice Lisbon L E M M O N S, a Hogshead of choice Jamaica Spirits, 2 Cases of Doctor's Instruments.

CUSTOM-HOUSE, *BOSTON.*

ENTETRD IN.

Church, Hammen, Rogers, abd Sparrell, Philadelphia. Morris, Virginia. Bernard and Weston, New-York. Rogers and Gray, Maryland. Oaks, Turks-Island. Greeley, St. Kitts, and Turks Island. Pearson, St. Lucia. Evans, Grenada. Angus, London. Wishart, Falmouth.

DEATHS in the Town of *Charlestown*, from *January* 1, 1773, to *January* 1, 1774.

65 Whites. 6 Blacks. In all, 71.

(Among which there are Ten White Persons, whose Ages added together, amount to 812 Years.)

Baptiz'd in the Church there, 43.

Last Year's Account stands thus:

Deaths—73 Whites, 8 Blacks, In all, 81.

Baptiz'd in the Church there, 52.

BURIALS and BAPTISMS in the Town of Boston, from January 1, 1773, to January 1, 1774.

Buried, Whites, 533. Blacks, 62. In all, 595.

Baptised in the several Churches, 485.

The Account for the Year 1772, stands thus:

Buried, Whites, 458 Blacks, 59. In all, 517.

Baptised in the several Churches, 393.

Burials in the Town of BOSTON, since our last.

Nine Whites. Two Blacks.

Baptiz'd in the several Churches, Ten.

High Water at BOSTON, *for the present Week.*

Monday, 44 min. aft. 3	Friday, 55 min. after 6
Tuesday, 30 min. aft. 4	Saturday, 47 min. af. 7
Wednesday 16 m. aft. 5	Lord's-Day, 48 m. aft. 8
Thursday, 5 min. aft. 6	☽'s last Q. 5 D. 1 A't.

A Quantity of large
Lignum Vitæ, Cotton Wool, } { Pitch per Barrel, And,
Excellent Madeira WINES in Quarter Caſks,
Will be Sold very cheap by
SAMUEL A. OTIS,
At Store No. 1, Butler's Row.

To be Sold cheap for Caſh, by

Cyrus Baldwin,

At his Shop in Cornhill, near the Town Houſe, *Boſton*,
Choice Bohea and Souchong Teas, beſt Hyſon ditto, at 18s. L. M. per Pound, Narraganſet CHEESE.

Cinnamon, Cloves, Mace, Nutmegs, Pepper, Allſpice, Kippen's Snuff and Indigo.

A Parcel of Parchment Deerſkins.

Alſo—A general Aſſortment of Engliſh, India and Scotch Goods, ſuitable for all Seaſons of the Year.

Wanted at the ſame Place, a Quantity of good large Lynn Shoes.

N. B. The above Teas were imported before the Eaſt India Company's Tea arsived, or it was known that they would ſend any here on their own Account.

To be Sold on board the Brig Suckey, William Brown, Maſter, now lying at JOHN ROWE, Eſq'rs Wharf,
The beſt *Newcaſtle* COALS, at Ten Dollars per Chaldron.

Alſo to be Sold by JOHN ROWE, at his Store,
Hemp, Ruſſia Engliſh and Ravens Duck, Ticklinburgs, Oznabrigs, Cod Lines, Cod Hooks, all Sorts of Nails and Window Glaſs, Gun Powder, Lead, Shot—The very beſt Sterling Madeira, by the Pipe or Quarter Caſk—very good Porter in Hampers 4 Dozen each, Liſbon and Liverpool Salt, with a Variety of other Goods. Boſton, December 20, 1773.

M. LEE,

(REMOVED from Cornhill to a Shop oppoſite Mr. *William Scott*'s Iriſh-Linnen Store in Ann-Street,)
Acquaints the Ladies ſhe has lately imported,
A Variety of Mercery and Millenery GOODS, amongſt which are a beautiful Aſſortment of Brocades, flower'd & plain Luteſtrings, Gorgoroons, and Taffaties, black Paduſoys and Armozeens, exceeding Cheap,

New Faſhion Cloaks and Bonnets, London made,	A large Variety of trolly, blond & bone Laces,
White, Grey, Leylock, Sky, Pink, Crimſon, Black & Fancy } Figured Modes & Sattins of the neweſt Patterns	Edgings, Lawns, and Cambricks,
	Silk Mitts and Gloves,
	Callicoes and Chinces,
	Schineal and Teſte black Hair-Pins,
	Paſte Sprigs and Pins,
	Silk Handkerchiefs,
Yard & ell-wide Mull Mull, Jaccnott, book & ſprig'd Muſlins,	Stomachers,
	White, blue and black Feathers, ſome very handſome,
Yard and ell-wide flower'd and plain Gauzes,	Childrens Morocco Shoes and Pumps,
Catguts, Queens Nett,	Skeleton and Cap Wire,
Parriſnett,	Brocaded Clogs,
A few ſuits of Blond Linen,	Court Plaiſter,
Rich Muffs, Tippets and Ermine,	Floſs Turbin Lappets,
Tambour work'd Aprons and Ruffles,	Italian Flowers,
Bruſſels & Mecklin Laces,	Chevaudefrize, and Snail Trimmings,

A Quantity of Ribbons, and many other Articles in the Millenery and Mercery Way. ALSO, Blue & white China Bowls, Cups & Saucers.

Imported in ſundry Veſſels lately arrived from England and Scotland,

By John Greenlaw,

A general Aſſortment of GOODS,
——Among which are the following viz.——

VERY rich black Sattins, Luteſtrings, Tobines, Brocades, Paduſoys, Modes, Sarſnets, Muſlins, Stuffs, very beſt Threads, and Women's Stays, to be diſpoſed of exceeding Cheap, at his Store South-End, Boſton.

N. B. Juſt come to Hand, very ſuitable Baizes, Coatings, Duffils, Ratteens and ſtrong Frizes, &c. &c.

All Perſons having any Demands againſt the Eſtate of Margaret Vintenon, late of Boſton, in the County of Suffolk, but laſt of Waltham in the County of Middleſex, Widow, deceaſed, are deſired to bring in the ſame to Jolley Allen, of Boſton, Merchant, Executor of the laſt Will of ſaid Deceaſed; and any Perſon indebted to ſaid Eſtate are deſired to make ſpeedy Payment to ſaid Allen, Executor as aforeſaid.

WANTED TO BUY,

A HORSE or MARE, from 14 to 16 Hands high, and between 4 and 8 Years old, Colour not much minded, muſt be a good Dealer, well broke in, quite gentletle, if uſed to the Road the better, and if clear of the Amble the more agreeable.——Apply to the Printers, with whom leave your Name, and Place of Abode.

TO BE SOLD

A Quantity of Barrel Beef, Pitch, Tarr and Turpentine, and a few Barrels of excellent Pickle Mackrel, alſo a Schooner about 50 Tons, almoſt new, to lett, Inquire of Nathaniel Waterman, near the South Battery.

To the Honorable SAMUEL DANFORTH, Eſq; one of his Majeſty's Juſtices of the Peace throughout the Province of the Maſſachuſetts-Bay.

WE the Subſcribers, ſome of the Proprietors of a Townſhip of Land called Silveſter-Canada, of the Contents of ſeven Miles ſquare, lying on a River called Androſcoggin River, and adjoining to Baker's Town, ſo called, in the County of Cumberland, the Plan of which, was confirmed to the Proprietors thereof by the General Court of ſaid Province in June 1768, humbly requeſt your Honor to iſſue a Warrant for calling a Meeting of ſaid Proprietors, to be held at the Dwelling-Houſe of Cornelius Turner, Innholder in Hanover, in the County of Plymouth, on Tueſday, the ninth Day of February next, at Ten o'Clock, in the Forenoon, then and there to act on the following Articles.

1. To chooſe a Moderator, Clerk, Treaſurer and Collector of Taxes.
2. To confirm any or all former Votes and Grants of ſaid Proprietors at any former Meeting or Meetings, as they ſhall ſee fit.
3. To raiſe a ſufficient Sum or Sums of Money by Tax or otherwiſe, for diſcharging their Debts due or that may become due.
4. To chooſe a Standing Committee to tranſact the Affairs of ſaid Proprietors, ſettle the Accounts, adjuſt the Debts that are or ſhall be due from the ſaid Proprietors, and order Payment of the ſame, and agreeable to Law to make Sale of thoſe Proprietors Land who are delinquent in paying their Taxes; and to determine where the Settling Lots ſhall be laid, and how much in a Lot, and about convenient Ways, and procure a Plan thereof, to be lodged with the Clerk as ſoon as may be.
5. To agree what ſhall be allowed the Clerk and Committee for their Service.
6. To chooſe a Committee for calling Meetings, for the future, and to agree on the Method thereof.
7. To appoint an Agent or Agents, Attorney or Attornies, with Power or Subſtitution, to commence an Action or Actions for ſaid Proprietors, and in their Names to proſecute the ſame in any Court of Law, or otherwiſe amply, to all Intents and Purpoſes, until final Judgment and Execution, and in like manner to defend them in all Actions brought or that may be brought againſt them.
8. And to agree on any other Thing which ſaid Proprietors ſhall judge neceſſary for carrying forward the Settlement of ſaid Townſhip.

Scituate, November 23d, 1773.

John Cuſhing,
Charles Turner
Wm. Sever
Ja's Warren
David Little, jun.

Province of the Maſſachuſetts-Bay.
To *Charles Turner*, of *Scituate*, in the County of *Plimouth*, in ſaid Province, Gentlemen, one of ſaid Proprietors.

{ Seal. }

In purſuance of the foregoing Application and Requeſt, you are hereby required to give Notice (in Time and Manner as the Law directs) to the ſaid Proprieors, That a Meeting of ſaid Proprietors is to be holden at the Time and Place, and for the Purpoſes mentioned in the afore-written Petition.

Given under my Hand and Seal, this 22d Day of December, A. D. 1773. S. DANFORTH, Juſtice of the Peace throughout the Province aforeſaid.
Scituate, December 23d, 1773.

BY Virtue of the afore-written Warrant, to me directed, I do hereby notify and warn the Proprietors of the aforeſaid Lands to meet at the Dwelling-Houſe of Cornelius Turner, Innholder in Hanover, on Tueſday, the Ninth Day of February next, at Ten o'Clock in the Forenoon, for the Purpoſes therein mentioned. CHARLES TURNER.

☞ Andrew Dexter,

Who keeps the CHEAP STORE, near the *Mill-Bridge*, acquaints People in general, and particularly ſuch as have been often *diſappointed* and *deceived*, when allured by pompous Advertiſements, they have gone to *Auction-Rooms*, to purchaſe either at *public* or *private* Sale, that he has juſt received by the *laſt Ship* from London, a *freſh* Parcel of GOODS, which for *Quality* and *extreme lowneſs of Price*, are not to be deſcribed by the Language in common Uſe among Traders; a Part of which Goods every Body who will pleaſe to come to his Shop, he hopes will be induced to buy; and he is very confident they will not have the leaſt Reaſon to repent of it afterwards.

Joſeph Peirce,

At his Shop the North Side of the Town Houſe, *Boſton*, —Informs his Cuſtomers and Others, that he has imported from LONDON per Capt. Scott,

A freſh Aſſortment of GOODS, which he will ſell at a *very reaſonable Profit, for ready Money.*

Amongſt his Goods are ſome Men's *exceeding neat 3 and 4 thread, plain and Patent Rib worſted Hoſe of various Colours,*—ſome *remarkable cheap ſcarlet Broad-Cloth*, Beaver-Coatings, Lambſkins, Kerſeys, Baizes, *ſcarlet Whitney—Corduſoy, Royal Rib, Crimſon Cape Velvet, Patens, beſt Engliſh made* Shoes, and Pumps, Clogs and Goloſhoes, Muffs, *Patent Cake Blacking, and Cake Ink*, Men's white, and coloured patent Rib, and plain Silk Hoſe, plain black ditto,—Boys black Hatts.—A few *elegant enamelled India China Punch-Bowls*, blue & white India half pint Bowls, ditto *with Saucers*, Breakfaſt, and Tea Cups and Saucers, blue and white Octagon Plates.—*True Sable Muffs and Tippets*,—together with more Articles than is convenient to enumerate in an Advertiſement.

AT a Meeting of the Proprietors of the Townſhip of Land granted to Samuel Livermore, Eſq; and others, and lying on both Sides Androſcoggin River, in the County of Cumberland, November 3, 1773,

VOTED and choſe Mr. Thomas Fiſh to proſecute, in Behalf of the Proprietors, to final Judgment and Execution (cum Facultate ſubſtituendi) any Perſon or Perſons who ſhall commit Treſpaſs on ſaid Propriety. Atteſt,
LEONARD WILLIAMS, Pro'rs Clerk.

PURSUANT to the above Vote, I do hereby notify all Perſons whom it may concern, that if any Perſon or Perſons ſhall commit Treſpaſs on ſaid Propriety, that they may depend upon being proſecuted with the utmoſt Severity of the Law. THOMAS FISH.
December 21, 1773.

TO BE LETT

A very neat convenient Dwelling-Houſe with large Yard-Room Entrance, an excellent Well of Water, &c. pleaſantly ſituated in Hanover-Street, by the head of Wings-Lane. Inquire of Edes and Gill.

H. Murdock
3/19/1919

JUST ARRIVED,
And now Opening,
A freſh ASSORTMENT of

Engliſh, India and Scotch Goods,

To be SOLD by

Parkman & Melvill,

At their Shop in Cornhill, formerly improved by Mrs. Mehitable Torrey.

N. B. They have juſt received in the laſt Veſſels from London, a handſome Aſſortment of Winter STUFFS for Ladies Gowns, which will be ſold extreme low.

TO BE SOLD CHEAP,

A ſuperfine Scarlet Cloth Riding Hood, almoſt new. Inquire of the Printers.

Juſt Arrived and to be Sold by

Archibald Cunningham,

At his Store in Ann Street, near the Draw Bridge, Boſton.
Liſbon Lemmons in exceeding good order per Box,—Malaga, Virgin and Claret Wine per Quarter Caſk,—Madeira Wine in Pipes and half Pipes,—Liſbon Oil in Caſks,—Anchovies per Bottle,—choice new Raiſins,—Turkey Figs,—Almonds,—Oil in ſquare Bottles,—Split Peaſe,—Dutch Hearth Bruſhes,—the very beſt of Souchong and Hyſon Tea per Dozen or ſingle Pound,—Green Capers per Caſk or Pound,—Barcelona Handkerchiefs per Dozen,—choice Bay Mackrel per Barrell,—and many other Articles in the Grocery way.

All Perſons that are indebted to the Eſtate of Mrs. LYDIA LEWIS, late of Boſton, Widow, deceas'd, are requeſted to make ſpeedy payment, and thoſe to whom ſaid Eſtate is indebted, are deſired to bring in their Accounts, in Order for Settlement, to ARCHIBALD CUNNINGHAM, Adminiſtrator.

To be Sold at private Sale,

The Manſion Houſe of the Deceaſed, in Middle-Street, conſiſting of three Rooms on the Floor, and three Story high, with a good Pump, Out-Houſe, Shop and paved Yard. For Particulars, inqrire of Archibald Cunningham, Adminiſtrator to ſaid Eſtate.

TO BE SOLD,
By EDWARD PROCTOR,
At the Sign of the Schooner, North-End.—Alſo,
By JOSEPH HALL, in *Cole-Lane*,
Choice *Malaga* LEMMONS at *Six Dollars* per ſingle Box, and leſs by the large Quantity; and *Three Pounds* per Hundred, and *Nine Shillings* per Dozen, Old Tenor.

IRISH LINNENS.

William Scott,

At his Iriſh Linnen Store in Ann-Street, between the Flat Conduit and Draw-Bridge, BOSTON.
HAS Imported from IRELAND,

A large Quantity of 3,4, 7-8 and yd-wide Linnens, Diapers, Clouting, Table Cloths, Sheetings, &c.

Said Store is alſo furniſh'd with a great Variety of European and India Goods ſuitable for the Seaſon, amongſt which are ſome nice Cinnamon-colour & mix'd Bath Coatings, ſuperfine blue and ſcarlet knap'd ditto, cloth-colour'd ſcarlet and crimſon Broad Cloths, Forreſt Cloths, Baizes, Duffils, &c.

Double Camblets, Cambleteens, Denmark & Pruſſian Luſtres, Crapes, Dorſetteens, Iriſh Camblets, Grizetts, Silveretts, Miſſionets, &c.

Black and cloth-colour'd India Taffities, flower'd and plain black, white, crimſon and pink Sattins, Capuchin Silks, Sarcenets and Modes of all Colours, Hoſiery plain and rib'd. His general aſſortment for Men's and Women's wear conſiſt of two great a multiplicity to be enumerated in a public advertiſement. All which will be ſold by wholeſale and retail at the loweſt reduced prices for ready Money only, a few very large Scotch Carpets 4 by 5, 4½ by 5½, 5 by 6.——

A freſh Importation of Doctor Hemmett's celebrated Eſſence of Pearl and Pearl Dentifrice for the preſervation of the Teeth and Gums, to be ſold at the London Prices, Cakes for the Liquid Shining Blacking for Shoes, Boots and Leather Botton Chairs.

A few Pieces of Ducapes, Luteſtrings and Engliſh Damaſks, to be ſold at the Sterling Coſt, a large Quantity of flower'd Scotch Lawns, on the ſame Terms.

RAN-AWAY from me the Subſcriber a Negro-Man named TOM, the 1ſt Inſt. had on when he went away, a light coloured Surtout, a Snuff coloured Coat with flower'd Braſs Buttons, a Chocolate coloured Jacket and black Hair, Pluſh Breeches and ſtriped Cotton and Linnen Shirt, black Stockings and Plated Buckles, about 5 Feet 7 or 8 Inches high. Whoever ſhall take up ſaid Negro and reture him to his Maſter, ſhall have 2 Dollars Reward, and all neceſſary Charges paid by me,—
SIMEON POLLEY.

Boſton, Dec. 1, 1773.

A Woman with a good Breaſt of Milk, would be glad to take a Child to Suckle.
Inquire of Edes and Gill.

Boſton: Printed, by EDES & GILL
in Queen-Street, 1774.

THE
Boston-Gazette,
AND
COUNTRY JOURNAL.

No. 979.

Containing the freshest Advices, Foreign and Domestic.

MONDAY, January 10, 1774.

NEDHAM'S REMEMB'RANCER, N. IV.

——— Think on thy country,
And die in terror of thy *guiltiness*.
SHAKESPEARE.

POLITICALLY speaking, the crime of betraying one's country is—the unpardonable sin. No guilt more deeply poisons the heart and embitters reflection. What pangs must swell the breast of a man, in the close of life, who looks back and sees himself—laboring to *abridge the liberties of his country*, enslaving it's inhabitants, and procuring the introduction of troops, which insult the civil magistrate and shed the blood of his brethren? What and how exquisite must be his feelings, when he hears young and old imprecate vengeance on his hoary head, and sees his name and progeny blasting with execrations and infamy.

The man who slanders his neighbour with dark insinuations and aims his distruction in secret, is obnoxious to general odium. But what must be our sentiments of him, who with these weapons deliberately renews the same attack on both individuals and the community?

In his excellency's letter of the 18th June 1768, "Mr. Hancock' is first noticed as "a representative of Boston, a wealthy merchant, of "*great influence over the* POPULACE," whose sloop being seized, the writer informs, "a mob "was *immediately* raised."

As *the populace* ever compose such assemblies, and Mr. Hancock being declared to have *great influence over them*, is there not the plainest insinuation, that this gentleman was the exciter of this tumult? Now as nothing could be more foreign from the truth, and scarce any thing more known to *this informer*, was not his design wicked and his mode of attack base?—

And when we advert to what the same writer says, in a subsequent letter, relative to resentment from Great Britain against PARTICULAR PERSONS, and compare it with a passage in the letter wrote a *few days* after by his brother Oliver, concerning the TAKING OFF *of incendiaries*, is there not great reason to believe, that this "*wealthy* merchant" was held up as a victim, and that hopes of sharing the plunder of his riches on a confiscation of his estate was the motive of action? Who can doubt that forfeitures and confiscations of this sort were the *penalties* of *another kind*, his excellency thought so *adequate*—so well *adapted* to the purpose. *

But we forget the injuries done the private character, when we contemplate the public.

Whoever reads governor Bernard's letters, of the 16, 17, and 18th of June 1768, Mr. Hutchinson's and Paxton's of the same date, and carefully compares them, can have no doubt, that *they wrote in concert*, and were each apprized of the purport of the other's letter: such a comparison will convince the intelligent reader, that *the conspiracy was joint*, and the guilt of the actors equal, unless the subtlety of Mr. Hutchinson, and his station as chief Justice, aggravate his crime above that of his fellows.

There is one instance of union between Paxton and our chief Justice which I do not recollect Bernard to have shared in. Paxton refers his correspondent to "Mr. Hallowell, the comptroller, to inform of *many particulars*". § Mr. Hutchinson "begs leave to refer to him (Hallowell) *for a more full account*." ‡ To give such a sanction to the stories of a man, who went over heated with party-rage and burning with resentment against this country, is such an instance of *unfairness* and *disingenuity*, *malice* and *cowardice*, as Bernard with all his enormity could not stoop to practice. †

We find in the 31st page of Mr. Hutchinson's history, that in 1634, Morton the infamous libeller and public enemy of this colony sent his *confidential* letters "by a *convenient* messenger": like principles and views in this and the last century produce similar actions: Thus we find Hallowell is letter-bearer to the chief Justice and Mr. Commissioner in 1768, as Paxton was for *brother* Oliver in 1767. ||

His honor Mr. Hutchinson in the above letter, which contains *his* account of a mob on the 10th of June, affirms, that "NO NOTICE was taken of their "extravagance in the time of it, NOR ANY ENDEAVOURS *by any authority except the governor*, "the next day to *discover* and *punish* the offenders." Now it is most certain, that not only the governor, but the council of this province the very next morning after the riot "agreed that an examination should be made into the affair, in order to the *discovery* and *punishment* of the offenders;" and "appointed a committee of such members of the board as were qualified to act as *justices of the peace in the county of Suffolk* to make enquiry into the facts." * Surely the council were *an authority*, and their proceedings *a notice* which militate with the account and veracity of this American correspondent.

In what way consistent with either conscience or honor can we acquit this letter-writer;—whose station as Chief Justice ought not only to have preserved him from such high crimes, but have kept him perfectly immaculate from the little base views and enterprizes of *party*. But so far was this gentleman from keeping his mind untinctured with the feuds of the times, he enters deeply into party pursuits, and in other passages of this very letter, his heart appears fraught with rancor against the council and the town of Boston, and his writings, *invite the resentment of the British administration*.

I know that it has been said; I know his Excellency has said, "that these were private letters—wrote before he came to the chair—and *expresly confidential*!" §

That the letters were written when Mr. Hutchinson was *not governor*, *but chief justice*, that they were *secret* and *confidential*, in my mind, adds a tenfold guilt. The gentleman to whom these writings were addressed was an active member of parliament and a zealous advocate of it's measures with the colonies. There can be no doubt, from many circumstances besides the letters themselves, that they were intended to have an operation against the people of this province. But I have one reason to suppose they *actually had* this effect, from certain resolutions of the house of lords, which I do not remember ever to have seen in print.

Among the Resolves of the Lords, sent by them to the House of Commons in December 1768, I find these following.

"Thirdly, Resolved by the lords spiritual and temporal in parliament assembled, that it appears that the town of Boston in the province of the Massachusetts Bay, has for some time past been in a state of great disorder and confusion, and that the peace of the said town has at several times been disturbed by riots and tumults of a dangerous nature, in which the officers of his majesty's revenue there have been obstructed by acts of violence in the execution of the laws, and their lives endangered.

Fourthly, Resolved by the lords spiritual and temporal in parliament assembled, that *it appears*, *that neither the council of the said province of Massachusetts Bay, nor the ordinary civil magistrates did exert their authority* for suppressing the said riots and tumults.

Fifthly, Resolved by the lords spiritual and temporal in parliament assembled, that IN THESE CIRCUMSTANCES of the province of the Massachusetts Bay, and of the town of Boston, the preservation of the public peace, & the due execution of the laws BECAME IMPRACTICABLE without the aid of a military force to support and protect the civil magistrate, and the officers of his majesty's revenue.

Sixthly, Resolved by the lords spiritual and temporal in parliament assembled, that the declarations, resolutions and proceedings in the town meetings at Boston, on the 14th of June and 12th of September, were illegal and unconstitutional, and calculated to excite sedition and insurrections in his majesty's province of the Massachusetts Bay.

Seventhly, Resolved by the lords spiritual and temporal in parliament assembled, that the appointment at the town meeting on the 12th of September, of a convention to be held in the town of Boston on the 22d of that month, to consist of deputies from the several towns and districts in the province of the Massachusetts-Bay, and the issuing a PRECEPT* by the selectmen of the town of Boston, to each of the said towns and districts, for the elections of such deputies, were proceedings subversive of his majesty's government, and evidently manifesting a design in the inhabitants of the said town of Boston, to set up a new and unconstitutional authority, independent of the crown of Great-Britain.

Eighthly, Resolved by the lords spiritual and temporal in parliament assembled, that the election by several towns & districts in the province of the Massachusetts-Bay, of deputies to sit in the said convention, and the meeting of such convention in consequence thereof, were daring insults offered to his majesty's authority, and audacious usurpations of the persons of government."

It is very observable, that the supposed neglect of council and the civil magistrate, of which Mr. Hutchinson gave information in his *confidential letters*, are *those very circumstances*, which induced the fifth resolution of the peers; in which they appear to be so grosly misinformed, as to solemnly resolve upon an impracticability which never existed in nature.

We can no longer doubt that Mr. Whately was of a like spirit with his friend, and made use of his American intelligence with a disposition congenial with his correspondent. And as we know, that *previous* to these resolutions, not only the letter of the 18th of June, but divers others of the same hand had reached England, so we are fully satisfied that the troops quartered in this town, the bloodshed and debauchery they introduced, are all placed to his Excellency's account,—and that in this world and the next he must stand the audit: and let me add in his own words "be"cause *it ought to be so*."

The introduction and establishment of British land-forces in this province are replete with the worst consequences: if not driven out from among us, they must in the end destroy not only public liberty and security, but all private morality and piety. They, therefore, who were the prime movers and instruments of this measure, are stained with a crime, that this people ought not—*they cannot*—*they will not* forget or forgive.

MARCHMONT NEDHAM.

[*To be continued.*]

* See his Excellency's Letters in 1769.
§ Letter 18 June, 1768. ‡ Letter of the same Day.
† Hutchinson is guilty of the same mean artifice, by referring to Hallowell for information against Mr. Temple in his Letter in August following.

|| See Secretary Oliver's Letter, 7 May, 1767.
* See the proceedings and records of Council heretofore published.
§ Message to the House of Representatives.

* This is another flagrant evidence of the base misinformation sent from people on this side the water to persons in authority on the other—Does not this whole province know, that no such precept was ever issued, and that there was not even a colour to pretend that there was?—What punishment too great for SUCH INFORMERS against their country!

Joseph Peirce,

At his Shop the North Side of the Town House, Boston,—Informs his Customers and Others, that he has imported from LONDON per Capt. Scott,

A fresh Assortment of GOODS,

which he will sell at a *very reasonable Profit, for ready Money*.

Amongst his Goods are some Men's *exceeding neat 3 and 4 thread, plain and Patent Rib worsted Hose of various Colours*,—some *remarkable cheap scarlet Broad-Cloth*, Beaver Coatings, Lambskins, Kerseys, Baize, *scarlet Whitney*—*Corduroy, Royal Rib, Crimson Cape Velvet Patens, best English made* Shoes, and Pumps, Clogs and Goloshoes, Muff, *Patent Cake Blacking, and Cake Ink*, Men's white, and coloured patent Rib, and plain Silk Hose, plain black ditto,—Boys black Hatts.—A few *elegant enamelled India China Punch-Bowls*, blue & white India half pint Bowls, ditto *with Saucers*, Breakfast, and Tea Cups and Saucers, blue and white Octagon Plates.—*True Sable Muffs and Tippets*,—together with more Articles than is convenient to enumerate.

Plymouth, January 1st, 1774.

To the PRINTER.

THERE are two very different species of men that pass under the general denomination of *tories*. The one sort totally devoid of the very ideas of honor or virtue, are the most despicable beings, that ever appear'd in human shape; the other are men of honest hearts, but deluded not by "sounds and declimations, but by the most palpable falshoods and fanciful ex stences, and possess so small a share of penetration and discernment, that they cannot (assisted by the united wisdom of the provinces) discover the imposition——these are rather objects of pity, than contempt. By the former, I mean those who are ever ready to prostitute their abilities on the altar of preferment, and to sacrifice their consciences, their Country, and their God to gratify the basest of all passions—an insatiable lust for gain—and consequently are exerting their influence to the utmost, to support measures of administration, which (should they succeed) will be fatal to the commerce, the liberties, and ultimately to the religion of this country. The latter are those who by reason of family connexion, great timidity of nature, or some unaccountable infatuation, view things thro' a false medium. They believe that the man who wants the liberties of his country abridged, is an inviolable friend to its constitution, that humble petitions are of wonderful efficacy to move the obdurate heart of oppression, and that 500 soldiers can crush America to atoms. Both of these respectable characters are among the number who signed our Plymouth protest; some of the youth among whom are weak and puerile enough to imagine, that, by having their names inserted in a public news paper with that of the once honorable name of W-----w, they have already reached the temple of immortal fame. There are (I say it with regret) names to the protest, of men who abhor slavery in every shape; but being immersed in the perplexing cares of the world, and not able to procure the necessary means of information were circumvented (to use the elegant language of the protest) by cunning stratagems. And indeed all the wily subtlety of the most serpentine heads, was practiced on this occasion. Men were told that the other provinces were perfectly quiet and easy—that the East-India teas came exempted from the American duty—that all this bluster was a mere expedient of the merchants in Boston, to augment their own coffers by enhancing the price of their own teas; large quantities of which it was said they had by them. Nor need any body be surprized that these things so destitute of the semblance of truth, should be insisted upon as irrefragable facts, since the venerable O— C— D—n (the veriest tool of the arch-traytor, and like him covering his traiterous designs under the garb of sanctity) frankly confess'd in a day of great zeal, that lying was the vice to which he was constitutionally addicted. And the young deputy waiter who boasted so much of the ingenuity of the composition, and was so affected with the beauties and masterly strokes in the protest, that he could not forbear publickly declaring himself to be the author of it; this ingenious compositor, if not constitutionally inclined to lie, is yet so habituated to the infamous practice that the use has in him become *second nature*. Nor is it necessary that the good-natur'd skipper should cross the atlantic in his ideal ship to imbibe the spirit of leasing, as it was the first principle taught him by a near relative, whose veracity is so unimpeachable, that a petit jury collected from various parts of the county unanimously agreed to pay no regard to his deposition, in a cause, in which he was not remotely interested. The hopeful child is now said to inherit the amiable virtues of his upright parent to a degree of perfection that could hardly have been wished. The Scotch pedlar with his budget of doggrel rhyme might have been spar'd, if he had not miraculously signed the protest at the distance of 70 leagues. The protest is dated the 13th of the month, and he arriv'd from Nova-Scotia on the 20th. They doubtless knew his spirit to be congenial to their own, and that he is always ready to captivate their senses with the melodious sound of his verse, or after evening prayers to risque his fortune at a social game of whist. The magical philosopher does not a little grace the illustrious catalogue—that essence of contradiction—that confused medley of law, divinity, and politicks, whose soul pants for the addition of 'squire, and whose sole qualification for it is intolerable conceit, and an happy versatility of disposition. That burlesque on the virtues and manners of a gentleman, the Yorkshire yeoman, brings up the rear of this respectable septem-virate; who leaving the sphere of life, for which nature originally designed him, and assuming the airs and importance of a man of worth, has become insupportable by his insolence. These are the distinguish'd partizans who have opposed themselves to the whole continent, and could I prevail upon myself to believe, that they aim'd at any less than wounding that cause, which it is their indispensable duty to support, and to bring reproach and obloquy upon this patriotic town, I should think them intitled to it's thanks; for this feeble effort, instead of answering the design for which it was intended, has, by creating a spirit of enquiry induced an almost universal conviction of the ridiculous absurdity of learning from the mere dupes of oppressors, the genuine principles of law, liberty, and reason.

CORNELIUS NEPOS.

N. B. If any tory or more dirty creature, if dirtier there can be, should have the effrontery to deny the abovemention'd facts, they shall be evinced to the satisfaction of the most prejudiced—and all the works of darkness of the whole group shall be exposed to light by C. N.

BALTIMORE, *December* 18.

A Gentleman just come to Town from Boston, assures us, That the East-India Company's TEA, lately arrived at that Place, in several Ships, from London, for the Purpose of *enslaving* and *impoverishing*, if not *poisoning*, the People, was all sent back to the Proprietors, conformable to the noble and spirited Resolves of the brave Inhabitants of the Town of Boston——and, it is hoped on its Arrival, *once more*, in Old England, that the Owners will set up Lord North, and his ministerial Brethren, in the *Grocery Business*—for tho' their late Manœuvres have proved them to be totally unfit to manage the Concerns of a great Nation, yet, contemptible as their Talents are, they may, *possibly*, be able to find out *Ways and Means* to barter away, or somewhow dispose of that *unmerchantable Article*, (like Mr. *Grenville's Stationary*) notwithstanding the Americans have *stamp'd* it as an *unconstitutional Drug*, and may refuse dealing with them.

A Letter from Boston mentions, That 2000 veteran Sons of Liberty were enrolled, in that Town, for the Purpose of destroying the detested Tea, in case any Measures were taken to land it. This Business they pledg'd themselves to execute, or perish in the Attempt.

Another Letter from Boston, says, "That 30 000 as brave Men as any in Britain, would have enforced the Resolves of that Town, respecting the Tea, had the Exigencies of their Country required their vigorous Aid.

NEW-YORK, December 30.

About 1 o'Clock last Thursday morning the house of the Hon. George D. Ludlow, Esq; third Justice of the Supreme Court of this Province, at Hampstead Plains, took Fire, and was burnt to the Ground, with almost every Thing therein contained, but providentially no Lives were lost.

Mr. Ludlow had been in New-York the Day before, and was scarce 3 Hours at home before his House was all Flames.—The Fire 'tis supposed originated by Means of some Sparks that found their Way thro' the Crack of an old Chimney, and communicated to the Wooden Work of one of the Rooms above.

The loss Mr. Ludlow sustains by this Accident, cannot be less than 3000l. for besides the Loss of his Furniture, Plate, &c. a Library worth 1200l. is entirely consumed.

Last Night a little before 11 o'Clock, a terrible Fire was discovered bursting out of the Governor's House in Fort George: Before the Town, or even the Family were alarmed, the Flames had risen to so great a Height, that it was impossible to save the House; and with Difficulty the Lives of the distressed Family were preserved. They were it seems all in Bed, and the Governor himself, with his Lady and Daughter, had Time to put on very few of their Clothes, before they were obliged to quit the House; so that it is not probable that the Papers, Books, Plate, Furniture, or any of the valuable Goods, &c. it contain'd, were sav'd: But providentially no Lives were lost.——The Flames spread with such Rapidity, that very soon after they were discovered, they universally filled the House in every Part, but appeared to rage most furiously on the Side next the Town, on which they were directly driven by a fresh Northwest Wind, which together with the Ramparts, which kept the Engines at too great a Distance, prevented the Water from reaching the House on that Side; therefore all that could be done was, to preserve the adjacent and other Houses in the City on which a fiery Shower of Flakes from the burning Shingles, &c. incessantly fell; but the Houses being covered with Snow, was a great Means of their Preservation; and on Col. Morris's House, which was most exposed, and where the Heat melted the Snow, several Engines were kept playing, which extinguished the Fire that fell on the House, before it had Time to kindle, and thereby happily prevented a general Conflagration, of which there was the most imminent Danger. The Confusion occasioned by this melancholy Event, and the Shortness of the Time since, hinders us from the Knowledge of the Cause of it, and many of the Circumstances that attended it. Every Countenance strongly express'd the deepest Concern for the Distress of the Persons principally affected by the Accident.

We have only Time to assure our Customers, that by Express just arrived from Philadelphia, we have authentic Intelligence, that the Tea Ship expected there, arrived on Saturday last, and on Sunday was sent back, with all the other Goods on board, for London. The Committee went to see her down to Reedy Island.

NEWPORT, December 27.

By a judicious calculation, the province of Massachusets-Bay can raise 80,000 fighting Men.

Notwithstanding the ridiculous boastings of the enemies of this country, "That the people have not virtue enough to quit India Tea, or any one superfluity, to save themselves and posterity from eternal slavery;" we have been informed by those who have the best opportunities to know, that more than 300 families in this town have lately abandoned the use of that noxious WEED: and that others are determined to buy no more, after using what small quantities they have by them. This we defy the rankest TORY to contradict.

The Ladies in Boston, to their immortal honour, are entering into an association against the use of India Tea; and we hope the Ladies in this town will universally do the same.

Mr. Aaron Lopez, owner of the ship Jacob, Captain Peters, has assured us in writing, that said ship has no India Tea on board, and that he thinks himself happy in giving such assurance.

On Tuesday last arrived the Snow —— Capt. Daverant, from Newfoundland, with whom came Passengers a number of Gentlemen belonging to Boston, and about 60 Irish persons to settle in these parts.

Last Monday was killed, at the country seat of Abraham Redwood, Esq; on this island, a hog, two years and a half old, which 24 hours after dressed, when dried fit for cutting up, weighing 512 pounds.

Ames's Almanack
For the Year 1774,
IS THIS DAY PUBLISHED,
And Sold by
R. Draper, Edes & Gill, and *T. & J. Fleet.*

TO-MORROW at One o'Clock, will be sold by Public Vendue at the Bunch of Grapes in King-Street,

17 Boxes LEMMONS.

J. RUSSELL, Auctioneer.

On WEDNESDAY NEXT, at Eleven o'Clock, will be Sold by public Vendue, at Mr. Jonathan Williams's Cloth Store in Ann-Street,

One Bale of damaged superfine Broad Cloths—for the Benefit of the Insurers.

J. RUSSELL, Auctioneer.

On THURSDAY NEXT,
At ELEVEN o'Clock,
Will be Sold by PUBLIC VENDUE,
At the Royal Exchange Tavern in King Street,
Ten Hogsheads choice Shop Sugars.

J. Russell, Auctioneer.

New AUCTION-ROOM, Cornhill,
TO-MORROW MORNING,
At TEN o'Clock,
Will be Sold by PUBLIC VENDUE,
At *Greenleaf's* Auction-Room,
A Variety of English GOODS,
Amongst which are

Broad Cloths, Kerseys, Ratteens, Forrest Cloths, Duffils, Strouds, Velvets and Velverets, Worsted Plushes, Lastings, Camblets, Shalloons, Durants, Mizenets, Grizetts, Brolios, Irish Linnens, flower'd and plain Lawns, Muslins, Silk Gauzes, Ribbons, Sattins, Figured Modes, Persians, Lutestrings, Taffaty's, Stamp'd and Check'd Linen Handkerchiefs, Callicoes, Table Cloths, Silver Watches, Beds, &c. &c.

W. GREENLEAF, Auctioneer.

To-Morrow Morning,
The sale will begin precisely at TEN o'Clock.

New AUCTION-ROOM, *Cornhill.*
On FRIDAY NEXT,
At TEN o'Clock in the Morning will be sold by
PUBLIC VENDUE,
At *Greenleaf's* Auction-Room,
A great variety of English GOODS as usual.

W. GREENLEAF, Auctioneer.

Choice Citron and *York* Biscuit,
To be Sold cheap, by
Mrs. *SHEAFFE*,
At her Shop the North Corner of Queen-Street—*Also*, Choice Brown Sugar by the Barrel, Rappee Snuff, Playing Cards; and all Kinds of Groceries.

IMPORTED in the last Ships from LONDON and SCOTLAND, and to be Sold at the cheapest Rates,

A general Assortment of English,

Scots and India GOODS, among which are a fine Choice of Men's and Women's Winter Cloathing of every kind, also Blankets, Rugs, &c. a parcel plain and spotted grey Muffs and Tippets, with a Variety Fur Trimings, Milled Gloves, &c.

☞ Just opening, an Assortment of Dutch Brushes, in sets and single, high iron Scates, Dutch Looking-Glasses, cheap Violins, Battledores, &c. &c.

Enquire at the Subscriber's Shop, near the Old South Meeting-House.

Dec. 29th, 1773.

Gilbert Deblois.

IMPORTED in Captains HALL and COFFIN from LONDON, and to be Sold by

Peter Hughes,
At his Store in King-Street;

Choice Newcastle Coals, Russia Duck, Oznabrigs, Ticklenburgs, Broad-Cloths, Duffils, Beaver-Coatings, Cod and Mackerel Lines and Hooks, Sein and Whipping Twine, 4d, 6d. 8d. 10 & 20d. Nails, sheathing and drawing ditto, 6 by 8, 7 by 9, & 8 by 10 Glass, Crates of Ware, 12, 15, 18 and 21, Inch Pipes, treble, double and single refin'd Loaf Sugar, Spices, Seive-Bottoms, Shot, Bar-Lead, White Lead per Cask, Porter in Hampers of 4 Dozen, Buntins, Writing-Paper, Durham Mustard, and a few Boxes Lemmons, &c. &c.

——A valuable FARM——

TO be sold, a valuable FARM, in Lancaster, in the county of Worcester, containing about 300 Acres, conveniently divided into Mowing, Pasturing and arable Land, with a fine Stream of Water running through it, making a large Tract of Interval Land belonging to the Farm. The Quality of the Land is exceeding good.—The Buildings are commodious, consisting of a large Dwelling House, and two Barns 50 Feet long, and other Out-Houses. The Price it is to be sold at, is very reasonable, and the Payment may be made on easy Terms. In Case it would better suit the Purchaser, the Husbandry Tools, and a Stock of Cattle, will be sold with the Farm. Enquire of Col Abijah Willard of said Lancaster, or the Printers hereof.

BOSTON, January 10, 1774.

** *The Rhode-Island Post with the Southern Mails, did not arrive till Tuesday last and set out again the next Day. He is expected next Saturday Evening.*

Yesterday arrived in this Town from Philadelphia Mr. *William Palfrey*, by whom we have the following important Intelligence.—

That late in the Night of Saturday the 25th of December last the Committee there was informed that their Tea Ship was at Anchor about 15 Miles from the City—That the next Morning the Committee appointed three of their Number to proceed to Chester, (where the Ship was) to prevail on the Captain to leave his Ship, come up to the Town himself, and settle the Matter with the Inhabitants, who would meet at 10 o'Clock on Monday—That the Gentlemen had but just left the Town, when Advice was received that the Ship had left Chester and was on her way to the City—That a very considerable Body immediately set off to prevent her coming up; and meeting with her about 4 Miles from the Town, brought her to Anchor, and conducted the Captain to the Coffee-Honse, where the Committee who were then sitting, obtained from him a solemn Promise not to Enter his Ship, until the Sentiments of the People could be known respecting her.—That on Monday there was a Meeting of the Town, which consisted of at least 5000, who collected in one Hour after Notice given—and that at this Meeting the following Resolves were passed.

RESOLVED, 1. *That the Tea on board Capt. Ayres shall not be landed.*

2. *That Captain Ayres shall neither enter nor report his Vessel at the Custom-House.*

3. *That Captain Ayres shall carry back the Tea immediately.*

4. *That he shall immediately send a Pilot on board his Vessel, with Orders to take Charge of her, and proceed with her to Reedy Island next high Water.*

5. *That he shall be allowed to stay in Town 'till To-Morrow, to provide Necessaries for his Voyage.*

6. *That he shall then be obliged to leave the Town and proceed to his Vessel, and make the best of his Way out of the River and Bay.*

7. *That Captain Heysham, Captain R. Whyte, Mr. Benjamin Loxley, Mr. Arthur Donaldson, be a Committee to see these Resolutions put in Execution.*

The Captain was then asked if he would conform himself to these Resolutions, he answered that he would.

The Assembly were then informed of the Spirit and Resolution of the People of New-York, and the Conduct of the People of Boston; whereupon it was unanimously Resolved,

8. *That this Assembly highly approve the Conduct and Spirit of the People of New York and Boston; and return their hearty Thanks to the People of Boston for their Resolution* in destroying the Tea, rather than suffering it to be landed.

One of the Consignees who came from London in the Ship, resigned without hesitation; the others who were resident there, had resigned before—We do not hear that the New-York Tea Ship had arriv'd; but we have the best assurance that Gov. Tryon will not obstruct the Resolution of the People there, that she shall be return'd with the Tea to London.—The united Spirit of the People of South Carolina, Philadelphia, New-York, this Province, &c. in opposing the subtle Design of the British Administration, to make the East India Company the Instruments in establishing the Revenue, and thus enslaving the Continent, forebodes a happy union of Councils among the several Colonies by means of their Committees of Correspondence.—The Tea Consignees in all the above places excepting this, chearfully resign'd their appointments rather than hold them to the Ruin of the common Liberty; by this their prudent Conduct, much of the East-India Company's Property is saved from destruction. *Our* Gentry, by their own obstinacy, supported by the Governor of the Province, the Commissioners of the Customs and others, reduced the people to the disagreeable Alternative, either of destroying a great part of that Property, or, of suffering it to be the sure means of destroying the Security of theirs. We have it on very good Authority, that *the Friends of Government*, as they are called, (that is the zealous Abettors of Ministerial Measures) in Philadelphia, New-York and Boston, *had engaged their Interest to carry this Measure thro', in America*: Gov. Tryon of New-York, and the Tea Consignees in the other Colonies, like wise Men, knew when to stop; Whether *our* Tea Consignees will be applauded for their Conduct by their Constituents, or whether this notable Instance of Zeal & Perseverance in Gov. Hutchinson will entitle him to the Thanks of the East India Company, or the Approbation of his Superiors, Time will 'ere long discover. The People in the respective Colonies seem generally to have determin'd their Judgment of the Actors in this Comic-Tragical Scene. The Conduct of TRYON is highly extolled, while that of HUTCHINSON is detested: And the Gentlemen to whom the Tea was Consigned in the other Colonies, are yet blessed with the Esteem of their Countrymen; while those of this Place, conscious that they have forfeited the Protection of their Fellow Citizens, have immured themselves in an Asylum for the reception of our inveterate Enemies.

It is reported that the Tea Consignees had better have had a Mill-Stone tied round their Necks, than suffer'd the Tea sav'd out of the Wreck of Capt. Loring to be landed at the Castle.

We hear from Gardinerston, in the County of Lincoln, that one Daniel M'Carthy, was lately committed to Goal for the supposed Murder of Josiah Parker; he is to have his Tryal at the Court of Assize to be held at Falmouth in July next.

MARRIED, by the Rev. Mr. Simeon Howard, Mr. Josiah Simpson, Cabinet-Maker, to Miss Betsey Potter.

The Trustees of the DUDLEIAN-Lecture have chosen the Rev. Mr. SAMUEL WEBSTER, of Salisbury, to preach the next Lecture on *The Validity of Presbyterian Ordination.*

Last Friday Evening died here, Mrs. Mary Whiting, Wife of Mr. Stephen Whiting, Æ. 55—Her Funeral will be To-Morrow Afternoon, half past 3 o'Clock, when it is hoped her Friends and Acquaintance will attend.

Saturday Morning departed this Life, the Rev. Mr. Thomas Balch of Dedham, in the 63d Year of his Age, and 38th Year of his Ministry.

His Funeral is to be on Thursday next.

Plymouth, 4 January 1774.

——"Perhaps you may think it odd that an Inhabitant of the Town of Plymouth should ask a Favor of a Bostonian after the Publication of so infamous a Protest as was sent down from here. But be it known, that a Recantation goes on as rapidly as did the cursed Original. Be it also known, that there is among the Signers thereof, one of the Name of L——, but he is not one of the Descendents of the Ancestors of Sir,

Your humble Servant, L——.

NEW FLOUR.

Choice new FLOUR to be sold cheap,
Enquire of JOHN CUSHING, at his Sugar-House, in Brattle-Street, near Doct. COOPER's Meeting-House.
Where also may be had as usual,
All Sorts of Refin'd Loaf and Brown SUGAR.

The Proprietors of Royalston, are hereby Notified to meet at the Dwelling House of Mr. Joshua Bracket, Innholder in Boston, on the Nineteenth Day of January current, at 5 o'Clock, P. M. to choose a Treasurer in Lieu of the Hon. *Thomas Hubbard*, Esq; deceas'd: And also to choose a Committee to settle the Proprietors Accounts, with the said Hubbard's Executors.

BENJA. KENT, Clerk.
Jan. 8, 1774. pro hac vice.

To be Sold on board the Brig Union, Sam. Williams Master, laying at South Side of Long Wharf,

Brandy in Pipes, a few Casks of excel-lent Muscovado Sugars, Redwood, choice Butter in Firkins, Hogs Fat, Barrel Beef, Flower, refin'd Iron, two packs Deer Skins, and three half Barrels of Honey, he will also take Freight for Salem.

WE the Subscribers, being appointed Commissioners by the Hon. Foster Hutchinson, Esq; Judge of Probate for the County of Suffolk, to receive and examine the Claims of the several Creditors to the Estate of Robert Jenkins, late of Boston, Merchant, deceased, represented insolvent, and six Months being allowed to receive said Claims, We do hereby Notify said Creditors, that we will attend upon said Business at the British Coffee-House in King-Street, from Six to Nine of the Clock, P. M. on the second Wednesday of this, and the five succeeding Months.

Boston, 8th January 1774.
Thomas Brown,
John Winniet,
Jacob Cooper.

TO BE SOLD,
250 Hogsheads Turks-Island SALT,
and about 60 Hogsheads St. Martin's Salt; a few Hogsheads Barbados Rum; Sugar per Barrel or smaller Quantity; Coffee by the 100 wt. or doz. Flour per Barrel, Eastern Peas per Bushell or smaller Quantity—Inquire of PETER CRAMMER, opposite the Sign of the Lamb, or of Capt. OAKS, at Wheeler's Point.

WANTED,
£.100 Lawful Money, for which good Security will be given—Enquire of Edes and Gill.

All Persons that have any Demands on the Estate of Capt. James Heath, late of Falmouth, deceas'd, are desired to bring in their Accounts to Enoch Ilsley and John Archer, Administrators on said Estate, and those Indebted to said Estate, are desired to make immediate Payment. *Falmouth Dec. 25, 1773.*

Was taken up in Charles's River, about a Month past, a small Moses Boat, about eleven Feet Keel. Whoever has lost the same, is desired to come to John Nutting of Charlestown, or to Charlestown Cryer. The Owner may have it again paying Charges.

A Woman with a good Breast of Milk, would take a Child to Suckle; for further Particulars inquire of the Printers.

TO BE SOLD
By Benjamin Church,
On THURSDAY next,
At THREE o'Clock in the Afternoon,
BY PUBLICK AUCTION,
A large Assortment of valuable Articles belonging to a Gentleman lately deceas'd. Consisting of

SUPERFINE midding and course Broad Cloths—Ratteens—Frizes—Half Thick—Kerseys—Shalloons—Calmancoes—Irish Linnens—Checks—Mens and Womens Hose—Velveretts—Handkerchiefs—Case Knives and Forks—Inkhorns—Penknives, &c. &c.—Sundry Articles of Household—Wearing Apparell—Watches, &c.&c. &c. Thursday next, 3 o'Clock P. M.

CHOICE MADDER, *the Produce of this Province*, to be Sold by JOHN BARRETT, at the Mill-Bridge, Boston.

For CASH, at the new Store, next Mr. Bracket's Tavern, Braintree——A fresh Assortment of Woolens, such as low-priz'd Cloths, Beavers, Ratteens, &c. just imported; and a variety of English Goods, all at the Boston Price.—Sugars at prime Cost, Groceries, &c.
N. B. Short Credit upon good Recommendation.

All Persons having Demands on the Estate of *John Mico Wendell*, late of Boston, Merchant, deceas'd, are desired to bring in their Accounts, in Order to settle, and those Persons Indebted, are desired to pay the same to *Katharine Wendell*, Administratrix.

Boston, January 6, 1774.

TO BE SOLD (or Exchanged for a Horse)
A black Mare about 7 Years old, very Gentle, and Trots well in a Chaise: Inquire at Mr. Macky's House in North School-Street, next the Rev. Doctor Byles's.

TO BE SOLD by PUBLIC AUCTION,
On WEDNESDAY the 12th Instant at Eleven o'Clock in the Forenoon.

A Quantity of West-India FISH,
now lying in a Store on Gray's Wharf.

N. B. The Fish may be seen any Time before the Sale, by applying to Mr. John Brewer, Block-Maker, on said Wharf.

At GOULD'*s Auction Office,*
In Back Street,
ON FRIDAY NEXT,
At TEN o'Clock in the Morning,
Will be Sold by PUBLIC VENDUE,
A large Assortment of English Goods,
as usual. R. GOULD, Auctioneer.

On Thursday next, at Ten o'Clock,
will be sold by Public Vendue, at the New Auction-Room South Side of the Town-House,

HOUSE Furniture, consisting of Mehogany Chest on Chest of Draws, Desks, round and square Dining and Spring Tables, Bureau ditto, Tea Trays, Black-walnut Chest of Draws and Tables, green Harrateen Curtains, easy Chairs, Feather Beds and Bedsteads, Glass Pictures, a pull up Clock. Also, Broad Cloths, Ratteens, Bearskins, Irish Linens, Jersey-knit Stockings, mill'd Caps, and a Number of other Articles.

A. OLIVER, Auctioneer.

For Private Sale,
At the NEW AUCTION ROOM, South Side of the Town House, viz.

HAndsome mahogany desks and book cases, chest on chest of draws, dining and spring tables, beaureau tables, mehogany hair and leather bottom chairs, straw bottom do. several handsome eight day clocks, silver and pinchbeck watches, chamber tables, harrateen curtains, feather beds and bedsteads, handsome sconce and other looking glasses, small dressing ditto. Also, blue, orange, lead, grey and cloth colour'd broad cloths; cotton velvets, shalloons tammies, ruffs of all colours, drab and mixt duffils, copper and mixt frizes, calamancoes, capuchin silks of all colours, buckskin breeches, men's silk and worsted hose, white baize, black handkerchiefs, black sattin and chip hats, silk gauze, black gauze handkerchiefs, black, blue, white and pink sarsnets. A small box of well assorted ribbons the newest fashion; Scotch carpets, superfine bottom hole twist, camp and basket buttons, blue frized cotton, glass pictures. A small quantity of choice Rhubarb, &c. A few Boxes of choice Lisbon LEMMONS, a Hogshead of choice Jamaica Spirits, 2 Cases of Doctor's Instruments.

At said Auction-Room constant attendance is given to receive all kinds of Goods for Public and Private Sale.

CUSTOM-HOUSE, *BOSTON.*
ENTERED IN.

Miller & Bangs, New-London; Bracket, Smith and Ross, Maryland; Hinckley, Philadelphia; Williams, New-York; Bradford, St. Martins; McLeod, Essequibo and Anguilla; Farrey, Cape-Nichola; Coulthard, Turks-Island; Loring, London; and Little, Falmouth.

Burials in the Town of BOSTON, since our last.
Nine Whites. No Blacks.
Baptiz'd in the several Churches, Eight.

High Water at BOSTON, *for the present Week.*

Monday, 50 min. aft. 9	Friday, 0 min. after 1
Tuesday, 51 min. aft. 10	Saturday, 51 min. af. 1
Wednesday, 55 m. aft. 11	Lord's-Day, 38 m. aft. 2
Thursday, 0 min. aft. 12	D's New 12 D. 4 M 10

This Day Published, Price 1s. 4d.

MILLS and HICKS's

BRITISH and AMERICAN

REGISTER,

With an ALMANACK for the present Year. Calculated for the Use of ALL the NEW-ENGLAND Governments.

And to be Sold at the Printing-Office in School-Street.

Brandy and Geneva.

A few Casks Old Brandy, and a few Cases Geneva to be Sold by CHARLES MILLER, at his Store in King-Street.

ALSO,

Superfine and common Philadelphia Flour,	Small Green Coffee, by large or small quantities,
Barr Iron,	A few Bales excellent Cotton,
Lisbon Wine,	Philadelphia Furkin Butter.
Lisbon Lemmons,	CHEAP FOR CASH.
Jamaica Spirits, &c. &c.	

To be Sold by *Jonathan Williams*, At Store No. 8, South Side Town Dock, Superfine and common Philadelphia Flour, Barr Iron, Cotton per Bag, Coffee, Cocoa, and Lisbon Salt, also a fine new SNOW of about 152 Tons Burthen, 11 Months old, with all her Appurtenances, as she now lies in said Town Dock.

Charles Sigourney

HAS just IMPORTED in Capt. Coulson, from BRISTOL, an additional Supply of Hard Ware

GOODS

of all Sorts, which will be Sold at his usual low Prices, at his Shop just above the Market. Also, Dutch Brushes in setts, Holland Scates, Looking Glasses, best English double refin'd Loaf Sugar, Brimstone, Copperas, &c. &c.

A few Crates of well assorted Earthen WARE, each Crate an Assortment for a Shop, the best of German Steel, and Brimstone, to be sold cheap for the Cash. Inquire of the Printers.

TO BE SOLD

A convenient BRICK-HOUSE, in good Repair, situate in Cold-Lane, accommodated with a retired Back Yard, and a Well of Water that never fails. Inquire of the Printers.

LIGNUMVITÆ.

A LARGE Quantity of LIGNUMVITÆ, of different sizes, uncommon straight and sound; to be sold Cheap for Cash, or Barter for any Merchandize that may offer & suit the Owner. Inquire of the Printers.

To be Sold by public Vendue, by Order of Court, by *Samuel Whitney* and *John Buttrick*, Administrators on the Estate of *John Homer*, late of Winchendon, deceased, on February 15, 1774, at One o'Clock Afternoon, at Levi Nichols's, Innholder in Winchendon aforesaid,——THE Real Estate of said *Homer*, consisting of a good Farm, containing 120 Acres, with a good House and Barn, with good Mowing, Ploughing and Pasturing, with a young Orchard. The whole of said Farm, or two Thirds, may be sold, as will best suit, saving to the Widow the Improvement of her Thirds during her Life.

Concord, Dec. 17, 1773. *Samuel Whitney*, *John Buttrick*, } Administrators on said Estate.

N. B. The above Farm lays upon the Great Road to No. 4, and within 80 Rods of the Meeting-House.

Just Published, (Price 11s. L. M. well Bound) and TO BE SOLD

By James Foster Condy,

At his BOOK-STORE in Union-Street, directly opposite the Cornfields, Boston,

AN Abridgement of Burn's Justice of the Peace, and Parish Officer: To which is added,

An APPENDIX, containing some general Rules and Directions, necessary to be known and observed by all Justices of the Peace.

Also to be sold at said Store (very reasonably) the following Books printed in America, viz.

Blackstone's Commentaries, 5 Vol. 4to.

Robertson's History of Charles 5th, 3 Vols. 8vo.

Hutchinson's History, 3 Vols. 8vo.

Palladium of Conscience, 4to.

Evans's Poems, 8vo. Vicar of Wakefield, 12mo.

Dissenting Gentleman's Answer to Mr. White's three Letters, 12mo.

PAMPHLETS.

Poem, Entitled the Grave.

Doddridge's Family Religion.

Smith's Essay on Universal Redemption.

Recovery from Sickness — Rush on Mineral Waters.

Critical Commentaries against Bishops.

Sermons to Doctors in Divinity.

(Lord Sommers) On Nations and King's.

Death) A Poetical Essay.

Letters from Yorrick to Eliza— Sermons to Asses.

History of Bellisarius, &c. &c. &c.

At said Store may be had, the most modern and esteemed Books, in every Branch of polite Literature, Arts and Sciences, (Catalogues may be had at said Store) at such Prices as will fully satisfy the Purchaser.

THE Subscriber having compleated a very large and extensive Survey of the New Ceded Countries to the Southward, which long wanted Discovery he has attained, at a vast Expence and bodily Fatigue, and now offers to the Public.

The Navigation through the Gulph Stream, over the Bahama Bank and in the Gulph of Mexico, is more particularly laid down therein than was ever done before, or than any Map Compiler has ever had an Opportunity to do. And as every Trader from North America, especially the Merchants who trade to Jamaica, Hispaniola, and to the two Floridas, are more particularly interested in this necessary Work, he addresses himself more immediately to them; and begs Leave to direct them to his printed Proposals, which have been put up & distributed through this Town.

He has come here to procure if possible, the Assistance of some Gentlemen (Lovers and Encouragers of American Literature) towards the Publication of this Work. He has for these eight Years past done it at his own Cost, but being now very near the Close of it, he finds the Expence to outrun his Expectation, and therefore thus throws himself on the generous Public.—New-York, Philadelphia and South-Carolina have given him Encouragement; he hopes therefore Boston will not withold her helping Hand.

A great Part of the Work is already printed, for that Reason he presumes the ordinary Thought of its falling through will not so much as be suspected, especially as our most esteemed Societies have thought it worthy of recommendation as beneficial to Mankind.

There is added to the Maps a Book of 500 Pages, in octavo, which will, no doubt, amuse the studious and learned, especially such as are Enquirers into the Wonders of the three Kingdoms of Nature, Botany more particularly; the inland Country is very minutely described, and the Maps will explain even the Land laid out on the river Missisippi; plain and ample directions to Navigators will likewise be given, and extensive Soundings on the Coast, pointed out, so as to render the Whole as desirable for the Sage in his Cabinet as for the Mariner in his Ship.

The elegance of the Map added to its large Size, of twelve Feet by seven, will likewise render it an ornamental Piece of Furniture.

In this exceeding difficult and dangerous Navigation are a great many watering Places not hitherto known, which will be described and directed to, and by which Means it is hoped many a poor distressed Crew will be saved from Ruin, even when they perhaps despair of Life.

His Stay will be short in Boston, therefore he begs the Well-wishers of American Science and Navigation to give their Names soon, in order that he may return to the compleating of the Work with redoubled Ardour.

About July, 1774, it is thought the Work will be compleated, and the Public may rest assured, that the Favours will be amply recompensed not only by this Work, but by one of much more extensive Nature, which he has now in Contemplation, he having devoted his Life to Pursuits of this Kind.

⁂ He may be heard of at Mess. Cox and Berry's; Mr. Knox's, Mr. Joshua Brackett's, Mr. Joseph Ingersoll's, and the Printers of this Paper. B. ROMANS.

Staffordshire, Nottingham and Bristol WARE.

William Porter,

ACQUAINTS his Friends and the Public in general, That he has imported in the last Ship from Bristol—A large and general Assortment of cream-coloured, enamell'd, black, white and brown Stone, Glass and Flint Ware, too many to be enumerated in an Advertisement, which are now open for Sale at his Shop lately opened, a little to the Southward of LIBERTY-TREE, *Boston*, either by the Crate, Groce, Dozen or single Article, as cheap as can be bought at any Shop or Store in the Province.

Likewise equally as cheap—A general Assortment of Groceries and West-India Goods.——Town and Country Traders are invited to call and see how extremely low they may be supply'd.

TO BE SOLD,

A Brigantine about 100 Tons, a Sloop about 92 Tons, and a Sloop about 84 Tons, built in Boston of the best white Oak. Inquire of the Printers.

A Woman with a choice young Breast of Milk, would be glad to go into a Gentleman's Family to Suckle. Inquire of Edes and Gill.

All Persons indebted to the Estate of Capt. John Hayward, late of Braintree, deceased, are desired without delay, to pay the same to David Person Hayward, or Ebenezer Hayward, of Braintree, Administrators on said Estate: And all Persons that have any Demands on said Estate, are desired to bring in their Accounts to said Administrators, in order for a speedy Settlement.

To be Sold cheap for Cash, by

Cyrus Baldwin,

At his Shop in Cornhill, near the Town House, *Boston*,

Choice Bohea and Souchong Teas, best Hyson ditto, at 18s. L. M. per Pound, Narraganset CHEESE.

Cinnamon, Cloves, Mace, Nutmegs, Pepper, Allspice, Kippen's Snuff and Indigo.

A Parcel of Parchment Deerskins.

Also—A general Assortment of English, India and Scotch Goods, suitable for all Seasons of the Year.

Wanted at the same Place, a Quantity of good large Lynn Shoes.

N. B. The above Teas were imported before the East India Company's Tea arrived, or it was known that they would send any here on their own Account.

All Persons having any Demands against the Estate of Margaret Vintendin, late of Boston, in the County of Suffolk, but last of Waltham in the County of Middlesex, Widow, deceased, are desired to bring in the same to Jolley Allen, of Boston, Merchant, Executor of the last Will of said Deceased; and any Person indebted to said Estate are desired to make speedy Payment to said Allen, Executor as aforesaid.

WANTED TO BUY,

A HORSE or MARE, from 14 to 16 Hands high, and between 4 and 8 Years old, Colour not much minded, must be a good Dealer, well broke in, quite gentiele, if used to the Road the better, and if clear of the Amble the more agreeable.—— Apply to the Printers, with whom leave your Name, and Place of Abode.

TO BE SOLD

A Quantity of Barrel Beef, Pitch, Tarr and Turpentine, and a few Barrels of excellent Pickle Mackrel, also a Schooner about 50 Tons, almost new, to lett, Inquire of Nathaniel Waterman, near the South Battery.

M. LEE,

REMOVED from Cornhill to a Shop opposite Mr. *William Scott's* Irish-Linnen Store in Ann-Street,) Acquaints the Ladies she has lately imported,

A Variety of Mercery and Millenery GOODS, amongst which are a beautiful Assortment of Brocades, flower'd & plain Lutestrings, Gorgoroons, and Taffaties, black Padusoys and Armozeens, exceeding Cheap,

New Fashion Cloaks and Bonnets, London made,	A large Variety of trolly, blond & bone Laces,
White, Grey, Leylock, Sky, Pink, Crimson, Black & Fancy } Figured Modes & Sattins of the newest Patterns	Edgings; Lawns, and Cambricks,
	Silk Mitts and Gloves,
	Callicoes and Chinces,
	Schineal and Teste black Hair-Pins,
	Paste Sprigs and Pins,
	Silk Handkerchiefs,
Yard & ell-wide Mull Mull, Jaconott, book & sprig'd Muslins,	Stomachers,
	White, blue and black Feathers, some very handsome,
Yard and ell-wide flower'd and plain Gauzes,	Childrens Morocco Shoes and Pumps,
Catguts, Queens Nett, Parrisnett,	Skeleton and Cap Wire,
A few suits of Blond Linen,	Brocaded Clogs,
Rich Muffs, Tippets and Ermine,	Court Plaister,
Tambour work'd Aprons and Ruffles,	Floss Turbin Lappets,
Brussels & Mecklin Laces,	Italian Flowers,
	Chevaudefrize, and Snail Trimmings,

A Quantity of Ribbons, and many other Articles in the Millenery and Mercery Way. ALSO, Blue & white China Bowls, Cups & Saucers.

To the Honorable SAMUEL DANFORTH, Esq; one of his Majesty's Justices of the Peace throughout the Province of the Massachusetts-Bay.

WE the Subscribers, some of the Proprietors of a Township of Land called Silvester-Canada, of the Contents of seven Miles square, lying on a River called Androscoggin River, and adjoining to Baker's Town, so called, in the County of Cumberland, the Plan of which, was confirmed to the Proprietors thereof by the General Court of said Province in June 1768, humbly request your Honor to issue a Warrant for calling a Meeting of said Proprietors, to be held at the Dwelling-House of Cornelius Turner, Innholder in Hanover, in the County of Plymouth, on Tuesday, the ninth Day of February next, at Ten o'Clock, in the Forenoon, then and there to act on the following Articles.

1. To choose a Moderator, Clerk, Treasurer and Collector of Taxes.

2. To confirm any or all former Votes and Grants of said Proprietors at any former Meeting or Meetings, as they shall see fit.

3. To raise a sufficient Sum or Sums of Money by Tax or otherwise, for discharging their Debts due or that may become due.

4. To choose a Standing Committee to transact the Affairs of said Proprietors, settle the Accounts, adjust the Debts that are or shall be due from the said Proprietors, and order Payment of the same, and agreeable to Law to make Sale of those Proprietors Land who are delinquent in paying their Taxes; and to determine where the Settling Lots shall be laid, and how much in a Lot, and about convenient Ways, and procure a Plan thereof, to be lodged with the Clerk as soon as may be.

5. To agree what shall be allowed the Clerk and Committee for their Service.

6. To choose a Committee for calling Meetings, for the future, and to agree on the Method thereof.

7. To appoint an Agent or Agents, Attorney or Attornies, with Power or Substitution, to commence an Action or Actions for said Proprietors, and in their Names to prosecute the same in any Court of Law, or otherwise amply, to all Intents and Purposes, until final Judgment and Execution, and in like manner to defend them in all Actions brought or that may be brought against them.

8. And to agree on any other Thing which said Proprietors shall judge necessary for carrying forward the Settlement of said Township.

Scituate, November 23d, 1773.

John Cushing,
Charles Turner
Wm. Sever
Ja's Warren
David Little, jun.

Province of the Massachusetts-Bay.

To *Charles Turner*, of *Scituate*, in the County of *Plimouth*, in said Province, Gentlemen, one of said Proprietors.

(Seal) In pursuance of the foregoing Application and Request, you are hereby required to give Notice (in Time and Manner as the Law directs) to the said Proprietors, That a Meeting of said Proprietors is to be holden at the Time and Place, and for the Purposes mentioned in the afore-written Petition.

Given under my Hand and Seal, this 22d Day of December, A. D. 1773. S. DANFORTH, Justice of the Peace throughout the Province aforesaid. Scituate, December 23d, 1773.

BY Virtue of the afore-written Warrant, to me directed, I do hereby notify and warn the Proprietors of the aforesaid Lands to meet at the Dwelling-House of Cornelius Turner, Innholder in Hanover, on Tuesday, the Ninth Day of February next, at Ten o'Clock in the Forenoon, for the Purposes therein mentioned. CHARLES TURNER.

Boston: Printed, by EDES & GILL.

No. 98

THE Boston-Gazette, AND COUNTRY JOURNAL.

Containing the freshest Advices, Foreign and Domestic.

MONDAY, January 17, 1774.

NEDHAM's REMEMB'RANCER, N° V.

Meet it is, I here set down,
That one may *smile*, & *smile*, and be A VILLAIN:
——And with this visage sugar o'er
THE DEVIL HIMSELF. SHAKESPEARE.

SUBTERFUGE and evasion are the true characteristics of a *little* mind;—and so are falshood and cowardice. Such artifices are but temporary expedients which great souls scorn to use: like base coin they may pass currently with the ignorant and incautious for a short time, but the cheat is soon discovered; and the impostor is punished and remains infamous for life. Thus he who practices the low arts of political cunning will in the end be detected and sink into contempt, unless his crimes and his station consign him to an *exemplary* punishment and everlasting infamy.

His excellency, in his message to the house of representatives of the 9th of June, affirms that "there is *not one passage* in them (his letters then lying on the speaker's table) which was ever *intended to respect* the particular *constitution of this government* as derived from the charter."

If his excellency had in contemplation the alteration of our form of government, and committed his sentiments to writing with a view to their being used in derogation of our liberties or annihilation of our charter; I should not be surprized to find *an ambiguity of expression with a plainess of meaning*: he would be too explicit for *his confident* to misunderstand his design, yet would retain a *characteristic* phraseology, which might stand him in stead in case his plan did not take, or his correspondent did not *keep the secret*. *

But the most wary knaves, when they enter into deep plots and perplex themselves with many plans, have their conduct attended with certain circumstances which seldom or ever fail to betray their guilt. And even where they have the exquisite caution to use an *intermediate instrument* for the purpose of self-concealment, the connexion between the *master-workman* and *the tool* is commonly discovered, by some *unlucky* accident which subtlety did not provide against.

But to return to his excellency, for whom I am in pain. He explicitly declares to his correspondent, that "there MUST BE an abridgment of what are called ENGLISH *liberties*."

Now I know of no liberties, emphatically called *English*, but what are as dear, if not more so, than any derived from our charter. Hence I suppose his excellency would not thank any one for *an endeavour to save his veracity*, by suggesting that he designed an excision of those liberties, which are peculiar to us as *Englishmen*, and not the abridgment of those that are recognized by *our provincial charter*. This would be to wreck him on Charybdis in order to deliver him from Sylla.—But, alas! what other subterfuge remains? Neither his excellency or his friends will say, that he did not "*intend to respect*" those subjects to which his reasonings were applied; and to which his words and the whole scope of his correspondence had a direct and plain tendency. Till, therefore, the above expedient—(poor indeed)—is adopted, or his excellency can show "*an abridgment* of what are called *English liberties*" which does *not* "*respect* the particular *constitution of this government* as derived from charter," he must *stand self-recorded* not only odiously wicked, but despicably mean.—Was not the dye of conspiracy against a whole people sufficiently deep, without adding the stain of falshood to the hateful hue?

But in order to determine the truth and sincerity of the preceeding message to the house, let us proceed with our considerations.

In the letter of the 20th of January 1769, Mr. Hutchinson says to his correspondent, that *it is most certain that marks* of PARLIAMENTARY *resentment will be placed somewhere*, and affirms that IT OUGHT TO BE *on the* PROVINCE IN GENERAL *or particular persons*. Now I have no doubt that if this resentment had extended to THE TAKING OFF those *particular persons* (which made his brother Oliver more explicitly pointed out) it had gratified the sanguine appetite of his excellency. But when the writer talks of *parliamentary resentment to the province in general* (and this after so much resentment had been shown as to send troops) I have no doubt, that he had "*respect*" to the "charter of this government," and that he had a more immediate reference to it's annihilation or *abridgment*, by an express act of parliament to that purpose. I am satisfied this was meant, because he soon after proceeds, "but if no measures (that is of parliament) shall have been taken to secure this *dependance*, (of this colony) or NOTHING MORE than some DECLARATORY acts or resolves, *it is all over with us*." And I am still more confirmed in this opinion, because with his peculiar hypocrisy he in the same letter soon after adds, "I never think of the measures *necessary* for the peace and good order of the colonies without pain:"—and then subjoins with his characteristic grace, "I wish the good of THE COLONY when I wish to see SOME FARTHER RESTRAINT OF LIBERTY, rather than the connexion with the parent-state should be broken." Now I should be glad to know what parliamentary measures could be taken *to secure our dependance* as a province without injury to our charter? I should be equally glad to be informed what additional *restraint of liberty* would prevent the breach of the before-mentioned connexion; or rather what *new restraint* would not dissolve it? And what *farther restraint of our liberties* could be effected, and especially by a parliamentary interposition, that would not capitally "*respect our constitution of government*," and destroy our "charter"?—Surely his excellency's *genius* failed him when he penned his message.

But I have not done with the matter yet. The manner in which his excellency and his advocates have endeavoured to *illude* the imputation of a design to subvert our constitution, shows that the guilt of the attempt is apparent. I have in a former number sufficiently intimated, that union of conduct and criminality which took place with the clan of our public enemies. I shall now take occasion to give one specimen (among many) which evinces the justness of my opinion.

It is worthy of notice, that there appears but 24 days difference in the date of the preceeding letter of Mr. Hutchinson, and one from his brother Oliver, which contains a most PREMEDITATED PLAN TO ALTER OUR CONSTITUTION AND ANNIHILATE THE CHARTER. It is far from being certain, that even that time intervened between the periods of the writing those letters: but be that as it may, whoever attends to the purport and expressions of both of them will have little doubt, that they were wrote in close concert, by parties who imbibed each others sentiments by an intimate communion upon the subject, if in fact they were not wrote by the same hand.

Mr. Hutchinson begins his letter to Mr. Whately with an acknowledgment of "very great obligations by a full and clear *account of proceedings in parliament*;" and Mr. Oliver informs the same gentleman that "the lieutenant governor (H.) had communicated to him the letter (of Mr. Whately) containing *an account of the debates in parliament*." Hutchinson "*expects* to be in suspence for three or four weeks, and then to hear "our *fate*," and Oliver "soon *expects* their *decision*, on American affairs."

Mr. Oliver writes "I have very lately had occasion to know, that be the *determination* of "*parliament* what it will, it is the determination "of some to agree to no terms that shall *remove* "*us from* OUR OLD FOUNDATION." Here is a plain intimation that it was then a matter of consideration with the members of that august body to *alter the foundation of this government*; and here is a key to what his colleague Mr. Hutchinson means by "marks of resentment the *parliament* will show to the *province in general*," and confirms my preceeding observation that he intended his "abridgment of English liberties" through the instrumentality of king, lords & commons.

Mr. Oliver directly after mentioning the above resolution to stand on the *old foundation*, immediately adds, "this confirms me in opinion, that if there be *no way* to TAKE OFF the original incendiaries, they will continue to instill their poison into the minds of the people." And his brother (Hutchinson) in league with him against the *community* and *individuals*, gives his sanction as we have before noticed, that *marks of resentment* OUGHT TO BE on the province in general or PARTICULAR PERSONS. The one adhering to his old *cunning*, is not explicit who those *particular persons are*, but from the words of the other, we may easily collect, they were those who wisely *determined not to be removed from their old foundation*.

His Excellency after expressing his "doubt whether it is *possible* to *project* a system of government in which a colony 3000 miles distant from "the parent state shall enjoy all the liberty of the "parent state," adds I am certain *I have seen no* "*such projection*." Now let the reader judge, where the mighty difficulty, nay *impossibility* of such a project for the government of a Colony, without a diminution of the liberties enjoyed by the mother-country, was not sent forward in order to make way for the favorable reception of a *joint projection* of this kind, which in a few days was to be forwarded under the signature of Andrew Oliver. A project which to be sure most notably *abridg'd* those *English* liberties enjoyed by the parent state; and which *an Englishman* needed some preparation in order to receive without horror, and which he never could read without cursing the projector. The plan transmitted, treated deliberately of proposed "alterations in the charters of the Colonies," and what is called "a reform of them."

Hutchinson begs "*pardon for his excursion*," and Oliver *apologizes* for what he affects to call "his *reveries*";—in which there is kept up that similarity of expression and sentiment which runs thro' both the letters; and so characteristically marks them, that few will doubt, they were the work of the same hand; and none will hesitate to pronounce them the *joint project* of two public conspirators against the rights and liberties, the happiness and peace of their native country.

MARCHMONT NEDHAM.

[*To be continued*.]

* See his Letter, 20 October 1769.

AT a legal Meeting of the Freeholders and Inhabitants of the Town of MEDWAY, *on the 27th of* December, 1773.

THE Town being well informed, That the East-India Company, in England, are by virtue and approbation of an Act of the British Parliament exporting their Teas to America, subject to Duties payable on its being landed, for the express Purpose of raising a Revenue in America, for the Support of Civil Government, &c. Therefore in Order to prevent the many Evils consequent upon the Success of this alarming and stubtle Attempt of Inslaving of us; the Town upon due Deliberation unanimously came into the following Resolves, viz.

1. That the Act of the British Parliament imposing a Duty on Tea payable in America, for the express Purpose of raising a Revenue, is in our Opinion, not only Unconstitutional, but its Consequences tends directly to involve us in Slavery, and therefore is an unreasonable and grievous Burden.

2. That the late Measures of the East-India Company in sending to these Colonies their Tea loaded with a Duty for raising a Revenue from America, as well as all those Employed by them, speak out their Intentions to involve and ruin us, and therefore deserve to be called and treated no better than Enemies to America, and are intitled to our highest Contempt, and every signal mark of Resentment.

3. That there is nothing in the Votes and Proceedings of the Town of Boston, at their several late legal Meetings on this alarming Occasion, but what we apprehend is Constitutional and Rational, yea, truly Generous and Just, and therefore the noble Inhabitants thereof, are highly honour'd and respected by this Town, for their great firmness in Support of, and earnest and expensive Contending for the general Liberty of America.

4. That we are willing on all proper Occasions, in Conjunction with our oppressed American Brethren, to exert ourselves according to our Ability and opportunity, in the Support and Defence of our Constitutional Rights, Liberties and Privileges, and that we will Vigorously oppose, and if possible, frustrate the present, and ever,

other Design, that shall appear to us to be subversive of the Constitutional Rights and Liberties of America.

5. That if any Head of a Family in this Town shall buy any Tea or Permit any to be used and Consumed in his Family while subject to Duties, for the Purposes and payable as aforesaid, ought to be viewed as an Enemy to the Country, and will be treated with Disrespect, by this Town.

6. That the Select Men of this Town for the Time being are directed and desired to withold and forbare their approbation for Innholders and Retailers of strong Liquors in this Town, from all such Persons that shall buy, use and consume any Tea in their Houses, while subject to Duties for the Purposes and payable as aforesaid.

7. That the Committee of Correspondence of this Town be favoured with an Attested Copy from the Town-Clerk, of this Day's Resolves, and that they be directed to forward the same to the Committee of Correspondence at Boston. True Copy,

Attest, ELIJAH CLARK, Town Clerk.

Messieurs EDES & GILL,

IT is proper that the whole American publick should be made acquainted with the circumstances attending the East-India Company's Tea, ship'd on board Capt. Loring's vessel, which was cast on shore on Cape Cod; and the the situation the tea is now in. The vessel belonged to *Richard Clarke* and sons, three of the consignees. Soon after they had heard that she was wrecked, one of the sons went down to the Cape to take care of the cargo. There he procured two Vessels to bring up the cargo, exclusive of the tea, but no one cared to be concern'd in receiving the detested article, till a Salem fishingSchooner arriv'd, the skipper of which, one COOK, was prevail'd upon by young *Clarke* to bring it toCastle William, which is situate on an Island a league from this town. The schooner laid several days under the protection of the Castle before the tea was landed. It now lies, as we are told, in the barracks. Whether it was landed by order of the Governor or of Col. Lasley, it was undoubtedly done *at the request* of the Consignees. They had petition'd the Governor and Council before either of the tea ships arriv'd, praying that "measures might be directed to for the *landing* and securing the teas until they could be at liberty openly and safely to dispose of the same, or until they could receive directions from their constituents". But this petition was rejected by the Council: they wisely observing upon it, that "the duty on the tea would become payable & must be paid or secured to be paid *on its being landed*; and should they direct or advise to any measure for landing it, they would of course advise to a measure for procuring the payment of the duty, and therefore be advising to a measure inconsistent with the declared sentiments of both houses in the last Winter session of the General Court, which they apprehended to be altogether inexpedient and improper".—It is given out by some of the relations of theConsignees, that after the vessel was wreck'd, the dutied article became the sole charge of the Custom-house officers, and they had nothing to do with it. If so, why did they not leave it to the care of those officers, at the Cape? Why did young *Clarke* take so much pains to provide a vessel to bring up the tea *in particular*; unless it was, that agreable to their original design, it might "be landed and secured at the Castle until they could be at liberty openly and safely to dispose of the same"? It was their own act; the officers of the Customs did not concern themselves in the tea while it was at Cape Cod. Young *Clarke*, no doubt by the joint direction of theConsignees, procured its freight. It appears by all their conduct, that having themselves design'd and effected its landing, they would now, by a piece of low cunning, shift the odium of it on the Custom-house officers; and one of those officers, who has heretofore fled from the displeasure of *his own* countrymen, in a distant part of this province, it is said, is so simple as to be willing to bear the odium and take the risque of it. The Consignees, by this last act, have, in the general opinion, *filled up the measure*, &c. The same watchfulness will be kept upon this tea, as was formerly on the accursed stamped papers, which were also lodg'd in the Castle; both being sent here with the same design. The obstinacy of *our* consignees has exceeded that of the STAMP-MASTERS; for they resigned their appointments, which the others did not do, but have resisted the solicitations of their countrymen to the very last. The *Stamp-Masters* by their resignation, made some atonement for their wickedness in suffering themselves to be made the instruments of carrying into effect a former parliamentary revenue act, for the sake of filthy lucre; and they have since lived quietly tho' neglected: But what power have these men left to themselves to make the least atonement to their injured country, for the indefatigable pains they have taken, with the same avaricious motives effectually to aid a corrupt and abandon'd administration, in carrying into effect a measure, equally unconstitutional, unjust and destructive, and therefore qually odious and abhorrent to a wise, spirited and free people.

R. S.

To Mr. HUTCHINSON.

TO commend Virtue, and to detest and oppose Vice, is the Perogative of every human Being, as thereby the Happiness of Society may be advanced; by the former in exciting to a Continuance and increase of it, and by the latter often in its restraint in some Degree at least: Suffer me then, Sir, to make a few Observations, refering them to you and others for a particular Application.

When the chief Magistrate administers his high Office for the Happiness of Society for which he was instituted by the Laws of God and Man, he justly has not only these Laws, but the highest Esteem and Regard of his Fellow-Men for his Security: On the contrary, when he prostitutes it to selfish Views, to accomplish which he becomes the Tool of wicked Men to enslave a People, he justly exposes himself to the Reproach of Mankind, is obnoxious to the Laws of God, and to those of Man were they not unrighteously executed, and therefore to be detested and opposed as having no Authority but the Submission of the People, which would be degrading themselves below the Brute Creation. Absolute and unlimited Submission is to be expected & required from them whose Nature is adapted only for that purpose: But mankind were design'd for an exalted and extensive Sphere; endow'd with an inestimable Variety of natural Rights, to enter into Society, all the Laws of which arise from Freedom of Choice and Determination, and under the Direction of the distinguishing Characteristick of their Nature, Reason and Understanding; the Result of which is to submit only to the Laws consented to for the Security of these natural Rights, and for the Happiness of Society which depends upon them. So that a proper Sense of the Dignity and Felicity of human Nature must excite Men when deprived of any of them, especially so essential a one as their Property, to appeal to the Laws of God & Nature, upon which those Laws were grafted that are executing for the Means of Slavery and Misery, when they were design'd to make Men free, and consequently happy, and not suffer such an infamous Tool to live: The Reverse of this is not Humanity, its the highest Act of Injustice to themselves and Posterity, as well as offensive to that Being who gave them Powers and Faculties to know and enjoy the Rights granted to them, for which they can rejoice in Existence as a Privilege, and which he has made it their Duty to support and defend, and to recover when wrested from them. Therefore such an unfaithful & unrighteous Magistrate cannot be treated with Severity equal to his Deserts; and it must be the Wish of all good Men, that if his own Reflections have not proved like a faithful Glass to give him back his own Image, thereby reducing him to such Distraction as *really to cut his own Throat*, that any one of the injured Community would do it for him, or that *some Shot* that should not prove Random, might take from the World (if God should not immediately in his ordinary Providence) such a Traitor and Rebel to the Laws of God and Man. Nor is it unreasonable to expect this might be the Case, for Man is often the Instrument in executing the Purposes of Heaven for the Punishment of Man.

Whether you Sir, are the amiable or abandon'd Character described, I leave to your own Conscience and Ninety-nine in a Hundred of the good People of this Province to determine.

In either Character that may be justly attributed to you, I hope you will experience the just Reward.

Milton, January 1774. FELTON.

Messieurs EDES & GILL,

Please to give the following a Place in your next.

NEVER since the first Settlement of this Country did there prevail so universal an Union in Sentiment as at this Time amongst its Inhabitants; and ill befall the Man who attempts to break it; they seem determined to oppose every attempt to tax us without our Consent; this general Resolution, like a Family Resemblance, proves our Descent from the same Stock; but as in Families there are distinguishing Features peculiar to each Individual, so amongst us, at this trying Time, there are different Opinions about the Mode of opposing. Some think putting a Stop to the Sale of dutied Tea sufficient; many think it necessary to put a Stop to the Sale and Use of all India Tea; aiming at the same Point, we will not quarrel about the Means of effecting our Purpose? Many Towns in this Province have determined to drop the Use of all India Tea: The Towns of Lexington and Charlestown have proceeded a Step further; they have, according to the True Whig in the last Evening-Post, burnt the Tea they had on Hand. This, after a sneering Remark, on the mighty Quantity each of these Towns have sacrificed, to what they undoubtedly think the general Good, is by him called a very ill-judged and ridiculous Scheme.—I beg Leave to set this Matter in a true Light. The Dealers in Tea of that Town, at a general Meeting, determined to destroy the Tea they had by them, and bear the Loss equally amongst themselves. The Town at a very full Meeting a few Days after, generously voted to pay for whatever might be destroyed, and that those Inhabitants who were not Dealers in Tea, and chose not to have their Tea lay dead by them, might have an Opportunity of disposing of it, a Committee was appointed to collect all the Tea from all the Inhabitants; no Compulsion was used; the Town-Cryer went about; those who had a Mind to part with their Tea, knew where to carry it, and be sure of their pay; those who had a Mind to keep it by them, were left at Liberty; the Town relying on their Honor, that it should be neither sold nor used. What was there so very ill-judged or ridiculous in this Scheme? Let me through the Channel of your Paper, propose to the public Consideration, the following Questions. Is it practicable to continue the Use and Sale of any India Tea amongst us, without the greatest Risque of consuming a considerable Quantity of dutied Tea, and by that Means assisting the Designs of our Enemies? If practicable, is it as Things are now circumstanced, prudent? The Subject is of the greatest Importance; and I wish some Gentlemen of Leisure and Ability, would cooly consider it, and favor the Public with their Sentiments. It seems the more necessary now, because the Dealers in Tea in the Town of Boston, having agreed amongst themselves, that from and after the 20th of January 1774, they will totally suspend the Sale of ALL TEAS, *untill the Sense and Determination of the Sea-Ports and other Towns can be known, with Respect to its total Expulsion, or untill a Repeal of the Revenue Act takes Place It becomes the Duty of every Town to let them know their Sense and Determination as soon as possible. A proper Discussion of these Questions, may enable them to determine with greater Propriety.*

PROBUS.

Joseph Coolidge,

At his Shop just above the Market, and directly opposite the Auction-Room in Cornhill, has just imported for Sale,

A Neat Assortment of GUNS,

compleat with Bayonets, Steel Rods and Swivels, a few neat Fowling Pieces, Pocket Pistols, Gun Locks, Violins, Fifes and Flutes, Cases with green and white Ivory Knives and Forks, Stag, Buck and Bone ditto, Pocket Books for Gentlemen and Ladies, Japan Trays and Waiters, neat Pinchbeck and black Shoe Buckles,

High Iron Scates,

Enamell'd Silver & Pinchbeck Watches, all Kinds of Goldsmiths and Jewellers Ware, with a Variety of Toys and Trinkets too many for an Advertisement.

N. B. CASH for old Gold and Silver Lace & Plate.

TO BE SOLD

By Benjamin Church,

On THURSDAY next,

At THREE o'Clock in the Afternoon,

BY PUBLICK AUCTION,

SUPERFINE middling and course BroadCloths—Ratteens—Frizes—Half Thicks—Kerseys—Shalloons—Calamancoes—Irish Linnens—Checks—Mens and Womens Hose—Velveretts—Handkerchiefs—Case Knives and Forks—Inkhorns—Penknives, &c. &c.—Sundry Articles of Household—Wearing Apparel—Watches, &c. &c. &c. Thursday next, 3 o'Clock P. M.

New AUCTION-ROOM, Cornhill,

TO-MORROW MORNING,

At TEN o'Clock,

Will be Sold by PUBLIC VENDUE,

At *Greenleaf*'s Auction-Room,

A Variety of English and Hard Ware

Goods, amongst which are, a Number of middling and low-prized Broad Cloths of various Colours, Forrest Cloths, Frizes, Duffils, Strouds, Kerseys, Plains, stamp and check Handkerchiefs, BookMuslin, Shalloon, Tammies, plain and figured Duroys, Velvets and Velverets, Stone Necklaces, Mouse-Traps, Brass Dividers, Springs for Bottles, Brass Locks for Doors, Till Locks, Marking Irons, Jack Chains, Curling and Pinching Tongs, Chest Hinges, Brass Wire, DeskLocks, singleReinBitts, Shoe Tacks, Brass Chimney Hooks, Girth Buckles, Steel Spring Snuffers, Powder Flasks, Metal Spoons, Silver Handle Knives and Forks, Bone and Buck ditto, Scalping, Butchers and Childrens Knives, Painters Patte do. Fleams in Cases, BlackLead Pencils, Hair Lines, Sleeve Buttons, &c. W. GREENLEAF, Auctioneer.

The sale will begin precisely at TEN o'Clock.

William Bant

Has to sell at his Store fronting Dock-Square,

A few Firkins of choice

PETERBOROUGH BUTTER,

That he can recommend for Family Use.

Also a large Assortment of Goods suitable for all Seasons, by Wholesale and Retail, at the lowest Rates for Cash.

☞ A fine Assortment of Broad Cloths.

TO-MORROW at *Twelve* o'Clock,

Will be Sold by PUBLIC VENDUE, on the Premises, in Milton, all the Real Estate of Mr. *Andrew McKensie*, deceased, which was Notified to be Sold the 10th Instant, by Order of Court, viz.

THE old SNUF MILL, with a Lot of LAND adjoining, 20 by 22 Feet, the said Mill has a Stack of Chimnies, which at a small Expence may be fitted for a Dwelling-House, to carry on the Snuff or any other Mill Business; said Mill is intitled to one half of Harris's Right to the Stream of Neponset River; also, a Pair of Mill-Stones fitted for to Grind Wheat, or any other Grain; likewise a small Lott of Land adjoining Mr. Ebenezer Vose's. R. GOULD, Auctioneer.

Muscongus Proprietary.

ALL Persons holding or claiming under the Ten Original Proprietors, are hereby notified, that their Committee's Meeting for the Sale of such of the Proprietor's Lands whose Taxes are yet unpaid, is further adjourned to THURSDAY the 17th Day of *February* next, at Ten o'Clock in the Forenoon, at the House of Colonel *Ingersoll's*, King-Street, *Boston*:—THE Committee flatter themselves that the several Delinquents cannot expect any further Indulgence by Adjournments, nothing will prevent so much of said Lands being then sold to the Highest Bidder, as will be sufficient to discharge said Taxes, but their being paid in, on or before said Day, unto *William Hunt*, Proprietor's Collector.

Boston, Jan. 6, 1774 WM. HUNT, Prop's Clerk.

TO BE SOLD VERY CHEAP

An exceeding genteel SLEY, made by

Major *Paddock*. Enquire of him, or of the Printers.

To be sold for want of Employ.

A very likely Negro Man about 22 Years of Age, used to Farming House-Work & taking Care of Horses. Inquire of Edes & Gill.

A Woman with a good Breast of Milk would be glad to go into a Gentleman's Family to Suckle.

Inquire of Edes and Gill.

Messieurs EDES and GILL,

WHEN we consider the notable exploit of the collector of the customs at Charlestown South Carolina, in seizing the East-India Company's tea, at the expiration of twenty days after its arrival there, we are confirm'd in our opinion, that after the tea consignees, the officers of the customs and the governor of the province had laid effectual bars in the way of returning the ships which arriv'd here with the detestable cargo, the same step would have been taken if the tea had not been destroyed before the twenty days after its arrival had expired. The consequence of this would in all probability have been bloodshed; for in the case supposed, the troops and ships of war which are stationed here for the odious purpose of aiding the crown officers in the execution of the Revenue-acts, might have been called upon, and the people were so united and determined against *the payment of the duty* on those Teas, which must have taken place on its being landed, that no danger would have intimidated them from attempting to prevent it. The following truths, says the Pensylvania Farmer, should be indelibly impress'd on our minds—"*that we cannot be* HAPPY *without being* FREE—that we cannot be free, *without being secure in our property*——that we cannot be secure in our property, *if without our consent others may as by Right take it away*——*that Taxes imposed upon us by parliament*, do thus take it away—*that duties laid for the sole purpose of raising money*, are taxes—and that attempts to lay such duties, SHOULD BE INSTANTLY OPPOSED." Have we not been opposing the revenue-acts by humble repeated petitions and remonstrances to the throne? And have not our petitions and remonstrances been disregarded, frowned upon, and laid aside? Did not the Merchants of New-York and Philadelphia, entirely, and those of this and other Colonies in a great Measure, refrain from importing Teas from England, because a duty was laid upon them for the purpose of raising money, or rather extorting a Revenue from us without our consent?——This mode of opposition quick'ned the East-India Company (as it was expected it would) to interest themselves for the repeal of the duty. The British administration, were resolv'd that the duty should not be repeal'd, and in order to pacify the company, procured an act of parliament to enable them to send their own tea to America, still subject to the payment of the duty. The design of which, as the patriotic town of *Rowley* have express'd it, was "to draw from the Americans an implicit acknowledgment of the authority of that parliament to impose a tax upon them without their consent". And that town as well as others, have resolv'd "that a determin'd and steady opposition unto their design is the duty of every American freeman". A manly and open opposition was made to the landing the tea when it arrived here, by the body of the people of this and the neighboring towns. The object of their endeavors was, not to destroy the Tea, but to have it return'd safe into the hands of the proprietors. These endeavors were frustrated by the arts of our enemies, who had engaged, by their interest, to carry the measure through, and therefore their reputation as *influential Tools*, and probably the political existence of ONE of them at least, depended upon it. Nothing then remain'd, but to submit to this "ministerial plan of governing America", as the town of *Exeter* in the province of New-Hampshire have justly called it, and to which, they have resolv'd that "a virtuous and steady opposition is absolutely necessary to preserve even *the shadow of Liberty*", or to destroy *that* property, for the preservation of which so much pains had been taken. It was destroyed; and under such circumstances, who can gainsay upon any rational or moral principle, the declaration of the town of *Dedham* in their late Resolves, that "whatever Blame may be incurred by it, must and will be imputed to those who prevented their (the peoples) *upright intention* from taking place. Upon the whole, the brave and virtuous Men, who with so much heroism have got us rid of this detestable Cargo, since our Consignees would not suffer it to be done in a more eligible way, may value themselves much upon the testimony of many in their favor; who are ready in the language of our brethren of Philadelphia, "to return them their thanks for their resolution in destroying the Tea, rather than suffer it be landed."

I am, Your's,

A COUNTRYMAN.

PHILADELPHIA, Dec. 27.

The following are the Particulars of the Proceedings of the Citizens of Philadelphia with Respect to Captain Ayres's Tea Ship. [After recapitulating in brief the Transactions of their former Meetings, they go on to say,] *viz*

On Saturday evening last, an express came up from Chester, to inform the town, that the tea ship, commanded by Captain Ayres, with her detested cargo, was arrived there, having followed another ship up the river so far.

The Committee met early the next morning, and being apprized of the arrival of Mr. Gilbert Barclay, the other consignee, who came passenger in the ship, they immediately went in a body to request his renunciation of the commission. Mr. Barclay politely attended the Committee, at the first request; and being made acquainted with the sentiments of the city, and the danger to which the public liberties of America were exposed by this measure, he, after expressing the peculiar hardship of his situation, also resigned the commission, in a mannner which affected every one present.

The Committee then appointed three of their members to go to Chester, and two others to go to Glocester Point, in order to have the earliest opportunity of meeting Capt. Ayres, and representing to him the sense of the public, respecting his voyage and cargo. The Gentlemen, who had set out for Chester, receiving intelligence that the vessel had weighed anchor about 12 o'Clock, and proceeded to town, returned. About two o'Clock she appeared in sight of Glocester Point, where a number of inhabitants from the town had assembled, with the Gentlemen from the Committee. As she passed along, she was hailed, and the Captain requested not to proceed farther, but to come on shore. This the Captain complied with, and was handed through a lane, made by the people, to the Gentlemen appointed to confer with him. They represented to him the general sentiments, together with the danger and difficulties, that would attend his refusal, to comply with the wishes of the inhabitants; and, finally, desired him to proceed with them to town, where he would be more fully informed of the temper and resolution of the people. He was accordingly accompanied to town by a number of persons, where he was soon convinced of the truth and propriety of the representations, which had been made to him—and agreed, that upon the desire of the inhabitants being publickly expressed, he would conduct himself accordingly.—Some small rudeness being offered to the Captain afterwards in the street by some boys, several gentlemen interposed, and suppressed it before he received the least injury. Upon an hour's notice this morning, a public meeting was called, and the State house not being sufficient to hold the numbers assembled, they adjourned into the Square. This meeting is allowed by all, to be the most respectable, both in the numbers and rank of those who attended it, that has been known in this City. After a short introduction, the Resolutions (inserted in our last) were not only agreed to, but the public approbation testified in the warmest manner.

The whole Business was conducted with a Decorum and Order worthy the Importance of the Cause. Capt. Ayres being present at this Meeting, solemnly and publickly engaged, that he would literally comply with the Sense of the City.

A proper Supply of Necessaries and fresh Provisions being then procured, in about two Hours the Tea Ship weighed Anchor from Gloucester Point, where she lay, within Sight of the Town, and has proceeded, with her whole Cargo, on her Return to the East India Company.

The Public think the Conduct of those Gentlemen, whose Goods are returned on board the Tea Ship, ought not to pass unnoticed, as they have, upon this Occasion, generously sacrificed their private Interest to the public Good.

Thus, this important Affair, in which there has been so glorious an Exertion of public Virtue and Spirit, has been brought to a happy Issue; by which the Force of a Law, so obstinately persisted in, to the Prejudice of the national Commerce, for the Sake of the Principle on which it is founded (a Right of taxing the Americans without their Consent) has been effectually broken—and the Foundation of American Liberty more deeply laid than ever.

WEDNESDAY, *Dec.* 28. The ground, which was covered by the people, on Monday last, in the State-House square, being measured, it was calculated by two different persons, unknown to each other, that there were near 8000 people collected there; and many hundreds who were on their way, were disappointed of reaching the place of meeting, before the business was over, owing to the short notice that was given.

Yesterday at three quarters of an hour after two o'Clock, Captain Ayres, of the Tea ship Polly, with Mr. Barclay, late one of the consignees, left Arch-street wharf, on board a pilot boat (having been 46 hours in town) to follow the ship to Reedy-Island, & from thence transport the East-India Company's adventure to its *old rotting place*, in Leaden-Hall street, London. They were attended to the wharf by a concourse of people, who wished them a good voyage.

From the New-York Journal *of January* 6, 1774.

To the PRINTER,

SIR, *New-York, Jan.* 3, 1774.

WE hear from Charles-Town, South Carolina, that the sending back the tea ship, having been by accident or design, delayed till the expiration of the 20 days, after which by the act, the duties are to become payable, the tea was then seized by the Custom-house Officers, and landed in their custody. We have no circumstantial account of the affair, nor by what means the patriotic designs, which, by our last accounts were so warmly and unanimously pursued by the Carolinians, were defeated, nor what is likely to be the consequences of landing the tea. It has been reported that a difference had arisen between the merchants and the planters, and that through private animosity, public duty was neglected. It is, however, conjectured, that both parties will recover their senses before it be too late, and unite in support of the rights & liberties of their country.

If the tea should be destroyed in the hands of the Custom-house officers, they will doubtless be liable, both for the duties and value of the tea, which otherwise would have gone back safe to the owners; & in such a difficult case, their officiousness was inexcuseable; not only as it may prove the sole cause of the loss of the tea, but as it may call the authority of the Custom house itself, Courts of Admiralty, Post Office, &c. into question. While they operate merely as regulators of trade, for public conveniency, people are not disposed to examine their foundations, but as soon as they begin to appear as instruments of tyranny to deprive the colonies of their rights, it is time to consider the authority on which they are established among us.

TACITUS.

NEW-YORK, Jan. 6. We received no Philadelphia Papers by the last Post, but hear the four Gentlemen of the Committee who went down with Capt. Ayres, to see the Departure of the Tea Ship, are returned, and report that they saw her under sail on her Passage for London.

SALEM, January 11.

We are informed that one John Cook, of this Town, Skipper of a Schooner belonging to Mr. George Bickford, accepted of the *infamous* Employment of transporting from Cape Cod to Castle-William the East-India Company's detestable Tea, saved out of the Wreck of Captain Loring's Brig.

Mr. Bickford is now a Patient at the Hospital; and we are assured that a Company of Natives, dressed in the Indian Manner, armed with Hatchets, Axes, &c. have already paid him a Visit; but he being under Innoculation, they deferred proceeding to Extremities.

What Punishment is to be inflicted on the Skipper is yet uncertain: But, if we may judge by the Expressions of Indignation at his Conduct, he will not escape with Impunity.

BOSTON, January 17, 1774.

(The Southern Post not arriv'd at this Publication.)

☞ In the 4th Paragh: of the Rememb'rancer of this Day, for the Word "ever", read *never*.

Thursday last died here, Deacon Shem Drowne, in his 91st Year—He was a sincere Christian and well respected amongst us—We hear his Funeral is intended on Wednesday next half after Three.

The several Committees of this Town we hear never had so much Business upon their Hands as at present. Three of them in their several departments it is said, sat late last Friday Evening: And the Committee of Correspondence the Evening before.

The Country Road Committees we are inform'd keep a very good look out, to prevent Teas coming into Town by Land. While the Night look-out Committees, are equally industrious in seeing none is Landed in this and the neighbouring Sea Ports.

One of the Tea Commissioners it is said narrowly escaped a Tarring and Feathering one Day last Week—Presumptuous Men to think of gaining a footing in this Town again—so says every Man high and low, rich and poor.

It is said by some of the Friends of the Tea Commissioners, that it is hard upon them to be kept confin'd at the Castle, while two of the Commissioners of the Customs who are more blameable are suffered to Walk the Streets at large.

The price of undutied tea we hear is in a few days to be fixed at 2s. 10d. per the Chest, and 3s. 4d. by the retailers by the single Pound. This president it must be said, is much to the honor of the Importers of that article—And these two great purposes will be answered—to prevent the other Governments throwing it in upon us—and the Country towns complaints that the late high Price took its rise from a few monopolers—Be that as it may, such practises will be effectually prevented in future.

Saturday Morning last, the following Hand-Bill was seen pasted up on the most public Places in this Town, viz.

Brethren, and Fellow-Citizens!

YOU may depend, that those odious Miscreants and detestable Tools to Ministry and Governor, the TEA CONSIGNEES, *(those Traitors to their Country, Butchers, who have done, and are doing every Thing to Murder and destroy all that shall stand in the Way of their private Interest,) are determined to come and reside again in the Town of Boston.*

I therefore give you this early Notice, that you may hold yourselves in Readiness, on the shortest Notice, to give them such a Reception, as such vile Ingrates deserve.

JOYCE, jun.

Chairman of the Committee for Tarring & Feathering.

☞ *If any Person should be so hardy as to Tear this down, they may expect my severest Resentment.* J jun.

WANTED,

A QUANTITY of damaged Feathers—Also an old one Horse Cart. Inquire of the Printers.

A young Woman of good Character is wanted to go with a Lady to the West-Indies—Handsome Wages will be given, Inquire of the Printers.

Those who have any Demands against the Estate of Col. David Burr, late of Fairfield, deceased, are requested to send an Account of the same to the Subscribers; and all Persons indebted to said Estate are desired to make Payment immediately to

Fairfield, Dec. 24. 1773.

Thaddeus Burr,
Jonathan Sturgis, } Administrators.
Eunice Burr.

On Thursday next, at Ten o'Clock, will be sold by Public Vendue, at the New Auction-Room South Side of the Town-House,

House Furniture,——Consisting of——

MEhogany Chest on Chest of Draws, Desks, round and square Dining and Spring Tables, Beauro ditto, Tea Trays, Blackwalnut Chest of Draws and Tables, Green Harrateen Curtains, Easy Chairs, Feather Beds and Bedsteads, Glass Pictures, a Pull up Clock,—ALSO—Broad Cloths, Ratteens, Bearskins, Irish Linnens, Jersey Knit Stockings, Mill'd Caps, & a Number of other Articles.

A OLIVER, Auctioneer.

Burials in the Town of BOSTON, since our last.

Six Whites. One Black.

Baptiz'd in the several Churches, Two.

High Water at BOSTON, *for the present Week.*

Monday, 24 min. aft. 3	Friday, 19 min. after 6
Tuesday, 7 min. aft. 7	Saturday, 6 min. af. 7
Wednesday, 51 m. aft. 4	Lord's-Day, 53 m. af. 7
Thursday, 34 min. aft. 5	D' fi [illegible] 19 D. 11 M.

NEW FLOUR.

Choice new FLOUR to be sold cheap, Enquire of JOHN CUSHING, at his Sugar-House, in Battle-Street, near Doct. COOPER's Meeting-House. Where also may be had as usual,

All Sorts of Refin'd Loaf and Brown SUGAR.

IMPORTED in Captains HALL and COFFIN from LONDON, and to be Sold by

Peter Hughes,

At his Store in King-Street;

Choice Newcastle Coals, Russia Duck, Oznabrigs, Ticklenburgs, Broad-Cloths, Duffils, Beaver-Coatings, Cod and Mackerel Lines and Hooks, Sein and Whipping Twine, 4d, 6d, 8d, 10d and 20d. Nails, sheathing and drawing ditto, 6 by 8, 7 by 9, & 8 by 10 Glass, Crates of Ware, 12, 15, 18 and 21, Inch Pipes, treble, double and single refin'd Loaf Sugar, Spices, Seive-Bottoms, Shot, Bar-Lead, White Lead per Cask, Porter in Hampers of 4 Dozen, Buntins, Writing Paper, Durham Mustard, and a few Boxes Lemmons, &c. &c.

IMPORTED in the last Ships from LONDON and SCOTLAND, and to be Sold at the cheapest Rates,

A general Assortment of English,

Scots and India GOODS, among which are a fine Choice of Men's and Women's Winter Cloathing of every kind, also Blankets, Rugs, &c. a parcel plain and spotted grey Muffs and Tippets, with a Variety Fur Trimings, Milled Gloves, &c.

☞ Just opening, an Assortment of Dutch Brushes, in setts and single, high iron Scates, Dutch Looking-Glasses, cheap Violins, Battledores, &c. &c.

Enquire at the Subscriber's Shop, near the Old South Meeting-House.

Dec. 29th, 1773. **Gilbert Deblois.**

Choice Citron and York Biscuit, To be sold cheap, by

Mrs. SHEAFFE,

At her Shop the North Corner of Queen-Street—Also, Choice Brown Sugar by the Barrel, Rappee Snuff, Playing Cards; and all Kinds of Groceries.

—A valuable FARM—

TO be sold, a valuable FARM, in Lancaster, in the county of Worcester, containing about 300 Acres, conveniently divided into Mowing, Pasturing and arable Land, with a fine Stream of Water running through it, making a large Tract of Interval Land belonging to the Farm. The Quality of the Land is exceeding good.—The Buildings are commodious, consisting of a large Dwelling House, and two Barns 50 Feet long, and other Out-Houses. The Price is to be sold at, is very reasonable, and the Payment may be made on easy Terms. In Case it would better suit the Purchaser, the Husbandry Tools, and a Stock of Cattle, will be sold with the Farm. Enquire of Col. Abijah Willard of said Lancaster, or the Printers hereof.

To be Sold on board the Brig Union, Sam. Williams Master, laying at South Side of Long Wharf,

Brandy in Pipes, a few Casks of excellent Muscovado Sugars, Redwood, choice Butter in Firkins, Hogs Fat, Barrel Beef, Flower, refin'd Iron, two packs Deer Skins, and three half Barrels of Honey, he will also take Freight for Salem.

TO BE SOLD,

250 Hogsheads Turks-Island SALT, and about 60 Hogsheads St. Martin's Salt; a few Hogsheads Barbad.s Rum; Sugar per Barrel or smaller Quantity; Coffee by the 100 wt. or doz. Flour per Barrel, Eastern Peas per Bushell or smaller Quantity—Inquire of PETER CRAMMER, opposite the Sign of the Lamb, or of Capt. OAKS, at Wheeler's Point.

WANTED,

£.100 Lawful Money, for which good Security will be given—Enquire of Edes and Gill.

WE the Subscribers, being appointed Commissioners by the Hon. Foster Hutchinson, Esq; Judge of Probate for the County of Suffolk, to receive and examine the Claims of the several Creditors to the Estate of Robert Jenkins, late of Boston, Merchant, deceased, represented insolvent, and six Months being allowed to receive said Claims, We do hereby Notify said Creditors, that we will attend upon said Business at the British Coffee-House in King-Street, from Six to Nine of the Clock, P.M. on the second Wednesday of this, and the five succeeding Months.

Boston, 8th January 1774.

Thomas Brown,
John Winniet,
Jacob Cooper.

The Proprietors of Royalston, are hereby Notified to meet at the Dwelling House of Mr. Joshua Bracket, Innholder in Boston, on the Nineteenth Day of January current, at 5 o'Clock. P. M. to choose a Treasurer in Lieu of the Hon. Thomas Hubbard, Esq; deceas'd: And also to choose a Committee to settle the Proprietors Accounts, with the said Hubbard's Executors.

BENJA. KENT, Clerk.
Jan. 8, 1774. pro hac vice.

A Woman with a good Breast of Milk, would take a Child to Suckle; for further Particulars inquire of the Printers.

IMPORTED from ENGLAND, By

JOHN WELSH,

And to be Sold at his Shop No. 6, Union-Street, BOSTON;

A general Assortment of English GOODS, suitable for all Seasons.

ALSO,

A large Assortment of Hard-Ware GOODS, Cutlery, Jewellery, Goldsmith's, Clock and Watch Articles, viz.

SUPERFINE, middling and low priz'd Broad cloths, with shalloons and trimmings to match, a fine assortment of serges, duffils, lambskins, bearskins, bath beavers knap'd and plain, cape velvet, clive velvet and velvereets, fire ratteens, green, crimson and red Colchester and drapery bays, flannels, swanskin, blankets, camblets, cambleteens, dorseteen, yd. wide fig'd stuffs, crapes, brilliants, missinets, grizet, Denmark lustres, worsted damasks, sagathies, duroys, everlastings, ruffells, callimancoes, durants, tammies, laces, snail, ermins, muffs, drawboys, sprig'd & plain sattins, figur'd mode, allamode, persians, tiffity, sarsnets and other silks, gauzes, catgut, cap wire, cambricks, plain and flower'd lawns, muslin, diapers, diaper table cloths, Irish linnens and cotton checks of all widths, furniture checks, bag holland, bed ticks, strip'd & brown holland, Russia drab, callicoes, bengalls and pennisicoes, chip hatts, silk, cotton and linnen handkerchiefs of all sorts, men's breeches pieces of all colours, men's & women's gloves & mitts, an assortment of men's and women's hose, women's English & Lynn shoes & pumps, silk knee straps, worsted ditto, sewing silk, silk twist and wax thread per lb. a large assortment of buttons, dowlass, ozenburgh, buckram, white and brown ditt. coat, shoe and quality bindings, and gartering per groce, silk ferrets, ribbons, fustians, thicksetts, wilton, pins, hair ditto, needles of all sorts, threads, tapes, cruels, men's worsted caps, indigo, cotton wool, English soles, &c. &c. &c.

Hard-Ware.

Bath stoves, tin plates, all sorts of glass, (in half and quarter boxes,) nails, tacks and brads, brass kettles, brass and bell metal skillets, warming pans, warming pan bottoms, ditto tops, frying pans, short handle ditto, English, German, blister'd and cast steel, bar lead, holsters and pocket pistols, English and French flints, gun hammers, London and Bristol pewter dishes, plates, basons, cans, spoons, &c. coffee mills, sugar knippers, chafin dishes, andirons, shovel & tongs, fire pans, brass and iron candlesticks, box irons and grates, flat irons, snuffers, bellows, velvet corks, cork pullers, cork screws, men's and women's thimbles, knitting kneedles, pinking irons, a large assortment of brass handles and escutcheons, locks, hinges, &c. for desks, chest draws, book cases and clock cases, carpenters, joiners and turners tools, shoe maker's hammers, knippers, pincers, knives, awl blades and hafts, tacks, punches, lasts & stretches, cross cut, hand and mill saw files, rasps, farrier's ditto, syckles, spook shaves, taylor's shears large and small, sheep and glover's ditto, men's and women's stirrup irons, snaffle & curb bitts, white setts, brass nails, girth and straining webb, throat lash buckles, tin tacks & bullion, brass cocks, brass scales, a fine assortment of coat and breast buttons, horn & ivory comb, pewter, brass, leather & paper ink pots, English glue, chalk lines, window pullies and lines, house bells, gimblets, chest, till, cubbard, and box locks, stock locks, padlocks, thumb latches, brass knob locks, hinges of all sorts, flat bolts, snuff and tobacco boxes, fiddle strings, mettal, steel and pinchback shoe knee and stock buckles, common and temple spectacles, carving knives, case knives, penknives, cutteaus, scissars, common and cast steel razors, ivory handle knives and forks in cases, curling irons, shaving boxes and brushes, hones and straps, brass dividers, iron compasses, cloak pins, nail knippers, center, dowling and pin bitts, pack and sewing thread, hunting and coach whips, farmer's iron shovels, devonshire ditto, bed castors, brass knobs and rings, steel key rings, money scales and weights, penny weights and grains separate, mops, broom brushes, painting brushes, masons brushes, lathing hammers and trowells, hearth, dust, cloth and table brushes, comb ditt. teeth and flesh ditto, hard and soft, shoe and buckle ditto, wheel ditto, fish hooks, chimney hooks, mouse traps, curry combs, iron pitch ladles, four and five blade fleems, jews-harps, small brass padlocks, metal cane-heads, marking irons, marking letters, &c. &c. &c.

Goldsmith's & Jewellery.

Anvills, hand standing and bench vices, a compleat assortment of women's plated buckles, men's shoe, knee and stock ditt. paste ditto, a large assortment of brilliant and cypher earings, button, brickle ring and locket stones, ruby and white foyl, steel top silver thimbles, stick coryl, hammers, skillets, crucibles, blue pots, casting sand, ting swages, screw & drawing plates, brass stamps, beak irons, blow pipes, borax boxes, thimble stamps, cutting knippers, plyers, shears, brass and iron wire of all sizes, steel ditto, files of all sorts, freezing pusches, gravers, black & white enamel, Turkey oil stones, shoe & knee chapes, emery and sand paper, corn and flour emery, per doz. pumice and rotten stone, sandover, borax, per dozen, allum, salt petre, speter sorder, glazier's diamonds, &c.

Clock & Watch Articles.

Watches, clock dial plates, ornaments &c. all sorts of clock and watch files, musical bells, clock-gut gilt balls, brass & iron scratch brushes, clock and watch riveting hammers, clock and watch hands, watch crystals, main springs, pendants, verges, silk strings, steel chains, seals and keys, watch dial plates, clock and watch screw drivers, broaches, endless screw keys, Turkey slips, Bohemia stones, &c. &c. &c.

ALSO,

An assortment of STATIONARY, and many other Articles.

CHOICE MADDER, the Produce of this Province, to be Sold by JOHN BARRETT, at the Mill-Bridge, Boston.

For CASH, at the new Store, next Mr. Bracket's Tavern, Braintree——A fresh Assortment of Woolens, such as low-priz'd Cloths, Beavers, Ratteens, &c. just imported; and a variety of English Goods, all at the Boston Price.——Sugars at prime Cost, Groceries, &c.

N. B. Short Credit upon good Recommendation.

All Persons having Demands on the Estate of John Mico Wendell, late of Boston, Merchant, deceas'd, are desired to bring in their Accounts, in Order to settle, and those Persons Indebted, are desired to pay the same to Katharine Wendell, Administratrix.

Boston, January 6, 1774.

TO BE SOLD (or Exchanged for a Horse)

A black Mare about 7 Years old, very Gentle, and Trots well in a Chaise: Inquire at Mr. Macky's House in North School-Street, next the Rev. Doctor Byles's.

All Persons that have any Demands on the Estate of Capt. James Heath, late of Falmouth, deceas'd, are desired to bring in their Accounts to Enoch Ilsley and John Archer, Administrators on said Estate, and those Indebted to said Estate, are desired to make immediate Payment. Falmouth Dec. 25, 1773.

For Private Sale, At the NEW AUCTION ROOM, South Side of the Town House, viz.

Handsome mahogany desks and book cases, chest on chest of draws, dining and spring tables, beaureau tables, mehogany hair and leather bottom chairs, straw bottom do. several handsome eight day clocks, silver and pinchbeck watches, chamber tables, harrateen curtains, feather beds and bedsteads, handsome sconce and other locking glasses, small dressing ditto. Also, blue, orange, lead, grey and cloth colour'd broad cloths; cotton velvets, shalloons tammies, stuffs of all colours, drab and mixt duffils, copper and mixt frizes, calamancoes, capuchin silks of all colours, buckskin breeches, men's silk and worsted hose, white baize, black handkerchiefs, black sattin and chip hats, silk gauze, black gauze handkerchiefs, black, blue, white and pink sarsnets. A small box of well assorted ribbons the newest fashion; Scotch carpets, superfine bottom hole twist, camp and basket buttons, blue frized cotton, glass pictures. A small quantity of choice Rhubarb, &c. A few Boxes of choice Lisbon LEMMONS, a Hogshead of choice Jamaica Spirits, 2 Cases of Doctor's Instruments.

At said Auction-Room constant attendance is given to receive all kinds of Goods for Public and Private Sale.

All Persons Indebted to the Estate of the late Mrs. Ruth Sinclair, Shopkeeper, deceas'd, are desired to pay their respective Ballances to Joseph Bradford or Joseph Bradford, junr. Administrators to the deceas'd's Estate, and all that have any Demands on the same are desired to bring in their Accounts to said Administrators.

To be Sold by public Vendue, by Order of Court, by Samuel Whitney and John Buttrick, Administrators on the Estate of John Homer, late of Winchendon, deceased, on February 15, 1774, at One o'Clock Afternoon, at Levi Nichole's, Innholder in Winchendon aforesaid, THE Real Estate of said Homer, consisting of a good Farm, containing 120 Acres, with a good House and Barn, with good Mowing, Ploughing and Pasturing, with a young Orchard. The whole of said Farm, or two Thirds, may be sold, as will best suit, saving to the Widow the Improvement of her Thirds during her Life.

Concord, Dec. 17, 1773. Samuel Whitney, } Administrators on
  John Buttrick, } said Estate.

N. B. The above Farm lays upon the Great Road to No. 4, and within 80 Rods of the Meeting-House.

To be Sold on board the Brig Suckey, William Brown, Master, now lying at JOHN ROWE, Esq'rs Wharf,

The best Newcastle COALS, at Ten Dollars per Chaldron.

Also to be Sold by JOHN ROWE, at his Store,

Hemp, Russia English and Ravens Duck, Ticklinburgs, Oznabrigs, Cod Lines, Cod Hooks, all Sorts of Nails and Window Glass, Gun Powder, Lead, Shot—The very best Sterling Madeira, by the Pipe or Quarter Cask—very good Porter in Hampers 4 Dozen each, Lisbon and Liverpool Salt, with a Variety of other Goods. Boston, December 20, 1773.

A Quantity of large Lignum Vitæ, Pitch per Barrel, Cotton Wool, And, Excellent Madeira WINES in Quarter Casks, Will be Sold very cheap by

SAMUEL A. OTIS,

At Store No. 1, Butler's Row.

Imported in sundry Vessels lately arrived from England and Scotland,

By John Greenlaw,

A general Assortment of GOODS,

Among which are the following viz.—

VERY rich black Sattins, Lutestrings, Tobines, Brocades, Padusoys, Modes, Sarsnets, Muslins, Stuffs, very best Threads, and Women's Stays, to be disposed of exceeding Cheap, at his Store South-End, Boston.

N. B. Just come to Hand, very suitable Baizes, Coatings, Duffils, Ratteens and strong Frizes, &c. &c.

Boston: Printed, by EDES & GILL

THE 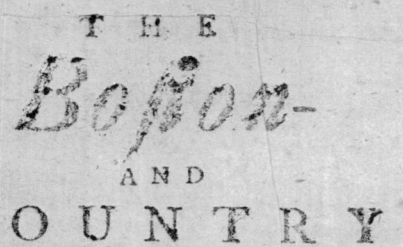 Boston  Gazette,
AND COUNTRY JOURNAL.

No. 981.

Containing the freshest Advices, Foreign and Domestic.

MONDAY, January 24, 1774.

ALL Persons indebted for this Paper, whose Accounts have been above 12 Months standing, are requested to make immediate Payment.

☞ Our Advertising Customers, are desired for the future to send their Advertisements by Saturday Sunset.

☞ WE have receiv'd THE REMEMB'RANCER, No. VI, intended for this Day's Paper; but as it publickly reveals very marvellous *Practices* of his Excellency, at the last Session of the General Assembly, we take the Liberty to defer it's Publication, till next Week, when the Members of both Houses will be more generally in Town.
The PRINTERS.

TO BE SOLD CHEAP,
A superfine Scarlet Cloth Riding Hood, almost new. Inquire of the Printers.

AT a meeting of the inhabitants of Townshend, regularly assembled at the public meeting-house in said town, upon Tuesday the 11th day of January, 1774. at one of the clock in the afternoon. Mr. JAMES LOCKE, chosen Moderator of said Meeting.

THE town taking into consideration certain intelligence received from the committee of correspondence in Boston, together with their request for intelligence and advice, from the several towns in this province, past the following votes and resolves, viz.

1. That being informed of the late proceedings of our fellow-countrymen in Philadelphia, relative to the East-India company's being allowed to send a large quantity of tea into these colonies, subject to the payment of a duty on its being landed here, we do firmly agree with them and readily adopt their sentiments upon this affair.

2. That we will on all fit occasions assert, and in all prudent measures agreeable to the constitution, the laws of nature, and natural rights of mankind, endeavor to vindicate our inestimable charter rights and privileges.

3. That we have ever been uneasy with the plan laid by the British ministry, for raising a revenue in America.

4. That the present situation of our public affairs, particularly in respect of a late act of parliament in favor of the East-India company, requires our attention, and therefore

5. We do in this way stand forth in the cause of liberty, in union with other Towns, and in gratitude to the leading spirited patriotic town of Boston in particular, especially are we pleased with their conduct towards the persons to whom the East-India company's tea was consigned, in earnestly soliciting them to resign.

6. We earnestly advise that no tea be imported into this or any other American colony, so long as it is subject to a duty payable here.

7. We are sorry for the unhappy disagreement between this and our mother-country, and earnestly wish to see harmony restored.

8. Voted that the preceeding votes and resolves be recorded, and a copy of the same attested by the town clerk be transmitted to the committee of correspondence for the town of Boston.

A true copy of the town votes.
Attest DANIEL ADAMS, Town-Clerk.

Fredk. Wm. Geyer,

ACQUAINTS the Public that he has for Sale at his Shop the Corner of Wing's Lane, near the Market, Boston,—A prime Assortment of Cut Goods—which he is determined to sell either in Whole or in Part, as may best suit the Purchaser or Purchasers, much lower than Goods are usually sold, as his purposes going into the Wholesale Branch only—Country Traders, and Town-Shop-keepers are invited to said Store, where they now have an Opportunity of buying great Pennyworths for Cash. (6w.)

At a Meeting of the Freeholders and other Inhabitants of the Town of Taunton, in the County of Bristol, on the 17th Day of May, 1773. And continued by Adjournments to the 20th Day of September then next.

THE committee appointed to take into consideration the pamphlet containing a state of the rights of the colonists and the violations of those rights; as also a copy of certain resolves of the house of Burgesses of the antient province of Virginia: As also a pamphlet containing copies of certain original letters sent from persons in this government to persons in Great Britain. All which were transmitted to this town by the town of Boston,

Report the following Resolves.

1. That the colonists have a right to have and enjoy all the liberties and immunities of free and natural subjects of our rightful sovereign king George the third to all intents constructions and purposes whatever, as if they had been born within the realm of England, and that the rights of the colonists as set forth in said pamphlet, are in our opinion in general well stated.

2. That it gives us great uneasiness to find from long observation that those rights, liberties and immunities, have been so repeatedly infringed upon, and that so many measures some secret and clandestine, others threatning and compulsive, have been used and are continually using to undermine the foundation of those liberties, and to introduce customs and regulations, not only unknown to and inconsistent with our charter and constitution, but also with those rights, liberties and immunities which belong to us as Englishmen, and for the enjoyment of which our ancestors emigrated to this remote, and then inhospitable wilderness.

3. That we are of opinion that it is our duty to assert and maintain those rights, privileges and immunities, from a principle of regard to ourselves, to our posterity, and also to Great Britain, whose union and harmony with the colonies is so essential to the happiness of the king's dominions, and whose liberties must eventually be affected by the loss of constitutional liberty in the colony.

4. That considering the importance and extent of those public grievances we are of opinion, that it is proper and very serviceable for the several towns to express their minds on the same, that so the opinion of the community may be known, and legal constitutional measures may be taken for the redress of them.

5. That as those rights and priviledges which are the most important and essential to the well-being of a community belong equally and in common to all his majesty's colonies in America: When therefore the colonies apprehend those liberties are invaded and in danger of being destroyed, we conceive it consistent with the laws of nature, society and the English constitution, that the colonies should correspond together and unite in such legal and constitutional measures as may have the best tendency to preserve their liberties, and therefore we approve of the resolves and proceedings of the house of Burgesses of the antient and patriotic province of Virginia, and of the doings of the houses of representatives of this and other governments consequent thereupon.

6. That as his majesty's council and the house of representatives for this province, have fully considered and acted on the letters before mentioned. We express our approbation of their conduct and careful attention to the welfare of this province.

The foregoing Report was read in said Meeting and accepted, and ordered to be Recorded.
Attest. JAMES WILLIAMS, jun.
Town-Clerk.

A true Copy attest, James Williams, jun. Clerk.

A young Woman of good Character is wanted to go with a Lady to the West-Indies—Handsome Wages will be given, Inquire of the Printers.

TO BE SOLD VERY CHEAP
An exceeding genteel SLEY, made by Major Paddock. Enquire of him, or of the Printers.

From the *New-York Journal*, of Jan. 6.
Mr. HOLT,

AS the House in Fort George has lately been burnt down by Accident; and it is highly probable that Application will be made to the General Assembly to rebuild it;—Though we sincerely condole with his Excellency, on Account of his Loss, we hope no such Step will be taken by the House of Assembly, before they have made themselves acquainted with the general Sense of their Constituents, upon this Subject.—You will therefore be pleased to insert, the following Quere, in your next Journal, and you will greatly oblige many of your Readers and Fellow Citizens.

As the Governors of this Province do no longer depend upon the People for their Salary, and Support; and as the Crown has rendered them, totally independent of us, (for Purposes too obvious, to need being mentioned) with what Propriety can the People be taxed, to provide a House, and furnish it, with Fire, and Candle, for the Accommodation of a Governor, under these Circumstances?

Ames's Almanack
For the Year 1774,
IS THIS DAY PUBLISHED,
And Sold by
R. *Draper*, *Edes & Gill*, and *T. & J. Fleet*.

William Bant
Has to sell at his Store fronting Dock-Square,
A few Firkins of choice
PETERBOROUGH BUTTER,
That he can recommend for Family Use.
Also a large Assortment of Goods suitable for all Seasons, by Wholesale and Retail, at the lowest Rates for Cash.
☞ A fine Assortment of Broad Cloths.

Joseph Coolidge,

At his Shop just above the Market, and directly opposite the Auction-Room in Cornhill, has just imported for Sale,

A Neat Assortment of GUNS, compleat with Bayonets, Steel Rods and Swivels, a few neat Fowling Pieces, Pocket Pistols, Gun Locks, Violins, Fifes and Flutes, Cases with green and white Ivory Knives and Forks, Stag, Buck and Bone ditto, Pocket Books for Gentlemen and Ladies, Japan Trays and Waiters, neat Pinchbeck and black Shoe Buckles,

High Iron Scates, Enamell'd Silver & Pinchbeck Watches, all Kinds of Goldsmiths and Jewellers Ware, with a Variety of Toys and Trinkets too many for an Advertisement.
N. B. CASH for old Gold and Silver Lace & Plate.

Those who have any Demands against the Estate of Col. David Burr, late of Fairfield, deceased, are requested to send an Account of the same to the Subscribers; and all Persons indebted to said Estate are desired to make Payment immediately to
Fairfield, Dec. 24. Thaddeus Burr,
1773. Jonathan Sturgis, } Administrators.
Eunice Burr,

Muscongus Proprietary.

ALL Persons holding or claiming under the Ten Original Proprietors, are hereby notified, that their Committee's Meeting for the Sale of such of the Proprietor's Lands whose Taxes are yet unpaid, is further adjourned to THURSDAY the 17th Day of February next, at Ten o'Clock in the Forenoon, at the House of Colonel Ingersoll's, King-Street, Boston:—THE Committee flatter themselves that the several Delinquents cannot expect any further Indulgence by Adjournments, nothing will prevent so much of said Lands being then sold to the Highest Bidder, as will be sufficient to discharge said Taxes, but their being paid in, on or before said Day, unto *William Hunt*, Proprietor's Collector.
Boston, Jan. 6, 1774. WM. HUNT, Propr's Clerk.

To be sold for want of Employ.
A very likely Negro Man about 22 Years of Age, used to Farming House-Work & the Care of Horses.
Inquire of Edes & Gill.

AT a legal Town-Meeting of the freeholders and other inhabitants of Watertown, duly warned and regularly assembled on Monday the 3d day of January, Anno Dom. 1774.

TAKING into consideration the distressed situation of this province, as well as the other British American Colonies, occasioned by the British parliament, claiming a right to tax the colonies and bind them in all cases whatsoever—thereby denying us an exclusive right of taxing ourselves, and disposing of our own properties—and have actually levied a tax upon the colonies, by imposing heavy duties on sundry articles imported by the colonies, for the express purpose of raising a revenue to the crown—and the injurious application of the revenues so unjustly extorted from us, viz. For the support of civil government, and defraying the charges of the administration of justice;—the bad effects whereof are already felt in this colony by rendering one branch of the legislative court intirely independant of the others for its support; and the aspect is no less threatning with respect to the executive part of government—having a tendency (as we apprehend) of saping and finally overthrowing our civil constitution of government, and introducing an arbitrary one.——The public distress is greatly increased by a late act of parliament, impowering the East India Company, to export their TEAS to America, subject to duties upon it, being landed, and the proceedings of said company in consequence of said act, in shipping a very large quantity for the colonies, a large quantity whereof hath lately arrived in Boston harbour, whereby the inhabitants of Boston and the neighbouring towns, has been greatly alarmed, which has occasioned the inhabitants of Boston and the neighbouring towns to assemble, to consult how the fatal consequence sof landing and vending said teas might be prevented; and we are fully of opinion that the people had a right thus to meet and consult for their common safety. We read that the Jews in a state of captivity and slavery, under an arbitrary King, when a decree was gone forth to destroy them, had liberty to assemble together and defend themselves, and consult how to ward off the blow that was coming on them, by preventing the wicked edict being carried into execution—Under providence they were wonderfully succeeded, having the kind influences of a good Mordecai in their favour, who not accusing them of riot, sought their welfare, and was accepted by the multitude of his brethren.

And we are also fully of opinion that the people assembled at Boston, on the 14th and 16th of December last, had no design or desire that the tea then on board the vessels in the harbour, should be destroyed or any way damaged, but on the contrary, were desirous and used their utmost endeavours that said tea might be safely returned to the owners thereof.

But that the destruction of the tea was occasioned by the custom-house officers, and the governor's refusing to grant a clearance and pass for the vessel that was designed to carry said tea back to the owners from whence it came.—Being influenced by the foregoing considerations—dreading of slavery with which we seem to be threatned, and being true friends to liberty, to which we have an undoubted right, we would exert ourselves to the utmost of our power, to avoid the former, and secure to ourselves the latter;—and we would be glad to be joined by all our brethren on the continent (in like tribulation) in this laudable attempt.—— For this purpose we Resolve,

1. To endeavour to discourage, and as far as it lies in our power, prevent the importation or bringing of tea into this province, by the East India company or any others, and accordingly declare that for the future we will purchase no tea, nor suffer it to be used in our families.

2. That we will have no dealings with any shopkeeper or tradesman, or any others, who shall persist in buying, selling, or using of tea in their families.

3. We give it in charge to our select-men for the time being, not to approbate any person for a tavern-keeper or a retailer, who shall supply any company or persons with tea, or shall persist in making use of it in their families—and that they use their endeavours to prevent any such having their licence renewed.

4. That in case any teas should be imported by the East-India company, or any others, into this province, we will to the utmost of our ability oppose the receiving and using said tea.

5. That if any persons in this town shall persist in selling, buying, or consuming any teas contrary to the true intent and meaning of the foregoing resolves, they shall be looked upon as inimical to their town and country, and treated accordingly.

6. That the foregoing resolves be in force and fully executed 'till the duties aforesaid are taken off, and no longer.

Then it was put to vote, Whether the foregoing resolves, &c. be agreeable to the town, and it passed in the affirmative, unanimously; and voted that the town-clerk record the same, and transmit a copy thereof to the committee of correspondence for the town of Boston.

A true copy as of record,

Attest, JONATHAN BROWN, Town Clerk.

AT a meeting of the inhabitants of the town of Beverley, held by adjournment, January 4, 1774, Capt. HENRY HERRICK, *being moderator, the following vote passed by a great majority, viz.*

THAT the Method of introducing Tea into this Province, in the Method propos'd by the British ministry for the Benefit of the East-India company, is justly and fairly stated by the inhabitants of the town of Boston, and that it is the sentiments of this Meeting that they will always in every salutary method chearfully join with our brethren of the town of Boston, and every other town in this province, in withstanding every unlawful measure tending to enslave us or to take our money from us in any unconstitutional manner. A true copy,

Attest, *Joseph Wood*, Town-Clerk.

Plymouth, January 14, 1774.

THAT the cause of Toryism in this country has been principally supported by the most barefaced misrepresentations, and flagitious falshoods, is a truth I have long been convinced of; for however great the influence of places, and the expectation of them may be; and however increased they have been of late, with design to answer the basest and most infamous purposes, the number of them (tho' dangerous) is yet too circumscribed to answer their ends, without that delusion and falshood which we see practiced on all occasions, great & small, not only through the several stages of revenue offices, where little else might be expected, but through those in the civil and military departments of this province. I don't however mean without exception, having myself the pleasure of being acquainted with several, who have never bowed the knee to Baal, and who scorn the conditions expected from them. It is yet a melancholy truth, more especially in this province, that the most of those who receive commissions of any kind, consider themselves as bound to erase from their minds every idea of liberty and truth, and not only to prostitute their own consciences, but to sacrifice the rights of the present and future generations to the views and purposes of him who bestows them. I am led into these reflections by seeing this day, in Draper's paper of the 6th instant (for the paper never reached us before) an account of the meeting of the inhabitants of Plymouth on the 29th of December last: an account in every part of it so wholly destitute of truth, that it may well be considered as a striking instance of what I have been observing. As I have both the honor & interest of this town much at heart, I beg leave to state the facts as they really were, in order to gratify the curiosity of the public, and to rescue the understanding and integrity of the inhabitants of Plymouth from the odium of being under the influence of the two magistrates there mentioned, whose sentiments and conduct they have long despised. The truth of the matter then is, that a number of persons in this town upon seeing in some of the papers the late proceedings of the Council of this Province, conceived that the reading them in public might answer the purpose of undeceiving some who had been deceived, and of confirming others who had entertained some doubts from the specious, solemn and confident manner in which the violent political principles, as well as basest misrepresentations, and frightful scarecrows were held up to the people, by some of those the author of that account calls respectable gentlemen, particularly by the Old Colony Deacon, with all the grimace and appearance of sanctity usually assumed by him upon such pious occasions. This joined to a curiosity in some to see if it was possible for that hardened countenance to feel that glow, which nature has designed should mark conscious guilt, induced them to set up two or three notifications for calling the people together for the special and *only* purpose of hearing those proceedings read; which notifications were conceived in such terms that even perverseness itself could not torture them to a design of any thing else. In consequence of this, a large number assembled, and among the rest the two magistrates mentioned in the account referr'd to, who with all the airs and pomposity of magistracy, endeavoured to frighten the people into the belief that their meeting was both irregular and unlawful, but without any kind of success; their townsmen being too well acquainted with them, and their dirty views, to suppose that the vanity and ignorance of the one, or the stupidity of the other, even in his brightest hours, could furnish one adequate idea of the origin of society, the nature and design of government, or the spirit of the constitution and laws of their country. They therefore proceeded as they at first designed; chose a gentleman to read the proceedings of the council, and had the pleasure of succeeding according to their wishes. In the course of the meeting a letter was mentioned, which Col. Watson had received, in such a manner as to induce the people to think some person here was the author of it, which upon the discovery of the truth, excited the only indignation on the occasion, distinct from what was generally entertained against all the protestors. The notable performance I am considering, is uniformly conducted throughout the various parts of it, and shews the author to be totally void of all regard for truth, or even the appearance of it. An instance of which marks strongly that paragraph relative to the conduct of (as he expresses it) a few persons in Boston, with respect to Capt. Hedge, which as it is totally unconnected with the account of the meeting, seems to be brought in to fill up the measure of the authors iniquities, and to show that he was ashamed of nothing. The sons of liberty in this town are so far from being lessened, that they are rather strengthened and increased. The author and the world may be assured, that more than nine tenths of the inhabitants of Plymouth, admire the spirit of the people in Boston, in the general cause of their country, and in the resentment shewn the protestors of this town, who they think have deserved it. The town of Plymouth has been, and is now very happy in having but a small number of tories in it, and those such, whose principles and conduct could be easily traced to their sources, by the offices, connections, and expectations they are marked with. The author of that account (if I mistake him not) is very sensible both of their small number, and insignificancy, and has used his best endeavours that they should supply by malignity, what is wanting in numbers. From thence originated the late protest; but the blow has reverted upon their own heads, and they are (if possible) more the subjects of contempt than ever. No less than 14 of the protestors, have made and signed a full recantation, after having expressed the strongest resentment and abhorrence of those, and their measures, who had so basely drawn them into their snare; and several others will very soon follow their example, and leave the cause of toryism here supported by none but a very few retainers and dependants.

P. S. The author of the account in Draper's paper (whether he be a new-made justice, while his character and conduct are a burlesque on, & reproach to the office, or an understrapper in the custom-house, or both) should have learnt that at least an appearance of truth will be thought by the most abandoned, a necessary qualification in a TOOL.

Messieurs EDES & GILL,

The following is a true copy of a RECANTATION of some of the late Protestors against the proceedings of the most ancient and patriotic town of PLYMOUTH. It is hoped that this frank and full Acknowledgment of the Subscribers, who were inadvertently seduced into an error by artifice and misrepresentation, will be satisfactory to the offended but candid public.

WHEREAS we the subscribers have by misrepresentations and a mistaken apprehension of things, been induced to sign a protest against the proceedings of this town, at their meeting on the 7th instant, which conduct of ours, we are now convinced, has reflected dishonor on the proceedings of our own town, the proceedings of that of a very large and respectable body of worthy patriots, who met at the Old South meeting-house in Boston, on the 29th November last, and on the common cause and interest of our country—do hereby freely express our sorrow for the error we were then led into, and the high estimation we entertain of the proceedings of that worthy assembly met at Boston, on the 29th of November, and of the proceedings of our own town, in defence of that liberty transmitted to us by our worthy ancestors, and which we think ourselves bound to support at the hazard of our lives & fortunes, and shall accordingly, when reinstated in the favor & good opinion of our countrymen, think ourselves obliged, on all occasions, to promote, support and defend our fellow-countrymen, in all such measures, as have a tendency to defend and secure us from that tyranny and oppression which threaten to involve us and our posterity in ruin and destruction.

James Doten, jun.	William Curtis,
William Weston,	Benjamin King,
Richard Cooper,	William Crombie,
David Lothrop,	Jonathan King,
Benjamin Rider, 3d.	Ebenezer Churchill,
Samuel Sherman,	Nathaniel Shirtlef,
Joseph Bartlet, jun.	*Plymouth, Dec.* 30, 1773.

W A N T E D

A genteel second-hand Turkey Carpet.

Inquire of Edes and Gill.

TO BE SOLD

By Benjamin Church,

On THURSDAY next,

At THREE o'Clock in the Afternoon,

BY PUBLICK AUCTION,

SUPERFINE middling and course Broad Cloths—Ratteens—Frizes—Half Thicks—Kerseys—Shalloons—Calamancoes—Irish Linnens—Checks—Mens and Womens Hose—Velveretts—Handkerchiefs—Case Knives and Forks—Inkhorns—Penknives, &c. &c.—Sundry Articles of Household—Wearing Apparel—Watches, &c. &c. &c. Thursday next, 3 o'Clock P. M.

Abraham Hunt, at his Celler under the Old Brick Meeting-House, has for sale the best old Sterling Madeira, Lisbon and Malaga WINE, also Fyal of a superior Quality, at the lowest Cash price.

Berry and Crane,

INFORM the Public, That they open their School this Evening for teaching Psalmody, at the House next Mr. Greenlaw's near Liberty Tree; where young Gentlemen and Youth may be instructed in the best Manner, and on the most reasonable Terms.

N. B. Said School will be kept every Monday and Wednesday Evenings.

A Woman with a good Breast of Milk would be glad to go into a Gentleman's Family to Suckle.

Inquire of Edes and Gill.

A few Casks very excellent Muscovado Sugars, to be Sold by GABRIEL JOHONNOT, at his Store South Side the Market house.

WANTED TO PURCHASE,

A single deck'd Schooner, burthen about 90 Tons, not more than two Year's old, for which the Cash will be paid immediately. Inquire of CONSTANT FREEMAN, School-Street.

B O S T O N, JANUARY 20.

THE Committee appointed at the late Meeting of the Dealers in Tea in this Town, joined by a Gentleman from the Committee of Correspondence in this Place, to repair to the Persons concerned in the Sale of that Article to obtain their Assent, and Subscription to the Resolves passed at said Meeting; have in Conformity, applied to the principal Dealers, and find the Numbers to stand thus,

79 against the Sale and Use of all Tea,
9 for the Sale and Use only of such, as may not be subjected to Duty,

This being the Day fixed when the Sale of Tea will cease, it is desired and expected that such who have agreed to, as well as those who have subscribed the Resolves offered to them by the Committee, will strictly adhere thereto; and it is wished that the Few who have not, will on a Reconsideration, perceive the Utility and Necessity of the Measure, and immediately join their disinterested Fellow-Citizens in the same Resolutions.

B O S T O N, January 24, 1774.

Wednesday next the Great and General Court or Assembly of this Province are to meet here.

Last Thursday a large Quantity of Bohea Tea, given up by some Gentlemen, was committed to the Flames in King-Street.

A considerable Quantity of Flour was brought to Market last Saturday upon Sleds, from Northampton.

A Schooner from South-Carolina for this Place was lately cast-away on Block-Island.

We hear from Milton, that a certain great Man in that town being at some distance from his seat heard a gun fired in the neighbourhood, and suspecting that instrument of death was aimed at him, ran trembling into his castle, whence we have had no further intelligence concerning him. —A miserable life this!—Always in fear and horror!

Last Monday evening Elisha Hutchinson one of the consignees arrived at the house of Col. Watson of Plymouth, his father-in-law. The people obtaining knowledge of it, they tolled the bells in a solemn manner, and there was speedily a great appearance of them before the house, demanding Mr. Hutchinson's instant departure from the town; but through the interposition of the committee of correspondence, so much traduced, because so much dreaded by the tories, he was suffered to tarry until the next morning. In the morning the young gentleman, either over-sleeping himself, or perhaps disposed to make an experiment on the tempers of the people, tarried beyond the limitted time; but was fully convinced that his safety depended on his departure and he decamped in a snow storm; making the best of his way to Cheesemetuck to relate the melancholy adventure to the very sympathetic Chief Justice HAZLEROD.

Tuesday last arrived here the Ship Lydia, Captain Hood, in 9 Weeks from London. Capt. Hood bro't Prints to the 13th of November, but no TEA.

Capt. Hood spoke the Brig Lydia, Capt. Winthrop, on Friday Morning the 14th Instant, 130 Leagues E. of Cape-Ann, out 3 Days from hence, bound to London.

Extract of a letter from Philadelphia, dated Dec. 28, 1773.

"The news of destroying the Tea at Boston was received here on Tuesday last with the ringing of bells, and every sign of joy and universal approbation; and at our meeting yesterday, it was proposed for the sentiments of our people, who voted it the most perfect approbation, with universal claps and huzzas; we all rejoice that the virtue of Boston appears firm and triumphant, we all allow you have had greater trials than any of the colonies, and we wonder much at your patience with the GREAT TRAITORS, who are the NATIVES of your country.—I am full of opinion the peaceable Pennsylvanians would have long ago demolished the biggest people we have, if they had acted such a part with the same contempt of the distresses and remonstrances of their fellow citizens."

Monday the 10th Instant, departed this Life, at Glocester the Honourable THOMAS SANDERS, Esq; with a paralytic Disorder, in the 45th Year of his Age; leaving a large Family, and many Friends, to lament his Exit.

On Friday last was respectfully interr'd, the Remains of WILLIAMS SMIBERT, Doctor in Physick, aged Forty One Years.

Last Friday died, much lamented, Mrs. Abigail Leverett, aged 70 Years. Her Remains are to be interred next Wednesday, at 4 o'Clock, P.M. from the House of her Son Thomas Leverett, in Cornhill, at which Time the Relations and Friends are desired to attend.

Friday last died Mrs. Rachel Homer, Wife of Mr. John Homer, Stone-Cutter.—Her remains are to be inter'd To-Morrow Afternoon, half past 3 o'Clock; when her Friends and Acquaintance are desired to attend.

Yesterday Morning, after a short Confinement, died, much lamented, Mrs. RUTH DAVIS, Wife of Mr. EDWARD DAVIS, Merchant, and oldest Daughter of the late Col. JOHN VASSALL. Her Funeral will be next *Wednesday* at 3 o'Clock, when her Friends and Acquaintance are desired to attend.

This Morning died here Widow Johonnot.

☞ *The Copy of the Letter said to be wrote by Mr.* George Leonard *to some Persons at* Haverhill, *we defer publishing this Week at his particular Request. We also defer the Letter he sent to Mrs.* [illegible]threll *last Saturday.*

WANTS EMPLOY,

A Person that understands book-keepkeeping, writes a good hand, and bears a fair Character, would be glad to serve any Gentleman by the Year, Month or Day.—Any Gentleman wanting such a Person may know his Name by Inquiring of the Printer.

THIS DAY IS PUBLISHED,
Adorn'd with an elegant Engraving of the Author.
[Price 3s. 4d. L. M. Bound.]

POEMS,

On various Subjects.—Religious and Moral.

By PHILLIS WHEATLEY,
A Negro Girl.

Sold by Mess'rs COX & BERRY,
At their Store in King Street, Boston.

N. B. The Subscribers are requested to apply for their Copies.

WHEREAS it has been falsely reported that I the subscriber have continued to sell tea since the 20th day of January instant, contrary to an agreement of the merchants and traders of this town:—I hereby declare that I have not directly or indirectly by myself or any body for me, bought or sold any tea of any kind, since said day, and challenge any person or persons whatever to say to the contrary.

Boston, Jan. 22, 1774. Wm. PORTER.

New AUCTION-ROOM, Cornhill,

TO-MORROW MORNING,

At TEN o'Clock,
Will be Sold by PUBLIC VENDUE,

At *Greenleaf's* Auction-Room,

A Variety of GOODS as usual, among which are,

MIDDLING and low priz'd Broad-Cloths of various Colours, Forrest Cloths, Frizes, Duffils, Strouds, Kerseys, Plains, stamp'd and check'd Handkerchiefs, Book Muslins, Tammies, Shalloons, plain and flower'd Modes, plain and flower'd Lawns, Gauzes, Aprons, Ribbons, Chintz and Callicoes, Muffs and Tippets, a Silver Cream Pott, Glass and Stone Necklaces. W. GREENLEAF, Auctioneer.

The sale will begin precisely at TEN o'Clock.

—For private Sale, *at prime Cost*—

Green, Blue, Rose and Cloth colour'd Padusoys, Taffaties of most Colours, Ducapes and Lutestrings, a Variety of plain and figur'd Sattins, Brocaded Silk Shoes and Clogs, Gauzes, Catguts, Worsted Damasks, Drawboys, Plushes, Shalloons, Tammies, Table Cloths, Clouting Diapers, Holland Threads, Pound Pins, Book-Muslins, Broad-Cloths, Serges, Plains, Bath-Beavers, fine Forrest Cloths, a Mehogany Desk and Book Case, one Beauro Table, a pair of elegant Sconce Glasses, some handsome Pictures, and a Variety of other Articles.

At GOULD'*s Auction Office*,
In Back Street,

ON FRIDAY NEXT,

At TEN o'Clock in the Morning,
Will be Sold by PUBLIC VENDUE,

A general Assortment of English Goods as usual. R. GOULD, Auctioneer.

Messieurs EDES and GILL,

AS I've an Acquaintance with the Person who advertis'd Delarivoir in the Newport Paper, I'm confident he is a Person of more Honor than to be guilty of Detraction. I beg therefore you'd give it a Place in your Paper, as I'm knowing to most of the Facts he has asserted of him, I think it a Piece of Justice done to the Public.

Your constant Reader.

Newport, December 23, 1773.

To the Printer of the NEWPORT MERCURY.

SIR,

EVERY man of honor and sentiment is careful to preserve a good reputation, as his happiness in life so greatly depends upon it; and it shows the highest degree of baseness for any one to rob another of so great a happiness, by aspersing his character unjustly: But there may be some instances where it would be in some degree criminal not to expose a scoundrel, and publish his villainies to the world for the benefit of society; and it may become the duty of an honest man to do it, in the same manner as a benevolent voyager describes the rocks and sands, upon a foreign coast; that others may shun the danger. Urged by the same laudible motive I thus publicly put all my countrymen trading to Hispaniola upon their guard, against one Delarivoir *a merchant at Cape-Francois;—who, by his matchless impudence, servile flattery, and base compliances, without a competent knowledge of the English tongue, is now their linguist at that place; in consequence of which office, together with his mountebank pretensions of extraordinary connexions with the Governor, and the officers of the customs there, which he made the English merchants in the different parts of America believe; by his false letters, wherein he informed them of his permit from the Governor to admit English vessels, with flour, and other contraband articles, when in truth he'd no such permission, he has monopolized almost all the English business at that place; when after finding himself established by the dint of impudence and falshood, without a rival in the English trade, the same baseness of heart, dishonest and avaricious principle that acquired him the office of King's interpreter without understanding English, and a principal factor without the knowledge of business, by progressive degrees, he has finished his character, and is now a rascal without honor or conscience.—It would be too long for a letter to descend into all the particular roguries that he has been guilty of, in his negotiating English business: But am ready, whenever I'm called upon, to produce my vouchers for what I say, when I inform the public, that some articles by him sold were credited for but two thirds the value, that he received for them, and many were accounted for only in gross, without an account of any particular sales; And in the late troubles at the Cape, where the English vessels were seized, his charges were more than double to those of Mr. Tardeau, for vessels under the same circumstances.——I desire therefore for the benefit of others, you'd please to give this letter a place in your useful paper; and in testimony to the truth of what I've wrote I subscribe myself the public's and your friend and humble servant.*

STANTON HAZARD.

On THURSDAY next, 27th Instant,
At Half after ONE o'Clock,
Will be Sold by PUBLIC VENDUE,
At the Royal Exchange Tavern, in King-Street,

TEN Quarter Casks choice Madera WINE, 2 Hogsheads and one Quarter-Cask Claret [illegible]: Also, a double SLEY. J. RUSSELL, Auctioneer.

On FRIDAY next,
Between the Hours of 1 and 2 o'Clock in the Afternoon
Will be Sold by PUBLIC VENDUE,
At the New Auction-Room South Side of the Town-House,——viz.

10 Quarter-Casks of choice West-India Madeira WINE.—Samples of each Cask to be seen at said Auction-Room the Day before the Sale.

A. OLIVER, Auctioneer.

N. B. A genteel Assortment of Looking-Glasses for private Sale.

☞ At said Auction-Room constant Attendance is given to receive all Kinds of Goods for public & private Sale.

The old Snuff-Mill and Lot of Land near *Milton* Bridge, which was advertised for Sale on the 18th Instant, but was postponed on Account of the Weather, will absolutely be Sold

On TUESDAY next
At TWELVE o'Clock on the Premises.

For PHILADELPHIA,

THE Brigantine Commerce, THOMAS DUNN, Master, will Sail this Week, for Freight or Passage inquire at the Store of BENJAMIN ANDREWS, near the Market, or of the Captain on board said Brig now lying at the Long Wharf. Boston Jan. 24, 1773.

To the Honorable SAMUEL DANFORTH, Esq; one of his Majesty's Justices of the Peace throughout the Province of the *Massachusetts-Bay*.

We the Subscribers, some of the Proprietors of a Township of Land called *Silvester-Canada*, of the Contents of seven Miles square, lying on a River called *Androscoggin* and adjoining to *Baker's-Town*, so called, in the County of *Cumberland*, the Plan of which was confirmed to the Proprietors thereof by the General Court of said Province in *June* 1768, humbly request your Honor to issue a Warrant for calling a Meeting of said Proprietors, to be held at the Dwelling-House of *Cornelius Turner*, Innholder in *Hanover*, in the County of *Plymouth*, on Tuesday the Eighth Day of *March* next, at Ten o'Clock in the Forenoon; then and there to act on the following Articles, *viz.*

1. To choose a Moderator, Clerk, Treasurer and Collector of Taxes.

2. To confirm any or all former Votes and Grants of said Proprietors at any former Meeting or Meetings, as they shall see fit.

3. To raise a sufficient Sum or Sums of Money by Tax or otherwise, for discharging their Debts due or that may become due.

4. To choose a Standing Committee to transact the Affairs of said Proprietors, settle the Accounts, adjust the Debts that are or shall be due from the said Proprietors, and order Payment of the same, and agreeable to Law to make Sale of those Proprietors Lands who are delinquent in paying their Taxes; and to determine where the Settling Lots shall be laid, and how much in a Lot, and about convenient Ways, and procure a Plan thereof, to be lodged with the Clerk as soon as may be.

5. To agree what shall be allowed the Clerk and the Committee for their Services.

6. To choose a Committee for calling Meetings for the future, and to agree on the Method thereof.

7. To appoint an Agent or Agents, Attorney or Attornies, with Power of Substitution, to commence an Action or Actions for said Proprietors, and in their Names to prosecute the same in any Court of Law, or otherwise amply, to all Intents and Purposes, until final Judgment and Execution, and in like manner to defend them in all Actions brought or that may be brought against them.

8. And to agree on any other Thing which said Proprietors shall judge necessary for carrying forward the Settlement of said Township.

Ja's Warren,
Wm. Sever,
Plymouth, January 12th, 1774. *John Cushing,*
David Little, jun.
Charles Turner.

Province of the Massachusetts-Bay,

TO CHARLES TURNER, of *Scituate*, in the County of *Plymouth*, in said Province, Gentleman, one of the principal Proprietors of the Land aforesaid, *Greeting*.

SEAL.

In pursuance of the foregoing Application and Request, you are hereby required to give Notice (in Time and Manner as the Law directs) to the Proprietors aforementioned, That they meet at the Time and Place and for the Purposes mentioned in the afore-written Petition.

Given under my Hand and Seal, this 19th Day of *January*, *A. D.* 1774. S. DANFORTH, Justice of the Peace throughout the Province aforesaid.

Scituate, January 20th, 1774.

By Virtue of the afore-written Warrant, to me directed, I do hereby notify and warn the Proprietors of the aforesaid Lands to meet at the Dwelling-House of *Cornelius Turner*, Innholder in *Hanover*, on Tuesday the Eighth Day of *March* next, at Ten o'Clock in the Forenoon, for the Purposes therein mentioned. CHARLES TURNER.

CUSTOM-HOUSE, *BOSTON.*
ENTETRD IN.

Laba from Halifax; Mackay from Gaudaloupe; Atwood from Anguilla; and Hood from London

---

Burials in the Town of BOSTON, since our last.
Five Whites. One Black.
Baptiz'd in the several Churches, Three.

High Water at BOSTON, for the present Week.

Monday, 42 min. aft. 8	Friday, 59 min. after 11
Tuesday, 28 min. aft. 9	Saturday 46 min. aft. 12
Wednesday, 17 m. aft. 10	Lord's-Day, 30 m. aft. 1
Thursday, 10 min. aft. 11	Full ☉ 27 Day 2 Aft.

NEW FLOUR.

Choice new FLOUR to be sold cheap, Enquire of JOHN CUSHING, at his Suga-House, in Battle-Street, near Doct. Cooper's Meeting-House. Where also may be had as usual,

All Sorts of Refin'd Loaf and Brown SUGAR.

IMPORTED in Captains HALL and COFFIN from LONDON, and to be Sold by

Peter Hughes,

At his Store in King-Street;

Choice Newcastle Coals, Russia Duck, Oznabrigs, Ticklenburgs, Broad-Cloths, Duffils, Beaver-Coatings, Cod and Mackerel Lines and Hooks, Sein and Whipping Twine, 4d, 6 I. 8J. 10 & 20 I. Nails, sheathing and drawing ditto, 6 by 8, 7 by 9, & 8 by 10 Glass, Crates of Ware, 12, 15, 18 and 21, Inch Pipes, treble, double and single refin'd Loaf Sugar, Spices, Seive-Bottoms, Shot, Bar-Lead, White Lead per Cask, Porter in Hampers of 4 Dozen, Buntins, Writing-Paper, Durham Mustard, and a few Boxes Lemmons, &c. &c.

IMPORTED in the last Ships from LONDON and SCOTLAND, and to be Sold at the cheapest Rates,

A general Assortment of English, Scots and India GOODS, among which are a fine Choice of Men's and Women's Winter Cloathing of every kind, also Blankets, Rugs, &c. a parcel plain and spotted grey Muffs and Tippets, with a Variety Fur Trimings, Milled Gloves, &c.

☞ Just opening, an Assortment of Dutch Brushes, in setts and single, high iron Scates, Dutch Looking-Glasses, cheap Violins, Battledores, &c. &c.

Enquire at the Subscriber's Shop, near the Old South Meeting-House.

Dec. 29th, 1773. Gilbert Deblois.

Choice Citron and York Biscuit, To be Sold cheap, by

Mrs. SHEAFFE,

At her Shop the North Corner of Queen-Street—Also, Choice Brown Sugar by the Barrel, Rappee Snuff, Playing Cards; and all Kinds of Groceries.

——A valuable FARM——

TO be sold, a valuable FARM, in Lancaster, in the county of Worcester, containing about 300 Acres, conveniently divided into Mowing, Pasturing and arable Land, with a fine Stream of Water running through it, making a large Tract of Interval Land belonging to the Farm. The Quality of the Land is exceeding good.—The Buildings are commodious, consisting of a large Dwelling House, and two Barns 50 Feet long, and other Out-Houses. The Price it is to be sold at, is very reasonable, and the Payment may be made on easy Terms. In Case it would better suit the Purchaser, the Husbandry Tools, and a Stock of Cattle, will be sold with the Farm. Enquire of Col. Abijah Willard of said Lancaster, or the Printers hereof.

To be Sold on board the Brig Union, Sam. Williams Master, lying at South Side of Long Wharf,

Brandy in Pipes, a few Casks of excellent Muscovado Sugars, Redwood, choice Butter in Firkins, Hogs Fat, Barrel Beef, Flower, refin'd Iron, two packs Deer Skins, and three half Barrels of Honey, he will also take Freight for Salem.

TO BE SOLD.

250 Hogsheads Turks-Island SALT, and about 60 Hogsheads St. Martin's Salt; a few Hogsheads Barbados Rum; Sugar per Barrel or smaller Quantity; Coffee by the 100 wt. or doz. Flour per Barrel, Eastern Peas per Bushell or smaller Quantity—Inquire of PETER CRAMMER, opposite the Sign of the Lamb, or of Capt. OAKS, at Wheeler's Point.

WANTED,

£.100 Lawful Money, for which good Security will be given—Enquire of Edes and Gill.

WE the Subscribers, being appointed Commissioners by the Hon. Foster Hutchinson, Esq; Judge of Probate for the County of Suffolk, to receive and examine the Claims of the several Creditors to the Estate of Robert Jenkins, late of Boston, Merchant, deceased, represented insolvent, and six Months being allowed to receive said Claims, We do hereby Notify said Creditors, that we will attend upon said Business at the British Coffee-House in King-Street, from Six to Nine of the Clock, P. M. on the second Wednesday of this, and the five succeeding Months.

Boston, 8th January 1774.

Thomas Brown,
John Winniet,
Jacob Cooper.

The Proprietors of Royalston, are hereby Notified to meet at the Dwelling House of Mr. Joshua Bracket, Innholder in Boston, on the Nineteenth Day of January current, at 5 o'Clock, P. M. to choose a Treasurer in Lieu of the Hon. Thomas Hubbard, Esq; deceas'd: And also to choose a Committee to settle the Proprietors Accounts, with the said Hubbard's Executors.

Jan. 8, 1774. Benja. Kent, Clerk. pro hac vice.

A Woman with a good Breast of Milk, would take a Child to Suckle; for further Particulars inquire of the Printers.

IMPORTED from ENGLAND, By

JOHN WELSH,

And to be Sold at his Shop No. 6, Union-Street, BOSTON;

A general Assortment of English GOODS, suitable for all Seasons.

ALSO,

A large Assortment of Hard-Ware GOODS, Cutlery, Jewellery, Goldsmith's, Clock and Watch Articles, viz.

SUPERFINE, middling and low priz'd broad cloths, with shalloons and trimmings to match, a fine assortment of serges, duffils, lambskins, bearskins, bath beavers knap'd and plain, cape velvet, olive velvet and velvereens, fine ratteens, green, crimson and red Colchester and drapery bays, flannels, swanskin, blankets, camblets, cambleteens, dorseteen, yd. wide fig'd stuffs, crapes, brilliants, missinets, grizet, Denmark lustres, worsted damasks, sagathies, duroys, everlastings, russells, callimancoes, durants, tammies, laces, snail, ermins, muffs, drawboys, sprig'd & plain sattins, figur'd mode, allamode, persians, tiffity, sarsnets and other silks, gauzes, catgut, cap wire, cambricks, plain and flower'd lawns, muslin, diapers, diaper table cloths, Irish linneas and cotton checks of all widths, furniture checks, bag holland, bed ticks, strip'd & brown holland, Russia drab, callicoes, bengalls and penniascoes, chip hats, silk, cotton and linnen handkerchiefs of all sorts, men's breeches pieces of all colours, men's & women's gloves & mitts, an assortment of men's and woman's hose, women's English & Lynn shoes & pumps, silk knee straps, worsted ditto, sewing silk, silk twist and wax thread per lb. a large assortment of buttons, dowlass, ozenburgh, buckram, white and brown dittoat, shoe and quality bindings, and gartering per groce, silk ferrets, ribbons, fustians, thicksetts, wilton, pins, hair ditto, needles of all sorts, threads, tapes, cruels, men's worsted caps, indigo, cotton wool, English soles, &c. &c. &c.

Hard-Ware.

Bath stoves, tin plates, all sorts of glass, (in half and quarter boxes,) nails, tacks and brads, brass kettles, brass and bell metal skillets, warming pans, warming pan bottoms, ditto tops, frying pans, short handle ditto, English, German, blister'd and cast steel, bar lead, holster and pocket pistols, English and French flints, gun hammers, London and Bristol pewter dishes, plates, basons, cans, spoons, &c. coffee mills, sugar knippers, chasin dishes, andirons, shovel & tongs, fire pans, brass and iron candlesticks, box irons and grates, flat irons, snuffers, bellows, velvet corks, cork pullers, cork screws, men's and women's thimbles, knitting kneedles, pinking irons, a large assortment of brass handles and escutcheons, locks, hinges, &c. for desks, chest drawrs, book cases and clock cases, carpenters, joiners and turners tools, shoe maker's hammers, knippers, pincers, knives, awl blades and hafts, tacks, punches, lasts & stretches, cross-cut, hand and mill saw files, rasps, farrier's ditto, sickles, spoak shaves, taylor's shears large and small, sheep and glover's ditto, men's and women's stirrup irons, snaffle & curb bitts, white setts, brass nails, girth and straining webb, throat lashbucklets, in tacks & bullion, brass cocks, brass scales, a fine assortment of coat and breast buttons, horn & ivory comb, pewter, brass, leather & paper ink pots, English glue, chalk lines, window pullies and lines, house bells, gimblets, chest, till, cubbard, and box locks, stock locks, padlocks, thumb latches, brass knob locks, hinges of all sorts, flat bolts, snuff and tobacco boxes, fiddle strings, mettal, steel and pinchback shoe knee and stock buckles, common and temple spectacles, carving knives, case knives, penknives, cutteaus, scissars, common and cast steel rasors, ivory handle knives and forks in cases, curling irons, shaving boxes and brushes, hones and traps, brass dividers, iron compasses, cloak pins, nail knippers, center, dowling and pin bitts, pack and sewing thread, hunting and coach whips, farmer's iron shovels, devonshire ditto, bed castors, brass knobs and rings, steel key rings, money scales and weights, penny weights and grains separate, mops, broom brushes, painting brushes, masons brushes, lathing hammers and trowells, hearth, duft, cloth and table brushes, comb ditto, teeth and flesh ditto, hard and soft, shoe and buckle ditto, wheel ditto, fish hooks, chimney hooks, mouse traps, curry combs, iron pitch ladles, four and five blade fleems, jews-harps, small brass padlocks, metal cane-heads, marking irons, marking letters, &c. &c. &c.——

Goldsmith's & Jewellery.

Anvils, hand standing and bench vices, a compleat assortment of women's plated buckles, men's shoe, knee and stock ditto, paste ditto, a large assortment of brilliant and cypher earings, button, brickle ring and locket stones, ruby and white foyl, steel top silver thimbles, stick coryl, hammers, skillets, crucibles, blue pots, casting sand, ring swages, screw & drawing plates, brass stamps, beak irons, blow pipes, borax boxes, thimble stamps, cutting knippers, plyers, shears, brass and iron wire of all sizes, steel ditto, files of all sorts, freezing punches, gravers, black & white enamel, Turkey oil stones, shoe & knee chapes, emery and sand paper, corn and flour emery, per doz. pumice and rotten stone, sandover, borax, per dozen, alium, salt petre, speter sorder, glazier's diamonds, &c.——

Clock & Watch Articles.

Watches, clock dial plates, ornaments &c. all sorts of clock and watch files, musical bells, clock-gut gilt balls, brass & iron scratch brushes, clock and watch rivetting hammers, clock and watch hands, watch crystals, main springs, pendants, verges, silk strings, steel chains, seals and keys, watch dial plates, clock and watch screw drivers, broaches, endless screw keys, Turkey slips, Bohemia stones, &c. &c. &c.

ALSO,

An assortment of STATIONARY, and many other Articles.

CHOICE MADDER, the Produce of this Province, to be Sold by JOHN BARRETT, at the Mill-Bridge, Boston.

For CASH, at the new Store, next Mr. Bracket's Tavern, Braintree——A fresh Assortment of Woolens, such as low-priz'd Cloths, Beavers, Ratteens, &c. just imported; and a variety of English Goods, all at the Boston Price.—Sugars at prime Cost, Groceries, &c. N. B. Short Credit upon good Recommendation.

All Persons having Demands on the Estate of John Mico Wendell, late of Boston, Merchant, deceas'd, are desired to bring in their Accounts, in Order to settle, and those Persons Indebted, are desired to pay the same to Katharine Wendell, Administratrix.

Boston, January 6, 1774.

TO BE SOLD (or Exchanged for a Horse)

A black Mare about 7 Years old, very Gentle, and Trots well in a Chaise: Inquire at Mr. Macky's House in North School-Street, next the Rev. Doctor Byles's.

All Persons that have any Demands on the Estate of Capt. James Heath, late of Falmouth, deceas'd, are desired to bring in their Accounts to Enoch Ilsley and John Archer, Administrators on said Estate, and those Indebted to said Estate, are desired to make immediate Payment. Falmouth Dec. 25, 1773.

For Private Sale,

At the NEW AUCTION ROOM, South Side of the Town House, viz.

Handsome mahogany desks and book cases, chest on chest of draws, dining and spring tables, beaureau tables, mehogany hair and leather bottom chairs, straw bottom do. several handsome eight day clocks, silver and pinchbeck watches, chamber tables, harrateen curtains, feather beds and bedsteads, handsome sconce and other looking glasses, small dressing ditto. Also, blue, orange, lead, grey and cloth colour'd broad cloths; cotton velvets, shalloons, tammies, stuffs of all colours, drab and mixt duffils, copper and mixt frizes, calamancoes, capuchin silks of all colours, buckskin breeches, men's silk and worsted hose, white baize, black handkerchiefs, black satin and chip hats, silk gauze, black gauze handkerchiefs, black, blue, white and pink sarsnets. A small box of well assorted ribbons the newest fashion; Scotch carpets, superfine bottom hole twist, camp and basket buttons, blue frized cotton, glass pictures. A small quantity of choice Rhubarb, &c. A few Boxes of choice Lisbon LEMMONS, a Hogshead of choice Jamaica Spirits, 2 Cases of Doctor's Instruments.

At said Auction-Room constant attendance is given to receive all kinds of Goods for Public and Private Sale.

To be Sold by Jonathan Williams,

At Store No. 8, South Side Town Dock,

Superfine and common Philadelphia Flour, Barr Iron, Cotton per Bag, Coffee, Cocoa, and Lisbon Salt, also a fine new SNOW of about 152 Tons Burthen, 11 Months old, with all her Appurtenances, as she now lies in said Town Dock.

Charles Sigourney

HAS just IMPORTED in Capt. Coulson, from BRISTOL, an additional Supply of Hard Ware

GOODS

of all Sorts, which will be Sold at his usual low Prices, at his Shop just above the Market. Also, Dutch Brushes in setts, Holland Scates, Looking Glasses, best English double refin'd Loaf Sugar, Brimstone, Copperas, &c. &c.

A few Crates of well assorted Earthen WARE, each Crate an Assortment for a Shop, the best of German Steel, and Brimstone, to be sold cheap for the Cash. Inquire of the Printers.

LIGNUMVITÆ.

A LARGE Quantity of LIGNUMVITÆ, of different sizes, uncommon straight and sound; to be sold Cheap for Cash, or Barter for any Merchandize that may offer & suit the Owner. Inquire of the Printers.

Brandy and Geneva.

A few Casks Old Brandy, and a few Cases Geneva to be Sold by CHARLES MILLER, at his Store in King-Street.

ALSO,

Superfine and common Philadelphia Flour,	Small Green Coffee, by large or small quantities,
Barr Iron,	A few Bales excellent Cotton,
Lisbon Wine,	Philadelphia Firkin Butter,
Lisbon Lemmons,	CHEAP FOR CASH.
Jamaica Spirits, &c. &c.	

All Persons Indebted to the Estate of the late Mrs. Ruth Sinclair, Shopkeeper, deceased, are desired to pay their respective Ballances to Joseph Bradford or Joseph Bradford, junr. Administrators to the deceased's Estate, and all that have any Demands on the same are desired to bring in their Accounts to said Administrators.

TO BE SOLD

A convenient BRICK-HOUSE, in good Repair, situate in Cold-Lane, accommodated with a retired Back Yard, and a Well of Water that never fails. Inquire of the Printers.

Boston: Printed, by EDES & GILL.

No. 982.

THE **Boston-Gazette,** AND COUNTRY JOURNAL.

Containing the freshest Advices, Foreign and Domestic.

MONDAY, January 31, 1774.

NEDHAM's REMEMB'RANCER, N. VI.

WEAKNESS is thy excuse,
And I believe it. *Weakness* to resist
Philistian gold.—If *weakness* may excuse,
What *murderer*, what TRAITOR, PARRICIDE,
Incestuous, sacrilegious, but may plead it?
All *wickedness* is WEAKNESS. Milton.

WISDOM and VIRTUE are not more nearly allied than VICE and *folly*. It falls to the lot of but few villains, among the many, to pass currently through life, with a reputation for sense and judgment. The common herd of rogues and knaves are soon penetrated by the sagacious:—For men of understanding and acquaintance with the world quickly discern *the real character*; while the simple-minded and credulous are later in their discoveries. But in the end the cheat is commonly found out; and, therefore, we may advance it as a general truth, that hypocrites and impostors, *finally* appear *weak and foolish* in proportion as they are *corrupt* and *wicked*.

The truth and integrity of Gov. Hutchinson in his message to the house in their last sessions has already been considered, and I believe his excellency will excuse me from any further illucidations on that subject.

We have already reviewed distinguishing parts of this gentleman's character, in which he appears aiming a fatal stroke at our political freedom and happiness, and in conjunction with his connexions and favourites concerting a plan, which he must know could never be carried into effect, without a waste of much precious blood and a most calamitous oppression of his countrymen.—Be astonished O earth!—This is the man who owed *his* ALL,—his exemption from obscurity and his advancement in honour and wealth, to the partiality of his native land:—And while he was thus plotting and *secretly* conspiring it's destruction, his mouth was as redundant with professions of tenderness and love, * as his heart replete with gaul and malevolence.—But what a singular fatality will attend our hero, if in the subsequent revision, he shall appear as eminently WEAK and RIDICULOUS, as he now does *vile* and *abominable*?

Whoever reads with attention my preceeding numbers, and especially if they consider the observations and resolves of the Council and House on his excellency's letters, will be convinced that *the former* were very lenient when they resolved, that those letters "had a tendency to effect AN "ALTERATION IN THE CONSTITUTION of the province," and that *the latter* were far from being severe, when they so unanimously † declared "that the tendency and DESIGN of said letters ‡ was *to subvert the constitution* of this government, and *to introduce arbitrary power* into this province."

And whoever considers his excellency's conduct in publickly affirming "he was *not conscious* of *any letters* which could have such an effect;" § and his express affirmation, that "there was not *one passage* in them *which was ever intended* TO RESPECT *the* particular *constitution of this government* as derived from charter," ‖ must suppose him given up to the strange delusion to believe a lie, or the more strange infatuation of believing all mankind, *except himself*, were fools and ideots.—But this weakness, with which I am afraid the gentleman is much contaminated, would not be greater than his having recourse to the little, temporary, futile expedient of procuring the following insignificant declaration from an old man.

I Wm Brattle do Declare that I heared the Go-
the copies of
vernor read ^ sundry letters which were wrote
by Him to Mr Whately & *the Governor said that those He* ~~or~~ *read were most exceptionable & in them* He read to me *there was nothing more contained than what He had expressed as his sentiments both*
very often
in Public & Private ^ the letters were wrote *AD* 1768 & were answers to letters wrote by Mr
sd Wately
Wately to the Governor that ^ first wrote to the Governor WBrattle
there was nothing in either of the letters as aforesd
any
that mentioned any thing relative to a ^ *petition of the Council* ~~or~~ to th— to the King or to the King & council or *to the Parliament* or any Petition of the House or the or of the House & Council to the King or King & Council or to the Parliament
June 1, 1773. WBrattle *

I am at a loss which to admire most; that his excellency should think such an expedient could do him any good, or that he should prostitute an *old* servant to such a mean office.—But I am not, in the least, surprized to see Brigadier Brattle meanly,—*meanly* stooping to this servility; nor the governor making *this use* of him, when he thought it would *serve his purposes*. It is not easy to say which of *the notable pair*, in this instance, appears the most odious—which the most contemptible.—

When *pristine* virtue and *ancient* honour are sullied and disgraced;—when *virgin* purity is *tem ed*, or *youthful* innocence *debauched*, sentiments of pity extinguish every other emotion.—But when an *old* TEMPTER *prostitutes* an *hackneyed bawd*—(whether the scene of iniquity is in the lustful recesses of a brothel, or the *political* chambers of state)—compassion takes it's flight, and the bosom of the spectator is alternately filled with scorn and derision, horror and indignation.

How difficult is it, for one who deviates from the way of truth & sincerity not to discover himself? The very windings and doublings practised in order to illude observation exhibit his path to full view.

Was his Excellency so used to dissimulation, that he could not be ingenuous with his friend;—one whom he pitched upon to give a certificate of his character? Why else does he read to him *only* those letters which were wrote *in* 1768, and affirm to *his confident* that *they* were the *most exceptionable*? Now was not this so far from the truth, that every one who saw the letters must discover the falshood? But was it not the design of this certificate, to have a *private operation* with the members to whom it was so industriously shown, previous to the resolves, in order to influence the judgment of the inconsiderate, and then, when it had taken some *little* effect and served some present purpose, to be pocketed or destroyed by this *singular duenna*? With all his weakness the Gov. could not imagine this petty artifice would avail, when his writings should be made public.

As to the Brigadier, he is certainly bound to confess himself imposed on and give up the impostor, or vindicate the truth and honor of his declaration. The general will not hesitate what is the part of a *man of arms*.—His honour is at stake;—the HONOR of a GENERAL must not be stained with impunity;—it must be wiped away by satisfaction—or avenged at *the point of the sword*.

General Brattle has pledged his word and *his honor*, that "there was *nothing more* contained in "those letters the governor read to him, than "what he had expressed as *his sentiments* both "*in public* and private *very often*." Now it is most certainly incumbent upon the Brigadier—he is *in honor bound*—to inform the world of *one* time out of those *many* in which the *sentiments* contained in the letters of 68, were *expressed in public*; or frankly tell the world, that the governor grossly deceived him, when he said, *those he read to him were the most exceptionable*.—There is no other alternative, General.—And what is more, the work will not end here.

It appears evident that the letter of the 10th of December 1768, gives intelligence of "a long ad-"dress or *petition* to *parliament*, agreed upon by "8 or 10 of the *council*, & signed by the president "—and appearing to be an act of council." The informer goes on to say "that the whole is no "more than the doings of a part of the council," whose meeting he declares "irregular and un-"constitutional, and ought to be discountenan-"ced and *censured*." Yet the Brigadier certifies under his hand, that "there was *nothing in ei-"ther* of the letters as aforesaid, that mentioned *any thing* relative to *any petition of the council* to *the parliament*." Surely his Excellency must have secreted this letter (tho' he declared he showed *the most exceptionable*) or the general is much impaired in sight and memory. A most unhappy alternative again occurs for the Brigadier's choice. This, this I say, is that very letter which THE COUNCIL have solemnly resolved "had a tendency to effect an *alteration in the constitution* of this province;" and therefore I hope for the sake of his Excellency, he wrote no letter *more exceptionable* in 68: if so, we shall find it impossible to save immaculate and entire the sincerity of his Excellency to the Brigadier, and the Brigadier's veracity in his written declaration. As the general is far advanced in life, it might prevent an unnecessary stain upon his reputation, if he would make his choice of the difficulties before him;—and if the truth is, that *the old game* was played with him, let him now make *one honest* declaration *before he dies*: he need not be afraid that the discovery will *sink his master* much lower in the esteem of all good men, or hope that an affected secrecy will *advance himself* even in the graces of bad men. An honest confession of the truth of fact will in the end certainly serve him more, than any subterfuge or concealment.

MARCHMONT NEDHAM.

[*To be continued.*]

* Resolved, that *while* the writer of these letters signed Tho. Hutchinson, has been thus exerting himself by his *secret and confidential* correspondence, *to introduce measures* DESTRUCTIVE *of our* CONSTITUTIONAL LIBERTIES; *he has been practising* EVERY METHOD among the people of this province, to fix in their minds an exalted opinion of *his warmest affection for them*, and *his unremitted endeavours* to promote their best interest at the court of Great-Britain.

The house of Representatives in their last session.

† 101 out of 106 members.

‡ Meaning those of the whole band of conspirators.

§ Message to the house 3d June 1773.

‖ Message 9th June 1773.

* The above we have compared with THE ORIGINAL in the Brigadier's *own Hand writing*; which was most industriously shown to Members of the General Court at their last Session; and it's Purport with equal Industry circulated abroad.

We have made the Copy as exact as is possible to do in Print. EDES & GILL.

Messieurs PRINTERS,

I Have made the Tour of the Colonies, and cannot but express the highest Satisfaction upon finding them all united with firm Resolution to defend the Liberties of America. I had heard (from Persons not friendly to this Country) that the Province of New-Hampshire would not unite with the other Colonies in the great Affair of Liberty; but I found by conversing with Gentlemen of Influence and Character in that Province, they were animated with the same Ardor for the Rights of America, and were equally determined to defend them, with their Brethren in other Parts of the Continent.—The late Proceedings of the principal Towns in New-Hampshire, breathe the same intrepid Spirit of Freedom which is the glorious Characteristic of Americans, and manifest to the World that they are not to be deceived nor subdued by the *Slave-Makers* in Britain.——I cannot forbear to congratulate the rising Millions of Freemen who possess this vast and fertile Continent of America——their Advantages, with their Wisdom and Fortitude, promises that they will be the first People in the World.

A TRAVELLER.

THIS DAY IS PUBLISHED,
Adorn'd with an elegant Engraving of the Author.
[Price 3s. 4d. L. M. Bound]

POEMS,

On various subjects,——Religious and Moral.
By PHILLIS WHEATLEY,
A Negro Girl.
Sold by Mess'rs COX & BERRY,
At their Store in King-Street, Boston.

N. B. The Subscribers are requested to apply for their Copies.

A few Casks very excellent Muscovado Sugars, to be Sold by GABRIEL JOHONNOT, at his Store South Side the Market house.

A Woman with a good Breast of Milk would be glad to go into a Gentleman's Family to Suckle. Inquire of Edes and Gill.

B O S T O N, January 31, 1774.

LAST Tueſday about 2 o'Clock Mr. George-Robert-Twelves Hewes was coming along Fore-ſtreet, near Capt. Rigway's, and found the redoubted JOHN MALCOM, ſtanding over a ſmall boy who was puſhing a little ſled before him, cuſing, damning, threatning and ſhaking a very large cane with a very heavy ferril on it over his head. The boy at that time was perfectly quiet, notwithſtanding which Malcom continued his threats of ſtriking him, which Mr. Hewes conceiving if he ſtruck him with that weapon he muſt have killed him out-right, came up to him and ſaid to him, Mr. Malcom, I hope you are not going to ſtrike this boy with that ſtick. Malcom returned you are an impertinent raſcal, it is none of your buſineſs. Mr. Hewes then aſked him, what had the child done to him? Malcom damned him and aſked him if he was going to take his part? Mr. Hughes anſwered no further than this, that he thought it was a ſhame for him to ſtrike the child with ſuch a club as that, if he intended to ſtrike him. Malcom on that damned Mr. Hewes, called him a vagabond, and ſaid he would let him know he ſhould not ſpeak to a gentleman in the ſtreet. Mr. Hewes returned to that, he was neither a raſcal nor vagabond, and though a poor man was in as good credit in town as he was. Malcom called him a liar, and ſaid he was not, nor ever would be. Mr. Hewes retorted, be that as it will, I never was tarred or feathered any how. On this Malcom ſtruck him, and wounded him deeply on the forehead, ſo that Mr. Hewes for ſome time loſt his ſenſes. Capt. Godfrey then preſent, interpoſed, and after ſome altercation, Malcom went home, where the people gathering round, he came out and abuſed them greatly, ſaying, you ſay I was tarred and feathered, and that it was not done in a proper manner, damn you let me ſee the man that dare do it better! I want to ſee it done in the new-faſhioned manner. After Malcom had thus bullied the people ſome time, and Mr. Uſher the conſtable had perſuaded him into the houſe, Mrs. Malcom threw up a ſaſh, and begged the people to go away, and Malcom come ſuddenly behind her and puſhed his naked ſword through the opening, pricked Mr. Waddel in the breaſt; the bone ſtopping its courſe, which would otherwiſe have reached his vitals. Mr. Waddel on this made a ſtroke at the window with his cane, and broke a ſquare of glaſs, through which breach he again made a paſs, and ſlightly wounded Mr. Waddel, who a ſecond time returned the blow, and Malcom withdrawing the people diſperſed.

Mr. Hewes after having his wound taken care of, went to Juſtice Quincy and took out a warrant for Malcom, and gave it to a conſtable, who went to Malcom's houſe to ſerve it, but found the doors ſhut againſt him, and was told by him, from a window, that he would not be taken that day, as he ſhould be followed by a damned mob, but would ſurrender to morrow afternoon. Here the matter appeared to ſubſide, till in the evening the people being informed of the outrages he had committed, the threatnings and defiances he had uttered, and among other things, that he would ſplit down the yankees by dozens, and receive 20l. ſterling a head for every one he deſtroyed, they muſtered and went to his houſe, which being barred againſt them, and he menacing with his loaded piſtols, which he declared he would fire upon them if they came near him, they got ladders and beating in an upper window, entered the houſe and took him without loſs of blood, and dragging him out put him on a ſled, and amidſt the huzzas of thouſand, brought him into King-ſtreet. Several Gentlemen endeavoured to divert the populace from their intention, alledging that he was open to the laws of the land which would undoubtedly award a reaſonable ſatisfaction to the parties he had abuſed; they anſwered he had been an old, impudent and miſchievous offender—he had joined in the murders at North-Carolina—he had ſeized veſſels on account of ſailors having a bottle or two of gin on board—he had in office, and otherwiſe, behaved in the moſt capricious, inſulting and daringly abuſive manner—and on every occaſion diſcovered the moſt rooted enmity to this country, and the defenders of its rights—that in caſe they let him go they might expect a like ſatisfaction as they had received in the caſes of Richardſon and the ſoldiers, and the other friends of government. With theſe and ſuch-like arguments, together with a gentle crouding of perſons not of their way of thinking out of the ring, they proceeded to elevate Mr. Malcom from his ſled into the cart, and ſtripping him to buff and breeches, gave him a modern jacket, and hurried him away to liberty-tree, where they propoſed to him to renounce his preſent commiſſion, and ſwear that he would never hold another inconſiſtent with the liberties of his country; but this he obſtinately refuſing, they then carted him to the gallows, paſſed a rope round his neck, and threw the other end over the beam as if they intended to hang him: But this manœuvre he ſet at defiance. They then baſted him for ſome time with a rope's end, and threatened to cut his ears off, and on this he complied, and they then brought him home.

See reader, the effects of a government in which the people have no confidence!

Let thoſe who pretend to dread anarchy and confuſion at length be perſuaded to join in the only meaſure to be depended on for their prevention, viz. to put the adminiſtration into the hands of men reverenced and beloved by the people.

From the Maſſachuſetts-Spy of Thurſday laſt.

You may be aſſured that the difficulty the Gentlemen in Boſton found in reſcuing Malcom from the modern mode of puniſhment preparing for him laſt evening, in conſequence of his ſtabbing a ſeaman aroſe from his falling into the hands of a great number of ſailors, from the Eaſtward and other parts, whom he had ſo often exaſperated that nothing could ſoften them. When they were told the law would have its courſe with him, they aſked what courſe had the law with Preſton or his ſoldiers, with Capt. Wilſon or Richardſon? And for their parts they had ſeen ſo much partiality to the ſoldiers and cuſtom-houſe officers by the preſent Judges, that while things remained as they were, they would, on all ſuch occaſions, take ſatisfaction their own way, and let them take it off.

A. Z.

The Honorable JOHN HANCOCK, *Eſq; is appointed to deliver the* ORATION, (*in Commemoration of the horrid Maſſacre*) *on the 5th of* March *next.*

Laſt Monday Morning, Jemima Lewis, Wife of Thomas Lewis, of this Town, Mariner, was found dead on the Floor of her Apartment; an Inquiſition was taken upon her Body, and it was fully proved to the Jurors, that the preceding Evening ſhe was intoxicated with ſpirituous Liquor, and being deſtitute of the common Neceſſaries of Life, and the Weather being extreme cold, was frozen, and by that Means came to her Death.

—The following we are aſſured is a Fact.—

Sometime in December laſt a man in a ſhabby dreſs, who called himſelf *Brown*, apply'd to a factor in the county of York, and inform'd him that there were ſundry cheſts of tea, that he (*Brown*) had taken out of a ſhip where the Eaſt-India company had freighted it, that the ſame tea was on board a coaſter, who would ſoon land it at Falmouth, which tea *Brown* offered very cheap—the trader pleaſed with the prize, (though a pretended ſon of liberty) after giving his correſpondent a ſhirt, agreed to buy the tea, paid conſiderable earneſt, and ſent a pilot to conduct the tea into a harbour in Wells—but on the road to Falmouth, *Brown* gave the pilot the ſlip and neither he or his tea has been heard of ſince.

We learn from New York, that early on Saturday Morning the 15th ult. the Brig Nancy, George Smith, Maſter, (lately arrived there from Scotland, whoſe inhuman Behavior to about 300 Highlanders who were ſo unfortunate as to be Paſſengers in his Veſſel, occaſioned the Death of near one third of them,) with equal prudence and precipitation, took her departure for Charleſtown, South Carolina, the Captain being apprehenſive that the Juſtice of this Country would bring him to condign Puniſhment.

We hear the Tea Ship was not arrived at New-York laſt Saturday ſe'nnight.

We hear from Marblehead, that laſt Tueſday Night the innoculating Hoſpital for the Small-Pox, lately erected on Cat-Iſland, near that Place, was intirely conſumed by Fire, together with upwards of 70 Beds, Bedding, and all the other Furniture:——'Tis ſuppoſed to have been purpoſely ſet on Fire by ſome of the Inhabitants; owing to their uneaſineſs and dread of having that Diſtemper ſpread among them, by the Patients and others not conforming to the Rules and Regulations by which the Hoſpital was at firſt permitted to be erected,—The Loſs to the Proprietors (ſaid to be only four in Number) is computed at £. 1500 Sterling.

THE infamous Advertiſement inſerted by G. LEONARD in the Boſton Evening Poſt of Monday laſt, which was moſt injuriouſly levelled at me, and deſign'd to vilify and abuſe my Character, demands an Anſwer, and which I ſhould now beg Leave to lay before the Public; but as Mr. Leonard has expreſs'd a Deſire of ſettling the Diſputes that have ariſen, I ſhall poſtpone increaſing the Difference, by an ample Refutation and Reply, of what he too haſtily I believe, I am ſure moſt groundleſsly has Charged me with. Should he refuſe according to the reaſonable Terms that have been offer'd him, I ſhall ſubmit the Matter in the next Thurſday's Papers to the Determination of the Public.

OBADIAH WETHERELL.

Meſſieurs EDES & GILL,

AS Mr. Leonard has given you Liberty to publiſh any Thing you have "in your Poſſeſſion of his hand writing," I here ſend you incloſ'd the Original Letter directed to me, which I deſire you would Print in your next, Word for Word, that any of your Readers, if they think fit, may compare with what he ſays in Mr. Draper's laſt Paper, was a Copy of the Original, that they may judge of the Strength of his Memory.

ALICE WETHERELL.

To Mrſs Allis Wethiell Preſent

Ma^d Boſton Jan 22 1774

I am writeing to you on a Subject which gives me Pain the Regard I have ever had for you, & your family, & alſo Mr Wethrell Relation; has Prevent my taken Notice of the Conduct of Mr Wethrell; for Some time Paſt; Something has Latety Turned up which oblidge me to Carrey the affair, which is Notorious to the Exſt eemity of the Law which I Dread the Conſequences

I thought Proper to mention the matter in this way to Prevent your thinking I Did it out of any Predugea to your am your friend & hum^e

Srt GEO LEONARD

Meſſieurs EDES & GILL,

HAVING unadviſedly put my name to a paper, called a Proteſt, &c. ſigned by about 40 perſons in the town of Plymouth, of which Town I am an inhabitant, without being ſo fully acquainted with the deſign and tendency of it, the nature of the ſtep I was then taking, as I ought to have been; and finding upon a more thorough conſideration of it, that I have been deceived, and that ſaid Proteſt is not only contrary to thoſe political principles in which I was educated, and by which I have ever been governed, but repugnant to that true ſpirit of liberty, which ſo happily, and almoſt univerſally prevails; and that it alſo more openly oppoſes, and in effect, cenſures, the juſt meaſures now purſuing, by every honeſt-hearted American, for the preſervation of our juſt rights and privileges, and the prevention of ſlavery and oppreſſion. I hereby, of my own free will and accord, make this public Recantation of the ſame.—Hoping, and not doubting, by this action, to receive the forgiveneſs and to be reinſtated in that favour which I have ſo juſtly forfeited—of the town of Plimouth in particular, and of the candid Community in general.

JAMES THOMAS.

Atteſt. January 13, 1773.

Peter Turner,

Jahaziel Fenne.

Beſides the foregoing, two others have ſigned the Recantation inſerted in our laſt, viz. Ebenezer Sampſon and John Kempton, jun.

In the Houſe of REPRESENTATIVES, June 26. 1773.

RESOLVED, That all that Tract of unappropriated Land lying together on both Sides of Deerfield-River, Weſt of Charlemont and Merrifield, and Eaſt of Bullock's Townſhip, ſo called, and ſo to extend the ſame Courſe Northerly with the Eaſt Line of Bullock's Townſhip to the North Line of the Province—Be ſold in three Pieces, at Public Vendue, on the fourth Wedneſday of the next Seſſion of the General Court, at the Dwelling-Houſe of Daniel Jones, Innholder in Boſton, at Three of the Clock in the Afternoon, viz. One Piece bounding Eaſt on Charlemont or Grants, Northerly on a Grant made to Samuel Pierce and Lock, on Hooſuck Mountain, and all the Province Land Southerly of ſaid Pierce's and Lock's Grants, and Eaſterly of Bullock's Grant, and Northerly of Number Seven. And alſo another Piece of Land lying Eaſt of Deerfield-River, and adjoining thereon, and Northerly of a Brook called Pelham's Mill-Brook, and Weſterly and Southerly on a Tract of Land called Merrifield and a Grant made to Fullam. The other Piece lying Weſt of Deerfield-River, and bounding thereon, and on Jones's Grant called Merrifield; and Southerly on ſaid Pierce's and Lock's Lands, and Eaſterly on ſaid Bullock's Grant, and to extend North from Bullock's North-Eaſt Corner the ſame Courſe with Bullock's Eaſt Line to the North Line of the Province: And that Mr. HANCOCK and Mr. PHILLIPS, with ſuch as the honorable Board ſhall join, be a Committee to ſell the ſame as aforeſaid; which Committee ſhall, in Behalf of this Province, make and execute a good Deed or Deeds of the ſame to the higheſt Bidder, when he ſhall pay the Purchaſe-Money into the Hands of ſaid Committee for the Uſe of this Province; which ſhall be by ſaid Committee paid into the Province Treaſury: And that the ſaid Purchaſer or Purchaſers at the Time of Sale ſhall pay one Eighth Part of the Sum ſo bidden as Earneſt; and in Caſe ſaid Purchaſer or Purchaſers do not pay the whole of the Purchaſe-Money within one Year from the Time of ſuch Sale, he ſhall not be entitled to ſuch Deed, or the Earneſt-Money paid at the Time of Sale. And the ſaid Committee ſhall give Notice of the Sale aforeſaid, by publiſhing in the *Maſſachuſetts* and *Boſton*-Gazette, an atteſted Copy of this Reſolve, three Weeks ſucceſſively, in the Month of September next, if the Court ſhould not ſit before that Time; and alſo the three Weeks next preceeding the Time of Sale: And that ſaid Committee, as ſoon as may be, employ *Samuel Taylor* of *Charlemont*, Surveyor, with two ſufficient Chainmen, (the ſaid Surveyor and Chainmen to be under Oath) to take an actual Survey of ſaid Lands, and return a Plan thereof to them at or before ſaid Time of Sale. Sent up for Concurrence.

T. CUSHING, Speaker.

IN COUNCIL, *June* 26, 1773.

Read and concurr'd, and *James Ruſſell*, Eſq; is joined.

JN^o. COTTON, D. Secr'y.

Conſented to, T. HUTCHINSON.

A true Copy, Teſt. JN^o. COTTON, D. Secr'y.

☞ The Committee will attend the Service above aſſigned them, on the fourth Wedneſday of the preſent Seſſion of the General Court, which will be the 16th Day of *February* next; the Plan of the Lands may be viewed, at any Time before the Sale, at the Secretary's-Office. *Boſton, January* 26, 1774.

To be ſold by PUBLIC VENDUE,

Purſuant to the Order of the Superior Court,

Part of the Real Eſtate of *William Bowdoin*, Eſq;

Late of Roxbury, deceaſed, viz.

A valuable Farm in Leiceſter, containing about 500 Acres, more or leſs, with a good Dwelling-Houſe and Barn thereon: A great Part of it under good Improvement, well fenced with a Number of Diviſions, watered by a large Fiſh Pond, and a great Quantity of Wood growing thereon; in the preſent Occupation of Mr. William Kilkee, jun. about half a Mile from Mr. Jonathan Sergeant's, Innholder in Leiceſter, and about 50 Miles from Boſton,—Alſo about 34 and three Quarter Acres of good Land in Leiceſter, bounded Northerly on the Country Road, and adjoining in the Rear on the aforeſaid 500 Acres, with a Dwelling Houſe thereon, in the Occupation of Mr. Nathaniel Richardſon, and near to the ſaid Sergeant's.—Theſe two Tracts of Land are to be Sold at the Public Houſe of the ſaid Sergeant's, in Leiceſter, at Noon, on Wedneſday the Ninth Day of February next.—At the ſame Time the Stock of Cattle, &c. on the ſaid Farms will be Sold.

The ſecond Lot of the great Allotments lying at the Head of Freetown in Pocaſſet Purchaſe, in the County of Briſtol, containing about 500 Acres, more or leſs, and is bounded on the South-Weſterly Side by the firſt Lot, and on the North-Weſterly Side with a Red Oak Tree, and a Red Oak in the Range both numbered 2, 3, ranging S. 28°. E. being 200 Rods wide.—This Tract is to be Sold at the Houſe of Mr. Strange, Innholder in Freetown, at Noon, on Wedneſday the Sixteenth Day of February next.

One Half of 950 Acres of Land, more or leſs, in Hadley, ſecond Precinct (now called Granby) bounded South by Springfield North Bounds, North by Land of Meſſi'rs Henchman and Downe, Eaſt by Belcherton, and Weſt by a High Way.—Capt. Nathaniel Dwight, of Belcherton, or Mr. Iſrael Cowls, who lives near it, can give Information about this Land; which is to be Sold at the Exchange Tavern in Boſton, at Eleven o'Clock before Noon, on Wedneſday the 23d Day of February next.

Alſo to be Sold at PRIVATE SALE,

By the Adminiſtrator on the ſaid Eſtate,

By Virtue of an Act of the Aſſembly of the Colony of Connecticut,

Several Farms in the ſaid Colony, being Part of the Eſtate of the ſaid Deceaſed, and particularly deſcribed in an Advertiſement lately publiſhed in this Paper.——

For the Terms apply to JAMES BOWDOIN, Eſq; Adminiſtrator: who once more requeſts, & earneſtly requeſts, thoſe that have Demands on, or Accounts open with the ſaid Eſtate, to exhibit them; and the Indebted to Pay what they owe, without further Application. Boſton, January 22, 1774.

T O B E S O L D,

A large Quantity of BRICKS, well made and burnt, of different Sizes, laying at New-Boſton, cheap for Caſh or ſhort Credit. Alſo a very good Iron Hearth about 1200 wt. with Coppers new tinn'd, ſuitable for a Ship of 400 Tons.

Enquire of Edes & Gill.

BOSTON, Jan. 31.

WEDENSDAY the Great and General Court or Assembly of this Province met here, agreeable to the last Prorogation, when His Excellency the Governor was pleased to make the following SPEECH to both Houses, viz.

Gentlemen of the Council, and
Gentlemen of the House of Representatives,

THE Letters which I have received since your last Session from the Right Honorable the Earl of DARTMOUTH, one of His Majesty's Principal Secretaries of State, have divers Matters in them which I am now to communicate to you.

The Indians of Martha's-Vineyard have, by their Agent, made their Application to His Majesty in Council, respecting their Claim to the Island Chobboquiddick. A Copy of their Petition shall be laid before you. No Determination has been yet made upon it. They are recommended to my Countenance and Protection. In the Year 1763 their Case was brought before the General Court and referred to a Committee of both Houses, by whom, I have Reason to think, it was fully and impartially considered; but, by some Means or other, no Report from that Committee was ever laid before the Court.— I am to desire you now to take the Affair into Consideration, and I hope you will prevent all Grounds or Pretence for any further Complaint of the Denial or Delay of Justice.

The Settlement of the Western Line of this Province where it is bounded by the Eastern Line of the Province of *New-York* has been laid before His Majesty. I have the Satisfaction of being informed, that the Part which I took in the Settlement of this Line is considered as an acceptable Service to the King, as it tended to bring to an Issue a Dispute which has been the Source of so much Mischief to two of His Colonies. I have Reason to expect His Majesty's Confirmation assoon as the necessary Formalities of Office will admit.

I gave the earliest Attention to the Request of the Council and House in their Address to me of the 23d of *January* last. I made the clearest and fullest Representation of the Case to which it referred, and I am encouraged to hope for such Determination and Order as shall be satisfactory to you.

The Judicial Proceedings of the Governor and Council as the Supreme Court of Probate and as the Court for determining in Cases of Marriage and Divorce having been impeded in many Instances where the Opinion of the Governor has been different from that of the Majority of Councellors present, the Governor having always considered his Consent as necessary to every Judicial Act: In the Year 1771, I stated the Arguments as well against as for the Claim of the Governor, and His Majesty having been pleased to order the Case thus stated to be laid before the Lords of His Majesty's most honorable Privy Council, I am now able to inform you that it has been signified to me, to be His Majesty's Pleasure that I do acquiesce in the Determination of the Majority of Councellors present, voting as a Court for proving Wills and Administration and deciding Controversies concerning Marriage and Divorce, although I should differ in Opinion from that Majority. This Order more immediately respects the Council; nevertheless, the tender Regard which His Majesty has shewn for the Interest and Convenience of His Subjects, in a Construction of the Charter, different from what had been made by all His Governors ever since its first Publication, make it proper for me to communicate the Order to both Houses.

I am required to signify to you His Majesty's Disapprobation of the Appointment of Committees of Correspondence in various Instances, which sit and act during the Recess of the General Court by Prorogation.

These are all the Matters which, from my public Letters, I am to lay before you, at present.

Gentlemen of the House of Representatives,

There never has been a Time since the first Settlement of the Country when the Treasury has been in so good a State as it is now. I may congratulate the Province upon its being entirely free from Debt, the Tax of the last Year, with the Stock in the Treasury, being equal to all the Securities due from the Government and to the Charges of the current Year. It is, at least, worth considering whether it may not be adviseable in your present Session by a moderate Duty on Spirituous Liquor, by an additional Impost or by such other Ways and Means as you may think more fit, to provide for the Charges of another Year. This will prevent the Necessity which the Assembly at the Session in *May* next will otherwise be under of contracting a new public Debt.

Gentlemen of the Council, and
Gentlemen of the House of Representatives,

There are certain Parts of the Public Business of the Province which have usually been omitted in the Session which by Charter must annually be held in *May*, in Expectation of another Session at this Season of the Year, and I need not particularly point them out to you. I may not neglect earnestly recommending to you to employ the Powers with which you are entrusted in promoting the Tranquility and good Order of the Government. You have no Reason to doubt of the Consent of the Chair to every Bill or Vote which shall have that Tendency.

Council-Chamber,
January 26, 1774. T. Hutchinson.

PROVIDENCE, January 22.

We are authorized to assure the Public, from the best Authority, that there have been but 9 Chests of Tea imported into this Town (on which the 3d Duty has been paid) since the memorable Non-Importation Agreement.

SALEM, January 21.

The Freeholders and other inhabitants of Salem, met on Thursday last, and adopted the Resolves of the City of Philadelphia, also Resolved to prevent the Sale of any Tea, or import any that is liable to a Duty, until the act imposing the same shall be repealed.—A Committee of 9 Persons were chosen for guarding against all attempts to introduce into this Town, any such Tea, &c.

We hear the Choice of a President for Harvard-College is to come on this Day.

It is said Mr. Faneuil has determined to come up to Town this Week, being so tired with the Treatment he receives from the beloved Soldiery, for which himself and Brethren had such a Veneration and Esteem, that he had rather run the risque of whatever his Fellow Citizens may be disposed to inflict on him, than submit any longer to continual Insult.

Remember Mr. Faneuil, this is the fruit of your own Nursery. You laughed at Town-meeting harangues against Military Tyranny. You are now perfectly welcome to the Monopoly both of it and the Tea Trade.

It is also said, Master Jackey Clarke was at Trinity Church Yesterday Afternoon.

The Weather for a Week past has been severely Cold.—Several Vessels who had been in the Vineyard are arrived below, but cannot get up by Reason of the Ice in the Harbour; so that our Navigation is now at a stand.

It is said Mr. Jack Frost has nearly compleated a Bridge from Castle-Island to the Main; so, that when finished, the Tea Consignees may, if dispos'd, have an Opportunity of walking to Land to see the Natives; or give them an Invitation to their City of Refuge.

'Tis said twenty Persons have been taken down with the Small-Pox in Marblehead since Tuesday last.

Yesterday Morning the following Hand-Bill was seen pasted up on the most public Places in this Town. viz.

Brethren, and Fellow-Citizens!

THIS is to Certify, That the modern Punishment lately inflicted on the ignoble JOHN MALCOM, was not done by our Order—We reserve that Method for bringing Villains of greater Consequence to a Sense of Guilt and Infamy. JOYCE, jun[r].

(*Chairman of the Committee for* Taring *and* Feathering.

☞ If any Person should be so hardy as to tear this down, they may expect my severest Resentment. J. jun.

(For the Benefit of the Insurers)

On TUESDAY next,

At ELEVEN o'clock,

Will be Sold by PUBLIC-VENDUE at Mr. SAMUEL BARRETT's Sail-Loft,

THE Sails, Rigging and Anchors, saved out of the Brig WILLIAM, lately cast-away.

TUESDAY next—Eleven o'Clock.

J. RUSSELL, Auctioneer.

Sam[l]. Abbot & Comp[y].

HEREBY Informs the Public, that their Co-partnership is this Day mutually dissolved, wherefore all Persons who have any Demands on, and all who are Indebted to said Company, are desired to call on *Samuel Abbot*, for an immediate settlement, at the Store on *Green's* Wharfe, near the Market, lately occupied by said Company, where is now selling off, an assortment of English Goods, on very low terms for Cash.

Boston 25th Jan. 1774.

CHESHIRE CHEESE.

A Quantity of Cheshire Cheese TO BE SOLD at a low Price by the Hundred or single Cheese, at the Store of

Penuel Bowen,

Opposite to the Golden Ball, *BOSTON*.

NAILS, &c.

A Quantity of 4d, 6d, 8d, 10d, & 20d Nails, a great variety of Looking Glasses, China, Taffaties and Gorgoroons, Velvet Corks, and a quantity of choice Pease, to be Sold cheap by

Lee & Jones,

Who have also for Sale,

A general Assortment of Piece Goods.

WANTED,

A good Spinet or Harpsichord.

Inquire of the Printers.

WANTED to Purchase

A Sloop or Schooner burthen from 70 to 80 Tons, not exceeding three Years old, for which the Cash will be immediately paid.

Inquire of Edward Davis.

WHEREAS the Proprietors of Land in the Township of *Leicester* on *Otter Creek*, (which Township was Granted by the Governor and Council of New-Hampshire) did at their Meeting in January 1773, Vote, That the Sum of 4 Dollars should be raised and levied on each original Right, and also at their Meeting in March following, Voted, That the Sum of 1 Dollar as aforesaid, for the Bounding and Lotting out said Township, and for the Managing and carrying on any other Affairs, for the common good of said Propriety, and that a Committee be appointed to assess the same.—Therefore we the Subscribers being appointed a Committee for the Purpose aforesaid, do a second Time Notify the Proprietors to pay the same to Mr. Isaac Stone, Collector, or to Capt. Elisha Child, Treasurer, at or before the adjourn'd Meeting of said Propriety, which will be on the second Day of March next, at one of the Clock on said Day, at the House of Nathaniel Child, Esq; of Woodstock, in the County of Windham, and Colony of Connecticut; otherwise their Rights will be exposed to Sale, at the House of the said Nathaniel Child, Esq; at 4 o'Clock P. M. on said Day, according to Law.

Woodstock, Nov. 16, 1773.

Nathaniel Child,
Elisha Child.
Samuel McClelland, } Committee.

TO BE SOLD

By Benjamin Church,

On THURSDAY next,

At THREE o'Clock in the Afternoon,

BY PUBLICK AUCTION,

SUPERFINE middling and course Broad Cloth—Ratteens—Frizes—Half Thicks—Kerseys—Shalloons—Calamancoes—Irish Linnens—Checks—Mens and Womens Hose—Velveretts—Handkerchiefs—Case Knives and Forks—Inkhorns—Penknives, &c. &c.—Sundry Articles of Household—Wearing Apparel—Watches, &c.&c. &c. Thursday next, 3 o'Clock P. M.

Nath[l]. & Will[m]. Coffin,

Have to Sell at the STORE lately occupied by Mr. WARD NICHOLAS BOYLSTON;

A Few Casks of good Sherry and Malaga WINE, Lisbon and Malaga LEMMONS in very good Order, COFFEE by the Hundred or larger Quantity, a few Hogsheads of West-India RUM, and some INDIGO of a remarkable Quality; besides a Variety of West-India GOODS, all which may be had Cheap.

New AUCTION-ROOM, Cornhill,

TO-MORROW MORNING,

At TEN o'Clock,

Will be Sold by PUBLIC VENDUE,

At *Greenleaf's* Auction-Room,

A large and valuable Assortment of Goods, being the effects of a Gentleman lately deceas'd.

——Among which are——

3-4, 7-8, and yard-wide Irish Linnens,

a quantity of nuns and colour'd threads, flower'd silk and thread gauzes, plain, strip'd and flower'd lawns, a few dozen worsted hose, blue and other colour'd broad cloths, drapery baizes, forrest cloths, duffils, plains, stamp'd and check'd handkerchiefs, duroys, velvets and velverets, lastings, plain and figur'd modes, and many other articles, and also a few casks rosin, 2 casks spirits of turpentine. W. GREENLEAF, Auctioneer.

The sale will begin precisely at TEN o'Clock.

FOR PRIVATE SALE,

A large assortment of silks, as damasks, padusoys, ducapes, lutestrings, taffaties, knapt beavers, fine broad cloths, best ravens duck, pip'd duffils, and a variety of other articles.

At GOULD's *Auction Office*,

In Back Street,

ON FRIDAY NEXT,

At TEN o'Clock in the Morning,

Will be Sold by PUBLIC VENDUE,

A general Assortment of English Goods as usual.—Also, a Quantity of Plate and a few setts of genteel Pictures, with sundry other Articles of Household Furniture. R. GOULD, Auctioneer.

At GOULD's Auction-Office in Back-Street, On Tuesday the 8th of February next, at Half past Nine o'Clock in the Morning, will be Sold by Public Vendue,

A Very large and valuable Collection of BOOKS, in Divinity, History, Law, Physic, Mathematics, Navigation, Philosophy, Travels, Voyages, Novels, Plays, &c.

The Books are all in good Order, and most Part of them new. R. GOULD, *Auctioneer*.

N. B. The Books may be viewed the Day before the Sale.——No Catalogues will be published.

On Thursday next, at Ten o'Clock,

will be sold by Public Vendue, at the New Auction-Room South Side of the Town-House, viz.

A Variety of GOODS as usual, among which are,

Mehogany chest on chest of draws,

round and square, dining and spring tables, beauro ditto, black walnut, chest of draws, tables and green bottom chairs, easy chairs, feather beds, bedsteds and beding, green harrateen curtains, glass pictures, metal, jacket buttons, a pull up clock: Also broad cloths, bearskins, ratteens, Irish linnens, Jersey knit hose, mil'd caps——And a number of other articles.

ANDREW OLIVER, Auctioneer.

N. B. For Private Sale, genteel looking glasses, and handsome muffs and tippets, and silver plated candlesticks.

At said Auction-Room constant attendance is given to receive all kinds of Goods for Public and Private Sale.

CUSTOM-HOUSE, *BOSTON*.

ENTETRD IN.

Dupuy from Gaudaloup.

CLEARED OUT.

Hudson for Dominica. Langdon and Downes for West-Indies. Sheppard for Jamaica. Coffin for London.

OUTWARD BOUND.

Andrews for West-Indies. Wood for London, Oakes for North-Carolina.

Burials in the Town of BOSTON, since our last.

Nine Whites. Two Blacks.

Baptiz'd in the several Churches, Six.

High Water at BOSTON, for the present Week.

Monday, 18 min. aft.	2	Friday, 34 min. after	5
Tuesday, 5 min. aft.	3	Saturday, 30 min. af.	6
Wednesday, 55m. aft.	3	Lord's-Day, 28 m. aft.	7
Thursday, 45 min. aft.	4	D's last Qr. 3 Da, 3 Af.	

W A N T E D
A genteel second hand Turkey Carpet.
Inquire of Edes and Gill.

WANTS EMPLOY,
A Person that understands book-keeping, writes a good hand, and bears a fair Character, would be glad to serve any Gentleman by the Year, Month or Day.—Any Gentleman wanting such a Person may know his Name by Inquiring of the Printer.

Abraham Hunt, at his Celler under the Old Brick Meeting-House, has for sale the best old Sterling Madeira, Lisbon and Malaga WINE, also Fyal of a superior Quality, at the lowest Cash price.

Berry and Crane,

INFORM the Public, That they open their School this Evening for teaching Psalmody, at the House of Mr. *Daniel Kneeland* in Queen-Street; where young Gentlemen and Youth may be instructed in the best Manner, and on the most reasonable Terms.

N. B. Said School will be kept every Monday and Wednesday Evenings.

WANTED TO PURCHASE,
A single deck'd Schooner, burthen about 90 Tons, not more than two Year's old, for which the Cash will be paid immediately. Inquire of CONSTANT FREEMAN, School-Street.

To the Honorable SAMUEL DANFORTH, Esq; one of his Majesty's Justices of the Peace throughout the Province of the *Massachusetts-Bay*.

We the Subscribers, some of the Proprietors of a Township of Land called *Silvester-Canada*, of the Contents of seven Miles square, lying on a River called *Androscoggin* and adjoining to *Baker's-Town*, so called, in the County of *Cumberland*, the Plan of which was confirmed to the Proprietors thereof by the General Court of said Province in *June* 1768, humbly request your Honor to issue a Warrant for calling a Meeting of said Proprietors, to be held at the Dwelling-House of *Cornelius Turner*, Innholder in *Hanover*, in the County of *Plymouth*, on Tuesday the Eighth Day of *March* next, at Ten o'Clock in the Forenoon; then and there to act on the following Articles, *viz.*

1. To choose a Moderator, Clerk, Treasurer and Collector of Taxes.
2. To confirm any or all former Votes and Grants of said Proprietors at any former Meeting or Meetings, as they shall see fit.
3. To raise a sufficient Sum or Sums of Money by Tax or otherwise, for discharging their Debts due or that may become due.
4. To choose a Standing Committee to transact the Affairs of said Proprietors, settle the Accounts, adjust the Debts that are or shall be due from the said Proprietors, and order Payment of the same, and agreeable to Law to make Sale of those Proprietors Lands who are delinquent in paying their Taxes; and to determine where the Settling Lots shall be laid, and how much in a Lot, and about convenient Ways, and procure a Plan thereof, to be lodged with the Clerk as soon as may be.
5. To agree what shall be allowed the Clerk and the Committee for their Services.
6. To choose a Committee for calling Meetings for the future, and to agree on the Method thereof.
7. To appoint an Agent or Agents, Attorney or Attornies, with Power of Substitution, to commence an Action or Actions for said Proprietors, and in their Names to prosecute the same in any Court of Law, or otherwise amply, to all Intents and Purposes, until final Judgment and Execution, and in like manner to defend them in all Actions brought or that may be brought against them.
8. And to agree on any other Thing which said Proprietors shall judge necessary for carrying forward the Settlement of said Township.

Plymouth, January 12th, 1774.
Ja's Warren,
Wm. Sever,
John Cushing,
David Little, jun.
Charles Turner.

Province of the Massachusets-Bay,
To CHARLES TURNER, of *Scituate*, in the County of *Plymouth*, in said Province, Gentleman, one of the principal Proprietors of the Land aforesaid, *Greeting*.

SEAL.

In pursuance of the foregoing Application and Request, you are hereby required to give Notice (in Time and Manner as the Law directs) to the Proprietors aforementioned, That they meet at the Time and Place and for the Purposes mentioned in the afore-written Petition.

Given under my Hand and Seal, this 19th Day of *January*, *A. D.* 1774. S. DANFORTH, Justice of the Peace throughout the Province aforesaid.

Scituate, January 20th, 1774.

By Virtue of the afore-written Warrant, to me directed, I do hereby notify and warn the Proprietors of the aforesaid Lands to meet at the Dwelling-House of *Cornelius Turner*, Innholder in *Hanover*, on Tuesday the Eighth Day of *March* next, at Ten o'Clock in the Forenoon, for the Purposes therein mentioned. CHARLES TURNER.

Muscongus Proprietary.

ALL Persons holding or claiming under the Ten Original Proprietors, are hereby notified, that their Committee's Meeting for the Sale of such of the Proprietor's Lands whose Taxes are yet unpaid, is further adjourned to THURSDAY the 17th Day of *February* next, at Ten o'Clock in the Forenoon, at the House of Colonel *Ingersoll's*, King Street, *Boston*:—THE Committee flatter themselves that the several Delinquents cannot expect any further Indulgence by Adjournments, nothing will prevent so much of said Lands being then sold to the Highest Bidder, as will be sufficient to discharge said Taxes, but their being paid in, on or before said Day, unto *William Hunt*, Proprietor's Collector.

Boston, Jan. 6, 1774. WM. HUNT, Prop's Clerk.

Joseph Coolidge,

At his Shop just above the Market, and directly opposite the Auction-Room in Cornhill, has just imported for Sale,

A Neat Assortment of GUNS, compleat with Bayonets, Steel Rods and Swivels, a few neat Fowling Pieces, Pocket Pistols, Gun Locks, Violins, Fifes and Flutes, Cases with green and white Ivory Knives and Forks, Stag, Buck and Bone ditto, Pocket Books for Gentlemen and Ladies, Japan Trays and Waiters, neat Pinchbeck and black Shoe Buckles,

High Iron Scates,

Enamell'd Silver & Pinchbeck Watches, all Kinds of Goldsmiths and Jewellers Ware, with a Variety of Toys and Trinkets too many for an Advertisement.

N. B. CASH for old Gold and Silver Lace & Plate.

Those who have any Demands against the Estate of Col. David Burr, late of Fairfield, deceased, are requested to send an Account of the same to the Subscribers; and all Persons indebted to said Estate are desired to make Payment immediately to

Fairfield, Dec. 24. 1773.
Thaddeus Burr, Jonathan Sturgis, Eunice Burr. } Administrators.

William Bant

Has to sell at his Store fronting Dock-Square, A few Firkins of choice
PETERBOROUGH BUTTER,
That he can recommend for Family Use.
Also a large Assortment of Goods suitable for all Seasons, by Wholesale and Retail, at the lowest Rates for Cash.
☞ A fine Assortment of Broad Cloths.

A young Woman of good Character is wanted to go with a Lady to the West-Indies—Handsome Wages will be given, Inquire of the Printers.

TO BE SOLD VERY CHEAP
An exceeding genteel SLEY, made by Major *Paddock*. Enquire of him, or of the Printers.

To be sold for want of Employ.
A very likely Negro Man about 22 Years of Age, used to Farming House-Work & taking Care of Horses. Inquire of Edes & Gill.

THIS DAY IS PUBLISHED AND SOLD BY

Cox and Berry,

At their Store in King-Street. [Price 6*s.* Lawful.]

THE
New Royal Harmony,
OR
Beauties of Church Music;

Containing a Number of Favorite Anthems, composed by some of the greatest Masters in the World, selected from the several Publications of *Williams, Arnold, Knapp, Stephenson, Lyon*, &c. some of them never before printed. Composed in Two, Three, Four and Five Parts: Carefully set in Score and neatly Engraved: And is designed for the Improvement of the Musical Societies, Country Choirs, &c.

By DANIEL BAYLEY, *PhiloMusico.*

*** At the same place may be had, *Tansur* and *Williams's* Singing Book.

Just Published, and to be sold by
JOSEPH GREENLEAF,
At his Printing Office in Hanover-Street, Boston,

AN Abridgment of Burn's Justice of the Peace, and Parish Officer:
To which is added,
An Appendix, containing some general rules and directions, necessary to be known and observed by all Justices of the Peace.

Subscribers for said book (Stitched) are desired to send for them. Those who are to have them bound, may have them the beginning of next week.

N. B This abridgment includes all that is applicable to the practice here, and may be had for nine Shillings stitched, or eleven shillings bound. The London edition of this book cannot be had under six dollars.

Also to be sold at said office,
The following PAMPHLETS, viz.

A calm Answer to the Question, Why are you a Dissenter from the Church of England.

The cause of the dissenting ministers; by Israel Morduit.

England's Warning Piece; a sermon occasioned by the Murder of Mr. William Allen, by a party of soldiers in George's Fields.

An anniversary sermon, being a sequel to the above.

The Adulateur; a Tragedy. By a Lady.

A Dissuasion from the Slave Trade. With a number of other pamphlets, also Testaments, Psalters, spelling books, Psalm books, Primers, Writing Paper, ink-pots, and other Stationary; also blanks of various sorts, some never before printed, particularly for the use of Justices of the Peace.

L I K E W I S E,
A Dissertation on the rise, progress, views, strength, interest and characters, of the two parties of the Whigs and Tories.

KEYSER's
FAMOUS PILLS

So well known all over *Europe*, and in *this* and the *neighbouring Colonies*, for their superior Efficacy and peculiar Mildness, in perfectly eradicating every Degree of a certain Disease, without the least Trouble or Confinement.

The Public may be assured, that this excellent Medicine is beyond any Thing in all Foulness and Impurities of the Blood, having performed many astonishing Cures in Scorbutic Eruptions, Leprosies, White Swellings, Stiff Joints, Gout and Rheumatic Disorders, &c.

THESE PILLS ARE NOW SOLD BY
EDES and GILL,
(In Boxes of 7/6. L. M. each, *fresh imported*)

Who have in their Hands a Letter from the Widow KEYSER, and a Certificate from under her own Hand of the Genuineness of the above Pills; which any Person may have the Perusal of by applying to them at their Printing-Office in *Queen-Street*: Where may be had a Variety of Books, &c.

Insurance on Vessels and Goods.

AT the Insurance-Office of EZEKIEL PRICE near the Exchange,
INSURANCE
May be made on Vessels, Cargoes, and private Adventures, at VERY LOW PREMIUMS, full one quarter Part less than formerly.

Note well—In Case of Loss the Insurance will be PUNCTUALLY PAID.

Lee & Jones,

Have Imported by the Haley, Capt. *Scott*, and other Vessels from ENGLAND,
A compleat Assortment of *Piece Goods* suitable for this Season, which are for Sale at their Store near the Swing-Bridge. ☞ *At the lowest Rates.*
Also a very great Variety of LOOKING GLASSES of all Sizes, *remarkably Cheap*.
A Quantity of Silver and Pinchbeck WATCHES.

JOHN MAUD, Taylor,

BEGS Leave to acquaint the Gentlemen who are his Customers, and others, That he carries on his Business as usual at his House the North Side of the Town House, in King-Street—Where all the various Branches of the Taylor's Business is executed in the neatest Manner, with Fidelity and Dispatch. And as he has now by him some of the newest Patterns, he flatters himself that no one can finish or cut Cloaths with greater Elegance and Taste. With Gentlemen who do not chuse to have their Cloaths Cut or finished according to the height of the Fashion, he will endeavour to observe a Medium, and will be particularly careful to follow any Directions given him. Regimental Cloathing, and Navy Uniform, he is well used to, having been employed these many Years by the Gentlemen of the Army and Navy. Any Cloaths which may happen not to fit, he will take back according to his former Advertisement. Gentlemen will be waited on immediately by sending Notice to the above Place.

For Private Sale,
At the NEW AUCTION ROOM, South Side of the Town House, viz.

HAndsome mahogany desks and book cases, chest on chest of draws, dining and spring tables, beaureau tables, mahogany hair and leather bottom chairs, straw bottom do. several handsome eight day clocks, silver and pinchbeck watches, chamber tables, harrateen curtains, feather beds and bedsteads, handsome sconce and other looking glasses, small dressing ditto. Also, blue, orange, lead, grey and cloth colour'd broad cloths; cotton velvets, shalloons, tammies, stuffs of all colours, drab and mixt duffils, copper and mixt frizes, calamancoes, capuchin silks of all colours, buckskin breeches, men's silk and worsted hose, white baize, black handkerchiefs, black sattin and chip hats, silk gauze, black gauze handkerchiefs, black, blue, white and pink sarsnets. A small box of well assorted ribbons the newest fashion; Scotch carpets, superfine bottom hole twist, camp and basket buttons, blue frized cotton, glass pictures. A small quantity of choice Rhubarb, &c. A few Boxes of choice Lisbon LEMMONS, a Hogshead of choice Jamaica Spirits, 2 Cases of Doctor's Instruments.

At said Auction-Room constant attendance is given to receive all kinds of Goods for Public and Private Sale.

——A valuable FARM——

TO be sold, a valuable FARM, in Lancaster, in the county of Worcester, containing about 300 Acres, conveniently divided into Mowing, Pasturing and arable Land, with a fine Stream of Water running through it, making a large Tract of Interval Land belonging to the Farm. The Quality of the Land is exceeding good.—The Buildings are commodious, consisting of a large Dwelling House, and two Barns 50 Feet long, and other Out-Houses. The Price it is to be sold at, is very reasonable, and the Payment may be made on easy Terms. In Case it would better suit the Purchaser, the Husbandry Tools, and a Stock of Cattle, will be sold with the Farm. Enquire of Col. Abijah Willard of said Lancaster, or the Printers hereof.

Boston: Printed, by EDES & GILL *in Queen-Street*, 1774.

THE
Boston-
AND
COUNTRY

No. 983.
Gazette,
JOURNAL.

Containing the freshest Advices, Foreign and Domestic.

MONDAY, February 7, 1774.

NEDHAM'S REMEMB'RANCER, N. VII.

Why, he can smile, *and* murder while he smiles;
And cry content to that which grieves his heart;
And wet his cheeks with artificial tears;
And frame his face to all occasions:
Deceive more slily, than Ulyses could;
And, like a Sinon, take another Troy:
Change shapes with PROTEUS, for advantages;
And set th' asp'ring CATALINE *to school.*

SHAKESPEARE'S HRNRY 6th.

IF we did not bear in mind the characteristic features of his Excellency, we should be surprized to find him continue a semblance of regard to this people and making declarations of his services to his country. At the very instant, that he is evading a disclosure of his letters to certain personages in England, the only way in which he could make attonement for his crimes;—at the very time that he must know his *secret and confidential* conduct was detected, and his character stood displayed in the face of all men; at the very moment, when the arrogance of a traitor, above the reach of law, ought to have given place to the humility of a convict;—at the very instant, I say, when the blushes of guilt and contrition ought to have precluded all effrontery and vain-glory;—his Excellency assumes his *wonted character*, shamelesly disavows any design of subverting the constitution of this government, affirms that his letters rather tended *to preserve it entire*, and positively declares he had reason to think they had *not been ineffectual to that purpose*. * Is it possible to give an example of an enemy to the Common-wealth, whose public behavior was so devoid of shame, with desperate conspiracies so conspicuous to view? He could never suppose, that a people, remarkable for their discernment and understanding, would be blind to the plenary evidence laid before them, or that so paltry an artifice could renovate their confidence in his professions. It must have been a credulity below the milkiness of infancy which could induce this people to suffer such declarations *from such a man* to delude them. His Excellency could, therefore, only intend to try the dangerous experiment of braving the scorn of mankind, and by sustaining the presure of an open conviction, without discovering remorse of conscience, secure his pre-emminence among his fellows. Thus by showing himself as destitute of the sense of shame, as of guilt, he preserved that *darling* prerogative of being *the chief* among *his brethren*; and by pushing a hardy front on this trying occasion, he gave ample testimony, that he was as capable of bearing universal odium and scorn, as of *leading* in secret conspiracies and desperate machinations.

Upon the fourth of June, the House by message desired "that his Excellency would be pleased to order, that copies be laid before them of such letters as he had written (of certain dates) relating to the public affairs of this province; *together with such other letters as his Excellency should think proper.*" Here was a fair opportunity for this gentleman, to discover *some one instance* of friendship to the country in the multitude of his corresspondencies. But so far from complying with this rational request, it was slighted with a deterity and air peculiar to the person to whom it was made.

The Governor in his answer to the Council, on the 17th of June last, informs them that they "could *not possibly* form a *right judgment* of ALL "the parts of those letters, unless they should also "be furnished with the letters to which his are "wrote in answer." But in the name of common sense, in whose power did it lay to furnish these letters; and against whom, and of what does the presumption lay, in case they are not produced? He who wanted *a right judgment to be formed of all parts* of the correspondence would give all the light he was able into the matter;—and he who thought it would be for his advantage, and had it in his power, would speedily give that light. But I have the uncommon happiness to fall in with the gentleman, and in this instance I see other reasons than his word to believe, and, therefore, I credit him. I verily believe that *a right judgment* cannot be formed of ALL PARTS of his excellency's letters, without an inspection into those of his correspondent: and what is more, I believe that the very reason, why the letters of Whately were not produced was because;—being produced & compared;—they would aid us much, not only in *forming a right judgment of the letters*, but also to determine with convincing certainty what were the machinations and views,—the *whole* hearts and souls of *the writers*.

In his Excellency's letter of the 4th of Oct. 68, he acknowledges the receipt of Mr. Whately's letter of the 31st of July, and then proceeds, "*It is not strange* that measures should be immediately taken *to reduce the colonies*," &c. Now I believe that his Excellency could help us to form a much *bett r judgment* of what those measures were which he thus acquiesces in, if he would exhibit the letter to which his is an answer. But he prefers leaving the matter to suspicion and conjecture, rather than gratify us with the whole truth of fact:—and manifestly for this reason, because concealment is of more advantage to him than such a discovery. I think he can never have cause to complain, if this people think *the worst* of him, 'till he shall remove their just suspicions by a frank and full disclosure of his whole correspondence.—And as the gentleman chuses to leave us at large to conjecture, I now form one, which will, probably, be not short of the truth.

His Excellency had informed his British friend so early as the 18th June, that "the com-"missioners, *four of them, being destitute of protec-"tion*, removed with their families on board the "Romney, & there remain and hold their board, "and next week intend to do the same, and also "open the Custom-house at the Castle." Now there can be no doubt, that this letter had reached England, previous to the 31st of July, and resolutions consequent upon it had been taken. If *a Chief Justice* informs that *the Subject*, especially a crown officer, *is destitute of protection*, the representation (however false) will be believed true in fact; and when this is the case, *all the aid which can be given to the officers of the crown* will be afforded; especially if it is credited, that with *all such aid they will have enough to do to maintain* THE AUTHORITY OF GOVERNMENT *and to carry* THE LAWS *into execution.* Now we all know that the extraordinary aid which is in Great-Britain ever afforded to the civil power, is that of *the military*:—Tho' it is a solemn truth, that *the civil power*, like every other, which calls in the aid of an ally stronger than itself, PERISHES *by the assistance it receives.*—This military aid was accordingly applied by the British administration to remedy the suggested evils; which from being almost wholly imaginary, became real, and from being trifling and temporary, became fixed and permanent. Of this *warlike*, and *hostile* application, Whately's letter to his Excellency of the 31st of July, no doubt gave full account:—And *these very measures*, there can be as little doubt, were those that *did not seem strange* to his Excellency;—tho' they appeared not only strange, but inhuman and mad, to every other good subject of his Majesty in the province. Instead of reducing the colonies to their former state of government, and order, they confirmed the more modern one of confusion and bloodshed, general oppression and universal murmur and discontent.

If such measures as these *did not really appear strange* to his Excellency, I can only attribute it to his thorough recollection of what he had done and wrote, and his good opinion of his own influence and weight with the British ministry: So that an *immediate* compliance with his inclinations and desire, was no more than *he expected*, and consequently, that this extravagant measure, which astonished all the world besides, was devested of all *strangeness* in the eye of his Excellency.

Thus have I considered Mr. Hutchinson, as degrading the highest station in the law to the lowest office of the inquisition; as descending from the rank of CHIEF JUSTICE to that of a common INFORMER:—An informer against "particular persons" & "THE PROVINCE IN GENERAL";—yes,—the *dark* assassin of *private characters* and HIS NATIVE COUNTRY.

Convinced, as I am, that governor Hutchinson, in defiance of every principal of right, every sentiment of honor and gratitude; convinced I say, that HE is the first, the most malignant and *insatiable* enemy of my country;—that he is the chief author and supporter of the severest calamities under which this people labor;—convinced that he has done more general mischiefs, and committed greater public crimes, than his *life* can repair or his *death* satisfy;—and that *he is the man*, against whom the blood of my slaughtered brethren cries from the ground:—I have, and shall, as strength is given me, pursue him. And if at this time of life I am too *old* for an AVENGER OF BLOOD, I am also too *young* to desert the service of my country. But it may be profitable now to leave him to the reflections of his own conscience—the anguish of a *departing* spirit.—And if he be not speedily called to the great bar of the universe; peradventure I shall once more call him—but with no *friendly* voice—to the highest, the most terrible tribunal on earth;—the tribunal of his injured countrymen.

Addressing to the contemplations of his pillow, I close for the present, with the words of a favorite author.

You have *lived long enough: thy way of life*
Is fallen into fear, the yellow leaf,
And that which should accompany old age,
As honor, love, obedience, troops of friends,
You must not look to have: But, in their stead,
CURSES, BOTH LOUD AND DEEP.

MARCHMONT NEDHAM.

* His message to the House, 9th June last, concludes with these words, "thus much however I may *assure* you, that it has not been the tendency and design of them (his letters) to subvert the constitution of this government, but rather *to preserve it entire*; and I have reason to think they have *not been altogether ineffectual to that purpose*."

(The following is but just come to Hand.)

Plimouth, January 7, 1774.

Messieurs EDES & GILL,

I HAVE been astonish'd that nobody has transmitted to you an account of the celebration of the 22d of December in this town, the anniversary of our ANCESTORS first landing in New-England; an event pregnant with empire, and ought to be commemorated, that we may keep in view the magnitude of their sufferings, and the cause which compell'd them to abandon their native country and begin a settlement (as it is elsewhere finely express'd) on bare creation. In the morning the committee of correspondence assembled at Mr. Howland's, and from thence proceeded to Mr. Robbins's meeting house, where the Rev'd Mr. Charles Turner deliver'd a discourse on the occasion from Zechariah 4th chapter, part of the 9th and 10th verses. It is difficult to say whether his discourse was most remarkable for the sublimity of the sentiment, the harmony of the periods, or the glorious spirit of liberty which breath'd thro' every sentence. After service the greater part of the people, together with five of the clergy conven'd at Mr. Howlands, and found an elegant and very suitable dinner prepar'd for their Entertainment. The whole day and evening were spent agreeably and to the honor of all present. Every countenance was expressive of gratitude and joy, and every tongue exuberant in blessing the memory of our fathers. The breast which had only one spark of patriotism must have been rais'd to a flame, to see a large circle of venerable old men, in contemplating the difficulties and hardships the first settlers waded through, animated to a degree that won'd have excited them to bleed at the shrine of freedom.

ALL Persons indebted for this Paper, whose Accounts have been above 12 Months standing, are requested to make immediate Payment.

B O S T O N, February 7, 1774.

ON Tuesday last his Majesty's Council unanimously passed the following ADDRESS to His Excellency the Governor, and on the same Day it was presented by the Hon. *James Pitts*, *Artemas Ward*, *Benjamin Greenleaf*, *Walter Spooner* and *Samuel Phillips*, Esqrs; a Committee for that Purpose, viz.

To his Excellency THOMAS HUTCHINSON, Esq; Governor and Commander in Chief in and over the Province of the MASSACHUSETTS-BAY.

The Address of his Majesty's COUNCIL of the said Province.

May it please your Excellency,

THE Board have attentively considered your Excellency's Speech to the two Houses at the opening of the present Session.

The Affair of the Indians of Martha's Vineyard has been repeatedly the Object of the Attention of the General Court, and at the last Session a new Committee was appointed to go thither to obtain a true State of the Facts; and it is expected at this Session they will make their Report. As soon as laid before us we shall take it into Consideration, and do our Part to "prevent all Grounds for Complaint of the Denial or Delay of Justice."

With respect to the late Settlement of the Western Line of this Province, where it is bounded by the Eastern Line of New-York, it gives us great Pleasure, as the Dispute has been the Source of so much Mischief to the two Colonies, that your Excellency has reason to expect his Majesty's Confirmation of that Settlement, as soon as the necessary Formalities of Office will admit. And with respect to the Subject of the Address of the two Houses in January last, we are glad your Excellency has reason to hope for a satisfactory Determination and Order concerning it.

The Order of his Majesty for regulating the future Conduct of the Governor in the Supreme Court of Probate, and in the Decision of Controversies concerning Marriage and Divorce, is founded in the highest Reason: for (as it is well observed by one of his Majesty's Council at Law, viz. *Richard Jackson*, Esq; to whom the Matter was referred for his Opinion in Point of Law) "it is so unsuitable to the Nature of a Court of Justice to consist of two Branches, each possessing a Negative on the other, that though something like it may be found, yet he conceives no Construction ought to be founded on the Possibility of the Existence of such a Court, because the Instances of such (if any) will be found to stand on Principles not applicable to the present Case. And he is of Opinion the Governor of the Province of the Massachusetts-Bay may lawfully acquiesce in the Determination of the Majority of the whole Number of Councellors present, although he should differ in Opinion from that Majority: because he conceives it to be past Doubt, that by the Clause in the Charter (which provides that in all Acts of Government by the General Assembly or in Council, the Governor shall have the negative voice) nothing more is intended by the Words, Acts of Government in Council, than executive Acts of State in Exclusion of judicial Acts, which though they are the Exercise of a Power derived under Government, are never, he believes, comprehended under the Description of Acts of Government." To which may be added, that it is plainly a Solecism that a Court of Justice should be so constituted, as in many Cases, properly cognizable by it, to be incapable, from the Nature of its Constitution, to give a Judgment. We agree with your Excellency, that in this Construction of the Charter, which you say is different from what has been made by all Governors ever since its first Publication, his Majesty has shewn a tender Regard for the Interest and Convenience of his Subjects.

Your Excellency is pleased to inform us, that you are "required to signify to the two Houses his Majesty's Disapprobation of the Appointment of Committees of Correspondence, in various Instances, which sit and act during the Recess of the General Court by Prorogation."—So far as this Matter relates to the Board, it can relate to them only in the Instance of Correspondence with Mr. Agent Bollan: With whom, since they chose him Agent, they have divers Times appointed a Committee to correspond during the Recess of the Court.

As this is a Matter of great Importance your Excellency will permit us to discuss it with Freedom—When Governor Bernard was in the Chair he early discovered a Disposition to infringe on the Rights of the Board: and this Disposition increased, till at length, regardless of the Dignity of his Station, he descended to the most ungentlemanly Treatment of them, when they either refused an Acquiescence with his unwarrantable Measures, or endeavoured to support their Rights against his Usurpation. They had long apprehended, that besides those personal Attacks in Council, he had by his Letters been misrepresenting them to his Majesty's Ministers; but they had not full Evidence of it, till they received authenticated Copies of some of his Letters to Lord Hillsborough, in which they found themselves personally abused, and all their Rights and Privileges in their public Capacity, and their very Existence in that Capacity, struck at. Those Letters having been laid before Parliament unjustly procured a Parliamentary Censure of the Council, and Threats of further Proceedings against them. Now though it had been usual in a regular State of Things for an Agent to be appointed with the Concurrence of the three Branches of the General Court, yet when that State became inverted, when the Governor was endeavouring to destroy the Rights of the Council, when our Constitutional Rights in general were in danger, and no Confidence could be placed in a Governor, the Principle of Self-Preservation and the Right of Defence, naturally inherent in Man, both individually and socially considered, required and justified the two Houses jointly or severally at their Option, to choose an Agent or Agents for the Defence of those Rights independent of the Governor. But it might frustrate the End of such Choice, if they had not the Power of appointing a Committee to correspond with their Agent when chosen: for although the Governor should permit them to sit till they had informed and instructed their Agent in every thing at that Time thought needful, yet after the fullest Information and Instructions at first given, many Things would probably arise during the General Court's Recess (which by successive Prorogations the Governor cou'd prolong) to make such a Correspondence necessary. If then there be sufficient Reason for the appointing an Agent independent of the Governor (as it clearly appears to us there was and still continues to be) there must be sufficient Reason for the Means necessary to effect the End of that Appointment: among which Means is the keeping up and maintaining with him a Correspondence, whereby he may be furnished from Time to Time, as he shall call for them, with all needful Information and Assistance: which in the Recess of the General Court cannot be done but by a Committee. Among those Means is also included a seasonable and just Compensation for his Services.

On this Occasion your Excellency will permit us to express our Concern, that you were not pleased to give your Assent to the first Grant made to Mr. Bollan for his Services since his being Agent by Appointment of the Council when you were not under the Obligation of an Instruction forbidding you to give such Assent.

If the Council had had Opportunity to state the Reasons of that Appointment, and those Reasons had been permitted to accompany the Representation which procured that Instruction, it is humbly apprehended they might have occasioned an essential Alteration in it, or wholly prevented it. But if the foregoing State of Facts should come to his Majesty's Knowledge, we humbly trust he will see sufficient Reason and be graciously pleased to revoke the said Instruction.

The procuring Instructions that are to affect the Rights of either House, or in any other way injure the Rights and Interests of the Province without giving them a Hearing, is a great Grievance. In the Law Courts, even in the smallest Concerns, the Parties may be heard before Judgment; and the Opportunity for it is founded in the highest Reason and Justice. Is there not equal Reason and Justice that a whole Province should be heard on the first Motion for, and through the Process of Instructions that are to affect them in their greatest Interests? But in what Instance of Instructions thus affecting them have they been heard?—When your Excellency was stating the Case of the Council's appointing a Committee to correspond with their Agent, which has procured his Majesty's Disapprobation of their Conduct, did not Justice require the Communication of it to the Council for their Observations on it, that from both together (if it was needful any Representation should have been made on that Head) his Majesty might have had the Means of forming a true Judgment concerning it? And does not Justice require a similar Proceeding in all Representations, on which are to be grounded any Instructions, that shall tend to lessen the Rights of either House, or any other Way affect the Interests of the Province?

On this Occasion it is obvious to observe that within these few Years the Ministry seem to have considered the Governors of this Province, not as Crown Officers with Commissions under the Great Seal, but as Officers within their Department and under their Direction. This remarkably appeared in the Administration of Governor Bernard, who very probably was the means of it: For there is Reason to suppose, and his Letters shew it, that he laid a Plan for depriving Americans in general, and this Province in particular, of their Liberties: And being a Volunteer in the executing it, in order to secure himself seems to have procured from the Minister Letters of Instruction from time to time, as he had occasion for them: Whereby without giving the Province an opportunity of being heard, its Rights, Interests and Character have been greatly injured. And as the same mode of proceeding has been continued, there is the same reason to complain of it. But it is humbly hoped from the Goodness and Justice of his Majesty, and the distinguished Virtues of the Earl of Dartmouth, (his Majesty's Minister for the American Department) that this Province will be made happy by the Removal of all its Grievances.

In the mean time the Board are affected with the deepest concern, that any part of their Conduct should be disapproved by his Majesty: but they humbly trust, that when his Majesty shall be informed of the Reasons on which it is grounded, it will notwithstanding be the Object of his Gracious Approbation.

Messieurs EDES & GILL,

FOR the information of posterity, who must undoubtedly be very much interested in transactions of such importance, it is publickly made known in Draper's Gazette of the 3d of February, that "*at a town-meeting*" held in Marshfield, the 31st of January 1774. Nathaniel Ray Thomas, was chosen Moderator *at said meeting*." After this we are told that "the vote was put to know the *town's mind*, whether the said moderator should have leave to speak *his mind*; and it passed in the affirmative." When the town's mind and the *moderator's mind* were thus discovered, we are informed, that then the vote was put to know *their minds*, (viz. both their minds) whether they would act;' and this also passed in the affirmative. Finding so remarkable an harmony, similarity and agreement between the *mind* of the town, and the *penetrating genius* of Nathaniel Ray Thomas, Esq; they proceeded next to choose a committee of SEVEN persons (after the pattern of the seven wise men of Gotham, the seven wise masters, and seven champions of Christendom.) viz. Doct. Isaac Winslow, Nathaniel Ray Thomas, Esq; Mess. Elisha Ford, Seth Bryant, William Stevens, John Baker and Ephraim Little, whose great names are there held up to the wonder and admiration of mankind. We are told that this committee was chosen to "draw up what they tho't proper to be voted by the town;" that "then the meeting was adjourned for half an hour, and at the expiration of that term made the report." Whether the meeting itself, or these glorious seven made the report, the accuracy of their draftsman has left in uncertainty. The report however is transmitted to us, as the opinion of the town of Marshfield, and which it is declared they voted to *except*. From the tenor of it, notwithstanding the favorable opinion we might before have imbibed both of the *town's mind* and the *moderator's mind*, it seems very doubtful whether either of them can at present be considered either of *sound mind or memory*. For by the very first declaration, it is voted and resolved as the opinion of the town, "that they *ever have and always will be* good and loyal subjects to our sovereign lord king George *the third*;" whereby they declare it as their opinion, that they were the subjects of king George the third, before he was born, and that for the future, whatever king shall reign, they will still be the subjects of *king George the third*. They then go on to declare "that they will observe, obey and *enforce* all good and wholesome laws of the legislature." It hath been usually thought sufficient for good subjects to *submit* to the laws; but the patriotic inhabitants of Marshfield, bent on works of supererogation, are so very good subjects, that they promise also to *enforce* them, not only to the utmost of their own power and ability, but, what is still more terrible, by the utmost endeavors of their representative, Abijah White; who is thereby empowered with full authority to detect and bring to justice the perpetrators of those horrible mischiefs, the detention and destruction of the teas belonging to the East India company; to oblige the people of Boston to pay for them, and secure the inhabitants of Marshfield, to carry all the laws of the province into due execution; to see that all offenders be properly punished, and to put their resolves into the public papers for the terror of evil-doers". They then go on to communicate a new discovery of the town of Marshfield with regard to the foundation and basis of Magna Charta; for they tell us, the grand basis of Magna Charta and the reformation is liberty of conscience and the right of private judgment;" an observation, which clearly shows that they have as compleat a knowledge of the foundation of Magna Charta and the reformation, as the indian had of the foundation of the earth, who imagined it stood upon a turtle. After these things, they declare "that the proceedings of the town of Boston have been illegal, tumultuous and of dangerous tendency, which they apprehend may *effect* their properties, if not their liberties; and that they think it their indispensible duty to show their disapprobation of such measures." They go on to protest against being tarred and feathered, and ratify all with the solemn attestation of Nehemiah Thomas, town clerk.

Had these Resolves originated in some obscure town, scarcely known or named, whose influence had been small, and whose threats despicable; or had the execution of them been committed to a man, whose utmost importance was confined to his ignorant adherents in a petty village; I should not have thought they deserved animadversion: But, when I hear these sentiments delivered by the great and glorious town of Marshfield, where liberty of conscience, and the right of private judgment, the grand basis of Magna Charta, and the Reformation, reside; when I see them committed to the hands of the ever memorable Abijah White, of whom it is enough to say that he is chosen the Representative of such a town; my concern predominates over my timidity, and I cannot but step forth to warn my fellow citizens of the town of Boston to take some speedy measures for avoiding the instant danger which hangs over their heads from the potent fulminations of the town of Marshfield, and the terrors of the puissant Abijah White.

I must nevertheless express my concern, that a town, who possess such a share of spirit and sentiment, should want a draftsman, able to write grammar and English. To throw in my mite towards their assistance, I would humbly offer and propose to their High Mightinesses, the two following Resolves, to be considered on and entered into at their next Town-Meeting.

First, Resolved, That the Draftsman of the last Resolves, in gratitude to him for his services, be sent to some public school, and maintained three years at the Town's charge, with a view to his learning to spell and write English; and we the Inhabitants of Marshfield do further declare that, notwithstanding the Blunder of our said Draftsman at the conclusion of said Resolves, which hath led many of our readers into mistakes and uncertainty, we did really mean to *accept* of the report of our committee, and not (as it might seem) to *except* against it.

Secondly, That whereas A——h W—e, Esq; our present R————e, setting forth on his adventure armed *Cap-a-pie* (as it is said) with a great appurtenance of swords, cutlasses, pistols, *Marshfield Resolves,* and other warlike Ammunition, hath very much dismayed, terrified and confounded the whole Town of Boston, and the Members of the General Court; and put all those people, who did not agree with him in sentiment, into the most violent fear of their lives; insomuch that it is expected that all, who "were acting, aiding and assisting, or *conniving at* the destruction of the Teas," and so had incurred our express resentment, are about to fly beyond the sea, to avoid the danger of his prosecutions: We the inhabitants of the said town of Marshfield, not wishing the *entire depopulation* of the province, do direct that the said A——h W—e do *surceose* from all further proceedings.

BOSTON, Feb. 7.

Monday last the Corporation of Harvard-College, made Choice of the Honorable JOHN WINTHROP, Esq; L. L. D. and F. R. S. to be PRESIDENT; but that he declined accepting that Office.

Thursday last the General Assembly made choice of the following Civil Officers for the Year ensuing.

The Hon. *Harrison Gray,* Esq; Treasurer and Receiver-General.

The Hon. *Thomas Cushing,* Esq; Commissary-General.

The Hon. *James Russell,* Esq; Impost-Officer.

Truck-Master for Fort *Pownall,* Mr. *Jedediah Prebble,* jun.

The great contest at present between the friends of Government and the friends of Liberty, seems to be, whether the Judges of the Superior Court shall receive their Salaries as usual by the Grants of the General Assembly of this Province, or be dependent upon the Crown for their Support. Both sides agree that if the latter takes place, our Courts of Justice will be turned into Courts of Politicks, and those who for the future are to hold the Stations of venerable Judges, will be, equally with Crown Officers, under too strong a temptation to pervert Law and Justice, in Compliance with the Humour or Interest of a weak or corrupt British Minister.

We hear that one G———, a new made Justice at Wellfleet, purchased two Chests of the East-India Company's Tea that was saved out of the *Brig* lately wreck'd at Cape Cod; one of which he carried to the Place of his abode; but before he had retailed one third of it, the People there took the Insult offered them into Consideration at a legal Town Meeting, where having expressed their Minds, they *demanded,* and got the Remainder into their Possession.——The other Chest was left at Province Town, at which Place (about a Fortnight since) there was an Ordination, when 7 Indians appeared, who, without much Ceremony, seiz'd upon the detested Drug and burnt it.——

Extract of a Letter from Plymouth, February 1, 1774.

"*JUDGE Oliver and Mr. Hutchinson came to Town last Thursday, no doubt with Intention to insult us, but to their great Mortification, they never before met with so warm a Reception.——On Friday Evening the Town appeared to be very uneasy, which alarmed the Tories, who gave out that Forty Men armed were ready to defend Col. Watson's House, and indeed a Number were there the greater Part of the Night, armed with loaded Guns and Kettles of hot Water; but notwithstanding their Vigilance, a Tribe of Indians met at Col. Watson's and* Boot-cap'd *Mr. Hutchinson's Sley.——Saturday Morning some sour Faces appeared, but not much said by the Tories, the Whigs continuing very uneasy that the Consignee did not decamp and retire to Chessamuttock.——Sunday, the* CONSIGNEE *went to Meeting, the People much dissatisfied: The worthy Veteran Capt. J——n with most of his Family and several others came to our Meeting, declaring they could not worship with a Man* who had done all in his Power to ruin his Country.*——Monday Morning a general Dissatisfaction thro' the Town; Col. Watson much alarm'd, made it his Business to talk with all he met, and assured them that Mr. Hutchinson should go out of Town assoon as the Sley could be repaired, and desired that the People would be patient till the Morrow. The People insisted that he should go out immediately; and if Mr. Hutchinson had not gone off that afternoon, I don't know what would have been the Consequence.*"

☞ Let the Enemies to their Country, from the Conduct and Fate of the fugitive *Consignees,* learn, that it is unsafe to aid a *Tyrant* in any Attempt to ENSLAVE a People BORN AND DETERMINED TO REMAIN FREE.

Extract of a Letter from Cambridge of the 5th Instant.

"*ALL the Persons in Captain* Marrett's *Family, who have had the* Small-Pox, *are recovered. There is no Person now sick of that Distemper, nor any who have the Symptoms of it, in this Town. Mr. Miller of Charlestown, who was taken ill with it a few Days since, caught it by visiting the sick Persons at Capt. Marrett's, before their Distemper was known to be the Small-Pox. Several other Persons, who were greatly exposed, have by a kind Providence escaped the Infection. It is apprehended the Students of the College may return to their Studies with Safety next Week.——Should anyThing intervene to prevent, Notice will be given of it in public.*"

Sundry Pieces omitted, will be in our next.

We are informed that the Resolves of the Town of Marshfield were carried by a Majority of only one Vote; and we soon expect a more *intelligible* account of the Meeting than has yet been given in a public paper.

The General Assembly of New York have appointed the Speaker, and twelve other Gentlemen of the House, or any seven of them, to be a standing Committee of Correspondence and Enquiry, with the other Colonies.

No Tea Ship arrived at New-York, by the last Papers.

DIED] On Friday last, Mr. David Moore Æ. 18, Son of Mr. Hugh Moore, deceased; his Funeral is to be attended this Afternoon from the House of his Mother's, near Oliver's Dock: His Friends and Relations are desired to attend.

Mrs. Sarah Field, Widow, her Funeral will be at half past 3 o'Clock, tomorrow Afternoon.

DIED Mrs. Rebecca Allen, aged 72, Widow of the late Mr. Jeremiah Allen, of this Town, Hatter, deceased.—She was a Woman of an unblemished Character in every Relation.

—At Haverhill, the Rev. Mr. Edward Barnard.

THIS DAY PUBLISHED, (by I. THOMAS,)
Number I. of
The Royal *American* MAGAZINE.

Joseph-Pearse Palmer,

At No. 18, South-Side of the Town-Dock.
HAS for Sale, very cheap for Cash, viz.

Chocolate, at 14*d.* 15*d.* & 20*d.* per lb. by the Box.

ALSO,

Nutmegs	Shalloons
Pepper	Beaver Coatings
Ginger	Breeches Patterns
Alspice	Water'd Tammies for Winter Gowns
Coffee (but no Tea)	Wine Glasses and Salts of several sorts
Loaf and Brown Sugar	Beer Glasses
Raisins	Wine and Water Glasses
N. E. and W. I. Rum	Tumblers of several sorts
Rice	Quart Decanters
Flour in large & small Bbls	Vinegar and Oil Cruets
Superfine Flour	Linnens and Threads
Dumb Fish	Drawboys &c.
Onions	Scotch Handkerchiefs
Bar-Iron	Paper
Nails	Nova-Scotia Oats
Irish Shovels	Redwood &c. &c. &c.
Narrow Axes	
Black Velvet	
Broad Cloths	

THIS DAY IS PUBLISHED BY
JOHN LANGDON,
Bookseller in Cornhill, (Price 2s. L. M.)

The Twelfth Edition of Lord *Somers*

Judgment of whole Kingdoms and Nations, concerning the Rights, Power and Prerogative of Kings, and the Rights, Privileges and Properties of the People. Shewing the Nature of Govergment in general, &c.

☞ This Pamphlet run thro' Ten Editions in London in less than twelve Months.

House-Furniture taken by Execution.
TO BE SOLD
By Benjamin Church,
On THURSDAY next,
At TEN o'Clock in the Forenoon,
BY PUBLICK AUCTION,

A Variety of House Furniture,—consisting of a neat Mehogany Case of Draws with an O G Top, a large Mehogany Desk with a swell'd Front, Mehogany and other Chairs, Ditto Tables, Looking Glasses, Feather Beds, Bedsteads and Bedding, sundry Pieces Plate, Pewter, Brass, &c. &c Also sundry European Articles, viz. Broad Cloths, Kerseys, Ratteens, Shalloons, Camblets, Linnens, Checks, Worsted Hose, Case Knives and Forks, Watches, a Fall-back Chaise and Harness, &c.

To begin at Ten o'Clock, A. M.

Penobscot Company.

ALL Persons claiming or holding under the Ten Original Proprietors of a certain Tract of Land granted by the Council of Plymouth, March 13th, 1629, to *John Beauchamp* of *London,* and *Thomas Leverett,* of *Boston,* in the County of *Lincoln;* situate in the Eastern Parts of the Province of the *Massachusetts-Bay,* commonly called MUSCONGUS, are hereby Notified, that their Meeting stands adjourned to Tuesday the Eighth Day of *March* next, at Six o'Clock P. M. at the House of Col. *Ingersol,* in King-Street, *Boston,* at which Time they will proceed to draw their several Shares or Lots of the Land surveyed and laid out on *Penobscot* River, called the Front or River Lots.

WM. HUNT, Prop'rs Clerk.

Boston, February 1, 1774.

On Thursday next, at Ten o'Clock,
will be sold by Public Vendue, at the New Auction-Room South Side of the Town House, viz.

HOUSE Furniture, consisting of Mehogany Chest of Draws, Desks, Dining and Spring Tables, Beauro ditto, Tea Trays, green Harrateen Curtains, green Bottom Chairs, Easy Chairs, Feather Beds and Bedsteds, Glass Pictures, Metal, Coat and Jacket Buttons: Also Broad Cloths, Bearskins, Ratteens, Irish Linnen, Jersey knit Hose, Killmarnock Caps, and a Number of other Articles.

ANDREW OLIVER, Auctioneer.

N. B. For private Sale at said Auction Room,——Handsome Looking Glasses, Muffs, a Silver Tankard, Porringers, Pepper Casters, Cups, Tea Spoons, a genteel Silver Salver, 10 Inches over, Silver plated Candlesticks, also a handsome full suit of Brocade, and a suit of black Grogram.

At said Auction-Room constant attendance is given to receive all kinds of Goods for Public and Private Sale.

WEDNESDAY next, *XI* o'Clock,
in the Morning, will be sold by PUBLIC VENDUE, at RUSSELL's Auction-Room in Queen-Street,
A Variety of English GOODS, —among which are,—

DRAB, mix'd, dark brown, blue and other coloured Broad-Cloths, Devonshire Kerseys, Duffils, strip'd Lutestrings, plain Sattins, rich black Taffaties, light Padusoys, Irish Linnens, a great Variety of lac'd Sattins, Missinets, yard-wide Poplins, Drawboys, Filleting Tapes, Pins, Mens and Womens Hose, &c. &c. Also, Mahogany Dining Tables, an Eight Day Clock, Looking-Glasses, several good Feather Beds, &c.

Wednesday next, XI o'Clock. J. RUSSELL, Auct'r.

New AUCTION-ROOM, Cornhill,
TO-MORROW MORNING,
At TEN o'Clock,
Will be Sold by PUBLIC VENDUE,
At *Greenleaf's* Auction-Room,

A Very great Assortment of Goods, being the Property of a Gentleman leaving the Province, amongst are 100 Pieces of Irish Linens, a Number Rheams of Writing Paper of differing fineness, Broad Cloths of various colours, Forrest Cloths, black, blue, and Claret colour Velvets, most sorts of Linnen Handkerchiefs, English and Raven's Duck, fashionable Muffs and Tippets, Men's Norway Doe Gloves, Worsted and Thread Hose, Worsted Breeches Pieces and Mitts, Lastings, coloured and Scotch Threads, Sewing Silks, Duffils, Ratteens, Kerseys, Ribbons, Tapes, Bobbins, a Variety of Penknives, Cuttoes, Scissars, Razors, Sleeve Buttons, Bags of Silk and Hair Buttons, Twist, plain and flower'd Silk Gauze, plain and figur'd Lawns, brown and strip'd Hollands, Callicoes, Shalloons, Tammies, Camblets, Duroys, Table Cloths and Napkins, also a few Barrels of Turpentine, Silver Watches, Past Necklaces, &c. &c.

W. GREENLEAF, Auctioneer.

The sale will begin precisely at TEN o'Clock.

The Sale of BOOKS begins
At GOULD's *Auction Office,*
In Back Street,
To-Morrow Morning at half past Nine o'Clock, precisely.

R. GOULD, Auctioneer.

To the Honorable SAMUEL DANFORTH, Esq; one of his Majesty's Justices of the Peace throughout the Province of the *Massachusetts-Bay.*

We the Subscribers, some of the Proprietors of a Township of Land called *Silvester-Canada,* of the Contents of seven Miles square, lying on a River called *Androscoggin* and adjoining to *Baker's-Town,* so called, in the County of *Cumberland,* the Plan of which was confirmed to the Proprietors thereof by the General Court of said Province in *June* 1768, humbly request your Honor to issue a Warrant for calling a Meeting of said Proprietors, to be held at the Dwelling-House of *Cornelius Turner,* Innholder in *Hanover,* in the County of *Plymouth,* on Tuesday the Eighth Day of *March* next, at Ten o'Clock in the Forenoon; then and there to act on the following Articles, *viz.*

1. To choose a Moderator, Clerk, Treasurer and Collector of Taxes.
2. To confirm any or all former Votes and Grants of said Proprietors at any former Meeting or Meetings, as they shall see fit.
3. To raise a sufficient Sum or Sums of Money by Tax or otherwise, for discharging their Debts due or that may become due.
4. To choose a Standing Committee to transact the Affairs of said Proprietors, settle the Accounts, adjust the Debts that are or shall be due from the said Proprietors, and order Payment of the same, and agreeable to Law to make Sale of those Proprietors Lands who are delinquent in paying their Taxes; and to determine where the Settling Lots shall be laid, and how much in a Lot, and about convenient Ways, and procure a Plan thereof, to be lodged with the Clerk as soon as may be.
5. To agree what shall be allowed the Clerk and the Committee for their Services.
6. To choose a Committee for calling Meetings for the future, and to agree on the Method thereof.
7. To appoint an Agent or Agents, Attorney or Attornies, with Power of Substitution, to commence an Action or Actions for said Proprietors, and in their Names to prosecute the same in any Court of Law, or otherwise amply, to all Intents and Purposes, until final Judgment and Execution, and in like manner to defend them in all Actions brought or that may be brought against them.
8. And to agree on any other Thing which said Proprietors shall judge necessary for carrying forward the Settlement of said Township.

Ja's Warren,
Wm. Sever,
Plymouth, January 12th, 1774. *John Cushing,*
David Little, jun.
Charles Turner.

Province of the Massachusetts-Bay,
TO CHARLES TURNER, of *Scituate,* in the County of *Plymouth,* in said Province, Gentleman, one of the principal Proprietors of the Land aforesaid, *Greeting.*

SEAL.

In pursuance of the foregoing Application and Request, you are hereby required to give Notice (in Time and Manner as the Law directs) to the Proprietors aforementioned, That they meet at the Time and Place and for the Purposes mentioned in the afore-written Petition.

Given under my Hand and Seal, this 19th Day of *January,* *A. D.* 1774. S. DANFORTH, Justice of the Peace throughout the Province aforesaid.

Scituate, January 20th, 1774.

By Virtue of the afore-written Warrant, to me directed, I do hereby notify and warn the Proprietors of the aforesaid Lands to meet at the Dwelling-House of *Cornelius Turner,* Innholder in *Hanover,* on Tuesday the Eighth Day of *March* next, at Ten o'Clock in the Forenoon, for the Purposes therein mentioned.

CHARLES TURNER.

Burials in the Town of BOSTON, since our last.
Eleven Whites. One Black.
Baptiz'd in the several Churches, Fourteen.

High Water at BOSTON, for the present Week.

Monday, 30 min. aft. 8	Friday, 0 min. after 12
Tuesday, 30 min. aft. 9	Saturday 28 min. af 12
Wednesday, 30m. aft. 10	Lord's-Day, 15 m. af 1
Thursday, 30 min. aft. 11	New ☽ 10 Day, 3 Aft.

WHEREAS the Proprietors of *Sudbury Canada*, (so called) being a Township granted to Josiah Richardson, Esq; and others, in the County of Cumberland, at a legal Meeting by adjournment, on the 17th Day of August, A. D. 1773, granted a Tax of 20/. L. M. on each single Right: Also, the said Proprietors at a legal Meeting by adjournment on the 7th Day of December, A. D. 1773, granted another Tax of 40/. L. M. on each single Right, to defray the Charges of clearing a Road to the said Township, and other necessary Charges: And although the said Taxes have been Published according to Law, and payment requested; nevertheless several of the said Proprietors are Delinquent in the payment of the said Taxes: Public Notice is therefore hereby given to said Delinquents, that unless their Taxes are paid to Cornelius Wood of Sudbury, Treasurer, or to us the Subscribers, by TEN o'Clock in the Morning of the 6th Day of April next, their Rights will be Sold as the Law directs, for the payment of their Taxes and Charges. The Sale to begin at Eleven o'Clock in said Morning, at the Dwelling-House of Captain Isaac Jones, Innholder in Weston, and continued by adjournment (if need be) 'till the whole be Sold.

Cornelius Wood, *Elijah Bent*, *Josiah Stone*, } Proprietor's Committee.

Saml Abbot & Com^y.

HEREBY Inform the Public, that their Co-partnership is this Day mutually dissolved, wherefore all Persons who have any Demads on, and all who are Indebted to said Company, are desired to call on

SAMUEL ABBOT,

for an immediate Settlement, at the Store on *Greene's* Wharf, near the Market, lately occupied by said Company, where is now selling off, an assortment of English & India Goods, on very low terms for Cash.

Boston 25th Jan. 1774.

CHESHIRE CHEESE.

A Quantity of Cheshire Cheese TO BE SOLD at a low Price by the Hundred or single Cheese, at the Store of

Penuel Bowen,

Opposite to the Golden Ball, *BOSTON.*

Nathl & Willm Coffin,

Have to Sell at the STORE lately occupied by Mr. WARD NICHOLAS BOYLSTON;

A Few Casks of good Sherry and Malaga WINE, Lisbon and Malaga LEMMONS in very good Order, COFFEE by the Hundred or larger Quantity, a few Hogsheads of West-India RUM, and some INDIGO of a remarkable Quality; besides a Variety of West-India GOODS, all which may be had Cheap.

NAILS, &c.

A Quantity of 4d, 6d, 8d, 10d, & 20d Nails, a great variety of Looking Glasses, China, Taffaties and Gorguroons, Velvet Corks, and a quantity of choice Pease, to be Sold cheap by

Lee & Jones,

Who have also for Sale,

A general Assortment of Piece Goods.

BRIMSTONE by the Cask.

WANTED,

A good Spinet or Harpsichord.

Inquire of the Printers.

WANTED to Purchase

A Sloop or Schooner burthen from 70 to 80 Tons, not exceeding three Years old, for which the Cash will be immediately paid.

Inquire of Edward Davis.

WHEREAS the Proprietors of Land in the Township of *Leicester* on *Otter Creek*, (which Township was Granted by the Governor and Council of New-Hampshire) did at their Meeting in January 1773, Vote, That the Sum of 4 Dollars should be raised and levied on each original Right, and also at their Meeting in March following, Voted, That the Sum of 1 Dollar as aforesaid, for the Bounding and Lotting out said Township, and for the Managing and carrying on any other Affairs, for the common good of said Propriety, and that a Committee be appointed to assess the same.— Therefore we the Subscribers being appointed a Committee for the Purpose aforesaid, do a second Time Notify the Proprietors to pay the same to Mr. Isaac Stone, Collector, or to Capt. Elisha Child, Treasurer, at or before the adjourn'd Meeting of said Propriety, which will be on the second Day of March next, at one of the Clock on said Day, at the House of Nathaniel Child, Esq; of Woodstock, in the County of Windham, and Colony of Connecticut; otherwise their Rights will be exposed to Sale, at the House of the said Nathaniel Child, Esq; at 4 o'Clock P. M. on said Day, according to Law.

Woodstock, Nov. 16, 1773. *Nathaniel Child*, *Elisha Child*, *Samuel McClelland*, } Committee.

A few Casks very excellent Muscovado Sugars, to be Sold by GABRIEL JOHONNOT, at his Store South Side the Market house.

In the House of REPRESENTATIVES, June 26, 1773.

RESOLVED, That all that Tract of unappropriated Land lying together on both Sides of Deerfield-River, West of Charlemont and Merrifield, and East of Bullock's Township, so called, and so to extend the same Course Northerly with the East Line of Bullock's Township to the North Line of the Province—Be sold in three Pieces, at Public Vendue, on the fourth Wednesday of the next Session of the General Court, at the Dwelling-House of Daniel Jones, Innholder in Boston, at Three of the Clock in the Afternoon, viz. One Piece bounding East on Charlemont or Grants, Northerly on a Grant made to Samuel Pierce and Lock, on Hoosuck Mountain, and all the Province Land Southerly of said Pierce's and Lock's Grants, and Easterly of Bullock's Grant, and Northerly of Number Seven. And also another Piece of Land lying East of Deerfield-River, and adjoining thereon, and Northerly of a Brook called Pelham's Mill-Brook, and Westerly and Southerly on a Tract of Land called Merrifield and a Grant made to Fullam. The other Piece lying West of Deerfield-River, and bounding thereon, and on Jones's Grant called Merrifield; and Southerly on said Pierce's and Lock's Lands, and Easterly on said Bullock's Grant, and to extend North from Bullock's North-East Corner the same Course with Bullock's East Line to the North Line of the Province: And that Mr. HANCOCK and Mr. PHILLIPS, with such as the honorable Board shall join, be a Committee to sell the same as aforesaid; which Committee shall, in Behalf of this Province, make and execute a good Deed or Deeds of the same to the highest Bidder, when he shall pay the Purchase-Money into the Hands of said Committee for the Use of this Province; which shall be by said Committee paid into the Province Treasury: And that the said Purchaser or Purchasers at the Time of Sale shall pay one Eighth Part of the Sum so bidden as Earnest; and in Case said Purchaser or Purchasers do not pay the whole of the Purchase-Money within one Year from the Time of such Sale, he shall not be entitled to such Deed, or the Earnest-Money paid at the Time of Sale. And the said Committee shall give Notice of the Sale aforesaid, by publishing in the *Massachusetts* and *Boston*-Gazette, an attested Copy of this Resolve, three Weeks successively, in the Month of September next, if the Court should not sit before that Time; and also the three Weeks next preceeding the Time of Sale: And that said Committee, as soon as may be, employ *Samuel Taylor* of *Charlemont*, Surveyor, with two sufficient Chainmen, (the said Surveyor and Chainmen to be under Oath) to take an actual Survey of said Lands, and return a Plan thereof to them at or before said Time of Sale.

Sent up for Concurrence.

T. CUSHING, Speaker.

IN COUNCIL, *June* 26, 1773.

Read and concurr'd, and *James Russell*, Esq; is joined.

JN^O. COTTON, D. Secr'y.

Consented to, T. HUTCHINSON.

A true Copy, Test. JN^O. COTTON, D. Secr'y.

☞ The Committee will attend the Service above assigned them, on the fourth Wednesday of the present Session of the General Court, which will be the 16th Day of *February* next; the Plan of the Lands may be viewed, at any Time before the Sale, at the Secretary's-Office. *Boston, January* 26, 1774.

TO BE SOLD,

A large Quantity of BRICKS, well made and burnt, of different Sizes, laying at New-Boston, cheap for Cash or short Credit. Also a very good Iron Hearth about 1200 wt. with Coppers new tinn'd, suitable for a Ship of 400 Tons.

Enquire of Edes & Gill.

To be sold by PUBLIC VENDUE,

Pursuant to the Order of the Superior Court,

Part of the Real Estate of *William Bowdoin*, Esq;

Late of Roxbury, deceased, viz.

A valuable Farm in Leicester, containing about 500 Acres, more or less, with a good Dwelling-House and Barn thereon: A great Part of it under good Improvement, well fenced with a Number of Divisions, watered by a large Fish Pond, and a great Quantity of Wood growing thereon; in the present Occupation of Mr. William Kilkee, jun. about half a Mile from Mr. Jonathan Sergeant's, Innholder in Leicester, and about 50 Miles from Boston,—Also about 34 and three Quarter Acres of good Land in Leicester, bounded Northerly on the Country Road, and adjoining in the Rear on the aforesaid 500 Acres, with a Dwelling House thereon, in the Occupation of Mr. Nathaniel Richardson, and near to the said Sergeant's.—These two Tracts of Land are to be Sold at the Public House of the said Sergeant's, in Leicester, at Noon, on Wednesday the Ninth Day of February next.—At the same Time the Stock of Cattle, &c. on the said Farms will be Sold.

The second Lot of the great Allotments lying at the Head of Freetown in Pocasset Purchase, in the County of Bristol, containing about 500 Acres, more or less, and is bounded on the South-Westerly Side by the first Lot, and on the North-Westerly Side with a Red Oak Tree, and a Red Oak in the Range both numbered 2, 3, ranging S. 28°. E. being 200 Rods wide.—This Tract is to be Sold at the House of Mr. Strange, Innholder in Freetown, at Noon, on Wednesday the Sixteenth Day of February next.

One Half of 950 Acres of Land, more or less, in Hadley second Precinct (now called Granby) bounded South by Springfield North Bounds, North by Land of Messi'rs Henchman and Downe, East by Belcherton, and West by a High Way.—Capt. Nathaniel Dwight, of Belcherton, or Mr. Israel Cowls, who lives near it, can give Information about this Land; which is to be Sold at the Exchange Tavern in Boston, at Eleven o'Clock before Noon, on Wednesday the 23d Day of February next.

Also to be Sold at PRIVATE SALE,

By the Administrator on the said Estate,

By Virtue of an Act of the Assembly of the Colony of Connecticut.

Several Farms in the said Colony, being Part of the Estate of the said Deceased, and particularly described in an Advertisement lately published in this Paper.——

For the Terms apply to JAMES BOWDOIN, Esq; Administrator: who once more requests, & earnestly requests, those that have Demands on, or Accounts open with the said Estate, to exhibit them; and the Indebted to Pay what they owe, without further Application. Boston, January 22, 1774.

KEYSER's FAMOUS PILLS

So well known all over *Europe*, and in *this* and the *neighbouring Colonies*, for their superior Efficacy and peculiar Mildness, in perfectly eradicating every Degree of a certain Disease, without the least Trouble or Confinement.

The Public may be assured, that this excellent Medicine is beyond any Thing in all Foulness and Impurities of the Blood, having performed many astonishing Cures in Scorbutic Eruptions, Leprosies, White Swellings, Stiff Joints, Gout and Rheumatic Disorders, &c.

THESE PILLS ARE NOW SOLD BY

EDES and GILL,

(In Boxes of 7/6. L. M. each, *fresh imported*)

Who have in their Hands a Letter from the Widow KEYSER, and a Certificate from under her own Hand of the Genuineness of the above Pills; which any Person may have the Perusal of by applying to them at their Printing-Office in *Queen-Street*: Where may be had a Variety of Books, &c.

THIS DAY IS PUBLISHED,

Adorn'd with an elegant Engraving of the Author

[Price 3s. 4d. L. M. Bound]

POEMS,

On various subjects,——Religious and Moral.

By PHILLIS WHEATLEY,

A Negro Girl.

Sold by Mess'rs COX & BERRY,

At their Store in King-Street, Boston.

N. B. The Subscribers are requested to apply for their Copies.

Abraham Hunt, at his Celler under the Old Brick Meeting-House, has for sale the best old Sterling Madeira, Lisbon and Malaga WINE, also Fyal of a superior Quality, at the lowest Cash price.

Berry and Crane,

INFORM the Public, That they open their School this Evening for teaching Psalmody, at the House of Mr. *Daniel Kneeland* in Queen-Street; where young Gentlemen and Youth may be instructed in the best Manner, and on the most reasonable Terms.

N. B. Said School will be kept every Monday and Wednesday Evenings.

For Private Sale,

At the NEW AUCTION ROOM, South Side of the Town House, viz.

HAndsome mahogany desks and book cases, chest on chest of draws, dining and spring tables, beaureau tables, mehogany hair and leather bottom chairs, straw bottom do. several handsome eight day clocks, silver and pinchbeck watches, chamber tables, harrateen curtains, feather beds and bedsteads, handsome sconce and other looking glasses, small dressing ditto. Also, blue, orange, lead, grey and cloth colour'd broad cloths; cotton velvets, shalloons, tammies, stuffs of all colours, drab and mixt duffils, copper and mixt frizes, calamancoes, capuchin silks of all colours, buckskin breeches, men's silk and worsted hose, white baize, black handkerchiefs, black sattin and chip hats, silk gauze, black gauze handkerchiefs, black, blue, white and pink sarsnets. A small box of well assorted ribbons the newest fashion; Scotch carpets, superfine bottom hole twist, camp and basket buttons, blue frized cotton, glass pictures. A small quantity of choice Rhubarb, &c. A few Boxes of choice Lisbon LEMMONS, a Hogshead of choice Jamaica Spirits, 2 Cases of Doctor's Instruments.

WANTED TO PURCHASE,

A single deck'd Schooner, burthen about 90 Tons, not more than two Year's old, for which the Cash will be paid immediately. Inquire of CONSTANT FREEMAN, School-Street.

Insurance on Vessels and Goods.

AT the Insurance-Office of EZEBIEL PRICE near the Exchange,

INSURANCE

May be made on Vessels, Cargoes, and private Adventures, at VERY LOW PREMIUMS, full one quarter Part less than formerly.

Note well—In Case of Loss the Insurance will be PUNCTUALLY PAID.

WANTED

A genteel second-hand Turkey Carpet.

Inquire of Edes and Gill.

WANTS EMPLOY,

A Person that understands book-keeping, writes a good hand, and bears a fair Character, would be glad to serve any Gentleman by the Year, Month or Day.—Any Gentleman wanting such a Person may know his Name by Inquiring of the Printer.

Boston: Printed, by EDES & GILL *in Queen-Street*, 1774.

THE Boston-Gazette, AND COUNTRY JOURNAL.

No. 984.

Containing the freshest Advices, Foreign and Domestic.

MONDAY, February 14, 1774.

Messieurs EDES and GILL, *Feb.* 4.

In Mill's and Hicks's Gazette of Monday last, I find the following piece of intelligence, viz.

"Last Week sailed from Portsmouth, bound to White Haven, the Brigantine Brothers, John Walker, Master, who had been seized (*on account of an information given by the noted* John Malcom, *for which he in November last received a Reward from the Sailors at Sheepscut River*) by one of his Majesty's Vessels, and cleared by Order of the Hon. Commissioners of his Majesty's Customs."

Now that the Publick may be acquainted with that whole Procedure, I beg you will publish the following Narrative, which I doubt not will be satisfactory to the bigger part of your Readers, as well as to your humble Servant, *A Friend to the Liberties of Mankind.*

THE Brigantine brothers, commanded by John Walker, was owned in Whitehaven in England, by several merchants of character and fortune, one of whom sold his part to another gentleman, who thinking his property in the vessel not entirely secure, while the sellers name remained in the register; inadvertently erased the name of the gentleman of whom he purchased, and inserted his own. With the register thus altered, Capt. Walker made several voyages to Sheepscut river, loaded the said brig with timber, cleared her at the custom house at Falmouth, Casco Bay, where it was not once suggested to him that his register was in any shape irregular; but about twelve months since, Capt. Walker was ordered to South-Carolina for a freight of rice for Zealand, where having loaded his brig, he applied to the custom-house for a clearance, and the collector being absent, who had cleared his vessel with the same register on a former voyage; his deputy its probable having an inclination to fleece the Capt. of three or four guineas, told him that his register was forged, and refused him a clearance, and upon his replying that the legality thereof was never questioned in any office before, the said officer with some warmth tore the said register and told him to take out a new one: he answered that as he was no part owner, nor could take upon him to swear who were the owners, it was impracticable for him to obtain a new register, and therefore demanded the old one; the officer, obstinately refused to let him have it, telling him to get a new one in England or elsewhere, but finally granted him a clearance, and he proceeded on his voyage. Having delivered his rice cargo at the destined port, he returned to Cowes in the Isle of Wight, and wrote to his owners respecting the loss of his register, and desired to be informed what voyage he should proceed on next; in reply thereto they directed him to sail for Sheepscut river and take in a cargo of timber, and from thence return to Whitehaven, and that he might depend upon their forwarding a new register to him by a vessel that was to sail soon after him. Capt. Walker immediately upon receiving this direction cleared out his brig, at the custom-house in Cowes, without any difficulty, and sailed *in ballast only*, for Sheepscut River, where he arrived some time in October last. Having got his vessel nearly loaded, he went to Falmouth by land, and cleared out the brig and cargo at the custom-house there for Whitehaven. But during his absence, a dirty scoundrel at Pownalborough, a native of Whitehaven, who was under the greatest obligations to the owners of this vessel, for peculiar favors he had received from them; had the ingratitude to send a letter fifteen miles to the —famous John Malcom, acquainting him that Capt. Walker had no register, and courting him to come over and make a seizure of the brigantine.

Malcom, without the least delay, sets out for the Informer's house, and demands a guard to protect him from insults; (he, I must beg pardon of the public for dubbing the Informer a dirty scoundrel, for in truth he holds a Captain's commission under the Governor of this province.) This informing Captain immediately orders his four serjeants to furnish themselves with such arms and ammunition as the law requires, and thus equipped, they set out to escort the great Malcom to Capt. Walker's brig, and having made the seizure he dismissed his guard; what pay they received for this very extraordinary military manoeuvre, has not transpired, but they soon became ashamed of their conduct. The heroic Malcom made a mark upon the mast, and commenced sole commander of the brig, ordered the laborers to desist from loading, heartily damned the sailors, menaced the mate, and behaved with great insolence to the gentleman who furnished the cargo, and who happened then to be on board; threatened to sheath his sword in the bowels of any one who dared dispute his authority, and in fact cut some tackling with which some timber was hoisting, by which means three or four people narrowly escaped instantaneous death. The brig's crew could not be reconciled to the treatment they received from their new commander, but soon told their grievances to about forty or fifty sailors then in the river, a council was held among the tars, and if common fame speaks true, Capt. Malcom verily received some inadequate reward.

Capt. Walker returned from Falmouth with his clearance, expecting to proceed on his voyage, but was told that his brigantine was seized by Malcom, and by him delivered to the custody of one Lieut. Mowit, commander of his Majesty's armed ship the Canceaux; Capt. Walker shewed his clearance from the office at Falmouth, and demanded his vessel, but Mowit told him, he would not deliver her unless he produced an order from the board of commissioners or from Admiral Montagu, and advised him to proceed immediately to Boston, and lay the matter before the board; Capt. Walker came to town the beginning of November, in good spirits, not doubting from the idea he had conceived in England, that this board was established for the regulation of trade, and of consequence that his vessel would be restored to him without hesitation; he soon waited upon their honors, informed them in what manner his register had been taken from him, and craved an order for the immediate delivery of his vessel; but how great was his astonishment at the reception he met with from their honors! some of them not only neglected treating him with common decency, but grossly insulted him, and charged him with bringing tea, china, and other contraband goods to Sheepscut: Which charges he denied, and offered them his affidavit, if they desired! however they finally told him their opinion was that no fraud was intended by him in the voyage: Upon this he again urged them to favor him with an order of delivery, but they absolutely refused doing it, telling him that Malcom had commenced a prosecution in the admiralty against him, that he might defend himself if he pleased, but they would not interfere in the matter, nor hear any thing he had to say farther upon the subject, and *really forced* him from their honorable presence.——

At length the day fixed by the Court of Admiralty for the decision of this grand cause arrived, when, behold! no libel had been served on the Brig, the Marshall it seems not relishing the thought of wearing a new-fashioned jacket so called at Pownalborough by the Tars, had deferred to serve the libel; upon which the court was adjourn'd for 20 days, and a gentleman of Pownalborough, a friend to Capt. Walker, was perswaded to accept of a Commission as Deputy Marshall, and to proceed to the Eastward and serve the Libel, and make his return during the adjournment; the evening before he was to take his departure, an officer took him with a warrant from Justice Quincy to answer to John Malcom, Esq; for a breach of the peace sworn against him by said Malcom; he obeyed the summons, by applying to the Justice for information when & where he had threatened Esq; Malcom with the loss of his life or members, the justice replied that Malcom had not sworn that his life was in danger by this gentleman, but that he was fearful this gentleman would either beat him himself or hire others to beat him; upon the whole the justice for reasons best known to himself, dismissed the deputy marshall, who the next morning set out for Pownalborough.

During this interval, Esq; Malcom became suspicious that the brig he had seized would not finally be condemned, and knowing that Capt. Walker was absent when the tars had their frolick at Pownalborough, and being determined at all events, to fleece this unfortunate man if he possibly could, repaired to his lodgings and threatned to take him with a libel for one hundred pounds sterling for taking in loading without a permit, and with a second libel for another hundred pounds for tendering him a bribe. Capt. Walker being an intire stranger here, and knowing he must be thrown into the common goal, if taken with these libels, though perfectly innocent, was under the disagreeable necessity of making himself a prisoner for near a fortnight. The solicitor being absent, Malcom assiduously applied to several gentlemen in the law for those two libels, and not obtaining them, he pressed the governor to recommend his hard case to some practitioner in the law, for every one he had apply'd to had refused him assistance, still the Esq; could not get possessed of his beloved libels, and being determined to make some bold push at Capt. Walker, got into his lodgings, and insulted and abused him with the most opprobrious language it was possible for a man to utter; Capt. Walker suspecting his drift, bore this treatment with all imaginable patience, and Malcom finding he could not provoke him either to threaten or strike a blow; challeng'd him to a single combat in Boston common with sword and postols; at all which Capt. Walker only laughed and the Esq; at last thought proper to depart.

The gentleman who went to execute the office of deputy marshall, return'd from Pownalborough and related that Lieut. Mowit had removed Capt. Walker's brig, about twenty miles from the place where Malcom seized her, and had just got her under sail in order to proceed for some other port, at the time he boarded her; that he had read the libel on board and delivered the vessel into the custody of the mate and crew; that after doing this he acquainted lieut. Mowit, with his proceedings and shewed him his authority for so doing, when the lieutenant began to insult him greatly, damned both the admiralty judge and commissioners, and swore if he had them there, he would put them all in irons; declared he would carry the brig to any port that he pleased in spite of any officer on the continent, and threatned to fire a broadside on the said deputy marshall if he attempted to go on board the brig a second time; the gentleman however despising his threats, went immediately on board and took an inventory of what articles were in the cabin; while he was on board, lieut. Mowit sent a boat from the Canceaux full of armed men, headed by one Hog, who was said to be master of the Canceaux, and by force took the greater part of the men, to whose custody the deputy marshall had committed the brig, and carried them on board the Canceaux, and he not thinking it prudent to contend with such tyrants, made the best of his way to Boston, and made a return of his warrant.

The court of admiralty set a second time, and Esq; Malcom fixing the value of the brig at 300l. L. M. and upon security being given for that sum, the final trial was postponed for six months, and a writ of delivery issued from the admiralty office; in consequence thereof, Capt. Walker left Boston to seek for his brig, not knowing where to find her: he at last got intelligence that she was in Piscataqua river, to which place he repair'd and found her in possession of Lieut. Mowit, who by removing her from harbour to harbour, had got her on shore and caused her to be very leaky, he had also rendered one of her new cables intirely useless, which had not long before cost the owners above 50l sterl. this he said was done in order to save the king's ship from going on shore: He still refused to deliver up the brig unless Capt. Walker would produce him an order from Admiral Montagu. Capt. Walker then applied to the custom-house at Portsmouth, and laid all his papers before the collector, who after keeping them for some time told him he would not meddle in the matter, but at the same time refusing to return his papers unless he would go immediately to Lieut. Mowit, and make up some differences with him; Capt. Walker replied that he never had any difference with Lieut. Mowit, and only wanted to obtain his vessel agreeable to the writ of delivery. At length being worn out with fatigue and vexation of mind, having no friend to consult, and meeting only with frowns and intimidations from those who ought to have treated him with some shadow of humanity, he was in fact compelled to sign a writing, of which the following is said to be a copy.——

"KNOW all men by these presents, that I John Walker master of the brigantine Brothers, of Whitehaven, in the county of Cumberland, for myself and for David Fletcher, owner of the said brigantine, and of the said county, and for all others claiming a property in the said brigantine;—Do hereby with one another surety firmly bind myself to William Hogs, * master of his Majesty's armed ship Canceaux, in the sum of 2000l. sterl. money, to be paid to the said William Hogs or his certain attorney, executors, administrators or assigns, for which payment well and truly to be made; we bind ourselves, our heirs, executors and administrators, and every of them, firmly by these presents, sealed with our seals, dated the 28th day of December, in the year of our Lord 1773, and in the 14th year of his Majesty's reign.

"Whereas the above named William Hogs did seize and detain the said brigantine Brothers, of Whitehaven, in the said county of Cumberland, the 30th of October last, and upon the said John Walker in behalf of the owners, having made application to the commissioners of his majesty's customs, and a request to him, he hath now restored to the said John Walker, master of the said brigantine Brothers, the same, with her cargo & all her appurtenances, as when seized by him.

"Now the condition of this obligation is such, that if they, said John Walker, David Fletcher, with all others claiming property in the said brigantine and cargo as aforementioned, their, and each of their heirs, executors, and administrators, do, and shall from time to time, and at all times hereafter, save, defend, keep harmless, and indemnify the said William Hogs, his heirs, executors, and administrators; as also Henry Mowat, Esq; commander of the said armed ship Canceaux, his executors and administrators; as also all other his superior officers in the navy, his, theirs, and every of their lands, tenements, goods, and chattles, of, from and against all accusations and actions, suits, costs, charges, damages and expences, which shall or may at any time be brought, commenced, prosecuted, happen or accrue to or against the said William Hogs, his heirs, &c. as aforesaid, for or by reason of detaining the said brigantine, or any matter or thing, relating thereto, since and before the seizure aforesaid. Then and in such case the above obligation to be utterly void, or else to be and remain in full force and virtue, according to the true intent & meaning thereof.

"Signed, sealed, delivered, and acknowledged, in presence of
Robert Traill,
John Marsh.

John Walker, for himself, owners, and all concerned.

Lieut. Mowat having extorted this very extraordinary bond from the distressed Capt. Walker, delivered him possession of his brigantine, and immediately presented him with an account of above 5l. sterl. for provision, butter and rum supplied his people and demanded payment.

(For remainder see the last page.)

* It is said the reason given why master Hogs was principally named in this bond was this; Lieut. Mowit had not been regularly initiated into the art, trade, and mystery of making seizures in America; but the other was stocked with a budget of oaths and acts of parliament which he brought from England.

BOSTON, Feb. 10.

In the House of REPRESENTATIVES, Feb. 5. 1774.

ORDERED, That Mr. *Adams*, Mr. *Phillips*, Col. *Bowers*, Col. *Warren*, and Col. *Lincoln*, be a Committee to wait on his Excellency the Governor with the following Answer to his Speech to both Houses at the Opening of this Session.

May it please your Excellency,

YOUR Speech to both Houses at the opening of this Session, has been duly considered in the House of Representatives.

The equitable Adjustment of the Disputes which have subsisted between the English Inhabitants of the Town of Edgartown, and the Indians of Martha's Vineyard, respecting their Claim to the Island Chappoquiddeck, had the particular Attention of the two Houses of this Assembly in the last Session. A Committee was then appointed to repair to the Place in the Recess of the Court, and report the Circumstances of that Affair. Their Report is daily expected, and we trust that the Difference will be settled to the reasonable Satisfaction of the Indians before the close of the present Session.

With Pleasure we hear from your Excellency, that there is Reason to expect his Majesty's Confirmation of the Settlement of the Western Line of this Province, where it is bounded on the Eastern Line of the Province of New-York. This Settlement, not only tends to bring to an issue, a Dispute which has been the Source of much Mischief, but also to establish Harmony between his Majesty's Colonies; upon which their own Safety and Welfare, as well as the Interest of Great-Britain, at this Juncture more especially, so much depends.

It affords great Satisfaction to this House, to find, that his Majesty has been pleased to put an End to an undue Claim heretofore made by the Governors of this Province; grounded upon a Supposition, that the Consent of the Chair was necessary to the Validity of the judicial Acts of the Governor and Council. Whereby their Proceedings, when sitting as the Supreme Court of Probate, and as the Court for determining in Cases of Marriage and Divorce, have been so often impeded. The Royal Order, that the Governor shall acquiesce in the Determination of the Majority of the Council, respects not the Council only, but the Body of the People of this Province. And his Majesty has therein shewn his Regard to *Justice*, as well as the Interest and Convenience of his Subjects, in rescuing a Clause in the Charter from a Construction, which in the Opinion of this House, was repugnant to the express Meaning and Intent of the Charter, inconsistent with the Idea of a Court of Justice, and dangerous to the Rights and Property of the Subject.

Your Excellency is pleas'd to inform the two Houses, that you are required to signify to them his Majesty's Disapprobation of the Appointment of Committees of Correspondence in various Instances which sit and act during the Recess of the General Court by Prorogation. You are not pleased to explain to us the Grounds and Reasons of his Majesty's Disapprobation: Until we shall have such explanation laid before us, a full Answer to this Part of your Speech will not be expected from us. We cannot however omit saying upon this Occasion, that while the common Rights of the American Subjects continue to be attacked in various Instances, and at times when the several Assemblies are not sitting, it is highly necessary that they should correspond with each other, in order to unite in the most effectual Means for the obtaining a Redress of their Grievances. And as the Sitting of the General Assemblies in this and most of the Colonies depends upon the Pleasure of the Governors, who hold themselves under the Direction of Administration, it is to be expected, that the Meeting of the Assemblies will be so ordered, as that the Intention proposed by a Correspondence between them will be impracticable, but by Committees to sit and act in the Recess. We would moreover observe, that as it has been the Practice for Years past, for the Governor and Lieutenant Governor of this Province, and other Officers of the Crown, at all Times to correspond with Ministers of State and Persons of Distinction and Influence in the Nation, in order to concert and carry on such Measures of the British Administration, as have been deemed by the Colonists to be grievous to them, it cannot be thought unreasonable or improper for the Colonists to correspond with their Agents as well as with each other; to the End that their Grievances may be so explained to his Majesty, as that in his Justice he may afford them necessary Relief. As this Province has heretofore felt the great Misfortune of the Displeasure of our Sovereign by Means of Misrepresentations, permit us further to say, there is Room to apprehend that his Majesty has in this Instance been misinformed: And that there are good Grounds to suspect, that those who may have misinformed him have had in Meditation further Measures destructive to the Colonies, which they were apprehensive would be defeated by Means of Committees of Correspondence sitting and acting in the Recess of the respective Assemblies.

It must be pleasing to the good People of this Province to find, that the heavy Debt which had been incurred by their liberal Aids through the Course of the late War, for the subduing his Majesty's inveterate Enemies and extending his Territory and Dominion in America, is so nearly discharged. Whenever the House of Representatives shall deem it incumbent upon them to provide for any future Charges, it will be done, as it ought, by such Ways and Means as, after due Deliberation, to them shall seem meet.

In the mean time, this House will employ the Powers with which they are intrusted, in supporting his Majesty's just Authority in the Province according to the Royal Charter, and in dispatching such publick Business as now properly lies before us. And while we pursue such Measures, as tend, by God's Blessing, to the Redress of Grievances, and to the Restoration and Establishment of the publick Liberty, we perswade ourselves that we shall at the same time, as far as in us lies, most effectually secure the Tranquility and good Order of the Government, and the great End for which it was instituted, the Safety and Welfare of the People.

On Friday last in the Forenoon, the Committee of the House of Representatives appointed to consider of further Proceedings necessary to be had on the Conduct of the Honorable PETER OLIVER, Esq; Chief Justice of the Superior Court of Judicature, brought in a Report, and desired Leave of the House to sit again. After a full Debate on the Report of the Committee, the House came into the following Resolves, by a Division of 96 to 9, viz.

WHEREAS it appears to this House, by a Writing under the Hand of the Hon. Peter Oliver, *Esq; the Chief Justice of the Superior Court of Judicature, Court of Assize and General Goal Delivery, over this Province, a Court wholly erected and constituted by the Great and General Court or Assembly of the same Province, by a Power granted to the said General Court by the Royal Charter, that he the said* Peter Oliver, *Esq; declining any more to take and receive the Grants of the General Assembly of this Province, for his Services as Chief Justice of the said Superior Court, hath, contrary to the Usage and Custom of the Justices of the said Court, ever since the erecting and constituting of the same invariably used and approved; and contrary to the plain Sense and Meaning of the said Royal Charter; and against the known Constitution of this Province, accepted received and taken a Salary and Reward granted him by his Majesty, for his Services as Chief Justice of the said Superior Court, from the fifth Day of July 1772, to the fifth Day of January 1774: And that he hath also plainly given this House to understand by the same Writing, under his Hand, his Resolution for the future to accept the Salary and Reward, which he affirms is granted to him by his Majesty, during his Residence in the Province, as Chief Justice of the said Superior Court.*

And whereas it appears to this House, that the said Peter Oliver, *Esq; hath received the said Salary and Reward, out of the Revenue unjustly and unconstitutionally levied and extorted from the Inhabitants of the American Colonies:*

And whereas the said Peter Oliver, *Esq; hath, perversely and corruptly done as aforesaid, against the known Sense of the Body of the People of this Province, most fully and expresly declared in the several Resolutions of divers Houses of Representatives, and otherwise:*

Therefore *Resolved*, That the said *Peter Oliver*, Esq; hath by his Conduct as aforesaid, proved himself an Enemy to the Constitution of this Province; that he has done that which hath an obvious and direct Tendency to the Perversion of Law and Justice in the said Court, and is become justly obnoxious to the good People of this Province.

Resolved, That the said *Peter Oliver*, Esq; hath by his Conduct as aforesaid, rendered himself totally disqualified, any longer to hold and act in the Office of a Justice of the said Court, and ought forthwith to be removed therefrom.

Resolved, That this House will remonstrate to his Excellency the Governor and Council of this Province, the said Conduct of the said *Peter Oliver*, Esq; praying that he may not be suffered any more to sit and act in his Office of Chief Justice of said Court, and that he may forthwith and without any Delay be removed therefrom.

YEAS.	YEAS.
Mr. Samuel Adams	Mr. Hezekiah Gay
Hon. John Hancock, Esq;	Mr. Enoch Ellis
William Phillips, Esq;	Mr. John Pickering, jun.
Capt. William Heath	Dr. Samuel Holten
Mr. Samuel Howe	Capt. Michael Farley
Mr. Josiah How	Hon. Joseph Gerrish, Esq;
Ebenezer Thayer, jun. Esq;	Ebenezer Burrell, Esq;
Mr. Nathaniel Bailey	Mr. Moody Bridges
Benjamin Lincoln, Esq;	Capt. Henry Herrick
Mr. Abner Ellis	Mr. Nathaniel Mighill
Mr. Moses Bullen	Mr. Samuel Smith
Mr. Jabez Fisher	Mr. Jonathan Webster
Capt. Benjamin Whit	Nathaniel Allen, Esq;

YEAS.	YEAS.
Mr. John Gould	Capt. Woodbridge Brown
Aaron Wood, Esq;	Capt. John Gray,
Isaac Merrill, Esq;	Edward Bacon, Esq;
Capt. Daniel Thurston	David Thatcher, Esq;
Capt. Thomas Gardner	Mr. Barnabas Freeman,
Mr. Nathaniel Gorham	Mr. Benjamin Freeman
Capt. Jonathan Browne	Mr. Moses Swift
Mr. Samuel Wyman	Mr. Joseph Doane
Abraham Fuller, Esq;	Robert-Treat Paine, Esq;
Samuel Bancroft, Esq;	Capt. Joseph Barney
Mr. Peter Bent	Jerathmeel Bowers, Esq;
William Stickney, Esq;	Benjamin Aikin, Esq;
Capt. Josiah Stone	George Wheeten, Esq;
Mr. Jonas Stone	Mr. John Dagget
Mr. Simeon Spaulding	Thomas Bragdon, Esq;
Capt. Joseph Twitchell	Edward Cutt, Esq;
Mr. Thomas Plympton	Mr. Ebenezer Sawyer
Capt. Ebenezer Harnden	Capt. Nathan Lord, jun.
Mr. Benjamin Hall	Mr. Joshua Bigelow
Jonas Dix, Esq;	Capt. Asa Whitcomb
James Prescott, Esq;	Mr. Edward Rawson
Henry Gardner, Esq;	Jedediah Foster, Esq;
Mr. John Bliss	Capt. Henry King
Hon. Joseph Hawley, Esq;	Mr. Thomas Denny
Mr. Josiah Pierce	Mr. Phineas Heywood
Dr. Moses Gunn	Dr. John Taylor
Tim. Danielson, Esq;	Hon. John Whitcomb, Esq;
Mr. Phinehas Wright	Capt. Ephraim Doolittle
Hon. James Warren, Esq;	Capt. Paul Mandell
Mr. Gideon Vinall	Mr. Samuel March
Mr. Ebenezer Sprout	David Ingersol, Esq;
Mr. Ebenezer White	Mr. Samuel Brown, junr.
Mr. Samuel Lucus	Mr. Charles Goodrich
Mr. John Turner	Mr. David Rossiter
Capt. Joseph Cushing	Mr. Peter Curtis

NAYS.	NAYS.
Elisha Jones Esq;	Thomas Gilbert, Esq;
Hon. J. Worthington, Esq;	Capt. Jeremiah Learned
Abijah White, Esq;	William Tyng, Esq;
Josiah Edson, Esq;	Mark Hopkins, Esq;
Daniel Leonard, Esq;	

In the Afternoon of the same Day, the House agreed upon a Remonstrance against the Conduct of the honorable PETER OLIVER, Esq; to the Governor and Council, praying that he may forthwith and without Delay, be removed from the Superior Court; and on the next Day the House directed the Secretary to deliver the same to the Governor.

In the House of REPRESENTATIVES, June 26, 1773.

RESOLVED, That all that Tract of unappropriated Land lying together on both Sides of Deerfield-River, West of Charlemont and Merrifield, and East of Bullock's Township, so called, and so to extend the same Course Northerly with the East Line of Bullock's Township to the North Line of the Province—Be sold in three Pieces, at Public Vendue, on the fourth Wednesday of the next Session of the General Court, at the Dwelling-House of Daniel Jones, Innholder in Boston, at Three of the Clock in the Afternoon, viz. One Piece bounding East on Charlemont or Grants, Northerly on a Grant made to Samuel Pierce and Lock, on Hoosuck Mountain, and all the Province Land Southerly of said Pierce's and Lock's Grants, and Easterly of Bullock's Grant, and Northerly of Number Seven. And also another Piece of Land lying East of Deerfield-River, and adjoining thereon, and Northerly of a Brook called Pelham's Mill-Brook, and Westerly and Southerly on a Tract of Land called Merrifield and a Grant made to Fullam. The other Piece lying West of Deerfield-River, and bounding thereon, and on Jones's Grant called Merrifield; and Southerly on said Pierce's and Lock's Lands, and Easterly on said Bullock's Grant, and to extend North from Bullock's North-East Corner the same Course with Bullock's East Line to the North Line of the Province: And that Mr. HANCOCK and Mr. PHILLIPS, with such as the honorable Board shall join, be a Committee to sell the same as aforesaid; which Committee shall, in Behalf of this Province, make and execute a good Deed or Deeds of the same to the highest Bidder, when he shall pay the Purchase-Money into the Hands of said Committee for the Use of this Province; which shall be by said Committee paid into the Province Treasury: And that the said Purchaser or Purchasers at the Time of Sale shall pay one Eighth Part of the Sum so bidden as Earnest; and in Case said Purchaser or Purchasers do not pay the whole of the Purchase-Money within one Year from the Time of such Sale, he shall not be entitled to such Deed, or the Earnest-Money paid at the Time of Sale. And the said Committee shall give Notice of the Sale aforesaid, by publishing in the *Massachusetts* and *Boston-Gazette*, an attested Copy of this Resolve, three Weeks successively, in the Month of September next, if the Court should not sit before that Time; and also the three Weeks next preceeding the Time of Sale: And that said Committee, as soon as may be, employ *Samuel Taylor of Charlemont*, Surveyor, with two sufficient Chainmen, (the said Surveyor and Chainmen to be under Oath) to take an actual Survey of said Lands, and return a Plan thereof to them at or before said Time of Sale.

Sent up for Concurrence.

T. CUSHING, Speaker.

IN COUNCIL, *June 26, 1773.*

Read and concurr'd, and *James Russell*, Esq; is joined.

JNO. COTTON, D. Secr'y.

Consented to, T. HUTCHINSON.

A true Copy, Test. JNO. COTTON, D. Secr'y.

☞ The Committee will attend the Service above assigned them, on the fourth Wednesday of the present Session of the General Court, which will be the 16th Day of *February* next; the Plan of the Lands may be viewed, at any Time before the Sale, at the Secretary's Office. *Boston, January 26, 1774.*

The Southern Post not arrived at the Publication of this Paper.

BOSTON, February 14.

The honorable House of Representatives have made Choice of the Rev. Mr. *Gad Hitchcock*, of Pembroke, to preach the Sermon on the Day of the General Election, the last Wednesday in May next.

It is a Matter of great Speculation whether the Chief Justice of the Superior Court will take his Seat in that Court, while he stands impeached by the Commons of this Province, of having proved himself to be an Enemy to the Constitution, and until the Governor and Council shall have decided upon the Remonstrance and Petition which now lies before them. It is the general opinion that he *will not*.

We are informed that Abijah White, Esq; the Member of the House of Representatives for Marshfield, was the only Dissentient in a full House of Ninety Members, when the Question was put on Tuesday last, Whether further Proceedings should be had on the Conduct of Chief Justice Oliver.

It is a Curiosity which the Public are impatient to be satisfied in, Whether the Grand Jury returned to the Superior Court will submit to be sworn to present any of his Majesty's Subjects to be tryed before that Court, unless they shall be assured that the Chief Justice will not take his Seat, until there is a final Decision of the Governor and Council on the Remonstrance of the House of Representatives.

We learn from Portsmouth, that thro' the assiduity of Col. John Fenton, Justice of the Peace for the County of Grafton, the famous or rather infamous Glazier Wheeler of Cohos, who some time since escaped from Worcester Goal, was apprehended in the Night of the 21st of last Month, for passing counterfeit Dollars; also one Peter Hobart, an Accomplice, who has turned King's Evidence and given such a Clue to Wheeler's Plans, as cannot fail of the most salutary Effects.

We hear from Shrewsbury, that one Day last Week a Pedlar was observed to go into a Tavern there, with a Bag containing about 30lb. Tea. Information of which being had at Northborough, about 5 Miles Distance, a Number of Indians went from the Great Swamp, or thereabouts, seized upon it, and committed it to the Flames on the Road facing said Tavern, where it was entirely consumed.

Extract of a Letter from Duxbury, Feb. 5, 1774.

"I imagine you have by this Time heard of the very remarkable Resolves of the Town of Marshfield, respecting the Destruction of Tea, &c. which was effected principally by the insinuating Art of a certain Man, who having lately rendered himself odious to the Province by his Conduct in a public Station, is endeavouring to wipe off the Infamy on the People of that Town. His Insinuations are (as I am informed by People of Veracity) that the Tea must be paid for; that any Town's remonstrating against the Destruction of it, will effectually secure them against paying any Part of the Expence; and if it is paid for, that his particular share will be 40l. who commonly pays scarce 3l. per ann. of the province tax. However the sentiments of the old Colony are not to be collected from those of Marshfield."

"We hear from Marshfield that the puissant A—— W——, Esq; lately went into a Neighbour's House, and being seated, tho' very uneasy, he was inquired of what made him so, when he instantly arose and drew forth a Sword, (being formerly a valiant Soldier) declaring he would make Day-light shine thro' 'em, but what he would carry his Point, giving as a Reason, that he was afraid of his Life without being arm'd, tho' never assaulted. Being thus accoutr'ed, one Day on going to his Barn, his Cattle being affrighted, and taking him to be a Stranger, surrounded him, and we hear 'twas with Difficulty that he escaped with his Life and the Loss of his Sword."

WE whose Names are hereto Subscribed, having been favored with a Copy of the Proceedings of the Town of Marshfield, at their late Meeting of the 31st Jan. and having to our great Admiration observed in these Proceedings a Clause to this effect.—We do renounce all Methods of Imposition, Violence and Persecution, such as has been most shamefully exercised upon a Number of Inhabitants of the Town of Plymouth, by obliging them to Sign a Recantation as called, and in Case of refusal, to have their Houses pulled down, or they Tarred and Feathered, and all this under the specious Mask of Liberty——*Do in this most public, explicit and solemn Manner, Declare that we Signed the Recantation therein referr'd to, from a Sense of Duty, and from a clear Conviction of the great Impropriety of our having Protested against the Proceedings of this Town, as well as those of the Town of Boston, and indeed of the whole Continent: When engaged in a Cause, to which we are now, and always have been, hearty Well-wishers—And we do further Declare that the Insinuations of the Town of Marshfield in the above cited Clause, are base, unjust, and void of Truth, and deserve in our Opinion, the Resentment of all, who wish well to this Country, and of us in particular.—We do therefore Resent such injurious Treatment, and do expect that the Committee of the Town of Marshfield, which Draughted the Resolve above refer'd to, do in the most unreserved Manner, favor us with the Name or Names of the Person or Persons, who gave them the above unjust and scandalous Information.*

Wm. Crombie,	William Curtis,
Benj. Rider the 3d.	David Lothrop,
Joseph Bartlett, Jun.	Wm. Weston,
John Kempton, Jun.	Nathaniel Shurtlef,
Ebenezer Churchill,	Ebenezer Sampson,
Benj. King,	Samuel Sherman,
James Doten, Jun.	Richard Cooper,
Plymouth, Feb. 7, 1774.	Jonathan King.

Plymouth, ss. Feb. 9, 1774. } THE above-named Persons appeared before me the Subscriber, and made Oath, that in signing the Recantation mentioned, they were not under any Imposition, Violence or Persecution, nor threaten'd therewith in Case of Refusal.

Sworn before me, THO. MAYHEW, Just. Pacis.

Monday last the Corporation of Harvard-College again met for the Choice of a PRESIDENT, when the Rev. Dr. COOPER of this Town was unanimously chosen, but we hear has since declin'd.

By a Gentleman just arrived from Princetown, in New-Jersey, we are informed, that the Students at Nassau College, being determined to contribute their Assistance towards discountenancing the Use of the detested Tea, collected all that was in the College, and voluntarily made a burnt Sacrifice of the same. They also burnt the Effigies of Governor H———n, amidst the repeated Acclamations of a large Crowd of Spectators.

The late much regretted Earl of Orrery in one of his Letters from Italy, dated January 1755, lately Published, writes in the following prophetic stile "*Tuscany was to Italy*, (says M. de Voltaire) *what Athens was to Greece.*" "What Greece is, Tuscany possibly may be, perhaps Italy, perhaps Europe. The ball of Empire may hereafter roll Westward, and may stop in America; a World unknown when Rome was in its meridian Glory; a World that may save the tears of some future Alexander."

DIED.] Mr. JOHN KNEELAND, in the 80th Year of his Age; for many Years one of the Assessors in this Town. His Funeral will be on Wednesday next at 4 o'Clock, when it is desired his Friends and Acquaintance would attend.

At Lunenburgh, Mrs. ANNA TAYLOR, Consort of Doctor JOHN TAYLOR, of that Place.

COTTON WOOL,

Of an excellent Quality, to be Sold by JONATHAN WILLIAMS, Junr. per Bag or smaller Quantity——VERY CHEAP.

N. B. Country Traders will find it advantageous to apply.

Wanted immediately to Hire,

A single decked Schooner or Brigantine, of 90 or 100 Tons Burthen. Inquire of Edes & Gill.

TO BE SOLD

By Benjamin Church,

On THURSDAY next,

At THREE o'Clock in the Afternoon,

BY PUBLICK AUCTION,

SUPERFINE middling and coarse Broad Cloths—Ratteens—Frizes—Half Thicks—Kerseys—Shalloons—Calamancoes—Irish Linnens—Checks—Mens and Womens Hose—Linnens—Velveretts—Handkerchiefs—Case Knives and Forks—Inkhorns—Penknives, &c.—Sundry Articles of Household—Wearing Apparel—Watches, Cutlery Ware, half a Dozen Mehogany Chair Frames—a Case of Draws—Feather Beds, &c. &c. &c.

Thursday next, 3 o'Clock P. M.

ALL Persons who have any Demands on the Estate of HANNAH DIX, late of Boston, Widow deceased, are desired to bring in their Accounts; and all who are Indebted are desired to make speedy payment to Elizabeth Orrok, Administratrix to said Estate.

FOR PHILADELPHIA,

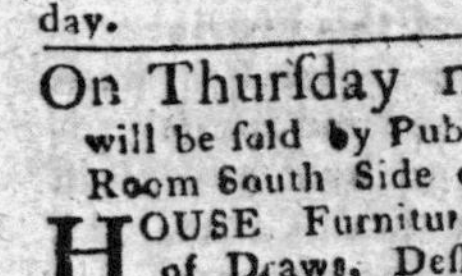

The BRIG BETSEY, CONSTANT FREEMAN, Master, Lying the South-Side Long-Wharff, will Sail in four or five Days; for Freight out, or home, inquire of the Master on Board, or at his House in School-Street.

New AUCTION-ROOM, Cornhill, TO-MORROW at TEN o'Clock will begin the Sale by PUBLIC VENDUE, at GREENLEAF's Auction-Room, of

A Very great Assortment of Goods, too many to be particularly mentioned, they being the Property of Persons leaving the Province. The Sale will be continued in the Afternoon, and on the Friday following.

Wm. GREENLEAF, Auctioner.

The Sales will begin precisely at Ten o'Clock, and at Three o'Clock to Morrow, and at Ten o'Clock on Friday.

On Thursday next, at Ten o'Clock, will be sold by Public Vendue, at the New Auction-Room South Side of the Town-House, viz.

HOUSE Furniture, consisting of Mehogany Chest of Draws, Desks, Dining and Spring Tables, Beauro ditto, Tea Trays, green Harrateen Curtains, green Bottom Chairs, Easy Chairs, Feather Beds and Bedsteads, Glass Pictures, Metal, Coat and Jacket Buttons: Also Broad Cloths, Bearskins, Ratteens, Irish Linnen, Jersey knit Hose, Killmarnock Caps, and a Number of other Articles,

ANDREW OLIVER, Auctioneer.

N. B. For private Sale at said Auction-Room,——Handsome Looking Glasses, Muffs, a Silver Tankard, Porringers, Pepper Castors, Cups, Tea Spoons, a genteel Silver Salver, 10 Inches over, Silver plated Candlesticks, also a handsome full suit of Brocade, and a suit of black Grogram.

At GOULD's Auction Office,

In Back Street,

ON FRIDAY NEXT,

At TEN o'Clock in the Morning.

Will be Sold by PUBLIC VENDUE, A Variety of English Goods, with sundry Articles of House Furniture.

R. GOULD, *Auctioneer.*

On FRIDAY next, the 18th Inst. at XI o'Clock in the Morning, will be Sold by PUBLIC VENDUE, at Store No. 16, on Tileston's Wharff,

ALL the Rigging and Stores saved out of the Sloop LITTLE BOB, lately cast away on the North-West Point of Lovell's Island, viz.

THREE Anchors, 3 Cables, 2 Mainsails, 2 Foresails, 2 Jibbs, and a Variety of other Sails, all her standing and running Rigging, and a great Variety of other Stores, also 3 Barrels of Irish Beef.—Inventory may be seen any Time before the Sale, in the Hands of

J. RUSSELL, Auctioneer.

N. B. The Sloop Little Bob, will be put up at the same Time and Place,—she now lays on the Rocks at Lovell's Island, has a very good Mast in her, a Number of Spars, &c.

Six Months longer are allowed the Creditors to the Estate of *Andrew McKensie*, late of Milton, Merchant, deceas'd, for bringing in their Claims, and proving their Debts, the Commissioners give Notice, that they shall attend that service at the British Coffee-house, in King-Street, from 6 to 9 o'Clock, the third Tuesday in this and the five following Months.

Boston Feb. 14th, 1774.

Wanted a Quantity of Shrums for the Caulkers Business, for which cash will be given; also to be SOLD a few Puncheons, and forty Gallon Casks of old choice Jamaica Rum. Enquire of the Printers.

NEW LONDON.

TO BE SOLD, a House and Land with good Accommodations, as our Houses &c. and well situated for a Tavern, and has been Improved as such for some Years past; with a Wharf adjoining, the best Accommodated and most Improved for Navigation in that Town, if not soon sold, to be Let, for Particulars Enquire of Richard Law & Duncan Stewart, Esquires; in New London or of Edes and Gill in Boston.

RAN-away from Jonathan Reed of Wrentham, on the seventh of this Instant, a Man Servant, calls his Name John Hopkins or James Gutridge, an Old Countryman, who Bound himself to said Reed, for Theft, about 30 Years of Age, a Shoemaker by Trade, mark'd with the Small-Pox, about 5 Feet & ½ high, his Hair red, and wears a darkish Wig, walks very upright, a well set Man: Had on when he went away a brown rusty short Coat, black Jacket, and old Leather Breeches, a thick Buff Cap, no Hat:—Whoever shall take up said Run-away and secure him, so that his Master may have him again shall have FIVE DOLLARS Reward, and necessary Charges paid by me.

JONATHAN REED.

Wrentham, Feb. 8, 1774.

WHEREAS the Proprietors of the Township of Land lying on both sides Androscogging River, in the County of Cumberland, and adjoining Sylvester Township, granted June 11th, 1771, to Samuel Livermore, Esq; and others: Voted and granted at their Meeting June 17th, 1772, a Tax of Forty Shillings on each Right, to defrey the Charges that had or might arise on said Propriety, to be paid unto Leonard Williams, Esq; their Treasurer, on or before the 4th of August 1772, which Tax has been made and published according to Law, notwithstanding which, several have neglected to pay said Tax. Public Notice is hereby given, that unless said Tax be paid by Wednesday the 16th Day of March next their Rights who are delinquent in paying said Tax, will be Sold at Public Vendue, at the House of Isaac Gleason, Innholder in Waltham, at 8 o'Clock in the Forenoon of said Day.

And whereas the Proprietors of said Township, at their Meeting Feb. 24th, 1773, Voted and Granted a Tax of Twenty-four Shillings on each Right, to be paid unto Leonard Williams, Esq; their Treasurer, on or before the 1st Day of Oct. 1773; and again on the 3d Day of Nov. 1773, the Proprietors aforesaid Voted and Granted a further Tax of Forty-eight Shillings on each Right, to defrey the Expences of said Propriety, to be paid their Treasurer as follows, viz. One half of said Tax on or before Wednesday the 16th Day of March next, and the other half on or before the 1st Day of August next, Public Notice is hereby given that if said Taxes be not paid by Wednesday the 16th Day of March next, and by the 1st Day of next August, their Rights, or so much of them as is sufficient to pay said Taxes, and the Charges arising thereon, will be Sold for Payment thereof, according to Law.

Waltham, Jan. 4, 1774. — *Leonard Williams, Elijah Livermore, Elisha Harrington,* } Assessors & Committee for Sale of delinquent Proprietors Rights.

The Proprietors of the Township aforesaid, are hereby Notified, that their Meeting stands adjourned to Wednesday the 16th Day of March next, at the House of Isaac Gleason, Innholder in Waltham, at Ten o'Clock A. M. at which Time it is desired there would be a general Attendance, as Affairs of the utmost Consequence to the Proprietors, are then to be transacted.

LEONARD WILLIAMS, Proprietor's Clerk.

Waltham, Jan. 4, 1774.

CUSTOM-HOUSE, *BOSTON.*

ENTERTD IN.

Fauner and Taylor, Anguilla. Corbet, St. Eustatia. Harlow, South-Carolina. Howard, Virginia. Alberson, Philadelphia, Harding, North-Carolina.

Burials in the Town of BOSTON, since our last.

Seven Whites. One Black.

Baptiz'd in the several Churches, Two.

High Water at BOSTON, for the present Week.

Monday, 56 min. aft. 1	Friday, 56 min. after 4
Tuesday, 40 min. aft. 2	Saturday, 43 min. af. 5
Wednesday, 24 m. aft. 3	Lord's-Day, 31 m. af. 6
Thursday, 10 min. aft. 4	D's F. Q. 18 Day 8 M.

thereof ; † Capt. Walker thinking his troubles were now at an end, applied to the cuſtom-houſe for leave to take his departure, but to his great ſurprize was informed by the collector that he muſt firſt wait on Gov. Wentworth ; he then applied to the Governor, and received as great a ſhock as ever, by being told that the Governor did not know but he ſhould ſeize the brig brothers again and bring on a new trial ; that there was light money for him to pay at Portſmouth, and finally that he ſaid Governor would not grant a paſs for the ſaid brig until Capt. Walker ſhould obtain an order from the commiſſioners for her delivery.—In this perplexed ſituation the poor man, concluded to take another journey to Boſton, and upon arriving here was obliged to make himſelf a priſoner for four days, for Eſq; Malcom ſoon got ſcent of his arrival, and uſed his moſt aſſiduous endeavors to get at him, but fortunately miſſed his aim : Capt. Walker at length obtaining an atteſted copy of Malcom's proſecution in the admiralty court, together with the order paſſed thereon, ‖ returned to Portſmouth, where it ſeems he ſatisfied both governor and collector, that it would not be prudent for them to interfere further in the matter, and having furniſhed his veſſel with proviſions embraced the firſt wind and ſailed for Whitehaven. ‡

From the polite, humane, and generous behavior of the —honorable board of commiſſioners ; from the tender mercies of the commanders of a number of floating caſtles which ſurround our ports, and from the kind offices diſcovered by the bigger part of the crown officers on this great continent, good Lord deliver every virtuous free-born American.

† Lieut. Mowat finally detained a valuable indented apprentice who had two years to ſerve Capt. Walker ; and what induced him to ſupply the brig's men with proviſions, &c. to the amount of five pounds ſterling, is ſurpriſing, as the veſſel was ſufficiently ſtocked with proviſions, for her intended voyage to England, at the time Malcom ſeized her.

‖ It muſt be ſaid to judge Auchmuty's honor, that he conducted with great impartiality in this whole procedure.

‡ The brig was detained three months on account of the ſeizure and the whole crew in pay, ſo that the charge of wages, proviſions, and the great coſts Capt. Walker was at while in Boſton, and at Portſmouth, for feeing attornies, &c. muſt fall very heavy upon his his owners.

From the Morning Chronicle, and *London Advertiſer*.

To the Worthy LIVERYMEN *of the* City *of* LONDON.

Gentlemen, *Manſion-Houſe, Nov.* 9.

CONSCIOUS of my inability to diſcharge adequately the important office of one of the Repreſentatives in Parliament of this great City, I had not preſumed to ſolicit the honour of your ſupport on the preſent vacancy, but in obedience to the commands of very many worthy and reſpectable gentlemen of the livery. It is their kind partiality to me which has now made me a candidate for your favor ; and, if I ſucceed, I truſt my conduct in parliament will bear evidence, that the obliging ſentiments, which they entertain of me, are not ill-founded.

I deſire, gentlemen, to ſtate to you what that conduct ſhall be on ſome points of the moſt eſſential importance to the free conſtitution of this kingdom. I think the ſhortening the duration of parliaments is indiſpenſible for the recovery of our antient conſtitution, and the integrity of the legiſlative body itſelf. Frequent appeals to the people are of the very eſſence of a government founded on liberty, and the ſureſt means of calling to a ſpeedy account all wicked and corrupt miniſters. Many other points likewiſe of high moment ought to engage our deepeſt attention. The excluſion of placemen and penſioners from ſitting in parliament, an equal repreſentation of the people, a law to ſubject each candidate to an oath, that he has not uſed bribery, or any other illegal means of compaſſing his election, the reſtoration of the American liberties to our meritorious brethren in the new world, and relief to the oppreſſed condition of our fellow ſubjects in Ireland, are points of extreme importance, which every member ought to endeavour to accompliſh. I will exert my poor abilities in this noble cauſe, in conjunction with all thoſe of every party, who purſue the public welfare with integrity, honeſty and ardour. I ſolemnly engage myſelf to you, my conſtituents, that I will promote, to the utmoſt of my power, the ſeveral acts of parliament neceſſary for the above great national purpoſes. As to myſelf, I ſhall always act from the conviction of a good conſcience, in the moſt pure and diſintereſted manner, for I will never accept from the crown, or any miniſter, place, penſion, contract, title, gratuity, or emolument of any kind.

Give me leave, gentlemen, to aſſure you, that if I am elected to this moſt important truſt, it ſhall be my conſtant aim to protect the rights and privileges of my conſtituents, to promote the manufactures, the trade, the commerce of this kingdom, and to ſupport our civil and religious liberties. In my preſent very honourable ſtation, I own, Gentlemen of the Livery, it would be an additional happineſs to me, that the ties between the head and the members of this great corporate body were ſtill more cemented by your making choice of me as one of your repreſentatives in parliament. If my wiſhes are gratified in this reſpect, it will become the primary object of my ambition, being cloſely connected with you for life as one of your magiſtrates, to act in ſuch a manner, that ſo deſirable an union with you may, till the ſame period, be indiſſoluble.

I am,
Gentlemen,
With gratitude and reſpect,
Your faithful and obedient humble ſervant,
FREDERICK BULL.

ALL Perſons indebted for this Paper, whoſe Accounts have been above 12 Months ſtanding, are requeſted to make immediate Payment.

THIS DAY PUBLISHED, (by I. THOMAS,)
Number I. of
The Royal *American* MAGAZINE.

Joſeph-Pearſe Palmer,

At No. 18, South-Side of the Town Dock.
HAS for Sale, very cheap for Caſh, viz.

Chocolate, at 14*d*. 15*d*. & 20*d*. per lb. by the Box. ALSO,

Nutmegs	Shalloons
Pepper	Beaver Coatings
Ginger	Breeches Patterns
Alſpice	Water'd Tammies for Winter Gowns
Coffee (but no Tea)	Wine Glaſſes and Salts of ſeveral ſorts
Loaf and Brown Sugar	Beer Glaſſes
Raiſins	Wine and Water Glaſſes
N. E. and W. I. Rum	Tumblers of ſeveral ſorts
Rice	Quart Decanters
Flour in large & ſmall Bbls	Vinegar and Oil Cruets
Superfine Flour	Linnens and Threads
Dumb Fiſh	Drawboys &c.
Onions	Scotch Handkerchiefs
Bar-Iron	Paper
Nails	Nova-Scotia Oats
Iriſh Shovels	Redwood &c. &c. &c.
Narrow Axes	
Black Velvet	
Broad Cloths	

THIS DAY IS PUBLISHED BY
JOHN LANGDON,
Bookſeller in Cornhill, (Price 2s. L. M.)
The Twelfth Edition of Lord *Somers*
Judgment of whole Kingdoms and Nations, concerning the Rights, Power and Prerogative of Kings, and the Rights, Privileges and Properties of the People. Shewing the Nature of Govergment in general, &c.

☞ This Pamphlet run thro' Ten Editions in London in leſs than twelve Months.

Penobſcot Company.

ALL Perſons claiming or holding under the Ten Original Proprietors of a certain Tract of Land granted by the Council of Plymouth, March 13th, 1629, to *John Beauchamp* of *London*, and *Thomas Leverett*, of *Boſton*, in the County of *Lincoln* ; ſituate in the Eaſtern Parts of the Province of the *Maſſachuſetts-Bay*, commonly called MUSCONGUS, are hereby Notified, that their Meeting ſtands adjourned to Tueſday the Eighth Day of *March* next, at Six o'Clock P. M. at the Houſe of Col. *Ingerſol*, in King-Street, *Boſton*, at which Time they will proceed to draw their ſeveral Shares or Lots of the Land ſurveyed and laid out on *Penobſcot* River, called the Front or River Lots.

WM. HUNT, Prop'rs Clerk.

Boſton, February 1, 1774.

WHEREAS the Proprietors of *Sudbury Canada*, (ſo called) being a Townſhip granted to Joſiah Richardſon, Eſq; and others, in the County of Cumberland, at a legal Meeting by adjournment, on the 17th Day of Auguſt, A. D. 1773, granted a Tax of 20ſ. L.M. on each ſingle Right : Alſo, the ſaid Proprietors at a legal Meeting by adjournment on the 7th Day of December, A. D. 1773, granted another Tax of 40ſ. L.M. on each ſingle Right, to defray the Charges of clearing a Road to the ſaid Townſhip, and other neceſſary Charges : And although the ſaid Taxes have been Publiſhed according to Law, and payment requeſted ; nevertheleſs ſeveral of the ſaid Proprietors are Delinquent in the payment of the ſaid Taxes : Public Notice is therefore hereby given to ſaid Delinquents, that unleſs their Taxes are paid to Cornelius Wood of Sudbury, Treaſurer, or to us the Subſcribers, by TEN o'Clock in the Morning of the 6th Day of April next, their Rights will be Sold as the Law directs, for the payment of their Taxes and Charges. The Sale to begin at Eleven o'Clock in ſaid Morning, at the Dwelling-Houſe of Captain Iſaac Jones, Innholder in Weſton, and continued by adjournment (if need be) 'till the whole be Sold.

Cornelius Wood,
Elijah Bent, } Proprietor's Committee.
Joſiah Stone,

WHEREAS the Proprietors of Land in the Townſhip of *Leiceſter* on *Otter Creek*, (which Townſhip was Granted by the Governor and Council of New-Hampſhire) did at their Meeting in January 1773, Vote, That the Sum of 4 Dollars ſhould be raiſed and levied on each original Right, and alſo at their Meeting in March following, Voted, That the Sum of 1 Dollar as aforeſaid, for the Bounding and Lotting out ſaid Townſhip, and for the Managing and carrying on any other Affairs, for the common good of ſaid Propriety, and that a Committee be appointed to aſſeſs the ſame.—Therefore we the Subſcribers being appointed a Committee for the Purpoſe aforeſaid, do a ſecond Time Notify the Proprietors to pay the ſame to Mr. Iſaac Stone, Collector, or to Capt. Eliſha Child, Treaſurer, at or before the adjourn'd Meeting of ſaid Propriety, which will be on the ſecond Day of March next, at one of the Clock on ſaid Day, at the Houſe of Nathanlel Child, Eſq; of Woodſtock, in the County of Windham, and Colony of Connecticut ; otherwiſe their Rights will be expoſed to Sale, at the Houſe of the ſaid Nathaniel Child, Eſq; at 4 o'Clock P. M. on ſaid Day, according to Law.

Woodſtock, Nov. 16, 1773.

Nathaniel Child,
Eliſha Child, } Committee.
Samuel McClelland,

A few Caſks very excellent Muſcovado Sugars, to be Sold by GABRIEL JOHONNOT, at his Store South Side the Market houſe.

Saml. Abbot & Comy.

HEREBY Inform the Public, that their Co-partnerſhip is this Day mutually diſſolved, wherefore all Perſons who have any Demads on, and all who are Indebted to ſaid Company, are deſired to call on

SAMUEL ABBOT,

for an immediate Settlement, at the Store on *Greene's* Wharf, near the Market, lately occupied by ſaid Company, where is now ſelling off, an aſſortment of Engliſh & India Goods, on very low terms for Caſh.

Boſton 25th Jan. 1774.

CHESHIRE CHEESE.

A Quantity of Cheſhire Cheeſe TO BE SOLD at a low Price by the Hundred or ſingle Cheeſe, at the Store of

Penuel Bowen,

Oppoſite to the Golden Ball, *BOSTON.*

Nathl. & Willm. Coffin,

Have to Sell at the STORE lately occupied by Mr. WARD NICHOLAS BOYLSTON ;

A Few Caſks of good Sherry and Malaga WINE, Liſbon and Malaga LEMMONS in very good Order, COFFEE by the Hundred or larger Quantity, a few Hogſheads of Weſt-India RUM, and ſome INDIGO of a remarkable Quality ; beſides a Variety of Weſt-India GOODS, all which may be had Cheap.

NAILS, &c.

A Quantity of 4d, 6d, 8d, 10d, & 20d Nails, a great variety of Looking Glaſſes, China, Taffaties and Gorgoroons, Velvet Corks, and a quantity of choice Peaſe, to be Sold cheap by

Lee & Jones,

Who have alſo for Sale,

A general Aſſortment of Piece Goods.

BRIMSTONE by the Caſk.

WANTED,

A good Spinet or Harpſichord.

Inquire of the Printers.

WANTED to Purchaſe

A Sloop or Schooner burthen from 70 to 80 Tons, not exceeding three Years old, for which the Caſh will be immediately paid.

Inquire of Edward Davis.

KEYSER's
FAMOUS PILLS

So well known all over *Europe*, and in *this* and the *neighbouring Colonies*, for their ſuperior Efficacy and peculiar Mildneſs, in perfectly eradicating every Degree of a certain Diſeaſe, without the leaſt Trouble or Confinement.

The Public may be aſſured, that this excellent Medicine is beyond any Thing in all Foulneſs and Impurities of the Blood, having performed many aſtoniſhing Cures in Scorbutic Eruptions, Leproſies, White Swellings, Stiff Joints, Gout and Rheumatic Diſorders, &c.

THESE PILLS ARE NOW SOLD BY
EDES and GILL,
(In Boxes of 7ſ6. L. M. each, *freſh imported*)

Who have in their Hands a Letter from the Widow KEYSER, and a Certificate from under her own Hand of the Genuineneſs of the above Pills ; which any Perſon may have the Peruſal of by applying to them at their Printing-Office in *Queen-Street* : Where may be had a Variety of Books, &c

---

TO BE SOLD,

A large Quantity of BRICKS, well made and burnt, of different Sizes, laying at New-Boſton, cheap for Caſh or ſhort Credit. Alſo a very good Iron Hearth about 1200 wt. with Coppers new tinn'd, ſuitable for a Ship of 400 Tons.

Enquire of Edes & Gill.

Inſurance on Veſſels and Goods.

AT the Inſurance-Office of EZEBIEL PRICE near the Exchange,

INSURANCE

May be made on Veſſels, Cargoes, and private Adventures, at VERY LOW PREMIUMS, full one quarter Part leſs than formerly.

Note well—In Caſe of Loſs the Inſurance will be PUNCTUALLY PAID.

A Woman with a good Breaſt of Milk would be glad to go into a Gentleman's Family to Suckle.

Inquire of Edes and Gill.

Boſton : Printed, by EDES & GILL
in Queen-Street, 1774.

No 985.

THE Boston-Gazette, AND COUNTRY JOURNAL.

Containing the freshest Advices, Foreign and Domestic.

MONDAY, February 21, 1774.

Messieurs EDES & GILL,
Please to insert the following.

TO THE PUBLIC.

WHOEVER will allow himself time *seriously* to reflect on the present unhappy situation of political affairs in this country, must *immediately* discern the *necessity* of its inhabitants being *united* not only in their sentiments concerning the *means they ought to use*, at this critical juncture, to extricate themselves from their present difficulties, and to *secure their common safety*, but also of a *fixt* and *inflexible resolution* to execute their purposes upon the first appearance of danger.—

The consideration of the success we have hitherto met with, under providence, in warding off the attacks of our enemies, ought to inspire us with *new courage*, and determine us to adhere *inflexibly* to our former *just* claims and pretensions.—Concession in a *single* point, at this present æra, will serve to accelerate the total destruction of AMERICAN LIBERTY, and would be opening with our *own* hands the flood-gate of oppression, which, like a mighty torrent, would soon sweep away whatever we esteem most valuable.—

A consciousness of *innocence* and of the *justice* of a cause which a man undertakes to defend, will ever give him a great superiority over another, whose strength, courage, and resolution undergo a sensible diminution from the sense of the *injustice* of his attack, and the *guilt* that attends him. If we can only *believe* it in our power to guard our rights against the efforts and stratagems of our sworn enemies, that *beleif* would be no *inconsiderable* step towards accomplishing our designs.—

And that period is now arrived when it is *impious* to be *lukewarm* in matters of the *last* moment to OURSELVES and POSTERITY, or for any of the inhabitants of this *injured* country to remain in a state of *silence* and INACTIVITY; for this would argue either a *stupid & criminal* insensibility to the dangers that are so evidently impending over us, or a *disgraceful* acquiescence in the measures taking by our TYRANNICAL RULERS. DISTRUST, DISCORD and IRRESOLUTION, either in council or in execution, at a time when our situation demands exactly the reverse, may prove fatal to the LIBERTIES of AMERICA.

The beneficent AUTHOR of our being must ever be pleased, when he beholds mankind *boldly* and *resolutely* exert themselves to preserve that liberty with which he endowed them, and which he never gave them power, under any pretence whatever, to alienate: For if thro' ignorance or inadvertence, any society of men should give up their liberty to another by voluntary contract or any other means, upon discovery of their error, it would immediately revert to them, and the contract, of course, become null and void.—

This principle, however discredited or disregarded by *arbitrary rulers*, is perfectly consentaneous to the immutable laws of nature, which none can violate without incurring guilt, and consequently meriting punishment.

Notwithstanding any thing that has been said, we do not pretend at *present*, to be a match for the parent state. That Britain is in possession of a great superiority of power, we have never yet disputed. We have already felt it's weight in a * peculiar manner; and were she in possession of a superior degree of *wisdom* and *justice* too, her power would have been exercised rather to the advantage, than detriment of America. Great-Britain, by her naval force, and by the dint of the sword, *may* extort from us some part of our property; but she may take this for her consolation, that she will lose millions in the *end*, where she gains a single pound at *present*, by oppressive measures, together with an everlasting alienation of our affections.—It is an eternal truth that a *forced* compliance to *unjustifiable* measures is *seldom* if *ever* productive of any beneficial consequences to the compelling party, but oftentimes exactly the reverse. We *certainly* cannot *long* love that parent, who, after having given us an existence, endeavours, *all that in her lies*, to make that existence *miserable*.—Britain's WORTHIES stationed in America have long subsisted, and that too most *luxuriously* on the *stolen* wealth of their oppressed neighbours; but certainly they cannot practice much longer on the same system *error & violence*; they must speedily reform their plan. Unr[illegible]med a *little longer*, they may ask forgiveness, but will ask in vain.—Americans as well as Britons are still men and FREEMEN too. They heartily *detest* and are equally *incapable* of submitting to the ARBITRARY and UNRIGHTEOUS DOMINATION of DESPOTS. Their courage still remains *undaunted*, and instead of being lessened or in the *least* degree relaxed, it has been greatly heighten'd and invigorated by recent acts of injustice;--and they are *determined* at all hazards to obtain redress.

But let us not forget to offer praise to those PATRONS of LIBERTY, who have long WORTHILY protected her. Among this number surely Mr. HUTCHINSON can never be forgotten; his unwearied zeal and industry, in his country's cause, have UNDOUBTEDLY given him a place among the first of PATRIOTS, and rendered him *peculiarly* meritorious. The *generous* and DISINTERESTED principles which he has *uniformly* acted upon, since elevated, by *superior* merit, to the first post of honor in the community, most convincingly prove that he is as great a PHILANTHROPIST and WELL-WISHER to his COUNTRY as *even* the PHILANTHROP at Cambridge.——His ready compliance on ALL OCCASIONS with the requests of his countrymen, and that too in direct *opposition* and *defiance* of MINISTERIAL MANDATES and INSTRUCTIONS, afford to every *unbiassed* mind the *clearest* and *most indubitable* evidence of the *rectitude* of his intentions; and that his COUNTRY's wellfare is much nearer his heart than either the AGGRANDIZEMENT of his *respectable offspring* or the honor, profits and privileges, however splendid, that are annexed to his office. His *fair* and *impartial* representations of the conduct of the Americans to his *confidential friend* on the other side the atlantic, is another shining proof of the *integrity* of the man, of his *friendly disposition* and *sincere attachment* to the RIGHTS and CONSTITUTION of his country. But it is needless, it is endless to describe his VIRTUES: they are amiable and glorious beyond *description* or *example*; may the *gratitude* of his countrymen find means to *requite* him. I am very conscious that my own genius and abilities are much too ordinary to do *justice* to the *merits* of his actions; but if they were not, that *alone* would be but a poor compensation for his immense services to this country, his name must ever be revered and blessed both by present and future generations, and after he is dead, a magnificent monument will doubtless be erected to his MEMORY, and inscribed with the GLORIOUS appellation of FATHER OF HIS COUNTRY. But what a mighty contrast is plainly discernable between the character of a HUTCHINSON and that of a number of ministerial tools and minions, who have *basely presumed* to call that GREAT and GOOD MAN their FRIEND and PATRON. How different from him in their disposition and views! The SCOURGES of Britain and PLUNDERERS of provinces are the odious and disgraceful epithets by which these ought ever to be distinguished. The LOCUSTS that once infested the *Egyptian* clime were far less noxious and burthensome than this numerous, *servile* and *despicable* train of VERMIN. Such an incomparable group of villains and sycophants never before plagued human society. Any *one* of them would thoroughly disgrace the age in which he lived; but a constellation of such malignant beings shed uncommon evils on the present day.

If any set of men under heaven deserve to be deprived of air and water, or any other of the common benefits of nature, it is *undoubtedly* that, which, by much good grace & obsequiousness, has distinguished itself by the *truly* honorable title of FRIENDS OF GOVERNMENT, especially the mercenary part, which by the way is much the greatest. But thanks be to Heaven the scene is well nigh over, and I will never attempt a *second* prediction if their latter-end is not *far* less joyful and triumphant with *them* than their beginning.

We have hitherto employed lenient measures *more* than enough; and there is *now* no other way (I fear) remaining, but with sword in hand to drive away that ravenous band of miscreants that infest the land, and totally to extirminate an infamous and lawless race of robbers, that have long since been rendered, by the allurements of gain, the devoted instruments of TYRANNY and OPPRESSION. BRITAIN! If you are truly anxious for the safety of your AMERICAN WOLVES, it now becomes you *speedily* to stretch forth your *compassionate arms* and kindly receive them; and *then* may the animosities that have long and unhappily subsisted between us, finally and for ever cease. May BRITAIN and her COLONIES henceforth be allied by much closer bands of union than heretofore. May they ever despise their *private* emoluments whenever it comes in competition with the *general good* of both, and may they be equally industrious in concerting measures most conducive to their *mutual interest* and *tranquility*.——

BRITAIN in FIRM UNION with her COLONIES may still keep the world in awe, and maintain her DIGNITY and INDEPENDENCE against the united powers of earth: But whenever she is *dis-connected* from them (Britain! tremble at the tho't!) that mighty empire which is now made rich by her American offspring, *must then bleed at every vein, and* WILL SOON EXPIRE. Thus unhappily disunited, tho' at present the GLORY and TERROR of the world, she must quickly condescend (to her eternal disgrace) to become a province of some neighbouring nation, and thus in part verifyng the prediction of the celebrated Montesqueieu many years agone, will afford a monument of folly and imprudence, like many other *once* flourishing kingdoms, for the warning and instruction of succeeding ages. In vain will she then deplore her unhappy fate, and curse too late those wanton hours that were miserably employed in forging chains for America.

O FORTUNATAS NIMIUM SUA SI BONA NORINT BRITANNICOS!

A PATAGONIAN.

* 5th of *March* 1770.

To AMERICAN FREEMEN.

SO rapid have been the strides of TYRANNY for a number of years past, that the continued succession of *new* injuries makes us forget the *former*; and a man must have the pen of a ready writer to record the abuses this people receive from a despotic administration; who have evidently nothing less in view than the total abolition of all American liberties. This is evident from a thousand instances of arbitrary plans and proceedings; and I would at this time call the attention of my countrymen to a most glaring and capital instance of tyranny, which ought to make every villain blush, and every free mind kindle with indignation against the abandoned herd of tyrants and their tools—viz. the *hydra* courts of admiralty. By the commission of a judge of one of these courts, published in the *Pennsylvania Journal* of January 26, (and re-published in the *Massachusetts Spy* of Thursday last) it appears that they were calculated, not only to annul the American charter, but *Magna Charta*, and to overturn the whole constitution of the nation.——Magna Charta, the Bill of Rights, and also the Charter of the Colonies, hold the persons & property of the subject sacred; and no one shall be *disseised of his property, nor imprisoned, without a trial by a jury of his peers, or equals*—But these commissions impower the *bribed judge* to trample upon all the fundamental laws of the constitution; and in the face of all that is sacred in LIBERTY & JUSTICE, give the said judge, power to *punish* and *imprison* all persons guilty of a breach of the acts of trade—and to *compel* all manner of persons to assist in carrying these laws into execution'——and this enormous power is extended not only to the seas and harbours, but to every "creek and stream of fresh water, and to *banks* and *shores* adjoining to them."——So that their powers have no bounds, for these judges being *enlightned* with a *bribe* of 600l. a year sterling, they will soon find that the whole earth, is a *bank* to the seas; and therefore their authority must be universal—I cannot doubt but this would be the case, if administration had mercenary troops enough to enforce their wicked plans. These unconstitutional and most abominable *courts of admiralty*, are a clear demonstration, that a system of tyranny has been formed to enslave the Americans; and if they had not made a resolute stand they would not at this day have had any thing which they might call their own. The united wisdom and power of every friend to this country, is now necessary to oppose the combined efforts of our enemies, who are using every art which the *father of lies* can suggest to them, to destroy the liberties of America.

This is not a time to be silent, *liberty* and *conscience* calls upon every man to speak and act in the cause of his country. May Heaven give us wisdom and power to preserve the rights of humanity.

AMERICA SOLON.

This Day is Published,
And Sold by EDES and GILL,
GAINE's
New Memorandum Book,
OR,
The MERCHANT's and TRADESMAN's
DAILY POCKET JOURNAL
For the Year 1774.
Disposed in a Method more useful and convenient for all Sorts of Business, than any of those who have pretended to imitate it. CONTAINING

FIFTY-two Pages for the Receipts and Expences of every Week in the Year; and Divisions for every Day in the Year—useful to enter any future Appointments, or shew when Notes or Payments will become due. Also a Genealogical List of the Royal Family of Great-Britain; the Births, Marriages, and Issue of the Sovereign Princes of Europe; English Nobility; Scots Nobility; Archbishops and Bishops of England; Members of the House of Commons of Great Britain; and the Counties, Cities, Boroughs, and Cinque Ports they represent; Summary of the House of Commons; His Majesty's most Hon. Privy Council; Knights of the most noble Order of the Thistle; Knights Companions of the most Hon. Order of the Bath; His Majesty's principal Secretaries of State; Lords Commissioners of the Treasury; Lords Commissioners of Trade and Plantations; Lords Commissioners of the Admiralty; His Majesty's Post Masters General; His Majesty's Land Forces; Royal Navy of Great-Britain; Of Precedency; Rank of Army and Navy; Irish Nobility; Archbishops and Bishops of Ireland; A List of the Commons of Ireland; Rank and Precedency in America; A List of his Majesty's Forces in North-America; and a List of the Officers of a Battalion consisting of seven Independent Companies of Militia, raised in the City of New-York; placed as they rank in the Field. To which is added a compleat Almanack.

TO BE LETT,
A large commodious Chamber, near the Market, fit for almost any Tradesman, or a Store.
Enquire of the Printers.

COTTON WOOL,
Of an excellent Quality, to be Sold by
JONATHAN WILLIAMS, Junr.
per Bag or smaller Quantity——VERY CHEAP.

BOSTON, *February* 21.

On Saturday February 12th, the Secretary of the Province was directed by the House of Representatives, without Delay, to deliver to his Excellency the Governor the following Remonstrance and Petition, for the Removal of PETER OLIVER, Esq; from the Superior Court; agreeable to their Resolve of the 11th, which was inserted in our last, viz.

Province of the MASSACHUSETTS-BAY.

To His Excellency the Governor and Council.

THE House of Representatives of this his Majesty's Province beg leave to remonstrate to your Excellency and Honors, That the Hon. Peter Oliver, Esq; the Chief Justice of the Superior Court of Judicature, Court of Assize and General Goal Delivery over the Province, a Court wholly erected and constituted by the Great and General Court or Assembly by a Power granted to the said General Court by the Royal Charter, declining any more to take and receive the Grants of the said General Assembly for his Services as Chief Justice of the said Superior Court, hath accepted, taken and received a Salary and Reward granted to him by his Majesty for his Services as aforesaid, from the 5th Day of July 1772, to the 5th Day of January 1774: And that the said Peter Oliver, Esq; Chief Justice of said Superior Court hath plainly given this House to understand by a Writing under his Hand, his Resolution for the future to accept the Salary and Reward for his Services as aforesaid, which he affirms is granted to him by his Majesty during his Residence in the Province as Chief Justice of said Superior Court. Now this House humbly conceive, that if his Majesty had not been misrepresented by his Ministers and Councellors touching the Way and Manner prescribed by the Royal Charter for the Support of his Government in this Province, he would not have ordered such Salary and Reward to be made to the said Peter Oliver, Esq;—Nevertheless he the said Peter Oliver, Esq; from *his own* Knowledge of the Charter and Constitution of the Province must have been assured that by accepting and receiving the same and resolving to continue so to do, he hath therein done and resolved to do, contrary to the Usage and Custom of the Justices of the said Superior Court, since the erecting of said Court invariably used and approved; contrary to the plain Sense and Meaning of the said Charter and against the known Constitution of this Province.

The House would further represent to your Excellency and Honors, That the said Peter Oliver, Esq; hath received the said Salary and Reward out of the Revenue unjustly and unconstitutionally levied and extorted from the Inhabitants of the American Colonies; and that he hath acted and done in Manner as aforesaid against the known Sense of the Body of the People of this Province most fully and expressly declared in the several Resolutions of divers Houses of Representatives and otherwise.

And it is the Opinion of this House, that the said Peter Oliver, Esq; hath by his Conduct as aforesaid perversely and corruptly done that which hath an obvious and direct Tendency to the Perversion of Law and Justice in the said Superior Court: That he hath thereby proved himself an Enemy to the Constitution of this Province; and has placed himself under an undue Bias, detached himself totally from his Connection with this People and lost their Confidence. And that he hath rendered himself altogether disqualified any longer to hold and act in the office of a Justice of the said Superior Court:

WHEREFORE it is the Prayer of the Representative Body of the People of this Province, That your Excellency and Honors would be pleased to Order that the said Peter Oliver, Esq; be not suffered any longer to sit and act in his Office of Chief Justice, and that he be forthwith and without Delay removed from said Court.

In the Name and by Order of the House,

T. CUSHING, *Speaker.*

On Monday following the two Houses passed a Resolve for the Adjournment of the Superior Court from Tuesday the 15th Instant, (being the Day on which it was by Law to be holden) to a further Day; it being judged by the two Houses altogether improper that the Chief Justice should sit and act under the present Circumstances, and uncertain what Opinion or Resolution he might have formed on the Matter. The Resolve was laid before the Governor, but his Excellency declining to give his Assent thereto, the Superior Court was of Course opened (the Chief Justice being absent) and adjourned itself till Tuesday the 22d Instant, which will be To-Morrow.

Tuesday Afternoon his Excellency the Governor was pleased to send the following Message to the Honorable House of Representatives, viz.

Gentlemen of the House of Representatives,

THE Secretary has presented to me a written Paper purporting a Remonstrance against *Peter Oliver*, Esq; Chief Justice of the Superior Court, for receiving and for having declared that he will continue to receive the Salary which has been granted to him by the King, and thereupon praying in the Words following, "That your Excellency and Honors would "be pleased to order that the said *Peter Oliver*, Esq; "be not suffered any longer to sit and act in his "Office of Chief Justice, and that he be forthwith "and without Delay removed from said Court." This Remonstrance the Speaker who has signed the same in the Name and by Order of the House, directed the Secretary to deliver to me.

Considering that some Expressions in your Remonstrance carry another Aspect, it may be necessary to observe to you that the Council, except when they are considered in their Legislative Capacity, or as a Court for the Probate of Wills and granting Administration, and for determining Cause of Marriage and Divorce, are by the Constitution to be advising and assisting to the Governor, and do not make one Court or Judiciary Body with the Governor; but the Governor is considered as an integral Part and has Authority from time to time at his Discretion to assemble and call the Council together. Any thing in your Remonstrance which has a contrary Aspect may have proceeded from Inadvertence.

There are other Parts of your Remonstrance which appear to me very exceptionable, but I chuse to avoid all Controversy with you except it shall be my indispensible Duty.

I think it proper to acquaint you that his Majesty having been pleased to direct Warrants to be prepared for the payment of Salaries to the Chief Justice and to the other Justices of the Superior Court, I received, as Governor of the Province, the earliest Notice of this Declaration of his Majesty's Pleasure, in order as I conceive that, as far as might appertain to me, I should conform thereto.

If I should comply with your Request or take any Steps in order to the Removal of the Chief Justice, from his Place, meerly for receiving what is thus granted him by the King, I should make myself chargeable with counteracting his Majesty and endeavouring to defeat his Royal Intentions expresly signified to me, with a Contempt of his Royal Authority, and with a Breach of the Trust reposed in me by my Commission, and I should fear some Mark of his Royal Displeasure. I am therefore in Duty to the King obliged to decline your Request.

I will by the first Opportunity transmit a Copy of your Remonstrance to be laid before the King, and I shall conform to such further Signification of his Majesty's Pleasure as I may hereafter receive.

Province-House,
15th Feb. 1774.

T. Hutchinson.

On Wednesday the 16th, the House ordered the following Message to be carried up to the Honorable Board, by Mr. *Hancock*, Mr. *Phillips*, Major *Hawley*, Capt. *Greenleaf*, and Mr. *Allen* of *Gloucester*, viz.

May it please the honorable Board,

THE House of Representatives beg Leave to acquaint the Honorable Board that *Peter Oliver*, Esq; Chief Justice of the Superior Court of Judicature over this Province, declining any more to accept and receive the Grants of this Assembly for his Services as a Justice of said Court, hath contrary to the known Constitution of the Province, and the invariable Usage and Custom of said Court, accepted and received a Salary and Reward granted to him by his Majesty for his said Service, from the 5th of July 1772, to the 5th Day of January 1774; which Salary and Reward he hath taken and received, as has been fully made to appear to this House, out of the Revenue unjustly and unconstitutionally levied and extorted from the Inhabitants of the American Colonies. And the said *Peter Oliver*, Esq; hath also given this House clearly to understand, by a Writing under his Hand, a true Copy of which, together with certain Resolutions of this House thereupon, will be laid on the Council Table, that he is determined for the future to accept the Salary and Reward, which he affirms is granted to him by his Majesty during his Residence in the Province as Chief Justice of the said Superior Court.

The House would further acquaint the honorable Board, that they did on the 12th of this Instant February, pass a Remonstance and Petition to his Excellency the Governor and Council, setting forth, that the said *Peter Oliver*, Esq; by his Conduct as aforesaid, acting against the known Sense of the Body of the People of this Province, most fully and expresly declared in the several Resolutions of divers Houses of Representatives and otherwise, had detached himself totally from his Connections with them, and lost their Confidence; and praying that he might not be suffered any longer to sit and act in the Office of Chief Justice of the said Superior Court; but that he might forthwith be removed therefrom: Which Remonstrance and Petition the House did on the same Day specially charge the Secretary to deliver to the Governor without Delay.

The honorable Board will please further to be informed, that his Excellency by his Message of Yesterday, acknowledged that the said Petition and Remonstrance had been laid before him, and expresly declared to this House, that "he was obliged in Duty to the King to decline their Request;" and also signified to the House, that he should not take any Step for the Removal of the said Chief Justice on that Account. A Copy of said Remonstrance and Petition, with his Excellency's said Message, will also be laid on the Council Table.

Now this House, having after the most mature Deliberation, judged the Matters aforementioned, to be of the most weighty Importance to this Province, do think themselves bound in Duty to their Constituents, thus explicitly to represent them to the honorable Board, that the honorable Board may duly advise thereon, and act and determine as in their own Wisdom they shall think proper.

The Papers referr'd to in the foregoing Message were afterwards by Order of the House laid on the Council Table.

And on Friday last the whole House of Representatives waited on his Excellency the Governor in the Council Chamber, where the Speaker delivered to him the following Petition for the immediate Removal of PETER OLIVER, Esq; from the Superior Court, viz.

Province of the
Massachusetts-Bay, }

To his Excellency the Governor.

THE House of Representatives being still deeply impressed with a Sense of the Importance and Necessity of Removing *Peter Oliver*, Esq; Chief Justice of the Superior Court, now wait on your Excellency with this repeated Petition, to which we hope your Excellency will not give a Denial: And pray that your Excellency would be pleased to take our Remonstrance and Petition to the Governor and Council of the 12th Instant into your further Consideration. And although your Excellency has signified to this House that you shall not take any Steps for the Removal of the Chief Justice from his Place; yet, as it is in the Judgment of this House a Matter of the most weighty Concernment to this Province, We pray that your Excellency would please to take the Advice of his Majesty's Council thereon. We do with the greatest Propriety urge this Matter, as we find in the Royal Charter that the principal End of the Institution of the Council is to be advising and assisting to the Governor in ordering and directing the Affairs of the Province, and that they are expresly appointed for that very End: And your Excellency's determining on this Matter by yourself, would be to order and direct one of the most important Affairs of this Province without the Advice and Assistance of the Council, and contrary to the most evident Design of the Charter.

We do assure your Excellency that the "written Paper" which you are pleased in your Message of Yesterday to say "purported a Remonstrance against Peter Oliver, Esq." was *in Truth*, the Remonstrance and Petition of this House, passed after the most mature Deliberation, by a very great Majority, in a very full House.

Your Excellency will please to consider that this House is well knowing to the general Sense of their Constituents in this Matter; and we can now assure you, that the Continuance of the Chief Justice in his Place, will increase the Uneasiness of the People without Doors, and endanger the publick Tranquility. We therefore earnestly intreat your Excellency, that while we are in this Instance "employing the Powers with which we are intrusted in promoting the Tranquility and good Order of the Government," we may agreable to your Declaration in your Speech to both Houses, find that you are ready to give your Consent to a Request of the House intended for that and other great and important Purposes; and that your Excellency will immediately take every Step for the Removal of the Chief Justice from the Superiour Court.

The List of the Members who voted for and against the above Petition, we are obliged to omit this Week, for want of Room.

Thus the Reader hath a true Account of this most momentous Affair, as it has hitherto been transacted among the several Branches of the Legislature. The House of Representatives press the Removal of the Chief Justice with a becoming Firmness and Decency: They expressly declare that his Continuance in his Place will *increase* the Uneasiness of the People, and *endanger the public Tranquility*. This alone would be a sufficient Reason, at least why a *prudent* Judge should remove himself by a Resignation, if he "dares not refuse the King's Grants" while he holds his Office. The Governor it is supposed will not remove him from a *Motive* said to be obvious. If his Excellency would condescend to take the Advice of a private and obscure Individual, *he would well consider* THE END *of an obstinate Refusal to comply with so* REASONABLE *a Request made to him by the* REPRESENTATIVE BODY *of a* FREE *and* DETERMINED *People.*

W A N T E D,

A Negro Man of an unexceptionable Character, warranted; for such an one a good Price will be given; one of a small Size, brought up in a Country Town, and who understands a little of House Business will be preferred. Inquire of the Printers.

Messieurs EDES & GILL,

IT has ever been a Complaint, That Ignorant Judges often dealt out Punishments disproportionate to Crimes. To remedy this Evil, I propose to make a SCALE of JUSTICE, numbered to 100 Degrees; and mark every Crime with a Number in Proportion to its real Criminality; that every Judge in future may adjust the Punishment to the Offence. But before I compleat my Scale, I would ask the Opinion of the learned Civilians, or any one who understands the Rules of Righteousness, what Number ought to be annexed to Treason against Liberty, and the Rights of Mankind? What Number against a Judge who receives a Bribe; endeavours to alter the Constitution of Government; or to introduce Tyranny? I should be glad to have an Answer to these Queries as soon as may be, from some of the Judgmatical Heads in America.

New-England, Feb. 6, 1774. ALFRED.

BOSTON, February 21.

By the Bill of Mortality last Year in the City and Liberties of Philadelphia, it appeared, that out of 1334 *who died there, above* 300 *of them perished with the Small-Pox in the natural Way; and as the chief of them were the Children of poor People, a Number of Gentlemen in that City have formed a Society for innoculating the Poor, free of Expence to them, and are providing a Fund for that Purpose.*

An Account is published of the Quantities of Flax-Seed exported from the Ports of New-York, and Philadelphia, to Ireland; by which it appears that there has been exported,

	Of the Growth of 1772.	
From New-York.	17187 *Hhds.*	29710
From Philadelphia.	12523	
	Of the Growth of 1773.	
From New-York,	14852 *Hhds.*	27012.
From Philadelphia,	12160.	

DIED] On Tuesday last Mrs. Mary Hubbard, Widow of the late Hon. Thomas Hubbard, Esq; deceased. Her Funeral is to be attended this Afternoon. [*The Character of this good Woman will be in our next.*]

Mrs. Sarah Boylston, Widow, Mother to Mr. Thomas Boylston, an eminent Merchant in this Place, in the 78th Year of her Age. Her Remains are to be inter'd To-Morrow Afternoon, when her Friends and Acquaintance are desired to attend.

At Roxbury Mrs. Katharine Greaton, aged 74, Consort of Mr. John Greaton.——At Charlestown, Mr. Miller, of the Small-Pox.——At Ipswich, two Persons of the Small-Pox.

On Friday Last departed this Life, at Pomechag in Connecticut, her Saffron coloured Majesty Ann, Queen Dowager of the Monahagan Indians, and Saturday her Remains were inter'd, in a Manner suitable to her high Rank, in the Indian Burying Ground, at Chelsea.

A CAPITAL CHANGE!

THE right well-born, the right valiant, stout and unconquerable A—h W—e, a high, canting, jesuitical Tool *of a* Tool, *either for Fear of being known by the Cattle, with whom thro' Mistake he had nearly come to a* brutal Engagement, *or from some warm Inclination to try the Principles of Whiggism, during his political Endeavours to serve his Master, has hired an old second-hand thread-bare* Bob Wig *of the ministerial Stamp, which being worn out in the Service, was left at the Barber's to be kicked up* alamode Toryo, *to be let, or sold to the most* suitable Head *in the Province——This curious* DonQuixot *being arm'd by Power of* Instruction, *with Sword, Pistol and dry Powder, for his great Safety, and to try a new Experiment, in Case he should dream of an Opposition in his Sleep, made a* Bed Companion *of his Cutlass, which was plac'd under his Pillow to keep Peace among the Freeholders of Headborough, that might come and disturb his Rest: But it so happened, that this Gentry beginning to Muster, some invisible Hand directed the Edge in such a Manner, that it cut off some of the* Capital Locks, *and so disfigured the Gravity of his venerable Phiz, that he was put to the great Expence of a new Roof to prevent the* March Winds *shaking the old hollow Fabric to Atoms.— On his Head may the Whig long flourish.*

James Swan

HAS for Sale at Store No. 6, leading to Treat's and Spear's Wharves,

A Quantity of *Indian Corn* very good and just arrived, choice Fine *Flour*, and a few Quoils of the best *Cordage*, all Cheap.

Dry'd OX HIDES,

Cotton and Piemento, just Imported from Jamaica, and to be Sold at GRIFFIN's Wharf.

TO BE SOLD

Utensils for the Tallow Chandler's

Business, a large Iron Kettle, Press, Tallow Tub, Chopping Knife, Trough, Candle Rods, &c.

Inquire of the Printers.

Lincolnshire Company 20 Associates.

WHEREAS there are divers Matters to be transacted by the 20 Associates of the *Lincolnshire* Company, respecting their Lands and Interest lying near *Penobscot-Bay* in the County of *Lincoln*:—The Committee of said Associates being duly authorised therefor, Hereby notify said Associates to meet on Wednesday the 9th Day of *March* next, at Mr. Hubbard's, the Vernon Tavern, in *Boston*, 6 o'Clock, P. M. then and there to act upon all such Matters as may properly come before them.

By Order of the Committee,

NATH APPLETON, Prop'rs Clerk.

February 16th, 1774.

Harvard-College LOTTERY,

5000 DOLLARS the highest Prize,

Not two Blanks to a Prize.

THE Public are hereby informed, That the Managers of HARVARD COLLEGE LOTTERY, are very desirous the Drawing of said LOTTERY should commence as soon as possible; they would therefore be glad those who have Subscribed for Tickets would send for them, and those who intend to be Adventurers, would purchase their Tickets immediately.

Choice Peas, Isle of Shoals dumb

Fish, Beef, Rye, a few Barrels Rye Flour, and Pork,

To be Sold by

JOHN BARRETT and SONS,

Near the Mill-Bridge.

GOODS under the Sterling Cost.

William Gale

Acquaints his Friends and Customers that he is now Selling the remainder of his Goods, under the *Sterling Cost*, (at his Shop opposite the Post-Office, in Cornhill, Boston.) ——Among them are following, viz.

Broad Cloths,	39. & 7-8 Garlix,
Flannels,	Figur'd Modes,
Lamb Skins,	Figur'd Sattins,
Plushes,	Pink, blue & white Sattins,
Kerseys,	Blond Laces,
Cotton Velvetts,	Black & white Sattin Pumps,
Womens Velvett,	Brocaded ditto,
Strip'd Swanskins,	White & color'd Russell dit.
Duffils,	Plain and sprig'd Muslin,
Felt Hatts,	Cambrick & sprig'd Muslin,
Shalloons,	English & flower'd Lawns,
Tammies,	Incle Lutestring,
Demaskus,	Silk Gauzes, &c. &c.
Irish Linnens,	

THE PUBLIC

ARE hereby informed, That JOHN JOY has just arrived from London, and brought with him a large and compleat Assortment of DRUGS and MEDICINES, of the best Quality. Also, Surgeons Instruments of every Kind finished in the neatest Manner, with a full Assortment of Groceries and Dye Stuffs; which as they were purchased by himself for the Cash, he will sell on very reasonable Terms, at his Shop the North Corner of Williams's Court, in Cornhill, Boston.

Practitioners and others, may be supplied with large or small Quantities, by Letter or otherwise, as well as though they were present.

Medicine Boxes of various Prices, for Ships or private Families, are put up in the neatest Manner.

TO BE SOLD very cheap for CASH, At the Shop next to the Sign of the Buck and Glove in Cornhill, BOSTON;

Superfine and common *Philadelphia* FLOUR,

COFFEE of an uncommon good Quality,

Very good Brown SUGAR,

Nutmegs,	Ginger,
Cinnamon,	Split Pease,
Cloves,	Velvet Corks,
Mace,	Powder Blue,
Pepper,	Salt Petre,
Allspice,	Allum,
Oil,	Olives,
New Raisins,	Durham Mustard,
Currants,	Chocolate,
London T D 18 Inch Pipes,	Rice,
Loaf Sugar,	Oatmeal,
Almonds,	Poland Starch,
Capers,	Crown Soap.

Best French INDIGO.

An Assortment of English GOODS, & Crockery Ware.

ALSO,

A large new Scale Beam, with Scales and Weights.

20 well made Draws in a Nest.

N. B. The above Shop and House will be Lett the first of April: Inquire of Samuel Minott, near the Draw-Bridge.

TO BE SOLD

MAY PLACE (the pleasant Seat of JOHN FENTON, Esq;) one Mile from *Charlestown* Ferry, upon the great Road leading to *Cambridge, Mistick*, &c. &c. (part of the remarkably fruitful Hill called *Bunkers*,) containing a handsome House, Out-Houses, Barn and Garden, stored with a great Variety of the choicest Fruit-Trees, all young and healthy.

Twenty-five Acres of choice Mowing and Pasturage, *(two thirds and more of which under Mowing)* newly Fenced off into proper Divisions, highly Drest and handsomly decorated with Locust Trees.

Between five and six Acres of Salt-Marsh; Also, a new Wharff adjacent to the Premises, very convenient for landing Wood, Manure, &c.

Whoever may incline to purchase the above Premises, may be informed of the Conditions by applying to ROBERT TEMPLE, Esq; of Ten Hills, near Charlestown: Mr. ISAAC MALLET at the Neck of Land near said Place, (who will at any Time shew the Premises): Or a Line directed to Col. JOHN FENTON, of Portsmouth, New Hampshire.

☞ If not Sold by the 2d of April—then the House, Warehouse, Barn, Garden, and a Pasture, containing about two and half Acres, to be Lett.

TO BE SOLD,

Next Wednesday the 23d Instant,

at Eleven o'Clock, A. M. by Public Vendue, at the Exchange Tavern in Boston, (pursuant to former Advertisement) one Half of about 950 Acres of Land in Granby, bounded S by Springfield North Bound, E by Belchertown, &c. being Part of the Real Estate of *William Bowdoin*, Esq; deceased.

In the Press and speedily will be Published, adorned with an elegant Frontispiece,

The Memoirs of the Life of the Rev. GEORGE WHITEFIELD, A. M,

Late Chaplain to the Countess of Huntingdon.

In which every circumstance worthy of notice, both in his private and public character is recorded. Faithfully selected from his original papers, journals and letters. Illustrated with a variety of interesting and entertaining Anecdotes, from the best authority.

The which is added, a particular account of his Death and Funeral; and Extracts from the Sermons which were Preached on that Occasion.

Compiled by the Rev. JOHN GILLIES, D. D.

CONDITIONS.

I. It shall be Printed in large Twelves, on good Paper, and with new Types.

II. It will consist of about 300 Pages, and the Price to Subscribers will be no more than Six Shillings, New-York currency, neatly Bound and Letter'd, although the London edition is nearly double that Price.

III. The Names of the Subscribers will be printed in the beginning, and no Money required until the delivery of the Book.

Subscriptions are taken in by EDES & GILL, Printers in Boston, and by all the other Printers and Booksellers on the Continent.

TO BE SOLD

By Benjamin Church,

On THURSDAY next,

At THREE o'Clock in the Afternoon,

BY PUBLICK AUCTION,

SUPERFINE middling and coarse Broad Cloths—Ratteens—Frizes—Half Thicks—Kerseys—Shalloons—Calamancoes—Irish Linnens—Checks—Mens and Womens Hose—Linneus—Velveretts—Handkerchiefs—Case Knives and Forks—Inkhorns—Penknives, &c.—Sundry Articles of Household—Wearing Apparel—Watches, Cutlery Ware, half a Dozen Mehogany Chair Frames—a Case of Draws—Feather Beds, &c. &c. &c

Thursday next, 3 o'Clock P. M.

JUST PUBLISHED, and to be Sold at GREENLEAF's Printing-Office in Hanover-Street, BOSTON;

A SERMON Preached at the Anniversary Thanksgiving at Plymouth, in commemoration of the first Landing of our Ancestors there, Anno Domini, 1720.

Nothing more need be said to recommend this Sermon to the perusal of the Public, than that it was Delivered by CHARLES TURNER, A. M. Pastor of the Church in Duxbury, who Preached the celebrated Election Sermon, the last Year.

New AUCTION-ROOM, Cornhill,

TO-MORROW at TEN o'Clock will be Sold by PUBLIC VENDUE, at GREENLEAF's Auction-Room,——A large Assortment of GOODS, the Property of a Gentleman leaving off Business;

——*Among which are*——

BLUE, Claret and Drab Broad Cloths, Kerseys Ratteens, Forrest Cloths, Shalloons, Tammies, Camblets, flower'd Russells, Poplins, Missionets, Grizets, worsted Mitts, Velvetts, and Velverets, Castor Hatts, Ribbons, Sattins, figur'd and plain Modes, 50 Pieces of 3/4 and 7/8 Irish Linnens, striped Hollands, Ginghams, check'd Handkerchiefs, Cambricks, Lawns, Muslins, Callicoes, Chintz, Scotch Threads, Metal and Horn Buttons, Cuttoes, Scizars, Razors, Penknives, Buckles, Sleeve Buttons, &c. &c. &c.

Wm. GREENLEAF, Auctioneer.

The Sale will begin Tomorrow at Ten o'Clock,

On Thursday next, at Ten o'Clock,

will be sold by Public Vendue, at the New Auction-Room South Side of the Town-House, viz.

BRoad-Cloths, Bearskins, Ratteens, Irish Linnens, Jersey-knit Hose, Kilmarnock Caps, and a Number of other Articles. Also a great Variety of House-Furniture.

ANDREW OLIVER, Auctioneer.

N. B. For private Sale at said Auction-Room,——Handsome Looking Glasses, Muffs, a Silver Tankard, Porringers, Pepper Castors, Cups, Tea Spoons, a genteel Silver Salver, 10 Inches over, Silver plated Candlesticks, also a handsome full suit of Brocade, and a suit of black Grogram.

CUSTOM-HOUSE, BOSTON.

ENTERED IN.

Chapman, Adams, and Davis Cape Nichola. Kissick, Demarara. Kent Jamaica. Cook, St. Lucia. Cook, Halifax. Smith, Virginia. Oakman, North Carolina.

Burials in the Town of BOSTON, since our last.

Nine Whites. None Black.

Baptiz'd in the several Churches, Twelve.

High Water at BOSTON, for the present Week.

Monday, 6 min. aft. 8	Friday, 20 min. after 11
Tuesday, 56 min. aft. 8	Saturday, 6 min. af. 12
Wednesday 42 m. aft. 9	Lord's-Day, 50 m. aft. 12
Thursday, 30 min. aft. 10	Full ◉ 26 Day 6 Morn.

PURSUANT to a Decree of the High Court of Chancery in England, William Rumbold, Mary the Wife of Alexander Laing, both of the Province of Maryland, Mary the Wife of Garrett Blackford, of the Province of New-Jersey, in North-America—Rumbold, of Cashell, in Ireland, Rodolphus Rumbold of Tipperary, in Ireland; William Rumbold of Jamaica; and William Rumbold of the Bay of Honduras; and all other Persons claiming to be Heirs at Law of Thomas Rumbold, late of Long-Alley, near Moorfields, in the County of Middlesex; or William Rumbold, of the same Place, his Brother, who were the Sons of Thomas Rumbold, formerly of the same Place, Stocking Trimer, deceased, who was the Son of William Rumbold, late of King's Clere, in the County of Southampton, Yeoman, deceased, are to come in and enter into Proof of their respective Claims of being Heirs at Law of the said Thomas Rumbold, and William Rumbold, before JOHN EAMES, Esq; one of the Masters of the said Court, at his Chambers in Symons Inn, Chancery-Lane, London, within twelve Months from the Publication hereof, or in Default thereof they will be absolutely excluded the Benefit of the said Decree.   J. EAMES.

WHEREAS the Great and General Court or Assembly at their Session begun and held on the 27th Day of May 1772, granted a Tax of *One Penny half Penny* per Acre, upon the Lands of the Non-resident Proprietors in the Town of *Ashby*, in the County of Middlesex; and whereas said Tax has been duly assessed and published agreeable to Law, and some Persons Proprietors or Owners of said Land, neglect or refuse to pay the same; and whereas the General Court by said Act did impower the Assessors chosen by the Town of Ashby, to Assess the same, to Sell so much of the Delinquent Proprietors Lands as shall be sufficient to pay and satisfy said Tax and other incidental Charges: And whereas the Owners of the following Lands are Delinquent in paying said Tax, viz.

Names of those who drew the Lots, or them who now own them.	What Division	What Right	No. Acre	l. s. d.
John Moffat			20	0 2 6
Col. Josiah Willard part	4 5 6	57 83 53	37	0 4 8
Henry Laughton part	4	32	14	0 1 9
Christopher Barrett			22	0 2 9
Cumings and Fletcher part	4		40	0 5 0
Rev'd Mr. Perry Two	3		133	16 7¼
Col. Wm. Lawrance	6	35	40	0 5 0
Hugh Hall, Esq; part	3	73	66	0 8 3
James Lawrance	5	70	40	0 5 0
Edward Emerson part	5	62	42	0 5 4
Ebenezer Southwick	6	19	50	0 6 3
Jona. Hill part	3	69	40	0 5 0
Samuel Brown	3	47	66	0 8 3
Simon Blood	4 part 6	14	124	15 6
David Melvin	6	58	42	0 5 3
James Nicholas	4 part 6	78	71	0 8 10¼
John Nichlas			20	0 2 6
— Gore part	3		62	0 7 9
Capt. Daniel Stickney part	3	58	40	0 5 0
Third Division, No.	60		66	0 8 3
Peter Atherton	3	37	66	0 8 3
Formerly belonging to Lunenburg				
Robert Paul	3 4	24	135	1 9 4¼
John Bridge, jun.			48	0 6 0
James Billings			53	0 6 7¼
Abraham Gibson			30	0 3 9
Joseph Lee			30	0 3 9
Heirs of Samuel Reed			100	12 6
Daniel Buttrick			32	0 4 0

NOTICE is hereby given to said Delinquents, that so much of their Lands will be exposed to Sale at Public Vendue, on the 31st Day of May next, at the House of Capt. Samuel Stone, Innholder in said Ashby, at 9 of the Clock in the Forenoon, and continued by Adjournments, if need be, until the second Day of June, as will be sufficient to pay said Tax, and other intervening Charges, unless prevented by Payment of said Tax, (and such Charges as have already arisen) unto the Assessors, before the aforesaid Time.

Ashby, Feb. 16, 1774.   James Locke, Samuel Stone, Jonathan Locke, } Assessors.

THIS DAY IS PUBLISHED BY

John Langdon,

Bookseller in Cornhill, (Price 2s. L. M.)

The Twelfth Edition of Lord *Somers* Judgment of whole Kingdoms and Nations, concerning the Rights, Power and Prerogative of Kings, and the Rights, Privileges and Properties of the People. Shewing the Nature of Government in general, both from God and Man. An Account of the British Government and the Rights and Privileges of the People in the Time of the *Saxons*, and since the Conquests. The Government which God ordained over the Children of *Israel*; and that all Magistrates and Governors proceed from the People, by many Examples in Scripture and History, and the Duty of Magistrates from Scripture and Reason. An Account of Eleven Emperors, and above Fifty Kings deprived for their evil Government. The *Rights* of the People and Parliament of *Britain*, to Resist and Deprive their Kings for evil Government, by King *Henry's* Charter, and likewise in *Scotland*, by many Examples.

The Prophets and ancient *Jews* were Strangers to absolute Passive-Obedience: Resisting of arbitrary Government is allowed by many Examples in Scripture, by most Nations, and by undeniable Reason.

A large Account of the Revolution; with several Speeches, Declarations, and Addresses, and the Names and Proceedings of Ten Bishops, and above Sixty Peers, concerned in the Revolution before King *James* went out of *England*.

Several Declarations in Queen *Elizabeth's* Time of the Clergy in Convocation, and the Parliament who assisted and justified the *Scotch*, *French* and *Dutch*, in resisting of their Evil and Destructive Princes.

☞ This Pamphlet run thro' Ten Editions in London in less than twelve Months.

KEYSER's FAMOUS PILLS

So well known all over *Europe*, and in *this* and the *neighbouring Colonies*, for their super or Efficacy and peculiar Mildness, in perfectly eradicating every Degree of a certain Disease, without the least Trouble or Confinement.

The Public may be assured, that this excellent Medicine is beyond any Thing in all Foulness and Impurities of the Blood, having performed many astonishing Cures in Scorbutic Eruptions, Leprosies, White Swellings, Stiff Joints, Gout and Rheumatic Disorders, &c.

THESE PILLS ARE NOW SOLD BY

EDES and GILL,

(In Boxes of 7/6. L. M. each, *fresh imported*)
Who have in their Hands a Letter from the Widow KEYSER, and a Certificate from under her own Hand of the Genuineness of the above Pills; which any Person may have the Perusal of by applying to them at their Printing-Office in Queen-Street: Where may be had a Variety of Books, &c.

Wanted immediately to Hire,

A single decked Schooner or Brigantine, of 90 or 100 Tons Burthen. Inquire of Edes & Gill.

FOR PHILADELPHIA,

The BRIG BETSEY, CONSTANT FREEMAN, Master, Lying the South-Side Long-Wharff, will Sail in four or five Days; for Freight out, or home, inquire of the Master on Board, or at his House in School-Street.

NEW LONDON.

TO BE SOLD, a House and Land with good Accommodations, as out Houses &c. and well situated for a Tavern, and has been Improved as such for some Years past; with a Wharf adjoining, the best Accommodated and most Improved for Navigation in that Town, if not soon Sold, to be Let, for Particulars Enquire of Richard Law & Duncan Stewart, Esquires; in New London or of Edes and Gill in Boston.

ALL Persons who have any Demands on the Estate of HANNAH DIX, late of Boston, Widow deceased, are desired to bring in their Accounts; and all who are Indebted are desired to make speedy payment to Elizabeth Orrok, Administratrix to said Estate.

Six Months longer are allowed the Creditors to the Estate of *Andrew McKenfie*, late of Milton, Merchant, deceas'd, for bringing in their Claims, and proving their Debts, the Commissioners give Notice, that they shall attend that service at the British Coffee-house, in King-Street, from 6 to 9 o'Clock, the third Tuesday in this and the five following Months.
Boston Feb. 14th, 1774.

Wanted a Quantity of Shrums for the Caulkers Business, for which cash will be given; also to be SOLD a few Puncheons, and forty Gallon Casks of old choice Jamaica Rum.   Enquire of the Printers.

WHEREAS the Proprietors of the Township of Land lying on both sides Androscoggin River, in the County of Cumberland, and adjoining Sylvester Township, granted June 11th, 1771, to Samuel Livermore, Esq; and others: Voted and granted at their Meeting June 17th, 1772, a Tax of Forty Shillings on each Right, to defray the Charges that had or might arise on said Propriety, to be paid unto Leonard Williams, Esq; their Treasurer, on or before the 4th of August 1772, which Tax has been made and published according to Law, notwithstanding which, several have neglected to pay said Tax. Public Notice is hereby given, that unless said Tax be paid by Wednesday the 16th Day of March next, their Rights who are delinquent in paying said Tax, will be Sold at Public Vendue, at the House of Isaac Gleason, Innholder in Waltham, at 8 o'Clock in the Forenoon of said Day.

And whereas the Proprietors of said Township, at their Meeting Feb. 24th, 1773, Voted and Granted a Tax of Twenty-four Shillings on each Right, to be paid unto Leonard Williams, Esq; their Treasurer, on or before the 1st Day of Oct. 1773; and again on the 3d Day of Nov. 1773, the Proprietors aforesaid Voted and Granted a further Tax of Forty-eight Shillings on each Right, to defray the Expences of said Propriety, to be paid their Treasurer as follows, viz. One half of said Tax on or before Wednesday the 16th Day of March next, and the other half on or before the 1st Day of August next, Public Notice is hereby given that if said Taxes be not paid by Wednesday the 16th Day of March next, and by the 1st Day of next August, their Rights, or so much of them as is sufficient to pay said Taxes, and the Charges arising thereon, will be Sold for Payment thereof, according to Law.

Waltham, Jan. 4, 1774.   Leonard Williams, Elijah Livermore, Elisha Harrington, } Assessors & Committee for Sale of delinquent Proprietors Rights.

The Proprietors of the Township aforesaid, are hereby Notified, that their Meeting stands adjourned to Wednesday the 16th Day of March next, at the House of Isaac Gleason, Innholder in Waltham, at Ten o'Clock A. M. at which Time it is desired there would be a general Attendance, as Affairs of the utmost Consequence to the Proprietors, are then to be transacted.

LEONARD WILLIAMS, Proprietor's Clerk.
Waltham, Jan. 4, 1774.

RAN-away from Jonathan Reed of Wrentham, on the seventh of this Instant, a Man Servant, calls his Name John Hopkins or James Gutridge, an Old Country-man, who Bound himself to said Reed, for Time, about 30 Years of Age, a Shoemaker by Trade, marked with the Small Pox, about 5 Feet & ½ high, his Hair red, and wears a dark Shirt wig, walks very upright, a well set Man: Had on when he went away a brown russy short Coat, black Jacket, and old Leather Breeches, a thick Buff Cap, no Hat:—Whoever shall take up said Run-away and secure him, so that his Master may have him again shall have FIVE DOLLARS Reward, and necessary Charges paid by me.
JONATHAN REED.
Wrentham, Feb. 8, 1774.

Joseph-Pearse Palmer,

At No. 18, South-Side of the Town-Dock.
HAS for Sale, very cheap for Cash, viz.
Chocolate, at 14d. 15d. & 20d. per lb. by the Box.   ALSO,

Nutmegs	Shalloons
Pepper	Beaver Coatings
Ginger	Breeches Patterns
Allspice	Water'd Tammies for Winter Gowns
Coffee (but no Tea)	Wine Glasses and Salts of several sorts
Loaf and Brown Sugar	Beer Glasses
Raisins	Wine and Water Glasses
N. E. and W. I. Rum	Tumblers of several sorts
Rice	Quart Decanters
Flour in large & small Bbls	Vinegar and Oil Cruets
Superfine Flour	Linnens and Threads
Dumb Fish	Drawboys &c.
Onions	Scotch Handkerchiefs
Bar-Iron	Paper
Nails	Nova-Scotia Oats
Irish Shovels	Redwood &c. &c. &c.
Narrow Axes	
Black Velvet	
Broad Cloths	

Saml. Abbot & Comy.

HEREBY Inform the Public, that their Co-partnership is this Day mutually dissolved, wherefore all Persons who have any Demands on, and all who are Indebted to said Company, are desired to call on
SAMUEL ABBOT,
for an immediate Settlement, at the Store on Greene's Wharf, near the Market, lately occupied by said Company, where is now selling off, an assortment of English & India Goods, on very low terms for Cash.
Boston 25th Jan. 1774.

Insurance on Vessels and Goods.

AT the Insurance-Office of EZEKIEL PRICE near the Exchange,
INSURANCE
May be made on Vessels, Cargoes, and private Adventures, at VERY LOW PREMIUMS, full one quarter Part less than formerly.
Note well—In Case of Loss the Insurance will be PUNCTUALLY PAID.

Penobscot Company.

ALL Persons claiming or holding under the Ten Original Proprietors of a certain Tract of Land granted by the Council of Plymouth, March 13th, 1629, to John Beauchamp of London, and Thomas Leverett, of Boston, in the County of Lincoln; situate in the Eastern Parts of the Province of the Massachusetts-Bay, commonly called MUSCONGUS, are hereby Notified, that their Meeting stands adjourned to Tuesday the Eighth Day of March next, at Six o'Clock P. M. at the House of Col. Ingersol, in King-Street, Boston, at which Time they will proceed to draw their several Shares or Lots of the Land surveyed and laid out on Penobscot River, called the Front or River Lots.
WM. HUNT, Prop'rs Clerk.
Boston, February 1, 1774.

WHEREAS the Proprietors of Sudbury Canada (so called) being a Township granted to Josiah Richardson, Esq; and others, in the County of Cumberland, at a legal Meeting by adjournment, on the 17th Day of August, A. D. 1773, granted a Tax of 20s. L.M. on each single Right: Also, the said Proprietors at a legal Meeting by adjournment on the 7th Day of December, A. D. 1773, granted another Tax of 40s. L.M. on each single Right, to defray the Charges of clearing a Road to the said Township, and other necessary Charges: And although the said Taxes have been Published according to Law, and payment requested; nevertheless several of the said Proprietors are Delinquent in the payment of the said Taxes: Public Notice is therefore hereby given to said Delinquents, that unless their Taxes are paid to Cornelius Wood of Sudbury, Treasurer, or to us the Subscribers, by TEN o'Clock in the Morning of the 6th Day of April next, their Rights will be Sold as the Law directs, for the payment of their Taxes and Charges. The Sale to begin at Eleven o'Clock in said Morning, at the Dwelling-House of Captain Isaac Jones, Innholder in Weston, and continued by adjournment (if need be) 'till the whole be Sold.
Cornelius Wood, Elijah Bent, Josiah Stone, } Proprietor's Committee.

Boston: Printed, by EDES & GILL in Queen-Street, 1774.

THE
Boston-
AND
COUNTRY

Gazette,
JOURNAL.

No. 98

Containing the freshest Advices, Foreign and Domestic.

MONDAY, February 28, 1774.

From the PUBLIC ADVERTISER, *of November* 16.

To Captain JOSEPH HARRISON,

Collector of the Customs at BOSTON.

YOU have questioned the Authenticity of the Letter from Boston, which I sent to the Press; yet you do not deny the Charge of your having been absent *four Years* from your Duty, but impeach my Cadour in not mentioning the Reason of your Absence. Since you demand it, I will give the real Reason. It is that *you and your Son* may both be quartered on the American Revenue, and that you may remain in London a pensioned Informer, being abhorred as a most detestable Hypocrite in Boston.

Without knowing your Person, I am perfectly acquainted with your Character. I know you to be a most unprincipalled Imposter. Your cunning and Hypocrisy may impose upon unsuspecting Minds in private, but will never stand the Test of public Inquiry.

Your Excuse for so shameful an Absence from your Post is, that you are 70 Years of Age—that you received a Blow from a Brick-bat 5 Years ago, of which you languished a Twelve Month, and that to return would be to hazard your Life in the Boston Mob.

Is this then the avowed Application of a Revenue extorted at the Risque of every Tie that is dear, and of our most important Commerce—to maintain in Idleness superannuated Spies? You should at least have proved by what Services you merited this Indulgence. Had your Craft and Dissimulation abated as your Years advanced, the Infirmities of your Age might have claimed our Compassion. But what Pity does he deserve who plays the Hypocrite under the Cloak of the Saint, and spends the Remainder of his Life in the Ruin of his Country?

You pretend to have received a Blow from a Brick-bat thrown by the Mob, of which you languished a Twelvemonth. You have forgot your own Affidavit, in which you impute that Blow to a Stick. Indeed it is well understood that you did not receive any Blow; for in four Days after the Fray you dined at Col. Phillips's apparently in perfect Health, and within a few Months was jaunting about the Country on Parties of Pleasure with your Friend Dr. M ffat. His Letters mention nothing of this Blow, or its languishing Effects, though he tells us you opened your Bosoms to each other. Pray, Sir, did you commune together upon the Catholic Faith, and piously wish the Re-establishment of that good old Religion, with her inseparable Companion—arbitrary Power?

But your Life you think would still be in Danger from the Mob. If they ever meditated any thing against it, what prevented them at that Time, when you was in their Power, or during the long Time you remained there afterwards, from executing their Design? Have you injured them more atrociously of late? Has any of your confidential Correspondence been detected? Would *you* be in danger where Hutchinson is safe?

How comes it, Sir, that in mentioning that Mob, you concealed the Cause of it? You do not wish it should be known, that it is proved by the Affidavits of fourteen reputable Persons, that the Tumult was occasioned by your seizing illegally, with an armed force, Mr. Hancock's Sloop, under a Pretence of Smuggling. Yet after this, from a Consciousness of your Inability to support the Charge, you dropt the Prosecution. In Truth your Purpose was answered. The Seizure made with such Circumstances of brutal Violence occasioned there, what it would have done here, a Tumult. This was precisely what you wished. I defy the warmest of your Friends to deny, from a full View of this Business, that the Seizure was made in consequence of a preconcerted Plan, between you, Governor Bernard and the Commissioners, to irritate the People to some Act of Violence that might justify the calling in a military Force to dragoon them into Slavery. By this Manœuvre, and a little hard swearing, you effected Part of the Plan; but the Spirit of the People disappointed the rest.

To that Outrage on the Property of Mr. Hancock you have added now another upon his Character, by joining the Name of that Gentleman with Smuggling; an Imputation for which you have not the least Colour of Truth, and to which every Action of that honourable Merchant's Life gives the Lye. You ought to be tender of this Charge, when you know it comes home to your Friend Governor Bernard.

I am almost ashamed of having wasted any Time on an Object so insignificant as you; but I hope it will prevent you from insulting the Public with such Apologies, and teach you to be satisfied with eating the Bread of Infamy in Silence.

PHILO-JUNIUS AMERICANUS.

OATS.
Quebec and Nova-Scotia Oats. Also, Nova-Scotia Peas, TO BE SOLD BY
JOSEPH P. PALMER,
At the lowest Store on the South Side of the Town-Dock.

BOSTON, Feb. 23.

A PROTEST *of a number of the inhabitants of the town of* MARSHFIELD, *against the proceedings of said town, on the 31st of January last.*

WE the subscribers think ourselves obliged, in faithfulness to the community, ourselves and posterity, on every proper occasion, to bear our publick testimony against every measure, calculated to destroy that harmony and unanimity which subsists through the colonies, and so eventually to the destruction of those liberties, wherewith the Author of Nature, and our happy constitution, has made us free: Were they not already notorious it would give us uneasiness to mention the resolves which were voted in this town the 31st of January last.

To the first of these Resolves we do not object; but do heartily join in recognizing our loyalty and subjection to the King of Great-Britain; and our readiness to be ever subject to the laws of *our* legislature.

In their second Resolve, they say that the "measures and proceedings in the town of Boston, in the detention and destruction of the teas, belonging to the East-India Company, are illegal, unjust, and of a dangerous tendency;"—against which we take the liberty to protest. We have long groaned under the weight of an American revenue act, and when by the virtue of the people, in not purchasing any goods loaded with a duty, the malignity of the act was, in some measure evaded, a scheme was devised and prosecuted by the ministry, to enforce said act by permitting the East-India company, to force their infectious teas upon us, whether we would or not. At this not only the inhabitants of Boston, but of the whole province, were very much, and very justly alarmed, and while they were prosecuting every method that human wisdom could devise, that the tea should be sent back undamaged, it was destroyed, but whether by the people of that town, or any other town of this province does not appear.

3dly, They resolved to instruct their Representative, 1st to endeavour that the perpetrators of these mischiefs be brought to justice. This appears to us to be the business of another department. We have executive courts and officers whose business it is to punish offenders, and we trust they are faithful.——2dly, They instruct him to endeavour that this town be excused from paying for said teas; which we think might have been omitted, at least, 'till there was a probability of a requisition from proper authority for payment.

They conclude with a renunciation "of all methods of imposition, violence, and persecution, such as has been most shamefully exercised upon a number of inhabitants of Plymouth, by obliging them to sign a recantation," &c.

Such bitter, virulent and injurious reflections, on our brethren at Plymouth, ought not to have taken place 'till some shadow of proof had been adduced to the town, that any such violence, &c. was ever practiced by them on a single person.

The occasion of this our protest has given us great uneasiness, and we were confident those extraordinary resolves would not have taken place, but by the insinuations of a certain gentleman who seems willing his constituents should share in the resentment of the whole country, which he has incurred by his conduct in a public character. We mean not to countenance riotous and disorderly conduct, but being convinced that liberty is the life and happiness of a community, are determined to contribute to our last mite in its defence, against the machinations of assuming arbitrary men, who stimulated with a lust of dominion, and unrighteous gain, are ever studying to subjugate this free people.

MARSHFIELD, *Feb.* 14, 1774.

Anthony Thomas,	*Benjamin White, jr.*	*John Shurman,*
Nehemiah Thomas,	*Lemuel Dilano,*	*Samuel Tilden, jr.*
William Thomas,	*Jabez Dingley,*	*Samuel Oakman,*
Thomas Foord,	*Isaac Carver,*	*Gersham Ewell,*
Thomas Waterman,	*Joshua Carver,*	*William Clift,*
Isaac Phillips,	*Lot H. Silvester,*	*Joseph Clift,*
Samuel Tilden,	*David Carver,*	*Joseph Bryant,*
Sam'l Williamson,	*Nathaniel Thomas,*	*John Oakman,*
Nathan Thomas,	*William Thomas, jr.*	*Joseph Oakman,*
John Dingley,	*Paul Sampson,*	*King Lapham*
Joseph Kent,	*John Bourn,*	*Barnard Tuels,*
Benjamin White,	*Thomas Dingley,*	*Peleg Kent,*
Joseph Hewit,	*Samuel Smith,*	*Zenas Thomas,*
Thomas Fish,	*Tho. Waterman, jr.*	*Luther Peterson,*
Jeremiah Low,	*Peleg Foord,*	*Briggs Thomas,*
Benjamin Tolman,	*Asa Waterman,*	*Elisha Kent,*
Jethro Taylor,	*John Waterman,*	*Timothy Williamson.*

WANTED,
A Negro Man of an unexceptionable Character, warranted; for such an one a good Price will be given; one of a small Size, brought up in a Country Town, and who understands a little of House Business will be preferred. Inquire of the Printers.

TO BE LETT,
A large commodious Chamber, near the Market, fit for almost any Tradesman, or a Store.
Enquire of the Printers.

Boston, Feb. 21. 1774.

LAST Tuesday, about sun-set, departed this life, after a short but painful disease, Mrs. MARY HUBBARD, widow of the late honorable THOMAS HUBBARD, Esq; and daughter of that "good man for whom one would even dare to die," Mr. JONATHAN JACKSON, late of this town. She nearly resembled her father in a naturally calm, even, placid, and sedate disposition of mind; which, being sanctified from her early days, became a permanent, strong, habitual principle; greatly conducing to her support under various pressing trials in life, and rendering her an example of christian patience, contentment and subjection to the alwise, righteous ruler of the world, highly worthy of the imitation of all that knew her.

Her piety was truly genuine; not expressing itself in ostentatious shew, which she abhorred; but in a serious, grave, solemn attendance on all the devotional services of religion, whether in the closet, the family, or the house of God. She laid no stress on such motions in the passions, to whatever height they might be raised, as were separable from an heart intirely devoted to God. Her religion was like that of the devout matrons in the first times of New-England, which did not consist in high talk, transient flights, and extraordinary sallies of affection; but in a steady, uniform, and universal regard to the governing authority of heaven.

She was a sound believer in the christian revelation; and "walked by faith, not by sight;" living above the world, and unconformed to it's gaities, amusements, fopperies, and vanities; adorning herself "in modest apparel, with sobriety; not with broidered hair, or gold; but (which becometh women professing godliness) with good works," ever appearing with "the ornament of a meek and quiet spirit, which is, in the sight of God, of great price."

Her benevolence, upon the gospel plan of love, placed her far above most of this present age. In imitation of God, of whom it is said, he is *love*, she loved her neighbour with undissembled affection; and made it evident she did so, not "in word and tongue" only, but "in deed and truth;" being ever "ready to communicate, willing to distribute," according to her ability, especially to those she trusted were of "the house of God."

Her faith in Christ was not an empty speculation, but influenced her to a becoming care of conducting well in all the relations she sustained in life. As a wife, she was tender, faithful and obedient: As a parent, wisely and affectionately concerned and careful, not meerly for the temporal happiness of her children, but that they might, by a good education, be fitted to be blessings in this world, and blessed in another: As a mistress, not rigorous and severe, but mild and gentle, behaving towards her servants with meekness and kindness; though not with imprudent indulgence: As a neighbour, condescending, obliging, and ever ready to all the offices of goodness. In a word, through the whole course of life, she conducted as having upon her mind an habitual deep sense of her accountableness to that Jesus, whom God has constituted the Judge of the world, and as being principally concerned that she might, at last, be able to give up her account with joy, and not with grief. Not that she imagined, after her best endeavours, that she was faultless. Far from this, she could, and did, exclaim with pious David. "If thou, Lord, shouldest mark iniquities, O Lord, who shall stand!" Her hope therefore, with reference to the joys of God's presence, was founded, not on her own worthiness, but the worthiness of that Jesus, who "became obedient to death," that he might atone for the sins of men, and make way for their "salvation with eternal glory," in God's kingdom that is above.

She appeared in her last sickness, which was severely trying, to be possessed of that calm, patient, humble, and resigned frame of spirit, which was honorary both to her, and to the grace of God which conspicuously operated in her. We have abundant reason to believe, that she may justly be reckoned among those "blessed dead," who died in the Lord, are rested from their labors, and whose works have followed them to the other world, where they are unspeakably happy.

BOSTON, February 28, 1774.

Tueſday laſt His Excellency the Governor ſent for the Houſe of Repreſentatives into the Council-Chamber and delivered them the following SPEECH.

Gentlemen of the Houſe of Repreſentatives,

IN my Anſwer to your Addreſs or Remonſtrance which you directed the Secretary to deliver to me, I acquainted you that to comply with your Requeſt would be to counteract the King in a Matter upon which His Majeſty's Pleaſure had been expreſsly ſignified to me, and, therefore, I was obliged to decline it.

In a ſecond Addreſs, preſented by your Speaker, the Houſe attending, you deſire me to take your Remonſtrance into my further Conſideration, and alſo to take the Advice of His Majeſty's Council thereon, of whoſe Inſtitution you ſay it was the principal End to be adviſing and aſſiſting to the Governor in ordering and directing the Affairs of the Province, and you add, that my determining on the Matter myſelf would be to order and direct one of the moſt important Affairs of the Province without the Advice and Aſſiſtance of the Council and contrary to the moſt evident Deſign of the Charter.

You have taken particular Parts or Clauſes of the Charter abſtracted from other Parts or Clauſes which relate to them, and which are intended to qualify and explain them, and in this way you are enabled to repreſent the Conſtitution very different from what it has always been underſtood to be.

You have paſſed over that Clauſe in the Charter which authorizes the Governor to aſſemble and call together the Council from time to time *at his diſcretion*, and likewiſe another Clauſe reſerving a negative Voice to the Governor as well in Council as in the General Aſſembly, and declaring that no Acts of Government whatſoever, either of the Council or Aſſembly ſhall be valid without his Conſent.

I am very ſenſible that beſides thoſe Acts of Government which the Charter authorizes the Governor to do by himſelf, there are others which are to be done by the Advice and Conſent of the Council; and, for the purpoſe of the laſt mentioned Acts, the Governor is authorized, from time to time, *at his diſcretion*, to aſſemble the Council, and no other Proviſion is made in the Charter for aſſembling or calling them together. It cannot be denied that the Governor may be requeſted to aſſemble the Council in order to the laying before them Matters of ſuch a nature, as that meerly agitating them in Council would derogate from the Honour of the King, and ſuffering a Queſtion to be put upon them would render the Governor highly culpable. Surely the Governor has a diſcretionary Power to refuſe to aſſemble the Council upon ſuch a Requeſt, otherwiſe the Clauſe in the Charter muſt be altogether nugatory and can have no force nor effect in any caſe whatſoever.

There is a Fallacy in your reaſoning, and you give a ſpecious Appearance to it by avoiding the Diſtinction between the Governor's doing an Act of Government without the Advice of Council and his declining to aſſemble the Council in order to their Advice upon an Act the ſubject matter whereof, according to his beſt Diſcretion, ought not to be made a Queſtion of or come into Debate.

That I may give you a full and, I hope, ſatisfactory Anſwer to your Addreſs I muſt repeat to you, what I have had occaſion to mention to former Houſes of Repreſentatives,—that I am the Servant of the King—that I have received no Inſtructions nor any Significations of His Majeſty's Pleaſure which are not perfectly conſiſtent with your Charter and which His Majeſty hath not an indiſputable Authority to give—that ſuch Inſtructions or Significations of His Majeſty's Pleaſure are, by my Commiſſion, the Rule of my Adminiſtration, and to depart from them would be a Breach of the Truſt which His Majeſty has repoſed in me.

I am nevertheleſs urged by you to bring this Queſtion, in effect, before His Majeſty's Council, whether I ſhall or ſhall not conform to His Majeſty's Pleaſure expreſsly ſignified to me, and to take their Advice upon it. *Taking* the Advice of his Majeſty's Council is an equivocal Expreſſion. If by *taking* the Advice you intend no more than conſulting or adviſing with them, in order to collect their Opinion, this would be trifling with the Council, as well as bringing before them an improper Subject of Debate, becauſe they would give their Advice to no purpoſe, ſeeing I am not at liberty, if they adviſe to it, to diſobey the King's Commands: If by *taking* their Advice you intend complying with it, though it ſhould be contrary to my own Senſe of my Duty to the King, this would be giving up the Power of a Negative granted or reſerved to me by the Charter; for if I do not uſe this Power to avoid a Breach of a ſpecial expreſs Truſt repoſed in me by the King, I know of no Caſe in which I ought to do it. In either Senſe of the Word I am not at liberty to comply with your Requeſt.

In a mixed Government, a Conformity of Sentiment in all the Parts of it, upon every Meaſure, is not to be expected. Every Part may, notwithſtanding, claim a right to Freedom of Judgment in the exerciſe of the Powers aſſigned to it by the Conſtitution. The Houſe of Repreſentatives, by long uſage, is in Poſſeſſion of the Power of originating all Grants of the Eſtate of the Province, whether in Lands or Money. I have often thought the Grants made by former Houſes much ſhort of an Equivalent to the Services which they were intended to compenſate. I have never urged inlarging them contrary to the free Judgment of the Houſe. The Power of aſſembling the Council in order to their Advice, is by Charter as well as uninterrupted uſage, in the Governor. I have a right to equal Freedom of Judgment in the exerciſe of this Power.

If I perſiſt in an erroneous Judgment, upon your humble Repreſentations to His Majeſty and making the Error to appear, you may be ſure of Redreſs; but until I am convinced of my Error I may not voluntarily depart from my own Judgment or Diſcretion and govern myſelf by the Diſcretion of the Houſe of Repreſeatatives, for I ſhould then be juſtly chargeable with ſubverting a material Part of the Conſtitution.

Province-Houſe, 22d Feb. 1774.   *T. Hutchinſon.*

Thus the Governor has declined complying with the ſecond Requeſt of the Houſe of Repreſentatives; which was to take the Advice of his Majeſty's Council upon their Petition for the Removal of Chief Juſtice OLIVER. "*That I may give you a* FULL *and I hope ſatisfactory Anſwer,*" *ſays his Excellency,* "*I muſt repeat to you,—that I am the Servant of the king—that I have receiv'd no Inſtructions nor any Significations of his Majeſty's Pleaſure, which are not perfectly conſiſtent with your Charter, and which his Majeſty has not an indiſputable Authority to give—and that ſuch Inſtructions or Significations of his Majeſty's Pleaſure are by my Commiſſion the Rule of my Adminiſtration.*". Whether all or either of theſe can be ſaid to be a pertinent or "full Anſwer" to the Requeſt of the Houſe, *every* Reader will judge. If indeed his Excellency has an Inſtruction from his Majeſty or any Signification of his Pleaſure, that he ſhall not take the Advice of his Council upon an Addreſs of the Houſe of Repreſentatives for the Removal of a Judge who they ſay has, in their Opinion founded on the Knowledge they have of the Sentiments of their Conſtituents, "loſt the Confidence of the People," if there be any ſuch Inſtruction, (which the Governor ſeems to hint, tho' he doth not aſſert it,) and that Inſtruction is the Rule of the Governor's Adminiſtration, his Excellency's Reaſoning may be thought by ſome Perſons to be not altogether impertinent and "fallacious"; but if there be no ſuch Inſtruction, he might at leaſt have gratified the Houſe ſo far as to have taken the Advice of the Council upon their Addreſs. The Houſe undoubtedly meant no more by *taking* the Advice of the Council, than "to adviſe and conſult with them" upon it. His Excellency might without a Queſtion have thus underſtood them. This he ſays "would be trifling with the Council—becauſe they would give their Advice to no Purpoſe, ſeeing he is not at Liberty, if they adviſe to it, *to diſobey his Majeſty's Command.*" The Governor, we judge, here expreſſeth himſelf ſomewhat *equivocally*. That he is not at Liberty to diſobey the King's Command, if the King's Command is indeed, as he ſays it is, the Rule of his Adminiſtration, muſt be allowed to be good Reaſoning; but whether the Governor here means that he ſhould diſobey the King's Command, if he ſhould by the Advice of the Council remove the Chief Juſtice, or whether he ſpeaks generally, is left uncertain, we will not ſay *deſignedly*. If he intends the former, which it is moſt natural to ſuppoſe, what he only hinted at before, he now plainly ſpeaks, that he is commanded by the King not to remove Chief Juſtice Oliver, upon the Requeſt of the Houſe of Repreſentatives, even though his Majeſty's Council ſhould adviſe him that the Addreſs of the Houſe was well founded, and for aught we know, tho' he ſhould be convinced of it himſelf.——— We cannot eaſily believe that our gracious Sovereign has ever laid him under ſuch a Command; eſpecially when we conſider that by Act of Parliament, it is lawful for the King to remove a Judge upon the Addreſs of both Houſes: But we obſerve that his Excellency ſpeaks of "Significations of the King's Pleaſure"; How we are to underſtand the King's pleaſure is *ſignified* to him, Whether by an Inſtruction under the Sign Manual, or in a Letter from one of his Miniſters or Servants, is one of the *Arcana Imperii* in this Country; his Excellency having formerly, if we miſtake not, inform'd the Houſe that he dared not diſcloſe it without his Majeſty's Leave. —Upon receiving this Meſſage from the Governor, the Houſe reſolved by a very great Majority to Impeach the Chief Juſtice, and appointed a Committee to prepare the Articles; which were afterwards brought in and agreed to in the Houſe by a Majority of 92 to 8. Whereupon the Houſe ſent a Meſſage to the Governor to deſire that his Excellency would be in the Chair; but he declining the *third* Requeſt of the Houſe, they immediately (on Saturday laſt) ſent up a Committee to Impeach the Chief Juſtice of High Crimes and Miſdemeaners. The Governor's Meſſage and the Articles of Impeachment we intend to give our Readers in our next.

On Friday laſt the Governor ſent the following Meſſage to both Houſes of Aſſembly, viz.

Gentlemen of the Council,

and of the Houſe of Repreſentatives,

HAVING received diſcretionary Leave from the King to go to England, I think it proper to acquaint you with this Inſtance of His Majeſty's moſt gracious Condeſcenſion, and that I intend to avail my ſelf of it aſſoon as His Service will admit.

I muſt deſire you to give all the Diſpatch poſſible to ſuch neceſſary publick Buſineſs as may yet lie before you, for I muſt ſoon, by an Adjournment or Prorogation, give the Court a Receſs that I may attend to that Preparation for my Voyage which His Majeſty's Service and my perſonal Affairs require.

Milton 24 *Feb.* 1774.   T. HUTCHINSON.

The Honorable the Superior Court is adjourn'd to Tueſday the 7th Day of June next, and not the 14th as mentioned in the Thurſday's Papers.

We hear from Marblehead that one Day laſt Week, two or three perſons were taken up there and committed to Salem Goal on ſuſpicion of being concerned in ſetting Fire to the Inoculating Hoſpital lately burnt at Cat Iſland, upon which 4 or 500 Perſons aſſembled from Marblehead and went to the Goal where they oblig'd the Keeper to deliver up the Keys, when they ſoon releaſed the Priſoners, and went off in triumph.

We hear from Martha's Vineyard, that on the 21ſt Inſtant put in there in Diſtreſs, the Ship Iſabella, Benja. Heming, Maſter, from Newcaſtle on Tyne bound to Philadelphia; ſhe ſail'd from England the 7th October laſt. Since the 29th of January their Stock of Water being exhauſted, they were oblig'd to ſubſiſt on ſuch ſmall matter as they could diſtil from the Sea Water in the Ships Kettle, and for a long time before that, they had been at a very ſhort allowance, by reaſon of which the Crew had become ſo exceeding ſick and weakly that they were unable to Work the Ship, and muſt inevitably have periſhed had they not met with Capt. Cutting Lunt in the Sloop Edmund from Newbury Port, bound to Greneda on Friday the 11th Inſt. lat. 39, 10. lon. 63W. who with great humanity and tenderneſs ſupplied them with Water, &c. by which means they were preſerved. Capt. Lunt and his Crew were all well.

DIED.] Mrs. Anna Vergooſe, aged 70.—Mrs. Elizabeth Hewes, Relict of the late Samuel Hewes, Eſq; of this Town, Merchant, in the 68th Year of her Age. —Mrs. Leaden, Widow, aged 69.—Mrs. Weſtwood, Widow.—Mrs. White, Widow.—Mr. —— Clough, Son of Mr. Clough, Gunſmith.—Mrs. Sarah Blake, aged 38, Wife of Mr. Joſeph Blake, Maſon.

At Charleſtown] Mrs. Sarah Auſtin, Widow of the late Capt. Thomas Auſtin.

TO BE SOLD,

By Benjamin Church,

On THURSDAY next,

At THREE o'Clock in the Afternoon,

SUPERFINE middling and coarſe Broad Cloths—Ratteens—Frizes—Half Thicks—Kerſeys—Shalloons—Calamancoes—Iriſh Linnens—Checks—Mens and Womens Hoſe—Linnens—Velveretts—Handkerchiefs—Caſe Knives and Forks—Inkhorns—Penknives, &c.—Sundry Articles of Houſehold—Wearing Apparel—Watches, Cutlery Ware, half a Dozen Mehogany Chair Frames—a Caſe of Draws—Feather Beds, &c. &c. &c

Thurſday next, 3 o'Clock P. M.

Whereas I the Subſcriber intend leaving off the Baking Buſineſs very ſoon, do take this opportunity of returning my Thanks to thoſe Gentlemen and Ladies who have favoured me with their Cuſtom, ſince my late Huſband's deceaſe. MARY SURCOMB.

The Buſineſs will be carried on as uſual by Mr. William Flagg.

N. B. *A very good Horſe and handſome Chaiſe to be Sold: Inquire of Mary Surcomb.*

Boſton, Feb. 28, 1774.

This is to Acquaint all Gentlemen and Ladies that the Baking Buſineſs will be carried on as uſual, by me the Subſcriber, who is determined to give univerſal Satisfaction. WILLIAM FLAGG.

PITCH.

A Quantity of Pitch and a few Chaldron of New Caſtle Coals, to be Sold by W. HOSKINS.

BARLEY.

WHOEVER is willing to engage a Quantity of *BARLEY*, to be delivered in Boſton next Fall, will find it of Advantage to leave their Propoſals in Writing with the Printers.

WANTED

A ſtrong active Perſon of a good Character, acquainted ſufficiently with the Diſtilling Buſineſs, ſo as to be able to undertake the Care of a large Diſtill-Houſe, out of Town: For further Particulars inquire of the Printers. *Boſton, Feb.* 28, 1774.

TO BE SOLD,

A Good Farm in Concord, containing about 80 Acres, with a good Houſe and two Barns, and a large new Store, two good Wells of Water upon the great Road, and within three Quarters of a Mile of the Meeting Houſe: Said Farm will be Sold for Engliſh and Weſt-India Goods, if applied for ſoon, Inquire of Mr. *Samuel Auſtin* in Boſton.

ALSO,

Another Farm in Lancaſter Pariſh, containing about 100 Acres, with a good Houſe and Barn on the ſame, will be Sold for Goods if apply'd for ſoon.

A Woman with a good Breaſt of Milk, would be glad to take a Child to Suckle.

Inquire of the Printers.

TO BE SOLD,

A healthy, active, Negro Boy, about 19 Years of Age, who is ſtrictly honeſt, and has had the Small Pox. For further Particulars, Inquire of the Printers.

All Perſons Indebted to *William Williams*, for the News-Papers and Carriage, are deſired to Pay the ſame by the Seventh Day of March next.

N. B. The ſaid *Williams* intends to Ride every other Week from Boſton to Fitchburg the enſuing Year, if proper Encouragement is given, and he will leave the Papers at the Stages as uſual.

BOSTON, February 28.

AS the Lamps for illuminating the Streets of this Town are now setting up, the following Extract from a late Law for the Regulating of said Lamps is now printed—that the Publick may be made more acquainted with the Fines and Penalties which will be incurred by such Person or Persons who either with Design or by Accident should any Ways destroy or Damage these Lamps.

BE it therefore further enacted, That if at any Time after the Publication of this Act, any Person or Persons shall and do wilfully and maliciously break, throw down, or extinguish any Lamp that is or shall be hung or set up to light the Streets, Lanes, Alleys or Passage-Ways, within said Town of Boston, either by said Town or by any private Inhabitant, or shall wilfully or maliciously damage the Post, Iron or other Furniture thereof, every Person so offending therein, and being thereof convicted by the lawful Testimony of one or more Witness or Witnesses, in any of his Majesty's Courts of General Sessions of the Peace, to be thereafter held within and for the County of Suffolk, who are hereby empowered to hear and determine the Offence, shall forfeit and pay the Sum of twenty Pounds, *for each Lamp so broken or damnified, and the like Sum for each Post or the Iron or other Furniture so broken or damaged, and Costs of Prosecution. And if any Person or Persons shall accidentally or undesignedly break, throw down, or otherwise damage any Post, Iron or Furniture of such Lamp, he shall pay so much as in the Judgment of the Selectmen of said Town for the Time being, shall fully repair the Damage done, into the Hands of the Selectmen, or to such Person as they may appoint to receive the same: And if any such Person or Persons shall refuse to pay said Selectmen or the Person they shall appoint in manner as aforesaid, the Treasurer of the Town of Boston is hereby empowered to prosecute any Person or Persons for said Damages, before any one of his Majesty's Justices of the Peace in said County of Suffolk, who is hereby empowered to hear and determine the same; provided the double Damages do not exceed Forty Shillings, if more then to be recovered in any Court proper to try the same; and upon Conviction to give Judgment for double Damages and for Costs of Prosecution, and award Execution accordingly. And if any Person or Persons sentenced to pay the aforesaid Fine of twenty Pounds and Costs, shall refuse to pay the same, he or they shall be punished for the Offence by being imprisoned not exceeding six Months, or by Whipping not exceeding twenty Stripes.*

Extract of a Letter from a Bookseller in London to a Gentleman of Musical turn here, dated Bagpipe-Ally Scotland Yard, November 5, 1773.

WE hear your Chief Governor is of late become *passionately* fond of Dancing! and to tunes of your composing, particularly well suited to our Scotch Instrument: Will you be so good as to send him one or two of my Musick Books, published for the current Year! PAXTON'S ALMANDE and HALLOWELL'S COTILLIONS that you write for, are quite old-fashion'd and out of Print; but new Editions of them with alterations, it is expected will appear the approaching Winter. THE HUTCHINSONIAN OPERA lately come out, called the Foxes unkennel'd, or Rascalls discover'd; is in high Vogue with the Great, at the West-end of the Town! and in truth all over the Kingdom. OLIVER'S GIGG is also thought much of, as being very uncommon, airy and gay, and well adapted to the name on both sides the Water; shall send one of each of these to his Honor and to his Excellency without waiting for orders, requesting them at the same time, to pay you the Value they may estimate the Work at, and in whatever Currency they please! though upon second thought *I may not do this without an Instruction.*

We hear much talk about a very great Dancing Master some where in your Country, a MR. DUNCAN MOFFATT MAC-DENBIGH! Who teaches grown folk to move the JEMMY forestep in the true ROME-AN HARRISONIAN stile, and that he has in a very short time taught ADMIRAL MACMOODY to move in the superlative degree, to that famous old tune, *the lamentations of Ireland.* Will you be so good as to recommend me to this great DOCTOR of Musick, that I may have his custom in my way; I publish 24 Country Dances every Year, besides Minuets and Reels, Horn Pipes and other Tunes, and all perfectly well suited to the *Wend Instrument* that's getting so much into fashion among you.

At a Town-Meeting in Sudbury, *legally Warned January 3d, 1774. The Town being met, proceeded and chose Mr.* JOHN MAYNARD, *Moderator.*

Then the papers sent us by the town of *Boston*, relating to the tea, sent here by the East India company, were read and taken into consideration by the town, and the town chose a committee to take into consideration the above papers and report their opinion thereon at the adjournment: Then the town adjourn'd their meeting to Monday the tenth day of January instant, at two o'clock, P. M. The town being met according to the aforesaid adjournment, proceeded, &c.—The committee appointed by the town, to take into consideration, the affair relating to the tea sent here by the East-India company; reported as follows, viz.

TAKING into consideration the late conduct of administration together with an act of parliament, enabling the East India company, to export their *teas* into America, free of all duties and customs in England; but liable to the rules, customs, regulations and penalties in America, as are provided by the revenue act: We are justly alarmed at this detestable craft and policy of the ministry, to deprive us of our American liberties, transmitted to us, by our worthy ancestors, at no less expence, than that of their blood and treasure, that price our renowned forefathers freely paid, that they might transmit those glorious liberties as a free, full and fair inheritance to posterity; which liberties, through the indulgent smiles of Heaven, we have possessed in peace and quietness, till within a few years past (excepting in the reign of the detestable Stuarts.) But now behold! the pleasing scene is changed, the British ministry, assisted by the inveterate enemies to American liberty, on this, as well as on the other side of the atlantick; combining together to rob us, of our dear bought freedom; have brought us to this sad dilemma either to resolve like men, in defence of our just rights and liberties, or sink under the weight of their arbitrary and unconstitutional measures, into a state of abject slavery. Therefore as freeborn Americans, intitled to all the immunities, liberties and privileges of free born Englishmen, we look upon ourselves under the strongest obligations, to use our utmost exertions, in the defence of our just rights, every constitutional method within our power, even though the cost of the defence should equal that of the purchase, therefore,

Resolved, 1st. That as we are intitled to all the privileges of British subjects; we have an undoubted and exclusive right to grant our own monies, for the support of government, and that no power on earth, has a right to tax, or make laws binding us, without our consent.

2d. That the British parliament's laying a duty on tea, payable in America, for the express purpose of raising a revenue, is in our opinion, an unjust taxation; and that the specious method of permitting the East-India company to export their *teas* into the colonies, has a direct tendency to rivet the chains of slavery upon us.

3d. That we will lend all the aid and assistance in our power, in every rational method, to hinder the importation of tea, so long as it is subject to a duty; and, that this town is well pleased with, and highly approve of the resolution in particular, entered into by the town of *Boston*, viz. That they will not suffer any tea to be imported into that town, while subject to an unrighteous duty, and it is the desire and expectation of this town, that said resolution be not relaxed in any degree, which if it should it would much lessen that confidence (which we hope we may justly say) we have reason to place in that reputable metropolis.

4th. That the persons appointed by the East-India company to receive and vend their *teas* (by their obstinate refusal to resign their odious commission) have shewn a ready disposition to become the tools of our enemies, to oppress and enslave their native country; and have manifested such stupidity and wickedness as to prefer private interest, to the good of their country; and therefore can expect no favor nor respect from us; but we leave them to accumulate a load of infamy, proportionate to their vileness.

5th. That whoever shall sell, buy, or otherwise use tea, while subject to and poisoned with a duty, shall be deemed by us enemies to their country's welfare; and shall be treated by us as such.

The town by their vote, ordered the foregoing resolves to be recorded in the town book, and copy of the same to be forwarded, to the committee of correspondence at *Boston*, with our sincere thanks to that respectable town, for their manly opposition to every ministerial measure to enslave America.

Thomas Plympton,
John Maynard,
Ezekiel How,
Sarson Belcher,
Phinehas Glezen,
Josiah Langdon. } Committee.

A true copy as on Record,

Attest. WILLIAM BALDWIN, Town Clerk.

N. B. The town by their vote chose the following gentlemen a committee of correspondence, viz. Deacon *Thomas Plympton*, Mr. *John Maynard*, Mr. *Sarson Belcher*, Capt. *Ezekiel How*, and Mr. *Phinehas Glezen.*

Attest. Wm. BALDWIN, Town-Clerk.

TO BE SOLD
AT PUBLICK AUCTION,
By Benjamin Church,
At his usual Place of Sale,
On Thursday the 17th Day of March,
Sundry Goods belonging to the Estate of Capt. Henry Omand, late deceas'd —— consisting of——
Tammies, Durants, Callamancoes, Crapes, Dorsetcens, Poplins, Persians, Sattins, Ribbons, Irish Linnens, Checks, German Serges, printed Handkerchiefs, Velverets, Worsted Plushes, striped Damascus, Moree Gowns, Threads, Qualities Pins, also a Variety of Wearing Apparel, and sundry other Articles.
N. B. The Sale to begin at 10 o'Clock A. M.

TO BE SOLD,
By Benjamin Dolbeare,
A Very good Fire Engine, London-made; old Jamaica Spirit by the Tierce, sundry Barrels of Jamaica Sugar, and Vinegar by the Barrel.

Wanted a Woman of a good Character, and one that can be well recommended, and that understands Cocking and other house Work; none need apply but such a one, and is Wanted immediately.—Good Wages will be given. Inquire of the Printers.

GARDEN SEEDS.
IMPORTED in Capt. SHEPHARD from LONDON
And TO BE SOLD By
Elizabeth Greenleaf,
At her Shop to the Southward of the Lane leading to Dr. Byles's Meeting House, Boston
EARLY Charlton, early golden Hotspur, early Hotspur, large Dwarf, and green Marrofats, white Rouncival, Ledman's Dwarf & Spanish Marratto Peas, large Windsor, Toker, early yellow, Dwarf Kidney, and large white Beans, red, purple, orange, and yellow Carrot seeds, early Yorkshire, early Dutch, early sugar loaf, early Battersea, red, large winter, green and yellow Savoy, early and late Colliflower, Cabbage, green and white Goss, brown Duck, Madeira, spotted and mogul Lettice seeds; red, white, Spanish, Portugal, and silver skin Onion seed; green and white endive, swelling Parsnip, red Beat, Time, Balm, sweet Marjoram, Sage, and summer-savory seeds; scarlet, salmon, short topt and turnip Radish seeds; summer and winter spinage, early and late Cucumber, early Dutch and French Turnip seeds; Parsley, Pepper Grass, Asparagus, Salery, Lavender and white Mustard seeds; Water and Musk Mellon seeds; summer and winter Squash seeds; Hemp, Rape and Canary Bird seed; choice split Pease by the large or smaller Quantity.——N. B. English GOODS.

IMPORTED in Capt. HOOD from LONDON,
And TO BE SOLD By
Susanna Renken
At her Shop near the Draw-Bridge, Fore-Street,
BOSTON:
EARLY Charlton, early golden Hotspur, green Marrows, white Rouncival, Spanish Morattoes, crooked Sugar, and Leadman's Dwarf Peas;—Toker, best Windsor, early Lisbon, large Dutch Kidney, Beans; Strasburgh, Spanish, Silverskin'd and Portugal Onion; Orange, early yellow, and scarlet Carrot; Parsnips; Early and late Turnip; Early short top'd, London, Salmon, turnip, Spanish, and scarlet Radish; Early frame, white goss, early green goss, large green goss, bloody goss, Aleppo goss, brown Dutch, marble, royal brown Dutch, imperial, tennisbal and Capuchin Lettice; Prickley and round Spinnage; Red Beats; Italian and solid Cellery; curl'd Pepper Grass; Indian Creses; Common, curld and large rooted Parsley; Early and late Coll-flower; Early York, large Battersea, early Dutch, large Scotch, large winter and turnip Cabbage; Yellow, green and white curl'd Savoy; long prickley, early prickley, green Turkey, and long Roman Cucumber; Baum, Sweet-Marjoram, Thyme, Rosemary, and Lavender Seed; Hemp and Canary Ditto; Broad red Clover; Fine white Ditto; Lucern and Rape Seed; Rye Grass, and other Grass Seeds; Sage Seed.
Durham's best Flour Mustard; —Groceries.
Also, *English* and *India* Goods: All which may be had cheap for Cash.

THE original Proprietors of a Township called Pennicook, now Concord, and the original Proprietors of a Township called Suncook, now Pembroke, (both in the Province of New-Hampshire) or the Heirs or Assigns of said original Proprietors; are hereby Notified that the General Court in their present Session, hath granted to each Propriety a Township in the late Province of Main, and appointed the Subscribers a Committee to exhibit a List to said Court, within 10 Months from the Date, of the Names of the Persons that have been Sufferers who have a just Claim to an Interest in the one or the other of said Townships:—This is therefore to give Notice to the said Pennicook Proprietors, and the said Suncook Proprietors, that the Committee will attend said Service at the House of Mrs. Hannah Osgood, Innholder in said Pennicook, on the second Wednesday in October next, ensuing, to receive authenticated Evidence of said Sufferers Claims to an interest in the Township granted to the said Pennicook Proprietors, and that they will attend said Service at the House of Mr. Samuel Conner, Innholder in said Suncook, on the third Wednesday in October aforesaid, to receive like Evidence of the said Sufferers Claims to an Interest in the Township granted to the said Suncook Proprietors.

Feb. 22, 1774.
Samuel Phillips,
Joseph Gerrish,
Jonathan Webster } Committee.

CUSTOM-HOUSE, *BOSTON.*

ENTETRD IN.

Willes, Surranam. Burnam. Harding and Jenkins, Cape-Nichola. Fletcher St. Eustatia. King, Esequibo. Clark and Waters St. Lucia, Stanwood and Hatch, Virginia. Hatch, Maryland

Burials in the Town of BOSTON, since our last.
Nine Whites. NO Black.
Baptiz'd in the several Churches, Eleven.

High Water at BOSTON, *for the present Week.*

Monday, 30 min. aft.	1	Friday, 34 min. after	4
Tuesday, 10 min. aft.	2	Saturday, 30 min. af.	5
Wednesday 50 m. aft.	2	Lord's-Day, 28 m. aft.	6
Thursday, 38 min. aft.	3	D's last Qr 5 Day 6 Morn.	

Harvard-College LOTTERY,

5000 DOLLARS the higheſt Prize,

Not two Blanks to a Prize.

THE Public are hereby informed, That the Managers of HARVARD-COLLEGE LOTTERY, are very deſirous the Drawing of ſaid LOTTERY ſhould commence as ſoon as poſſible; they would therefore be glad thoſe who have Subſcribed for Tickets would ſend for them, and thoſe who intend to be Adventurers, would purchaſe their Tickets immediately.

Choice Peas, Iſle of Shoals dumb

Fiſh, Beef, Rye, a few Barrels Rye Flour, and Pork,

To be Sold by

JOHN BARRETT and SONS,

Near the Mill-Bridge.

GOODS under the Sterling Coſt.

William Gale

Acquaints his Friends and Cuſtomers that he is now Selling the remainder of his Goods, under the *Sterling Coſt*, (at his Shop oppoſite the Poſt-Office, in Cornhill, Boſton.) ——Among them are following, viz.

Broad Cloths,	3q. & 7-8 Garlix,
Flannels,	Figur'd Modes,
Lamb Skins,	Figur'd Sattins,
Pluſhes,	Pink, blue & white Sattins,
Kerſeys,	Blond Laces,
Cotton Velvetts,	Black & white Sattin Pumps,
Womens Velvett,	Brocaded ditto,
Strip'd Swanſkins,	White & color'd Ruſſell dit.
Duffils,	Plain and ſprig'd Muſlin,
Felt Hatts,	Cambrick & ſprig'd Muſlin,
Shalloons,	Engliſh & flower'd Lawns,
Tammies,	Incle Luteſtring,
Demaſkus,	Silk Gauzes, &c. &c.
Iriſh Linnens,	

TO BE SOLD

MAY PLACE (the pleaſant Seat of JOHN FENTON, Eſq;) one Mile from *Charleſtown* Ferry, upon the great Road leading to *Cambridge*, *Miſtick*, &c. &c. (part of the remarkably fruitful Hill called *Bunkers*,) containing a handſome Houſe, Out-Houſes, Barn and Garden, ſtored with a great Variety of the choiceſt Fruit-Trees, all young and healthy.

Twenty-five Acres of choice Mowing and Paſturage, (*two thirds and more of which under Mowing*) newly Fenced off into proper Diviſions, highly Dreſt and handſomly decorated with Locuſt Trees.

Between five and ſix Acres of Salt Marſh; Alſo, a new Wharff adjacent to the Premiſes, very convenient for landing Wood Manure, &c.

Whoever may incline to purchaſe the above Premiſes, may be informed of the Conditions by applying to ROBERT TEMPLE, Eſq; of Ten Hills, near Charleſtown; Mr. ISAAC MALLET at the Neck of Land near ſaid Place, (who will at any Time ſhew the Premiſes): Or a Line directed to Col. JOHN FENTON, of Portſmouth, New-Hampſhire.

☞ If not Sold by the 2d of April—then the Houſe, Warehouſe, Barn, Garden, and a Paſture, containing about two and half Acres, to be Lett.

THE PUBLIC

ARE hereby informed, That JOHN JOY has juſt arrived from London, and brought with him a large and compleat Aſſortment of DRUGS and MEDICINES, of the beſt Quality. Alſo, Surgeons Inſtruments of every Kind finiſhed in the neateſt Manner, with a full Aſſortment of Groceries and Dye Stuffs; which as they were purchaſed by himſelf for the Caſh, he will ſell on very reaſonable Terms, at his Shop the North Corner of Williams's Court, in Cornhill, Boſton.

Practitioners and others, may be ſupplied with large or ſmall Quantities, by Letter or otherwiſe, as well as though they were preſent.

Medicine Boxes of various Prices, for Ships or private Families, are put up in the neateſt Manner.

TO BE SOLD very cheap for CASH, At the Shop next to the Sign of the Buck and Glove in Cornhill, BOSTON;

Superfine and common *Philadelphia* FLOUR,

COFFEE of an uncommon good Quality,

Very good Brown SUGAR,

Nutmegs,	Ginger,
Cinnamon,	Split Peaſe,
Cloves,	Velvet Corks,
Mace,	Powder Blue,
Pepper,	Salt Petre,
Allſpice,	Allum,
Oil,	Olives,
New Raiſins,	Durham Muſtard,
Currants,	Chocolate,
London T D 18 Inch Pipes,	Rice,
Loaf Sugar,	Oatmeal,
Almonds,	Poland Starch,
Capers,	Crown Soap.

Beſt French INDIGO.

An Aſſortment of Engliſh GOODS, & Crockery Ware.

ALSO,

A large new Scale Beam, with Scales and Weights.

20 well made Draws in a Neſt.

N. B. The above Shop and Houſe will be Lett the firſt of April: Inquire of Samuel Minott, near the Draw-Bridge.

PURSUANT to a Decree of the High Court of Chancery in England, William Rumbold, Mary the Wife of Alexander Laing, both of the Province of Maryland, Mary the Wife of Garrett Blackford, of the Province of New-Jerſey, in North-America—Rumbold, of Caſhell, in Ireland, Rodolphus Rumbold of Tipperary, in Ireland; William Rumbold of Jamaica; and William Rumbold of the Bay of Honduras; and all other Perſons claiming to be Heirs at Law of Thomas Rumbold, late of Long-Alley, near Moorfields, in the County of Middleſex; or William Rumbold, of the ſame Place, his Brother, who were the Sons of Thomas Rumbold, formerly of the ſame Place, Stocking Trimer, deceaſed, who was the Son of William Rumbold, late of King's Clere, in the County of Southampton, Yeoman, deceaſed, are to come in and enter into Proof of their reſpective Claims of being Heirs at Law of the ſaid Thomas Rumbold, and William Rumbold, before JOHN EAMES, Eſq; one of the Maſters of the ſaid Court, at his Chambers in Symons Inn, Chancery-Lane, London, within twelve Months from the Publication hereof, or in Default thereof they will be abſolutely excluded the Benefit of the ſaid Decree. J. EAMES.

James Swan

HAS for Sale at Store No. 6, leading to Treat's and Spear's Wharves,

A Quantity of *Indian Corn* very good and juſt arrived, choice Fine Flour, and a few Quoils of the beſt *Cordage*, all Cheap.

Dry'd OX HIDES,

Cotton and Piemento, juſt Imported from Jamaica, and to be Sold at GRIFFIN's Wharf.

TO BE SOLD

Utenſils for the Tallow Chandler's

Buſineſs, a large Iron Kettle, Preſs, Tallow Tub, Chopping Knife, Trough, Candle Rods, &c.

Inquire of the Printers.

Lincolnſhire Company 20 Aſſociates.

WHEREAS there are divers Matters to be tranſacted by the 20 Aſſociates of the *Lincolnſhire* Company, reſpecting their Lands and Intereſt lying near *Penobſcot-Bay* in the County of *Lincoln*:—The Committee of ſaid Aſſociates being duly authorſed therefor, Hereby notify ſaid Aſſociates to meet on Wedneſday the 9th Day of *March* next, at Mr. Hubbard's, the Vernon Tavern, in *Boſton*, 6 o'Clock, P. M. then and there to act upon all ſuch Matters as may properly come before them. By Order of the Committee,

NATH. APPLETON, Prop'rs Clerk.

February 16th, 1774.

WHEREAS the Great and General Court or Aſſembly at their Seſſion begun and held on the 27th Day of May 1772, granted a Tax of *One Penny half Penny* per Acre, upon the Lands of the Non-reſident Proprietors in the Town of *Aſhby*, in the County of Middleſex; and whereas ſaid Tax has been duly aſſeſſed and publiſhed agreeable to Law, and ſome Perſons Proprietors or Owners of ſaid Land, neglect or refuſe to pay the ſame; and whereas the General Court by ſaid Act did impower the Aſſeſſors choſen by the Town of Aſhby, to Aſſeſs the ſame, to Sell ſo much of the Delinquent Proprietors Lands as ſhall be ſufficient to pay and ſatisfy ſaid Tax and other incidental Charges: And whereas the Owners of the following Lands are Delinquent in paying ſaid Tax, viz.

Names of thoſe who drew the Lots, or them who now own them.	What Diviſion	What Right.	No. Acre	*l.*	*s.*	*d.*
John Moffat			20	0	2	6
Col. Joſiah Willard part	4 5 6	57 83 53	37	0	4	8
Henry Laughton part	4	32	14	0	1	9
Chriſtopher Barrett			22	0	2	9
Cumings and Fletcher	part 4		40	0	5	0
Rev'd Mr. Perry Two	3		133		16	7½
Col. Wm. Lawrance	6	35	40	0	5	0
Hugh Hall, Eſq;	part 3	73	66	0	8	3
James Lawrance	5	70	40	0	5	0
Edward Emerſon part	5	62	42	0	5	4
Ebenezer Southwick	6	19	50	0	6	3
Jona. Hill part	3	69	40	0	5	0
Samuel Brown	3	47	66	0	8	3
Simon Blood	4 part 6	14	124		15	6
David Melvin	6	58	42	0	5	3
James Nicholas	4 part 6	78	71	0	8	10½
John Nichlas			20	0	2	6
—— Gore part	3		62	0	7	9
Capt. Daniel Stickney part	3	58	40	0	5	0
Third Diviſion, No.		60	66	0	8	3
Peter Atherton	3	37	66	0	8	3
Formerly belonging to Lunenburg						
Robert Paul	3 4	24	235	1	9	4¾
John Bridge, jun.			48	0	6	0
James Billings			53	0	6	7¾
Abraham Gibſon			30	0	3	9
Joſeph Lee			30	0	3	9
Heirs of Samuel Reed			100		12	6
Daniel Buttrick			32	0	4	0

NOTICE is hereby given to ſaid Delinquents, that ſo much of their Lands will be expoſed to Sale at Public Vendue, on the 31ſt Day of May next, at the Houſe of Capt. Samuel Stone, Innholder in ſaid Aſhby, at 9 of the Clock in the Forenoon, and continued by Adjournments, if need be, until the ſecond Day of June, as will be ſufficient to pay ſaid Tax, and other intervening Charges, unleſs prevented by Payment of ſaid Tax, (and ſuch Charges as have already ariſen) unto the Aſſeſſors, before the aboveſaid Time.

Aſhby, Feb. 16, 1774.

James Locke, *Samuel Stone*, *Jonathan Locke*, } Aſſeſſors.

JUST PUBLISHED, and to be Sold at GREENLEAF'S Printing-Office in Hanover-Street, BOSTON;

A SERMON Preached at the Anniverſary Thankſgiving at Plymouth, in commemoration of the firſt Landing of our Anceſtors there, Anno Domini, 1720.

Nothing more need be ſaid to recommend this Sermon to the peruſal of the Public, than that it was Delivered by CHARLES TURNER, A. M. Paſtor of the Church in Duxbury, who Preached the celebrated Election Sermon, the laſt Year.

Wanted immediately to Hire,

A ſingle decked Schooner or Brigantine,

of 90 or 100 Tons Burthen. Inquire of Edes & Gill.

NEW LONDON.

TO BE SOLD, a Houſe and Land with good Accommodations, as out Houſes &c. and well ſituated for a Tavern, and has been Improved as ſuch for ſome Years paſt; with a Wharf adjoining, the beſt Accommedated and moſt Improved for Navigation in that Town, if not ſoon Sold, to be Let, for Particulars Enquire of Richard Law & Duncan Stewart, Eſquires; in New London or of Edes and Gill in Boſton.

ALL Perſons who have any Demands on the Eſtate of HANNAH DIX, late of Boſton, Widow deceaſed, are deſired to bring in their Accounts; and all who are Indebted are deſired to make ſpeedy payment to Elizabeth Orrok, Adminiſtratrix to ſaid Eſtate.

Six Months longer are allowed the

Creditors to the Eſtate of *Andrew McKenſie*, late of Milton, Merchant, deceas'd, for bringing in their Claims, and proving their Debts, the Commiſſioners give Notice, that they ſhall attend that ſervice at the Britiſh Coffee-houſe, in King-Street, from 6 to 9 o'Clock, the third Tueſday in this and the five following Months.

Boſton Feb. 14th, 1774.

Wanted a Quantity of Thrums for the

Caulkers Buſineſs, for which caſh will be given; alſo to be SOLD a few Puncheons, and forty Gallon Caſks of old choice Jamaica Rum. Enquire of the Printers.

WHEREAS the Proprietors of the Townſhip of Land lying on both ſides Androſcogging River, in the County of Cumberland, and adjoining Sylveſter Townſhip, granted June 11th, 1771, to Samuel Livermore, Eſq; and others: Voted and granted at their Meeting June 17th, 1772, a Tax of Forty Shillings on each Right, to defray the Charges that had or might ariſe on ſaid Propriety, to be paid unto Leonard Williams, Eſq; their Treaſurer, on or before the 4th of Auguſt 1772, which Tax has been made and publiſhed according to Law, notwithſtanding which, ſeveral have neglected to pay ſaid Tax. Public Notice is hereby given, that unleſs ſaid Tax be paid by Wedneſday the 16th Day of March next, their Rights who are delinquent in paying ſaid Tax, will be Sold at Public Vendue, at the Houſe of Iſaac Gleaſon, Innholder in Waltham, at 8 o'Clock in the Forenoon of ſaid Day.

And whereas the Proprietors of ſaid Townſhip, at their Meeting Feb. 24th, 1773, Voted and Granted a Tax of Twenty-four Shillings on each Right, to be paid unto Leonard Williams, Eſq; their Treaſurer, on or before the 1ſt Day of Oct. 1773; and again on the 3d Day of Nov. 1773, the Proprietors aforeſaid Voted and Granted a further Tax of Forty-eight Shillings on each Right, to defray the Expences of ſaid Propriety, to be paid their Treaſurer as follows, viz. One half of ſaid Tax on or before Wedneſday the 16th Day of March next, and the other half on or before the 1ſt Day of Auguſt next, Public Notice is hereby given that if ſaid Taxes be not paid by Wedneſday the 16th Day of March next, and by the 1ſt Day of next Auguſt, their Rights, or ſo much of them as is ſufficient to pay ſaid Taxes, and the Charges ariſing thereon, will be Sold for Payment thereof, according to Law.

Waltham, Jan. 4, 1774.

Leonard Williams, *Elijah Livermore*, *Eliſha Harrington*, } Aſſeſſors & Committee for Sale of delinquent Proprietors Rights.

The Proprietors of the Townſhip aforeſaid,

are hereby Notified, that their Meeting ſtands adjourned to Wedneſday the 16th Day of March next, at the Houſe of Iſaac Gleaſon, Innholder in Waltham, at Ten o'Clock A. M. at which Time it is deſired there would be a general Attendance, as Affairs of the utmoſt Conſequence to the Proprietors, are then to be tranſacted.

LEONARD WILLIAMS, Proprietor's Clerk.

Waltham, Jan. 4, 1774.

RAN-away from Jonathan Reed of Wrentham, on the ſeventh of this Inſtant, a Man-Servant, calls his Name John Hopkins or James Gutridge, an Old Countryman, who Bound himſelf to ſaid Reed, for Theft, about 30 Years of Age, a Shoemaker by Trade, mark'd with the Small-Pox, about 5 Feet & ½ high, his Hair red, and wears a darkiſh Wig, walks very upright, a well ſet Man: Had on when he went away a brown ruſty ſhort Coat, black Jacket, and old Leather Breeches, a thick Buff Cap, no Hat:—Whoever ſhall take up ſaid Run-away and ſecure him, ſo that his Maſter may have him again ſhall have FIVE DOLLARS Reward, and neceſſary Charges paid by me.

JONATHAN REED.

Wrentham, Feb. 8, 1774.

Boſton: *Printed, by* EDES & GILL *in Queen-Street*, 1774.

THE Boston- AND COUNTRY

Gazette, JOURNAL.

No. 987.

Containing the freshest Advices, Foreign and Domestic.

MONDAY, March 7, 1774.

IN our last we gave our Readers Reason to expect this Week a Publication of the Impeachment laid by the Honorable House of Representatives against PETER OLIVER, *Esq; of High Crimes and Misdemeanours, before the Governor and Council. It is as follows, viz.*

Province of MASSACHUSETTS-BAY.

ARTICLES of Impeachment of High Crimes and Misdemeanours against *PETER OLIVER*, Esq; Chief Justice of the Superior Court of Judicature, Court of Assize and General Goal Delivery over this Province, by the House of REPRESENTATIVES, in General Court Assembled, in their own Name, and in the Name of all the Inhabitants of this Province, *February* 24, 1774.

WHEREAS their late Majesties King William and Queen Mary of glorious memory, from their great regard to the English constitution, and earnest desire to establish the same in this his Majesty's province, did by their charter made and granted in the third year of their reign, establish and ordain, that all and every of the subjects of them their heirs and successors, which should come to and inhabit within this province and territory, and every of their children which should happen to be born there, or on the seas in coming thither or returning from hence, should have and enjoy all liberties and immunities of free and natural subjects within any of the dominions of them their heirs and successors, to all intents constructions and purposes whatever, as if they and every of them were born within the realm of England.

And in the said charter it is further granted and ordained, that the Great and General Court or Assembly of the province, which is before established in the same charter, shall forever have full power and authority to erect and constitute judicatories and courts of record, or other courts, for the hearing, trying and determining of all manner of crimes, &c.

And the said General Court or Assembly hath by the same charter, full power and authority to impose and levy proportionable and reasonable assessments, rates and taxes, upon the estates and persons of all and every the proprietors and inhabitants of the province, for his Majesty's service in the necessary defence and support of his Majesty's government of the province, and the protection and preservation of the inhabitants thereof: To the intent that the inhabitants of this his Majesty's province might always have and enjoy that essential privilege of the English constitution, of supporting the executive and judicial officers in the government of this province by THE FREE GRANTS OF THE PEOPLE.

And whereas the Great and General Court or Assembly of this province, in pursuance of the power and authority granted as aforesaid, and of the good intention thereof, have uninterruptedly and exclusively from the granting of the said charter, made provision by their own grants for the support of his Majesty's said Superior Court: But many evil-minded persons, not regarding the said charter nor the good intentions of the same, have of late years combined and conspired together, to put divers constructions on the said charter, wholly inconsistent with the aforesaid manifest intent and purpose of the same, and destructive of English Liberties; and to introduce and establish another form of government, and a new mode of supporting the executive and judicial officers of the government. For which intent they did by false representations, procure to be made and passed by the parliament of Great-Britain, an act for the establishment of a revenue to be levied in America, and appropriated among other things for the defraying of the charges of the administration of justice in such colonies where his Majesty should judge proper; and also by false representations and evil advice, have procured the royal grant of large sums of money, to be paid annually out of the said revenue, to the justices of the said superior court; by the establishment of which the said Justices of the said Superior Court would be aliened from any connection with the people of this province, for whose benefit they are and ought to be appointed, and would be indebted to his Majesty for his grants made to them for their services; and by means thereof become subject to the influence and direction of his Majesty's Ministers of state, in matters appertaining to the distribution of justice in this province; whereby a foundation will be laid of a union of the department of the judicial powers here, with that of the King's ministers of state in Great-Britain, than which nothing is more to be dreaded by a free people.

And whereas Peter Oliver, Esq; chief justice of the superior court of judicature, court of assize and general goal delivery over this province, a court wholly erected and constituted by the great and general court or assembly by a power granted to the said general court by the clause in said charter aforementioned, well knowing the premises but not regarding the same, with design to subvert the constitution of this province as established by the said royal charter, and to introduce into the said court a partial arbitrary and corrupt administration of justice, declining to take and receive any more the grants of the general assembly of this province, did on or about the tenth day of January, 1774, at Boston, in the county of Suffolk, take and receive, and resolve for the future to take and receive from his Majesty's ministers and servants, a grant or salary for his services as chief justice of the said superior court, against his own knowledge of the said charter, and of the way and manner prescribed therein for the support of his Majesty's government in the province, and contrary to uninterrupted and approved usage and custom since the erecting and constituting of the said court. And the said Peter Oliver, Esq; continues in his said resolution so to do, against the opinion and conduct of the other judges of the said court, each of whom has declared respecting himself his resolution to the contrary. And whereas the unmerited sum of four hundred pounds sterling granted by his Majesty and annually to be paid to the said Peter Oliver Esq; for his services as chief justice of the said superior court, together with the hopes of it's augmentation, if he is still suffered to continue in his said office, cannot fail to have the effect of a continual bribe in his judicial proceedings, and expose him to a violation of his oath. And by his accepting and receiving the said sum, he hath betrayed the corruption and baseness of his heart, and the sordid lust of coveteousness: In breach of his engagements to rely solely upon the grants of the general assembly, necessarily implied and involved in his accepting said office.——

And the said Peter Oliver, Esq; by his taking and receiving the said grant out of the revenue unjustly levied and extorted from the inhabitants of the American colonies, hath as far forth as lay in his power, put a sanction on and established the said revenue, which is a most destructive infraction of the constitution of this province, and a violation of the natural and most essential rights of the people,—the exclusive right of giving, granting and appropriating their own property, and of judging of the merits of their own servants. And hath counteracted the reasonable petitions of the Representatives of the people to his Majesty, and other their constitutional endeavours to obtain the redress of this grievance.

And the said Peter Oliver, Esq; by his conduct as aforesaid, in defiance and contempt of the known sense of the body of this people, expresly and repeatedly declared and published by their Representatives and otherwise, hath wickedly and perversely endeavoured to continue and increase the discontent and jealousies of this people, and the grievance aforementioned, at a time when there is ground to hope that his Majesty, if not otherwise determined by the said conduct of the said Peter Oliver, Esq; and the continued false representations of others, will be graciously pleased to revoke said Grant, and order a full redress.

And the said Peter Oliver, Esq; did on the Eighth Day of February Instant, direct and cause to be delivered to this House, a Writing under his own Hand, dated Middleborough, February 3, 1774; the Tenor of which Writing is in the Words and Figures following, viz.

To the Honorable the House of Representatives in General Court convened February 1774.

May it please your Honors,

ON the second Instant I received the Resolves of the Honorable House of the first Instant, requiring me to declare whether I had receiv'd in full of the Grants of the General Assembly made to me the last Year, and to declare explicitly whether I would for the future accept the Grants of the General Assembly of this Province as a Justice of the Superior Court, without accepting any Grant from the Crown for my Service as a Justice of said Court. Permit me, May it please your Honors! *to state the Circumstances of my Case, as a Justice of the Superior Court.*

In the Year 1756 I was appointed as a Justice of that Court, and accepted the Office contrary to my own Inclination, but by the Perswasion of Gentlemen who were then Members of the General Assembly. In this Office I have continued for above seventeen Years; and I hope your Honors will excuse me if I say, that I was never yet conscious that I had ever been guilty of any Violations of the Laws of my Country in a judicial Capacity, but have always endeavor'd to act with that Fidelity required in so important a Character; and with this Sentiment I doubt not of ever consoling myself in the Approbation of my own Mind.

During these seventeen Years, I have annually felt the great Inconveniencies of serving in my judicial Office, by suffering in my private Business, and not having a Salary which would any Ways support my Family, which was large, and I cannot charge myself with any Degree of Extravagance in the Support of it: and I wish I may not have been too parsimonious for the Dignity of the Province, in my judicial Character.

May it please your Honors!

I can with the strictest Truth assert, that I have suffer'd, since I have been upon the Bench of the Superior Court, in the Loss of my Business and not having sufficient to maintain my Family from my Salaries, above THREE THOUSAND POUNDS STERLING! —— *I have repeatedly thrown myself on former Assemblies for Relief, but never have obtain'd any Redress: I have repeatedly attempted to resign my Office, but have been disswaded from it, by respectable Gentlemen of former Assemblies, who encouraged me with Hopes of a Support, but I never receiv'd any Relief in that Way.*

When his Majesty, of his great Goodness and Favor granted me a Salary (as he did to several others on the Continent in my Station) it was without any Application of mine; and when it was granted, I thought it my incumbent Duty, from the Respect and Gratitude which I owed to his Majesty: from a Sense of that Fidelity which I owed to my Country, by being enabled to discharge the Duty of my Office in being less embarrass'd in my Mind whilst in the Execution of it, and being more at Liberty to qualify myself for the Duties of it in Vacation Time: as also from a Principle of Justice due to my Family and to others: On these Accounts, and not from any avaricious Views, I was oblig'd to take his Majesty's Grant from the 5th of July 1772 to 5th of January 1774, and have taken the Grant of the Province only until July 1772.

These Considerations, May it please your Honors! *urg'd me to take his Majesty's Grant; and I cannot but hope that the Candor of the honorable House of Representatives will excuse me in so doing, as what proceeded from Necessity and not Avarice or the least Disregard to the Sentiments of the honorable House.*

May it please your Honors!

With Respect to my not taking any future Grant from his Majesty; permit me to say, that without his Majesty's Leave I dare not refuse it, lest I should incurr a Censure from the best of Sovereigns. And as the Tenor of the Grant is during my Residence in the Province as Chief Justice, I receive it as during good Behavior, which in my Opinion preserves me from any undue Bias in the Execution of my Office.

I am with the most profound Respect
for the Honorable House of Representatives,
their most obedient humble Servant,
PETER OLIVER.

Middleborough, Feb. 3, 1774.

In which Writing the said Peter Oliver, Esq; hath ungratefully, falsly and maliciously laboured to lay Imputation and Scandal upon this his Majesty's Government, insolently and contemptuously insinuating, that by the Parsimony, Injustice and Ingratitude of the said Government, in with-holding from him an adequate and due Reward for his Services as a Justice of the said Superior Court, he hath been greatly impoverished, and that therefore, he was obliged to take his Majesty's Grant from a Principle of Justice due to his Family and others. Whereas in Fact, the Rewards granted to him by this Government, were always fully equal to the Merit of his Services as a Justice of the said Court; as it is well known that the said Peter Oliver, Esq; before his Advancement to a Seat in the Superior Court, had been usually employed in the Business of Trade, Husbandry, and Manufactures, to which he had applied his Mind, And that he was appointed to said Office without previous Education and regular Study in the Law.

And the said Peter Oliver, Esq; by his Conduct as aforesaid, hath misrepresented and traduced this Government, and endeavoured to alienate the Hearts of his Majesty's liege People of this Province from his Majesty, and set a Division between them, to introduce into said Court a partial and corrupt Administration of Justice, destroy the present Form of Government in this Province, and establish an arbitrary and tyrannical Government in its Stead.

Wherefore this House of Representatives, in their own Name, and in the Name of all the Inhabitants of this Province, DO IMPEACH THE SAID PETER OLIVER, Esq; of the high Crimes and Misdemeanors aforesaid. And saving to themselves by Protestation the Liberty of exhibiting at any Time hereafter, to the Governor and Council, or to the Council only, any Complaints or Allegations against the said Peter Oliver, Esq; for any Incompetency, Incapacity or Disability for the Execution of his high Office; or any other Accusation or Impeachment against the said Peter Oliver, Esq; for any other Crimes and Misdemeanours by him done and committed. And also of replying to the Answer which the said Peter Oliver, Esq; shall make to the said Articles, or any of them; and of offering Proof of the Premises, or any of their Impeachments, Accusations and Complaints that shall be exhibited by them, as the Case shall require. They pray that the said Peter Oliver, Esq; Chief Justice of the Superior Court of Judicature, Court of Assize and General Goal Delivery over this whole Province, may be put to Answer to all and every of the Premises; and that such Proceedings, Examinations, Tryals and Judgments may be had and ordered thereon, as may be agreeable to Law and Justice.

YEAS.	YEAS.
Mr. Samuel Adams,	Jonas Dix, Esq;
Hon. John Hancock, Esq;	James Prescot, Esq;
William Phillips, Esq;	Henry Gardner, Esq;
Capt. William Heath,	Hon. Joseph Hawley, Esq;
Mr. Samuel Howe,	Mr. Josiah Pierce,
Ebenezer Thayer, jun. Esq;	Capt. John Moseley,
Mr. Nathaniel Bailey,	Dr. Moses Gunn,
Benjamin Lincoln, Esq;	Mr. Phinehas Wright,
Mr. Abner Ellis,	Mr. Isaac Lothrop,
Mr. Moses Bullen,	Mr. Gideon Vinall,
Mr. Jabez Fisher,	Mr. Ebenezer Sprout,
Capt. Benjamin White,	Mr. Ebenezer White,
Mr. Hezekiah Gay,	Mr. John Turner,
Mr. Enoch Ellis,	Capt. Joseph Cushing,
Mr. John Pickering, jun.	Capt. Woodbridge Brown,
Dr. Samuel Holton,	Capt. John Gray,
Capt. Michael Farley,	Mr. Stephen Nye,
Hon. Joseph Gerrish, Esq;	David Thatcher, Esq;
Capt. Jonathan Greenleaf,	Mr. Barnabas Freeman,
Ebenezer Burrell, Esq;	Mr. Benjamin Freeman,
Mr. Moody Bridges,	Mr. Moses Swift,
Capt. Henry Herrick,	Mr. Joseph Doane,
Mr. Nathaniel Mighill,	Robert-Treat Paine, Esq;
Mr. Samuel Smith,	Capt. Joseph Barney,
Mr. Jonathan Webster,	Jerathmeel Bowers, Esq;
Nathaniel Allen, Esq;	Benjamin Aikin, Esq;
Mr. John Gould,	Mr. John Dagget,
Aaron Wood, Esq;	Elnathan Walker, Esq;
Isaac Merrill, Esq;	Thomas Bragdon, Esq;
Capt. Daniel Thurston,	Edward Cutt, Esq;
Capt. Thomas Gardner,	Thomas Perkins, Esq;
Mr. Nathaniel Gorham,	Mr. Joshua Bigelow,
Capt. Jonathan Brown,	Mr. Edward Rawson,
Mr. Samuel Wyman,	Jedediah Foster, Esq;
Capt. James Barrett,	Capt. Henry King,
Abraham Fuller, Esq;	Mr. Thomas Denny,
Samuel Bancroft, Esq;	Capt. Stephen Maynard,
Mr. Peter Bent,	Mr. Phineas Heywood,
William Stickney, Esq;	Dr. John Taylor,
Capt. Josiah Stone,	Israel Taylor, Esq;
Mr. Jonas Stone,	Hon John Whitcomb, Esq;
Mr. Simeon Spaulding,	Capt. Ephraim Doolittle,
Capt. Joseph Twitchell,	Timothy Brigham, Esq;
Mr. Thomas Plympton,	Mr. Paul Mandell,
Capt. Ebenezer Harnden,	Mr. Samuel Brown, jun.
Mr. Benjamin Hall,	Mr. Peter Curtis.
NAYS.	**NAYS.**
Elisha Jones, Esq;	Thomas Gilbert, Esq;
Abijah White, Esq;	Capt. Jeremiah Learned,
Josiah Edson, Esq;	William Tyng, Esq;
Edward Bacon, Esq;	Mr. Samuel March.

The Number of YEAS, NINETY-TWO, *and* Eight Nays.

The House having previous to the carrying up this Impeachment, acquainted the Governor of their Resolution and desired he would then be in the Chair; his Excellency was pleas'd to send them the following Message, viz.

Gentlemen of the House of Representatives,

BY your Message of Yesterday you informed me that you had resolved to impeach *Peter Oliver*, Esq; Chief Justice of the Superior Court, &c. before the Governor and Council of High Crimes and Misdemeanors, and that you had prepared the Articles of Impeachment, and you prayed that I would be in the Chair that you might then have an Opportunity of laying them before the Governor and Council.

I know of no Species of High Crimes and Misdemeanors nor any Offence against the Law committed within this Province, let the Rank or Condition of the Offender be what it may, which is not cognizable by some Judicatory or Judicatories, and I do not know that the Governor and Council have a concurrent Jurisdiction with any Judicatory in Criminal Cases, or any Authority to try and determine any Species of High Crimes and Misdemeanors whatsoever.

If I should assume a Jurisdiction and with the Council try Offenders against the Law without Authority granted by the Charter or by a Law of the Province in pursuance of the Charter, I should make myself liable to answer before a Judicatory which would have cognizance of my Offence, and His Majesty's Subjects would have just Cause to complain of being deprived of a Trial by Jury, the general Claim of Englishmen except in those Cases where the Law may have made special Provision to the contrary.

Whilst such Process as you have attempted to commence shall appear to me to be unconstitutional, I cannot shew any countenance to it.

Milton, 26 Feb. 1774. T. HUTCHINSON.

The House upon Consideration of this Message, wherein it plainly appears to be the Opinion of the Governor, that the Governor and Council are not a Court competent for the Tryal of High Crimes and Misdemeanors, done and committed by an Officer of their own Appointment, and being resolved to take every Method for the Removal of the Chief Justice, did afterwards send up to the Governor and Council the same Articles with an Introduction and Conclusion in a different Form from the other; by no Means however retracting their Impeachment, or their original Address for the Removal of the Chief Justice: In Order that the Matter might be taken up by the Governor and Council in which Way soever to them it should seem meet.

The Introduction is in the following Words, viz.

In the House of REPRESENTATIVES, *March* 1, 1774.

WHEREAS this House did on the Twelfth Day of February last, address his Excellency the Governor, and Council, for the Removal of PETER OLIVER, Esq; Chief Justice of his Majesty's Superior Court of Judicature, Court of Assize and General Goal Delivery over this whole Province, for certain Reasons therein set forth, and did afterwards address the Governor, praying that he would further consider the said former Address for the Removal of the said Chief Justice, and that he would take the Advice of the Council thereon: And his Excellency did utterly refuse to comply with the Request of the House, and lay the same before the Council for Advice:

And *Whereas* this House did also on the 24th Day of February proceed to *Impeach* the said PETER OLIVER, Esq; of certain high Crimes & Misdemeanors, before the Governor and Council, a Court competent in the opinion of this House, for the Trial of the same, to the Intent of the determining the Necessity of the Removal of the said PETER OLIVER, Esq; from his said Office: But his Excellency hath in his Message of the 26th of February declared, that "whilst such Process as this House has attempted to commence, appears to him to be Unconstitutional, he cannot shew any Countenance to it". *Therefore*, to prevent any Doubts or Delays or Advantages being taken—on Account of the mere Informality of any of our former Proceedings, this House hath thought proper to exhibit the same Articles of Charge and Complaint against the said *Peter Oliver*, Esq; in such Form as will remove all Color or Pretence of Exception, viz.

Province of Massachusetts-Bay.

To his Excellency THOMAS HUTCHINSON, *Esq; Governor and Commander in Chief in and over his Majesty's Province of the Massachusetts-Bay, and to the honorable his Majesty's Council.*

ARTICLES of high Crimes and Misdemeanors offer'd and presented to his Excellency the said Governor, and to the Honorable his Majesty's said Council, against PETER OLIVER, Esq; Chief Justice of the Superior Court of Judicature, Court of Assize and General Goal Delivery over this whole Province, this first Day of March Anno Domini 1774, and in the fourteenth Year of his Majesty's Reign.

[*Here the Articles were brought in in* totidem Verbis, *as they stood in the Impeachment, and the Conclusion was as follows*, viz.]

All which Matters contained in the foregoing Articles, the said House of Representatives are ready to verify and prove. They therefore pray, in their own Name, and in the Name of all the Inhabitants of this Province, that the Governor and Council would give Orders that the said PETER OLIVER, Esq; may be Notified to make Answer to the Charges contained in the foregoing Articles, and be brought to a Hearing and Trial thereon; that if he be found Guilty thereof, he may by the Governor and Council, be forthwith removed from his said Office, and some other more worthy be Nominated and Appointed in his stead.

Sent up by Mr. Adams, Col. Bowers, Mr. Phillips, Mr. Hancock, Mr. Pickering, Mr. Paine, Col. Thayer, Capt. Heath, and Capt. Greenleaf.

There were 78 Members present in the House, and the Division was 71 to 7.

N. B. *Forty Members make a Quorum of the House.*

Thus we have given our readers an account of the transactions of the House of Representatives upon this most interesting matter. A matter, which though it more immediately affects this province, is justly alarming to *every other colony*. For it is apparently the design of the British Administration, to render the most important branches of the *executive* powers in America subservient to their purpose of *extorting* a TRIBUTE from us, even by force of ARMS if necessary. We have too often seen in this province the names of gentlemen appointed to the lower offices in the executive department, such as Justices of the Peace, Sheriffs, &c. whose principles and manners would lead one to think that they were appointed principally for that purpose; & it will be well if it can betruly said of some of them that they have any tolerable idea of the Constitution of the Free Government under which they live, and of others, that they have taken the most cursory View even of the Province Law Book! Such Appointments tend, more than any thing else, to bring Government into Contempt. When Men are appointed to the Magistracy, who for want of sufficient understanding or Morals are contemptible in the Eyes of the People, the discerning People will think that those who had any Concern in their Appointment, had, to say the least, a Design to insult them; and Men in general will not make a distinction between the Persons and the Offices they sustain. Religion as well as the Cause of Liberty requires, that men of *adequate* knowledge and *exemplary* Virtue, and those *only*, should be advanced to the Office and Dignity of Magistrates; and it is to be hoped, that his Majesty's Council will never for the *future*, give the least Occasion for any *justly* to say, that they have suffer'd their Attention to nod, when Persons of the *opposite* Characters are nominated! Our readers, we trust, will pardon this Digression.—We hear that the Council are in deep Consultation, upon the Papers laid before them by the House of Representatives, relating to the Chief Justice; and if any thing transpires, we shall continue to give the Readers a faithful Narrative in our next Paper.

We hear that his Excellency the Governor on Friday last, nominated & appointed George Bethune, Benjamin Gridley, Samuel Barret, Nathaniel Taylor and Edward Lyde, Esq'rs; to be Justices of the Peace, for the County of Suffolk; to which Nomination, his Majesty's Conncil did advise and consent.

Last Saturday the House of Representatives ordered the Secretary of the Province to lay on their Table, a complete List of the Appointments of Civil Officers, which have been made, during the Administration of Governor HUTCHINSON; together with the Names of the Councellors present at each Appointment.

Thursday Morning last, between 5 and 6 o'Clock, died here, the Hon. ANDREW OLIVER, Esq; Lieutenant-Governor of this Province, in the 68th Year of his Age.—His Remains are to be interr'd To-Morrow Afternoon.

On the Evening of the 17th of last Month, a Pedlar, with a Budget of Tea, made his Appearance at Montague, in the County of Hampshire, and put up at the Tavern there; which taking Air, a Number of Persons (well fraught with *Tar and Feathers*) went to the Inn, determined to give him the modern Dress, thinking this a more lenient as well as ready Measure to put an immediate Stop to a Conduct so injurious to the Community, than to the *Rigour of Law*; but as the Man appeared very humble, plead Innocence, promised to return the Tea to the Place from whence it came, not to offend in the like Manner for the future, and to submit to whatever Terms they should think reasonable to impose; they dismissed him, determining to apply *an effectual Remedy* to the next Offender.

The following melancholly Accident happened on Wednesday, viz. As a Sleigh with two Horses and five People, were returning from a Wedding at Haddam, and crossing Connecticut-River a few Rods above East Haddam Landing, the Ice broke through, when one young Woman, named Lydia Gates, Daughter of Mr. Joshua Gates of East-Haddam, was drowned, together with both the Horses, who were carried under the Ice by the Current.

Saturday last the Cooper's Shop and Barn belonging to Mr. Gideon Allen, of Sandwich, was consumed by Fire, together with a large Quantity of Hay.

Married at New-York by the Rev. Dr. Auchmuty, Mr. Paschal Nelson Smith, Partner with Mr. Aspinwall, to Miss Hester Sears, Daughter of Mr. Isaac Sears, an eminent Merchant of that City.

Married at Hollis, in New-Hampshire, by the Rev. Mr. Emerson, Mr. John Kneeland, of this Town, Merchant, to Miss Nancy Hobart, eldest Daughter of Samuel Hobart, Esq; of that Place.

YEsterday Afternoon Capt. Gorham arrived here in a Brig in 9 Weeks from London, by whom we have advice of the arrival of the Captains Folger, White, Symmes, Callahan and Calef, from this Place, also the Earl of Halifax Packet in 36 Days from New-York.—By Capt. Gorham we have the public Prints to the 31st of December, which contain but few Articles of Intelligence; the most material are—That the Parliament was not to meet till some time in January: That Frederick Bull, Esq; the present Lord Mayor, was chosen Member for the City of London in the Room of Sir Robert Ladbrook, deceased: That the Philadelphia Resolves and the Proceedings of the People with the Consignees at Liberty-Tree were received and published in the News-Papers there: That the Opinion of all the Judges had been required on some Questions relative to North-America, which was a prelude to something of Consequence concerning that Country being brought before Parliament next Sessions: That Governor Pownal will positively go over to Boston early in the spring, in order to take the management of that quarter under his care: Orders have been dispatched in the course of the last week to Ireland, for the immediate embarkation of three regiments to be sent to Boston and New-York: That the Board of Trade had also come to several resolution relative to American Affairs, to be recommended at the same time: The latter End of December some Advices were received at Lord Dartmouth's Office from Boston in New-England, which were kept a profound secret: That the Susanna, Smith from Boston and Gouldsborough, was lost on an Island near Scotland: And that there had been a Duel fought between JOHN TEMPLE, Esq; late of this Town and Mr. WHATELY, a Broker in London, in which the latter was much wounded, but the former not hurt; they first discharged their Pistols, but miss'd each other, and then drew their Swords, with which they finished the Fray; the Quarrel was occasioned by Mr. Whately's publickly insinuating that Mr. Temple was the Person who sent over some original Letters from Gentlemen in America to his late

Brother, of which Mr. Oliver in a Letter to him had since complained of their being laid before the General Assembly; and tho' Mr. Temple gave every Assurance that a gentleman could give, that he had not taken any one Letter, nor a line of one, but what he saw, and gave leave, and had no concern in procuring or transmitting them to Boston; yet being still charged with the same, notwithstanding these Protestations, and receiving from Mr. Whately, as he apprehended, the Lie direct, he took the above Method, which the Feelings of Honor, and Impatience under such an Imputation, to call upon Mr. Whately for honorable Amends.—They fought without Seconds, as Mr. Whately declined it on his Part.

From the Morning Chronicle, *&c. of* December 27, 1773.

To the PRINTER.

SIR.

FINDING that two Gentlemen have been unfortunately engaged in a duel, about a transaction and its circumstances of which both of them are totally ignorant and innocent, I think it incumbent on me to declare (for the prevention of farther mischief, as far as such a declaration may contribute to prevent it) that I alone am the person who obtained and transmitted to Boston the letters in question,—Mr. W. could not communicate them, because they were never in his possession; and, for the same reason, they could not be taken from him by Mr. T.——They were not of the nature of "*private letters between friends*:" They were written by public officers to persons in public station, on public affairs, and intended to procure public measures; they were therefore handed to other public persons who might be influenced by them to produce those measures: their tendency was to incense the Mother Country against her colonies, and, by the steps recommended, to widen the breach, which they effected. The chief caution expressed with regard to privacy, was, to keep their contents from the *Colony Agents*, who the writers apprehended might return them, or copies of them, to America. That apprehension was, it seems, well founded; for the first agent who laid his hands on them, thought it his duty to transmit them to his constituents.

B. FRANKLIN, *Agent for the House of Representatives of the Massachusett's-Bay.*

Craven-street, Dec. 25, 1773.

Saturday last being the Anniversary of the 5th of March, upon which Day, agreeable to a Vote of the Town last Year, the Freeholders and other Inhabitants of this Town met at Faneuil-Hall at Ten o'Clock in the Forenoon, and after choosing Mr. SAMUEL ADAMS Moderator, they adjourned to the Old South Meeting House; where, after the Moderator had informed them of the Occasion of the Meeting, the Honorable JOHN HANCOCK, Esq; delivered an ORATION, on the dangerous Tendency of Standing Armies being placed in free and populous Cities, and to perpetuate the Memory of the horrid Massacre on the 5th of March 1770, by a Party of Soldiers belonging to the 29th Regiment, commanded by Capt. Thomas Preston.—A prodigious Crowd of People attended to hear the Oration, which was received with universal Applause, and a Committee was appointed to return the Orator the Thanks of the Town for his elegant and spirited Oration, and also to request a Copy of it for the Press.—Another Committee was also chosen to engage a suitable Person to pronounce an Oration at the next Anniversary; after which the Meeting was Dissolved.

At the breaking up of the above Meeting a very generous Collection was made for the poor unfortunate Christopher Monk, now about 23 Years of Age, (then present) who was wounded on the fatal Evening of the Massacre, and now remains a shocking Monument of that horrid Transaction.

As this Anniversary happened on Saturday, the Evening of which is considered by many Persons as the Commencement of the Sabbath, the Exhibition Portraits of the Murderers, and the slaughtered Citizens, was put off till this Evening, when they will be exposed to publick View at Mrs. Clapham's in King-Street.

Capt. Gorham, we are told, has about 30 Chests of Tea on board, said to be private Property, and consigned to some Persons here; but what will be the Fate thereof, a short time will discover——Certainly not suffered to be landed in Boston.

Messi'rs Edes & Gill, PUBLISH THIS!

IT is said that Capt. Gorham who is just arrived from London, has brought Forty Chests of that *baneful, detested, dutied Article* TEA, shipped by the East-India Company, their Brokers or Employers, and consigned to HENRY LLOYD, Esq; of this Town, Merchant. Justice to ourselves and to AMERICA—Justice even to the *other* Consignees—A Regard to our own Reputation and Honor—Every Obligation binds us most SOLEMNLY, at once to DETERMINE ABSOLUTELY to oppose its Landing—Experience has fully convinced us that the Governor and the Custom-House Officers concern'd *will* lay INSUPERABLE Bars in the Way of sending it back to London. The Consent of the Consignee to have it return'd would be to no Purpose, if he be waited upon to request it. The SACHEMS must have a *Talk* upon this Matter—Upon THEM we depend to extricate us out of this *fresh* Difficulty; and to THEIR Decisions all the GOOD People will say, AMEN!

Captain Allen in Ten Days from Charlestown South Carolina, informs, That the East India Company's Tea landed there is entirely destroyed.

Captain Allen of Salem informs of the following Vessels being at the Vineyard, last Friday, viz. The Capts. Smith, Dennison, Pearson, Gee & Burnham of Cape-Ann—Barnes of Plymouth—Hill of Portsmouth——Ingersol and Phelps of Salem—Cochran, Valentine, Sweat and White of Boston—and 6 Fishing Schooners—Capt. Allen in crossing the Sound saw a Ship standing to the Westward, which he took to be a Packet by her Pendant's flying.

Last Thursday Morning Died of a lingering Sickness, Mrs. Susanna Wheatly, Wife of Mr. John Wheatly Merchant, of this Town, in the 65th Year of her Age. Her funeral will be on Wednesday next if the Weather permits: When her Friends and Relations are desired to attend.

On Thursday next,
At Eleven o'Clock, will be Sold by PUBLIC VENDUE, at the Bunch of Grapes, King-Street;
A Few Hogsheads choice Shop SUGARS, and few Bags of COTTON. J. RUSSELL, Auct'r.

On Friday next,
At Eleven o'Clock, will be Sold by PUBLIC VENDUE, at Capt. Brrrett's Sail Loft,
SEVERAL Suits of SAILS, and a Quantity of RIGGING. J. RUSSELL, Auctioneer.

VELVET-CORKS.
Choice VELVET CORKS by the Quantity or single Groce,
TO BE SOLD By
Samuel Elliot,
At his Shop near the Head of Dock-Square, just above the Market:
Also, a general Assortment of *English* and *India* Goods; with a very fine Assortment of *Irish* LINNENS.

Lisbon Wine in Quarter Casks, and Sperma Cæti Candles, warranted pure, to be Sold very Cheap, By Francis Rotch, in King-Street.

For LONDON,
The Brigantine HOPE,
A Fine new Vessel, has excellent Accommodations, and will sail as soon as loaded.
For Freight or Passage, apply to JONATHAN WILLIAMS, jun. in Ann-Street.

To be Sold or Let,
The large House, and about 20 Acres of Upland and Meadow adjoining upon Boston Neck so called, well known by the Name of the George or King's-Arms Tavern, now in the Occupation of Mr. *Thomas Bracket*: The House, Out-Houses, Barns, Gardens and Fences in good Repair. Inquire for the Terms of *Melatiah Bourn*, Esq; in *Boston*.

WANTED TO CHARTER for Twelve Months,
A double Deck'd Vessel of 130 Tons, for which a good Price will be given. Inquire of Edes and Gill. ALSO, TO BE SOLD
A well Built Schooner, of about 70 Tons, almost new, well found.

For the Benefit of Mr. MORGAN,
At Concert Hall on Wednesday 23d Inst.
Will be a Concert of Vocal and Instrumental Music.—Tickets to be had at the British Coffee House, at Mrs. Cummins's in Cornhill, and Mrs. Taylor's in Winter Street, at half a Dollar each.
To begin at half after Six o'Clock.

TO BE SOLD
By Benjamin Church,
On THURSDAY next,
At THREE o'Clock in the Afternoon,
SUPERFINE middling and coarse Broad Cloths—Ratteens—Frizes—Half Thicks—Kerseys—Shalloons—Calamancoes—Irish Linnens—Checks—Mens and Womens Hose—Linnens—Velveretts—Handkerchiefs—Case Knives and Forks—Inkhorns—Penknives, &c.—Sundry Articles of Household—Wearing Apparel—Watches, Cutlery Ware, half a Dozen Mehogany Chairs Leather botomt—a Case of Draws—Feather Beds, &c. &c. &c
Thursday next, 3 o'Clock P. M.

Garden Seeds.
A fresh Assortment just arrived, in the Lydia, Captain Hood, from London, and to be sold by
EBENEZER OLIVER,
At his Shop nearly opposite the Old-South Meeting-House, BOSTON.
The Seeds, Peas and Beans, he can recommend to be good, and warrants them all of the last Year's Growth.
(The Particulars of which we are oblig'd to omit)

JOHN ADAMS,
(Opposite the Old-South Meeting-House, BOSTON,)
Hath received by the last Vessel from LONDON, A fresh Supply of GARDEN SEEDS,
Which he doubts not will be satisfactory to the Purchaser, as they are warranted good, and of the last Year's Growth. (The Particulars in our next.)

WANTED immediately, an Anchor of 110 wt. Inquire of the Printers.

Nathaniel Seaver,
INFORMS the Publick and his Customers in Particular, that he continues to keep the Shop lately improved by *Seaver & Carnes*, where may be had a large Assortment of English, India and Scotch Goods, Suitable for all Seasons, upon the lowest terms for Cash.
N. B. Said *Seaver* returns his hearty Thanks to his Friends & Customers for the favours already shown, and further assures them that he will do every thing in his power to serve them.

New AUCTION-ROOM, Cornhill,
TO-MORROW at TEN o'Clock will be Sold by PUBLIC VENDUE, at GREENLEAF'S Auction-Room,——
A very large Assortment of Goods as usual. Wm. GREENLEAF, Auctioneer.
The Sale will begin Tomorrow at Ten o'Clock,

TO BE LETT,

A Farm in Watertown, and entered on the first of April next, the Farm contains about 65 Acres of good Land, well accommodated for Plowing, Pasturing, and Mowing, with a plenty of Fruit. For further Particulars, Inquire of Mr. *Elijah Bond*, or Capt. *Jonathan Brown*, living in said Town. *Watertown, Feb. 28, 1774.*

A Farm to be Sold in Watertown, very pleasantly situated, and within two Miles of the Colledge, contains about 40 Acres of choice good Land, has on it a good House and Barn, is well accommodated for Mowing, Pasturage and Tillage, has on it a variety of all kinds of Fruits, and will very well accommodate a Gentleman: Whoever is inclined to Purchase the same may apply to JOHN STRALLON of said Watertown.
Feb. 28, 1774.

TO BE SOLD or LETT,
A small Farm in Newton, about ten Miles from Boston, with a House and Barn thereon, and may be enter'd on the first of April next. Enquire of John Newell Living in Wings-Lane, Boston.
N.B. About 40 or 50,000 red Oak Hhd. Staves, and 13 Thousand white Oak ditto to be sold by said Newell.
Boston, March 5th, 1774.

TO BE SOLD
AT PUBLICK AUCTION,
By Benjamin Church,
At his usual Place of Sale,
On Thursday the 17th Day of March,
Sundry Goods belonging to the Estate of Capt. *Henry Oman*, late deceas'd——consisting of——
Tammies, Durants, Callamancoes, Crapes, Dorsteens, Poplins, Persians, Sattins, Ribbons, Irish Linnens, Checks, German Serges, printed Handkerchiefs, Velverets, Worsted Plushes, striped Damascus, Moree Gowns, Threads, Qualities Pins, also a Variety of Wearing Apparel, and sundry other Articles.
N. B. The Sale to begin at 10 o'Clock, A. M.

WANTED IMMEDIATELY,
One Thousand Pounds Old Tenor, for which good Security will be given. For further Particulars inquire of the Printers.

GARDEN-SEEDS,
IMPORTED from LONDON, in Capt. HOOD, and TO BE SOLD BY
Elizabeth Clark and *Nowell*,
At their Shop Six Doors to the Southward of the Mill-Bridge, BOSTON:
EARLY Chalton, early hotspur, golden hotspur, large marrowfat, dwarf, large sugar, Spanish morratto, blue marrowfat, and marster's hotspur PEAS; large Windsor, green Norfolk, early yellow, dwarf, kidney, and large white dwarf BEANS; early Yorkshire, early Dutch, green Savoy, large Winter, early Sugar-Loaf, and Battersea Cabbage Seeds; Eearly and Late Colliflower; large Orange, early yellow, and purple Carrot; Swelling Parsnip, and red Beat Seeds; Green and white gols Cabbage; Marble, Breton, brown, Dutch, and grand Admiral Lettice Seeds; Thyme, Balm, Sweet-Marjoram, Sage and Fennel Seeds; Silverskin and Portugal Onion Seeds; early Salmon, scarlet and Turnip Radish Seeds; curl'd Parsley, curld Creses; Early Dutch Turnip Seeds; Early, long prickley Cucumber; white Mustard; green curld Endive; round Spinnage; best Mallon, Gourd Squash, solid Cellery, red Clover, and Canary Seeds.
☞ All warranted New of the genuine Sort,

CUSTOM-HOUSE, *BOSTON.*

ENTETRD IN.

Thorp from New-Haven. Smith from Virginia. Freeman from Halifax. Lewis from Lisbon, and Babson for St. Lucia.

Burials in the Town of BOSTON, since our last,
Eight Whites. One Black.
Baptiz'd in the several Churches, Seven.

High Water at BOSTON, *for the present Week.*

Monday, 26 min. aft. 7	Friday, 54 min. afternoo
Tuesday, 21 min. aft. 8	Saturday, 38 min. af. 11
Wednesday, 15 m. aft. 9	Lord's-Day, 16 min. aft. 12
Thursday, 5 min. aft. 10	D's New 12 Day 5 Morn

Whereas I the Subscriber intend

leaving off the Baking Business very soon, do take this opportunity of returning my Thanks to those Gentlemen and Ladies who have favoured me with their Custom, since my late Husband's decease. MARY SURCOMB.

The Business will be carried on as usual by Mr. William Flagg.

N. B. *A very good Horse and handsome Chaise to be Sold: Inquire of Mary Surcomb.*

Boston, Feb. 28, 1774.

This is to Acquaint all Gentlemen and Ladies that the Baking Business will be carried on as usual, by me the Subscriber, who is determined to give universal Satisfaction. WILLIAM FLAGG.

PITCH.

A Quantity of Pitch and a few Chaldron of New Castle Coals, to be Sold by W. HOSKINS.

BARLEY.

WHOEVER is willing to engage a Quantity of *BARLEY*, to be delivered in Boston next Fall, will find it of Advantage to leave their Proposals in Writing with the Printers.

WANTED

A strong active Person of a good Character, acquainted sufficiently with the Distilling Business, so as to be able to undertake the Care of a large Distill-House, out of Town: For further Particulars inquire of the Printers. *Boston, Feb. 28, 1774.*

TO BE SOLD,

A Good Farm in Concord, containing about 80 Acres, with a good House and two Barns, and a large new Store, two good Wells of Water upon the great Road, and within three Quarters of a Mile of the Meeting House; Said Farm will be Sold for English and West-India Goods, if applied for soon, Inquire of Mr. *Samuel Whitney* of Concord, or of Mr. *Samuel Austin* in Boston.

ALSO,

Another Farm in Lancaster Parish, containing about 100 Acres, with a good House and Barn on the same, will be Sold for Goods if apply'd for soon.

Wanted a Woman of a good Character, and one that can be well recommended, and that understands Cooking and other house Work; none need apply but such a one, and is Wanted immediately.—Good Wages will be given. Inquire of the Printers.

GARDEN SEEDS,

IMPORTED in Capt. SHEPHARD from LONDON And TO BE SOLD By

Elizabeth Greenleaf,

At her Shop to the Southward of the Lane leading to Dr. Byles's Meeting House, Boston.

EARLY Charlton, early golden Hotspur, early Hotspur, large Dwarf, and green Marrofats, white Rouncival, Ledman's Dwarf & Spanish Marratto Peas, large Windsor, Toker, early yellow, Dwarf Kidney, and large white Beans, red, purple, orange, and yellow Carrot seeds, early Yorkshire, early Dutch, early sugar loaf, early Battersea, red, large winter, green and yellow Savoy, early and late Colliflower, Cabbage, green and white Goss, brown Duck, Madeira, spotted and mogul Lettice seeds; red, white, Spanish, Portugal, and silver skin Onion seed; green and white endive, swelling Parsnip, red Beat, Time, Balm, sweet Marjoram, Sage, and summer savory seeds; scarlet, salmon, short topt and turnip Radish seeds; summer and winter Spinage, early and late Cucumber, early Dutch and French Turnip seeds; Parsley, Pepper-Grass, Asparagus, Salery, Lavender and white Mustard seeds; Water and Musk Melon seeds; summer and winter Squash seeds; Hemp, Rape and Canary Bird seed; choice split Pease by the large or smaller Quantity.—N. B. English GOODS.

IMPORTED in Capt. HOOD from LONDON, And TO BE SOLD By

Susanna Renken

At her Shop near the Draw-Bridge, Fore-Street, BOSTON:

EARLY Charlton, early golden Hotspur, green Marrows, white Rouncival, Spanish Morattoes, crooked Sugar, and Leadman's Dwarf Peas;—Toker, best Windsor, early Lisbon, large Dutch Kidney, Beans; Strasburgh, Spanish, Silverskin'd and Portugal Onion; Orange, early yellow, and scarlet Carrot; Parsnips; Early and late Turnip; Early short top'd, London, Salmon, turnip, Spanish, and scarlet Radish; Early frame, white goss, early green goss, large green goss, bloody goss, Aleppo goss, brown Dutch, marble, royal brown Dutch, imperial, tennisbal and Capuchin Lettice; Prickley and round Spinnage; Red Beats; Italian and solid Cellery; curl'd Pepper Grass; Indian Creses; Common, curld and large rooted Parsley; Early and late Colliflower; Early York, large Battersea, early Dutch, large Scotch, large winter and turnip Cabbage; Yellow, green and white curl'd Savoy; long prickley, early prickley, green Turkey, and long Roman Cucumber; Baum, Sweet-Marjoram, Thyme, Rosemary, and Lavender Seed; Hemp and Canary Ditto; Broad red Clover; Fine white Ditto; Lucern and Rape Seed; Rye Grass, and other Grass Seeds; Sage Seed.

Durham's best Flour Mustard; —Groceries.

Also, *English* and *India* Goods; All which may be had cheap for Cash.

TO BE SOLD,

By Benjamin Dolbeare,

A Very good Fire Engine, London-made; old Jamaica Spirit by the Tierce, sundry Barrels of Jamaica Sugar, and Vinegar by the Barrel.

A Woman with a good Breast of Milk, would be glad to take a Child to Suckle. Inquire of the Printers.

THE original Proprietors of a Township called Pennicook, now Concord, and the original Proprietors of a Township called Suncook, now Pembroke, (both in the Province of New-Hampshire) or the Heirs or Assigns of said original Proprietors; are hereby Notified that the General Court in their present Session, hath granted to each Propriety a Township in the late Province of Main, and appointed the Subscribers a Committee to exhibit a List to said Court, within 10 Months from the Date, of the Names of the Persons that have been Sufferers who have a just Claim to an Interest in the one or the other of said Townships:—This is therefore to give Notice to the said Pennicook Proprietors, and the said Suncook Proprietors, that the Committee will attend said Service at the House of Mrs. Hannah Osgood, Innholder in said Pennicook, on the second Wednesday in October next, ensuing, to receive authenticated Evidence of said Sufferers Claims to an Interest in the Township granted to the said Pennicook Proprietors, and that they will attend said Service at the House of Mr. Samuel Conner, Innholder in said Suncook, on the third Wednesday in October aforesaid, to receive like Evidence of the said Sufferers Claims to an Interest in the Township granted to the said Suncook Proprietors.

Feb. 22, 1774. *Samuel Phillips, Joseph Gerrish, Jonathan Webster* } Committee.

WHEREAS the Great and General Court of Assembly at their Session begun and held on the 27th Day of May 1772, granted a Tax of *One Penny half Penny* per Acre, upon the Lands of the Non-resident Proprietors in the Town of *Ashby*, in the County of Middlesex; and whereas said Tax has been duly assessed and published agreeable to Law, and some Persons Proprietors or Owners of said Land, neglect or refuse to pay the same; and whereas the General Court by said Act did impower the Assessors chosen by the Town of Ashby, to Assess the same, to Sell so much of the Delinquent Proprietors Lands as shall be sufficient to pay and satisfy said Tax and other incidental Charges: And whereas the Owners of the following Lands are Delinquent in paying said Tax, viz.

Names of those who drew the Lots, or them who now own them.	What Division.	What Right	No. Acre	*l.*	*s.*	*d.*
John Moffat			20	0	2	6
Col. Josiah Willard part	4 5 6	57 83 53	37	0	4	8
Henry Laughton part	4	32	14	0	1	9
Christopher Barrett			22	0	2	9
Cumings and Fletcher	part 4		40	0	5	0
Rev'd Mr. Perry Two	3		133		16	7½
Col. Wm. Lawrance	6	35	40	0	5	0
Hugh Hall, Esq;	part 3	73	66	0	8	3
James Lawrance	5	70	40	0	5	0
Edward Emerson part	5	62	42	0	5	4
Ebenezer Southwick	6	19	50	0	6	3
Jona. Hill part	3	69	40	0	5	0
Samuel Brown	3	47	66	0	8	3
Simon Blood	4 part 6	14	124		15	6
David Melvin	6	58	42	0	5	3
James Nicholas	4 part 6	78	71	0	8	10½
John Nichlas			20	0	2	6
—— Gore part	3		62	0	7	9
Capt. Daniel Stickney part	3	58	40	0	5	0
Third Division, No.		60	66	0	8	3
Peter Atherton	3	37	66	0	8	3
Formerly belonging to Lunenburg						
Robert Paul	3 4	24	235	1	9	4½
John Bridge, jun.			48	0	6	0
James Billings			53	0	6	7½
Abraham Gibson			30	0	3	9
Joseph Lee			30	0	3	9
Heirs of Samuel Reed			100		12	6
Daniel Buttrick			32	0	4	0

NOTICE is hereby given to said Delinquents, that so much of their Lands will be exposed to Sale at Public Vendue, on the 31st Day of May next, at the House of Capt. Samuel Stone, Innholder in said Ashby, at 9 of the Clock in the Forenoon, and continued by Adjournments, if need be, until the second Day of June, as will be sufficient to pay said Tax, and other intervening Charges, unless prevented by Payment of said Tax, (and such Charges as have already arisen) unto the Assessors, before the abovesaid Time.

Ashby, Feb. 16, 1774. *James Locke, Samuel Stone, Jonathan Locke,* } Assessors.

TO BE SOLD

Utensils for the Tallow Chandler's Business, a large Iron Kettle, Press, Tallow Tub, Chopping Knife, Trough, Candle Rods, &c. Inquire of the Printers.

Lincolnshire Company 20 Associates.

WHEREAS there are divers Matters to be transacted by the 20 Associates of the *Lincolnshire* Company, respecting their Lands and Interest lying near *Penobscot-Bay* in the County of *Lincoln*:—The Committee of said Associates being duly authorised therefor, Hereby notify said Associates to meet on Wednesday the 9th Day of *March* next, at Mr. Hubbard's, the Vernon Tavern, in *Boston*, 6 o'Clock, P. M. then and there to act upon all such Matters as may properly come before them. By Order of the Committee,

NATH. APPLETON, Prop'rs Clerk.

February 16th, 1774.

James Swan

HAS for Sale at Store No. 6, leading to Tread's and Spear's Wharves,

A Quantity of *Indian Corn* very good and just arrived, choice Fine *Flour*, and a few Quoils of the best *Cordage*, all Cheap.

Dry'd OX HIDES,

Cotton and Piemento, just Imported from Jamaica, and to be Sold at GRIFFIN's Wharf.

PURSUANT to a Decree of the High Court of Chancery in England, William Rumbold, Mary the Wife of Alexander Laing, both of the Province of Maryland, Mary the Wife of Garrett Blackford, of the Province of New-Jersey, in North-America—Rumbold, of Cashell, in Ireland, Rodolphus Rumbold of Tipperary, in Ireland; William Rumbold of Jamaica; and William Rumbold of the Bay of Honduras; and all other Persons claiming to be Heirs at Law of Thomas Rumbold, late of Long-Alley, near Moorfields, in the County of Middlesex; or William Rumbold, of the same Place, his Brother, who were the Sons of Thomas Rumbold, formerly of the same Place, Stocking Trimmer deceased, who was the Son of William Rumbold, late of King's Clere, in the County of Southampton, Yeoman deceased, are to come in and enter into Proof of their respective Claims of being Heirs at Law of the said Thomas Rumbold, and William Rumbold, before JOHN EAMES, Esq; one of the Masters of the said Court, at his Chambers in Symons Inn, Chancery-Lane, London, within twelve Months from the Publication hereof, or in Default thereof they will be absolutely excluded the Benefit of the said Decree. J. EAMES.

Choice Peas, Isle of Shoals dumb Fish, Beef, Rye, a few Barrels Rye Flour, and Pork, To be Sold by JOHN BARRETT and SONS, Near the Mill-Bridge.

GOODS under the Sterling Cost.

William Gale

Acquaints his Friends and Customers that he is now Selling the remainder of his Goods, under the *Sterling Cost*, (at his Shop opposite the Post-Office, in Cornhill, Boston.) ——Among them are following, viz.——

Broad Cloths,	39. & 7-8 Garlix,
Flannels,	Figur'd Modes,
Lamb Skins,	Figur'd Sattins,
Plushes,	Pink, blue & white Sattins,
Kerseys,	Blond Laces,
Cotton Velvetts,	Black & white Sattin Pumps,
Womens Velvett,	Brocaded ditto,
Strip'd Swanskins,	White & color'd Russell dit.
Duffils,	Plain and sprig'd Muslin,
Felt Hatts,	Cambrick & sprig'd Muslin,
Shalloons,	English & flower'd Lawns,
Tammies,	Incle Lutestring,
Demaskus,	Silk Gauzes, &c. &c.
Irish Linnens,	

TO BE SOLD

MAY PLACE (the pleasant Seat of JOHN FENTON, Esq;) one Mile from *Charlestown*-Ferry, upon the great Road leading to *Cambridge*, *Mistick*, &c. &c. (part of the remarkably fruitful Hill called *Bunkers*,) containing a handsome House, Out-Houses, Barn and Garden, stored with a great Variety of the choicest Fruit-Trees, all young and healthy.

Twenty-five Acres of choice Mowing and Pasturage, *(two thirds and more of which under Mowing)* newly Fenced off into proper Divisions, highly Drest and handsomly decorated with Locust Trees.

Between five and six Acres of Salt Marsh; Also, a new Wharff adjacent to the Premises, very convenient for landing Wood, Manure, &c.

Whoever may incline to purchase the above Premises, may be informed of the Conditions by applying to ROBERT TEMPLE, Esq; of Ten Hills, near Charlestown: Mr. ISAAC MALLET at the Neck of Land near said Place, (who will at any Time shew the Premises) Or a Line directed to Col. JOHN FENTON, of Portsmouth, New-Hampshire.

☞ If not Sold by the 2d of April—then the House, Warehouse, Barn, Garden, and a Pasture, containing about two and half Acres, to be Lett.

THE PUBLIC

ARE hereby informed, That JOHN JOY has just arrived from London, and brought with him a large and compleat Assortment of DRUGS and MEDICINES, of the best Quality. Also, Surgeons Instruments of every Kind finished in the neatest Manner, with a full Assortment of Groceries and Dye Stuffs; which as they were purchased by himself for the Cash, he will sell on very reasonable Terms, at his Shop the North Corner of Williams's Court, in Cornhill, Boston.

Practitioners and others, may be supplied with large or small Quantities, by Letter or otherwise, as well as though they were present.

Medicine Boxes of various Prices, for Ships or private Families, are put up in the neatest Manner.

Boston: Printed, by EDES & GILL *in Queen-Street,* 1774.

THE Boston-Gazette, AND COUNTRY JOURNAL.

Containing the freshest Advices, Foreign and Domestic.

MONDAY, March 14, 1774.

Mess'rs EDES & GILL,

AT a late interment, great numbers of People were collected to see the Cadet Company perform their Exercises; and by the unusual Joy which appeared in their Countenances, it was apprehended they had forgot the Command, "*Rejoice not when thine Enemy falleth*".

LONDON, November 13.

In the Irish Parliament, notwithstanding the favourable opinion conceived of Lord Harcourt, on his arrival in Ireland, the ministerial party are as powerful as ever, and carry every question as they please—so that that poor devoted nation seems to have no chance to avoid ruin and slavery.

A most affecting picture of their oppression and general distress was exhibited by several of the members in the debates, on motions for laying new taxes and impositions upon them, when they are already burden'd with more than they are able to bear. Mr. Fitzgibbon, in his speech against new taxes, among many other affecting passages, has these words,—"I find at last, that the "Ministry of England, jealous of our abridged privileges, have their eye on a general land tax, for all other "schemes they see are ineffectual; if they tax our soap, "the poor must rot in filth, for they would not have "wherewith to wash the rags of wretchedness;—if a "tax was laid on leather, even the hardened brogue they "wear at present must be laid aside; if a tax on candles, the dreary night of winter must be a night of "darkness to them;—and if on malt, the cold cup of "water must allay their thirst; upward, Sir, of two "millions of our poor people are unable to pay any tax "at all, whose distresses are so great, and whose poverty "is so well known, that instead of the two shillings exacted for their single hearth, when to them the tremendous gatherers appear, they have often been obliged to part with the pot that was to boil their potatoes."

Besides the expences of government, augmented by extravagant salaries to a great number of useless officers, these poor people are burthened with the payment of a list of Pensions amounting to about £.79,000 per ann. to persons with whom they have no concern, and from whom they never received any benefit.—[AMERICANS! *Beware of the deplorable State of your long-abused Brethren of Ireland!*]

BOSTON, MARCH 14.

His Majesty OKNOOKORTUNKOGOG King of the Narraganset Tribe of Indians, on receiving Information of the arrival of another Cargo of that Cursed Weed TEA, immediately Summoned his Council at the Great Swamp by the River Jordan, who did Advise and Consent to the immediate Destruction thereof, after Resolving that the IMPORTATION of this Herb, by ANY Persons whatever, was attended with pernicious Consequences to the Lives and Properties of all his Subjects throughout America. Orders were then issued to their Seizor & Destroyer-General, and their Deputies to assemble the executive Body under their Command, to proceed directly to the Place where the noxious Herb was. They arrived last Monday Evening in Town, and finding the Vessel, they emptied every Chest, into the Great Pacific Ocean, and effectually Destroyed the whole, (Twenty-eight Chests and an half.) They are now returned to Narragansett to make Report of their doings to his Majesty, who we hear is determined to honour them with Commissions for the Peace.

On Monday evening the horrid tragedy of the 5th of March was observed with the usual solemnity, by exhibiting to public view a portrait of that inhuman and cruel Massacre perpetrated by Preston, and his infamous butchers: on the right, a figure of America pointing to her slaughtered sons, on the left, a monument to the memory of Gray, Attucks, Maverick, Caldwell and Carr. In one of the windows was a representation of H——n and J—e O—r, in the horrors, occasioned by the appearance of the two ghosts of Empson and Dudley, advising them to think of their fate. They appeared to be worshipping their ill-gotting gold the modern deity of the *North*.

Ye TRAITORS; "Is there not some chosen curse,
Some hidden thunder in the stores of heaven,
Red with uncommon wrath, to blast the man
Who owe their greatness to their country's ruin!

His Excellency has signed 20 public and private Acts, passed the late Sessions of the General Assembly.

REFUSED

A Bill against Bribery and Corruption in the Election of Representatives.

A Bill for obliging the Sheriffs of the several Counties to give Bond for the faithful Discharge of their respective Offices.

A Bill to prevent the further Importation of Negroes.

It appears by an *Advertisement* in the last Court Gazette, that his Excellency the Governor, has, "in Imitation of the pious & laudable Example" "of the Authority of this Province," by "long and uninterrupted Practice," appointed Thursday the 14th of April next, to be *religiously* observed as a Day of Fasting and Prayer throughout this Province; to implore certain "enumerated Mercies, and other public and private Blessings."—*Pray for the Peace of Jerusalem! May those that seek her Prosperity prosper; and those who have sought or shall still seek to procure* "an abridgment of what are called English Liberties" *be ashamed, confounded and melt away.* AMEN.

The Assembly of New-York have granted his Excellency Governor Tryon £.5000 Currency, in some Measure to compensate his Loss at the late Fire.

Capt. Sweet arrived at Newport, brings Advice, that the New-York Tea Ship was arrived at Antigua, in a very shattered Condition; and a Number of other Vessels, having been blown off this Coast, were also arrived in the West-Indies.

In our last paper we published an account of Capt. Gorham's bringing forty chests of the East India company's tea consigned to Henry Lloyd, Esq; of this Town, Merchant. Better information obliges us to inform the public that Mr. Lloyd on the fifth and seventh of November last wrote to his correspondent to send him no tea on any account whatever, till further orders. Mr. Lloyd's correspondent concluding (as he wrote) that the people opposed the importation only on account of the monopoly, sent 16 chests on the joint account of Mr. Lloyd and himself. Thus Mr. Lloyd directly contrary to his order and expectation has been drawn into view in a light very disagreeable to himself, and wishes nothing more ardently than to have his conduct truly represented to his Country, with whom his highest ambition is to stand fair and agreeably.

Married.] Mr. *Samuel Gore*, to Miss *Polly Pierce.*

DIED.] Yesterday, at Charlestown, greatly lamented, THOMAS BRIGDEN, Esq; of Westminster, in the 29th Year of his Age. His Remains are to be interr'd on Wednesday next.

MARCH 6. *Last Friday se'nnight, in the Forenoon, Mr. Brown, of Salem, Deputy Sheriff, went on board a Fishing Vessel, at Marblehead, and arrested John Watts and John Guillard, in an Action of Damages for £.3000, commenced by the Gentlemen who were Proprietors of the late Essex Hospital, on Suspicion that the said two Persons were concerned in burning that Building on the 26th of January last.—The Prisoners were committed to his Majesty's Goal in Salem, about 2 o'Clock, P. M. Almost as soon as the Keys were turned upon them, the People began, in small Companies, to enter the Town from Marblehead, and continued coming over in this Manner, 'till near Night, Rendezvouzing near the Goal. The Magistrates were busy in consulting upon Measures for preserving the Peace, and dispersing the People who were assembling from Marblehead; from whence a still greater Number was expected after dark. About Sunset, on Application to the Colonel of the Militia, the Drums were ordered out, and beat to* Arms.—*Immediately upon hearing this, the Mob, to the Number of* 4 *or* 500, *arming themselves with Clubs, Sticks of Wood,* &c. *and while it was yet Day-light, made a most furious Attack upon the Goal.—They first burst open the Doors, and broke most of the lower Windows in that Part of the Building which is the Prison-Keeper's Dwelling; and then, with Iron-Crows, Axes, &c. they soon beat their Way thro' four of the Prison Doors, each of which was very strong, & well secured with many large Locks. Thus having got into two Apartments of the Prison, in less than ten Minutes from the first onset, carried off the abovementioned two Prisoners in Triumph, and went immediately to Marblehead, where they soon dispersed.——They assembled again the next Day, and obliged the Gentlemen abovementioned to Declare, that no Prosecution should ever after be Commenced on Account of burning the Hospital.*

TO BE SOLD,

A large handsome & convenient Brick Dwelling House, situate in Hanover-Street, Boston, late the Estate of Jacob Royall, Esq; deceased, containing three Rooms upon a Floor, three upright Stories, the Cellar pav'd and ceil'd, a large Yard and Garden, an excellent Well of Water, Stable and Chaise House, with every Convenience suitable for a Gentleman. Any Person inclining to purchase the Premisses, may apply to RICHARD LECHMERE, Esq;

To be Sold for want of Employ,

A likely, healthy, strong Negro Girl, about 12 *Years of Age, can be well recommended.*

Inquire of the Printers.

New AUCTION-ROOM, Cornhill.

TO-MORROW at TEN o'Clock will be Sold by PUBLIC VENDUE, at GREENLEAF'S Auction-Room,——

A very large Assortment of Goods as usual. Wm. GREENLEAF, Auctioner.

The Sale will begin Tomorrow at Ten o'Clock,

[For the Benefit of the Insurers]

To-Morrow Morning, Ten o'Clock,

Will be Sold by PUBLIC VENDUE,

At the Sail-Loft of Mr. William Kimble, at the North-End.

16 Pieces of damaged *RUSSIA* DUCK.

J. RUSSELL, Auctioneer.

TO-MORROW,

At ELEVEN o'Clock, will be Sold by PUBLIC VENDUE, at the Store of Mr. *John Head*,

A few Bags of damaged PEPPER.

J. RUSSELL, Auctioneer.

TO-MORROW, at ONE o'Clock,

Will be Sold by PUBLIC VENDUE, at the Bunch of Grapes Tavern in King-Street,

Six Half Pipes Madeira and Four Quarter Casks Claret WINE.—Likewise a very handsome Chaise and Harness, almost new.

J. RUSSELL, Auctioneer.

(For the Benefit of Insurers.)

ON WEDNESDAY NEXT,

At ELEVEN o'Clock in the Morning, will be sold by PUBLIC VENDUE, at Mr. *Job Gray's* Rope-Walk,

A Quantity of damaged HEMP.

J. RUSSELL, Auctioneer.

ON THURSDAY NEXT,

At ONE o'Clock, will *absolutely* be sold, by PUBLIC AUCTION, at the Bunch of Grapes-Tavern in King-Street.

A Large Brick Dwelling-House, belonging to the Estate of Thomas Tyler, Esq; deceased, situated on the Town-Dock, now occupied by Mr. Thomss Lee; also a Warehouse and Shed on Wentworth's Wharff.

At GOULD's Auction-Office in Back-Street,

On Friday next,

At TEN a'Clock in the Morning,

Will be Sold by PUBLIC VENDUE,

A Variety of English and Hard Ware Goods, as usual.

Also, a Green Harrateen Bed compleat, Feather Beds, Bedsteads, Mehogany Tables, Looking Glasses, &c.&c.

R. GOULD, Auctioneer.

N. B. Cash given for Merchantable & un-Merchantable Potash, and Potash Salts, at said Office.

GARDEN SEEDS

IMPORTED in Capt GORHAM, from LONDON, And TO BE SOLD

By *Lydia Dyar*,

At her Shop near the North Battery, BOSTON;

Early Charlton, Early Hotspur, Golden Hotspur, large Marrowfatts, Dwarf Marrow, blue Marrow, and Spanish Moratto PEAS; large Windsor, large Toker, early Lisbon, early Hotspur, early yellow Dwarf, early speckled Dwarf, and early white BEANS, with black Eyes; early Yorkshire, early Dutch, Sugar-loaf, large Winter, Battersea, green and yellow Savoy, early and late Colliflower Seeds; Best Cabbage Lettice, White Goss, Green Goss, Marble and Brown Dutch Lettuce, Seeds, Double Peppper Grass, round Spinage, short top, Scarlet and Salmon Radish, double Parsley, white Spanish, silver skin and red Onion seeds, long green prickly Cucumber, and early ditto, sweet Marjoram, Thyme, Baum, Sage, Hysop, Summer and Winter Squash, early and late Dutch Turnip, long French ditto, red Beets, large swelling Parsnip, Orange, golden colour'd, early yellow Carrot, & Canary Seeds, warranted to be new and good. LIKEWISE,

A Variety of Flower SEEDS.

GARDEN SEEDS imported in Capt. Hood, from LONDON, and Sold

By ANN JOHNSON,

At the Head of Black-Horse Lane, near the Rev. Dr. Pemberton's Meeting-House.—Particulars in our next.

HACKNEY COACH, drove by George Hamlin, will attend Gentlemen and Ladies to, or from any Part of the Town, at any Time in the Day or Evening, at 1*s.* each, a single Person for 2*s.*

N. B. Said Hamlin gives constant attendance at Mr. Paddock's Coach Yard, Long-Acre.

We shall in this Paper conclude our Narrative of the Proceedings of the several Branches of the General Assembly relating to Chief Justice OLIVER. The Council having on the 28th of February by a Message acquainted the Governor that the House of Representatives had laid on the Table Articles of Impeachment of high Crimes and Misdemeanors against the Chief Justice, and that they had also laid on the Table Articles of Charge and Complaint against him, his Excellency on the 3d March sent them the following Message, viz.

Gentlemen of the Council,

YOU acquaint me, in your Message of the 28th of the last Month, that the House of Representatives, in their own Name and the Name of the Inhabitants of this Province, by a Committee, had Impeached Peter Oliver, Esq; Chief Justice of the Superior Court, of high Crimes and Misdemeanors, and had laid on the Council Table Articles of Impeachment against the said Peter Oliver, Esq; and Prayed that the Governor and the Council would appoint a Time to proceed with, try, and judge the said Peter Oliver, Esq; as may be agreeable to Law and Justice; and you, therefore, pray that I will be pleased to inform you when I will be present, with the Council, to proceed upon this Business.

The House of Representatives having, by a Message to me, desired that I would be present, in Council, that they might have an Opportunity of laying Articles of Impeachment which they had prepared against the Chief Justice, for High Crimes and Misdemeanors before the Governor and Council, I declined complying with the Request, for Reasons which I thought proper to give in a Message to the House; and this Message was first communicated to you, agreeable to my uninterrupted Practice, that you may be acquainted with every Thing which passes from me to the House. You seem, nevertheless, to consider my being present in Council, to proceed with you upon a Trial for High Crimes and Misdemeanors, as a meer Matter of Course.

You have made it necessary for me to give you my Sense of the Powers of the Governor and Council as they stand related to each other, that you may know upon what Principles I have governed my past, and must govern my future Conduct:—Except in Cases of Wills and Administration, and Marriage and Divorce, the Governor and Council have no Jurisdiction, either civil or criminal, as a Court of Judicature, and the assuming the Powers of such a Court, without Authority derived from the Crown, will undoubtedly be considered as an Offence against his Majesty's Prerogative. In those judicial Proceedings, the Governor is a necessary though not an integral Part. The Council, except in a judiciary Capacity or as a Branch of the Legislature, are, by the Constitution, to be advising and assisting to the Governor, and are to be convened for that Purpose, from Time to Time, at the Discretion of the Governor, and not by their own Act nor by any other Authority whatsoever. I have never thought myself warranted to do, or attempt to do, any Act of Government by myself alone, where the Advice and Assistance of the Council is, by the Charter, made necessary. In all Cases where Acts have been expedient, and also where it has been doubtful whether they were or were not expedient, I have convened the Council in order to their Advice and Assistance: But when any Act has been suggested to be necessary which would counteract and tend to defeat the Acts and doings of the King, or which would be in any other Respect contrary to the Duty which I owe to the King, I have not thought it consistent with Discretion to convene the Council to ask their Advice, whether I should or should not do such an Act, seeing, I dare not do it although they should advise to it. Indeed an Act may be suggested of such a Nature that it would be an Indignity to the King to propose a Question upon it.

Milton, March 3, 1773. T. HUTCHINSON.

As the Governor in this Message takes no Notice of the Paper containing the Articles of Charge and Complaint exhibited by the House against the Chief Justice, the Council the next Day sent him another Message in the Words following.

May it please your Excellency,

SINCE the Message which the Board sent to your Excellency on the 28th of the last Month, to acquaint you, that the House of Representatives had impeached Peter Oliver, Esq; Chief Justice of the Superior Court, of high Crimes and Misdemeanors; and had laid on the Council Table Articles of Impeachment against him, and prayed that the Governor and the Council would appoint a Time to proceed with, examine, try and judge the said Peter Oliver, Esq; as may be agreeable to Law and Justice; the House of Representatives have laid upon the Council Table Articles of Charge and Complaint against the said Peter Oliver, Esq; and pray that the Governor & Council would give Order that the said Peter Oliver, Esq; may be notified to make Answer to the Charges contained in the foregoing Articles, and he brought to a Hearing and Trial thereon: That if he should be found guilty thereof, he may by the Governor and Council, be forthwith removed from his said Office, and some other more worthy be nominated and appointed in his Stead.

These Articles of Charge and Complaint the Board directed the Secretary to lay before your Excellency, together with the Articles of Impeachment aforesaid, and the Secretary informs the Board that he has done it accordingly. In your Message of Yesterday, your Excellency has declined joining with the Board, in any Proceedings with Relation to the Articles of Impeachment, but have not signified your Mind with Respect to the last-mentioned Articles of Charge and Complaint. The Board therefore desire your Excellency would be pleased to inform them, what your Determination is, with Regard to those Articles of Charge and Complaint.

On Monday the 7th March, the Council sent a Committee to his Excellency the Governor with the following Message, viz.

May it please your Excellency,

YOUR Message of the 3d instant to this Board relative to the Chief Justice of the Superior Court, and your several Messages to the House of Representatives relative also to him (which with other papers the House by Message have laid before the Board for their consideration) are on a subject of great importance. They contain declarations from your Excellency which we think do not comport with the spirit of the Charter, and tend to take away or lessen the jurisdiction of the Governor and Council, considered as a judiciary body or court of justice, and therefore it is incumbent on this Board in faithfulness to the province, and in justice to themselves, to take notice of some of them.

Among those papers we find a copy of the Remonstrance of the House addressed to your Excellency and the Council, and your Excellency's answer to it. By the former they pray for the removal of the Chief Justice from his office, and by the latter you declare, that in duty to the King you are obliged to decline their request; and you are pleased repeatedly to decline it on their repeated applications.

But before your Excellency had proceeded thus far, was it not proper, as the Remonstrance is addressed to the Council in conjunction with your Excellency, that it should have been communicated to them for their consideration of it? Is not your undertaking to determine solely on a matter that falls under the cognizance of the Governor and Council jointly, and is so addressed to them by the House, an unkind and disrespectful treatment of the representative body of the province, and an infringement on the rights of the Council? Or rather does it not annihilate the Council, considered either in their capacity of being advising and assisting to the Governor, or as a court of justice with, or without the Governor? And being done under a profession of duty to the King, does it not tend to alienate the affections of his Majesty's subjects from him? Though such be the tendency, such an effect will not flow from it. If it had been communicated to the Board, they assure your Excellency they would not have done any thing concerning it inconsistent with their duty to the King, notwithstanding any indirect or constructive intimation to the contrary.

Your Excellency's apprehension, that your taking any steps in this business would be counteracting his Majesty, and inconsistent with your duty to him, is founded on the facts mentioned in this clause in your first Message to the House, viz. "His Majesty having been pleased to direct warrants to be prepared for the payment of salaries to the Chief Justice, and to the other Justices of the superior court I received as Governor of the province the earliest notice of this declaration of his Majesty's pleasure, in order as I conceive that, as far as might appertain to me, I should conform thereto."——This notice (that warrants were directed to be prepared) which appears to be intended only as an article of intelligence, your Excellency, by this and your other Messages on the same subject, construes as an instruction obliging you, not to do any thing to prevent the effect of those warrants, or inconsistent with the intention of them. But what room is there for such a construction, or to suppose you were under such an obligation, when the Justices themselves (at least four of them) whom this affair immediately respected, thought themselves not obliged to take his Majesty's grant, but at liberty to refuse it, and accordingly have refused it from July 1772 (when their stipends were to commence) to the present time, and very lately in the fullest and most explicit manner? As in their refusal, which was a more effectual counteracting the intention of those warrants than any thing your Excellency could do, those gentlemen did not think they acted inconsistently with their duty to his Majesty, why should your Excellency think your laying before the Council the Remonstrance of the House inconsistent with your duty to him? Especially when your duty to the province, with which your duty to the King cannot militate, required it.

But supposing the notice of those warrants implied an instruction, or had been accompanied with an instruction, that you should do nothing directly or indirectly inconsistent with the intention of them, why should it operate to prevent your Excellency's even hearing the Remonstrance, and not operate to prevent your consenting to and signing the grants made by the assembly, not only to those four justices, but also to the chief justice, for their services during the same time, for which those warrants were intended to pay them; and for which, by virtue of one of those warrants, the chief justice has in fact been paid? Does not this give room for the apprehension, that your Excellency was not influenced solely by a sense of duty to the King, in refusing to lay before the Board the Remonstrance of the House?

The reasons why it was not laid before them seem to be given in that paragraph of your Message to the House, wherein you are pleased to tell them "that the Council, except when they are considered in their legislative capacity, or as a court for the probate of wills and granting administration, and for determining causes of marriage and divorce, are by the constitution to be advising and assisting to the governor, and do not make one Court or judiciary body with the governor, but the governor is considered as an integral part, and has authority from time to time at his discretion to assemble and call the Council together."—We shall presently consider whether there be not other cases than those here mentioned by your Excellency, in which the Council make one court or judiciary body with the Governor, and in which the Governor is not to be considered as an integral part; but first beg leave to make a few observations on another part of the foregoing paragraph.

We agree with your Excellency, that the Council by the constitution are to be advising and assisting to the Governor. The Governor also with them, or seven of them at the least, shall and may from time to time hold and keep a council for the ordering and directing the affairs of the province. But we humbly ask, what advantages would be derived to the province from this part of the constitution, if the Governor, even in the most important cases, should refuse to hold a council, wherein he might be advised and assisted; and wherein also the Governor with the Council jointly, according to the nature of the case, might take the needful measures for the ordering (that is the well ordering) and directing the affairs of the province?——These clauses of the Charter were doubtless intended for some beneficial purpose. They were intended more effectually to secure to the province a permanent good government, not subject to the will and caprice of a Governor: who, left to act wholly independent of a council, might bring upon the province the greatest mischiefs. Happy it was for the province, that the late Governor Sir Francis Bernard was not thus independent! But the benefits intended by the appointment of a council would be defeated, if the Governor should not call them together when affairs of the greatest importance to the province demanded it; and indeed this would frustrate the end of their appointment in every capacity in which they cannot act without him. To apply this to the subject of the Remonstrance, and to all cases, in which complaint is made to the Governor and Council against officers of their appointment,---It appears to us, that when complaint is thus made, and the Governor refuses or neglects to lay it before the council, he thereby counteracts the spirit and intention of the charter, which the honour and faith of the crown are pledged to maintain, and gives just reason for uneasiness.

We shall pass over the intermediate messages, and come to the last message your Excellency sent to the House of Representatives: On which it is necessary to make some observations.

We find by it the House had informed you, that they had resolved to impeach Peter Oliver, Esq; Chief Justice of the Superior Court, before the Governor and Council, of high crimes and misdemeanors; that they had prepared articles of impeachment, and prayed your Excellency would be in the chair, that they might have an opportunity of laying them before the Governor and Council.

But your Excellency, after making divers observations concerning the manner of trial for crimes and misdemeanors, declined granting their request, by declaring, that "whilst such process as the House have attempted to commence shall appear to you to be unconstitutional, you cannot shew any countenance to it."——It is with great reluctance the Board have entered into the consideration of a subject, on which they are obliged to dissent from your Excellency. But a vindication of their right of jurisdiction as a Court makes it necessary.——The complaint and process abovementioned are against an executive officer appointed by the Governor and Council. Complaints of this sort are no novelty. Many instances of them have taken place since your Excellency was first a member of the General-Court; and some of them, while you were Speaker of the House of Representatives, preferred by the House. The Governor and Council have always been esteemed the proper Judicature, before whom officers appointed by them have been triable for crimes or misdemeanors, so far as that, when found guilty, judgment has been given against them, with respect to their continuance in office; and thus far your Excellency has yourself supported the jurisdiction of that Court; which, when your Excellency presided, gave judgment in a recent case for the removal of an executive officer appointed by the Governor and Council. If such cases, in order to such a judgment, are not cognizable by that Court, there is no other Court in the province, by which they are cognizable for the purpose of removal from office. Divers such judgments have been obtained in consequence of the complaint of private persons. If private persons have a right to complain of mal-administration of officers, the representative body, who are the grand inquest for the province, must *a fortiori* have that right. But your Excellency intimates, that the process the House of Representatives have now attempted to commence is unconstitutional. The process they first attempted with regard to the Chief Justice was by remonstrance, addressed to the Governor and Council, which your Excellency, without communicating it to the Council, thought proper to suppress. The process next attempted was by impeachment, which you think unconstitutional. If it be unconstitutional, it cannot be cognizable by the Court: The jurisdiction of which being affected by the denial of the constitutionality of impeachments, it becomes needful to examine the reasons of that denial. They are given in your Excellency's message, in which you are pleased to say, "that there are no species of crimes committed within this province, which are not cognizable by some established Judicatory, and that the Governor and Council have no concurrent jurisdiction with any Judicatory in criminal cases, nor any authority to try and determine any species of high crimes and misdemeanors whatsoever," [except at least for the purpose of removal from office, as your Excellency might have added.] "That if you should assume a jurisdiction, and with the Council try offenders against the law without authority granted by the Charter, or by a law of the province in pursuance of the Charter, you should make yourself liable to answer for it; and his Majesty's subjects would have just cause to complain of being deprived of a trial by jury, the general claim of Englishmen, except in those cases, where the law may have made special provision to the contrary."

All this may be true, and yet we humbly apprehend it will not support the conclusion, that a process by impeachment is unconstitutional.

The records and papers, containing the transactions of the General-Court, having divers times greatly suffered by fire, it is very difficult to apply to them for precedents; nor is it necessary; for if they abounded with them, the first precedent would be, or ought to be, grounded on the reason and nature of the case, which still remain for a guide. But if precedents should be necessary, the most respectable authority (the British parliament) as your Excellency well knows, furnishes a multitude of them. The Commons may exhibit an accusation to the Lords in parliament, by petition, complaint, or impeachment. The House of Representatives are in this province, what the House of Commons are in Britain. The constitutional rights of the latter (among which is indisputably the right of impeachment) belong to the former. Between the House of Lords, and the Council of this province, there is not so near a resemblance: But with respect to legislation, and so far as the Council with or without the Governor are a judiciary body, there is a resemblance. It is now settled by a late determination of his Majesty, that the Governor and Council are a judiciary body, with regard to the Probate of Wills, and granting administration, and for determining causes of marriage and divorce: And it is humbly apprehended they also are, with regard to the removal of all officers from offices, to which appointments are made by the Governor and Council. The impeachment made by the House of Representatives, concludes with praying, "that such proceedings, examinations, trials and judgments may be had and ordered on the premises, as may be agreeable to law and justice." This prayer is consistent with the jurisdiction of the Court; who have lawful power to remove from office, or confirm in it, as may be agreeable to law and justice; and therefore may go into such proceedings, examinations, and trials, and form such judgments in and upon the premises, as are incidental and necessarily preparatory to a final decision. We humbly apprehend therefore your Excellency's reasoning does not extend to the present case: For even though the impeachment had been for such high crimes and misdemeanors, as are made felony, it would not induce, or involve in it, an obligation on the court to give an extrajudicial sentence. An executive officer appointed by the Governor and council may be guilty of crimes, for which by law he is punishable in a variety of ways by the common law courts: If he be impeached for those crimes before the Governor and Council, it is for the purpose of his removal from office, which the other courts have no power to decree. As those courts cannot invade the jurisdiction of the Governor and Council, so the Governor and Council, in any other than their legislative capacity, it is presumed will never attempt to interfere in the jurisdiction of the other courts. It might be supposed the Governor and Council could (and if they act at all they must) trust themselves in the exercise of their jurisdictive powers: Though your Excellency, in reference to that exercise, seems unwilling to trust yourself in the case of the present Impeachment, notwithstanding you consider yourself as having a right of negative on the judgment of the Council. With regard to the Governor's right of negative on the Council, it operates in all acts of government, pursuant to the Charter, "in exclusion of judicial acts," in which it can have no operation: "It being utterly unsuitable to the nature of a court of justice to consist of two branches, each possessing a negative on the other," whereby in many cases, if such was the constitution of the court, it could not give a judgment: Which is incompatible with every idea of a court of justice. On these reasons the late determination of his Majesty in council, with regard to the supreme court of probate, &c. was grounded; and they extend with equal force to the Governor and Council, considered as a court for hearing all complaints, remonstrances and impeachments, relative to the executive officers of the government, and giving judgment thereon, either for or against the defendant, by acquitting him, or removing him from his office.

But it may be objected, that the same power, which appointed, should remove.

On which it may be observed, that the appointment is to a trust for the public good, and vests a property (the lawful emoluments of the office) in the trustee. The mode of appointment is particularly directed by the Charter. It is by the Governor with the advice and consent of the Council; neither of whom act in this matter in a judicial character. But the mode of removal, the Charter being silent about it, must depend on the reason and nature of the thing. These require that the removing power should be considered, and in fact be, a court of justice. Property, both public and private, being depending and to be settled by that power, determine the nature of it to be specifically judicial, or that it must be a court of justice; which excludes the idea of one of its members, where there is a plurality, being an integral part.—There is therefore an essential difference between the appointing and removing power, though consisting of the same persons, when they act in those different characters. To apply this to the Governor and Council,---in the first character they have a reciprocal controul of each other, agreeable to the Charter. In the latter character, there is no such controul, but they together do constitute a court of justice, with powers to form and regulate themselves incidental to all courts, where law has not made provision for that purpose. There is nothing in the Charter inconsistent with this reasoning, but on the contrary, this reasoning is grounded on the Charter. The clause of the Charter, that relates to the subject under consideration runs thus, "The Governor with the assistants or councellors, or seven of them at least, shall and may from time to time hold and keep a council for the ordering and directing the affairs of our said province."---The Governor and Councellors are here blended, and together constitute a council, which in all cases, proper for their cognizance, are jointly (and not as two branches having a negative on each other) authorized and appointed for the ordering and directing the affairs of the province, except in certain cases (particularly mentioned in other parts of the Charter) wherein seven or more councellors are to be advising and assisting to the Governor. The end of this appointment, viz. the ordering and directing the affairs of the province, includes among other things, the removal of bad officers from office, and consequently includes a jurisdiction to hear, try and determine on all complaints, remonstrances and impeachments, for that purpose, which perfectly coincides with the idea of a court of judicature; and therefore, according to the spirit and intention of the Charter, the Governor and Council must have that jurisdiction, without which their power for the well ordering and directing the affairs of the province would be essentially deficient.

Upon the whole, we are humbly of opinion, that although "there are no species of crimes committed within this province, which are not cognizable by some established judicatory"---although "the Governor and Council have no concurrent jurisdiction with any judicatory in criminal cases, nor any authority to try and determine any species of crimes" [except at least for the purpose of removal from office] it does not thence follow, that "the process by impeachment," or the Governor and Council's proceeding and determining upon it, "is unconstitutional;" nor that their so doing "will be an assuming of a new or unwarrantable jurisdiction, and make your Excellency liable to answer for it;" nor that "his Majesty's subjects would have just cause to complain of being deprived of a trial by jury." And we are further of opinion, that a denial of the right of complaining, or remonstrating against, and impeaching for, mal-administration of office, and a refusal to hear and determineon such complaint, remonstrance or impeachment, are unconstitutional; will have an unhappy tendency to encourage the executive officers of the government to deviations from their duty; and are incompatible with the safety and happiness of the people. Wherefore this Board declare their readiness to hear, and determine on the impeachment abovementioned, or to hear and determine on the charge and complaint since exhibited by the House of Representatives on the same subject, and desire that your Excellency with the Council would appoint a time for that purpose.

And on the next Day a Committee of the House of Representatives waited on the Governor with a Message as follows, viz.

May it please your Excellency,

THE House of Representatives have attentively considered your Message of the twenty-sixth of February, in which your Excellency is pleased to say, "That you know of no species of high crimes and misdemeanors, nor of any offences against the law, committed within this province, let the rank of the offenders be what it may, which is not cognizable by some established judicatory or judicatories, and you do not know that the Governor and Council have concurrent jurisdiction with any judicatories in criminal cases, or any authority to try and determine any species of high crimes and misdemeanors whatsoever." And you also add, that "if you should assume a jurisdiction, and with the Council try offenders against the law, without authority granted by the Charter or by a law of the province in pursuance of the Charter, you should make yourself liable to answer," &c.

We assure your Excellency, that as we would not willfully neglect any constitutional endeavours for a redress of grievances which this province labours under, so neither would we desire you to assume any jurisdiction not authorized by the constitution of the province. But your Excellency will allow us to say, that the sentiments advanced in your message, and on which you ground your refusal to comply with our requests, are new and very alarming to us. And as the point in question is of weighty importance to the province, we cannot refrain from freely expressing our minds upon it.

By the charter of this province, the Governor with the advice and consent of the Council, has the sole power of appointing Judges and other civil officers; and though there is no power of removal expressed in the charter, yet such power is necessarily therein implied, and the greatest evils and inconsistencies would arise from a want of it. As no officer ought to hold his office, when his crimes and misdemeanors have rendered him unfit for it, the Governor and Council who have the power of removal, will naturally enquire into the truth of the charges against the officer, previous to the removal; the contrary of which proceedure must suppose, either that an officer *cannot* be, or *is not to be* removed from his office, or else, that he may be removed upon the bare allegation of crimes and misdemeanors, without enquiry into the truth of them; neither of which your Excellency can be supposed to assert. As therefore officers must be removed for crimes and misdemeanors, and previous to such removal there must be an enquiry into the truth of such allegations, such enquiry must involve in it the power of notifying and hearing the officer accused; and it must issue in a judgment and determination, that the officer ought, or ought not, to be removed.

This proceedure, necessarily involved in the power of appointing officers, is in essence a judicatory; and to this purpose the Governor and Council must have cognizance and jurisdiction of crimes and misdemeanors charged upon officers, as it is on the truth of such a charge that the officer is to be removed. This jurisdiction of crimes and misdemeanors, being for a particular purpose, may not be said to be concurrent with the other judicatories; as the only punishment to be inflicted in consequence of conviction is removal, and other judicatories, as the case may be, may take cognizance of such crimes and misdemeanors, and punish them as breaches of law. But, it is not consistent with the dignity and importance of the Governor and Council, vested with the power of removing officers, that they should wait the event of a trial by a jury (which may never take place) before they proceed to enquire into the reasons and necessity of such removal. And we would further observe, that there are high misdemeanors respecting the execution of an office, which may disqualify the officer and render him liable to removal by the power which appoints him, but yet may not be of such a nature as to subject the officer to punishment by the ordinary courts of justice. Should a judge dismiss a Grand Jury soon after their being impanneled, without permitting them to find any bills of presentment---Should he be charged with gross negligence and inattention to the duties of his office, or with great partiality or other corrupt practices, no one, we trust, will say, that such a judge should not be punished: But we do not know that the ordinary courts of judicatory would take cognizance of such offence, neither can we suppose, that the Governor and Council would remove such a judge, without due enquiry into the truth of the charge. From the very nature of our constitution, there must be some where a supreme court who have cognizance of the crimes and misdemeanors of high officers, so far at least, as is necessary for their removal: This supreme court, we take to be the Governor and Council; and to this court are to be presented, all complaints touching the misdemeanors of judges. When complaint is thus made of the crimes and misdemeanors of a judge to the Governor and Council, who have cognizance of his conduct and power of removal, we think the Governor and Council will and ought to enquire into the charge, previous to the removal; and that for this purpose, from the nature and necessity of the thing, the Governor with the Council do "make one Court or justiciary body:" And that, for the same reasons that the Governor and Council are a court for the probate of wills, and deciding controversies concerning marriage and divorce; because, though the removal, in it self considered, may be an act of government, yet, when the proof of misdemeanors is necessary, the enquiring into and determining on such misdemeanors, involves in it, a judicial act, which constitutes a court.

If this be not the true description of our constitution, respecting the removal of officers, we are at a loss to know, of what use the Council are, or what their department is in Council; for, to suppose that the Council, are to be advising and consenting to the removal of an officer, without enquiring into the truth of any charge against him, is inconsistent and incongruous. If it is intirely in the *discretion* of the Governor, whether the misdemeanors of an officer shall be enquired into or not, it is then in the power of the Governor to give a sanction to the most flagrant corruption of a Judge, and by screening a misbehaving officer from examination, to subvert the Justice of the province.

We therefore apprehend, that when a charge is thus made against a Judge before the Governor and Council, it ought to be examined; and if it be not proved, or, if what is proved be not sufficient ground of removal, the determination will be accordingly.

We are not disposed "to ground our construction of the charter on detached paragraphs;" but to consider all the parts, the intents and purview of the whole. And to us it therein appears, that we are expresly intitled to all the liberties enjoyed by the parent state, though "at the distance of three thousand miles from the said parent state"; and that the constitution of our government was designed as "an epitomeof the English constitution"; and that such proceedures as we now pray for, have always been had and used in this government, as the case required.

Your Excellency in your message of the fifteenth of February is pleased, to say, "If you should comply with our request, or take any steps in order to the removal of the chief justice from his place merely for receiving a salary thus granted him by the King, you should make yourself chargeable with counteracting his Majesty, and endeavouring to defeat his Royal intention expresly signified to you, and you should fear some mark of his Royal displeasure"; and therefore you say "In duty to the King you are obliged to decline our request." To this we beg leave to answer; that the articles of impeachment referred to, in your Excellency's message of the twenty sixth of February, and which your Excellency therein signified your refusal to receive, contain *other* matters besides merely receiving the grants of the King; and such matters as the representative body of this province thought themselves in duty bound to complain of to your Excellency and the Council, in order that enquiry and determination might be had thereon. We apprehend that we can clearly prove, that the articles of our complaint, are of the same kind with great numbers made by the House of Commons in England, against high officers. As instances of this kind must be fresh in your Excellency's memory, we think it needless at present to adduce them. And as it never was supposed in England, that the dignity of the King was affected by any charges against his officers, we cannot conceive why it should here; for though it is a maxim, that the King can do no wrong, yet, by the misrepresentations of his officers much wrong hath been and may again be brought to pass. If any person may by his conduct, break through the constitution of the province grounded on the charter and confirmed by constant usage, without being liable to be called to account by any judicatory here, merely because the Royal assent to such construction hath been procured, we do not know where such practices will stop; and we fear, that by degrees, without our even having an opportunity of being heard, one innovation after another may be forced upon us, till there will be not only "an abridgment of what are called English liberties," but a total subversion of the constitution.

We assure ourselves, that were the nature of our grieveances fully understood by our sovereign, we should soon have reason to rejoice in the redress of them. But, if we must still be exposed to the continual false representations of persons who get themselves advanced to places of honour and profit by means of such false representations, and when we complain we cannot even be heard, we have yet the pleasure of contemplating, that posterity for whom we are now struggling will do us justice, by abhoring the memory of those men "who owe their greatness to their country's ruin."

On the 9th Instant his Excellency the Governor, without the usual and Parliamentary Notice from the several Houses of their having finished all the necessary public Business that lay before them, and without allowing himself Time to consider several important Bills which had passed the two Houses, was Pleased to put an End to the Session, after having directed the Secretary to read in each House the following short but very *extraordinary* Message, viz.

Gentlemen of the Council, and
Gentlemen of the House of Representatives,

I Have omitted nothing in my power, consistent with my duty to the King, which had a tendency to promote harmony and good agreement in the legislature, the present session. I have passed over without notice the groundless, unkind and illiberal charges and insinuations made by each of the other branches against the Governor, rather than any part of the publick business of the province should be left unfinished; but as some of your votes, resolves, and other proceedings, which you have suffered to be made publick, strike directly atthe honour and authority of the King and of the Parliament, I may not neglect bearing publick testimony against them, and making use of the powers vested in me by the constitution to prevent you from proceeding any further in the same way.

Province-House,
March 8, 1774.

T. HUTCHINSON.

We are informed that the House of Representatives had some previous Notice of the Governor's Design to put an End suddenly to the Session, and ordered their Door to be locked, till they finished some important Business; among which was a Resolve that they had the Satisfaction of having done all in their Power in the Capacity of Representatives, to effect the Removal of Chief Justice OLIVER, and the Governor's Refusal was presumed to be, "because he himself received his Support from the Crown" independent of the People The Assembly however was prorouged before the House could compleate all the necessary Business.

From the PUBLIC LEDGER, of December 31.

To the PRINTER.

SIR, *Great George-street, December 18, 1773.*

WHEN the malice of my enemies, by falsely impeaching my character, had put me to the hazard of my life, I flattered myself it would have rested silent and satisfied: But as I understand they are still busy with my reputation, and are endeavouring by a thousand misrepresentations to destroy that good name, which to me is inestimable, I am compelled to trouble the public with a detail of those circumstances which obliged me to appeal to the sword. I hope to shew that my conduct in so doing was proper, as far as complying with a custom, the tyranny of which I confess, I have not fortitude to resist, can be justified.

It it with infinite regret I find myself obliged to mention Mr. Whately, and that sometimes in terms of censure. The part he took in the question made me feel myself aggrieved by him. He answered me in the field like a man of spirit and a Gentleman. It is with pleasure I do this justice to his character.

When Mr. Whately was apprized of some original Letters from Gentlemen in America to his late Brother having been sent over and made public at Boston, he called upon me, read part of a Letter from Mr. Oliver, complaining of the publication of his Letters, and mentioned that he had given me access to some of his Brother's Letters from his Correspondents in America. He accompanied this with a declaration, that he had not the least suspicion of me, and did not know that those published Letters were ever in his possession; but he wished I would authorize him to say I had them not from him. I gave Mr. Whately every assurance that a Gentleman could give, that I had not taken any one Letter, nor a line of one, from among those he shewed me, but such as he saw and gave me leave to take, and which were all written by my Brother and myself. I did this repeatedly, and in the most explicit terms. Mr. Whately appeared perfectly satisfied; and I own, I did not expect he would have mentioned that transaction again in any manner that could throw a possibility of suspicion on my character. For in my apprehension, when a Gentlemen has pledged his honor to another, to insinuate, or countenance a suspicion of him afterwards, leads inevitably to the consequences which have attended this transaction. Some time after this explanation between Mr. Whately and myself, several paragraphs appeared in the News-papers highly injurious and dishonourable to me. I was held forth as a monster of ingratitude, and as a villain, who, under the cover of friendship, watched for an opportunity, when Mr. Whately's back was turned, to rob him of papers which were in confidence put into my hands. Of these things I took no public notice, not because they gave me no uneasiness, but because I knew not how to redress myself. A search after the Authors of them I conceived would be vain. Such malevolent attacks could have been made by none but cowards, who would take care to conceal themselves. It seemed impossible that Mr. Whately could have had any knowledge of the Authors, or could have given any countenance to such aspersions, after the solemn assurances which I had given him; nor should I have troubled him on the subject if his name had not been used as an authority to support these false and malicious assertions.------These Writers artfully suppressed three very material circumstances in their representations; that Mr. Whately did not know the Letters sent to Boston were ever in his possession; that of those which he put into my hands none appeared to be missing, which could not have been the case if seventeen Letters, and some of them very long, had been taken away; and that I had given him every assurance which a Gentleman could require or receive, that no such Letters had been taken by me. Without the use of Mr. Whately's name, the charge would have had no effect upon the Public. That Gentleman suffered the unfair and injurious representations, under the sanction of his name, to pass unexplained. I not expect when he saw the purpose to which the men who gained intelligence from him were applying it, that he would in justice to truth, and to me, have stated the whole as above. If he had done so, I appeal to the judgment of the Public, whether any suspicion would have rested upon me, or any serious consequences followed. I did not ask this of him, because I thought he ought to have done it unasked. There is an indelicacy in urging a Gentleman to do that which is his duty, and owes its merit to its being voluntary.-- ---The suspicion against me upon so unfair a state of facts, aided, I suppose, by the private slanders of those who raised it, secretly gained ground; and on the 8th of this month a Writer, under the Signature of *Antenor*, renewed the accusation of me by name, vouching it with a conversation which he seems to have himself held upon the subject with Mr. Whately.

Under so direct a charge, I thought it would not become me to be any longer silent. I went with the paper to Mr. Whately, and received from him, as I imagined, a satisfactory denial of those pretended facts, which materially supported the suspicion. This I made public: Mr. Whately then came forward with his name. He omitted to state what was solely essential, that he did not know the Letters in question were among those he put into my hands, and that none of those with which he had entrusted me appeared to be missing, but related the matter in such a manner as strongly to corroborate the anonymous charge, and gave me, to my understanding, the lie direct. They who have any feelings of honor will not wonder that I was impatient under such an imputation, and thought every moment miserable, till I had called upon him, from whom I received such an affront, for honorable amends. The Public is acquainted with the sequel: But the circumstances of that affair have been so falsely represented to my dishonor, that I am obliged to beg a moment's indulgence, till I state that transaction fairly.

The Gentleman, who waited upon Mr. Whately with my invitation, told him he would attend me as a Second, if Mr. Whately would have one on his part. Mr. Whately declined having any Second, and therefore I brought none. He appeared at the place appointed with a sword only. I gave him one of my pistols. We discharged them mutually; mine being, at his request the first, without effect. If his was not directed at me, it escaped my observation. I then drew my sword, and approached him, who had also unsheathed his, with a persuasion, grounded on his coming with a sword only, when the choice of weapons was in him, that I was to encounter an adversary much superior to myself in skill. I soon found my mistake; and, as far as I could reason in such a situation, determined, by wounding him in the sword-arm, to end the business, without a fatal stroke, But my skill was not equal to my intention; it soon became a struggle, instead of a regular combat, and I could only avoid making a full lange, which probably would have wounded him mortally. The contortions of my antagonist's body, during the struggle, exposed parts, which in a regular encounter could never have been touched. When he turned himself to seize the blade of my sword, with his left hand, I supposed he received the wounds in his left side; and in some violent effort his shoulder must have been exposed. The extreme smallness of the wound in that part being, as I am well informed, a mere puncture, proves it to have been accidental. Had my purpose been unfair, I should have taken the life that was in my power; had it been mortal, every wound would not have been superficial, and one only dangerous, not from its depth, but its direction. I understand it has been said he was down. In such circumstances it is as impossible to account for every thing that happens, as to remember every thing that passes. But of this I am very sure, that, though he slipt once, he never fell.

It is proper to apprize the reader that I am unfortunately very deaf. If any words of accommodation, as has been represented, were really used by Mr. Whately, I did not hear them. They who expect coolness in the midst of such a conflict, and deliberation in the moment of a deadly point being at one's breast, require too much. It is well that the passion, which rises fast on such an occasion, did not alter imperceptibly my general determination not to push so forcibly as to make a deep wound. It is with confidence I can affirm, I was not guilty of any unfair action, because I never had an unfair thought—nor of a cruel one, because my purpose was the reverse.

I have received no bodily wound; but they whose minds can feel for consequences, which they could not with honor avoid, will understand me when I say, that I have felt those wounds which far surpass in anguish every bodily pain.

The anonymous assassins, who have been really the cause of this mischief, remain unknown; but time, I trust, will drag them forth to the punishment they deserve.

Of those to whom I am unknown, the candid and honorable, are, I hope, convinced, that the injurious charges which have been brought against me, are totally without foundation.—With those to whom I am known, I flatter myself, the constant tenor of my life has rendered a defence of my conduct unnecessary.

I have but a few words more to say up on the subject.—As Mr. Whately's narrative tends to confirm the suspicion of my having taken from him the letters which were sent to Boston, I do again most solemnly affirm, that I neither took from him those, nor any other letters, but such as were written by my brother and myself to the late Mr. Whately, and that with his knowledge and consent; nor had I any concern, directly or indirectly, in procuring or transmitting the letters which were sent to Boston.

J. TEMPLE.

Russia Duck, best Petersburgh Hemp, Dutch Rope Yarns, also a Quantity of *choice Junk*, fit to make into Cordage of any Size, great part of which will do for rigging small Vessels without working over—

To be Sold at *Thomas Walley's* Store on Dock-Square,

—Where is to Sell by Wholesale or Retail—

Dutch Looking Glasses of various Sizes,
Dutch Brushes, single or by the sett,
Hampers Stone Ware, viz. Qt. & Pt. Mugs and Chamber Pots,
A few Casks Choice Rice,
All sorts of Spices *very low*, *Oatmeal per Bushel*,
A parcel of fine Narraganset and Pomfret Cheese,
New Raisins, Currants, and all sorts of Groceries as usual——*Except TEA.*

N. B. A Quantity of choice 3 threaded Sein Twine, for Salmon, Mackrel or Herring Nets.

ALSO, White Beans per Bushel.

All Persons indebted to the Estate of John Ruddock, *late of Boston, Esq; deceas'd, are desired to settle the same with* Abiel Ruddock, *Administrator, or they will be Sued at next April Court: And all who have any demands on said Estate, are desired to bring their Accounts to said Administrator for Adjustment.*

To be SOLD at the Store of

ABIEL RUDDOCK,

At the North End, cheap for Cash or short Credit,

St. Martins Salt, Lignum Vitæ, Anchors, Grapling WhaleWarp, Whale IronLances, Blubber, Hooks and Spades, a Slay and Harness, an Engine in good Order with it's Appurtenances; and also a Brig of 105 Tons, Boston Built, about Four Years old, has always been in the Whale Fishery: Also a Sloop of 84 Tons, about Five Years old, both in good Order.

GUN POWDER.

Choice Gun Powder just Imported in Capt. GORHAM, And to be SOLD by

Amory's, Taylor & Rogers,

At their Store in Marlborough Street, where may be had as usual a general Assortment of

English, India and Hard Ware GOODS on reasonable Terms by Wholesale and Retail——

——VELVET CORKS.——

A few Casks of very good Sherry Wine, and a few Hogsheads of old West-India Rum, to be sold Cheap at *Nathaniel & William Coffins* Store.

John & Eleanor Druitt,

Most respectfully acquaint their Friends and the Public, they continue to keep School as usual, in Hanover-Street, near Concert-Hall.

JOHN DRUITT, Instructs Young Ladies in the Rudiments of English, Epistolary-writing, Writing, and Arithmetick:—for their more speedy Improvement, intends to devote himself intirely to their Service, and not take Boys.

ELEANOR DRUITT, Instructs them in French Grammatically, Reading English, and Orthography; likewise the following Needleworks, viz

Point, Brussells, (Gold, Silver and Silk) Embroidery's, Dresden, Tambour, Feather-Stitch, & Darning, with a great variety of Open-work; Tapestry, Catgut, diaper and plain Darning, Knitting, Marking, Plain-work and Baby-linnen, &c.

As it has been apprehended by some Ladies, that said *Druitt* don't teach Plain-work; now Informs them she does, and with equal care and assiduity, as she performs the rest of her undertakings.

They tender their most grateful thanks to those who have favour'd them with the care of their Children; and assures the Public, they will exert their utmost abilities in the improvement of their Pupils.

It has been rumour'd, they were leaving the Province; but is intirely false.

TO BE SOLD

By Joseph Hall,

At his Shop in *Cole-Lane*,

New-England and *West-India* RUM, by Wholesale and Retail; Old Jamaica Spirits, Brandy, Madeira, Teneriff, Malaga, and Claret WINES, by the Gallon & Kegg, Cinnamon, Clove, Annisееd, Snakeroot and Orange WATERS; GENEVA by the Gallon; LEMMONS by the Box, Hundred or Dozen; and a few Firkins of BUTTER.

HABIJAH SAVAGE

HAS for Sale at his Store No. 16. on the Long Wharff,

A Quantity of FLOUR just arrived, new Rice, Cocoa, West-India & New-England Rum, French Brandy, Loaf and Brown Sugar, Cotton Wool, Indigo, Coffee, Window Glass, Pipes, Cases with Bottles, Case Bottles, Red Wood, Log Wood, Brimstone, and a Quantity of Corn, &c.

N. B. Fifty Barrells FLOUR light, fit for the West-Indies.

PUBLICK AUCTION.

On TUESDAY the 29th MARCH will be Sold by PUBLICK AUCTION, at the Dwelling House of Mr. JOHN MICO WENDELL, deceas'd, a variety of Houshold Furniture—consisting of—

Tables, Chairs, Pier Glasses, Mehogony Case of Draws, Beauros, Feather Beds, Bedsteads, Houshold Linnen, Kitchen Furniture, Plate. &c.

The Sale will begin at 9 o'Clock, A. M.

PUBLIC VENDUE of House Furniture,

On WEDNESDAY next, the 16th Instant, at NINE o'Clock will be sold by PUBLIC VENDUE, at the Dwelling-House of the Widow ELIZABETH HEWES, deceas'd, near Trinity-Church, in Summer-Street; All the Household Furniture of said deceas'd, consisting of

A good Eight-Day Clock, Looking-Glasses, Chest of Draws, Tables, Chairs, Beds and Bedding, sundry Pieces of Plate, Glass, China and Delph Ware, Andirons, Shovels and Tongs, a good Jack, Pewter, Brass, and sundry Kitchen Furniture.

Wm. GREENLEAF, Auctioneer.

The Furniture may be viewed the Day before the Sale.

TO BE SOLD,

Laying in the Province of *New Hampshire*,

Three valuable Tracts of Land, consisting chiefly of Interval and high Interval Land, the Growth of which is mostly Rockmaple, Beach and yellow Birch Trees, containing in the Whole about 4000 Acres, lying on *Saco* and *Ellis's* Rivers, distant from *Falmouth* about 50 Miles, from *Dover* about 45 Miles, from *Frye's*-Town only 8 Miles: Each Tract lying on a County Road. For further Particulars inquire of WILLIAM GREENLEAF of Boston.

TO BE SOLD OR LETT,

A good FARM in Newton, and entered upon the first Day of April, containing One Hundred Acres of good Land, with a House and Barn thereon, all in good Repair, well proportioned for Mowing, Plowing and Orcharding, &c. with a Stream that runs thro' said Farm, never known to be dry.—For further Particulars inquire of Abraham Fuller, Esq; living near said Farm, or of Amariah Fuller, living on said Premises.

MILLENARY.

Sundry Articles of MILLENARY to be Sold at Mrs. MECOM's, a little to the Northward of Concert-Hall, opposite GREENLEAF's Printing-Office; Sattins of the newest Fashion for Cloaks and Bonnets, the nicest chip Hats and the common Sort for covering. An Assortment of genteel Ribbons, Persians, Allamodes, Sewing Silk, Muslins, Gloves and Mits, Gimp-trimings, Gauzes, Blond Lace & Edgings, black ditto, Cap-wire, Tooth-brushes, Silk Laces for Stays, Pins, Needles, Threads, Tapes, Bindings, Durants and Tammies. Also, ready-made Caps and Hoods, &c. &c. &c.

☞ ALL Sorts of MILLENARY Work done with Care and Expedition, as usual.

All Persons indebted to, or that have any Demands on the Estate of Mr. Edward Brick, jun. late of Dorchester, Yeoman, deceas'd, are desired to bring in their Accounts to Dr. Thomas Williams, of Roxbury, Administrator, in Order for Settlement.

Whereas the Copartnership of Simon Whipple and Company is mutually Dissolved—These are to Desire all Persons that have Accounts open, and are indebted to said Company, to settle and pay the same as soon as may be; and those that have any Demands on said Company, are desired to apply to Simon Whipple, who will discharge them immediately.

⁂ Choice St. Georges Stone Lime, to be sold by WHIPPLE and WHEATON, at Dawes's Wharff.

WANTED TO HIRE,

A Sloop or Schooner, between 50 and 60 Tons Burthen. Enquire of CHARLES LOW, in Marshall's Lane, opposite the Boston Stone, near the Mill-Bridge.

Just IMPORTED, and TO BE SOLD by

John Decosta

In Milk-Street, a little below the Old South Meeting House; Beans, Peas, and a Variety of other Garden Seeds; Fresh and Good; also a Variety of young Fruit Trees, Grafted and Innoculated; also Roots and Plants, all at Reasonable Rates.

TO BE SOLD

AT PUBLICK AUCTION,

By Benjamin Church

At his usual Place of Sale,

On Thursday the 17th Day of March,

Sundry Goods belonging to the Estate of Capt. *Henry Oman*, late deceas'd——consisting of——

Tammies, Durants, Callamancoes, Crapes, Dorseteens, Poplins, Persians, Sattins, Ribbons, Irish Linnens, Checks, German Serges, printed Handkerchiefs, Velverets, Worsted Plushes, striped Damascus, Moree Gowns, Threads, Qualities, Pins, also a Variety of Wearing Apparel, and sundry other Articles.

N. B. The Sale to begin at 10 o'Clock, A. M.

Wanted a Quantity of Thrumbs for the Caulkers Business, for which cash will be given; also to be SOLD a few Puncheons, and forty Gallon Casks of old choice Jamaica Rum. Inquire of the Printers.

WANTED,

A Boy about 14 or 15 Years old, to a Mason's Trade. Inquire of the Printers.

By Virtue of an Act of the General Court, in the Province of New-Hampshire, the Proprietors of the Lands in Francestown, formerly New-Boston adition, are desired to Pay the Tax due, by Virtue of said Act, unto John Quigly, *Esq; who is empowered to Collect the same, in Order for Building a Meeting House in said Town, the Tax being One Pound Five Shillings, Lawful Money, on the Lott or Hundred Acres: And if the said Tax is not paid on, or before the Eleventh Day of April, so much of the Delinquents Land will be Sold at Public Vendue as will Pay the Taxes with cost of Sale, at the House of* Mr. Pierce, *Innholder in Groton, on Monday the 11th Day of April, at* 3 *o'Clock in the Afternoon of said Day.*

Francestown March 7, 1774.

WHEREAS the Proprietors of Land in the Township of *Leicester* on *Otter Creek*, (which Township was granted by the Governor and Council of New-Hampshire) did at their Meeting in January 1773, Vote, That the Sum of Four Dollars should be raised and levied on each original Right; and also at their Meeting in March following, Voted, That the Sum of One Dollar as aforesaid, for the Bounding and Lotting out said Township, and for the managing and carrying on any other Affairs for the common Good of said Propriety, and that a Committee be appointed to assess the same.—Therefore we the Subscribers being appointed a Committee for the Purpose aforesaid, do a third Time notify the Proprietors to pay the same to Mr. Isaac Stone, Collector, or to Capt. Elisha Child, Treasurer, at or before the adjourn'd Meeting of said Propriety, which will be on the last Tuesday in April, which will be the 26th Day of said Month, at Nine o'Clock in the Morning, at the House of Nathaniel Child, Esq; of Woodstock, in the County of Windham, and Colony of Connecticut; otherwise their Rights will be exposed to Sale, at the House of the said Nathaniel Child, Esq; at Ten o'Clock on said Day, according to Law.

Woodstock, March 3, 1773.

Nathaniel Child,
Elisha Child,
Samuel McClelland. } Committee.

THE original Proprietors of a Township called Pennicook, now Concord, and the original Proprietors of a Township called Suncook, now Pembroke, (both in the Province of New-Hampshire) or the Heirs or Assigns of said original Proprietors; are hereby Notified that the General Court in their present Session, hath granted to each Propriety a Township in the late Province of Main, and appointed the Subscribers a Committee to exhibit a List to said Court, within 10 Months from the Date, of the Names of the Persons that have been Sufferers who have a just Claim to an Interest in the one or the other of said Townships:—This is therefore to give Notice to the said Pennicook Proprietors, and the said Suncook Proprietors, that the Committee will attend said Service at the House of Mrs. Hannah Osgood, Innholder in said Pennicook, on the second Wednesday in October next, ensuing, to receive authenticated Evidence of said Sufferers Claims to an interest in the Township granted to the said Pennicook Proprietors, and that they will attend said Service at the House of Mr. Samuel Conner, Innholder in said Suncook, on the third Wednesday in October aforesaid, to receive like Evidence of the said Sufferers Claims to an Interest in the Township granted to the said Suncook Proprietors.

Feb. 22, 1774.

Samuel Phillips,
Joseph Gerrish,
Jonathan Webster } Committee.

(*Advertisements omitted will be in our next.*

CUSTOM-HOUSE, *BOSTON.*

ENTETRD IN.

Nicolson. Jamaica and Cape Nichola; Orne, Guadaloup and St. Eustatia; Caswell, Madeira; Cockran, Folger, Eldridge and Howes, Cape Nichola; Ayres, Grenades and St. Lucia; Rich, Hopkins, White, Ridley, Collings, Godfrey and Pulling, North-Carolina; Smith and Paine, Maryland; Summers, Hawley and Burroughs, New-Haven.

Burials in the Town of BOSTON, since our last.

Eight Whites. Three Blacks.

Baptiz'd in the several Churches, Nine.

High Water at BOSTON, *for the present Week.*

Monday, 26 min. aft. 7	Friday, 54 min. after 10
Tuesday, 21 min. aft. 8	Saturday, 38 min. aft. 11
Wednesday, 15 m. aft. 9	Lord's-Day, 16m. aft. 12
Thursday, 5 min. aft. 10	☽'s New 12 Day 5 Morn.

Boston: Printed, by EDES & GILL

THE Boston-AND COUNTRY Gazette, JOURNAL.

Containing the freshest Advices, Foreign and Domestic.

MONDAY, March 21, 1774.

No. 989.

Written at the Request of a Gentleman, (who described the late Sacrifice of TEA to the public Welfare,) as a squabble among the Cœlestials of the Sea, arising from a Scarcity of Nectar and Ambrosia.

Bright Phœbus drove, his rapid Carr, amain
But baits his Steeds, beyond the Western Plain;
Behind a Golden-skirted Cloud to rest,
E'er Ebon Night had spread her sable Vest;
And drawn her Curtain o'er the fragrant Vale
Or Cynthia's Shadow, drest the lonely Dale.

The Hero's of the Tuskarora Tribe,
Who scorn alike a Fetter or a Bribe:
In order rang'd, and waiting Freedom's Nod,
To make an Offering to the wat'ry God.
Grey Neptune rising, from his Sea-green Bed,
Wav'd his bright Trident, o'er his ousy Head:
Stretching from Shore to Shore, his regal Wand
Bids all the River Deities attend.
But lest Refusal, from some distant Dame
Tryton's, hoarse Clarion, summon'd them by Name.
In Council met t' adjust Affairs of State,
Among their Godships rose a warm Debate,
What luscious Draught, they next should substitute,
That might the Palates of Cœlestials suit.
As Nectar's Stream, no more, meand'ring rolls,
And rich Ambrosia, quaff'd in flowing Bowls
Profusely's spent; nor can Scamander's Shore,
Yield the fair, Sea Nymphs, one short Banquet more.

The Titan's all, with one accord, arous'd,
To Travail o'er Columba's Coast, propos'd
To rob and plunder, ev'ry neighb'ring Vine,
Regardless of Nemisis sacred Shrine.
Nor leave untouch'd the Peasant's little Store,
Or think of Right, while Demi-Gods have Pow'r.

But they on no Alternative agreed,
Nor e'en great Neptune further could proceed;
'Till ev'ry Goddess of the Streams and Lakes,
And lesser Deities of Fens and Brakes,
With all the Nymphs that Swim, around the Isles
Deign to give Sanction, by approving Smiles;
For Females have their Influence o'er Kings,
Nor Wives, nor Mistresses, were useless Things.
E'en to the Gods, of ancient Homer's Page,
Nor when in weighty Matters they engage:
Could they neglect the Sex's sage Advice,
And least of all in any Point so nice,
As to forbid the choice Ambrosial Sip,
And offer Bohea to the rosy Lip?
Proud Amphitrite rejects it, in disdain
Refus'd the Gift, and quits the wat'ry Main,
With servile Proteus lagging by her side
To take Advantage of the shifting Tide,
To catch a smile, or pick up golden Sands
Either from Plutus, or the naked Strands,
Long practic'd, easy he assumes the shape
Of Fox, of Panther, Crokodile, or Ape:
If 'tis his Interest, his Step-dame he'll aid
One Pebble more, and Amphitrites betray'd.

A flaming Torch she took in either Hand
And as fell Discord, reign'd thro'out the Land,
Was well appriz'd the Centaurs would conspire
Resolv'd to set the Northern World on Fire,
By scattering the Weeds of Indian Shores
Or else to lodge them in Pigmalion's Stores,
But if the Artifice should not succeed,
Then in Revenge attempt some bolder Deed:
For while old Ocean's mighty Billows roar,
Or foaming Surges lash the distant Shore;
Shall Goddesses regale, like Woodland Dames,
First let Chinesean Herbage feed the Flames.
But all the Nereads, whisper'd Murmurs round,
And craggy Cliffs, re-echo back the Sound
Till fair Salacia, perch'd upon the Rocks,
The rival Goddess, waves her yellow Locks
Proclaims, that HYSON, shall assuage their Grief
With choice SOUCHONG, and the Imperial Leaf.

The Hero's of the Tuskarora Race
(Who neither hold, nor even wish for Place)
While Faction reigns, and Tyranny presides
And base Oppression o'er the Virtues rides,
While venal Measures dance in Silken Sails
And Avarice, o'er Sea and Earth prevails,
And Luxury, creates such mighty Feuds,
E'en in the Bosoms of the Demi-Gods)
Lent their strong Arm, in pity to the fair,
To aid, the bright Salacia's generous Care,
Pour'd a Profusion of delicious Teas,
Which wafted by a soft favonian Breeze
Supply'd the wat'ry Deities in Spite
Of all the Rage of jealous Amphitrite.
The fair Salacia, *Vict'ry! Vict'ry!* sings
In spite of Heroes, Demigods, and Kings!
She bids Defiance, to the servile Train
The Pimps, and Sychophants of G——'s Reign
The virtuous Daughters of the neighbouring Mead
In graceful Smiles, approve the glorious Deed,
And (tho' the Syrens left their coral Beds)
Just o'er the Surface lifted up their Heads,
And sung soft Pæans to the brave and fair,
'Till almost caught in the delusive Snare,
To sink securely in a Golden Dream,
And taste the sweet inebriating Stream:
Which tho' a Repast for the wa'try Naiades
Is baneful Poison to the mountain Dryades
They saw, delighted, from the Inland Rocks
O'er the broad Deep, pour'd out Pandora's Box,
And join Salacia Victory to sing,
Ocean rebounds, and Songs of Triumph ring,
From Southern Rivers, down to Northern Rills,
And spreads Confusion round NEPONSIT Hills.

TO BE SOLD,
A new Vessel about 60 Tons burthen, new on the Stocks at Cohasset, may be launched within a Month. For further Particulars, enquire of BRECK and HAMMETT, at their Store the Head of GREEN'S Wharff, or of DANIEL TOWER at Cohasset.

TO BE SOLD and entered upon immediately,
A House in Milton, with a Malt House and five Acres of Orcharding and Mowing Land, about 10 Miles distant from Boston, and 2 from the Meeting-House, on the main Road that leads to Stoughton. It is known by the Name of Samuel Soper's, lately tenanted by Rufus Bent. Any Person inclining to Purchase may apply to Ralph Inman, Esq; at his Warehouse in Boston.

TO BE SOLD,
A Farm lying on Squanton-Neck, late the Estate of Remember Preston, deceased, containing about 50 Acres of good Land, with a House and Barn thereon. For further Particulars, enquire of John Preston of Boston, or of Ebenezer Baker of Dorchester.

TAKEN up on Monday last, a Moses Boat, about 8 or 9 Feet Keel, almost new, painted red, with an Iron Loop to set the Mast in, Straps in the Stern with Iron. Whoever has lost the same, may have Information of her, by inquiring of the Printers.

A Wet Nurse, with a good Breast of Milk, would take a Child to suckle. Inquire of the Printers.

WHEREAS the Proprietors of Land in the Township of Leicester on Otter Creek, (which Township was granted by the Governor and Council of New-Hampshire) did at their Meeting in January 1773. Vote, That the Sum of Four Dollars should be raised and levied on each original Right; and also at their Meeting in March following, Voted, That the Sum of One Dollar as aforesaid, for the Bounding and Lotting out said Township, and for the managing and carrying on any other Affairs for the common Good of said Propriety, and that a Committee be appointed to assess the same.—Therefore we the Subscribers being appointed a Committee for the Purpose aforesaid, do a third Time notify the Proprietors to pay the same to Mr. Isaac Stone, Collector, or to Capt. Elisha Child, Treasurer, at or before the adjourn'd Meeting of said Propriety, which will be on the last Tuesday in April, which will be the 26th Day of said Month, at Nine o'Clock in the Morning, at the House of Nathaniel Child, Esq; of Woodstock, in the County of Windham, and Colony of Connecticut; otherwise their Rights will be exposed to Sale, at the House of the said Nathaniel Child, Esq; at Ten o'Clock on said Day, according to Law.

Woodstock,   Nathaniel Child,
March 3,   Elisha Child, } Committee.
1773.   Samuel McClelland,

WANTED,
A Boy about 14 or 15 Years old, to a Mason's Trade. Inquire of the Printers.

Russia Duck, best Petersburgh Hemp, Dutch Rope Yarns, also a Quantity of choice Junk, fit to make into Cordage of any Size, great part of which will do for rigging small Vessels without working over—
To be Sold at *Thomas Walley's* Store on Dock-Square,
—Where is to Sell by Wholesale or Retail—
Dutch Looking Glasses of various Sizes,
Dutch Brushes, single or by the sett,
Hampers Stone Ware, viz. Qt. & Pt. Mugs and Chamber Pots,
A few Casks Choice Rice,
All sorts of Spices very low, Oatmeal per Bushel,
A parcel of fine Narraganset and Pomfret Cheese,
New Raisins, Currants, and all sorts of Groceries as usual—Except TEA.
N. B. A Quantity of choice 3 threaded Sein Twine, for Salmon, Mackrel or Herring Nets.
ALSO, White Beans per Bushel.

THE original Proprietors of a Township called Pennicook, now Concord, and the original Proprietors of a Township called Suncook, now Pembroke, (both in the Province of New-Hampshire) or the Heirs or Assigns of said original Proprietors; are hereby Notified that the General Court in their present Session, hath granted to each Propriety a Township in the late Province of Main, and appointed the Subscribers a Committee to exhibit a List to said Court, within 10 Months from the Date, of the Names of the Persons that have been Sufferers who have a just Claim to an Interest in the one or the other of said Townships:—This is therefore to give Notice to the said Pennicook Proprietors, and the said Suncook Proprietors, that the Committee will attend said Service at the House of Mrs. Hannah Osgood, Innholder in said Pennicook, on the second Wednesday in October next, ensuing, to receive authenticated Evidence of said Sufferers Claims to an interest in the Township granted to the said Pennicook Proprietors, and that they will attend said Service at the House of Mr. Samuel Conner, Innholder in said Suncook, on the third Wednesday in October aforesaid, to receive like Evidence of the said Sufferers Claims to an Interest in the Township granted to the said Suncook Proprietors.

Feb. 22, 1774.   Samuel Phillips, Joseph Gerrish, Jonathan Webster, } Committee.

By Virtue of an Act of the General Court, in the Province of New-Hampshire, the Proprietors of the Lands in Francestown, formerly New-Boston addition, are desired to Pay the Tax due, by Virtue of said Act, unto John Quigly, Esq; who is empowered to Collect the same, in Order for Building a Meeting House in said Town, the Tax being One Pound Five Shillings, Lawful Money, on the Lott or Hundred Acres: And if the said Tax is not paid on, or before the Eleventh Day of April so much of the Delinquents Land will be Sold at Public Vendue as will Pay the Taxes with cost of Sale, at the House of Mr. Pierce, Innholder in Groton, on Monday the 11th Day of April, at 3 o'Clock in the Afternoon of said Day.

Francestown March 7, 1774.

TO BE SOLD,
Laying in the Province of New Hampshire, Three valuable Tracts of Land, consisting chiefly of Interval and high Interval Land, the Growth of which is mostly Rockmaple, Beach and yellow Birch Trees, containing in the Whole about 4000 Acres, lying on Saco and Ellis's Rivers, distant from Falmouth about 50 Miles, from Dover about 45 Miles, from Frye's Town only 8 Miles. Each Tract lying on a County Road. For further Particulars inquire of WILLIAM GREENLEAF of Boston.

GARDEN SEEDS.
IMPORTED in Capt. HOOD from LONDON, and Sold
By ANN JOHNSON,
At the Head of Black-Horse Lane, near the Rev. Dr. Pemberton's Meeting-House:
A large Assortment of
GARDEN SEEDS,
Peas, Beans, &c. among which are,
EARLY charlton, early golden hospur, Ormand hotspur, Spanish moratto, white rouncival, dwarf marrowfat and bush pease, large Windsor, true early Lisbon, early yellow six weeks white kidney and six o'clock beans, early Yorkshire, Dutch Sugar loaf, battersea, savoy, red and brocoli cabbage seed, coliflower, cucumber, onion, carrot, turnip, raddish and lettice of all sorts, round spinnage, endive, cellery and asparagus, thyme, baum, sweet marjoram, broad clover, white Dutch clover, la lucern, rape, canary, and an assortment of flower seeds: Also a variety of other seeds not mentioned; all which are imported from the seedsmen in London, and are warranted to be fresh & good, and of the last year's produce.

On Thursday next,

At Ten o'Clock, will be sold by Public Vendue, at the New Auction Office, South Side of the Town House,

HOUSE Furniture, consisting of Mehogany Chest on Chest of Draws, Desks, dining, spring, bureau and card Tables, Mehogany stiff-back Chairs, Leather and Straw Bottom ditto, Black Walnut Chest of Draws, Dining and Chamber Tables, Feather Beds, Bedsteads, and Coverlids, Brass Andisons, large Brass Kettles, Copper Dish Kettles, Iron Skillets and Sauce-pans, Frying Pans, Green Harrateen lazy Chairs.—Also, Broad Cloths, Bearskins, Ratteens, Irish Linnens, Mill'd Caps, Shalloons, Jersey knit Hose, Worsted Caps, Chip Hatts, all sorts of colour'd Cruels, Eye Glasses small and large, and a number of other Articles.

A. OLIVER, Auctioneer.

Just Imported from London in Capt. Gorham, and sold

By Rebeckah Walker,

At her Shop at the Bottom of Black-Horse Lane, over against Mr. Harrod's turning down to Charlestown Ferry

A fresh Assortment of Garden SEEDS, of the last Year's Produce, viz.

EARLY Golden Hotspur Peas, early Charlton, large Marrowfats, dwarf Marrowfats, early Ormond Hotspurs, early Masters Hotspurs, Spanish Moratto, Leadman's dwarf Peas, large Winsor Beans, early Lisbon, early yellow Dwarf, and several other Sorts of Beans, early Yorkshire Cabbage Seed, early Dutch, early Sugar Loaf, early Battersea, large Winter Cabbage, red Cabbage, Savoy Cabbage, Spanish Onions, Silver Skin ditto, several Sorts of Carrot Seeds, several Sorts of Lettice Seed, Swelling Parsnip, scarlet and Salmon Raddish, early and late Cucumber, early and late Turnip, double-curl Parsley, double-curl Pepper-Grass, early and late Colliflower, Summer Savory, white Mustard, red Beat, Summer Spinage, Sweet Marjoram, hard Thyme, Sage, Cellery and Endive, Carraway and Corriander Seed, Hemp, Rape, Canary Seed and Split Peas.

NEW-YORK, March 10.

Tuesday afternoon arrived, in 6 weeks and 5 days, from Falmouth, the Mercury Packet-Boat, Captain Dillon, by whom we have the following Advices.

LONDON.

Jan. 11. It is said, that the French King is in a state of mind very little removed from idiotcy or insensibility, so much, that neither the charms of his favorite's conversation, nor the pleasures of the chace, are capable of rouzing him. This, it is said, has caused several cabals, and given birth to a spirit of intrigue extremely alarming to the mistress and the minister.

It is now generally believed that the Parliament will not be dissolved till March twelvemonth.

Extract of a Letter from Warsaw, Dec. 15

"WE have just now received a full and authentic confirmation of the great and important victory gained by the Russian army on the other side the Danube, over the army of the Grand Vizir on the 16th ult. The whole Turkish grand army being defeated, the Russians made themselves masters of all the Turkish artillery, baggages, and military chest, to an immense value. The Grand Vizir was missing, and it was reported, and generally believed (when the courier who brought the intelligence from the army came away) that he is among the number of the dead. The Russians were still in pursuit of the enemy; and the rest of the Russian army who were yet on this side of the Danube, have received orders to pass the river, and give the last blow to the enemy. The garrison at Silistria are at present left to themselves, without the least hope of receiving succour from the Turkish army; nor are the fugitive Turks able to fly into that fortress, as all the passes are cut off by the Turks, which give the Russians great hopes of being masters of that important fortress very soon, which will open the passage to Adrianople; so that there is the greatest reason to hope, that the present winter campaign will finish the struggle, before the Turks are able to compose themselves; and in all probability, the Porte will be obliged to comply with the terms of peace proposed by Russia in the late congress, before the expiration of another month, unless some Christian powers (as is expected) should throw off the mask, and publicly declare themselves for the Porte; against which event not less than half a million of Austrian and Prussian troops are in readiness."

Proceedings of the Town of HINGHAM.

At a legal Town-Meeting held at Hingham, on the 31st Day of January, A. D. 1774, the Town appointed a Committee to take into Consideration a Letter sent to them by the Committee of Correspondence of the Town of Boston; as also a Number of Papers inclos'd, and Report to the Town at the Adjournment; and then the Meeting was adjourned to the Annual Meeting in March next. The Town being met according to Adjournment, their Committee Reported as follows, viz.

WHEN we call to mind a late Act of the British Parliament, expresly declaring, That the King, Lords and Commons, in Parliament assembled, "have, ever had, and of Right ought to have full Power and Authority to make Laws and Statutes of sufficient force and validity to bind the Colonies and People of America, subject to the Crown of Great-Britain, in all Cases whatever": And in Consequence thereof an Act of Parliament made for the express Purpose of raising a Revenue in America, for defraying the Charge of the Administration of Justice, &c. in the Colonies. And when we also consider that the more effectually to carry into execution the same Act, the Councils of the Nation, in a late Session of the British Parliament, have empowered the East-India Company to export their Teas into America, free of all Duties in England, but still liable to a Duty on its being landed in the Colonies. And comparing those Acts and others similar to them, with several Clauses in the Charter granted to this Province, by their late Majesties King William and Queen Mary of blessed Memory; in which it is among other Things established and ordained, that "all and every of the Subjects of us, our Heirs and Successors, which shall go to Inhabit in our said Province and Territory, and every of their Children which shall happen to be born there, or on the Seas in going thither, or returning from thence, shall have and enjoy, all Liberties and Immunities of free and natural born Subjects within any of the Dominions of us, our Heirs and Successors, TO ALL INTENTS, CONSTRUCTIONS AND PURPOSES WHATEVER, as if they and every of them were born within this our Realm of England." And whereas by the said Royal Charter it is also especially ordained, that the GREAT AND GENERAL COURT OR ASSEMBLY therein constituted, shall have full Power and Authority to impose and levy proportionable & reasonable assessments, Rates and Taxes, upon the Estates and Persons of all and every of the Proprietors and Inhabitants of the said Province and Territory, for the service of the King, in the necessary defence and support of his Government in the Province, and protection and preservation of his Subjects therein.

The Design and Tendency of the said Acts of Parliament appear in too conspicuous a point of Light to need any comment: And are too alarming to admit of silence, since silence might be construed into Acquiescence.—We therefore Resolve,

[*Then follow a Number of Resolves in the Words of those enter'd into by the Citizens of Philadelphia before publish'd in this Paper, to which is added,* viz.]

Resolved, That it affords the greatest satisfaction the Inhabitants of this Town, to find that his Majesty's Subjects of the American Colonies and of this Province in particular, are so throughly awakened to a sense of their Danger arising from Incroachments made on their Constitutional Rights and Liberties, and that so firm a union is establish'd among them. And that we will be ever ready to join our fellow Subjects in all laudable Measures for the Redress of the many Grievances we labor under.

The said Report having been several Times read; upon a Motion made, the Question was put, whether the same be Accepted, and be Recorded in the Town's Book of Records, and a Copy thereof sent by the Town-Clerk to the Committee of Correspondence of the Town of Boston, and passed in the Affirmative.

A true Copy,

Attest. BENJ^a LINCOLN, Town-Clerk.

NEW-YORK, March 14.

The 21st ultimo, about two o'Clock a smart Shock of an Earthquake was felt at Westover, the Seat of the Hon. William Byrd, Esq; in Virginia. The Motion of the Earth was so great at Petersburgh and Blanford as to move Houses off their Foundation.

His Excellency our Governor, with his Lady, and Miss TRYON, take their Passage for England in the Mercury Packet, Capt. Dillon, who will sail the first Wednesday in April next, for Falmouth.

BOSTON, MARCH 21.

DIED. Mrs. *Ann Pierpont*, aged 45, Wife of Mr. *Robert Pierpont*.

At Salem, the Hon. Nathaniel Ropes, Esq; one of the Justices of the Superior Court, Court of Assize, &c. for this Province.

Last Monday arrived in this Town, Mr. WILLIAM GODDARD, Printer in Philadelphia and Baltimore—The cause of that Gentleman's tour is interesting to all the Colonies, and we are happy to find that all through which he has come are so thoroughly engaged in it. Every Colony to the Southward of us, manifest their readiness to come into the measure, provided we adopt it, and we are informed there is not the shadow of a doubt of its being as warmly patronized here as any where. How chearfully will every well wisher to his Country lay hold of an opportunity to risque the channel of public and private intelligence out of the hands of a power openly inimical to its Rights and Liberties. Several Meetings have already been held on the interesting subject, and on the Morrow Evening it is hoped to be concluded so far that Mr. Goddard may proceed Eastward, with a moral certainty of carrying his point throughout the Colonies.

To ——— ———, Esq;

SIR,

I Have heard that in circles where you depend upon your influence, you are very industrious in starting objections against the propriety and feasibility of Mr. ——'s scheme of establishing a constitutional Post Office. The objections I have heard are the following, viz. That at present the office can but barely support itself, and affords no revenue: 2. That the establishment of Postmasters and Riders in the manner proposed will render the public uncertain of the monies, bills, &c. committed to their care: 3. That in case such an office should be set up, the keeper of it may expect to be prosecuted at the suit of the Postmaster-General, and tho' no damages be found by a jury on this side the water, yet the matter in debate being above three hundred sterl. an appeal will lie to the King in council, who will undoubtedly award the appellant the sum he sues for, with costs of prosecution. The other trifling consideration of its being an improper time, while we have already so much business on hand, and this *manœuvre* being owing to a private pique between Mr. —— and the P— M— G. may be taken up hereafter, should any one appear to urge them in earnest.

1. To the first head I answer, that I can hardly conceive the other riders to run the office in debt, while Mr. Silent Wilde, Mr. William Williams, and a rider between Hartford and Nine Partners, maintain themselves. The profits along the sea coast must be tensold.

2. To the second I answer that both masters and riders will, on the present plan, be under the controul of a committee of the subscribers throout the continent, and can be displaced by them in case of unfaithfulness, which is more than we can promise ourselves in the present state of things.

3. Respecting prosecution, and appeal; this in my opinion is a meer bugbear. The Postmaster's damages must lie for intrusion, upon an estate which he lawfully holds. All Europe and America know he can hold no such estate in the colonies without the consent of their parliaments; new offices with new fees, or even the augmentation of fees to old offices being in such case void and contrary to Magna Charta. No jury can therefore find damages where they find no estate: No court can give *judgment* or *sentence* contrary to the verdict of a jury: If no judgment therefore can be made up on damages found, there can be no judgment to appeal from. This reasoning must appear to every one so incontestible that to offer any thing further in support of so plain a case would imply a question of the good sense of my countrymen. HORTENSIUS.

At the same Time Mr. Goddard's Plan of establishing an American Post-Office by Subscription, meets with the greatest Encouragement imaginable in this Metropolis, we are informed the Patriotic Doctor Franklin is severely threatened with the loss of that Place under the British Minister. Should such a thing really take Place it would multiply the Satisfaction of every Friend to this Country in disappointing the Revenge of that inveterate Enemy to the Rights of America. Many of the Patrons of this new Scheme were much concerned lest it should appear ungrateful to Doctor Franklin, especially at a Period when he has given such signal Proof of faithfulness to his Trust, in obtaining and sending over the treasonable Letters of Hutchinson, Oliver, &c. But perhaps the new Post-Office may be beneficial and more agreeable to the Doctor than ever was the old one.

The Superior Court for the County of Middlesex, which was to have been held at Charlestown on the second Tuesday of April next, is, by a late Act, appointed to be held there on the first Tuesday of April annually.

Capt. Silas Atkins, jun. arrived here on Thursday last, informs us, That on Saturday the 6th Instant, in Lat. 36 : 37. Long. 70 : 38 West, he spoke with the Brig Barbados Packet, William Hawkins, Master, bound from Philadelphia for Barbados, who the Day before lost his Foremast and Bowsprit, having had very bad Weather, and was putting back for Philadelphia in order to refit.

Capt. Maccarty is arrived at Barbados from the Coast of Africa.

We hear from Nantucket, that on Wednesday the 9th of March Instant, at about 8 o'clock in the Morning, they had the most violent Gust of Wind that perhaps was ever known there, but it lasted only about a Minute, it seem'd to come in a narrow Vein, and in its progress blew down and totally destroyed the *Light-House* on that Island, besides several Shops, Barns, &c. had the Gust continued fifteen Minutes it's thought it would not have left more than one half the Buildings standing, in the Course that it passed, but we don't hear of any Persons receiving much hurt, nor much Damage done, except the loss of the Light-House which in every respect is considerable.

Thursday Night last a Number of Prisoners set Fire to the Goal in this Town, and had it got a little more Head before it was discovered, it would have entirely consumed the same.—This is the fourth Time the Goal Watch have preserv'd the same.

AT a Meeting of the Freeholders and other Inhabitants of this Town at Faneuil-Hall on Monday last, the Honorable JOHN HANCOCK, Esq; was chosen Moderator, but Indisposition prevented his attending: The Honorable THOMAS CUSHING, Esq; was then chosen Moderator and the following Town-Officers for the Year ensuing, viz.

Town-Clerk; Mr. William Cooper.

Select-Men. John Scollay, Esq; Hon. John Hancock, Esq; Mr. Timothy Newell, Thomas Marshall, Esq; Mr. Samuel Austin, Mr. Oliver Wendell, Mr. John Pitts.

Town Treasurer; Mr. David Jeffries.

Overseers of the Poor. John Barrett, Esq; William Phillips, Esq; Mr. Benjamin Dolbeare, Mr. William Whitwell, Mr. William Greenleaf, William White, Esq; John Leverett, Esq; John Gore, Esq; Capt. Samuel Partridge, Mr. Samuel Whitwell, Mr. Samuel Abbot, Mr. Daniel Waldo.

Firewards. John Scollay, Esq; Newman Greenough, Esq; Mr. William Cooper, Thomas Marshall, Esq; Mr. Joseph Tyler, Adino Paddock, Esq; Capt. Benjamin Waldo, Hon. John Hancock, Esq; Mr. Samuel Adams, Capt. Martin Gay, Francis Shaw, Esq; Capt. Job Prince, Capt. Edward Procter, Mr. John Coffin, Deacon Caleb Davis, and Capt. John Pullen.

Wardens. Francis Green, Esq; Mr. Ebenezer Sever, Capt. Samuel Dagget, Mr. Ebenezer Hancock, Mr. Thomas Kimble, Mr. George Bright, Mr. William M'Niel, Capt. Samuel Sellon, Mr. John Cotton, Mr. Samuel Bass, Capt. Nehemiah Somes, Alexander Edwards, Esq;

Committee for purchasing Grain, Joseph Jackson, Esq; John Leverett, Esq; Mr. John Sweetser, jun'r.

Surveyors of Wheat: Mr. John Lucas, and Mr. John White.

Surveyor of Hemp. John Gray, Esq;

Assessors. Mr. Benjamin Church, Mr. Jonathan Brown, Mr. Daniel Pecker, Capt. Samuel Downes Giles Harris, Esq; Mr. William Lowder, and Mr. Samuel Johnson.

Collectors of Taxes. Mr. Edward Holliday, Mr. Abraham Savage, Mr. Benjamin Henderson, Mr. Benja. Gray,

Clerks of the Market. Messir's. Richard Billings, jun. Andrew Brimmer, Samuel Parkman, Thomas Melvill, Joshua Blanchard, jun. John Barrett, jun. Benjamin Hammatt, jun. Duncan Ingraham, jun. John Coffin Jones, David Sears, Daniel Bell, Henry Prentice.

Informers of Deer. Messir's Thomas Edes, and Adam Colson.

Assay Masters. Capt. Martin Gay, & Mr. John Skinner.

Fence Viewers. Mr. John Dyer, Mr. Samuel Dyer, Mr. Obadiah Lowe, Capt. John Joy, Mr. William Crafts.

Surveyors of Boards. Messirs William Nichols, Clement Collins, Jacob Thayer, Joseph Edmunds, John Greenough, Isaac Vergoose, Clement Collins, jun'r. John Champney, Andrew Symmes, Henry Allen, Edmund Ranger, Richard Walker, Thomas Uran, John Bulfinch, Abraham Howard, Joseph Butler, Joseph Ayers, Andrew Townsend, Joseph Ballard, Elisha Homes, Thomas Bayley, John Holland, John Rogers, Obadiah Low, Benj. Page, Dinely Wing, Henry Blaesdell, Abraham Rogers, Benjamin White, and James Blake.

Cullers of Staves. Messirs. Peter Cotta, Joseph Dyer, Manasseh Masters, Capt. John Haskins, Capt. David Spear, Jonathan Jenkins, Caleb Hayden, Capt. Job Wheelwright, Joshua Pico, Benjamin Sault, Paul Baxter, John Owen, Thomas Knox, Samuel White, Edward Cowell, Peter Ellis, Nathan Spear, Timothy Pease, Jacob Williams, Nathaniel Waterman, Samuel Barnard, John Newell, Joseph Phillips, Henry Lucas, James Beard, Richard Flood, William Rogers, Samuel Peck.

Scavangers. Wards, N°. 1. Messir's. Josiah Vose, 2. Joseph Snelling, 3. Caleb Champney, 4. Freeman Pulcifer, 5 John Lowell, 6. Joseph Loring, 7. Charles Perin, 8. John Langdon, 9. Samuel Warden, 10. John Fullerton, 11. Thomas Chace, 12. Benjamin Wheeler.

Sealers of Leather. Messirs. Samuel Bangs, Joseph Clark, Thomas Knowlan, Benjamin Bass, Daniel Parks.

Hayward. Mr. Willliam M'Fadden.

Hogreeves. Messirs. Benjamin Blake, Elijah Searl.

Constables. Messieurs Augustus Hale, John Wells, John Coverly, Stephen Simmes, George Thomas, John Bennet, Samuel Greenleaf, John Hammat, Joseph Foye, William Todd, Thomas Bell, and Mathew Nazro.

The Meeting stands Adjourned to Wednesday the 30th Instant, at 10 o'Clock, Beforenoon.

ON WEDNESDAY NEXT,
AT ELEVEN o'Clock,
THE
ORATION,
DELIVER'D BY THE
Hon. JOHN HANCOCK, Esq;
Will be PUBLISHED,
And SOLD by EDES & GILL in Queen-Street.

FIFTY DOLLARS REWARD.

LAST Night the Dwelling-House of the Subscriber was broke open, and from thence were taken the following Articles of Plate, viz.

1 Pair of Silver Chaffingdishes, 1 pair of Butter-cups, 1 silver can, 2 large soup-spoons, 1 pepper-box, 6 large table-spoons, 6 tea-do. and a strainer, marked E. D. maker's name, D. Henchman all except the spoons, which have a Hand for a Crest.—A silver tea-pot, 1 do. sugar-dish, a boat for tea spoons, 1 pair tea-tongs, 5 tea-spoons and a cream-cup. Two porringers and two salt-cellars, all mark'd E. S. 1 silver Tankard without a lid, marked

S
J. S. *1 silver canmarked* I.
D
E. *an old fashion'd pepper-box*
D
mark'd A. E. *6 large table spoons marked* E. S. *1 silver salver, no mark upon it, the foot resembling the mouth of a tunnel, a silver tankard marked* A. B. *1 silver porringer without any mark, 3 table spoons marked* A. B. *1 old spoon*
S.
marked I. S. *4 tea spoons no mark, 1 pair tea tongs, Makers names of these not made by D. Henchman, I. Hurd some of them, and some B. W—with several other small articles.——Whoever will take up the Thief or Thieves, so as he or they may be brought to Justice and the Plate recovered, shall be paid the above Reward, and a reasonable Reward for any Part of the Plate, in Proportion to its Value.* per me, THADDEUS BURR.

Fairfield, Connecticut, 15 *March,* 1774.

N. B. *If any of the above Plate should be discovered in Boston, please to give Notice to* JOHN HANCOCK, *Esq; and an adequate Reward shall be given.*

All Persons that have any Demands on

the Estate of the late Elizabeth Hewes, *Widow, deceas'd, are desired immediately to bring in their Accounts for Settlement; and all Persons indebted to said Estate, are desired to make speedy Payment to*

Boston, March 21, 1774. HENDERSON INCHES, AND, NATH. APPLETON, } Executors.

The best Turks Island SALT,

To be SOLD on board the Schooner Sally. Capt. Rogers, lying at Griffins Wharf.

STOLEN out of the Barn of me the Subscriber on Wednesday Night the 16th of March Inst. a red Mare, Saddle and Bridle, with a Blaze in her Face, about 13 Hands high, and about 12 Years old or upwards, carries her Head very low.——Whoever will take up the said Mare and bring her with the Saddle and Bridle to the Owner, shall have two Dollars Reward, and all necessary Charges paid, by RALPH DEVEREAUX.

Marblehead, March 16, 1774.

TO BE LETT,

A commodious Brick Messuage, situate

in Brattle Square. Inquire of Edes and Gill.

THERE is to be sold, a genteel Horse and Chaise, with or without a Negro Boy of 16 Years old, that can be well recommended, understands taking Care of Horse and Chaise, and cleaning them in the neatest Manner; drives with great Care; can do House-work and Cook as well as any one of his Age; is good-temper'd lively and spry. The above to be sold for no other Reason than that the Gentleman to whom they did belong is deceas'd. If any Gentleman or Lady inclines to purchase the above, and it is not convenient to pay the Money, it may lay on good Security. Inquire of the Printers.

TO BE SOLD
AT PUBLICK AUCTION,
By Benjamin Church,
At his usual Place of Sale,
On THURSDAY next,
At THREE o'Clock in the Afternoon,

SUPERFINE middling and coarse Broad Cloths—Ratteens—Frizes—Half Thicks—Kerseys—Shalloons—Calamancoes—Irish Linnens—Checks—Mens and Womens Hose—Linnens—Velvesetts—Handkerchiefs—Case Knives and Forks—Inkhorns—Penknives, &c.—Sundry Articles of Household—Wearing Apparel—Watches, Cutlery Ware, half a Dozen Mehogany Chairs Leather botomt—a Case of Draws—Feather Beds, &c. &c. &c

Thursday next, 3 o'Clock P. M.

PUBLICK AUCTION.

On TUESDAY the 29th MARCH will be Sold by PUBLICK AUCTION, at the Dwelling House of Mr. JOHN MICO WENDELL, deceas'd, a variety of Houshold Furniture—consisting of—

Tables, Chairs, Pier Glasses, Mehogony Case of Draws, Beauros, Feather Beds, Bedsteads, Houshold Linnen, Kitchen Furniture, Plate, &c.

The Sale will begin at 9 o'Clock, A. M.

M. DESHON, Auctioneer.

All Persons that have any De-

mands on the Estate of Mr. Andrew Cunningham, late of Boston, Hatter, deceased, are desired to bring in their Accounts to Mary Greenleaf and John Cunningham, Administrators on said Estate, for Adjustment.——And all Persons indebted to said Estate, are desired to make immediate Payment to said Administrators.

John Cunningham,

HAS for Sale at his Shop near the Corner of School-Street, opposite Mr. Deblois's,

A Large Assortment of English and India Goods, suitable for all Seasons, which he is determined to sell at the Sterling Cost (clear of Charges) he being determined to quit the Business.

ENGLISH GOODS CHEAP.

Imported from LONDON, by

Samuel Dashwood,

And to be Sold at his Shop next Door to Dr. Silvester Gardner's in Marlborough-Street, Boston.

A Great Variety of English, India and Scotch Goods, among which are,—Irish Linnens of all widths, Chinces and Callicoes, great Variety of Silks, best Royal Ribbs, best English Shoes at One Dollar per Pair, and many other Articles too tedious to mention, which will be sold by Wholesale at the Sterling Cost, and by Retail at the Cost and Charges, as he is going into another Branch of Business.

N. B. Spices of all Kinds, great Variety of Glass, China and Earthen Ware, sold remarkable cheap for Cash.

TO BE LET,

A large commodious Brick Distilling-

House, in a very good Part of the Town, with three Stills, one of 1200 Gallons, one of 400 ditto, and one of 300 ditto, with Cisterns in Proportion to the same, and has every Convenience requisite for the Distilling-Business.—It may be entered upon and set to work immediately. Enquire of Edes & Gill.

N. B. There has been more than 700 Hogsheads of Rum distilled in the above House, in one Year.

TO BE LETT,

The Back Part of the large Brick House

in King-Street, at the Corner of Quaker-Lane, containing a very large and pleasant Parlour, convenient Chambers, and a good Kitchen, accommodated with a good Yard and large Brick Stable.————Enquire of Amory's, Taylor & Rogers, Marlborough-Street.

All Persons that are indebted to, or

have any Demands on the late Company of Aaron Davis, *jun. and Company, are desired to make speedy Settlement with* Wales *and* Somes, *the two surviving Partners, at their Store the upper Corner going on* Minot's T.——At which Store is to be sold, good Bait Mackrell, Salmon in Barrels or Kegs, new Flour, Bar Iron, a Quantity of Twice-laid Rigging and Junk.

Wednesday Next at X in the Morning

Will be sold by PUBLIC VENDUE, at the Auction-Room in Queen-Street,

A Variety of House-Furniture,

belonging to a Gentleman lately deceased,

Among which are,

A Mahogany Desk & Book Case with glass Doors, Tables, Chairs, Feather Beds, Bedsteads, Beding,——a Suit of white Curtains, crimson Curtains, painted canvass floor Cloth, Turkey Carpet, Scotch Carpet, Couch & Squab, Glass & China Ware, a neat Sophy, a Set of Lolling Chairs, a very good Sett of Chairs, Mehogany Frames, carved Feet, and Copper-plate Bottoms, an 8 Day Clock, Womens Wearing Apparel, Kitchen Furniture,—Also, a Variety of Plate, Butter-Boats, Porringers, Table Spoons, Punch-Ladles, Cream-Pot and Sugar-Dish, Tankards, *Tea*-Pots, Salvers, Tea-Tongs, Tea-Spoons and Strainers, &c. &c.

J. Russell, Auctioneer.

On THURSDAY NEXT,

At ONE o'Clock,

Will *certainly* be SOLD by PUBLIC VENDUE, at the Bunch of Grapes Tavern in King-Street.

A Brick House, Land, Wharff and Dock

near the Swing Bridge, now improved by Mr. Thomas Lee—the House is large and well built, and has every Accommodation needed by a Gentleman in Trade——Also, a new Store, Chaise House and Barn on Wentworth's Wharff near the Draw-Bridge, with Part of the Wharff and Dock.

N. B. The above Premisses are Part of the Real Estate of Thomas Tyler, Esq; late of Boston, deceased, and are the same that was design'd to have been sold last Thursday.

TO BE SOLD IMMEDIATELY,

By *Margaret Newman,* Administratrix

to the Estate of Mrs. *Margaret Fletcher,* deceased——A BRICK HOUSE situate in Ann-street, making the Corner of the new Street lately made from Ann to Middle-street, at present occupied by Mr. Jeremiah Allen—it has two Rooms on a Floor, with a good Celler, Yard and Pump; the whole in good Repair.——Said *Newman* has to Let, a Store nearly opposite the above.

CALLICOES.

A Small Invoice of newest-fashion Callicoes, to be sold for less than the Sterling Cost and Charges.

Inquire of Edes and Gill.

To be Sold cheap, for Cash only,

50 Acres of choice Land, lying in the

Town of Lunenburgh, in the County of Worcester—in the Third Division Land (so called) near Manoosenett-Hill, which was originally laid out to John Scott.——Enquire of John Gray, Esq; Rope-Maker in Boston.

To be SOLD or LET,

A Farm in Cambridge Neck so called, (and entered upon the first of April next) containing between Seventy and Eighty Acres, consisting of Mowing Land, both English and Salt, with good Plowland, and Pasturage, and a good Orchard of choice Fruit thereon, the same being well watered. Said Farm lying within one Mile from the College, and about three Miles from Charlestown Ferry. For further Particulars, enquire of Samuel Soden of Watertown, or of Seth Hastings of said Cambridge.

TO BE SOLD,

A Pleasant FARM at Newton, about a Mile from Watertown Bridge, containing about 30 Acres:—Also a Wood Lot nearly adjoining, of about 30 Acres:—Three Years will be allowed for the Payment, good Security being given. If more Land should be wanted, the adjoining Farm of 30 Acres is also to be Sold. Enquire of the Printers.

TO BE SOLD OR LETT,

A good FARM in Newton, and entered

upon the first Day of April, containing One Hundred Acres of good Land, with a House and Barn thereon, all in good Repair, well proportioned for Mowing, Plowing and Orcharding, &c. with a Stream that runs thro' said Farm, never known to be dry.—For further Particulars inquire of Abraham Fuller, Esq; or of Amariah Fuller, living near said Premises.

Hackney Coach

Drove by GEORGE HAMBLIN,

Will attend Gentlemen and Ladies to

or from any Part of the Town, at any Time in the Day or Evening, at *One Shilling* each—A single Person for *Two Shillings.*

N. B. Said Hamlin gives constant Attendance at Major PADDOCK's Coach-Yard, Long-Acre.

CUSTOM-HOUSE, *BOSTON.*

ENTETRD IN.

Coffin and Adams, North Carolina; Hinckley, South Carolina; Higgins and Kemp, Maryland; Whitney, New-Haven; Ewell, Virginia; Harris, New-London; Valantine and Whitmarsh Suranam; Barnes, Grenada and Saltertuda; Atkins, St. Lucia; Rogers, Turks-Island; and Peabody, Hispaniola.

Burials in the Town of BOSTON, since our last.

Nine Whites. No Blacks

Baptiz'd in the several Churches, Eight.

High Water at BOSTON, for the present Week.

Monday, 10 min. aft. 6	Friday, 15 min. after 9
Tuesday, 55 min. aft. 6	Saturday, 2 min. af. 10
Wednesday 42 m. aft. 7	Lord's-Day, 50m aft 10
Thursday, 30 min. aft. 8	☽'s first Qr. 20 Day 5 [illegible]

Just IMPORTED, and TO BE SOLD by

John Decosta

In Milk-Street, a little below the Old South Meeting House; Beans, Peas, and a Variety of other Garden Seeds; Fresh and Good; also a Variety of young Fruit Trees, Grafted and Innoculated; also Roots and Plants, all at Reasonable Rates.

W A N T E D,

A Negro Man of an unexceptionable Character, warranted; for such an one a good Price will be given; one of a small Size, brought up in a Country Town, and who understands a little of House Business will be preferred. Inquire of the Printers.

TO BE LETT,

A large commodious Chamber, near the Market, fit for almost any Tradesman, or a Store. Enquire of the Printers.

COTTON WOOL,

Of an excellent Quality, to be Sold by JONATHAN WILLIAMS, Junr. per Bag or smaller Quantity——VERY CHEAP.

Nathaniel Seaver,

INFORMS the Publick and his Customers in Particular, that he continues to keep the Shop lately improved by *Seaver & Carnes*, where may be had a large Assortment of English, India and Scotch Goods, Suitable for all Seasons, upon the lowest terms for Cash.

N. B. Said *Seaver* returns his hearty Thanks to his Friends & Customers for the favours already shown, and further assures them that he will do every thing in his power to serve them.

For the Benefit of Mr. MORGAN,

At Concert Hall on Wednesday 23d Inst.

Will be a Concert of Vocal and Instrumental Music.—Tickets to be had at the British Coffee-House, at Mrs. Cummins's in Cornhill, and Mrs. Taylor's in Winter Street, at half a Dollar each.

To begin at half after Six o'Clock.

GARDEN-SEEDS,

IMPORTED from LONDON, in Capt. HOOD, and TO BE SOLD BY

Elizabeth Clark and Nowell,

At their Shop Six Doors to the Southward of the Mill-Bridge, BOSTON:

EARLY Charlton, early hotspur, golden hotspur, large marrowfat, dwarf, large sugar, Spanish moratto, blue marrowfat, and marster's hotspur PEAS; large Windsor, green Norfolk, early yellow, dwarf, kidney, and large white dwarf BEANS; early Yorkshire, early Dutch, green Savoy, large Winter, early Sugar-Loaf, and Battersea Cabbage Seeds; early and late Collifiower; large Orange, early yellow, and purple Carrot; Swelling Parsnip, and red Beat Seeds; green and white gofs Cabbage; Marble, Breton, brown, Dutch, and grand Admiral Lettice Seeds; Thyme, Balm, Sweet-Marjoram, Sage and Fennel Seeds; Silverskin and Portugal Onion Seeds; early Salmon, Scarlet and Turnip Radish Seeds; curl'd Parsley, curld Creses; Early Dutch Turnip Seeds; Early, long prickley Cucumber; white Mustard; green curld Endive; round Spinnage; best Mallon, Gourd Squash, solid Cellery, red Clover, and Canary Seeds.

☞ All warranted New of the genuine Sort.

WANTED IMMEDIATELY,

One Thousand Pounds Old Tenor, for which good Security will be given. For further Particulars inquire of the Printers.

TO BE LETT,

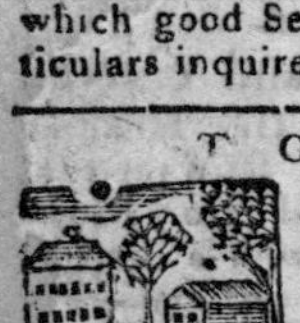

A Farm in Watertown, and entered on the first of April next, the Farm contains about 65 Acres of good Land, well accommodated for Plowing, Pasturing, and Mowing, with a plenty of Fruit. For further Particulars, Inquire of Mr. *Elijah Bond*, or Capt. *Jonathan Brown*, living in said Town. *Watertown, Feb. 28, 1774.*

A Farm to be Sold in Watertown, very pleasantly situated, and within two Miles of the College, contains about 40 Acres of choice good Land, has on it a good House and Barn, is well accommodated for Mowing, Pasturage and Tillage, has on it a variety of all kinds of Fruits, and will very well accommodate a Gentleman: Whoever is inclined to Purchase the same may apply to JOHN STRALLON of said Watertown.

Feb. 28, 1774.

TO BE SOLD *or* LETT,

A small Farm in Newton, about ten Miles from Boston, with a House and Barn thereon, and may be enter'd on the first of April next. Enquire of John Newell Living in Wings-Lane, Boston.

N B. About 40 or 50,000 red Oak Hhd Staves, and 13 Thousand white Oak ditto to be sold by said Newell.

Boston, March 5th, 1774

O A T S.

Quebec and Nova-Scotia Oats. Also, Nova-Scotia Peas, TO BE SOLD BY

JOSEPH P. PALMER,

At the lowest Store on the South Side of the Town-Dock.

To be Sold or Let,

The large House, and about 20 Acres of Upland and Meadow adjoining upon Boston Neck so called, well known by the Name of the George or King's-Arms Tavern, now in the Occupation of Mr. *Thomas Bracket*: The House, Out-Houses, Barns, Gardens and Fences in good Repair. Inquire for the Terms of *Melatiah Bourn, Esq*; in *Boston*.

For LONDON,

The Brigantine HOPE,

A Fine new Vessel, has excellent Accommodations, and will sail as soon as loaded.

For Freight or Passage, apply to JONATHAN WILLIAMS, jun. in Ann Street.

WANTED TO CHARTER for Twelve Months, A double Deck'd Vessel of 130 Tons, for which a good Price will be given. Inquire of Edes and Gill. ALSO, TO BE SOLD

A well Built Schooner, of about 70 Tons, almost new, well found.

VELVET-CORKS.

Choice VELVET CORKS by the Quantity or single Groce,

TO BE SOLD By

Samuel Elliot,

At his Shop near the Head of Dock-Square, just above the Market:

Also, a general Assortment of *English* and *India* Goods; with a very fine Assortment of *Irish* LINNENS.

Lisbon Wine in Quarter Casks, and Sperma Cæti Candles, warranted pure, to be Sold very Cheap, By Francis Rotch, in King-Street.

TO BE SOLD very cheap for CASH, At the Shop next to the Sign of the Buck and Glove in Cornhill, BOSTON;

Superfine and common *Philadelphia* FLOUR,

COFFEE of an uncommon good Quality, Very good Brown SUGAR,

Nutmegs,	Ginger,
Cinnamon,	Split Pease,
Cloves,	Velvet Corks,
Mace,	Powder Blue,
Pepper,	Salt Petre,
Allspice,	Allum,
Oil,	Olives,
New Raisins,	Durham Mustard,
Currants,	Chocolate,
London T D 18 Inch Pipes,	Rice,
Loaf Sugar,	Oatmeal,
Almonds,	Poland Starch,
Capers,	Crown Soap.

Best French INDIGO.

An Assortment of English GOODS, & Crockery Ware.

ALSO,

A large new Scale Beam, with Scales and Weights. 20 well made Draws in a Nest.

N. B. The above Shop and House will be Lett the first of April: Inquire of Samuel Minott, near the Draw-Bridge.

PITCH.

A Quantity of Pitch and a few Chaldron of New Castle Coals, to be Sold by W. HOSKINS.

BARLEY.

WHOEVER is willing to engage a Quantity of *BARLEY*, to be delivered in Boston next Fall, will find it of Advantage to leave their Proposals in Writing with the Printers.

W A N T E D

A strong active Person of a good Character, acquainted sufficiently with the Distilling Business, so as to be able to undertake the Care of a large Distill-House, out of Town: For further Particulars inquire of the Printers. *Boston, Feb. 28, 1774.*

TO BE SOLD,

A Good Farm in Concord, containing about 80 Acres, with a good House and two Barns, and a large new Store, two good Wells of Water upon the great Road, and within three Quarters of a Mile of the Meeting House: Said Farm will be Sold for English and West-India Goods, if applied for soon, Inquire of Mr. *Samuel Whitney* of Concord, or of Mr. *Samuel Austin* in Boston.

ALSO,

Another Farm in Lancaster Parish, containing about 100 Acres, with a good House and Barn on the same, will be Sold for Goods if apply'd for soon.

Wanted a Woman of a good Character, and one that can be well recommended, and that understands Cooking and other house Work; none need apply but such a one, and is Wanted immediately.—Good Wages will be given. Inquire of the Printers.

WANTED immediately, an Anchor of 1100 wt. Inquire of the Printers.

Whereas I the Subscriber intend leaving off the Baking Business very soon, do take this opportunity of returning my Thanks to those Gentlemen and Ladies who have favoured me with their Custom, since my late Husband's decease. MARY SURCOMB.

The Business will be carried on as usual by Mr. William Flagg.

N. B. *A very good Horse and handsome Chaise to be Sold: Inquire of Mary Surcomb.*

Boston, Feb. 28, 1774.

This is to Acquaint all Gentlemen and Ladies that the Baking Business will be carried on as usual, by me the Subscriber, who is determined to give universal Satisfaction. WILLIAM FLAGG.

GARDEN SEEDS,

IMPORTED in Capt. SHEPHARD from LONDON And TO BE SOLD By

Elizabeth Greenleaf,

At her Shop to the Southward of the Lane leading to Dr. Byles's Meeting House, Boston.

EARLY Charlton, early golden Hotspur, early Hotspur, large Dwarf, and green Marrofats, white Rouncival, Ledman's Dwarf & Spanish Marratto Peas, large Windsor, Toker, early yellow, Dwarf Kidney, and large white Beans, red, purple, orange, and yellow Carrot seeds, early Yorkshire, early Dutch, early sugar loaf, early Battersea, red, large winter, green and yellow Savoy, early and late Collifiower, Cabbage, green and white Goss, brown Duck, Madeira, spotted and mogul Lettice seeds; red, white, Spanish, Portugal, and silver skin Onion seed; green and white endive, swelling Parsnip, red Beat, Time, Balm, sweet Marjoram, Sage, and summer-savory seeds; scarlet, salmon, short topt and turnip Radish seeds; summer and winter spinage, early and late Cucumber, early Dutch and French Turnip seeds; Parsley, Pepper-Grass, Asparagus, Salery, Lavender and white Mustard seeds; Water and Musk Mellon seeds; summer and winter Squash seeds; Hemp, Rape and Canary Bird seed; choice split Pease by the large or smaller Quantity.——N. B. English GOODS.

IMPORTED in Capt. HOOD from LONDON, And TO BE SOLD By

Susanna Renken

At her Shop near the Draw-Bridge, Fore-Street, BOSTON:

EARLY Charlton, early golden Hotspur, green Marrows, white Rouncival, Spanish Morattoes, crooked Sugar, and Leadman's Dwarf Peas;—Toker, best Windsor, early Lisbon, large Dutch Kidney, Beans; Strasburgh, Spanish, Silverskin'd and Portugal Onion; Orange, early yellow, and scarlet Carrot; Parsnips; Early and late Turnip; Early short top'd, London, Salmon, turnip, Spanish, and scarlet Radish; Early frame, white gofs, early green gofs, large green gofs, bloody gofs, Aleppo gofs, brown Dutch, marble, royal brown Dutch, imperial, tennisbal and Capuchin Lettice; Prickley and round Spinnage; Red Beats; Italian and solid Cellery; curl'd Pepper Grass; Indian Creses; Common, curld and large rooted Parsley; Early and late Colliflower; Early York, large Battersea, early Dutch, large Scotch, large winter and turnip Cabbage; Yellow, green and white curl'd Savoy; long prickley, early prickley, green Turkey, and long Roman Cucumber; Baum, Sweet-Marjoram, Thyme, Rosemary, and Lavender Seed; Hemp and Canary Ditto; Broad red Clover; Fine white Ditto; Lucern and Rape Seed; Rye Grass, and other Grass Seeds; Sage Seed.

Durham's best Flour Mustard; —Groceries.

Also, *English* and *India* Goods: All which may be had cheap for Cash.

TO BE SOLD,

By Benjamin Dolbeare,

A Very good Fire Engine, London-made; old Jamaica Spirit by the Tierce, sundry Barrels of Jamaica Sugar, and Vinegar by the Barrel.

A Woman with a good Breast of Milk, would be glad to take a Child to Suckle. Inquire of the Printers.

GARDEN SEEDS

IMPORTED in Capt GORHAM, from LONDON, And TO BE SOLD

By *Lydia Dyar*,

At her Shop near the North Battery, BOSTON;

Early Charlton, Early Hotspur, Golden Hotspur, large Marrowfatts, Dwarf Marrow, blue Marrow, and Spanish Moratto PEAS; large Windsor, large Toker, early Lisbon, early Hotspur, early yellow Dwarf, early speckled Dwarf, and early white BEANS, with black Eyes; early Yorkshire, early Dutch, Sugar-loaf, large Winter, Battersea, green and yellow Savoy, early and late Colliflower Seeds; Best Cabbage Lettice, White Goss, Green Goss, Marble and Brown Dutch Lettuce, Seeds, Double Peppper Grass, round Spinage, short top, Scarlet and Salmon Radish, double Parsley, white Spanish, silver skin and red Onion seeds, long green prickly Cucumber, and early ditto, sweet Marjoram, Thyme, Baum, Sage, Hysop, Summer and Winter Squash, early and late Dutch Turnip, long French ditto, red Beets, large swelling Parsnip, Orange, golden colour'd, early yellow Carrot, & Canary Seeds, warranted to be new and good. LIKEWISE,

A Variety of Flower SEEDS.

Boston: Printed, by EDES & GILL in QUEEN STREET.

THE
Boston-
AND
COUNTRY

Gazette,
JOURNAL.

No. 990.

Containing the freshest Advices, Foreign and Domestic.

MONDAY, March 28, 1774.

A PUBLIC VENDUE
OF THE
Present MINISTRY.*

Extracted from a piece published sometime since, which appeared with several copperplate prints designed to represent their beads in the medallion taste—The first engraving is of an Ass, which the Auctioneer applies to the prime Minister, Lord N**TH ; *the second is the figure of a Newmarket Jockey, perfectly accommodated to ride a match over the Beacon, and designed to represent his Grace the Duke of* G**F**N ; *the third is the portait of* TH***S BR*****W, *Esq* ; *the fourth, a Negro, by way of caricatura, of* JE*****H DY**N, *Esq*; *and the fifth the head of the Hon.*CH***S F*X, *Esq*; a la macaroni.

I NOW entered the auction room, and Christie had just mounted the rostrum.—He seized his hammer, and throwing his eyes round the room with that activity and bewitching ease peculiar to great men, called for the first lot, and began.

AUCTIONEER.

Hand it up there—hum—the first lot, gellmen, carries its own *weight* with it ; it is an Ass's head.—that is to say the head of an ass—or of a minister. For various reasons have we chosen to give these terms as synonymous, and to make the one represent the other. Our *minister* has long acted like an *ass*, and he has got his reward; for like an *ass* they have used him.—Is an *ass* endued with great *gravity* ?—So is the *minister*. Hence that deep, important plodding air—those stiff, unbending features—that solemn, soporific, mystic countenance, which mark him with eternal business.—Hence it is, that you see him prodigiously thoughtful, and prodigiously forgetful ; now musing with his arms a kembo, and now making calculations with his fore-finger upon his nose, now measuring his paces like a city militiaman, or like the man in black before a funeral, slow and stately, one, two, three—and now galloping, like the fiery Phæton, from the court to the Cockpit—and from the Cockpit to the court. Is the *ass obstinate ?* So is the *minister*, for he is always willing to *have his own way*. Hence it is that our ships are rigged one week, and unrigged the next—that our stocks are rising to day, and falling tomorrow—that our couriers are eternally on the wing to Versailles, & that the dispatches of to day flatly contradict the dispatches of yesterday. Did our *ass* ever *prophecy ?* Yes, Balaam's did——Our *minister* will match him there too, for he too has *propesied.* But his prophesies are as brittle as his promises, for his *ten years peace* begins to expire already. Is the *ass patient ?* So is the *minister.* How else could he support his burdens, and hold his post, so long ?——In the mean time somebody put him in. O he is a very state *Grizel*, and outdoes Job and the evangelist, for humility and long suffering. How has he been torn and worried by the hawks of power and the dogs of office—now buffeted by the Bloomsbury gang, and now pelted by the junto—the companion of clerks, the slave of slaves, and the butt of Scotsmen and favourites !—But do you think that he ever murmured ? No, never. He gulped every thing. Like a true christian he did to them as he did to the Spaniards—*when they smote him upon one cheek, he turned unto them the other also.*—Who'll bid for him ? You must not be surprised that he hangs his ears so much, for stocks are greatly fallen of late.—And yet, for an ass, he's a smooth, well com'd creature.—But then he's a court ass, and must wear the fashion there.—Who bids ? "Eighteen pence for him."—Well said, Mr. Goodluck.—He was always fond of speculation, schemeing, and financing, and will do well for a lottery office. Once, twice, eighteen pence for him—Nobody more than eighteen pence ?—Thrice—He's your's, Mr. Goodluck, and a cheap bargain he is. A prime minister for eighteen pence !—Bless me ! you might at least have given one of his own lottery tickets for him.

Lot 2. was now called for. He was a Newmarket academician, and was handed up to the auctioneer in his proper dress.

AUCTIONEER.

There, gellmen, is one of the race of Nimrod for you——a duke, a privy-councellor, and a skeleton !——Well, who bids for this equestrian figure ? or rather, who *betts* for him ? for he is a complete Newmarket-boy. He winks, and nods, and whispers, and starts, and deals about "*Done*" and "*Damme*" with such volubility, that his tongue seems fleeter than the fleet Bay Malton. O he's a deep whip and spurman—one of the mystical black-legs, and a member of the august Jockey-club. For shame, Sirs ! say something for him. Though his figure, like one of his own race-horses, is long and slender, we can warrant him found in *some* of his limbs, and tolerably sure in his paces : his greatest fault is, that he is sometimes very foolish ; but you need not be surprised at that, as there is some *royal* blood in his veins.—"Five guineas for him."—Well said, Lady Bab ! But he is too much debilitated to be a good *cicisbeo :* the Irish for that. Look at his forlorn appearance, and you'd swear the crows had been picking him.—And so they were, but they were the *fair Crows* of Covent-Garden. Many a warm evening has he stood the hot fires of the bagnio—many a bleak night has he run the round of riot and midnight frolicks—now pelted by watchmen and constables, and now pelting them—now hunted from Princes street to King-Street, from Drury lane to long acre, and now romping with whores, or fondling with demi-reps.——O he has been a fellow of hard service, and his bones bespeak it. Where are the venerable members of the Jockey club ? He is deeply skilled in the science of jostling, and would make a good rider of matches.—"Fifteen guineas for him !——Excellent, my Lords ! a true Newmarket bett ! Fifteen guineas for a duke and a jockey. Nobody more than fifteen guineas ?—Ladies and Lords, he'll fit either of you—he'll do for the turff or the bed chamber, for he's a good judge of *flesh*—whether it be horse flesh or womans flesh. Once, twice, fifteen guineas. No more than fifteen ?—Thrice.——The Jockey club have got him to ride their matches.——He's ripe for use, my Lords ; for he is ready sweated down for the course, and as lean as a Scotch oyster.

My Lord Duke was handed down to the grooms, and Lot 3. was called for ; and the moment he made his appearance, the room resounded with tittering and horse laughs.

AUCTIONEER.

You may well laugh, ladies and gellmen, for here comes the miraculous BR——w himself, alias Cream colour'd Tommy. We have introdced him with great propriety next to the former lot, for he has been long accustomed to page it at his heels, and to follow his footsteps. We could recommend him to you in many characters, for many are his talents, and little is his pride.—he will stoop to do any thing for any man ; but we chuse to confine ourselves at present to his own favourite character.—a Convenient man ; in plain English, a pimp.—Stand forth, my Lord Duke and Lady Dutchess—ye Earls, Countesses, and Secretaries of States—ye female romps of quality, and ye nobles of shallow heads and deep purses—stand forth, I say, and vouch for your faithful servant and slave.—Bear witness for him who has so often watched the motion of your eyes, studied the bent of your passions administered to your pleasures, and fed the voracious stomach of your carnal cravings.—Who says for him ? Laugh at him who will, he's no blusher ; he parted with all his blushes when he was a child, and left them in the cradle. Bid away, bid away, for this is no every day's bargain.—You might search all the hundreds of Middlesex before you could meet with his match.—None but himself can be his parallel.—He's deep in the science of fornication and intrigue, and knows all the laws of adultery, from tipping the wink up to delivering a billet-doux or bribing a lady's maid. "Half a guinea for him." Good : half a guinea for a notorious pimp, once, twice—nobody more than half a guinea ?—One would think he would fetch a better price, when adultery is so much in fashion. Will no rampant member of the Carlisle-house Coterie, with a soft, asking eye, and a roving heart, buy him off for the service of the winter campaign ? Have we here no prim procuress, no Bond-street milliner, to hire him for the secret business of the back-room ? Do but mark the lascivious roll of his eye, the suppleness of his joints, and the flexibility of his muscles. He is a complete Mercury—will cringe, fawn, and flatter like a Parisian, and fetch and carry like a spaniel. Nobody more than half a guinea for a new grown gentleman and lord ? Oh fie ! fie ! knavery has lost its value. "A guinea for him !" Well spoke Charlotte ! a true whore's price !—One guinea for cream colour'd Tommy,—once, twice—thrice. Charlotte Hayes has got him, to be chaplain to her nunnery.

The next lot raised high the expectations of the audience. It was *Mungo.*

AUCTIONEER.

Black as he is, he is very honest, for his heart shines through his face. Who'll put him in ? This is not the first *market* he has been at, and he always *sold* well—and if he lives another *session*, it will not be the last. Buy him who will, they will not loose by him—for he is a man of *all work*, and has long been used to hard services. Poor soul he was long the political foot-ball, the game of green statesmen, and the understrapper of understrappers—the dupe of dunces, and the butt of weathercock wits—strappado'd by this one, and bastinado'd by that one—"Say this," said the master ; and he said it.—"Do this," said the servant ; and he did it.—Poor Mungo ! some kind soul say six pence for him—He bustled long in the storm—they used him like the foul fiend, and drove him from hedge to stile, and from ditch to dank—through bogs, and fens, and fogs and foul places—now kennelled with parasites, and now pillowing upon thorns. Poor Mungo ! put him in. They trod upon his heart, and well for him that it was callous, or he could never have supported it. Poor *black* man ! long he led the life of a dog, and it was a great mercy he had neither a spark of pride or of virtue, or he would have died under the load. Foul day or fair day, Mungo was the word—from morning to night, and from night to morning, it was nothing but Mungo ! Mungo ! Was a junto to be assembled, or an election to be carried ? "Do this Mungo." Was a lord to be bribed, or a commoner corrupted ? "Do this Mungo." Was the city to be counteracted, a job negociated, or a question smuggled in the house ? "Where are you Mungo." An outcast from heaven, a knave of knaves, and a devil of devils, he was up, and down, and every where.—He is now here, and would he were off my hands. "A *thirteener* for him." Well said my jewels of Ireland—a thirteener for Mungo, once, twice—nobody more than a thirteener for a *great black ?* Once, twice, thrice. The Irish patriots have bought him to hang him in effigy.

Hand up the next lot there, and don't ruffle his head-dress. (*Hon. C——s F—, Esq;*)

AUCTIONEER.

Bless me ! whom have we here ?---He with the full, unbashful feature's---the affected stagger---and the unruly roll of the eye ?---O---'tis he himself--'tis the CUB.--the true begotten son of peculation and cunning—the man of mode---and the beardless senator ! This lot, gellmen, does not at present absolutely belong to the ministry ; but as we were ranging through the purlieus of St. Stephen's, we found him standing in the *market*, ready to join the *best bidder* ; we have therefore huddled in the *corrupted* with the *corrupting*, for they have a natural right to each other's

(*Turn to the last Page.*)

* It is probable the next *Public Sale*, or *Outcry*, will *expose* the POSTMASTERS GENERAL and *some* of her DEPUTIES, if not the present BOARD OF COMMISSIONERS, at *Boston* who, since *their Masters* have got *new Places*, must be *taken Care of*, to prevent their falling into the Hands of the *grim Subjects* of his Majesty OKNOOKORTUNKOGOG, the *inflexible Monarch* of *Narraganset*, who hath discovered a *great Aversion* to *foreign Tax-Gatherers*, as well as to the *Poisonous Herbage* of *more Eastern Indians*. It is the opinion of the most *judicious Auctioners* that the *Lot* which is sold *first*, will come to the *best Market*.

Proceedings of the Town of BRAINTREE.

March 11th, 1774. THE Town of *Braintree* being legally assembled by Adjournment from the 24th of *February* last.

The following Draught was laid before the Town with Respect to the present Situation of our publick Affairs, viz.

WE have Reason to be alarm'd when all that is dear to us is at Stake; and there can be nothing more influencing than the danger of losing our Civil and Religious Privileges: Benefits in themselves truly valuable, and obtain'd by such expence of treasure and toil, attended with such hazards and hardships, as are not parallel'd in history. The recovery of such as are abridg'd, and the preserving those that remain, will undoubtedly be judg'd objects worthy the highest attention. The declarative right of the British Parliament to Tax the American Colonies without their consent, and to make Laws binding on them in all Cases whatsoever, is evidently repugnant to the views our Predecessors had of their Privileges; and should it take place must leave us, and our Posterity nothing to hope, but every thing to fear, that a corrupt or prejudic'd Ministry, may see Cause at any Time to impose on us. And as the doctrine of passive obedience and non-resistance, is not less mischievous in Politicks, than Religion; and as we have an unquestionable right to use every lawful Means to ward off impending Dangers, &c. We Resolve—

1st. That the great end and design for which Men first formed themselves into Governmental Society, and submitted to Government, was the greater good of the whole, and not to enrich, or aggrandize one or a few.

2d. That it is essential to this great end, the greater good of the whole, that all Laws be by the Consent of the People, either Personally or by their Representatives; since without this Right they must be ever exposed to oppression from their Rulers.

3d. That it necessarily follows that no British Law can justly be binding on us, who neither have, or (from our local situation) possibly can have, either Personally, or by Representation, any equal share in enacting them. And we therefore resolve in the spirit of the Law of the late Colony of New-Plymouth, above an Hundred Years ago; "That no Act, Imposition, Law, or "Ordinance, be made, or imposed upon us at "present, or to come, but such as (has or) shall "be enacted by the consent of the Body of Freemen, or their Associates, or their Representatives legally assembled; which is according "to the free Liberties, of the free born People "of England." And of the same purport have been the Resolves of our Parliaments, or General Assemblies to the present Day.

4th. That we have reason therefore to complain that there are now in being sundry Laws of the British Legislature; the professed design of which is to raise a revenue in America, and by which our Property is by unconstitutional measures extorted from us, and applied not to pay Britain's Debts, but to support Revenue Commissioners in Idleness and Luxury, to the waste of our Property, and danger of our Morals. And in particular the late Act of the British Parliament, which thro' artful Ministerial contrivance, allows the East India Company to export Teas to America, charged with a duty payable here, is craftily calculated to establish a revenue, which if effected, will probably render abortive all further opposition; and we must then be liable to the variety of Taxation which Britain now pays, upon a number of articles most necessary for the conveniencies of Life; besides a large Tax upon our Lands. For the preventing whereof, we Resolve as far as in us lies, to put an end to the use of all East-India Teas and Piece Goods; and to consider every Person among us who shall hereafter buy, sell, or use said Teas, or Piece Goods, until our Grievances are redress'd, (if not intentional) yet practical Enemies, to our Rights and Privileges.

5. That the declarative Right of the British Parliament, that they have a Right to make Laws binding on the Colonies, in all Cases whatever, is very alarming; the Universality of this Declaration evinces, that our religious Rights are in danger, as well as our civil; for as agreeable to this Declaration they have in fact deprived us of some of our civil Rights, and imposed Taxes upon us, so in Conformity to the same Declaration, by an Act of Uniformity, or otherwise, they may impose any religious Shackles upon us: and we know of no Instance wherein a People have been deprived of their civil Rights, but they have lost their religious Rights also; and in the Nature of Things they must stand or fall together.

6. That at the same Time we so freely resolve and determine against submitting to all foreign Taxation, and that we are determin'd by the Will of God, to stand fast in the Liberty wherewith we are made free; and to hazard Life itself rather than submit to foreign Taxation. We also resolve to pay all Obedience to our provincial Laws, and that we will not use our Liberty, as a Cloak of Licentiousness.

7. We greatly lament the want of a truly patriotic Spirit; and that private Views and Interest are so apparently the governing Motive of so great a Part, in this Day of Distress and Danger; while every Individual is interested; or can we have, notwithstanding all our Resolves and Determinations, any Prospect of a favourable Issue, unless our private Interest give Place to the general Good, and we unitedly engage, and use our utmost Efforts to promote it. And to that End we shall readily join, not only with our Brethren in this Province, but thro' this wide extended Continent, in every lawful, just and constitutional Measure for the recovering and preserving inviolate all our civil and religious Rights & Privileges. And by this Means (to use the Words of his Majesty's Council) we hope to see Happiness and Tranquility restored to the Colonies and especially to see betwixt Great-Britain and them a Union establish'd on such an equitable Basis, as neither of them shall ever wish to destroy. We humbly supplicate the sovereign Arbiter of human Affairs for these happy Events.

The foregoing was voted, accepted, and ordered that the same be enter'd in the Town's Book of Records; and that an attested Copy of the same be transmitted to the Committee of Correspondence at Boston.

A true Copy from the Town's Book of Record,
Attest. ELISHA NILES, Town-Clerk.

Braintree, March 15, 1774.

BOSTON, MARCH 28.

The patriotic Inhabitants of the ancient Town of PLYMOUTH, in Town-Meeting legally assembled on the 24th Instant, in Addition to their truly spirited Votes and Proceedings a few Months ago, relating to the *united* Attempts of the British Administration and the East India Company to establish the detested Duty on Tea in America, have declared, That whoever shall for the future expose to Sale in that Town any Tea while the Duty continues, is and ought to be considered, as an Enemy to America; and that they will have no Dealings with such Men, nor with any others who shall countenance them in so doing.—There is only *one* Person in that Town, who contrary to, and in Defiance of the Sense of his Fellow Townsmen, is so hardy as to continue the Practice of vending this infamous Drug. His Name is exposed in the Votes of the Town, which came too late to be inserted at large in this Paper.

Messieurs EDES and GILL, *March 17, 1774.*

TIME eradicates the Horrors of Guilt, and effaces the Apprehensions of Danger: In Confidence of the Truth of these Maxims, it is said a Number of the most eminent of the Plymouth Protestors are preparing to make a Visit to the Metropolis.

The following is a List of those who have not recanted.

Lemuel Jackson	John Thomas, jun.
Lemuel Goddard	Elkanah Cushman
William Trenholm	Thomas Mathews
Isaac LeBarron	Capt. Benja. Churchill
William LeBarron	John Russell
Ichabod Shaw	Thomas Foster, Esq;
Samuel Harlow	George Watson, Esq;
John Kempton	Edward Winslow, Esq;
Gideon White	Edw. Winslow, jun. Esq;
Cornelius White	Pelham Winslow, Esq;
John Wattson	James Hovey, Esq;
Thomas Foster, 3d	

A CARD.

THE Plymouth Protestors present their Compliments to JOYCE, jun. and ask the Favor of him to make Preparation for a Reception of a select Committee from their Body, who propose to honor the Metropolis with a Visit very soon.

Last Saturday *Richard Clark*, one of the Tea Consignees was seen stroling on the Road between Milton and Roxbury; he was on Horseback and alone. There are various Conjectures as to the Reason of this Excursion. Some say it was to secure an Interest for a Seat in the Superior Court lately vacant; for which it is confidently affirm'd he is (exclusive of the Character of a Friend of Government) as well qualified in all Respects as Chief Justice *Oliver*. Others think his only Design was to feel the Pulse of the true-born Sons of Liberty in the neighboring Towns.

A generous Price will be given for an easy-going Saddle-Horse, that shall be warranted sound Wind and Limb. Inquire of Edes and Gill.

For *Quebec*,

The Schooner Polly, Capt. PEPPER, will sail in all the Month of April, having two Thirds of her Cargo engaged: For Freight or Passage apply to said Master on Board at Long-Wharff; or of *Edward Davis*, at his Store, who wants to Charter a single deck'd Vessel from 70 to 100 Tons Burthen to load at Quebec for the West-Indies.

TO BE SOLD
AT PUBLICK AUCTION,
By Benjamin Church,
At his usual Place of Sale,
On THURSDAY next,
At THREE o'Clock in the Afternoon,
A Variety of valuable House Furniture;
a Number of large Looking-Glasses—Chairs, Tables, Feather Beds—Pewter, &c. Some Plate—A Variety of European Goods, viz. Broad Cloths—Plains—Kerseys—Shalloons—Tammies—Calamancoes—Irish Linnens—Checks—Mens Horse——a large Quantity of Buttons double wash'd and others—Buckles—Knives and Forks—Watches——&c. &c. &c.
At Three o'Clock Afternoon.

PUBLICK AUCTION.
On TUESDAY the 29th MARCH will be Sold by PUBLICK AUCTION, at the Dwelling House of Mr. JOHN MICO WENDELL, deceas'd, a variety of Houshold Furniture—consisting of—
Tables, Chairs, Pier Glasses, Mehogony Case of Draws, Beauros, Feather Beds, Bedsteads, Houshold Linnen, Kitchen Furniture, Plate, &c.
The Sale will begin at 9 o'Clock, A. M.
M. DESHON, Auctioneer.

Bar Iron and Anchors,
Warranted of a prime Quality, and SOLD by
SAM^L. A. OTIS,
At Store No. 1, Butler's Row, ALSO,
New-England RUM, CHOCOLATE, and many other Articles.
☞ A few Quarter Casks Madeira WINES very cheap.

POT-ASH.
CASH given for *POT-ASH*,
By JONATHAN MASON,
At his Shop next Door to the Sign of the *Buck & Glove*, Near the Town-House, BOSTON.
N. B. To be Sold by said MASON,
A Quantity of choice Connecticut Pork.

LAND TO BE SOLD
Five Hundred Acres of LAND,
in the Town of *Granville*, to be Sold, either the whole at once, or such Lots as may best suit the Purchaser.—
Inquire of
Richard Salter,
At his Shop in Cornhill;
Who continues to Sell on the most reasonable Terms, English and India GOODS suitable for all Seasons——The best French and Spanish Indigo, Pepper and Spices: Also a fine Assortment of Women's and Children's Stays made in the neatest and best manner: Best russel, callamanco and everlasting Women and Children Shoes, Pumps, Goloshoes, &c.

Stolen one Evening last Week
from a House in Union-Street, one Scarlet Cloth Riding-hood, one Scarlet Cloth Cloak, one black Russell quilted Petticoat, one Tippet and one Holland Apron. A handsome Reward will be given to any Person that can give Information to the Printer, so that the Thief may be detected and the Things recover'd. 28 March 1774.

TO be Sold by Publick Vendue, on Wednesday the Sixth Day of April next—The Farm of Samuel Woolly late of Bedford, deceased, containing 152 Acres of excellent Plough-Land, Mowing, Pasturing, Orcharding and Woodland, upwards of an 100 Acres under Improvement, with a large Dwelling-House, two Barns a Mill-House, Cyder-Mill, and Corn House, about eight Acres of Winter Rye, pleasantly situated on a publick Road, within two Miles of the Meeting House.—The Sale to begin at One of the Clock Afternoon, at the Dwelling-House on the Premises in said Bedford.

WANTED,
A Woman of a good Character,
and one that can be well recommended, and that understands Cooking and other House Work; none need apply but such a one, and is wanted immediately.—Good Wages will be given. Inquire of Edes & Gill.

A FARM to be Sold in Watertown, very pleasantly situated, and within two Miles of the College, contains about 40 Acres of choice good Land, has on it a good House and Barn, is well accommodated for Mowing, Pasturage and Tillage, has on it a Variety of all kinds of Fruits, and will very well accommodate a Gentleman: Whoever is inclined to Purchase the same may apply to *John Stratton* of said Watertown. *Feb. 28. 1774.*

TO BE SOLD VERY REASONABLY,
By ISRAEL HUNTING, of *Dedham*,
All his Interest in the first Parish in said Town, viz.
HIS Homestead, containing 15 Acres of choice Mowing and Tillage Land, having some excellent Apple-Trees thereon; there being a good House and Barn on the Premises, and but a quarter of a Mile from the Meeting-House.—*Also*, 4 Acres of Pasturing and Orchard, one Mile and an half from said Homestead.

LONDON,

Jan. 13. The Turks are hastily raising 60,000 men at Constantinople, as a last effort against the Russians.

This day his Majesty went to the House of Peers, and opened the Session of Parliament with a most gracious SPEECH, the substance of which was :

HE took notice of the good effects that had succeeded the temporary distress which had been created by the regulations they had made last Session respecting the Gold Coin ; and recommended to them in the strongest terms, to prosecute their enquiries still farther, into the adulteration of the coin, as a duty they owed their country. He said, he had the pleasure to inform them, that his neighbours and allies entertained the same pacifick sentiments as himself ; and lamented that the war still raged between the Russians and Turks. He concluded in the usual manner, with his hope that they would chearfully grant the usual supplies, the estimates of which should be laid before them.

Lord Sandwich has left town for a month, and has commissioned six new Captains for 6 guardships ; he has likewise generously lessened the expences of Millar the Printer, and has taken off 1500l. of the 2000 . fine.

NEW-YORK, March 21.

Extract of a Letter from Philadelphia, dated March 17, 1774.

Capt. Love arrived here left London the 19th of January and the Isle of White the 30th. We have a few Papers, one as late as the 27th of January,—The Accounts of the Destruction of the Tea at Boston is published in the Papers of the 22d of January ; and our Tea Ship, the Polly, Capt. Ayres, arrived off Dover 25th January ; no Remarks in the Papers about either. The Paper of the 20th January, says the Affairs of America will not be taken up by Parliament till the Session is pretty far advanced. By the Papers there has been a great Insurrection at Petersburgh, but cannot find out Particulars. The Russian Troops are ordered out of Poland, and many Regiments from the Grand Army on the Turkish Frontiers, are going for Petersburg ; the Remainder of the Russian Troops are gone to Winter Quarters, and a Letter from Paris, dated 17th January, says, it is positively asserted that Orders are given to all our Regiments to hold themselves in Readiness to take the Field upon the earliest Notice, and that an Army of 100,000 Men will be assembled on the Rhine in the Spring. Our London Ships were to sail about 20th February, and yours the Beginning of March. Not one Arrival from your Port.

A Gentleman in England, writes his Friend in Philadelphia, " The warlike Preparations of the French I imagine will alarm all Europe ; what their Designs are Time must bring forth : The Insurrection at Petersburg, we imagine is set on Foot by them, and his Prussian Majesty is at the Bottom of the Scheme. We expect soon to hear of the fitting out Fleets and sending Armies to different Parts, as we certainly will not be tame Spectators."

Our Tea-Ship is hourly expected, she having sailed from Antigua for this Port, 28 Days since.

NEWPORT, March 21.

We hear the blustering, hectoring Lindzee was lately broke, that the murderous Capt. Preston died at a bleeding at the mouth, and that the infamous Duddingston took his departure from France to the realms of darkness a few months past. *So may all our enemies perish ! !*

BOSTON, March 28.

Extract of a Letter from a Gentleman of Distinction in North-Carolina, dated, Pitt, Feb. 18, 1774.

" I read with much Satisfaction the Account of the Destruction of the Tea, as it was, I think, the only Remedy left to rescue the Colonies from their destined Slavery. You labour under some Difficulties more than your Neighbours ; but the Satisfaction of a consciencious Discharge of the Duty you owe Posterity, together with *the Approbation of the whole Continent*, of your Conduct, is a sufficient Reward."

We hear that the Jamaica-Planter, a large new Ship that sailed from this Place last Winter for Jamaica, John M'Fadzean, Master, was cast-away on a Reef of Rocks as she was going up the Harbour of Kingston, and beat to Pieces : The People and most of the Cargo were saved.

We hear two Printers, with Printing Materials, are expected in one of the Spring Ships from London, to carry on the Business in this Town ; and that several other Tradesmen and Factors are expected in the Course of the Summer : Likewise, that a Number of Manufacturers and Husbandmen were preparing to embark for the Southern Colonies from Great-Britain and Ireland.

DIED.] On Tuesday last Mr. Joseph Gale, aged 64, his Remains were decently interr'd on Thursday last.

Mess'rs EDES & GILL,

SOME People believing that the American Post-Office was first instituted by an Act of the British Parliament, it may be necessary to acquaint them that it was, in its Origin, established by a private Gentleman, one Mr. Benger, of Fredericksburg, Virginia, who was *permitted* to continue it under his own Direction, until a British Ministry, by Means of a *Letter-writer*, discovered that a Revenue might be raised therefrom—and, in Consequence, we were *restrained* in our Liberties, and taxed without our Consent, in the IXth Year of the Reign of Queen Anne, for the express Purpose of raising a Revenue, to ease her Majesty's Subjects, the *Lawmakers*, on the other Side of the Atlantic.

As the Plan for establishing New Post-Offices in America meets with so great Encouragement, it is imagined that several of the Deputy-Post-Masters will have the Virtue and Spirit to resign their Appointments, from a Conviction that the Post Masters General have no more *Right* to erect Offices here, than a Nabob of Indostan.

Messieurs EDES and GILL,

IT is really surprizing that Mr. Draper, who, on all Occasions, *plumes himself* on the *Accuracy* and *Authenticity* of *his* Intelligence, should venture on a FALSHOOD, the Detection of which is so easy, and so scandalously unbecoming a Man, whose Duty it is, at least, to *read* the public Papers. Will not Enmity to the Liberties of *his* Country, so conspicuous in all his public Conduct, account for this foul Proceeding of his Excellency's PRINTER ?

G.

County of L———n, March 14, 1774.

Messieurs EDES & GILL,

AS it is the Custom, at opening a Court, to read the G———r's Proclamation for the suppressing of Vice and Immorality, and he promises to do all in his Power to carry the Proclamation into Effect, I could not but be much surprised at a late Nomination of a Justice for this County——Instead of looking out for one of a moral and religious Character, it seems one is pitched upon who is tho't to be quite the reverse of every Thing of that Nature. If Whoring, Lying, profane Swearing, if not Perjury, are to be the Ingredients in the Composition of a Justice of the Peace, I never desire to be one. If such are the Guardians of our Laws and Morals, its probable we soon shall be as Sodom and Gomorrha, and ripe for the Destruction design'd for us by those in Power.

A former Justice.

LYME, March 17th, 1774.

Yesterday one William Lamson, of Martha's-Vineyard, came to this Town with a Bag of TEA, (about 100 Wt) on Horse back, which he was peddling about the Country. It appeared that he was about Business which (he supposed) would render him obnoxious to the People, which gave Reason to suspect that he had some of the detested Tea lately landed at Cape Cod ; and upon Examination it appeared to the Satisfaction of all present, to be part of that very Tea ; (though he declared that he purchased it of two Gentlemen in Newport, one of them it is said is a Custom House Officer, and the other Captain of the Fort,) Whereupon a Number of the Sons of Liberty assembled in the Evening, kindled a Fire and committed the Bag with its Contents to the Flames, where it was all consumed and the Ashes buried on the Spot, in Testimony of their utter Abhorrence of all Tea subject to a Duty for the Purpose of raising a Revenue in America.

A laudable Example for our Brethren in *Connecticut*.

Marlborough, March 3, 1774. This morning died here Mrs. Elizabeth Harrington, Widow of Mr. Daniel Harrington, late deceased, aged 101 Years, wanting a few Months ; she lived in this Town in the Time of the Indian War, and often went to Garrison to escape the Cruelty of the aboriginal Barbarians, and towards the Close of Life saw a gloomy Scene arising from those born and educated amongst us, more brutish and unnatural than the very Aboriginals themselves ; and tho' she could not continue to see the End of these troublesome Times, yet she doubted not that the Wickedness of the Wicked would shortly come to an End : She sustained a *good Name* thro' Life, and retained her *Reason* to the last, and was gathered in, as a full ripe Sheaff of Corn, and is now where the Wicked cease from troubling and the weary be at Rest.

Woburn, March 19, 1774.

Last Sabbath died very suddenly of a Paralytick disorder, the Rev'd *Thomas Jones*, Pastor of the second Church in this Town, in the 52d Year of his Age, and 24th of his Ministry : His Seizure was while in Public Worship, concluding his Morning Prayer. He was very soon depriv'd of his Speech and Reason, and expir'd at the going down of the Sun. He was a good Divine, a clear and profitable Preacher, cloathed with humility, of a pacific mind, benevolent disposition, amiable in the practice of virtue, a lover of all good Men, and one who walked within his House with an upright Heart. He has left a disconsolate Widow and three Daughters, to lament his Death ; an afflicted People and mourning Vicinity.

All Persons having any Demands

on the Estate of Mr. JOHN KNEELAND, late of Boston, Shopkeeper, deceased, are desired to bring in their Accounts in Order for Adjustment ; and all who are indebted to said Estate, are desired to pay their respective Dues.

ABIGAIL KNEELAND,
BARTHOW' KNEELAND,
EDWARD KNEELAND.

Executors of the Deceased's last Will.

At the Sterling Cost, are now selling off,

THE Shop Goods belonging to the Estate of Mr. *John Kneeland*, deceased, at the Shop lately kept by him in Union-Street, near the Market. Any Person minded to purchase the whole Stock together, will find it for their Interest to apply soon, as the Sales must be closed in a short Time.

N. B. A small Parcel of Gold and Silver Lace to be Sold at extreme low Rates.

TO BE SOLD

By *Joseph Belknap*,

In Ann-Street, near the Draw-Bridge, Boston,

White CALVE SKINS,

by the Dozen or single Skin.

Just Imported, and to be Sold by

GEORGE ERVING,

A Large Quantity of Russia Duck, Dutch Rope Yarns, Junk, Looking-Glasses, Linseed Oyl, Stone Ware, &c. &c. Boston, March 28, 1774.

CASH

GIVEN for Merchantable and Unmerchantable Pot-ash, and Potash Salts, at GOULD's Auction Office in Back Street, Boston.

SEVEN good HORSES, one Stage Coach, with Harness compleat for four Horses, and two Fall-back Chaise, to be Sold very reasonable for the Cash or West-India Goods. Inquire of JOHN WALDO, at his House third Door South of the Lamb Tavern.

Wednesday Next at X in the Morning

Will be sold by PUBLIC VENDUE, at the Auction-Room in Queen-Street,

A great Variety of English Goods—among which are,

BROAD Cloths, Shalloons, Tammies, Callimancoes, fine Cotton Velvets, Denmark Lustres, Popplins, Brolioes, Sergedenims, Venetians, Cambleteens, Missinets, Tabourets, Lutestrings, Ducape, laced Sattins, Silk Gloves, Mens and Womens Hose, Swanskins, a Quantity of Velvet Corks, a large Parcel of Twine, a few Groce of Bank Cod-Hooks, &c. &c.

J. Russell, Auctioneer.

On THURSDAY NEXT,

At ONE o'Clock,

Will be SOLD by PUBLIC VENDUE, at the Bunch of Grapes Tavern in King-Street.

TWO Half Pipes, and Twelve Quarter Casks of Madeira Wine, one Quarter Cask of Claret do. a few Boxes Malaga Lemmons, and a Quantity of unginn'd Cotton. J. RUSSELL, Auctioneer.

Thursday next, 1 o'Clock

TO BE SOLD CHEAP,

A Brig called the NANCY, about

Eighteen Months old, 124 Tons Burthen, a prime Sailer and well found, now lying at John Hancock, Esq'rs Wharf. For further Particulars, Inquire of Mr. *Thomas Boylston*.

WANTED,

£.400 Lawful Money, for which good

Real Security will be given in Boston. Inquire of Edes and Gill.

All Persons having Demands on

the Estate of *Pitts Hall*, late of Boston, Merchant deceased, are requested to bring in their Accounts for Adjustment, to the Subscriber, who is appointed Administrator on said Estate. JOHN ERVING, jun.

For Annapolis-Royal in Cumberland,

The Schooner RAVEN, DAVID CROWELL, Master, will sail in 6 Days : For Freight or Passage apply to CHARLES LOWE, at his Shop opposite the Boston Stone, near the Mill-Bridge, or on board said Schooner lying at Pitts's Wharf.

TO BE SOLD,

A Schooner about 35 Tons, lying at *Minot*'s

T. employ'd in the Fishing Business. Enquire at Mr. *Munro*'s Notary-Publick, near the Court-House, King-Street.

TWENTY DOLLARS Reward.

STOLEN out of the Stable of Capt. NATHAN BRIGHAM in Southborough, on the Night of the 22d Instant, a valuable Sorrel Horse, with a Blaze in his Face, and several red Spots among the white near his Nose, Trotts and Paces well, one of his hind Feet is Part white, he is five Years old, and about fifteen Hands high, his Hair is wore off of his sides with the Saddle Skirts on his Loins with the Housing. Whoever shall Secure the said Horse so as the Owner may have him again, and also Secure the Thief so that he may be brought to Justice shall receive the above Reward ; and Eight Dollars Reward for the Horse only.

Southborough, March 24, 1774.

Nathan Brigham.

For private Sale,

At the NEW AUCTION-ROOM, South Side of the Town-House, viz.

Three handsome Mehogany Desks

and Book Cases, Chest on Chests of Draws, Desks, round and square Dining & Spring Tables, Beauro ditto, Card and Chamber Tables, Mehogany Chairs with Copper-plate yellow and Leather Bottoms, round-about Chairs, black Walnut Leather bottom Chairs, handsome Clocks, Pinchbeck Watches, handsome Sconce Looking-Glasses of all sorts and sizes, a Suit of Harrateen Curtains, a Suit of yellow Morien Curtains, with Window Curtains, Squabbs and Easy Chair, 6 green bottom Chamber Chairs, Window Shades, small handsome Spinnett, Mehogany and Maple four Post Bedsteads, small Mehogany Sugar Chests, 2 Cases of Doctor's Instruments, small Handmaids, a large Scale Beam, with Scales & Chains, Plate, handsome Silver Terreen Tankard, large Salver, Chaffin-dishes, Porringers, Cups, Pepper Boxes, large and small Spoons, silver hilted Swords, silver and Ivory Handle Knives and Forks, silver plated Candlesticks, a genteel brass reading Candlestick, a very neat pair of steel Pistols, Gun and Bayonet, Barometer, also, orange, blue and green collour'd Broad Cloths, Cotton Velvetts, Shalloons, Tammies, Stuffs and Durants, white Baize, Irish Linnens, Men's silk Hose, Capuchine Silks of all colours, black, blue, red and white Sarsnets, Patch Work Coverlids, a Box of well assorted and handsome Ribbonds, Poplins, Buckskin Breeches, handsome Muffs, a large Globe, silk Gauzes, black Sattin and Chip Hatts, a handsome full suit of Brocade, and suit of black Grogram, small Pocket Glasses, and Lisbon Lemmons by the Box, a Variety of other Articles.

N. B. At said Auction-Office constant Attendance is given to receive all kind of Goods for public and private Sale.

CUSTOM-HOUSE, *BOSTON*.

ENTETRD IN.

Blaney & Sobier, Cape Nichola ; *Collier, St. Vincents and St. Lucia* ; *Parrish, New-Haven* ; *Clap, North-Carolina* ; *Thatcher, South-Carolina.*

Burials in the Town of BOSTON, since our last.

Eleven Whites. One Black.

Baptiz'd in the several Churches, Fourteen.

High Water at BOSTON, *for the present Week.*

Monday, 46 min. aft. 11	Friday, 32 min. after 3
Tuesday, 40 min. aft. 12	Saturday, 28 min. af. 4
Wednesday, 36 m. aft. 1	Lord's-Day, 25m. aft 5
Thursday, 34 min. aft. 2	Full ● 27 Day 6 After.

ther's company. He looks drowsy, for he has been up at Arthur's all night. Turn round, sirrah, and stare them all in the face, as usual -- and as usual, shew your teeth. There's a figure for you, gellmen and ladies! Who bids for it? There's an ungodly composition of powder, vanity, pomatum and folly! Do but mark his languishing attitudes, the womanishness of his dress, and the arch of his eye brow. O he's a puppy of the right race -- of the original kennel --- of the true Maccaroni breed --- for ever mouthing, grinning, sneering -- the dupe of beauty, and the bubble of wit. Where are ye, ye tender, weak, and puppy-loving fair ones? If ye want a meet companion for a vapourish morning, or a rainy evening, here it is. --- This is he, or she, or it, that can lisp lies into a lady's ear, and hum minuets, and lounge on laps, and talk scandal, and ogle a Countess, or bilk a whore, with any he, she, or it at Arthur's. This is he, that trim, tripping, smooth faced, black hearted thing, that assumes more changes than the changeful Cynthia --- now sighing with ladies, and now swearing with gamblers and lordlings --- now deep in politicks at St. Stephen's, and now deeper in Arthur's. Do good people, put him in. O he's a fellow of profound plans and keen execution. He once carried a bill into the senate for the repeal of the marriage act, and well was the work begun --- Keen, vigilant, and active, he sweated, he beseeched, he harrangued, and he argued --- all was ripe for the *fiat*; but one unlucky morning ruined all --- for this keen, vigilant, and active young man, had sat three hours and an half under the fingers of his hair dresser, and was absent: the bill was lost, and the North road is still the only cure for love. Bless me! will nobody bid for him? What! for this man of glitter, of powder and silk? Do but smell him, gellmen --- he breathes odours like a hyacinth. There is a *rank* smell runs through all the family of the *Reynards*, but he has quite overpowered it with perfumery. --- Oh! somebody bid for him -- He'd be a good bargain to a minister or a taylor, for he can lead a debate or a fashion with equal success --- What nobody? Not even a hair-dresser, to hang his head in the front window? Pshaw! throw him aside: for all people seem to be of opinion, *That a macaroni is worth nothing.*

TO BE SOLD IMMEDIATELY,

By *Margaret Newman*, Administratrix

to the Estate of Mrs. *Margaret Fletcher*, deceased—— A BRICK HOUSE situate in Ann-street, making the Corner of the new Street lately made from Ann to Middle-street, at present occupied by Mr. Jeremiah Allen —it has two Rooms on a Floor, with a good Celler, Yard and Pump; the whole in good Repair.——Said *Newmzn* has to Let, a Store nearly opposite the above.

To be Sold cheap, for Cash only,

50 Acres of choice Land, lying in the Town of Lunenburgh, in the County of Worcester—in the Third Division Land (so called) near Manoosenett-Hill, which was originally laid out to John Scott.—— Enquire of John Gray, Esq; Rope-Maker in Boston.

To be SOLD or LET;

A Farm in Cambridge Neck so called, (and entered upon the first of April next) containing between Seventy and Eighty Acres, consisting of Mowing Land, both English and Salt, with good Plowland, and Pasturage, and a good Orchard of choice Fruit thereon, the same being well watered. Said Farm lying within one Mile from the College, and about three Miles from Charlestown Ferry. For further Particulars, enquire of Samuel Soden of Watertown, or of Seth Hastings of said Cambridge.

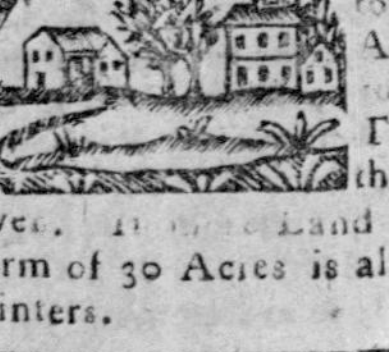

TO BE SOLD,

A Pleasant FARM at Newton, about a Mile from Watertown Bridge, containing about 30 Acres:—Also a Wood Lot nearly adjoining, of about 30 Acres:— Three Years will be allowed for the Payment, good Security being given. If more Land should be wanted, the adjoining Farm of 30 Acres is also to be Sold. Enquire of the Printers.

TO BE SOLD OR LETT,

A good FARM in Newton, and entered upon the first Day of April, containing One Hundred Acres of good Land, with a House and Barn thereon, all in good Repair, well proportioned for Mowing, Plowing and Orcharding, &c. with a Stream that runs thro' said Farm, never known to be dry.—For further Particulars inquire of Abraham Fuller, Esq; or of Amariah Fuller, living near said Premises.

Hackney Coach

Drove by GEORGE HAMBLIN,

Will attend Gentlemen and Ladies to or from any Part of the Town, at any Time in the Day or Evening, at *One Shilling* each—A single Person for *Two Shillings*.

N. B. Said Hamlin gives constant Attendance at Mr. PADDOCK's Coach-Yard, Long-Acre.

All Persons that have any Demands on the Estate of Mr. Andrew Cunningham, late of Boston, Hatter, deceased, are desired to bring in their Accounts to Mary Greenleaf and John Cunningham, Administrators on said Estate, for Adjustment.——And all Persons indebted to said Estate, are desired to make immediate Payment to said Administrators.

John Cunningham,

HAS for Sale at his Shop near the Corner of School-Street, opposite Mr. Deblois's,

A Large Assortment of English and India Goods, suitable for all Seasons, which he is determined to sell at the Sterling Cost (clear of Charges) he being determined to quit the Business.

FIFTY DOLLARS REWARD.

LAST Night the Dwelling-House of the Subscriber was broke open, and from thence were taken the following Articles of Plate, viz.

1 Pair of Silver Chaffingdishes, 1 pair of Butter-cups, 1 silver can, 2 large soup-spoons, 1 pepper-box, 6 large table-spoons, 6 tea do. and a strainer, marked E. D. maker's name, D. Henchman all except the spoons, which have a Hand for a Crest.—A silver tea-pot, 1 do. sugar-dish, a boat for tea spoons, 1 pair tea-tongs, 5 tea-spoons and a cream-cup. Two porringers and two salt-cellars. all mark'd E. S. 1 silver Tankard without a lid, marked S / I. S. *1 silver can marked* D / I. E. *an old fashion'd pepper-box mark'd* D / A. E. *6 large table spoons marked E. S. 1 silver salver, no mark upon it, the foot resembling the mouth of a tunnel, a silver tankard marked A. B. 1 silver porringer without any mark, 3 table spoons marked A. B. 1 old spoon marked* S / I. S. *4 tea spoons no mark, 1 pair tea tongs, Makers names of these not made by D. Henchman, I. Hurd some of them, and some B. W—with several other small articles.——Whoever will take up the Thief or Thieves, so as he or they may be brought to Justice and the Plate recovered, shall be paid the above Reward, and a reasonable Reward for any Part of the Plate, in Proportion to its Value.* *per me,* THADDEUS BURR.

Fairfield, Connecticut, 15 March, 1774.

N. B. *If any of the above Plate should be discovered in Boston, please to give Notice to* JOHN HANCOCK, *Esq; and an adequate Reward shall be given.*

TO BE SOLD,

A new Vessel about 60 Tons burthen, now on the Stocks at Cohasset, may be launched within a Month. For further Particulars, enquire of BRECK and HAMMETT, at their Store the Head of GREEN's Wharff, or of DANIEL TOWER at Cohasset.

TO BE SOLD and entered upon immediately,

A House in Milton, with a Malt House and five Acres of Orcharding and Mowing Land, about 10 Miles distant from Boston, and 2 from the Meeting-House, on the main Road that leads to Stoughton. It is known by the Name of Samuel Soper's, lately tenanted by Rufus Bent. Any Person inclining to Purchase may apply to *Ralph Inman*, Esq; at his Warehouse in Boston.

TO BE SOLD,

A Farm lying on Squanton-Neck, late the Estate of Remember Preston, deceased, containing about 50 Acres of good Land, with a House and Barn thereon. For further Particulars, enquire of John Preston of Boston, or of Ebenezer Baker of Dorchester.

Russia Duck, best Petersburgh Hemp, Dutch Rope Yarns, also a Quantity of *choice Junk*, fit to make into Cordage of any Size, great part of which will do for rigging small Vessels without working over— To be Sold at *Thomas Walley*'s Store on Dock-Square,

—Where is to Sell by Wholesole or Retail—

Dutch Looking Glasses of various Sizes,
Dutch Brushes, single or by the sett,
Hampers Stone Ware, viz. Qt. & Pt. Mugs and Chamber Pots,
A few Casks Choice Rice,
All sorts of Spices *very low, Oatmeal per Bushel,*
A parcel of fine Narraganset and Pomfret Cheese,
New Raisins, Currants, and all sorts of Groceries as usual——*Except TEA.*

N. B. A Quantity of choice 3 threaded Sein Twine, for Salmon, Mackrel or Herring Nets.

ALSO, White Beans per Bushel.

A Wet Nurse, with a good Breast of Milk, would take a Child to suckle. Inquire of the Printers.

WANTED,

A Boy about 14 or 15 Years old, to a Mason's Trade. Inquire of the Printers.

TO BE SOLD,

By Benjamin Dolbeare,

A Very good Fire Engine, London-made; old Jamaica Spirit by the Tierce, sundry Barrels of Jamaica Sugar, and Vinegar by the Barrel.

WANTED;

A Negro Man of an unexceptionable Character, warranted; for such an one a good Price will be given; one of a small Size, brought up in a Country Town, and who understands a little of House Business will be preferred. Inquire of the Printers.

Just IMPORTED, and TO BE SOLD by

John Decosta

In Milk-Street, a little below the Old South Meeting House; Beans, Peas, and a Variety of other Garden Seeds; Fresh and Good; also a Variety of young Fruit Trees, Grafted and Innoculated; also Roots and Plants, all at Reasonable Rates.

GARDEN SEEDS.

IMPORTED in Capt. HOOD from LONDON, and Sold

By ANN JOHNSON,

At the Head of Black-Horse Lane, near the Rev. Dr. Pemberton's Meeting-House:

A large Assortment of

GARDEN SEEDS,

Peas, Beans, &c. among which are,

EARLY charlton, early golden hospur, Ormand hotspur, Spanish moratto, white rouncival, dwarf marrowfat and bush pease, large Windsor, true early Lisbon, early yellow six weeks white kidney and fine toker beans, early Yorkshire, Dutch Sugar loaf, battersea, savoy, red and brocoli cabbage seed, collyflower, cucumber, onion, carrot, turnip, raddish and lettice of all sorts, round spinnage endive, cellery and asparagus, thyme, baum, sweet marjoram, broad clover, white Dutch clover, la lucern, rape, canary, and an assortment of flower seeds: Also a variety of other seeds not mentioned; all which are imported from the seedmen in London, and are warranted to be fresh & good, and of the last year's produce.

TO BE SOLD,

Laying in the Province of *New Hampshire*,

Three valuable Tracts of Land, consisting chiefly of Interval and high Interval Land, the Growth of which is mostly Rockmaple, Beach and yellow Birch Trees, containing in the Whole about 4000 Acres, lying on *Saco* and *Fllis*'s Rivers, distant from *Falmouth* about 50 Miles, from *Dover* about 45 Miles, from *Frye's* Town only 8 Miles: Each Tract lying on a County Road. For further Particulars inquire of WILLIAM GREENLEAF of Boston.

WHEREAS the Proprietors of Land in the Township of *Leicester* on *Otter Creek*, (which Township was granted by the Governor and Council of New-Hampshire) did at their Meeting in January 1773, Vote, That the Sum of Four Dollars should be raised and levied on each original Right; and also at their Meeting in March following, Voted, That the Sum of One Dollar as aforesaid, for the Bounding and Lotting out said Township, and for the managing and carrying on any other Affairs for the common Good of said Propriety, and that a Committee be appointed to assess the same.—Therefore we the Subscribers being appointed a Committee for the Purpose aforesaid, do a third Time, notify the Proprietors to pay the same to Mr. Isaac Stone, Collector, or to Capt. Elisha Child, Treasurer, at or before the adjourn'd Meeting of said Propriety which will be on the last Tuesday in April, which will be the 26th Day of said Month, at Nine o'Clock in the Morning, at the House of Nathaniel Child, Esq; of Woodstock, in the County of Windham, and Colony of Connecticut; otherwise their Rights will be exposed to Sale, at the House of the said Nathaniel Child, Esq; at Ten o'Clock on said Day, according to Law.

Woodstock, March 3, 1773.
Nathaniel Child,
Elisha Child,
Samuel McClelland, } Committee.

THE original Proprietors of a Township called Pennicook, now Concord, and the original Proprietors of a Township called Suncook, now Pembroke, (both in the Province of New-Hampshire) or the Heirs or Assigns of said original Proprietors; are hereby Notified that the General Court in their present Session, hath granted to each Propriety a Township in the late Province of Main, and appointed the Subscribers a Committee to exhibit a List to said Court, within 10 Months from the Date, of the Names of the Persons that have been Sufferers who have a just Claim to an Interest in the one or the other of said Townships:—This is therefore to give Notice to the said Pennicook Proprietors, and the said Suncook Proprietors, that the Committee will attend said Service at the House of Mrs. Hannah Osgood, Innholder in said Pennicook, on the second Wednesday in October next, ensuing, to receive authenticated Evidence of said Sufferers Claims to an interest in the Township granted to the said Pennicook Proprietors, and that they will attend said Service at the House of Mr. Samuel Conner, Innholder in said Suncook, on the third Wednesday in October aforesaid, to receive like Evidence of the said Sufferers Claims to an Interest in the Township granted to the said Suncook Proprietors.

Feb. 22, 1774.
Samuel Phillips,
Joseph Gerrish,
Jonathan Webster } Committee.

By Virtue of an Act of the General Court, in the Province of New-Hampshire, the Proprietors of the Lands in Francestown, formerly New-Boston adition, are desired to Pay the Tax due, by Virtue of said Act, unto John Quigly, *Esq; who is empowered to Collect the same, in Order for Building a Meeting House in said Town, the Tax being One Pound Five Shillings, Lawful Money, on the Lott or Hundred Acres: And if the said Tax is not paid on, or before the Eleventh Day of April so much of the Delinquents Land will be Sold at Public Vendue as will Pay the Taxes with cost of Sale, at the House of Mr. Pierce, Innholder in Groton, on Monday the 11th Day of April, at 3 o'Clock in the Afternoon of said Day.*

Francestown March 7, 1774.

Boston: Printed, by EDES & GILL

in QUEEN STREET.

THE Boston- AND COUNTRY Gazette, JOURNAL.

Containing the freshest Advices,   *Foreign and Domestic.*

No. 991.

MONDAY, April 4, 1774.

AT a legal meeting of the town of Hull, held on Monday March 14, 1774. Mr. Thomas Jones chosen moderator, &c.——

Voted, That the letter from the committee of correspondence at Boston, be taken into consideration, and that Lieut. *Daniel Souther*, Mr. *Caleb Goold*, and Mr. *Amos Binney*, jun. be a committee to give the sense of the town thereon, and make report at the adjournment of the meeting, &c.

March 28, 1774, then met upon the adjournment, &c.—The committee bro't in their report, which was then read and accepted, and the town-clerk directed to transmit a fair copy thereof to said committee at Boston for publication, if they think fit.

From the Records, &c.
Attest,   *John Goold*, Town-Clerk.

WE the freeholders and other inhabitants of Hull, being impressed with a just sense of the inestimable value of our rights, liberties and privileges; and with deep concern at the many attacks made on them of late years, through the influence and misrepresentations of corrupt and evil minded men, in the administration of government under the King, both here and in Great-Britain; take the liberty at this truly alarming and critical situation of public affairs, to deliver our sentiments of our rights, and the infringements on those rights, more particularly in the article of tea.—This article is at present subjected to a tribute payable here, imposed by a parliament in which, from our local situation and circumstances we neither are or can be present in person, or by our representative to give our free consent, which is essential to every just tax on a people. This tribute on tea, as that on sugar, wines, and other articles, and as was intended in the stamp act, is collected by an odious band of placemen and pensioners, supported by an armed force, both by sea and land, to over-awe the continent into a compliance, or enforce it by fire and sword, as is evident by the destruction of the people in Boston, on the fatal fifth of March 1770. Thus we see the spoils and plunder of our estates are to be torn from us, and lavished away on those task-masters, who seem as unrelenting as those employed by Pharoah of old, or by the Grand Turk at present. On the whole, it is manifest that we are all in eminent danger of losing not only our estates, but that fairest and best inheritance on earth, so nobly purchased with the toil, blood and treasure, of our pious and worthy ancestors; we mean the rights, liberties and privileges, *civil and religious*, transmitted to their posterity. Therefore,

Resolved, That in our opinion, every man by the law of *God* and *nature*, has a right to life, liberty, and property, and to the peaceable and quiet enjoyment of each, while he injures not others; and that the true and ultimate end of government is for the security and protection of our rights, liberties and privileges.

2. That where there is no protection given, there can be no subjection justly demanded, or due, much less when those who are intrusted with the powers of government, make use of those powers only to oppress.

3. It is essential to the nature of a free government, and adopted as the *basis* or groundwork of the British constitution, that no man should be bound by any human laws, but such as he, or his ancestors have consented to in person, or by representative.

4. That the imposition on tea by parliament, and on other articles, and by means of an armed force, over awing, or dragooning the inhabitants into a compliance, differs in nothing essential, if at all to the subject, between a tribute demanded of vassals and slaves, or a military contribution.

5. That the professed purpose in the acts laying impositions on the Americans, namely, for the support of government, and administration of justice, is specious but delusive; for it is explained by the practice of giving salaries to governors and judges, thereby making them dependant on a minister of state for their bread, while they should act,

and fit, as free as possible, from temptation in all cases, whether between the King and the subject, or between subject and subject.

6. If the parliament have a right to take from us our money without our consent, all general assemblies are quite useless; for when our property is gone, liberty is gone, and life of no further value than to give us an opportunity to prepare for a better.

7. That whoever shall directly or indirectly aid or assist in landing, buying or selling any tea sent, or to be sent, by or through the East-India company, while subjected to imposition here, shall be deemed an enemy to America.

8. That while the imposition on the East-India tea from England remains, we will not use, or suffer any such tea to be used in our families.

9. That on taking off the imposition on tea, we will on equal terms, in that and in all other articles, give the preference to England, whose true interest we have always considered as our own; and sincerely lament the animosities that have arisen in Britain and America, and that breach of cordiality in all respects which once so happily subsisted between the two countries.—We ardently wish and pray for the life, health, and prosperity of his Majesty and family, and that his ministers and councellors may be endued with more wisdom, that all grievances may in due time be redressed, and that every blessing of peace, civil and religious, may be enjoyed by him and all his subjects.

DANIEL SOUTHER, }
CALEB GOOLD,   } Committee
AMOS BINNEY, jun. }

A true Copy,
per JOHN GOOLD, Town Clerk.

All Persons having any Demands on the Estate of Mr. JOHN KNEELAND, late of Boston, Shopkeeper, deceased, are desired to bring in their Accounts in Order for Adjustment; and all who are indebted to said Estate, are desired to pay their respective Dues.   ABIGAIL KNEELAND,
    BARTHOW' KNEELAND,
    EDWARD KNEELAND.
Executors of the Deceased's last Will.

At the Sterling Cost, are now selling off, THE Shop Goods belonging to the Estate of Mr. *John Kneeland*, deceased, at the Shop lately kept by him in Union-Street, near the Market. Any Person minded to purchase the whole Stock together, will find it for their Interest to apply soon, as the Sales must be closed in a short Time.

N. B. A small Parcel of Gold and Silver Lace to be Sold at extreme low Rates.

TO BE SOLD By *Joseph Belknap*, In Ann-Street, near the Draw-Bridge, Boston, White CALVE SKINS, by the Dozen or single Skin.

Just Imported, and to be Sold by GEORGE ERVING, A Large Quantity of Russia Duck, Dutch Rope Yarns, Junk, Looking-Glasses, Linseed Oyl, Stone Ware, &c. &c.
Boston, March 28. 1774.

CASH GIVEN for Merchantable and Unmerchantable Pot-ash, and Potash Salts, at GOULD's Auction Office in Back Street, Boston.

POT-ASH. CASH given for POT-ASH, By JONATHAN MASON, At his Shop next Door to the Sign of the *Buck & Glove*, Near the Town-House, BOSTON.
N. B. To be Sold by said MASON.
A Quantity of choice Connecticut Pork.

For *Quebec*, The Schooner Polly, Capt. PEPPER, will sail in all the Month of April, having two Thirds of her Cargo engaged: For Freight or Passage apply to said Master on Board at Long-Wharff; or of *Edward Davis*, at his Store, who wants to Charter a single deck'd Vessel from 70 to 100 Tons Burthen to load at Quebec for the West-Indies.

Bar Iron and Anchors, Warranted of a prime Quality, and SOLD by SAM^l. A. OTIS, At Store No. 1, Butler's Row, ALSO, New-England RUM, CHOCOLATE, and many other Articles.
☞ A few Quarter Casks Madeira WINES very cheap.

TO BE SOLD CHEAP, A Brig called the NANCY, about Eighteen Months old, 129 Tons Burthen, a prime Sailer and well found, now lying at John Hancock, Esq's Wharf. For further Particulars, Inquire of Mr. *Thomas Boylston*.

WANTED, £.400 Lawful Money, for which good Real Security will be given in Boston. Inquire of Edes and Gill.

TO BE SOLD, A Schooner about 35 Tons, lying at *Minot*'s T. employ'd in the Fishing Business. Enquire at Mr. *Munro*'s Notary-Publick, near the Court-House, King-Street.

A generous Price will be given for an easy-going Saddle Horse, that shall be warranted sound Wind and Limb. Inquire of Edes and Gill.

SEVEN good HORSES, one Stage Coach, with Harness compleat for four Horses, and a Fall-back Chaise, to be Sold very reasonable for the Cash or West-Indies Goods. Inquire of JOHN WALDO, at his House third Door South of the Lamb Tavern.

All Persons having Demands on the Estate of *Pitts Hall*, late of Boston, Merchant deceased, are requested to bring in their Accounts for Adjustment, to the Subscriber, who is appointed Administrator on said Estate.   JOHN ERVING, jun.

Stolen one Evening last Week from a House in Union-Street, one Scarlet Cloth Riding-hood, one Scarlet Cloth Cloak, one black Russell quilted Petticoat, one Tippet and one Holland Apron. A handsome Reward will be given to any Person that can give Information to the Printer, so that the Thief may be detected and the Things recover'd.   28 March 1774.

TO be Sold by Publick Vendue, on Wednesday the Sixth Day of April next—The Farm of Samuel Woolly late of Bedford, deceased, containing 152 Acres of excellent Plough Land, Mowing, Pasturing, Orcharding and Woodland, upwards of an 100 Acres under Improvement, with a large Dwelling-House, two Barns a Mill-House, Cyder-Mill, and CornHouse, about eight Acres of Winter Rye, pleasantly situated on a publick Road, within two Miles of the Meeting House.—The Sale to begin at One of the Clock Afternoon, at the Dwelling-House on the Premises in said Bedford.

TWENTY DOLLARS Reward. STOLEN out of the Stable of Capt. NATHAN BRIGHAM in Southborough, on the Night of the 22d Instant, a valuable Sorrel Horse, with a Blaze in his Face, and several red Spots among the white near his Nose, Trotts and Paces well, one of his hind Feet is part white, he is five Years old, and about fifteen Hands high, his Hair is wore off of his sides with the Saddle Skirts on his Loins with the Houling. Whoever shall Secure the said Horse so as the Owner may have him again, and also Secure the Thief so that he may be brought to Justice shall receive the above Reward; and Eight Dollars Reward for the Horse only.   Nathan Brigham.
Southborough, March 24. 1774.

A FARM to be Sold in Watertown, very pleasantly situated, and within two Miles of the College, contains about 40 Acres of choice good Land, has on it a good House and Barn, is well accommodated for Mowing, Pasturage and Tillage, has on it a Variety of all kinds of Fruits, and will very well accommodate a Gentleman: Whoever is inclined to Purchase the same may apply to *John Stratton* of said Watertown.   Feb. 28. 1774.

TO BE SOLD VERY REASONABLY. By ISRAEL HUNTING, of *Dedham*, All his Interest in the first Parish in said Town, viz. HIS Homestead, containing 15 Acres of choice Mowing and Tillage Land, having fine excellent Apple Trees thereon, there being a good House and Barn on the Premises, and but a quarter of a Mile from the Meeting House.—Also, 4 Acres of Pasturing and Orchard, one [illegible] Homestead.

The following is a Letter from the Committee of Correspondence of the Town of Hadley, *in the County of* Hampshire.

GENTLEMEN, *Hadley, January 24, 1774.*

WE, by Order of the Town of Hadley, here inclose to you a Copy of their Proceedings at their Meeting, on Adjournment January 3, 1774.

To the Gentlemen Committee of Correspondence in Boston.	*Phinehas Lyman,* *Josiah Pierce,* *Oliver Smith,* *Jonathan Warner*	Committe

At a legal Meeting of the Freeholders and other Inhabitants of the Town of Hadley, *assembled at the School House in said* Hadley; *begun Sept. 24, 1773, and continued by Adjournments to* January 3, 1774.

The Committee appointed the 7th Day of *October* 1773, reported as follows.

UPON the Information given us by the Committee of Correspondence at *Boston*, in their Letter and Copies inclosed, transmitted to the Town-Clerk, and laid before this Town, We can no longer suppress our Uneasiness at the many Infringements and Violations of our Rights, so often enumerated by other Towns, that they need not be mentioned particularly by us; and we must express our Concern for the Charter-Privileges of this Province, and of the other Colonies in America.

Resolved, That it is the Opinion of this Town, that the Grievances we labour under, are owing, in a great Measure, to Methods taken by Persons among us, of an arbitrary Turn of Mind, to set the Temper and Behavior of the People of this Province in an unfavourable Light at Great-Britain, and insinuating that "*there must be an Abridgement of what are called English Liberties.*"

Resolved, That this Town will use all such Measures as shall appear to them consistent with their Duty, in order to obtain a Redress of the Grievances we feel; and to prevent, if possible, any further Violations of our natural and constitutional Rights, that our invaluable Liberties, Civil and Religious, may be enjoyed by us, and transmitted to Posterity inviolate; always hoping in the Goodness of divine Providence, that the Machinations of designing Persons, to effect a Change in our happy Constitution, will be rendered abortive, from Time to Time, to the latest Generation.

Resolved, That a standing Committee of Correspondence be appointed, consisting of five Inhabitants of this Town, to keep up and maintain a Correspondence with the Committee of Correspondence in other Towns within this Province, respecting this important Concern.

John Eastman, *Phinehas Lyman,*	*Josiah Pierce,* *Moses Marsh,* *John Chester Williams,* *Jonathan Cooke,* *Jonathan Warner.*	Committee.

Voted, That said Report be accepted, and that Mr. Phinehas Lyman, Doctor Giles Crouch Kellogg, Messi'rs. Oliver Smith, Josiah Pierce and Jonathan Warner, be a standing Committee to keep up and maintain a Correspondence in other Towns within this Province.

Voted. That said Report be recorded in the Town-Book, by the Town Clerk, and that a Copy thereof, and of the Votes of this Meeting, attested by the Town-Clerk, be transmitted to the Committee of Correspondence in Boston, by the standing Committee appointed at this Meeting. Attest. *Jonathan Warner*, Moderator.

A true Copy. Attest.
Josiah Pierce, Town-Clerk.

A LETTER from the Committee of Correspondence at Chatham, *to the Committee of Correspondence of this Town,*

GENTLEMEN,

WE with Gratitude return you our most hearty Thanks for your unwearied Diligence and Steadfastness in our glorious Cause of Liberty, which to every virtuous Man, is esteemed dearer than Life itself.

We congratulate you on the happy Union that prevails throughout America, excepting a few Individuals that will keep their Eyes clos'd, till they are opened by the upbraiding of their Children in the next World. We heartily approve of the Patriotic Resolves of your Meetings; and we are determined to use our most strenuous Endeavours, in a constitutional Way, to ward off all impending Evils, &c. and will by all possible Means, use our small Endeavours, to the uttermost of our power, to oppose, and, if possible, to frustrate the evil Designs of our Enemies on both Sides the Water. As to suffering any Teas to be landed in this Town subject to Duty, our Friends have put it out of our Power, even if we would: Neither can we find, by the most strict Enquiry, that there hath been Ten Pounds bro't into this Town from the Wreck at Cape-Cod, and that was by those that never understood, and we fear never will, 'till they are convinced as abovementioned. We would not forget our thankful Acknowledgment to the adjacent Towns near Boston, as well as to the Gentlemen our Brethren in Boston, for their vigorous Assistance in so important an Affair. And we further add, that we have an Heart and Disposition to be as free as our Charter will permit, and to stand by the Rights of our most gracious Sovereign King George, as free born Subjects; but if we do it as Slaves, the Lord must turn our Hearts from what they now are. We are, Gentlemen, with great Esteem,

Your sincere Friends,
and very humble Servants,

Dated, *Chatham,* *February* 15, 1774.	*James Covel,* *Seth Smith,* *Joseph Attwood,* *Thos. Hamilton.*

At a Meeting of the Freeholders and other Inhabitants of the Town of Scarborough, *duly qualified and legally Warned in public Town Meeting, assembled at the Meeting House in the first Parish in said Town, on Thursday the* 20th *Day* January 1774, *at* 10 *o'Clock, A. M.* Samuel Small, jun. *Moderator.*

THE Inhabitants of this Town taking into Consideration the impending Evils upon us and our Posterity with our Brethren in the Colonies, respecting the Importation of *Tea*, or any other Article from Great-Britain subject to Duties payable by us, are justly alarmed at the same, and considering our Privileges which were purchased by our Forefathers, and handed down to us, and if by Mal-administration are attempted to be taken from us without our consent; we are determined in all justifiable Methods, even to the risk of our Lives and Fortunes, to ward off all such unrighteous Taxations, and Resolve as follows, viz.

Res. 1st. That we will not Import or Purchase any *Tea* or any other Article subject to Duties imposed by a late act of Parliament, nor suffer any to be Landed in said Town.

Res. 2d. That the Thanks of this Town be given to the Town of Boston, for their late noble Exertions in the Cause of American Liberties.

Voted, That the Town Clerk transmit a Copy of the Proceedings of this Meeting to the Corresponding Committee of the Town of Boston.

Voted, That there be a Corresponding Committee chosen for this Town, and accordingly Seven was Nominated and Appointed, viz.

Samuel Small, jun. Mr. *Reuben Fogg*, Mr. *Samuel March*, Mr. *Timothy McDaniel*, *William Thompson* Esq; Mr. *Nath. Milliken*, Mr. *Joshua Fayben.* Corresponding Committee.

A true Copy of the Proceedings of the Town Meeting as above. *Attest,*
SAMUEL SMALL, Town-Clerk.

By the Ship Richmond, *arrived at Philadelphia, from London, we have the following Advices.*

Paris, Jan. 17. It is very positively asserted, that orders are given to all our regiments to hold themselves in readiness to take the field on the earliest notice, and that an army of 100,000 men will be assembled on the Rhine in the spring.

L O N D O N, *January* 14.

We hear from Potzdam, that his Prussian Majesty is ever in close conference with the Russian and Austrian Ministers; courier upon courier are sending to their triumvirate Courts: Upon the late defeat of the Turks, two expresses came within four hours of each other; when it was the next day propagated at Berlin, that a revolution was daily expected at Constantinople, and all the Christian merchants were removing their effects with the utmost secrecy and expedition from that capital. The rage of the Turks is so great at this time against the Christians and Jews, that there is no walking the streets of Constantinople for fear of their fury. The Grand Signior hourly distributes large sums of money among his Janissaries, to hinder their revolt; but without he marches in person at their head, and leads them on to battle (which is what they cry aloud for) all his temporising will avail him nothing.

Jan, 13. Six ships, from 400 to 500 tons each, are fitting out at Portsmouth, for the purpose of importing timber from America, for the use of his Majesty's dock-yards.

A petition it is said, has been presented to the Privy Council from the General Assembly of the province of Massachusetts Bay, requesting the removal of the Governor and Lieutenant-Governor of that province from their posts, on account of the discoveries made in their conduct by the publication of some letters lately.

Jan. 15, Yesterday morning at eleven o'clock, commissions passed the great seal, impowering his Excellency Simon Earl Harcourt, his Majesty's Lieutenant Governor and General Governor of Ireland, to give the royal assent to the Stamp and Annuity bills, without any alteration being made therein; and as soon as they were sealed, they were dispatched by a messenger, as were duplicates by another, the one by way of Holyhead, and the other by that of Port Patrick, in Scotland.

Dr. Franklin was on Thursday last examined before the Privy Council, touching the unfortunate letters that have given occasion to a late duel, by which that mysterious business is likely to be cleared up.

The grand committee of North-America merchants are expected to present their petition at the bar of the Lower House some time next week, on affairs of the utmost importance to the interests of the colonies.

Jan. 19. The affairs of America, it is now said, will not be taken up by Parliament till the sessions is pretty far advanced.

We hear from the West-Indies, that the lands taken from the Caraibs at St. Vincent, are divided among the officers who served in that expedition, and that General Monckton is to have 10,000 acres, and a captain, lieutenant, &c. 100 acres each.

Jan. 21. Lord Viscount Pitt, son to the Earl of Chatham, is to embark next month for North-America to make the tour of the British colonies on that continent.

Jan. 26. A letter from the Lower Elbe, dated Jan. 13, says, "The insurrection in Russia is at present the topic of every conversation. It seems to have happened in the most critical time, when fresh troops were greatly wanted; but by this unhappy event they are not only disabled from raising any new troops, but have been obliged to recall many regiments that were upon their march for Moldavia; and the troops which were cantoned about Warsaw have received sudden orders to march for Petersburgh. It is suspected that many of the principal men in the empire will lay hold of this opportunity, & that a total revolution will be the consequence of it. In the mean time, couriers to Vienna, Berlin and Copenhagen, from Petersburgh, are more frequent than ever; and the current reports are very disagreeable."

Jan. 27. One of the morning papers says, "The cause of the late commotions in Russia is owing to the appearance of the Czarina's husband, real, or pretended, we know not, as that Monarch was said to have been degraded and died in confinement.——The report, however, is credited at the west end of the Town."

By a private letter just received from Paris, we are informed, that the French King is so ill that his life is despaired of.

It is confidently asserted at the Hague, when the last letters came from thence, that a new congress was appointed for negociating a peace between the Russians and Turks.

Jan. 27. Mr. Van said in the House of Commons, that great sums were expended to protect the Bostonians, &c. who by their conduct did not deserve protection; that instead of keeping troops there at a vast expence, we might only send them over able officers, and teach them how to fight; that they were numerous enough to defend themselves against an enemy, but not strong enough to rebel against us.

Our letters by yesterday's mail give us a circumstantial account of what happened between the Russians and the Turks near Varna on the 12th of November last, according to which Gen. Ungern-Sternberg lost 6000 men, among whom are General Reize, and 21 officers; and that Gen. Dolgorucki who marched with his corps on another road, in order to join the former, when he was informed of the unhappy event, turned back; but his foreguard, consisting of near 3000 Cossacks, who were advanced too far, fell into the hands of the Bassa of Adrianople, who was just come to defend the fortress of Varna, and all these 3000 Cossacks were cut to pieces by his troops. They add, that notwithstanding the loss which that General sustained, yet his undertaking was very laudable; and if he had come two hours sooner, he would have rendered himself master of that important fortress, which would have proved very fatal to the enemy; nevertheless his way of retiring with the rest of the troops, did him great honor.

We are informed, that 18,024 effective men are to be employed for the land service, for guards and garrisons in Great Britain, including 1522 invalids, for the present year.

We also hear, that 638,630 l. will be granted towards the maintenance of the army.

Monday evening Mr. Alderman Trecothick was seized with a paralytic stroke, and we are informed continues very ill.

The Americans are about to vote the East India company the sum of 16,000 l. as a compensation for the rejection and destruction of the Tea sent out by that body. [*But it is doubtful whether Governor H——n, who employed all his Power and Art to prevent the Return of the TEA in Safety to the Company, will now give his Consent to a Grant for the Reparation of their Damages.*]

St. James's, Jan. 25. The King has been pleased to appoint Soame Jenyns, Edward Elliot, and Bamber Gascoyne, Esquires, the Hon. Robert Spencer, commonly called Lord Robert Spencer, William Joliffe, Whitshed Keene, Esqrs. and the Hon. Charles Grenville, Esq; to be his Majesty's Commissioners for Trade and Plantations.

Jan. 22. A correspondent observes, that if government does not, with a becoming spirit, instantly embark a few regiments on a visit to the rebellious Bostonians--- it will be entitled to the execration of every Englishman, for such an infamous instance of servile pusillanimity.

They write from Paris, that a body of 50,000 French troops have been ordered to be formed immediately; the object of this force is kept secret.

NEW-YORK, March 28.

Saturday Morning last the Ship John Galley, Capt. Quick, arrived here from London, in 8 Weeks, but has brought no later Prints than what we had received before; and by Letters from thence we learn, That the Conduct of the Americans with Regard to the Tea sent to this Country, is much applauded, but it is generally said all that Commodity destroyed at Boston must be paid for by somebody; [So said Admiral Montagu the next Morning after;] and that Hints had been dropped the act imposing the Duty of 3d. per lb. on all Teas sent to America from Great Britain, would be repealed this present Session of Parliament.

Extract of a Letter from Baltimore dated March 18, 1774.

"Captain Lawrence, in the Jenny and Polly, in four Weeks from London, acquaints us, that the News of the Destruction of the Tea at Boston was arrived there before he sailed, and says, instead of their being exasperated, they much applaud the noble Spirit of the Americans, and were resolved to let the East-India Comaany get the Matter settled in the best Manner they can."

BOSTON, April 4.

Wednesday last the Governor issued a Proclamation for Dissolving the General Assembly of this Province.

Wednesday the Inhabitants of this Town met according to adjournment.

The Hon. John Hancock, Esq; having on account of Health, declined serving as a Fire-ward, it was Voted unanimously, that the Thanks of the Town be given him for his good Services in that Office a Number of Years past.

Mr. John Smith and Mr. Joseph-Pierce Palmer, were at the above-mentioned adjournment chosen Clerks of the Market.

The last Meeting stands adjourned to Friday the 8th of April, at three o'Clock.

The Town chose a Committee to purchase the Clock of Gawen Brown, and to have the same fixed on the Old South Meeting-House.

The insolence of a certain Publican at Westown, has drawn on him the Indignation of the People in that and the neighbouring Towns, a Number of whom lately assembled to *Compliment* his Person, but he having fled, we are informed they broke his windows and shewed other tokens of their resentment.

The Ship Haley, Capt. Scot, from this Port, arrived at Gravesend the 20th of January.

The following clause of the Law relative to Lamps is published for the further information of those who neglect to remove such Posts or Sign Board, which intercept or lessen the light of these Lamps.

And be it further enacted, That the Selectmen of the Town of *Boston* for the Time being be, and they are hereby empowered to take down or remove any Post or Sign thereon in any Street, Lanes, Alleys or Passage-Ways in said Town, or that now are or hereafter may be fixed, or that adjoin to any Dwelling-House or Building, in Case they shall judge any such Post or Sign tends to intercept or any ways lessen the Light in said Lamp; or said Selectmen may direct and order the Owner of such Posts or Signs to take down or remove the same, and if such Owner or Owners shall refuse so to do for the space of forty-eight Hours after such Order or Notice given, he, she or they shall forfeit and pay the Sum of *six Shillings* for every twenty-four Hours the same shall remain standing or fixed to any Building.

March 31.

JOICE, jun.

PRESENTS his Compliments to the Plymouth Protestors, and acknowledges the Sight of their Card; also informs them that he has made Preparations to receive their select Committee, in a Manner suitable to their Character, Lady Birch having absolutely engag'd to honor them, assoon as she knows of their Arrival, with her immediate Presence.

Her Ladyship would have waited on Mr. T—s when he was last in Town, wou'd Decency have permitted, while he was in such—— Circumstances.

This Day Published, and to be sold by *Edes & Gill*, The SECOND EDITION of

Mr. HANCOCK's

ORATION

Deliver'd *March 5th, 1774.*

TO BE SOLD

At John Winthrop, jun'rs Store, on Treat's Wharff near the Market, very cheap *Philadelphia* and *Baltimore* FLOUR.

BOTTLES with and without Cases. IRON, &c. &c.

Wanted to Hire by the Year,

An industrious Man of a good Character, that understands Gardening, and to wait on a Gentleman's Family. Inquire of the Printers.

TO BE LETT, and enter'd upon immediately,

A FARM in Leicester, *consisting of Mowing, Arrable and Pasture Land, &c. Enquire of* Capt. Nathaniel Scott, *living near the Premises, or the Printers hereof.*

A Negro Child to be given away, of an excellent Breed. Inquire of Edes & Gill.

CHOICE *MADDER*,

The Growth of this Province,

TO BE SOLD BY,

John Barrett,

Near the Mill-Bridge, BOSTON.

GUN-POWDER,

To be Sold by HENRY BROMFIELD, at his Store opposite the Custom-House in King-Street,

ALSO,

Pepper, a few Barrels Pork, and Cod-Lines very cheap.

TO BE SOLD

A BRIG of about 170 Tons, now on the Stocks at York, and will be Launch'd in ten Days;—She is built of the best Materials, and is extremely well calculated for the Guinea or Streights Trade.—For further Particulars inquire of WILLIAM PALFREY, Who has for sale,

Spermacæti Candles,

Warranted genuine and pure.

A Quantity of FLOUR, and a few Barrels of Middling ditto, to be sold cheap. Also a Parcel of *Newfoundland* BREAD;—Inquire of JOHN CUSHING, at his Sugar-House, Brattle-Street, near Doctor Cooper's Meeting-House, Boston.

TO BE SOLD CHEAP,

About 100 Quintals of good Jamaica Cod Fish.—Two Foresails suitable for a Brig of 100 Tons.—One new Foresail and Mainsail, suitable for a Schooner of 50 or 60 Tons, and a small quantity of new Cordage. Inquire of the Printers.

WANTED,

£. 200 Lawful Money, for which good Security will be given. Inquire of the Printers.

For *Quebec*,

THE Brigantine BETSEY, CONSTANT FREEMAN, Master, lying the South side the Long-Wharff, will sail in about 15 Days:—For Freight or Passage apply to said Freeman, on board, or at his House in South School-Street.

For *Quebec*,

THE Schooner EUNICE, NATHANIEL ATKINS, Master, lying the South-side the Long-Wharff, will sail in about 15 Days:—For Freight or Passage apply to said Master on board, or to Constant Freeman, at his House in South School-Street.

For *Annapolis Royal*,

THE SLOOP Jenny, GEORGE MITCHELL, Master, Lying at Wentworth's Wharf, having good Accommodations for Passengers, will Sail in Ten Days. For Frieght or Passage Inquire of the Master on said Wharf.

TO BE SOLD

AT PUBLICK AUCTION,

By Benjamin Church,

At his usual Place of Sale,

On THURSDAY next,

At THREE o'Clock in the Afternoon,

A Variety of valuable House Furniture, a Number of large Looking-Glasses—Chairs, Tables, Feather Beds—Pewter, &c. Some Plate—A Variety of European Goods, viz. Broad Cloths—Plains—Kerseys—Shalloons—Tammies—Calamancoes—Irish Linnens—Checks—Mens Hose—a large Quantity of Buttons double wash'd and others—Buckles—Knives and Forks—Watches———&c. &c. &c.

At Three o'Clock Afternoon.

WANTED *immediately*,

A sober active Lad, as an Apprentice to the Goldsmith's Business. Inquire of the Printers.

TO BE SOLD

A likely Negro Lad, 17 Years old, speaks English and French. Inquire of *Jean Francois Magellon*, at the House of Capt. *Isaac McDaniel*, New-Boston.

LAND TO BE SOLD

Five Hundred Acres of LAND, in the Town of *Granville*, to be Sold, either the whole at once, or such Lots as may best suit the Purchaser.—Inquire of

Richard Salter,

At his Shop in Cornhill;

Who continues to Sell on the most reasonable Terms, English and India GOODS suitable for all Seasons.—The best French and Spanish Indigo, Pepper and Spices: Also a fine Assortment of Women's and Children's Stays made in the neatest and best manner: Best russel, callamanco and everlasting Women and Children Shoes, Pumps, Goloshoes, &c.

TO BE LETT,

A commodious Brick Messuage, situate in Brattle Square. Inquire of Edes and Gill.

FLOUR.

A Quantity of the newest *Baltimore* FINE FLOUR, and *Philadelphia* fine and superfine Ditto, *Philadelphia* BAR IRON.

A few Hogsheads of choice BRAN, and Quarter Casks of WINE.

To be sold as cheap, if not cheaper than at any Store in Town by *James Swan*,

At his Store leading to *Treat's* Wharff, next the South side of the Town Dock.

At GOULD's *Auction Office*,

In Back-Street,

On FRIDAY next, at Ten o'Clock in the Morning, Will be Sold by PUBLIC VENDUE,

A Variety of genteel House Furniture, amongst which are, one Mahogany Chest upon Chest of Draws, two Chest Walnut ditto, one Mahogany Bureau Table, one Sett Leather-bottom'd Mahogany Chairs, one Sett Walnut ditto, common ditto, Mahogany and Walnut Dining and Tea Tables, one Mahogany 4 Post Bedstead, common ditto, Feather Beds, Looking-Glasses, Pictures, one Marble Slab, one Riding Chair, a Quantity of new Sash Windows.

Also ENGLISH GOODS, viz.

Callicoes & printed Linnens, Muslins, figur'd & plain Lawns, Gauze Handkerchiefs, black and white Catgut, ribbed and plain Hose, silk and worsted Knee Garters, a Quantity of Table Knives, plated & common Buckles, 12 dozen Kippen's Snuff, with a Variety of Woolens and many other Articles. R. Gould, Auctioneer.

N. B. For private Sale, one very handsome new Chaise and Harness, two good second-hand ditto.

On WEDNESDAY next, at Eleven o'Clock, Will be Sold by PUBLIC VENDUE, on Capt. *David Spear's* Wharff.

Between 150 and 200 Quintals of Jamaica Fish.

LIKEWISE,

At XII o'Clock—Between 150 and 200 Quintals more on *Minot's* T.

A. OLIVER, Auctioneer.

On Thursday next,

At Ten o'Clock,

Will be Sold by PUBLIC VENDUE, at the New Auction-Office, South Side of the Town-House.

A large and valuable Assortment of ENGLISH GOODS, belonging to a Gentleman leaving off the Business——*Consisting of*,

Callicoes, Chints and Patches, mixt, cinnamon and cloth-colour'd Bengalls, Long Lawns, Diaper Table Cloths, Irish Linnens, Dimothys, Mens Cotton and Worsted Hose, Brolio's, pink, crimson, cloth-colour'd and black Callamancoes, cloth-colour'd Durants and Camblereens, green, red and blue Mecklenburgs, green, blue and cloth-colour'd Shalloons, pink, black, brown, green, white and cloth-colour'd Tammies, Pensacolas, green and red worsted Brocades, pink, blue, purple and orange Missinets, pink, blue, purple and yellow Silveritts, cloth colour'd Breeches Patterns, Cotton Velvets, handsome Ribbons, white handle Knives and Forks, Broad Cloths, Ratteens, Bearskins, Jersey-knit Hose, mill'd Caps, white Quality Binding, Crewels, worsted Caps, check Handkerchiefs—Plate—Handsome Tankard, Porringers, Tureen, Chaffindishes, large & small Spoons, Pepper Boxes, Cream-pots, Cups, &c. And a Variety of other Articles, too numerous for an Advertisement. ANDREW OLIVER, Auctioneer.

To the PUBLIC.

AS the Method lately practis'd by the Subscriber, in having a Person at his Door to invite Gentlemen and others to his public Sales——has given Dissatisfaction to some——(Gentlemen Shopkeepers in particular) to avoid giving Offence for the future, he shall desist from that Practice, and pursue one (as follows) which he flatters himself cannot fail giving universal Satisfaction, as he sincerely wishes so to do. The Public are most earnestly requested to remember (for *their own Advantage*) that for the future Notice will be given by sounding of a Bell which he has purchased for that Purpose, which will be erected over his Auction-Room Door near the Market, Boston, where constant Attendance is given both early and late to receive the Favors of all such who are pleas'd to confer on their

Much obliged, most obedient, and very humble Servant,

M. BICKER.

∴ Said BICKER sells as cheap as ever.

On THURSDAY NEXT,

Will be Sold by PUBLIC VENDUE, at BICKER's Auction-Room near the Market, Boston.

A large Quantity of cut and other Goods belonging to the Estate of a Gentleman lately deceased, among which are a large Quantity of Callicoes, printed Cottons, stamp'd Linnen, Patches, corded Poplins, half yard Crapes, Dorsetteens, Irish Camblets, Cambleteens, Missenetts, Grezetts, Drawboys, figur'd & plain Lawns, Gauzes, Kenting & Linnen Handkerchiefs, No. 12 Pins, Callamancoes, Shalloons, Tammies, figur'd Modes, Quality Binding, Ribbons, &c. &c. &c.

M. BICKER.

No Entries receiv'd this Week.

Burials in the Town of BOSTON, since our last.

Eight Whites. One Black.

Baptiz'd in the several Churches, Twelve.

High Water at BOSTON, *for the present Week.*

Monday, 22 min. aft.	6	Friday, 44 min. after	9
Tuesday, 18 min. aft.	7	Saturday, 30 min. aft.	10
Wednesday, 10 m. aft.	8	Lord's-Day, 12m. aft	11
Thursday, 0 min. aft.	9	D's last Qr. 3 Day	1 M.

The best Turks Island SALT,
To be SOLD on board the Schooner Sally. Capt. Rogers, lying at Griffins Wharf.

All Persons that have any Demands on the Estate of the late Elizabeth Hewes, Widow, deceas'd, are desired immediately to bring in their Accounts for Settlement; and all Persons indebted to said Estate, are desired to make speedy Payment to

Boston, March 21, 1774. HENDERSON INCHES, AND, NATH. APPLETON, } Executors.

THERE is to be sold, a genteel Horse and Chaise, with or without a Negro Boy of 16 Years old, that can be well recommended, understands taking Care of Horse and Chaise, and cleaning them in the neatest Manner; drives with great Care; can do House-work and Cook as well as any one of his Age; is good-temper'd lively and spry. The above to be sold for no other Reason than that the Gentleman to whom they did belong is deceas'd. If any Gentleman or Lady inclines to purchase the above, and it is not convenient to pay the Money, it may lay on good Security. Inquire of the Printers.

STOLEN out of the Barn of me the Subscriber on Wednesday Night the 16th of March Inst. a red Mare, Saddle and Bridle, with a Blaze in her Face, about 13 Hands high, and about 12 Years old or upwards, carries her Head very low.——Whoever will take up the said Mare and bring her with the Saddle and Bridle to the Owner, shall have two Dollars Reward, and all necessary Charges paid, by RALPH DEVEREAUX.
Marblehead, March 16, 1774.

All Persons that have any Demands on the Estate of Mr. Andrew Cunningham, late of Boston, Hatter, deceased, are desired to bring in their Accounts to Mary Greenleaf and John Cunningham, Administrators on said Estate, for Adjustment.——And all Persons indebted to said Estate, are desired to make immediate Payment to said Administrators.

John Cunningham,

HAS for Sale at his Shop near the Corner of School-Street, opposite Mr. Deblois's,

A Large Assortment of English and India Goods, suitable for all Seasons, which he is determined to sell at the Sterling Cost (clear of Charges) he being determined to quit the Business.

FIFTY DOLLARS REWARD.

LAST Night the Dwelling-House of the Subscriber was broke open, and from thence were taken the following Articles of Plate, viz.

1 Pair of Silver Chaffingdishes, 1 pair of Butter-cups, 1 silver can, 2 large soup-spoons, 1 pepper-box, 6 large table-spoons, 6 tea-do. and a strainer, marked E. D. maker's name, D. Henchman all except the spoons, which have a Hand for a Crest.—A silver tea-pot, 1 do. sugar-dish, a boat for tea spoons, 1 pair tea-tongs, 5 tea-spoons and a cream-cup. Two porringers and two salt-cellars, all mark'd E. S. 1 silver Tankard without a lid, marked S / I. S. *1 silver can marked* D / I. E. *an old fashion'd pepper-box mark'd* D / A. E. *6 large table spoons marked E. S. 1 silver salver, no mark upon it, the foot resembling the mouth of a tunnel, a silver tankard marked A. B. 1 silver porringer without any mark, 3 table spoons marked A. B. 1 old spoon marked* S / I. S. *4 tea spoons no mark, 1 pair tea tongs, Makers names of these not made by D. Henchman, I. Hurd some of them, and some B. W—with several other small articles.——Whoever will take up the Thief or Thieves, so as he or they may be brought to Justice and the Plate recovered, shall be paid the above Reward, and a reasonable Reward for any Part of the Plate, in Proportion to its Value.* per me, THADDEUS BURR.
Fairfield, Connecticut, 15 March, 1774.

N. B. *If any of the above Plate should be discovered in Boston, please to give Notice to* JOHN HANCOCK, *Esq; and an adequate Reward shall be given.*

TO BE SOLD IMMEDIATELY,
By *Margaret Newman*, Administratrix to the Estate of Mrs. *Margaret Fletcher*, deceased——
A BRICK HOUSE situate in Ann-street, making the Corner of the new Street lately made from Ann to Middle-street, at present occupied by Mr. Jeremiah Allen—it has two Rooms on a Floor, with a good Celler, Yard and Pump; the whole in good Repair.——Said *Newman* has to Let, a Store nearly opposite the above.

To be Sold cheap, for Cash only,
50 Acres of choice Land, lying in the Town of Lunenburgh, in the County of Worcester—in the Third Division Land (so called) near Manoosenett-Hill, which was originally laid out to John Scott.——Enquire of John Gray, Esq; Rope-Maker in Boston.

TO BE SOLD,
A new Vessel about 60 Tons burthen, now on the Stocks at Cohasset, may be launched within a Month. For further Particulars, enquire of BRECK and HAMMETT, at their Store the Head of GREEN'S Wharff, or of DANIEL TOWER at Cohasset.

TO BE SOLD,
A Farm lying on Squanton-Neck, late the Estate of Remember Preston, deceased, containing about 50 Acres of good Land, with a House and Barn thereon. For further Particulars, enquire of John Preston of Boston, or of Ebenezer Baker of Dorchester.

All Persons indebted to the Estate of John Ruddock, *late of Boston, Esq; deceas'd, are desired to settle the same with* Abiel Ruddock, *Administrator, or they will be Sued at next April Court: And all who have any demands on said Estate, are desired to bring their Accounts to said Administrator for Adjustment.*

To be SOLD at the Store of
ABIEL RUDDOCK,
At the North End, cheap for Cash or short Credit,
St. Martins Salt, Lignum Vitæ, Anchors, Grapling Whale Warp, Whale Iron Lances, Blubber, Hooks and Spades, a Slay and Harness, an Engine in good Order with it's Appurtenances; and also a Brig of 105 Tons, Boston Built, about Four Years old, has always been in the Whale Fishery: Also a Sloop of 84 Tons, about Five Years old, both in good Order.

TO BE SOLD
By Joseph Hall,
At his Shop in Cole-Lane,
New-England and *West-India* RUM, by Wholesale and Retail; Old Jamaica Spirits, Brandy, Madeira, Teneriff, Malaga, and Claret WINES, by the Gallon & Kegg, Cinnamon, Clove, Anniseed, Snakeroot and Orange WATERS; GENEVA by the Gallon; LEMMONS by the Box, Hundred or Dozen; and a few Firkins of BUTTER.

TO BE SOLD and entered upon immediately,
A House in Milton, with a Malt House and five Acres of Orcharding and Mowing Land, about 10 Miles distant from Boston, and 2 from the Meeting-House, on the main Road that leads to Stoughton. It is known by the Name of Samuel Soper's, lately tenanted by Rufus Bent. Any Person inclining to Purchase may apply to *Ralph Inman*, Esq; at his Warehouse in Boston.

To be SOLD or LET,
A Farm in Cambridge Neck so called, (and entered upon the first of April next) containing between Seventy and Eighty Acres, consisting of Mowing Land, both English and Salt, with good Plowland, and Pasturage, and a good Orchard of choice Fruit thereon, the same being well watered. Said Farm lying within one Mile from the College, and about three Miles from Charlestown Ferry. For further Particulars, enquire of Samuel Soden of Watertown, or of Seth Hastings of said Cambridge.

TO BE SOLD,
A Pleasant FARM at Newton, about a Mile from Watertown Bridge, containing about 30 Acres:—Also a Wood Lot nearly adjoining, of about 30 Acres:—Three Years will be allowed for the Payment, good Security being given. If more Land should be wanted, the adjoining Farm of 30 Acres is also to be Sold. Enquire of the Printers.

CALLICOES.
A Small Invoice of newest-fashion Callicoes, to be sold for less than the Sterling Cost and Charges. Inquire of Edes and Gill.

——VELVET CORKS.——
A few Casks of very good Sherry Wine, and a few Hogsheads of old West-India Rum, to be sold Cheap at *Nathaniel & William Coffins* Store.

All Persons indebted to, or that have any Demands on the Estate of Mr. Edward Brick, jun. late of Dorchester, Yeoman, deceas'd, are desired to bring in their Accounts to Dr. Thomas Williams, of Roxbury, Administrator, in Order for Settlement.

Whereas the Copartnership of Simon Whipple and Company is mutually Dissolved—These are to Desire all Persons that have Accounts open, and are indebted to said Company, to settle and pay the same as soon as may be; and those that have any Demands on said Company, are desired to apply to Simon Whipple, who will discharge them immediately.
*** Choice St. Georges Stone Lime, to be sold by WHIPPLE and WHEATON, at Dawes's Wharff.

MILLENARY.
Sundry Articles of MILLENARY to be Sold at Mrs. MECOM's, a little to the Northward of Concert-Hall, opposite GREENLEAF's Printing-Office; Sattins of the newest Fashion for Cloaks and Bonnets, the nicest chip Hats and the common Sort for covering. An Assortment of genteel Ribbons, Persians, Allamodes, Sewing Silk, Muslins, Gloves and Mits, Gimp-trimings, Gauzes, Blond Lace & Edgings, black ditto, Cap-wire, Tooth-brushes, Silk Laces for Stays, Pins, Needles, Threads, Tapes, Bindings, Durants and Tammies. Also, ready-made Caps and Hoods. &c. &c. &c.
☞ ALL Sorts of MILLENARY Work done with Care and Expedition, as usual.

WANTED TO HIRE,
A Sloop or Schooner, between 50 and 60 Tons Burthen. Enquire of CHARLES LOW, in Marshall's Lane, opposite the Boston Stone, near the Mill-Bridge.

To be Sold for want of Employ,
A likely, healthy, strong Negro Girl, about 12 Years of Age, can be well recommended.
Inquire of the Printers.

HABIJAH SAVAGE
HAS for Sale at his Store No. 16, on the Long Wharff, A Quantity of FLOUR just arrived, new Rice, Cocoa, West-India & New-England Rum, French Brandy, Loaf and Brown Sugar, Cotton Wool, Indigo, Coffee, Window Glass, Pipes, Cases with Bottles, Case Bottles, Red Wood, Log Wood, Brimstone, and a Quantity of Corn.
N. B. Fifty Barrels FLOUR light, fit for the West-Indies.

ENGLISH GOODS CHEAP.
Imported from LONDON, by
Samuel Dashwood,
And to be Sold at his Shop next Door to Dr. Silvester Gardner's in Marlborough-Street, Boston.
A Great Variety of English, India and Scotch Goods, among which are,—Irish Linnens of all widths, Chinces and Callicoes, great Variety of Silks, best Royal Ribbs, best English Shoes at One Dollar per Pair, and many other Articles too tedious to mention, which will be sold by Wholesale at the Sterling Cost, and by Retail at the Cost and Charges, as he is going into another Branch of Business.
N. B. Spices of all Kinds, great Variety of Glass, China and Earthen Ware, sold remarkable cheap for Cash.

GUN POWDER.
Choice Gun Powder just Imported in Capt. GORHAM, And to be SOLD by
Amory's, Taylor & Rogers,
At their Store in Marlborough Street, where may be had as usual a general Assortment of English, India and Hard Ware GOODS on reasonable Terms by Wholesale and Retail——

TO BE LET,
The Back Part of the large Brick House in King-Street, at the Corner of Quaker-Lane, containing a very large and pleasant Parlour, convenient Chambers, and a good Kitchen, accommodated with a good Yard and large Brick Stable.——Enquire of Amory's, Taylor & Rogers, Marlborough-Street.

TO BE SOLD,
A large handsome & convenient Brick Dwelling House, situate in Hanover-Street, Boston, late the Estate of Jacob Royall, Esq; deceased, containing three Rooms upon a Floor, three upright Stories, the Cellar pav'd and ceil'd, a large Yard and Garden, an excellent Well of Water, Stable and Chaise-House, with every Convenience suitable for a Gentleman. Any Person inclining to purchase the Premisses, may apply to RICHARD LECHMERE, Esq;

All Persons that are indebted to, or have any Demands on the late Company of Aaron Davis, jun. and Company, are desired to make speedy Settlement with Wales and Somes, the two surviving Partners, at their Store the upper Corner going on Minot's T.—At which Store is to be sold, good Bait Mackrell, Salmon in Barrels or Kegs, new Flour, Bar Iron, a Quantity of Twice-laid Rigging and Junk.

TO BE LET,
A large commodious Brick Distilling-House, in a very good Part of the Town, with three Stills, one of 1200 Gallons, one of 400 ditto, and one of 300 ditto, with Cisterns in Proportion to the same, and has every Convenience requisite for the Distilling-Business.—It may be entered upon and set to work immediately. Enquire of Edes & Gill.
N. B. There has been more than 700 Hogsheads of Rum distilled in the above House, in one Year.

Wanted a Quantity of Thrumbs for the Caulkers Business, for which cash will be given; also to be SOLD a few Puncheons, and forty Gallon Casks of old choice Jamaica Rum. Inquire of the Printers.

John & Eleanor Druitt,
Most respectfully acquaint their Friends and the Public, they continue to keep School as usual, in Hanover-Street, near Concert-Hall.
JOHN DRUITT, Instructs Young Ladies in the Rudiments of English, Epistolary-writing, Writing, and Arithmetick:—for their more speedy Improvement, intends to devote himself intirely to their Service, and not take Boys.
ELEANOR DRUITT, Instructs them in French Grammatically, Reading English, and Orthography likewise the following Needleworks, viz.
Point, Brussells, (Gold, Silver and Silk) Embroidery's, Dresden, Tambour, Feather-Stitch, & Darning, with a great variety of Open-work; Tapestry, Catgut, diaper and plain Darning, Knitting, Marking, Plain-work and Baby-linnen, &c.
As it has been apprehended by some Ladies, that said *Druitt* don't teach Plain-work; now Informs them she does, and with equal care and assiduity, as she performs the rest of her undertakings.
They tender their most grateful thanks to those who have favour'd them with the care of their Children; and assures the Public, they will exert their utmost abilities in the improvement of their Pupils.
It has been rumour'd, they were leaving the Province; but is intirely false.

Boston: Printed, by EDES & GILL.

THE
Boston-Gazette,
AND
COUNTRY JOURNAL.

No. 992.

Containing the freshest Advices, Foreign and Domestic.

MONDAY, April 11, 1774.

Mess'rs EDES & GILL,

AS there is now a vacant Seat on the Bench at the Superior Court, it is the earnest Desire and Expectation of the good People of this Province, that the vacancy may be filled by a Gentleman of approved Wisdom and Integrity,—one who is a firm friend to the rights of America, and a genuine Patriot. As this is a Matter of great Importance to the Public, it is presumed that no Gentleman who has the Honor to sit at the Council Board, will give his Vote for any one who has not merited the Esteem and Confidence of the People.

A Judge ought to have a Character pure and unspotted, distinguished for Virtue, Religion, Wisdom, Humanity, Benevolence, and Patriotism. Without these, he is unworthy to sit on the Judgment Seat. Nor let it be objected, that such noble Characters are not to be found; there are many such in this Province; and let it ever be remembered, that in any Government where Virtue and Merit are made requisite Qualifications for a public Office, good Men never will be wanting. To substitute other Things in the Room of Virtue and Merit, is the Bane of Society, and poisons the Vitals of Government.

Notwithstanding worthy Men have ever been plenty in this Province, yet in *some* Periods there have been Men advanced to Offices in Government who ought to have been forever hid in the silent Vale of Obscurity; but we hope that no Man in future Time will be distinguished by a public Office until he has first distinguished himself by a noble Attachment to the Liberties of his Country and the Rights of Mankind; and by a virtuous beneficent Life has demonstrated that the public Weal is the great Object at which he aims, and that sublime Ideas of Honour and Religion govern and animate the Springs of his Mind—— Then will Justice and Judgment run through the Land like a pure Stream, and Righteousness shine forth like chearing Beams of the Sun.

AMERICA SOLON.

Massachusetts, March 1774.

Messieurs EDES & GILL,

The LORD *reigns, let America rejoice! If* HE *is for us, it matters not who is against us.*

IT has been an animating consideration, in every succeeding period of New-England, that GOD has ever smiled upon this People, and in all their Distresses hath appeared for their relief. When *Satan* stirred up *Gog* and *Magog* against them, they triumphed over their savage Foes; and when the same *evil Spirit* instigated the *French* to attempt their destruction, Heaven destroyed their Enemies. From the first Settlement in 1620, to this Day, GOD has frowned upon the Enemies to the Rights and Liberties of this Country; those who have been influenced by *Satan* to be active and plotting against them, have come to disgrace and ruin; and remain on Record as Monuments of Divine Vengeance——Therefore let all the Friends to Liberty and their Country, still trust in GOD, and He will tread down their Enemies and cause Liberty to triumph over all her Foes in America.

Whoso is wise and will observe these Things, shall understand the Loving-kindness of the Lord.

The PREACHER.

M ssieurs EDES and GILL,

WHEN we consider the vast Quantity of Oak Timber, Plank, &c. that has of late Years been sent from this Continent to Great Britain, may we not take it to be a Plan of the British Ministry. Perhaps they have in View, as soon as opportunity offers, the entire suppression of Ship-Building in the Colonies; and, in Time, a corrupt Administration may bring in a Bill, and have it established by Parliament, for preventing the Building any Vessels in America:—What seems to confirm this is, a Clause in the Commission to the Judge of the Admiralty, whereby Ship Carpenters are liable to be called before said Judge of Admiralty and be fin'd, imprison'd, or punished at the Pleasure of the Judge:—It therefore behoves every American, (especially our worthy Brethren the Ship Carpenters) to oppose at the risque of Life itself, every such Usurpation; and expel from this Continent every Villain who dares accept such a diabolical Commission.

N. B. Every Carpenter in America ought to be acquainted with the Tenor of the above mentioned Commission, and it would be well for him to have one in his possession, and the further Exportation of Timber, Plank, &c. ought to be prevented.

CAUTULUS.

LONDON.

Jan. 21. Fresh instructions, it is said, have been dispatched to our several American Governors containing very detailed & specific directions for their future conduct.

The above instructions, it is believed, unless supported by the full strength of the British legislature, will rather serve to create fresh troubles than to appease those already subsisting.

Jan. 22. A correspondent says, that unless some very *effectual* measures are taken with the rabble at Boston, their insolence may be expected to increase; he recommends, instead of tea, a cargo of manufactured hemp, to be immediately forwarded to that loyal colony, the disposition of which, with a suitable support, to be in the hands of Governor *Hutchinson*.

Jan. 24. The following is at present a favorite toast among the friends of their country: "Detested be the man who shall form a scheme for abridging the Liberty of the Press, and for ever detested be the Minister who shall patronize it."

Jan. 24. The Ministry received the account of the mischief done to the East-India Company, in the destruction of the tea at Boston, with the utmost insensibility. Lord North proposes to refer the Directions or redress, on their complaining of the violence done them, to the consumers in the Massachusets. The Company will find very few friends in the nation, as they have endeavored to saddle the Colonies with a duty that would prove equally oppressive to them, with the many hardships they pretended to meet with from the present administration.

The account of the proceedings at Boston, against landing the East India Company's Tea, is introduced in the Public Ledger, of the 22st January, in the following manner.

AMERICAN AFFAIRS

☞ The following Account of the Proceedings of the Bostonians will serve to shew the spirit and resentment of a people who have undergone every species of injurious treatment, and have sustained, with exemplary patience, every species of indignity, offered them by an Administration so infatuated with the idea of Despotism, as to be qualified only to SUBVERT, instead of MAINTAIN, the Liberties of a brave and free people.

Lord Sandwich, we hear, has proposed to the Cabinet, an increase of twenty ships of the line, but the expence being objected to, his Lordship observed, that it was an act of prudence not only to establish a permanent peace, but a certain superiority over the united strength of Europe.

Jan. 25. The report of the Rev. Mr. Rosenhagen being the author of Junius's papers is without foundation.

The last letters from the Cape of Good-Hope say, that Captain David Roche, formerly one of the candidates at the Middlesex election, having quarrelled, during his continuance at that port, with ——— Farquharson, Esq; a duel ensued, in which the latter was unfortunately run through the breast, and died in a few hours after. The surviver was an Ensign, and in 1757 was broke at Halifax.

We hear that the Sheriffs Sayer & Lee, will send notice to John Wilkes, Esq; member for Middlesex to attend the House of Commons, according to the order of the Speaker.

WILLIAMSBURG (Virginia) *March* 17.

We are favoured with the following remarkable intelligence, which we hope may be the means of bringing to light so mysterious an occurrence, and prove serviceable to those who are concerned in it. Some time last December a sloop of about 100 hogsheads burthen stood in for Machotick Creek, on Potowmack, and ran aground on a mud bank, a little way up the creek. Soon after a decent well looking man, dressed in black, with a gold laced hat, came on shore from the sloop, and calling at a Gentlewoman's house in the neighbourhood, told her he was bound for Alexandria, to purchase a load of wheat, but that his hands had left him, and he wanted the loan of a horse to carry him to Leeds Town, to engage others. Being disappointed in getting a horse, he went to a planter's house a few miles distant, where he lodged all night, went off in the morning, and has never been heard of since. On his way he stopped at a petty ordinary, where he left three ruffled shirts, a neat fowling piece, and a great coat; but carried with him a pair of saddlebags, which the landlord concluded, from their weight, contained a considerable sum of money.——After the vessel had continued near a fortnight in the creek, with her sails standing, some of the Gentlemen in the neighbourhood went on board; and, upon searching her, found neither provisions, water, chests, papers, or any other effects, than one feather bed, a gold laced hat, a sailor's jacket, a pair of trousers, some cooking utensils, and two sea compasses made in Salem. She is a long sharp built vessel, with only a cabin, containing five births, and hold. On her stern is painted, in white letters, FALMOUTH PACKET; and the same words, in letters made of cloth are on her pendant.

NEW-YORK, March 28.

It is reported that His Majesty's 64th regiment now in garrison at Castle-William, near Boston, will relieve the 14th regiment at St. Augustine and the Bahamas; that part of the relief from England, expected out in the ensuing summer, will be stationed at Boston: And it is said that neither the royal regiment of Welch Fusileers nor the 47th regiment in New-Jersey, will be removed from their present situations, unless his Majesty's service should more immediately require their presence elsewhere.

The intentions of the British Administration relative to the American duty on tea, are not fixed; the Minister has many weighty subjects to lay before the Lower House before that article will be brought into debate, and the session will be far expended 'ere any alteration in the revenue laws will be attended to.

NEW-LONDON, April 1.

The following are the Heads of a Subscription which were laid before the Committee of Correspondence at Boston.

WHEREAS in our present struggles with the British Administration, it is of the last importance to have a free and safe Communication throughout the whole extent of English America—a channel established by an act of the British Parliament for the express purpose of raising a revenue here, & under the absolute controul of the British minister, being both in principle and operation, highly dangerous; and whereas we are certified from several of the southern colonies, that a post-office has been erected in Maryland and Pennsylvania, on the principles of a voluntary subscription; and we have good reason to believe the salutary institution, will be generally adopted by all the intermediate colonies, as well as those on both extremes; and whereas the said institution, if generally adopted, will defeat one *revenue act*, and obviate all its pernicious consequences; will unite all the friends of America in one common bond of alliance, and reduce the postage of letters one third, as well as ensure the transmission of interesting advice to the place of destination,

—WE the Subscribers do severally promise to pay to the post-master who shall be hereafter appointed by major vote of our body, the several sums annexed to our names, or to the successor in said office, to be by him or them employed in furnishing post-riders to the several stages we may agree upon, and securing himself or deputies from any losses and damages that may acrue unto him or them by means of their offices, meaning and understanding this present instrument to be a deposit and security to the said post-master to be recoverable by him in whole or in proportion to the sums subscribed, and to make up the deficiencies, if any there appear to a committee of our body chosen to inspect accounts, after the whole amount of the monies received for postage shall have been placed to our credit.

In testimony, &c.

NORWICH, March 31.

On the 27th of January last, a severe Shock of an Earthquake was felt all over the Island of Jamaica, and very perceptibly on board the Vessels at Anchor in Kingston Harbour, however it did no other Damage than putting the Inhabitants in great Terror.

On Monday the 21st. a Report prevailed in New-York, That Mr. Henry White, of that City, Merchant, to whom the Cargo of the so long expected Tea Ship is consigned, had received a Letter from Capt. Lockyer, who commands her, dated at Antigua the 15th of February last, the Purport of which is, that said Lockyer having heard of the proceedings of the People at Boston and Philadelphia, and the Resolution of the New-Yorkers; with Regard to the Tea Shipped for America by the East-India Company; has determined, that upon his Arrival at Sandy-Hook he will Anchor the Vessel and proceed to the City in his Boat; he requests that Mr. White will provide the necessary Supplies of Stores and Provisions for for him, as (if the People will not suffer the Tea to be landed) he intends imediately to sail for England. He desires that these his Resolutions may be communicated to the Publick, that he may not be exposed, upon his Arrival in New-York, to personal Insults.

On Thursday the 12th Inst. Allan Wood, of this Town, set off from Chelsea in a Canoe; he was missing until Sunday Forenoon, when his Body was found in the River about two Miles below Chelsea-Bridge.

PROVIDENCE, March 26.

Tuesday last a Boy about six Years of Age, Son of Mr. Benedict Tabor, having eaten of a poisonous Root which he had found, was soon after seized with Fits, and died. A Daughter of Mr Tabor's, about four Years of Age, likewise partook of the Root, which her Brother had given her, and was taken ill: but an Emetic being timely administered, she recovered.

This Day Published, and to be sold by Edes & Gill,

The SECOND EDITION of

Mr. HANCOCK'S

ORATION

Deliver'd *March* 5th, 1774.

LONDON, January 20.

The House of Commons yesterday broke up at half past three o'clock, having agreed to the report of the resolution of Monday last for granting a supply to his Majesty, and ordering it to be called over on the 15th of February; and the Speaker to write circular letters to all the Members, to acquaint them therewith; informing them, that those that did not attend, otherwise than by leave of the House, should be taken into custody of the House. This order for calling over the House was on the motion of Alderman Sawbridge, on which day he will make a motion for shortening the duration of Parliaments.

India stock, we hear, fell considerably yesterday, on account of the American proceedings with the tea, of which report saith no less than 300 000 . worth was shipped from England.

Extract of a Letter from Inverness, December 30.

"The emigration of the inhabitants of this part of Scotland is very alarming; but considering the situation of things in this country, it is not to be wondered at. The following reasons are assigned for it:

"The tyrannical, oppressive, and impolitic conduct of the landholders in this country, hath at last driven the labouring poor to despair. Nothing is now seen among that class of men but beggary and ruin. These many years past provisions have been so dear, that even when work was got, the labourer could scarcely earn bread for his family. What can he do now, when manufactures were so low, but fly from a country where want and misery are his only portion? He hath no alternative, but to starve, or emigrate.

"The following are the motives given for emigration to North-America by a body of Highlanders, who embarked last summer for that part of the British empire:

"1. The price of land is so low in some of the British colonies, that 40 or 50 pounds will purchase as much ground there, as 1000 in this country.

"2. There are few or no taxes at present in the colonies, most of their publick debt being paid off since the last peace.

"3. The climate in general is very healthy, and provisions of all kinds extraordinary good, and so cheap, that a shilling will go as far in America, as four shillings in Scotland.

"4. The price of labour (from the scarcity of hands, and great plenty of land) is high in the colonies: A day labourer can gain there thrice the wages he can earn in this country.

"5. There are no beggars in North-America, the poor, when they appear, are amply provided for.

"Lastly, There are no titled proud Lords, to tyrannize over the lower sort of people, men being upon a level, and more valued, in proportion to their abilities, than they are in Scotland."

WILLIAMSBURGH, (Virginia) March 17.

By a gentleman just arrived from New-River, in Fincastle county, we are informed, thet about 40 families were lately murdered on the Okonies by the Indians. Capt. Russell, from the same county, who a few days ago came to this city, reports, that the people are in the most dreadful consternation, on account of the outrages committed by those savage people.

NEWBERN, (*North Carolina,*) *March* 11.

Last Week we had a severe Gale of Wind at North and Northeast, attended with the most heavy Rains that has ever been remembered in this Country; the Waters came down in such Torrents as to sweep away Mills, Bridges, and every Thing that obstructed its Passage, and has done incredible Damage to the Roads; a very great Inconvenience at present, as we have no County Courts, or Overseers of the Roads, to order the speedy Reparation of them.

PHILADELPHIA, March 30.

Extract of a Letter from London, January 24.

"*Three* Men of War are ordered to be in Readiness to sail for Boston, and exact Payment for the TEA."

NEWPORT, April 4.

Extract of a Letter from the West-Indies, March 9.

"It is reported that after Admiral Perry left Crab Island, and renewed the English Claim, an English Vessel belonging to St. Kitts, went there to cut Lignumvitæ, &c. after tarrying there a little Time, they were surprized by a Number of armed Spaniards, from Porto Rico, who took the Vessel, and murdered every Soul on board, except one Man, who made his Escape; in Consequence of which, a Man of War sailed from St. Kitts last Saturday, for London. It is an Affair of great Importance; it is certain a Packet sailed from Porto Rico for Old-Spain, in Consequence of this Crab-Island Expedition."

It is pretty certain, by Advice received Yesterday from New-York, that the India Company have applied to Administration to adopt some Measures for obtaining Satisfaction for the TEA sent to this Country; that they met with a cold Reception, and were told that they must apply to the AMERICANS for Compensation.

PORTSMOUTH, April 8.

The Merchants and Traders in this Town, are desired to meet at Union-Hall, this Afternoon, at 4 o'Clock, to consult upon a Matter very interesting to them, and the Public.

Last Friday came to Town Mr. *William Goddard*, Printer to the City of Philadelphia, and at Baltimore in Maryland. The Cause of that Gentleman's Tour is interesting to all the Colonies, and we are happy to find, that ALL thro' which he has come are thoroughly engaged in the glorious Cause, every Colony to the Southward of us manifest their readiness to come into the Measure: and we are informed there is not the Shadow of a doubt of its being warmly patronized by the genuine Sons of Liberty in Portsmouth, who are to meet at Union-Hall this Afternoon.—How cheerfully will every well Wisher to his Country lay hold of an Opportunity to rescue the Channel of Public and Private Intelligence out of the Hands of a Power, openly inimical to its Rights and Liberties.

Yesterday the General Assembly met here.

SALEM, April 5.

We hear from Marblehead, that a Person, named Clark, went to Cat-Island last Wednesday, and took away some Cloaths, (said to be his own) which he brought up to the Town. As they had been infected with the small-Pox, and it was uncertain whether they were cleansed or not, he was immediately ordered, by the Selectmen, round to the Ferry, back of the Town, where the Cloaths were to be examined. He accordingly obeyed: But returning to Town again, he was surrounded by a considerable Number of People; and lest they should proceed to any Violence with him, the Selectmen appeared, and promised that he should be properly and legally punished, if deserving of it, the next Day. This seemed to satisfy the People: But about 10 or 11 o'Clock at Night, 20 or 30 of them went and pulled him out of his House, carried him to the public Whipping-Post, and whipped him most cruelly. The next Day he went to Ipswich, made his Complaint to the Justices of the Inferior Court, then sitting, and told who the Persons were that had abused him. A Warrant was issued, one of the Criminals was taken up and committed to Goal, and a good Look-Out is kept for apprehending the others? one of whom, as he was returning from Meeting on the last Sabbath, an Officer gave Chace to, but could not catch him.——The abovementioned Clark is one of the Persons who were tarred and feathered some Time since.

Last Tuesday the Superior Court of Judicature &c. Open'd in Charlestown in and for the County of Middlesex. The Grand Jurors were sworn, and the Charge was deliver'd to them by the Hon. Judge TROWBRIDGE. *And on Thursday they delivered in their Bills, together with the following* REMONSTRANCE *aud* PROTEST, *viz.*

Charlestown, April 7, 1774.

To the honorable his Majesty's Justices of the Superior Court of Judicature, Court of Assize, &c. now sitting at Charlestown, *in and for the County of* Middlesex.

WE the Subscribers being of the Grand Jury for said Court, beg Leave to represent, That whereas the Venire's for choosing Jurymen bear Test *Peter Oliver*, Esq; who stands Impeached by the Grand Inquest of this Province, the honorable House of Commons, for High Crimes and Misdemeanors, we were under great Doubts about taking the Oath; but foreseeing the insuperable Difficulties that would take Place from the Course of Justice being impeded, were constrained to take the Oath and proceed to Business, and have, to the best of our Knowledge, conscienciously discharged our Trust. But we think it our incumbent Duty to Remonstrate and Protest against the honorable *Peter Oliver*, Esq; his sitting as Chief Justice on the Trial of any of the Offences by us presented, until he shall be acquitted of the Crimes he is charged with.——The Impropriety of the Chief Justice sitting to judge of the Crimes of others, while he himself lies under an Impeachment for High Crimes and Misdemeanors—will, we flatter ourselves, sufficiently apologize to the honorable Court for this our Remonstrance.

The Jury present consisted of 18. *This Remonstrance was signed by* 14—*the other* 4 *declined.*

To the PRINTERS.

THE respectable Grand Jury of Middlesex have exhibited an Example, worthy to be followed by those of the other Counties in this Pronince, in nobly bearing their Testimony against the Chief Justice of the Superior Court his sitting in the Trial on any of the Offences presented by them, until he shall be acquitted of the High Crimes and Misdemeanours whereof he has been impeached by the Representative Body of the Province, altho' Governor Hutchinson feeling no doubt, his own Independency, or rather more properly speaking, his Dependence upon Ministers of State, has refused to admit the Conduct of the Judge to an Examination. Would the Governor's *Royal Master* have thought it prudent to have thus *screened a Favourite* from answering to an Impeachment of the House of Commons in the Name of all the People of England? But the Governor of this Province is made less dependent on the General Assembly, than the King is upon the Parliament. If a Man who has had his Birth and Education in the Province, and owes all his Greatness to the former Indulgence of his Fellow-Citizens, which as his own Letters evince, he has ungratefully forgot, I say, if such a Man can go to so great a Length in endeavouring to establish an Executive independent of the Legislative in his own Country, what may we not expect from a Stranger who will have the Conduct of a *Native* to plead as a Precedent.—But the Eyes of this People, for which we are indebted to the Freedom of the Press, and the indefatigable Industry of our Patriots, are at length open: They clearly see the Designs of a corrupt Administration, not barely to "abridge the Liberties of Englishmen" but to annihilate the free Part of the Constitution. They are convinc'd by Experience, that the absolute Dependence of the Governor upon the Crown for his Being and Support is a leading Step towards it, as it alienes him from the People, and renders him meanly subservient to Ministers of State; in short that it shifts the Government into their Hands. They contemplate their Condition with deep Resentment. They will never patiently submit to it. Their Opposition to Tyranny grows daily more into a System. And that Man will do eminent Service to his Country, who instead of flattering the British Administration, with the least degree of Hope that their Plans will finally succeed, shall convince them, that let who will be advanced to the Chair of this Government, he will assuredly meet with the Contempt and Hatred *at least* of a very spirited People, if he comes clogg'd with such Conditions and Instructions as will degrade him from the Character of a constitutional Governor, down to that of the meanest and most despicable of the human Species, a ***dependant Tool of a Man in Power.***

BOSTON, April 11.

We hear from the county of Worcester, that the friends of GOOD government are under some apprehensions that Peter Oliver, Esq; will attempt to take the seat of Chief Justice, and act as such, at the Superior Court which is to sit in that county in April Instant; notwithstanding the impeachment against him in the name of the whole people of this province by their representatives: But that the people are upon their guard. And to prevent any persons being tried, fined, or otherways punished by the judgment or sentence of a judge, accused of being under the influence of a bribe. It is expected the Grand Jurors, returned to serve at that court, will meet very early in the Morning before the Court sits, at the House of Mr. Asa Ward in Worcester; and agree not to be impanneled, nor serve as Grand Jurors with the said Peter Oliver on the Bench as Chief Justice, or Judge of said Court, until he hath been tried and acquitted of the Charges against him. And that the Grand Jurors will be justified, and, if need be, defended by the People, who look upon this Way much better than Opposition by *Violence*, but are determined upon the *last Resort*, if necessary.

Monday last the Ancient and Honorable Artillery Company made Choice of the Rev. Mr. Hunt of this Town to preach a Sermon to them on the first Monday of June next, being the Anniversary of the Election of Officers for that Company the ensuing Year.

The same Day arrived here his Majesty's Frigate King's Fisher, Capt. G. Montague, from Halifax.

Yesterday sail'd the Lydia, Capt. Hood, for London.

We are informed from Halifax, that in Consequence of the King's Mandamus, dated the 3d January, James Burrow, Esq; Comptroller of the Customs for Nova-Scotia, and Register of Chancery there, was sworn in one of His Majesty's Council in the Room of the Hon. Benjamin Green, Esq; deceased.

Extract of a letter from an eminent house in London, to a correspondent in this town, dated 24th December, 1773.

"We are sorry the government under cover of the East India company are taking such strides to establish a revenue in the colonies,—and if the tea should be consumed with you *that they have and do intend* sending out if no obstruction, we fear the colonies will be drained of a great part of their cash to suport revenue officers—we see no remedy but the people determining not to make use of the article, if they can, tho' this we fear wont be done."

We are inform'd that at a General Council on Thursday last, Governor Hutchinson nominated Jonathan Sayward, Esq; as a Justice of the Inferior Court of Common Pleas for the County of York; and that his Majesty's Council did *advise* and *consent* thereto. This Person was one of the seventeen RESCINDERS in the Year 1768; and as we are inform'd there was no Objection at the Board to his Appointment, doubtless his Excellency is encourag'd to hope that the same Respect will be shown to a Nomination of another *Rescinder* who is talk'd of to fill up the Vacancy in the Superior Court by the Death of Judge Ropes.

Last Thursday was killed at Charlestown, an Ox (bred and fatted by Robert Temple, Esq; of Ten-Hills) weighing as follows, viz. Beef 1261lbs. Hyde 144 lbs. Tallow 200 Total 1605lbs.

MARRIED] Sampson Salter Blowers, Esq; Barrister at Law, to Miss Sally Kent, youngest Daugher of Benjamin Kent, Esq;

Mr. Robert G. Cranch, to Miss Polly Clemmons Daughter of Capt. Clemmons.

Mr. Daniel Ingersol, to Miss Polly Gridley.

Died at Saco. Dr. Cummins.

At Wells. Waldo Emerson, Merchant.

TAKEN out of a Wallet in the new Court-House in Queen-Street on Friday last, 5 yards of black Taffaty, $3\frac{1}{2}$ yds black Tammy, $\frac{1}{2}$ yd black Cyprus, &c. wrapt up in one yard check Linnen. The Person who took them is desir'd to leave them with Edes & Gill.

PROCEEDINGS *of the Town of* Wells.

At a Meeting of the Freeholders and other Inhabitants of the Town of Wells, *duly warned and legally assembled at the Meeting-House in the first Parish in said* Wells, January 6, 1774, *and continued by Adjournment to the 28th Day of* March, *being legally assembled, according to Adjournment, Voted the following Resolves.*

1. RESOLVED, That Freedom is essential to the Happiness of a State, which no Nation can give up without violating the Laws of Nature, Reason and Religion, ruining Millions, and entailing the deepest Misery upon Posterity.

2dly. *Resolved*, That the late Act of British Parliament, empowering the East-India Company to export their Teas to America, subject to a Duty, is a daring Infringement upon our invaluable Rights and Privileges, is a Measure replete with every Evil, Political & Commercial; therefore it is incumbent on every Man who values his Birthright and would support the Constitution, to oppose every such Attempt in all lawful and constitutional Ways.

3dly. *Resolved*, That we will not receive any Teas whereon an unconstitutional Duty may be laid, whether shipp'd by the East India Company or private Merchants; and will esteem every Person who shall or may receive any such Teas, as unfriendly to the Town, and inimical to the Country and Constitution; and will treat them with that Contempt which such Conduct deserves.

4thly. *Resolved*, That we will bear faithful and true Allegiance to our Sovereign Lord George the Third, and are ready at all Times to support his Crown and Dignity, at the Expence of our Lives and Fortunes; but by no Means to support the oppressive Measures of Parliament, which have and still continue to threaten total Destruction to the Liberties of all America.

5thly. *Resolved*, That the Thanks of this Town be given to our worthy Brethren the patriotic Inhabitants of the Town of Boston, for their early Intelligence, and steady Perseverance in the common Cause. Posterity we doubt not will applaud their Conduct, and their Children will rise up and call them Blessed.

Voted, That an attested Copy of these our Proceedings be transmitted to the Committee of Correspondence in Boston.

A true Copy. Attest.

NATH. WELLS, Town-Clerk.

WHEREAS *the Co-parnership of* Scott *and* Gill *was mutually Dissolved the 21st of* February *last*——ALL Persons indebted are requested to make immediate Payment to *Moses Gill*: And all to whom the Company is indebted, are desired to bring in their Accounts to said *Gill*, for Adjustment, and receive their Balances.

Boston, 6*th* April 1774.

N. B. *The Business is carried on as usual, by* Moses Gill, *where the Customers of the late Company, and all others, may be well served.*

TO BE LETT,

A House with 3 Acres of Land,

within 4 Miles of Boston, upon the Cambridge Road, conveniently situated for a Gentleman's Seat.

Enquire of *Eliphalet Downer* of Brookline.

Wanted to Hire Immediately,

A Faithful honest Man, that understands the Leather Dressing Business, for which a good Price will be given. For further Particulars, enquire of Edes & Gill.

West-India RUM,

A few Casks of TORTOLA & St. VINCENTS RUM, and choice old JAMAICA SPIRITS, to be SOLD by

Jonathan Davis,

At his Store on Bull's Wharff; who has also for Sale, INDIAN CORN, BEEF and PORK, by the Barrell; and a Quantity of very good Country made OARS.

CHOICE WINES,

per Quarter-Cask, just arrived and to be SOLD

By Archibald Cunningham,

At his Store in Ann-Street, near the Draw-Bridge, *Boston*.

Lisbon,	ALSO, Olives per Jarr.
Calcavilla,	Anchovies in Kegs or Bottles.
Malaga,	Capers per Cask.
Sherry,	Almonds in or out of the Shell, per Hundred or single Pound.
Shallow,	Cases of Bottles, and Case Bottles.
Madeira, and	Hampers of Dutch Ware, Quart Chamber Potts and Muggs.
Fayal Wine.	Dutch Brushes in Setts or single, Wicker'd Quart and Pint Bottles.

Lisbon and French Oil, per Cask, Velvet Corks, best French Indigo per Hundred Dozen or single Pound, Spices, split Peas, Coffee, Raisins, Currants, Turkey Figgs.——N. B. Barcelona Handkerchiefs of different sorts, by the Quantity or single Dozen, very cheap.

Cash given at said Store for small Olive Jarrs, and empty Bottles of every kind. OLIVES per Jarr.

TO BE SOLD

A double HOUSE, pleasantly situated in Sudbury-Street, next to Mr. William Crafts's, the Purchaser may have the half or the whole.

This Day the Subscriber will open his School for Young Ladies. The Hours for Attendance will be Eleven o'Clock in the Morning, and Five o'Clock in the Afternoon.

Boston, 11 *April* 1774. JOSEPH WARD.

FLOUR.

Fine Burr Flour, also, Ship Bread of the best Quality, to be Sold at Mr. CHEEVER's Store in King-Street.

TO BE SOLD,

(and entered upon immediately)

A Handsome well finished Dwelling House, in Brookfield, with a large Store, Barn, &c. all in very good Repair, together with thirty Acres of Land, is pleasantly situated on the great Post Road, and is in a fine place for carrying on Trade—Any Person inclining to purchase the same may apply to THEOPHILUS LILLIE, at Boston.

COFFEE,

In handy Casks for

EXPORTATION,

And a few Tierces RICE of a Quality fit for the London Market, to be SOLD cheap for Cash, at POWELL's Warehouse, No. 14, Long-Wharff.

ALL Persons indebted to, or that have any Demands on the Estate of Mr. Joshua Seaver late of Roxbury, Yeoman, deceas'd, are desired to bring in their Accounts to John Newell, of Newton, or Ebenezer Seaver, of Roxbury, Administrators on said Estate, in Order for Settlement.

WANTED,

A Woman of a good Character,

and one that can be well recommended, and that understands Cooking and other House Work; none need apply but such a one, and is wanted immediately.—Good Wages will be given. Inquire of Edes & Gill.

Mrs. *Oliver* (at her School a little below the Mill-Bridge, leading to the new Grist-Mill) informs the young Ladies both in Town & Country, That she still continues teaching Embroidery, Queen, Tenth and Irish Stitching, Coats of Arms, Marking and plain Sewing. Whoever pleases to favour her with their Custom, may depend on being as well and faithfully instructed in the above Branches, as at any School without Exception, in Town.

N. B. Children instructed in Spelling, Reading and Sewing, as usual.

TO BE SOLD

AT PUBLICK AUCTION,

By Benjamin Church,

At his usual Place of Sale,

On FRIDAY next,

At THREE o'Clock in the Afternoon,

A valuable Assortment of European Articles, consisting of Broad Cloths—Plains—Ratteens—Shalloons——Irish Linnens—Checks—Oznabrigs,—Handkerchiefs, &c. &c. Likewise House Furniture, as Glasses,—Feather Beds,—Tables,——Chairs, &c.——Watches——&c.

On FRIDAY, at Three o'Clock, P. Mr.

TO BE SOLD

At John Winthrop, jun'rs Store, on Treat's Wharff near the Market, very cheap *Philadelphia* and *Baltimore* FLOUR.

BOTTLES with and without Cases. IRON, &c. &c

FLOUR.

A Quantity of the newest *Baltimore* FINE FLOUR, and *Philadelphia* fine and superfine Ditto.

Ditto in Half Barrels.

Philadelphia BAR IRON.

A few Hogsheads of choice BRAN, and Quarter Casks of WINE.

To be sold as cheap, if not cheaper than at any Store in Town by *JAMES SWAN*,

At his Store leading to *Treat*'s Wharff, next the South-side of the Town Dock.

Messi'rs *Morgan* and *Stieglitz*,

Request Permission to inform the Ladies and Gentlemen of Boston, that, having received assurance of the Patronage and Assistance of the Musical Gentlemen, they purpose having at Concert-Hall, on Wednesday the 20th of April, a GRAND CONCERT of Vocal and Instrumental MUSIC assisted by the Band of the 64th Regiment.

ACT 1st.	ACT 2d.
Overture—Stamitz 1st.	Overture—Stamitz 4th.
Concerto.—German Flute,	Hunting Song.
Song.—'My dear Mistress,' &c	Solo, German Flute.
Harpsic. Concerto by Mr. *Selby*	Song, Oh! my Delia, &c.
Simphony—Artaxerexes,	Solo Violin.

To conclude with a grand Military Simphony accompanied by Kettle Drums, &c. compos'd by Mr. *Morgan*.

TICKETS at Half a Dollar each, to be had at the *British Coffee-House*, at Miss *Cumming*'s in Cornhill, at Messi'rs *Cox* and *Berry* in King-Street, and of Messi'rs *Stieglitz* and *Morgan*.

N. B. Copies of the Songs to be delivered out (*gratis*) with the Tickets.—To begin at 7 o'Clock precisely.—

ANCHORS

Of all Sizes from 100 to 1000 wt. well wrought, and warranted good, to be Sold by

Benjamin Andrews,

Who has for Sale also, Choice GREEN COFFEE, by the Hogshead or Hundred wt. Indigo, Snuff, Mustard, Crown Soap, Roll Brimstone, Pitch, Cordage, white Beans, Peas, *Philadelphia* new Flour, common & superfine, Bar Iron, Nova-Scotia Grindstones, Potash Kettles, a large Assortment of Iron Ware, Crates of Crockery Ware, and English Goods as usual——*all at the very lowest Rates for Cash.*

All Persons that have any Demands on the Estate of Mr. Andrew Cunningham, late of Boston, Hatter, deceased, are desired to bring in their Accounts to Mary Greenleaf and John Cunningham, Administrators on said Estate, for Adjustment.——And all Persons indebted to said Estate, are desired to make immediate Payment to said Administrators.

John Cunningham,

HAS for Sale at his Shop near the Corner of School-Street, opposite Mr. Deblois's.

A Large Assortment of English and India Goods, suitable for all Seasons, which he is determined to sell at the Sterling Cost, (clear of Charges) he being determined to quit the Business.

New AUCTION-ROOM, Cornhill.

TO-MORROW at TEN o'Clock will be Sold by PUBLIC VENDUE, at GREENLEAF's Auction-Room,——

A large Assortment of English and Hard-Ware Goods, as usual.

Wm. GREENLEAF, Auctioneer.

The Sale will begin Tomorrow at Ten o'Clock.

For private Sale,

Handsome Sconce Glasses, a Mehogany Book Case, two 8-Day Clocks, a Mehogany Dining and Beauro Table, Bone and Buck-Handle Table Knives and Forks, two Setts of handsome Glaz'd Pictures, cream-colour'd Terreens, a Parcel of Beer and Cyder Glasses, Beaver Hats, some small Boxes of well-assorted Ribbons, rich black Padusoys, a Variety of Damasks, Ducapes, Lutestrings, Taffaties, fine Chints, Velverets, Brocade Silk Shoes and Clogs, Cambrick and Book Muslins, and many other Articles.

On Wednesday next,

At Ten o'Clock,

Will be Sold by PUBLIC VENDUE, at the New Auction-Office, South Side of the Town-House.

A large and valuable Assortment of English Goods, belonging to a Gentleman leaving off Business,

Consisting of,

CALLICOS, Chints and Patches, mixt Cinnamon and cloth-coloured Bengalls, Long Lawns, Diaper Table Cloths, Irish Linnens, Dimothees, Mens silk and cotton Hose, Womens pink Hose, Muslin and printed Linnen Handkerchiefs, Brolioes, Everlastings; pink, crimson, black and cloth-coloured Callimancoes, cloth-coloured Durants & Cambleteens, Irish Cambletts, green red and blue Mecklinburgs, green, blue and cloth-coloured Shalloons, pink, black, brown, white and cloth-coloured Tammys, Pensacoley's, green and red worsted Brocades, pink, blue, purple and orange Messinetts, pink, blue, purple and yellow Silveritts, cloth-coloured Breeches Patterns, cotton Velvets, handsome Ribbons, white handle Knives and Forks, Broad Cloths, Ratteens, Bearskins, Jersey knit Hose, mill'd Caps, white Quality Binding.—Plate, handsome Tureen, Tankard, Porringers, Chaffindishes, large and small Spoons, Pepper Boxes, Creampotts, Cups, &c. and a variety of House Furniture, and a number of other Articles, too numerous for an Advertisement. A. OLIVER, Auctioneer.

To the PUBLIC.

AS the Method lately practiced by the Subscriber, in having a Person at his Door to invite Gentlemen and others to his public Sales—has given Dissatisfaction to some—(Gentlemen Shopkeepkers in particular) to avoid giving Offence for the future, he shall desist from that Practice, and pursue one (as follows) which he flatters himself cannot fail giving universal Satisfaction, as he sincerely wishes so to do. The Public are most earnestly requested to remember (for *their own Advantage*) that for the future Notice will be given by sounding a Bell which he has purchased for that Purpose, which is erected over his Auction-Room Door near the Market, Boston, where constant Attendance is given both early and late to receive the Favours of all, such who are pleased to confer on their *Much obliged*,

Most obedient, and very humble Servant.

M. BICKER.

*** Said BICKER sells as cheap as ever.

CUSTOM-HOUSE, *BOSTON*.

ENTETRD IN.

Rider and Partridge, from North-Carolina. Eldridge, Olds, Brooks and Birdsey, New-Haven. Cook, Halifax. Hurd, New-London, Prince, Philadelphia. Smart, Jamaica and Turks-Island. Lovit, Tortola. Boardman, Guadaloup. Tucker, Martinico. Brown, St. Martins.

Burials in the Town of BOSTON, since our last.

Twelve Whites. One Black.

Baptiz'd in the several Churches, Seven.

High Water at BOSTON, for the present Week.

Monday, 0 min. aft. 12	Friday, 36 min. after 2
Tuesday, 30 min. aft. 12	Saturday, 23 min. af. 3
Wednesday, 1 m. aft. 1	Lord's-Day, 12m. aft 4
Thursday, 46 min. aft. 1	New D 10Day 8 Aftern.

CHOICE *MADDER*,
The Growth of this Province,
TO BE SOLD BY,
John Barrett,
Near the Mill-Bridge, BOSTON.

GUN-POWDER,
To be Sold by HENRY BROMFIELD, at his Store opposite the Custom-House in King-Street,
ALSO,
Pepper, a few Barrels Pork, and Cod-Lines very cheap.

TO BE SOLD
A BRIG of about 170 Tons, now on the Stocks at York, and will be Launch'd in ten Days;—She is built of the best Materials, and is extremely well calculated for the Guinea or Streights Trade.—For further Particulars inquire of WILLIAM PALFREY,
Who has for sale,
Spermacæti Candles,
Warranted genuine and pure.

A Quantity of FLOUR, and a few Barrels of Middling ditto, to be sold cheap. Also a Parcel of *Newfoundland* BREAD:—Inquire of JOHN CUSHING, at his Sugar-House, Brattle-Street, near Doctor Cooper's Meeting-House, Boston.

TO BE SOLD CHEAP,
About 100 Quintals of good Jamaica Cod Fish.—Two Foresails suitable for a Brig of 100 Tons—One new Foresail and Mainsail, suitable for a Schooner of 50 or 60 Tons, and a small quantity of new Cordage.
Inquire of the Printers.

WANTED,
£. 200 Lawful Money, for which good Security will be given. Inquire of the Printers.

For *Quebec*,
THE Brigantine BETSEY, CONSTANT FREEMAN, Master, lying the South-side the Long-Wharff, will sail in about 15 Days:—For Freight or Passage apply to said Freeman, on board, or at his House in South School-Street.

For *Quebec*,
THE Schooner EUNICE, NATHANIEL ATKINS, Master, lying the South-side the Long-Wharff, will sail in about 15 Days:—For Freight or Passage apply to said Master on board, or to Constant Freeman, at his House in South School-Srreet.

For *Annapolis Royal*,
THE SLOOP Jenny, GEORGE MITCHELL, Master, Lying at Wentworth's Wharf, having good Accommodations for Passengers, will Sail in Ten Days. For Frieght or Passage Inquire of the Master on said Wharf.

Wanted to Hire by the Year,
An industrious Man of a good Character, that understands Gardening, and to wait on a Gentleman's Family. Inquire of the Printers.

WANTED *immediately*,
A sober active Lad, as an Apprentice to the Goldsmith's Business. Inquire of the Printers.

A Negro Child to be given away, of an excellent Breed. Inquire of Edes & Gill.

For private Sale,
At the NEW AUCTION-ROOM,
South Side of the Town-House, viz.
Three handsome Mehogany Desks and Book Cases, Chest on Chests of Draws, Desks, round and square Dining & Spring Tables, Beauro ditto, Card and Chamber Tables, Mehogany Chairs with Copper-plate yellow and Leather Bottoms, round-about Chairs, black Walnut Leather bottom Chairs, handsome Clocks, Pinchbeck Watches, handsome Sconce Looking-Glasses of all sorts and sizes, a Suit of Harrateen Curtains, a Suit of yellow Morien Curtains, with Window Curtains, Squabbs and Easy Chair, 6 green bottom Chamber Chairs, Window Shades, small handsome Spinnett, Mehogany and Maple four Post Bedsteads, small Mghogany Sugar Chests, 2 Cases of Doctor's Instruments, small Handmaids, a large Scale Beam, with Scales & Chains, Plate, handsome Silver Terreen Tankard, large Salver, Chaffindishes, Porringers, Cups, Pepper Boxes, large and small Spoons, silver hilted Swords, silver and Ivory Handle Knives and Forks, silver plated Candlesticks, a genteel brass reading Candlestick, a very neat pair of steel Pistols, Gun and Bayonet, Baremeter, also, orange, blue and green collour'd Broad Cloths, Cotton Velvetts, Shalloons, Tammies, Stuffs and Durants, white Baize, Irish Linnens, Men's silk Hose, Capuchine Silks of all colours, black, blue, red and white Sarsnets, Patch Work Coverlids, a Box of well assorted and handsome Ribbonds, Poplins, Buckskin Breeches, handsome Muffs, a large Globe, silk Gauzes, black Sattin and Chip Hatts, a handsome full suit of Brocade, and suit of black Grogram, small Pocket Glasses, and Lisbon Lemmons by the Box, a Variety of other Articles.
N. B. At said Auction-Office constant Attendance is given to receive all kind of Goods for public and private Sale.

TO BE LETT, and enter'd upon immediately,
A FARM in Leicester, *consisting of Mowing, Arrable and Pasture Land, &c. Inquire of Capt.* Nathaniel Scot, *living near the Premises, or the Printers hereof.*

TO BE SOLD
A likely Negro Lad, 17 Years old, speaks English and French. Inquire of *Jean Francois Magellon*, at the House of Capt. *Isaac McDaniel*, New-Boston.

LAND TO BE SOLD
Five Hundred Acres of LAND, in the Town of *Granville*, to be Sold, either the whole at once, or such Lots as may best suit the Purchaser.—
Inquire of
Richard Salter,
At his Shop in Cornhill;
Who continues to Sell on the most reasonable Terms,
English and India GOODS suitable for all Seasons—The best French and Spanish Indigo, Pepper and Spices: Also a fine Assortment of Women's and Children's Stays made in the neatest and best manner: Best russel, callamanco and everlasting Women and Children Shoes, Pumps, Goloshoes, &c.

TO BE LETT,
A commodious Brick Messuage, situate in Brattle Square. Inquire of Edes and Gill.

TO BE SOLD
By *Joseph Belknap*,
In Ann-Street, near the Draw-Bridge, Boston,
White CALVE SKINS,
by the Dozen or single Skin.

Just Imported, and to be Sold by
GEORGE ERVING,
A Large Quantity of Russia Duck, Dutch Rope Yarns, Junk, Looking-Glasses, Linseed Oyl, Stone Ware, &c. &c. Boston, March 28, 1774.

CASH
GIVEN for Merchantable and Unmerchantable Pot-ash, and Potash Salts, at GOULD's Auction Office in Back Street, Boston.

POT-ASH.
CASH given for *POT-ASH*,
By JONATHAN MASON,
At his Shop next Door to the Sign of the *Buck & Glove*,
Near the Town-House, BOSTON.
N. B. To be Sold by said MASON,
A Quantity of choice Connecticut Pork.

The best Turks Island SALT,
To be SOLD on board the Schooner Sally. Capt. Rogers, lying at Griffins Wharf.

All Persons that have any Demands on the Estate of the late Elizabeth Hewes, *Widow, deceas'd, are desired immediately to bring in their Accounts for Settlement; and all Persons indebted to said Estate, are desired to make speedy Payment to*

Boston, March 21, 1774. HENDERSON INCHES, AND, NATH. APPLETON, } Executors.

ENGLISH GOODS CHEAP.
Imported from LONDON, by
Samuel Dashwood,
And to be Sold at his Shop next Door to Dr. Silvester Gardner's in Marlborough-Street, Boston.
A Great Variety of English, India and Scotch Goods, among which are,—Irish Linnens of all widths, Chinces and Callicoes, great Variety of Silks, best Royal Ribbs, best English Shoes at One Dollar per Pair, and many other Articles too tedious to mention, which will be sold by Wholesale at the Sterling Cost, and by Retail at the Cost and Charges, as he is going into another Branch of Business.
N. B. Spices of all Kinds, great Variety of Glass, China and Earthen Ware, sold remarkable cheap for Cash.

THERE is to be sold, a genteel Horse and Chaise, with or without a Negro Boy of 16 Years old, that can be well recommended, understands taking Care of Horse and Chaise, and cleaning them in the neatest Manner; drives with great Care; can do House-work and Cook as well as any one of his Age; is good-temper'd lively and spry. The above to be sold for no other Reason than that the Gentleman to whom they did belong is deceas'd. If any Gentleman or Lady inclines, to purchase the above, and it is not convenient to pay the Money, it may lay on good Security. Inquire of the Printers.

STOLEN out of the Barn of me the Subscriber on Wednesday Night the 16th of March Inst. a red Mare, Saddle and Bridle, with a Blaze in her Face, about 13 Hands high, and about 12 Years old or upwards, carries her Head very low.——Whoever will take up the said Mare and bring her with the Saddle and Bridle to the Owner, shall have two Dollars Reward, and all necessary Charges paid, by RALPH DEVEREAUX.
Marblehead, March 16, 1774.

All Persons having any Demands on the Estate of Mr. JOHN KNEELAND, late of Boston, Shopkeeper, deceased, are desired to bring in their Accounts in Order for Adjustment; and all who are indebted to said Estate, are desired to pay their respective Dues.
ABIGAIL KNEELAND,
BARTHOW' KNEELAND,
EDWARD KNEELAND.
Executors of the Deceased's last Will.
At the Sterling Cost, are now selling off,
THE Shop Goods belonging to the Estate of Mr. *John Kneeland*, deceased, at the Shop lately kept by him in Union-Street, near the Market. Any Person minded to purchase the whole Stock together, will find it for their Interest to apply soon, as the Sales must be closed in a short Time.
N. B. A small Parcel of Gold and Silver Lace to be Sold at extreme low Rates.

For *Quebec*,
The Schooner Polly, Capt. PEPPER, will sail in all the Month of April, having two Thirds of her Cargo engaged: For Freight or Passage apply to said Master on Board at Long-Wharff; or of *Edward Davis*, at his Store, who wants to Charter a single deck'd Vessel from 70 to 100 Tons Burthen to load at Quebec for the West-Indies.

Bar Iron and Anchors,
Warranted of a prime Quality, and SOLD by
SAM^L. A. OTIS,
At Store No. 1, Butler's Row, ALSO,
New-England RUM, CHOCOLATE, and many other Articles.
☞ A few Quarter Casks Madeira WINES very cheap.

TO BE SOLD CHEAP,
A Brig called the NANCY, about Eighteen Months old, 129 Tons Burthen, a prime Sailer and well found, now lying at John Hancock, Esq'rs Wharf. For further Particulars, Inquire of Mr. *Thomas Boylston*.

WANTED,
£.400 Lawful Money, for which good Real Security will be given in Boston. Inquire of Edes and Gill.

TO BE SOLD,
A Schooner about 35 Tons, lying at *Minot's* T. employ'd in the Fishing Business. Enquire at Mr. *Munro's* Notary-Publick, near the Court-House, King-Street.

A generous Price will be given for an easy-going Saddle-Horse, that shall be warranted sound Wind and Limb. Inquire of Edes and Gill.

SEVEN good HORSES, one Stage Coach, with Harness compleat for four Horses, and two Fall-back Chaise, to be Sold very reasonable for the Cash or West-India Goods. Inquire of JOHN WALDO, at his House third Door South of the Lamb Tavern.

All Persons having Demands on the Estate of *Pitts Hall*, late of Boston, Merchant deceased, are requested to bring in their Accounts for Adjustment, to the Subscriber, who is appointed Administrator on said Estate. JOHN ERVING, jun.

Stolen one Evening last Week from a House in Union-Street, one Scarlet Cloth Riding-hood, one Scarlet Cloth Cloak, one black Russell quilted Petticoat, one Tippet and one Holland Apron. A handsome Reward will be given to any Person that can give Information to the Printer, so that the Thief may be detected and the Things recover'd. 28 March 1774.

TWENTY DOLLARS Reward.
STOLEN out of the Stable of Capt. NATHAN BRIGHAM in Southborough, on the Night of the 22d Instant, a valuable Sorrel Horse, with a Blaze in his Face, and several red Spots among the white near his Nose, Trotts and Paces well, one of his hind Feet is Part white, he is five Years old, and about fifteen Hands high, his Hair is wore off of his sides with the Saddle Skirts on his Loins with the Housing. Whoever shall Secure the said Horse so as the Owner may have him again, and also Secure the Thief so that he may be brought to Justice shall receive the above Reward; and Eight Dollars Reward for the Horse only.
Southborough, March 24, 1774. Nathan Brigham.

A FARM to be Sold in Watertown, very pleasantly situated, and within two Miles of the College, contains about 40 Acres of choice good Land, has on it a good House and Barn, is well accommodated for Mowing, Pasturage and Tillage, has on it a Variety of all kinds of Fruits, and will very well accommodate a Gentleman: Whoever is iuclined to Purchase the same may apply to *John Stratton* of said Watertown. *Feb.* 28, 1774.

TO BE SOLD VERY REASONABLY,
By ISRAEL HUNTING, of *Dedham*,
All his Interest in the first Parish in said Town, viz.
HIS Homestead, containing 15 Acres of choice Mowing and Tillage Land, having some excellent Apple-Trees thereon; there being a good House and Barn on the Premises, and but a quarter of a Mile from the Meeting-House.—*Also*, 4 Acres of Pasturing and Orchard, one Mile and an half from said Homestead.

Boston: Printed, by EDES & GILL.

THE

Boston-Gazette, AND COUNTRY JOURNAL.

No. 993.

Containing the freshest Advices, Foreign and Domestic.

MONDAY, April 18, 1774.

Messieurs EDES & GILL,

I make it a principle to accept instruction from every quarter that offers it; and have often been entertained and informed by the productions of an almanack maker. I am also willing to contribute my mite in detecting any errors that are published to the world. It is for this reason I trouble you with this. Mr. Stearns, in his almanack for this year, has printed a series of calculations of the times of the sun's rising and setting founded on a principle noticed in his preface. This principle, I believe, is erroneous; but if I labour under a mistake, am desirous of having it rectified by that gentleman, or any of your astronomical correspondents. He thinks the sun, at the times of the equinoxes, rises before and sets after six o'clock, in the latitude of Boston— He acknowledges that, at the equator, he rises and sets precisely at six; but, because he is seen a whole day by a spectator at the pole, and only 12 hours by one at the equator, he concludes that he rises at different times, during the equinoxes, in the intermediate latitudes—I am of opinion that the sun, at those seasons, rises precisely at 6 o'clock, in all latitudes where he rises at all— I say, *rises at all*, because the horizons of spectators placed under the pole, coincide with the equator, which is then the sun's diurnal path, and to them his centre would appear to move in their horizons the whole day, supposing the earth had no progressive motion in her orbit, and the atmosphere destitute of a refracting power; which supposition I make in the present remark—The reason of my opinion is this—The sun's diurnal path, at the equinoxes, is a great circle, and so is the horizon of every spectator wherever he is placed; now every astronomer knows that all great circles either coincide with, or bisect, each other, consequently the sun, at those seasons, is half the day above, and half below, the horizon, and therefore must rise and set at six o'clock.

A lover of Truth.

Extract from a book publish'd a few years since in London, entituled "the present state of Great-Britain *and* North-America, *with Regard to Agriculture, Population, Trade, and Manufactures, impartially considered." Remarking on a Book before published, intitled "the Regulation of the Colonies." The Author says,*

"THAT it appears (from the Reasons he had been giving) that the common Opinions received and propagated in *Britain* concerning the Colonies, are no more than so many vulgar errors, by which means most People there seem not to know their own Interest in the Colonies, and mistake the one for the other: But they must certainly have good Reason to be satisfied, that all the Regulations mention'd are directly contrary to the Interest of *Britain*; and that the Colonies, and all others, have shewn a sincere Zeal for the Welfare of the Nation, in opposing them; if they have been exposed to Blame and Censure for their Pains. A bare mention of these Regulations will shew it. They were intended

1st. To confine the Colonies to their present Bounds, and cut them off from all the more fruitful Parts of that Continent, the Lands on the Missisippi and the Ohio, which would produce any Thing for *Britain*, or enable the Colonies to make Remittance to her.

2dly. To lay Duties on many of the Goods they have from Britain, which so enhanced their Price, that the Merchants could not deal in them; and at any Rate such Duties could only be an additional Premium on the Manufactures of the Colonies, which is already very great from the dearness of British Goods.

3dly. To restrain their Trade, which is already so limitted, that it will not maintain a Tenth Part of the People; and to lay new Impositions on that Trade, by which they are already Losers, although many of the Colonies have no other Source of Remittances to *Britain*.

4thly. To levy Money upon them, when they have none, even to pay their Debts in *Britain*; and to lay Taxes on them, when they cannot even purchase the absolute Necessaries they want from *Britain*.

The Result and Drift of all which Regulations, and of the Oppositions which the Colonies have shewn to them, are, whether they shall purchase their Manufactures and other Necessaries from *Britain*, go without them, or make them for themselves; which is a Matter of no small Consequence to this Nation, if we consider the Number of People in the Colonies, and their daily Increase, and must concern the Nation at Home, much more than the Colonies themselves. The true Interests of both indeed is inseperable, and you cannot hurt the Colonies without doing double Damage to *Great Britain*; notwithstanding the Author of these Regulations, and others, would make them a separate Interest, that the Burthens which they would lay upon the Colonies, may not be thought to fall on *Great Britain*, as they have done with a double Loss. It is this that sets the Colonies and their Mother Country at Variance, to the Loss and Detriment of both.——Yet notwithstanding all these Regulations have been exploded and repealed, they are still defended; and we are told, in *the Conduct of the late Ministry*, who exerted themselves so gloriously in that Service of their Country, "the *Principles* and *the Intentions* of the Stamp-Act, however they may be "treated in *America*, deserve the Approbation "of every Inhabitant of *Great Britain*." As for the *Principles*, on which that Act was founded, they are well known to have been only a Piece of Chicanery; by which it is pretended, that the Colonies are no other than Corporations *in England*. Were they in England, it is true, they would be upon the same Footing with the Corporations here; but as they are at the Distance of Three Thousand Miles, the Difference must be as wide as that Distance.—The Members of Corporations here act in a double Capacity; they are both Freemen of Boroughs or Counties, and Members of their particular Corporations, by which they are entitled to, and enjoy, all the *Privileges* of other British Subjects, and the Advantages of their Corporations likewise: Whereas the Inhabitants of the Colonies enjoy neither of these Privileges. The one may be both Electors of Representatives in Parliament, and elected, as they generally are; when the other can be neither. To put them therefore on the same Footing, which was the *Principle* of the Stamp-Act, and the only one on which it was founded, is an Argument only fit for some Attorney to advance in a Court of *nisi prius*, and not to determine the Rights of Mankind, or Privileges of BRITISH SUBJECTS.—These their undoubted Privileges the Inhabitants of the Colonies derive from their *Birthright* as *Englishmen*; but it was the Principle of the Stamp-Act to deprive them of those Privileges, to which Nature herself, as well as the Laws of the Land entitle them.—It is this happy Constitution, which the Colonies derive from their Mother Country, that attaches them to her.——But it was the Principle of the Stamp Act to deprive them of.——— Besides this first principle of Right, there is another of Justice and Equity, which the Votaries of this Act seem never to have understood, or at least to have regarded. The Inhabitants of the Colonies do not so much as enjoy the Benefits and Profits of their own Labour; we are told by one of the best Judges we have had (Gee on Trade) "That not one fourth Part of their Produce redounds to their own Profits," all the rest is reaped by the Inhabitants of *Britain*. To put them therefore on the same footing, and to make them pay Taxes, is as contrary to Reason and Justice, as to their natural Rights and sound Policy. Before they can pay Taxes, they must reap all the Profits of their own Labour, which is the certain Way to deprive *Great Britain* of the Advantage she does and may receive from them. —But if the Inhabitants of Great Britain thus enjoy the Profits of the Labour of the People in the Colonies, what can any just and reasonable Man think, of the first imposing Taxes on the last, in Order to relieve themselves?—Such a Mode of Taxation is contrary to the first Principles of Liberty; and we meet with no Instances of it in any Part of the World; all People are Taxed either by themselves or Sovereign, and not by their Fellow-Subjects, to relieve themselves—this seems to be a Power too great for Mankind to be intrusted with.—Were any of the Subjects of *Great-Britain* to submit to such a Power, which is commonly exercised by a Minister, they would only be fit Tools to make Slaves of all the rest.--Thus the Colonies, by defending their own, preserve the Liberty of their Mother Country. Deprive an Englishman of the Right of being Taxed by Representatives of his own choosing, he ceases to be one, and will never reckon himself a Member of the Community; but if you will not allow them to be *Englishmen*, consider in Time, what they are to be.—It was depriving the People of their Liberties and Privileges, that *Flanders* cost *Spain* Three Millions of Money, for no other Purpose but to lose it at last; and take Care that Britain does not sustain the like Loss from *North America*; which will certainly be the Case, sooner or later, if you deprive the People of their Liberties and Privileges. Whereas by letting them enjoy these their Natural Rights, you may reap all the Benefits of them, without any Thing more to do; and have that for the most certain Pledge of their Allegiance and Dependance."

NEW FLOUR.

Philadelphia FLOUR, Bar Iron,

and a few Pairs of best

LEATHER BREECHES,

TO BE SOLD BY

Joseph-Pearse Palmer,

At the lowest Store, South Side of the Town-Dock.

TO BE *SOLD, OR LETT,*

A Dwelling-House in *Roxbury*, with large and very good Accommodations, now, or late, in the Occupation of Messrs. Monroe and Willard; being as good a Situation for Trade, or any public Business, as any in the Town. Enquire, for farther Particulars, of any of the Select-Men of Braintree, or of *Joseph-Pearse Palmer, of Boston.*

Samuel Garnett,

Taylor and Habit-Maker from LONDON,

TAKES this Method to acquaint the Public in General, and his Friends in Particular, that he carries on the aforesaid Business in all its Branches, in *Green's* Lane.———Ladies and Gentlemen that pleases to Favour him with their Custom may be served in the best Manner, and in the most reasonable Terms and shortest Notice.

Garden Seeds.

JOHN ADAMS,

(Opposite the Old-South Meeting-House, BOSTON,)

Hath received by the last Vessel from LONDON,

A fresh Supply of GARDEN SEEDS,

Which he doubts not will be satisfactory to the Purchaser, as they are warranted good, and of the last Year's Growth.

EARLY Golden Hotspur PEAS; early Chalton ditto. Ormorods Hotspur, blue Rouncivals, Spanish Morattoes, large black Ey'd, and Dwarff Marrowfat Peas; large Windsor, early Lisbon, and early Yellow Bush Beans; large and small White Dwarffs, White and Speckled Pole, and Kidney Beans, Silver-skin'd, White Spanish, Portugal White, and Blood-red Onion; early Yorkshire, early Dutch, early Battersea, Sugar-loaf, best Red, and large Winter Cabbage; Greenland Yellow, curl'd Savoy Cabbage; early and late Colliflower; best Cabbage; Green & White Coss; Brown Dutch, hardy Green, Silesia, Marble and Honey Lettuce; early Yellow, Orange and Purple Carrot; Early Dutch, long French, large White, and Winter Turnip; best double Parsley, and Pepper Grass; Summer and Winter Spinnage, White Mustard; Salmon, Scarlet, short Top't, Sallad and Turnip Raddish; Italian, and Sollid Cellery; Warranted Beet and Parsnip; Greenland White Endive; best early and long Prickley Cucumber; large Musk and Water Mellon; Summer and Winter Squash; Squash Pepper Seed; Asparagus; Sweet Marjoram; Thyme; Summer Savory; Baum; Sage; Rosemary; Bush Basil; Hemp; Rape and Canary; with a large Assortment of FLOWER SEEDS; Red & White Clover, & Herd's Grass Seed; Split Peas, &c.—Likewise a great Variety of Glass and Earthen Ware, Groceries, with a Number of other Articles, very Cheap.

Messieurs EDES and GILL,

WHEN the late House of Representatives impeach'd Chief Justice Oliver before the Governor and Council, his Excellency was pleas'd to observe in a subsequent Message to the House, that "he knew of no Species of high Crimes and Misdemeanors, nor any Offence against the Law committed within this Province, let the Rank or Condition of the Offender be what it may, which is not cognizable by some Judicatory or Judicatories, &c. From hence we may conclude that it is the Opinion of the Governor, that the high Crimes and Misdemeanors of which the Chief Justice stood charg'd, were subject to an Enquiry of a Grand Jury, and if presented were cognizable by the Superior Court. The House in their Bill of Impeachment alledg'd that "the said Peter Oliver, Esq; had endeavor'd to introduce into the Court" viz. the Superior Court, "a partial Administration of Justice, destroy the present Form of Government in this Province and establish an arbitrary and tyrannical Government in its Stead." These are certainly Crimes of the highest Nature, and, as such, ought to be taken Notice of by every Man who takes the Oath of a Grand Juror; more especially as the Governor hath publickly declared, that "he doth not know that the Governor and Council have any Authority to try & determine any Species of high Crimes and Misdemeanors whatever." The House appear to have had in View, not the *Punishment* so much as the REMOVAL of the Chief Justice; and for *this Purpose* they prayed that Tryal and Determination might be had on the Articles of their Complaint: But the Governor told them that the Process they had attempted to commence against him was unconstitutional, and he should not shew any Countenance to it. It seems to be the Language of Reason, and the two Houses in their several Messages have made it abundantly evident, that it is the Duty of the Governor and Council, who alone can remove a Judge, to take Cognizance of, hear and determine upon all Matters alledged against him, which, if proved, will render him utterly disqualified for his Office, and afford the strongest Reason why he ought to be removed. But the Governor treated their Messages with ineffable Contempt, not to say Insult and Abuse; putting an immediate End to the Session in the Midst of Business, to prevent them from proceeding any further, as he himself expressed it, by their Resolves, &c. "*to strike directly at the* AUTHORITY *of the King*"; which in Effect is charging them with little short of High Treason.

In the Administration of Governor Shirley, who I dare say will be allowed by all impartial Judges to have had *more* Knowledge of the Law and of the Constitution than Governor Hutchinson, the late Justice Hall was impeached by the House of Representatives of certain Crimes and Misdemeanors. The Governor did not hesitate to appoint a Time for the Hearing, which lasted *de Die in Diem* for more than a Week, and finally the Governor and Council removed the Justice from his Office. And Governor Bernard, who never was more friendly to our Constitution *perhaps* than Governor Hutchinson, has discovered himself to be, upon a Complaint made of a Justice of the Peace, even by a *private* Man, called the Council together, and with them heard and determined thereon; and the Justice, though as well qualified for a Tool of Power as the Chief Justice, was censured by the Governor and Council. These are notorious Facts, and I suppose stand on the publick Records, and they serve to show that the Doctrine of late advanced by Governor Hutchinson is novel, and can no more be supported by Usage and Practice, than Reason. But a *Relation* and a *Favourite* must be screened; and it is thought sufficient to tell the House, that there are Judicatories by which all Crimes and Misdemeanors are cognizable, and with which the Governor and Council have no concurrent Jurisdiction. Let us now suppose a Grand Jury should indict the Chief Justice; would not the King's Attorney, who is as much *dependent on the Crown* as Gov. Hutchinson, find out *another* Way to prevent a Trial in the Superior Court, by entering *Nolle Prosequi*?——— There have been Instances of this kind frequently since the Conspiracy to "abridge what are called English Liberties," was hatch'd by a Cabal on this Side the Water. But supposing he should be tryed and convicted of high Crimes and Misdemeanors; the Superior Court can order him to be punished, but they cannot *remove* him. We should then see a Judge and a Convict in the same Person. Even in this Case however there is a Remedy for a *Favorite*; for his Excellency may *remit* the Punishment; perhaps he may think that the Ends of Government would be as well serv'd by it as they were by pardoning *Ebenezer Richardson, Esq*; and then in the Opinion of some the one would be as duly qualified for the Office of a Judge as the other is to hold a Place under the Right Honorable the Commissioners of the Customs in America, or an immaculate Administration in Great or *little* Britain.

Oppression maketh a WISE MAN *mad, how much more the* SIMPLE *and* FOOLISH!

Your old Friend, B. Y.

Lancaster, April 7, 1774.

PHILADELPHIA.

Extract of a Letter from Norfolk, Virginia, March, 23.

"A few days ago arrived here the brig Abby, Captain Herbert, from London, by whom we learn, that the fate of the East-India Company's Tea at Boston had reached England some time before his departure, but did not make that stir as was at first expected. There have been several meetings of the Company to consider in what manner they shall proceed with respect to this noisy affair, the result of which, it is imagined, will be the taking off the duty lately imposed on the afforesaid article. We also learn the Tower of London caught fire, by some accident, about the beginning of January last, which consumed some come considerable part of it, as also two or three houses that were at a little distance therefrom.—Luckily the fire, through the activity of the people, did not reach the ammunition, as, if it had, great part of London must inevitably have perished. And that on Saturday the 15th of January last, Lord Townshend, Sir Jeffery Amherst, and Sir Charles Frederick, went to the Tower, viewed the place were the fire happened and expressed their anger at a large quantity of powder being clandestinely lodged in the cellar of one of the houses, as it might have been attended with the most dangerous consequences. Lord Townshend ordered several new cisterns, firecocks, and buckets, to be fixed in different parts of the Tower, to be in readiness to supply the engines, if a like accident should happen; likewise that the Stationer's shop should be removed from the White Tower, as it was dangerous to keep so large a quantity of paper near the Magazine. Lord Townshend mentioned the great impropriety of having but one entrance into the Tower, and proposed building another Drawbridge from the Devil's Battery to Irongate; as, should a fire happen at the present entrance, it would be impossible either to convey engines to it, or for the inhabitants to escape."

NEW-YORK, April 28.

Last Thursday Morning about 10 o'Clock, his Excellency our most worthy Governor, (with his Lady, Daughter and Family) embarked on board, and sailed immediately in the Mercury Packet, for England, accompanied with the best Wishes of all the good People of this Province.

On Monday Evening there was a very numerous and most brilliant Appearance of Ladies at a Ball in Hull's Assembly-Room, on occasion of Mrs. Tryon's, and his Excellency our GRACIOUS Governor's Departure for England.

Capt. Kennedy in 43 Days from Madeira, informs us, That a Brig belonging to Liverpool, bound for the Coast of Africa, late commanded by Capt. Spencer, arrived at that Island a few Days before he sailed, and that the People on board gave the following Account, viz. That in the Month of February, the Boatswain and Part of the Crew, had formed a Plan to run-away with the Vessel; to effect which, in the Night, the Watch upon Deck went below and murdered the Captain, Chief Mate, and Carpenter, and threw them overboard, when the Command was taken by the Boatswain, who ordered out the Boat with a Number of the Hands to look for Madeira, (there being too many on board to his Mind, the Number 35) but one of the Crew left behind being in the Captain's Interest, and who expected to share the Fate of his Master, soon gave the Boatswain his Quietus with a Hammer, assumed the Command of the Brig, followed the Boat, took out those concerned in the Murder, secured them, and arrived safe at Madeira a few Days after.

The Upper House of the Assembly of Georgia having rejected the Memorial sent them by the Lower House, for the Re-appointment of Benjamin Franklin, Esq; Agent in Great-Britain, for the said Colony, during another Year. The Lower House have insisted upon their Appointment, resolved that the Right is solely in them, that the Thanks of the House for his faithful Services, be transmitted to him, with Notice of his Appointment for another Year, commencing the second of March, and 150l. Sterl. Salary for the same, over and above his Charges and Disbursements, incurred on Account of his Agency.

NEW-PORT, *April* 11.

We hear that a Whale Sloop, belonging to Mr. Gideon Almy, of Tiverton, and another owned in Boston, as they were Watering in a Harbour at Hispaniola, were Seized by a French Frigate, carried into Portau Prince and Condemned.

BOSTON, April 18.

Thursday last four young Men went in a Canoe to Braintree about some Business of their own, and on their Return stopt to Fish between Castle-William and Dorchester-Bay, but meeting with no Success, endeavoured to hoist up the Kellick, in doing which they overset her, whereby one of them, an Apprentice to Mr. Geyer, Stone-cutter, at the South-End, aged about 19, was unfortunately drowned; the others were saved by a Boat that was going from this Town to the Castle, who took them off the Canoe's Bottom, to which they had held, till they were almost spent.

Extract of a Letter from St. Croix, March 14th 1774.

"To complete the ruin of this Island, we have a stamp-act, which has just taken place; and is perhaps the most oppressive order ever imposed, even in oppressive governments, every man in common business is obliged to use stamp-papers; a running account is forfeited, if on common paper, and the party rendering it severely fined; receipts are not valid, unless stampt; paper for obligations are excessive high——some sheets cost two hundred pieces of eight; a sheet for a bill of sale is 4 pieces of eight, for an account 4 royals. At this rate the country will soon lose all the English inhabitants; for no true Englishmen will ever live under such oppression. These stamps are not all we are to expect, a few months will convince us that the expences of that kind of paper will be trivial to other burthens and taxes we shall be made to pay, such as a heavy poll tax on the white people,—All dry goods are and must be stamp, and such as are not, are forfeited; also an additional duty on produce is expected. There are great hardships on the continent as well as us here; and I don't know what way to bring our Tyrants to reason, but by your withholding your trade from us one year. I believe the inhabitants would suffer a temporary inconvenience for a lasting establishment on good footing, for by a stagnation of trade from America, even for a few months, little or no money would go into the King's treasury.

Cambridge, April 15. Last Night died Deacon *Samuel Sparhawk*, in the 76th Year of his Age, and in the 40th of his Deaconship. He feared God from his Youth. In very early Life, by the Death of his Father, he had the Care of a Family devolved upon him; in which, at the Desire of his pious Mother, he kept up the Worship of God. With uncommon Care, Wisdom and Prudence, he conducted all the Concerns of the Family, to the great Comfort and Benefit of the same. His whole Life, in the various Stations, Relations, and peculiar Trials of it, has been such an Exhibition of Wisdom and Prudence, Patience, Piety and Goodness, as hath greatly recommended him to the Esteem and Respect, the Love and Confidence of all who were acquainted with him.

Being in a languishing State for some Months, he saw Death approaching; but it was with the Calmness, Composure and Comfort, that became a Christian, whose Views are carried beyond the Grave, and who is 'begotton to a lively Hope, by the Resurrection of Jesus Christ from the Dead.'

It is said his Funeral will be To-Morrow Afternoon.

DIED.] Miss Mackey, aged 12 Years, Daughter of Capt. Mackey at the North End.

Mrs. Brooks.—Mr. Thomas Chapman, aged 66.—Mrs. Thankful Jepson, Wife of Mr. Jepson, Taylor.

On his Passage from St. Croix, Capt. Samuel Perkins aged 39 Years.

THOMAS CARNES, Broker,

HAS for Sale, at a very low Rate for Cash—Three new Fall-back Chaise, a new Sulkey compleat, fit for a Gentleman Traveller.——Goods of any Kind will be taken for them, if there is a Prospect of turning them into Cash by July Court.

He is to be found near the Old North Meeting House.

N. B. Also to be Sold three Casks of Indigo, a Quantity of Salt Fish, and 1000 Weight of Piemento.

An Invoice of £.100 Ster. is wanted to be purchased.

TO BE SOLD
AT PUBLICK AUCTION,
By Benjamin Church,
At his usual Place of Sale,
On THURSDAY next,
At THREE o'Clock in the Afternoon,

A valuable Assortment of European Articles, consisting of Broad Cloths—Plains—Ratteens—Shalloons——Irish Linnens—Checks—Oznabrigs,—Handkerchiefs, &c. &c. Likewise House Furniture, as Glasses,—Feather Beds,—Tables,——Chairs, &c.——Watches———&c.

On THURSDAY, at Three o'Clock, P. M.

TO BE SOLD
By Gawen Brown, *in King Street*,
Sundry new CLOCKS,

One Second-Hand ditto, with Japann'd Case,—genteel Silver WATCHES, *some go on Diamonds, and some with a Cap over the Work, finish'd by the best Hands, Cheap for Cash.*

At GOULD's *Auction Office*,
In Back Street,
On FRIDAY next, at Ten o'Clock in the Morning.
Will be Sold by PUBLIC VENDUE,
A Variety of valuable House Furniture,
Also an Assortment of English Goods, as usual.
ROBt. GOULD, Auctioneer.

Just Published, and to be Sold opposite the New Court-House, in Queen-Street.

A TABLE, shewing the Value of *Old Tenor* in *Lawful Money*, to the 15th Part of a *Farthing*, from *one Penny* to £. 10 000 ——To which is added,—A TABLE to reckon DOLLARS in *Old Tenor* and *Lawful Money*.——ALSO,—A TABLE of the Weight and Value of COINS, as they pass in *Massachusetts-Bay, New-York*, and *Philadelphia*.

All Persons having any Demands on the Estate of William Bulfinch, *late of Boston, Sail Maker, deceas'd, are desired to bring in their Accounts to* Samuel Bulfinch *and* David Hyde, *Administrators on said Estate,—and those that are Indebted, are desired to make speedy Payment to said Administrators.*

Soap Coppers to be Lett.

Coppers to make Soap in, of all Sizes, from One Barrel up to Six, to be Let by the Day, at the Golden Cock, Marlborough-Street, BOSTON.

To be Sold for no Fault,
A likely Negro Lad, about 13 Years of Age.
Inquire of the Printers.

To the Inhabitants of the County of Worcester.

Gentlemen,

WHEN the tools of power are making use of every machination to trample your rights and liberties under foot; in defiance of the good and wholesome laws of the province; and set themselves and their dependants above the law; it is your duty to double your guard and keep a good look-out for the future, or you may soon see the day when every privilege you have shall be turned to the emolument of your worst enemies, with all the parade and formality of law and good order.

What induced me at this time to address you upon this subject, is the conduct of our court of General essions of the peace in their late session at *Worcester*, in not having the votes for a county treasurer opened, sorted and counted, in presence of the justices as the law expresly requires it shall be done, at the next quarter session after the choice. However trifling it may appear to some, that the business is only adjourned to our next quarter session, which will sit in *June* next; and that the person who was chosen for the last year, and who hath serv'd to acceptance, will continue in said office until another be chosen and sworn in his room. Let such persons consider that the office of county treasurer is an office of considerable profit and importance, and the people have a *Right* to chuse whom they esteem are best qualified to serve. And the sessions are obliged by law to count the votes openly, and publickly; that the people may be satisfied of the equity of the proceeding and choice.

Though every town in the county has an equal right to bring in their votes for a county-treasurer, they have generally neglected it, and the town of Worcester, with one or two of the adjacent towns, have chosen a person into that office, for a number of years past, and no objection has been made, so long as they chose one of a certain family, famous for holding all the lucrative offices in the county; and one of the honorable justices, who it is thought, has great influence over the rest. But as the Shire town this year, at their annual Meeting in March, (the usual time for chusing a County-Treasurer,) by a considerable majority of votes, made choice of one of their friends, of a fair character, and undoubted ability, to discharge the duties of the office to acceptance, in preference to the person aforesaid; and it is thought that the sessions, being under the influence and directions of the *old one*, adjourned counting the votes, until he could write to the several towns in the county for their votes, which I make no doubt of his obtaining, if he reigns in the hearts of a majority of the children of the county. But if he should fail of acquiring votes enough to hazard a public counting, according to the province law, the following precedent may serve him and his friends in the dilemma.

When we last chose a Register of Deeds for the County of *Worcester*, the votes was pretty much divided between three persons (some say near equally) and it was expected that when the votes came to be counted it would not be a choice, neither of them having a majority of votes, as the law requires. One of the three candidates had serv'd in the office a number of years and was what is called a Friend to Government, and in affinity with the right family. Another was termed a friend to the people and constitutional liberty, and had been broke from being a Colonel for the crime. The third was suspected not to be orthodox in the faith, but placed too much dependance upon good works.

The sessions, therefore, that the office might be kept in the right channel, chose a committee consisting of one of his brothers-in-law, and two others his peculiar friends, to open, sort and count the votes; which they performed in private, in the lobby; and whether all the votes were ever delivered to them, or whether they made account of any but such as were for their friends, and a friend to government is very uncertain. And we have nothing to satisfy us but the bare word of the committee, for had we their oaths in the case, it would not mend the matter; for I can take their words as soon as their oaths, it being an unlawful act, at least appears to me such—both in the committee and in the sessions that received their report. For the law expresly requires that the votes for a register of deeds shall be opened, sorted and counted, in the presence of the justices, or "as in the election of county treasurer," but this law seem'd to be degraded in the case I am speaking of, and no doubt may again, when it is like to operate in favor of a vote of the people, and against a court favorite; or (according to modern tory language) a friend to government.

Quere, Would not the grand jurors do well to present such an open breach of the law, and will not their neglect of it perjure them?

VIGORNIENSIS.

Narraganset Cheese,

To be Sold by JOSEPH PEARSE PALMER, At the lowest Store on the Southside of the Town Dock.

Sperma-Cæti CANDLES

Warranted Pure,—

Excellent Dorchester and

Taunton ALE,

Packed in Casks, very handy for Transportation, To be Sold CHEAP for CASH by

William Palfrey.

A Quantity of Turpentine, Pitch and Tar,

To be Sold at JOHN PECK's Wharf, Near Hallowell's Ship Yard.

Inquire of Mr. JOHN PECK.

WANTED IMMEDIATELY,

A Schooner from 100 to 130 Tons burthen; any Person having such a Vessel (single Deck'd) and inclining to Charter her, may apply to

JAMES SWAN,

At his Store leading to *Treat's* Wharff, next the Southside of the Town Dock.

Wanted to Hire,

A pleasant and genteel Tenement at New-Boston. Enquire of Edes and Gill.

To be LETT, and entered upon immediately;

A large House, with about an Acre and an Half of Land, with convenient Out buildings, adjoining the Seat of Robert Auchmuty, Esq; late in the Occupation of Captain Nathaniel Williams, deceas'd, in Roxbury, being a very pleasant Situation for a Gentleman. Enquire of Captain Jeremiah Tucker of Milton, or Samuel Warren of Roxbury.

New *Baltimore* FLOUR,

Philadelphia common ditto,

ditto — superfine ditto in half Barrels, and a Quantity of BAR IRON, just Imported, and to be Sold by DANIEL BELL, (at his Store near the East End of Faneuil-Hall) very low for Cash.

N.B. WEST INDIA GOODS to be had at the same Place, as cheap as at any Store in Town without Exception.

TO be exposed to Sale by Publick Vendue at the House of Capt. *Ephraim Jones*, Innholder in Concord, on Thursday the 28th Day of April Current, at 3 o'Clock, P. M. viz.——A good House Licenced for Retailing Spirituous Liquors, with a Shop adjoining. —Also a Barn and about 6 Acres of Land, situate within about 20 Rods of the Meeting-House, in said Concord, now in the Possession of *Ezekiel Brown*: Said House is well accommodated for a Trader's. For further Particulars inquire of Lieut. *John Butbick* and Mr. *Nathaniel Stearns*, in said Concord, or of said *Brown*, now Residing in Boston.

WE the Subscribers, appointed Commissioners by the honorable Foster Hutchinson, Esq; Judge of Probates, &c. for the County of Suffolk, to receive and examine the Claims of the several Creditors to the Estate of Mr. Richard Walker, Mariner, deceased, represented insolvent—Notify said Creditors that we shall attend that Service at the House of Mr. Jonathan Brown, near Charlestown Ferry, on the last Monday in this, and the five following Months, from Six to Eight o'Clock, P. M.

Boston, 16 April, 1774.

BENJA. HARROD,
GILES HARRIS.

WHEREAS the Proprietors of Land in the Township of Sudbury, on Otter Creek, which Township was granted by the Governor and Council of New-Hampshire, did at their Meeting the Eighth Day of March 1774, Vote that the Sum of One Pound Lawful Money should be raised and levied on each Original Right, for the Bounding and carrying on the Settlement of said Township for the common Good of said Propriety; and that a Committee be appointed to assess the same; which has accordingly been done.—Therefore we the Subscribers being appointed a Committee to notify the Proprietors aforesaid, to pay the same, together with their former delinquent Taxes—We do hereby notify them, that unless they pay the same, on or before the 17th Day of May next, to Thomas Miller, of Newton, in the County of Middlesex, and Province of the Massachusetts-Bay, Collector, their Rights will be sold according to Law for Payment of said Taxes.

April 15, 1774.

JOSHUA FULLER,
THOMAS MILLER,
NATHl. SPARHAWK } Committee.

New AUCTION-ROOM, Cornhill.

TO-MORROW at TEN o'Clock will be Sold by PUBLIC VENDUE, at GREENLEAF's Auction-Room,——

A Variety of English Goods and Hard Ware as usual, and a Number of Pieces of New-England Manufactures, as Sagathy's, double and single Callamancoes, Lastings, Sattins, red Buntings, and some House Furniture.

Wm. GREENLEAF, Auctioneer.

The Sale will begin Tomorrow at Ten o'Clock.

For private Sale,

A genteel Curricle almost new, with Harness compleat, Sconce Glasses, a Mehogany Desk and Book Case, 3 8. Day Clocks, with a Variety of English Goods.

On Thursday Next, the 21st Instant,

At ONE o'Clock.

Will be SOLD by PUBLIC VENDUE, at the Bunch of Grapes Tavern in King-Street.

The Brigantine *Nancy*, 130 Tons Burthen, now laying at Col. HANCOCK's Wharff, about 18 Months old, has been only two Voyages at Sea, is a fast sailing Vessel, and well fitted and was built by as good a Workman as any in the Province.

☞ For the Inventory of her Stores and other Particulars, apply to J. Russell, Auctioneer.

At the same Time and Place will also be Sold at Vendue, a few Boxes of LISBON LEMMONS.

William Homes,

HAS to Sell a few Hogshead and Barrels of SUGARS, Cheap and good. Inquire at his Shop opposite the Golden Key.

Excellent Brown SUGARS,

TO BE SOLD CHEAP,

By Mrs. Sheaffe,

At her Shop the North Corner of Queen-Street.

Also, Philadelphia Rusk, New-York Biscuit, choice French Indigo, Citron, &c. &c.

She has a compleat Assortment of Groceries that are the best of their Kinds, which she hopes will induce her Friends to continue their Kindness.

To be Sold by PUBLIC VENDUE, TO MORROW,

One Quarter Part of the Schooner TRITON, with her Appurtenances, now laying at CRUFT's Wharff, North-End, being Part of the Estate of Captain Benjamin Chadwell, late of Boston, Mariner, deceased, Intestate. The Sale to begin precisely at XII o'Clock. The Premises may be view'd the Day before Sale, by applying to JACOB COOPER.

WE the Subscribers being appointed by the honorable Foster Hutchinson, Esq; Judge of Probates, &c. for the County of Suffolk, Commissioners to receive and examine the Claims of the several Creditors to the Estate of Benjamin Chadwell, late of Boston, Mariner, deceased, Intestate, represented Insolvent—Do hereby give Notice, That we shall attend said Service at the British Coffee-House, on the Third Tuesday of this and the five following Months, from the Hours of Six to Nine o'Clock in the Evenings of said Days.

Boston, April 18, 1774.

EZEKIEL LEWIS,
JOSEPH TURELL,
JACOB COOPER,

A Wet Nurse with a good Breast of Milk, would be glad to go into a Gentleman's Family to Suckle. Inquire of the Printers.

WANTS EMPLOYMENT,

A young Man who will be well recommended, and capable of tending and waiting on any Gentleman, or Tutoring in any private Family; understands Lattin, Riding, Nicking, Docking, Bleeding and Curing Lameness in Horses, and is no Novice in Gardening. Whoever wants any such, will be informed by the Printers hereof.

On Thursday next,

At Ten o'Clock,

Will be Sold by PUBLIC VENDUE, at the New Auction-Office, South Side of the Town-House.

A Large and valuable Assortment of English Goods as usual——ALSO, a Variety of House Furniture, consisting, of Mehogany Desks, Dining, Spring and Beauro Tables, small Spinet, Leather and Strawbottom Chairs, Feather Beds and Bedsteads, Pewter, Brass Kettles, Brass and Iron Kitchen Shovel & Tongs, white Handle Knives and Forks, &c. &c. Some Plate.

ANDREW OLIVER, Auctioneer.

Thursday next at Ten o'Clock.

Also for private Sale,

A convenient Dwelling-House, two Story high, with two Rooms on a Floor, with a good Yard & Necessary-House, near the Draw-Bridge, leading down the Wharff opposite Mr. Peter Sigourney's, Braizer, very suitable for a private Family. For further Particulars, enquire of

ANDREW OLIVER, Auctioneer.

CUSTOM-HOUSE, BOSTON.

ENTERED IN.

Thompson from Halifax. Leighton, Maryland. Ryder, Morris & Linds, New-Haven. Moore, New York. Williams, New-London. Johnson & Goddard, St. Lucia. Hallett, St. Croix. Blake, Demarara. Moore, Cape-Nichola.

OUTWARD BOUND.

Doane, Newfoundland. Parnish and Olds, New-London. McCluer, Quebec, Miller and Higgins, New London. Boardman, Dominica. Hallett, St. Croix.

Burials in the Town of BOSTON, since our last.

Four Whites. NO Black.

Baptiz'd in the several Churches, Twelve.

High Water at BOSTON, for the present Week.

Monday, 0 min. aft. 5	Friday, 3 min. after 8
Tuesday, 43 min. aft. 5	Saturday, 50 min. af. 8
Wednesday, 30 m. aft. 6	Lord's-Day, 36 m. aft 9
Thursday, 18 min. aft. 7	D. FirstQ 18D. 10 aft.

To the PUBLIC.

AS the Method lately practiced by the Subscriber, in having a Person at his Door to invite Gentlemen and others to his public Sales—has given Dissatisfaction to some—(Gentlemen Shopkeepers in particular) to avoid giving Offence for the future, he shall desist from that Practice, and pursue one (as follows) which he flatters himself cannot fail giving universal Satisfaction, as he sincerely wishes so to do. The Public are most earnestly requested to remember (for *their own Advantage*) that for the future Notice will be given by founding a Bell which he has purchased for that Purpose, which is erected over his Auction-Room Door near the Market, Boston, where constant Attendance is given both early and late to receive the Favours of all such who are pleased to confer on their *Much obliged, Most obedient, and very humble Servant,*
M. BICKER.

West-India RUM,
A few Casks of TORTOLA & St. VINCENTS RUM, and choice old JAMAICA SPIRITS, to be SOLD by
Jonathan Davis,
At his Store on Bull's Wharff; who has also for Sale, INDIAN CORN, BEEF and PORK, by the Barrell; and a Quantity of very good County made OARS.

This Day the Subscriber will open his School for Young Ladies. The Hours for Attendance will be Eleven o'Clock in the Morning, and Five o'Clock in the Afternoon.
Boston, 11 *April* 1774. JOSEPH WARD.

FLOUR.
Fine Burr Flour, also, Ship Bread of the best Quality, to be Sold at Mr. CHEEVER'S Store in King-Street.

ANCHORS
Of all Sizes from 100 to 1000 wt. well wrought, and warranted good, to be Sold by
Benjamin Andrews,
Who has for Sale also, Choice GREEN COFFEE, by the Hogshead or Hundred wt. Indigo, Snuff, Mustard, Crown Soap, Roll Brimstone, Pitch, Cordage, white Beans, Peas, Philadelphia new Flour, common & superfine, Bar Iron, Nova-Scotia Grindstones, Potash Kettles, a large Assortment of Iron Ware, Crates of Crockery Ware, and English Goods as usual—all at the very lowest Rates for Cash.

All Persons that have any Demands on the Estate of Mr. Andrew Cunningham, late of Boston, deceased, are desired to bring in their Accounts to Mary Greenleaf and John Cunningham, Administrators on said Estate, for Adjustment.—And all Persons indebted to said Estate, are desired to make immediate Payment to said Administrators.

John Cunningham,
HAS for Sale at his Shop near the Corner of School-Street, opposite Mr. Deblois's.
A Large Assortment of English and India Goods, suitable for all Seasons, which he is determined to sell at the Sterling Cost, (clear of Charges) he being determined to quit the Business.

CHOICE WINES,
per Quarter-Cask, just arrived and to be SOLD
By Archibald Cunningham,
At his Store in Ann-Street, near the Draw-Bridge, Boston.

Lisbon,
Calcavilla,
Malaga,
Sherry,
Shallow,
Madeira, and
Fayal Wine.

ALSO, Olives per Jarr.
Anchovies in Kegs or Bottles.
Capers per Cask.
Almonds in or out of the Shell, per Hundred or single Pound.
Cases of Bottles, and Case Bottles.
Hampers of Dutch Ware, Quart Chamber Potts and Muggs.
Dutch Brushes in Setts or single,
Vicker'd Quart and Pint Bottles.

Lisbon and French Oil, per Cask, Velvet Corks, best French Indigo per Hundred Dozen or single Pound, Spices, split Peas, Coffee, Raisins, Currants, Turkey Figgs.——N. B. Barcelona Handkerchiefs of different sorts, by the Quantity or single Dozen, very cheap. Cash given at said Store for small Olive Jarrs, and empty Bottles of every kind. OLIVES per Jarr.

TO BE SOLD
A double HOUSE, pleasantly situated in Sudbury-Street, next to Mr. William Crafts's, the Purchaser may have the half or the whole.

Messrs *Morgan* and *Stieglitz,*
Request Permission to inform the Ladies and Gentlemen of Boston, that, having received assurance of the Patronage and Assistance of the Musical Gentlemen, they purpose having a Concert-Hall, on Wednesday the 20th of April, a GRAND CONCERT of Vocal and Instrumental MUSIC assisted by the Band of the 64th Regiment.

ACT 1st.
Overture—Stamitz 1st.
Concerto—German Flute.
Song.—My dear Mistress, &c
Harpsi. Concerto by Mr. Selby
Simphony—Artaxerxes;

ACT 2d.
Overture—Stamitz 4th.
Hunting Song.
Solo, German Flute.
Song, Oh! my Delia, &c.
Solo Violin.

To conclude with a grand Military Simphony accompanied by Kettle Drums, &c. compos'd by Mr. Morgan.
TICKETS at Half a Dollar each, to be had at the *British* Coffee-House, at Miss *Cumming's* in Cornhill, at Messrs Cox and Berry in King-Street, and of Messrs Stieglitz and Morgan.
V. B. Copies of the Songs to be delivered out (gratis) the Tickets.—To begin at 7 o'Clock precisely.—

WHEREAS the Copartnership of Scott and Gill was mutually Dissolved the 21st of February last——ALL Persons indebted are requested to make immediate Payment to Moses Gill;—And all to whom the Company is indebted, are desired to bring in their Accounts to said Gill, for Adjustment, and receive their Balances.
Boston, 6th *April* 1774.
N. B. The Business is carried on as usual, by Moses Gill, where the Customers of the late Company, and all others, may be well served.

TO BE LETT,
A House with 3 Acres of Land, within 4 Miles of Boston, upon the Cambridge Road, conveniently situated for a Gentleman's Seat.
Enquire of *Eliphalet Downer* of Brookline.

Wanted to Hire Immediately,
A Faithful honest Man, that understands the Leather Dressing Business, for which a good Price will be given. For further Particulars, enquire of Edes & Gill.

TO BE SOLD,
(and entered upon immediately)
A Handsome well finished Dwelling House, in Brookfield, with a large Store, Barn, &c. all in very good Repair, together with thirty Acres of Land, is pleasantly situated on the great Post Road, and is in a fine place for carrying on Trade.—Any Person inclining to purchase the same may apply to THEOPHILUS LILLIE, at Boston.

COFFEE,
In handy Casks for
EXPORTATION,
And a few Tierces RICE of a Quality fit for the London Market, to be SOLD cheap for Cash, at POWELL'S Warehouse, No. 14, Long-Wharff.

ALL Persons indebted to, or that have any Demands on the Estate of Mr. Joshua Seaver late of Roxbury, Yeoman, deceas'd, are desired to bring in their Accounts to John Newell, of Newton, or Ebenezer Seaver, of Roxbury, Administrators on said Estate, in Order for Settlement.

Mrs. Oliver (at her School a little below the Mill-Bridge, leading to the new Grist-Mill) informs the young Ladies both in Town & Country, That she still continues teaching Embroidery Queen, Tenth and Irish Stitching, Coats of Arms, Marking and plain Sewing. Whoever pleases to favour her with their Custom, may depend on being as well and faithfully instructed in the above Branches, as at any School without Exception, in Town.
N. B. Children instructed in Spelling, Reading and Sewing, as usual.

TO BE SOLD
At John Winthrop, jun's Store, on Treat's Wharff near the Market, very cheap Philadelphia and Baltimore FLOUR.
BOTTLES with and without Cases. IRON, &c. &c.

FLOUR.
A Quantity of the newest *Baltimore* FINE FLOUR, and *Philadelphia* fine and superfine Ditto.
Ditto in Half Barrels.
Philadelphia BAR IRON.
A few Hogsheads of choice BRAN, and Quarter Casks of WINE.
To be sold as cheap, if not cheaper than at any Store in Town by *JAMES SWAN,*
At his Store leading to *Treat's Wharff,* next the South-side of the Town Dock.

WANTED,
A Woman of a good Character, and one that can be well recommended, and that understands Cooking and other House Work; none need apply but such a one, and is wanted immediately.—Good Wages will be given. Inquire of Edes & Gill.

ENGLISH GOODS CHEAP.
Imported from LONDON, by
Samuel Dashwood,
And to be Sold at his Shop next Door to Dr. Silvester Gardner's in Marlborough-Street, Boston.
A Great Variety of English, India and Scotch Goods, among which are,—Irish Linnens of all widths, Chinces and Callicoes, great Variety of Silks, best Royal Ribbs, best English Shoes at One Dollar per Pair, and many other Articles too tedious to mention, which will be sold by Wholesale at the Sterling Cost, and by Retail at the Cost and Charges, as he is going into another Branch of Business.
N. B. Spices of all Kinds, great Variety of Glass, China and Earthen Ware, sold remarkable cheap for Cash.

TO BE LETT, and enter'd upon immediately,
A FARM in Leicester, consisting of Mowing, Arrable and Pasture Land, &c. Enquire of Capt. Nathaniel Scott, living near the Premises, or the Printers hereof.

CHOICE MADDER,
The Growth of this Province,
TO BE SOLD BY,
John Barrett,
Near the Mill-Bridge, BOSTON.

GUN-POWDER,
To be Sold by HENRY BROMFIELD, at his Store opposite the Custom-House in King-Street,
ALSO,
Pepper, a few Barrels Pork, and Cod-Lines very cheap.

A Quantity of FLOUR, and a few Barrels of Middling ditto, to be sold cheap. Also a Parcel of *Newfoundland* BREAD:—Inquire of JOHN CUSHING, at his Sugar-House, Brattle-Street, near Doctor Cooper's Meeting-House, Boston.

TO BE SOLD CHEAP,
About 100 Quintals of good Jamaica Cod Fish.—Two Foresails suitable for a Brig of 100 Tons.—One new Foresail and Mainsail, suitable for a Schooner of 50 or 60 Tons, and a small quantity of new Cordage.
Inquire of the Printers.

WANTED,
£. 200 Lawful Money, for which good Security will be given. Inquire of the Printers.

For Quebec,
THE Brigantine BETSEY, CONSTANT FREEMAN, Master, lying the South-side the Long-Wharff, will sail in about 15 Days:—For Freight or Passage apply to said Freeman, on board, or at his House in South School-Street.

For Quebec,
THE Schooner EUNICE, NATHANIEL ATKINS, Master, lying the South-side the Long-Wharff, will sail in about 15 Days:—For Freight or Passage apply to said Master on board, or to Constant Freeman, at his House in South School-Street.

For Annapolis Royal,
THE SLOOP Jenny, GEORGE MITCHELL, Master, Lying at Wentworth's Wharff, having good Accommodations for Passengers, will Sail in Ten Days. For Freight or Passage Inquire of the Master on said Wharf.

Wanted for the Year,
An industrious Man of a good Character, that understands Gardening, and to wait on a Gentleman's Family. Inquire of the Printers.

WANTED *immediately,*
A sober active Lad, as an Apprentice to the Goldsmith's Business. Inquire of the Printers.

For private Sale,
At the NEW AUCTION-ROOM,
South Side of the Town-House, viz.
Three handsome Mehogany Desks and Book Cases, Chest on Chests of Draws, Desks, round and square Dining & Spring Tables, Beauro ditto, Card and Chamber Tables, Mehogany Chairs with Copper-plate yellow and Leather Bottoms, round-about Chairs, black Walnut Leather bottom Chairs, handsome Clocks, Pinchbeck Watches, handsome Sconce Looking-Glasses of all sorts and sizes, a Suit of Harrateen Curtains, a Suit of yellow Morien Curtains, with Window Curtains, Squabbs and Easy Chair, 6 green bottom Chamber Chairs, Window Shades, small handsome Spinnets, Mehogany and Maple four Post Bedsteads, small Mehogany Sugar Chests, 2 Cases of Doctor's Instruments, small Handmaids, a large Scale Beam, with scales & Chains, Plate, handsome Silver Terreen Tankard, large Salver, Chaffindishes, Porringers, Cups, Pepper Boxes, large and small Spoons, silver hilted Swords, silver and Ivory Handle Knives and Forks, silver plated Candlesticks, a genteel brass reading Candlestick, a very neat pair of steel Pistols, Gun and Bayonet, Barometer, also, orange, blue and green colour'd Broad Cloths, Cotton Velvetts, Shalloons, Tammies, Stuffs and Durants, white Baize, Irish Linnens, Men's Silk Hose, Capuchine Silks of all colours, black, blue, red and white Sarsnets, Patch Work Coverlids, a Box of well assorted and handsome Ribbonds, Poplins, Buckskin Breeches, handsome Muffs, a large Globe, silk Gauzes, black Sattin and Chip Hatts, a handsome full suit of Brocade, and suit of black Grogram, small Pocket Glasses, and Lisbon Lemmons by the Box, a Variety of other Articles.
N. B. At said Auction-Office constant Attendance is given to receive all kind of Goods for public and private Sale.

TO BE SOLD
A likely Negro Lad, 17 Years old, speaks English and French. Inquire of *Jean Francois Magellen,* at the House of Capt. *Isaac McDaniel,* New-Boston.

A Negro Child to be given away, of an excellent Breed. Inquire of Edes & Gill.

Boston: Printed, by EDES & GILL
in Queen-Street, 1774.

No. 994

THE Boston-Gazette, AND COUNTRY JOURNAL.

Containing the freshest Advices, Foreign and Domestic.

MONDAY, April 25, 1774.

Messieurs EDES & GILL,

BY the Charter of this Province we find that the Governor "shall have Authority, from "time to time, at his Discretion to assemble and "call together the Councellors or Assistants, of "the said Province for the time being: And "that the said Governor, with the said Assistants "or Councellors, or seven of them at the least, "shall and may from time to time hold and keep "a Council for the ordering and directing the "Affairs of the said Province."

It cannot however be suppos'd that the spirit and meaning of the Charter is, that the Governor with seven only, or at most a third part of the Council, shall assemble together and transact the most weighty affairs of the province; among which the appointment of Judges and other Magistrates ought to be reckoned, though one would think by the appointments that have been generally made, they are design'd as mere compliments to gentlemen who are entitled to the sunshine of court favors. No one I believe will say, that every gentleman who has been appointed to the office of a justice of the peace during the present administration, can be suppos'd to have a competent knowledge of the law to qualify him for such Appointment; it is probable that some of them never opened a law book in the course of their lives. And the late House of Representatives in their impeachment, by a very strong hint lead us to think, that in their opinion, even the Chief Justice of the province, of whom it is justly to be expected that he be a most able lawyer, would upon a thorough enquiry be found deficient. They expressly declare that "before his advancement to a seat in the Superior Court he had been usually employed in the business of trade, husbandry and manufactures, to which he had principally applied his mind, and that he was appointed to said office without previous education and regular study in the law." What proficiency he has made in the study of the law since his appointment, or whether the care of his iron works at Middleboro' leaves him "at liberty to qualify himself for the duties of his office in vacation times," I pretend not to say—It is to be hoped we shall before long be bless'd with a Governor, who will turn his eyes elsewhere, than to an insurance office or a compting house to seek for a judge. As learning has increas'd in the province, the publick has a right to expect that men of learning and integrity will be piched upon to fill up vacances on the sacred Bench of Justice; otherwise government may be brought into contempt and deservedly so. There are men of genius to be found, who have taken great pains and made deep researches into the law; and it would be a pity if such men should be over look'd or as it were turn'd aside to give place to a favourite, a party man, or at best a mere smatterer in law.

I have had an opportunity of seeing a list of civil Officers appointed since Mr. Hutchinson came to the Chair of this government, which I have tho'ts of publishing, as I am satisfied it will afford matter of speculation, and serve very much to shew the genius of the present administration in this province. At this time I can only point out a few instances. And the first nomination that was made by Mr. Hutchinson was that of *his own brother Foster Hutchinson*, Esq; to be Judge of the probate for the county of Suffolk; and this appointment was made, present only seven Councellors; three of whom then held lucrative Offices, for which they annually depended upon the smiles of the Governor. Not long after *Nath. Hatch*, Esq; was appointed a Justice of the court of common pleas for the same County, when there were only eight Councellors' present—And soon after the Hon. *Benja. Lynde*, Esq; was appointed Chief Justice of the Superior Court, *Foster Hutchinson*, Esq; (though a Judge of probate) a Justice of the same Court, and *Josiah Edson*, Esq; a Justice of the Inferior Court of common pleas for the county of Plymouth. And what is somewhat extraordinary, an office was erected, for no other purpose that can be thought of by many, but to hold up a friend in view, and introduce him into a place to which a *pension* or *grant from the crown* might hereafter be annexed, under the name of *Solicitor General*. These appointments were made when there were present only nine councellors.—At another council, *James Russell*, Esq; was appointed a Justice of the inferior court of common pleas for the county of Middlesex, present only seven councellors, of whom the appointee himself was one. If this gentleman was not in *that instance* to be accounted as one of the board, which is a very natural supposition, there was not a quorum, and consequently the appointment was illegal. Be that as it may, it is presumed he was silent when the question was put. But I have been told that silence is taken for consent; and I have heard that officers have sometimes been appointed with the explicit consent of less than a majority of seven, and perhaps the majority present expressed their dissatisfaction in a few hours after, when it was too late to declare their minds. I have nothing to say against the gentleman whose name I have last mentioned, not having the honor of his acqauintance, and having never heard but that, whether he was legally appointed or not, he fills his place with integrity; and whether he does or not, is not my present business to inquire.—At another time *Thomas Goldthwait*, Esq; was appointed a Justice of the common pleas for Lincoln, present seven councellors only. And the next month there came out such a large emission of justices (with the name of *Elisha Hutchinson*, second son of his Excellency, at the head of them) as led me to inquire whether most of the justices had not been taken off by some contagious distemper—there were present at this time ten councellors. These were for the most part justices of the peace and coroners; there being among them only one justice and one special justice of a court of common pleas. But at the next council were appointed, *Peter Oliver*, Esq; chief justice of the superior court, *Nathaniel Ropes* and *William Cushing*, Esq'rs; justices of the same court, and *Benjamin Lynde*, Esq; (who resigned the office of chief justice, which made room for Mr. *Oliver*,) was appointed judge of probate for the county of Essex. These four important offices were filled up when there were only seven councellors present at the board. It would be tedious to go through the list. I shall therefore conclude with one instance more; and that is the appointment of *Thomas Hutchinson*, Esq; his Excellency's eldest Son, to the Office of a Justice of the Court of common pleas for the county of Suffolk, present only seven Councellors. And if fame speaks true, for want of a Quorum, his Excellency and six Councellors mov'd (for it cannot be said they adjourn'd) from the Council chamber to the House of one of the Councellors who was in an ill state of health and could not go abroad, and there the appointment was made: This I will not vouch for, but so I have been informed; let him gainsay it who can.—The appointment of such Officers as *Judges*, is of more importance to the Community than some are apt to consider it to be. The design of it is not to put feathers into the caps of gentlemen, or to procure them bread, or merely to give them rank. If such appointments are ordinarily made, or ever unless in cases of absolute necessity, when two thirds or three quarters of the number of his Majesty's Council are, and it is to be presumed the like proportion of the *wisdom* and *integrity* of the Board is, wanting, if this, I say, be agreeable to the true spirit of the Charter, I acquiesce with all my heart; but if not, *the publick have a right to expect an immediate reformation.*

PRATT.

Since our last arrived here from London, *the Captains* Folgier *and* Symmes; *by them we have Prints to the 3d of March, from which we have extracted the following Advices, viz.*

LONDON, Jan. 28.

THE twelve men of war now fitting out are to be disposed of as follows: Four for America, two for Antigua, two for Jamaica, three for the Mediterranean, and one for the East-Indies.

Letters from Boston complain much of the taste of their fish being altered: Four or five hundred chests of tea may have so contaminated the water in the harbour, that the fish may have contracted a disorder not unlike the nervous complaints of the human body. Should this complaint extend itself as far as the Banks of Newfoundland, our Spanish and Portugal fish trade may be much affected by it.

Council last week, only voted two regiments to America. His Majesty has ordered five more from Ireland. The Bostonians are to be chastised, and are to drink tea, though ever so great an emetic.

A short time since, Dr. Benjamin Franklin, agent to the House of Assembly of New-England, presented a petition from the House of Assembly to the King, assuring his Majesty, that the people of New-England had no confidence in their Governor; that they considered him as an enemy to the province; that the breach between them and him was so open and avowed, and the enmity between them so declared and positive, the public business of the province was thereby so essentially injured and impeded, that it was necessary for the public service, as well as their happiness, to remove him; and concluded with a request to remove him from that government. The King gave no answer to the petition; and it was imagined no notice would be taken of it; but upon reconsidering the matter, it was thought most prudent to refer it to the privy council. Administration were thus obliged to take it up; a sort of mock-trial was resolved upon, that the truth of the allegations might be affectedly enquired into; and upon which some judgment was to be formed, and reported to the King.—The enquiry came on last Saturday, before the privy council. Dr. Franklin attended according to order; and the Attorney and Solicitor-General being, by order of administration, counsel for Governor Hutchinson, Dr. Franklin was allowed counsel likewise.—He had Mr. Serjeant Glynn, and Mr. Dunning.—The matter turned chiefly upon the extraordinary letters (which have been published) of the Governor and Lieutenant-Governor to the late Mr. Whately. It was some time doubted whether copies of them could be admitted as evidence; but it being impossible to obtain the originals, they being before the House of Assembly, the copies were at length admitted. The event of the enquiry is not yet made public.—The fate of America, and in that, of Great-Britain, depends upon the advice or rather report, which the privy council shall make to the King upon this occasion. The situation of affairs in America is become more truly alarming than ever. The union throughout that continent, to reject the tea, while it is subject to a duty to be paid there, shews that the ministers, or rather the cabinet junto, in whom only the King thinks proper to confide, are as cordially despised in America, as they are detested in England. If the tax is attempted to be imposed, which can only be by force, the remmittances to England of tobacco, naval stores, &c. &c. will of course be stopped, and thereby the immense debt (not less than FIVE MILLIONS!) which the North-Americans owe to the merchants in Great-Britain must remain unpaid. This will inevitably so materially injure our merchants, traders, and mechanics at home, that a general bankruptcy will, in all probability, succeed. The passion for power on one side, and the resolution to preserve liberty on the other, give a very serious, and in many people's apprehension, a very dreadful complexion to this dispute. The throwing the tea into the sea in Boston, irritates the court extremely, and while it shews the indignity with which the legislative authority of this country is treated in America, gives room to apprehend, if force is attempted it will be opposed. The other colonies, particularly Carolina, where no stratagem to land the tea was projected, have not indeed shewn the same indignity, because there was not the same provocation, but have acted with the same spirit and firmness; and besides sending the tea back, have guarded against the possibility of its being introduced by trick or stealth amongst them; for they have agreed not to have any dealings, or connections of any kind whatsoever, with any person who shall offer to sell any. So resolved and determined are these people to defend and preserve their liberties, that they will relinquish this favourite part of their diet.

Jan. 30. It is said that the Tea thrown into the sea at Boston, is valued at 18,000 l. at 1s. 6d. per pound. The whole sent to America is said to be about 300,000 l. worth, which is returning home, not being suffered to be landed.

On Saturday last the privy council met to hear the arguments for and against the petition of the assembly of Boston, (which was some time since presented by their agent Dr. Franklin) "praying that his majesty would be pleased to remove the Governor, &c." Serjeant Glynn, and Mr. Dunning were counsel for the petition, and urged very strongly the expediency and necessity of granting the prayer of it. Mr. Solicitor General was employed on the other side, and instead of answering the learned arguments of his brethren, or refuting the allegations of the petition, contented himself with pronouncing a most severe *Philippic* on the celebrated American philosopher, in which he loaded him with all the *licensed* scurrility of the bar, and decked his harangue with the choicest flowers of Billingsgate.——The Doctor seemed to receive the thunder of his eloquence with philosophic tranquility, and sovereign contempt, whilst the approving smiles of those at the board clearly shewed that the *coarsest language* can be grateful to the *politest ears*.

Feb. 3. A Correspondent recollects, that there was the same rout made in 1769, about sending to Boston the copies of Governor Bernard's thirty-three letters, that there now is about the sending Hutchinson's & Oliver's. The honest fair-minded Lord North, went so far then, as even to exclaim about it in Parliament, and very disrespectfully mentioned Mr. Agent Bollan by name. That Gentleman, it seems, had the letters IN CONFIDENCE from Mr. Alderman Beckford, and conformably to his duty, transmitted them to his Constituents, who immediately acted upon them, and resolved, (both Houses of Parliament there) "That the letters were "FALSE AND SCANDALOUS, tending to incense the "Mother Country against the Colonies, and unnecessa"rily to introduce a fleet and army;" yet the VIRTUOUS Ministry, instead of punishing, screened and rewarded THAT infamous Governor, as they seem now disposed (if one may judge from DeG--'s conduct) to acquit Hutchinson and Oliver; however, on the decision of this business, the Americans will, no doubt, be confirmed in an opinion, that has for some years laid heavy on their minds, viz. "that there is NO JUSTICE AT "THE FOUNTAIN HEAD;" and that the best recommendation is, to be a CRAFTY LYING KNAVE, ever ready to write and say what may tend the most to irritate and inflame. O blessed Ministry! your time, your time, however is almost expired! You have LOST THE COLONIES, and will soon see it; when you will begin to impeach and behead one another, for having been the cause of it; nor will any thing less satisfy the nation, when they FEEL the great and IRRETRIEVABLE losses occasioned by your execrable measures.

Feb. 5. Yesterday there was a great Levee, at St. James's but no Council; and General Gage, Commander in Chief of his Majesty's Forces in North-America, had a long conference with his Majesty, and it is said he will soon set out again in that station.

Feb. 9. Hugh Finlay, Esq; Surveyor of the Posts in North America, is appointed Deputy-Post-Master General, in the Room of Dr. Franklin.

Feb. 16. On Thursday last, about half an hour after six in the evening, the Queen was delivered of a Prince.

BOSTON, April 25.

Last Wednesday arrived in this Town from the Eastward, Mr. William Goddard, by whom Letters are received from the Committees of Correspondence of Portsmouth, Newbury, Newbury-Port, Salem, &c. expressive of the hearty Concurrence of the Gentlemen in those Towns with the Proposal of erecting a Post-Office upon constitutional Principles, throughout this Continent. Subscriptions are set on foot in each of them, and they have already succeeded beyond the most sanguine Expectation in all.——The Removal of Dr. Franklin from the Post-Office has added fresh Spirit to the Promoters of this salutary Plan, as several viewed an Opposition to his Interest, at a Time when he had signally served the Cause of America, as a very disagreeable Object; but all Reluctance from that Quarter must now vanish, and all the Friends of Liberty rejoice that they have now an Opportunity of taking up a Gentleman discarded by an *unrighteous* Ministry for the faithful Discharge of his Duty, and placing him above a Dependance on their Caprice, in the grateful Arms of his applauding Countrymen.

Capt. Folgier, on his Passage, the 17th of March, in Long. 20 met with a very hard Gale of Wind in which he shipp'd several Seas, and the next Day being more moderate, he spoke with a Brig bound from Biddeford to Newfoundland, who in the same Gale had both her Masts carried away, and every Thing wash'd off her Deck: Capt Folgier supplied them with some spare Spars, &c. and lay by them part of the Night in order to give them further Assistance, but the Weather proving so boisterous before the Morning, he was obliged to leave them:—They intended to return to England.

We hear that upon the first News of the Tea's being destroyed at Boston, and the dreadful Denunciations which were given out against that obnoxious *Carthage*, a Committee from the North-American Merchants waited on Lord Dartmouth to be informed, Whether their Property might be safe if shipped to that apparently devoted Capital?—The large Cargoes on board half a Dozen Ships come and hourly expected, seem a pretty satisfactory Answer that the Town will not yet be *laid in Ashes*, whatever might be the Fate of the *Committee*, who are again *talked of* to be sent for and tried on the *bugbear* Statute of Henry the Eighth.

A Passenger in Captain Folgier says, that as Lord Dartmouth was busily examining Evidences concerning the Destruction of the Tea at Boston, a Clerk of the House of Commons came to him and informing him of the Arrival of the Philadelphia Tea Ship, observed it was in vain to make further Enquiry about it, for the Continent was all in a Flame; and upon this his Lordship immediately dismissed the Examinants.

Extract of a Letter from London, dated Jan. 31.

"I was last Saturday at the Grand hearing before the Lords of the Privy Council, when the Massachusetts Petition and Gov. Hutchinson's Letters was read, and Dr. Franklin was treated with unparreled abuse by the Council for the Governor.—Mr. Hutchinson's best Friends allow that the Dr. was scandalously treated, and he has since had his place taken from him.

Extract of a Letter from a Gentleman of Rank in London, dated Feb. 15, to his Friend here.

"It is not yet known what Steps will be taken by Government with Regard to the Colonies, or your Province in particular. But as Enquiries are making of all that come from thence concerning the destruction of the Tea and the Meetings that preceded it, and who were Speakers and Movers at said Meetings, &c. I suppose there is some Intention of seizing Persons, and perhaps of sending them hither. But of this I have no Certainty." *So the Rhode-Island Game is to be play'd here, and Chief Justice O—r will again find something to do in Times of Vacations besides applying his Mind to Trade, Husbandry and* Iron *Manufactures.*

Extract of a Letter from London, *Feb.* 19, 1774.

—"Few seem to condemn the returning the Tea, but many think the destroying of it at Boston as an attrocious Act, taking it in the light of an avowed Insult—Frequent Councils are held, but little transpires—Puffing Politicians talk of violent Measures; forcing Tea upon the Americans with a Fleet, and Troops to guard it—But to what Purpose this, unless determined to knock out the Brains of those who refuse to buy and drink it—They talk of blocking up all your Ports; but to what Purpose that! the Colonists can't be starv'd in a plentiful Country; the Merchants and Manufacturers in England would suffer, and be the first to complain—Judicious people consider forcible Measures baneful and ruinous to both Countries; and I am persuaded Administration will avoid such as far as they can—'Tis said Government is to indemnify the East India Company and make a Demand upon Boston, and 'tis probable they will exact it under some Menace—'Tis said here, you are willing to make Restitution, provided the Act is repealed; but how Government will take such an alternative, is a Question—It seems the general opinion here, that the Controversy with America is at such a Crisis, that if something solid is not speedily devised and pursued, the Colonies must be absolutely lost—There is good Sense in the Observation, and I doubt not Government sees it—The present Ministry are called timid, be that as it will, I am much inclined to think from their private Characters, they would of themselves much prefer conciliating to hostile Measures, could they see their Way—It were to be wished, some unprejudiced Person of Abilities, would just now candidly dilate the Merits of the Controversy in a Letter to Lord Dartmouth, and by an Investigation of the several and relative Interests of the two Countries, to frame at least the Outlines of a conciliating Plan; it is no doubt an arduous Task, (as the Field is wide) yet not impracticable. I am perswaded such an attempt candidly and well done, would prove as acceptable at present to Administration as a Lanthorn to a Man groping in the Dark—Some harsh Steps were resolved on, and would have taken place, in the Affair of the Schooner at Rhode-Island, but a well wrote Letter to his Lordship, pointing out the Consequences, seasonably arrived to prevent it, of two Evils his Lordship chose the least—Administration no doubt sees the impolicy of exasperating a People already too much disgusted, and a People on whom this Country's Strength and Wealth so much depends; but what shall they do! Things are not thoroughly understood here in regard to the Colonies, and on the other Hand your Jealousy and Prejudicies are grown strong—'Tis said Government means to engage some principal People in each of your Capitals to give a lead to their Measures—I can hardly credit this, such principal People had best take care, Liberty Boys are unmanageable Folks—I hope a kind Providence will superintend and direct all for the best."

We learn, (via. Rhode-Island,) that the Tea-Ship, which has been so long expected at New-York, arrived there from the West Indies last Monday after the Post came away.—It is also said that about a Dozen Chests of the same detestable Commodity was smuggled there in one of their last Ships from London as *Bales of Woollens*; but being detected, they were taken *proper Care of*, in order to be returned with the East India Company's Ship Load.—Further Particulars may be expected by our next.

A Correspondent observes, that there is a very remarkable Coincidence between the Proceedings of the Americans and the Measures of the British Administration:—While the Ministry are dismissing the Post-Master General from his Place, the Americans are DISMISSING THE OFFICE—FOREVER.——The Designs of Providence and the Policy of Britain, from the beginning, have cooperated to accellerate that amazing Velocity with which *the Ball of Empire* rolls to this Western World.

Last Tuesday died at Charlestown, the Rev. HULL ABBOTT, senior Pastor of the Church and Congregation in that Town, after a long Confinement, in the 72d Year of his Age, and 51st of his Ministry.—He was a faithful Servant of Christ.—His Remains were respectfully interr'd on Thursday last.

By Capt. Folgier we learn, that Capt. Adam Winthrop, Son of the Hon. John Winthrop, Esq; of Cambridge was unfortunately knock'd overboard by the boom of his Vessel, on his Passage from hence to London, and was drowned.

Te, WINTHROP, nobis jam jam sperare licebat,
Velis inadversis, decorantem Littora nostra
Sed fatum infælix! nunc Mortis frigida Manus
Florentem tetigit, madido tradidit(q); sepulchro
Non mihi si centum Linguæ sint oraque centum
Ferrea vox, omnes virtutes dicere possim.

DIED] Miss Elizabeth Newell, aged 21, Daughter of Capt. Thomas Newell, Warfinger.

At Scituate. General Winslow.

At New-York, Dr. James Magrah, an eminent Physician.

At Barbados, Mr. Elisha Thayer, graduated at Harvard-College 1767, Son of Ebenezer Thayer, Esq; of Braintree: A young Gentleman who lately went thither as Preceptor to Madam Holder's Children.

JUST IMPORTED,
By Josiah Waters & Son,
And to be Sold at their Store in Ann-Street;
Painter's Oil and Colours of all Kinds,
in large or small Quantities, Window Glass, Brushes, &c. All Kinds of Pipes, Spices, and Groceries as usual, a few Kegs Split Peas, Powder, &c.

At the same Place may be had a most elegant Assortment of
PAPER HANGINGS,
N. B. Paints prepared for House, or Ship Painting.
House & Ship Painting perform'd with Care & Dispatch.

Samuel Parkman,
Informs his Friends and Customers, he has rece v'd per the Captains *Folgier & Symmes* from London,
A compleat Assortment of Spring GOODS,
Which will be Sold by Wholesale or Retail, (at his Shop in Union-Street) at a very low advance for Cash.

John Kneeland,
Informs his Friends and the Public, that he has opened a Store of West-India GOODS, at the Head of *Green's* Wharf, opposite to *John Rowe*, Esq's; near the Market; where he has for Sale,

W. India and N. England RUM,	Choice Green COFFEE,
Leaf & Brown SUGARS,	CHOCOLATE warranted pure,
New RICE,	RAISINS;

With most kinds of other Articles in the West-India and Grocery Way, by large or small Quantities, on as low Terms for Cash, as at any Store in Town.

He likewise Acquaints his Friends and others, that he proposes to Sell GOODS on Commissions, as he is very conveniently situated for such Business, and engages to exert his utmost Abilities for the Interest of all those who may Favour him with their Commands in this Way.

N. B. To be Sold *very low*, a small Invoice of English, India and Hard Ware GOODS, containing a very good Assortment for a Country Trader, about £.150 Sterl. Value.

Philadelphia superfine FLOUR,
BAR-IRON, and ANCHORS; a Quantity of each to be SOLD very low (if apply'd for soon,)
By Edward Gray,
At Store No. 2, South side the Town Dock; where may be had all kinds West India GOODS, and Iron WARE, very cheap for Cash or Produce.

TO BE SOLD,
By Moses Peck *in King-Street*,
NEW & second-hand Clocks—One elegant Church Clock, plain & engrav'd genteel Silver Watches, Metal and enamel'd ditto, Gold Diamon'd ditto, Watch Glass, Main Springs, Steel and Metal Chains, Keys and Seals, &c. &c.

Just Arriv'd in the Ship NICHOLAS, Capt. FOLGIER, from LONDON,
A grand Assortment of Paper Hangings, Painters Oil and Colours, &c. &c. And to be Sold
By *William* Gooch,
At the Sign of Admiral *Vernon* in King-Street.
N. B. A good Store in *Butler's* Rowe to be Let. Inquire of WILLIAM GOOCH.

Choice Fayal Wines,
Just arrived, and to be Sold at
Nathaniel & William Coffin's Store,
Near Oliver's Dock.

Excellent Florence Oil,
Just Imported & to be Sold cheap by the Chest or Flask,
By Daniel Silsby,
At his Shop opposite South Side *Faneuil-Hall*; Where may be had, West-India Goods and Groceries of all Sorts, at as reasonable Rate as at any Store in *Boston*.

A Negro Boy, likely, tractable and good Temper'd, 12 Years old, to be sold to any Gentleman that will treat him kindly—He has been a Year in the Country, and if sold it will be for no other Reason than the Owner leaving the Province may not find it convenient to carry him.

To the PRINTERS.

THE Petition of the late House of Representatives for the removal of Hutchinson and Oliver, has shared the same fate with most if not all other petitions which have been offered to the throne during the present reign. I have endeavoured to collect some of the particulars.—On Saturday the 8th of January in the *Afternoon* Dr. Franklin the agent of the house, unexpectedly received notice from the clerk of the council, that the lords of the committee for plantation affairs would on the *Tuesday* following at 12, meet at the Cock-Pit to take it under consideration——The agent sent directly to Dr. Lee, to consult with him, but he was at Bath. Mr. Bollan, the agent of his Majesty's Council of this province, having had similar notice, and consulting with Dr. Franklin, whether it would be best to employ council, they concluded that it would be needless; but that Mr. Bollan should move to be heard in behalf of the council of the province. On Monday following *very late in the afternoon*, the agent of the house received another notice that Israel Mauduit agent for the governor and lieutenant-governor, had asked, and had obtained leave to be heard by council on the morrow in their behalf. The short notice seemed as if it was intended to surprize them.

On Tuesday they attended at the Cock-Pit; and the petition being read, Dr. Franklin was called upon for what he had to offer in support of it: Who acquainted them that Mr. Bollan then present, in pursuance of their notice, would speak to it. He began to speak; but objections were immediately made by some of the lords, that he being only agent for the council, which was not a party to this petition, could not properly be heard upon it. He however repeatedly endeavoured to obtain leave to speak, but without effect; they would scarce hear him out a sentence, and finally set him aside. Dr. Franklin laid before the Board the resolutions of the house which preceded the petition, and a copy of the letters on which the resolutions and petitions were founded. When the letters were taken up, Mr. Wedderburn, the solicitor-general, bro't there as council for the governors, was allowed to object. He enquired how they were authenticated? This appeared by the authentication annexed. Lord chief justice DeGrey asked to whom the letters were directed? observing that there was no address prefixed to any of them. Dr. Franklin said, that tho' it did not appear to whom they were directed, it appeared *who had written them*; their names were subscribed; the originals had been shewn to the gentlemen themselves, and they had not denied their hand-writing; and the testifications annexed proved them to be true copies. The solicitor-general then proceeded to make observations as council for the governors. Dr. Franklin said to the council, that it was some surprize to him to find council employed against the petition, having had no notice of that intention till late the preceding day; that he had not purposed troubling their lordships with the hearing of council, because he did not conceive that any point of law or right could arise out of the petition, that might require the discussion of lawyers; but if council was to be heard on the other side, he must request leave to bring council in behalf of the assembly; and that a farther day might be appointed. The solicitor general finding that his *cavils* against the admission of the letters were not supportable, at last said, he would admit the copies to be true manuscripts of the originals; but he should reserve to himself the right of asking certain questions when the matter came on again; such as, How the assembly came into the possession of them? Through what hands? And by what means they were procured? Certainly; (replied lord chief justice DeGrey) and to whom they were directed? Thus ended the first meeting. Dr. Franklin had leave to be heard by council, and the day appointed was the 29th of January.

While the agent's mind was thus taken up with this business, he was harrassed with a subpæna from the chancellor, to attend *his* court the next day, at the suit of Mr. Whately, concerning the letters.

On the 29th of January the hearing began. The council for the petition opened the matter with great strength of argument as well as propriety & decency. The solicitor-general then went into what he called a *history of the province* for the last ten years, and bestowed plenty of *abuse* upon it, mingled with encomium on the governors. But the favorite part of his discourse was levelled at Dr. Franklin, who stood the butt of his invective and ribaldry for near an hour. He totally departed from the question, and was *permitted* to wander into a new case, the accusation of the person who *merely delivered* the petition, with the consideration of which no part of *his* conduct had any concern; charging him with *stealing the letters*; which if he had done, *that* was not the tribunal where he was to be accused and tried; the cause was already before the chancellor. Not a single lord checked and recalled this orator to the business before them; but on the contrary (a very few excepted) they seemed to *enjoy highly* the *entertainment*, and frequently burst out into *loud applause*. The reply of Mr. Dunning concluded; and their lordships report is dated *the same day*. Whether it had been *preconcerted* or not, every one will judge from the *manner* of the tryal. It contains the same kind of censure upon the petition and the petitioners, as that which was passed formerly on the petition for the removal of Bernard. This is no more than what all expected, who had *proper* ideas of the *disposition* of the King's ministers; therefore they are not disappointed or chagrin'd. It will not perhaps be deem'd extraordinary that their lordships should conclude, as it appears they have done, that the charge against Dr Franklin of having *surreptitiously* obtained the governors letters is true, merely from his silence; altho' a single justice of the peace in America, would have seen thro' the impropriety of passing any such censure upon such a trial; to be sure he would have tho't it *unjust & partial* to have done it upon a bare charge without the least shadow of evidence. Even the Solicitor General himself, *virulent* as he was against the Doctor, had acquainted them, that that matter was before the Chancellor; and the impropriety of his answering before their Lordships to charges then lying in *another* court had been stated to them. To what purpose was it to insert this conclusion in the report, unless it was to wound the Doctor's character. But the shaft is pointless, and indeed they have missed the mark; his character is not so vulnerable as they imagined. But supposing he had *infamously* obtain'd the letters, would that have alter'd the nature of them, their tendency and design? Would that have made them innocent? How weak and ridiculous is this? The truth is, the Doctor came by the letters *honorably*; his intention in sending them was *virtuous*; to lessen the breach between Britain & the Colonies, by showing that the injuries complained of by *one* of them did not proceed from *the other*, but from *Traitors among themselves*. The *Treason* thus discover'd, the *Conspirators* were complain'd of. The Agent is suffer'd to be abus'd by a *Solicitor*; the Complaint *called*, I had like to have said *judg'd*, false, vexatious, scandalous; and the Complainers, factious and seditious. The pain we feel on Dr. Franklin's account is lost in what we feel for America and for Britain. When Petitions and Complaints of Grievances are so odious to Government, that even the mere hand that conveys them becomes obnoxious, how is peace and union to be maintain'd or restored? Grievances cannot be redress'd unless they are known; and they cannot be known but thro' complaint and petitions; if these are deem'd *affronts*, and the messengers punish'd as *offending*, who will henceforth send petitions? Who will deliver them? The consequences are plain!

The day following the hearing, Dr. Franklin was *dismiss'd* from his office of Deputy Postmaster. The Post Office in America thro' *his* care and management of it alone, is rais'd from *nothing*, to produce £.3000 sterl. annually, *clear* to the treasury. This comes out of the pockets of the Colonists. Though it is not a revenue in principle, it is in effect. It grows daily more and more valuable by the increase of correspondence. By the conduct of Administration towards Dr. Franklin, it appears as if the managers of the Post-Office, and all their train of dependants must promote *their* measures, or they must not expect to be continued. The post officers will in a little time become as formidable as the Commissioners of the Customes and their numerous levee. Orders have already been given (*this may be depended on as a fact*) to the American Postmasters General, who used to have the disposition of all places under them, not to fill vacancies of value till notice of such vacancies be sent to England, and *instructions* thereupon receiv'd from thence. It is plain from hence, that *such influence* is to be a part of the system; and probable, that those vacancies will for the future be filled by officers from thence. How safe the correspondence of *committees* along the continent will be, thro' the hands of *such* officers, is now worth consideration: especially as the Post-Office act of parliament allows a Postmaster to open letters, if warranted so to do by the order of the Secretary of State; and every provincial Secretary may be deem'd a Secretary of State in his Province. *Behold Americans where matters are driving!*

The Speech of Mr. Solicitor General Wedderburn before his Majesty's Privy Council, relative to the obtaining and sending away Mr. Whately's Letters, may be had at the Printing Office in School-Street To-Morrow Afternoon.

Caleb Blanchard,

In UNION-STREET.

Begs Leave to inform his Friends and Customers, That he has Imported by Capt. SYMMES, from LONDON,

A Fresh Assortment of Summer GOODS, which he will sell at the very lowest Prices for ready Money, *viz.* *Dutch Laces*, Cheavaux de Frize & Blond Laces, Gauzes, Gauze Handkerchiefs, a fine Assortment of Callicoes, &c. India Dimothys, Jackonet, sprig'd and striped Muslins, Bengalls, Nankeens, Lungee Romalls, black and blue Ostritch Plumes, Skeleton & Cap Wire, Allamode, Sarsnets, Ribbons, Gown Trimmings. *Hoses* best Pumps, Silk ditto, Girls & Misses Morrecco Pumps, Cambricks, Lawns, a fine Assortment of Mens & Womens Worsted, Thread & Cotton Hose, Breeches Pieces, Morris's Patent Gloves and Mitts, superfine and other Cloths, Duroys, Wiltons, Serges, Ravens Duck, Dowlass, China Ware, Paper, Nests red Trunks, Irish Linnens of all Widths, Spices, &c. &c. &c.

BRAZILETTO per Ton,
COTTON WOOL per Pack, and,
A Quantity of most excellent
LIGNUM VITÆ,
On Board the BRIG SUCKEY, at Capt. *Spear*'s Wharf,
Inquire of Saml. A. Otis,
At his Store next Door to Mr. *Thomas H. Peck's*:

Barr-Iron and Anchors,	New-England Rum per Barrell,
Pitch, Twine,	Chocolate per Box,
Hollow Ware,	Lines, Hooks:

And many other Articles Sold by said OTIS, as Cheap at least as at any Store in Town.
Also, a Quantity of COFFEE, if applied for directly.

CADIZ SALT

To be Sold on Board the Brig SEA NYMPH, JAMES McEWEN, Master, Lying at the End of the Long-Wharff, Apply to the Master on Board, or at *Bethune & Prince's* Store in King-Street——Where is to be Sold,— A few Pipes of Sterling MADEIRA, and empty Quart Bottles, in Crates of a Groce each.

TO BE SOLD
AT PUBLICK AUCTION,
By Benjamin Church,
At his usual Place of Sale,
On THURSDAY next,
At THREE o'Clock in the Afternoon,

A Variety of valuable Articles, *viz.* Broad Cloths, Checks, Irish Linnens, Callicoes, Serges, Sagathees, Mens & Womens Hose, Lawns, Cambricks, Bone Lace, Sewing Silks, Silk Mitts, Handkerchiefs, &c. &c. Likewise House Furniture, as Tables, Chairs, Glasses, Beds, &c. an 8-Day Clock, Watches, &c. &c.

On THURSDAY, at Three o'Clock, P. M.

N. B. On the 5th of next Month, to begin at Ten o'Clock in the Forenoon, a large and valuable Assortment of Spring Goods, being a Consignment—the Particulars to be inserted in the next Paper.

New AUCTION-ROOM, Cornhill.

TO-MORROW at TEN o'Clock will be Sold by PUBLIC VENDUE, at GREENLEAF's Auction-Room,——

A large Assortment of English Goods, amongst which are, Callicoes, Chints, printed Linnens, stamped Linnen Handkerchiefs, flower'd & plain Lawns, silk Gauzes, Ribbons, Taffities, Irish Linnens, white Threads, Silk Twist, Silk and Hair Duroys, Shalloons, Calamancoes, Manchester Velvets, Broad Cloths, Forrest Cloths, German Serges, Ratteens, Duffils, Kerseys, Buck, Bone, Coco Handled Table Knives and Forks, Pen Knives.—Also some House Furniture, as Looking-Glasses, one Desk, one Jack, Brass Kettles, Sause Pans, Andirons, Frying Pans, &c. &c. &c.

WILLIAM GREENLEAF, Auctioneer.

The Sale to begin To-Morrow Morning Ten o'Clock.

On Thursday next,
Between One and Two o'Clock,
Will be Sold by PUBLIC VENDUE, at the New Auction-Office, South Side of the Town-House.

A Genteel new Chaise, with Harness compleat ANDREW OLIVER, Auctioneer.

At GOULD's *Auction Office,*
In Back-Street,
On FRIDAY next, at ONE o'Clock.
Will be Sold by PUBLIC VENDUE,

Three or four Chaises both new and second Hand, with Harnesses compleat, if not sold before at private Sale.

ROBt. GOULD, Auctioneer.

No Entries receiv'd this Week.

Burials in the Town of BOSTON since our last.
Nine Whites. Three Blacks
Baptiz'd in the several Churches, Twelve.

High Water at BOSTON, *for the present Week.*

Monday, 25 min. aft. 10	Friday, 30 min. after 2
Tuesday, 17 min. aft. 11	Saturday, 29 min. aft. 3
Wednesday 20 m. aft. 12	Lord's-Day, 26m. aft. 4
Thursday, 28 min. aft. 1	Full ● 26 D. 5 Morn.

Mess'rs EDES & GILL,

GOVERNOR HUTCHINSON's public character seems at present so well settled, that few need further information concerning it, the following story may serve to give the public a specimen of the behaviour of this great, excellent and honorable gentleman, *in private life*.

ON the evening of the 25th of March last past, Thomas Hutchinson, junr. being at Milton, sent for a young man in that neighbourhood, and asked him to go to Woburn on an errand for him on the next day, being Saturday, to which the young man consented. On Saturday a servant came and told him he must come to the governor's for his orders, which he did, and was instructed to take a horse at Milton and ride to the lieut. governor's in Boston, and leaving that to take one thence to Charlestown, there he was to take a second horse and proceed with both to Woburn. With these orders, half a pistareen was offered him to bear his expences. The young man told the servant that half a pistareen was by no means sufficient for his expences: the servant replied Mr. Hutchinson desires you would bear your own expences and bring in your account of expences and trouble together. To this the young man agreed, proceeded to Boston and Charlestown as directed, where he took the horse one Mrs. Bruce had left there, to lead to Woburn. Mr. DeL'Isle teacher of French, seeing him have a led horse told him he would treat him in case he would let him ride him to Cambridge, to which he consented, and they rode together. At Cambridge the young man mist Mrs. Bruce's saddle bags, which he enquired for in vain; and finding the horse stripped he asked DeL'Isle what all this meant? DeL'Isle told him it was because that he had mentioned he was on the governor's business. However he found the saddle, but not the bags. He then went on to Woburn and thence to Milton that night, where he told the story and no body found much fault with his conduct; till on saturday the 2nd of this month T. Hutchinson, jun. sent to him to find the bags and return them; on which he went to the governor's; and the governor asked him what this story was about Mrs. Bruce's saddle bags? He answered he knew no more about them than that they were lost. The governor asked him what he intended to do about them? He answered that Mrs. Bruce must bear the loss for any thing he knew. The governor proceeded to enquire how they were lost, and whether any one was in company with him when they were lost? He answered Mr. DeL'Isle was in company, that he rode the lieut. governor's horse, reciting the agreement. The governor asked where might it be that Mr. DeL'Isle asked him him to drink with him? He answer'd between Capt. Goodwin's and the meeting-house. To this his excellency very politely replied he lied: and further observed that he had rather lie than speak truth; for that he knew every house between the ferry and Cambridge, and there was not a dram shop between Goodwin's and the meeting-house. Besides that Mr. DeL'Isle was a man of polite education and would not be seen with him in a publick house; therefore he must have lied. He then called in his son Thomas, and Mrs. Bruce, and told the young man that he had told a story different from what he had told Thomas. The young man replied he had never exchanged a word with Thomas about it, which Thomas confirmed. He then called him a villain and a liar, and said he should pay for the bags; and turning to Mrs. Bruce told her his advice to her was to go right to Boston and take out a writ for him, and he would see to the action; adding that he, the young man, should be punished for his tricks. The young man told them they might prosecute at pleasure, as he would not pay a half-penny for the bags. Thomas (our worthy judge of the inferior court) observed that many men had been taken up and convicted for less crimes than that was. The young man answered that might be, and at the same time convict murderers turned loose among the people, and no authority take notice of them. Thomas said then he had no more to say than that he should pay for the bags. The young man retorted he requested his pay for his time & expences in his service; to which Thomas replied he was richly paid already. On Wednesday the 6th current, the young man went to Charlestown to inquire for the bags and found them advertised at the ferry-house, and redeeming them for a pistareen, came back to Charlestown, to see whether his Excellency or himself was most out in their guess of there being a publick-house between Goodwin's and the meeting-house; and he readily found the three cranes and two others besides. He then proceeded to Milton with the bags which he bro't to the governor's, told him that he had spent two days and an half in his son's service, which he tho't hard to do for nothing; withall reminding his Excellency, that instead of there being no publick house between Goodwin's and the meeting-house, he had found three. The governor answered his son had paid him. The young man acknowledged the receipt of two pistareens, which was no more than his expences on the road the first day; and besides he had expended another the second day. He then said his son would pay him; the young man replied he wanted his money and came off. Thomas then followed him and handed him three pistareens, asking if that would do? He answered no. He then gave another and said it was all he would give, as he could get any one to do the business for that money. So that upon the final settlement of this pleasant affair the young man had *three shillings & seven pence half-penny* clear for two days and an half's service, besides the abuse and anxiety such *rascally* treatment exposed him to, which no man of spirit would have suffered for ten times the sum.

To be SOLD or LET,

A neat and very convenient House, with a Barn and Chaise House, and about two Acres of Land, including a rich Garden Spot, very pleasantly situated, and a fine healthy Place—not five Miles from Boston Town-House—on a great Road where most Kinds of Provisions can easily be procured.

Enquire of Edes & Gill.

ALL Persons Indebted to, or that have any Demands on the Estate of Mr. *John Hunter*, late of Marlborough, in the County of Middlesex, Victualler, deceas'd, are desired to bring in their Accounts to *Edward Hunter*, Administrator on said Estate, (or to *Andrew Campbell* of Boston, Attorney to said Hunter) in Order for Settlement.

TO be Sold at Publick Vendue on the first Day of June next, at the House of Mr. *Edward Richardson*, Innholder in Watertown, if not Sold before at Private Sale.——A FARM lying in said Watertown, contains about 40 Acres of choice good Land, is all well Fenced into suitable Apartments, with good Stone Walls, has on it, a good House and Barn, two good Wells of Water, a Variety of all kinds of Fruit, is well accommodated for Mowing, Pasturage and Tillage, &c. For the Particulars of the Sale inquire of Mr. JOHN STRATTON, now living on the Premises.——

—The Sale to begin at 3 o'Clock Afternoon.

April 18th, 1774.

Stop Thief and Runaway Man Servant.

WHEREAS WILLIAM HAYWARD, Baker, absconded himself from my Service 16th March, 1774, and took with him to the Value of *Eight Pounds*, L. M. and he being taken and convicted, voluntarily Bound himself, to serve me Six Months, to Pay Damages & Cost; and he lastNight absconded himself again; had on an old Felt Hat, an old cloth colour'd Coat and Waistcoat, check'd Woolen Shirt, a Pair of new cloth colour'd Breeches, a Pair of old pale blue Stockings, and a Pair of singleSole Shoes.—Said Hayward is about Thirty-three Years of Age, Five Feet Five Inches high, darkish short Hair, and down look like a Rogue and Thief.——Whosoever will take up said Servant and Notify me the Subscriber so that I may have him again, shall have FIVE DOLLARS Reward, paid by me,

Marlboro' April 9, 1774. ISAAC SHERMAN.

All Bakers are hereby Cautioned against Employing said Servant.

RAN-away from the Subscriber the 18th Instant, a Negro Man named *David*, about 27 Years of Age, six Feet high, a very slender Make, Complection a little upon the yellow:——Had on when he went away, an old flopt Hat with a Hole in the Crown, a Homspun grey Coat and Jacket, and Hose, and goes a little lame. Whoever will take up said Negro, or secure him, so that his Master may have him again, shall have EIGHT DOLLARS Reward, and all necessary Charges paid.

JOSIAH STARR.

All Masters of Vessels, and others, are hereby caution'd against harbouring, concealing or carrying off said Negro on Penalty of the Law.

N. B. He was seen in Kingstreet last Tuesday.

WHEREAS the Co-parnership of Scott *and* Gill *was mutually Dissolved the 21st of February last.*——ALL Persons indebted are requested to make immediate Payment to *Moses Gill*: And all to whom the Company is indebted, are desired to bring in their Accounts to said *Gill*, for Adjustment, and receive their Balances. *Boston, 6th April 1774.*

*** GUN POWDER, just arrived, and Choice Connecticut Pork, to be sold by said *Gill*.

N. B. *The Business is carried on as usual, by* Moses Gill, *where the Customers of the late Company, and all others, may be well served.*

POT-ASH.

CASH given for *POT-ASH*,

By JONATHAN MASON,

At his Shop nextDoor to the Sign of the Buck & Glove, Near the Town-House, BOSTON.

N. B. To be Sold by said MASON, choice Gun Powder and best Philadelphia Bar Iron.

WHEREAS there are divers Matters to be transacted by the 20 Associates of the Lincolnshire Company respecting their Lands and Interest, laying near Penobscut Bay in the County of Lincoln—The Committee of said Associates being duely authorised therefor, hereby notify said Associates to meet on Wednesday the 11th Day of May next, at the BritishCoffee-House in King-Street, Boston, at 6 o'Clock P. M. then & there to act on the following Articles viz.

1st. To choose a Moderator, Clerk, Treasurer, standing Committee and any other Officers that may be thought necessary, and to appoint them such Salaries, Fees or Rewards by Money, or unappropriated Lands, as they shall think needful, from Time to Time for the Benefit of the Propriety.

2d. To determine upon any further Surveys of their Lands.

3d. To impower the standing Committee to compleat the Conditions of Settlement on the Part of the Proprietors when any Settler has performed the Conditions on his Part, by executing such Deed or Deeds as the Proprietors stand obliged to by their Permissions to Settlers.

4th. To determine whether they will make Sale of any more of their Lands to defray the necessary Charges of the Propriety, or raise such Monies as may be wanted by taxing the Proprietors in Proportion to their Interest in said Propriety.

5th. To determine upon any further Division of their Lands among the Proprietors.

6th To determine whether they will Lease any of their Lands, Islands, or Streams.

7th. To fix upon a suitable Piece of Land to place a Meeting-House for publick Worship and a publick School.

8th. To sequester a Lot of Land for the Support of the Gospel-Ministry within the first Township forever.

9th. To fix upon a Lot of Land to be given to the first Minister of the Gospel, that shall be settled in the first Township by a free Choice of a Majority of the Inhabitants, and shall reside in said Township and Officiate for the Space of seven Years if living.

10th. To sequester a Lot of Land for the Support of a School or Schools in the first Township for Learning to Read, Write and Cypher.

11th. To determine whether they will lay out any more Lots of Land to be given or sold to Settlers.

12th. To consider whether a further Grant shall be made to the Persons who were of the Committee for conferring with the Heirs of the late Brigadier *Waldo* as appointed Sept. 6th. 1766.

Pr. Order of the Committee,

NATH. APPLETON, Prop. Clerk.

Boston, *April* 12th. 1774.

TO BE SOLD

By Gawen Brown, *in King-Street*,

Sundry new CLOCKS,

One Second-Hand ditto, with Japann'd Case,—genteel Silver WATCHES, *some go on Diamonds, and some with a Cap over the Work, finish'd by the best Hands, Cheap for Cash.*

WHEREAS the Proprietors of Land in the Township of Sudbury, on Otter Creek, which Township was granted by the Governor and Council of New-Hampshire, did at their Meeting the Eighth Day of March 1774, Vote that the Sum of One Pound Lawful Money should be raised and levied on each Original Right, for the Bounding and carrying on theSettlement of said Township for the common Good of said Propriety; and that a Committee be appointed to assess the same; which has accordingly been done.—Therefore we the Subscribers being appointed a Committee to notify the Proprietors aforesaid, to pay the same, together with their former delinquent Taxes—We do hereby notify them, that unless they pay the same, on or before the 17th Day of May next, to Thomas Miller, of Newton, in the County of Middlesex, and Province of the Massachusetts-Bay, Collector, their Rights will be sold according to Law for Payment of said Taxes.

April 15, 1774. JOSHUA FULLER, THOMAS MILLER, NATHl. SPARHAWK, } Committee.

TO be exposed to Sale by Publick Vendue at the House of Capt. *Ephraim Jones*, Innholder in Concord, on Thursday the 28th Day of April Current, at 3 o'Clock, P. M. viz.——A good House Licenced for Retailing Spirituous Liquors, with a Shop adjoining. —Also a Barn and about 6 Acres of Land, situate within about 20 Rods of the Meeting-House, in said Concord, now in the Possession of *Ezekiel Brown*: Said House is well accommodated for a Trader's. For further Particulars inquire of Lieut. *John Butrick* and Mr. *Nathaniel Stearns*, in said Concord, or of said *Brown*, now Residing in Boston.

All Persons having any Demands on the Estate of William Bulfinch, *late of Boston, Sail Maker, deceas'd, are desired to bring in their Accounts to* Samuel Bulfinch *and* David Hyde, *Administrators on said Estate,—and those that are Indebted, are desired to make speedy Payment to said Administrators.*

Soap Coppers to be Lett.

Coppers to make Soap in, of all Sizes, from One Barrel up to Six, to be Let by the Day, at the Golden Cock, Marlborough-Street, BOSTON.

To be Sold for no Fault,

A likely NegroLad, about 13 Years of Age.

Inquire of the Printers.

A Wet Nurse with a good Breast of Milk, would be glad to go into a Gentleman's Family to Suckle. Inquire of the Printers.

Boston: Printed, by EDES & GILL.

THE Boston AND COUNTRY Gazette, JOURNAL.

Containing the freshest Advices, Foreign and Domestic.

No. 995.

MONDAY, May 2, 1774.

From the Public Advertiser, Feb. 3.
To ALEXANDER WEDDERBURNE, Esq;
SIR,

IT is not without a Sense of Abasement, that I descend to a Contest with one so utterly destitute of Character as you. The Vices and Treachery which have advanced you, from Indigence to Opulence, from a menial Office in Chancery to the respectable Post of Solicitor-General, has not dignified you enough, in my Opinion, to render you a reputable Antagonist for a Gentleman. But the Opportunity you lately had of calumniating those I esteem, and the Manner in which you used it, compel me to the irreputable Contest.

Your Defence of Mr. Hutchinson and Mr. Oliver, against the Petition of the House of Representatives of Massachusetts Bay, consisted of an elaborate Invective against the People, a studied Eulogium of the Governors, and the foulest Abuse of the Agent Dr. Franklin.

It shall be my Business to shew, that hardly one Word of what you uttered, was true—hardly a Conclusion you drew, was fair.

You began with affirming, that their Lordships were desired to condemn your Clients upon an Accusation only, without Proof being offered, in Violation of a fundamental Rule of English Justice, that Innocence is to be presumed. It was impossible but you must have known this Assertion to be untrue, because you had the Moment before heard the authenticated Letters read as Evidence of their Guilt. Their own Letters were the Witnesses, upon which the Accusation was founded, from which their Guilt was apparent. Where then was the Resemblance between this Case, and that of the Roman Satyrist? He supposes a Man, who was covered with Crimes, * the detested Favorite of a detestable Prince, accused by a Letter from that very Prince, and upon that Evidence only condemned to die. The Satyr arises from the Populace applauding his Punishment, without knowing whether it was just, or founded on any other Proof than the *verbosa & grandis epistola* of the Emperor, merely because the Man was odious, and had fallen from the Favor, under the Enmity of his Prince.

Turba Remi, sequitur fortunam semper, et odit Damnatos.

What Colour of Similitude is there here? Nothing but a Similarity of Sound in the Word Letters. But what Letters?—Not of another, but of themselves—their own acknowledged Letters—the Men not fallen from, but in the Zenith of Power—not hated, but, if we may believe you, beloved, respected, and honoured. Such is the aptness of your Allusions, such the Clearness of your Ideas, such the Proofs of your Scholarship. I remember a similar Misapplication upon this very Subject, of a Passage in Cicero, by a worthy Gentleman, under the Signature of Antenor, whom I suspect to have an intimate Communication with you. Your Imitation of him induces me to conjecture, that he furnished you with the Quotations, and led you to expose yourself, by repeating, like an ignorant School Boy, what you did not understand.

You proceeded to charge the Assembly with having accused the Governors of bringing upon them those Calamities, of which they complained, when they knew it to be false, because they themselves published the Letters of Governor Bernard, General Gage, and others, which did produce those Effects.

To use your own Words, Sir, you knew it was false when you made this Charge against the Assembly. You had a Copy of their Petition. You had heard it read. The Words are, that the Letters had a *Tendency* to produce such and such Effects, not that they had actually produced them. It was the Malignity of the Intention, not the Mischief of the Execution, which rendered the Writers Criminal. Is there no Difference between the Tendency & the Operation of a Thing?

* Seianus, whose Character see in Tacit. Annal. lib. 4.

Suppose I were to say, that the Scurrility of a certain impudent Lawyer, not very unlike the Solicitor General, had a Tendency to bring upon him personal Chastisement, would any one who heard me understand me to mean that he had actually suffered a Caning? Was there then any Inconsistency in saying those Letters had a Tendency to effect that which they knew had been effected by other Letters? Did not this very Knowledge convince them of the Propriety of the Charge, as those Letters, which did actually occasion the Measures, were, in Sentiment and Misrepresentation, exactly similar to these?

To aggravate your Charge, you made a false Quotation from General Gage's Letter. Your Words were, "there is no Government in Boston." The Letter, Sir, is in Print, and I defy you to shew such a Passage in it. Where was the Veracity of a Man, the Character of a Gentleman, the Dignity of a Solicitor General, when you presumed thus to impose a Forgery upon your Hearers?

Your Observation on the Proceedings of the Town Meeting in Boston hardly deserves an Answer. You take half a Sentence, and set it up for Ridicule. The whole of the Proposition is this: All Men have a Right to remain in a State of Nature as long as they please; therefore as their entering into Society is a voluntary Act, in case of intolerable Oppression in it, Civil or Religious, they have a Right to leave that Society, and form another. The Position is undeniable, the Conclusion clear. Ferguson on Civil Society, nor yet Macdowell's Institutes, do not contain a Position more pertinent and important. It is not your Tongue, Sir, and much less your Sword, that will subdue Men so thoroughly grounded in the Principles of that Constitution for which they are contending, though their Efforts appear to you, when in Place, rebellious Phrenzy, which, when out of Place, you softened into a *successful Resistance.*

You had the Confidence to assert on the Information of Mr. Hutchinson, that the Odium against him, and the Opposition to the Tyranny of this Country, was confined to a few; for that the People in general had seen their Error, and were ashamed of their Conduct. We are told directly the Reverse by the public Resolutions of all the Town-Meetings, by the unanimous Resolves of his Majesty's Council, and those of the House of Representatives, in which there were but twelve Negatives to eighty-two Affirmatives. To which of these Testimonies shall we give Credit concerning the Disposition of the Province—to the People themselves, and both Houses of Assembly; or to this solitary Trumpeter of his own Popularity and Praise?

Of the same Impression was the Declaration that Mr. Otis was the only Enemy he had in the Province, and the Cause of all the Insults offered him. Why did you not, Sir, relate a Truth concerning Mr. Otis, which should have put to Shame many that were present, would have kindled every Spark of virtuous Indignation, and excited every Feeling of Humanity in the Audience, that Mr. Otis, at Noon-day, in the midst of that City, in which he was accused of being the Demagogue, was attacked by a Band of Ruffians with Swords and Sticks, headed by Mr. Robinson, a Commissioner of the Customs, from whom though he escaped with his Life, yet he has ever since been cut off by this barbarous and brutal Outrage from every Enjoyment, every Advancement, every Happiness to which his uncommon Abilities and his Virtues entitled him. Why did you not relate that this Crime was not pursued by the Fury of an ungovernable Populace, partial to their Leader, and unjust to his Enemy, but was examined into by the deliberate Course of Law: That when Mr. Robinson was convicted by the Law, he was forgiven, upon acknowledging a Contrition for his Offence. But so far was he from receiving any Rebuke from Government, that when he was obliged to fly for other Malefactions, he was suffered to enjoy here the Profits of his Place as a Sinecure, and still retains it, though he is pursuing his Fortune in the West Indies.

This is the Town which you have represented as being under the Rule of a democratic Despotism, where none but Demagogues are safe, where his Majesty's Government and Officers are hereby insulted with Impunity, and where a Military Force is necessary to support Justice, and subdue the licentious Spirit of the People. O audaciam! sive illa tibi nota non sunt (nihil enim boni nosti) sive sunt, quæ apud tales viros, tam impudenter loquare!* A BOSTONIAN.

P. S. I will not fatigue Mr. Wedderburne with too much at a Time; but he may depend upon it that not one Word which fell from him shall pass without the Reproof it deserves.
* Second Philippic.

[Several other Letters to Mr. Wedderburne, sign'd A Bostonian, are in a SUPPLEMENT which accompanies this Day's Gazette.]

Joseph Peirce

HAS IMPORTED by Captain SYMMES, (who is just arrived from LONDON) and is now opening at his Shop in Kingstreet, nearly opposite the North Door of the Town-House, BOSTON,
DUTCH LACES
Of all Widths,
INDIA CALICOES (very low)
A beautiful variety of
CHINTZ and CALICOE PATTERNS,
Royal Rib,
Cotton Denim,
Spotted Jean,
CORDUROYS,
Silk Corcusoys,
Crimson Silk SASHES for Officers,
New Gorgets for ditto,
Brocades,
Rich { Blue, Black and White } Sattins,
Rich Leather mounted and other Fans,
Brussels and Mecklin Laces,
English brocaded and other Pumps,
Mens and Youths white and brown Holland and Beaver Gloves,
Ladies white Beaver furred Riding Hats,
Mens white Beaver Hats,
Boys white and black turn-up Brim Hats,
Irish Linens of all Widths and Prices,
Checks ditto ditto,
Ravens Duck,
Dowlass,
Sheeting,
Russia Drabs,
Muslins and Cambricks,
A large Assortment of Mens, Womens and Childrens Thread, Cotton and Silk Hose,
White and Black Silk Breeches Patterns,
All Colours Worsted ditto,
White KERSEYMERE,
Black embroidered Coat Loops,
Neat Patent Wove Stays.
With a great Variety of other Articles, all which his Customers and others may be assured he will sell at a very small Profit for READY MONEY.

CHINA WARE,

Nathaniel Greenough

HAS just imported in Captain Calef——With a large Assortment of Goods suitable for the Season, which he is determined to sell at his usual very low Price. There are too many Articles to mention particularly here. Besides it would be rather tedious for his good Friends to read a long Advertisement. If they will again favour him with their Presence at his Store, two Doors Northward of the Post-Office in Cornhill, he will esteem it an Honour to wait on them himself; and assures them they shall be well rewarded for Pains and Kindness.

N. B. Irish Linens from 6s. to 40s. per Yard. Nutmegs, Cloves, Cinnamon and Mace, fresh, good and cheap.

ALL Persons indebted for this Paper, whose Accounts have been above 12 Months standing are requested to make immediate Payment.

BOSTON.

The grand Design of establishing a new American Post Office, seems now to engage the Attention of all Ranks. In our present Situation, it is allowed to be consistent, important and indispensible. Several Meetings have been lately held here in order so to regulate the Plan, as to remove and prevent Objections. This has been compleated, and is as follows, viz.

The PLAN *for establishing a New* American POST-OFFICE.

THE present American Post-Office was first set up by a private Gentleman in one of the Southern Colonies, and the Ministry of Great-Britain finding that a Revenue might arise from it, procured an Act of Parliament in the 9th Year of the Reign of Queen Anne, to enable them to take it into their own Hands; and succeeding Administrations have, ever since, taken upon them to regulate it—have committed the Management of it to whom they pleased, and availed themselves of its Income, now said to be at least £.3000 Sterling per Annum clear. By this Means a Set of Officers, *Ministerial* indeed, in their Creation, Direction and Dependance are maintained in the Colonies, into whose Hands all the social, commercial & political Intelligence of the Continent is necessarily committed; which, at this Time, every one must consider as dangerous in the extreme. It is not only our Letters that are liable to be stopt and opened by a Ministerial Mandate, and their Contents construed into treasonable Conspiracies, but our News-Papers, those necessary and important Alarms in Time of public Danger, may be rendered of little Consequence for want of Circulation. Whenever it shall be thought proper to restrain the Liberty of the Press, or injure an Individual, how easily may it be effected! A Post-Master General may dismiss a Rider, and substitute his Hostler in his Place, who may tax the News-Papers to a Prohibition; and when the Master is remonstrated to upon the Head, he may deny he has any Concern in the Matter, and tell the Printer he must make his Terms with the Post.

As, therefore, the Maintenance of this dangerous and unconstitutional Precedent of Taxation without Consent—as the parting with very considerable Sums of our Money to support Officers, of whom it seems to be expected that they should be inimical to our Rights—as the great Danger of the Increase of such Interest and its Connections, added to the Considerations abovementioned, must be alarming to a People thoroughly convinced of the fatal Tendency of this Parliamentary Establishment, it is therefore proposed,

1. That Subscriptions be opened for the Establishment and Maintenance of a Post-Office; and for the necessary Defence of Post-Officers and Riders employed in the same.

2. That the Subscribers, in each Colony, shall annually appoint a Committee from among themselves, consisting of seven Persons, whose Business it shall be to appoint Post-Masters in all Places within their respective Provinces, where such Offices have hitherto been kept, or may hereafter be judged necessary; and to regulate the Postage of Letters and Packets, with the Terms on which News Papers are to be carried; which Regulations shall be printed and set up in each respective Office.

3. That the Post-Masters shall contract with, and take Bonds, with sufficient Sureties, of suitable Persons to perform the same Duty as hath heretofore been performed by Post Riders; subject to the Regulation and Controul of the Committee.

4. That the several Mails shall be under Lock and Key, and liable to the Inspection of no Person but the respective Post-Masters to whom directed, who shall be under Oath for the faithful Discharge of the Trust reposed in them.

5. That a Post-Master General shall be annually chosen, by the written Votes of all the Provincial Committees, inclosed and sent to the Chairman of the New-York Committee, who on receiving all the Votes, and giving one Month's public Notice in all the New-York Papers, of the Time and Place appointed for that Purpose, shall open them in Committee, in Presence of all such Subscribers as shall choose to attend, and declare the Choice, which Choice shall be immediately communicated to all the other Provincial Committees by a Certificate under the Hand of the said Chairman.

6. That the Post-Master General shall be empowered to demand & receive the Accounts from the several Post-Masters throughout the Colonies connected with this Post-Office, and shall adjust and liquidate the same, and by his Order transfer, in just Proportion, the Surplusages of one Office to make good the Deficiencies of another, if any such should appear; and in Case of a Deficiency upon the Whole, he shall have Power to draw for the same upon the several Committees, in Proportion to the Amount of the Subscriptions in their Departments: And, at the Year's End, transmit to the said Committees a fair and just Account of the whole Post Office under his Inspection.

7. That the several Post-Masters shall charge   per Cent. on all the Monies received into their respective Offices, for their Services, and also   per Cent. for the Use of the Post-Master-General, which they shall remit to him Quarterly with their Accounts.

8. That whatever Balances may remain in the Hands of the several Post-Masters, after all Charges are paid, shall, by the Direction of the Subscribers in the Province or Provinces where such Post-Masters reside, be appropriated to the Enlargement of the present Institution within their respective Provinces.

In Order that the foregoing Plan may be carried into Execution, We the Subscribers do severally promise to pay the several Sums annexed to our Names, to the Chairman of the Committee to be appointed in Pursuance of said Plan, whenever, according to the Conditions thereof, they shall be called for by him or his Successor in Office. BOSTON, APRIL 30, 1774.

We have the Pleasure of assuring the Public, that the above Subscription, (in this Form) was opened late on Saturday last; and hath been patronized by the first Gentlemen for Character and Fortune in the Town. The second Gentleman to whom it was presented, generously engaged *Fifty Pounds*, Lawful Money, and many others have done as handsomely in proportion to their Circumstances—With this indubitable Evidence of the Disposition of the Bostonians, added to the noble Conduct of the patriotic Inhabitants of Portsmouth, Newbury, Newbury Port, Salem, &c. Mr. Goddard, will set out on his Return homewards this Week, rejoicing in the great Success which hath attended his Endeavours to rescue the Channel of *public* and *private* Intelligence from the horrid Fangs of ministerial Dependants.

Mess'rs EDES & GILL,

Please to insert the following, and you'll oblige a Number of the Inhabitants of the County of York.

WHEREAS the Governor's *Soothsayer*, and *Grand Oracle of Infallibility* for this County, hath uttered his Prediction in the Town of Boston, that Sir PETER LACK LEARNING intends to take his Seat in this County, on an Invitation of the said Soothsayer and his Friends; this is to inform the said Sir PETER LACK LEARNING, that he will GRIEVOUSLY AFFRONT by far the greater and most respectable Part of the Inhabitants of this County, if he *presumes* to take his Seat here; and he is hereby ADVISED not to do it, untill he hath fully acquitted himself, if he is able so to do, of the High Crimes and Misdemeanors, of which he stands *justly* charged by the highest Authority.

SPRING GOODS,

extremely cheap,

JUST IMPORTED BY

John Barrett and Sons,

Near the Mill-Bridge,

A most elegant and compleat Assortment of

English, India and *Scotch* GOODS,

Suited to the Season,

With all Kinds of *London Bristol, Sheffield & Birmingham* Hard-Ware and Cutlary Goods.

(The Particulars in our next.)

China Ware.

IMPORTED in the John, Capt. White, from LONDON,

By *Elizabeth Perkins*,

And now opening at her Shop, two Doors below the British Coffee-House, North Side of King-Street,

A large Assortment of China and Glass Ware,

amongst which are blue and white and enamel'd China Dishes, Plates, Pattes, Sauce Boats, Custard Cups, Tea Cups and Saucers, Coffee ditto, Coffee Pots, Tea ditto, Sugar Dishes, Cannisters, Milk Pots, Bowls, &c. Plain, cut, enamel'd and engraved Wine Glasses, Wine and Water Glasses, Ale Glasses, Tumblers, Cruets, Jellies, Syllabubs, Salts, Mustards, Proof Glasses, Chamber Lamps, Bird Boxes, Sugar Dishes, Salvers, Decanters, Nipple Shells, Breast Pipes, Cream Buckets, &c.——— And a great Variety of Liverpool Ware.

ALSO, Spices of all Sorts,

Cheshire Cheese	Durham Mustard
Rhode-Island ditto	Olives
Allspice	Capers
Pepper	Anchovies
Currants	Split Peas
Raisins	Round ditto
Rice, ground ditto	White Beans
Coffie, Chocolate	Oatmeal
Snuff	Common & Poland Starch
Velvet Corks	Choice French Indigo
Single, midling & double refin'd Loaf Sugar	Spanish ditto
	Hard Soap
Salt Petre	Crown ditto
Dumb Fish	15 & 18 Inch Pipes
Flask Oil	Hunter's.

An Assortment of Holland Stone Ware.

The above Articles, with many others, by Wholesale or Retail, as cheap as at any Place in Town.

ON FRIDAY NEXT,

At TEN in the Morning,

Will be SOLD by PUBLIC VENDUE at RUSSELL's Auction-Room in Queen-Street,

A Variety of genteel House Furniture, among which are a neat Mahogany Desk and Book-Case, Chest of Draws, Bureau Dining Tables, Tea Tables, Card Table, crimson Harrateen Bed with Window Curtains and Easy-Chair, Sconce, Pier and Dressing Glasses, Leather Bottom and Chamber Chairs, a neat eight Day Clock, Silver handled Knives & Forks, and white Ivory handled ditto in Shagreen Cases; a great Variety of China, among which is a Tea sett, enameled; Cream coloured, Stone and Delph Ware; Kitchen Furniture, &c. &c.—Also the Wearing Apparel and other Effects of an Officer lately deceased; Sulkey and Harness. J. RUSSELL, Auctioneer.

Nathan Frazier,

(Just returned from LONDON,)

BEGS Leave, respectfully to inform the Public, that he has brought with him,

An Assortment of GOODS suitable for the Spring Trade, which he will sell, by Wholesale and Retail, at his Store the Corner of Wing's Lane, near the Market, BOSTON.

*** Said Frazier has for Sale an extraordinary good Gold Watch.

TO BE LETT,

A Tenement in Wing's Lane, adjoining to the Store of said Frazier, of whom please to enquire.

Smith & Atkinson

ACQUAINT their Customers and others, in Town and Country, they have IMPORTED in sundry Vessels lately arrived from LONDON,

A Compleat and General Assortment of SPRING GOODS, which will be Sold (by WHOLESALE only) on such Terms as must appear reasonable to every Judge of the different Articles.

N. B. A few Barrels of choice Connecticut Pork, Pig and Bar Iron of the best Quality, with POTASH KETTLES cast from the best Mountain Ore. (tbcif)

Jeremiah Allen,

Informs his Friends and the PUBLIC,

That he has received by the LONDON, Capt. CALEF,

And is now opening for Sale,

At his Shop in Ann Street a little North of the Draw Bridge, by Wholesale and Retail.

A compleat Assortment of Braziery, Cutlery and Ironmongery GOODS, purchased from the most approved Manufacturers in Great Britain, and which he doubts not will give satisfaction both in Price and Quality to those who please to favour him with their Custom.

(The Particulars in our next.)

William Hawes,

COACH and CHAISE Maker,

BEGS Leave to inform his Friends and the Public, That he carries on the Business as usual in its various Branches at his Shop at the Sign of the Coach-Makers Arms, opposite the Friend's Meeting-House, Boston;—where may be had a second-hand CHARRIOT, and a Number of second-hand CHAISES, a SULKEY, Neat's-Foot OYL, &c.—He takes second-hand CHAISES in Part for New ones.

N. B. Said HAWES has just receiv'd from LONDON, a fresh Supply of High Copal Oyl VARNISH for Coaches and Chaise, fine black Japan Laker for the Leather of Coaches and Chariots, which he will Warrant to look as well as on any Carriage that has came from England.

RAN-away from William Thompson of Billerica, on the 24th ult. a Negro Man named Cæsar, about 5 Feet 7 Inches high, carried with him two Suits of Cleaths, homespun all Wool, light coloured, with white Lining and plain Brass Buttons, the other homespun Cotton and Linnen Twisted. Whoever takes up said Negro and secures him, or returns him to his Master, shall be handsomely rewarded, and all necessary Charges paid by JONATHAN STICKNEY.

N. B. All Masters of Vessels and others, are cautioned from carrying off or concealing said Negro, as they would avoid the Penalty of the Law.

Province of MASSACHUSETTS-BAY *April 29*, 1774.

WHEREAS Application hath been made to me the Subscriber, by more than one Sixteenth Part of the Proprietors of the Township of Neshobe, in the Province of New-York, to grant a Warrant for calling a Proprietors Meeting for Neshobe, for the following Purposes, viz.—To give public Notice to all the Proprietors of the Township of said Neshobe, which was granted by his Excellency *Benning Wentworth*, Esq; late Governor of *New-Hampshire*, to Capt. *Josiah Powers* and his Associates in the Year 1771, that there is to be a Proprietors Meeting for said Neshobe, held at the Dwelling-House of *Benjamin Simons*, of *Williamstown*, in the County of *Berkshire*, and Province of *Massachusetts-Bay*, Innholder, on the third Wednesday of *June* in this present Year 1774, at One of the Clock in the Afternoon, then and there to do the following Business, viz. 1st. To choose a Moderator. 2dly. To choose a Proprietor's Clerk. 3dly. To see what Measures the Proprietors will come into for the Division of said Neshobe, and what will be most for the Benefit of said Propriety, and to act thereon as they shall judge best and most proper for the good of said Propriety.

W. BRATTLE,

Justice of the Peace thro' said Province.

IN Pursuance of the above Warrant the Proprietors are hereby Notified to meet at the Time and Place appointed, to transact the above Articles.

BENJA. POWERS, Proprietor's Clerk.

Boston, April 29th, 1774.

Yesterday arrived here Capt. Callahan in 6 Weeks from London, by whom we have Papers to the 16th of March, but have only Time to extract the following Articles.

L O N D O N.

March 14. All forcible, as well as pacific measures will be nugatory and ineffectual with the Boston rebels, unless their *Charter is vacated.* It is the spring and source of all their insolent and unjustifiable acts. The council being chosen by the people yearly, must vote according to their pleasure, so that, in fact, they are not the *Counsellors* of the King, but the *Tools* of the Faction. The People of the Massachusetts Province are also over represented; the number ought to be reduced to a fourth part of the present. Boston, instead of sending four members should send but *two* at most, tho' *one* would do better. Without this previous necessary step, every other attempt to bring them to reason will be fruitless, nay, will be inflammatory, whether the method be gentle or vigorous; it will only be pruning and watering the tree of sedition, instead of striking at its root.

March 15. Yesterday Lord North made the following motion in the House of Commons, "That leave be given to bring in a Bill for the immediate removal of the Officers concerned in the collection and management of his majesty's duties and customs from the Town of Boston in the Province of Massachusetts-Bay, in North-America, and to discontinue the landing & discharging, lading & shipping of goods, wares and merchandize at the said Town of Boston, or within the harbour thereof."

Lord North supported the motion in a Speech of near an hour. He was supported by Mr. R. Fuller, Mr. Cavendish, Capt. Phipps, Mr. C. Fox, Col. Barre, Governor Pownall and Mr. Calvert.

The motion was strongly opposed by Col. Jennings, Mr. Dempster, Mr. Sawbridge, Mr. Byng, Mr. Dowdswell and Lord Cavendish.

Friday next the whole House will resolve itself into a committee for a further consideration of American affairs.

It is thought by many that the proceedings against the Americans will not be so harsh as generally reported, as the trade of this kingdom with her colonies is still thought worth cherishing, little being left to the other parts of the world. The grand question that will admit of debate, is, whether, considering them as not represented they can legally be taxed by any other than by their own assemblies.

N E W - Y O R K, April 25.

On Monday last Advice was received from Philadelphia, that Capt. Chambers of the Ship London, of this Port, had taken on board at the Port of London, 18 Boxes of fine Tea, which were regularly cleared, and the Mark and Numbers were taken from the Cocket by Capt. All, of Philadelphia. As Capt. Chambers was one of the First who refused to take the India Company's Tea on Freight the last Summer, for which he received the Thanks of the Citizens, they could not believe that he knew of the Teas being on board, and therefore supposed it to have been shipt by some ministerial Tool, under another Denomination, in order to injure the Owners, or the Reputation of the Master, or to make an Experiment of this Mode of introducing the Teas to America. The Committee and the Inhabitants were therefore determined to examine into the Matter with great Vigilance. In the Night the long expected Tea Ship, Nancy, Captain Lockyer, arrived at Sandy Hook, without her Mizen Mast and one of her Anchors, which were lost in a Gale of Wind the 2d Instant, when her Main Top Mast was sprung, and she thrown on her Beam Ends. Letters being delivered to him by the Pilot, from sundry Gentlemen of this City, informing him of the determined Resolution of the Citizens not to suffer the Tea on board his Ship to be landed, he requested the Pilot to bring him up to procure Necessaries and make a Protest, but they would not do it 'till Leave was obtained. Early the next Morning this was communicated to the Committee, and it appearing to them to be Sense of the City that such Leave should be granted to him, the Ship to remain at the Hook, the Pilot was immediately dispatched to bring him up. This Intelligence was immediately communicated to the Public by an Hand Bill. At 6 P. M. the Pilot Boat returned with Capt. Lockyer on board, and altho' the People had but a very short Notice of it the Wharf was crouded with the Citizens, to see the Man whose Arrival they long and impatiently wished, to give them an Opportunity to co-operate with the other Colonies. The Committee conducted him to the House of the Hon. Henry White, Esq; one of the Consignees, and there informed Capt. Lockyer that it was the Sense of the Citizens that he should not presume to go near the Custom-House, and to make the utmost Dispatch in procuring the necessary Articles he wanted for his Voyage. To this he answered, "That as the Consignees would not receive his Cargo, he would not go to the Custom-House, and would make all the Dispatch he could to leave the City." A Committee of Observation was immediately appointed to go down in a Sloop to the Hook, to remain there near the Tea Ship till she departs for London.

Wednesday Night arrived Capt. Lawrence, from London, who confirmed the Account received from Philadelphia, of Capt. Chambers having on board 18 Boxes of Fine Tea, but could not tell who was the Shipper, or to whom it was addressed. Thursday the Committee interrogated Capt. Lawrence relative to what he knew of the Tea's being on board of Capt. Chambers, when he shewed them a Memorandum in his Pocket Book, which he took from the Cocket in the Middle of Capt. Chambers's File of Papers in the Searcher's Office at Gravesend, corresponding with the Advice transmitted from Philadelphia, except some Variation in the Mark. This Morning the following Hand Bill was distributed.

To the P U B L I C.

"The Sense of the City relative to the Landing the "India Company's Tea, being signified to Capt. Lockyer, by the Committee, nevertheless, it is the Desire "of a Number of the Citizens, that at his Departure "from hence, he should see, with his own Eyes, their "Detestation of the Measures pursued by the Ministry "and the India Company, to enslave this Country.— "This will be declared by the Convention of the People at his Departure from this City; which will be "next Saturday Morning, about nine o'Clock, when "no Doubt every Friend to this Country will attend. "The Bells will give the Notice about an Hour before "he embarks from Murray's Wharf."

New York, April 21, 1774

By Order of the Committee.

Friday at Noon Capt. Chambers came into the Hook; the Pilot asked him if he had any Tea on board. He declared he had none. Two of the Committee of Observation went on board of Captain Chambers, and informed him of the Advices received of his having Tea on board, and demanded a sight of all his Cockets, which was accordingly given them, but the Cocket for the Tea was not found among them, nor was the Mark or Number on his Manifest.

About 4 P. M. the Ship came to the Wharf, when she was boarded by a Number of Citizens. Capt. Chambers was interrogated relative to his having the Tea on board, but he still denied it. He was then told it was vain to deny it, for there was good Proof of its being on board; for it would be found, as there were Committees appointed to open every Package, and that he had better be candid and open about it; and demanded the Cocket for the Tea; upon which he confessed it was on board, and delivered the Cocket. The Owners and the Committee immediately met at Mr. Francis's where Capt. Chambers was ordered to attend. Upon examining him who was the Shipper and Owner of the Tea, he declared that he was the sole Owner of it.—After mature Deliberation, it was determined to communicate the whole State of the Matter to the People, who were convened near the Ship; which was accordingly done. The Mohawks were prepared to do their Duty at a proper Hour, but the Body of the People were so impatient that before it arrived a Number of them entered the Ship, about 8 P. M. took out the Tea, which was at Hand, broke the Cases and started their Contents in the River, without doing any Damage to the Ship or Cargo. Several Persons of Reputation were placed below to keep Talley and about the Companions to prevent ill disposed Persons from going below the Deck. At 10 the People all dispersed in good Order, but in great Wrath against the Captain; and it was not without some Risque of his Life that he escaped. Saturday at 8 A. M. all the Bells of the City rang, pursuant to the Notice published on Thursday.——About nine, the greatest Number of People were collected at and near the Coffee-House, that was ever known in this City. At a Quarter past nine the Committee came out of the Coffee-House with Captain Lockyer, upon which the Band of Musick attending, played, God save the King. Immediately there was a Call for Captain Chambers,—where is he? where is he? Capt. Lockyer must not go till we find Capt. Chambers to send him with the Tea Ship. This produced Marks of Fear in Capt. Lockyer, who imagined some Mischief was intended him; but upon Assurances being given him to the contrary, he appeared composed. The Committee with the Musick, conducted him through the Multitude, to the End of Murray's Wharf, where he was put on board the Pilot Boat, and wished a safe Passage; upon which the Multitude gave loud Huzza's, and many Guns were fired, expressive of their Joy at his Departure. The Committee of Observation at the Hook, have Cognizance of him till a fair Wind offers for his Departure from thence. Thus to the great Mortification of the secret and open Enemies of America, and the Joy of all the Friends of Liberty and human Nature, the Union of these Colonies is maintained in a Contest of the utmost Importance to their Safety and Felicity.

B O S T O N, May 2, 1774.

His Majesty's Writ is issued for calling a Great and General Court or Assembly to be convened here on Wednesday the 25th of May Instant, being the last Wednesday in the Month, agreeable to the Royal Charter.

In Capt. Callahan came Passengers, Francis Huger, Esq; of South Carolina, Mr. James Henderson, and Mr. John Semple, of this Town, Merchants, Miss Lee, Mr. Sprowel, and Mr. Morewood.

At a Court Marshal held on board the Active Man of War, on Friday 7-night, the Boatswain of the Tamer was tried for Mutiny, found guilty, and is now under Sentence of Death.

On Tuesday the 19th Instant the Superior Court of Judicature open'd at Worcester in and for the County of Worcester. Chief Justice Oliver was not present in Court. The good Men return'd to serve as Grand-jurymen had a Meeting together previous to the opening of the Court, and fifteen of their Number, being in all twenty, agreed to and subscribed a Paper, and deliver'd the same to the Court; wherein they express'd a Doubt of the Legality of their Return the Venire bearing the Test of Peter Oliver, Esq; who had been impeach'd of high Crimes and Misdemeanors; and they refus'd to take the Oath unless they should be assured that the said Peter Oliver would not take his Seat on the Bench. The Court remov'd their Doubt by telling them that the Law requir'd that all Writs and Summonses be tested by the Chief Justice, and that Mr. Oliver had not been remov'd by the Governor & Council; and they further said that though they knew not whether he intended to take his Seat on the Bench or not, they apprehended that he did not, as he had not attended when the Court was held lately in the several Counties of Suffolk and Middlesex. The Jury mov'd that they might retire further to consider the Matter, and the Court adjourn'd till Afternoon. The Jury then came in again and said that in Consideration of what the Court had offer'd in the Forenoon, and also of certain Intelligence which they had themselves received they were ready to be sworn; but declaring at the same Time that it was upon a Presumption that the Chief Justice would not appear on the Bench, for they could not present their Bills to the Court while Mr. Oliver sat therein, who had himself been impeach'd of high Crimes and Misdemeanors, whereof he had not been acquitted nor tryed. The Chief Justice did not attend during the Term.

Married. At Atkinson, by the Rev. Mr. Peabody, Capt. James Tileston, of this Town, to Miss Polly Bryant, eldest Daughter of Capt. John Bryant——A most amiable young Lady.

TEN DOLLARS Reward upon the Conviction of the THIEF.

Stolen out of the Entry of the Subscriber last Wednesday in the Forenoon, a blue Huzzar Cloak, lined with Red, and Buttons made at the Factory. If such a one should be offer'd for Sale it is desired Notice may be given to HABIJAH SAVAGE.

N. B. The same Afternoon it was brought and offered for Sale by a Man in a Sailor's Habit at Mr. Bicker's Auction-Room, but he declining to be concerned with it, the Man went away with it on his Arm through the Market Square.

Just IMPORTED from LONDON, and to be Sold

By Daniel Boyer, *Jeweller,*

At his Shop opposite the Province-House in Boston.

A large Assortment of Articles for the Jewellers and Goldsmith's Use; Also a good Assortment of Guns, with and without Bayonets, Trooping Pistols, wash'd Swords, Sword Belts, Plated Spurs, Plated and Pinchbeck Shoe, Knee and Neck Buckles, black Ditto, black Sleeve Buttons, Silver Watches, Steel Chains, Seals, Brass and Steel Watch Keys, Watch Christials, large and small Money Scales.—ALSO, At said Shop may be had most sorts Jewellery and Goldsmiths Work.

Amory's, Taylor & Rogers,

ACQUAINT their Customers, and others, That they have Imported in the last Vessels from England and Scotland,

A fresh Supply of Spring Goods, which they sell as usual on the lowest Terms, by

Wholesale and Retail,

At their Store in Marlborough-Street.

JOHN SEMPLE

—Just Arriv'd in Capt. CALLAHAN from London—Begs leave to inform the Public that he has brought with him a compleat Assortment of Goods suitable for the Season—all which he will Sell at the lowest advance—Wholesale or Retail at his Shop in Cornhill.—

N. B.—Among his Assortment is a Variety of Silks and Muslins.——

For *LONDON,*

The Ship LONDON,

ROBERT CALEF, Master,

Now laying at the Long Wharf,

Will sail with all Expedition.

For Freight or Passage,

apply to PETER HUGHES, at his Store in King Street.——Where is to be sold, viz. English, Russia and Ravens Duck, Pickles in Hampers and Cases, Cheshire Cheese, Loaf Sugar, Chip Hatts.

T O B E S O L D

AT PUBLICK AUCTION,

By Benjamin Church,

On THURSDAY next,

At Ten o'Clock in the Forenoon,

At the usual Place of Sale,

A very large and general Assortment of new and very fashionable Silks—just imported, consisting of strip'd and plain Lutestrings—Mantuas—Brocades—Sattins—Modes—Persians, &c.——ALSO,——Tammies—Durants—Calamancoes—Missinetts—Broglioes—Also an Assortment of Check—Bed Ticks—Ozenbrigs, &c. &c.———At Ten o'Clock, A. M.

To be Sold for want of Employ,

A healthy, strong, good-temper'd Negro Man, about 22 Years old. He will make an excellent Servant for a Farmer, and can be well recommended. For further Particulars, inquire of Edes and Gill.

New AUCTION-ROOM, Cornhill.

TO-MORROW at TEN o'Clock will be Sold by PUBLIC VENDUE, at GREENLEAF's Auction-Room,——

A large Assortment of English Goods, as usual. Also a Quantity of Table Knives and Forks, a handsome Harpsichord, a Bureau Table, Looking Glasses, and one Cask Kippen's Snuff.

WILLIAM GREENLEAF, Auctioneer.

The Sale to begin To-Morrow Morning Ten o'Clock.

To be Sold, Wholesale or Retail, by public or private Sale, at BICKER's Auction-Room, near the Market, BOSTON.

CALLICOES, Patches, Printed Linnens, Cotton and Linnens, India Chints, Silver and Pinchbeck Watches, Cotton Checks, plain Lawns, plain Muslins.

A very great Choice of the above-mentioned Articles. Those who intend to have the Advantage of purchasing, had better apply soon, lest they be disappointed.

CUSTOM-HOUSE, *BOSTON.*

ENTETRD IN.

White and Calef, London: Morrison, Greenock: Bacon, St. Christopher's & St. Eustatia: Drinkwater, Turks Islands: Morton, Cape Nichola: Kendrick, New-London: Horsey & Summers, New-Haven.

Burials in the Town of BOSTON, since our last.

Eight Whites. Two Blacks.

Baptiz'd in the several Churches, Seven.

High Water at BOSTON, for the present Week.

Monday, 25 min. aft. 5	Friday, 32 min. aft. 8
Tuesday, 14 min. aft. 6	Saturday, 18 min. aft. 9
Wednesday, 10 m. aft. 7	Lord's-Dy, 5 m. aft. 10
Thursday, 50 min. aft. 7	D's last Qtr. 2 D 2 Aft.

JUST IMPORTED,

By Joſiah Waters *&* Son,

And to be Sold at their Store in Ann-Street;

Painter's Oil and Colours of all Kinds,

in large or ſmal Quantities, Window Glaſs, Bruſhes, &c. All Kinds of Pipes, Spices, and Groceries as uſual, a few Kegs Split Peas, Powder, &c.

At the ſame Place may be had a moſt elegant Aſſortment of

PAPER HANGINGS,

N. B. Paints prepared for Houſe, or Ship Painting. Houſe & Ship Painting perform'd with Care & Diſpatch.

Samuel Parkman,

Informs his Friends and Cuſtomers, he has receiv'd per the Captains *Folgier* & *Symmes* from London, A compleat Aſſortment of Spring GOODS, Which will be Sold by Wholeſale or Retail, (at his Shop in Union-Street) at a very low advance for Caſh.

Philadelphia ſuperfine FLOUR,

BAR-IRON, and ANCHORS; a Quantity of each to be SOLD very low (if apply'd for ſoon,)

By Edward Gray,

At Store No. 2, South-ſide the Town Dock; where may be had all kinds Weſt-India GOODS, and Iron WARE, very cheap for Caſh or Produce.

TO BE SOLD,

By Moſes Peck *in King-Street,*

NEW & ſecond-hand Clocks—One elegant Church Clock, plain & engrav'd genteel Silver Watches, Metal and enamel'd ditto, Gold Diamon'd ditto, Watch Glaſs, Main Springs, Steel and Metal Chains, Keys and Seals, &c. &c.

Juſt Arriv'd in the Ship NICHOLAS, Capt. FOLGIER, from LONDON,

A grand Aſſortment of Paper Hangings, Painters Oil and Colours, &c. &c. And to be Sold

By *William* Gooch,

At the Sign of Admiral *Vernon* in King-Street.

N. B. A good Store in *Butler's* Rowe, to be Let. Inquire of WILLIAM GOOCH.

Choice Fayal Wines,

Juſt arrived, and to be Sold at

Nathaniel & William Coffin's Store,

Near Oliver's Dock.

Excellent Florence Oil,

Juſt Imported & to be Sold cheap by the Cheſt or Flaſk,

By Daniel Silſby,

At his Shop oppoſite South-Side *Faneuil-Hall*; Where may be had, Weſt India Goods and Groceries of all Sorts, at as reaſonable Rate as at any Store in *Boſton*.

A Negro Boy, likely, tractable and good Temper'd, 12 Years old, to be ſold to any Gentleman that will treat him kindly—He has been a Year in the Country, and if ſold it will be for no other Reaſon than the Owner leaving the Province may not find it convenient to carry him.

POT-ASH.

CASH given for *POT-ASH,*

By JONATHAN MASON,

At his Shop next Door to the Sign of the Buck & Glove, Near the Town-Houſe, BOSTON.

N. B. To be Sold by ſaid MASON, choice Gun Powder and beſt Philadelphia Bar Iron.

To be SOLD or LET,

A neat and very convenient Houſe, with a Barn and Chaiſe Houſe, and about two Acres of Land, including a rich Garden Spot, very pleaſantly ſituated, and a fine healthy Place—not five Miles from Boſton Town-Houſe—on a great Road where moſt Kinds of Proviſions can eaſily be procured.

Enquire of Edes & Gill.

ALL Perſons Indebted to, or that have any Demands on the Eſtate of Mr. *John Hunter*, late of Marlborough, in the County of Middleſex, Victualler, deceas'd, are deſired to bring in their Accounts to *Edward Hunter*, Adminiſtrator on ſaid Eſtate, (or to *Andrew Campbell* of Boſton, Attorney to ſaid Hunter) in Order for Settlement.

TO be Sold at Publick Vendue on the firſt Day of June next, at the Houſe of Mr. *Edward Richardſon*, Innholder in Watertown, if not Sold before at Private Sale ——A FARM lying in ſaid Watertown, contains about 40 Acres of choice good Land, is all well Fenced into ſuitable Apartments, with good Stone Walls, has on it, a good Houſe and Barn, two good Wells of Water, a Variety of all kinds of Fruit, is well accommodated for Mowing, Paſturage and Tillage, &c. For the Particulars of the Sale inquire of Mr. JOHN STRATTON, now living on the Premiſes.——

—The Sale to begin at 3 o'Clock Afternoon.—

April 18th, 1774.

Stop Thief and Runaway Man Servant.

WHEREAS WILLIAM HAYWARD, Baker, abſconded himſelf from my Service 16th March, 1774. and took with him to the Value of *Eight Pounds*, L. M. and he being taken and convicted, voluntarily Bound himſelf, to ſerve me Six Months, to Pay Damages & Coſt; and he laſt Night abſconded himſelf again; had on an old Felt Hat, an old cloth colour'd Coat and Waiſtcoat, check'd Woolen Shirt, a Pair of new cloth colour'd Breeches, a Pair of old pale blue Stockings, and a Pair of ſinglebole Shoes.—Said Hayward is about Thirty-three Years of Age, Five Feet Five Inches high, darkiſh ſhort Hair, and down look like a Rogue and Thief.———Whoſoever will take up ſaid Servant and Notify me the Subſcriber ſo that I may have him again, ſhall have FIVE DOLLARS Reward, paid by me,

Marlboro' April 9, 1774. ISAAC SHERMAN.

All Bakers are hereby Cautioned againſt Employing ſaid Servant.

A Quantity of Turpentine, Pitch and Tar, To be Sold at Store No. 5, on PECK's Wharf.

Narraganſet Cheeſe,

To be Sold by JOSEPH PEARSE PALMER, At the loweſt Store on the South Side of the Town-Dock.

Sperma Cæti CANDLES

Warranted PURE.—

Excellent Dorcheſter and

Taunton ALE,

Packed in Caſks, very handy for Tranſportation, To be Sold CHEAP for CASH by

William Palfrey.

THOMAS CARNES, Broker,

HAS for Sale, at a very low Rate for Caſh—Three new Fall-back Chaiſe, a new Sulkey compleat, fit for a Gentleman Traveller.——Goods of any Kind will be taken for them, if there is a Proſpect of turning them into Caſh by July Court.

He is to be found near the Old North Meeting House.

N. B. Alſo to be Sold three Caſks of Indigo, a Quantity of Salt-Fiſh, and 1000 Weight of Piemento.

An Invoice of £.100 Ster. is wanted to be purchaſed.

William Homes,

HAS to Sell a few Hogſheads and Barrels of SUGARS, Cheap and good. Inquire at his Shop oppoſite the Golden Key.

Excellent Brown SUGARS,

TO BE SOLD CHEAP,

By Mrs. Sheaffe,

At her Shop the North Corner of Queen-Street,

Alſo, Philadelphia Ruſk, New-York Biſcuit, choice French Indigo, Citron, &c. &c.

She has a compleat Aſſortment of Groceries that are the beſt of their Kinds, which ſhe hopes will induce her Friends to continue their Kindneſs.

New *Baltimore* FLOUR,

Philadelphia common ditto,

ditto — ſuperfine ditto in half Barrels, and a Quantity of BAR IRON, juſt Imported, and to be Sold by DANIEL BELL, (at his Store near the Eaſt End of Faneuil-Hall) very low for Caſh.

N. B. WEST INDIA GOODS to be had at the ſame Place, as cheap as at any Store in Town without Exception.

Wanted to Hire,

A pleaſant and genteel Tenement

at New-Boſton. Enquire of Edes and Gill.

To be LETT, and entered upon immediately,

A large Houſe, with about an Acre and an Half of Land, with convenient Out buildings, adjoining the Seat of Robert Auchmuty, Eſq; late in the Occupation of Captain Nathaniel Williams, deceas'd, in Roxbury, being a very pleaſant Situation for a Gentleman. Enquire of Captain Jeremiah Tucker of Milton, or Samuel Warren of Roxbury.

WANTS EMPLOYMENT,

A young Man who will be well recommended, and capable of tending and waiting on any Gentleman, or Tutoring in any private Family; underſtands Lattin, Riding Nicking, Docking, Bleeding and Curing Lameneſs in Horſes, and is no Novice in Gardening. Whoever wants any ſuch, will be informed by the Printers hereof.

WE the Subſcribers being appointed by the honorable Foſter Hutchinſon, Eſq; Judge of Probates, &c. for the County of Suffolk, Commiſſioners to receive and examine the Claims of the ſeveral Creditors to the Eſtate of Benjamin Chadwell, late of Boſton, Mariner, deceaſed, Inteſtate, repreſented Inſolvent—Do hereby give Notice, That we ſhall attend ſaid Service at the Britiſh Coffee-Houſe, on the Third Thurſday of this and the five following Months, from the Hours of Six to Nine o'Clock in the Evenings of ſaid Days.

EZEKIEL LEWIS,
Boſton, April 18, 1774. JOSEPH TURELL,
JACOB COOPER,

WHEREAS there are divers Matters to be tranſacted by the 20 Aſſociates of the Lincolnſhire Company reſpecting their Lands and Intereſt, laying near Penobſcut Bay in the County of Lincoln—The Committee of ſaid Aſſociates being duly authoriſed therefor, hereby notify ſaid Aſſociates to meet on Wedneſday the 11th Day of May next, at the Britiſh Coffee-Houſe in King-Street, Boſton, at 6 o'Clock P. M. then & there to act on the following Articles viz.

1ſt. To chooſe a Moderator, Clerk, Treaſurer, ſtanding Committee and any other Officers that may be thought neceſſary, and to appoint them ſuch Salaries, Fees or Rewards by Money, or unappropriated Lands as they ſhall think needful, from Time to Time for the Benefit of the Propriety.

2d. To determine upon any further Surveys of their Lands.

3d. To impower the ſtanding Committee to compleat the Conditions of Settlement on the Part of the Proprietors when any Settler has performed the Conditions on his Part, by executing ſuch Deed or Deeds as the Proprietors ſtand obliged to by their Permiſſions to Settlers.

4th. To determine whether they will make Sale of any more of their Lands to defrey the neceſſary Charges of the Propriety, or raiſe ſuch Monies as may be wanted by taxing the Proprietors in Proportion to their Intereſt in ſaid Propriety.

5th. To determine upon any further Diviſion of their Lands among the Proprietors.

6th To determine whether they will Leaſe any of their Lands, Iſlands, or Streams.

7th. To fix upon a ſuitable Piece of Land to place Meeting-Houſe for publick Worſhip and a publick School.

8th. To ſequeſter a Lot of Land for the Support of the Goſpel-Miniſtry within the firſt Townſhip forever.

9th. To fix upon a Lot of Land to be given to the firſt Miniſter of the Goſpel, that ſhall be ſettled in the firſt Townſhip by a free Choice of a Majority of the Inhabitants, and ſhall reſide in ſaid Townſhip and Officiate for the Space of ſeven Years if living.

10th. To ſequeſter a Lot of Land for the Support of a School or Schools in the firſt Townſhip for Learning to Read, Write and Cypher.

12th. To determine whether they will lay out any more Lots of Land to be given or ſold to Settlers.

12th. To conſider whether a further Grant ſhall be made to the Perſons who were of the Committee for conferring with the Heirs of the late Brigadier *Waldo* as appointed Sept. 6th. 1766.

Pr. Order of the Committee,
NATH. APPLETON, Prop. Clerk.

Boſton, *April* 12th. 1774.

WE the Subſcribers, appointed Commiſſioners by the honorable Foſter Hutchinſon, Eſq; Judge of Probates, &c. for the County of Suffolk, to receive and examine the Claims of the ſeveral Creditors to the Eſtate of Mr. Richard Walker, Mariner, deceaſed, repreſented inſolvent—Notify ſaid Creditors that we ſhall attend that Service at the Houſe of Mr. Jonathan Brown, near Charleſtown Ferry, on the laſt Monday in this, and the five following Months, from Six to Eight o'Clock, P. M.

BENJA. HARROD,
Boſton 16 April, 1774. GILES HARRIS

TO BE SOLD

By Gawen Brown, *in King-Street,*

Sundry new CLOCKS,

One Second-Hand ditto, with Japann'd Caſe,—genteel Silver WATCHES, *ſome go on Diamonds, and ſome with a Cap over the Work, finiſh'd by the beſt Hands, Cheap for Caſh.*

All Perſons having any Demands on the Eſtate of William Bulfinch, *late of Boſton, Sail Maker, deceas'd, are deſired to bring in their Accounts to* Samuel Bulfinch *and* David Hyde, *Adminiſtrators on ſaid Eſtate,—and thoſe that are Indebted, are deſired to make ſpeedy Payment to ſaid Adminiſtrators.*

Soap Coppers to be Lett.

Coppers to make Soap in, of all Sizes, from One Barrel up to Six, to be Let by the Day, at the Golden Cock, Marlborough Street, BOSTON.

To be Sold for no Fault,

A likely Negro Lad, about 13 Years of Age.

Inquire of the Printers.

A Wet Nurſe with a good Breaſt of Milk, would be glad to go into a Gentleman's Family to Suckle. Inquire of the Printers.

WHEREAS the Proprietors of Land in the Townſhip of Sudbury, on Otter Creek, which Townſhip was granted by the Governor and Council of New-Hampſhire, did at their Meeting the Eighth Day of March 1774, Vote that the Sum of One Pound Lawful Money ſhould be raiſed and levied on each Original Right, for the Bounding and carrying on the Settlement of ſaid Townſhip for the common Good of ſaid Propriety; and that a Committee be appointed to aſſeſs the ſame; which has accordingly been done—Therefore we the Subſcribers being appointed a Committee to notify the Proprietors aforeſaid, to pay the ſame, together with their former delinquent Taxes—We do hereby notify them, that unleſs they pay the ſame, on or before the 17th Day of May next, to Thomas Miller, of Newton, in the County of Middleſex, and Province of the Maſſachuſetts-Bay, Collector, their Rights will be ſold according to Law for Payment of ſaid Taxes.

JOSHUA FULLER,
April 15, 1774. THOMAS MILLER, } Committee.
NATHL. SPARHAWK

Boſton: Printed, by EDES & GILL.

SUPPLEMENT to the *Boston-Gazette*, &c. of No. (995.)

MONDAY, May 2, 1774.

From the Public Advertiser, *Feb.* 6.

To ALEXANDER WEDDERBURNE, *Esq;*

SIR,

I HAVE entered into some Part of your Harrangue against the Province of Massachusetts-Bay, and have proved it totally destitute of Truth. I am much mistaken if what remains be not equally reprehensible.

You founded your next Charge against the House of Representatives, on a Misrepresentation framed long since by Governor Bernard, and ecchoed back by that Parrot of a Minister the Earl of Hillsborough. It is your Merit to revive this which has been fully refuted and consigned among other Untruths from the Nettleham Baronet to Oblivion. The Charge is, that after a Motion for sending a circular Letter to the rest of the Provinces had been rejected, it was, in Violation of parliamentary Order, revived and voted in a thin House of the same Session. It is true it was revived and carried during the same Session, but neither in a thin House nor against their Rules. Their Rules admit the proposing the same Question twice in the same Session, provided the same Number of Members are present. This Rule was complied with in the Instance in Question. Eighty-two Members were present when the Motion was first made, and exactly the same Number on moving it a second Time. There was therefore nothing unusual, nothing out of Order in the Proceeding.

Your Reflection upon the Assembly for complaining of the dangerous Innovation in directing the Salaries of the Judges to be paid by the Crown was equally just. You stated it as a strange Thing that the Judges should depend on those whom they were to judge. This is similar to the rest of your Sophistry and Misrepresentation. The Truth is, that the Judges were dependant upon the King's Pleasure, as well for the Continuance in their Places as for their Appointment; but their Salaries were voted by the Assembly, so that depending equally on the Crown and the People, they held the Scales of Justice even and unbiassed. This did not answer the iniquitous Purposes of Governors Bernard and Hutchinson, and therefore they planned the paying their Salaries by the Crown, which, with their holding their Places at Pleasure, renders them totally dependant. This is the dangerous Innovation, this is the Grievance of which they complain, and which I promise you they will not suffer to continue, though at the Hazard of their Lives. Had an Alteration been made with a good Intention it would have been to fix their Places and Salaries as in this Country, for Life, revocable only on an Address of either House of Assembly. Upon the late Establishment it is impossible there should be an impartial Administration of Justice between the Crown and the People; which being of the utmost Danger to Life, Liberties and Property, the Innovation is alarming, and the Complaint is just.

With this ended your invective against the Province, so far as it was reducible to particular Positions. We are next to consider you as chanting the Praises of the two Governors. You triumphed much in the acknowledgment of the Petitioners, that they once enjoyed the Confidence of the People, which they had lost by the discovery of these insidious and incendiary Letters. But what matter of Joy there can be in this, except from the Similarity of their Situations and your own, cannot be conceived. Their Professions of Regard for that Public, and those Liberties, of which they were privately planning the Destruction, aggravated their Guilt. Do you flatter yourself, Sir, that your Apostacy from the Principles which you publicly and privately professed, does not increase the Infamy of being the Pander of those ministerial Measures, which are fatal to all public Virtue and public Good? Do you pretend, in spite of your own Experience, not to know that Hypocrisy deepens the Die of every Crime?

To endear Mr. Hutchinson to you the more, know that he is exactly similar to yourself, in deep Dissimulation, plausible Hypocrisy, detestable Treachery. He has violated every Profession, political and religious, to gratify his Ambition and his Avarice in the Possession of the Government. No Man more positively questioned the Right of Parliament to tax America, at the Commencement of the Stamp-Act. But Governor Bernard soon touched his visual Nerve, and he began to see all political Objects through the Medium of his own Interest and Ambition.

As to Mr. Oliver, on whom, with equal Justice, you bestowed the highest Encomiums, let his Majesty's Council speak to his Character;

Council, Oct. 4. 1770.

Resolved unanimously, that Andrew Oliver, Esq; Secretary of this Province, by *secretly* taking Minutes at Council of what was said by the Members in their Debates, also by signing a Paper containing those Minutes, and further by giving his Deposition to the Truth of it, has in each of those Instances acted *inconsistent with the Duty of his Office*, and is thereby *guilty of a Breach of Trust*.

Lord Hillsborough discovering an Earnest of future Faithfulness in former Treachery, immediately promoted him to be Lieutenant Governor.

Your Justification of the Letters, on which these Men were impeached, contained nothing but positive Assertions, that they were not only innocent but highly praise-worthy, and such as did Honour to their Authors. They have been laid before the Public, and the Public will judge of them. But if they contain nothing more than the declaration that there must be an "Abridgement of English Liberty," would it not be enough to subject the Writer to the severest Censure? Is not this a treasonable Sentiment, and what every Man, who deserves the Name of Englishman, ought to hear with abhorrence? But containing, as they do, the strongest Representations against the People, inculcating the Necessity of subduing them by Military Force, proposing Plans for subverting the Constitution, and proscriptive Insinuations against Individuals——can there be a doubt of the deliberate and malignant Purpose of those who wrote them? When you magnified the Wisdom of these Men, you rendered your own Apology for them unavailing; that their Letters were oceanas, innocent, unmeaning Speculations. It is the Fool alone, Sir, who scatters Firebrands and Death, and saith, am not I in sport. Chuse which character you please for your Friends, that of mischievous Folly, or malignant Knowledge.

A BOSTONIAN.

From the Publick Advertiser, *Feb.* 8.

To ALEXANDER WEDDERBURNE, *Esq;*

SIR,

I AM now, Sir, come to that Part of your Speech which contained the most unjust, the most illiberal, the most indecent personal Abuse that ever disgraced the Lips of a Pleader, or dishonoured the Decency of a Court. Some little Difference there is between your Character and that of the Object of your rancorous Revenge.

A long Life of Virtue has rendered him respectable; a short one of Baseness has made you the Reproach of your Time. The great, but modest Merit of a true Philosopher, has rendered him amiable and illustrious in the Estimation of Europe and America. A ridiculous Affectation of Science makes you the Contempt of the little Circles in which you move, as a pragmatical Pretender to universal Knowledge. He had a high and untouched Reputation to be wounded; you have prostituted yours below the Reach of Resentment.

Your first Charge against him was founded on his having transmitted to Boston, as Agent to the House of Representatives, the flagitious Letters of Mr. Hutchinson and Mr. Oliver. These Letters, you affirmed, were transmitted "for Purposes the most malignant, and procured by Means the most infamous and corrupt." But on what Evidence did you found so opprobrious an Accusation, quibus indiciis, quo teste? nil horum. Mr. Wedderburne's Suspicion was the Accuser; Mr. Wedderburne's Suspicion was the Witness; Mr. Wedderburne's Suspicion pronounced Sentence. In Defiance of that Rule of English Justice, which you yourself had laid down for your Clients, you presumed Guilt without a Shadow of Proof; for what were your pretended Proofs? impudent Assertions, a Combination of Chances, a Conundrum, or something more contemptible —your Opinion; the Opinion of a Witling, a Punster, and a Prig:

> A pert, prim Lawyer of the Northern Race;
> Guilt in his Heart, and Famine in his Face.

Hear him in the infernal Spirit of Iago, and led like him to diet his Revenge:

> ——"I know not if't be true;
> "But I for mere Suspicion in that Sort
> "Will do as if for Surety."——

But even this Character, high wrought by Shakespeare's powerful Fancy, falls infinitely short of yours. The Subject of his Suspicion was the highest Injury a Man can receive. The Subject of yours was, if we may believe you, a Favour, or at worst an impotent Attempt to injure, futile in the Instrument, favourable in the Issue. You affirm the Letters were not only innocent, but did Honour and Credit to the Persons by whom they were written. Where then was the Injury of detecting them? Whence this Complaint, this Rage, this Rancour, this Revenge? By what strange Perversion of Judgment could a Man transmit, for Purposes the most malignant against the Authors, Letters, the Contents of which were laudable and meritorious?

But admitting the Purpose had been malignant, you cannot on your own stating pretend to say that the Means were adequate, or the Event answerable. Why then such Anger, why such a Thirst of Revenge? Would the Man who threw a Straw at you excite the same Degree of Enmity with him who aimed a Javelin at your Heart, tho' the Intention that actuated them were equal? Are you so weak as not to perceive, that all this Passion is a powerful Proof, how much you and your Clients feel the Infamy of those detested Letters? It is my Humanity that makes this Apology for you, lest you should appear too far to surpass the blackest Character of Fiction in diabolical Revenge.

I cannot do your argument so much Justice, as by repeating it Word for Word: "My Lords, I beg you will attend to this Argument; it is close; it is irrefragable to shew that the Letters must have been stolen. I am confident neither the late, nor the present Mr. Whately gave them, they must therefore have been stolen, & Dr. Franklin must have stolen them from him who stole them, for he says he obtained them."

This is the Logic of a Solicitor General; this the Language of an Orator; this the close, the irrefragable Argument, to which the Attention of your noble Hearers was so emphatically called. From whence your Confidence in the Retention of your Friends flows, I know not; but of this I am certain, there are numbers of most confidential Letters to the late Mr. Whately in the Hands of those for whom they were never intended.

Concerning the Writers of those Letters which were sent to Boston, I cannot speak in Words more apt than those of Ciceco: "Etenim cum homines nefarii de patriæ parricidio confiterentur, consciorum indiciis, *sua manu, voce pene literarum* coacti, se urbem inflammare, cives trucidare, vastare Italiam, delere rempublicam consensisse; quis esset, qui ad salutem communem defendendam, non exciteretur?" The Introduction of a Military Force, the Abridgment of their Liberties, the Destruction of their Charter, which was the Purpose of those Letters, threatened all the Miseries which are here described.

The Transmission of such Letters was therefore an Act of Duty, prompted by the most laudable of all Motives, a detestation of parricidal Treachery, and an earnest Desire of healing those unhappy Divisions which have too long subsisted between the Parent State and her Colonies, by discovering to the Colonists that the Measures, which have alienated their Affections, originated not so much in any oppressive Views of this Country, as from the Misrepresentations of some Men high in Trust and Confidence among themselves. The Discovery of these Letters operated this Effect; and had not our Ministers been more unwise than Ignorance made drunk, they would have embraced that Opportunity of burying in Oblivion forever the baneful Cause of our late Dissentions. The Punishment of two Men, who deserved to be punished, the Discovery of whose treacherous and malignant Intentions had rendered them odious and infamous, would have been a Propitiation for what is past, would have manifested a Spirit of Justice and Temper here which might happily have prepared the Way for a perfect Reconciliation.

But it has pleased the Wisdom and Moderation of our Ministers to inflame the Heat of that Distemperature, which threatned the worst of all Evils, a Civil War, and to attempt the extinguishing that Fire which already burnt too fierce, by throwing Oil upon the Flames.

A BOSTONIAN.

For the Public Advertiser, *Feb.* 10.

To ALEXANDER WEDDERBURNE, *Esq;*

I BEG your Pardon, Mr. Solicitor, for having left you a Moment. You deserve every Attention of virtuous Indignation. If you are made of penet[illegible]le Stuff, if you have Sense, any feeling, you shall be ashamed, you shall be repentant of what you have done; you shall feel that Calumny, unsupported by Truth, recoils with double Shame on him who utters it. You will learn from Dr. Franklin, what your own Feelings can never teach you, that the Testimony of a good Conscience is a sevenfold Shield against the Malice of Man.

You stated as a Fact, that he sent the Letters in an anonymous Cover, with Injunctions of Secrecy, written in a Hand, however, well known there; not to the Speaker, as officially he ought to have done, but to private Persons. From hence you drew a Conclusion, that he was conscious of Villainy, and ashamed of having it known.

The weakness of this Stating, were it true, would defeat the Wickedness of the Conclusion. How could you suppose a Man would expect Concealment from suppressing his Name, if his Hand were well known; or if, by some strange Confusion of Ideas, he did think himself concealed, to what End should he enjoin Secrecy? Wherefore should he have wished for Concealment? Was there such Terror in the Hatred of those he detected, Mr. Hutchinson and Mr. Oliver? Could he possibly have conceived that any Set of Ministers would be so weak and wicked as to persecute him for a Measure, which ministred to them the fairest Opportunity of healing graciously those unhappy Divisions with which they were perplexed in the Extreme?

But what will your Hearers, what will the World think of you, when I affirm, that the Whole of what you stated was an absolute Falshood? I defy you to prove a Word of it. I feel the Harshness of the Terms I use, but I appeal to every one who heard you, whether the Language you uttered intitles you to be treated like a Gentleman?

The Letters were enclosed to the Speaker; that which accompanied them was signed by the Agent; nor was there a single Injunction of Secrecy with regard to the Sender. He apprehended that the immediate Publication of them would raise the popular Indignation so as to be fatal to the Writers. Out of Humanity to them he desired they might not be made public. He has met with that Return, which wicked and ungratefulMen forever make to theirBenefactors.

Dr. Franklin's Declaration was the next Subject of your Abuse. You enveighed against it as marking the most inhuman Apathy that the Imagination could conceive made to insult over theDistress,& aggravate the Wounds which his Villainy had occasioned.

Let us state the Fact, and see how far it will support the Charge.

On the 8th of December a Letter, under the Signature of *Antetor*, accused Mr. Temple of dishonourably taking the letters in Question from Mr. Whately, whose name was vouch'd for the Truth of the Charge. The next Day Mr. Temple's Answer appeared, declaring Mr. Whately's Concurrence with him in denying the Facts on which the Charge was founded. So far was there in this Stage of the Business an Appearance of any Quarrel likely to happen between these two Gentlemen, it seemed as if they were united in contradicting a malignant, anonymous Accusation: But on the 11th Mr. Whately contradicted Mr. Temple, and at Four o'Clock that Day the Duel was fought. What Time or Opportunity was there here for the Intervention of Dr. Franklin, especially as Mr. Temple's Challenge was grounded on the other's flatly denying what he had given to the Public under his Hand? The original Cause too of the Dispute was, Mr. Whately's having given Rise to and countenanced a most false, unjust and cruel Accusation against Mr. Temple.

In a few Days it appeared that the Friends of Mr. Whately had been exceedingly industrious, not only in attempting to fix the first Charge upon Mr. Temple, but to blacken it by an Imputation of unfair Behaviour in the Duel. Dr. Franklin conceived, that his intervention would not be of use; that shewing neither of the Gentlemen was concerned in the Detection of those Letters, could be the most probable Means of preventing further Mischief, and of relieving the two Gentlemen who were subject to the suspicion. The Sense of that Suspicion he knew must rankle in the Wounds of Mr. Whately, and must greatly distress Mr. Temple, who, from the precarious State of his Adversary's Health, was withheld from vindicating himself to the Public. In this distressful Moment Dr. Franklin came forward with his healing Declaration. The Concealment of the Person who really procured and transmitted the Letters, was the Ground-work of all this Distress, which his Avowal of it effectually removed.

He knew the Danger to which this Step exposed him. He could not but have heard the Threats which were thrown out against the Author of this Detection. He was apprized that all the private and public Friends of Mr. Hutchinson and Mr. Oliver, with every Scoundrel, who felt himself equally guilty, were determined to prosecute with implacable Vengeance,theMan who was instrumental in disclosing to the Public the Iniquity which those Letters contained: But Honour and Humanity called upon him for a Declaration, and, at every Hazard to himself, he obeyed. These are the Facts.

By what more than hellish Rancour were you actuated, in attempting to convert the Balm, which Dr.Franklin'sHumanity had poured upon theWounds of others, into a poisonous Mineral for his Destruction? To whatCharacter in Times past shall I compare you? what Fiction will furnish your Equal? I will not insult Zanga by a Comparison that will dishonour him; I will not compare the Dignity of insulted Worth with the Meanness of cowardly Revenge. No, Sir,—the exquisite Villainy of Iago, in the blackest Purposes of his Heart, will best delineate yours.

* "So will I turn his Virtue into Pitch,
"And, out of his own Goodness, make the Net
"That shall enmesh him."

Is it the Act of a Coward to insult an old Man? Is it the Act of a Villain to accuse falsely, and stab the Character of an innocent Man? Mr. Wedderburne is the Man who insults Age. Mr. Wedderburne is the Man who stabs Innocence.

I have now exposed the Falshoods you uttered. They were Falshoods not hastily, but deliberately uttered; not wantonly, but maliciously; not whispered, but proclaimed; not to a few, but to a high and numerous Audience.

And now after being thus arraigned and thus convicted, where will you shew your opprobrious Head? —κυνος ομματ' εχων, κρ διην δ' ελαφοιο—Who will again believe, who will listen to a Man capable of uttering the worst of Falshoods for the worst of Purposes? Wherever you appear, it must be with this Stigma upon your front; Quiconque est capable de menter, est indigne d'etre compti parmi les hommes.

Go now and boast your Abilities—Go boast your Eloquence—but let it be among Wretches like your self, destitute of every sense of Honor, of every Feeling of Humanity. Go try if the indecent and unprecedented Exclamation of hear him, hear him, from Men pretending to sit in criminal Judgment, can console you under the contempt & Detestation of every virtuous Mind. It is you on whom a Mark will be fixed——Hic niger est hunc tu Romane caveto. It is your Name that will in future point the Sting of the bitterest Invective. When every other Epithet of Opprobrium is exhausted, it will be the last Effort of Abuse against a Man to say—He is the Wedderburne of his Day. A BOSTONIAN.

* Shakespear's Othello.

For the Public Advertiser, *Feb.* 21.

To Alexander Wedderburne, *Esq*;

I HAD determined to despise you for the future in Silence. Some Indignity there must be in contending with a Character like yours. Yet I was restrained by the Moderation of my Friends, not by my own Prudence. I know of no Consideration that should withhold a Friend of Virtue from exposing its Foes, to the detestation they deserve. I would therefore plant your pillow with incessant Thorns; pursue you from private into public, from public into private Life, till no Hole should hide your Head from universal Reproach.

A Publication of your Speech, by, I suppose, the squeaking Wretch who is your Informer, convinces me that some Parts of it had escaped my Memory. In others, I am glad to see that even he is ashamed of the Weakness of your Argument, and the Indecency of your Language. He has omitted the contemptible Conundrum, by which you attempted to prove, that Dr. Franklin had *stolen*, that was *your Word*, the Letters in question. I will tell you, had it been my Case how I would have answered you.—My Lords, you have heard Mr. Wedderburne say, I stole these Letters—I hope it will not be construed into any Disrespect of your Lordships, when, in the only Terms adequate to such Language, I tell him, he is an infamous Liar.

The Retailer of your Speech, has softened the Charge into a firm Belief, that "without Fraud, they could not have been got out of the Custody of the Person, whose Hands they fell into." But on what Foundation did you ground this Belief? Will that Person deny, that he gave a great Number of his late Brother's Letters and Papers to the Earl of Suffolk? Will he deny, that he has not given them to other People? Had these identical Letters, therefore, ever been in his Custody, nothing would have been more probable, than their getting abroad with his Consent.

You say Dr. Franklin "very nearly occasioned the Murder of Mr. Whately." The World, I believe, is pretty well convinced, that his own unfair Conduct, in unjustly impeaching the Character of a Gentleman, brought upon him the Chastisement he received. I proved in my last Letter, that Dr. Franklin did avow the Act, as soon as it appeared that such a Discovery was necessary; and that therefore your Abuse of him, on that Ground, was false and malignant.

It is impossible any Thing can be more weak, than your Attempt to prove, that these Letters were not on public Subjects, and to a public Person. What are your Reasons—because one of them contains the Writer's Compliments to an old Lady; and because a Member of Parliament, is not a public Man.——What! a Member of the Legislature, not only for these three Kingdoms, but, according to the new fangled Doctrine, of all America too,—a Member of that Parliament, which Mr. Hutchinson's Letters repeatedly call upon to interpose, to censure the public Measures he represents, and shew Marks of Resentment against his Countrymen was not he a public Man? Is it not an Insult on Common-sense to say, such a Man is not in a public Character, and is it only by confounding our Ideas, that you hope to defend these wicked Men? You chose to omit the strongest Proof of these being private Letters, that is the repeated Stipulations of the avaricious Authors of them for Rewards and Emoluments to themselves. This, and what relates to the old Lady excepted, the rest is entirely on public Subjects. They state, and misstate all the public Proceedings of the Province; they expect and implore the Vengeance of Parliament against the People; they enter minutely into the Constitution of the Colony, and point out what Alterations should be made effectually to abridge their Liberties; every public Event is detailed with a suitable Comment, and all this is to an active Member of that Parliament, from which they expected the Alterations they proposed, and the Vengeance they denounced. "What Marks of Resentment Parliament will shew, says the mild and affectionate Mr. Hutchinson, whether they will be on the Province in general, or particular Persons, is extremely uncertain, but that they will be placed somewhere is most certain." "We soon expect, says Mr. Oliver, the decision of Parliament upon American Affairs, some, I doubt, not without Fear and Trembling." Yet Mr. Wedderburne is the Man, who has the Effrontery to affirm, that these Letters were not written on public Affairs, nor intended to produce public Measures.—But of what Degree of Impudence and Falshood is he incapable? He says they were the Communications of private Friends. Now I affirm, and let him, or any of his Creatures, disprove it if they can, that Mr. Whately never saw Mr. Hutchinson, that they were utterly unknown to each other, that they entered into a Correspondence solely on public Affairs, and with no other earthly View, till that of the latter's private Interest opened to him, but to gratify their mutual Malignity against the Colonies.—With what Colour of Truth then can these be treated as private Letters of Friendship?

But this incautious Advocate has discovered to us a Principle in these Letter Writers, which ought to bring upon them the Resentment of the King as well as of the People. He tells us Mr. Oliver justly observes in one of his Letters, "that they could not be supposed to apply to Mr. Whately, as having an interest with the Ministers, when they knew that he was all that Time voting in Opposition to them." Here then is an Acknowledgment, that Mr. Hutchinson and Mr. Oliver, his Majesty's Lieutenant Governor and Secretary, kept up a secret and factious Correspondence with a Member of Parliament, whom they knew to be voting in Opposition to the Measures of his Majesty's Ministers. They were intended therefore to promote the Purposes of Faction & Opposition to the King's Servants. They were to compel them into hostile Measures with America, however injudicious they might have deemed them. These Men knew, that they were, at that time, many of his Majesty's Servants, who were utterly averse to Hostilities with America; who wished to heal the unhappy Divisions between the two Countries, and by lenient conciliating Measures to restore that Harmony, which the violent and preposterous Councils of Mr. Whately and his Faction had interrupted. Lord Chatham, Lord Shelburne, Lord Granby, and Sir Edward Hawke, were those respectable Persons.—It was for this Reason, the Depth of Machiavelian Politics to furnish a powerful Opposition in Parliament with such Representations as should force the King's Servants from their pacific Purposes. Mr. Whately was only the Jackal to Mr. G. Grenville, on whom the Letters were, in Reality, to operate. Yet these are the Letters which Mr. Wedderburne and his Associates will tell you, contain nothing reprehensible or unworthy the Station and Trust of those who wrote them. These are the Letters which we are to be told do not in any Degree impeach the Honor, Integrity, or Conduct of his Majesty's Governor and Secretary. This then is the Doctrine to be held forth—that the King's Servants in America may by every secret, false, wicked and insidious Art spirit up a Faction here to oppose and embarrass his Majesty's Ministers, not only with Impunity, but with Praise; provided it ultimately tend to injure, oppress and enslave their Countrymen.

A BOSTONIAN.

NEW FLOUR.

Philadelphia FLOUR, Bar Iron,

and a few Pairs of best

LEATHER BREECHES,

TO BE SOLD BY

Joseph-Pearse Palmer,

At the lowest Store, South Side of the Town-Dock.

TO BE *SOLD*, OR *LETT*,

A Dwelling-House in *Roxbury*, with large and very good Accommodations, now, or late, in the Occupation of Messi s. M nroe and Willard; being as good a Situation for Trade, or any public Business, as any in the Town. Enquire, for farther Particulars, of any of the Select-Men of Braintree, or of *Joseph-Pearse Palmer*, of *Boston*.

Boston: Printed, by Edes & Gill *in Queen-Street*, 1774.

THE
Boston-
AND
COUNTRY

No. 996.
Gazette,
JOURNAL.

Containing the freshest Advices, Foreign and Domestic.

MONDAY, May 9, 1774.

REASONS *offer'd to show that the Public had an indisputable Right to Mr.* Hutchinson's *Letters to the late Mr. Whately.*

BECAUSE they were written by a Man in a *public* Station, he being Lieutenant Governor and Chief Justice of this Province; and were addressed to a Man who was also in a *public* Station, a Member of Parliament who was and had been very *influential* in promoting the Stamp Act and every other public Measure relating to America.

Because they were written with a manifest Intention to promote further *public* Measures with Regard to America in general, and this Province in particular; the Writer declaring in one of them in these Words, "My *chief Inducement* in making this Representation is a Regard to the *public* Interest."

Because it is manifest that Mr. Hutchinson considered Mr. Whately as capable of doing much as a *public* Person, in carrying violent Measures against the *public*; and urges his utmost Exertions in the following Words, "With all the Aid you can give," and "if they (the Commissioners, &c.) fail of Support from you," that is, from the Parliament of which you are an active and leading Member, "it is all over with us."

Because the Letters had the most pernicious Tendency and Design towards the *public*; containing not only the most exaggerated Accounts of Facts, but the most palpable Falshoods. Among many others which doubtless the Reader has taken Notice of, I shall only mention one, "A *Barrel of Tar*, says Mr. Hutchinson, was placed on the Beacon in the Night to bring in the Country, when the Troops appeared, and all the Authority of Government was not strong enough to remove it." Mr. Hutchinson could not be Ignorant while he was Writing this, that the *Barrel of Tar* had turned out to be a Nail Cask. He must also have known, for it was notorious long enough before the Date of this Letter, that the Sheriff with not more than three Assistants upon the first Attempt, removed it without the least Opposition; so far was it from being true that the whole Authority of Government was not strong enough to remove it. I mention this Instance, because I think no other Misrepresentation could have shown a more malevolent Design. He knew full well, the difference between representing this as a *Barrel of Tar*, and as it really was an empty Cask. He *knew* that he could not have given a stronger Colouring of a *rebellious* Intention in the People, and consequently that such a Representation would best answer his Design.

Because the public Measures intended to be procured by Mr. Hutchinson were of no less Importance than the posting a standing Army, and an Abridgment of the Liberties of the Charter. That he intended to procure Regiments, appears from the following Circumstances considered collectively, viz. 1st. Hallowell by whom his Letters were sent, carried also the Commissioners Letters to Government, as Paxton tells us in his Letter. 2d. The Commissioners in their Letters strongly urge the sending Troops, "Nothing, say they, but an immediate Exertion of military Force will prevent an open Revolt in this Town which may probably spread thro' the Provinces," and, "It is impossible for us to set Foot in Boston until there are two or three Regiments in Town." 3d. Mr. Hutchinson recommends Hallowell who he knew had this Budget of Letters and refers Mr. Whately to him "for a more full Account" than he chose to give. 4th. Mr. Hutchinson himself, to strengthen and confirm the Commissioners Letters, and compleat the Design of them, tells the Ministry through Hallowell and Whately (for which there was not the least Foundation) that the Council declined to assist the Governor with their Advice; artfully insinuating his own Opinion, that this *ought* to be greatly resented in England, by saying that the Council "*did not consider how much it must be resented* there;" and concluding, with a Representation that we were in a state of *Anarchy*, by saying "It is not possible that this *Anarchy* should last always." And how should a stop be put to it but by external Force from England, that is, *a military Force*, when in this Letter he had told them that "all the internal Authority of the Province took no Notice of it."

Because the publick have a Right to know *who the Person is* that has been the Instrument of bringing upon them the worst of all Calamities. Hallowell went to England in the Month of June, and in October following, a suitable Time to expect the fatal Effects of the Letters, the Troops arrived. It is plain that the Governor expected the Nation would be inflamed, as well he might, when Administration should receive his own Accounts as well as those from the Commissioners, to which *he had given his Sanction*, by his Recommendation of Hallowell the Bearer, as an impartial Intelligencer, tho' he knew he went home burning with Rage against his native Country. I say Mr. Hutchinson expected that his, and the Commissioners Letters sent by Mr. Hollowel, would inflame the Nation against the Province; for he says in his next Letter after the Troops had arrived, "I never dared to think what the Resentment of the Nation would be upon Hallowell's Arrival," whom he had recommended; but he immediately recollects himself and justifies the Measure which he had so great an Influence in promoting; "it is not strange, says he, that Measures should be taken to reduce *the Colonies* to the former State of *Government*." And to be sure it was not strange when so warm a Friend as Mr. Hutchinson had been *suppos'd* to be, had join'd with Bernard and the Commissioners in soliciting such Measures. He then goes on in the same and subsequent Letters to press the Necessity of *continuing* the Troops, by representing "the common People" as "in a Frenzy," "Men in public Posts" as "encouraging them in what is highly Criminal," the Legislature as "Influenced by them," the Executive Power as "having *intirely* lost their Force," His Majesty's Council as a Set of Men "of the most contracted Minds," who "ought to be Censured for their Conduct," and the Crown Officers, himself in particular, as in Danger of being "knock'd in the Head," and that "there was no Security for him but by his quitting his Post" of Chief Justice. And in order that the Troops might be continued, he tells Whately and the Ministry, that "it will be a Work *of Time* to reduce the People back to *just Notions* of Government; that is, as he explains it, to oblige them to submit to "an Abridgment of what are call'd," or they call, "English Liberties."

Because it was best that such Intelligence should be known to come from *him* in a very particular Manner. When he desired in his Letters "that every Thing he Wrote might be kept Secret," the Reason he gave was "because it was best that such Intelligence should *not* be known to come *from him*," lest his Countrymen should be upon their Guard against him, and put it out of his Power any more to Stab them in the Dark. For this very Reason it was right to make them public. Tho' *some* knew him before, there were *but few* that even suspected him. The Commissioners had acted an open Part in Comparison with him, who put on and wore the Guise of Friendship. *Their* Letters were known to be Inimical; *His* were said to be "replete with Tenderness to the People", and many believed it. *They* were kept at Arms distance from the People; but *he* was taken into their Bosom; and while his Designs were undetected, if he had not done it before, might have wounded their very Vitals. Hence it was not only *right*, but it became *necessary* that the Public should know what he had written. Mr. Wedderburne calls them *private Letters*, which is an affront to common Sense; and the Lords of the Committee of Council reported that there was nothing in them unworthy of the Situation Mr. Hutchinson is in, and so it has been determined by *one* Tribunal. They are *still* before the *great Tribunal* of the Public. All impartial Men will agree that there is nothing in them inconsistent with the Character of a Man who is the Instrument in the Hands of a corrupt Administration to carry on the Purposes of despotick Power in America.

The following REMONSTRANCE *was presented to the Justices of the Superior Court at their Sessions in April 1774, by those returned as Grand Jurors of Inquest for the County of* Worcester; *and after some Debate was received by the Court, and ordered to be read publickly by the Clerk.*

WORCESTER, *April* 19, 1774.

To the Honorable His Majesty's Justices of the Superior Court of Judicature, &c. now sitting at Worcester, in and for said County.

WE the Subscribers being returned by our respective Towns to serve as Jurors of Inquest for this Court, beg leave humbly to inform your Honors, that it is agreeable to the sense of those whom we represent, we should not Empannel nor be Sworn into this important Office, provided Peter Oliver, Esq; sits as Chief Justice of this Court; and we would further add, that our own Sentiments perfectly coincide with those of our Constituents, respecting this Matter; so that to whatever inconveniences we expose ourselves, we are firmly Resolved not to Empannel, unless we are first assured that the abovesaid Gentleman will not Act as a Judge in this Court, for the following Reasons.

1st. Because the Honble House of Commons of this Province in their last Sessions, among other Things, Resolved, That Peter Oliver, Esq; hath by his Conduct, rendered himself totally disqualified any longer to Hold and Act in the Office of a Justice of said Court, and ought forthwith to be Removed therefrom.

2d. Because the said House of Commons in their said Sessions did impeach the said Peter Oliver, Esq; of High Crimes and Misdemeanors, (the particulars of said Impeachment we apprehend are known to your Honors, which will excuse us from reciting them at large) to which Impeachment the said Peter Oliver, Esq; hath not yet been brought to Answer; and therefore we apprehend that the Venire bearing Test Peter Oliver, Esq; is illegal: But if we should be mistaken, nevertheless we Remonstrate and Protest against the said Peter Oliver, Esq; acting as Judge on any of the Bills we may find at this Sessions, unless he is Constitutionally acquitted of said Impeachment: Because we apprehend it would be highly injurious to subject a Fellow-Countryman to a Trial at a Bar where one of the Judges is not only Disqualified as aforesaid, but by his own Confession stands convicted in the Minds of the People of a Crime more heinous (in all Probability) than any that might come before him.

These, with other Reasons that might be offered, we hope your Honors will Esteem sufficient to Justify us for Presenting the foregoing Remonstrance.

Joshua Bigelow,	*Silas Bailey,*
Thomas Robinson,	*John Sherman,*
Phinehas Heywood,	*William Henshaw,*
Nathan Walker,	*Nathaniel Carriel,*
Ephraim Doolittle,	*Moses Livermore,*
John Fuller,	*Timothy Bigelow,*
John Tyler,	*William Campbell.*
Daniel Clap,	

After the before-going Remonstrance was read, the Hon. Edmund Trowbridge, Esq; acquainted the Jury, that it was altogether unlikely that Mr. Oliver would attend and take his Seat; and being also informed that the high Sheriff had been a Number of Miles out, in Order to wait on him to Town as is usual, and had returned without him, they retired; and further considering the Inconveniences which might attend a final Refusal, to take their Oaths, on Account of the Delay of Justice it might Occasion, and being unwilling to cast the least Disrespect on the Constitutional Judges present; in the Afternoon were induced to take their Oaths; and accordingly at half after Four o'Clock, P. M. were Sworn, and received the Charge from the Honble Edmund Trowbridge. A JUROR.

THE Grand Jury at the present Term, Voted unanimously, That if Peter Oliver, Esq; should appear and Act as Judge at this present Court, that they would not proceed to Business, but would utterly refuse.

Attest. DAVID WILDER, Foreman.

LONDON.

March 8. Yesterday the Speaker of the House of Commons took the Chair at two o'Clock; and after his Majesty's message to them, relative to the unhappy disturbances in America, was read, Mr. Rice moved, that an address be presented to his Majesty for his great goodness in ordering his message, and the American papers to be laid before that House, and to assure his Majesty that his faithful Commons would, without delay, exert every means in their power to see the laws duly executed in America, &c. He prefaced his motion with a long account of the rise and progress of the American rebellious proceedings, and was much for using spirited measures to bring them to a compliance.

Lord Clare said, he agreed with the Honourable Gentleman, hoped he should find this measure carried thro' with unanimity, therefore seconded the motion.

Mr. Dowdeswell spoke greatly against the propriety of measures that had been heretofore adopted, and said, let those wise heads who brought us into the trouble now extricate us. He was very severe on Administration throughout his speech.

Col. Jennings said he should object to the words "*every* means," and should move an amendment, that "*proper* means."

Colonel Barre, in a *spirited* speech, arraigned the ill advice of using spirited measures, and said, their being thus factious, proved more strongly, that they were bone of our bone, and flesh of our flesh.

The Question concerning the Address was put, and carried.

So much depends upon the measures adopted respecting the Colonies, that it is not hyperbole to say, our very political existence is at stake. The Minister should not advert to those Counsellors who advise severity. The Americans are too powerful to endure with implicit reverence an hostile attack, even from what is called the parent state: they are too spirited to kiss the hand which smites them, and should Administration, by an appeal to the sword, dare to risque the consequence of American allegiance upon the fate of a combat. The mercantile part of this country will have but too much reason to execrate the folly prevalent in the British Councils.

Mar. 9. The assertion of Colonel Barré in the House on Monday, "that the expence of our Military Establishment was at least equal, if it did not exceed that "of FRANCE," must afford matter of astonishment to those who feel for the unnecessary burthens with which their unhappy country is loaded. That a free people should be taxed most insupportably for the maintenance of an immense standing army in a time of profound peace; that the expences incurred by the support of such infamous drones, who fatten on the vitals of the laborious, that these should amount to as much as the FRENCH disburse for the support of their Military Arrangement, is a fact too melancholy to dwell one moment upon, without execrating the hand, head, and heart of the Minister, and wishing the speedy extirpation of a Parliament base enough to countenance the existence of an evil of such magnitude.

Mr. Edmund Burke, in the House of Commons on Monday, vehemently declaimed against the adoption of hostile measures with respect to the Colonies. He affirmed, that the evils subsisting in America were of a CIVIL nature, and that, to propose military remedies for the correction of civil abuses, was to act in direct contradiction to every principle of sound policy; besides the execution of a plan of the kind had been, and would be in every popular Government, found impracticable. The Magistrate must act in concert with the Military, or every effort of the latter would prove futile and abortive. Every law process relative to the life, liberty or property of an English subject, bespoke a POPULAR origin, from the presentment of the Grand Jury to the final adjudication of a Petit Jury. The principles of Government, therefore, should have respect to the DEMOCRACY OF THE CONSTITUTION; and, as that allowed of no appeal to the Sword but in conjunction with the Civil Power, where the Magistracy REFUSED to co-operate, a military force must turn to little account. These positions, applied to America would, Mr. Burke said, hold good in every respect: The introduction of an army would not change the OPINIONS of the Colonists; the men who thought themselves ill-treated now, would not be of different sentiments when the boyonets were pointed to their breasts; and unless, by an alteration of measures, you effected a change in the OPINIONS of men, you might destroy numbers, without being able to establish any permanent sovereignty over the multitudes who survived the sanguinary policy. Mr. Burke concluded by advising a CHANGE OF AMERICAN GOVERNORS, the folly of the present having brought on the mischiefs of which we now complained; and, when the Colonists seemed averse to contend the authority of the Mother Country, one of the Governors [HUTCHINSON] at once to gratify his VANITY & expose his IGNORANCE, absolutely CHALLENGED the Assembly to a dispute about the Right of Taxation, and the first Principles of Legislation! like DUNS SCOTUS, and the Schoolmen of old, who stuck up papers challenging men who held espoused opposite tenets to a public disputation! Was not this TO SINK THE DIGNITY OF A REPRESENTATIVE OF MAJESTY IN THE LOGICAL QUIBBLES OF A WORD CATCHER? Nor was it otherwise than natural that men of this stamp must be CONTEMNED by the wise, and LAUGHED AT EVEN BY THE VULGAR.

NEW-YORK, April 28.

On Sunday night, at 8 P. M. the Committee of Observation returned from the Hook. They inform us, that the sailors of the Tea-Ship, unwilling to proceed with her to London, made a raft of spars and boards, in order to quit the ship with the tide of flood, but were observed by the Captain, and being aided by the Committee, who offered their Assistance to him, they desisted from their project.—That on Sunday at 10 A. M. the ship and sloop, with the Committee, weighed their Anchors and stood to sea; and at 2 P. M. the pilot boat and the Committee's sloop left her at the distance of three leagues from the Hook.

With Capt. Lockyer, in the ship Nancy, went passenger, Capt. James Chambers.

Many persons still suspecting that Capt James Chambers continues privately in this city, they may be assured that he sailed out of the Hook, for London, on Sunday last, on board the Naucey, Capt. Lockyer, who afforded him a very hospital and gentlemanly reception. And whose whole behaviour, during his stay in this city proved him to be a sensible, discreet, and a very well-bred man.

BOSTON, May 9.

FROM the English Papers, Letters, &c. it appears that the Ministry are not a little confounded that the good sense and spirit of the colonies had rendered abortive their late scheme to establish a revenue and monopolize their trade.—That they were at a loss which way to shew their resentment without a greater injury to themselves and the NATION *than to us—That the people in general applaud our conduct, as well as the members of the greatest honor and abilities in both Houses; and our friends say, that if we continue firm and united, we shall ward off the slavery intended, and escape the condition of the people of Ireland and many in England, who can hardly get one meal of flesh for a dinner in a twelvemonth, by reason of taxes, duty, &c. to support placemen and pensioners——that the illiberal treatment of the great Dr. Franklin when he appeared before the Privy Council as the Representative of a great Province, and acted* wholly officially, *is despised by foreigners as well as the independant part of the nation, who now look upon the friends of America in the present dispute with the ministry as the wisest and best friends of Great-Britain—that the commissioners and their tribe were to be removed from this town, and a new Governor and Lieutenant Governor soon appointed—that all parties appeared against risquing any more troops amongst us upon a hostile intention.—Notwithstanding the false and inflammatory accounts transmitted Administration by the Incendiaries of Boston to induce them to take so rash a measure; and that it was questioned whether Ministry would venture to carry into execution the other part of the Incendiaries Scheme for what they call an amending or altering the Constitution, which in plain English is nothing more or less than* vacating or destroying *the Charter of this Province;—that however this may be, the Colonies have acted* a rational *as well as* manly *part in their opposition to measures calculated to reduce them to the most abject and ruinous Slavery; for if in a day of trial, Ministerial force should carry it against the Colonies, in opposition to Law and Right, redress may hereafter be obtained by their own growing Strength if not from the Justice of the nation; but Rights and Privileges once* surrendered *are lost for ever.*

The Conduct of the patriotick Citizens of New-York, with respect to the Teas sent them, after they had been fully apprized of the bluster made by the Friends of Tyranny and Enemies of the Colonies on the other side of the Water, appears as *generous* as it was *spirited* and *necessary*, and may serve to convince Administration, that when Americans perceive Insult added to Oppression and Injustice, they will always resent it in manner becoming the Character of a wise and great People.

The removal of Dr. Franklin from his Place in the Post-Office, for his Faithfulness to Provinces for which he was Agent, is a most injudicious Step of Administration, as it manifests to the World their Intention that no one shall hold a Place, but in subserviency to their detestable Views; and may fully teach the Colonies what is the Design of Ministry in the multiplication of Revenue, Custom-House and Monopoly Officers, and what Americans are to expect from the present set of Placemen and Pensioners.

Let us suppose, says an English Paper, that the Governor and Lieutenant Governor (Hutchinson and Oliver) had written as warmly against the Powers and Prerogative of the King, as they *did write* against the Liberties of the People; let us suppose that these Letters had fallen into the Hands of Sollicitor Wedderburn, what would his System of Morality have led him to do then? Would he have conceal'd or would he have denounced them? He would perhaps in that Case talk of Treason & Misprision of Treason. Tho' the technical Learning of Westminster-Hall may not have taught it to him, yet *there is such a Thing as Treason against the People.* The Rebel to his King is not a greater Culprit, than he who can advise a Minister to deprive three Millions of Subjects of their Birth Rights, and to "abridge those Liberties" which were purchas'd by our Ancestors at the Expence of their best Blood.

Since the Arrival of the last Ships from London, it has been confidently reported that Part of the Contents of one of the Letters written by our *great Man to his Superiors in England, the last Winter, is nearly if not precisely in the following Words,* "There is an absolute Necessity of of 5 or 6 Regiments here; for, let the Faction now say what they will, this Province is in a State of Rebellion; my Daughter was oblig'd to fly with her Infant in her Arms." *This corresponds with what the Ministerial Writers in the Whitehall Evening Post expresly say* "*is Governor Hutchinson's settled Opinion*", *as appears by his Letters read before the House of Commons, viz.* "That no Effort in the Colonies by any Body of Men, Civil or Military, can remove the Evils that now reign among them." *Mr. Hutchinson, in his printed Letters, private and confidential, seems to have principally aim'd at* an Alteration of our Charter; *if then an Alteration should be attempted, we know already to whose Account to place it.* "*There must be an Abridgement of what are called English Liberties.*" "*I wish the Good of the Colony, when I wish to see a further Restraint of Liberty.*" *This was his Language. And in his Letter which was laid before Parliament, we are told that he added,* "Parliament and Parliament only can restore that Country (*America*) to Peace," &c. *And we are further told,* "that his Letters for these six Years past have uniformly inculcated and held forth *the same Doctrine.*" *But though the Destruction of the free Part of our Constitution might be the principal Intention, yet a military Force might be strenuously sollicited, as a necessary Means of effecting it.*

Some of our inquisitive Folks lately asked a certain Patriot, what we were to do, if Troops should be *again* sent to this Town——Do, do says the Patriot, why go *again* to the Old South Meeting-House.

At a General Council last Wednesday the Governor was pleased to nominate *William Brown*, Esq; to be a Justice of the Superior Court in the room of *Nathaniel Ropes*, Esq; deceased; but there being but *seven* Counsellors present, they declined to act on a Matter in which the Lives, Liberties and Properties of the People were so deeply Interested, and it was put off 'till after the next Election of Counsellors.

There is no appointment in this Government, especially under the present situation of our public Affairs, of greater Importance than that of a Judge. It is the *reasonable* Expectation of this People, that Men who are thorough Judges, and have had too much Honor to be made the Instruments in carrying on the Measures of a corrupt Court, should be promoted to the Bench of Justice; and it is *universally* known that there are *such* Men to be found. This depends upon the Circumspection of the Representatives that are now to be chosen *by the People*; for let it be remembered that if only *eight* out of the *twenty-eight* Counsellors to be Elected are such as the Governor can manage, it will be in his Power by exercising his Prerogative of *Negativing* (and possibly this may be his *Intentions* of making those *eight* a *Majority* of a legal Council,) and Consequently of *appointing* such Judges as he shall be pleased to *nominate.*

Yesterday arrived here his Majesty's Ship Mercury from London.

This Day Mr. William Goddard set out on his Return Homewards, taking Providence, Newport and the principal Towns in Connecticut in his Way. The last mentioned Colony is the only one in New-England who has not greatly encouraged his Undertaking, and there can hardly be a Question whether a Plan, so conservative of American Liberty, will be favoured by that patriotic People or no, when laid before them.

We hear the Boatswain of his Majesty's Ship Tamer, who was under Sentence of Death for Mutiny, is pardon'd by Admiral Mantagu.

MARRIED.] *Richard Boynton*, Esq; to Mrs. *Annapell Greene*, Widow of the late Capt. *Nathaniel Greene.*—Mr. *Stickney* to Miss *Nabby Blodget*, Daughter of *Samuel Blodget*, Esq; of Goff-Town in New-Hampshire.

DIED.] Mrs. Elizabeth Welch, aged 38 Years, Consort of Capt. Hezekiah Welch, Distiller.

Mr. Isaac Vergoose, aged 69. His Funeral is to be attended on Wednesday next.

In London. Thomas Hollis, Esq; F. R. S.

At Woburn. Mr. Nathan Brooks, Aged 20.

At Dunstable in New-Hampshire, Mrs. Rebecca Blanchard, aged 63, Widow of the late Hon. Joseph Blanchard, Esq; of that Place.

For *LONDON*,

The Brig LEOPARD, BENJAMIN GORHAM, Master, Laying at Col. HANCOCK's Wharf, has genteel Accommodations, and will sail with all possible Dispatch One Third Part of her Cargo being already engaged: For Frieght or Passage apply to JONATHAN WILLIAMS, jun'r. in Ann-Street.

☞ As said WILLIAMS proposes to embark in the above Vessel he earnestly requests those Gentlemen who are Indebted to him to make immediate Payment.

TO BE SOLD,

BY Order of Court, a Dwelling-House, Sail-Loft, Cooper's Shop, Wharff and Flatts, &c. scituate, lying and being near Fish-Street, at the Northerly Part of Boston, being Part of the Estate of Captain John Dobel, late of Boston, Mariner, deceas'd. For Terms, apply to JACOB COOPER, Attorney to Joseph Doble, Executor to said Estate.

TO BE SOLD,

BY Order of Court, a Dwelling-House and two Acres and one Quarter of Land, in the Town of Lynn, being Part of the Estate of Capt. Benjamin Chadwell, late of Boston, Mariner, deseased, Intestate. For Terms of Sale, apply to JACOB COOPER.

TO BE SOLD

A TOPSAIL SCHOONER with her Appurtenances, now lying at Spear's Wharff.—Also, a Parcel of Rye, Beans and Flour, being Part of the Estate of Capt. Samuel Snow.——Inquire of Jacob Cooper, Attorney to Sarah Snow, Administratrix to said Estate.

ALL Persons indebted to the Estate of Capt. Samuel Snow, late of Boston, Mariner deceased, Intestate, are desired to make speedy Payment to Jacob Cooper, Attorney to the Administratrix.

TO BE SOLD at Publick VENDUE,

On Wednesday the Eighth of June next,

At five o'Clock in the Afternoon,

on the Premises, unless Sold before at Private Sale.

Two Dwelling Houses, very conveniently Scituated in BOSTON, the one near the Draw Bridge in Ann-Street; and the other in Bennett Street, near Dr. Elliot's Meeting-House. They being Part of the Real Estate of *James Halsey*, late of said Boston deceased.—For Particulars, apply to *Anna Halsey* Widow, Relict of said *James Halsey*.

TO be Sold, a SLOOP 80 Tons Burthen, Four Years old, a fast Sailer, and extremely well found, laying at *Minot*'s T. Inquire of ELISHA THATCHER.

To the FREE ELECTORS of the MASSACHUSETTS-BAY.

Friends and Brethren,

FOR some Years past I have thought myself able, from a local Advantage only, to offer some Things not unworthy your Attention at the Season of your Choice of Representatives. But, the happy Establishment of Correspondence by Town-Committees bringing every *secret* Plot of the Enemies of our Constitution speedily to Light, and being also an extensive Channel of the wisest Counsels, I thought my usual Appearance in this Gazette would not fail to receive the Brand of VANITY. This accounts for my Silence thus far lately. My Fears on that Score are at Length superseded by the Dread of a more severe Stigma, that of TIMIDITY. In the first Case, Self-Love only would be pained; in the last, my Patriotism would be deeply wounded. For, insignificant as I may really be, yet having repeatedly exalted myself before the public Eye, Timidity, just at this Time, even in *me* might chance to have *public* ill Consequences: I therefore fly from the very Appearance of it.

While the most crude and frantic Menaces are uttered with more than papal Insolence by some in Britain, there are not wanting here a Number of basely imitative Wretches to eccho in our Ears *Fleets, Armies* and *Annihilation*. Nor is it to be expected but that the British Ministry's Servant, our detected, pension'd Enemy, who to the Scandal of all well-planned Government *continues* in the Chair, should give all possible Height of Colouring to that Picture of Terror. We have experienced much Insult, the natural Fruit of his Situation, ever since the Day his Interest was changed, and made opposite to that of the Province; and surely additional Haughtiness may be expected now, when he stalks in a fresh Suit of Tinsel Honor, derived from his late Mock-Tryal.

You will therefore, Brethren in one common Cause, look out for Men of *known Resolution* for your Representatives in *our* Parliament. It is hard, I think, to find any who do not *know* your Rights and Privileges, but you may meet unhappily with some who are too timorous properly to *claim* and *defend* them.

It is said publickly in England that you elect "too many Representatives." The Parchments of Commission and the appropriated Chest of Bribery are found insufficient to debauch a Majority of the present Number; therefore the more frugal Method of Intimidation will probably be attempted to bring about base Compliances and Resignation. Guard well against such an Attempt by giving your Votes for those Men only whose *sound Principles* are backed with a *resolute Spirit*; and confirm them still further by your INSTRUCTIONS.

AN ELECTOR, 1774.

WANTED *immediately*,

A long, strong BOOM,

that will reach from Cape-Cod to Cape-Ann.——Any Person having such an One to dispose of, will meet with a good Price, by applying to

N***H.

N. B. *The Distance is only 18 Leagues.*

Samuel Abbot

INFORMS his Customers and others, That he has IMPORTED in the last Ships from LONDON, An Assortment of *English* and *India* GOODS, Cutlery Ware, Nails, Glasses, &c. which he is now selling off on very low Terms for Cash, at his Store on Green's Wharff, near the East-End of the Market.

N. B. He once more Requests all Persons indebted to the late Co-partnership of Samuel Abbot, and Company, to call on him for an immediate Settlement.

David Sears

Acquaints his Friends and the Publick that he has Just receiv'd by Capt. *Calef*,

A large and fresh Assortment, of European and India GOODS, which were bought on the very best terms, and are now Opening at his shop directly opposite Liberty-Tree, where he is determined to dispose of them on as good terms as they can be bought in Town by Wholesail or Retail for CASH only.

N. B. He returns his hearty Thanks to his Customers for their Favours the Year past, and assures them he will shew them his gratitude in the lowness of his Prices.

Cyrus Baldwin,

HEREBY notifies his Customers and others, That he purposes to embark for London early next Fall; and that he is now selling off his Stock in Trade, consisting of large and valuable Assortments of ENGLISH, INDIA, and SCOTCH GOODS, very cheap for Cash at his Store in Cornhill, near the Town-House in Boston. (The Particulars in our next.)

Samuel Grant and Son,

ACQUAINT their Customers and others, that they have IMPORTED in the last Vessels from LONDON, a fresh Supply of ENGLISH and INDIA GOODS;

ALSO—all sorts of UPHOLSTERY, which they will sell at the lowest advance for Cash, at their Shop in Union-Street, near the Market, BOSTON.

☞ A good assortment of PAPER HANGINGS.

Lee and Jones,

HAVE Imported in the several Vessels this Spring, from England, and have for Sale at their Store near the Swing-Bridge, very cheap,——A general Assortment of *Piece Goods*, suitable for the Season.

Also, A few Cases of *blue and white China Cups and Saucers*.

A large Assortment of *Paper Hangings*.

Looking Glasses.

Silver and Pichbeck Watches.

Gold & Silver Lace, and Gold & Silver Buttons.

A beautiful Variety of Brocades and flower'd Lutestrings, coloured Taffaties and Grograms.

A few exceeding neat Tambour-work'd Ruffles and Aprons.

TO BE SOLD

Forty Thousand Red-Oak Hogshead STAVES, and *Thirty Thousand* White-Oak ditto:—Inquire of JOHN NEWEL, near the Draw-Bridge, Boston.

TO BE SOLD

AT PUBLICK AUCTION,

By Benjamin Church,

On THURSDAY next,

At Ten o'Clock in the Forenoon,

At the usual Place of Sale,

Irish Linnens—Cotton and Linnen Checks—Bed Ticks—Ozenbrigs—Shalloons—Tammies—Calamancoes—a variety of beautiful Silks—Damascus—Tobines—Cordesoys—Lorettees—Superfine Moree Gowns—Mens & Womens Hose—Cutlery Wares, &c. House Furniture—an eight Day Clock—a second hand Chaise—Watches, &c. &c. &c.

At THREE o'Clock, P. M.

N. B. On Thursday the 26th Instant, there will be Sold a large and valuable Assortment of Silks, Linnens, Woolens, &c. —The Particulars in the next Paper.—

New AUCTION-ROOM, Cornhill.

TO-MORROW at TEN o'Clock will be Sold by PUBLIC VENDUE, at GREENLEAF's Auction-Room,—

An Assortment of English Goods, some Cutlery, Hard Ware, House Furniture & Apparel.

WILLIAM GREENLEAF, Auctioneer.

The Sale will begin precisely at Ten o'Clock.

All Persons having Demands on the Estate of John Goodwin, Mariner, late of Boston, deceased, are desired to bring in their Accounts to Levi Beal, Administrator on said Estate: And all those indebted to said Estate are desired to pay the same immediately.

All Persons indebted to, or that have any Demands on the Estate of Mr. John Parker, late of Sandwich, Merchant, deceased, are desired to bring in their Accounts to Joseph Parker, of Falmouth, sole Executor to said Estate, in Order for Settlement.

TO BE SOLD the Real Estate of said Deceased, consisting of a large Dwelling-House, Barn, &c. lying in said Sandwich, very suitable for a Gentleman's Seat, or Trader. For Particulars, inquire of said Executor.

Any Person or Persons who would undertake to erect a Saw Mill, or Grist Mill, or both, on the Township Granted to *Samuel Livermore*, Esq; and others, lying on both Sides *Androscogging*-River, adjoining Sylvester Township in the County of Cumberland, are desired to send the Terms on which they would undertake to erect either, or both of said Mills to *Leonard Williams*, Esq; Lieut. *Elijah Livermore* of Waltham, *Richard Woodward* of Dedham, *William Campbell* of Oxford, *Seth Adams* of Boston, *Ebenezer Marshall* of Framingham, or of *Jeremiah Whittemore* of Spencer, or ether of them (they being a Committee appointed by the Proprietors of said Township, to receive the Proposals of any Person or Persons who would undertake said Service) on or before the last Wednesday of June next.

TO BE SOLD,

A Farm adjoining to Kennebunk-River, in the Township of Wells, containing about 50 Acres, two Thirds of it under good Improvement, and in due Proportion for Tillage, Mowing and Pasturage.—The Situation exceeding convenient for a Trader or Tradesman, lying at the Head of the Tide. The House and Barn well finished, within 15 Rods of the principal Landing for Boards and other Lumber, and adjoining the Interest of Waldo Emerson, deceased, a late prosperous Merchant in those Parts. Also within a Mile of the Meeting-House, and near two Grist-Mills, Saw-Mill, Iron-Works and Building Yard.——Conditions of Sale, &c. may be known at Capt. Kimball's in said Wells, Innholder, or of Moses Little, Esq; Merchant in Newbury-Port. Wells, April 25, 1774.

On WEDNESDAY 11th Inst.

At Ten in the Morning,

Will be Sold by PUBLIC VENDUE,

At RUSSELL's Auction Room in Queen-Street,

Callicoes, Chinces and printed Cottons, Irish Linnens, lac'd Sattins, figur'd and plain Lawns, fine Damask Table Cloths, Diaper ditto, 3 qrs. and 6-qrs, Huckabucks, Silk & Linnen Handkerchiefs, fine and coarse Sheetings, Dowlasses, a variety of beautiful Ribbons, a fine assortment of best double gilt Buttons, Buckrams, Oznabrigs, colour'd Threads, a large Quantity of Straw Hatts, a quantity of Cod Lines and Twine, Cod Hooks, Velvet Coks, Men's Wearing Apparell, &c. &c. J. RUSSELL, Auctioneer.

ALL Persons having Demands on, or are Indebted to the Estate of the late Mrs. *Mary Grice*, deceased, are desired to bring in their Accompts as soon as may be, to *Ebenezer Torry*, Administator on said Estate, in order for a speedy Settlement.

ON FRIDAY NEXT,

At TEN in the Morning,

Will be Sold by PUBLIC VENDUE,

At the House of the late Mrs. *Mary Grice*, deceas'd,

Near the Old Brick Meeting;

All the Wearing Apparel and House Furniture of said deceas'd——consisting of——

Silk Gowns, &c. &c. Also, Tables, Chairs, Looking Glasses, Chest of Draws, Desks, Feather Beds, Bedsteds and Bedding, a variety of China and Glass Ware—some Plate, Kitchen Furniture, &c. &c.—Also,—a large Copper of at least Three Barrels.—

J. RUSSELL, Auctioneer.

_ The Goods may be viewed the Day before the Sale. FRIDAY next—at X o'Clock.

☞ A very genteel new Chaise and Harness, at private Sale.

On THURSDAY the 26th Instant,

At NINE in the Morning,

Will begin the Sale at PUBLIC VENDUE,

At RUSSELL's Auction-Room in Queen-Street,

A large and valuable Collection of new and old BOOKS, in almost every Branch of polite Literature.

_ Printed Catalogues may be had gratis the Monday preceeding the Sale, of J. RUSSELL, Auct'r.

At GOULD's *Auction-Office*, In Back-Street.

On Friday next, at Ten o'Clock in the Morning,

Will be Sold by PUBLIC VENDUE,

A Variety of *English, Scotch*, and Hard Ware GOODS.

ALSO—At ONE o'Clock precisely, will be put up A very handsome new Chaise, one Second Hand Ditto, both with Harnesses compleat.

R. GOULD, Auctioneer.

N. B. At said Office may be had at PRIVATE SALE, genuine Scotch SNUFF, by the Cask or Dozen, and a small Invoice of white Threads, from No. 6, at 50, exceeding low.

At GOULD's *Auction Office*,

In Back-Street,

On THURSDAY the 26th Inst. at Nine o'Clock in the Morning will be Sold by PUBLIC VENDUE,——A large and valuable Collection of

BOOKS, chiefly new & neatly Bound.

—Amongst the many celebrated Authors that Compose this truly Valuable Collection, I shall only insert the few following, viz.——Milton—Pope—Swift—Addison—Young—Stearns—Thompson—Smollet—Rollin—Guthrie—Salmon—Flavell—Hervey—Doddridge—Stackhouse—Owen—Fordyce—Ambrose—Burkett—Willson—Boston—Sherlock, &c. &c. &c.

N. B. The BOOKS may be viewed two Days before the Sale. R. GOULD, Auctionesr.

To be sold at private Sale,

At FALLASS's VENDUE-OFFICE,

Square and round Mehogany Tables, an 8-Day Clock, a second-hand Chaise & Harness, and as neat a genteel Chaise and Harness as any in Boston, hangs on Steel Springs, to be sold very cheap.

Wm. FALLASS, Auctioneer.

The Subscriber begs Leave to acquaint the Publick, That he being appointed by the Select-Men one of the Vendue Masters in this Town, has opened his Room on Dock-Square, next the King's Arms Tavern, where he us'd formerly to keep; has to sell on Monday and Tuesday next, English and Scotch Goods, Houshold Furniture, Wearing Apparel, &c. &c.—and those Gentlemen who are disposed to offer Goods, Merchandize, &c. at public Sale, may depend upon his best and constant Endeavours, by his Industry and Fidelity, to recommend himself to the Continuance of their Favours. DAVID SYMONDS.

CUSTOM-HOUSE, *BOSTON*.

ENTETRD IN.

Callahan, London; Bubier, Fa'mouth; Ross, St. Croix; Coit, Cape Nichola; Bass, Jamaica and Cape Nichola; Baker Jamaica; Lee, Martinico; Wilbur, Rhode-Island; Gorham & Brecket, Maryland; Sqiuer, Burrough, Harrison, Hull and Rice, Newhaven; Bernard, New-York.

Burials in the Town of BOSTON, since our last.

Six Whites. Three Blacks.

Baptiz'd in the several Churches, Nine.

High Water at BOSTON, for the present Week.

Monday, 45 min. aft. 10	Friday, 17 min. after 1
Tuesday, 20 min. aft. 11	Saturday, 8 min. af. 2
Wednesday, 0 m. aft. 12	Lord's-Day, 59 m af. 2
Thursday, 20 min. aft. 12	D's New 10 D 11 M rn

From the Public Ledger, *March* 9, 1774.

To ALEXANDER WEDDERBURNE, *Esq*;

WE left your mild, your honest, your amiable friend. Mr. Hutchinson employing the secret correspondence, which is now deemed so sacred for the public purposes of driving the people to despair. The aim of all his actions, the object of all his wishes was to provoke the people to some act of violence, which might effectually prevent a reconciliation, and bring upon them the utmost indignation of Great Britain. In the eyes of America what can be worse, in the eyes of England what ought to be worse, than such principles and such practices? Who is it can more deserve the collected indignation of the whole Community than the man who is secretly labouring to prevent that accommodation between Great Britain and her Colonies, which alone can render us happy at home and formidable abroad? Is it an act of atrocious wickedness to sow dissentions in a private family, and fatally to inflame the mind of a Father against a Son?—What name then shall we find for Mr. Hutchinson's crime, in kindling an unextinguishable animosity in the great family of the Nation, and urging the Parent state to plunge the sword into the bosom of her Children?

Yet this is the man whom you had the effrontery to declare to us was "obnoxious only because he had stopt the train, which Dr. Franklin's constituents had laid to blow up the Province into a flame." This avowed Incendiary, whose own acknowledged Letters witness, that what Dr. Franklin's Constituents wished, was to be restored to their former tranquility and peace, which it was his hope and aim to prevent. Because he successfully employed that hypocrisy, which Milton justly describes, as the—— only evil, that walks invisible through heaven and earth, to deceive the people into an opinion of his good intentions towards them, at the moment in which he was contriving their destruction; therefore, when his wicked schemes are detected, they ought not to complain of him. The very circumstance which aggravates his guilt, is by the peculiar propriety of your logic, produced in his defence.

But his enmity to the Liberties of the People atones for every crime. That Impudence and scurrility, which was driven with indignation from the Scotch bar, is therefore brought forward here to defend him, and calumniate his accusers.—What an indeliable stain to the decency and justice of an English Court? Yet who else could have been found hardy and indecent enough to justify Mr. Hutchinson in the face of his own factious and inflammatory Letters? But it seems his "private Letters now breath nothing but moderation. He loves the Soil, the Constitution, the People of New England; he looks with reverence to this Country, and with affection to that. For the sake of the People he wishes some faults corrected, Anarchy abolished, and Government re-established; but these salutary ends he wishes to promote by the gentlest means; and the abridging of no Liberties, which a People can possibly use to its own advantage."——Amiable, artless, upright man! But has not this been his constant cant? Is not his hypocrisy now unveiled? And does he again expect to deceive? Will you assure us that Mr. Hutchinson has not, on this occasion, practised the Art which he has on others, and sent two sets of letters, totally different, to be produced here at the discretion of his friends? When the whole of this honest Gentleman's manœuvres are unfolded, as they shall be, the world will stand astonished at the cunning and wickedness of his conduct. You, Mr. Solicitor, will then recommend him, as Sir Francis Bernard, from an intimate knowledge of him, has already done as *one* who may be *trusted like yourself*. Such a recommendation will finish his character, and render his infamy immortal.

Governor Hutchinson has given us upon record, a flagrant proof of the honesty of his professions when the Assembly were in possession of his letters, he publicly declared in his message to them, "that he was not conscious of any letters which could have a tendency to subvert the constitution, and that he never wrote any *public* or *private* letters with such intention."

This assertion was made at a time when it was given out, and he believed, the letters would be made public: He therefore determined to meet the resolves of the Assembly, with a desperate declaration, which might put the people at large in doubt whether he merited the imputation thrown upon him: But he was taken in his own snare, for, when the letters were published, the people reading a direct declaration that "their liberties must be abridged," beheld him universally in the detestable light of a pernicious hypocrite, a secret plotter against their chartered rights, and a criminal capable of the most hardy and atrocious falshoods. His adherents, for friends he has none, were struck dumb, and he himself, overwhelmed with confusion, and bereft for once of his faculties, stood the silent mark of universal detestation.

After this, Sir, do you expect that his arts will ever again influence the People, or render them the dupes of his hypocrisy? Do you conceive his professions will regain their confidence, however aided by the decent and conciliating perswasives of their speech? For my part, Sir, I have my fears, that even the very mild and candid report of his Majesty's Privy Council, which you have affixed to the second edition of your much admired speech, upon the Petition of their Representatives, will not entirely convince them that their Governor is innocent, and they themselves misled. I am apprehensive, that, deaf to his profession, to your arguments, and to this report you have procured, the people will still think Governor Hutchinson an infamous hypocrite, and a dangerous enemy to their rights and the liberties of his country.

A BOSTONIAN.

CHARLESTOWN, (*South-Carolina*) *March* 28.

The following is a copy of the agreement at the general meeting of the people on the 16th instant, and is now signing in different parts of the province, most of the Representatives having set the example, viz.

WHEREAS an insidious attempt hath been made, by the Ministry, to promote the sale of Teas burthened with a duty laid without our consent, and thereby to tax the good people of America contrary to the constitution thereof: We, the subscribers, being determined to secure to ourselves, and to our posterity, that liberty which our ancestors have obtained and secured, at the expence of their lives and properties, have, this 16th day of March, 1774, *come to the following resolutions, viz,*

1. *That NO TEAS (except such as, having been order'd before the 3d of December last, shall arrive on or before the 16th of April next) shall be imported, landed, bought or sold, until the Act of the 7th of* GEO. III. *Chap.* 46, *commonly called the American Revenue Tea Act, be totally and clearly repealed.*

2. *That the East-India Company's Tea now lying in a cellar under the Exchange, shall not be sold in this province, or removed from the place where it now lies, unless to be put on ship board to be carried off the province, while subject to such duty: And, that we will, by every means in our power, prevent such sale or removal.*

III. *If any person shall import, buy or sell any Tea, contrary to the first abovementioned resolution, That we will have no dealings with such person.*

F L O U R.

A Quantity of the Newest Philadelphia FLOUR, to be SOLD uncommonly Cheap by

Joshua Blanchard, jun'r.

At his Store on Dock Square, Boston. ALSO,
Choice Florence Oil per Chest or Flask,
Cheshire and Gloucester Cheese,
2000 of Narragansett Ditto,
Lisbon Oil per Cask, Gallon or less,
Cocoa and Chocolate warranted pure,
Raisins and best Turkey Figs, per Cask,
French, Spanish and Carolina Indigo,
A Quantity of excellent Bacon, and
All kinds of West-India Goods and Groceries as Cheap as at any Store or Shop in Town.

SPRING GOODS

Extreamly Cheap.

JUST IMPORTED BY

John Barrett & Sons,

Near the MILL-BRIDGE,

A most elegant and compleat Assortment of

English, India and Scotch

GOODS,

Suited to the Season,

With all Kinds of *London, Bristol, Sheffield,* and *Birmingham*

Hard Ware and Cutlery Goods,

Which being excellent in Quality, and advantageously purchased, they can engage to sell, by Wholesale and Retail, on such Terms, for *Cash or short Credit,* as cannot fail to give universal Satisfaction to their Customers.——

The Variety is such as to render an Enumeration of the Articles *rather tedious* to their Friends; they shall therefore only quote a *few,* which may serve as some Specimen of their Assortment, viz.

Chints, Calicoes and *Patches* of all Kinds and Prices, and of the newest Fashion,
Nankeens, Fustians,
Jeans, Damascus,
Lorettos, Brunswicks,
Mozeens, *Bengals,*
White Dimothy striped, plain and figured,
Book, strip'd, *check'd* and *sprig'd Muslin,*
Cambricks and Lawns,
Flowering & Nuns Thread,
Gauzes, Catgut,
Patent and Spider Net,
Dutch Laces,
Silk & Muslin Gauze Aprons and Handkerchiefs,
Lawn Ditto,
Fine Chip Hats,
A very great Variety of black Bone & blond Lace,
White blond & *Thread ditto* and *Edging,*
Black, blue, crow & great Variety of brown, olive & cloth coloured *Padusoys,*
Grey, green, crow, olive, barre and cloth colour'd Ducapes,
Cloth colour'd, black, pink, grey, blue, straw, and the most beautiful shot or changeable *Lutestrings* and *Mantuas,*
Striped and brocaded ditto,
Rich black Sattin,
White ditto,
English Damasks,
A great Variety of plain and figur'd, wide and Pelong Sattins of all Colours,
Skeleton and Cap Wire,
Cinnamon, Mace,
Nutmegs, Cloves.

An Assortment of the most fashionable fine and SUPERFINE BROAD-CLOTHS,—with suitable Linings and Trimmings,
White, pink, straw, blue and black narrow *Modes, Persians & Sarsnets,* ditto wide English and India,
A Variety of English and India Taffeties,
Rich Double Allopeen, plain and changeable,
Silk & Worsted Sagathees,
Silk and *Thread Mitts,* and *Gloves,*
Silk, Thread & Cotton Hose of all Prices,
Black Breeches Patterns,
Duroys, *Corduroys,* or *Royal Rib,*
Cantoon, Stay Tick,
White & col'd *Russia Drab,*
Russia Diaper, Clouting do.
Checks of all Kinds,
Ravens Duck, Huckabuck,
A large Assortment of *Irish Linens,* exceeding low,
Handkerchiefs of every sort,
Marking Canvass,
Table Linen, Shirt Buttons,
Superfine plated & Gold and Silver Thread Buttons,
Tiffany, Hat-Crape,
French & English Necklaces,
A large & elegant Assortment of Ribbons, &c. &c.
Nails, Pewter, Steel,
GUN-POWDER & Shot,
Glass 6 by 8, 10 by 8, and 7 by 9,
A fine Assortment of Looking-Glasses,
Writing-Paper,
Ink-Powder, *&c. &c.*

Province of MASSACHUSETTS-BAY. *April* 29, 1774.

WHEREAS Application hath been made to me the Subscriber, by more than one Sixteenth Part of the Proprietors of the Township of Neshobe, in the Province of New-York, to grant a Warrant for calling a Proprietors Meeting for Neshobe, for the following Purposes, viz.—To give public Notice to all the Proprietors of the Township of said Neshobe, which was granted by his Excellency *Benning Wentworth,* Esq; late Governor of *New-Hampshire,* to Capt. *Josiah Powers* and his Associates in the Year 1771, that there is to be a Proprietors Meeting for said Neshobe, held at the Dwelling-House of *Benjamin Simons,* of *Williamstown,* in the County of *Berkshire,* and Province of *Massachusetts-Bay,* Innholder, on the third Wednesday of *June* in this present Year 1774, at One of the Clock in the Afternoon, then and there to do the following Business, viz. 1st. To choose a Moderator. 2dly. To choose a Proprietor's Clerk. 3dly. To see what Measures the Proprietors will come into for the Division of said Neshobe, and what will be most for the Benefit of said Propriety, and to act thereon as they shall judge best and most proper for the good of said Propriety.

W. BRATTLE,
Justice of the Peace thro' said Province.

IN Pursuance of the above Warrant the Proprietors are hereby Notified to meet at the Time and Place appointed, to transact the above Articles

BENJA. POWERS, Proprietor's Clerk.

Boston, April 29th, 1774.

Joseph Peirce

HAS IMPORTED by Captain SYMMES, (who is just arrived from LONDON) and is now opening at his Shop in Kingstreet, nearly opposite the North Door of the Town-House, BOSTON,

DUTCH LACES
Of all Widths,
INDIA CALICOES (very low)
A *beautiful variety* of
CHINTZ and CALICOE PATTERNS,
Royal Rib,
Cotton Denim,
Spotted Jean,
CORDUROYS,
Silk COREUSOYS,
Crimson Silk SASHES for Officers,
New GORGETS for ditto,
Brocades,
Rich Blue, Black and White Sattins,
Rich Leather mounted and other Fans,
Brussels and Mecklin Laces,
English brocaded and other Pumps,
Mens and Youths white and brown Holland and Beaver Gloves,
Ladies white Beaver furred Riding Hats,
Mens white Beaver Hats,
Boys white and black turn-up Brim Hats,
Irish Linens of all Widths and Prices,
Checks ditto ditto,
Ravens Duck,
Dowlass,
Sheeting,
Russia Drabs,
Muslins and Cambricks,
A large Assortment of Mens, Womens and Childrens Thread, Cotton and Silk Hose,
White and Black Silk Breeches Patterns,
All Colours Worsted ditto,
White KERSEYMERE,
Black embroidered Coat Loops,
Neat Patent Wove Stays.

With a great Variety of other Articles, all which his Customers and others may be assured he will sell at a very small Profit for READY MONEY.

CHINA WARE,

Nathaniel Greenough

HAS just imported in Captain Calef——With a large Assortment of Goods suitable for the Season, which he is determined to sell at his usual very low Price. There are too many Articles to mention particularly here. Besides it would be rather tedious for his good Friends to read a long Advertisement. If they will again favour him with their Presence at his Store, two Doors Northward of the Post-Office in Cornhill, he will esteem it an Honour to wait on them himself; and assures them they shall be well rewarded for Pains and Kindness.

N. B. Irish Linnens from 6s. to 40s. per Yard.——Nutmegs, Cloves, Cinnamon and Mace, fresh, good and cheap.

TO be Sold at Publick Vendue on the first Day of June next, at the House of Mr. *Edward Richardson,* Innholder in Watertown, if not Sold before at Private Sale.——A FARM lying in said Watertown, contains about 40 Acres of choice good Land, is all well Fenced into suitable Apartments, with good Stone Walls, has on it, a good House and Barn, two good Wells of Water, a Variety of all kinds of Fruit, is well accommodated for Mowing, Pasturage and Tillage, &c. For the Particulars of the Sale inquire of Mr. JOHN STRATTON, now living on the Premises.——

—The Sale to begin at 3 o'Clock Afternoon.—

April 18th, 1774.

ALL Persons Indebted to, or that have any Demands on the Estate of Mr. *John Hunter,* late of Marlborough, in the County of Middlesex, Victualler, deceas'd, are desired to bring in their Accounts to *Edward Hunter,* Administrator on said Estate, (or to *Andrew Campbell* of Boston, Attorney to said Hunter) in Order for Settlement.

Stop Thief and Runaway Man Servant.

WHEREAS WILLIAM HAYWARD, Baker, absconded himself from my Service 16th March, 1774, and took with him to the Value of *Eight Pounds,* L. M. and he being taken and convicted, voluntarily Bound himself, to serve me Six Months, to Pay Damages & Cost; and he last Night absconded himself again; had on an old Felt Hat, an old cloth colour'd Coat and Waistcoat, check'd Woolen Shirt, a Pair of new cloth colour'd Breeches, a Pair of old pale blue Stockings, and a Pair of single Sole Shoes.—Said Hayward is about Thirty-three Years of Age, Five Feet Five Inches high, darkish short Hair, and down look like a Rogue and Thief.——Whosoever will take up said Servant and Notify me the Subscriber so that I may have him again, shall have FIVE DOLLARS Reward, paid by me,

Marlboro' April 9, 1774. ISAAC SHERMAN.

All Bakers are hereby Cautioned against Employing said Servant.

Boston: Printed, by EDES & GILL,

THE
Boston-
AND
COUNTRY

No. 996.
Gazette,
JOURNAL.
Containing the freshest Advices, Foreign and Domestic.

MONDAY, May 16, 1774.

Since our last arrived here from London, *the Captains* Jenkins, Shayler, Mowat, Scott, *and* Lyde, *by whom we have the following very* interesting *and* important *Advices, viz.*

LONDON, *March* 28.

HOUSE of COMMONS.

Substance of the DEBATES on the BOSTON PORT-BILL.

THE House on Wednesday resolved itself into a Committee on the Boston port-bill. Sir Charles Whitworth having taken the chair the debates opened in the following manner.———Mr. Fuller said, his wish was to make an alteration in the bill by exacting a fine previous to blockading the port. He agreed that the port of Boston was of infinite consequence and the greatest utility imaginable to Great Britain, that the bill under consideration was without a precedent, as the instances of Edinburgh and Glasgow which had been adduced, were not by any means cases in point, that blocking up the port was a punishment infinitely too severe for the first offences; that the Bostonians, upon the first resistance, will refuse to remit the money they owe you; that nothing but confederacies would spring up among them; that he was strongly of opinion, that this bill could not be carried into execution without a military force; that if a small number of men were sent over, the Boston militia would immediately cut them to pieces; that if you send over a larger number, 6 or 7000, the Americans will debauch them; and by these means we should only hurt ourselves. I would begin (says he) by an amercement; nor would I wish this bill to take place, until they had refused the payment of it; I apprehend that about 15,000l. would make amends to the India Company, and in some measure be a relief to the Custom-house officer, who has been tarred and feathered, and where damages are done by unknown persons, the community should be made to pay; he therefore wished that the House would adopt the amendment he had proposed.

MR. HERBERT opposed the measure which Mr. Fuller proposed; said the proposition would by no means relieve us, but throw us into greater difficulties. He said, the Bostonians would certainly resist the payment of the fine; that we must then have recourse to this method; the measure proposed was still more likely to be resisted than the bill, because the fine would be laid on all America; this would induce others to join in the opposition, who before were not concerned in it; he said the Americans were a strange set of people, and that it was in vain to expect any degree of reasoning from them; that instead of making their claim by argument, they always chose to decide the matter by *tarring* and *feathering*; that the method now proposed in the Bill would become more a punishment by their refusal, than by their compliance; that the Americans alone were the persons by whose behaviour the lenity or severity of the measure was to be proved; he therefore should agree to the Bill, in preference to the amendment proposed.

LORD NORTH said, however great his obligations were to the candour and public spirit of the honourable Gentleman who made the motion, yet he differed very much from him in the amendment proposed. His Lordship observed, that though the honourable Gentleman had said it was the *first* offence, yet upon recollection he was very sure he would not be of that opinion, as the people at Boston had began many years ago to endeavour to throw off all obedience to this Country; that indeed this was the first time Parliament had proceeded to punish them. He added, "I am "by no means an enemy to lenient measures, but I find that re-"solutions of censure and warning will avail nothing; we must "therefore proceed to some immediate remedy;—now is our "time to stand out—to defy them to proceed with firmness, and "without fear;" that they would never reform until we take a measure of this kind. Let this Bill produce a conviction to all America, that we are now in earnest, and that we will proceed with firmness and vigour; that conviction would be lost, if they see us hesitating and doubting; that it would be enough to shew, that Great Britain is in earnest. The merchandize now will be landed at *Marble Head, in the Province of Salem,* which is putting Boston 17 miles from the sea with respect to foreign trade; this restriction will be continued as long as they persist in their present proceedings; it will operate severely or mildly against them, according to their behaviour; if they are obstinate the measure will be severe; if not, mild. He believed that Boston would not immediately submit to a fine, nor to the intention of the present bill, unless it came attended with a mark of resolution and firmness that we mean to punish them, and assert our right; it is impossible to suppose, but some of our own people may in some degree suffer a little, but we must compare those temporary inconveniencies with the loss of that country, and its due obedience to us; they bear no comparison, and the preference must certainly be given to the latter, and attended to. The honorable Gentleman tells us, "that the Americans will not pay their "debts due to this Country, unless we comply with their dispo-"sition." I believe (says his Lordship) things will remain much in the same state as they did upon a like occasion; they threatned us with the same thing if we did not repeal the Stamp Act; we repealed that Act, and they did not pay their debts. If this threat is yielded to, we may as well take no remedy at all; threats will hold equally good to the fine proposed by the honourable Gentleman, as to the operation of this Bill. I hope that we every one feel that it is the common cause of us all, and such an unanimity will go half way to their obedience to this Bill. The honourable Gentleman tells us, "that the Act will be a waste piece of pa-"per, and that an army will be required to put it in execution." The good of this Act is, that four or five frigates will do the business without any military force; but if it is necessary, I should not hesitate a moment to enforce a due obedience to the laws of this country. The situation of the troops in that country has been such, that no Magistrate or Civil Officer of the Peace has been willing to call forth their strength on proper occasions; it will become us to find out some method whereby the military force may act with effect, and without bloodshed, in endeavouring to support and maintain the authority of Great-Britain; but I hope that this Act will not, in any shape, require a military force to put it in execution; the rest of the Colonies will not take fire at the proper punishment inflicted on those who have disobeyed your authority; we shall then be nearly in a situation, that all lenient measures will be at an end if they do; but if we exert ourselves now with firmness and intrepidity, it is the more likely they will submit to our authority. If the consequences of their not obeying this Act are likely to produce rebellion, that consequence belongs to them, and not to us; it is not what we have brought on, but what they alone have occasioned; we are only answerable that our measures are just and equitable. Let us continue to proceed with firmness, justice, and resolution; which, if pursued, will certainly produce that due obedience and respect to the laws of this country, and the security of the trade of it's people, which I, so ardently wish for.

MR. GASCOIGNE differed much from the proposition made (by Mr. Fuller) as an amendment to the Bill. Will Gentlemen consider what sort of Acts of Assembly the Bostonians have lately passed? They have sent over one law, to be approved of by his Majesty, for the *raising* and purchasing 12 pieces of brass cannon; these, he said, were to be produced against the present proposition of amendment. Do these proceedings look with a peaceable eye? It is not the acts of tarring and feathering only that shew their dipleasure to persons who have offended them, but they have other modes of punishment which they make use of by way of argument and reason; the house of any person with whom they are displeased, they immediately daub over with excrement and tar, by which means the whole family is obliged to quit it. That the Bill before them now, he apprehended, would bring these tarring and feathering casuists to a little better reason; nor did he imagine that a military force would be in the least necessary; that as their meetings were chiefly made up of Merchants, the prescribing limitations to their trade would be the only way to bring such Merchants to their senses.

MR. MONTAGUE (second son of Lord Sandwich) expatiated much on the load of debt which this country had incurred on obtaining America in Germany; that we had spilt the dearest and best blood we had in the attainment of it; that it had been the result and deliberations of our councils to obtain the possession of it by any means, and at any risque whatsoever; that it had been he darling object of this country, ever since we possessed it, to cherish and nourish it as the main prop and support of the constitutional body of Great-Britain; that after all these struggles for the possession of such a jewel in the crown of this country, it would be madness, it would be folly indeed to the last extremity, were we not to pursue the most determined conduct to preserve it hereafter; the giving up that gem which we have so carefully and dilligently polished, or neglecting to enforce that due obedience, and cultivate the friendship, would be as it were an actual surrender of all our right and claim. He affirmed that the disorders abroad had entirely been owing to our weak councils at home, and condemned much the tame, unmanly proceedings of government towards the Americans. Those acts of the Americans call loudly for that power and that interposition which has been long, and with so much danger to this country withheld.—The bill before them, he said, would operate as a restorative and palliative; but if the amendment was adopted, it would indeed produce a punishment, the sting of which Great Britain would in some measure feel. He concluded with giving his hearty approbation to the bill now before the House, as it bore on its face those distinguishing lines which ought to be the true characteristic of every British Minister, *moderation* and *courage*.

MR. BYNG said, the bill would effectually put an end to all importation of British goods to Boston, and thus, besides materially injuring our exports, it would give rise to that very association amongst the Americans which we have hitherto so cautiously endeavored to annihilate and destroy. This was not to punish the *Bostonians* but the *British Merchants*; men who would, in a body, unite in petitioning the House, were they not confident that their Petition would be disregarded. Mr. Byng concluded, by declaring himself against both the proposed Amendment and the Bill itself; but if an Act of the kind must pass, he should propose that, after the Clause prohibiting the Bostonians from importing goods, the words, Except of "*British Merchants*," be inserted.

MR. STANLEY said, that the place where trade and merchandize could not be landed in safety was not a port, it was therefore proper that some other port should be found out, where the subjects of this country might land their merchandize in safety.

MR. DEMPSTER said, that he knew of no Act to which he gave his hearty consent in a more willing manner, than to that which was for the *repeal of the Stamp Act*. He said, our disorders had arisen from our attempts to tax the Americans by that odious Stamp Act; and he was very sure the destruction of America would be certain, if we should offer to tax it. Have we not given an extent of power to his Majesty, to prevent the port of Boston from ever being reinstated, if the King should think proper? What limit or line is drawn, to define *when* it will be proper, right, and just, that the port of Boston should be reinstated? He said, the dignity of Parliament was by no mean concerned in the disputes with our Colonies; that we should treat them as our children, nourish and protect them.

LORD NORTH arose to explain himself. When he mentioned the threats of Boston were not to be depended upon at the repeal of the Stamp Act; that he begged to be understood in that light, only to shew that the threats of Boston, at that time, in not paying their debts unless the Stamp Act was repealed, were not always to be depended upon.

MR. WARD approved (he said) of this Bill, because there was no other resource left: but he disagreed to the amendment.

MR. JENKINSON much commended the measure of the Stamp Act. What (says he) is to become of all your trade, if the proceedings of the Bostonians are to become a precedent to the rest of the Colonies; we have gone into a very expensive war for the attainment of America; the struggle we shall now have to keep it, will be but of little expence.

GENERAL CONWAY observed in favour of the Bill, that he was happy in the mode of punishment adopted by it, but disclaimed a wish to recall past measures; he acknowledged himself to have voted for the repeal of the Samp Act; he was not ashamed of the part he took in the business, nor did he believe that the present disorders were occasioned by a repeal of that Act.

The Debate ended, and the blanks were filled up in the Bill.

The Bill was then read, and when the question was put on the clause which "vests the power in the Crown to restore the port."

MR. C. FOX said, he should give his negative, as it was trusting the Crown with that power, which Parliament were afraid to trust themselves with, and if he did not succeed in his negative to this clause, he should object to the clause following, which seemed to militate against the measure adopted in this, as a restraint was there laid upon the Crown, until the India Company were made satisfaction. This bill, he said, was calculated for three purposes, the *first* for securing the trade, the *second* for punishing the Bostonians, and the *third* for satisfaction to the East India Company. He said, the first clause did not give a true and exact distinction by what means, and at what period the Crown was to exercise that power vested in it; he thought that application for relief should come to Parliament only, and that the power of such relief should not be lodged in the Crown. The quarrel, he said, was with Parliament, and Parliament was the proper power to end it; not that, says he (in a sneer) there is any reason to distrust his Majesty's Ministers, that they will *not* restore the port when it shall be proper, but I want to hear the reason why this clause should be so left in the judgment of the Crown, and the next clause should be so particularly granted, with such a guard upon his Majesty, to prevent him from restoring the port, until the East India Company shall be fully satisfied.

MR. PHIPPS contended that nothing was so proper, as to allow the Crown that power which always had been attributed to it, that of *mercy*; his Majesty cannot deprive the people of a port without the leave of Parliament, but he may certainly give one; as to the power being lodged in the Crown, of restoring the port upon proper contrition, it is highly proper, and not in Parliament, for Parliament may not be sitting at the time when the trade of Boston ought to be restored; that power which has a right to give a port, has also a power of appointing quays and wharfs; if the power was not lodged in the crown, quays and wharfs might be made at places totally inconvenient to the Custom House Officers, and thereby prevent the collection of his Majesty's revenues.

Lord NORTH (to explain) said, that the test of the Bostonians will not be the indemnification of the East India Company alone, it will remain in the breast of the King not to restore the Port, until *peace* and *obedience* shall be observed in the port of Boston. I am ready to admit a clause to secure those wharfs and quays which are now in use, to be the same when the port is restored. He observed, he had been charged with changing his opinion, for that the declaration which he had made, tended chiefly to the *punishment* of the Bostonians, and that the bill particularly adhered to the views of making the India Company satisfaction.—He believed the House would do him the justice to say, that he had declared *both* those measures to be his intention, at the first setting out of the business, as well as to restore the trade to a proper footing; that he hoped he had never deviated from them, notwithstanding what the honourable Gentleman (Mr. Fox) had charged him with; that he should never be ashamed, at any time, to give up his opinion upon good grounds; it would be the height of obstinacy not to do it, when he saw any good reasons to guide his opinion to better judgment.

MR. VAN agreed to the flagitiousness of the offence in the Americans, and therefore was of opinion, that the town of Boston ought to be knocked about their ears, and destroyed, "*delenda* "*est Carthago.*" Says he, I am of opinion you will never meet with that proper obedience to the laws of this country, until you have destroyed that nest of locusts.

COLONEL BARRE said, he had very little thought of troubling the Committee upon this Clause, but for an expression which fell from an honourable Gentleman under the gallery, *delenda est Carthago*. I should not have rose, says he, had it not been for those words—The bill before you is the first vengeful step that you have taken. We ought to go cooly to this business, and not trouble our heads with who passed, or who repealed the Stamp Act, or other Taxes. We are to proceed *rebus sic talibus*. I hate the word *Fine*; it is a Tax, and as long as I sit here among you I will oppose the taxing of America. This bill, I am afraid, draws in the fatal doctrine of submitting to taxation; it is also a doubt, by this bill, whether the port is to be restored to its full extent. Keep your hands out of the pockets of the Americans, and they will be obedient subjects. I have not a doubt, but a very small part of our strength will, at any time, over-power them—I think this bill a moderate one; but I augur that the next proposition will be a black one. You have not a loom nor an anvil but what is stamped with America; it is the main prop of your trade. Parliament may fancy they have rights in *theory*, which they can never reduce to *practice*. America employs all your workmen here; nourish and protect it, that they may be supported.

The clauses objected to passed in the affirmative without any division but one or two negatives.

The Committee broke up, and the bill was reported that night, and ordered to be engrossed.

LONDON,

March 29. Yesterday the House of Commons went into a Committee on the further consideration of the American papers, and after some time spent therein, Sir Charles Whitworth acquainted the House that the Committee had come to one resolution, which will be reported this day, and the Committee to sit again on Wednesday fortnight. The resolution is said to be, to move for leave to bring in a bill to regulate the Civil Government of Massachuset's Bay. As such a bill, is imagined, will interfere with some of the American charters, there is no doubt but it will be strongly opposed.

Messieurs EDES & GILL,

THE Act of Parliament for Blockading the Town of Boston, cannot be parallell'd in all the English history: the passion, the cruelty, the tyranny, appearing at first glance in the very face of it, were never equall'd in any reign of the Stuarts. It exhibits to every town in this province, to every colony upon this extensive continent, and to the whole world, what is to be expected from a government that claims an unbounded authority over us, that still calls itself, and we till of late have been wont to call, with true filial affection, the parent state. *It aims to reduce us to the last distress, for what every friend to the rights of humanity, will highly applaud us, because we abhor Slavery, and devoted to destruction an article, after endeavouring with all our might to send it back safe to the proprietors, the vending of which among us must have rivetted our chains. It is notorious, that the opposition to the EastIndiaCompany's sending their Tea to America, first began among the Merchants of England.—It then appeared in the provinces of Pennsylvania and New-York; and was last adopted here. The reasons for such an opposition are indisputable—They never have been, and never can be answered but by meer brutal force——and of this force Boston is destined to be the first example. It was expected that a requisition would have been made for the payment of the price of the tea, and time allowed for an answer to such a requisition. Instead of this, vengeance to the highest extreme immediately falls upon us—no time allowed to make submission were we dispos'd to do it—no terms of security for us defin'd——but the many thousands in this town must be at once ruined; and persons of all political sentiments without distinction, the aged and the young, the widow and the orphan, the mother and the suckling, all reduc'd at once, to a distress that the sternest Prince would have spared to a conquered town of the most obstinate rebels.*

But who could imagine that this cruel edict should be plann'd by a native of the town of Boston? and yet there is no room to doubt that the hypocritical, smiling, ambitious, avaricious Hutchinson; *a man born for the distress of his country, and to be the object of it's execrations in all times to come, aided by the* Olivers, Sewall, Auchmuty, Paxton, Hallowell, *&c. &c. contriv'd and urg'd with all their sophistry, low-cunning, and malice, this instrument for desolating the town of Boston. Their tools and minions gave out soon after the destruction of the tea, that the sea-ports, and particularly Boston, would soon be managed in such a manner as to set all things right: that all our trade would be ruined—that the inhabitants would then divide among themselves and cut one anothers throats——that the other towns thro' the province would desert the cause, and grow exasperated with the capital—that the other colonies unchastis'd, and glad at their own security, would leave Boston and Massachusetts to the mercy of the ministry; and bluster no more for American Rights: And that this stroke would scatter terror through the continent, and annihilate all opposition to the authority of parliament. The reverse of all this is likely to take place. There is now little or no distinction of parties among us—all are anxious for the common safety, and the town never so well united.——Our brethren in the country behold the approaching misery of a capital that has been exemplarily vigilant, and generously expos'd itself to ministerial vengeance, for the preservation of their Rights, as well as its own, with pity to the distress'd, and indignation at the authors. They value above every earthly thing the Rights for which we suffer, and send us from all quarters the most encouraging assurances of their aid and support. Our sister colonies behold in this metropolis a specimen of what they may expect after we are subdued—they know that the Renunciation of Rights demanded of us by military torture, is what must essentially affect them; and that our perseverance greatly depends upon their assistance and aid, which we may be assured they will most readily afford. This union will secure the success of the American cause, and establish Liberty & Happiness in this rising Empire, in spite of all the efforts of an unnatural Mother.*

From the Public Advertiser *of March* 30.

THE Public is not acquainted with the full Merits of the Bill against the Town of Boston, and the Manner in which it has been conducted; yet nothing can be more worthy of their Curiosity; being the most extraordinary that this or any other Country ever produced.

From the Beginning of this Business, every Hearer has been excluded, and every Door barred with uncommon Anxiety. It was conceived, that this was to prevent the Accusers of the Town and the Evidence against it from being known. Even this would have been a Mode of Proceeding unknown to the Court of Star Chamber, and of which no Example could be found, but in the Courts of Inquisition abroad.

Now however it appears, that there neither is any Accuser, nor any Evidence against the Town. On the contrary, Admiral Montagu charges the Fault of suffering the Tea to be destroyed upon the avowed Enemies of Boston. These are his Words: "During the Whole of this Transaction, neither the Governor, Magistrates (who are appointed by the Governor) Owners, or Revenue Officers of this Place, ever called for my Assistance; if they had, I could easily have prevented the Execution of this Plan." Dated Boston, Dec. 17, 1773, & addressed to the Lords of the Admiralty.

It is plain from this Information of the Admiral, that Governor Hutchinson and the Commissioners connived, at least, at the Destruction of the Tea, for which the Town is to be punished: And as the Perpetrators of this Outrage were disguised and unknown, perhaps it may hereafter appear that they were hired by the Enemies of the Town, on purpose to bring a Reproach upon it. To strengthen this Suspicion, it is observable that the People of the Town wished to have the Tea returned to England, not destroyed. This was the Resolution of all their Meetings, and this the Governor prevented by refusing to let the Ship pass the Castle which commands the Harbour. He could have had but two possible Views in this, to drive the People to Extremities, or to throw the Blame of destroying the Tea upon them, which others were employed to effect. Had not Governor Hutchinson been influenced by some such View, he would have desired the Admiral to protect the Tea, or he would have agreed, as General Haldiman writes was the Resolution of Governor Tryon, to permit that the Tea should be sent back to England to prevent dangerous Extremities.

It is therefore manifest, even from the mutilated Papers the Ministry have been pleased to give us, that it was a settled Plan beeween the Governor, Commissioners, &c. to urge the Mob to such Violence which might be visited upon the Town. Surely these were Circumstances sufficient to authorize a farther Enquiry into the Transaction before Parliament proceeded to a Bill of the severest Pains and Penalties against the Town, which is so far from appearing guilty that Governor Hutchinson himself writes on the 4th of November, that nothing had been done "which could bring any Imputation upon the Town in general."

Yet without the Shadow of Evidence, without any direct Accusation against the Town, with all the Circumstances of Suspicion that their Enemies were the Authors of this Outrage, the Town of Boston is to be punished with a Severity, of which the worst Times of this Country cannot furnish a single Example. JUSTICE.

L O N D O N.

March 11. The miscreant Ministerial Writers labour hard to misrepresent the present controversy between Great-Britain and her Colonies. It is not, as they shamefully insist, reduceable to the following question, "Whether the Mother Country shall or shall not retain her supremacy?" Her right of supremacy is indisputable; but if she abuses that right by every effort of illegal taxation; if she protects a set of scoundrel Governors in their base designs to enslave a brave, and, by Charter, a free people; if Great-Britain does all this, and the Bostonians, rouzed with sensibility at the injuries they sustain, happen to express their resentments in an imprudent manner, the question then is, "Whether they shall or shall not be put to the sword?" This is the query; the debates on which now occupy the British Councils.

March 22. It may be depended on that a Sloop of War sailed from Plymouth 14 Days since for Boston, with Orders to bring to England, in Irons, Mess. Hancock, Row, Adams, and McIntosh. McIntosh has been very Active among the lower order of People, the others among the higher.

Should Government kidnap and bring over as Prisoners the leading Patriots at Boston, 'tis much feared it will cause an Insurrection.

April 7. The Effrontery of the Gentlemen in Office is such as will render Ministerial Audacity proverbial. There was a Time when Administration, whatever might have been their private Inclinations, would yet not have dared Publickly to talk of annihilating the political Constitution of either the Mother Country or her Colonies; designs black as Hell would have been kept secret as the Grave. The Times, however, are altered, and every Miscreant Treasury Runner, every Coffee House Spy in the Pay of the Minister can now harrangue upon "the absolute Necessity of new-modelling (as it is called) the American Charters."—Lord North is an excellent Hand at this Work; he hath new-modelled the Charter of the East-India Company, that is, he hath eventually destroyed it. An Experiment with America is wanting, and if the Minister succeeds in his Plan of overturning the political Constitution of the Colonies, there remains but one glorious Effort to new model, alias annihilate the English Constitution to compleat the Happiness of the best of Kings, and the Views of the best of Poppy-headed Ministers.

P H I L A D E L P H I A, May 4.

Yesterday, about 3 o'clock in the afternoon, the effigies of Alexander Wedderburne, Esq; convicted of traducing the Americans and insulting their Agent, before his Majesty's Privy Council, for doing his duty, and of Thomas Hutchinson, Esq; Governor of Massachusett's Bay, convicted of an attempt to incense Great Britain against her Colonies, were put into a cart and conducted through the streets of this city. On the breast of Wedderburne was the following label:——

"*The infamous* WEDDERBURNE,
"A pert prime Prater, of a scabby race,
"Guilt in his heart, and famine in his face.
CHURCHILL, *altered*.
"Similis *Proteo* mutet, at fallaci [illegible] *Catalina*.
"Hunc vos, Britanni cavete!

"*He availed himself of the license of the bar to insult the venerable Dr.* FRANKLIN, *whose knowledge in philosophy, universal benevolence, just sentiments of liberty, and indefatigable labours to promote harmony between Britain and her Colonies, entitle him to the esteem of the learned of every nation, the love of all good men, and the sincere affection of every* honest *Briton and American.*

"*But the base born* SOLLICITOR, *who attempted to turn his learning, benevolence, and patriotism, into ridicule, is (like Hutchinson) a Parricide of the first rank, who would sacrifice his country, his liberty and his God, and delight in the carnage of the most faithful British subjects in America, to gain promotion at Court.*

"*Such horrid monsters are a disgrace to human nature, and justly merit our utmost detestation, and the* GALLOWS, *to which they are assigned, & then burnt by Electric Fire.*"

Among others, the following lines were taken from Hudibras:

So a wild Tartar, when he spies
A man that's handsome, valiant, wise,
If he can kill him, thinks t'inherit
His wit, his beauty, and his spirit:
As if just so much he enjoy'd,
As in another is destroy'd.

Governor Hutchinson, who was represented with a double face, had affixed on his breast the following label:—"Governor HUTCHINSON, *whom we now consign to the gallows and flames, as the only proper reward for double-dealing and treachery to his native country."*

After being exposed for several hours, they were hung on a Gallows erected near the Coffee House, set in flames by electric fire, *and consumed to ashes, about 6 o'clock, amidst a vast concourse of people, who testified their resentment against the* ORIGINALS *by the loudest acclamations.*

B O S T O N, May 16.

Eztract of a Letter from London, March 28, 1774.

CONCERNING public Matters, I am sorry to say that Things are going from bad to worse, and a Breach between Great-Britain and her Colonies seems approaching very fast. This *accursed Tea* is the very *Match* that is appointed to set fire to a *Train of Gun-Powder*, that has been long, tho' secretly, laid by *our Ministry and your Governor*, JOINT AGENTS in that *most infernal Business* of destroying the Liberties of three Millions of British Subjects.——

I write and speak boldly on these Matters, and I care not who knows it: Life would be reduced to mere Existence if Liberty was taken away—and I hope to hear that there are some Remains of Virtue among you, tho' it is almost extinguish'd here, swallowed up by our Luxury, Effeminacy and Avarice—Could the PIMS and the HAMDENS of a former Period but take a View of the *base degeneracy of their Successors*, it would make them weep TEARS OF BLOOD.

In Respect to the present State of Affairs, it grieves me to find such an Outcry against your Townsmen, and to hear some moderate People that I daily converse with carried away by the Current; and to speak the Truth *(for these are not Times for Dissimulation)* the Chicanery and Misbehavior of some of your Impostors, in a Mercantile View, gives great additional Weight to the public Clamour, and takes off the Zeal with which our Merchants and Traders supported you in the Repeal of the Stamp-Act.——

For myself, if I was intirely deserted I would not fear to maintain my Old Principles, that all the Subjects of the British Crown have an equal Right to Liberty, to Favour, and to Protection; that *Taxation* implies *Representation*, that *Legislation and Taxation* are different Things—that a King should have no Partiality or Personal Resentment—that our House of Commons are not *omnipotent*, but *limitted*—that the *Americans* are our *best Customers*, our FAST FRIENDS—that the enormous Expences of the late War ought not to be charg'd to them, and that they already, as Consumers of our Manufactures, pay *their full Quota of the Taxes*.

But at last we must leave these Matters to Providence, and comfort ourselves with doing what is Right in our own Consciences, and in this Spirit, I salute you, and am, &c."

TO BE SOLD,
By *BENJAMIN CHURCH*,
On FRIDAY NEXT,
At Three o'Clock in the Afte noon.
A Variety of valuable Articles, viz. Callicoes—Checks—Linnens—Shalloons—Durants—Calmancoes—Brussels—Taberits—Venetians—Antilloor——Camblets—Cambleteens——plated Buckles————Handkerchiefs, &c. &c.——Also House Furniture as Tables—Chairs—Glasses—an 8 Day Clock, Watch
At 3 o'Clock, P. M.

Messieurs EDES & GILL,

I Inclose Rivington's Gazetteer of the 21st of April 1774, in which you will find an Address to the Hon. Mr. Hancock, which was apparently designed to injure him and the Cause of Freedom which he supports with so much Firmness and Dignity. I thought it proper to give a more just Account to the Public of the Affair there treated of, than the Writer of that Piece has exhibited—I therefore request you would republish the Address in your next Gazette, and the Answer which I send with the Gazetteer in the succeeding Paper. Your's,

RHADAMANTHUS.

[*The Address, together with the Answer, we shall endeavor to give our Readers next Week.*]

B O S T O N, May 15.

Tuesday last the Freeholders and other Inhabitants of this Town met at Faneuil Hall for the Choice of Representatives, the Number of Votes were 536.

The Hon. Thomas Cushing, Esq; had	524 Votes.
Mr. Samuel Adams,	535
Hon. John Hancock, Esq;	536
William Phillips, Esq;	534

After which, Mr. SAMUEL ADAMS was chosen Moderator, and the usual Business Transacted.

Friday last arrived here his Majesty's Ship Lively, Capt. Bishop, in 26 Days from England, in whom came his Excellency General GAGE, who is appointed Governor and Commander in Chief of this Province:—His Excellency landed at Castle William under a Discharge of the Cannon of that Fortress. And we hear that the next Day the following Advice was given by his Majesty's Council to his Excellency Governor Hutchinson.——That General GAGE's Commission for Governor of this Province be read on Tuesday next; the Boston Regiment, the Troop of Guards and the Cadet Company to be in Arms; his Excellency to land at the End of the Long Wharf, from thence to be escorted, attended by his Majesty's Council, to the Court-House; and an elegant Dinner to be prepared, which we hear is to be at Faneuil-Hall.

It is worthy of remark, that nothing is said by the East India company, or their friends, in England, of the Destruction of the Tea as being their property, or any damages accruing to them thereby. It is solely taken up by the British parliament, and the friends of the British ministry, which plainly evinces, that the introducing said Tea into America upon that plan, was a scheme of the present Administration.

It appears that the drift of Administration and their *good friends* in England, is to break the union of the American colonies, and that devoted Boston shall feel the unparallelled tokens of their displeasure. But let us not be dismayed, let us persevere to the end, and resolve to yield our lives and fortunes, before we will submit to the iron yoke of tyranny! And let this sacred truth be borne in the mind of every American, "By *Uniting* we *Stand*, by *Dividing* we *Fall*!"

Extract of a Letter from a Gentleman of the first Character in London, *dated* April 2, 1774, *to his Friend in this Town.*

"A Motion has been made in the House of Commons, with a View to conciliate as is said, that all the Duty Acts should be revised, and in Revision and re-enacting without *formally* or *expressly* repealing the Tea Duty (which would hurt the Dignity of Parliament) sink or omit it, and add an equal Value in some of the Coasting Port Duties, and the Tea Duty being thus taken out the Way, *it is supposed will have the salutary Effect of preventing the other Colonies from making a common Cause with that of your Town and Province*"——Some Advantages in Trade are at the same Time to be given to America for the same Purpose, such as carrying Wine and Fruit directly from Spain and Portugal without touching in England."

Extract of a letter from one of the first character in London, dated April 2.

"Alterations in the constitution of the Massachusetts are now greatly talked of, though what they are to be seems hardly yet settled. One thing mentioned is the appointment of a Council by mandamus; another giving power to the Governor to appoint magistrates without consent of Council; another the abolishing of town meetings or making it unlawful to hold them till the business to be proposed has been certified to the Governor and his permission obtained."

DIED.] Last Night, Mrs. Mary Symmes, Consort of Capt. Andrew Symmes, aged 22.

O A T S.

OATS, Pease, Philadelphia Flour, and Bar-Iron, *Also*, warranted Scythes and Axes, a few neat Fowling Pieces, and a small Quantity of good Snuff, to be sold cheap, at the lowest Store on the South Side of the Town Dock, by Joseph-Pearse Palmer.

(For New Advertisements see Postscript)

ON Friday last there was a numerous and respectable Meeting of the Freeholders and other Inhabitants of this Town, legally warned and assembled in Faneuil-Hall, to consider an *Edict* lately passed by the British Parliament for shutting up the Harbour and otherwise punishing the Inhabitants, and to determine upon proper Measures to be taken by the Town thereon.

After making Choice of Mr. SAMUEL ADAMS Moderator of the Meeting, the Edict was distinctly read by the Clerk; and the Nature & Tendency as well as the *Design* of it being explained in the Observations of several Gentlemen upon it, the Town came into the following Vote. Nem. Con.

VOTED, That it is the Opinion of this Town, that if the other Colonies come into a JOINT Resolution to stop all Importations from Great-Britain, and Exportations to Great-Britain, and every Part of the West-Indies, till the Act for blocking up this Harbour be repealed, the same will prove the Salvation of North America & her Liberties: On the other Hand, if they continue their Exports and Imports, there is high reason to fear that Fraud, Power, and the most odious Oppression will rise triumphant over Right, Justice, social Happiness and Freedom. And Ordered, that this Vote be forthwith transmitted by the Moderator to all our Sister Colonies, in the Name & Behalf of this Town.

Then it was moved for Consideration, what Measures were proper for the Town to take on the present Emergency; whereupon several judicious, spirited and manly Proposals were made; which being debated with a Candor, Moderation and Firmness of Mind becoming a People resolved to preserve their Liberty, it was Voted, that the *Moderator*, with *John Rowe*, Esq; Mr. *Thomas Boylston*, *William Phillips*, Esq; Doctor *Joseph Warren*, *John Adams*, Esq; *Josiah Quincy*, Esq; *Thomas Cushing*, Esq; Mr. *Henderson Inches*, Mr. *William Mollineux*, and Mr. *Nathaniel Appleton*, be a Committee to take the several Proposals that have been, and others that may be made, into Consideration, and report to the Town as soon as may be.

After which the Town made Choice of Mr. *Oliver Wendell*, *Isaac Smith*, Esq; Mr. *William Dennie*, Mr. *William Powell*, and Mr. *John Pitts*, to repair immediately to the Towns of *Salem* and *Marblehead*, to communicate the Sentiments of this Metropolis to the Gentlemen there, consult with them, and make report at the Adjournment.

Then the Meeting was adjourned 'till WEDNESDAY NEXT at Ten of the Clock in the Forenoon. The Meeting was opened with an excellent *Prayer* by the Rev. Dr. COOPER.

A Correspondent observes that there was never more *unanimity* than appeared in Faneuil Hall last Friday; and he adds, that it was as perfect as human Society can admit of.

It is an inexpressible Grief that Mr. HANCOCK's ill state of Health would not permit his attendance in Faneuil-Hall on Friday last. We pray GOD he may be able to attend the General Assembly at the approaching Session.

Last Saturday our worthy fellow Citizen, Mr. *Paul Revere*, was dispatch'd by the Committee of Correspondence of this Town with *important* Letters to the Southern Colonies.

To the Inhabitants of BOSTON.

Friends and Brethren,

PReserve your *Unanimity*, keep up your *Spirits*, and above all put your Trust in GOD, and seek to him for *Wisdom* and *Fortitude*, and you need not fear what Man can do unto you.

A. B. of Charlestown.

A Correspondent tells us, that if the Colonies will now *unite* in a total Suspension of Trade with Great Britain and the West-Indies, they may "*Stand still and see the Salvation of the* Lord."

By Letters from Marblehead and Salem we are assured that a Number of the capital Merchants in those Towns are resolved to haul up their Vessels till the Harbour of Boston shall be free.

The patriotic Merchants of Newbury Port *have exhibited a noble Example in the following spirited Resolution*, viz. THAT we will, in Case the other Provinces on the Continent shall join in the Measure, or even if all the other Sea Ports in this Province will come in to it, lay up all our Vessels (as they come in) after the 14th June next, and that we will neither Import or Export any one Article of Merchandize or Produce to the Southward of South-Carolina, more especially that we will break off all Trade to and from the West-Indies, or any Part of Great Britain or Ireland, and that this Resolution we will continue in till the Town and Port of Boston is again opened and free to go in and out of, or till the Disputes between this Continent and Great-Britain are settled upon such a Basis as that we and our Children may enjoy all those Privileges we are contending, and reasonable Men ought to contend for?

It is Fact that Faneuil-Hall was so throng'd last Friday that several hundred Persons were unable to attend the Meeting.

Now in the Press,

OBSERVATIONS ON THE ACT OF PARLIAMENT For Blocking up the Harbour of *Boston*; WITH THOUGHTS ON CIVIL SOCIETY AND STANDING ARMIES.

BRITONS *arise!*
And show you have the virtue to be mov'd.
POPE.

NULLA FIDES, pietasq; viris, qui CASTRA sequuntur,
VENALESQUE MANUS: ibi fas, ubi maxima merces.
LUCAN.

BY *JOSIAH QUINCY*, Junr

The following Passage, towards the Close of the Performance, is extracted for the Satisfaction of our Readers.

"*YET be not amused, my Countrymen!—the extirpation of bondage, and the re-establishment of freedom are not of easy acquisition. The worst passions of the human heart and the most subtile projects of the human mind are leagued against you; and principalities and powers have acceded to the combination. Trials and conflicts you must, therefore, endure;—hazards and jeopardies—of life and fortune—will attend the struggle. Such is the fate of all noble exertions for public liberty and social happiness.——Enter not the lists without thought and consideration, lest you arm with timidity and combat with irresolution. Having engaged in the conflict, let nothing discourage your vigour, or repel your perseverance:—Remember that submission to the yoke of bondage is the worst that can befall a people, after the most fierce and unsuccessful resistance. What can the misfortune of vanquishment take away, which despotism and rapine would spare? It had been easy (said the great law-giver Solon to the Athenians) to repress the advances of tyranny, and prevent it's establishment,* but now it is established and grown to some heighth, *it would be* MORE GLORIOUS to *demolish* it.

To be sold upon reasonable Terms,

A Quantity of choice good Lisbon LEMMONS, by the Box or smaller Quantity, by CHARLES PERRIN, at the Granby's Head in Wing's-Lane, or JOHN MADDEN, near the Market.

Spring GOODS.

Cheap for Cash or short Credit, just Imported
By JOHN WHITE,
Near the Cornfields, Union-Street;

A compleat Assortment of newest-fashion'd Callicoes and India Chints, Nankeens, Russia Drabs, yd-wide, 7-8 and 3-4 Irish Linnen, Cambricks and Lawns, Gauzes and Catgut, Patent & Spider's Net, Book Muslin, black, bone and blond Lace, white blond and thread ditto, Cheveaux de Frize, strip'd and sprig'd silk Gauze, silk Gloves and Mitts, a compleat Assortment of newest fashioned Ribbons, Mode Sarsnet and Sattin of all Colours, Cotton Hose, Handkerchiefs of Sorts, English and French Necklaces, Womens English Shoes and Clogs, Looking Glasses, a large Assortment of China, Glass and Earthen Ware, &c. &c. &c.

N. B. A few Casks of English Cheese, and a few Hampers of exceeding fine Porter.

This Day Published, (by I. Thomas)
[Embellished with elegant Engravings. I. The Bust of Mr. SAMUEL ADAMS. II. The Hill-Tops: A new Hunting Song, set to Music, with a Representation of the Death of the Stag.]

NUMBER IV. of
THE ROYAL
American MAGAZINE
OR UNIVERSAL
Repository of Instruction and Amusement.
For APRIL, 1774.

WANTED immediately

A SHIP from 200 to 300 Tons burthen: Any Person having such a one, and inclining to Charter her, may apply at Store No. 6 on *Treat's* Wharf, or to The Printers.

N. B. A BRIG of 200 Tons may answer.

CUSTOM-HOUSE, *BOSTON.*

ENTETRD IN.

Geddinge, from St. Lucia. Cleaves, Fayal. Frazier, Cape-Nichola. Hay, Jamaica. Luthert North Carolina. Baker and Barnes, Bristol. Erskine and Walker, Greenock. Chevalier, Jersey. Shayler, Jenkins, Lyde, Mowat, and Scott, London.

Burials in the Town of BOSTON, since our last.
Seven Whites. No Blacks.
Baptiz'd in the several Churches, Five.

High Water at BOSTON, for the present Week.

Monday, 45 min. aft.	3	Friday, 50 min. after	6
Tuesday, 32 min. aft.	4	Saturday, 38 min. aft.	7
Wednesday, 17 m. aft.	5	Lord's-Day, 25 m af.	8
Thursday, 3 min. aft.	6	D's first Qu. 18 D. 2 Af.	

LONDON, April 4.

The following is the much-talked-of BOSTON PORT-BILL, which on Thursday last received the Royal Assent, and after the FIRST of JUNE becomes a Law.

Anno Regni GEORGII III. Regis Magnæ Britanniæ, Franciæ, & Hiberniæ,

An ACT to discontinue, in such manner, and for such time as are therein mentioned, the landing and discharging, lading or shipping, of Goods, Wares, and Merchandise, at the town, and within the harbour of Boston, in the Province of Massachusetts-Bay, in North America.

WHEREAS dangerous commotions and insurrections have been fomented and raised in the town of Boston, in the Province of Massachusetts-Bay, in New England, by divers ill-affected persons, to the subversion of his Majesty's government, and to the utter destruction of the public peace, and good order of the said Town; in which commotions and insurrections certain valuable cargoes of Teas, being the property of the East-India Company, and on board certain Vessels lying within the bay or harbour of Boston, were seized and destroyed: And whereas, in the present condition of the said town and harbour, the commerce of his Majesty's subjects cannot be safely carried on there, nor the customs payable to his Majesty duly collected; and it is therefore expedient that the officers of his Majesty's Customs should be forthwith removed from the said town: May it please your Majesty that it may be enacted; and be it enacted by the King's most excellent Majesty, by and with the advice and consent of the Lords spiritual and temporal, and commons, in this present Parliament assembled, and by the authority of the same, That from and after the FIRST DAY OF JUNE, One thousand seven hundred and seventy-four, it shall not be lawful for any person or persons whatsoever to lade or put, or cause or procure to be laden or put, off or from any quay, wharf, or other place, within the said town of Boston, or in or upon any part of the shore of the bay, commonly called the harbour of Boston, between a certain headland or point called NAHANT POINT, on the Eastern side of the entrance into the said bay, and a certain other headland or point called ALDERTON POINT, on the western side of the entrance into the said bay, or in or upon any island, creek, landing-place, bank, or other place, within the said bay or headlands, into any ship, vessel, lighter, boat, or bottom, any goods, wares, or merchandise whatsoever, to be transported or carried into any other country, province, or place whatsoever, or into any other part of the said province of the Massachusetts-Bay, in New-England; or to take up, discharge, or lay on land, or cause or procure to be taken up, discharged, or laid on land, within the said town, or in or upon any of the places aforesaid, out of any boat, lighter, ship, vessel, or bottom, any goods, wares, or merchandise whatsoever, to be brought from any other country, province or place, or any other part of the said province of the Massachusetts-Bay, in New-England, upon pain of the forfeiture of the said goods, wares, and merchandise, and of the said boat, lighter, ship, vessel, or other bottom into which the same shall be put, or out of which the same shall be taken, and of the guns, ammunition, tackle, furniture, and stores, in or belonging to the same: And if any such goods, wares, or merchandise, shall, within the said town, or in any the places aforesaid, be laden or taken in from the shore into any barge, hoy, lighter, wherry, or boat, to be carried on board any ship or vessel outward-bound to any other country or province, or other part of the said province of the Massachusetts Bay, in New-England, or be laden or taken into such barge, hoy, lighter, wherry, or boat, from or out of any ship or vessel coming in and arriving from any other country or province, or other part of the said province of the Massachusetts-Bay, in New-England, such barge, hoy, lighter, wherry, or boat, shall be forfeited and lost.

And be it further enacted by the authority aforesaid, That if any wharfinger, or keeper of any wharf, crane, or quay, or their Servants, or any of them, shall take up or land, or knowingly suffer to be taken up or landed, or shall ship off, or suffer to be waterborne, at or from any of their said wharfs, cranes, or quays, any such goods wares, or merchandise; in every such case, all and every such wharfinger, and keeper of such wharf; crane, or quay, and every person whatever who shall be assisting, or otherwise concerned in the shipping or in the loading or putting on board any boat, or other vessel, for that purpose, or in the unshipping such goods, wares, and merchandise, or to whose hands the same shall knowingly come after the loading, shipping, or unshipping thereof, shall forfeit and lose treble the value thereof, to be computed at the highest price which such sort of goods, wares, and merchandise, shall bear at the place where such offence shall be committed, at the time when the same shall be so committed, together with the vessels and boats, and all the horses, cattle, and carriages, whatsoever made use of in the shipping, unshipping, landing, removing, carriage, or conveyance of any of the aforesaid goods, wares, and merchandise.

And be it further enacted by the authority aforesaid, That if any ship or vessel shall be moored or lie at anchor, or be seen hovering within the said bay, described and bounded as aforesaid, or within one league from the said bay so described, or the said headlands, or any of the islands lying between or within the same, it shall and may be lawful for any Admiral, Chief Commander, or commissioned Officer of his Majesty's fleet or ships of war, or for any Officer of his Majesty's Customs, to compel such ship or vessel to depart to some other port or harbour, or to such station as the said officer shall appoint, and to use such force for that purpose as shall be found necessary: And if such ship or vessel shall not depart accordingly, within six hours after notice for that purpose given by such person as aforesaid, such ship or vessel, together with all the goods laden on board thereon, and all the guns, ammunition, tackle, and furniture, shall be forfeited and lost, whether bulk shall have been broken or not.

Provided always, That nothing in this act contained shall extend, or be construed to extend, to any military or other stores for his Majesty's use, or to the ships or vessels whereon the same shall be laden, which shall be commissioned by, and in the immediate pay of, his Majesty, his heirs or successors; nor to any fuel or victual brought coastwise from any part of the Continent of America, for the necessary use and sustenance of the inhabitants of the said town of Boston, provided the vessel wherein the same are to be carried shall be duly furnished with a cocket and let-pass, after having been duly searched by the proper Officers of his Majesty's custom's at Marblehead, in the port of Salem, in the said province of Massachusetts-Bay; and that some Officer of his Majesty's customs be also there put on board the said vessel, who is hereby authorised to go on board, and proceed with the said vessel, together with a sufficient number of persons, properly armed, for his defence, to the said town or harbour of Boston; nor to any ships or vessels which may happen to be within the said harbour of Boston on or before the first day of June, One thousand seven hundred and seventy-four, and may have either laden or taken on board, or be there with intent to load or take on board, or to land or discharge any goods, wares, and merchandise, provided the said ships and vessels do depart the said harbour within fourteen days after the said first Day of June, One thousand seven hundred and seventy-four.

And be it further enacted by the authority aforesaid, That all seizures, penalties and forfeitures, inflicted by this act, shall be made and prosecuted by any Admiral, Chief Commander, or commissioned Officer, of his Majesty's fleet, or ships of war, or by the Officers of his Majesty's Customs, or some of them, or by some other person deputed or authorised, by warrant from the Lord High Treasurer, or the Commissioners of his Majesty's Treasury for the time being, and by no other person whatsoever: And if any such Officer, or other person authorised as aforesaid, shall, directly or indirectly, take or receive any bribe or reward, to connive at such lading or unlading, or shall make or commence any collusive seizure, information, or agreement for that purpose, or shall do any other act whatsoever, whereby the goods, wares or merchandise, prohibited as aforesaid, shall be suffered to pass either inwards or outwards, or whereby the forfeitures and penalties inflicted by this act may be evaded, every such offender shall forfeit the sum of FIVE HUNDRED POUNDS for every such offence, and shall become incapable of any office or employment, civil or military; and every person who shall give, offer or promise any such bribe or reward, or shall contract, agree, or treat with any person, so authorised as aforesaid, to commit any such offence, shall forfeit the sum of FIFTY POUNDS.

And be it further enacted by the authority aforesaid, That the forfeitures and penalties inflicted by this act shall and may be prosecuted, sued for, and recovered, and be divided, paid and applied, in like manner as other penalties and forfeitures inflicted by any act or acts of Parliament, relating to the trade or revenues of the British colonies or plantations in America, are directed to be prosecuted, sued for, or recovered, divided, paid and applied by two special acts of Parliament, the one passed in the fourth year of his present Majesty (intitled an act for granting certain duties in the British colonies and plantations in America; for continuing, amending, and making perpetual, an act passed in the sixth year of the reign of his late Majesty King George the Second, intitled An act for the better securing and encouraging the trade of his Majesty's sugar colonies in America; for applying the produce of such duties, and of the duties to arise by virtue of the said act, towards defraying the expences of defending, protecting, and securing, the said colonies and plantations; for explaining an act made in the twenty-fifth year of the reign of King Charles the Second, intitled An act for the encouragement of the Greenland and Eastland Trades, and for the better securing the plantation trade; and for altering and disallowing several drawbacks on exports from this kingdom, and more effectually preventing the clandestine conveyance of goods to and from the said colonies and plantations, and improving and securing the trade between the same and Great-Britain) the other passed in the eighth year of his present Majesty's reign (intitled An act for the more easy and effectual recovery of the penalties and forfeitures inflicted by the acts of Parliament relating to the trade or revenues of the British colonies and plantations in America.)

And be it further enacted by the authority aforesaid, That every charter party bill of lading, and other contract for consigning, shipping, or carrying any goods, wares, and merchandise whatsoever, to or from the said town of Boston, or any part of the bay or harbour thereof, described as aforesaid, which have been made or entered into, or which shall be made or entered into, so long as this act shall remain in full force, relating to any ship which shall arrive at the said town or harbour, after the first day of June, One thousand seven hundred and seventy-four, shall be, and the same are hereby declared to be, utterly void, to all intents and purposes whatsoever.

And be it further enacted by the authority aforesaid, That whenever it shall be made to appear to his Majesty, in his Privy Council, that peace and obedience to the laws shall be so far restored in the said town of Boston, that the trade of Great-Britain may safely be carried on there, and his Majesty's Customs duly collected, and his Majesty, in his Privy Council, shall adjudge the same to be true, it shall and may be lawful for his Majesty, by proclamation, or order of Council, to assign and appoint the extent, bounds and limits, of the port or harbour of Boston, and of every creek or haven within the same, or in the islands within the precinct thereof; and also to assign and appoint such and so many open places, quays and wharfs, within the said harbour, creeks, havens and islands, for the landing, discharging, lading, and shipping of goods, as his Majesty, his heirs or successors, shall judge necessary and expedient; and also to appoint such and so many officers of the Customs therein, as his Majesty shall think fit; after which it shall be lawful for any person or persons to lade or put off from, or to discharge and land upon, such wharfs, quays, and places, so appointed within the said harbour, and none other, any goods, wares, and merchandise whatever.

Provided always, That if any goods, wares, or merchandise, shall be laden or put off from, or discharged or landed upon, any other place than the quays, wharfs, or places, so to be appointed, the same, together with the ships, boats, and other vessels employed therein, and the horses, or other cattle and carriages used to convey the same, and the person or persons concerned or assisting therein, or to whose hands the same shall knowingly come, shall suffer all the forfeitures and penalties imposed by this or any other act on the illegal shipping or landing of goods.

Provided also, and it is hereby declared and enacted, That nothing herein contained shall extend, or be construed, to enable his Majesty to appoint such port, harbour, creeks, quays, wharfs, places, or officers, in the said town of Boston, or in the said bay or islands, until it shall sufficiently appear to his Majesty that full satisfaction hath been made by or on behalf of the inhabitants of the said town of Boston to the united company of merchants of England trading to the East-Indies, for the damage sustained by the said company by the destruction of their goods sent to the said town of Boston, on board certain ships or vessels as aforesaid; and until it shall be certified to his Majesty, in Council, by the Governor, or Lieutenant Governor, of the said province, that reasonable satisfaction hath been made to the officers of his Majesty's revenue, and others, who suffered by the riots and insurrections above mentioned, in the months of November and December, in the year one thousand seven hundred and seventy-three, and in the month of January, in the year of one thousand seven hundred and seventy-four.

And be it further enacted by the authority aforesaid, That if any action or suit shall be commenced, either in Great-Britain or America, against any person or persons, for any thing done in pursuance of this act of Parliament, the defendant or defendants, in such action or suit, may plead the general issue, and give the said act, and the general matter, in evidence, at any trial to be had thereupon, and that the same was done in pursuance and by the authority of this act: And if it shall appear to have been done, the jury shall find for the defendant or defendants; and if the plaintiff shall be nonsuited, or discontinue his action, after the defendant or defendants shall have appeared; or if judgment shall be given upon any verdict or demurrer, against the plaintiff, the defendant or defendants shall recover treble costs, and have the like remedy for the same, as defendants have in other cases by law.

Boston: Printed, by EDES & GILL, *in Queen-Street,* 1774.

THE Boston-Gazette, AND COUNTRY JOURNAL. No. 997.

Containing the freshest Advices, Foreign and Domestic.

MONDAY, May 23, 1774.

Extracts of private Letters from London, *dated April 7 and 8, to Persons in* New-York *and* Philadelphia.

WITH the most anxious and deep concern, I sit down to give you some account of the bitter things that are meditated against America, and through her against England itself, and that constitution, by which it has long been distinguished among the nations, as a land of freedom and happiness, and an asylum against tyranny and oppression—A distinction, alas! that now subsists no more! and must be forever lost—unless kind Providence should interpose, to save us from that slavery and darkness, which has well nigh overspread the face of the whole earth. *America*, the last resort of retiring *Freedom*, is now to be invaded, and the fugitive driven from her peaceful recesses there, that so she may find no resting place on this side Heaven.

A plan of despotism and arbitrary power, has incessantly been pursued, during the present reign; thro' all the ministerial changes and manœvres, *that* has still been the grand object in view; and may explain all those intricate movements of government, which otherwise appear quite mysterious and unaccountable; especially with regard to the colonies, it may account for that obstinate perseverance in measures palpably inconsistent with every principle of the English constitution, of justice, and of common sense; which have been attended with almost infinite expence, trouble and difficulty, both to the colonies and Great-Britain itself; when at the same time a plain, easy and certain way to peace, harmony and prosperity lies so open before us, that none can mistake it, and yet offers itself in vain. An absolute, arbitrary government, has infinite charms for a multitude of haughty luxurious parasites and flatterers that ever surround a throne and hope to share with it in tyrannizing over the people and rioting on their spoils. No wonder that such as these should prevail on a young Monarch to be pleased with, to countenance and adopt their plan. Unlimited power is generally a most desirable object, especially to youth and inexperience—and few are distrustful of themselves, or imagine that it would be unsafe in their hands.

In England almost every obstruction to the execution of this plan, is removed; places of high trust and importance, are bestowed upon those who will act in subserviency to the views of the court; those who might impede those views, are divested of power, and disabled from any effectual opposition. Experience has shewn, that the pensions and places in the gift of the Crown have as great an influence on the Nobility, whose estates might set them above dependance, as upon common men—for luxury is boundless, and can render the possessor of the greatest estate as needy as a beggar, and, as vulnerable to the influence of a bribe. As for the Commons, those natural guardians of the liberties and properties of the people, tho' there are many worthy men among them, who do their utmost to stem the torrent of corruption, and preserve their country; yet their number is too small to answer the end: The eloquence of Cicero, the most consummate knowledge of the interests of their country, and zeal for its service, the greatest abilities and integrity, are all render'd entirely useless by a corrupt majority of ministerial tools, who vote just as they are directed: This House, therefore, which used to be the bulwark of the people's security, serves now only to give the form or appearance of legality to acts of real tyranny and oppression, by which they are deprived of their liberty and property. A great majority of the house are return'd by little venal Burroughs, bribed by the nation's own money, to elect such men as the Ministry choose, and afterwards command to vote as they please. A friend well acquainted with the internal state of Great-Britain, assures me, "that many burroughs in the "kingdom have scarce 10 persons qualified to "vote for a representative in parliament, and "that all who are qualified are under the influ"ence of some Nobleman, or Squire, who, if he "has no person of his own family to put in, "transfers the election, or rather nomination, to "such adventurers as choose to purchase a seat "as a means of climbing the hill of preferment. "In some places there is not even the sha"dow of an election or town-meeting.—— "The sovereign, bailiff, or rather returning offi"cer, with two or three burgesses, go privately "to the session house, and in a moment name "such a one, as duly elected, without the ap"pearance of a candidate.

"What a farce are such transactions, when the liberties of the people are thus played away at a game, wherein a corrupt government, and an ambitious covetous landlord are the only gainers!" All things being thus ripe in England for the open introduction of arbitrary power, nothing seems to have prevented it, but the struggles of the Americans to preserve their liberties. These struggles have been doubly mortifying to the ministry, as they have thereby been not only prevented from levying a revenue upon America, but from executing their scheme, in its full extent upon England. And unless that scheme be very soon executed, it is in danger of being blown up entirely; for matters have risen to such a crisis, the uneasiness and distress of the nation are become so general, that some violent commotion seems inevitable, and near at hand; and if a revolution should happen, and fail to establish despotism in England, it would probably be fatal to those who have attempted to introduce it. The most strenuous efforts therefore will now be made, both by force and fraud to reduce the Americans to a conformity with the measures of the ministry, who are enraged & distracted at the obstructions they meet with from that quarter.

I therefore earnestly warn you to firmness and vigilance, every art will be used, both to intimidate, and to deceive you, may God direct you to be wise and faithful to yourselves and to your country, and crown your endeavours with success. You have every thing at stake that can be dear to reasonable creatures; your freedom, your property, your posterity, your honour.——— The very ministry who are striving to enslave you, in spight of themselves, both honour and fear you; but if they succeed against you, will despise and spurn you.

About a fortnight ago an act of Parliament of a most extraordinary kind, to shut up the port of Boston, was passed in a most extraordinary manner, being smuggled through the House, in 17 days only from its introduction. The Evidence before the Privy Council was suppressed, the agents refused a hearing at the bar, and no member for Boston or America in either House. Nor had the merchants and manufacturers in England, who will be deeply affected by the execution of this act, any proper notice of it, or opportunity to remonstrate against it. Indeed it is openly said that many a thousand pounds were issued from the Treasury to obtain a majority in the House, and hurry it through before there should be time for opposition: So that when a body of merchants trading to Boston and America, waited on Lord North with a request that a petition might be heard against the bill, before it passed into a law; they had the mortification to find they were too late, and that the bill had already passed. As his Majesty has, by the act, a conditional power to suspend its operation, in case the tea destroyed at Boston should be paid for, the merchants offered Lord North £. 19,000, or a security to the India Company, to pay for the tea, if that suspension of the act might be procured from his Majesty. But these offers were refused, and the merchants went away much dissatisfied——as thinking people are in general, against the proceedings of the Ministry, especially in respect to this law, and the manner of getting it passed, which was with as much privacy and haste as possible, so that it is hardly yet known in the manufacturing towns which will be hurt by it. It is expected to raise great clamour and uneasiness as soon as it comes to be generally known, and felt, by the labouring people, and the trade, the stoppage of which, it is imagined, in a few months will convince the Ministry they have acted wrong.

Another new bill, as extraordinary as the Boston bill, only more general in its operation, is in agitation, in the Privy Council; and like the Boston bill it is intended to be smuggled through the House. God grant it may be stopped in its progress, or defeated of its design. It is expected here that America will be surprised or frightened into a compliance with it, by the intended alarming clauses in it, and the spirited manner of enforcing it.

God give you vigilance, fortitude, and wisdom to avoid the snares laid for you, and enable you to escape them.

General Gage is appointed Governor and Commander in Chief of Massachusetts Bay, with very extensive powers. Under him are to be a set of officers, approved by the Ministry, to be made Councellors, and enforce the parliamentary laws, with the (apparent) consent of the people.

In short, every art will be used to deceive you, and either cheat or frighten you out of your freedom and property: However, I can assure you the commanders have private orders not to fight, unless they can provoke you to appear the aggressors,—nay they have orders not to commence hostilities, without further orders. But how soon that restriction may be taken off, God only knows; nor do I think that it was from any regard to justice, or tenderness to you, that such a restraint was laid; but purely from fear of the consequences of sanguinary orders; Therefore I think, if you are firm and prudent, you have no occasion at this time, to fear any tragical consequences from a refusal to be taxed by the British parliament, who have really no right at all to tax you; —not that I would persuade you to this refusal merely upon a supposition, that the ministry will not proceed to hostile and sanguinary measures— for my opinion is, that there is nothing too absurd or wicked for them to do; but that if they should proceed to such measures, it will be better for you to die than submit to them: However as your cause is just, and all the world must see that you are injured and oppressed, your oppressors will be condemned by all the world, both at home and abroad; and if you are but firm and prudent in your opposition, fear not but providence will interpose in your behalf, and raise you up friends to support and assist you. Some of the greatest and wisest, as well as best men in England, are already on your side, and will stand by you; your enemies have nothing but mere power, unjustly obtained, and applied, to support their cause; reason and justice are altogether against them; they therefore stand on slippery ground, and totter in their stations. Lord Camden, exerted himself nobly in the House of Lords, in your favour—He told them the Boston bill would be productive of a train of evils, and that they would certainly have cause to repent it. Great care is taken to prevent copies of his speech from getting to America, as well as to deceive you by false intelligence. Every tool of power in America will be called upon, and furnished with means to mislead you by a misrepresentation of facts, and giving a false turn and colouring to every thing that it concerns you to know. Six hundred pounds per annum, are paid to writers of false intelligence, and letters as well as news papers, that might give you such intelligence as the ministry desire to conceal from you, are all stopped.

It is given out that severe measures are only intended against Boston, to punish their refractory conduct; but depend upon it, if they succeed against Boston, the like measures will be extended to every colony in America; they only begin with Boston, hoping the other colonies will not interpose. But you are all to be visited in turn, and devoured one after another. You may depend upon my intelligence—my office gives me access to the principals, concerned in the measures, and I think it my duty to warn the innocent against the wicked devices that I know to be meditated against them. It behoves the colonies, to be united, in their intelligence, councils and measures; it is a matter of the last importance to them, to stand by and support one another; the most favoured can only expect to be last devoured. The

(*Turn to the last Page.*)

ministry

From the London Evening Post, *April* 9.

PROCEEDINGS AGAINST

EDINBURGH.	BOSTON.
Began the 10th of February, 1737, and ended the 21st of June, having continued near four months.	Began the 14th, and ended the 31st of March, 1774, being in all seventeen days.
The Provost and Magistrates of Edinburgh, the Judges of Scotland, and many other witnesses examined at the bar.	Witnesses examined at the Privy Council, and their evidence suppressed.
Council and evidence for the Magistrates and City fully heard at the bar.	The Agent refused a hearing at the bar.
Two Members for Edinburgh, forty five for Scotland in the Lower House, and sixteen in Upper House.	Not one Member for Boston in either House, nor for all or any part of America, nor even a voice in electing one.
Charge, an overt act of rebellion, and an attrocious murder—— proved on a full hearing, and by competent evidence.	Charge, a riot and trespass—no evidence, and no hearing.
Frequent conferences held between the two Houses to compare the evidence, &c.	Not one conference.
Punishment—A fine 2000l.	Punishment——The loss of their port to the injury of the town, at the lowest and most favourable estimate, of 500,000l. The restoration of their port, and the use of their property, left at the King's mercy, after they shall have paid for rotten tea the full price of that which is found, and all damages, to the amount, we may presume, of 30,000l.
For proof, see the Journals of the Lords and Commons in 1737, and the bill against Edinburgh.	Journals of the Lords and Commons 1774, and the Boston port bill.

B O S T O N, May 23.

WE cannot but gratefully acknowledge the generous and brotherly Interposition of our Brethren of the other Colonies on the present desperate Attack of the British Parliament on the Town of Boston, *among our warmest Friends we are happy to enumerate the respectable Inhabitants of the Towns of* New-York, Hartford, Newport, Portsmouth *and* Westerly, *who have thus early assured us of their readiness to unite in every Measure of Self Denial and Hazard to extricate themselves as well as us from impending Slavery.*

Extracts of a Letter from New-York, May 14, 1774, *addres'd to the* COMMITTEE OF CORRESPONDENCE *in* BOSTON.

" Last Thursday Capt. Couper arriv'd from London in 27 Days. By him we have receiv'd the shocking and detestable Act of Parliament, that shuts up your Port the first of June. We want Language to express our Abhorrence of this additional Act of Tyranny to America; we clearly see that she is to be attack'd and enslav'd by distressing and subduing you—We are perswaded that the sensible People of the Town of Boston anticipate the Object of the Act in all its dire Events; and therefore, that a Compliance with the Provision of it will only be a *temporary* Relief from a *particular* Evil, which must end in a general Calamity. Impress'd with this, a great Number of our Citizens wish our Port to be in the same State with yours. And as the Ministry have put it out of your Power to continue your Trade with Great-Britain, the Merchants are to have a Meeting To Morrow Evening to agree upon a general Non-Importation and Non-Exportation of Goods to and from Great-Britain; also to stop the Exportation of all Hoops, Staves, Heading and Lumber to the English Islands, and to export no more of the first Articles to the foreign Islands than will be sufficient to bring Home the Sugar, Rum and Molasses for the Return of American Cargoes. We shall advise you of the Result of the Meeting.——————————

We can with great Truth assure you, that many timid People in this City, who have interested themselves but very little in the Controversy with Great-Britain, express the greatest Resentment and Indignation at the Conduct of the Ministry to your Town, and consider the Treatment to it *as if done in this City*; and this is the general Sense of the Inhabitants. The Express is a true Friend to the Liberties of this Country, and will wait your Directions for his Return."

At a Town Meeting legally called, and held at Newport, in the Colony of Rhode Island, the 20th Day of May, 1774.

VOTED, *That we have the deepest Sense of the Injuries done to the Town of Boston, by the Act of Parliament lately passed for putting an End to their Trade, and destroying the Port; and that we consider this Attack upon them as utterly Subversive of American Liberty: For the same Power may at Pleasure destroy the Trade and shut up the Ports of every other Colony in its Turn, so that there will be a total End of all Property.*

VOTED, *That we will unite with the other Colonies in all reasonable and proper Measures, to procure the Establishment of the Rights of the Colonies upon a just and permanent Foundation; and particularly in Case the other Colonies shall upon this most alarming Occasion put a Stop to their Trade to Great-Briain and the West-Indies, that we will heartily join with them in the Measure.*

VOTED, *That the Committee of Correspondence for the Town immediately transmit a Copy of these Resolutions to the Committee of Correspondence for the Town of Boston.*

VOTED, *That the Committee of Correspondence for this Town, immediately send a Copy of the above Resolutions to each Town in this Colony.*

A true Copy,

Witness, Wm. Coddington, *Town-Clerk.*

Gentlemen, *Westerly, 19th May,* 1774.

WITH mingled Concern and Indignation the Committee of Correspondence for this Town have seen an Act for blocking up the Harbour of Boston.

Rome designing to destroy the City of Carthage, barbarously required of the Carthaginians that they should forsake their City and remove their Habitations twelve Miles from the Sea: The Consideration of the inveterate Hatred occasioned by the long and bloody Wars which had subsisted between Rome and Carthage, the Remembrance of several Hundred Thousand Romans killed in those Wars, and several Hundred Towns plundered by the Carthaginians is some Excuse for the Roman Severity.

But the cruel and unnatural Treatment which the Town of Boston has received from Great-Britain, will admit of no Kind of Palliation; the Metropolis of a most affectionate and loyal Colony, which in all the Wars of Great-Britain hath gloriously supported the British Interest in America, and even by their wise and vigorous Efforts made a Conquest which gave Peace to Europe, is now threatened with Destruction, for no other Cause but because the People have bravely determined not to become Slaves.

We have long felt for the Town of Boston: We heartily sympathize with our Brethren upon this alarming Occasion: We are much pleased with the noble Firmness with which this cruel Edict is received in Boston! We highly approve the Measures taken by the Town, and are entirely of Opinion that the joint Resolution of the Colonies to stop all Importations from and Exportations to Great-Britain and the West-Indies, until the Act is repealed, will infallibly produce the desired Effect.

The Country which we possess, blessed be God, affords every necessary of Life; We are morally certain that with the common Blessings of Heaven upon our Industry and Frugality, we can live comfortably without importing a single Article from Britain or the W. Indies: And we are equally certain that neither England or the West-Indies can subsist long without us. Their own Preservation therefore will compel them to do us Justice.

This horrid Attack upon the Town of Boston we consider not as an Attempt upon that Town singly, but upon the whole Continent. We are therefore determined to use our whole Influence for the Support of the Town of Boston in the same Manner as if the Attack had been made in the Metropolis of this Colony. And we doubt not but the other Colonies will consider this arbitrary and tyrannical Edict in the same Light, and heartily unite with the Friends of Liberty in Boston in Support of the common Cause.

That infinite Wisdom may direct and preserve all the Colonies, is the ardent Prayer of,

(Sign'd by the Committee of Correspondence.)

Extract of a Letter fom the Committee of Correspondence for Portsmouth, *dated May* 19, 1774, *to the Committee of Correspondence for the Town of* Boston.

"WE think the late Act of Parliament to shut up the Port of Boston of a most extraordinaoy Nature and fatal Tendency; Administration are taking every Method to disunite the Colonies, thereby to render the noble opposition to their arbitrary and destructive Measures abortive: We hope a firm Union of all the Colonies will still subsist, and that such a Plan may be devised and resolutely pursued by all, as may prevent the cruel Effects of this Act.

We heartily sympathize with you, under your present difficult and alarming situation.—We will exert ourselves to carry any Plan into Effect which may be concerted by the Colonies for the general Relief —We sincerely wish you Resolution and Prosperity in the common Cause, and shall ever view your Interest as our own, and are with the highest Esteem, &c."

It may be depended upon that Mr. William Jones of Bristol, intending this Summer for Boston, engaged a Ship, and went down to the Manufacturing Towns to engage a Cargo for her to bring out with Him; and on his Return homewards he met with the Boston Port Bill, which Influenced him at considerable Expence to contradict all Orders. These disappointments, with the many Countermands and other Letters declarative of the present Disposition of the Colonists in general, must throw the Manufacturers into a worse Consternation than any thing of the Kind that has ever yet happened; as all Ranks and Degrees of Men can now plainly perceive the Designs of Administration.

Friday 7-night arrived here his Majesty's Ship Lively, Capt. Bishop, in 26 Days from England, in whom came his Excellency General GAGE, who is appointed Governor and Commander in Chief of this Province:—His Excellency landed at Castle William under a Discharge of the Cannon of that Fortress. And on Tuesday the Troop of Guards, Regiment of Militia, Company of Artillery and Grenadiers, as also the Company of Cadets, appeared under Arms in King-Street. At 11 o'Clock his Excellency left the Castle under discharge of the Cannon of that Fortress, and proceeded on board his Majesty's Ship Captain, having previously given Notice of his Intention to Land on the Long Wharf. At Twelve His Majesty's Council, the Secretary of the Province, the Magistrates High Sheriff, Marshall of the Court of Vice Admiralty, the Selectmen, and many other Gentlemen, preceded by the Cadet Company, received him there upon his Landing, and under the Discharge of the Cannon of the Admiral's Ship and the Batteries in the Town. Upon his passing up King-Street his Excellency received the standing Salutes from the officers of the respective Corps.

His Majesty's Commissions appointing him Captain General and Governor in Chief of this Province, &c. were then published in the Council Chamber, and after the usual Oaths were administered, his Excellency was pleased to Issue a Proclamation requiring all Officers whose Commissions would otherwise cease and determine, to continue in the exercise of their respective Commissions until further Orders. Three Vollies were then fired, and three Cheers given by a vast Concourse of People collected on this Occasion.

After his Excellency had received the Compliments of his Majesty's Council, of the Gentlemen in Commission of the Peace, the Episcopal and Dissenting Clergy, Military Officers, and a great number of other Gentlemen, he proceeded (escorted by the Company of Cadets) to Faneuil Hall, where an elegant Dinner was provided for his Welcome Reception.

Thursday Evening died, Mr. Samuel Stedman, Printer, Son of Capt. Ebenezer Stedman of Cambridge, aged 21, wanting only 9 Days. He was a young Man of great Sobriety and Faithfulness—very modest in his Manners & Conversation—remarkable for avoiding the Follies of Youth. He bore his Illness with great Patience and Resignation, and his latter End was Peace.

† *The Piece prom[illegible] in our last, together with a Number of other speculative Pieces, new Advertisements, &c. we are obliged to omit for want of room.*

To the Addressors of the late Governor Hutchinson.

GENTLEMEN,

TO forward you in your generous Undertaking, to contradict the general Voice of the two Branches of your own Legislature, and of every honest and sensible Man in the Empire, you are informed, That this same excellent Patriot, some few Years ago in Conversation with Lord William Campbell, then Governor of Nova-Scotia, on a Tour this Way, expressed his Approbation of the Expediency of having this Country reduced to Lordships, and thereby the People brought into due Subordination; and subjoined, That "he had been endeavouring to bring this Matter about for many Years."—If you question the Truth of this publickly, I will produce you an Affidavit to the full Amount of what is here set forth.

W. K.

For L O N D O N,

The Ship Thomas,

Thomas Robson, Master,

Will sail with all Expedition.

For Freight or Passage apply to PETER HUGHES, at his Store in King-Street.

Where there is to be Sold,

ENGLISH, Russia and Ravens Duck, Ticklinburgs, Oznabrigs, Broad Cloths, Duffils, Beaver Coatings, Cod and Mackrel Lines and Hooks, Sail, Sein & Wharpping Twine, 4d. 6d. 8d. 10d. & 20d Nails, Sheathing and Drawing ditto, 6 by 8, 7 by 9 & 8 by 10 Glass, Florence Oil, Gun Powder in Half and Quarter Barrels, Crates of Ware, 12, 15, 18 & 21 Inch Pipes, treble, double and single refin'd Loaf Sugar, Buntins, Shot, Barr Lead, Writing Paper, Spices, Turkey Figgs, Porter in Hampers of 4 Dozen Bottles, Durham Mustard, choice Newcastle Coals. Boston, May 21, 1774.

Messieurs EDES and GILL,

THE late act of Parliament for shutting up this Harbour has taken up the attention of every inhabitant, and various schemes have been proposed for preventing the threatened calamity—Some honest but timid persons have been led to think that it wou'd be best to pay for the Tea, but they who are of that opinion must not have attended to the act; for it is enacted that the port shall not be opened "until it shall sufficient-"ly appear to his Majesty that full Satisfaction "hath been made by or on behalf of the inha-"bitants of the said town of Boston to the united "company of merchants of England trading to "the East Indies, for the damage sustained by the "said company by the destruction of their goods "sent to the town of Boston", and "until it "shall be certified to his Majesty in Council by "the Governor or Lieut. Governor of said Pro-"vince, that reasonable satisfaction hath been "made to the officers of his Majesty's revenue, "and others, who suffered by the riots and in-"surrections abovementioned, in the months of "November and December, in the Year 1773, "and in the Month of January, in the Year 1774."
So that it is impossible that paying for the tea alone shou'd answer any valuable purpose; and it is impossible to say what will be judged reasonable satisfaction to those who suffer'd, or pretend they suffered at the times mentioned in the act.—Nay, if all this was done it wou'd be impossible to know what steps we must take in order that it may "appear that peace and obedience to the "laws shall be so far restored in the said town of "Boston, that the trade of Great-Britain may be "safely carried on there, and his Majesty's customs "duly collected, and his Majesty in his Privy "Council shall adjudge the same to be true." But even if we knew and had taken those steps at this moment, we must suffer all the penalties in-flicted by the act; for we shall have suffer'd the loss of all our summer trade before his Majesty can be acquainted with our submission, and his orders for opening the port have reached America. So that no advantage can possibly be derived from this scheme of paying for the Tea; it wou'd only make us contemptible in the eyes of the Colonies, and invite the Ministry to lay still heavier burdens upon us. But if we come into a manly resolution to suspend our trade with Great-Britain until our Rights are restored, and are heartily joined by our sister Colonies, (as we have the best reason to believe we shall be) the world will be convinced that the virtue of America is superior to all the attacks of corruption and tyranny.

G.

Messieurs EDES & GILL,

THIS country never yet saw a time, in which the People—and of course their FATHERS and REPRESENTATIVES—ought to *stand more firm* and play the man. Never was there a time in which a wise, upright and steady COUNCIL OF THE LAND was more necessary to our common safety.—A weak and pusillanimous COUNSELLOR at this period may do more mischief than many wise and intrepid ones will be able to remedy in an age.

Let us throw aside personal attachment and private connexion; let us consider the evils which we may do by a bad choice—evils that it will never be in our power to correct, tho' we weep tears of blood.

If we have ever given our suffrages for wicked, base or unworthy characters, let us now repent of that great sin, and make the best reparation to our injured brethren and posterity, that we have now power and opportunity, by giving our voices to none, but such who have *understanding, integrity* and *zeal* to guide the COMMONWEALTH—in this storm of power and oppression.—Should we be careless and unconcerned, indifferent or in-active, at this season, we not only endanger the great ship of THE STATE, in which our treasures are laden;—but let us bear *weightily* on our mind, that WE ARE ALL *embarked* in one COMMON BOTTOM—lives and fortune, children and posterity must be overwhelmed and sink in case of *shipwreck.*

Let none of us, therefore, make *shipwreck* of OUR CONSCIENCES, lest we not only perish in this world—but *most miserably perish* in that which is to come.

AN OLD COMMONER.

TO THE INHABITANTS
OF THE TOWN OF
NEW-HAVEN:

YESTERDAY a special Messenger arrived from Boston, with a Letter to this Town, containing In-telligence of the utmost Importance.—Also another from New-York.

THIS is therefore to desire the Inhabitants of this Town to meet at the Court-House at 3 o'Clock P. M. to consider what Measures to adopt on this alarming Occasion.

Tuesday Morning, 17th *of May,* 1774.

THE Merchants, and all concerned in Trade in this Place, are requested to meet at the British Coffee-House, at 6 o'Clock this Evening, on Matters of general and important Concern.
Boston, May 23, 1774.

Teneriffe WINE.

CHOICE Teneriffe WINE, just arrived, in Pipes, half Pipes and Quarter Casks, TO BE SOLD. Inquire at SOLOMON DAVIS or THOMAS WAL-LEY's Store.

All Persons that have any Concerns with JONATHAN WILLIAMS, Junr. are desired to apply to JONATHAN WILLIAMS, Senior, Esq; who is impower'd to transact his Business during his absence.

William Bant

Has Imported in the last Vessels from LONDON, a Ge-neral Assortment of Spring and Summer Goods, which he will sell by Wholesale and Retail at his Store front-ing Dock Square, at the very lowest Rates for Cash.
Boston April 21st.   (6 w.)

Edward Church

Has Imported in the last Ships from LONDON, An Assortment of Spring Goods, which he is now selling at his Usual low Rate at his Store in New-bury Street.

Imported in the last Ships from LONDON & GLASGOW,

By Samuel Parkman,

And are now selling at his Shop in Union-Street,
A compleat Assortment of English, India and Scotch GOODS, among which are a Variety of stript, plain and changeable Lutestrings and Mantua's, Sarsnet, Sattins and Modes, plain, spotted, stript and flower'd Gauze, Gauze Aprons & Handkerchiefs, Lawn Aprons and Handkerchiefs, Callicoes and Patches, Ben-galls, Brolio, Missinets, &c. A large Assortment of Ho-siery, Corderoys, black and white Cotton Denim, brown Thread Breeches Pieces, Nankeen, Taffities & Persians, a great Variety of black & white Bone Blond & Trolly Lace and Edgings, and many other Articles.
⁂ He asks the Favour of those who have Money to lay out to call and see him, that he may have an Opportunity to prove to them that his Goods are really very *cheap.*

TO BE SOLD,
By BENJAMIN CHURCH,
ON THURSDAY NEXT,
At THREE o'Clock in the Afternoon.
A Variety of valuable Articles, viz.

CALLICOES—Checks—Linnens—Shalloons—Du-rants—Calamancoes—Bussels—Taberits—Veneti-ans—Antiloons—Camblet—Cambleteens—platedBuc-kles—Handkerchiefs, &c. &c.——Also House Furni-ture, as Tables—Chairs—Glasses—an Eight-Day Clock, Watches, &c.   At 3 o'Clock. P. M.

Andrew Newell,

Mathematical Instrument Maker,
At his Shop next Door below the Sign of the Globe, in King-Street, has just imported and ready for Sale, All sorts of Mathematical Instruments in every Branch.——ALSO, STATIONARY of every kind; and continues to make, mend and repair all sorts of Instruments in the Mathematical Branches; Spy Glasses, &c. &c.
N. B. The present prospect of Affairs in the Town induces him to sell cheap for Cash only.

Just Published, and to be Sold by J. EDWARDS, next Door to the Post-Office in Cornhill, (Price 9*d.*)
A Rational Explication of
St. John's Vision of the two Beasts,
in the 13th Chapter of the Revelation.
Shewing that the Beginning, Power, and Dura-tion of POPERY are plainly predicted in that Vision, and that these Predictions have hitherto been punctually verified. By SAMUEL LANGDON, D.D. Pastor of the first Church in *Portsmouth, New Hampshire.*
Blessed is he that readeth, and they that hear the Words of this Prophecy, and keep these Things that are written therein, for the Time is at Hand, Rev. 1. 3.

TO BE LETT
A large commodious Shop, pleasantly situated in Cornhill, directly opposite John Semple's, and at the same place may be had genteel Boarding and Lodging for Gentlemen and Ladies, by MARY TAI-LER.

Shipping Timber.

ABOUT 80 Tons of good white Oak Shipping Timber, to be Sold cheap. Inquire of Edes & Gill.

TO BE SOLD
A ROPE WALK, the Buildings in good repair, with all the Tools and Implements necessary for carrying on the Rope Making Business, it is very plea-santly and conveniently situated, and has the Advantage of a Water Carriage—The Business may be carried on in this Town to as much Advantage, as perhaps it can be in any Town upon the Continent.——Any Person that inclines to purchase, may know the Terms by applying to JOHN ADAMS, opposite the Old South Meeting-House in Boston.

Portsmouth in New Hampshire, May 18.

The Commissioners of His Majesty's Customs hereby give Notice, that from and after the first day of June 1774, the Officers of the Customs for the Port and Harbour, will be removed from the Town of Boston, to the Town of Plymouth, within the limits of the Port of Boston; then and there to proceed to carry on in the usual Manner the Business of their respective Departments, in the Collection and Management of His Majesty's Customs and the Execution of the Laws of Trade. And no Officer of the Customs will be permit-ted to remain in the Town or Harbour of Boston from and after the first Day of June next—during the Continu-ance of said Act.   By Order of the Commissioners,
SAMUEL MATHER,
Custom-House, BOSTON,   pro Secretary.
May 20. 1774.

JUST ARRIVED,
New Philadelphia Flour in large and small Barrels, (suitable for a family) a quantity of best Pigg and Barr Iron—Anchors and a few Barrels of Pitch, to be Sold very cheap by
Edward Gray,
At Store No. 2, South Side the Town Dock,
Where may be had as usual,
West India Goods and Iron Ware.

WATCHES.
RICHARD CRANCH,
Near the Mill Bridge, BOSTON,
INforms his Customers, that he has received a fresh Assortment of Watches (some of them with Day of Month) which he will sell at his usual Prices.

TO BE SOLD,
A genteel new Fall-back Chaise, with Harness compleat.   Inquire of Edes & Gill.

✕✕✕✕✕✕✕✕✕✕✕✕✕✕✕✕✕✕✕✕✕✕

To be Sold on TUESDAY the Twenty-first Day of June next, at Two o'Clock in the Afternoon, by PUBLIC VENDUE, at the House of Mr. Edward Low in Leominster, by Philip Sweetser, of said Leo-minster,

A Good Farm situated in said Town, containing a-bout 140 Acres of choice Land, consisting of Plow-ing, Pasturing and Mowing, with a fine young Orchard, and is well Wooded and excellently Watered, upon a great Road, suitable for a Tavern or Trader, with a good House, Barn, and other valuable Accommodations, which renders it a very desirable Farm. It will be sold at a reasonable Price; and if it should be sold at private Sale before the Day above-mentioned, publick Notice shall be given.
May 5. 1774

TO be Sold by Virtue of an Order of the Inferior Court of Common Pleas for the County of Suf-folk,—A Brick Dwelling-House and Land, situate in Queen-Street in Boston, now improved by Mr. Henry Bass. Also, six Lots of Land at Penobscot, in the Coun-ty of Lincoln; all late belonging to the Estate of Mr. John Proctor, late of said Boston, School-Master, de-ceased.—For further Particulars, inquire of Eunice Proctor, of said Boston, Widow and Administratrix of the said Deceased's Estate, at her Dwelling-House on Copp's Hill, who is fully authorised and impowered by the said Court to sell the same.   May 20. (5w.)

New AUCTION-ROOM, Cornhill.

TO-MORROW at TEN o'Clock will be Sold by PUBLIC VENDUE, at GREENLEAF's Auction-Room,——
A large Assortment of GOODS,
——Amongst which are——
3-4, 7-8 and yard-wide Irish Linnens, callicoes, chints, striped flowered and plain lawns, lawn aprons, sprigg'd muslins, silk gauzes, catgutts, ribbons, plain modes, silk twist, damask and diaper table cloths, kenting and linnen handkerchiefs, checks, stript hol-lands, bedticks, broad cloths, kerseys, ratteens, duffils, Manchester velvets, shalloons, tammies, thread & worsted hose, breeches patterns, mens and boys castor and felt hatts, table knives and forks, silver-plated buckles, sleeve buttons, stone shoe knee and neck buckles, silver watches, cream coloured and white stone dishes and plates, and a quantity of glass ware, &c. &c.
WILLIAM GREENLEAF, Auctioneer.
The Sale will begin precisely at Ten o'Clock.
For private Sale, an 8-Day Clock, a Desk and Book-Case, a new Chaise and Harness, a handsome Curricle, some Looking-Glasses, and a Variety of English Goods.

At GOULD's *Auction Office,* In Back-Street,
ON FRIDAY NEXT,
At TEN in the Morning,
Will be Sold by PUBLIC VENDUE,
A Variety of English Goods, with a general Assortment of Hard Ware. Also a Number of Articles taken by Execution, both in the English Goods and Grocery Way.   R. GOULD, Auctioneer.

A Sale of FURNITURE,
At GOULD's *Auction Office,* in Back-Street,
On Tuesday the 31st Instant, at Ten in the Morn-ing.   R. GOULD, Auctioneer.

Burials in the Town of BOSTON, since our last.
Ten Whites.   No Blacks.
Baptiz'd in the several Churches,   Six.

High Water at BOSTON, *for the present Week.*
Monday, 5 min. aft. 9 } Friday, 2 min. after. 1
Tuesday, 4 min. aft. 10 } Saturday, 1 min. aft. 2
Wednesday, 3 m. aft. 11 } Lord's-Day, 1 m af. 3
Thursday, 2 min. aft. 12 } ☉'s Full 25 D. 1 Aft.

ministry are determined to try your metal to the utmost. Mansfield and Bute are supposed to be the prime directors, and to influence the royal ear as they please. The spoils of England are insufficient to support the luxury of the minions of power, they have fixed their voracious appetites upon the possessions of the Americans, and intend to make a prey of them, in defiance of reason and justice, of the charters of kings, and the divine laws of nature. Depend upon it, every colony is to be subdued into a slavish obedience to the tyrannical impositions of Great-Britain; nothing less will suffice, nothing less is intended. After the subjection of Boston, and perhaps all the New England Governments, New Jersey and New-York, are to be the next in course; and they talk of taking away Penn's charter. Look to yourselves, exert all your faculties to the utmost, your virtues will be put to a severe trial, and if they are not genuine and well founded, they will not stand the test.

Alas! how is my soul shock'd at the present situation of England, my native country—a great, a generous, & late a happy people—but now, how changed, how fallen! The men who are really wise and good, deprived of opportunities of acting—The poor and middling people ruin'd and oppressed, the rich, lost in luxury and dissipation, a set of weak and wicked men, misguiding the reins of government, the people tax'd to death without mercy, placemen and pensioners without number, &c.

Many of the officers on the intended expedition against Boston and America, have nobly thrown up their commissions, and refused to fight against their brethren in the colonies, without a just cause; and it is expected the soldiers will desert in multitudes, from a mere sense of honour and justice.

April 8. News is just now arrived, by a private hand, that the discontent of the people has so far prevailed, that orders are sent to unman the fleet, or at least that it should not sail till further orders. I hope the news will prove true.

The Scots in the House of Commons have been your great enemies. I think it would be but just in the Bostonians to withold every farthing due to them in that town, which I am told is very considerable, especially to the city of Glasgow. Indeed I think as the port is shut up, the whole debt due from them to Great-Britain should be stopped, and reprisals be made by every means in your power. The preservation of England itself and her excellent constitution, require it of you. May God direct and prosper your counsels.

T.

Spring GOODS.

Cheap for Cash or short Credit, just Imported

By JOHN WHITE,

Near the Cornfields, Union-Street;

A compleat Assortment of newest-fashion'd Callicoes and India Chints, Nankeens, Russia Drabs, yd-wide, 7-8 and 3-4 Irish Linnen, Cambricks and Lawns, Gauzes and Catgut, Patent & Spider's Net, Book Muslin, black, bone and blond Lace, white blond and thread ditto, Cheveaux de Frize, strip'd and sprig'd silk Gauze, silk Gloves and Mitts, a compleat Assortment of newest fashioned Ribbons, Mode Sarsnet and Sattin of all Colours, Cotton Hose, Handkerchiefs of Sorts, English and French Necklaces, Womens English Shoes and Clogs, Looking Glasses, a large Assortment of China, Glass and Earthen Ware, &c. &c. &c.

N. B. A few Casks of English Cheese, and a few Hampers of exceeding fine Porter.

All Persons that have any Demands on the Estate of Mr. Andrew Cunningham, late of Boston, Hatter, deceased, are desired to bring in their Accounts to Mary Greenleaf and John Cunningham, Administrators on said Estate, for Adjustment.—And all Persons indebted to said Estate, are desired to make immediate Payment to said Administrators.

John Cunningham

HAS for Sale at his Shop near the Corner of School-Street, opposite Mr. Deblois's.

A Large Assortment of English and India Goods, suitable for all Seasons, which he is determined to sell at the Sterling Cost (clear of Charges) he being determined to quit the Business.

☞ *King's Arms Tavern.*

THE large, commodious and pleasant House on Boston Neck, which has been occupied as a public Tavern for many Years past, is to be let and may be entered upon within a Fortnight, or is to be sold, with Land enough to accommodate the same, if applied for within ten Days.

Enquire of Edes & Gill.

All Persons indebted to, or that have any Demands on the Estate of Mr. John Parker, late of Sandwich, Merchant, deceased, are desired to bring in their Accounts to Joseph Parker, of Falmouth, sole Executor to said Estate, in Order for Settlement.

Cyrus Baldwin,

HEREBY notifies his Customers and others, That he purposes to embark for London early next Fall; and that he is now selling off his Stock in Trade, consisting of large and valuable Assortments of ENGLISH, INDIA, and SCOTCH GOODS, very cheap for Cash at his Store in Cornhill, near the Town-House in Boston.

——*Among which are*——

Royal Ribb, Jennets, Denim, Cotton Velvets, and A large Assortment of superfine, midling, and low-pric'd BROAD-CLOTHS, with Trimmings; German Serges, Wiltons, Jeans, Fustians, Cotton Velvets, Hair and Worsted Plushes, Furniture and other Calicoes, Furniture Checks, Irish Linnens, Cambricks, Lawns, thick Muslin, Book ditto, Silks for Ladies Gowns of various sorts and colours, (some of them at the first Cost) a beautiful Assortment of Ribbons, Quality and Shoe Bindings, Garterings and Tapes; a fine Assortment of Silk, Thread, Worsted and Cotton Hosiery, Carpets and Carpeting, Looking Glasses, &c. with *a Thousand other Articles*, not here mentioned.—Very neat superfine Chip Hats at the sterling Cost.

*† Those who have the Cash to pay will most surely find it to their Advantage to apply to said Baldwin.—He earnestly Requests all Persons that are indebted to him, to make speedy Payment.

John Welsh

INFORMS his Friends and Customers, that he has Imported in the last Vessels from England,

A General Assortment of English, India, Hard-Ware and Cutlery Goods; also Jewellery, Goldsmiths, Clock and Watchmaker's Articles, which will be sold by Wholesale and Retail, at a very low Advance for Cash, at his Shop No. 6, Union-Street, Boston.

IMPORTED in the last ships from LONDON,

And TO BE SOLD By

Luke Baker,

At his VARIETY STORE, nearly opposite Capt. Cobb's Distill-House, at the South-End,

A very large, genteel, and fashionable Assortment of

S I L K S,

Consisting of

BROCADES, Sattins, Lutestring, ½ Ell and ¾ wide plain and strip'd Mantuas, Modes, Persians, &c. &c. which he will sell under the *Sterling Cost*.

ALSO—A great Variety of all other kinds of Spring GOODS, suitable for Ladies and Gentlemen, which he is determin'd to sell as low as can be bought at any Shop or Store in Boston.

Liverpool WARE exceeding Cheap.

TO BE SOLD,

THE Estate late belonging to Wheeler and Morse, lying in Grafton, in this Province, of Massachusets-Bay, about 32 Miles from Providence, and 40 from Boston, consisting of a Dwelling-House, a large Shop, Store, two Barns, and other Outhouses, about one Acre and ½ of Land adjoining, with a good Garden, also about 30 Acres of good Pasture, Meadow or Tillage Land, with about 50 Acres of Woodland, in Sight of the House. It is a very pleasant and convenient Situation for a Country Trader, being on the great Country Road, and within 15 Rods of the Meeting House.

Any Person inclining to purchase, may have Time for Payment, on giving good Security, and may also have the Goods now in said Store, and be supplied with others, on as good Terms as can be purchased anywhere in America. For Terms, apply to NICHOLAS BROWN and Company, in Providence, or JOSEPH ROGERS, who is now in Possession of the Premises.

N. B. The Outland may be Sold separate from the House, Shop, &c.

Colony of Rhode-Island, &c. Newport, May 12, 1774.

WHEREAS Matthew Cozzens of Newport aforesaid, Merchant, by Petition represented unto the General Assembly of the Colony aforesaid, that he is an insolvent Debtor, and prayed that he might be admitted to the Benefit of an Act passed in June, A. D. 1756, entitled, "An Act for the Relief of Insolvent Debtors". Upon which the General Assembly referred the said Petition to the next Sessions, and ordered that in the mean Time the Creditors of the said Matthew Cozzens shall be Notified by Advertisement, to be inserted in the Massachusetts, New-York and Rhode-Island News Papers, to appear at the next Session to answer the same:

I do therefore hereby Notify the Creditors of the said Matthew Cozzens to appear (if they shall think fit) at the General Assembly to be holden at said Newport, on the second Monday in June next, then and there to shew Cause (if any they have) why the said Petition should not be granted. HENRY WARD, *Secretary.*

Samuel Garnett,

Taylor and Habit-Maker from LONDON,

TAKES this Method to acquaint the Public in General, and his Friends in Particular, that he carries on the aforesaid Business in all its Branches in Green's Lane.—Ladies and Gentlemen that please to favour him with their Custom may be served in the best Manner, and on the most reasonable Terms and shortest Notice.

Amory's, Taylor & Rogers,

ACQUAINT their Customers, and others, That they have Imported in the last Vessels from England and Scotland,

A fresh Supply of Spring Goods, which they sell as usual on the lowest Terms, by

Wholesale and Retail,

At their Store in Marlborough-Street.

UMBRELLAS

of all Sizes and Prices, made in the neatest Manner with Ivory and Bone Handles to screw, also more common Mahogany or Maple Handled ditto, Ladies that would buy Cheap and good, call at ISAAC GREENWOOD, Ivory Turner's Shop, next Shop to Dr. CLARKS, North-End, Boston; where you may have your old Umbrella's ... mended and covered, your Ivory and bone stick Fan mended, Gentlemen may have India Canes, neat Ivory and Bone, headed, Hickery Stick, Ivory or Bone, handled, Chaise Whips, Hidrometers for proving Spirits, German Flutes, ditto Tiped with Ivory Fife, Billiard Balls, and many other Articles. Such Gentlemen as are Building may have their Banisters and Posts, Pillers for Fronticepieces and Porticoes, Balls and Flower Pots, or any other Ornaments, turned or twisted in the neatest Manner with Fidelity and Dispatch at the above Shop, all Favours from those that have and shall Imploy duly acknowledged, by their humble Servant,

ISAAC GREENWOOD.

TO BE SOLD

On Board the Sloop *London Expedition*, NICHOLAS CHEVALIER, Master, laying at Wibert's Wharf, New-Boston.

A Number of Indented Jersey Servants of both Sexes: Likewise a Quantity of Cordage of all Sorts, and Hosiery.

All Persons indebted to the Estate of Thomas Brigden, Esq; late of Westminster, in the County of Worcester, deceased, either on Book, Bond or Note, are desired to make immediate Payment to Moses Gill, of Boston, Executor to said Estate. And all to whom the Estate is indebted, are requested to bring in their Accounts for Adjustment.

300 Quintails Cod Fish, 60 Quintails Pollack, 30 Quintails Haddick, and 20 Quintals Cusk

TO BE SOLD CHEAP

By *John Newell*, Cooper.

Nathaniel and *Joseph Cranch,*

Ironmongers and Gunsmiths,

Nearly opposite the Sign of the Lamb, South-End, Boston, have just receiv'd from the Makers, an additional Supply of

FIRE ARMS.

Among which, together with their Stock on Hand, are the following, viz.

VERY neat Fusees, proper for Field-Officers, Mounted in white Copper, with Bayonets, Steel Rods, and Swivels, Ditto Mounted in Brass, Ditto Brass Barrell'd, Coach Guns or Blunderbusses, Holster or Trooping Pistols, some very neat Pocket Ditto,—Gun Locks, Gun Barrels, Brass Mounting Forg'd Work for Gun Locks, &c. &c.—A handsome rifled Barrell Gun, Guns proper for Fowling, Birding, &c. of most Kinds and Prices.

N. B. At the above Shop all Kinds of Gun Work are taken in and executed in the neatest Manner.

Also, Razors, Scissars, Case and Penknives, Ground and Polish'd, so as to satisfy every Reasonable employer.

TO BE SOLD,

BY Order of Court, a Dwelling-House, Sail-Loft, Cooper's Shop, Wharff and Flatts, &c. scituate, lying and being near Fish-Street, at the Northerly Part of Boston, being Part of the Estate of Captain John Dobel, late of Boston, Mariner, deceas'd. For Terms, apply to JACOB COOPER, Attorney to Joseph Doble, Executor to said Estate.

TO BE SOLD,

BY Order of Court, a Dwelling-House and two Acres and one Quarter of Land, in the Town of Lynn, being Part of the Estate of Capt. Benjamin Chadwell, late of Boston, Mariner, deceased, Intestate. For Terms of Sale, apply to JACOB COOPER.

TO BE SOLD

A TOPSAIL SCHOONER with her Appurtenances, now lying at Spear's Wharff.—Also, a Parcel of Rye, Beans and Flour, being Part of the Estate of Capt. Samuel Snow.——Inquire of Jacob Cooper, Attorney to Sarah Snow, Administratrix to said Estate.

ALL Persons indebted to the Estate of Capt. Samuel Snow, late of Boston, Mariner deceased, Intestate, are desired to make speedy Payment to Jacob Cooper, Attorney to the Administratrix.

ALL Persons having Demands on, or are Indebted to the Estate of the late Mrs. *Mary Grice*, deceased, are desired to bring in their Accompts as soon as may be, to *Ebenezer Torry*, Administator on said Estate, in order for a speedy Settlement.

Samuel Grant and Son,

ACQUAINT their Customers and others, that they have IMPORTED in the last Vessels from LONDON, a fresh Supply of ENGLISH and INDIA

G O O D S;

ALSO—all sorts of UPHOLSTERY, which they will sell at the lowest advance for Cash, at their Shop in Union-Street, near the Market, BOSTON.

☞ A good assortment of PAPER HANGINGS.

Boston: Printed, by EDES & GILL.

No. 998.

THE Boſton-Gazette, AND COUNTRY JOURNAL.

Containing the freſheſt Advices, Foreign and Domeſtic.

MONDAY, May 30, 1774.

BOSTON May 30.

WEDNESDAY being the Anniverſary of the Day appointed by Royal Charter for Convening a Great and General Court or Aſſembly of this Province, and for the Election of His Majeſty's Council, the Gentlemen who were returned to ſerve and repreſent the ſeveral Towns, met agreeable to the Precepts at the Town-Houſe in Boſton, at Nine o'Clock in the Morning: A Committee from the Honorable Board, authorized and appointed by his Excellency the Governor, adminiſtred the Oaths required by Act of Parliament, to the Members of the Houſe, who after having taken the Oath of Abjuration and ſubſcribed the Declaration, they unanimouſly choſe Mr. SAMUEL ADAMS, for their Clerk: The Houſe then proceeded to the Choice of a Speaker, when the Honorable THOMAS CUSHING, Eſq. was unanimouſly choſen.

At Eleven o'Clock, His Excellency the Governor accompanied by the Honorable His Majeſty's Council, and a Number of other Gentlemen, preceded by the Company of Cadets, went from the Province Houſe in Proceſſion to the Council Chamber, His Excellency being in the Chair, a Committee of the Houſe preſented to him the Speaker Elect, who afterwards ſent a Meſſage in Writing, agreable to the Royal Explanatory Charter, that he approved of their Choice.

This Buſineſs being finiſhed, His Excellency, His Majeſty's Council, and the Honorable Houſe of Repreſentatives, &c. went in Proceſſion to the Old Brick Meeting-Houſe, where a Sermon was preached before them by the Rev. Mr. GAD HITCHCOCK of Pembroke, from thoſe Words in Proverbs, chap. xxix. v. 2 *When the righteous are in authority, the people rejoice: but when the wicked beareth rule, the people mourn.*

After Divine Service, the Proceſſion, eſcorted by the Cadet Company, went to Faneuil-Hall where an Entertainment was provided for them.

At Noon the Guns at the Batteries were fired, and at One o'Clock thoſe of His Majeſty's Ships in the Harbour.

The following Gentlemen were elected Counſellors for the enſuing Year.

For the late Colony of MASSACHUSETTS-BAY.

The HONORABLE

SAMUEL DANFORTH, Eſq;	JOHN WINTHROP, Eſq;
JOHN ERVING, Eſq;	* WILLIAM PHILLIPS, Eſq;
JAMES BOWDOIN, Eſq;	* JOHN ADAMS, Eſq;
JAMES PITTS, Eſq;	* JAMES PRESCOTT, Eſq;
SAMUEL DEXTER, Eſq;	* TIMO. DANIELSON, Eſq;
ARTEMUS WARD, Eſq;	* RICH. DERBY jun. Eſq;
BENJA. GREENLEAF, Eſq;	* MICHAEL FARLEY, Eſq;
CALEB CUSHING, Eſq;	* BENJAMIN AUSTIN, Eſq;
SAMUEL PHILLIPS, Eſq;	* NORTON QUINCY, Eſq;

For the late Colony of PLYMOUTH.

JAMES OTIS, Eſq;	WALTER SPOONER, Eſq;
WILLIAM SEVER, Eſq;	* JERATHMEEL BOWERS, Eſ.

For the late Province of MAINE.

JEREMIAH POWELL, Eſq;	* ENOCH FREEMAN, Eſq;
JEDEDIAH PREBBLE, Eſq;	

For SAGADAHOCK, | * BENJA. CHADBURNE, Eſq;

At Large.

GEORGE LEONARD, jun. Eſq; | * JEDEDIAH FOSTER, Eſ.

The Gentlemen with this [*] Mark, were not of the Council laſt Year.

Before the Election of Counſellors, Letters were received from the Hon. ISAAC ROYALL, and JAMES GOWEN, Eſq'rs. Reſigning their Seats at the Board.

The Liſt of Counſellors choſen being on Thurſday, agreeable to the Direction of the Royal Charter, preſented to his Excellency the Governor, His Excellency was pleaſed to conſent to the Election of the Gentlemen before mentioned, except

James Bowdoin, Eſq;	Michael Farley, Eſq;
Samuel Dexter, Eſq;	Benjamin Auſtin, Eſq;
John Winthrop, Eſq;	Norton Quincy, Eſq;
William Phillips, Eſq;	Jerathmeel Bowers, Eſq;
John Adams, Eſq;	Enoch Freeman, Eſq;
James Preſcott, Eſq;	Jedediah Foſter, Eſq;
Timothy Danielſon, Eſq;	

On Wedneſday His Excellency was pleaſed to make the following SPEECH to both Houſes.

Gentlemen of the Council, and
Gentlemen of the Houſe of Repreſentatives,

HIS Majeſty having been pleaſed to appoint me Governor and Captain General of his Province of the Maſſachuſetts-Bay, and my Commiſſions having been read and publiſhed, I have met you for the Election of Councellors for the enſuing Year; on which Buſineſs you have been convened agreeably to your Charter. And as that Work is finiſhed you will proceed as you ſhall judge fit, to the Conſideration of ſuch other Matters as may properly come before you, and that you judge ought ought to be entered upon pevious to the firſt of next Month. And you will be aſſured that I ſhall with Pleaſure concur with you to the utmoſt of my Power in all Matters that tend to the Welfare and Proſperity of the Province.

I make mention of the firſt of next Month, becauſe I have the King's particular Commands for holding the General Court at Salem from that Day, until His Majeſty ſhall have ſignified his Royal Will and Pleaſure for holding it again at Boſton.

The honor of my Appointment to the Command of this Government being ſo lately conferred, and the time ſince I took it upon me ſo very ſhort, I have not at preſent any Matter to lay before you, farther than to acquaint you, that the Provincial Treaſurer having informed me, that ſufficient Proviſion is made for the Redemption of the Government Securities that are now, and will become due in June 1775, you will have no other Burden upon you but to ſupply the Treaſury for the Support of Government for the enſuing Year.

Council Chamber,
May 26, 1774.

T. GAGE.

The following Gentlemen are returned to repreſent the ſeveral Towns and Diſtricts to which their Names are affixed. Thoſe with this [*] Mark, were not of the Houſe laſt Year.

For the County of SUFFOLK.

BOSTON, Hon. THOMAS CUSHING, Eſq. (*Speaker.*)
Mr. Samuel Adams
Hon. John Hancock, Eſq.
William Phillips, Eſq.
Roxbury, Capt. William Heath
Dorcheſter, * Capt. Lemuel Robinſon
Milton, * Mr. Stephen Miller
Braintree, Ebenezer Thayer, jun. Eſq.
Weymouth, Mr. Nathaniel Bayley
Hingham & Cohaſſet, Benjamin Lincoln, Eſq.
Dedham, Mr. Abner Ellis
Medfield, Mr. Moſes Bullen
Wrentham, Mr. Jabez Fiſher
Brookline, Capt. Benjamin White
Stoughton, and *Stoughtonham* D. Mr. Hezekiah Gay,
Walpole, Mr. Enoch Ellis
Medway, * Capt. Jonathan Adams
Needham, *Bellingham*, *Hull*, *Chelſea.*

For the County of ESSEX.

Salem, Richard Derby, jun. Eſq.
Mr. John Pickering, jun.
Danvers, Dr. Samuel Holten
Ipſwich, Capt. Michael Farley,
Newbury, Joſeph Gerriſh, Eſq.
Newbury-Port, Mr. Jonathan Greenleaf
Marblehead, * John Galliſon, Eſq.
Lynn, Ebenezer Burrill, Eſq.
Andover, Capt. Moody Bridges
Beverly, * Mr. Joſiah Bachellor, jun.
Rowley, * Mr. Nathaniel Myghill
Sailſbury, Mr. Samuel Smith
Haverhill, Mr. Jonathan Webſter
Glouceſter, * Capt. Peter Coffin
Topsfield, Mr. John Gould
Boxford, Aaron Wood, Eſq.
Almſbury, Iſaac Merrill, Eſq.
Bradford, Capt. Daniel Thurſton
Wenham, *Mancheſter*, *Methuen*, *Middleton.*

For the County of MIDDLESEX.

Cambridge, Capt. Thomas Gardner
Charleſtown, Mr. Nathaniel Gorham
Watertown, Capt. Jonathan Browne
Woburn, Mr. Samuel Wyman
Concord, Capt. James Barrett
Newton, Abraham Fuller, Eſq.
Reading, Samuel Bancroft, Eſq.
Marlborough, Mr. Peter Bent
Billerica, William Stickney, Eſq.
Framingham, Capt. Joſiah Stone
Lexington, Mr. Jonas Stone
Chelmſford, Mr. Simeon Spaulding
* *Sherburne*, Mr. Samuel Bullard
Sudbury, Mr. Thomas Plympton
Malden, Capt. Ebenezer Harnden
Medford, Mr. Benjamin Hall
Weſton, Eliſha Jones, Eſq.
Hopkinton,
Waltham, Jonas Dix, Eſq.
Groton, *Shirley* D. *Pepperrell* D. James Preſcott, Eſq.
Stow, *Townſhend*, *Aſhby*, & *Stoneham*
Wilmington, *Natick*, *Dracut*,
Bedford, *Holliſton*, *Tewkſbury.*
Acton, * Mr. Joſiah Hayward
Weſtford, * Capt. Joſeph Reed
Littleton, * Mr. Joſiah Hartwell
Dunſtable, * John Tyng, Eſq.
Lincoln, * Capt. Eleazer Brooks

For the County of HAMPSHIRE.

Springfield, *Willbraham*, *Ludlow*, D. Hon. John Worthington, Eſ. Mr. John Bliſs
Weſt-Springfield, * Benjamin Day, Eſq.
Northampotn, & *Southampton*, Joſeph Hawley, Eſq.
Hadley, *South-Hadley*, D. *Amherſt*, *Granby*, Mr. Joſiah Pierce
Hatfield, *Whately* & *Williamſburgh*, Mr. John Dickinſon
Deerfield, *Greenfield*, D. *Shelburne*, D. *Conway*, D. Mr. Samuel Field
Weſtfield, & *Southwick*, Mr. John Moſeley
Sunderland & *Montague*, Mr. Moſes Gunn
Brimfield, *South-Brimfield*, & *Monſon*, Mr. Tim. Danielſon
Northfield, Mr. Phineas Wright
Pelham, *Granville*, *New-Salem*, *Colrain*,
Belcherſton, *Ware*, *Warwick*, *Bernardſton*,
Murrayfield, *Charlemont*, *Aſhfield*,
Worthington, *Shuteſbury*, *Cheſterfield*,
Suffield, *Enfield*, *Somers*, *Norwich*
Edgcomb, *Leverett*,

For the County of PLYMOUTH.

Plymouth, Hon. James Warren, Eſq.
Mr. Iſaac Lothrop
Scituate, Mr. Gideon Vinal
Marſhfield, Abijah White, Eſq.
Middleborough, Capt. Ebenezer Sprout
Rocheſter, Mr. Ebenezer White
Plympton, Mr. Samuel Lucas
Pembroke, Mr. John Turner
Hanover, Capt. Joſeph Cuſhing
Abington, Woodbridge Brown, Eſq.
Bridgwater, * Capt. Edward Mitchell
Kingſton, Capt. John Gray
Duxbury, * Mr. George Partridge
Halifax, *Wareham.*

For the County of BARNSTABLE.

Barnſtable, Edward Bacon Eſq.
Sandwich, Mr, Stephen Nye
Yarmouth, David Thatcher, Eſq.
Eaſtham & *Wellfleet*, Mr. Barnabas Freeman
Harwich, Mr. Benjamin Freeman
Falmouth, Mr. Moſes Swift
Chatham, Mr. Joſeph Doane
Truro.

For the County of BRISTOL.

Taunton, Daniel Leonard, jun. Eſq.
Robert-Treat Pain, Eſq.
Rehoboth, Cap. Joſeph Barney
Swanzey, with *Shawamet*, Jerathmeel Bowers, Eſq.
Dartmouth, Benjamin Aikin, Eſq.
Norton, & *Mansfield*, * Thomas Morey, Eſq.
Attleborough, Mr. John Daggett
Dighton, Elnathan Walker, Eſq.
* Mr. William Baylies
Freetown, * Capt. Thomas Durphey
Eaſton, Capt. Matthew Hayward
Raynham, *Berkley.*

For the County of YORK.

York, * Mr. Daniel Bragdon
Kittery, Edward Cutt, Eſq;
Wells, Mr. Ebenezer Sayer
Berwick, Capt. Nathan Lord, jun.
Arundell, Thomas Perkins, Eſq.
Biddeford, & *Pepperrelborough*,
Lebanon, *Stanford*, *Buxton.*

For the County of DUKES-COUNTY.

Edgarton, Mr. Thomas Cooke
Chilmark,
Tiſbury,

For the County of NANTUCKET.

Sherburne, Mr. Stephen Huſſey.

For the County of WORCESTER.

Worceſter, Mr. Joſhua Bigelow,
Lancaſter, Capt. Aſa Whitcomb
Mendon Mr. Edward Rawſon
Brookfield, Jedediah Foſter, Eſq;
Oxford, & *Charlton*, * Edward Davis, Eſq.
Sutton, Capt. Henry King
Leiceſter, *Spencer* D. *Paxton* D. Mr. Thomas Denny
Rutland, *Rutland* D. *Oakham*, *Hubbardſton* John Murray, Eſq.
Weſtborough, *Northborough*, Capt. Stephen Maynard
Shrewſbury, Mr. Phineas Heywood
Lunenburgh, *Fitchburgh*, Mr. John Taylor
Uxbridge, Mr. Joſeph Read
Harvard, Iſrael Taylor, Eſq.
Bolton, John Whitcomb, Eſq.
Peterſham, Capt. Ephraim Doolittle
Southborough,
Hardwick, Mr. Paul Mandell
Weſtern,
Sturbridge, * Moſes Mercey, Eſq.
Leominſter, * Mr. Iſrael Nicholas
Dudley,
Upton, * Mr. Abiel Sadler
New-Braintree, *Holden*, *Douglaſs*,
Graſton, * Mr. John Shearman
Royalſton, *Weſtminſter*, *Templeton*,
Athol, *Princeton*, *Aſhburnham*, *Winchendon*,
Woodſtock:

For the County of CUMBERLAND,

Falmouth, & *Cape-Elizabeth*, * Enoch Freeman, Eſq.
Scarborough, Mr. Samuel March
North-Yarmouth, Mr. John Lewis,
Gorham,
Brunſwick, & *Harpſwell*, *New-Gloceſter*,
Windham, *New-Gloceſter*, *New-Boſton.*

For the County LINCOLN.

Georgetown, & *Woolwich*,
Pownalborough, *Newcaſtle*, *Topſham*,
Boothbay, *Briſtol*, *Bowdoinham*, *Edgcomb*,
Medumcook, *Broad-Bay*, *St. Georges*,
Vaſſalborough, *Winthrop*, *Winſlow*,
Gardinerſton. *Belfaſt*. *Waldoborough.*

For the County of BERKSHIRE.

Sheffield, *Great-Barrrington*, *Egremont*, and *Alſord*, David Ingerſoll, jun. Eſq.
Stockbridge, * Mr. Thomas Williams
Weſt-Stockbridge.
Tyringham, * Capt. Gyles Jackſon
Pittsfield, * Mr. James Eaſton
Richmont, *Lenox*, Mr. * John Patterſon
Laneſborough, Mr. Peter Curtis
Williamſtown, * Capt. Iſaac Searl
Sandisfield, *New-Marlborough*, *Becket*
Gageborough, * Capt. William Clark.
Partridgefield, *Loudon*
Plantation, N°. 5. *Plantation*, N°. 7.
Plantation Hartwood, *Eaſt-Hooſuck*, *Jericho.*

Messrs. EDES and GILL,

THE Address of the Episcopal Clergy to the disgraced and execrated TRAITOR; is Matter of much Speculation; for myself I am not surprized to find Sycophants in Cassocks; but that they should have the Effrontery to Tax the legislative Body of the Province with Misapprehension, after they had deliberately Scanned and publickly Protested against the Conduct of this infamous Culprit, is superlatively arrogant. —'Tis to be hoped these Reverend Gentlemen will not forget, in their Paroxysms of Prayer, to offer up a Petition that the Idol of their present Address may be furnished with the Grace of Repentance, for involving his Country in her present Calamity; otherwise 'tis presumed he may fall short of *an Eternity of Happiness in the Life to come.* A. B.

P. S. The Apostate at the North with his mimic Majesty of Manhood, is requested to inform the Publick whether his Wardens were applied to, and whether they excused themselves by saying they could not conveniently attend?

At a Town Meeting held at Providence, on the 17th Day of May, 1774 called by Warrant.
RESOLVED,
THAT this Town will heartily join with the Province of Massachusetts-Bay, and the other Colonies, in such Measures as shall be generally agreed on by the Colonies, for the protecting and securing their invaluable natural Rights and Privileges, and transmitting the same to the latest Posterity.

That the Deputies of this Town be requested to use their Influence, at the approaching Session of the General Assembly of this Colony, for promoting a CONGRESS, as soon as may be, of the Representatives of the General Assemblies of the several Colonies and Provinces of North-America, for establishing the firmest Union, and adopting such Measures as to them shall appear the most effectual to answer that important Purpose; and to agree upon proper Methods for executing the same.

That the Committee of Correspondence of this Town be desired to assure the Town of Boston, that we consider ourselves greatly interested in the present alarming Conduct of the British Parliament towards them, and view the whole English American Colonies equally concerned in the Event; and that we will, with the utmost Firmness, act accordingly, whenever any Plan shall be agreed on. In the mean Time, we are of Opinion, that an universal Stoppage of all Trade with Great Britain, Ireland, Africa, and the West-Indies, until such Time as the Port of Boston shall be reinstated in its former Privileges, &c. will be the best Expedient in the Case, and that a proper Time should be agreed on for the same universally to take Place.

WHEREAS John Shoemaker, late of Providence, died intestate, and hath left six Negroes, four of whom are Infants: And there being no Heir to the said Jacob in this Town or Colony, the said Negroes have fallen to this Town by Law, provided no Heir should appear. Therefore,
It is VOTED by this Meeting, That it is unbecoming the Character of Freemen to enslave the said Negroes, and they do hereby give up all Claim of Right or Property in them the said Negroes or either of them. And it is hereby recommended to the Town Council to take the said Negroes under their Protection, and to bind the small Children to some proper Masters and Mistresses: And in Case there should not be personal Estate of the said John Shoemaker, sufficient to pay his just Debts, it is further recommended to said Council to bind out either or both of the adult Negroes for that Purpose.

WHEREAS the Inhabitants of America are engaged in the Preservation of their Rights and Liberties; and as personal Liberty is an essential Part of the natural Rights of Mankind, the Deputies of the Town are directed to use their Endeavours to obtain an Act of the General Assembly, prohibiting the Importation of Negro Slaves into this Colony; and that all Negroes born in the Colony should be free, after attaining a certain Age.

A true Copy, JAMES ANGELL, *Town-Clerk.*

At a Meeting of the Freeholders and other Inhabitants of this Town, qualified to vote according to Law, duly warned and legally convened the Twenty-third Day of May, 1773.
Deacon STEPHEN PHILLIPS, Moderator.
VOTED, THAT the Thanks of this Town are hereby returned to the respectable Citizens of Boston, for sundry Papers, this Day communicated to the Town by the Desire of the Gentlemen their Committee, and that they may be assured of the Readiness of this Town to join this and the other Colonies in a Non-Exportation and Non-Importation Agreement, to and from Great-Britain, and in any other rational Agreements that shall be generally adopted and can be carried into Execution by this Community, for the Preservation of American invaded Rights and Liberties.

Voted, There shall be a Committee of Correspondence chosen for this Town, of several Persons to correspond with the Committee of Correspondence of Boston, and of the neighbouring Towns within this Province.

Voted, That Joshua Orne, William Doliber, Stephen Phillips, Edward Fitteplace, John Nutt, John Gerry and John Prince to be the Committee.

Voted, That the Select Men of this Town be desired to transmit as soon as may be, to the Committee of Correspondence for Boston, an attested Copy of this Day's Proceedings of the Town. A true Copy, attest.
Marblehead, May 24. EBE. BODEN, *Town-Clerk.*

A Copy of an Address from sundry Persons in Boston to Gov. Hutchinson, being read at the above Meeting, and containing Matters that appeared to the Inhabitants palpably absurd, was honoured with a *general Hiss.*

NEWPORT, May 23.
'Tis proposed, that a number of gentlemen immediately form a company, for carrying on the woolen manufacture in this colony, in the most extensive manner; there being quite wool enough raised here to cloath all the inhabitants.

We hear the people of Connecticut are about exhibiting a glorious example of patriotism, by raising a large sum of money for the support of those persons in Boston who may become sufferers by the horrid act for blocking up that port.

Last Thursday the Magdalen Schooner sailed for Boston, supposed to assist in blockading the port of Boston.

BOSTON, May 30.
The following is a PROTEST of the Merchants and Traders of this Town, unanimously Voted at a very full Meeting the 24th Instant, viz.

"WHEREAS a Paper called an Address to Governor Hutchinson, has been handed about and Signed in a Private Manner by sundry Persons, which it is said stile themselves Merchants, Traders and others of the Town of Boston; and whereas the Merchants and Traders duly notified and met, having been refused a copy of said Paper, although requested by their Committee, and apprehending said Address is intended to justify the Administration of Mr. Hutchinson when Governor of this Province, we hereby utterly disclaim said Address, and disavow a Measure so clandestinely conducted, and so injurious in its Tendency."

On Saturday last Mr. PAUL REVERE returned from Philadelphia, having been sent express to the Southern Colonies with Intelligence of the late rash, impolitick and vindictive Measures of the British Parliament, who by the execrable Port-Bill have held out to us a most incontestible. Argument why we ought to submit to their Jurisdiction; and what rich Blessings we may secure to Ourselves and Posterity, by an absolute Acquiescence in their *Lenity, Wisdom* and *Justice.* Nothing can exceed the Indignation with which our Brethren in Rhode-Island, Connecticut, New-York and Philadelphia have received this Proof of Ministerial Madness.——
They universally declare their Resolution to stand by us to the last extremity; they esteem the Cause to be their own, and highly applaud the Resolution of this People, not to be awed into Acquiescence by a mad exertion of mere Power on the Part of our Enemies;—they adjure us for *their* sakes as well as *our own* to persevere; much approve the Plan of an entire suspension of Trade with Great-Britain, and advise to a Committee of Merchants from all the trading Towns to convene at New-York to form a restrictive Plan for their Trade to the West-Indies—Expresses are gone from Philadelphia for this Purpose to the Colonies Southward of them, who no doubt will concur in the same Measure, and view the Subjugation of Boston, as in Fact it is, the enslaving the whole Continent.

It was noticed to Mr. Revere, that in this Meeting Mr. Dickinson spoke longer and with more Life and Energy than ever he had done on any former Occasion. The Spirits of the People were raised to an high Degree; and they declare in their Letter, that, "if satisfying the East India Company for the Damage they have sustained, would put an End to the Controversy, and leave us on the Footing of Constitutional Liberty for the future, that neither they nor we could continue a Moment in Doubt what Part to act; for, say they, it is not the Tax, but the indefeasible Right of giving and granting our own Money, *from which we never can recede,* that is the Matter now in Consideration."

And from New-York, they write,
"Your Port-Bill has given us infinite Trouble and Concern. A Pack of selfish, prejudiced Wretches would have sacrificed you and all America to their sordid Views and uncharitable Designs. But Thanks to an over-ruling Hand, they have not been able to effect their Machinations. You will receive, by your worthy Messenger, Mr. Revere, a very consolatory Letter, that will have a direct Tendency to put the Affairs of America on a better footing than ever they have been.—You may be assured every Thing in our Power will be done, for we are as deeply concerned in the Event as yourselves.—Comfort and strengthen the weak-hearted; many have declared here, that they will contribute largely to the Support of your Poor. Some have said they would go as far as £.1000, others £.100, &c."

And from another Hand,
"Your Favour came duly to Hand; by which I have the inexpressible Pleasure to find, that the Ministry are like to be disappointed in their Expectations, that the Town of Boston would have meanly complied with their Demands.——I am pleased with your Firmness; and I trust you will not fail to have all the Aid and Assistance of all the Colonies upon this trying Occasion.——Mr. Revere has Letters from the Committees of Philadelphia and this City, which I hope will animate our Brethren in Boston, and induce them to think they will not be deserted in the Hour of Difficulty."

At a Meeting of many respectable Inhabitants of the City of Philadelphia, May 20, 1774.
The following Persons were nominated a Committee to correspond with Committees of the other Colonies.
John Dickinson, Dr. William Smith, Edward Pennington, Joseph Fox, John Nixon, John Nesbit, Samuel Howell, Joseph Read, Thomas Wharton, jun. Benjamin Marshall, Joseph Moulder, Thomas Barclay, Charles Thomson, Jeremiah Warder, jun. John Cox, John Gibson, George Clymer, Thomas Mifflin,
until some Alteration is made by a more general Meeting of the Inhabitants of this City.

The Committee were instructed to apply to the Governor, and to request him to call a Meeting of the Assembly of this Province.

They were likewise instructed to write to the Town of Boston, informing them, that the Inhabitants now met, truly feel for their unhappy Situation, and recommend to them Firmness, Prudence and Moderation; and that we will continue to evince our firm Adherence to the Cause of American Liberty.

The Committee were also directed to acquaint our Brethren of New-York, and the other Colonies, with the foregoing Resolutions.

By the Tenor of these Advices, it is determined whether Mr. Dudley the Collector of Newport was right in his Judgment, that the other Colonies would by no Means have any Thing to do with the Bostonians.

We hear that a certain Person who has appeared divers Times as a Scribbler, in Favor of the late Administration, and once, if not oftner, under Signature of A.B.C, in Consideration of which an aged Esquire, with whom the said A. B. C. is connected, was appointed of the Quorum, has very lately visited his *excellent* Friend, at a neighbouring Fortress, and sympathized most cordially with him under the cruel Treatment he has met with from both Houses of Assembly, and the whole Body of this People, in Return for his very kind Letters to Great Britain in Favor of the Province, and for other worthy Deeds by him performed: And knowing it would be the last Time he should *take* Sight of his grinning Benefactor, he said ten Thousand sweet Things to him; repeating some favourite Words and Expressions, *over and over, and over* again; and fawning and cringing with all the Appearances of ineffable Servility; as if Fortune, Life, and *even a Diploma* depended on the Favor of the Man for whom he was then expressing *disinterested* Regards.

Since our last arrived from New-York, Capt. Lamoine, and the Lieutenants Shand, Grant and Shuttleworth, of his Majesty's Royal Regiment of Artillery, with six Field Pieces, two Howits, and a Quantity of Military Stores, and 60 private Men.

We are told that when his Excellency Governor Gage mentioned the Instruction from his Majesty to negative James Bowdoin, Samuel Dexter and John Winthrop, Esquires, the last of the three honorable Gentlemen was not in the Council Chamber. The other two, in their Speeches to the Governor on the Occasion, intimated a strong Suspicion that there had been base and unjust Representations made against them to the Ministry, by the late Governor Hutchinson; and Mr. Dexter, in particular, expressed his Satisfaction at falling under the Disapprobation of such A DETERMINED ENEMY TO HIS NATIVE COUNTRY.

The Lady and Family of his Excellency Governor Gage, attended by Major Kemble, were to embark for New-York, from London, the beginning of this month.
We hear Governor Hutchinson, Elisha Hutchinson, Esq; his second Son, and Miss Hutchinson, his Daughter, will sail To-morrow in Capt. Callahan for London.

A Gentleman of the most unimpeachable Character affirms, that at the Time General Gage was here in the Year 1769, Governor Hutchinson told him that he was the most ignorant & contemptible of human beings.

It is reported that the late Governor, now immured at Castle-William, has solemnly declared, ON THE WORD OF AN HONEST MAN, that he never gave his Advice, nor Opinion, to Governor Gage, with Respect to his approving or disapproving any Gentlemen chosen Counsellors on Wednesday last; and that his Excellency *never shewed* to him his Instruction from the King to negative Mr. Bowdoin, Mr. Dexter and Doctor Winthrop; nor gave him the *least* Hint that he had such an Instruction; and that *he knew* Nothing of the Governor's Intention previous to his putting it into Execution! To the Surprize of all that heard him, ONE GENTLEMAN said upon the Exchange, on Friday last, that he believed the Declaration to be *true.*

It was reported by Hutchinson's bosom Friends, that he had told them that if the Tea could be paid for, which would be stated at the lowest Rate by the East-India Company, he should upon his Arrival be able to set aside the Port-Bill, and remove every other Difficulty—this accounts for the Names of some honest tho' weak Men in the late Address.

About 120 Signers, pick'd up with Secrecy and Industry from Town and Country, including the Sandemanians, Importers at the Time of Non-Importation Agreement—Crown Officers, new-made Justices, &c. to the late Address, is too contemptible to give the Pensioner the least Shadow of Importance on the other Side the Water, which was the main Design of the Labourers, and appears to be the last Effort of a detested and expiring Faction.

A Padlock once fixed on American Pockets with respect to British Superfluities, will allow us to set still and see the Salvation of our God.

Saturday last his Excellency the Governor was pleased to adjourn'd the General Court to the 7th of June next, then to meet at Salem.

Last Saturday was brought to this Market by Oliver Vose, a Sheep that weigh'd 120 lb. the four Quarters, it being allowed to be the best that was ever brought into this Market. Said Vose has also a Sheep that has brought 7 Lambs within Eleven Months, 4 at one Time and 3 at the other.

This Day Mr. BRADFORD is dispatched on his Return to New-York, with such Answers to the Proposals of our Brethren at New-York and Philadelphia, from the Committee of Correspondence of this Town, as will probably tend to facilitate the Plan of Redemption from Ministerial Tyranny.

The Meeting of this Town stands adjourn'd to Ten o'Clock this Day.

To the PRINTERS.

IN Draper's last Gazette, we have a remarkable Letter from Philadelphia calculated to discourage the Plan of Non Importation, so much dreaded by the Enemies of America. I know from the palpable Falshoods contained in it, that it must have been forged, but looking at the Date, every one must be convinced of this. The Letter is dated May 17, and begins thus, " The Post has just brought us an Account of General Gage's Arrival." *Now General Gage arrived on Friday the 13th of May,* and how the Post could carry in four Days this Account to Philadelphia, is beyond my Comprehension.—This is one Instance among many of the lying Tricks of our Enemies, and should teach the Friends of Liberty in the several Colonies, at the present Crisis, not to give Credit to Reports circulated with Design to break the Union, and interrupt the present happy Harmony of the American Colonies. Letters and Informations from Towns, Committees of Correspondence, or from Gentlemen of established Characters in the several Provinces, may alone be depended upon.*

IT has been circulated from great Authority, and confidently believed by many, that Mr. Hutchinson at the time of his removal received Letters from Administration acquainting him, that he stood in high Favour at Court—that the Work now to be performed in Boston, &c. was too severe for his tender and benevolent Spirit. Administration has therefore graciously eased him of this harsh and unpleasant task, and appointed a more suitable Person for it—That General Gage's Administration would be very short, and that when he had gone through his rough Work he would be recalled, and Mr. Hutchinson, if he chose it, might then return to his Government. What compliment this is to our present Governor, and how well adapted to quiet the Minds of the People under his Administration, the world will judge.—Should it now be asked, from whence this Report originated, the Reader may be assured it came from Mr. Hutchinson himself, it being communicated by him to his Confidents, and by them propagated with no little Industry, and has in fact already made upon numbers the Impressions intended. It is certain however, that 99 out of 100 in this Province believe that there is much more Generosity and Moderation in General Gage than ever existed in his Predecessor, and that the present severe and unjust Measures are principally owing to the latter.

The Artillery lately play'd with so much execution against the Members of his Majesty's Council, it is not doubted was pointed by the amiable, the tender hearted and weeping Hutchinson.

* *The first Post which set out for the Southward after the Governor's arrival was on Monday afternoon the 16th Inst. so that according to the Writer the Post travelled 350 Miles, and crost at least 6 considerable Ferries in 24 Hours.*

To-Morrow will be Published,

And Sold by EDES *and* GILL, *in Queen-Street,*

[*Price,* 1s. 6d.]

OBSERVATIONS
ON
THE ACT OF PARLIAMENT
For Blocking up the Harbour of *Boston*;
WITH
THOUGHTS
ON
CIVIL SOCIETY
AND
STANDING ARMIES.
BY *JOSIAH QUINCY*, Jun.r

William Turner

Lately arrived from LONDON,

Begs Leave to acquaint the Gentlemen and Ladies of the Town and Country, that he continues to teach the polite Art of Dancing and Fencing in the newest and most approved Method, at Concert-Hall:——Those Gentlemen and Ladies who propose sending their Children to be instructed may depend the best Care will be taken as to their Behaviour.

N. B. Cotillons taught as they are performed at all polite Balls and Assemblies in England.

——Figure Dances likewise.——

Mr. *Turner* will attend two Days in the Week at any House from 6 o'Clock in the Morning till 6 o'Clock in the Evening on grown Gentlemen and Ladies, and assures the utmost Secrecy shall be kept till they are capable of exhibiting in high Taste.

UMBRILLOES.

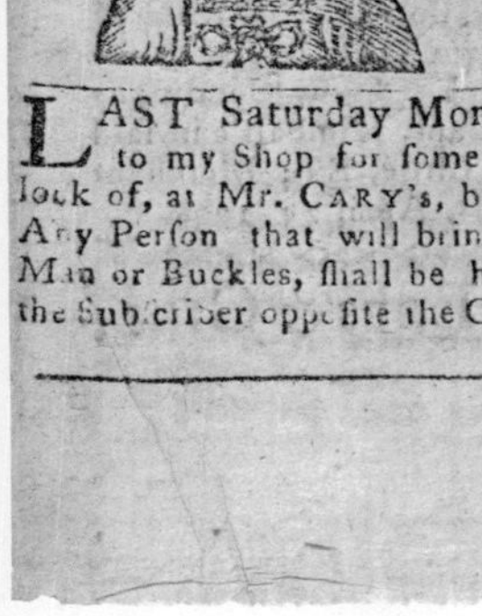

Umbrilloes of all sorts for Ladies & Gentlemen; made in the best Manner and to be sold by JOHN CUTLER, at the *Golden Cock*, in Marlborough-Street, Boston.——

ALSO,

Umbrillo Sticks to sell uncovered, old Umbrilloes may be mended and covered at the same Place. All done at a low Rate.

LAST Saturday Morning came a Negro Man to my Shop for some Buckles for some Ladies to look of, at Mr. CARY's, but which proves a deception. Any Person that will bring information of the Negro Man or Buckles, shall be handsomely Rewarded by me the Subscriber opposite the Golden Key.

WILLIAM HOMES.

THE Merchants and Traders of this Town are desired to remember that their Meeting stands adjourned to Thursday next, at Five o'Clock in the Afternoon, to the West Chamber in the Town-House, where they are desired to attend, on Matters of great Importance.

WATCHES,

Plain, Skeleton and Horrizontal in Gold, Silver and Pinchbeck Case—in particular a great Variety of Silver Watches from Ten Dollars to Ten Guineas—some of which shew the Day of the Month, and others with Seconds, are very suitable for Physicians—Likewise Spring and Pendulum Eight Day Clocks, also an Assortment of Tools and Materials used by Clock and Watch Makers—To be sold by DAVID MITCHELSON, at the House of Mr. Benjamin Davis, Merchant, near the Mill Bridge.

N. B. The above Articles are of the best Kinds, newly Imported from the Makers, and will be sold at the most reasonable Prices for Cash only.

ALL Persons that have any Concerns with JONATHAN WILLIAMS, Junr. are desired to apply to JONATHAN WILLIAMS, Senr. Esq; who is impowered to transact his Business during his Absence.

TO BE SOLD,
By *BENJAMIN CHURCH*,
ON THURSDAY NEXT,
At THREE o'Clock in the Afternoon.

A Variety of European Articles—as Cloths—Serges—Linnens—Checks—Tammies—Camblets—Calicoes—Venetians—Oznabrigs—Handkerchiefs—House Furniture, viz. Mahogany Tables—Desks—a Case of Draws—Beds &c. &c. &c. A new Chaise and Harness compleat—an 8 Day Clock, Watches, &c. &c.

At Three o'Clock, P. M.

TO BE SOLD CHEAP,

A choice Lot of Land in the Town of Granvile, consisting of Forty-three Acres, near the Centre of the Town, there are 200 Families settled in said Town.—For further intelligence inquire of the Printers.

WE the Subscribers being appointed by the honorable Foster Hutchinson, Esq; Judge of Probates for the County of Suffolk, Commissioners to receive and examine the Claims of the several Creditors to the Estate of JACOB ROYALL, late of Boston, Esq; deceased, intestate, represented insolvent, do hereby give Notice, that we shall attend said service at the British Coffee House, on the last Tuesday of this and the five following Months, from Six to Nine o'Clock of the Evening of said Days.

SAMUEL DOWNE,
Boston, May 27, 1774. JACOB COOPER.

ALL Persons indebted to the Estate of Richard Surcomb, late of Boston, Baker, deceased, are once more requested to make immediate to Mary Surcomb, Executrix, as they would avoid being sued at July Court.

TO BE LETT,

A handsome House with an excellent Garden well stocked with Vegetables, in a delightful Situation, within two Miles of Boston, fit for a small or large genteel Family, on the most reasonable Terms, may be entered on immediately, enquire of Edes & Gill.

Lemuel Pattingall of Norwich, in Connecticut, Brick Layer and Mason, wants to Hire Two or Three Workmen at that Business, during the Season. Norwich, 20th May, 1774.

WANTED,

A sober, faithful honest Man, that understands taking Care of a Tavern; one of this Character that can be well recommended, by inquiring of the Printers will be inform'd of the Place, where he will have good Wages.

A Wet Nurse with a good Breast of Milk would take a Child to Suckle.

Inquire of the Printers.

WANTS EMPLOYMENT,

A young Man who is capable of tending a Gentleman's Family, taking care of Horses and driving a Chariot; can be well recommended.

Inquire of the Printers.

RAN away from his Master on Friday Evening last, a Negro Boy, named GOREE, about 16 Years of Age, 5 Feet, 3 Inches High, had on when he went away, a brown Cloth Coat, dark Velvet Waistcoat, white Shirt, white Linen Breeches, grey Yarn Stockings, a pair of Shoes tore at the Heels, with Pinchbeck Buckles, an old Felt Hat. Whoever will take up said Runaway, and secure him, and give information to the Subscriber, so that he may have him again, shall have a handsome Reward and necessary Charges paid by

DANIEL VOSE.

All Masters of Vessels and others, are hereby cautioned against harbouring, concealing, or carrying off the above Negro, as they would avoid the Penalty of the Law.

Milton, May 30, 1774.

To be Sold by PUBLIC VENDUE,
On Tuesday the Seventh Day of June next,

A Dwelling House, Sail Loft, Cooper's Shop with the Land and Wharff thereto belonging, situate, lying and being near Fish-street, at the Northerly part of Boston: Said Premises are part of the Estate of Capt. John Doble, late of Boston, Mariner, deceased.

N. B. The Sale to begin at 11 o'Clock, at the said Dwelling-House. J. RUSSELL, Auctioneer.

TAKEN up off the Graves a Lighter between 25 and 30 Tons; she had on Board a Foresail, one Cable and Anchor: Whoever has lost her, may apply to Mr. John Larkin at Charlestown, or Edes & Gill.

New AUCTION-ROOM, Cornhill.

TO-MORROW at TEN o'Clock will be Sold by PUBLIC VENDUE, at GREENLEAF's Auction-Room,——

A large Assortment of GOODS, amongst which are—3.4, 7 8 & yd-wide Irish Linens, Callicoes, Chints, strip'd, flower'd and plain Lawns, Lawn Aprons, sprig'd Muslins, silk Gauzes, Catguts, Ribbons, plain Modes, Silk Twist, Damask and Diaper TableCloths, Kenting & Linnen Handkerchiefs, Checks, strip'd Hollands, Bed Ticks, Broad Cloths, Velvets, Shalloons, Tammies, Thread & Worsted Hose, Breeches Patterns, Mens and Boys Castor and Felt Hatts, Table Knives & Forks, Silver-plated Buckles, Sleeve Buttons, Stone, Shoe, Knee and Neck Buckles, Silver Watches, &c. &c. WILLIAM GREENLEAF, Auctioneer.

The Sale will begin precisely at Ten o'Clock.

For private Sale,

An 8-Day Clock, a Desk and Book Case, a new Chaise and Harness, a handsome Curricle, some Looking Glasses, and a Variety of English Goods.

At GOULD's *Auction-Office*, In Back-Street,
On TUESDAY next,
At TEN in the Morning,
Will be Sold by PUBLIC VENDUE,
A Variety of House Furniture,
—Amongst which are—

One Mahogany Desk and Book Case, one Mahogany Chest upon Chest of Draws, Mahogany Dining, Tea and Card Tables, Walnut and Maple ditto, a Variety of looking Glasses, Chairs, Mahogany and other Bedsteads, Feather Beds, Curtains, China, Stone and Glass Ware, Pictures, Kitchen Furniture of all Sorts, two large Writing Desks, &c. &c.—Also,—One second-hand chaise and Harness to be put up at One o'Clock. R. GOULD, Auctioneer.

At GOULD's *Auction Office in Back Street*,
ON FRIDAY NEXT,
At TEN o'Clock in the Morning,
Will be Sold by PUBLIC VENDUE,

A large and Valuable Assortment of English and other GOODS.

R. GOULD, Auctioneer.

At GOULD's *Auction-Office*,
In Back-Street,
On TUESDAY the 7th Day of June next,
Will be Sold by PUBLIC VENDUE,

THE remaining Part of the Library of the late Mr. MOREHEAD, consisting of about 200 Volumes of valuable Books, both ancient and modern (many of which are in Folio) also 200 Volumes received from different Hands, which makes a very fine Collection.—No Catalogues—The Books may be viewed next Saturday and Monday.

Josiah Willard Gibbs

BEGS Leave to acquaint his Friends and the Public, That he has just imported a compleat and elegant Assortment of *London, Bristol, Bermingham & Sheffield*

Hard Ware GOODS,

All which were purchas'd of the several Manufacturers upon the best Terms, and which he will sell for ready Money either by Wholesale or Retail, at such reasonable Rates, as he doubts not will give entire Satisfaction to all who may please to favour him with their Custom, at his Shop in Cornhill, near the State-House, Boston.

OATS.

OATS, Pease, Philadelphia Flour, and Bar-Iron, *Also*, warranted Scythes and Axes, a few neat Fowling Pieces, and a small Quantity of good Snuff, to be sold cheap, at the lowest Store on the South-Side of the Town Dock, by Joseph-Pearse Palmer.

CUSTOM-HOUSE, *BOSTON*.

ENTERED IN.

Lambert, Gaudaloup; Robinson, Saltertudas; Smith, Turks Islands; Fulford, Maryland; Topping, Philadelphia; Robinson, Harris, Higgins and Williams, New-London; Thorp & Summers, Newhaven; White, Crocker, Thayer, Hall and Kirk, North-Carolina; Crowell, Virginia.

Burials in the Town of BOSTON, since our last.
Twelve Whites. One Blacks.
Baptiz'd in the several Churches, Ten.

High Water at BOSTON, *for the present Week.*

Monday, 5 min. aft.	9	Friday, 2 min. after.	1
Tuesday, 4 min. aft.	10	Saturday, 1 min. aft.	2
Wednesday, 3 m. aft.	11	Lord's-Day, 1 m af.	3
Thursday, 2 min. aft.	12	☉'s Full 25 D. 1 Afte.	

Messieurs EDES & GILL,

As the following Reflections taken from a Manuscript proposed for the Press may seem somewhat seasonable at this Period, be pleased to offer them to the Public. I am, Gentlemen Your's, &c.

CATO OF UTICA.

" Sha'l at this Æra all our Hopes expire,"
And weeping *Freedom* from her Fanes retire,
Shall proud *Oppression* still our Peace pursue,
" From the pain'd Eyebrow drink the Vital Dew."
One of our own Poets.

"HAVING Remarked in particular, I take leave to observe in general, that profligate ministers think in the same train, and sacrifice the state to personal gratification, hence empires have been oftner destroyed by false policy, than the sword, the arms of Cæsar were not more fatal to the liberties of the Roman republic, than the ill policy of the imperial ministry to the existence of the Empire.——Arbitrary ministers regard the People as their property, and open the scenes of depredation at a distance from the capital, therefore, the remote provinces of great states have ever been the theatres of ministerial rapine, but intolerable oppressions have always worked the independence of the subject, often the dethronement of the sovereign ; thus false ministers by oppressing the one betray the diadems of the other, whence the memorable caution of Mr. Pitt to the British ministry, if said that wise statesman " *you drive America* to *extremes, she will pull down the pillars of the state.*"—The conflagration that devoured the Roman world was kindled in the provinces, and a similar catastrophe daily threatens the Ottoman empire ; 'tis indeed impertinent to multiply instances of revolutions induced by false policy, they are too many and too obvious to have escaped the attention of Mr. Hutchinson or the Chief Justice, they have engaged the notice of less sensible readers, and are even the subjects of vulgar reflection ; a pity it is they have not employed their eminent abilities and knowledge for the public utility, if his Excellency in particular, had not perverted the purpose of his studies, he would have sedately considered the connection of causes, and from parity of circumstance, inferred similarity of effect, he would have foreseen that the oppressions of America must work her independence, weaken the Empire, and, perhaps, to recite the *prediction* of Mr. Pitt, " pull down the pillars of the state." If with that great and good man he had espoused the cause of the constitution, and been the friend of his country, the blessings of the age, and the reverence of posterity had been his portion, instead of the curse of the one and the contemptuous derision of the other.——I was once the partizan of his Excellency, I was facinated with his reasoning, and anticipated by his authority, his judgment indeed was the medium thro' which I perceived political objects, and as attachment of opinion forms personal affection, and as gentle dispositions loose with reluctance those agreeable feelings, my country will indulge the frailty of too tender a temper, and permit me to wish the divine Benignity may work wonders in his heart, and restore him, at least, to the compassions of his countrymen.—But I leave this melancholly subject for more agreeable reflections.——Many and remarkable have been the exertions of oppress'd states in support of original constitution.—*Liberty is inspiration*, it is, to speak the language of Cato, " *the divinity that stirs within us*," 'tis the very principle of *self valuation*, 'tis the source of *virtue and true glory*, without it a man is the *companion of brutes*, & on a par with the very cattle he feeds :—The heroic ages were the most free, and in proportion to the progress of tyranny, pusilanimity and barbarism have prevailed, liberty invigorates the spirit and refines the understanding, while slavery debilitates the one, and stupifies the other.——Where have been the seats of science, where the nurseries of heroism ? in the courts of absolute princes, or the communities of freedom? who are wiser in council the minions of a monarch, or the substitutes of a free people? which more victorious in war, the mercenary troops of a despot, or the voluntary bands of free states ? What stimulates the one, tyranny and the scourge ; what inspires the other, patriotism and true glory?—Who defended the pass of Themopolæ against millions of armed slaves, commanded by their emperor—a single cohort of Sparta—who were an over match for the eastern empire, and at length annihilated that over-grown state of slaves—the common wealths of Greece—who subdued the world, the Roman republic?——Where are the Nimrods of mankind, forgotten with their slaves, or remembered with execration ; but who are idolized by intelligent posterity, the citizens of Athens and Rome ; nor have antient ages alone been illustrious for free spirit and liberal constitution, modern periods have shewn very exemplary instances.——I will recite a very pertinent one in the Vicinity of Great-Britain.

When, says Doctor Robertson, " the people of the united Netherlands threw off the Spanish yoke and asserted their antient liberty and laws, these they defended with a persevering valour, ruined the reputation of that monarchy, and at last constrained their antient masters to recognize and to treat with them as a free independent state. This state founded on liberty, and reared by industry and œconomy, had grown into reputation even while struggling for its existence, but when peace and security allowed it to expend its views, and to enlarge its commerce, it rose to be one of the most respectable as well as enterprizing powers in Europe."——Such is the character given us of the states of Holland, by the celebrated Dr. Robertson, and whose military history is splendid and glorious, as their civil policy illustrious and admirable.——If their fleets have swept the seas, and more than once driven the British navy from the ocean, their armies have defeated the whole puissance of Lewis le Grand.—While they triumphed abroad, the palladium of the state, its civil constitution was inviolate at home, and around the cap of liberty flourished the laurels of military renown.——This republic of patriots were even the guarantees of English liberty, when the rights of Britain were infringed by James the 1st, they drove that tyrant from the throne, and seated in his stead William of blessed memory.—Thus have these magnanimous states preserved the liberties of our own parent, and from *their* citizens given her a King. This royal republican it was who recognized our own constitution and form'd the pacta conventa that connects us with the English crown.—'Tis a sure earnest, 'tis a glorious omen of freedom to resemble those illustrious republicans, 'tis therefore an agreeable reflection, that our own spirits are congenial with theirs.—Our religious and civil sentiments are the same, both were nurtured in the school of *Calvin*, & both idolize the *deified William*, this sympathy of principle hath been woven with the indearments of personal friendship and the duties of gratitude,—they were our sanctuary when we were driven from home, they consoled our afflictions, they invited us to participate the fruits of their own freedom, but we were following Heaven to this western world, we were predestined to found a new empire, in whose map the British isles e'er long will be discerned as a SPECK, thence the impolicy, &c. &c. &c.

For LONDON,
The Ship Thomas,
Thomas Robson, Master,
Will sail with all Expedition.
For Freight or Passage apply to PETER HUGHES, at his Store in King-Street.
Where there is to be Sold,

ENGLISH, Russia and Ravens Duck, Ticklinburgs, Oznabrigs, Broad Cloths, Duffils, Beaver Coatings, Cod and Mackrel Lines and Hooks, Sail, Sein & Wharpping Twine, 4d. 6d. 8d. 10d. & 20d Nails, Sheathing and Drawing ditto, 6 by 8, 7 by 9 & 8 by 10 Glass, Florence Oil, Gun Powder in Half and Quarter Barrels, Crates of Ware, 12, 15, 18 & 21 Inch Pipes, treble, double and single refin'd Loaf Sugar, Buntins, Shot, Barr Lead, Writing Paper, Spices, Turkey Figgs, Porter in Hampers of 4 Dozen Bottles, Durham Mustard, choice Newcastle Coals. Boston, May 21, 1774.

The Commissioners of His Majesty's Customs hereby give Notice, that from and after the first day of June 1774, the Officers of the Customs for this Port and Harbour, will be removed from the Town of Boston, to the Town of Plymouth, within the limits of the Port of Boston ; then and there to proceed to carry on in the usual Manner the Business of their respective Departments, in the Collection and Management of His Majesty's Customs and the Execution of the Laws of Trade. And no Officer of the Customs will be permitted to remain in the Town or Harbour of Boston from and after the first Day of June next—during the Continuance of said Act. By Order of the Commissioners,

SAMUEL MATHER, pro Secretary.

Custom House, BOSTON, *May 20. 1774.*

Shipping Timber.

ABOUT 80 Tons of good white Oak Shipping Timber, to be Sold cheap. Inquire of Edes & Gill.

TO BE SOLD

A ROPE WALK, the Buildings in good repair, with all the Tools and Implements necessary for carrying on the Rope Making Business, it is very pleasantly and conveniently situated, and has the Advantage of a Water Carriage.—The Business may be carried on in this Town to as much Advantage, as perhaps it can be in any Town upon the Continent.——Any Person that inclines to purchase, may know the Terms by applying to JOHN ADAMS, opposite the Old South Meeting-House in Boston.

Portsmouth in New-Hampshire, May 18.

Teneriffe WINE.

CHOICE *Teneriffe* WINE, just arrived, in Pipes, half Pipes and Quarter Casks, TO BE SOLD, Inquire at SOLOMON DAVIS or THOMAS WALLEY's Store.

Edward Church

Has Imported in the last Ships from LONDON, An Assortment of Spring Goods, which he is now selling at his Usual low Rate at his Store in Newbury Street.

To be Sold on TUESDAY the Twenty-first Day of June next, at Two o'Clock in the Afternoon, by PUBLIC VENDUE, at the House of Mr. Edward Low in Leominster, by Philip Sweetser, of said Leominster,

A Good Farm situated in said Town, containing about 140 Acres of choice Land, consisting of Plowing, Pasturing and Mowing, with a fine young Orchard, and is well Wooded and excellently Watered, upon a great Road, suitable for a Tavern or Trader, with a good House, Barn, and other valuable Accommodations, which renders it a very desirable Farm. It will be sold at a reasonable Price ; and if it should be sold at private Sale before the Day above-mentioned, publick Notice shall be given. May 5, 1774.

All Persons indebted to the Estate of Thomas Brigden, Esq; late of Westminster, in the County of Worcester, deceased, either on Book, Bond or Note, are desired to make immediate Payment to Moses Gill, of Boston, Executor to said Estate. And all to whom the Estate is indebted, are requested to bring in their Accounts for Adjustment.

TO BE SOLD,

THE Estate late belonging to Wheeler and Morse, lying in Grafton, in this Province, of Massachusets Bay, about 32 Miles from Providence, and 40 from Boston, consisting of a Dwelling-House, a large Shop, Store, two Barns, and other Outhouses, about one Acre and ¼ of Land adjoining, with a good Garden, also about 30 Acres of good Pasture, Meadow or Tillage Land, with about 50 Acres of Woodland, in Sight of the House. It is a very pleasant and convenient Situation for a Country Trader, being on the great Country Road, and within 15 Rods of the Meeting House.

Any Person inclining to purchase, may have Time for Payment, on giving good Security, and may also have the Goods now in said Store, and be supplied with others, on as good Terms as can be purchased anywhere in America. For Terms, apply to NICHOLAS BROWN and Company, in Providence, or JOSEPH ROGERS, who is now in Possession of the Premises.

N. B. The Outland may be Sold separate from the House, Shop, &c.

Colony of Rhode-Island, &c. Newport, May 12, 1774.

WHEREAS Matthew Cozzens of Newport aforesaid, Merchant, by Petition represented unto the General Assembly of the Colony aforesaid, that he is an insolvent Debtor, and prayed that he might be admitted to the Benefit of an Act passed in June, A. D. 1756, entitled, "An Act for the Relief of Insolvent Debtors". Upon which the General Assembly referred the said Petition to the next Sessions, and ordered that in the mean Time the Creditors of the said Matthew Cozzens shall be Notified by Advertisement, to be inserted in the Massachusetts, New-York and Rhode-Island News Papers, to appear at the next Session to answer the same :

I do therefore hereby Notify the Creditors of the said Matthew Cozzens to appear (if they shall think fit) at the General Assembly to be holden at said Newport, on the second Monday in June next, then and there to shew Cause (if any they have) why the said Petition should not be granted. HENRY WARD, *Secretary.*

Any Person or Persons who would undertake to erect a Saw Mill, or Grist Mill, or both, on the Township Granted to *Samuel Livermore*, Esq; and others, lying on both Sides *Androscogging-River*, adjoining Sylvester Township in the County of Cumberland, are desired to send the Terms on which they would undertake to erect either, or both of said Mills to *Leonard Williams*, Esq; Lieut. *Elijah Livermore* of Waltham, *Richard Woodward* of Dedham, *William Campbell* of Oxford, *Seth Adams* of Boston, *Ebenezer Marshall* of Framingham, or of *Jeremiah Whittemore* of Spencer, or either of them (they being a Committee appointed by the Proprietors of said Township, to receive the Proposals of any Person or Persons who would undertake said Service) on or before the last Wednesday of June next.

TO BE SOLD,

A Farm adjoining to Kennebunk-River, in the Township of Wells, containing about 50 Acres, two Thirds of it under good Improvement, and in due Proportion for Tillage, Mowing and Pasturage—The Situation exceeding convenient for a Trader or Tradesman, lying at the Head of the Tide. The House and Barn well finished, within 15 Rods of the principal Landing for Boards and other Lumber, and adjoining the Interest of Waldo Emerson, deceased, a late prosperous Merchant in those Parts. Also within a Mile of the Meeting-House, and near two Grist-Mills, Saw-Mill, Iron-Works and Building-Yard.—Conditions of Sale, &c. may be known at Capt. Kimball's in said Wells, Innholder, or of Moses Little, Esq; Merchant in Newbury-Port. Wells, April 25 1774.

Boston: Printed, by EDES & GILL.

No. 999.

THE Boston-Gazette, AND COUNTRY JOURNAL.

Containing the freshest Advices, Foreign and Domestic.

MONDAY, June 6, 1774.

BOSTON, June 6.

THE Corporation of Harvard College, considering the present dark Aspect of publick Affairs, have voted that there shall be no Commencement this Year.

We hear that an Address hath been industriously circulated among the honest Yeomen of Milton: But they were so thoroughly acquainted with Mr. Hutchinson, that the Matter went on *slowly indeed*. For after many Days trial, only three could be deluded to Sign it, viz. The worshipful Justices Murray and Miller, and Capt. Davenport.

Thomas Hutchinson, Esq; sailed Wednesday Morning with Capt. Callahan for London. *Jonah laid three days in the Whale's Belly, on his Passage to Nineveh, that great City.*

Business was finished at the Custom-House at 12 o'Clock Wednesday noon, and this Harbour is now Shut against all Vessels bound hither, and on the 15th instant none will be allowed to depart hence. *Be it forever remembered, to thy great grief and shame, O Britain!*

Thursday last Captain Williamson arrived at Marblehead, in 36 Days from Bristol; by whom we have London Papers to the 26th of April, from which we have extracted the following interesting Advices, viz.

CORK, *April* 11.

WE are informed, that the four regiments that are going to America, are ordered to be encamped at Boston.

LONDON,

April 14. There is a report that parliament will not be prorogued this year, but be kept sitting during the summer by adjournment, from an apprehension that the affairs of Europe or America, or both, may require their sudden interposition and assistance.

Governor Hutchinson, we hear, has already been acquainted that he must prepare himself for a parliamentary inquiry as soon as he arrives in this kingdom.

April 18. Monday last a commission, during pleasure, passed the Great Seal, "Granting unto Thomas Gage, Esq; Lieutenant-General of his Majesty's forces, Governor of the Massachusetts-Bay, full Power and authority, where he shall see cause, or shall judge any offender or offenders to be fit objects of his Majesty's mercy, to pardon and remit all treasons, petit treasons, murders, felonies, crimes, contempts, and misdemeanors whatsoever, done or committed; and all fines, forfeitures, or penalties whatsoever, incurred or imposed."

We are assured that the arrest of General Gage, last Friday, at the suit of Major Robert Rogers, was for a trespass, damages, and false imprisonment of the Major, by the contrivance of the General when he was Commandant of Michilimackinac, in North America, in the month of December 1767, where he was loaded with irons, and confined in a cold room all the winter, and was dragged in irons for near 1200 miles the next summer to Montreal, where he was honorably acquitted by a General Court Martial of every charge brought against him by General Gage.

Proceedings in the House of Commons,

The order of the day for taking into consideration his Majesty's message, and the American papers were then read; after which the Clerks read several extracts of letters from Boston, which took up a considerable time.

As soon as the papers were read, the House resolved into a Committee, and Lord North made the following motion;—"That the Chairman be directed to move the House, that leave be given to bring in a bill for the impartial administration of justice, in the cases of persons questioned for any acts done by them in the execution of the law, or for the suppression of riots and tumults, in the Province of Massachusetts-Bay, in New-England."

This motion occasioned a very warm and well-supported debate, which continued 'till within a few minutes of nine o'clock, when the question being put, it was agreed to without a division, and a bill ordered to be brought in accordingly.

Previous to the motion being delivered to the chairman, Lord North explained the intentions of the bill, traced its several outlines, and obviated many of the probable objections that might be made to it; said, in particular, that he proposed that offenders should be removed for trial to the other Colonies, or, if government thought that justice could not be had there, that in that case they should be brought to Great Britain, the expence to be defrayed by the public. He informed the committee, that it was intended to send four regiments of foot to Boston; that General Gage was to be invested with the civil and military command of the province; and, in conformity to this arrangement, Governor Hutchinson has already taken his passage for Europe.

Yesterday the Panther of 60 guns, and Aldborough frigate, bent their sails, and will go to Spithead in a few days: They are both of the Newfoundland station.

April 19. His Majesty having been pleased to appoint the Right Hon. Frederick North, commonly called Lord North, to be Lord Lieutenant of the county of Somerset, he this day took the oaths appointed to be taken thereupon, instead of the oaths of allegiance and supremacy.

April 23. It is said, the reason of sending so many forces from hence, and from Ireland, to Boston, is because it is thought improper to draw the force from other parts of America, as was at first intended.

The Quakers are at length roused in defence of their rights in the colonies, and have prepared a most spirited petition to the Throne, which they mean to present at St. James's in full procession. They have also, in case of the failure of this Petition, subscribed a very large sum, which they mean to present to a certain great and amiable commoner to bear his expences to America, that they may reap the benefit of his advice for their future conduct.

Two vessels which sailed this week out of the river, one for Philadelphia, and the other for Boston, are full of passengers, tradesmen, and their families, who have been out of employ for some time.

House of Commons, April 21.

The House sat for near half an hour without any business before them, when Lord North came, and presented to the Speaker several extracts of letters, &c. and the third Boston bill, "for the impartial administration of justice in the cases of persons questioned "for any acts done by them in the execution of the "law, or for the suppression of riots and tumults, in "the province of Massachusetts-Bay, in New-England."

The Bill was read a first time; upon which Mr. Sawbridge arose, saying, "Sir, I am astonished at the noble Lord's proceeding, in bringing in a bill of the utmost consequence, at a time when there is so thin a House. [There was only forty-one Members] It is an improper time; it is taking us by surprize; it is cowardly. But, Sir, I should think myself highly unworthy a seat in this Assembly, was I to suffer so pernicious a bill to pass in any stage, without giving my hearty negative to it. I will oppose it every time I have an opportunity, although I do not imagine I shall be much attended to. This is a bill, Sir, of such a ridiculous and cruel nature, that I am really astonished how any person could think of making it. Does the noble Lord think that a man who chances to see a person murdered in America, will come over here as an evidence against the aggressor? Does the noble Lord think, that any American would hazard a trial here, or that he should expect to have justice done him, if he was to come over? Then, Sir, a person would be brought over here to be tried, and you would have evidences only on one side; but I imagine if these evidences should not be sufficient, evidence here, who never saw the transaction, would be procured, and the criminal acquitted. I plainly foresee the dangerous consequences of this bill; IT IS MEANT TO ENSLAVE AMERICA, and the same Minister who means to enslave them, would if he had it in his power, enslave England; it is his aim, and what he wishes to do; but I sincerely hope the Americans will not admit of the execution of these destructive bills, but nobly refuse them; if they do not, they are the most abject slaves that ever the earth produced, and nothing that the Minister can do, is base enough for them.

Lord North.—Sir, I think myself called upon to vindicate my conduct for bringing in the bill at so thin a house. Sir, Was I to know there would be but few Members attend? I did as I promised I would do, which was to bring in a bill as soon as it was ready; it was but just finished when I brought it, and I little expected to have any debate upon it in this stage: I thought Sir, the debate would be upon the second reading; it usually is so; and I sincerely hope, when this bill is read a second time, that we shall have a very full House, and let every gentleman give his opinion upon it. I wish to have it thoroughly discussed, and if it should be found to be a bad bill, in God's name throw it out; but if found otherwise, you cannot be too unanimous in assenting to it; the more unanimity there is, the stronger effect it will have. As to its being meant to enslave America, I deny it, I have no such intention; it is an unpleasant, but necessary step to bring them to a sense of their duty; that assertion has much the same truth in it as what has been before said, that the Americans had seen their error, and were willing to satisfy the India Company. Sir, there is a ship arrived, I think her name is the Fortune, Captain Gorham; she arrived in Boston harbour the latter end of February, or beginning of March 1774, I cannot say which; she was loaded with tea; the inhabitants came immediately and unloaded her, and emptied the contents of her cargo into the sea. Is this Sir, seeing their error? Is this Sir reforming? Is this making restitution to the India company? Surely no gentleman will, after this, urge any in their defence. The honorable gentleman has said this bill is a pernicious one; I trust, when gentlemen come to consider it, they will see it is quite otherwise.

Sir Thomas Frankland arose only to acquaint the House, that he, yesterday afternoon, after the House broke up, was shewn a letter which a friend of his received from Boston, dated March 1774, which mentioned the tea being destroyed, which was the cargo of Captain Gorham, as the noble Lord had mentioned.

Mr. Fyng.—Sir, I cannot help rising to oppose this bill. I agree with my worthy friend, that it is a most pernicious bill, and I fear made with no good intention. I really am surprised at the noble Lord, who said, his wish was to make their laws in America as near as possible to our own. Is this bill any thing like it? No, it is quite the reverse; dragging people from one country to another to give evidence, is such a proposition I never heard before, nor could have thought of; but, Sir, every person must know, and will allow, that the noble Lord finds his other two bills are so defective and dangerous, that no person will venture to put them into execution; he is therefore obliged to have recourse to a third, to indemnify such persons as shall be concerned in executing his destructive project. I shall oppose this bill every time I have an opportunity, and I trust every lover of his country will do the same.

He further said, that whatever professions of candor were thrown out, he should trust to them with great caution; that for his part these attacks made abroad, seemed to be intended to prepare mens minds for measures of a similar nature to be enforced at home; and that the conduct and complexion of public measures in general wore the appearance of a systematic design of enslaving the people, as well in Great-Britain as the colonies.

Lord Beauchamp.—I really am surprised, Sir, to hear an honorable gentleman say, that every person must know that the two former bills are defective. Sir, I will venture to say the fact is otherwise; every person must allow they are necessary for the preservation of peace, and restoring the Americans to a sense of their duty. Does the hon. gentleman think the soldiery at Boston will act without they are indemnified? No; they could not. No person would execute the laws half so well, was this bill not to pass. I think it a necessary bill; it will make their trials by Juries like ours, which are so much approved of; and I shall give my hearty affirmative to it.

Mr. Sawbridge.—Sir, I rise to explain to the noble Lord why I think it a pernicious bill. I am certain, that however willing I might be to bring an offender to justice, was I to see murder committed in London, my love of justice might induce me to go to any part of the country to appear as an evidence; but I assure the noble Lord I would not go over to America on any account, not for any mandate he could issue; and I believe that noble Lord will allow that not any sum would induce him to go over now; therefore we have the same right to imagine that people in America will not come over here. I make no doubt but government will take care to bring over evidence in support of their side, but they will not trouble themselves with evidence on the contrary; therefore all your trials will be *ex parte*, and nothing but a mockery of justice. I do not mention this as an advocate America, but as an Englishman.

The question was then put that this bill be read a second time on Monday next.

Mr. Sawbridge desired to know of the noble Lord if he had any objections to having it printed.

Lord North answered, No.

Mr. Sawbridge then said, Monday would be too soon for the second reading, there would not be time to print it by that day.

The question was again put, and carried without a division.

House of Commons, April 22.

Orders were given to clear the gallery, and to enforce them the more expeditiously the Serjeant at Arms attended himself. At four o'clock the order for the second reading of the bill for regulating the government of Massachusetts-Bay came on, which produced a warm debate that continued till almost seven o'clock; and a motion being made for committing the said bill, it passed in the affirmative without a division. The principal speakers were Mr. Welbore Ellis, Sir George Savile, Lord North, Gen. Conway, Mr. Jenkinson, Gov. Johnstone, Mr. Harris, Sir George Young, Mr. Ward, Gov Pownal, Mr. Rigby, Mr. C. Fox, and Sir G. Elliot.

April 26. It is said —— —— is so far flattered and satisfied, the measures begun and to be pursued with America, will produce perfect tranquility there, that Parliament, it is now given out, will rise on the 3d June.

The duty on Tea, it is said, will be repealed.

A gentleman lately observed, that the Bostonians had purchased a *temporary* relief from taxation, at the expence of their liberty.

We are assured from a gentleman's own mouth, who heard Lord Chatham declare since he came to town, that so far from altering his sentiments as to America, he is more than ever confirmed in the system he has so often held in public, relative to that country.

Lord Chatham's ideas are, that as the people of America are not represented here, there is no foundation to tax them; but that from necessity, we must regulate and direct the system of commerce.—*The people of America think so too.*

DUBLIN, *April* 19. We learn from Belfast, that no less than three ships sailed from thence last week with emigrants for America; in one of which there were near 500 passengers. Nothing but a speedy revival to the linnen trade can save this country, for without money and people it will be exhausted.

A BILL for the impartial Administration of Justice in the Cases of Persons questioned for any Acts done by them in the Execution of the Law, or for the Suppression of Riots and Tumults, in the Province of the Massachusetts-Bay *in* New-England.

WHEREAS in His Majesty's Province of *Massachusetts-Bay*, in *New-England*, an Attempt hath lately been made to throw off the Authority of the Parliament of *Great Britain* over the said Province; and an actual and avowed Resistance, by open Force, to the Execution of certain Acts of Parliament, hath been suffered to take place, uncontrouled and unpunished, in Defiance of His Majesty's Authority, and to the utter Subversion of all lawful Government:

And whereas, in the present disordered State of the said Province, it is of the utmost Importance to the general Welfare thereof, and to the Re-establishment of lawful Authority throughout the same, that neither the Magistrates acting in Support of the Laws, nor any of His Majesty's Subjects aiding and assisting them therein, or in the Suppression of Riots and Tumults, raised in Opposition to the Execution of the Laws and Statutes of this Realm, should be discouraged from the proper Discharge of their Duty, by an Apprehension, that in case of their being questioned for any Acts done therein, they may be liable to be brought to Trial for the same, before Persons who do not acknowledge the Validity of the Laws in the Execution whereof, or the Authority of the Magistrate in the Support of whom such Acts had been done:

In order therefore to remove every such Discouragement from the Minds of His Majesty's Subjects, and to induce them, upon all proper Occasions, to exert themselves in Support of the Publick Peace of the Province, and of the Authority of the King and Parliament of *Great Britain* over the same; *Be it enacted* by the King's Most Excellent Majesty, by and with the Advice and Consent of the Lords Spiritual and Temporal, and Commons, in this present Parliament assembled, and by the Authority of the same, That if at any Time, within the Space of Years from and after the any Bill or Bills of Indictment shall be found against any Person for Murther, or other capital Offence, in the Province of the *Massachusetts Bay*, and it shall appear, by Information given upon Oath to the Governor, or in his Absence to the Lieutenant Governor, of the said Province, that the Fact was committed by the Person indicted, while he was either in the Execution of his Duty as a Magistrate, for the Suppression of Riots, or in the Support of the Laws of Revenue, or that he was acting in his Duty as an Officer of Revenue, or acting under the Direction and Order of any Magistrate for the Suppression of Riots, or for the carrying into Effect the Laws of Revenue, or aiding and assisting in any of the Purposes aforesaid; and if it shall also appear, to the Satisfaction of the said Governor or Lieutenant Governor respectively, that an indifferent Trial cannot be had within the said Province, in that Case it shall and may be lawful for the Governor or Lieutenant Governor to direct, that the Indictment shall be tried in some other of his Majesty's Colonies, or in *Great Britain*, and for that Purpose to order the Person indicted to be sent under a sufficient Custody to the Place appointed for his Trial; and that there may be no Failure of Justice from the want of Evidence in such Cases, it shall and may be lawful for the Governor, or in his Absence the Lieutenant Governor, to settle and assess a reasonable Sum to be allowed for the Expences of such Witnesses as the Prosecutor, or the Person indicted, shall desire to be summoned; which Sum shall be advanced by the Commissioners of His Majesty's Customs, to the Witness, who, upon the Receipt thereof, shall enter into a Recognizance before a Judge of the Superior Court, to appear and give Evidence upon the Trial of such Indictment.

And be it further Enacted, That the Governor, or in his Absence the Lieutenant Governor, if he shall direct the Trial to be had in any other of His Majesty's Colonies, shall transmit the Indictment, together with the Recognizances of the Witnesses, under the Seal of the Province, to the Governor of such other Colony; who shall immediately issue a Commission of Oyer and Terminer, and deliver or cause to be delivered the said Indictment, with the said Recognizances, to the Chief Justice, and such other Persons as have usually been Commissioners of Oyer and Terminer there; who shall have Power to proceed upon the said Indictment, as if the same had been found before them, and the Trial shall thereupon proceed in like Manner, to all Intents and Purposes, as if the Offence had been committed in such Place: And in case the Governor, or in his Absence the Lieutenant Governor, shall direct the Trial to be had in *Great Britain*, he shall then transmit the Indictment, together with the Recognizances of the Witnesses, under the Seal of the Province, to one of his Majesty's principal Secretaries of State, who shall deliver or cause to be delivered the same, to the Master of the Crown Office, and the Indictment shall be tried in the next Term, at the Bar of the Court of *King's Bench*, in like Manner, to all Intents and Purposes, as if the Offence had been committed in the County of *Middlesex*.

A BILL for the better regulating the Government of the Province of the Massachusetts-Bay *in* North-America.

WHEREAS by Letters Patent under the Great Seal of *England*, made in the Third Year of the Reign of their late Majesties King *William* and Queen *Mary*, for uniting, erecting, and incorporating, the several Colonies, Territories, and Tracts of Land therein mentioned, into One real Province, by the Name of their Majesties Province of the *Massachusetts-Bay*, in *New-England*, whereby it was amongst other Things ordained and established, That the Governor of the said Province should from thenceforth be appointed and commissionated by their Majesties, their Heirs and Successors, it was however granted and ordained, That from the Expiration of the Term, for, and during which the Eight and Twenty Persons, named in the said Letters Patent, were appointed to be the First Counsellors or Assistants to the Governor of the said Province for the Time being, the aforesaid Number of Eight and Twenty Counsellors or Assistants should yearly Once every Year, for ever thereafter, be, by the General Court or Assembly, newly chosen:

And whereas the said Method of electing such Counsellors or Assistants, to be vested with the several Powers, Authorities, and Privileges therein mentioned, although conformable to the Practice, theretofore used, in such of the Colonies thereby united, in which the Appointment of the respective Governors had been vested in the General Courts or Assemblies of the said Colonies, hath by repeated Experience, been found to be extremely ill adapted to the Plan of Government established in the Province of the *Massachusetts-Bay*, by the said Letters Patent hereinbefore mentioned, and hath been so far from contributing to the Attainment of the good Ends and Purposes thereby intended, and to the promoting of the internal Welfare, Peace, and good Government, or to the Maintenance of that just Subordination to, and Conformity with, the Laws of *Great Britain*, that the Manner of exercising the Powers, Authorities, and Privileges, aforesaid, by the Persons so annually elected, hath for some Time past been such as had the most manifest Tendency to obstruct, and in great Measure defeat the Execution of the Laws, to weaken the Attachment of His Majesty's well-disposed Subjects, in the said Province, to His Majesty's Government, and to encourage the ill disposed among them to proceed even to Acts of direct Resistance to, and Defiance of, His Majesty's Authority; and it hath accordingly happened, that an open Resistance to the Execution of the Laws hath actually taken place in the Town of *Boston* and the Neighbourhood thereof, within the said Province:

And whereas it is, under these Circumstances, become absolutely necessary, in order to the Preservation of the Peace and good Order of the said Province, the Protection of His Majesty's well-disposed Subjects therein resident, the Continuance of the mutual Benefits arising from the Commerce and Correspondence between this Kingdom and the said Province, and the maintaining of the just Dependance of the said Province upon the Crown and Parliament of *Great Britain*, that the said Method of annually electing the Counsellors or Assistants of the said Province should no longer be suffered to continue, but that the Appointment of the said Counsellors or Assistants should henceforth be put upon the like Footing as is established in such other of His Majesty's Colonies or Plantations in *America*, the Governors whereof are appointed by His Majesty's Commission under the Great Seal of *Great Britain*:

Be it therefore Enacted, by the KING's most Excellent MAJESTY, by and with the Advice and Consent of the Lords Spiritual and Temporal, and Commons, in this present Parliament assembled, and by the Authority of the same, That from and after the

so much of the Charter granted by their Majesties King *William* and Queen *Mary*, to the Inhabitants of the said Province of the *Massachusetts Bay*, in *New England*, and all and every Clause, Matter, and Thing, therein contained, which relates to the Time and Manner of electing the Assistants, or Counsellors, for the said Province, and all Elections and Appointments of such Counsellors and Assistants made in pursuance thereof, shall

and that from and after the said the Council or Court of Assistants of the said Province for the Time being, shall be composed of such of the Inhabitants or Proprietors of Lands within the same, as shall be thereunto nominated and appointed by His Majesty, his Heirs & Successors by Warrant under his or their Signet or Sign Manual, and with the Advice of the Privy Council, agreeable to the Practice now used in Respect to the Appointment of Counsellors in such of His Majesty's other Colonies in *America*, the Governors whereof are appointed by Commission under the Great Seal of *Great Britain*: Provided that the Number of the said Assistants or Counsellors shall not at any One Time exceed nor be less than

And it is hereby further Enacted, That the said Assistants or Counsellors so to be appointed as aforesaid, shall hold their Offices respectively, for and during the Pleasure of His Majesty, his Heirs or Successors, and shall have and enjoy all the Powers, Privileges, and Immunities, at present held, exercised, and enjoyed by the Assistants or Counsellors of the said Province, constituted and elected from Time to Time, under the said Charter, except as hereinafter excepted; and shall also, upon their Admission into the said Council, and before they enter upon the Execution of their Offices, respectively take the Oaths, and make, repeat, and subscribe, the Declarations required, as well by the said Charter as by any Law or Laws of the said Province now in force, to be taken by the Assistants or Counsellors, which have been so elected and constituted as aforesaid.

And be it further Enacted by the Authority aforesaid, That from and after the it shall and may be lawful for His Majesty's Governor, for the Time being, of the said Province, or, in his absence, for the Lieutenant Governor, to nominate and appoint, under the Seal of the Province, from Time to Time, the Judges of the Inferior Courts of Common Pleas, Commissioners of Oyer and Terminer, the Attorney General, Sheriffs, Provosts Marshals, Justices of the Peace, and other Officers to the Council or Courts of Justice belonging, and to remove the same without the Consent of the Council; and that all Judges of the Inferior Courts of Common Pleas, Commissioners of Oyer and Terminer, the Attorney General, Sheriffs, Provosts Marshals, Justices, and other Officers so appointed by the Governor, or, in his absence, by the Lieutenant Governor alone, and shall and may have, hold and exercise, the said Offices, Powers, and Authorities as fully and completely, to all Intents and Purposes, as any Judges of the Inferior Courts of Common Pleas, Commissioners of Oyer and Terminer, Attorney General, Sheriffs, Provosts Marshals, or other Officers, have or might have done heretofore under the said Letters Patent, in the Third Year of the Reign of their late Majesties King *William* and Queen *Mary*, any Law, Statute, or Usage, to the contrary notwithstanding.

Provided always, and be it Enacted, That nothing herein contained shall extend, or be construed to extend to annul or make void the Commission granted before the

to any Judges of the Inferior Courts of Common Pleas, Commissioners of Oyer and Terminer, the Attorney General, Sheriffs, Provosts Marshals, Justices of the Peace, or other Officers; but that they may hold and exercise the same, as if this Act had never been made, until the same shall be determined by Death, Removal by the Governor, or other Avoidance, as the Case may happen.

And be it further Enacted by the Authority aforesaid, That upon every Vacancy of the Offices of Chief Justice and Judges of the superior Court of the said Province, from and after the

the Governor for the Time being, or in his Absence the Lieutenant Governor, without the Consent of the Council, shall have full Power and Authority to nominate and appoint the Persons to succeed to the said Offices, who shall hold their Commissions during the Pleasure of His Majesty, his Heirs and Successors; and that neither the Chief Justice and Judges appointed before the said nor those who shall hereafter be appointed pursuant to this Act, shall be removed, unless by the Order of his Majesty, his Heirs or Successors, under his or their Sign Manual.

And be it further Enacted by the Authority aforesaid, That the Governor, Lieutenant Governor, Chief Justice, the Judges of the Superior Court, and the Secretary of the said Province, for the Time being, shall be, and they are hereby appointed, during their Continuance in their respective Offices, Justices of the Peace in and for every County of the said Province, and shall and may have, hold, and enjoy, all the Powers and

Authorities given to the Juſtices of the Peace by virtue of their Commiſſion, or by any Act of the General Court of the ſaid Province.

And whereas, by an Act of the General Court of the ſaid Province, made in the Fourth Year of the Reign of their late Majeſties King *William* and Queen *Mary*, intituled, "An Act for regulating of Townſhips, Choice of Town Officers, and ſetting forth their Power," the Freeholders and Inhabitants of the ſeveral Townſhips, rateable at Twenty Pounds Eſtate, are authorized to aſſemble together, in the Month of *March* in every Year, upon Notice given by the Conſtable, or ſuch other as the Select Men of the Town ſhall appoint, for the Choice of Select Men, Conſtables, and other Officers; and the Freeholders and Inhabitants are alſo impowered to make and agree upon ſuch neceſſary Rules, Orders, and Bye-laws, for the directing, managing, and ordering, the prudential Affairs, and to annex Penalties for the Non-obſervance of the ſame, not exceeding Twenty Shillings for one Offence; provided they be not repugnant to the General Laws of the ſaid Province:

And whereas a great Abuſe has been made of the Power of calling ſuch Meetings, and the Inhabitants have, contrary to the Deſign of their Inſtitution, been miſled to treat upon Matters of the moſt general Concern, and to paſs many dangerous and unwarrantable Reſolves; *For* Remedy whereof, *Be it enacted*, That from and after the

no Town Meeting ſhall be called by the Select Men, or at the Requeſt of any Number of Freeholders, without the leave of the Governor in Writing, expreſſing the ſpecial Buſineſs of the ſaid Meeting, firſt had and obtained, except the Annual Meeting, in the Month of *March*, for the Choice of Select Men, Conſtables, and other Officers; and that no other Matter ſhall be treated of at ſuch Meeting, except the Election of their aforeſaid Officers, nor at any other Meeting, except the Buſineſs expreſſed in the Leave given by the Governor.

And whereas, in purſuance of an Act of Aſſembly of the ſaid Province, made in the Seventh Year of the Reign of *William* the Third, and Three other Acts of Aſſembly, made in the Eleventh Year of the ſame Reign, Jurors, as well Grand as Petty, have been uſually ſummoned and returned by the Conſtables of the ſeveral Towns, by virtue of Writs or Warrants directed to them, by the Clerks of the ſeveral Courts, requiring them to aſſemble the Inhabitants of the ſaid Towns, to chuſe fit Perſons to ſerve as Jurors for ſuch Towns, and to ſummon and return ſuch Perſons ſo choſen; which Practice of chuſing Jurors, and returning them, without the Intervention of the Sheriff, has been found to be detrimental to the Adminiſtration of Juſtice; *Be it therefore Enacted* by the Authority aforeſaid, That from and after the

next enſuing, ſo much of the ſaid Acts of Aſſembly, and of all other Laws now in force, within the ſaid Province, as directs the Returns of Juries to be made by the Conſtables, by an Election of the Inhabitants of the ſeveral Towns, ſhall

and all Jurors, as well Grand as Petty, ſhall be returned by the Sheriffs of the ſeveral Counties, and no otherwiſe; and the Juſtices of the Superior Court of the ſaid Province, at a convenient Time before the Sitting of the Superior Court in every County, and the Juſtices of the Peace for every County in the ſaid Province, at a convenient Time before the Sitting of the Quarter Seſſion of ſuch County, ſhall iſſue their Precepts or Warrants to the Sheriff of ſuch County, for ſuch ſeveral Courts reſpectively to ſummon, out of the Freeholders and Inhabitants of ſuch County qualified to ſerve upon Juries, ſuch a Number of good and lawful Men as ſuch Precept or Warrant ſhall direct, to ſerve upon the Grand Jury at ſuch reſpective Court; and ſuch Perſons ſo ſummoned and returned by the ſaid Sheriff, or ſuch of them as ſhall appear, ſhall be impannelled and ſworn the Grand Inqueſt for the Body of the County, and ſhall continue as ſuch during the Sitting of ſuch reſpective Court, and until they ſhall be diſmiſſed by the ſame; and in all Indictments, Informations, Actions, and Cauſes, depending before the Superior Court, or any Court of Quarter Seſſion, or Court of Common Pleas, in the ſaid Province, which ſhall be at Iſſue, and ordered for Trial, the Juries ſhall be ſummoned, impannelled, and returned, by the Sheriff of the County, out of the Freeholders and Inhabitants of the ſaid County qualified to ſerve upon Juries, and ſhall be choſen and arrayed in ſuch Manner and Form, and by and with ſuch Regulations and Reſtrictions, as is directed and ordered in and by an Act of Parliament, made in the Seventh and Eighth Years of the Reign of his late Majeſty King *William* the Third, intituled, "An Act for the Eaſe of Jurors, "and better regulating of Juries;" and One other Act, made in the Eighth and Ninth Years of the ſame Reign, intitled "An Act to enable the "Returns of Juries as formerly, until the Firſt "Day of *November*, One thouſand Six hundred and Ninety-ſeven;" and One other Act of Parliament, made in the Third Year of the Reign of his late Majeſty King *George* the Second, intituled "An "Act for the better Regulation of Juries; and One other Act, made in the Twenty fourth Year of the ſame Reign, intituled, "An Act for the "better Regulation of Trials by Jury, and for "enlarging the Time for Trials by *Niſi Prius*, "in the County of *Middleſex*."

And be it further Enacted by the Authority aforeſaid, that Liſts of the Freeholders and Inhabitants of the ſeveral Towns, qualified to ſerve upon Juries, ſhall be returned to, and recorded at, the Quarter Seſſions for the ſeveral Counties, and ſhall be delivered to the ſeveral Sheriffs in Manner and Form as directed by the ſaid Acts of Parliament, or any of them; and until ſuch Liſts of ſuch Freeholders and Inhabitants ſhall be delivered as aforeſaid, the Sheriff of any County ſhall and may ſummon and return fit Perſons to ſerve upon Juries as aforeſaid, out of the Body of the Freeholders and Inhabitants of the County, qualified to ſerve upon Juries, according to his Judgment and Diſcretion; and whenever the Judges of the Superior Court ſhall Award a Special Jury to be ſtruck (which they are hereby authorized and impowered to do in ſuch Manner as Special Juries have been uſually ſtruck in the Court at *Weſtminſter* at Trials at Bar) and if the Sheriff of the County in which ſuch Jury ſhall be awarded, ſhall not have received Liſts of the Freeholders and Inhabitants qualified to ſerve upon Juries as hereinbefore ordered and directed, ſuch Sheriff ſhall attend the proper Office of the ſaid Court, with a Liſt of   of the principal Freeholders & Inhabitants of the ſaid County qualified to ſerve upon Juries, and the ſaid Special Jury ſhall be ſtruck out of the ſaid Liſt; and it ſhall and may be lawful for the Juſtices of the ſaid Superior Court, and they are hereby authorized and impowered, upon the Motion of either of the Parties, in any Cauſe or Action which ſhall be brought to iſſue, to order the ſaid Cauſe or Action to be tried in any County, other than the County in which the ſaid Cauſe or Action ſhall have been brought or laid, by a Jury of ſuch other County, as they ſhall judge fit and proper, any Act of Aſſembly or Provincial Law to the contrary notwithſtanding.

And be it further Enacted by the authority aforeſaid, That all Clerks of Courts, Sheriffs, Conſtables, and other Perſons within the ſaid Province, to whom the ordering, making, delivering, or recording, the Liſts of the Freeholders and Inhabitants qualified to ſerve upon Juries as aforeſaid, ſhall belong or appertain, according to the true Intent and Meaning of this preſent Act, and the ſaid Acts hereby referred to, who ſhall be guilty of any wilful Neglect, Default, or Miſfeazance, in the carrying into Execution this Act, according to its true Intent and Meaning, ſhall incur and ſuffer ſuch Fines and Penalties as are ſeverally mentioned in the ſaid Acts of Parliament hereby referred to; and all Perſons who, being duly qualified as aforeſaid, ſhall be duly ſummoned to ſerve upon Juries in Manner aforeſaid, and ſhall not attend ſuch Service, ſhall incur and ſuffer ſuch Fines and Penalties as, by the Laws of the ſaid Province, Jurors making Default are now ſubject to.

And be it further Enacted by the Authority aforeſaid, That if any Action ſhall be brought againſt any Sheriff, for what he ſhall do in Execution, or by virtue of this Act, he may plead the general Iſſue, and give the ſpecial Matter in Evidence; and if a Verdict ſhall be found for him, he ſhall recover   Coſts.

ALL Perſons indebted for this Paper, whoſe Accounts have been above 12 Months ſtanding, are requeſted to make immediate Payment.

RAN-away from the Subſcriber, living in Gorham, which joins Falmouth, Cumberland County, in the Maſſachuſetts Province, a ſhort Negro Man named Prince, about 26 Years of Age, 5 Feet ſome Inches high, talks broken Engliſh, has remarkable ſmall Ears and a Jewel Hole in one of them. Had on almoſt a new Felt Hat, a reddiſh grey home-made Cloth Coat Jacket and Breeches, with ſilk knee Garters, a dark Callicoe under Jacket, a white Linnen Shirt, red Collar and Cuffs to his Coat with Metal Buttons, white Cotton Stocking, Calf-ſkin Pumps. It may be he has a Paſs. Said Negro plays tolerable well on a Violin. Whoever will take up ſaid Negro, or bring him to his Maſter ſhall have Sixteen Dollars Reward, and all Charges paid, by

WILLIAM M'LENNEN.

N. B. *Said Negro having done ſome Damage at the Houſe where the Negroes met to hold their Frolick on Election Day, did not return to his Maſter again.*

All Maſters of Veſſels are forewarned not to carry him off at their Peril. *May 26, 1774.*

Juſt Publiſhed,

And Sold by EDES *and* GILL, *in Queen Street,*

[*Price*, 1s. 6d.]

OBSERVATIONS

ON

THE ACT OF PARLIAMENT

COMMONLY CALLED

THE

BOSTON PORT-BILL;

WITH

THOUGHTS

ON

CIVIL SOCIETY

AND

STANDING ARMIES.

Dedicated to the FREEHOLDERS and YEOMANRY of the COUNTRY,

BY *JOSIAH QUINCY*, Junr.

BRITONS *ariſe!*——
And ſhow you have the virtue to be mov'd.
POPE.

NULLA FIDES, pietaſq; viris, qui CASTRA ſequuntur,
VENALESQUE MANUS: ibi fas, ubi maxima merces.
LUCAN.

Our necks are under PERSECUTION. LAM. v. 5.

What MAN can do againſt them, *not afraid*,
Though to THE DEATH; againſt ſuch CRUELTIES
With *inward conſolation* recompenc'd:
And oft ſupported ſo, *as ſhall amaze*
Their PROUDEST PERSECUTORS. MILTON.

They that be ſlain by THE SWORD are better than they that be ſlain *with hunger*. LAM. iv. 9.

Mill-Saws.

A Number of fine Engliſh Steel-Plate Mill-Saws, ſuitable for the Eaſtward Uſe, ſuperior to any ever in America before, and made on an entire new Model,

Is juſt open'd, and to be Sold by

Charles Sigourney,

At his Shop at the Head of Dock-Square Market, BOSTON. ALSO,

Guns, Swords, Trooping-Piſtols, Fuzees, with Spring Pipes, Steel Rods and Bayonets, Gun Locks, ſpare Gun-Barrels. ALSO,

2d, 3d, 4d, 6d, 8d, 10d, 20d & 24d. Nails, ſheathing, drawing and deck nails, tacks and brads of all ſorts, glaſs, lead, powder, ſhot, ſteel, French and Engliſh flints, Engliſh glue, pewter diſhes, plates, baſons, porringers, tankards, canns, ſpoons, braſs kettles, ſkillets, warming pans, ſkimmers, copper and iron tea-kettles, knives and forks of all ſorts, penknives, ſciſſars, razors, cuttoes, and every other article in the Hard-Ware Branch, that is imported into this Place. ALSO,

TIN-Plates, Lanthorn-Leaves, Allum, Copperas, Brimſtone, Engliſh double refin'd Loaf-Sugar, &c.

PAINTER's OYL and COLOURS.

Juſt arrived——An Aſſortment of Painters Oyl and Colours, and will be ſold at the loweſt Rates. ALSO,

An Invoice of Colours, conſiſting of Red Lead, Spaniſh Brown, White Lead, Spaniſh White, and a few Caſks of Oyl, very cheap, being a Conſignment.

To the Honorable JEREMIAH POWELL, Eſq; one of his Majeſty's Juſtices of the Peace throughout the Province of the Maſſachuſetts-Bay, humbly Shew,

THE the Subſcribers, more than five of the Proprietors of a Tract of Land, lying in the County of York, ſituate between the Rivers of Great Oſſipee and Little-Oſſipee, within the County aforeſaid, containing the Breadth of all that Space between the ſaid Rivers, and ſo running Southweſterly from Saco-River, more than twelve Miles, which ſame Tract was purchaſed of one Captain Sunday, an Indian Sagamore, by Francis Small, who lived on the ſame Land a long Time, and had a quiet Poſſeſſion thereof, and the ſaid Petitioners being now in the Poſſeſſion of the ſame, and being deſirous of being an acting Propriety, according to the Law in that Caſe made and provided: Do requeſt your Worſhip to call a Meeting to be at the Houſe of Mr. Samuel March, Innholder in Scarborough, in the County of Cumberland, on the firſt Monday of Auguſt next, at Ten of the Clock in the Forenoon, to Act on the following Articles, to wit:

1ſt, To chooſe a Moderator.

2dly. To chooſe a Proprietors Clerk.

3dly. To chooſe a Committee to tranſact the prudential Affairs of ſaid Proprietors.

4thly. To chooſe Agents to proſecute and defend Suits in behalf of ſaid Proprietors.

5thly. To agree on any Method for raiſing Money or ſettling the ſame Land, as alſo to agree on any Method for calling future Meetings.

May 17th, 1774.

SAMUEL SMALL.
SAMUEL SMALL, jun.
SAMUEL MARCH,
JOSHUA SMALL,
BENJAMIN SMALL,
NATHANIEL MILLIKEN,
JOHN WRIGHT,
NATHAN CHICKE,
JOSEPH SMALL,
JAMES SMALL,
BENJAMIN MEAD LORD,

Province of the Maſſachuſetts-Bay.

(L. S.)

To SAMUEUEL MARCH, of Scarborough, in the County of Cumberland, in ſaid Province, Gentleman, one of ſaid Proprietors,

Greeting.

IN purſuance of the foregoing Application and Requeſt, you are hereby required to give Notice (in Time and Manner as the Law directs) to the ſaid Proprietors, that a Meeting of ſaid Proprietors is to be holden at the Time and Place, and for the Purpoſes mentioned in the afore-written Petition.

Given under my Hand and Seal, this 28th Day of May, A. D. 1774. JERE. POWELL, Juſtice of the Peace throughout the Province aforeſaid.

May the 28th, 1774.

BY Virtue of the afore-written Warrant to me directed, I do hereby notify and warn the Proprietors of the aforeſaid Lands, to meet at the Dwelling-Houſe of Samuel March, Innholder in Scarborough aforeſaid, on the firſt Monday of Auguſt next, at Ten of the Clock in the Forenoon, for the Purpoſes therein mentioned.

SAMUEL MARCH.

The DECLARATION of Marblehead, relative to the Address from sundry Inhabitants of the Town to Governor HUTCHINSON.

"BE it known to the whole World, its present Generation, and every future one: That the Town of Marblehead now legally assembled, pursuant to Adjournment, taking into Consideration an Address which appeared in the last Essex Gazette from sundry Inhabitants of this Town to the late Governor Hutchinson, is clearly of opinion,

1st. That, as the Address did originate since the commencement of this Meeting, and as the Warrant for the Meeting enbled the Inhabitants to take any suitable Steps upon the present critical Situation of public Affairs, whether by Addressing, Instructing or otherwise; the Addressers by the secret and clandestine Manner in which they have conducted this Address, have manifested a Disposition to destroy the Harmony of the Town in its public Affairs; and thus planted the Seeds of Dissentions, Annimosities, and Discords.

2d. That a public Address to a person just leaving a high and public Office in the Province, who is not only neglected by the two honorable Branches of the present Legislature of it, but has likewise been censur'd by both Houses of a former Assembly as an inveterate Enemy to the Liberties of the Province; is such an Indignity offered to those Branches of the Government as this Town is in Duty and Gratitude bound to bear Testimony against——more especially, as it conceives itself under lasting Obligations to them for their steady and virtuous attachment to the Liberties and true Interest of the Province, which they have strenuously contended for.

3d. That the Addressers have to the utmost of their Power strengthened the Hands of a subtle Enemy to the Province by their Address; and this Instrument, altho' but a *fantastical Shadow* of public Respect, will be naturally improved by Mr. Hutchinson to justify his own Conduct, and raise still higher the Prejudices which so unjustly rage against this injured Province & Continent.

4th. That the Address aforesaid is not only in Substance exceptionable, but insulting and affrontive to this Town; as the Addressers first say to Mr. Hutchinson, "in your public Administration, we are fully convinced that the general good was the mark you ever aimed at," (which however this Town could never believe, and having been "fully convinced" of the contrary, hath publickly declared it) and then they go on to assert, *that* this their Sentiment is likewise the Opinion of all "*dispassionate thinking* Men, within the Circle of their Observation, notwithstanding many Publications would have taught the World to think the contrary;" by which Paragraph this Town conceives, that the Addressers have plainly adjudg'd all the Inhabitants of it who are not in this their Opinion, relative to Mr. Hutchinson, to be *passionate thoughtless* Men; and that at least nineteen twentieths of the Inhabitants must fall under this indecent Censure.

5th. That the thirty three Inhabitants of this Town, who could publickly pass such an Encomium on an Opinion of their own, which appears to the Town both flattering and absurd, as that "it is likewise the Opinion of all dispassionate thinking Men:" Who could not only declare themselves and those in their Opinion intitled to the Characters mentioned, but that no other Persons in the Community of which they were a Part, were deserving of them; and who could in the public Papers appear Subscribers of such a Conduct; have exposed themselves to be censured by the World, as Persons in this Instance both *Vain* and *Inattentive*.

6th. That the Addressers have needlesly agitated the Matter of "Fishermen's paying Hospital Money;" which being an Affair that nearly affects many considerable Towns in this Province, could not with propriety have been taken up so publickly by any particular *Town* without consulting the other Towns, as it has been by the *Addressers*. And without noticing an Error in the Address, Mr. Hutchinson is told by the Signers, "that they believe it is owing to his Representation of the Matter, that we are *hitherto* free from that Burden:" by which Clause the Government of Great Britain may have great Reason to think that a Demand of Hospital Money from the Fishery is expected here, and should the poor Men who can now scarcely support themselves and Families alive by Fishing, have an encreased Burden of Hospital Money brought on them hereafter, they may have great Reason to condemn this imprudent Measure of the Addressers.

This Town cannot but express on the present occasion, a great Satisfaction at the Unanimity which appears in the collective Body of this Province, with respect to its Enemies; the Numbers addressing Mr. Hutchinson, compared with the Body of *Freeholders* in the Province, are but as a Drop in the Bucket. May it continue to be the fixed Principle of the *latter*, "that the Persons who are declared by the righteous Government of a *People* to be *their* inveterate Enemies, ought to be esteemed and treated by *them*; and may we heartily join with our Brethren in this Province, in supporting the Honor and Dignity of our General Assembly, by treating with Neglect and Contempt those Persons who are or may be under its just Censuress."——

The preceeding is a true Copy of a Declaration this Day unanimously Voted at a legal Meeting of this Town, and published by its Order. Marblehead, June 3, 1774.

Copy attest. BENJ. BODEN, Town Clerk.

BOSTON, JUNE 6.

Tell it in GATH, publish it in ASKELON, that the Boston Port-Bill, in all its Parts is now carrying into Execution, and that Boston is thereby got into greater Distress, and is more insulted by an English armament than she ever was by a French or Spanish Fleet in the hottest War, when left without one British Ship for her protection. The Town is become a Spectacle to ANGELS and MEN, GOD grant that it may not be intimidated by the present Horrors to make a surrender of the Rights of Americans; or in any Respect to dishonour herself at this Day of Tryal and Perplexity.

The regiment on board the transports arrived Wednesday we are informed, is the 4th, or King's own.

Two or three Regiments more are hourly expected. One is to relieve that at Halifax.

Wednesday his Excellency Governor Gage, attended by the Secretary of the Province and other Gentlemen, sat out for Salem.

Died. Yesterday Afternoon, Mr. RICHARD DRAPER, Printer, aged 47. We hear his Remains are to be interr'd on Wednesday next.

*** Advertisements &c. omitted will be in our next.

Charlestown Stage Coach No. 1.

Sets off for *Salem* This Day at 8 o'Clock in the Morning, from Mr. *Woart's* Tavern at the Sign of the Three Cranes near the Ferry in *Charlestown*, and to put up at Mr. *Goodhue's* Tavern in *Salem*, and to continue to return the same Day on every Day in the Week, Sunday's only excepted, with four good Horses, and as neat a Coach as perhaps was ever drove in *America*: All Persons who shall please to favour the Subscriber with their Custom, by leaving their Names at Mr. *Hubbard's* in King-Street, Boston, or at Mr. *Woart's* in *Charlestown*, may depend on the best Usage: the strictest Care will be taken of all Bundles, and the smallest Favours acknowledged,

By their most humble Servant,

SAMUEL LORD.

Charlestown, June 6, 1774.

Messieurs EDES and GILL,

AS some of my worthy friends have thought (not a little to my disadvantage) that I was a Signer to the address to the late governor Mr. Hutchinson, I beg leave thro' the channel of your paper, to acquaint them, that it is a mistake, and easily to be accounted for, when the resentment is allowed for which the reading of this list raises in the breast of every friend to the community, together with the near sound, Nathaniel Greenwood bears with that of Nathaniel Greenough; but his friends may be assured he never saw the address, till it was in the paper of 30th instant, and consequently never signed it. The said

NATHANIEL GREENOUGH

Has imported in the several Vessels arrived here this spring a large Assortment of English Goods, suited to the season, among his goods are CHINA WARE, SPICES, and a grand assortment of HOSIERY. Mens Silk Hose, Plain White Ribb'd and Random, Men's Women's and Children's Thread and Cotton ditto. Men's and Women's Black and White Silk Gloves, Women's and Children's Black, White and Colour'd Silk Mitts, &c. &c. &c. The smallest favour of those who will please to favour him with their Custom shall be esteemed and regarded by him.

Wanted to Purchase,

An Estate in this Province, Rhode-Island, or Connecticut Provinces, in some good Situation, either clear'd or woody. Any Person having such to dispose of, and leaving a Line within 7 Days from this Date, directed for John Thompson, to the Care of the Printer, mentioning the Situation, will be treated with.

TO BE SOLD,

By *BENJAMIN CHURCH*,

ON THURSDAY NEXT,

At THREE o'Clock in the Afternoon.

A Couch Bed crimson Harrateen compleat, a new green ditto, square Mahogany Tables, a Mehogany Case of Draws, OG Top, a Walnut Ditto, Looking Glasses, Beds, &c. &c. Sundry European Articles, as Cloths, Linnens, Checks, Callicoes, some Silks, Tammies, Camblets, Handkerchiefs, &c. &c. a warranted 8-Day Clock, a new Chaise and Harness, Watches, &c.

At Three o'Clock, P. M.

Joshua Warner

HEREBY begs Leave to inform the Public, That whereas Capt. John Phelps of Stafford, has for a Number of Years past refused to take in Boarders who used to resort there, for the Use and Benefit of the Mineral Spring or Pool in said Town, that he is now in the possession of a House with good Accommodations, and will Entertain those Gentlemen and Ladies that have Occasion to Resort there in the best Manner he is capable of.

ON the third Night of this Instant, was committed to Goal by the North Watch, a Man who says his Name is Richard Peters, having a Bag, the Contents of which is as follows, viz.—Sundry Cut Cloths—one old white Shirt—two Pair Hose—some Mettle Buttons—one small Bag of Copperas—one large Jack Knife new—one Pair of Sizars—which Articles were suppos'd to have been Stolen; they may be seen at Mr. Otis's, Goal-Keeper.

WHEREAS publick Notice has been given to the Proprietors of a Township lying on both Sides Amarascoggin-*River, in the County of* Cumberland, *in the late Province of* Main, *granted by the Great and General Court on the 11th Day of* June, *A. D.* 1771. *to* David Phips, *Esq; and others, of the Taxes that have been assessed on the Rights of said Proprietors; several of which are delinquent in the Payment of said Taxes:*

Said Delinquents are therefore hereby Notified that unless said Taxes are paid to *Seth Hastings*, of *Cambridge*, or to *Samuel Harrington*, of *Waltham*, Collectors of Taxes for said Proprietors, by 7 o'Clock in the Morning of the 29th Day of *June* next, their Rights will be sold (as the Law directs) for the Payment of their Taxes and incidental Charges. The Sale to begin at 8 o'Clock on said Morning, at the Dwelling-House of Capt. *Jonathan Brewer*, Innholder in *Waltham*, and continued by Adjournment (if need be) till the whole be sold: To which Time and Place said Proprietors Meeting stands adjourned.

May 29, 1774.

Braddyl Smith,
Alex. Shepard,
Nathaniel Bridge.
} Committee for Sale.

To be Sold by PUBLIC VENDUE,

On Tuesday the Seventh Day of June Inst.

A Dwelling House, Sail Loft, Cooper's Shop with the Land and Wharff thereto belonging, situate, lying and being near Fish-street, at the Northerly part of Boston: Said Premises are part of the Estate of Capt. John Doble, late of Boston, Mariner, deceased.

N. B. The Sale to begin at 11 o'Clock, at the said Dwelling-House. J. RUSSELL, Auctioneer.

On WEDNESDAY 8th Inst.

At Ten in the Morning,

Will be Sold by PUBLIC VENDUE,

At RUSSELL's Auction-Room in Queen-Street,

A Variety of Summer Goods, some House Furniture,—a good 8-Day Clock—a neat Sulkey and Harness, &c. J. Russell, Auctioneer.

TO BE SOLD at Publick VENDUE,

On Wednesday the Eighth of June Inst.

At five o'Clock in the Afternoon,

on the Premises, unless Sold before at Private Sale.

Two Dwelling Houses, very conveniently Scituated in BOSTON, the one near the Draw Bridge in Ann-Street; and the other in Bennett Street, neae Dr. Elliot's Meeting-House. They being Part of the Real Estate of *James Halsey*, late of said Boston deceased. —For Particulars, apply to *Anna Halsey* Widow, Relict of said *James Halsey*.

WHEREAS the Proprietors of a Township called Sudbury, lying on both Sides Otter Creek, granted by the Governor and Council of New-Hampshire, on the 6th Day of August, A. D. 1773, to Capt. Silas Brown and others, at their legal Meeting on the 8th Day of March last, granted a Tax of Twenty Shillings lawful Money on each Right in said Township, towards defreying the Charges of the Propriety, which has been published agreeable to Law, and the Payment thereof requested; notwithstanding several of said Proprietors are delinquent in the Payment of said Tax, and in their former Taxes.—PUBLIC NOTICE is therefore hereby given to such delinquent Proprietors, that unless they pay their Taxes to Thomas Miller of Newton, in the County of Middlesex, and Province of Massachusetts-Innholder, and Collector of said Taxes, by One o'Clock in the Afternoon of the 5th Day of July next, their Rights will be sold (as the Law directs) for the Payment of their Taxes and incidental Charges. The Sale to begin at Two o'Clock in said Afternoon (and continued by adjournment, if need be) at the Dwelling-House of said Thomas Miller; to which Time and Place, the said Proprietors Meeting stands adjourned.

May 18, 1774.

Joshua Fuller,
Thomas Miller,
Nathl. Sparhawk.
} Proprietors Committee.

New AUCTION-ROOM, Cornhill.

TO-MORROW at TEN o'Clock will be Sold by PUBLIC VENDUE, at GREENLEAF's Auction-Room,——

A large Assortment of GOODS, The Property of a Gentleman leaving the Province

——*Amongst which are*——

A Variety of genteel chints and callicoes in patterns for gowns, (some of which have darns in them, but not so as to hurt the garment,) Irish linnens, long lawns, striped flowered and plain lawns, lawn aprons, sprig'd muslins, queens gauze, ribbons, modes, damask table cloths, checks, stript hollands, bedticks, thread and worsted hose, castor and felt hats, thicksets, royal ribs, silk jacket patterns, white laces, gauze handkerchiefs, black patches, broad cloths, velverets, shalloons, lasting, coloured jeans, plated buckles, handsome stone shoe knee and stock buckles, and sleeve buttons, silver watches, &c. WILLIAM GREENLEAF, Auctioneer.

The Sale will begin precisely at Ten o'Clock, and be continued in the Afternoon, as many of the above Goods belong to a Gentleman going out of the Province this Week.

At GOULD's *Auction Office*, In Back-Street,

IS now selling off by private Sale,

A very fine Assortment of Hosiery GOODS, consisting of Mens and Womens Worsted Thread and Cotton Hose, Black and Cloth-coloured Breeches Patterns, Worsted Mitts, &c. &c.

At GOULD's *Auction Office in Back Street,*

ON FRIDAY NEXT,

At TEN o'Clock in the Morning,

Will be Sold by PUBLIC VENDUE,

A General Assortment of English GOODS, as usual. R. Gould, Auctioneer.

N. B. For private Sale at said Office, a few Setts of very handsome and valuable Table Knives.

Moses Deshon

TAKES this Method to acquaint the PUBLICK, That he has remov'd his Auction-Room, to his Dwelling-House in Royal Exchange Lane, formerly improv'd by Mr. Hamock, deceas'd, where he is ready to receive all Sort of Goods and Merchandize for public or private Sale; and all those Gentlemen Merchants, and others, who will favour him with their Employ, will be greatfully acknowleged——At the same Place may be had genteel Boarding and Lodgings for Gentlemen and Ladies.

Burials in the Town of BOSTON, since our last.

Nine Whites. Two Blacks.

Baptiz'd in the several Churches, Eight

High Water at BOSTON, for the present Week.

Monday, 20 min. aft. 9	Friday, 18 min. after 12
Tuesday, 10 min. aft. 10	Saturday, 52 min. aft. 12
Wednesday, 54 m. aft. 10	Lord's-Day, 40 m af. 1
Thursday, 38 min. aft. 11	D's New 9 D. 2 Morn.

BOSTON: Printed by EDES and GILL.

THE

Boston-Gazette, AND COUNTRY JOURNAL.

No. 1000.

Containing the freshest Advices, Foreign and Domestic.

MONDAY, June 13, 1774.

LONDON, April 26.

An Authentic Account of Friday's Debate on the second Reading of the Bill for regulating the civil goverment of Massachusetts-Bay.

MR. *Fuller* said, he did not rise to make any debate, for he was not enabled as yet to form any opinion whether the bill before the House was a proper bill, or not; as copies of the charters which had been ordered before the House were not yet laid, he would venture to say, that no man knew the constitution of that government; it was therefore impossible for him to say in what manner he would correct or amend it.

Sir George Savile said, he had not troubled the House before on the occasion, but he could not help observing, that the measure now before the House, was a very doubtful and dangerous one; doubtful as to the propriety of regulation, and dangerous as to its consequence; that charters by government were sacred things, and are only to be taken away by a due course of law, either as a punishment for an offence, or for a breach of the contract, and that can only be by evidence of the facts; nor could he conceive that in either of those cases there could be any such thing as proceeding without a fair hearing of *both* parties. This measure before us seems to be a most extraordinary exertion of legislative power. Let us suppose a lease granted to a man, wherein was a covenant, the breach of which would subject him to a forfeiture of his lease—would not a court of justice require evidence of the fact? why, then, will you proceed different from the line which is always observed in courts of justice? You are now going to alter the charter, because it is convenient. In what manner does the House mean to take away this charter, when in fact they refuse to hear the parties, or to go thro' a legal course of evidence of the facts. Chartered rights have, at all times, when attempted to be altered or taken away, occasioned much bloodshed and strife; and whatever persons in this House have advanced, that they do not proceed upon this business but with trembling hands, I do also assure them that I have shewn my fears upon this occasion, for I have run away from every question, except one, to which I gave my negative. I do not like to be present at a business, which I think inconsistent with the dignity and justice of this House; I tremble when I am, for fear of the consequences; and I think it a little extraordinary that *Mr. Bollan* should be admitted to be heard as an American agent in the *House of Lords*, when in the *House of Commons* he was refused. I believe it is true that the facts set forth in his petition to this House, were different from those which he presented to the House of Lords; in one declaring himself an inhabitant of Boston, and in the other omitting it. I cannot conceive it possible to proceed on this bill upon the small ground of evidence which you have had.

Mr. W. Ellis. I must rise, Sir, with great confidence, when I differ from the honorable gentleman who spoke last, whose abilities are so eminently great; but I think, Sir, that chartered rights are by no means those sacred things which never can be altered; they are vested in the Crown, as a prerogative, for the good of the people at large; if the supreme legislature find that those Charters so granted, are both unfit and inconvenient for the public utility, they have a right to make them fit and convenient; wherever private property is concerned, the legislature will not take it away without making a full recompence, but wherever the regulation of public matter is the object, they have a right to correct, controul, or take it away as may best suit the public welfare. The Crown may sometimes grant improper powers with regard to governments that are to be established, will it not be highly proper and necessary that the legislature, seeing in what manner the Crown has been ill-advised, should take it into their consideration, and alter it as far as necessary. It is the legislature's duty to correct the errors that have been established in the infancy of that constitution, and regulate them for the public welfare. Is a charter, not consistent with the public good, to be continued? The honorable gentleman says, much bloodshed has been occasioned by taking away or altering of chartered rights; I grant it; but it has always been where encroachments have been made by improper parties, and the attack has been carried on by improper powers. He also says, this form of government in America ought not to be altered without hearing the parties;——the papers on your table, surely, are sufficient evidence of what they have to say in their defence;——look only into the letter dated the 19th of November 1773, wherein the Governor applied to the Council for advice, and they neglected giving it to him! and also wherein a petition was presented to the Council by certain persons who applied for protection to their property during these disturbances, the Council, without giving any answer, adjourned for 10 days, and the Governor was not able to do any thing himself without their opinion. Look again, Sir, into the resolution which the Council came to when they met again, stating the total insufficiency of their power. This, surely, Sir, is an evidence competent to ground this bill upon. We have now got no farther than just to alter these two parts, as stated by themselves. Surely Sir, that form of government which will not protect your property, ought to be altered in such a manner as it may be able to do it.

Gen. Conway. What I intend to say will not delay the House long. I am very sure what I intend to say will little deserve the attention of the House; but the subject is of that importance, that it requires it. The consequence of this bill will be very important and dangerous. Parliament cannot break into a right without hearing the parties. The question then is simply this: Have they been heard? What! because the papers say a murder had been committed, does it follow they have proved it? *Audi alteram partem*, is a maxim I have long adhered to; but it is something so inconsistent with parliamentary proceedings not to do it, that I am astonished at it. The Council are blamed, because they did not give that advice to the Governor which he wanted. I think, Sir, the Governor might have acted alone, without their assistance. Gentlemen will consider, that this is not only the charter of Boston, or of any particular part, but the charter of ALL America. Are the Americans not to be heard?—Don't chuse to consent and agree about appointing an agent? I think there is no harm, upon this occasion, in stretching a point; and I would rather have Mr. Bollan, as an agent of America (though he is a little irregular in his appointment) sooner than leave it to be said, that this bill passed without it. *The House being vociferous*, he said, I am afraid I tire the House with my weak voice; if that is the case, I will not proceed, but I do think, and it is my sincere opinion, that *we* are the *aggressors* and *innovators*, and *not* the *colonies*. We have *irritated* and *forced* laws upon them for these six or seven years last past. We have enacted such a *variety* of laws, with these new taxes, together with a refusal to repeal the *trifling* duty on tea; all these things have served no other purpose but to *distress* and *perplex*. I think the Americans have done *no more* than *every* subject *would* do in an *arbitrary* state, where laws are imposed against their will. In my conscience, I think, *taxation* and *legislation* are in this case *inconsistent*. Have you not a legislative right over Ireland? And yet no one will *dare* to say we have a right to tax. These acts, respecting America, will *involve* this country and its Ministers in *misfortunes*, and I wish I may not add, in *ruin*.

Lord North. I do not consider this matter of *regulation* to be taking away their charters in such manner as is represented; it is a *regulation of government* to *assist* the *crown*; it appears to me not to be a matter of political expediency, but of *necessity*. If it does not stand upon that ground, it stands on nothing. The account which has just now been read to you is an authentic paper, transmitted to government here, shewing that the Council refused in every case their assistance and advice; and will this country sit still when they see the colony proceeding against your own subjects, *tarring* and *feathering* your servants; denying your laws and authority; refusing every direction and advice which you send? Are we, Sir, seeing all this, to be silent, and give the Governor no support? Gentlemen say, let the colony come to your bar, and be heard in their defence; though it is not likely that they will come, when they deny your authority in every instance, can we remain in this situation long? We must effectually take some measures to correct and amend the defects of that government. I have heard so many different opinions in regard to our conduct in America, I hardly know how to answer them. The honorable gentleman, who spoke last, formerly blamed the tame and insipid conduct of government; now he condemns this measure as harsh and severe. The Americans have tarred and feathered your subjects, plundered your merchants, burnt your ships, denied all obedience to your laws and authority; yet so clement and so long-forbearing has our conduct been, that it is incumbent upon us now to take a different course. *Whatever may be the consequence, we must risque something; if we do not*, ALL IS OVER. The measure now proposed, is nothing more than taking the election of Counsellors out of the hands of those people, who are continually acting in defiance and resistance of your laws. It has also been said by gentlemen---send for the Americans to your bar---give them redress a twelvemonth hence. Surely, Sir, this cannot be the language that is to give effectual relief to America; it is not, I say again, political *convenience*, it is political *necessity* that urges this measure; if this is not the proper method, shew me any other which is preferable, and I will postpone it.

Sir George Younge. It remains to me, Sir, that it is unanswered and unanswerable, what has been advanced by the honorable gentleman who spoke second, that the parties should be heard, though even at a twelvemonth hence. Nothiug, Sir, but *fatal* necessity can countenance this measure. No body of men ought to be proceeded against without being heard, much less ought the regulation of a whole government to take place, without the parties attending in their defence against such alterations.

Governor Johnston. I see, Sir, a great disposition in this house to proceed in this business without knowing any thing of the constitution of America; several inconveniencies will arise if the Sheriff is to be appointed by the Governor; the jury will, of course, be biassed by some influence or other; special Juries will be most liable to this. [Here the Governor gave an account of the different riots which had happened in England, and compared them with what he called the false accounts of those from America.] I impute, says he, all the misfortunes which have happened in America, to the taking away the power of the Governor. No man, of common sense, can apprehend that the Governor would ever have gone two or three days into the country, during these disturbances, if he had had the command of the military power. The natural spirit of man would be fired, in such a manner, as to actuate himself to shew resistance; but in this Governor no power was lodged. I disapprove much of the measure which is before us, and I cannot think but its consequences will be prejudicial.

Mr. C. Jenkinson. I rise, Sir, only to observe, that if the colony has not that power within itself to maintain its own peace and order, the legislature should, and ought to have. Let me ask, Sir, whether the colony took any step, in any shape, to quell the riots and disturbances? No, they took none. Let me ask again, whether all the checks and controul that are necessary, are not put into the commission of the governments? Much has been said about hearing the parties, and taking away their chartered rights; I am of opinion, that where the right is a high political regulation, you are not in that instance bound to hear them; but the hearing of parties is necessary where private property is concerned. It is not only in the late proceedings, but in all former, that they have denied your authority over them; they have refused protection to his Majesty's subjects, and in every instance disobeyed the laws of this country; either let this country forsake its trade with America, or let us give that due protection to it which safety requires.

Mr. Harris. I cannot see, Sir, any reason for so wide a separation between America and England as other gentlemen are apt to think there ought to be; that country, Sir, was hatched from this; and I hope we shall always keep it under the shadow of our wings. It has been said, no representation, no taxation. This was the system formerly adopted, but I do not find it authorised in any book of jurisprudence, nor do I deem it to be a doctrine either reasonable or constitutional. I insist upon it they are bound to obey both the crown and parliament. The last twelve years of our proceedings have been a scene of lenity and inactivity. Let us proceed and mend our method, or else I shall believe, as an honorable gentleman has observed, that we are the aggressors.

Sir Edward Astley. If we have had a twelve year's *lenity* and *inactivity*, I hope we shall not now proceed to have a twelve year's *cruelty* and *oppression*. By the resolution and firmness which I perceive in the House, it seems to indicate a perseverance in the measure now proposed, which I deem to be a *harsh one*, and *unworthy* of a British legislature.

Mr. Ward. [The House was very noisy during the few words which he said.]---- --He found fault with the charter being left too much as to the execution of its powers in the people, and he could not think the legislature was doing any thing which it had not a right to do, as he had looked upon all charters to be granted with a particular clause in it, expressing that it should not be taken away but by the parliament.

Governor Pownal. I beg leave to set some gentlemen right, who have erred with regard to the charters of America. The appointment of several of the officers is in the Governor. The charter of Boston directs that the Governor shall ask the Council for advice, but it does not say he shall not act without it, if they refuse to give it. It is said it is criminal to do any thing without advice of the Council; I differ greatly, Sir, from that doctrine; for I myself have acted without it in putting an end to disturbances, in preserving the peace and good order of the place; if I had been Governor during the late disturbances, I would have given an order for the military power to attend, and then let me have seen what officer dare disobey. I think the Council are much to blame for not co-operating and assisting the Governor, but I think the Governor might have acted without the Council. The Council are inexcuseable, though not criminal, as they are not obliged to give it. I, Sir, for my part, shall give my last opinion. I have always been in one way of thinking with regard to America, which I have both given here and wrote to America. They have all along tended to one point; but it is now no longer matter of opinion. Things are now come to *action*; and I must be free to tell the House, that the Americans WILL RESIST these measures. They are PREPARED to do it. I do not mean by arms, but by the conversation of public town-meetings; they now send their letters by couriers, instead of the post, from one town to another; and I can say your POST-OFFICE will very soon be deprived of its revenue. With regard to the officers who command the militia of that country, they WILL HAVE them of their OWN appointment, and NOT from government; *but I will never more give an opinion concerning America in this House; those I have given have been disregarded.*

Mr. R. Rigby. Upon my word, Sir, what was just now said is very worthy the consideration of this house; and if, from what the honorable gentleman says, it is true, and I believe he is well informed, it appears, *that America is preparing to arms; and that the deliberations of their town meetings tend chiefly to oppose the measures of this country by force.* He has told you, Sir, that the Americans will appoint other officers than those sent by government to command their troops. He has told you that a Post-office is established on their account from town to town, in order to carry their traiterous correspondence from one to another. He has told you, the Post-office revenue will soon be annihilated. If these things are true, Sir, I find we have been the aggressors, by continually doing acts of lenity for these twelve years last past. I think, Sir, *and I speak out boldly when I say it*, that this country *has a right to tax America*; but, Sir, it is matter of astonishment to me, how an honorable gentleman (Mr. Conway) can be the author or bringer in of a declaratory law over all America, and yet saying at one and the same time, that we have no right to tax America! If I was to begin to say that America should not be taxed, and that these measures were not proper, I would first desire my own declaratory law to be repealed; but being of opinion that the Americans are the subjects of this country, I will declare freely, that I think this country has a right to tax America; but I do not say I would put any new tax on at this particular crisis; but when things are returned to a peaceable state, I would then begin to exercise it. And I am free to declare my opinion, that I think we have a right to tax Ireland, if there was a necessity so to do, in order to help the mother country. If Ireland was to rebel and resist our laws, I would tax it. The mother country has an undoubted right and controul over the whole of its colonies. Again, Sir, a great deal has been said concerning requisition. Pray, in what manner is it to be obtained? Is the King to demand it, or are we, the legislative power of this country, to send a very *civil polite gentleman* over to treat with their Assemblies? How and in what manner is he to address that assembly? Is he to tell the Speaker of it that we have been extremly ill used by our neighbours, the French; that they have attacked us in several quarters; that the financies of this country are in a bad state; and therefore we desire you'll be *kind* enough to assist us, and give us some money? Is this to be the language of this country to that; and are we thus to go cap in hand? I am of opinion, that if the administration of this country had not been changed soon after the passing of the Stamp Act, that tax would have been collected with as much ease as the land tax is in Great Britain. I have acted, with regard to America, one consistant part, and shall continue in it till I hear better reason to convince me to the contrary.

Gov. Pownal (to explain) I apprehend I have been totally misunderstood. I did not assert the Americans were *now* in rebellion, but that they are *going* to rebel; when that comes to pass, the question will be who was the occasion of it. Something has been said relative to requisition; I think I gave several instances wherein the same had been complied with in time of war.

Mr. C. Fox. I am glad to hear from the honorable gentleman who spoke last, that *now* is not the time to tax America; that the only time for that is, when all these disturbances are quelled, and they are returned to their duty; so, I find, taxes are to be the reward of obedience; and the Americans who are considered to have been in open rebellion, are to be rewarded by acquiescing to their measures. When will be the time when America ought to have heavy taxes laid upon it? The honorable gentleman (Mr. Rigby) tells you, that that time is when the Americans are returned to peace and quietness. The honorable gentleman tells us also, that we have a right to tax Ireland; however I may agree with him in regard to the principle, it would not be policy to exercise it; I believe we have no more right to tax the one than the other. I believe America is wrong in resisting against this country, with regard to its legislative authority. It was an old opinion, and I believe a very true one, that there was a dispensing power in the crown, but whenever that dispensing power was pretended to be exercised, it was always rejected and opposed to the utmost, because it operated to me as a subject, as a detriment to my property and liberty; but, Sir, there has been a constant conduct practised in this country, consisting of violence and weakness, I wish those measures may not continue; nor can I think that the stamp-act would have been submitted to without resistance, if the administration had not been changed; the present bill before you is not *tanti* to what you want; it irritates the minds of the people, but does not correct the deficiencies of that government.

Sir Gilbert Elliot arose to answer Mr. C. Fox, which he did in a very masterly manner, by stating, that there was not the least degree of absurdity in taxing your own subjects, over whom you have declared you had an absolute right; though that tax should, through necessity, be enacted at a time when peace and quietness were the reigning system of the times; you declare you have that right, where is the absurdity in the exercise of it.

Sir Richard Sutton read a copy of a letter relative to the government of America, from the Governor of America to the Board of Trade, shewing, that at the most quiet times, the disposition to oppose the laws of this country were strongly ingrafted in them, and that all their actions conveyed a spirit and wish for independence. If you ask an American who is his master, he will tell you he has none, nor any governor but Jesus Christ. I do believe it, and it is my firm opinion, that the opposition to the measures of the legislature of this country, is a determined prepossession of the idea of total independence.

After which the bill was committed for Friday next without a division.

WILLIAMSBURG, (*in Virginia*) May 26.

ON Tuesday last the Honourable the House of Burgesses came to the following Resolution, which was directed to be forthwith printed and published: "This House being deeply impressed with apprehension of the great dangers to be derived to British America from the hostile invasion of the city of Boston, in our sister colony of Massachusetts-Bay, whose commerce and harbour are, on the first of June next, to be stopped by an armed force, deem it highly necessary that the said 1st of June be set apart by the Members of this House as a day of Fasting, Humiliation, and Prayer, devoutly to implore the divine interposition for averting the heavy calamity which threatens destruction to our civil rights, and the evils of civil war; to give us one heart, and one mind, firmly to oppose, by all just and proper means, every injury to American rights; and that the minds of his Majesty, and his Parliament, may be inspired from above with wisdom, moderation & justice, to remove from the loyal people of America all cause of danger from a continued pursuit of Measures pregnant with their ruin.

"*Ordered*, therefore, That the Members of this House do attend in their places at the hour of ten in the forenoon, on the 1st day of June next, in order to proceed with the Speaker and Mace to the Church in this city for the purpose aforesaid; and that the Rev. Mr. Price be appointed to read Prayers, and the Rev. Mr. Gwatkin to preach a Sermon suitable to the occasion."

Upon the Rev. Mr. Gwatkin's petitioning to be excused from complying with the appointment, the Rev. Mr. Price, Chaplain to the House, was directed to preach in his stead.

Friday, May 27. Yesterday, between three and four o'clock, P.M. the Right Honourable the Earl of Dunmore sent a message to the Honourable the House of Burgesses, by the Clerk of the Council, requiring their immediate attendance in the Council Chamber, when his Excellency spoke to them as follows:

Mr. Speaker, and Gentlemen of the House of Burgesses,

"I have in my hand a paper, published by order of your House, conceived in such terms as reflect highly upon his Majesty and the Parliament of Great-Britain; which makes it necessary for me to dissolve you, and you are dissolved accordingly."——

And this day, at ten o'clock, the Honourable Members of the late House of Burgesses met, by agreement, at the long room in the Raleigh tavern, in this city, called the Apollo, when the following was unanimously entered into by that patriotic Assembly, in support of the constitutional Liberties of AMERICA, against the late oppressive act of the British Parliament respecting the town of Boston, which, in the end, must affect all the other Colonies.

"We his Majesty's most dutiful and loyal subjects, the late representatives of the good people of this country, having been deprived, by the sudden interposition of the executive part of this government, from giving our countrymen the advice we wished to convey to them in a legislative capacity, find ourselves under the hard necessity of adopting this, the only method we have left, of pointing out to our countrymen such measures as, in our opinion, are best fitted to secure our dearest rights and liberties from destruction, by the heavy hand of power now lifted against North-America. With much grief we find that our dutiful applications to Great-Britain for security of our just, antient, and constitutional rights, have been not only disregarded, but that a determined system is formed, and pressed, for reducing the inhabitants of British America to slavery, by subjecting them to the payment of taxes, imposed without the consent of the people or their representatives; and that, in pursuit of this system, we find an Act of the British Parliament, lately passed for the stopping the harbour and commerce of the town of Boston, in our sister colony of Massachusetts Bay, until the people there, submit to the payment of such unconstitutional taxes, and which Act most violently and arbitrarily deprives them of their property, in wharves erected by private persons, at their own great and proper expence; which Act is, in our opinion, a most dangerous attempt to destroy the constitutional liberty and rights of all North-America. It is farther our opinion, that as TEA, on its importation into America, is charged with a duty, imposed by Parliament for the purpose of raising a revenue, without the consent of the people, it ought not to be used by any person who wishes well to the constitutional rights and liberty of British America. And whereas the India Company have ungenerously attempted the ruin of America, by sending many ships loaded with Tea into the Colonies, thereby intending to fix a precedent in favour of arbitrary taxation, we deem it highly proper, and do accordingly recommend it strongly to our country, not to purchase or use any kind of East-India commodity whatsoever, except saltpetre and spices, until the grievances of America are redressed. We are farther clearly of opinion, that an attack made on one of our sister colonies, to compel submission to arbitrary taxes, is an attack made on all British America, and threatens ruin to the rights of all, unless the united wisdom of the whole be applied. And for this purpose it is recommended to the Committee of Correspondence, that they communicate, with their several corresponding Committees, on the expediency of appointing deputies from the several colonies of British America, to meet in a general congress, at such a place annually as shall be thought most convenient; there to deliberate on those general measures which the united interest of America may from time to time require.

"A tender regard for the interest of our fellow subjects, the Merchants and Manufacturers of Great-Britain, prevents us from going further at this time; most earnestly hoping, that the unconstitutional principle of taxing the colonies without their consent will not be persisted in, thereby to compel us, against our wills, to avoid all commercial intercourse with Britain. Wishing them and our people free and happy, we are their affectionate friends, the late Representatives of Virginia."

The above was immediately signed by the Honorable the Speaker and ALL the members of the late House of Burgesses, as well as by a number of Clergymen and other inhabitants of the colony, who, after having maturely considered the contents of the Association, did most cordially approve and accede thereto.

Extract of a Letter from London.

"*There is a persuasion here, that America will see, without any interposition, the ruin of Boston. It is of the last importance to the general cause that your conduct should prove the opinion erroneous. If once it is perceived that you may be attacked and destroyed piecemeal, it is certain that every part, in turn, will feel the vengeance which it would not unite to repel, and a general slavery must ensue. The Colonies should never forget Lord North's declaration in the House of Commons, that he would not listen to the complaint of America till she was at h's feet. The character of Lord North, and a consideration of what surprising things he has effected towards enslaving this country, makes me own that I tremble for yours. Plausible, deep, and treacherous, he has no passions to divert him, no pursuits of pleasure to withdraw him, from the accursed design of deliberately destroying the liberty of his country. A perfect adept in the arts of corruption, and indefatigable in the application of them, he effects great ends by means almost magical; because they are unseen. In four years he has overcome the most formidable opposition in this country, from which the Duke of Grafton fled with terror. At the same time, he has effectually enslaved the East India Company, and made the vast revenue and territory of India, in effect, a royal patronage. Flushed with these successes, he now attacks America; and certainly, if we are not both firm, united, and wise, he will triumph in the same manner over us. In my opinion, a general resolution of the Colonies to break off all commercial intercourse with this country, till they are secured in their liberties, is the only adviseable and sure mode of defence.*

WILLIAMSBURG (Virginia) May 19.

☞ We have not been able to procure the acts of Parliament, relating to the town of Boston, for this week's paper; but our readers have the substance of it, and will see the whole in our next, as we know it is arrived.——Not a single news paper came from the northward last week by the post, therefore it is not known whether the men of war and troops are yet arrived before Boston; altho', from the circumstances of our not receiving papers as usual, it would seem as if this armament had laid an embargo upon the northern intelligence.

ANNAPOLIS, (*in Maryland.*) May 26

At a Meeting of the Inhabitants of this City, on Wednesday the 25th Day of May 1774, after Notice given of the Time, Place, and Occasion of this Meeting;

RESOLVED, *that it is the unanimous opinion of this meeting, that the town of Boston is now suffering in the common cause of America to unite in effectual means to obtain a repeal of the late act of Parliament for blocking up the harbour of Boston.*

That it is the opinion of this meeting that the colonies come into a joint resolution to stop all importations from and exportations to Great-Britain, till the said act be repealed, the same will preserve North-America and her liberties.

RESOLVED *therefore, that the inhabitants of this city will join in an association with the several counties of this province, and the principal colonies of America, to put an immediate stop to all exports to Great-Britain, and that after a short day hereafter to be agreed, that there be no imports from Great-Britain 'till the said act be repealed, and that such associations be on oath.*

That it is the opinion of this meeting, that the Gentlemen of the law of this province bring no suit for the recovery of any debt due from any inhabitant of this province to any inhabitant of Great-Britain, until the said act be repealed.

That the inhabitants of this city will, and it is the opinion of this meeting, that this province ought immediately to break off all trade and dealings with that colony or province which shall refuse to decline to come into similar resolutions with a majority of the colonies.

That Messieurs John Hall, Charles Carroll, Thomas Johnson, jun. William Paca, Matthias Hammond, and Samuel Chase, be a committee for this city to join with those who shall be appointed for Baltimore town, and other parts of this province, to constitute one general committee, and that the gentlemen appointed for this city immediately correspond with Baltimore town, and other parts of this province, to effect such associations as will best secure American liberty.

QUEEN ANN's COUNTY, (Maryland.)

At a Meeting of a considerable Number of the Magistrates and other respectable Inhabitants of Queen Ann's *County, at* Queen's-Town, *on the 30th Day of May, 1774, in Order to deliberate upon the Tendency and Effect of the Act of Parliament* for blocking up the port and harbour of Boston.

DULY considering and deeply affected with the prospect of the unhappy situation of Great-Britain and British America, under any kind of disunion. This Meeting think themselves obliged by all the ties which ever ought to preserve a firm union amongst Americans, as speedily as possible to make known their sentiments to their distressed brethren of Boston, and therefore publish to the world—

"That they look upon the cause of Boston, in its consequences, to be the common cause of America.

"That the Act of Parliament, for blocking up the port and harbour of Boston, appears to them a cruel and oppressive invasion of their natural rights as men, and constitutional rights as English subjects; and if not repealed will be a foundation for the utter destruction of American freedom.

"That all legal and constitutional means ought to be used by all America for procuring a repeal of the said Act of Parliament.

"That the only effectual means for obtaining such repeal, they are at present of opinion, is an association under the strongest ties, for breaking off all commercial connexions with Great Britain, until the said Act of Parliament be repealed, and the right ASSUMED by Parliament of taxing America *in all Cases whatsoever* be given up, and American freedom ascertained, and settled upon a permanent and constitutional foundation.

"That the most practicable mode of forming such an effectual association they conceive to be, a general meeting of the gentlemen who are already, or shall be appointed Committees, to form an American intercourse and correspondence upon this most interesting occasion.

"That in the mean time, they will form such particular association, as to them shall seem effectual, yet professing themselves ready to join in any reasonable general one, that may be devised as aforesaid.

"That these sentiments be immediately forwarded, to be printed in the next Maryland and Pensylvania Gazettes.

"That Edward Tilgham, Solomon Wright, Turbut Wright, John Browne, Richard Tilghman Earle, James Hollyday, Thomas Wright, William Amesley, Adam Gray, Clement Sewell, Richard Tilgham, James Kent, John Kerr, James Bordley and William Burff, be a Committee of Correspondence and Intercourse until some alteration is made in this appointment by a more general Meeting." Attested, by

James Earle, Clerk of the Committee.

BOSTON, June 13.

The Honorable House of Representatives, before they proceeded to Business in *Salem*, on Wednesday last, came into the following Resolutions, and ordered the same to be entered on their Journal, viz.

RESOLVED, *That by the Royal Charter of this Province, the Power of convening, proroguing and adjourning the Great and General Court or Assembly, from Time to Time, is vested in the Governor, to be exercised as he shall judge necessary, and for the Good of the People.*——The Clause,

RESOLVED, *That it is clearly the Opinion of this House, That whensoever the Governor of the Province doth convene or hold the General Assembly at any Time or Place unnecessarily, or merely in Obedience to an Instruction, and without exercising that Judgment and Discretion of his own, with which by Charter he is specially vested for the Good of the Province, it is manifestly inconsistent with the Letter, as well as the Spirit and Intention of the Charter.*

RESOLVED, That the Town of Boston hath from the earliest Times of this Province been judged, and still is on various Accounts the most convenient Place for holding the General Assembly, and according y ample Provision is there made for the Accommodation of the said General Assembly, at a very great Expence to the People of this Province.

RESOLVED as the clear Opinion of this House, That the General Assembly cannot be removed from its ancient Seat the Court House in Boston, and held in any other Place, without great and manifold Inconvenience to the Members thereof, and Injury and Damage to those who have necessary Business to transact with the said General Assembly; many of which Inconveniencies have been clearly stated, and expressed by former Houses of Representatives, as appears by their Journals.

RESOLVED, That this House can see no Necessity for the Removal of the General Assembly from its ancient and only convenient Place the Court-House in Boston, to the Town of Salem; and the Removal of the said Assembly from the Court-House in Boston, without Necessity, is at all Times to be considered as a very great Grievance

Last Thursday a Committee of the House of Representatives waited on the Governor with the following Answer to his Speech at the Opening of the Session.

May it please your Excellency,

YOUR Speech to both Houses of the General Assembly at the opening of this Session has been read and considered with all due Attention in the House of Representatives.

Your Excellency has therein signified to us that his Majesty has been pleased "to appoint you Governor and Captain-General of his Province of Massachusetts-Bay, and that your Commission has been read and published;" We congratulate your Excellency on your safe Arrival, and honour you in the most exalted Station in this Province; and confiding in your Excellency, that you will make the known Constitution and Charter of the Province the Rule of your Administration, We beg Leave to assure you that nothing on our Part shall be wanting that may contribute to render the same easy and happy to yourself, and to aid your Excellency in promoting the Prosperity of his Majesty's Government and the Welfare of our Constituents; and we thank your Excellency for the Assurances you are pleased to give of your Concurrence with us therein.

It gives us Pain to be informed by your Excellency, that "you have the King's particular Commands for holding the General Court at Salem, from the first Day of this Instant June, until his Majesty shall have signified his royal Will and Pleasure for holding it again at Boston". We are intirely at a Loss for the Cause of this Command, as we cannot conceive any public Utility arising from it, and both we and our Constituents are now suffering the great Inconveniencies of it.

The Removal of the Assembly from the Court House in Boston, its ancient and only convenient Seat, has very lately given great Discontent to the good People of this Province; and we cannot but think that Misrepresentations from Persons residing in this Province have induced his Majesty's Ministers to advise his Majesty to lay your Excellency under an Injunction whereby the People are in this Instance deprived of the Benefit of that discretionary Power, which is vested in the Governor by the Charter, and has been exercised by former Governors, of determining in such Case for the Good of the Province: We confide, however, in your Excellency's Impartiality and Justice, that the true State of this Province, and the Character of his Majesty's Subjects in it, their Loyalty to their Sovereign, their Affection for the parent Country, as well as their invincible Attachment to their just Rights and Liberties, will be laid before his Majesty, and we hope that by this Means your Excellency will be the happy Instrument of removing the Displeasure of his Majesty, and restoring Harmony, which has too long been interrupted by the Artifices of interested and designing Men.

Your Excellency has laid no particular Business before us, excepting the Supply of the Treasury for the Support of Government, for the ensuing Year; to which we shall give our immediate Attention; as also to any other Matters your Excellency may please to lay before us, and give that dispatch to the public Business which the manifold and great Inconveniences of our present Situation will admit.

We are assured that the House of Representatives, notwithstanding what was given out by the inveterate Enemies of this Country, are as firm in the Cause of Liberty at Salem as they have been in this Town.

Wednesday last his Excellency Governor Wentworth, of Portsmouth, sent the following Message to the Hon. House of Representatives, then sitting there, viz.

Mr. Speaker, and Gentlemen of the Assembly,

AS I look upon the Measures entered upon by the House of Assembly, to be inconsistent with his Majesty's Service, and the Good of this Government, it is my Duty, as far as in me lies, to prevent any Detriment that might arise from such Proceedings —I do therefore hereby DISSOLVE *the General Assembly of this Province; and it is Dissolved accordingly.*

J. WENTWORTH.

Province of New Hampshire, Council Chamber, June 8, 1774.

The late worthy Mr. HOLLIS, distinguished by his universal Regard to the Liberties and Happiness of Mankind, and well known in this Country for his generous Benefactions to HARVARD-COLLEGE, in the Frontice-piece of a Volume presented to that Society, inscribed with his own Hand, this prophetic Admonition to the Inhabitants of this Land.

"*People of* MASSACHUSETTS.

"*When your Country shall be cultivated, adorned like this Country, and ye shall become elegant, refined in all civil Life,——then, if not before,*

'WARE TO YOUR LIBERTIES."

Monday last being the Anniversary for the Election of Officers for the ancient and honourable Artillery Company, the following Gentlemen were chosen for the Year, viz. Captain, Lieut. William Bell,
Lieutenant, Mr. John Stutson,
Ensign. Mr. Asa Stoddard.

Mr. Jonathan Ropes of Salem, is chosen a Representative for that Town in the room of the Hon. Richard Derby, Esq; elected a Member of his Majesty's Council.

BOSTON, Behold! a few Months ago the united Force of Great-Britain, at the Expence of a Million sterling, levelled against the poor innocent, uninlighten'd Carebs at St. Vincents. Fleets and Armies sent to Conquer and take Possession of every Thing dear to that poor devoted People. But remember the invincible Behavior, and to the everlasting Honor of that injur d Nation, let it be sounded in your Ears, they Struggled in the glorious Cause of Liberty till they put to Shame their Oppressors, who silently call'd off their Forces, and left them to enjoy their Birthrights unmolested. Let it never be said, that America's Sons have given Carebs reason to exult in their own Superior Virtue.

O Americans! play the Men for the People and City of your God. Give not up, but at the Expence of your choicest Blood and Treasure, these inestimable Privileges purchased by your Ancestors, who waded thro' Seas of Blood to secure them to themselves and their Posterity.

Wednesday last the Dwelling-House of the Rev. Joseph Jackson of Brookline was consumed by Fire; most of his Furniture was saved.

Since our last arrived here the King's own or IVth Regiment, which we hear is to Encamp on the Common this Day.

Extract of a Letter from Connecticut, dated June 9.

"Our Assembly have recommended a Congress of all the Colonies, and appointed Commissioners to attend it."

ARTICLES FROM OUR CORRESPONDENTS.

To the Consumers of British Manufactures thro' this whole Continent——The poor persecuted and almost ruin'd Inhabitants of this once flourishing Town of Boston, send Greeting.

KNOW ye, good Americans and true, that it is in the Power of a few selfish Merchants, emboldned and protected by Fleets and Armies, and encouraged by the Officers to render abortive the salutary Design the greater Part of that Order of Men had in View, by entering into a Non Importation Agreement. If therefore the honest Yeomanry of the several Colonies will one and all or in general solemnly engage not to purchase for their own or Families Use, from and after a certain Time, any Goods imported from Great-Britain; and will also suspend their Trade with such as continue to import or purchase such Merchandize; then the civil Rights of the Colonies will be restored, and our religious Privileges still continued to us; but in Default hereof, an absolute Despotism in Church and State will take Place, and this once happy and free People, will become the most abject and miserable Slaves in all Christendom.

We learn from divers Parts of the Country, that the People in general, having become quite impatient by not hearing a Non-Importation Agreement has yet been come into by the Merchants, are now taking the good Work into their own Hands, and have and are solemnly engaging not to purchase any Goods imported from Great-Britain, or to trade with those who do import or purchase such Goods:—This is the most effectual Method that the Wit of Man can devise to counterwork the Designs of our Enemies, and to effect the Salvation of this distressed and much injured People.

We are credibly informed that Subscriptions are handing about in the inland Parts of this Province, engaging to forbear the purchase or Use of British Manufactures, 'till the Rights of America are restored. Thousands it is said have Signed.

JUST IMPORTED from LONDON
And to be Sold by

John Gore & Son,

At the PAINTER'S ARMS, in Queen Street,
A large and compleat Assortment of
Painters Oils, Colours, Brushes and
Tools, of all Sizes:

Likewise, Gum Copal, Anamæ, Sandriack, Shell Lack, Seed Lack, Arabic and Amber, half Length, Kitt Katt and three Quarter Cloths, brown and white Varnish and Lacker; also Martin's best Copal Oil Varnish, which will enable them to finish Coach and Chaise Bodies as high as any ever imported from London.

TO BE SOLD,
ON THURSDAY NEXT,
By *BENJAMIN CHURCH,*
At FOUR o'Clock in the Afternoon,

A General Assortment of European Articles, Linnens, Woolens, Checks, &c. &c. Some House Furniture, an 8-Day Clock, Mehogany Case of Draws, Watches, &c. &c.—At Four o'Clock, P. M.—

The Proprietors of the Township

granted to *Samuel Livermore*, Esq; and others, are hereby Notified, that their Meeting stands adjourned to Wednesday the 29th Instant, to the House of Isaac Gleason, Innholder in Waltham, at Ten o'Clock, A.M.
per LEONARD WILLIAMS, Prop'rs Clerk.
Waltham, June 10, 1774.

Frederick William Geyer

Acquaints his Friends and others, that he has removed from the Corner of Wings-Lane to the Store lately improved by Mr. Ward Nicholas Boylston, the door below Messi's Bethune and Prince, in King-street,
BOSTON:

Where he continues selling English, India and Scotch Piece Goods, by Wholesale only, on the lowest Terms, for Cash or short Credit.

To be Sold by *William Jennison*, of Mendon, a valuable FARM, containing 100 Acres, consisting of Plowland, Mowing, Pasturing, Orcharding and Woodland; divided into fifteen seperate inclosures, Fenc'd chiefly with Stone Wall, together with two Dwelling Houses on the Premises, one a large commodious Mansion House 6 Rooms on a Floor, half a Mile from the Rev. Mr. *Frost's* Meeting House, pleasantly situated for a Gentleman or Trader, with a large new Barn, Potash Works, Shop for Goods, Warehouse, Grainery and other out Buildings, 24 Miles from Providence and 34 from Boston, is on the nearest Road from Connecticut to Cambridge, Salem, &c. is now, and has been a number of Year's improv'd as a Tavern: Said Interest to be Sold for 1000l. only. West-India Goods will be accepted for one half, the other half may lie a number of Years on good Security.

Ten Dollars Reward.

RAN AWAY from the Subscriber, *Joseph Moors*, of Groton, in the County of Middlesex, and Province of Massachusetts-Bay, a Molatto Man Servant, named TITUS, about 20 Years of Age, of a midling Stature, wears short curl'd Hair, has one of his Fore-Teeth broke out, took with him a blue Surdan, a Snuff-coloured Coat, and a Pair of white wash'd Leather Breeches, a Pair of new Cow-Hide Pumps and a Fur'd Hat with large Brims, and sundry other Articles of Wearing Apparel.——Whoever will take up said Servant and confine him in any of his Majesty's Goals, so that the Owner may have him again, shall have TEN DOLLARS Reward and all necessary Charges paid, by
JOSEPH MOORS.

☞ *All Masters of Vessels and others, are hereby Caution'd against Harbouring, Concealing, or carrying off said Servant, as they would thereby avoid the Penalty of the Law.*

TO BE LETT,

A House with 3 Acres of Land, within 4 Miles of Boston, upon the Cambridge Road, conveniently situated for a Gentleman's Seat. Inquire of *Eliphalet Downer* of Brookline.

N. B. The House will be Let with or without the Land.

WE the Subscribers being appointed by the Hon. Foster Hutchinson, Esq; Judge of Probate for the County of Suffolk, Commissioners to receive and examine the Claims of the several Creditors to the Estate of SAMUEL SNOW, late of Boston, Mariner, deceas'd, intestate, represented Insolvent, Do hereby give Notice, that we shall attend said Service, at the British Coffee House, on the second Tuesday of this and the Five following Months, from Six 'till Nine o'Clock of the Evening of said Days.
JOB PRINCE,
Boston, June 11, 1774.
JOHN CARNES.

Waltham, June 6, 1774.

RAN-away from the Subscriber, a Servant Boy, named Silence Robinson, between 17 and 18 Years old, large of his Age. Any Person who will secure said Servant, so that his Master may have him again, shall have Five Shillings, O. T. Reward for their Trouble, paid by
JOSEPH WELLINGTON.

All Masters of Vessels and others, are hereby cautioned against Concealing or Harbouring said Servant, as they will avoid the Penalty of the Law.

RAN-away from the Subscriber on the Eighth of June Instant, at Night, a Negro Boy, about Seventeen Years of Age: Had on when he went off, a dark coloured cloth Jacket and Trowsers, and is branded on the Breast Delamote, very remarkable: said Fellow speaks tolerable good English, and some French. Whoever takes up said Fellow and Secures him in any of his Majesty's Goals, or Returns him to the Subscriber, shall have FIVE DOLLARS Reward, and all necessary Charges paid by
ALLIN BROWN.
Providence, June 10 1774.

New AUCTION-ROOM, Cornhill:

TO-MORROW at TEN o'Clock will be Sold by PUBLIC VENDUE, at GREENLEAF'S Auction-Room,——

A large Assortment of GOODS,
(Part of which belonged to a Gentleman lately deceased)
Amongst which are,

A Variety of genteel chints and callicoes, in patterns for gowns, some of which are damaged; long lawns, stript flower'd and plain lawns, lawn aprons, sprig'd muslins, gauzes, ribbons, modes; silk mitts and gloves, &c.
WILLIAM GREENLEAF, Auctioneer.

The Sale will begin precisely at Ten o'Clock, and be continued in the Afternoon.

Burials in the Town of BOSTON, since our last.
Ten Whites. No Blacks.
Baptiz'd in the several Churches, Ten.

High Water at BOSTON, for the present Week.

Monday, 22 min. aft. 2	Friday, 24 min. after. 5
Tuesday, 10 min. aft. 3	Saturday, 7 min. aft. 6
Wednesday, 50 m. aft. 3	Lord's-Day, 53 m af. 6
Thursday, 38 min. aft. 4	D's First Qr. 17 D. 3 M. 5

Messieurs EDES and GILL,

AS some of my worthy friends have thought (not a little to my disadvantage) that I was a Signer to the address to the late governor Mr. Hutchinson, I beg leave thro' the channel of your paper, to acquaint them, that it is a mistake, and easily to be accounted for, when the resentment is allowed for which the reading of this list raises in the breast of every friend to the community, together with the near sound, Nathaniel Greenwood bears with that of Nathaniel Greenough; but his friends may be assured he never saw the address, till it was in the paper of 30th instant, and consequently never signed it. The said

NATHANIEL GREENOUGH

Has imported in the several Vessels arrived here this spring a large Assortment of English Goods, suited to the season, among his goods are CHINA WARE, SPICES, and a grand assortment of HOSIERY. Mens Silk Hose, Plain White Ribb'd and Random, Men's Women's and Children's Thread and Cotton ditto. Men's and Women's Black and White Silk Gloves, Women's and Children's Black, White and Colour'd Silk Mits, &c. &c. &c. The smallest favour of those who will please to favour him with their Custom shall be esteemed and regarded by him.

WHEREAS the Proprietors of a Township called Sudbury, lying on both Sides Otter Creek, granted by the Governor and Council of New-Hampshire, on the 6th Day of August, A. D. 1773, to Capt. Silas Brown and others, at their legal Meeting on the 8th Day of March last, granted a Tax of Twenty Shillings lawful Money on each Right in said Township, towards defreying the Charges of the Propriety, which has been published agreeable to Law, and the Payment thereof requested; notwithstanding several of said Proprietors are delinquent in the Payment of said Tax, and in their former Taxes.—PUBLIC NOTICE is therefore hereby given to such delinquent Proprietors, that unless they pay their Taxes to Thomas Miller of Newton, in the County of Middlesex, and Province of Massachusetts-Bay, Innholder, and Collector of said Taxes, by One o'Clock in the Afternoon of the 5th Day of July next, their Rights will be sold (as the Law directs) for the Payment of their Taxes and incidental Charges. The Sale to begin at Two o'Clock in said Afternoon (and continued by adjournment, if need be) at the Dwelling-House of said Thomas Miller; to which Time and Place, the said Proprietors Meeting stands adjourned.

May 18, 1774. *Joshua Fuller, Thomas Miller, Nathl. Sparhawk,* } Proprietors Committee.

WHEREAS *publick Notice has been given to the Proprietors of a Township lying on both Sides Amariscoggin-River, in the County of Cumberland, in the late Province of Main, granted by the Great and General Court on the 11th Day of June, A. D. 1771. to David Phips, Esq; and others, of the Taxes that have been assessed on the Rights of said Proprietors; several of which are delinquent in the Payment of said Taxes:* Said Delinquents are therefore hereby Notified that unless said Taxes are paid to *Seth Hastings*, of *Cambridge*, or to *Samuel Harrington*, of *Waltham*, Collectors of Taxes for said Proprietors, by 7 o'Clock in the Morning of the 29th Day of *June* next, their Rights will be sold (as the Law directs) for the Payment of their Taxes and incidental Charges. The Sale to begin at 8 o'Clock on said Morning, at the Dwelling-House of Capt. *Jonathan Brewer*, Innholder in *Waltham*, and continued by Adjournment, (if need be) till the whole be sold: To which Time and Place said Proprietors Meeting stands adjourned.

May 29, 1774. *Braddyl Smith, Alex. Shepard, Nathaniel Bridge.* } Committee for Sale.

Joshua Warner

HEREBY begs Leave to inform the Public, That whereas Capt. John Phelps of Stafford, has for a Number of Years past refused to take in Boarders who used to resort there, for the Use and Benefit of the Mineral Spring or Pool in said Town, that he is now in the possession of a House with good Accommodations, and will Entertain those Gentlemen and Ladies that have Occasion to Resort there in the best Manner he is capable of.

ON the third Night of this Instant, was committed to Goal by the North Watch, a Man who says his Name is Richard Peters, having a Bag, the Contents of which is as follows, viz.—Sundry Cut Cloths—one old white Shirt—two Pair Hose—some Mettle Buttons—one small Bag of Coppers—one large Jack Knife new—one Pair of Sizars—which Articles were suppos'd to have been Stolen; they may be seen at Mr. Otis's, Goal-Keeper.

Wanted to Purchase,

An Estate in this Province, Rhode-Island, or Connecticut Provinces, in some good Situation, either clear'd or woody. Any Person having such to dispose of, and leaving a Line within 7 Days from this Date, directed for John Thompson, to the Care of the Printer, mentioning the Situation, will be treated with.

RAN-away from the Subscriber, living in Gorham, which joins Falmouth, Cumberland County, in the Massachusetts Province, a short Negro Man named Prince, about 26 Years of Age, 5 Feet some Inches high, talks broken English, has remarkable small Ears and a Jewel Hole in one of them. Had on almost a new Felt Hat, a reddish grey home-made Cloth Coat Jacket and Breeches, with silk knee Garters, a dark Callicoe under Jacket, a white Linnen Shirt, red Collar and Cuffs to his Coat with Metal Buttons, white Cotton Stocking, Calf-skin Pumps. It may be he has a Pass. Said Negro plays tolerable well on a Violin. Whoever will take up said Negro, or bring him to his Master, shall have Sixteen Dollars Reward, and all Charges paid, by

WILLIAM M'LENNEN.

N. B. Said Negro having done some Damage at the House where the Negroes met to hold their Frolick on Election Day, did not return to his Master again.

All Masters of Vessels are forewarned not to carry him off at their Peril. *May 26, 1774.*

William Turner

Lately arrived from LONDON,

Begs Leave to acquaint the Gentlemen and Ladies of the Town and Country, that he continues to teach the polite Art of Dancing and Fencing in the newest and most approved Method, at Concert-Hall:——Those Gentlemen and Ladies who propose sending their Children to be instructed may depend the best Care will be taken as to their Behaviour.

N. B. Cotillons taught as they are performed at all polite Balls and Assemblies in England.

——Figure Dances likewise.——

Mr. *Turner* will attend two Days in the Week at any House from 6 o'Clock in the Morning till 6 o'Clock in the Evening on grown Gentlemen and Ladies, and assures the utmost Secrecy shall be kept till they are capable of exhibiting in high Taste.

Mill-Saws.

A Number of fine English Steel-Plate Mill-Saws, suitable for the Eastward Use, superior to any ever in America before, and made on an entire new Model, Is just open'd, and to be Sold by

Charles Sigourney,

At his Shop at the Head of Dock-Square Market, BOSTON. ALSO,

Guns, Swords, Trooping Pistols, Fuzees, with Spring Pipes, Steel Rods and Bayonets, Gun Locks, spare Gun-Barrels. ALSO,

2d, 3d, 4d, 6d, 8d, 10d, 20d & 24d. Nails, sheathing, drawing and deck nails, tacks and brads of all sorts, glass, lead, powder, shot, steel, French and English flints, English glue, pewter dishes, plates, basons, porringers, tankards, canns, spoons, brass kettles, skillets, warming pans, skimmers, copper and iron tea-kettles, knives and forks of all sorts, penknives, scissars, razors, cuttoes, and every other article in the Hard-Ware Branch, that is imported into this Place. ALSO,

TIN-Plates, Lanthorn-Leaves, Allom, Copperas, Brimstone, English double refin'd Loaf-Sugar, &c.

PAINTER's OYL and COLOURS.

Just arrived——An Assortment of Painters Oyl and Colours, and will be sold at the lowest Rates. ALSO,

An Invoice of Colours, consisting of Red Lead, Spanish Brown, White Lead, Spanish White, and a few Casks of Oyl, very cheap, being a Consignment.

To the Honorable JEREMIAH POWELL, Esq; one of His Majesty's Justices of the Peace throughout the Province of the *Massachusetts-Bay*, humbly shew,

The Subscribers, more than five of the Proprietors of a Tract of Land lying in the County of *York*, situate between the Rivers *Great-Ossipee* and *Little-Ossipee*, within the County aforesaid, containing the Breadth of all that Space between the said Rivers, and so running Southwesterly from *Saco* River, more than Twelve Miles, which same Tract was purchased of one Captain *Sunday*, an Indian Sagamore, by *Francis Small*, who lived on the same Land a long Time, and had a quiet Possession thereof, and the said Petitioners being now in the Possession of the same, and being desirous of being an acting Propriety, according to the Law in that Case made and provided; do request your Worship to call a Meeting to be held at the House of Mr. *Samuel March*, Innholder in *Scarborough*, in the County of *Cumberland*, on the first Monday of *August* next, at Ten of the Clock in the Forenoon, to act on the following Articles, to wit:

1st, To choose a Moderator.

2dly, To choose a Proprietors Clerk.

3dly, To choose a Committee to transact the prudential Affairs of said Proprietors.

4thly, To choose Agents to prosecute and defend Suits in behalf of said Proprietors.

5thly, To agree on any Method for raising Money or settling the same Land, as also to agree on any Method for calling future Meetings.

May 17th, 1774.

Samuel Small,
Samuel Small, jun.
Samuel March,
Joshua Small,
Benjamin Small,
Nathaniel Milliken,
John Wright,
Nathan Chicke,
Joseph Small,
James Small,
Benjamin Mead Lord.

Province of the Massachusetts Bay.

L. S.

To SAMUEL MARCH of *Scarborough*, in the County of *Cumberland*, in said Province, Gentleman, one of said Proprietors, Greeting.

In pursuance of the foregoing Application and Request, you are hereby required to give Notice (in Time and Manner as the Law directs) to the said Proprietors, that a Meeting of said Proprietors is to be holden at the Time and Place, and for the Purposes mentioned in the afore-written Petition.

Given under my Hand and Seal, this 28th Day of *May*, A. D. 1774. JERE. POWELL, Justice of the Peace throughout the Province aforesaid.

May the 28th, 1774.

By Virtue of the afore-written Warrant to me directed, I do hereby notify and warn the Proprietors of the aforesaid Lands, to meet at the Dwelling-House of *Samuel March*, Innholder in *Scarborough* aforesaid, on the first Monday of *August* next, at Ten of the Clock in the Forenoon, for the Purposes therein mentioned. SAMUEL MARCH.

WE the Subscribers being appointed by the honorable Foster Hutchinson, Esq; Judge of Probates for the County of Suffolk, Commissioners to receive and examine the Claims of the several Creditors to the Estate of JACOB ROYALL, late of Boston, Esq; deceased, intestate, represented insolvent, do hereby give Notice, that we shall attend said service at the British Coffee House, on the last Tuesday of this and the five following Months, from Six to Nine o'Clock of the Evening of said Days.

Boston, May 27, 1774. SAMUEL DOWNE, JACOB COOPER.

WATCHES,

Plain, Skeleton and Horrizontal in Gold, Silver and Kinchbeck Case—in particular a great Variety of Silver Watches from Ten Dollars to Ten Guineas—some of which shew the Day of the Month, and others with Seconds, are very suitable for Physicians—Likewise Spring and Pendulum Eight Day Clocks, also an Assortment of Tools and Materials used by Clock and Watch Makers—To be sold by DAVID MITCHELSON, at the House of Mr. Benjamin Davis, Merchant, near the Mill Bridge.

N. B. The above Articles are of the best Kinds, newly Imported from the Makers, and will be sold at the most reasonable Prices for Cash only.

ALL Persons that have any Concerns with JONATHAN WILLIAMS, Junr. are desired to apply to JONATHAN WILLIAMS, Senr. Esq; who is impowered to transact his Business during his Absence.

TO BE SOLD CHEAP,

A choice Lot of Land in the Town of Granvile, consisting of Forty-three Acres, near the Centre of the Town, there are 200 Families settled in said Town.—For further intelligence inquire of the Printers.

ALL Persons indebted to the Estate of Richard Surcomb, late of Boston, Baker, deceased, are once more requested to make immediate Payment to Mary Surcomb, Executrix, as they would avoid being sued at July Court.

TO BE LETT,

A handsome House with an excellent Garden well stocked with Vegetables, in a delightful Situation, within two Miles of Boston, fit for a small or large genteel Family, on the most reasonable Terms, may be entered on immediately, enquire of Edes & Gill.

Lemuel Pattingall of Norwich,

in Connecticut, Brick Layer and Mason, wants to Hire Two or Three Workmen at that Business, during the Season. Norwich, 20th May, 1774.

WANTED,

A sober, faithful honest Man, that understands taking Care of a Tavern; one of this Character that can be well recommended, by inquiring of the Printers will be inform'd of the Place, where he will have good Wages.

A Wet Nurse with a good Breast of Milk would take a Child to Suckle.

Inquire of the Printers.

WANTS EMPLOYMENT,

A young Man who is capable of tending a Gentleman's Family, taking care of Horses and driving a Chariot; can be well recommended.

Inquire of the Printers.

RAN away from his Master on Friday Evening last, a Negro Boy, named GOREE, about 16 Years of Age, 5 Feet, 3 Inches High, had on when he went away, a brown Cloth Coat, dark Velvet Waistcoat, white Shirt, white Linen Breeches, grey Yarn Stockings, a pair of Shoes tore at the Heels, with Pinchbeck Buckles, an old Felt Hat. Whoever will take up said Runaway, and secure him, and give information to the Subscriber, so that he may have him again, shall have a handsome Reward and necessary Charges paid by

DANIEL VOSE.

All Masters of Vessels and others, are hereby cautioned against harbouring, concealing, or carrying off the above Negro, as they would avoid the Penalty of the Law. Milton, May 30 1774.

OATS.

OATS, Pease, Philadelphia Flour, and Bar-Iron, *Also*, war anted Scythes and Axes, a few neat Fowling Pieces, and a small Quantity of good Snuff, to be sold cheap, at the lowest Store on the South Side of the Town Dock, by Joseph-Pearse Palmer.

To be Sold on TUESDAY the Twenty-first Day of June next, at Two o'Clock in the Afternoon, by PUBLIC VENDUE, at the House of Mr. Edward Low in Leominster, by Philip Sweetser, of said Leominster,

A Good Farm situated in said Town, containing about 140 Acres of choice Land, consisting of Plowing, Pasturing and Mowing, with a fine young Orchard, and is well Wooded and excellently Watered, upon a great Road, suitable for a Tavern or Trader, with a good House, Barn, and other valuable Accommodations, which renders it a very desirable Farm. It will be sold at a reasonable Price; and if it should be sold at private Sale before the Day above-mentioned, publick Notice shall be given. *May 5, 1774.*

TO BE SOLD

A ROPE WALK, the Buildings in good repair, with all the Tools and Implements necessary for carrying on the Rope Making Business, it is very pleasantly and conveniently situated, and has the Advantage of a Water Carriage.—The Business may be carried on in this Town to as much Advantage, as perhaps it can be in any Town upon the Continent.——Any Person that inclines to purchase, may know the Terms by applying to JOHN ADAMS, opposite the Old South Meeting-House in Boston.

Portsmouth in New-Hampshire, May 18.

Boston: Printed, by EDES & GILL.

THE Boston-Gazette, AND COUNTRY JOURNAL.

No. 1001.

Containing the freshest Advices, Foreign and Domestic.

MONDAY, June 20, 1774.

We have the grateful Advices from Philadelphia, that the ILLUSTRIOUS FARMER *is once more exerting his* GENIUS——FOR HIS OPPRESSED COUNTRYMEN.—*And we have two Letters, printed in the publick Papers, directed "To the Inhabitants of the British Colonies in "America", come to Hand, containing the strongest internal Evidence of being the Work of that great and good Man,* JOHN DICKINSON *of* Philadelphia;—*whose Name will be revered and loved, while Knowledge, Sentiment and Spirit invigorate this Northern World. And we shall inspire our Readers with a Republication of them in their Order.*

PHILADELPHIA, May 24. 1774.

LETTER I.

To the INHABITANTS *of the* British Colonies *in* AMERICA.

BRETHREN,

DIVINE Providence has been pleased to place us in this age and country under such circumstances as to be reduced to the necessity of chusing one of these conditions—either to submit to the dominion of others, holding our lives, liberties, and properties, by the *precarious tenure* of their will---or to exert that understanding, resolution and power, with which Heaven has favoured us, in striving to maintain our rank in the class of freemen.

The importance of these objects is so immensely great, and the treatment of one of these colonies so extremely alarming, as to call for your most earnest and immediate consideration.

The subject of the present dispute between Great-Britain and us is so generally understood, that to enlarge upon it is needless. We know the *Extent* of her claims. We begin to feel the *Enforcement* of those claims. We may foresee the consequences of them; for reason, teaching us to infer actions from principles, and events from examples, should convince us what a perfection of servitude is to be fixed on us and our posterity. I call it perfection---because the wit of man, it is apprehended, cannot devise a plan of domination more compleatly tending to bear down the governed into the lowest and meanest state in society, than that now meditated, avowed, and in part executed on this continent.

If this system becomes established, it may, with truth, be said of the inhabitants of these colonies, "that they hold their lives, liberties, and properties, by the precarious tenure of the will of others."*

Allowing the danger to be real---At the prospect of so abject and so lasting a subjection, what must be the sentiments of judicious and virtuous Americans? They will quickly determine whether the first part of the alternative should be adopted.

Here arguments would be absurd. Not more ridiculous would be an attempt to prove vice preferable to virtue---the climate of St. Vincent more pleasant than that of Pennsylvania---the natives of Indostan under the government of the East-India Company, as happy as English Freeholders---or the inhabitants of Great-Britain more loyal subjects than those of the colonies.

That liberty is inestimable---and should, if possible, be preserved---you *know*. To pretend to convince you of the truth of the former proposition, or of the duty of the latter, would be to insult you.

You must be, you are resolved to observe the properest conduct for securing your best and dearest interests. What *that* may be deserves-- demands---your closest attention---your calmest deliberation.

On this head I venture to submit some observations to your consideration. I am, by every tye of interest and duty, an American; and unless my heart deceives me, I am an American in affection My fortunes, hopes, and wishes, are bound up in your prosperity. With my countrymen I must mourn or rejoice; and, therefore, though I am perfectly sensible I cannot present to them reflections arising from great abilities, or extensive learning, and adorned by elegance of composition, yet I trust they will lend a careful and candid attention to plain thoughts, dictated by honest intentions, and a participation of afflictions. Aiming solely at your welfare, and not at the trifling reputation of a writer, far be from me the overweening presumption, that my opinions are free from error. Conscious of my frailties, I desire those opinions to be severely examined. The correction of them will confer a real obligation upon me, if it serves my country; and happy shall I esteem myself, if the detection of my mistakes shall open to you a clear view of the most expedient measures to be pursued.

There are some men who say, that the late Act of Parliament, abolishing the privileges of the port of Boston, was occasioned by the particular imprudence of the inhabitants, and in no manner concerns the other colonies.

To form a true judgment on this point, it will be proper to take a short review of some other transactions.

Great-Britain, triumphant by your assistance in the late war, found, at the conclusion of it, by a peace hastily bestowed on her haughty and hereditary foes, her dominions enlarged---her fleets formidable—her armies disciplined—her trade flourishing—her enemies intimidated and exhausted—her colonies thriving, affectionate and dutiful.

The cup of prosperity, large and full, courted her lips. Deep she drank of the enchanted beverage, as if the vessel, like the cruise of *Sarepta's* widow, could not fail. After a short, but feverish repose, she roused herself, may I say---as one of *Homer's* giants---a race---

"By whom no statutes and no rights were known."

to injure those who never injured her, She had conquered her *enemies*. *That* other kingdoms had done. Should no exploits of a transcendent energy illustrate the annals of GEORGE the third? No atchievements so shockingly great and advantageous, that even the pensioned historians of the animated Æra must weep in tracing them, and blush in reciting them? Luckily for her fame---*perhaps for her profit*---the near sighted policy and low spirited humanity of every state, in every period, had left untouched, for her, the novel glory of conquering *Friends---Children---Flesh of her Flesh*, and *Bone of her Bone*, unstained by any former reproach ---resting in a perfect tranquility, acknowledged loyalty, and actual obedience to every kind of authority hitherto exercised by her over them---perpetually pouring into her lap those fruits of their labour and industry, which she would permit them to collect from the different parts of the world---proud of their connection with her---confiding in her---loving---revering---almost adoring her---and ready and willing, as they ever had been, to spend their treasure and their blood at her request---in her cause.

† "Parcere *Superbis*, et debellare *Subjectos*"

was a thought that had escaped the sagacity of statesmen, and even the fancy of poets. The subtilty of *Machiavel's* Italian brain had missed it---and no Bæotian had blundered upon it.

The temptation was too great to be resisted---The parent resolved to *seize that treasure*, and, if not tamely resigned, to spill that blood herself. ‡ "O *sapiens* et *beata* Regina."

The greatest § ministers, who had heretofore conducted her affairs, had discovered and declared that we were continually toiling for her benefit---that she was sure of receiving, in the course of commerce, all those emoluments of our labour, which reason could require---and tenderly cherished and supported us. Notions too dull! and advantages too just! to merit the slightest regard from his Majesty's enlightened and magnanimous counsellors.

"They lavish gold out of the bag, and weigh silver in the balance---they fall down, yea, they worship (them)---remember this, and shew yourselves men." *Isaiah*, Cha. xlvi.

F. P.

* "*Non nobis nati sumus. It is for our posterity we desire to provide---that they may not be in worse case than villains: For a* FREE-MAN *to be* TENANT AT WILL *for his* LIBERTY! *I will not agree to it. It is a tenure not to be found in all* Littleton." *Speech of Sir Edward Cooke, Lord Chief Justice. Parliamentary History, Vol. 8, Page 61.*

"† *To spare the proud, and to subdue the subject.*"

"‡ *O* wise *and* happy *Queen.*"

"§ *Sir* Robert Walpole, *and every other minister to whom the project of taxing the Colonies was mentioned, rejected it.*

"*When I had the honour of serving his Majesty I availed myself of the means of information, which I derived from my office.* I speak, therefore, from knowledge. *My materials were good. I was at pains to* collect, *to* digest, *to* consider *them; and I will* be bold to affirm, *that the profit of* Great-Britain *from the trade of the Colonies, through all its branches*, is two millions a year. This *is the fund that carried you triumphantly through the last war. The estates that were rented at two thousand pounds a year, three-score years ago, are three thousand pounds at present. Those estates sold then from fifteen to eighteen years purchase; the same may now be sold for thirty.* You owe this to America. This is the price that America pays you for her protection. *I dare not say how much higher these profits may be augmented---Upon the whole, I will beg leave to tell the House what is really my opinion; it is, that the* Stamp-Act *be repealed absolutely, totally and immediately. That the reason for the repeal be assigned, because it was founded on an* erroneous principle." *Mr.* PITT's *Speech.*

All the most distinguished writers on the trade of Great-Britain, *previous to the present reign, held a language entirely agreeing with Mr.* Pitt's *sentiments. See Davenant, Child, Tucker, Beawes, Postlethwaite, &c.*

TO BE SOLD at the Royal Exchange Tavern in King-Street, Boston,

At PUBLIC VENDUE,

On Wednesday the Fourteenth Day of September next, at Ten o'Clock in the Forenoon,

The following Lots of Land, viz.

Lot marked F. 2. in the first range of Lots, containing about six Thousand Acres (exclusive of Settlers Lots interspersed) being near one Mile wide and fifteen Miles long, and fronting on *Kennebeck*-River, on the West-side of it, about ten Miles above Fort Halifax: to be divided and Sold in two Parts.

Lot marked B. D. 1. in the second range of Lots, about six Miles above *Norridgwalk*, on the West Side of *Kennebeck*-River, and fronting thereon, containing about seven Thousand Acres, exclusive of Settlers Lots interspersed, being one Mile wide, & 15 Miles long.

Lot marked C. A. 1. in the third range of Lots, near the Falls of *Cariotonka*, about twelve Miles above *Norridgwalk*, on the West Side of *Kennebeck*-River, and fronting thereon, containing about seven Thousand Acres, exclusive of Settler's Lots interspersed, being one Mile wide and fifteen Miles long.

Lot No. 20, called a Ten Mile back Lot, on the West Side of *Kennebeck* River, containing about four Thousand eight Hundred Acres.

Three Lots of Land, viz. Lot No. 32, on the East Side of *Kennebeck*-River, about 300 Poles above *Fort Western*, N°. 86, on the East Side of said River, about nine Miles, and 120 Poles above *Fort-Western*, and also Lot N°. 20, on the West Side of said River, about one Mile and 230 Poles above *Fort-Western*, containing 400 Acres each.

Also all the Islands in Cobbiseconte Pond, and all the Islands in *Kennebeck*-River, above *Fort-Halifax*. The Pay will be made easy to the Purchasers.

For further Particulars enquire of *Henry Alline*, jun. at his Office in King-Street, *Boston*, *June* 10. 1774.

ALL Persons indebted for this Paper, whose Accounts have been above 12 Months standing, are requested to make immediate Payment.

SALEM, June 14.

The Provision and Wood Vessels bound to Boston since the tyrannical Port Bill has taken Place, are obliged to unload and load again at Marblehead before they can proceed to Boston.

Captain Coffin from London, but last from Halifax, arrived at Marblehead last Wednesday. He brings nothing new.

BOSTON.

In COUNCIL, June 9, 1774.

ORDERED, that *Jeremiah Powell*, *William Sever*, and *Jedediah Preble*, Esq'rs. be a Committee to wait on his Excellency the Governor with the following Address in Answer to his Speech at the Opening of the present General Court. THO'S FLUCKER, Secr'y.

To his Excellency THOMAS GAGE, Esq; Captain-General and Governor in Chief of the Province of Massachusetts-Bay, &c. &c.

The Address of the Council of the said Province.

May it please your Excellency,

YOUR Speech to the two Houses at the Opening of this Session has been duly considered by this Board. His Majesty having been pleased to appoint you to the Government of this Province, We take this Opportunity to wait on you with our Congratulations on that Occasion.

Your Excellency has arrived at a Juncture when the Harmony between Great-Britain and the Colonies is greatly interrupted, whereby your Station, though elevated, must needs be rendered less agreeable to you than otherwise it would have been: But if you should be the happy Instrument of restoring in any Measure that Harmony, and of extricating the Province from their present Embarrassments, you will doubtless consider these happy Effects as more than a Compensation for any inconveniences arising to you from the peculiar Circumstances of the Times. His Majesty's faithful Council will on all Occasions chearfully co-operate with your Excellency in every Attempt for accomplishing those desirable Ends. We wish your Excellency every Felicity: The greatest of a Political Nature, both to yourself and the Province is, that your Administration in the Principles and general Conduct of it, may be a happy Contrast to that of your two immediate Predecessors.—It is irksome to us to Censure any one, but we are constrained to say there is the greatest Reason to apprehend that from their Machinations (both in concert and apart) are derived the Origin and Progress of the Disunion between Britain and the Colonies, and the present distressed State of this Province —a Province, to which the latter of them, in an especial Manner, owed his best Services, and whose Liberties and Rights he was under every Obligation of Duty and Gratitude to Support.

The Inhabitants of this Province claim no more than the Rights of Englishmen, without Diminution or "Abridgement." These as it is our indispensible Duty, so it shall be our constant Endeavor to maintain to the utmost of our Power, in perfect consistence however with the truest Loyalty to the Crown; the just Prerogatives of which your Excellency will ever find this Board zealous to Support.

Permit us Sir, on this Occasion, to express the firmest Confidence that, under their present Grievances, the People of this Province will not in vain look to your Excellency for your paternal Aid and Assistance; and, as the great End of Government is the good of the People, that your Experience and Abilities will be applied to attain that End; the steady Pursuit of which, at the same Time it insures their Confidence and Esteem will be a source of the truest Enjoyment, self Approbation.

We thank your Excellency for the Assurance you have given "that you shall with Pleasure concur with the two Houses to the utmost of your Power in all Matters that tend to the Welfare and Prosperity of the Province;" and your Excellency may be assured that we shall contribute every Thing on our Part to promote Measures of so salutary a Tendency.

JUNE 14.

The Committee appointed to present the foregoing Address, waited on his Excellency therewith Yesterday, and read as far as that Part which reflects on the Administration of his Excellency's two immediate Predecessors, when he desired the Chairman not to proceed any further, and that he would assign his Reasons for refusing to receive it, in a Message to the Council, and on the same Day sent by the Secretary the following Message:

Gentlemen of the Council,

I CANNOT *receive an Address which contains indecent Reflections on my Predecessors who have been tried and honourably acquitted by the Lords of the Privy Council, and their Conduct approved by the King.*

I consider this Address as an Insult upon his Majesty and the Lords of his Privy-Council, and an Affront to my self.

T. GAGE.

BOSTON, June 20.

The late Hon. House of Representatives of this Province having finished all the ordinary public Business of Importance that had been before them, on Friday last came into the following Resolutions, present 129 Members and only 12 Dissentients, viz.

In the House of REPRESENTATIVES, *June 17, 1774.*

THIS House having duly considered, and being deeply affected with the unhappy Differences which have long subsisted & are increasing between Great Britain & the American Colonies, do RESOLVE, That a Meeting of Committees from the several Colonies on this Continent is highly expedient and necessary, to consult upon the present State of the Colonies, and the Miseries to which they are and must be reduced by the Operation of certain Acts of Parliament respecting *AMERICA*; and to deliberate and determine upon wise and proper Measures to be by them recommended to all the Colonies, for the Recovery and Establishment of their just Rights and Liberties, Civil and Religious, and the Restoration of Union and Harmony between Great Britain and the Colonies, most ardently desired by all good Men.

Therefore, *RESOLVED*, That the honorable *James Bowdoin*, Esq; the Hon. *Thomas Cushing*, Esq; Mr. *Samuel Adams*, *John Adams*, and *Robert Treat Paine*, Esq'rs; be and they are hereby appointed a Committee on the Part of this Province, for the Purposes aforesaid, any Three of whom to be a Quorum; to meet such Committees or Delegates from the other Colonies, as have been or may be appointed, either by their respective Houses of Burgesses, or Representatives, or by Convention, or by the Committees of Correspondence, appointed by the respective Houses of Assembly, in the City of *Philadelphia*, or any other Place that shall be judg'd most suitable by the Committee, on the First Day of *September* next; and that the Speaker of the House be directed, in a Letter to the Speakers of the Houses of Burgesses or Representatives in the several Colonies, to inform them of the Substance of these Resolves.

In the House of REPRESENTATIVES, *June 17, 1774.*

WHEREAS this House, taking into Consideration the many Distresses and Difficulties to which the American Colonies, and this Province in particular, are and must be reduced by the Operation of certain late Acts of Parliament, have determined that it is highly expedient that a Committee should be appointed to meet as soon as may be the Committees that are or shall be appointed by the several Colonies on this Continent, to consult together upon the present State of the Colonies, and to deliberate and determine upon wise and proper Measures to be by them recommended to all the Colonies for the Recovery and Establishment of their just Rights and Liberties, Civil and Religious, and the Restoration of that Union and Harmony between Great-Britain and the Colonies, most ardently desired by all good Men. And the Honorable JAMES BOWDOIN, Esq; the Hon. THOMAS CUSHING, Esq; Mr. SAMUEL ADAMS, JOHN ADAMS, and ROBERT-TREAT PAINE, Esquires, are appointed a Committee on the Part of this Province, for the Purposes aforesaid; any three of whom to be a Quorum, to meet such Committees or Delegates from the other Colonies, as have been or may be appointed, either by their respective Houses of Burgesses, or Representatives, or by Convention, or by Committees of Correspondence appointed by the respective Houses of Assembly, in the City of *Philadelphia*, or any other Place that shall be judged most suitable by the joint Committees, on the 1st Day of *September* next. And whereas this House did *Resolve*, That there be paid to said Committee out of the public Treasury, the Sum of *FIVE HUNDRED POUNDS*, to enable them to discharge the important Trust to which they are appointed; they upon their Return to be accountable for the same.—And said Resolve was sent up to the honorable Board for their Concurrence, who accordingly concurred the Resolve of the House, but his Excellency the Governor declined his Consent to the same.——Wherefore this House would Recommend, and they do accordingly hereby recommend to the several Towns and Districts within this Province, that each Town and District, raise, collect and pay, to the Honorable *Thomas Cushing*, Esq; of *Boston*, the Sum of *FIVE HUNDRED POUNDS* by the Fifteenth Day of *August* next, agreeable to a List herewith exhibited,* being each Town's and District's Proportion of said Sum, according to the last Province Tax, to enable them to discharge the important Trust to which they are appointed; they upon their Return to be accountable for the same.

* The List will be sent to the Selectmen of said Towns and Districts.

In the House of Representatives, June 17, 1774.

WHEREAS the Towns of Boston *and* Charlestown, *are at this Time suffering under the Hand of Power, by the shutting up the Harbour by an armed Force, which in the Opinion of this House is an Invasion of the said Towns, evidently design'd to compel the Inhabitants thereof to a Submission to Taxes imposed upon them without their Consent: And whereas it appears to this House that this Attack upon the said Towns for the Purpose aforesaid is an Attack made upon this whole Province and Continent, which threatens the total Destruction of the Liberties of all British America:*

It is therefore *RESOLVED*, as the clear Opinion of this House, that the Inhabitants of the said Towns ought to be relieved; and this House do recommend to all, and more especially to the Inhabitants of this Province, to afford them speedy and constant Relief in such Way and Manner as shall be most suitable to their Circumstances, 'till the Sense and Advice of our Sister Colonies shall be known: In full Confidence that they will exhibit Examples of Patience, Fortitude and Perseverance, while they are thus called to endure this Oppression, for the Preservation of the Liberties of their Country.

In the House of REPRESENTATIVES, *June 17, 1774.*

WHEREAS this and his Majesty's other Colonies in North America have long been struggling under the heavy Hand of Power; and our dutiful Petitions for the Redress of our intolerable Grievances have not only been disregarded and frown'd upon, but the Design totally to alter the free Constitutions of Civil Government in British America, and establish arbitrary Governments, and reduce the Inhabitants to Slavery, appears more and more to be fixed and determined. It is therefore strongly recommended by this House to the Inhabitants of the Province, that they renounce altogether the Consumption of India Teas, and as far as in them lies, discontinue the use of all Goods and Manufactures whatever, that shall be imported from the East Indies and Great-Britain, until the publick Grievances of America shall be radically and totally redress'd. And it is also further recommended to all, that they give all possible Encouragement to the Manufactures of America. And it is moreover strongly recommended to the Inhabitants aforesaid, that they use their utmost Endeavours to suppress Pedlars and Petty Chapmen (who are of late become a very great Nuisance) by putting in Execution the good and wholesome Laws of this Province for that Purpose.

His Excellency the Governor having directed the Secretary to acquaint the two Houses it was his Excellency's pleasure the General Assembly should be dissolved and to declare the same dissolved accordingly; the Secretary went to the Court House and finding the Door of the Representatives Chamber locked, directed the Messenger to go in and acquaint the Speaker that the Secretary had a Message from his Excellency to the Hon. House, and desired he might be admitted to deliver it; the Messenger returned, and said he had acquainted the Speaker therewith, who mentioned it to the House, and their Orders were to keep the Door fast:—Whereupon the following Proclamation was published on the Stairs leading to the Representatives Chamber, in presence of a Number of the Members of the House and a Number of other Persons, and immediately after in Council.

Province of MASSACHUSETTS-BAY.

By the GOVERNOR.

A PROCLAMATION

For dissolving the General Court.

WHEREAS the Proceedings of the House of Representatives, in the present Session of the General Court, make it necessary, for his Majesty's Service, that the said General Court should be dissolved.

I have therefore thought fit to dissolve the said General Court, and the same is hereby dissolved accordingly, and the Members thereof are discharged from any further Attendance.

GIVEN under my Hand at Salem the 17th Day of June, 1774, in the Fourteenth Yea of his Majesty's Reign.

By his Excellency's Command, } T. GAGE.
THO's FLUCKER, Secretary.

GOD SAVE THE KING.

In the House of Representatives, June 14 1774.

WHEREAS there will become due in this Month, sundry Notes given by the Province Treasurer, and sufficient Provision having been made for the paying off the same, and if the Possessors of such Notes should not bring them in to the Treasurer to be paid, the Province will suffer Damage by such Neglect:

Therefore RESOLVED, That the Possessors of such Notes, who shall not bring them to the Province Treasurer, to be paid by the last Day of *July* next, shall not receive any Interest on the same, after that Time, and the Province Treasurer is hereby directed forthwith to cause this Order to be published in all the *Boston* News-Papers, three Weeks successively, that every one concerned may be Notified hereof. Sent up for Concurrence.

T. CUSHING, Speaker.

In Council, June 15th. Read and concurred.
JOHN COTTON, D. Sec'ry.

Consented to, THOs. GAGE.

A true Copy attest. JOHN COTTON, D. Sec'ry.

THE Treasurer of the Province hereby gives public Notice to the delinquent Constables and Collectors of the Province Taxes, that they pay the same into the Treasury by the 31st of *July* next.

Treasury-Office, July 18, 1774.

In the House of Representatives it was resolv'd on Friday last as the Opinion of the House, that considering the present State of the publick Affairs, it is highly proper that a Day of Prayer be observ'd in the several religious Assemblies, throughout the Province; and that the Members of the House recommend the same to their respective Parish Ministers.

The following Act, among others, passed the late Sessions of the General Assembly, viz.

An Act for incorporating a Tract of Land in the County of Worcester, known by the Name of Rutland-District, into a Town by the Name of HUTCHINSON.

We are authorized to inform the World, that at the the last Winter Session, a Bill passed both Houses of Assembly, for incorporating the above District into a Town, by the Name of BARRE;—which being presented to his Excellency *Governor Hutchinson, he refused his Assent to the Bill.*—The House of Representatives for the future will take Care to avoid the *ill timed* Complaisance of leaving a Blank for the Governor to insert *the Name of the Town.*

The following is said to be a true List of the Names of Eleven of the Gentlemen who voted AGAINST a Congress; the remaining one is *at present* uncertain.

Col. Worthington, Col. Murray, Col. Jones, Major Ingersol, David Thatcher, Esq; Abijah White, Esq; Col. Bacon, Col. Day, Capt. Hayward of Easton, Mr. Samuel Feild and Barnabas Freeman.

AT a legal and very full Meeting of the Freeholders and other Inhabitants of the Town of Boston, *by Adjournment at* Faneuil-Hall, June 17, 1774.

The Hon. JOHN ADAMS, *Esq; Moderator.*

UPON a Motion made, the Town again entered into the Consideration of that Article in the Warrant, viz. "To consider and determine what Measures are proper to be taken upon the present Exigency of our public Affairs, more especially relative to the late Edict of a British Parliament for blocking up the Harbour of Boston, and annihilating the Trade of the Town": And after very serious Debates thereon,

VOTED, (With only one dissentient) That the Committee of Correspondence be enjoined forthwith to write to all the other Colonies, acquainting them that we are not idle, that we are deliberating upon the Steps to be taken on the present Exigencies of our public affairs; that our Brethren the landed Interest of this province, with an unexampled Spirit and Unanimity, are entering into a Non-consumption Agreement; and that we are waiting with anxious Expectation for the Result of a Continental Congress, whose Meeting we impatiently desire, in whose wisdom and Firmness we can confide, and in whose Determinations we shall chearfully acquiesce.

Agreeable to Order, the Committee of Correspondence laid before the Town such Letters as they had received in Answer to the Circular Letters wrote by them to the several Colonies, and also the Sea Port Towns in this Province, since the Reception of the Boston Port Bill; and the same being publicly read,

VOTED, unanimously, That our warmest Thanks be transmitted to our Brethren on the Continent, for that Humanity, Sympathy and Affection with which they have been inspired, and which they have expressed towards this distressed Town at this important Season.

VOTED, unanimously, That the Thanks of this Town be, and hereby are, given to the Committee of Correspondence, for their Faithfulness, in the Discharge of their Trust; and that they be desired to continue their Vigilance and Activity in that Service.

Whereas the Overseers of the Poor in the Town of Boston *are a Body politic, by Law constituted for the Reception and Distribution of all charitable Donations for the Use of the Poor of said Town:*

VOTED, That all Grants and Donations to this Town, and the Poor thereof, at this distressing Season, be paid and delivered into the Hands of said Overseers, and by them appropriated and distributed in Concert with the Committee lately appointed by this Town for the Consideration of Ways and Means of employing the Poor.

VOTED, That the Town Clerk be directed to publish the Proceedings of this Meeting in the several News Papers.

The Meeting was then adjourned to Monday the 27th of June Instant. Attest,

WILLIAM COOPER, *Town-Clerk.*

The late Town-Meeting was as full and respectable as ever was known—their unanimity and firmness was never exceeded; not one, tho' often called upon, had any Thing to offer in favor of paying for the Tea in compliance with the Boston Port Bill; all appeared disposed to stand the utmost efforts of Tyranny, rather than make a free surrender of the Rights of America.—The Speeches made on the State of American Affairs would do honour to any Assembly.

A Merchant in one of our Sea-Ports, who has £. 500[illegible] Sterling in London, which was to have been remitte[d] him in British Manufactures, has now ordered the sam[e] to be sent him in Money; many others are doing the same——The Boston Port Bill is certainly as anti-commercial a[s] it is anti-charteral and inhuman.

The Solemn League & Covenant *for a non-consumptio[n] of British Merchandize is an Ax to the Root of the tree; by coming into it we establish our own Manufactures, sav[e] our Money, and finally our Country from the destructio[n] that threatens it.*

On Saturday last the following Address from the Merchants and Freeholders of the Town of Salem, was presented to his Excellency Governor GAGE, viz.

May it please your Excellency,

WE who are Merchants and Freeholders in the Town of Salem beg Leave to present you our dutiful Respects on your Appointment to the Government of this Province. The universal Tribute of Thanks and Applause paid you for the Wisdom, Mildness and exact Regularity of your Conduct in another Command, cannot fail to excite the most just Expectations that this Province will enjoy the happy Fruits of your Benignity.

We are deeply affected with a Sense of our public Calamities: but the Miseries that are now rapidly hastening on our Brethren in the Capital of the Province, greatly excite our Commiseration; and we hope your Excellency will use your Endeavours to prevent a further Accumulation of Evils on that already sorely distressed People.

By shutting up the Port of Boston some imagine that the Course of Trade might be turned hither, and to our Benefit: but Nature in the Formation of our Harbour forbids our becoming Rivals in Commerce to that convenient Mart. And were it otherwise,—we must be dead to every Idea of Justice—lost to all the Feelings of Humanity—could we indulge one Thought to seize on Wealth and raise our Fortunes on the ruin of our suffering Neighbours. But so far from receiving a Benefit, we are greatly injured by the shutting up the Harbour of Boston, as it deprives us of a Market for much the largest Part of our West-India Imports; and there is not a Town in the Province but will feel the ill Effects of it. Permit us then, Sir, to apply to your Clemency and Justice to afford us every Alleviation in your Power, and to procure for us every possible Relief from this extensive Mischief.

We account it the greatest Unhappiness that this Province, which has ever been foremost in Loyalty to the Kings of Britain—in its Efforts to defend their Territories and enlarge their Dominions—should be the first to feel our Sovereign's severest Displeasure. Our Fathers fled from Oppression, braved every Danger, and here began a Settlement on bare Creation. Almost incredible are the Fatigues and Difficulties they encountered to subdue a dreary Wilderness filled with Savage Beasts, and yet more Savage Men: but by their invincible Resolutions they rose superior to them all; and by their astonishing Efforts greatly facilitated the Settlement of the other British Colonies in America. Yet, Sir, we speak it with Grief, the Sons are checked and dishonored for exhibiting Proofs of their inheriting some portion of that Spirit which in their Fathers produced such astonishing Effects.

A happy Union with Great Britain is the Wish of all the Colonies. 'Tis their unspeakable Grief that it has in any Degree been interrupted. We earnestly desire to repair the breach. We ardently pray that Harmony may be restored. And for these Ends, every measure compatible with the Dignity and Safety of British Subjects we shall gladly adopt.

We assure your Excellency we shall make it our constant Endeavour to preserve the Peace and promote the Welfare of the Province; and hereby we shall best advance the Interest of our Sovereign.

In these Times the Administration of Government must be peculiarly arduous and difficult; but yours we wish may be as easy as the Nature of Things will possibly admit, and the Event happy; and that your public Labours may be crowned with the noblest Reward—the voluntary, disinterested Applause of a whole free People.

[This Address was signed by 125 Persons.]

His EXCELLENCY's ANSWER.

GENTLEMEN,

I Thank you for the obliging Expressions towards me, contained in your Address, and be assured, it will always afford me sincere Pleasure to be of Use to the Inhabitants of this Town, or any Individuals in the Province.

I feel, as well as you, the Inconveniencies that the Inhabitants must suffer from shutting up the Port of Boston; and should be glad they would co-operate with my Endeavours to extricate themselves from them; but without their Assistance, I can take no Step towards their relief; I am sorry that the People of that Capital should have given such repeated Provocations to the King and the British Nation, as to force them to take the present Measures in Support of their Authority. Great Britain is equally desirous as yourselves, of a happy Union with this, as well as every other Colony, and inheriting the Spirit of her Ancestors, finds it necessary to support her Rights, as the supreme Head of her extended Empire: She strives not to check that Spirit which you say you inherit from your Fathers, but to inculcate that due Obedience to the King in his Parliament, which your Fathers acknowledged.

Salem, June 18, 1774.

THE present aspect of public affairs is highly favorable to the liberties of America: The whole continent seems inspired by one soul, and that soul a vigorous and determined one.

Before the dissolution of the patriotic house of Burgesses of Virginia, they had drawn up a number of very spirited resolves, of which we have room only for the last, viz. "Resolved, That be appointed deputies from this house to meet at , such deputies as shall be appointed from the other colonies, there to consider and determine on ways the most effectual to stop the exports from North-America, and such other methods as shall be most decisive for saving the liberties of America against the systematic plan formed for their destruction." That whole province is in motion; and Maryland has made amazing progress for the short space since they have taken this fresh alarm from the Boston port bill. Meetings of towns, counties, and by delegates of the whole province, either have been held or are going rapidly on. Besides the doings of Annapolis and Baltimore, those of Chester are deserving of our warmest acknowledgments. Subscription papers have been set on foot in that County, and considerable sums already subscribed for the relief of our poor in this devoted town. Philadelphia is following the generous example, as well as the Jerseys, New-York and Connecticut. A most respectable meeting of the trademen was held at Philadelphia, on the afternoon of the 9th current, wherein the dissatisfaction of that body at the indecision of the proceedings of the parties who have hitherto acted, was so great that the committee sometime since appointed, resigned and agreed to call a general meeting of all the people on the 15th, to choose a joint and more extensive committee, with a view to bring about a congress and in re decisive measures. This body has begun a correspondence with their brethren the tradesmen of New-York, another intrepid and determined set of MEN. New-Jersey is very forward, and are on the point of choosing their deputies for the Congress by a very regular method, viz. of meeting in towns and neighbourhoods, sending deputies from those meetings to county meetings, and others from those to a provincial one. Committees of correspondence are not now confined to the province of the Massachusetts-Bay. Lord North's administration is become so important that nearly every subject of the empire feels himself deeply interested in it, and insists upon being acquainted with the very *minutiæ* of all his plans.

The colony of Rhode-Island have appointed the Hon. STEPHEN HOPKINS, and SAMUEL WARD, Esq'rs; to represent them in the general congress.

The zeal, firmness, and unanimity of our late house of representatives, and the steady support they received from the honorable his Majesty's council, does honor to the good sense and patriotism of the parties who at this trying season committed the conservation of their inestimable and now much endangered rights into such worthy hands. Some exceptions we must allow there have been; but ignorance, ambition, for the fancied honors of commissions, civil and military, and rank cowardice respecting the event of contending to blood for our rights, daily giving way to the better information abounding thro' all ranks of people, afford us the comfortable hope that in a little time our house of representatives shall emulate that of Virginia, in which a gentleman lately from thence says, there was not so much as a luckewarm member, much less a dissentient from the cause of his country.

NEWPORT, June 13.

The behaviour of the Americans, at this alarming crisis, will most probably *stamp* their characters, and hand them down to posterity, as a brave generation of patriots, or sink them into contempt in the opinion of all future ages. Life and death, or, which are tantamount thereto, *liberty* and *slavery* are now before them, and it is in their power to chuse which they please. If they submit, says a writer, they deserve more than man can lay upon them.

It has been lately proposed, by some writers in England, to have an American LAND TAX, equal to what it is in Great-Britain.

This day the honorable the general assembly of this colony meet in this town, who 'tis hoped, will grant a sum of money for the relief of the poor of Boston, who may be reduced to distress by the present *worse* than *savage* treatment, which that town suffers from a people for whom they have often spent their best blood and treasure.

The number of Governor Hutchinson's addressers, consisting of merchants, shopkeepers, pedlars, pettifoggers, &c. amounted to 140; and it is said, great pains were taken throughout Boston, and many other towns, to procure that number, which must certainly appear very contemptible, when 'tis considered, that there are full *four hundred thousand* inhabitants in that province.

BOSTON, June 20.

We hear that the Patriotic Inhabitants of Philadelphia have generously Voted to give the Poor of this Town 1500 Barrels of Flour, 500 of which, it is said, may be soon expected.

Tuesday last the 4th, or King's own Regiment landed from on board the Transports, lying at the Long-Wharff, and Marched to the Common, where they are Encamped.

Wednesday the 43d Regiment landed on the Long-Wharff, and are now Encamped in the Common.

We are informed that the 5th and 38th Regiments are Hourly expected to arrive here.

We hear from Salem, that at a Council held there on Wednesday last, the Hon. *William Brown*, Esq; was appointed a Justice of the Superior Court in the Room of *Nathaniel Ropes*, Esq; deceased.

The following VOTE was passed by the Corporation of Harvard College on May 31st, and on June 2d 1774 confirmed by the Honorable and Reverend Board of Overseers, viz.

CONsidering the present dark Aspect of our publick Affairs, *Voted*, that there be no public COMMENCEMENT this Year, and that the Candidates for their first and second Degrees, after having been presented, *nominatim* to, and approved by the Honorable and Reverend Board of Overseers, shall receive their Degrees in a general Diploma signed by the Corporation. Provided that on or before the 13th Day of July next, they bring to Dr. Appleton, Senior Fellow of the Corporation, a Certificate from the Steward, that they have paid the stated Fee for a Degree, and have discharged all College Dues required by Law, except for the public Dinner on Commencement Day; also a Certificate from the Librarian, that they have returned in good Order or replaced all the Books they have borrowed from the Library.

A true Copy,

Attest. NATH. APPLETON, Senior Fellow of the Corporation of Harvard-College.

N. B. The Meeting of the Overseers is adjourned to the 14th of July, so that they who do not apply before that Time, cannot have their Names inserted in the general Diploma, nor be admitted to their Degrees this Year.

The first of June when the Boston Port Bill took Place, was observed by the Inhabitants of Hartford, in Connecticut, as a Day of Mourning; the Bells began to Toll early in the Morning, and continued 'till Evening; the Town-House was hung with black, and the Edict affixed thereto; the Shops were all shut, and their Windows covered with black & other Ensigns of Distress.

TO BE SOLD,

By Thomas Handasyd Peck,

At his Shop in Merchant's-Row, near the Golden Ball.

ALL Sorts of Linnen Linings suitable for Beaver, Beaveritt, Castor & Felt Hatts, black, blue and green Tabby Linings, Mohair Looping and Bands Silk ditto, Buttons and Loops newest Fashion, sundry Sorts of Chain and Shapes for Button Loops, Gold and Silver Buttons and Loops, white and yellow Triming for Childrens Hatts, white and yellow Bands & Buckles, Gold and Silver Chain, Brushes, Cards, Velures, Bowstrings, Luping-Needles, Nus skins, Camels Hair, Irons, Verdegreale, Copperas, Logwood, Beaver, Beaveritt, Castor and Felt Hatts, Childrens black turn-up Hatts, white ditto, also Strouds and Blankets suitable for the Indian Trade, Powder, Shot, and Russia Duck.

N. B. Cash given for Beaver, and all Sorts of Furs as usual.

S & S Salisbury

Acquaint their Friends, they have just Imported in the last Ships from LONDON and BRISTOL,

A fresh Assortment of

—*Hard Ware GOODS*—

N. B. They have an Assortment of Nails in the Town of Marblehead, which they would be glad to dispose of, to be delivered there.

TO BE SOLD,

ON THURSDAY NEXT,

By *BENJAMIN CHURCH*,

At FOUR o'Clock in the Afternoon,

A General Assortment of European Articles, Linnens, Woolens, Checks, &c. &c. Some House Furniture, an 8-Day Clock, Mehogany Case of Draws, Watches, &c. &c.—At Four o'Clock, P. M.—

For LONDON,

The Ship DARTMOUTH,

JOS. ROTCH, Commander,

Will Sail in 20 Days from Dartmouth. For Passage apply to

FRANCIS ROTCH,

At his Store in King-Street;

Where is to be had,

A few Boxes choice Spermæ Candles, a few Casks genuine Lisbon Wine, Barr Lead, and a Quantity of Brass Kettles.

To be sold upon reasonable Terms,

A HOUSE well situated, and well accommodated for a small Family, within 8 or 10 Miles of Boston. There is as much Land adjoining to the House as may be thought convenient. Enquire of Edes & Gill.

To be Sold for Want of Employ,

A Likely young Negro Man, who can shave and dress Hair, and is otherways well qualified for a Gentleman's Servant. Inquire of Edes & Gill.

New AUCTION-ROOM, Cornhill.

TO-MORROW at TEN o'Clock will be Sold by PUBLIC VENDUE, at GREENLEAF's Auction-Room,

—A great Variety of GOODS as usual—

Part of which taken by Execution,—consisting of—

Yard wide, 7-8, & 3-4 Irish Linnens,

Callicoes, fine Chints, strip'd and flower'd, Cotton and Linnens, stamp'd Linens, strip'd, flower'd and plain Lawns, flower'd Lawn and Muslin Aprons, a variety of Ribbons, plain Modes, Table Cloths, Kenting, Linnen and Lawn Handkerchiefs, Check, strip'd Hollands, Bed Ticks, Thread and Worsted Hose, Castor and Felt Hatts, Broad Cloths, Velverets, Shalloons, silver shoe and knee Buckles, stone ditto set in silver, silver Watches, a variety of Hard Ware, consisting of Pinchbeck and other Mettal shoe and knee buckles, Thimbles, brass Lenks, an assortment of Penknives, Cuttoes, Razors, Scissars, Table Knives and Forks, Gimblets, Rings, &c. &c. also a Parcel of choice INDIGO.

An elegant 8-Day Clock at private Sale.

WILLIAM GREENLEAF, Auctioneer.

The Sale will begin precisely at Ten o'Clock, and be continued in the Afternoon.

At GOULD's Auction-Office, In Back-Street,

On TUESDAY next,

At TEN in the Morning,

Will be Sold by PUBLIC VENDUE,

A Variety of House Furniture,

—Amongst which are—

Desks, Chest of Draws, leather bottom'd and common Chairs, Dining and Tea Tables, looking Glasses, Feather Beds, Bedsteads, Curtains, China and Stone Ware, Brass Kettles, Andirons, &c. &c. &c. Also, A Quantity of Wearing Apparel.

R. GOULD, Auctioneer.

Burials in the Town of BOSTON, since our last.
Ten Whites. ONo Blacks.
Baptiz'd in the several Churches, Five.

High Water at BOSTON, for the present Week.

Monday, 44 min. aft. 7	Friday, 30 min. after 11
Tuesday, 36 min. aft. 8	Saturday, 32 min. aft. 12
Wednesday, 30 m. aft. 9	Lord's-Day, 36 m. aft. 1
Thursday, 30 min. aft. 10	Full ◉ 23 D. 8 After.

ALL who deſire Admiſſion into HARVARD-COLLEGE this Year, are hereby Notified, That the Tutors have determined to attend the Buſineſs of Examination on Tueſday and Wedneſday, the 19th and 20th Days of July next.

J. WADSWORTH, per Order.

Harvard-College, June 15, 1774.

Halifax, Nova-Scotia, May 19, 1774.

TO BE SOLD at PUBLIC AUCTION,
On TUESDAY the Second Day of Auguſt next in the Town of Halifax, at the Houſe of Mr. *John Rider*,

A VALUABLE Tract of Land or Townſhip, commonly known by the Name of New-Jeruſalem, or Port-Roſaway, on the Southern Shore of the Province of Nova-Scotia, containing One Hundred Thouſand Acres of Land, granted by his Majeſty to ALEXANDER MACNUTT, Eſq; but lately the Property and Eſtate of BENJAMIN GERRISH, Eſq; deceaſed, and contain ſeveral fine Harbours for Veſſels or Ships of any Draught of Water and full of all Sorts of Fiſh, as Cod, Salmon, Mackrel, Herring, &c. &c. &c. extending about twelve Miles on the Sea Coaſt, well wooded and watered.

Conditions of Pay, viz. To pay 10 per cent. down in Caſh, and the Remainder on executing the Deed of Sale for the ſame, which ſhall be within one Month after the Sale.

Alſo, a Lot of Land, an old Houſe and Bake-Houſe on the Beach, with a large Baking Oven, late in the Occupation of Mr. RICHARD JACOBS.

Alſo, a Lot of Land walled in with Stone, containing five Acres of Land more or leſs, lying on the Road to RICHARD JACOBS Farm.

Alſo, one Half of the Meeting-Houſe Cellar.

Alſo, the late Dwelling-Houſe of BENJAMIN GERRISH, Eſq; deceaſed, with the front Yard and back Gardens and Out Houſes.

Alſo, a Wharf with four Stores thereon and a Coach-Houſe and Stable.

Alſo, a Tract of Land, containing ten Thouſand Acres, granted to BENJAMIN GERRISH, Eſq; deceaſed, ſituate on the North Side of the Baſon of Mines in the Province of Nova Scotia, comprehending the three Rivers commonly called and known by the Names of the Baſs Rivers abounding with Shad, Salmon, Baſs and other Kinds of Fiſh, and contains upwards of two Hundred Acres of Marſh Land, and was formerly a Settlement by the Accadeans. And alſo an Iſland called Mooſe-Iſland about one Mile diſtant, containing about one Hundred and Ninety Acres of rich Land. The aforeſaid Baſs Rivers are navigable for Veſſels of 50 or 60 Tons and good Harbours.

Alſo, ſixty one and half Acres of Dike Land in the Townſhip of Horton on the Grand Pree.

Alſo, a Farm in the Townſhip of Falmouth, now under good Improvement with a Dwelling-Houſe and Barn and other Out-Houſes, containing about Twelve Hundred and Fifty Acres of Land more or leſs, and all other Lands belonging to ſaid Eſtate of BENJAMIN GERRISH, Eſq;

N. B. In all the above Eſtates the Widow's Dower is to be excepted and treated for with her in Particulars for her Thirds during Life.

Conditions of Pay as aforeſaid.

MARTIN BICKER,

Has juſt received for Sale at his Auction-Room near the Conduit, Boſton, A very large and valuable Aſſortment of

ENGLISH GOODS,

which are the Property of a Gentleman leaving off the Buſineſs, therefore they will be ſold very low,——

Among which are

A very large Aſſortment of Iriſh Linnens, and Mancheſter Cotton Velvets,—Cotton Checks,—India and Engliſh Callicoes,—Sheeting Linnens,—Lawns,—Cambrick—Cotton—and Thread and Worſted Hoſe,—Handkerchiefs of all kinds,—Dowlaſs and Oznabrigs,—Bedticking,—German Serges,—black Sattins,—Engliſh black Taffity,—Breeches Pieces,—Pins,—ſome Hard-Ware,—Silver and Pinchbeck Watches, &c. &c. (t.f.)

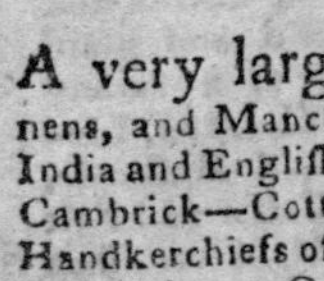

TO BE SOLD,

A Farm with a Dwelling Houſe, Barn & Shop thereon, lying in the Town of Braintree, North Precinct, ſituated on the Main Road to Plymouth, between the Meeting Houſe and Brackett's Tavern, conſiſting of nine Acres of arrable Land, well Watered, five Acres of Freſh Meadow, and three or four Acres of Salt Marſh.——Any Perſon inclining to purchaſe the ſame may apply to Mr. John Mills, living on the Premiſes.

UMBRILLOES.

Umbrilloes of all ſorts for Ladies & Gentlemen; made in the beſt Manner and to be ſold by JOHN CUTLER, at the *Golden Cock*, in Marlborough-Street, Boſton.——

ALSO,

Umbrillo Sticks to ſell uncovered, old Umbrilloes may be mended and covered at the ſame Place. All done at a low Rate.

All Perſons that have any Concerns with JONATHAN WILLIAMS, Junr. are deſired to apply to JONATHAN WILLIAMS, Senior, Eſq; who is impower'd to tranſact his Buſineſs during his abſence.

JOHN NOBLE,

(Poſt Rider from *Boſton* to *Portſmouth*)

INFORMS the Public, That he has remov'd from Mr. Hubbard's at the Sign of Admiral Vernon, to Deacon Jones's at the Royal Exchange Tavern, in King-Street.

N B. He arrives at Boſton on Saturday Evenings and ſits out for Portſmouth, early on Tueſday Mornings. Any Buſineſs and Packages delivered to him ſhall be executed with Care and Fidellity.

Province of the Maſſachuſetts-Bay, } *To the Hon.* James Otis, *Eſq;* *one of his Majeſty's Juſtices of the Peace through the ſaid Province.*

We the Subſcribers, Proprietors of a Tract of Land lying at *Broad-Bay*, in the County of *Lincoln*, in ſaid Province, and bounded as followeth, viz.—beginning at *Pemaquid-Falls* and ſo running a direct Courſe to the Head of *New-Harbour*, from thence to the South End of *Miſconcus-Iſland*, taking in the Iſland, ſo running five and twenty Miles into the Country North by Eaſt, and thence eight Miles North Weſt by Weſt, and thence turning and running South by Weſt to *Pemaquid*, where it firſt began——pray that your Honour would iſſue a Warrant to one of us to call a Meeting of the Proprietors of ſaid Land, to be on the third Day of *Auguſt* next, at Ten of the Clock in the Forenoon, at the Houſe of *William Goodhue*, Innholder in *Salem*; then and there to chuſe a Moderator of ſaid Meeting, a Clerk of ſaid Proprietors, a Committee to tranſact the Affairs of ſaid Proprietors as Occaſion may require, and any other needful Officers; to agree upon a Method for calling of Meetings for the future; to take under Conſideration the Diviſion that the Proprietors of ſaid Land made ſome Years ago and confirm the ſame, or order a new Diviſion and run the boundary Line; to ſettle with thoſe Perſons who have made Settlements of ſaid Land on reaſonable Terms, by ſelling them the Land or otherways, but in caſe they refuſe to ſettle as aforeſaid, to ſue them off and proſecute any Perſon or Perſons who ſhall treſpaſs on ſaid Land; to paſs any Orders that are neceſſary to bring forward the Settlement of ſaid Land, by giving away Land or otherways, and to raiſe Money on ſaid Land for neceſſary Charges and order the collecting the ſame.

Salem, June 15. 1774.

Daniel Sargent,
his
John + *Brown,*
Mark
John Choate,
Jona. Cogſwell, jun.
John Sargent.

Province of the Maſſachuſetts-Bay.

(Seal.) *To* John Choate *of* Ipſwich, *in the County of* Eſſex, *in ſaid Province, one of the principal Proprietors of the Land aforeſaid,* Greeting.

In purſuance of the foregoing Application and Requeſt, you are hereby required to give Notice, in Time and Manner as the Law directs, to the Proprietors afore-mentioned, that they meet at the Time and Place and for the Purpoſes mentioned in the afore-written Petition. Given under my Hand and Seal this 15th Day of June, Anno Domini, 1774.

JAMES OTIS, a Juſtice of the Peace through the Province of the Maſſachuſets-Bay.

Ipſwich, June 15, 1774.

By Virtue of the afore-written Warrant to me directed, I do hereby notify and warn the Proprietors of the aforeſaid Land to meet at the Dwelling Houſe of *William Goodhue*, Innholder at Salem, on the 3d Day of Auguſt next, at Ten of the Clock in the Forenoon, for the Purpoſes therein mentioned.

JOHN CHOATE.

To the Honorable JEREMIAH POWELL, Eſq; one of His Majeſty's Juſtices of the Peace throughout the Province of the *Maſſachuſetts-Bay*, humbly ſhew,

The Subſcribers, more than five of the Proprietors of a Tract of Land lying in the County of *York*, ſituate between the Rivers *Great-Oſſipee* and *Little-Oſſipee*, within the County aforeſaid, containing the Breadth of all that Space between the ſaid Rivers, and ſo running Southweſterly from *Saco* River, more than Twelve Miles, which ſame Tract was purchaſed of one Captain *Sunday*, an Indian Sagamore, by *Francis Small*, who lived on the ſame Land a long Time, and had a quiet Poſſeſſion thereof, and the ſaid Petitioners being now in the Poſſeſſion of the ſame, and being deſirous of being an acting Propriety, according to the Law in that Caſe made and provided; do requeſt your Worſhip to call a Meeting to be held at the Houſe of Mr. *Samuel March*, Innholder in *Scarborough*, in the County of *Cumberland*, on the firſt Monday of *Auguſt* next, at Ten of the Clock in the Forenoon, to act on the following Articles, to wit:

1ſt, To chooſe a Moderator.
2dly, To chooſe a Proprietors Clerk.
3dly, To chooſe a Committee to tranſact the prudential Affairs of ſaid Proprietors.
4thly, To chooſe Agents to proſecute and defend Suits in behalf of ſaid Proprietors.
5thly, To agree on any Method for raiſing Money or ſettling the ſame Land, as alſo to agree on any Method for calling future Meetings.

May 17th, 1774.

Samuel Small,
Samuel Small, jun.
Samuel March,
Joſhua Small,
Benjamin Small,
Nathaniel Milliken,
John Wright,
Nathan Chicke,
Joſeph Small,
James Small,
Benjamin Mead Lord.

Province of the Maſſachuſets-Bay.

L. S. To SAMUEL MARCH of *Scarborough*, in the County of *Cumberland*, in ſaid Province, Gentleman, one of ſaid Proprietors, Greeting.

In purſuance of the foregoing Application and Requeſt, you are hereby required to give Notice (in Time and Manner as the Law directs) to the ſaid Proprietors, that a Meeting of ſaid Proprietors is to be holden at the Time and Place, and for the Purpoſes mentioned in the afore-written Petition.

Given under my Hand and Seal, this 28th Day of *May*, A. D. 1774.

JERE. POWELL, Juſtice of the Peace throughout the Province aforeſaid.

May the 28th, 1774.

By Virtue of the afore-written Warrant to me directed, I do hereby notify and warn the Proprietors of the aforeſaid Lands, to meet at the Dwelling-Houſe of *Samuel March*, Innholder in *Scarborough* aforeſaid, on the firſt Monday of *Auguſt* next, at Ten of the Clock in the Forenoon, for the Purpoſes therein mentioned.

SAMUEL MARCH.

To be Sold by *William Jenniſon*, of Mendon, a valuable FARM, containing 100 Acres, conſiſting of Plowland, Mowing, Paſturing, Orcharding and Woodland; divided into fifteen ſeperate incloſures, Fenc'd chiefly with Stone Wall, together with two Dwelling Houſes on the Premiſes, one a large commodious Manſion Houſe 6 Rooms on a Floor, half a Mile from the Rev. Mr. *Froſt*'s Meeting Houſe, pleaſantly ſituated for a Gentleman or Trader, with a large new Barn, Potaſh Works, Shop for Goods, Warehouſe, Grainery and other out Buildings, 24 Miles from Providence and 34 from Boſton, is on the neareſt Road from Connecticut to Cambridge, Salem, &c. is now, and has been a number of Year's improv'd as a Tavern: Said Intereſt to be Sold for 1000l. only. Weſt-India Goods will be accepted for one half, the other half may lie a number of Years on good Security.

RAN-away from the Subſcriber on the Eighth of June Inſtant, at Night, a Negro Boy, about Seventeen Years of Age: Had on when he went off, a dark coloured cloth Jacket and Trowſers, and is branded on the Breaſt Delamote, very remarkable: ſaid Fellow ſpeaks tolerable good Engliſh, and ſome French. Whoever takes up ſaid Fellow and Secures him in any of his Majeſty's Goals, or Returns him to the Subſcriber, ſhall have FIVE DOLLARS Reward, and all neceſſary Charges paid by

ALLIN BROWN.

Providence, June 10, 1774.

The Proprietors of the Townſhip granted to *Samuel Livermore*, Eſq; and others, are hereby Notified, that their Meeting ſtands adjourned to Wedneſday the 29th Inſtant, to the Houſe of Iſaac Gleaſon, Innholder in Waltham, at Ten o'Clock, A.M.

per LEONARD WILLIAMS, Prop'rs Clerk.

Waltham, June 10, 1774.

Joſhua Warner

HEREBY begs Leave to inform the Public, That whereas Capt. John Phelps of Stafford, has for a Number of Years paſt refuſed to take in Boarders who uſed to reſort there, for the Uſe and Benefit of the Mineral Spring or Pool in ſaid Town, that he is now in the poſſeſſion of a Houſe with good Accommodations, and will Entertain thoſe Gentlemen and Ladies that have Occaſion to Reſort there in the beſt Manner he is capable of.

Wanted to Purchaſe,

An Eſtate in this Province, Rhode-Iſland, or Connecticut Provinces, in ſome good Situation, either clear'd or woody. Any Perſon having ſuch to diſpoſe of, and leaving a Line within 7 Days from this Date, directed for John Thompſon, to the Care of the Printer, mentioning the Situation, will be treated with.

Lemuel Pattingall of Norwich, in Connecticut, Brick Layer and Maſon, wants to Hire Two or Three Workmen at that Buſineſs, during the Seaſon. Norwich, 20th May, 1774.

WHEREAS the Proprietors of a Townſhip called Sudbury, lying on both Sides Otter Creek, granted by the Governor and Council of New-Hampſhire, on the 6th Day of Auguſt, A. D. 1763, to Capt. Silas Brown and others, at their legal Meeting on the 8th Day of March laſt, granted a Tax of Twenty Shillings lawful Money on each Right in ſaid Townſhip, towards defreying the Charges of the Propriety, which has been publiſhed agreeable to Law, and the Payment thereof requeſted; notwithſtanding ſeveral of ſaid Proprietors are delinquent in the Payment of ſaid Tax, and in their former Taxes.—PUBLIC NOTICE is therefore hereby given to ſuch delinquent Proprietors, that unleſs they pay their Taxes to Thomas Miller of Newton, in the County of Middleſex, and Province of Maſſachuſetts-Innholder, and Collector of ſaid Taxes, by One o'Clock in the Afternoon of the 5th Day of July next, their Rights will be ſold (as the Law directs) for the Payment of their Taxes and incidental Charges. The Sale to begin at Two o'Clock in ſaid Afternoon (and continued by adjournment, if need be) at the Dwelling-Houſe of ſaid Thomas Miller; to which Time and Place, the ſaid Proprietors Meeting ſtands adjourned.

May 18, 1774.

Joſhua Fuller,
Thomas Miller,
Nathl. Sparhawk, } Proprietors Committee.

WHEREAS *publick Notice has been given to the Proprietors of a Townſhip lying on both Sides* Amaraſcoggin-*River, in the County of* Cumberland, *in the late Province of* Main, *granted by the Great and General Court on the 11th Day of* June, *A. D.* 1771. *to* David Phips, *Eſq; and others, of the Taxes that have been aſſeſſed on the Rights of ſaid Proprietors; ſeveral of which are delinquent in the Payment of ſaid Taxes:*

Said Delinquents are therefore hereby Notified that unleſs ſaid Taxes are paid to *Seth Haſtings*, of *Cambridge*, or to *Samuel Harrington*, of *Waltham*, Collectors of Taxes for ſaid Proprietors, by 7 o'Clock in the Morning of the 29th Day of *June* next, their Rights will be ſold (as the Law directs) for the Payment of their Taxes and incidental Charges. The Sale to begin at 8 o'Clock on ſaid Morning, at the Dwelling-Houſe of Capt. *Jonathan Brewer*, Innholder in *Waltham*, and continued by Adjournment, (if need be) till the whole be ſold: To which Time and Place ſaid Proprietors Meeting ſtands adjourned.

May 29, 1774.

Braddyl Smith,
Alex Shepard,
Nathaniel Bridge. } Committee for Sale.

Boſton: Printed, by EDES & GILL, *in Queen-Street,* 1774.

SUPPLEMENT to the *Boston-Gazette*, &c. of *June 20, 1774.*

ALL Persons that have any Concerns with JONATHAN WILLIAMS, Junr. are desired to apply to JONATHAN WILLIAMS, Senr. Esq; who is impowered to transact his Business during his Absence.

Messieurs EDES and GILL,

AS some of my worthy friends have thought (not a little to my disadvantage) that I was a Signer to the address to the late governor Mr. Hutchinson, I beg leave thro' the channel of your paper, to acquaint them, that it is a mistake, and easily to be accounted for, when the resentment is allowed for which the reading of this list raises in the breast of every friend to the community, together with the near sound, Nathaniel Greenwood bears with that of Nathaniel Greenough; but his friends may be assured he never saw the address, till it was in the paper of 30th instant, and consequently never signed it. The said

NATHANIEL GREENOUGH

Has imported in the several Vessels arrived here this spring a large Assortment of English Goods, suited to the season, among his goods are CHINA WARE, SPICES, and a grand assortment of HOSIERY. Mens Silk Hose, Plain White Ribb'd and Random, Men's Women's and Children's Thread and Cotton ditto. Men's and Women's Black and White Silk Gloves, Women's and Children's Black, White and Colour'd Silk Mitts, &c. &c. &c. The smallest favour of those who will please to favour him with their Custom shall be esteemed and regarded by him.

William Turner

Lately arrived from LONDON,

Begs Leave to acquaint the Gentlemen and Ladies of the Town and Country, that he continues to teach the polite Art of Dancing and Fencing in the newest and most approved Method, at Concert-Hall:——Those Gentlemen and Ladies who propose sending their Children to be instructed may depend the best Care will be taken as to their Behaviour.

N. B. Cotillons taught as they are performed at all polite Balls and Assemblies in England.

——Figure Dances likewise.

Mr. Turner will attend two Days in the Week at any House from 6 o'Clock in the Morning till 6 o'Clock in the Evening on grown Gentlemen and Ladies, and assures the utmost Secrecy shall be kept till they are capable of exhibiting in high Taste.

TO BE SOLD CHEAP,

A choice Lot of Land in the Town of Granvile, consisting of Forty-three Acres, near the Centre of the Town, there are 200 Families settled in said Town.——For further intelligence inquire of the Printers.

ALL Persons indebted to the Estate of Richard Surcomb, late of Boston, Baker, deceased, are once more requested to make immediate Payment to Mary Surcomb, Executrix, as they would avoid being sued at July Co'rt.

TO BE LETT,

A handsome House with an excellent Garden well stocked with Vegetables, in a delightful Situation, within two Miles of Boston, fit for a small or large genteel Family, on the most reasonable Terms, may be entered on immediately, enquire of Edes & Gill.

WANTED,

A sober, faithful honest Man, that understands taking Care of a Tavern; one of this Character that can be well recommended, by inquiring of the Printers will be inform'd of the Place, where he will have good Wages.

A Wet Nurse with a good Breast of Milk would take a Child to Suckle.

Inquire of the Printers.

WANTS EMPLOYMENT,

A young Man who is capable of tending a Gentleman's Family, taking care of Horses and driving a Chariot; can be well recommended.

Inquire of the Printers.

ON the third Night of this Instant, was committed to Goal by the North Watch, a Man who says his Name is Richard Peters, having a Bag, the Contents of which is as follows, viz.——Sundry C. Cloths——one old white Shirt——two Pair Hose——some Mettle Buttons——one small Bag of Coppers——one large Jack Knife new——one Pair of Sizars——which Articles were suppos'd to have been Stolen; they may be seen at Mr. Otis's, Goal-Keeper.

JUST IMPORTED from LONDON
And to be Sold by

John Gore & Son,

At the PAINTER's ARMS, in Queen-Street,

A large and compleat Assortment of

Painters Oils, Colours, Brushes and Tools, of all Sizes;

Likewise, Gum Copal, Anamæ, Sandarack, Shell Lack, Seed Lack, Arabic and Amber, half Length, Kitt Katt and three Quarter Cloths, brown and white Varnish and Lacker; also Martin's best Copal Oil Varnish, which will enable them to finish Coach and Chaise Bodies as high as any ever imported from London.

Frederick William Geyer

Acquaints his Friends and others, that he has removed from the Corner of Wings-Lane to the Store lately improved by Mr. Ward Nicholas Boylston, the door below Messi'rs Bethune and Prince, in King-street,
BOSTON:

Where he continues selling English, India and Scotch Piece Goods, by Wholesale only, on the lowest Terms, for Cash or short Credit.

TO BE LETT,

A House with 3 Acres of Land, within 4 Miles of Boston, upon the Cambridge Road, conveniently situated for a Gentleman's Seat. Inquire of *Eliphalet Downer* of Brookline.

N. B. The House will be Let with or without the Land.

WE the Subscribers being appointed by the Hon. Foster Hutchinson, Esq; Judge of Probate for the County of Suffolk, Commissioners to receive and examine the Claims of the several Creditors to the Estate of SAMUEL SNOW, late of Boston, Mariner, deceas'd, intestate, represented Insolvent, Do hereby give Notice, that we shall attend said Service, at the British Coffee House, on the second Tuesday of this and the Five following Months, from Six 'till Nine o'Clock of the Evening of said Days.
JOB PRINCE,
Boston, June 11, 1774.   JOHN CARNES.

Waltham, June 6, 1774.

RAN-away from the Subscriber, a Servant Boy, named Silence Robinson, between 17 and 18 Years old, large of his Age. Any Person who will secure said Servant, so that his Master may have him again, shall have Five Shillings, O. T. Reward for their Trouble, paid by JOSEPH WELLINGTON.

All Masters of Vessels and others, are hereby cautioned against Concealing or Harbouring said Servant, as they will avoid the Penalty of the Law.

RAN-away from the Subscriber, living in Gorham, which joins Falmouth, Cumberland County, in the Massachusetts Province, a short Negro Man nomed Prince, about 26 Years of Age, 5 Feet some Inches high, talks broken English, has remarkable small Ears and a Jewel Hole in one of them. Had on almost a new Felt Hat, a reddish grey home made Cloth Coat Jacket and Breeches, with silk knee Garters, a dark Callico under Jacket, a white Linnen Shirt, red Collar and Cuffs to his Coat with Metal Buttons, white Cotton Stocking, Calf-skin Pumps. It may be he has a Pass. Said Negro plays tolerable well on a Violin. Whoever will take up said Negro, or bring him to his Master shall have Sixteen Dollars Reward, and all Charges paid, by
WILLIAM M'LENNEN.

N. B. Said Negro having done some Damage at the House where the Negroes met to hold their Frolick on Election Day, did not return to his Master again.

All Masters of Vessels are forewarned not to carry him off at their Peril.

May 26, 1774.

Ten Dollars Reward.

RAN AWAY from the Subscriber, Joseph Moors, of Groton, in the County of Middlesex, and Province of Massachusetts-Bay, a Mulatto Man Servant, named TITUS, about 20 Years of Age, of a midling Stature, wears short curl'd Hair, has one of his Fore-Teeth broke out, took with him a blue Surtus, a Snuff-coloured Coat, and a Pair of white wash'd Leather Breeches, a Pair of new Cow-Hide Pumps and a Fur'd Hat with large Brims, and sundry other Articles of Wearing Apparel.——Whoever will take up said Servant and confine him in any of his Majesty's Goals, so that the Owner may have him again, shall have TEN DOLLARS Reward and all necessary Charges paid, by
JOSEPH MOORS.

☞ All Masters of Vessels and others, are hereby Caution'd against Harbouring, Concealing, or carrying off said Servant, as they would thereby avoid the Penalty of the Law.

William Bant

Has Imported in the last Vessels from LONDON, a General Assortment of Spring and Summer Goods, which he will sell by Wholesale and Retail at his Store fronting Dock Square, at the very lowest Rates for Cash.
Boston April 21st. (6 w.)

TO BE LETT

A large commodious Shop, pleasantly situated in Cornhill, directly opposite John Semple's, and at the same place may be had genteel Boarding and Lodging for Gentlemen and Ladies, by MARY TAILER.

Mill-Saws.

A Number of fine English Steel-Plate Mill-Saws, suitable for the Eastward Use, superior to any ever in America before, and made on an entire new Model, Is just open'd, and to be Sold by

Charles Sigourney,

At his Shop at the Head of Dock-Square Market, BOSTON. ALSO,
Guns, Swords, Trooping-Pistols, Fuzees, with Spring Pipes, Steel Rods and Bayonets, Gun Locks, spare Gun-Barrels. ALSO,
2d, 3d, 4d, 6d, 8d, 10d, 20d & 24d. Nails, sheathing, drawing and deck nails, tacks and brads of all sorts, glass, lead, powder, shot, steel, French and English flints, English glue, pewter dishes, plates, basons, porringers, tankards, canns, spoons, brass kettles, skillets, warming pans, skimmers, copper and iron tea-kettles, knives and forks of all sorts, penknives, scissars, razors, cutloes, and every other article in the Hard-Ware Branch, that is imported into this Place. ALSO,
TIN-Plates, Lanthorn-Leaves, Alum, Copperas, Brimstone, English double refin'd Leaf Sugar, &c.
PAINTER's OYL and COLOURS.
Just arrived——An Assortment of Painters Oyl and Colours, and will be sold at the lowest Rates. ALSO,
An Invoice of Colours, consisting of Red Lead, Spanish Brown, White Lead, Spanish White, and a few Casks of Oyl, very cheap, being a Consignment.

To be Sold on TUESDAY the Twenty-first Day of June next, at Two o'Clock in the Afternoon, be PUBLIC VENDUE, at the House of Mr. Edward Low in Leominster, by Philip Sweetser, of said Leominster,

A Good Farm situated in said Town, containing about 140 Acres of choice Land, consisting of Plowing, Pasturing and Mowing, with a fine young Orchard, and is well Wooded and excellently Watered, upon a great Road, suitable for a Tavern or Trader, with a good House, Barn, and other valuable Accommodations, which renders it a very desirable Farm. It will be sold at a reasonable Price; and if it should be sold at private Sale before the Day above-mentioned, publick Notice shall be given. May 5, 1774.

WATCHES,

Plain, Skeleton and Horizontal in Gold, Silver and Pinchbeck Case—in particular a great Variety of Silver Watches from Ten Dollars to Ten Guineas—some of which shew the Day of the Month, and others with Seconds, are very suitable for Physicians—Likewise Spring and Pendulum Eight Day Clocks, also an Assortment of Tools and Materials used by Clock and Watch Makers—To be sold by DAVID MITCHELSON, at the House of Mr. Benjamin Davis, Merchant, near the Mill Bridge.

N. B. The above Articles are of the best Kinds, newly Imported, from the Makers, and will be sold at the most reasonable Prices for Cash only.

UMBRELLAS

of all Sizes and Prices, made in the neatest Manner with Ivory and Bone Handles to screw, also more common Mahogany or Maple Handled ditto, Ladies that would buy Cheap and good, call at ISAAC GREENWOOD, Ivory Turner's Shop, next Shop to Dr. CLARKS, North-End, Boston; where you may have your old Umbrella sticks mended and covered, your Ivory and bone stick Fans mended, Gentlemen may have India Canes, neat Ivory and Bone, headed, Hickery Stick, Ivory or Bone, handled, Chaise Whips, Hidrometers for proving Spirits, German Flutes, ditto Tiped with Ivory Fife, Billiard Balls, and many other Articles. Such Gentlemen as are Building may have their Banisters and Posts, Pillers for Fronticepieces and Porticoes, Bails and Flower Pots, or any other Ornaments, turned or twisted in the neatest Manner with Fidelity and Dispatch at the above Shop, all Favours from those that have and shall Imploy duly acknowledged, by their humble Servant,
ISAAC GREENWOOD.

TO BE SOLD.

A genteel new Fall-back Chaise, with Harness compleat. Inquire of Edes & Gill.

Imported in the last ships from LONDON & GLASGOW,

By Samuel Parkman,

And are now selling at his Shop in Union-Street,
A compleat Assortment of English, India and Scotch GOODS, among which are a Variety of stript, plain and changeable Lutestrings and Mantua's, Sarsnet, Sattins and Modes, plain, spotted, stript and flower'd Gauze, Gauze Aprons & Handkerchiefs, Lawn Aprons and Handkerchiefs, Callicoes and Patches, Bengalls, Brolio, Messinets, &c. A large Assortment of Hosiery, Corderoys, black and white Cotton Denim, brown Thread Breeches Pieces, Nankeen, Taffities & Persians, a great Variety of black & white Bone Blond & Ticlly Lace and Edgings, and many other Articles.

※ He asks the Favour of those who have Money to lay out to call and see him, that he may have an Opportunity to prove to them that his Goods are really very cheap.

Andrew Newell,

Mathematical Instrument Maker,
At his Shop, next Door below the Sign of the Globe, in King-Street, has just imported and ready for Sale,
All sorts of Mathematical Instruments in every Branch.——ALSO, STATIONARY of every kind; and continues to make, mend and repair all sorts of Instruments in the Mathematical Branches; Spy Glasses, &c. &c.

N. B. The present prospect of Affairs in the Town induces him to sell cheap for Cash only.

WATCHES.

RICHARD CRANCH,

Near the Mill Bridge, BOSTON,

INforms his Customers, that he has received a fresh Assortment of Watches (some of them with Day of Month) which he will sell at his usual Prices.

TO be Sold by Virtue of an Order of the Inferior Court of Common Pleas for the County of Suffolk,—A Brick Dwelling-House and Land, situate in Queen-Street in Boston; now improved by Mr. Henry Bass. Also, six Lots of Land at Penobscot, in the County of Lincoln; all late belonging to the Estate of Mr. John Proctor, late of said Boston, School-Master, deceased.—For further Particulars, inquire of Eunice Proctor, of said Boston, Widow and Administratrix of the said Deceased's Estate, at her Dwelling House on Copp's Hill, who is fully authorised and impowered by the said Court to sell the same. May 26. (5 w.)

Smith & Atkinson

ACQUAINT their Customers and others, in Town and Country, they have IMPORTED in sundry Vessels lately arrived from LONDON,

A Compleat and General Assortment of SPRING GOODS, which will be Sold (by WHOLESALE only) on such Terms as must appear reasonable to every Judge of the different Articles.

N. B. A few Barrels of choice Connecticut Pork, Pig and Bar Iron of the best Quality, with POTASH KETTLES cast from the best Mountain Ore. (tberf)

WE the Subscribers being appointed by the honourable Foster Hutchinson, Esq; Judge of Probates for the County of Suffolk, Commissioners to receive and examine the Claims of the several Creditors to the Estate of JACOB ROYALL, late of Boston, Esq; deceased, intestate, represented insolvent, do hereby give Notice, that we shall attend said service at the British Coffee House, on the last Tuesday of this and the five following Months, from Six to Nine o'Clock of the Evening of said Days.
SAMUEL DOWNE,
JACOB COOPER.
Boston, May 27, 1774.

RAN away from his Master on Friday Evening last, a Negro Boy, named GOREE, about 16 Years of Age, 5 Feet, 3 Inches High, had on when he went away, a brown Cloth Coat, dark Velvet Waistcoat, white Shirt, white Linen Breeches, grey Yarn Stockings, a pair of Shoes toe at the Heels, with Pinchbeck Buckies, an old Felt Hat. Whoever will take up said Runaway, and secure him, and give information to the subscriber, so that he may have him again, shall have a handsome Reward and necessary Charges paid by
DANIEL VOSE.

All Masters of Vessels and others, are hereby cautioned against harbouring, concealing, or carrying off the above Negro, as they would avoid the Penalty of the Law. Milton, May 30. 1774.

Boston: Printed by EDES & GILL.

No. 1002.

THE Boſton-Gazette, AND COUNTRY JOURNAL.

Containing the freſheſt Advices, Foreign and Domeſtic.

MONDAY, June 27, 1774.

FROM THE BATH CHRONICLE, OF APRIL 28.

Col. BARRE's SPEECH on Lord North's motion for leave to bring in a bill, empowering a Governor of North America to ſend any Officer, who ſhall commit murder in the Province, to another Colony, or to England, to be tried.

Mr. SPEAKER,

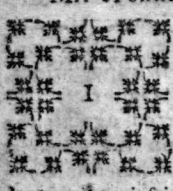

I RISE with great unwillingneſs, to oppoſe this meaſure in its very infancy, before its features are well formed, or to claim that attention which this Houſe ſeems to beſtow with ſo much reluctance on any arguments in behalf of America. But I muſt call you to witneſs, that I have hitherto been ſilent, or acquieſcing to an unexpected degree of moderation. While your proceedings, ſevere as they were, had the leaſt colour of foundation in juſtice, I deſiſted from oppoſing them; nay more—though your bill for ſtopping up the port of Boſton contained in it many things moſt cruel, unwarrantable, and unjuſt, yet as they were couched under thoſe general principles of juſtice, retribution for injury, and compenſation for loſs ſuſtained, I not only deſiſted from oppoſing but aſſented to its paſſing. The bill was a bad way of doing what was right; but ſtill it was doing what was right. I would not therefore by oppoſing it ſeem to countenance thoſe violences which had been committed abroad; and of which no man diſapproves more than I do.

Upon the preſent queſtion I am totally unprepared. The motion itſelf bears no ſort of reſemblance to what was formerly announced. The noble Lord and his friends have had every advantage of preparation. They have reconnoitred the field, and choſen their ground. To attack them in theſe circumſtances may, perhaps, ſavour more of the gallantry of a ſoldier, than of the wiſdom of the Senator.

But, Sir, the propoſition is ſo glaring; ſo unprecedented in any former proceedings of Parliament; ſo unwarranted by any delay, denial, or perverſion of juſtice in America; ſo big with miſery and oppreſſion to that country, and with danger to this—that the firſt bluſh of it is ſufficient to alarm and rouze me to oppoſition.

It is propoſed to ſtigmatize a whole people as perſecutors of innocence, and men incapable of doing juſtice; yet you have not a ſingle fact on which to ground that imputation. I expected the noble Lord would have ſupported this motion by producing inſtances of the Officers of Government in America having been proſecuted with unremiting vengeance, and brought to cruel and diſhonorable deaths by the violence and injuſtice of American juries. But he has not produced one ſuch inſtance; and I will tell you more, Sir,—he cannot produce one. The inſtances which have happened are directly in the teeth of his propoſition. Capt. Preſton and the ſoldiers, who ſhed the blood of the people, were fairly tried, and fully acquitted. It was an American Jury, a New-England Jury, a Boſton Jury, which tried and acquitted them. Captain Preſton has, under his hand, publickly declared, that the inhabitants of the very town, in which their fellow citizens had been ſacrificed, were his advocates and defenders. Is this the return you make them? Is this the encouragement you give them to perſevere in ſo laudable a ſpirit of juſtice and moderation? When a Commiſſioner of the Cuſtoms, aided by a number of ruffians, aſſaulted the celebrated Mr. Otis in the midſt of the town of Boſton, and with the moſt barbarous violence almoſt murdered him, did the mob, which is ſaid to rule that town, take vengeance on the perpetrators of this inhuman outrage againſt a perſon who is ſuppoſed to be their Demagogue? No, Sir, the law tried them; the law gave heavy damages againſt them; which the irreparably injured Mr. Otis moſt generouſly forgave upon an acknowledgement of the offence. Can you expect any more ſuch inſtances of magnanimity, under the principle of the bill now propoſed?

But the noble Lord ſays, "We muſt now ſhew the Americans that we will no longer ſit quiet under their inſults." Sir, I am ſorry to ſay that this is declamation, unbecoming the character and place of him who utters it. In what moment have you been quiet? Has not your government for many years paſt been a ſeries of irritating and offenſive meaſures, without policy, principle, or moderation? Have not your troops and your ſhips made a vain and inſulting parade in their ſtreets and in their harbours? It has ſeemed to be your ſtudy to irritate and inflame them. You have ſtimulated diſcontent into diſaffection, and you are now goading that diſaffection into rebellion. Can you expect to be well inform'd when you liſten only to partizans? Can you expect to do juſtice when you will not hear the accuſed?

Let us conſider, Sir, the precedents which are offered to warrant this proceeding.—The ſuſpenſion of the Habeas Corpus Act in 1745—the making Smugglers triable in Middleſex, and the Scotch rebels in England. Sir, the firſt was done upon the moſt preſſing neceſſity *flagrante Bello*, with a dangerous rebellion in the very heart of the kingdom. The ſecond you well know, was warranted by the moſt evident facts: Armed bodies of ſmugglers marched publickly without preſentment or moleſtation from the people of the county of Suſſex; who, even to their Magiſtrates, were notoriouſly connected with them. They murdered the officers of Revenue, engaged your troops, and openly violated the laws. Experience convinced you, that the Juries of that, and of the counties ſimilarly circumſtanced, would never find ſuch criminals guilty; and upon the conviction of this neceſſity you paſſed the act. The ſame neceſſity juſtified the trying of Scotch rebels in England. Rebellion had reared its dangerous ſtandard in Scotland, and the principles of it had ſo univerſally tainted that people, that it was manifeſtly in vain to expect juſtice from them againſt their countrymen.—But in America not a ſingle act of rebellion has been committed. Let the Crown Law Officers, who ſit by the noble Lord, declare, if they can, that there is upon your table a ſingle evidence of treaſon or rebellion in America. They know, Sir, there is not one, & yet we are proceeding as if there were a thouſand.

Having thus proved, Sir, that the propoſed bill is without precedent to ſupport, and without facts to warrant it; let us now view the conſequences it is likely to produce. A ſoldier feels himſelf ſo much above the reſt of mankind, that the ſtrict hand of the civil power is neceſſary to controul the haughtineſs of diſpoſition which ſuch ſuperiority inſpires. You know, Sir, what conſtant care is taken in this country to remind the military that they are under the reſtraint of the Civil Power. In America their ſuperiority is felt ſtill greater. Remove the check of the law, as this bill intends, and what inſolence and outrage may you not expect? Every paſſion that is pernicious to ſociety will be let looſe upon a people unaccuſtomed to licentiouſneſs and intemperance. On the one hand will be a people who have been long complaining of oppreſſion, and ſee in the ſoldiery, thoſe who are to enforce it upon them; on the other hand, an army ſtudiouſly prepoſſeſſed with the idea of that people being rebellious, unawed by the apprehenſion of civil controul, and actuated by that ſpirit which prevails ever among the beſt of troops. In this ſituation, the prudent officer will find it impoſſible to reſtrain his ſoldiers, or prevent that provocation which will rouſe the tameſt people to reſiſtance. The inevitable conſequence will be, that you will produce the rebellion you pretend to obviate.

I have been bred a ſoldier, have ſerved long. I reſpect the profeſſion, and live in the ſtricteſt habits of friendſhip with a great many officers; but there is not a country gentleman of you all, who looks upon the army with a more jealous eye, or would more ſtrenuouſly reſiſt the ſetting them above the controul of the Civil Power. No man is to be truſted in ſuch a ſituation. It is not the fault of the ſoldier, but the vice of human nature, which, unbridled by law, becomes inſolent and licentious, wantonly violates the peace of ſociety, and tramples upon the rights of human kind.

With reſpect to thoſe gentlemen who are deſtined to this ſervice, they are much to be pitied. It is a ſervice which an officer of feeling and of worth muſt enter upon with infinite reluctance; a ſervice, in which his only merit muſt be, to *bear much, and do little*. With the melancholy proſpect before him of commencing a civil war, and embruing his hands in the blood of his fellow ſubjects; his feelings, his honour, his life are hazarded, without a poſſibility of any equivalent or compenſation. You may perhaps think a law, founded upon this motion, will be his protection. I am miſtaken if it will. Who is to execute it? He muſt be a bold man indeed who makes the attempt. If the people are ſo exaſperated, that it is unſafe to bring the man who has injured them to trial, let the Governor who withdraws him from juſtice look to himſelf. The people will not endure it; they would no longer deſerve the reputation of being deſcended from the loins of Engliſhmen, if they did endure it.

When I ſtand up as an advocate for America, I feel myſelf the firmeſt friend of this country. We ſtand upon the commerce of America. Alienate your Colonies, and you will ſubvert the foundation of your riches and your ſtrength. Let the banners of rebellion be once ſpread in America, and you are an undone people. You are urging this deſperate, this deſtructive iſſue. You are urging it with ſuch violence, and by meaſures tending ſo manifeſtly to that fatal point, that, but that a ſtate of madneſs only could inſpire ſuch an intention, it would appear to be your deliberate purpoſe. In aſſenting to your late bill, I reſiſted the violence of America, at the hazard of my popularity there. I now reſiſt your phrenzy at the ſame riſque here. You have changed your ground. You are becoming the aggreſſors, and offering the laſt of human outrages to the people of America, by ſubjecting them, in effect, to military execution. I know the vaſt ſuperiority of your diſciplined troops over the provincial; but beware how you ſupply the want of diſcipline by deſperation. Inſtead of ſending them the olive branch you have ſent the naked ſword. By the olive branch, I mean a repeal of all the late laws, fruitleſs to you, and oppreſſive to them.

Aſk their aid in a conſtitutional manner, and they will give it to the utmoſt of their ability. They never yet refuſed it, when properly required. Your journals bear the recorded acknowledgments of the zeal with which they have contributed to the general neceſſities of the ſtate. What madneſs is it that prompts you to attempt obtaining that by force which you may more certainly procure by requiſition? They may be flattered into any thing, but they are too much like your ſelves to be driven. Have ſome indulgence for your own likeneſs; reſpect their ſturdy Engliſh virtue; retract your odious exertions of authority, and remember—that the firſt ſtep towards making them contribute to your wants, is to reconcile them to your government.

PHILADELPHIA, June 1. 1774.

LETTER II.

To the INHABITANTS *of the* Britiſh Colonies *in* AMERICA.

BRETHREN,

IT is not my Deſign to travel through all the miniſterial Manœuvres reſpecting us, ſince the Commencement of this Reign. It is not neceſſary. Sufficient, I truſt, it will prove, to lay before you ſuch a Series of correſpondent facts, as will thoroughly convince you,---that a Plan has been deliberately framed, and pertinaciouſly adhered to, unchanged even by frequent Changes of Miniſters, unchecked by any intervening Gleam of Humanity, to ſacrifice to a Paſſion for arbitrary Dominion, the univerſal Property, Liberty, Safety, Honour, Happineſs and Proſperity of us, unoffending yet devoted Americans---And that every Man of us is deeply intereſted in the Fate of our Brethren of *Boſton*.

If ſuch a Series is not laid before you, the combined Force of which ſhall tear up by the Roots, and throw out of your Boſoms, every lurking Doubt, cenſure me as an Enthuſiaſt, too violently warmed by a Senſe of the Injuſtice practiſed againſt my beloved Country.

The Danger of a Father's Life, once racked Words from a dumb Son. Worſe than Death, in my View, threatens our common Mother. Pardon, therefore, a Brother's Imperfections.

Amidſt a Volume of Inſtitutions, called Regulations---wrong at firſt---corrected into other Errors---again corrected---ſtill requiring Regulation---and remaining, after all their Editions, if not like *Draco*'s Codes of Blood, yet Codes of Plunder---confounding by the Intricacy and Multiplicity of their Inventions---and confiſcating for having confounded*----appears the Fourth of *George* the Third, Chap. 15th, ſtiled "An Act for granting certain Duties in the Britiſh Colonies and Plantations in *America*, &c." This was the firſt Comet of the Kind that glared over theſe Colonies ſince their Exiſtence. Here firſt we find the Commons of *Great-Britain*, "giving and granting" our Money, *for the expreſs Purpoſe* of "raiſing a Revenue in *America*."

We, buſy in guiding our Ploughs, felling our Timber, or ſailing in the Circuits of Traffic preſcribed us, and ſtill veering like Bees to their Hive, with Millions of our Gains to *Great-Britain*, the Center of our Toils by Land and Sea, poor harmleſs Huſbandmen and Traders! ſcarce obſerved the Blow given us. Our Hearts filled with Confidence by contemplating the pleaſing Images of her generous diſtinguiſhed Virtues, from the Splendor of which, in our Judgment, thoſe of ancient *Greece* and *Rome* hid their diminiſhed Heads---Suſpicion could find no Entrance. We ſaw, in the Preamble, ſomething of the uſual Forms "for extending and "ſecuring Navigation and Commerce,"---were lulled into Security, nor could ſuppoſe the Stroke was aimed at our Vitals. An Infant, that had tottered along a directed Walk in a Garden, and loaded with Flowers had preſented them to a Mother, would as ſoon have expected to be knocked down by her.---

Not long were we ſuffered to enjoy our Tranquility. The 5th of *George* the Third, Chap. the 12th, the ever memorable Stamp-Act, quickly followed. By this, reciting the former Act, the Commons of *Great-Britain* "gave and granted" Duties, ſo called, of our Money on almoſt every Piece of Parchment, Vellum or Paper to be uſed in theſe Colonies, and declared every Inſtrument of Writing without a Stamp to be void. Tax-gatherers of a new Kind were appointed to collect theſe Duties. The Petitions of our Aſſemblies, previous to its paſſing, on Notice received of the Deſign, aſſerting our Rights, and ſupplicating a Reſpect for them, were treated with Contempt. You remember the Time and its Diſtreſs. You behaved as you ought.† Convinced that a People, who *wiſh* to be free, muſt *reſolve* to be free, you aboliſhed the "abominable Thing"----and proceeded in your uſual Buſineſs, without any Regard to the illegal Edict obtruded upon you.

Permit me to add two Obſervations, relating to remarkable Attendants on the Taxation comprized in that Act, the Memory of which is perhaps grown faint, from Length of Time, in ſome Minds.

By the Statutes granting Stamp-duties in *England* or *Great-Britain*, eſpecial Caution has been taken, that nothing more ſhould be levied upon the Subject, under any Pretence whatſoever, than the Duties themſelves. Theſe Words run through thoſe Acts---"That the Officers ſhall receive the ſeveral Duties---and "ſtamp and mark the Vellum, Parchment and Paper, &c. *with-"out any other Fee or Reward*---which Stamp or Mark ſhall be "a ſufficient Diſcharge for the reſpective Duties, &c." And "the Commiſſioners ſhall take Care, that the ſeveral Parts of the "Kingdom ſhall, from Time to Time, be ſufficiently furniſhed "with Vellum, Parchment and Paper, ſtamped and marked as is "directed, TO THE END, that the Subjects, &c. MAY HAVE

* "*Omitting the immenſe Increaſe of People by natural Population, in the more northern Colonies, and the Migration from every Part of* Europe, *I am convinced the whole commercial Syſtem of* America *may be altered to Advantage. You have prohibited where you ought to have encouraged; and you have encouraged, where you ought to have prohibited. Improper Reſtraints have been laid on the Continent in Favour of the Iſlands. You have but two Nations to trade with in* America. *Would you had twenty! Let acts of Parliament in Conſequence of Treaties remain, but let not an* Engliſh Miniſter *become* a Cuſtom-Houſe Officer *for* Spain, *or for any foreign Power. Much is wrong, much may be amended for the general Good of the whole.*" *Mr.* PITT's *Speech.*

† "*I rejoice that America has reſiſted. Three Millions of People, ſo dead to all the Feelings of Liberty, as voluntarily to conſent to be Slaves, would have been fit Inſtruments to make Slaves of the reſt.*" *Mr.* PITT's *Speech.*

"IT IN THEIR ELECTION, *either to buy* the same of the Officers and Persons to be employed, &c. at the *usual* and *most common Rates* above the said Duties, or *to bring* THEIR OWN Vellum, Parchment or Paper, to be stamped or marked as aforesaid." ‡

Was the Stamp-Act for *America* like those Statutes? Judge. By this it is enacted, "that the High Treasurer, or any three or more of the Commissioners of the Treasury, shall once in every Year SET THE PRICES, at which all Sorts of stamped Vellum, Parchment and Paper, shall be sold," &c.

The Stamps were kept in *England*. Ship loads of "all Sorts of stamped Vellum, Parchment and Paper," were sent over to us. We had no *Choice*, either to take these or to carry other Vellum, Parchment or Paper to be stamped. We must not only have paid the certain Duties imposed, but the uncertain "Prices," which the Commissioners should please to "set" for the Value of their "Vellum, Parchment and Paper;" and "Penalties and Forfeitures" fell upon us, every Step we took, without paying these *Impositions*. This surely was not only to be taxed by the Parliament, but over again for the same Articles by the Commissioners.

Here some Men, whose Minds are strongly impressed with Ideas of Equity, may ask, if it is possible that even a British Parliament should so wantonly degrade us? It is as true, as that the Port of *Boston* is THIS DAY shut up.

The "Forfeitures and Penalties thereby imposed were to be sued for and recovered in any Court of Record, or in ANY COURT OF ADMIRALTY OR VICE ADMIRALTY, appointed or to be appointed, and having Jurisdiction in the respective Colony where the Offence should be committed, &c."

THIS was no Regulation of Trade. The Facts, to be tried in any Dispute, must have arisen on Land---within the Body of a County--as remote from Admiralty Jurisdiction on every constitutional Principle, as a Suit on a Bond, or an Ejectment for a Freehold. Yet thus, by a few Lines, was the inestimable Privilege of Trial by Jury to be torn from you and your Posterity.---Thus the Decision of the Rights of Property, not in Controversies between Man and Man, on the Question of "meum vel tuum." where though wrung by Oppression, the wretched Loser might draw a degree of Consolation, by reflecting that he had received some Consideration for the Substance taken away, or at least that a Countryman gained his Spoils---but in Litigations founded on rigid *Forfeitures* and arbitrary *Penalties*---was to be referred to the incorrupt Tribunals of single Judges----appointed from another Country---filled with its Prejudices---holding their Commissions during Pleasure---totally independant on you---claiming Fees and Salaries to be paid out of your Money, condemned by themselves. §

---

‡ *5th and 6th Will. and Mar. ch. 21. 30th G. 2d. ch. 19. and other Statutes.*

§ "*When the jury have delivered their verdict, and it is recorded in court, they are then discharged. And so ends the trial by jury: a trial, which besides the other vast advantages which we have occasionally observed in its progress, is also as expeditious and cheap, as it is convenient, equitable, and certain; for a commission out of chancery, or the civil law courts, for examining witnesses in one cause will frequently last as long, and of course be full as expensive, as the trial of a hundred issues at* nisi prius*: and yet the fact cannot be determined by such commissioners at all; no, nor till the depositions are published and read at the hearing of the cause in court.*

"*Upon these accounts the trial by jury ever has been, and I trust ever will be, looked upon as the glory of the English law. And, if it has so great an advantage over others in regulating civil property, how much must that advantage be heightened, when it is applied to criminal cases! But this we must refer to the ensuing book of these commentaries: only observing for the present, that it is the most transcendent privilege which any subject can enjoy, or wish for, that he cannot be affected either in his property, his liberty or his person, but by the unanimous consent of twelve of his neighbours and equals. A constitution, that I may venture to affirm has, under providence, secured the just liberties of this nation for a long succession of ages. And therefore a celebrated French writer,* * *who concludes, that because Rome, Sparta and Carthage have lost their liberties, therefore those of England in time must perish, should have recollected, that Rome, Sparta, and Carthage, at the time when their liberties were lost, were strangers, to the trial by jury.*

"*Great as this eulogium may seem, it is no more than this admirable constitution, when traced to its principles, will be found in sober reason to deserve. The impartial administration of justice which secures both our persons and our properties, is the great end of civil society. But if that be entirely entrusted to the magistracy, a select body of men, and those generally selected by the prince or such as enjoy the highest offices in the state, their decisions, in spite of their own natural integrity, will have frequently an involuntary bias towards those of their own rank and dignity: it is not to be expected from human nature, that the* few *should be always attentive to the interests and good of* the many. *On the other hand, if the power of judicature were placed at random in the hands of the multitude, their decisions would be wild and capricious, and a new rule of action would be every day established in our courts. It is wisely therefore ordered, that the principles and axioms of law, which are general propositions, flowing from abstracted reason, and not accommodated to times or to men, should be deposited in the breasts of the judges, to be occasionally applied to such facts as come properly ascertained before them. For here partiality can have little scope: the law is well known, and is the same for all ranks and degrees; it follows as a regular conclusion from the premises of fact pre-established. But in settling and adjusting a question of fact, when intrusted to any single magistrate, partiality and injustice have an ample field to range in; either by boldly asserting that to be proved which is not so, or more artfully by suppressing some circumstances, stretching and warping others, and distinguishing away the remainder. Here therefore a competent number of sensible and upright jurymen, chosen by lot from among those of the middle rank, will be found the best investigators of truth, and the surest guardians of public justice. For the most powerful individual in the state will be cautious of committing any flagrant invasion of another's right, when he knows that the fact of his oppression must be examined and decided by twelve indifferent men; and that when once the fact is ascertained, the law must of course redress it. This therefore preserves in the hands of the people that share, which they ought to have in the administration of public justice, and prevents the encroachments of the more powerful & wealthy citizens. Every new tribunal, erected for the decision of facts, without the intervention of a jury, (whether composed of justices of the peace, commissioners of the revenue, judges of a court of conscience, or any other standing magistrates) is a step towards establishing aristocracy, the most oppressive of absolute governments. The feodal system, which, for the sake of military subordination, pursued an aristocratical plan in all its arrangements of property, had been intolerable in times of peace, had it not been wisely counterpoised by that privilege, so universally diffused through every part of it, the trial by the feodal peers. And in every country on the continent, as the trial by the peers has been gradually disused, so the nobles have increased in power, till the state has been torn to pieces by rival factions, and oligarchy in effect has been established, though under the shadow of regal government; unless where the miserable commons have taken shelter under absolute monarchy, as the lighter evil of the two. And particularly, it is a circumstance well worthy an Englishman's observation, that in Sweden the trial by jury, that bulwark of northern liberty, which continued in its full vigour so lately as the middle of the last century,* † *is now fallen into disuse* || *and that there, though the regal power is in no country so closely limitted, yet the liberties of the commons are extinguished, and the government is degenerated into a mere aristocracy.* ‡ *It is therefore, upon the whole, a duty which every man owes to his country, his friends, his posterity, and himself, to maintain to the utmost of his power this valuable constitution in all its rights; to restore it to its antient dignity, if at all impaired by the different value of property, or otherwise deviated from its first institution; to amend it, wherever it is defective; and, above all, to guard with the most jealous circumspection against the introduction of new and arbitrary methods of trial, which, under a variety of plausible pretences, may in time imperceptibly undermine this best preservative of English liberty.*" Blackstone's Com. 3d Vol. Page 378---381.

* Montesq. Sp. L. xi. 6.

† Whitelock of parl. 427. || Mod. Un. Hist. xxxiii. 22. ‡ Ibid. 17.

If this be "Wisdom," it is not of that Kind, the "Ways whereof are *past finding out*."

The Act, thus revoked by you, received soon after a formal Repeal in Parliament. This was done by the 6th of *George* the Third, Chapter the 11th. Because it was unconstitutional, as we were not and could not be represented there? No. Because it deprived "three Millions" of loyal Subjects of their darling Privilege of Trial by Jury, "the best Preservative of English Liberty?" No. Because "the Continuance of the said Act would be attended with many Inconveniences, and might be productive of Consequences greatly detrimental to the commercial Interests of" *Great-Britain*.

Cool, guarded Expressions! breathing the true Spirit of the modern Philosophy, so prevailing among the higher Ranks in that polished Kingdom. How much Care to avoid *Inconveniences* and *Detriment* to their own *commercial* Interests! How sovereign a Contempt for all the Agonies, that bowed us down to the Earth, while Indignation, Shame, Grief, Affection, Veneration and Gratitude, combated within our Breasts! They were advised to speak Peace to our Souls, by nobly assigning an "*erroneous Principle*," for the Repeal. ¶ No. The Freedom of *America* is the *Carthage* of *Great-Britain*---DELENDA EST. Let us repeal the Act, but never resign the Principle, on which it was founded.

One *generous* step, however, they did take, becoming *Britons*. It demands our acknowledgments: Nor should we withold them. Why will they not suffer us to thank them for other Favours?

The repealing Act spoke an indecisive Language, subject to Comments, that might differ on different Sides of the *Atlantic*. We might have been too much agitated between Hopes and Apprehensions. It would have been unkind to leave us in such a State of Anxiety. It would have been unworthy of a free People, who were determined to subjugate another free People. *Parmenios* may steal Victories. *Alexander* scorns it.

Therefore, the same Day, I think, in which they repealed the Stamp-Act, in the next Chapter, however, they *candidly* explained to us their Sentiments and Resolutions, beyond Possibility of a Mistake, by the "Act for the better securing the Dependency of his Majesty's Dominions in *America* upon the Crown and Parliament of *Great-Britain*."

"Lift up thine Eyes round about, and behold: All these gather themselves together, AND COME TO THEE: Thou shalt SURELY CLOTHE thee with them all, as with an Ornament, and BIND them on thee as a Bride doth." Isaiah, Chap. 49.

¶ "*Upon the whole, I beg leave to tell the House, what is really my opinion; it is, that the Stamp-Act be repealed, absolutely, totally, and immediately; that the reason for the repeal be assigned,* because it was founded on an ERRONEOUS PRINCIPLE."

Mr. PITT's *Speech*.

Messieurs EDES & GILL,

FROM an Extract of a Letter from a Southern Colony, and the Publications in last Thursday's Gazette, it is very evident a Scheme has been concerted by some Persons to frustrate any Attempts that might be made to suspend our Trade with Great-Britain, till our most intolerable Grievances are redressed. The Scheme appears to be, to *seem* to agree to the Suspension in Case all agreed, and then by construing some Passage in a Letter from the Committee of another Province, that they had *not agreed*, to declare that the conditional Signers were *not holden*. A GAME or two of such Mercantile Policy would soon have convinced the World that Lord North had a just Idea of the Colonies; and that notwithstanding their real Power to prove a Rope of Hemp to him, they were a Rope of Sand in Reality, among themselves. I would beg Leave to ask the voluminous Querists referr'd to, whether they conceive a Non-consumption Agreement would ever have been tho't of in the Country, could our Brethren there have persuaded themselves that the Merchants were in earnest to suspend Trade the little Time there was between our receiving the Port-Bill, and the Appointment of a Congress, or any other general Measure come into, from which a radical Relief might be expected? 2. Whether the Trade in their last Meeting declaring, That their *conditional* Agreement was *dissolved*, on Pretence that Advices from New-York and Philadelphia were totally discouraging, was not highly unbecoming a People, whose peculiar Circumstances rendered it their duty to stop their Trade to Great Britain the Moment the Port-Bill reached the Shore of America? 3. Whether they conceive the Committee of Boston planned the Non-consumption Agreement, and sent it first into the Country for their Adoption? or rather, whether the Country, enraged at their preposterous Management, did not originate the Plan and press the Committee to have it digested, printed and recommended throughout the Colony? 4. I would enquire whether a Backwardness in the Province, actually suffering, to come into the only peaceful Measure that remains for our Extrication from Slavery, would not naturally excuse every other Province from taking one Step for the common Salvation? 5. Whether in that Case all the Trade of the Province, whether consisting of Spring, Summer or Fall Importations, would in the End be worth an Oyster Shell? 6. Whether all the Bugbears started against the Worcester Covenant, as holding up the taking a solemn Oath to "withdraw all Commercial Connexions", which our honest Commentators tell the People means even to deny buying or selling Greens or Potatoes to them, does not betray a great want of that Candor and manly Generosity, which is expected from well-bred and reasonable Citizens? 7. Whether the Suggestion that the Boston Merchants ceasing to Import, will throw the Trade into the Hands of Importers in other Provinces, is not utterly unbecoming an Inhabitant of that Town, into which the Beneficence of the whole Continent is ready to flow in the most exemplary Manner? For Shame! Self Interested Mortals, cease to draw upon your worthy Fellow Citizens the just Resentment of Millions. If there may be some Punctilios wrong in the Non-consumption Agreement, the united Wisdom of the Continent will surely be capable of setting Matters right at the general Congress; and no Gentleman Trader, be his Haste ever so great to get Rich, need distress himself so mightily about the Profits of one Fall-Importation, if the constant Clamour of the Trade for two Years past, that they did Business for nothing, had any Foundation.

CANDIDUS.

WILLIAMSBURG, (Virginia,) June 2.

In our last we mentioned the intention of the late respectable House of Burgesses to solemnize the 1st of June with fasting, humiliation & prayer; and it is with pleasure we assure our readers that every inhabitant of this city, and numbers from the country, testified their gratitude, in the most expressive manner, by attending the worthy and patriotic Speaker at the court-house, and proceeded from thence, with the utmost decency and decorum, to the church, where prayers were accordingly read, and a sermon, suitable to the occasion, was delivered, by the Rev. Mr. Price, from the 103d psalm and 19th verse. *The Lord hath prepared his seat in Heaven, and his kingdom ruleth over all.*

The following text being so extremely applicable, we are requested to insert it.

GENESIS, 18 chap. 32 ver.

"And he (*Abraham*) said, Oh, let not the Lord be angry, and I will speak yet but this once; peradventure *ten* (righteous) *shall be found there.* And HE said, I will not destroy it for ten's sake."—*Reader, revise this whole chapter; behold! and adore the goodness and mercy of God.*

FREDERICSBURG, (*Virginia,*) June 2.

Yesterday being the Day set apart by the Members of the late House of Burgesses as a Day of Fasting, Humiliation, and Prayer, devoutly to implore the Divine Interposition for averting the heavy Calamity which threatens Destruction to the Civil Rights of America, the same was very devoutly observed by the Inhabitants of this Place, who repaired to Church and heard an excellent Sermon preached by the Rev. Mr. James Mayre, from Psalm xii. Verse 1 *Help, Lord, for the godly Man ceaseth, for the faithful fail from among the Children of Men.* The Reverend Mr. Wilson read Prayers.——Much [illegible] is due to the Ladies for the Part they took in our Association, and it does Honor to their Sex; for no [illegible] were they made acquainted with the Resolution to prohibit the Use of TEA, after the first of June, but, before the Day came, they sealed up the Stock which they had on Hand, and vowed never more to use it till the oppressive Act imposing a Duty thereon should be repealed.—*May their Example be followed by all the Ladies on the Continent!*

A Young Woman with a good Breast of Milk, would go into a Family to Suckle a Child, or take it Home, as it may suit; her Character for Honesty is indisputable. Inquire of the Printers.

CHALES-TOWN SOUTH-CAROLINA, June 6.

Last Wednesday, JUNE the 1st, the memorable Day on which the Blockade of the Town of Boston was to commence, the very Elements, at *this Distance*, were in such Commotion, between four and five o'Clock in the Afternoon, that all the Vessels lying at the Wharves were torne from them in an Instant, several of them much damaged, four Schooners were oversett, and it was scarce possible to see across even the narrowest Street in Town. A great deal of Damage was also done in the Country, where Abundance of growing Corn, many Fences, and some slight Houses were thrown down. During this Commotion, in our Air, there was more sharp Lightning, and less Thunder heard than usual—and we have had no settled Weather since.

PHILADELPHIA, June 15.

Last Thursday Evening about 1200 Mechanics of this city and suburbs, assembled at the State-House, to hear a letter and other papers read, from the Mechanics of the city of New York, and to form such resolutions, as should be judged proper, for their future conduct at this most alarming and critical time, when American liberty is so deeply wounded, and her rights so unjustly invaded, by levying taxes on us without our consent for the purpose of raising a revenue, and for refusing payment of those illegal taxes, blocking up, with divers ships of war, the port and town of Boston, thereby most unjustly depriving that once flourishing and loyal town of its whole trade, the inhabitants of their private property, and the labouring poor of the means of subsisting themselves and families. These proceedings of the parent state against her American children, call aloud upon all Americans to assemble, consult, and determine firmly to pursue such measures for their own and neighbours security, as shall be judged most likely to avert the present calamity, and secure to them the perfect enjoyment of their liberties and properties upon a fixed and lasting foundation; for which purpose, the Mechanics of this city have chosen 11 Gentlemen as a Committee of Correspondence, with the Mechanics of New-York, to cooperate with the Committee of Merchants, & to strengthen their hands, as will convince the world Americans were born and determined to live free, and that they never will be slaves; that liberty is thir birth-right—they cannot, they will not give it up.

But after sending out the hand-bills for calling that great assembly, information was received, that the present Committee have sent expresses to all the southern Colonies for their advice on this alarming occasion, and returns to those expresses are expected in a few days. That the Committee had determined to call a general meeting of all the inhabitants in the city and county, to correspond with the Committees of the neighbouring provinces, and to adopt such measures to be pursued by all, as their united wisdom shall direct; wherefore it was judged best not to enter into any particular resolves.

As it was judged, there would not be sufficient time to give proper notice to the country, it was agreed on Saturday last, by the Committee and a number of the most respectable inhabitants called to advise on the present occasion, that the GENERAL MEETING be postponed to Saturday next, at or near the State-House, at three o'clock, P. M. at which time and place, the inhabitants of this city and county, qualified to vote for representatives, are desired to attend, in order to take into their consideration, certain propositions prepared to be laid before them.

We hear from sundry Parts of Maryland, that the Inhabitants are so alarmed at the dangerous tendency of the British Councils, that they are disposed to plant no more Tobacco: As from this Article is raised a considerable part of the American revenue.

We learn from Alexandria, in Virginia, that on Wednesday the first of June, the Inhabitants of that place *unanimously* shewed their Sympathy, with their Brethren in Boston, by suspending all Business; and that Sermons were preached, on that day, in their Episcopal Church, and at the Court-House.

We hear that the Tradesmen and Farmers of the city and county of Philadelphia are DETERMINED to enter into an Association to purchase no more British Goods, (till the late Acts of Parliament are repealed) if the voice of the proposed Congress should be in Favour of a Non-Importation Agreement.

A correspondent remarks, that to oppose the British Parliament, (which has declared itself absolute, *in all cases whatever*, over the American Colonies) by refusing to import nothing but *dutied Articles*, will be as ineffectual a step to establish the liberties of America upon a permanent foundation, at the present juncture, a it would be to attempt to restrain a mad bull, by cutting off his tail, without aiming a blow at his vitals.

NEW-YORK, June 16.

Last Night a Gallows with the Figures of 3 Men suspended by the Neck, said to be intended to represent Lord North, Governor Hutchinson, and Solicitor Wedderburn, with another Figure representing the Devil, were carried thro' the principal Streets of the City, attended by several Thousand People, and at last burnt before the Coffee-House Door. It is said they were decorated with suitable Emblems, Devices & Inscriptions.

BOSTON, June 27.

On the 17th Instant, the following Resolve passed the House of Representatives, viz.

WHEREAS the two Houses of this General Assembly on the 27th Day of *May* 1774, did Address his Excellency the Governor praying that he would be pleased to appoint a Day of Fasting and Prayer, and his Excellency hath not yet thought proper in Compliance with said Request, to issue a Proclamation for the Purpose thereof—It is Resolved as the Sense of this House, that it is highly seasonable that such a Day of Prayer should be observed in the several Religious Assemblies throughout this Province, and in Case the Governor shall not be pleased by Proclamation to appoint a Day before the End of this Session, *It is Ordered*, That the Members of the House do recommend to their respective Parish Ministers the setting apart some convenient Day for the same Purpose.

AS the above Recommendation of the Hon. House of Representatives appears seasonable and proper, —The associated Ministers of Boston have agreed to propose to their several Congregations, that Thursday the 14th Day of July next, may be set apart and religiously kept as a Day of Fasting and Prayer. And this public Notice is given, that there may be a voluntary Union of the Churches through the Province, in the Devotions of that Day, so far as it may be deem'd expedient.

We hear three Gentlemen are appointed to attend the general Congress for the Province of New-Hampshire.

We hear a Ship is lading with Rice at South-Carolina for Rhode Island, in order to be sent to this Town.

Extract of a Letter from a Gentleman at Chester-Town, Kent-County, Maryland, *dated 7th June*, 1774, *to his Friend in this Town.*

"The Inhabitants of this County had a general Meeting the second Instant, and it gave much Pleasure to see how heartily they sympathized with Boston. Twenty-five Gentlemen were appointed a Committee of Correspondence, among whom I have the Honour to be named: After the Business was over, a Subscription was proposed to the Committee, which was most chearfully adopted, and they subscribed some 20l. others 10l. and none less than 5l. * to be laid out in Provisions, and forwarded for the Use of such poor People as are reduced to Necessity by the cruel Hand of Oppression. My advice was, to send off a Load of Corn, without giving any Notice of it, which I concluded would be an agreeable surprize to Boston. Words are said to be cheap, but it is universally allowed, that when a Man parts with his Money, he is in earnest. Subscription Papers are sent out into the Country, and I dare say will be filled up to a large amount. Those who cannot give Money can give Corn. The People of Boston need not be afraid of being starv'd to a Compliance. If they will only give a short Notice, they may make their Town THE GRAINERY OF AMERICA. We all hope they will stand to their Integrity, and not sully the Honour which they have so justly acquired. An Account of our Proceedings, accompanied with a Letter, is sent to the Committee, and I suppose will be published."

* Maryland Currency is 7/6 to a Dollar.

Worcester ss. Inferior Court of Common Pleas, &c. second Tuesday of June, A. D. 1774. Mr. Samuel Paine was appointed and sworn as joint Clerk of the Inferior Court of Common Pleas and Court of General Sessions of the Peace for the County of Worcester, with the Hon. Timothy Paine, Esq;

Last Thursday was Married by the Rev. Dr CANER, Mr. HENRY KNOX, of this Town, to Miss LUCY FLUCKER, second Daughter to the Honorable THOMAS FLUCKER, Esq; Secretary of the Province.

We hear from Natick that on Sunday the 20th Instant, departed this Life, Mr. Stephen Badger, aged 79, formerly of Charlestown, he bore the Character of a good Man, and we trust he is gone to receive the Rewards of a good and faithful Servant.—His Funeral was attended by the Militia Company of that Town who were under Arms, and behaved with the greatest Decency.

Last Wednesday Evening died here, Miss Elizabeth Greenleaf.

Boston, June 24, 1774.

THE Committee of Correspondence for this Town have just received the following Notification *from their patriotic and truly disinterested Friends and Brethren of* Marblehead, *who are thereby intitled to the unfeigned Thanks of every one who regards the Interest of his Country, and wishes to promote that Harmony & friendly Intercourse so important at this critical Juncture.*

NOTIFICATION.

TO the Merchants, Traders and other Inhabitants of Boston, and the Towns thereto adjacent, whose Interest is affected by the detested Port Bill, are hereby Notified, that Provision is made by sundry Merchants and Traders of this Town, for saving them the Expence of Storage, Wharfage and Commissions, in Case of their landing or vending Goods here, during the continuance of the oppressive Act mentioned; and they are desired to be at no Expence on these accounts, but to apply to the Committee of Correspondence of this Place, who will esteem such Application friendly, and according to Desire of many of the Trade here, will shew them suitable Accommodations for the Purposes mentioned.

MARBLEHEAD, June 23, 1774.

Messieurs PRINTERS,

THE present Tyranny produces glorious Effects in the Country Towns—The Passion for American Manufactures, and a Dislike to every Thing British, grows rapidly. I am convinced that the Oppressions we now suffer, will, in the Event, be vastly advantageous; and promote the Growth, Wealth and Independance of America. The *Non-Consumption Agreement*, will cut up the whole System of Tyranny by the Roots, and fix the Freedom of this Country on a sure foundation——This the Faction who are conspiring to enslave us are fully sensible of; and therefore every Art which *Satan* can devise or *his under Tyrants* execute, will be employed to defeat this most salutary Measure. It is most certain, that there are but *three Choices* left for the Americans; they must either preserve their Rights by breaking off all Commerce with Britain, or defend them with the Sword, or submit to the horrors of Slavery.—Therefore every Man ought immediately to determine what Part he will act, and declare his Opinion openly. At this Day, when the relentless Hand of Oppression is tearing out the Vitals of *Freedom*, and mocking Justice, *silence* is Guilt, and *inaction* is Infamy; the great Contention ought to be, who shall do most for the Salvation of his Country. The greatest Crime Man can commit against Man, is to destroy his Liberty—and consequently to Defend it, must be the highest Virtue. Therefore whoever in this important Day when the Liberty of America trembles on the brink of Ruin, shall not exert all his Powers to preserve it, must be regarded as an abandoned Wretch.

A COUNTRYMAN.

To be Sold cheap for CASH.

A few Casks of good Sugars;

West-India Rum, and a few Casks of Coffee.——Inquire at Cruft's Store, a little to the Northward of Hancock's Wharf, North-End.

CHARLESTOWN Stage No. 1. sets out with four good Horses for Salem, from Mr. WOART's Tavern every Morning at 8 o'Clock, and returns the same Day; it puts up at Mr. Goodhue's in Salem. Any Gentlemen or Ladies who wants a Passage are desired to call at Admiral Vernon's, in King-street, Boston; or Mr. Woart's, in Charlestown, and leave their Names.—Also at the same Place, Stage No. 2. with four good Horses may be had to convey any Gentleman or Lady to any Part of this, or any other Province, or at so small a Distance as five or six Miles.

Any Gentlemen or Ladies who choose to go in either of the above Stages, will be accommodated in the best Manner, and the smallest Favour will be acknowledged,

By their humble Servant,

SAMUEL LORD.

Charlestown, June 22, 1774

Doctor *Lagord*, Originally from France, practices Physick, surgery and Midwifry, practised some Years at Braintree, but has lately removed to that Part of Cambridge called Menotomy, near the Meeting-House, at the Masons Arms Tavern, now kept by Benjamin Cooper from Boston; any Person who please to employ the said *Lagord* in any of the Branches, may speak with him at the above mentioned Place, where may be had good Entertainment for Gentlemen Travellers.—Near said Cooper's is the famous Menotomy Pond, where he keeps a neat Boat for Fishery.

TO BE SOLD,
ON THURSDAY NEXT,
By *BENJAMIN CHURCH*,
At FOUR o'Clock in the Afternoon,

A General Assortment of European Articles, Linnens, Woollens, Checks, &c. &c. Some House Furniture, an 8-Day Clock, Mehogany Case of Draws, Watches, &c. &c.—At Four o Clock, P. M—

GOODS at the *Sterling Cost*.

John Cunningham

HAS yet remaining a good Assortment of English and India GOODS, which he continues to sell at the Sterling Cost clear of Charges, at his Shop opposite to Mr. Gilbert Deblois's, near School-Street.

Choice Muscovado Sugars, Grenada Rum, Coffee, &c. &c. To be Sold by GABRIEL JOHONNOTT, at his Store South Side of Faneuil-Hall Market.

New AUCTION-ROOM, Cornhill.

TO-MORROW at TEN o'Clock will be Sold by PUBLIC VENDUE, at GREENLEAF's Auction-Room,——

—A great Variety of GOODS as usual—

——*Amongst which are,*——

A Number of very fine Chints, stript flower'd and plain Laws, Lawn Aprons, flower'd Muslin, a Variety of Ribbonds, wide and narrow plain Modes, Damask and Diaper Table-cloths, some Irish Linnens, Long Lawns, Checks, strip'd Hollands, Bed Ticks, Broad Cloths, Forrest Cloths, Velverets, Thicksets, Sagathees, Shalloons, Worsted and Thread Hose, Castor and Felt Hatts. Also, a Variety of Hard Ware, as Penknives, Cuttoes, Razors, Buckles, Scissars, Table Knives and Forks, &c. Also a Cask of choice Indigo.

An elegant 8 Day Clock at private Sale.

WILLIAM GREENLEAF, Auctioneer.

The Sale will begin precisely at Ten o'Clock, and be continued in the Afternoon.

To MORROW,
At TEN o'Clock in the Morning,
Will be Sold by PUBLIC VENDUE,
At the House of Mr. Joseph Glidden, *deceased, near the the Sign of Ship in Distress, in Fore-Street,*

All the Houshuld Furniture of the *said* Glidden, *consisting of Desks, Chest of Draws, Mahogany and other Tables, Looking Glasses, Pictures, Feather Beds, Bedding and Beadsteads, Leather Bottomed and common Chairs, Table Linnen, Brass, Copper, Tin and Iron Ware of all Sorts.* R. GOULD, Auctioneer.

RAN-away from the Subscriber on the Eighth of June Instant, at Night, a Negro Boy, about Seventeen Years of Age: Had on when he went off, a dark coloured cloth Jacket and Trowsers, and is branded on the Breast Delamote, very remarkable: said Fellow speaks tolerable good English, and some French. Whoever takes up said Fellow and Secures him in any of his Majesty's Goals, or Returns him to the Subscriber, shall have FIVE DOLLARS Reward, and all necessary Charges paid by ALLIN BROWN.

Providence, June 10, 1774.

THESE are to desire those Persons who make Coffins for the Dead, that they would out of Humanity to the Living, especially to the Undertakers of Funerals, That they take Care to make them so close, as not to leak, which is much to the Prejudice of them and their Clothes in hot Weather, and which is often the Case. THE SEXTONS.

Burials in the Town of BOSTON, since our last.
Seven Whites. No Blacks.
Baptiz'd in the several Churches, Seventeen.

High Water at BOSTON, for the present Week.

Monday, 35 min. aft.	2		Friday, 6 min. after.	6
Tuesday, 34 min. aft.	3		Saturday, 38 min. aft.	6
Wednesday, 30 m. aft.	4		Lord's-Day, 25 m. af.	7
Thursday, 29 min. aft.	5		D's Last Q. 30D. 2 AS	

In the House of Representatives, June 14, 1774.

WHEREAS there will become due in this Month, sundry Notes given by the Province Treasurer, and sufficient Provision having been made for the paying off the same, and if the Possessors of such Notes should not bring them in to the Treasurer to be paid, the Province will suffer Damage by such Neglect:

Therefore, RESOLVED, That the Possessors of such Notes, who shall not bring them to the Province Treasurer, to be paid by the last Day of *July* next, shall not receive any Interest on the same, after that Time, and the Province Treasurer is hereby directed forthwith to cause this Order to be published in all the *Boston* News-Papers, three Weeks successively, that every one concerned may be Notified hereof. Sent up for Concurrence.

T. CUSHING, Speaker.

In Council, June 15th. Read and concurred.

JOHN COTTON, D. Sec'ry.

Consented to, THOS. GAGE.

A true Copy attest. JOHN COTTON, D. Sec'ry.

☞ *THE Treasurer of the Province* hereby gives public Notice to the delinquent Constables and Collectors of the Province Taxes, that they pay the same into the Treasury by the 31st of *July* next.

Treasury-Office, July 18, 1774.

TO BE SOLD,

By Thomas Handasyd Peck,

At his Shop in Merchant's-Row, near the Golden-Ball.

ALL Sorts of Linnen Linings suitable for Beaver, Beaveritt, Castor & Felt Hatts, black, blue and green Tabby Linings, Mohair Looping and Bands Silk ditto, Buttons and Loops newest Fashion, sundry Sorts of Chain and Shapes for Button Loops, Gold and Silver Buttons and Loops, white and yellow Triming for Childrens Hatts, white and yellow Bands & Buckles, Gold and Silver Chain, Brushes, Cards, Velures, Bowstrings, Luping-Needles, Nus-skins, Camels Hair, Irons, Verdegrease, Coppera, Logwood, Beaver, Beaveritt, Castor and Felt Hatts, Childrens black turn-up Hatts, white ditto, also Strouds and Blankets suitable for the Indian Trade, Powder, Shot, and Russia Duck.

N. B. Cash given for Beaver, and all Sorts of Furs as usual.

TO BE SOLD,

A Farm with a Dwelling House, Barn & Shop thereon, lying in the Town of Braintree, North Precinct, situated on the Main Road to Plymouth, between the Meeting House and Brackett's Tavern, consisting of nine Acres of arrable Land, well Watered, five Acres of Fresh Meadow, and three or four Acres of Salt Marsh.——Any Person inclining to purchase the same may apply to Mr. John Mills, living on the Premises.

Halifax, Nova-Scotia, May 19, 1774.

TO BE SOLD at PUBLIC AUCTION,

On TUESDAY the Second Day of August next in the Town of Halifax, at the House of Mr. *John Rider*,

A VALUABLE Tract of Land or Township, commonly known by the Name of New-Jerusalem, or Port-Rosaway, on the Southern Shore of the Province of Nova-Scotia, containing One Hundred Thousand Acres of Land, granted by his Majesty to ALEXANDER MACNUTT, Esq; but lately the Property and Estate of BENJAMIN GERRISH, Esq; deceased, and contain several fine Harbours for Vessels or Ships of any Draught of Water and full of all Sorts of Fish, as Cod, Salmon, Mackrel, Herring, &c. &c. &c. extending about twelve Miles on the Sea Coast, well wooded and watered.

Conditions of Pay, viz. To pay 10 per cent. down in Cash, and the Remainder on executing the Deed of Sale for the same, which shall be within one Month after the Sale.

Also, a Lot of Land, an old House and Bake-House on the Beach, with a large Baking Oven, late in the Occupation of Mr. RICHARD JACOBS.

Also, a Lot of Land walled in with Stone, containing five Acres of Land more or less, lying on the Road to RICHARD JACOBS Farm.

Also, one Half of the Meeting-House Cellar.

Also, the late Dwelling-House of BENJAMIN GERRISH, Esq; deceased, with the front Yard and back Gardens and Out-Houses.

Also, a Wharf with four Stores thereon and a Coach-House and Stable.

Also, a Tract of Land, containing ten Thousand Acres, granted to BENJAMIN GERRISH, Esq; deceased, situate on the North Side of the Bason of Mines in the Province of Nova Scotia, comprehending the three Rivers commonly called and known by the Names of the Bass Rivers abounding with Shad, Salmon, Bass and other Kinds of Fish, and contains upwards of two Hundred Acres of Marsh Land, and was formerly a Settlement by the Accadeans. And also an Island called Moose-Island about one Mile distant, containing about one Hundred and Ninety Acres of rich Land. The aforesaid Bass Rivers are navigable for Vessels of 50 or 60 Tons and good Harbours.

Also, sixty one and half Acres of Dike Land in the Township of Horton on the Grand Pree.

Also, a Farm in the Township of Falmouth, now under good Improvement with a Dwelling-House and Barn and other Out-Houses, containing about Twelve Hundred and Fifty Acres of Land more or less, and all other Lands belonging to said Estate of BENJAMIN GERRISH, Esq;

N. B. In all the above Estates the Widow's Dower is to be excepted and treated for with her in Particulars for her Thirds during Life.

Conditions of Pay as aforesaid.

TO BE SOLD at the Royal Exchange Tavern in King-Street, Boston,

At PUBLIC VENDUE,

On Wednesday the Fourteenth Day of September next, at Ten o'Clock in the Forenoon,

The following Lots of Land, viz.

Lot marked F. 2. in the first range of Lots, containing about six Thousand Acres (exclusive of Settlers Lots interspersed) being near one Mile wide and fifteen Miles long, and fronting on *Kennebeck*-River, on the West-side of it, about ten Miles above Fort Halifax: to be divided and Sold in two Parts.

Lot marked B. D. 1. in the second range of Lots, about six Miles above *Norridgwalk*, on the West Side of *Kennebeck*-River, and fronting thereon, containing about seven Thousand Acres, exclusive of Settlers Lots interspersed, being one Mile wide, & 15 Miles long.

Lot marked C. A. 1. in the third range of Lots, near the Falls of *Cariotonka*, about twelve Miles above *Norridgwalk*, on the West Side of *Kennebeck*-River, and fronting thereon, containing about seven Thousand Acres, exclusive of Settler's Lots interspersed, being one Mile wide and fifteen Miles long.

Lot No. 20, called a Ten Mile back Lot, on the West Side of *Kennebeck* River, containing about four Thousand eight Hundred Acres.

Three Lots of Land, viz. Lot No. 32, on the East Side of *Kennebeck*-River, about 300 Poles above *Fort-Western*, No. 86, on the East Side of said River, about nine Miles, and 120 Poles above *Fort-Western*, and also Lot No. 20, on the West Side of said River, about one Mile and 230 Poles above *Fort-Western*, containing 400 Acres each.

Also all the Islands in Cobbisecontee Pond, and all the Islands in *Kennebeck*-River, above *Fort-Halifax*. The Pay will be made easy to the Purchasers.

For further Particulars enquire of *Henry Alline*, jun. at his Office in King-Street, *Boston, June 10. 1774.*

Province of the Massachusetts-Bay, } *To the Hon.* James Otis, *Esq; one of his Majesty's Justices of the Peace through the said Province.*

We the Subscribers, Proprietors of a Tract of Land lying at *Broad-Bay*, in the County of *Lincoln*, in said Province, and bounded as followeth, viz.—beginning at *Pemaquid-Falls* and so running a direct Course to the Head of *New-Harbour*, from thence to the South End of *Misconcus-Island*, taking in the Island, so running five and twenty Miles into the Country North by East, and thence eight Miles North West by West, and thence turning and running South by West to *Pemaquid*, where it first began——pray that your Honour would issue a Warrant to one of us to call a Meeting of the Proprietors of said Land, to be on the third Day of *August* next, at Ten of the Clock in the Forenoon, at the House of *William Goodhue*, Innholder in *Salem*; then and there to chuse a Moderator of said Meeting, a Clerk of said Proprietors, a Committee to transact the Affairs of said Proprietors as Occasion may require, and any other needful Officers; to agree upon a Method for calling of Meetings for the future; to take under Consideration the Division that the Proprietors of said Land made some Years ago and confirm the same, or order a new Division and run the boundary Line; to settle with those Persons who have made Settlements of said Land on reasonable Terms, by selling them the Land or otherways, but in case they refuse to settle as aforesaid, to sue them off and prosecute any Person or Persons who shall trespass on said Land; to pass any Orders that are necessary to bring forward the Settlement of said Land, by giving away Land or otherways, and to raise Money on said Land for necessary Charges and order the collecting the same.

Daniel Sargent,
his
John + *Brown,*
Mark
John Choate,
Jona. Cogswell, jun.
John Sargent.

Salem, June 15. 1774.

(Seal.) *Province of the Massachusetts-Bay.*
To John Choate *of* Ipswich, *in the County of Essex, in said Province, one of the principal Proprietors of the Land aforesaid,* Greeting.

In pursuance of the foregoing Application and Request, you are hereby required to give Notice, in Time and Manner as the Law directs, to the Proprietors afore-mentioned, that they meet at the Time and Place and for the Purposes mentioned in the afore-written Petition. Given under my Hand and Seal this 15th Day of June, Anno Domini, 1774.

JAMES OTIS, a Justice of the Peace through the Province of the Massachusetts-Bay.

Ipswich, June 15, 1774.

By Virtue of the afore-written Warrant to me directed, I do hereby notify and warn the Proprietors of the aforesaid Land to meet at the Dwelling House of *William Goodhue*, Innholder at Salem, on the 3d Day of August next, at Ten of the Clock in the Forenoon, for the Purposes therein mentioned.

JOHN CHOATE.

To be Sold by *William Jennison*, of Mendon, a valuable FARM, containing 100 Acres, consisting of Plowland, Mowing, Pasturing, Orcharding and Woodland; divided into fifteen seperate inclosures, Fenc'd chiefly with Stone Wall, together with two Dwelling Houses on the Premises, one a large commodious Mansion House 6 Rooms on a Floor, half a Mile from the Rev. Mr. *Frost's* Meeting House, pleasantly situated for a Gentleman or Trader, with a large new Barn, Potash Works, Shop for Goods, Warehouse, Grainery and other out Buildings, 24 Miles from Providence and 34 from Boston, is on the nearest Road from Connecticut to Cambridge, Salem, &c. is now, and has been a number of Year's improv'd as a Tavern: Said Interest to be Sold for 1000l. only. West-India Goods will be accepted for one half, the other half may lie a number of Years on good Security.

ALL who desire Admission into HARVARD-COLLEGE this Year, are hereby Notified, That the Tutors have determined to attend the Business of Examination on Tuesday and Wednesday, the 19th and 20th Days of July next.

J. WADSWORTH, per Order.

Harvard-College, June 15, 1774.

S & S Salisbury

Acquaint their Friends, they have just Imported in the last Ships from LONDON and BRISTOL,

A fresh Assortment of

—Hard Ware GOODS—

N. B. They have an Assortment of Nails in the Town of Marblehead, which they would be glad to dispose of, to be delivered there.

For LONDON,
The Ship DARTMOUTH,
JAS. ROTCH, Commander,
Will Sail in 20 Days from Dartmouth. For Passage apply to
FRANCIS ROTCH,
At his Store in King-Street;
Where is to be had,
A few Boxes choice Spermæ Candles, a few Casks genuine Lisbon Wine, Barr Lead, and a Quantity of Brass Kettles.

To be sold upon reasonable Terms,

A HOUSE well situated, and well accommodated for a small Family, within 8 or 10 Miles of Boston. There is as much Land adjoining to the House as may be thought convenient. Enquire of Edes & Gill.

To be Sold for Want of Employ,

A Likely young Negro Man, who can shave and dress Hair, and is otherways well qualified for a Gentleman's Servant. Inquire of Edes & Gill.

JOHN NOBLE,

(*Post-Rider from Boston to Portsmouth*)

INFORMS the Public, That he has remov'd from Mr. Hubbard's at the Sign of Admiral Vernon, to Deacon Jones's at the Royal Exchange Tavern, in King-Street.

N. B. He arrives at Boston on Saturday Evenings and sets out for Portsmouth, early on Tuesday Mornings. Any Business and Packages delivered to him shall be executed with Care and Fidellity.

JUST IMPORTED from LONDON
And to be Sold by

John Gore & Son,

At the PAINTER'S ARMS, in Queen Street,

A large and compleat Assortment of

Painters Oils, Colours, Brushes and Tools, of all Sizes:

Likewise, Gum Copal, Anamiæ, Sandriack, Shell Lack, Seed Lack, Arabic and Amber, half Length, Kitt Katt and three Quarter Cloths, brown and white Varnish and Lacker; also Martin's best Copal Oil Varnish, which will enable them to finish Coach and Chaise Bodies as high as any ever imported from London.

WE the Subscribers being appointed by the Hon. Foster Hutchinson, Esq; Judge of Probate for the County of Suffolk, Commissioners to receive and examine the Claims of the several Creditors to the Estate of SAMUEL SNOW, late of Boston, Mariner, deceas'd, intestate, represented Insolvent, Do hereby give Notice, that we shall attend said Service, at the British Coffee House, on the second Tuesday of this and the Five following Months, from Six 'till Nine o'Clock of the Evening of said Days.

JOB PRINCE,
JOHN CARNES.

Boston, June 11, 1774.

Waltham, June 6, 1774.

RAN-away from the Subscriber, a Servant Boy, named Silence Robinson, between 17 and 18 Years old, large of his Age. Any Person who will secure said Servant, so that his Master may have him again, shall have Five Shillings, O. T. Reward for their Trouble, paid by JOSEPH WELLINGTON.

All Masters of Vessels and others, are hereby cautioned against Concealing or Harbouring said Servant, as they will avoid the Penalty of the Law.

Ten Dollars Reward.

RAN AWAY from the Subscriber, *Joseph Moors*, of Groton, in the County of Middlesex, and Province of Massachusetts-Bay, a Molatto Man Servant, named TITUS, about 20 Years of Age, of a midling Stature, wears short curl'd Hair, has one of his Fore-Teeth broke out, took with him a blue Surdan, a Snuff-coloured Coat, and a Pair of white wash'd Leather Breeches, a Pair of new Cow-Hide Pumps and a Furr'd Hat with large Brims, and sundry other Articles of Wearing Apparel.——Whoever will take up said Servant and confine him in any of his Majesty's Goals, so that the Owner may have him again, shall have TEN DOLLARS Reward and all necessary Charges paid, by JOSEPH MOORS.

☞ *All Masters of Vessels and others, are hereby Caution'd against Harbouring, Concealing, or carrying off said Servant, as they would thereby avoid the Penalty of the Law.*

Boston: Printed, by EDES & GILL, *in Queen-Street,* 1774.

THE

Boston-Gazette,

AND

COUNTRY JOURNAL.

No. 1003.

Containing the freshest Advices, Foreign and Domestic.

MONDAY, *July* 4, 1774.

ALL Persons indebted for this Paper, whose Accounts have been above 12 Months standing, are requested to make immediate Payment.

PHILADELPHIA, June 8. 1774.

LETTER III.

To the INHABITANTS *of the* British Colonies *in* AMERICA.

BRETHREN,

THESE are the Words of the declaratory Act, mentioned in the last Letter, "Whereas several of the Houses of Representatives in his Majesty's Colonies and Plantations in *America* have of late, AGAINST LAW, claimed to themselves, or to the General Assemblies of the same, the SOLE and EXCLUSIVE Right of imposing Duties and Taxes upon his Majesty's SUBJECTS IN THE SAID COLONIES AND PLANTATIONS; and have, in Pursuance of such Claim, passed certain Votes, Resolutions and Orders, DEROGATORY TO THE LEGISLATIVE AUTHORITY OF PARLIAMENT, and inconsistent with the Dependency of the said Colonies and Plantations, &c. therefore be it declared, &c. that the said Colonies and Plantations in *America* have been, are, and of Right ought to be, subordinate unto, and dependent upon the imperial Crown and Parliament of *Great-Britain* and that the King's Majesty, by and with the Advice and Consent of the Lords Spiritual and Temporal, and Commons of *Great-Britain*, in Parliament assembled, had, HATH, and OF RIGHT OUGHT TO HAVE, full Power and Authority to make Laws and Statutes, of sufficient Force and Validity to BIND the Colonies and People of AMERICA, Subjects of the Crown of *Great-Britain*, IN ALL CASES WHATSOEVER."

From the Croud of Objects, each pressing for Attention, that present themselves to the Mind of a *British American*, on reading this Act, I beg Leave to select and particularly mention only two, that you collecting them, and taking a just View of your present Situations, may feel *that* and only *that* Resentment, springing from Virtue, and guided by Wisdom, which the most worthy and the most peaceable Men must approve.

The Resolutions, &c. mentioned in this Act, were those caused by the Stamp-act. These principal Points are firmly asserted in them.---*the exclusive Right of Taxation*, and the *Right of Trial by Jury*. The Parliament, well knowing how harsh and jarring it would sound in English Ears to say, the Right of Trial by Jury was "*derogatory to the legislative Authority of Parliament*, and INCONSISTENT *with the Dependency of the Colonies*, planted their most direct Battery against the Right of Taxation ---Common-Sense and the Experience of all Nations, AS NOT A SINGLE INSTANCE OCCURS TO THE CONTRARY, convincing them, if *that* gave Way, a general Ruin would soon ensue, and all the rest would follow in the Train of the Chief, like captive *Nobles* attending their conquered *Prince*.

However, not quite satisfied with the slow Work of exterminating them in Detail, but improving upon an impartial Hint, it was judged fittest, upon the whole, so to consolidate them, that, as if the *British-Americans* had but "ONE NECK," a SINGLE *Stroke* might dispatch Millions---by subjecting us *at once* to the Decrees of Parliament, IN ALL CASES WHATSOEVER.

Widely different was the Act of the 6th of George the First, Chap. 5th, "for the better securing the Dependency of the Kingdom of *Ireland*," &c. By that Act *Ireland* was declared "to be subordinate unto and dependent upon the Imperial CROWN* of *Great-Britain*." These Words "and Parliament" are not in it. It is said indeed, that "the King, with the Advice and Consent of the Lords and Commons of *Great-Britain*, in Parliament assembled, had, and of Right ought to have, Power and Authority to make Laws and Statutes, of sufficient Force and Validity to bind the Kingdom and People of *Ireland*."

Compare the Acts, and you will find the Act for *America* copied from that of *Ireland*; but in the last mentioned, the annihilating Words----"IN ALL CASES WHATSOEVER" are not to be found. The People of Ireland have been for several Centuries bound by *English* Statutes for regulating their Trade, and for other Purposes, and this Statute, therefore, only asserted the USUAL Authority over them. Their Vitals, the exclusive Right of Taxation, and the Right of Trial by Jury, have been preserved. If it was the Intention of the British Parliament to exercise a "Power and Authority" over that Kingdom, destructive of these Rights, it is not expressed----it is not implied. Why were the unlimited Words omitted in that Act? Or, why when the Lords and Commons were copying a Pattern which their Fathers set them, did they deform the Transcript by such Eastern Flourishes.

The Truth is--the Fathers too much revered the English Principles, for which they had been upon the Point of shedding their Blood in placing their Sovereign on his Throne, so flagrantly to violate them---or, if their Conduct was not directed by Justice, they dared not thus to provoke the brave, generous Inhabitants of that ancient Kingdom.

"*Are there yet the Treasures of Wickedness in the House, and the scant Measure, that is abominable, The rich Men thereof are full of Violence.*" MICAH, Chap. vi,

* "*A Tax granted by the Parliament of England shall not bind those of* Ireland, *because they are not summoned to our Parliament*;" *and again*, "Ireland *hath a Parliament of its own, and maketh and altereth Laws; and Statutes do not bind them, because they do not send Knights to our Parliament: But their Persons are the* King's Subjects, *like as the Inhabitants of* Calais, Gascoigny, *and* Guienne, *while they continued under the* King's *Subjection*."

LETTER IV.

To the INHABITANTS *of the* British Colonies *in* AMERICA.

Brethren,

THE intelligence received, since the preceeding letter was written, seems to render needless every attempt to prove from *former transactions*,—my first intention, if health had permitted—that a regular plan has been invariably pursued to enslave these Colonies, and that the Act of Parliament for blocking up the port of *Boston* is a part of the plan. However unprecedented and cruel that measure is, yet some persons among us might have flattered themselves, that the resentment of the Parliament is directed solely against that town. The last advices mention two bills to be passing in Parliament; one, changing the chartered constitution of the province of *Massachusets-Bay* into a military government; and another, for empowering administration to send for and try persons in *England* for actions committed in that colony.*

By these instances we perceive, that administration has not only renounced all respect, and all appearance of respect, for the rights of these colonies, but even the plainest principles of justice and humanity. Were the representatives of the people of *Massachusets-Bay* called upon to make satisfaction for the damage done to private property in any late tumult there? No. Yet it was known, that those representatives had made ample reparation for the injuries committed on occasion of the stamp act. It was known, that the like reparation had been made by the Assemblies of *New-York* and *Rhode-Island*. In short, it was known, that notwithstanding the incessant pains taken by many Ministers to teaze the colonists by oppressions and insults into madness, yet they have with difficulty excited only a few tumults, for which the popular branch of the legislature in the several colonies has ever been ready to attone, upon requisitions from the crown.

Great clamour has been raised at home against *Massachusets-Bay*, on account of resolutions at some of their town meetings, and other writings published in that Colony; and better it were, that many of them had been suppressed. The truth is—that people animated by an ardent and generous love of liberty saw and peculiarly felt the projects against the freedom and happiness of *America*. I know them well: and if ever a state deserved the character, they are a moral, religious, quiet and loyal people, affectionately attached to the welfare and honour of *Great-Britain* and dearly valuing their dependence on her. Observant and sensible, as they were, of the present and approaching evils, some of them adopted a very imprudent, but what appeared to them a very peaceable and justifiable method of discouraging Aministration from proceeding in such alarming and dangerous measures, —that of speaking in a high tone. Words were opposed to injuries, and menaces, never designed for execution, to insults intollerable. What could they do? Their *humble petitions* were haughtily and contemptuously rejected. The more they *supplicated*, the more they were *abused*. By their tears, and Heaven knows many they have shed, their persecutions flourished, as trees by water poured on their roots. Their very virtue and passionate fondness for concord, for their Mother-Country occasioned this objected error. "Surely" says Solomon, "oppression maketh a wise man mad," a silly man may disregard it. In playing the fool they shewed their wisdom. This is the true history of those futile pieces, that produced so much solid eloquence in *Great-Britain*.

Riots and weak publications, by a small number of individuals, are sufficient reasons with Parliament to ruin many thousands of a truly respectable town, to dissolve charters, to abolish the benefits of the writ of *habeas corpus*,† and extirpate American liberty—For the principle reaches all. But in *England* the press groans with publications, seditious, treasonable and even blasphemous, The discontented swarm over the kingdom, proclaiming their resentments. Many enormous riots have disturbed the public peace. The Sovereign has been insulted in passing from his Palace to the Parliament-house, on the business of the nation. Is it to be concluded from these facts, that the BODY OF THE POEPLE is seditious and traiterous? Can his Majesty believe, that he is thought by his English subjects in *general* to be such a Prince, as some of them have represented him? Will the two Houses of Parliament acknowledge what has been spoken and written and acted against them in *England*, expresses the sentiments of the kingdom? Or will they say, that the *People* of *England* have forfeited their liberty, because *some of them* have run into licentiousness? Let a judgment be formed in *both* cases by the *same* rule. Let them condemn *those*, or acquit *us*.

Pretences and reasons are totally different. The provocations, said to be given by our sister colony, are but *Pretences* for the exorbitant severity exercised against her. The *Reasons* are these —the policy, despicable and detestable as it is, of suppressing the freedom of *America* by a military force, to be supported by money taken out of our own pockets, and the supposed conveniency of opportunity for attaining this end. The *Reasons* are evident from the Minister's speech. The system is formed with art, but the art is discoverable. Indeed I do not believe it was expected, we should have such early and exact intelligence of the schemes agitated against us, as we have received. Any person, who examines the multitude of invectives published in pamphlets and news papers in *Great-Britain*, or the speeches made in either House of Parliament, will find them directed *against the Colonies in general*. The people in that kingdom have been with great cunning and labour,§ inflamed *against the Colonies in general*.—They are deluded into a belief, that we are in a state of rebellion and aiming directly at a state of independency; though the first is a noxious weed that never grew in our climates; and the latter is universally regarded with the deepest execrations by us—a poison we never can be compelled to touch, but as an antidote to a worse, if a worse can be—a curse, that if any Colony on this continent should be so mad as to aim at reaching, the rest of the body would have virtue and wisdom enough to draw their swords, and hew the traitors into submission, if not into loyalty. It would be our interest and our duty thus to guarrantee the public peace.

The Minister addressing the House of Commons, uses several expressions relating to *all the Colonies*, and calls the stoppage of the port of *Boston* "a punishment inflicted on those, *who have disobeyed your Authority*." Is it not extremely remarkable, after such a variety of charges affecting *all* the Colonies, that the statute of vengeance should be levelled against a *single* Colony?—*New-York*, *Philadelphia* and *Charlestown* have denied freedom of Trade to ships sailing *under the protection of Acts of Parliament*. Will not the House of Commons think the inhabitants of these places "have disobeyed their authority," and that "a punishment should be inflicted on them?" Why do we not hear of some measure pursued against those Cities? Are *they* immaculate in the eyes of Administration and Parliament? Has not each of these places done *real damage* to the *East-India* Company? Has there been ever a requisition of compensation for that damage from any of them? Why is there such a *profound silence* observed with respect to them? Because they are judged by Administration and Parliament, more innocent than the Colony of *Massachusets-Bay*? No. Because Administration and Parliament do us *Americans* the honour to think, we are such very idects, that we shall not believe ourselves interested in the fate of *Boston*, but that one Colony may be attacked and humbled after another, without shewing the sense or spirit of beasts themselves, many of which unite against a common danger.

Why were the states of *Greece* broken down into the tamest submission by *Philip* of *Macedon*, and afterwards by the *Romans*? Because they contended for freedom *separately*. Why were the states of *Spain* subdued by the *Carthaginians* and afterwards by the *Romans*? Because they contended for freedom *separately*.—Why were the antient inhabitants of the kingdom, that now harrasses us, conquered by their invaders? *Tacitus* will inform us. "Nec aliud adversus validissimas gentes pro nobis utilius, quam quod in *Commune Non consulunt*. Rarus ad propulsandum *commune periculum* conventus. Ita dum *singuli* pugnant *omnes* vincuntur. ‡

Why did the little *Swiss* cantons, and seven small provinces of the Low Countries, so successfully oppose the tyrants, that not contented with an empire founded in humanity and mutual advantages, *unnecessarily* and arrogantly strove to "*lay*" the faithful and affectionate wretches "*at their feet*? Because, they wisely regarded the interest of *each* as the interest of *all*,

Our own experience furnishes a mournful additional proof of an observation made by a great and good man, Lord President *Forbes*. "It is a certain truth," says he, "that all states and kingdoms, in proportion as they grow great, wealthy and powerful, grow wanton, wicked, and oppressive, and the history of all ages gives evidence of the fatal catastrophe of *all such* states and kingdoms, when the cup of their iniquity is full." Another "truth" as "certain" is—that "such states and kingdoms" never have been, and never will be checked in the career of their "wantonness, wickedness and oppression" by a people in any degree dependent upon them, but by the prudent, virtuous and steady *unanimity* of that people. To employ more words to elucidate a point so manifest, would be the idle attempt of gilding gold.

* *By the first of these bills, the* Governor *is to be invested with the power of a* Justice of the Peace, *to call out the military to effect, though the Minister says, in his speech,*——"*I shall always consider that a military power acting* under *the authority and controul of a civil magistrate*, Is a part of the constitution." *By the second*, Americans *are to be seized, confined, and carried to* England *to be tried, that is hanged on charges for acts done in a colony. This is not all. Soldiers and others, who shall commit* any offence, *such as murdering the colonists, under the pretence of supporting the authority of Parliament, shall be carried to England to be tried—that is—acquitted. Of the* Habeas Corpus *and* trial *by* peers, "*stat nominis umbra*."

"*That the absolute powers* claimed & exercised *in a neighbouring nation, is more tolerable than that of the Eastern empires, is in a great measure owing to their having united the judicial power in their parliaments, a body separate and distinct from both the legislative and executive, and if ever that nation recovers its former liberty, it will owe it to the efforts of those assemblies. In* Turkey *where* every Thing *is centered in the* Sultan *or* his Minister, Despotic power *is in its meridian, and* wears a most dreadful aspect." 1 Blackstone, 269, 270.

† *Both Houses of Parliament resolved two or three years ago, that persons might be sent for from* any of the colonies *for acts done there, and tried in* England, *under the old statute of Henry the 8th—made before the colonies existed. The late court at* Rhode-Island *was established on that principle. The intention of Parliament in passing the bill above-mentioned, is chiefly to screen persons, acting in support of their unconstitutional claims. They have declared, they have no doubt but that the 35th of* Henry *has established a just and legal method of cutting* American *throats*.

"*I can live, altho' another who has no right be put to live with me; nay, I can live, altho' I pay* excises *and* impositions *more than I do; but to have my* Liberty, *which is the* Soul *of my* Life, *taken from me by* power, *and to have my body pent up in a goal*," (*then thrown into a ship of war, transported three thousand miles across the ocean, to a land of bitter, selfish, furious and revengeful enemies, there thrust into the jaws of dungeons*) "without remedy by law, *and to be so adjudged: O improvident ancestors! O unwise forefathers! to be so curious in providing for the quiet possession of our laws, and the liberties of Parliament, and to neglect our persons and bodies, and to let them lie in prison, and that* durante bene placito, *remediless! If this be law, why do we talk of liberties? Why do we trouble ourselves with a dispute about law, franchises, property of goods, and the like?* What *may any man call* his own *if not the liberty of his person? I am weary of treading these ways.*" Speech *of Robert Phillips*, a member of the wise and moderate Parliament that met in the year 1627.

§ *Private letters give a further proof of this fact.*

‡ "*Nor was any thing more advantageous to us against very powerful nations, than their imprudence in not* consulting together for the interest of the whole. *Conventions for repelling a* common danger *were rare. Thus while* each *State resisted* singly, all *were subdued*. Tacit. in vit. Agric.

[The Remainder of the FARMER's 4th Letter will be in our next.]

PROVINCE of the MASSACHUSETTS-BAY.

By the GOVERNOR.

A PROCLAMATION

For discouraging certain illegal Combinations.

WHEREAS certain Persons, calling themselves a Committee of Correspondence for the Town of Boston, have lately presumed to make or cause to be made, a certain unlawful Instrument, purporting to be *a solemn League and Covenant*, intended to be signed by the Inhabitants of this Province; whereby they are most solemnly to covenant and engage, to suspend all commercial Intercourse with the Island of Great-Britain, until certain Acts of the British Parliament shall be repealed: And whereas printed Copies of the said unlawful Instrument have been transmitted, by the aforesaid Committee of Correspondence, so called, to the several Towns in this Province accompanied with a scandalous, traiterous, and seditious Letter, calculated to inflame the Minds of the People, to disturb them with ill-grounded Fears and Jealousies, and to excite them to enter into an unwarrantable, hostile, and traiterous Combination, to distress the British Nation, by interrupting, obstructing, and destroying her Trade with the Colonies, contrary to their Allegiance due to the King; and to the Form and Effect of divers Statutes made for securing, encouraging, protecting, and regulating the said Trade; and destructive of the lawful Authority of the British Parliament, and of the Peace, good Order, and Safety of the Community. And whereas the Inhabitants of this Province, not duly considering the high Criminality, and dangerous Consequences to themselves of such alarming and unprecedented Combinations, may incautiously be tempted to join in the aforesaid unlawful League and Covenant, and thereby expose themselves to the fatal Consequences of being considered as the declared and open Enemies of the King, Parliament, and Kingdom of Great-Britain.

In Observance therefore of my Duty to the King; in Tenderness to the Inhabitants of this Province; and to the End that none who may hereafter engage in such dangerous Combinations, may plead, in Excuse of their Conduct, that they were ignorant of the Crime in which they were involving themselves; I have thought fit to issue this Proclamation, hereby earnestly cautioning all Persons whatsoever within this Province, against signing the aforesaid, or a similar Covenant, or in any Manner entering into, or being concerned in such unlawful, hostile, and traiterous Combinations, as they would avoid the Pains and Penalties due to such aggravated and dangerous Offences.

And I do hereby strictly enjoin and command all Magistrates, and other Officers, within the several Counties in this Province, that they take effectual Care to apprehend and secure for Trial, all and every Person who may hereafter presume to publish, or offer to others to be signed, or shall themselves sign the aforesaid, or a similar Covenant; or be in any wise aiding, abetting, advising, or assisting therein.

And the respective Sheriffs of the several Counties within this Province, are hereby required to cause this Proclamation forthwith to be posted up, in some public Place, in each Town, within their respective Districts.

GIVEN under my Hand at Salem, the 29th Day of June, 1774, in the Fourteenth Year of His Majesty's Reign.

THOS. GAGE.

By His Excellency's Command,
THO'S. FLUCKER, Sec'ry.

GOD Save the KING.

The following Articles are taken from the London Papers to May 9, bro't by Captain Tittle, *who arrived at* Marblehead *last Thursday Night from* Falmouth, *viz.*

LONDON.

April 29. Ordered, that the bill for the better regulating the government of Massachusetts-Bay, in North-America, be read a third time on Monday, if it shall be then ingrossed.

Extract of a Letter from Norwich, April 23.

"It touches one's heart to see the misery of our poor weavers. There used to be orders from the American Merchants; but those being stopped, prevent our manufactures from being able to employ the poor workmen."

LONDON, *May* 6. The Order of the Day for the third Reading of the Bill for the more impartial Administration of Justice in Persons questioned for Acts done by them in the Execution of the Law for the Suppression of Riots and Tumults in the Province of Massachusetts Bay, being called for, the Bill was read, and a very warm Debate ensued:—The Friends of the Bill said but little in its Praise, resolving to shew its Merit by a Division; but the Enemies resolving to give it the last Stroke they could, condemned it in the severest Manner possible. At Six o'Clock a Motion was made that the Bill do pass; the Question being put, the House divided, Ayes 127, Noes 24. The principal Speakers were Lord North, Mr. Bourke, Mr. Wallce, Mr. Cowper Mr. Sawbridge, Governor Pownal, and Mr. Pulteney.

PHILADELPHIA, June 22.

A Correspondent remarks, that instead of complying with the Plan proposed by some People, for sending Members from America, to represent us in Parliament, it would be much better to delegate the MANUFACTURERS of Britain (by stopping our Imports,) for that Office; a Sett of Men whose Eloquence has never been exerted in vain, in Behalf of the Liberties of their Country.

NEWPORT, June 27.

Notwithstanding the many falsehoods propagated by the inveterate enemies to American freedom, that the people of Boston are divided into numerous parties, that they are intimidated, and just ready to submit, with a deal of such stuff; we can assure our readers that, except a few miscreant tools of blind power, who would curse father and mother, tamely see their wives and daughters debauch'd, and sell their souls to the devil for a little pelf; the people of Boston stand firm and resolute, undauntedly determined to free their country from the yoke of bondage, now fastening on them, or die gloriously in the attempt.

PORTSMOUTH, (New-Hampshire,) July 1.

Last Saturday arrived here Capt. Brown in a Mast-Ship, in 8 Weeks from London, who brings no later News than we have had already; in whom came Ten Passengers; and unluckily, for this Place, there were on Board 27 Chests of that pernicious, destructive, troublesome Commodity, called TEA, which for a long Time has, and still keeps the whole Continent in a Ferment, the Duty on which, operates in so violent a Manner on the Minds of the Inhabitants, not only in the Sea-Port Towns, but the whole Country in general, that it will require the most cooling Medicines, and the best Skill of the ablest political Physicians, to prevent the Body Politic from great Convulsions.—However, upon its being certified that there actually were 27 Chests of Tea consigned to Edward Parry, Esq; of this Town, a Meeting of the Inhabitants of the Town was immediately called, and a special Committee chosen to wait upon Mr. Parry, the Consignee, to know whether he would consent to certain Proposals which were made to him, that the Tea might not be sold here, but reshipped, who in a genteel Manner gave them all the reasonable Satisfaction they could desire, and a Watch of 25 Men were appointed by the Town to watch it two Days and two Nights, and the third Day it was put on board another Vessel, and sent out of this Harbour, with a fair Wind, committed to the watry Element, and hope in due Time the Owners thereof will receive the nett Proceeds, and for the future take Care how they send any disagreeable Commodity to this Province, with a Duty thereon.

Every Transaction was conducted with the greatest Decency and good Order possible, which could have done Honour to any Society—The Whole being of one Heart and one Mind that the Tea should go out of this Port and Harbour immediately, and not be landed in this Province.

Town-Meetings have been every Day this Week held, and not yet over, we could not procure an Account of all the regular Proceedings relative to the TEA, but shall endeavor to do it in Season for our next Paper.

BOSTON.

AT a meeting of the freeholders and other inhabitants of the town of BOSTON, by adjournment, at Faneuil-Hall, June 27, 1774.

Mr. SAMUEL ADAMS, Moderator.

Upon a motion made, Voted, That the committee of correspondence be directed to lay before the town the letters which they have wrote to the other colonies, as well as those sent to the other towns in his province, since the receipt of the Boston Port-Bill.

The Hall not being sufficient to contain all the inhabitants assembled, the meeting was adjourned to the Old South Meeting-House.

The town being again met according to adjournment. A motion was made and passed, that all letters received, as well as the answers returned, be laid before the town, and read.

After the Town-Clerk had accordingly read a number of said letters, a motion was made that the said vote be so far reconsidered as that the reading of all other letters previous to the covenant sent into the country by the committee of correspondence, and the letters accompanying the same, be suspended for the present, and that the town proceed to the reading of the said letter and covenant, and any other letters that may be particularly called for.

The said covenant and a number of letters having been read, a motion was made, that some censure be now passed by the town, on the conduct of the committee of correspondence, and that said committee be annihilated.

Mr. Adams, the Moderator, then moved that as the conduct of the committee of correspondence, for this town, of which he had the honor of being a member, is now to be considered, another Moderator might be chosen pro temp.

The Hon. THOMAS CUSHING, Esq; was accordingly chosen Moderator during that debate.

The motion for censuring and annihilating the committee of correspondence was considered, and the gentlemen in favor of the motion patiently heard, but it being dark, and these declaring that they had further to offer, it was voted that the consideration thereof be referred to the next meeting; and the meeting was accordingly adjourned.

TUESDAY, June 28, 10 o'clock. Met according to adjournment.

The motion for censuring and annihilating the committee of correspondence again considered, and after long debates, the question was accordingly put, which passed in the negative by a vast majority.

It was then moved, that the following vote, be passed, viz. "That this town bear open testimony that they are abundantly satisfied of the upright intentions, and much approved the honest zeal of the committee of correspondence, and desire that they would persevere with their usual activity and firmness, continuing steadfast in the way of well doing."——And the question being put, passed in the affirmative by a vast majority.

The committee on ways and means for employing the poor, acquainted the town, that they had met, and had received very encouraging accounts of the readiness of their sister colonies to assist us, and various proposals from sundry persons for employing the poor, upon which they were deliberating, but were not yet prepared to report, required further time, which was allowed them.

Mr. ADAMS again in the Chair.

A motion made that this meeting be adjourned to Tuesday the 19th of July, at 10 o'clock, A. M. to meet at Faneuil-Hall; and the meeting was adjourned accordingly.

Attest. WILLIAM COOPER, Town-Clerk.

Mr. Treasurer Gray asserted in the last Town Meeting that many Towns had rejected the Covenant not to consume British Manufactures with Indignation; upon being pressed to name one, he named the Town of Worcester—*But we have the most undoubted Authority to assure the Publick, that the Covenant has been adopted and already signed by more than three Quarters of the Freeholders of that Town. Some other Parts of that Gentleman's extraordinary Speech will probably be animadverted on, particularly his very whimsical Declaration, that there were amongst the Addressers to Governor Hutchinson, one Hundred Men equal in Wealth to any other Hundred in the Town of Boston.* Nimium ne crede.

To his Excellency Governor GAGE.

SIR,

YOU have been appointed by his Majesty to preside over this colony at a time when the most extensive abilities as well as the greatest integrity are required. The eyes not only of this Continent but of Britain and all Europe are fixed upon you; it is therefore of the last importance, that you shou'd form a just judgment of the genius of the people whom you are sent to govern. If you mistake in this, you will certainly be unsuccessful in your endeavors to restore harmony between great Britain and the colonies; and if that harmony is not restored, 'tis not necessary to say what fatal consequences must ensue. Permit me, Sir, to tell you that I think myself bound as a liege subject of king George the third, to make some friendly remarks in this public manner which I am not at present in a situation to communicate to you in any other way.

You have spent the greatest part of your life in attending to military affairs. In the army the commands of the superior are considered by the inferior as a law by which he is absolutely bound. In civil life we know not of any authority but that which is derived from the law of the land, which every man is presumed to be acquainted with; and whenever a magistrate goes beyond the limits of the law, or *attempts* to do that which the law does not authorize him to do, he cannot in that *attempt* be considered as a magistrate; it is therefore necessary in order to keep up the dignity of a magistrate, that he make the law of the land the rule of his conduct.

It is also requisite that a man placed at the head of a government should gain, if possible, the confidence of the subjects. A tender regard to the welfare of the people will never fail to conciliate their affections—to be careful of their rights is the sure way to make them careful that a due respect & obedience is paid to their rulers.

Your excellency is at the head of a province whose loyalty to their sovereign has been frequently testified in the most honorable manner; their affection to their brethren in Britain is innate and has been cultivated by that intercourse which friendship and our commercial connection have occasioned; and whoever destroys this *affection*, does an irreparable injury both to great Britain and her colonies; for he may be assured, that, this tie once broken, no other will ever be found sufficient to bind the two countries together.

Our ancestors came to America to enjoy the rights of men and christians; many of them left fair possessions in England for which they never did and never desired to receive any sort of compensation; but their estates went to the next heirs, or perhaps some of them fell into the hands of the crown. Their posterity still consider their lives and fortunes less dear than their liberties and religion, and, whilst animated with a sense of the justice of their cause, they will be able to endure such hardships and such conflicts as far surpass the belief of those who are unacquainted with those principles from whence such invincible resolution is derived. The harbour of Boston, is shut——the inhabitants suffer——does not the gracefulness with which they suffer convince you that a consciousness of their innocence supports them under this severe trial?——You have encamped your troops in the town of Boston——Is any one intimidated? Has any one deserted from the *American cause*, whom you wou'd not think a disgrace to *any cause*?—— You have issued your proclamation, and in it have told a truth which the enemies of Britain and America have for many years strenuously denied, viz. that a combination not to consume British manufactures tends to distress the trade of Great Britain. But, Sir, it is unusual that Proclamations shou'd be issued without the advice of the council; and if the common formality *had* been attended to, no Proclamation can alter the established laws of the land; and though, I doubt not, this Proclamation will have its due weight, it might be well to consider into which scale it will fall. Public measures, at this time especially, shou'd be founded in wisdom, and executed with discretion.—My hearty wish is that your Excellency may act such a part as may endear you to this people, and render you deserving of the approbation and confidence of our sovereign.

I am your Excellency's respectful servant,

A freeholder in the County of SUFFOLK.

Messieurs PRINTERS, *That the Public may see how much Governors differ in their Sentiments, relative to Non-Importation and Non-Consumption Associations, please to give the following Extracts from a Speech of Governor Pownall's in the House of Commons, at the Time of the late Non Importation Agreement, a Place in your Paper.*

Mr. SPEAKER,

" It has been said, that the associations under which this trade is suspended, are unwarrantable and illegal. Associations, to illegal purposes, are unwarrantable and illegal.—But so long as one British subject hath a right to purchase, or to refrain from purchasing, of another his fellow-subject, any article, the terms of the sale of which he does not approve, so long will the Americans, agreeing with one another in associations of œconomy against the unbounded rates now fixed upon them, be not only warrantable towards others, but justifiable towards themselves.

" This measure is in its consequences, a species of resistance to your taxes, which the law of God & nature hath armed them with; & which the law of man cannot take out of their hands. There is nothing in this resistance, which is either illegal or unwarrantable. What irregular proceedings may have been gone into by some imprudent people, in carrying these designs into execution, I neither know, nor will take upon me to justify.—But I will maintain, that associations of œconomy, and self-restraint in withholding from purchasing, are justifiable, and may be prudent.

Last Week were driven to the neighbouring Town of Roxbury, *Two Hundred and fifty-eight Sheep, a generous Donation of our sympathising Brethren of the Town of* Windham *in the Colony of* Connecticut; *to be distributed for the Employment or Relief of those who may be Sufferers by Means of the Act of Parliament called the Boston Port Bill. The Letter from our Friends cannot be inserted this Week, for want of Room; the following is an Extract from the Proceedings of the Town of* Windham, *June 23d, 1774. viz.*

" We cannot close this Meeting without expressing our utmost Abhorrence and Detestation of those Few in a devoted Province, stiling themselves, Ministers, Merchants, Barristers and Attornies, who have against the Sense and Opinion of the rest of that extensive Government, as also of this vast Continent, distinguished themselves in their late fawning, adulating Address to Governor HUTCHINSON, the Scourge of the Province which gave him Birth, and the Pest of America. His Principles and Conduct, evidenced by his Letters, and those under his Approbation, are so replete with Treason against his Country, and with the meanest of Self-exaltation, as cannot be palliated by Art, nor disguised by Subtilty.

" In general we esteem those addresses a high-handed Insult on the Town of Boston, and the Province of the Massachusetts-Bay in particular, and all the American Colonies in general. Those stiled Merchants may plead their profound Ignorance of the constitutional Rights of Englishmen as an Excuse in some Degree. But for those who stile themselves Barristers & Attornies, they have either assumed a false Character, or they must in some Measure be acquainted with the constitutional Rights of Englishmen, and those of their own Province. For them to present such an Address is a daring Affront to common Sense, a high Insult on all others of the Profession, and Treason against Law. And from that learned Profession, who are supposed to be well acquainted with the English Constitution, and have the best Means, and are under the greatest Advantages to defend the Rights of Society, and who have been famed as the greatest Supporters of English Liberties, for any of them to make a Sacrifice of all to their Pagod, of Vanity and fulsome Adulation, is mean, vile and unpardonable; and cannot be accounted for upon any other Principles, but those of their Master, who would sacrifice his Country to become the independant Head of a respectable Province, and the few Leaders of this infamous Law Band would it seems give their Aid and Support therein to obtain the first Places in his new Kingdom. The addressing Clergy we leave to the Reproaches of their own Consciences, but lament to find they are the first in their ignominious Homage to their Idol."

So far are the People of this Province from discovering the "high Criminality" of "a certain Instrument purporting to be a *solemn League and Covenant*," that it has made more rapid Progress through many Towns *since Thursday last*, than ever before. By what Act of the British Parliament or Clause in the Oath of Allegiance are we inhibited from raising our own Flax and Wool, or encouraging our own Manufactures in preference to those of any other Country? If there be no Act of the British Parliament or of the Province against it, what are the "dangerous Consequences" which we are told will ensue? A cool observer of the Times cannot but smile to hear some Connisseurs say, that the Trade of the Colonies is of no more Importance to the Mother Country than a single Thread in a whole Piece, while others with as *high a Tone* assures us, that to "suspend all Comercial Intercourse" with her in *one Province* only, will "*distress the British Nation*" ! ! !

Mills and Hicks's Paper of last Monday, announces that the Governor has assurance that 10000 Cannadians are ready to march hither upon the shortest Warning, to support Government. HUM!

Nothing could equal the virulent Abuse offered to the Committee of Correspondence at the Town-Meeting last Monday, but the Calmness those Gentlemen discovered under it; the foul Language used with unlimitted Freedom by their Accusers is not to be palliated as being hastily uttered in the warmth of Debate, for it had been committed to Writing in a cool Hour, and was read in the Meeting. The Committee have repeatedly received the fullest Approbation of the Town, in a very crouded Meeting within a Fortnight; and the last Time after the severest Scrutiny into their Conduct.

Extract of a Letter from Charlestown, South Carolina, dated June 13, 1774.

" Our Committee have met and deliberated this Evening upon the Virginia Packet—We have thereupon unanimously agreed to call a general Meeting of the Inhabitants of the *whole Province*.—The Day fixed on is Tuesday the 5th July.—In the mean Time we are to write to leading Men in every Part of the Country, acquainting them with the present State of America, and to influence them to attend at or consult their several Districts, and send Deputies with their Sentiments, to the General Meeting.——*Even the Merchants now seem generally dispos'd for a* NON-IMPORTATION.—A general Congress will be readily adopted here."

We hear from the Westward, that Brigadier R—— having openly declared, upon a Sight of the solemn League and Covenant, that he would commit the Man to Goal that would presume to sign it, upwards of a Hundred Persons immediately put their Names to it——A wise Man might easily have foreseen that this would have been the Consequence of such an imprudent Threat.

The Episcopalian Parsons are too deeply in the Designs of Administration to expect to gain many Proselytes: an honest Non Conformist wou'd be glad to be informed whether these pious Gentlemen are careful to transmit home a true State of the Numbers who have lately revolted from the Legend of Modes and Forms.—We were not surprized at the Complaints of the little Man at the North, that he was compelled to preach to bare Walls; and it is probable that one B-s—t, an equally despicable Predicator in Newport, for lately reviling and scurrilously abusing the Inhabitants of Boston in their present distressed Circumstances, may be reduced to the same miserable Situation. However he may stand a tolerable good Chance to be prefered to a Welsh-Curacy, where Gambling and Toping are no Objections to the Character of a worthy Pastor.

We hear that a certain L. G——r has informed G. G—e that his Province is in a State of Anarchy and Confusion—That the Mayor and Aldermen who opposed the Inhabitants, were tumbled in the Dirt for their Exertions; and that Ships and Troops are absolutely necessary to restore Peace and good Order.

It is said the Tea at Portsmouth has been sent off by the Governor, to prevent the Consequences of the Resentment of the Inhabitants.

Extract of a Letter from New York, dated 26th June 1774.

" I am extremely well pleas'd with the Spirit and glorious Conduct of your General Court. They are a Band of Patriots, fit to be entrusted with the Rights and Liberties of a People; and whose resolution and good Sense, would do them honor in any Country under Heaven; and at the same time I felicitate you on the pleasing prospect of American Affairs, and the unanimity which apparently subsists, throughout this wide extended Continent; which cannot fail to conduct us, to the summit of our wishes, by procuring us a Restoration of our inestimable Rights and Liberties; and an ample Redress of all our Grievances.—I am well informed, that Subscriptions are rapidly going on in Philadelphia, and some of the other Southern Colonies, for the Relief of the suffering Poor in your Town; and a Motion will be made To-morrow Evening at our grand Committee, for the same laudable Purpose, which I am well assur'd will be carried, and a Subscription immediately open'd."

Since our last arrived a Number of Transports from Ireland, having on board the 5th and 38th Regiments of Foot.

Friday last arrived here from England, Vice Admiral Graves, in the Preston Man of War of 50 Guns.

A Company of the Royal Train of Artillery, with 8 Pieces of Cannon, landed here from the Castle on Saturday last, and are encamped on Powder House Hill in the Common.

TO BE SOLD,

Several good Farms, with Dwelling-Houses, Barns, &c. thereon, pleasantly situated about 10 Miles from Boston, on a considerable Road——The Payment may be made very easy.——Also several Rights of Land in a new Township. Enquire of Edes & Gill.

To be sold for Cash only,

A small Quantity of good dry Mehogany, fit for immediate Use: Inquire of Edes & Gill.

To be sold on very reasonable Terms,

The Hull of a double-deck'd Brigantine about 146 Tons Burthen, now launched in Taunton-River. Farther enquire of ABIEL SMITH, nearly opposite to the Head of Orange Tree-Lane, Boston, or Mr. JOB SMITH, at Taunton.

To be Sold at Public Vendue, by Order of his Majesty's Justices of the Inferior Court, on the first Wednesday in August,

PART of the Real Estate of SAMUEL WELD, late of Roxbury, Joiner, decease'd, viz. Half of a House, known by the Name of the Greyhound Tavern, and 8 Acres of Land, near the Rev. Mr. Gordon's Meeting House. The Sale to be at said House on Wednesday the 3d of August, at Three o'Clock, P. M.

TO BE SOLD

ON THURSDAY NEXT,

By BENJAMIN CHURCH,

At FOUR o'Clock in the Afternoon,

A General Assortment of European Articles, Linnens Woollens, Checks, &c. &c. Some House Furniture, an 8-Day Clock, Mehogany Case of Draws, Watches, &c. &c.—At Four o Clock, P. M.—

TO BE LETT,

A convenient Brick Tenement, near the Orange-Tree. Inquire of the Printers.

The Sloop JENNY, lying at the Long-Wharff at Salem, will sail in 10 Days, for Annapolis-Royal.——For Freight or Passage apply to GEORGE MITCHEL, on board said Sloop, or to his House on Winter's Wharff, Boston.

CHoice Lisbon LEMMONS per Box. Lisbon, Madeira, Malaga, Virgin, Sherry, Shullowe WINE, per Quarter Cask.—Raisins per Cask. Citron per Box. Lisbon Oil per Cask, Dutch Brushes, Barcelona Handkerchiefs per Dozen, TO BE SOLD

By Archibald Cunningham,

At his Store in Ann-Street, Boston.

ON TUESDAY the Twelfth Day of July Inst. at Ten o Clock in the Forenoon, will be Sold by PUBLICK VENDUE, at the Dwelling House of Mr. Experience Brewer, deceased, being the Northward of Doctor Cutler's Church, and near the Dwelling House of Capt. William White.

ALL the House Furniture of the said Brewer, consisting of Desks, Chests of Draws, Mehogany and other Tables, Chairs, Looking Glasses, Pictures, Feather Beds, Bedding and Bedsteads, Brass, Copper, Pewter, Tin and Iron Ware; also some Remnants of Shop Goods, some Peices of Plate and other Articles.

TO BE SOLD,

A large and convenient Dwelling House, situate on Spring Hill so called, in Portsmouth, in the Province of New Hampshire, near the Market, in the most principal Part of the Town for any Gentleman to carry on Trade, both by Sea & Land. Said House is almost New, and almost finished, with an excellent Cellar, and a back Yard, and a Garden, also a Warehouse and Stable, with many other Conveniences suitable for a Family. Inquire of the Printers.

IMPORTED in the last Ships from LONDON, and to be Sold by JOHN WHITE, near the Cornfield, Union Street.

AN Assortment of Goods, amongst which are 7-8 and yard-wide Irish Linnen, Cotton and Linnen Check, newest fashioned Callicoes, Ribbons of all Sorts, Handkerchiefs of all sorts, Diaper Table Cloaths, Clouting Diaper, Russia Drabs, Nankeens, Women's Shoes and Clogs, silk Gloves and Mitts, Book Muslin, Cambricks and Lawns, Catgut, Patent and Spiders Net, Black, Bone and Blond Lace, White Blond and Thread ditto, Cheveaux de Frize, sprig'd and strip'd Silk Gauze, English and French Necklaces, Sarsnets and Sattins of all Colours, Cotton Hose.—A large Assortment of Looking Glasses, China, Glass and Earthern Ware, English Loaf Sugar, and a few fine Cheshire Cheeses.

A young Woman, with a good Breast of Milk would be glad to take a Child to Suckle.——Inquire of Edes and Gill.

New AUCTION-ROOM, Cornhill.

TO-MORROW at TEN o'Clock will be Sold by PUBLIC VENDUE, at GREENLEAF's Auction-Room,——

—A great Assortment of GOODS—

——Amongst which are,——

Irish Linnens, fine Chints, Callicoes, flower'd and plain Lawns, Lawn Aprons, sprig'd Muslins, Ribbons, plain Modes, Table Cloths, Checks, strip'd Hollands, Bed Ticks, silk Twist, Broad Cloths, Velverets, Shalloons, Durants, Tammys, Worsted Hose, Felt and Castor Hats, stamp'd and check'd Handkerchiefs. Also a Quantity of Hard Ware, and some Indigo. WILLIAM GREENLEAF, Auctioneer.

The Sale will begin at Ten o'Clock precisely.

At GOULD's Auction Office in Back Street,

TO-MORROW MORNING,

At TEN o'Clock,

Will be Sold by PUBLIC VENDUE,

A Variety of genteel House Furniture,

Belonging to a Gentleman leaving the Province immediately.——Amongst which are——

Mahogany Dining, Tea and Card Tables, Mahogany Four Post and other Bedsteads, Looking Glasses, Feather Beds, Chairs, Desks, Chests of Draws. Curtains, Parlour and Kitchen Andirons, and all sorts Kitchen Furniture.——Also all the Wearing Apparel, and other Personal Effects of a Gentleman deceas'd. R. GOULD, Auctioneer.

Burials in the Town of BOSTON, since our last.

Six Whites. No Blacks.

Baptiz'd in the several Churches, Six.

High Water at BOSTON, for the present Week.

Monday, 10 min. aft. 8	Friday, 16 min. after 11
Tuesday, 54 min. aft. 8	Saturday, 3 min. aft. 12
Wednesday, 40 m. aft. 9	Lord's-Day, 30 m. af. 12
Thursday, 30 min. aft. 10	D's New 8 Day 5 After.

VIRGINIA.

At a meeting of the freeholders and other inhabitants of the county of Frederick, and gentlemen practising at the bar, held at the town of Winchester the 8th of June, 1774, to consider of the best mode to be fallen upon to secure their liberties and properties, and also to prevent the dangerous tendency of an act of Parliament passed in the fourteenth year of his present Majesty's reign, intitled, An act to discontinue in such manner and for such time as are therein mentioned, the landing and discharging, lading and shipping of goods, wares and merchandize at the town, and within the harbour of Boston, in the Province of Massachusetts-Bay, in North-America, evidently has to invade & deprive us of the same.

The Rev. Mr. Charles M. Thurston, being voted Moderator, a committee of the following gentlemen, viz. the Rev. Charles M. Thurston, Isaac Zane, George Rootes, Angus M'Donal, Alexander White, George Johnson, and Samuel Beall, 3d, were appointed to draw up resolves suitable to the same occasion, who withdrawing for a short time, returned with the following votes, viz.

VOTED,

I. THAT we will always cheerfully pay due submission to such acts of government as his Majesty has a right by law to exercise over his subjects as sovereign of the British dominions, and to such only.

II. That it is the inherent right of British subjects to be governed and taxed by representatives chosen by themselves only; and that every act of the British Parliament respecting the internal policy of North-America, is a daring and unconstitutional invasion of our said rights and privileges.

III. That the act of Parliament is not only in itself repugnant to the fundamental laws of natural justice, in condemning persons for a supposed crime unheard, but also a despotic exertion of unconstitutional power, calculated to enslave a free and loyal people.

IV. That the enforcing the execution of the said act of parliament by a military power, will have a necessary tendency to raise a civil war, thereby dissolving that union which has so long happily subsisted between the mother country and her colonies; and that we will most heartily and unanimously concur with our suffering brethren of Boston, and every other part of North-America that may be the immediate victims of tyranny, in promoting all proper measures to avert such dreadful calamities, to procure a redress of our grievances, and to secure our common liberties.

V. It is the unanimous opinion of this meeting, that a joint resolution of all the colonies to stop all importations from Great-Britain, and exportations to it, till the said act be repealed, will prove the salvation of North-America and her liberties: On the other hand, if they continue their imports and exports, there is the greatest reason to fear that fraud, power, and the most odious oppression, will rise triumphant over right, justice, social happiness and freedom.

VI. That the East-India company, those servile tools of arbitrary power, have justly forfeited the esteem and regard of all honest men; and that the better to manifest our abhorrence of such abject compliance with the will of a venal ministry in ministering all in their power, an increase of the fund of peculation; we will not purchase tea, or any other kind of East-India commodities, either imported now, or hereafter to be imported, except saltpetre, spices and medicinal drugs.

VII. That it is the opinion of this meeting that committees ought to be appointed for the purpose of affecting a general association, that the same measures may be pursued thro' the whole continent: That the committees ought to correspond with each other, and to meet at such places and times as shall be agreed on, in order to form such general association, and that when the same shall be formed and agreed on by the several committees, we will strictly adhere thereto; and till the general sense of the continent shall be known, we do pledge ourselves to each other and our country, that we will inviolably adhere to the votes of this day.

VIII. That Charles M. Thurston, Isaac Zane, Angus M'Donal, Samuel Beall, 3d, Alexander White, and George Rootes, be appointed a committee for the purposes aforesaid; and that they, or any three of them, are hereby fully empowered to act.

Which being read, were unanimously assented to and subscribed.

PAILADELPHIA.

At a very large and respectable Meeting of the Freeholders and Freemen of the City and County of Philadelphia, on Saturday, June 18, 1774.

THOMAS WILLING, } Esquires, CHAIRMEN.
JOHN DICKINSON, }

RESOLVED,

I. THAT the act of Parliament, for shutting up the port of Boston, is unconstitutional; oppressive to the inhabitants of that town; dangerous to the liberties of the British colonies; and that, therefore, we consider our brethren, at Boston, as suffering in the common cause of America.

II. That a congress of deputies from the several colonies in North-America, is the most probable and proper mode of procuring relief for our suffering brethren, obtaining redress of American greviances, securing our rights and liberties and re-establishing peace and harmony between Great-Britain and these colonies, on a constitutional foundation.

III. That a large and respectable Committee be immediately appointed for the city and county of Philadelphia, to correspond with the sister colonies, and with the several counties in this province, in order that all may unite in promoting and endeavoring to attain the great and valuable ends mentioned in the foregoing resolution.

IV. That the Committee nominated by this meeting, shall consult together, and on mature deliberation determine, what is the most proper mode of collecting the sense of this province, and appointing deputies for the same, to attend a general congress; and having determined thereupon, shall take such measures, as by them shall be judged most expedient, for procuring this province to be represented at the said congress, in the best manner that can be devised for promoting the public welfare.

V. That the Committee be instructed immediately to set on foot a subscription for the relief of such poor inhabitants of the town of Boston, as may be deprived of the means of subsistence by the operation of the act of Parliament, commonly stiled the Boston Port Bill. The money arising from such subscription to be laid out as the committee shall think will best answer the ends proposed.

VI. That the Committee, consist of forty-four persons, viz. *John Dickinson*, [the reputed author of the excellent letters from a Pennsylvania Farmer] *James Pemberton, Edward Pennington, John Nixon, Thomas Willing, George Clymer, Samuel Howell, Joseph Read, John Roberts, (Miller) Thomas Wharton jun. Charles Thompson, Jacob Barge, Thomas Barclay, William Rush, Robert Smith, (Carpenter) Thomas Fitzimons, George Roberts, Samuel Ervin, Thomas Miflin, John Cox, George Gray, Robert Morris, Samuel Miles, John M. Nesbitt, Peter Cheavalier, William Moulder, Joseph Moulder, Anthony Morris, jun. John Allen, Jerimiah Warder, jun. Rev. Dr. William Smith, Paul Engle, Thomas Penrose, James Mease, Benjamin Marshall, Ruben Hains, John Bayard, Jonathan B. Smith, Thomas Wharton, Isaac Howell, Michael, Hillegas, Adam Hudley, George Schlosser*, and *Christopher Ludwick*:——To whose approved integrity, abilities and sincere affection for the interest of this immense empire, their constituents look up for the most propitious events.

At this meeting, and suitable to the interesting occasion of it, an eloquent oration, expressed in the finest language ever heard in Pennsylvania, was delivered by the Reverend Doctor Smith.

ALL who desire Admission into HARVARD-COLLEGE this Year, are hereby Notified, That the Tutors have determined to attend the Business of Examination on Tuesday and Wednesday, the 19th and 20th Days of July next.

J. WADSWORTH, per Order.

Harvard-College, June 15, 1774.

To be Sold cheap for CASH.

A few Casks of good Sugars, West-India Rum, and a few Casks of Coffee.——Inquire at Cruft's Store, a little to the Northward of Hancock's Wharf, North-End.

GOODS at the *Sterling Cost*.

John Cunningham

HAS yet remaining a good Assortment of English and India GOODS, which he continues to sell at the Sterling Cost clear of Charges, at his Shop opposite to Mr. Gilbert Deblois's, near School-Street.

Choice Muscovado Sugars, Grenada Rum, Coffee, &c. &c. To be Sold by GABRIEL JOHONNOTT, at his Store South Side of Faneuil-Hall Market.

Doctor *Lagord*, Originally from France, practices Physick, Surgery and Midwifry, practised some Years at Braintree, but has lately removed to that Part of Cambridge called Menotomy, near the Meeting-House, at the Masons Arms Tavern, now kept by Benjamin Cooper from Boston; any Person who please to employ the said *Lagord* in any of the Branches, may speak with him at the above mentioned Place, where may be had good Entertainment for Gentlemen Trevellers.—Near said Cooper's is the famous Menotomy Pond, where he keeps a neat Boat for Fishery.

In the House of Representatives, June 14 1774.

WHEREAS there will become due in this Month, sundry Notes given by the Province Treasurer, and sufficient Provision having been made for the paying off the same, and if the Possessors of such Notes should not bring them in to the Treasurer to be paid, the Province will suffer Damage by such Neglect:

Therefore, RESOLVED, That the Possessors of such Notes, who shall not bring them to the Province Treasurer, to be paid by the last Day of *July* next, shall not receive any Interest on the same, after that Time, and the Province Treasurer is hereby directed forthwith to cause this Order to be published in all the *Boston* News-Papers, three Weeks successively, that every one concerned may be Notified hereof. Sent up for Concurrence.

T. CUSHING, Speaker.

In Council, June 15th. Read and concurred.

JOHN COTTON, D. Sec'ry.

Consented to, THOs. GAGE.

A true Copy attest. JOHN COTTON, D. Sec'ry.

☞ *THE Treasurer of the Province* hereby gives public Notice to the delinquent Constables and Collectors of the Province Taxes, that they pay the same into the Treasury by the 31st of *July* next.

Treasury-Office, July 18, 1774.

A Young Woman with a good Breast of Milk, would go into a Family to Suckle a Child, or take it Home, as it may suit; her Character for Honesty is indisputable. Inquire of the Printers.

RAN-away from the Subscriber on the Eighth of June Instant, at Night, a Negro Boy, about Seventeen Years of Age: Had on when he went off, a dark coloured cloth Jacket and Trowsers, and is branded on the Breast Delamote, very remarkable: said Fellow speaks tolerable good English, and some French. Whoever takes up said Fellow and Secures him in any of his Majesty's Goals, or Returns him to the Subscriber, shall have FIVE DOLLARS Reward, and all necessary Charges paid by ALLIN BROWN.

Providence, June 10, 1774.

CHARLESTOWN Stage No. 1. sets out with four good Horses for Salem, from Mr. WOART's Tavern every Morning at 8 o'Clock, and returns the same Day; it puts up at Mr. Goodhue's in Salem. Any Gentlemen or Ladies who wants a Passage are desired to call at Admiral Vernon's, in King-street, Boston; or Mr. Woart's, in Charlestown, and leave their Names.—Also at the same Place, Stage No. 2. with four good Horses may be had to convey any Gentleman or Lady to any Part of this, or any other Province, or at so small a Distance as five or six Miles.

Any Gentlemen or Ladies who choose to go in either of the above Stages, will be accommodated in the best Manner, and the smallest Favour will be acknowledged,

By their humble Servant,

SAMUEL LORD.

Charlestown, June 22, 1774.

Province of the Massachusetts-Bay, } *To the Hon.* James Otis, *Esq*; *one of his Majesty's Justices of the Peace through the said Province.*

We the Subscribers, Proprietors of a Tract of Land lying at *Broad-Bay*, in the County of *Lincoln*, in said Province, and bounded as followeth, viz.—beginning at *Pemaquid-Falls* and so running a direct Course to the Head of *New-Harbour*, from thence to the South End of *Misconcus-Island*, taking in the Island, so running five and twenty Miles into the Country North by East, and thence eight Miles North West by West, and thence turning and running South by West to *Pemaquid*, where it first began——pray that your Honour would issue a Warrant to one of us to call a Meeting of the Proprietors of said Land, to be on the third Day of *August* next, at Ten of the Clock in the Forenoon, at the House of *William Goodhue*, Innholder in *Salem*; then and there to chuse a Moderator of said Meeting, a Clerk of said Proprietors, a Committee to transact the Affairs of said Proprietors as Occasion may require, and any other needful Officers; to agree upon a Method for calling of Meetings for the future; to take under Consideration the Division that the Proprietors of said Land made some Years ago and confirm the same, or order a new Division and run the boundary Line; to settle with those Persons who have made Settlements of said Land on reasonable Terms, by selling them the Land or otherways, but in case they refuse to settle as aforesaid, to sue them off and prosecute any Person or Persons who shall trespass on said Land; to pass any Orders that are necessary to bring forward the Settlement of said Land, by giving away Land or otherways, and to raise Money on said Land for necessary Charges and order the collecting the same.

Salem, June 15. 1774.

Daniel Sargent,
his
John + *Brown,*
Mark
John Choate,
Jona. Cogswell, jun.
John Sargent.

Province of the Massachusetts-Bay.

(Seal.) *To* John Choate *of* Ipswich, *in the County of* Essex, *in said Province, one of the principal Proprietors of the Land aforesaid,* Greeting.

In pursuance of the foregoing Application and Request, you are hereby required to give Notice, in Time and Manner as the Law directs, to the Proprietors afore-mentioned, that they meet at the Time and Place and for the Purposes mentioned in the afore-written Petition. Given under my Hand and Seal this 15th Day of June, Anno Domini, 1774.

JAMES OTIS, a Justice of the Peace through the Province of the Massachusets-Bay.

Ipswich, June 15, 1774.

By Virtue of the afore-written Warrant to me directed, I do hereby notify and warn the Proprietors of the aforesaid Land to meet at the Dwelling House of *William Goodhue*, Innholder at Salem, on the 3d Day of August next, at Ten of the Clock in the Forenoon, for the Purposes therein mentioned.

JOHN CHOATE.

TO BE SOLD at the Royal Exchange Tavern in King-Street, Boston,

At PUBLIC VENDUE,

On Wednesday the Fourteenth Day of September next, at Ten o'Clock in the Forenoon,

The following Lots of Land, viz.

Lot marked F. 2. in the first range of Lots, containing about six Thousand Acres (exclusive of Settlers Lots interspersed) being near one Mile wide and fifteen Miles long, and fronting on *Kennebeck*-River, on the West-side of it, about ten Miles above Fort Halifax: to be divided and Sold in two Parts.

Lot marked B. D. 1. in the second range of Lots, about six Miles above *Norridgwalk*, on the West Side of *Kennebeck*-River, and fronting thereon, containing about seven Thousand Acres, exclusive of Settlers Lots interspersed, being one Mile wide, & 15 Miles long.

Lot marked C. A. 1. in the third range of Lots, near the Falls of *Cariotonka*, about twelve Miles above *Norridgwalk*, on the West Side of *Kennebeck*-River, and fronting thereon, containing about seven Thousand Acres, exclusive of Settler's Lots interspersed, being one Mile wide and fifteen Miles long.

Lot No. 20, called a Ten Mile back Lot, on the West Side of *Kennebeck* River, containing about four Thousand eight Hundred Acres.

Three Lots of Land, viz. Lot No. 32, on the East Side of *Kennebeck*-River, about 300 Poles above *Fort Western*, No. 86, on the East Side of said River, about nine Miles, and 120 Poles above *Fort Western*, and also Lot No. 20, on the West Side of said River, about one Mile and 230 Poles above *Fort-Western*, containing 400 Acres each.

Also all the Islands in Cobbiseconte Pond, and all the Islands in *Kennebeck* River, above *Fort Halifax*. The Pay will be made easy to the Purchasers.

For further Particulars enquire of *Henry Alline*, jun. at his Office in King Street, *Boston*, *June* 10. 1774.

Boston: Printed, by EDES & GILL, *in Queen-Street*, 1774.

THE Boston-Gazette, AND COUNTRY JOURNAL.

No. 1004.

Containing the freshest Advices, Foreign and Domestic.

MONDAY, July 11, 1774.

Remainder of LETTER IV.

To the INHABITANTS of the British Colonies in AMERICA.

BRETHREN,

SURELY you cannot doubt at this time, my countrymen, but that the people of the *Massachusets-Bay* are suffering in a cause ‖ common to us all; and therefore, that we ought immediately to concert the most prudent measures for their relief and our own safety.

Our interest depending on the present controversy is unspeakably valuable. We have not the least prospect of human assistance. The passion of despotism raging like a plague, for about seven years past, has spread with unusual malignity through *Europe*. *Corsica*, *Poland* and *Sweden*, have sunk beneath it. The remaining spirit of freedom, that lingered and languished in the Parliaments of *France*, has lately expired, by the new modelling their Parliaments. What kingdom or state interposed for the relief of their distressed fellow creatures? The contagion has at length reached *Great-Britain*. Her statesmen emulate the *Nimrods* of the earth and wish to become "mighty hunters" in the woods of *America*. What kingdom or state will interpose for our relief? The preservation of our freedom and every attendant blessing must be wrought out, under Providence, *by ourselves*. Let not this consideration discourage us. We cannot be false to each other, without being false to ourselves. We have the firmest foundation of union and fidelity—that we wish to attain the same things—to avoid the same things. The friendship of others might be precarious, suspected, deceitful.

The infinitely great, wise, and good being, who gave us our existence, certainly formed us for a state of society. He certainly designed us for such a state of society, as would be productive of happiness. Liberty is essential to the happiness of a society, and therefore is our right. The father of mercies never intended men to hold *unlimited* authority over men. ¶ Craft and cruelty have indeed triumphed over simplicity and innocence, in disobedience to his holy laws. The father of mercies never intended *us* for the slaves of *Britons*. Craft and cruelty indeed are striving to brand us with marks infamously denoting us to be their property, as absolutely as their cattle. Their pretensions to a right of such power, not only oppose constitutional principles, but even partake of impiety. The sentence of bondage against us is only issued by the frail OMNIPOTENCE* of *Parliament*.

> "*Non sic inflectere sensus*
> "*Humanos edicta valent.*" §

We cannot question the *justice* of our cause. This consideration will afford comfort and encouragement to our minds.

Let us therefore, in the first place, humbling ourselves before our gracious creator, devoutly beseech his divine protection of us his afflicted servants, most unreasonably and cruelly oppressed.—Let us seriously reflect on our manifold transgressions, and by a sincere repentance, and an entire amendment of our lives, strive to recommend ourselves to divine favour.

In the next place, let us cherish and cultivate sentiments of brotherly love and tenderness amongst us. To whom under the cope of Heaven, can we look for help in these days of "darkness and trouble," but one to another. O my countrymen! have pity one on another—Have pity on yourselves, and your children. Let us—by every tender tie, I implore you—let us, mutually excuse and forgive each other our weaknesses and prejudices, (for who is free from weaknesses and prejudices?)—and utterly abolishing all former dissentions and distinctions, wisely and kindly unite in one firm band, in one common cause.

If there are any men or any bodies of men on this continent, who think that an accommodation between us and *Great-Britain*, or that their own particular interest, may be advanced by withdrawing themselves from the councils of their countrymen, I would wish them most deliberately to consider the consequences, that may attend such a conduct. What step can possibly be taken more directly tending to *prevent* an accommodation between us and *Great-Britain*, than supplying administration with *proofs of our intestine division*? What do our enemies so ardently wish for, as for these divisions? Has not the *expectation* of these events encouraged the ministry to treat us with such unexampled contempt and barbarity? Will not the *certainty* of these events excite resolutions in them to press us—to take every advantage of a people so industriously studying and labouring to weaken and destroy themselves? Then a minister may with reason call upon the House of Commons—"*now is our time to* stand—to *defy* them—to proceed with *firmness* and *without fear*—to produce a conviction to ALL *America*, that we are now *in earnest*; and that we will proceed with firmness and rigour——until SHE SHALL BE LAID AT OUR FEET."†

I appeal to every man of common sense, whether any measures will be so likely to induce administration to think of an accommodation with us, as our *unanimity*. Must not, therefore, every measure impeaching the credit and weight of this unanimity in the same degree obstruct all accommodation? Will not every such measure naturally produce *haughtiness*, *perseverance* and *fresh rigour* in our oppressors? Will not *these* still more enrage us, and place us farther from an accommodation? If the *Protection* and *Peace*, we wish to derive from our unanimity be taken from us, by the imprudence of our brethren, who break that unanimity or destroy all respect for it in *Great-Britain*, and thereby encourage her to seize, what she will certainly think, the lucky opportunity for pursuing her blows, what must be the consequence? We held up a shield for our defence. If our brethren have pierced it through and rendered it useless—their indiscretion will, according to the usual course of human affairs, compel us to change the mode of defence, and drive us into all the evils of civil discords.

What advantages can they gain, that can compensate to men of any understanding or virtue, for the miseries occasioned by their bad policy. Their numbers will be too small, in any manner whatever, to controul the sentiments or measures of the people of *America*. Their conduct never can prevent the exertions of these colonies in vindication of their liberty. It may, by provocations, render those exertions more rash and imprudent. But their numbers will be so extravagantly exaggerated, as all facts have been against us, on the other side of the *Atlantic*, that *Great-Britain* may be *deceived* and *emboldned* into measures destructive to herself and to us. We are now strenuously endeavouring, *in a peaceable manner*, by this single *power*—the force of *Unanimity*---to preserve our freedom. Those, who *lessen* that unanimity, *detract* from its force---will *prevent* its *effect*---and must be, therefore, justly chargeable with all the dreadful consequences to these colonies.

The third important consideration, I beg leave to recommend to my countrymen, is to draw such reflections from their situation as will confirm their minds in that manly noble fortitude, so absolutely necessary, for the maintenance of those inestimable privileges, for which they are now contending. The man, who fears difficulties arising in the defence of freedom, is unworthy of freedom. God has given the right and the means of asserting it. We may reasonably ask and expect his gracious assistance in the reasonable employment of those means. To look for miracles, while we abusively neglect the powers afforded us by divine goodness, is not only stupid, but criminal. We are yet free---let us think like freemen.

In the last place I beg leave to offer some observations concerning the measures that may be most expedient in the present emergency. Other nations have contended in blood for their liberty, and have judged the jewel worth the price that was paid for it. These colonies are not reduced to the dreadful necessity. So dependent is *Great-Britain* on us for supplies, that Heaven seems to have placed in our hands means of an effectual, yet peaceable resistence, if we have sense and integrity to make a proper use of them. A general agreement between these colonies of non-importation and non-exportation faithfully observed would certainly be attended with success. But is it now proper to enter into such an agreement? Let us consider that we are contending with our antient venerable and beloved parent-country. Let us treat her with all possible *respect* and reverence: ‡ Though the rulers there have had no compassion upon us, let us have compassion on the people of that kingdom: And if to give weight to our supplications and to obtain relief for our suffering brethren, it shall be judged necessary to lay ourselves under some restrictions with regard to our imports and exports, let it be done with tenderness, so as to convince our brethren in *Great-Britain* of the importance of a connection and harmony between them and us, and of the danger of driving us into despair. Their true interests and our own are the same; nor should we admit any notion of a distinction, till we *know* their *resolutions* to be *unalterably hostile*.

In the mean time, let us pursue the most proper methods for collecting the sentiments of all the British colonies in *North-America*, on the present situation of affairs---the first point, it is apprehended, to which attention should be paid. This may be effected in various ways. The assemblies that may have opportunities of meeting, may appoint deputies to attend a general congress at such time and place as shall be agreed on. Where assemblies cannot meet, such of the people as are qualified by law to vote in election of representatives may meet and appoint---or may request their representatives to meet and appoint.

When the inhabitants of this extended continent observe that regular measures are prosecuted for re-establishing harmony between *Great-Britain* and these colonies, their minds will grow more calm. Prospects of accommodation, it is hoped, will engage them patiently and peaceably to attend the result of the public councils and such applications as by the joint sense of America may be judged proper to be made to his Majesty and both Houses of Parliament.

"Better is a little with righteousness, than great revenues without right." Proverbs xvi.——

‖ *The act for shutting up the port of* Boston *orders, that it shall not be opened until peace and* obedience to the laws *shall be so far restored in the said town of* Boston, *that the trade of* Great-Britain *may safely be carried on there, and his Majesty's* DUTIES DULY COLLECTED,"*&c. Thus it appears, if the inhabitants* renounce *the common cause of the colonies, the port may be* opened——*if they* adhere *to that cause it will remain* shut.

¶ "*To live by one man's* WILL *became the cause of all men's misery*" HOOKER'S *Eccles. Pol.*

"*Is not* universal misery *and* ruin *the* SAME, *whether it comes from the hands of* many *or of* one?" Bishop HOADLY'S Disc. on Gov.

"*Of so contrary an opinion was this good man* (Hooker) *to that of some others, who can never oppose one* extreme, *without running to* another, *as bad, if not* worse, *and think they cannot enough condemn* rebellion, *without giving the divine sanction to* tyranny *and* oppression. *This judgment ought likewise to be of the more weight with such as profess the most profound veneration for the memory of Charles the first, and the honour of the* old Church of England: *Because this treatise in which it is to be found, was chosen out of many others by that* Prince, *to be recommended to his* children, *as the best* instructor *they could converse with; and was had in such* estimation *by all* churchmen, *from the time of its appearance, that it may well pass, not only for his own* judgment *in particular, but for the judgment of the whole* Church *of England at that time.*" Bishop HOADLY ibid.

"*Would not the* unhappiness *of this nation in particular have been the same, whether a late King* alone, *or by a* FORMAL LAW, *had subjected it to the religion of* Rome, *and the* MAXIMS OF FRANCE? *And upon supposition of such an* attempt, *would not our* late deliverance *have been as* glorious, *as great and* justifiable, *as much wanted, and as truly beneficial, as it was upon the attempt of the* King alone? *Would not* the invitation of the Prince of Orange, *the* election *and* meeting *of the persons, who made the* convention, *and the* consequent establishment *in the* Protestant line, *have been as requisite and* useful? *Nay, would not the* ends of government *have been more effectually answered this way, than by* SUBMISSION *to a* TOTAL DISSOLUTION OF ALL HAPPINESS *at* present, *and of* ALL HOPES *for the* future? *How then can it be said, that the* ends of government *require that degree of* submission *upon the* one *supposition, which they are allowed not to do upon the* other, *when the same* MISERY *and* DESTRUCTION *must follow a* submission *in both cases, and the same* UNIVERSAL HAPPINESS *must, in both, be the* consequence *of a* just *and* well-managed defence? *Or would the* ends of government *be destroyed should the miserable condition of the whole people of* France, *which hath proceeded from the King's being absolute, awaken the thoughts of the* wisest heads *amongst them, and move them all to exert themselves,* so as that those ends should be better answered for the time to come." Bishop HOADLY, ibid.

It was resolved by the House of Commons, that this Bishop, then Mr. Hoadly, *and rector of* St. Peter's Poor, *London,* "*for having often strenuously justified the* principles, *on which her* Majesty *and the* Nation *proceeded in the late happy revolution, had justly merited the favour and recommendation of the House.*" *And accordingly addressed Queen Anne,* "*that she would be graciously pleased to bestow some dignity in the church on the said* Mr. Hoadly, *for his eminent services both to the* church & state."

"*Whatsoever dishonours human nature, dishonours the policy of a government which permits it; and a free state, which does not communicate the natural right of liberty to all its subjects* who have not deserved by their crimes to lose it, *hardly seems to be worthy of that honourable name.*" Lord LITTLETON'S History of HEN. II.

"*Without goodness, power would be* tyranny *and* oppression, *and wisdom would degenerate into craft and mischievous contrivance,*" Archbishop TILLOTSON'S sermons.

"*Etiamsi non sit molestus dominus, tamen est miserimum, posse, si velit.*" Cicero. *Even if a sovereign does not oppress, yet it is a most miserable condition for the subjects, that he has the* power, *if he has the* will.

* 1 *Blackstone*, 161.

§ *Edicts cannot so bend the common sense of human nature.*

† *Lord North's Speech.*

‡ "*By justice (saith the scripture) the throne is established,*" *and* "*by justice a nation shall be exalted.*" *I resemble justice to* Nebuchadnezzar's *tree, shading not only the palace of the King and the house of nobles, but sheltering also the cottage of the poorest beggar. Wherefore if now the blast of indignation hath so bruised any of the branches of this tree, that either our persons or goods, or possessions have not the same shelter as before, let us not therefore* neglect the root of this great tree; *but rather, with all our possible means, endeavours and unfeigned duties, both apply fresh and fertile mould unto it, and also water it even with our tears, that so those bruised branches may be recovered, and the whole tree prosper again and flourish.*" Mr. Creskeld's speech in the Parliament that met in 1727.

NEW-YORK, June 30.

His Honour Governor Penn hath required the Attendance of the Members of the Assembly of Pennsylvania to meet the 18th July.

A Committee of Gentlemen, inhabitants of this province, will in a few days be appointed to meet the Representatives of the other colonies, at the ensuing grand continential congress, to be held on the 1st day of September next, at a place that shall in the interim be fixed on, agreeable to the measures lately concerted by the Hon. House of Representatives of the Massachusets-Bay.

The Right Honorable the Earl of Dunmore has ordered writs to be issued for the election of a new Assembly, to meet as speedily as possible, at Williamsburg in Virginia: When the distracted state of affairs on the Ohio, will be laid before the Members.

JUST PUBLISHED,
And to be sold by JOHN KNEELAND,
Remarks on the Rev. Mr. *Hopkin's* Answer to a Tract, intitled, "A Vindication of the Power, Obligation and Encouragement of the Unregenate to attend the Means of Grace, &c
By MOSES HEMMINGWAY, A.M.
Pastor of the first Church in Wells.
N. B. A few of the above Author's Vindication may be had at said *Kneeland's* Office.
*** *Those who have Subscriptions in their Hands are requested to return them immediately.*

CREAM WARE.
Two Crates of elegant Cream Pencil Ware, one Crate of Gally Pots, several Bags Spikes, Deck and Sheathing Nails of different sizes, six Barrels of Durham Mustard in quarter Pound Bottles, a few Boxes 18 Inch Tip'd Pipes, one Case of Hats from Beaver to Felts, with a few Pipes of quarter Casks of Fyal Wines, to be Sold cheap, By
William Hoskins.

W A N T E D,
A Negro Man from 18 to 30 Years of Age, that will steal, lie and get Drunk. Any Person having such an one to dispose of, may hear of a Purchaser by applying to the Printers hereof.

L O N D O N.

Die Mercurij, 11° Maij, 1774.

THE order of the day being read for the third reading of the bill, intituled, "An Act for the better regulating the Government of the Province of the Massachusetts-Bay, in New-England;" and for the Lords to be summoned:

The said bill was accordingly read the third time. Moved, That the bill, with the amendments, do pass. Which being objected to, After a long debate, the question was put thereupon.

It was resolved in the affirmative.

Contents	——	69	
Proxies	——	23	92
Not contents	——	20	20
Proxies	——	0	

Dissentient;

BECAUSE this bill, forming a principal part in a system of punishment and regulation, has been carried through the House without a due regard to those indispensible rules of public proceeding, without the observance of which no regulation can be prudently made, and no punishment justly inflicted. Before it can be pretended, that those rights of the colony of Massachusetts-Bay, in the election of Counsellors, Magistrates, and Judges, and in the return of Jurors, which they derive from their charter, could with propriety be taken away, the definite legal offence, by which a forfeiture of that charter is incurred, ought to have been clearly stated and fully proved; notice of this adverse proceeding ought to have been given to the parties affected; and they ought to have been heard in their own defence. Such a principle of proceeding would have been inviolably observed in the Courts below. It is not technical formality, but substantial justice. When therefore the *magnitude* of such a cause transfers it from the cognizance of the inferior Courts, to the high judicature of Parliament, the Lords are so far from being authorized to reject this equitable principle, that we are bound to an extraordinary and religious strictness in the observance of it. The subject ought to be indemnified by a more liberal and beneficial justice in Parliament, for what he must inevitably suffer by being deprived of many of the *forms* which are wisely established in the Courts of ordinary resort for his protection against the dangerous promptitude of arbitrary discretion.

2dly. Because the *necessity* alledged for this precipitate mode of judicial proceeding cannot exist. If the numerous land and marine forces, which are ordered to assemble in Massachusets-Bay, are not sufficient to keep that single colony in any tolerable state of order, until the cause of its charter can be fairly and equally tried, no regulation in this bill, or in any of those hitherto brought into the House, are sufficient for that purpose; and we conceive, that the mere celerity of a decision against the charter of that province, will not reconcile the minds of the people to that mode of government which is to be established upon its ruins.

3dly. Because the Lords are not in a situation to determine how far the regulations of which this bill is composed, agree or disagree with those parts of the constitution of the colony that are not altered, with the circumstance of the people, and with the whole detail of their municipal institutions. Neither the charter of the colony, nor any account whatsoever of its Courts and judicial proceedings, their mode, or the exercise of their present powers, have been produced to the House. The slightest evidence concerning any one of the many inconveniencies, stated in the preamble of the bill to have arisen from the present constitution of the colony judicatures, has not been produced, or even attempted. On the same general allegations of a declaratory preamble, any other right, or all the rights of this or any other public body, may be taken away, and any visionary scheme of government substituted in their place.

4thly. Because we think, that the appointment of all the members of the council, which by this bill is vested in the crown, is not a proper provision for preserving the equilibrium of the colony constitution. The power given to the crown of occasionally increasing or lessening the number of the council on the report of governors, and at the pleasure of ministers, must make these governors and ministers masters of every question in that assembly; and by destroying its freedom of deliberation, will wholly annihilate its use. The intention avowed in this bill, of bringing the council to the platform of other colonies, is not likely to answer its own end; as the colonies, where the council is named by the crown, are not at all better disposed to a submission to the practice of taxing for supply without their consent, than this of Massachusetts-Bay. And no pretence of bringing it to the model of the English constitution can be supported, as none of those American councils have the least resemblance to the House of Peers. So that this new scheme of a council stands upon no sort of foundation, which the proposers of it think proper to acknowledge.

5thly. Because the new constitution of judicature provided by this bill is improper, and incongruous with the plan of the administration of justice in Great-Britain. All the Judges are to be henceforth nominated (not by the Crown but) by the Governor; and all (except the Judges of the Superior Court) are to be removable at his pleasure, and expresly *without* the consent of that very Council which has been nominated by the Crown.

The appointment of the Sheriff is by the will of the Governor only, and without requiring in the person appointed any local or other qualification; that Sheriff, a magistrate of great importance to the whole adminstration and execution of all justice, civil and criminal, and who in England is not removable even by the royal authority, during the continuance of the term of his office, is by this bill made changeable by the Governor and Council, as often, and for such purposes as they shall think expedient.

The Governor and Council, thus intrusted with powers, with which the British constitution has not trusted his Majesty and his Privy-Council, have the means of returning such a jury in each particular cause, as may best suit with the gratification of their passions, and interests. The lives, liberties, and properties of the subject are put into their hands without controul; and the invaluable right of trial by jury, is turned into a snare for the people, who have hitherto looked upon it as their main security against the licentiousness of power.

6thly. Because we see in this bill the same scheme of strengthening the authority of the officers and Ministers of State, *at the expence of the rights and liberties of the subject* which was indicated by the inauspicious act for shutting up the harbour of Boston.

By that act, which is immediately connected with this bill, the example was set of a large important city (containing vast multitudes of people, many of whom must be innocent, and all of whom are unheard) by an arbitrary sentence, deprived of the advantage of that port, upon which all their means of livelihood did immediately depend.

This proscription is not made determinable on the payment of a fine for an offence, or a compensation for an injury; but is to continue until the Ministers of the Crown shall think fit to advise the King in Council to revoke it.

The legal condition of the subject (standing unattainted by conviction, for treason or felony) ought never to depend upon the arbitrary will of any person whatsoever.

This act, unexampled on the records of Parliament, has been entered on the Journals of this House as voted *nemine dissentiente*, and has been stated in the debate of this day, to have been sent to the colonies, as passed without a division in either House, and therefore as conveying the uncontroverted universal sense of the nation.

The despair of making effectual opposition to an unjust measure, has been construed into an approbation of it.

An unfair advantage has been taken on the final question for passing that penal bill, of the absence of those Lords who had debated it for several hours, and strongly dissented from it on the second reading; that period on which it is most usual to debate the principle of a bill.

If this proceeding were to pass without animadversion, the Lords might think themselves obliged to reiterate their debates, at every stage of every bill which they oppose, and to make a formal division whenever they debate.

7thly, Because this bill, and the other proceedings that accompany it, are intended for the support of that unadvised scheme of taxing the colonies, in a manner new, and unsuitable to their situation and constitutional circumstances.

Parliament has asserted the authority of the legislature of this kingdom, supreme and unlimited, over all the Members of the British empire.

But the legal extent of this authority furnishes no argument in favour of an unwarrantable use of it.

The sense of the nation on the repeal of the stamp act was, *that in equity and sound policy, the taxation of the colonies for the ordinary purposes of supply, ought to be forborn*; and that this kingdom ought to satisfy itself with the advantages to be derived from a flourishing and increasing trade, and with the free grants of the American assemblies; as being far more beneficial, far more easily obtained, less oppressive, and more likely to be lasting than any revenue to be acquired by parliamentary taxes, accompanied by a total alienation of the affections of those who were to pay them. This principle of repeal was nothing more than a return to the ancient standing policy of this empire. The unhappy departure from it, has led to that course of shifting and contradictory measures, which have since given rise to such continued distractions; by which unadvised plan, new duties have been imposed in the very year after the former had been repealed; these new duties afterwards in part repealed, and in part continued, in contradiction to the principles upon which those repealed were given up; all which, with many weak, injudicious, and precipitate steps taken to enforce a compliance, have kept up that jealousy, which on the repeal of the stamp-act was subsiding; revived dangerous questions, and gradually estranged the affections of the colonies from the mother country, without any object of advantage to either. If the force proposed should have its full effect, that effect we greatly apprehend may not continue longer than whilst the sword is held up. To render the colonies permanently advantageous, they must be satisfied with their condition. That satisfaction we see no chance of restoring, whatever measures may be pursued, except by recurring in the whole, to the wise and salutary principles on which the stamp-act was repealed.

RICHMOND,
PORTLAND,
ABINGDON,
KING,
EFFINGHAM,
PONSONBY,
ROCKINGHAM,
ABERGAVENNY,
LEINSTER,
CRAVEN,
FITZWILLIAM.

From the Supplement to the Pennsylvania Journal, June 29.

All the Printers of News-Papers in the British Colonies, are requested to publish the following Act of Parliament; which it is said, will be passed the End of the present Session, or Beginning of the next.

"*An Act for the more effectual keeping of his Majesty's American Colonies* dependent *on the* Crown of Great-Britain, *and to enforce their Obedience to all such Acts of Parliament as may be necessary for that Purpose.*"

WHEREAS *it is found by experience that Colonies which are planted by Governments, or otherwise dependent on them do at some time or other, form themselves into unwarrantable and rebellious Associations, and by their perseverance therein, entirely throw off their dependence and subjection to such Parent State: And whereas the British Plantations, in America, have of late, discovered a disposition to follow the same steps and, in all likelihood, will if not speedily prevented, form themselves into a separate and independent Government, to the great detriment of the other parts of the British Empire, to the dishonour of his Majesty, and to the prejudice of the trade of this Kingdom in particular:* And whereas the great ENCREASE of People, in said Colonies, has an immediate tendency to produce this effect—*To the end therefore that such evil designs may not be carried into execution, and that the said Colonies and Plantations may be, at all times hereafter, kept in due subordination to the authority of the British Parliament. Be it enacted by the King's most excellent Majesty, by, and with the advice and consent of the Lords spiritual and temporal, and Commons in this present Parliament assembled, and by authority of the same.*

1. That no person whatever who shall, from and after the passing of this Act, transport him or herself, from the Kingdoms of Great-Britain and Ireland, or the Islands thereunto belonging, to any of his Majesty's Plantations in America, with intent to settle and dwell therein for any *longer* time than the space of seven years, shall presume to depart from the said Kingdoms, until he or she, so transporting him or herself, shall pay, at the Custom-House of the Port, from which such vessel shall take out her clearance, the sum of Fifty Pounds, sterling money of Great-Britain: And be it further enacted that for every child, or servant, which shall be so transported by the parent, or master, the like sum of Fifty Pounds shall be paid in manner aforesaid.—And be it further enacted by the authority aforesaid, that if any person shall transport him, or herself, or procure themselves to be transported, contrary to this Act, every person, so offending, shall be adjudged guilty of felony without benefit of clergy—and that the Captain of the vessel, in which such person shall be so transported, contrary to this Act, shall forfeit and pay, for any such person, the sum of £500 sterling money aforesaid.

2. And be it further enacted by the authority aforesaid, that if any person, who shall transport him, or herself, from the Kingdoms aforesaid, to any of his Majesty's Plantations, in America, with intent to stay and dwell therein, for any space of time *less* than seven years, shall nevertheless stay, dwell, and abide therein, beyond the said space of seven years, such person so staying, dwelling, and abiding, in any of his Majesty's Plantations, in America, shall be adjudged guilty of felony without benefit of clergy.

3. *Provided always, and be it further enacted, that nothing in this Act shall extend, or be construed to extend to his Majesty's Governors of the said Plantations, or to any other person, or persons, in the actual service and employ of his Majesty, as aforesaid*

4. And be it further enacted by the authority aforesaid, that all Marriages in his Majesty's said Plantations shall be performed in consequence of a Licence from the Governor where such Marriage shall be celebrated, for which Licence the sum of Twenty Pounds shall be paid, and no more, and that all Marriages had without such Licence, shall be void in law to all intent and purpose whatever.

5. And be it further enacted, that on the birth of every male child, the sum of Fifteen Pounds, and on the birth of every female child, the sum of Ten Pounds sterling money shall be paid to the Governor of the Colony or plantation in which such children shall be born.

6. And be it further enacted by the authority aforesaid, that on the birth of every bastard child in any of his Majesty's said Plantations, the sum of Fifty Pounds sterling money shall be paid by the *Mother* of such bastard child, to the Governor where such bastard child shall happen to be born, and that in case any person, shall hereafter, either with malice prepense, or otherwise kill or destroy any child or children; such killing or destroying shall not henceforth be deemed or adjudged to be murder in any Court or Courts, nor shall such killing be punished in any way or manner whatever.

7. *Provided always and it is hereby further enacted, that nothing in this Act shall extend to make any such killing legal, or justifiable, if the child, so killed or destroyed, be above the age of twelve months, but that every such killing and destroying shall be punished as heretofore, any thing in this Act to the contrary in any wise notwithstanding.*

8. And be it further enacted by the authority aforesaid, that from and after the Day in the year upon the exportation of each and every barrel of FLOUR from any of his Majesty's said Plantations to any port or place beyond sea, a duty of *Five Shillings* sterling shall be paid to the Custom-House of the respective Colony, from which such FLOUR shall be so shipped or exported.

9. And be it further enacted, that on the exportation of any WHEAT from his Majesty's said Plantations to any port or place beyond the sea, a duty of *Two Shillings* sterling per *bushel* shall be paid as aforesaid, for every quantity which shall be so shipped or exported. And that if any person, shall export any wheat or flour contrary to the directions of this Act, all such wheat or flour together with the ship in which it is exported as aforesaid, shall be seized and forfeited to the use of his Majesty, and condemned in any of his Majesty's Courts of Admiralty where such vessel shall happen to be seized as aforesaid.

10. *Provided always, and be it further enacted, that if any such flour or wheat, which shall be exported from any of his Majesty's said Plantations, and carried to any port of Great-Britain, with design to re-ship the same to any other port or place beyond the sea, there shall be allowed upon every barrel of flour so re-shipped, a bounty of Two Shillings and Six Pence sterling, and for every bushel of wheat, a bounty of One Shilling sterling.*

11. And be it further enacted by the authority aforesaid, that the duties imposed by this Act, shall be applied towards RAISING A REVENUE the better to ENABLE his MAJESTY to BUILD FORTS and to GARRISON the same, and to support and maintain such a REGULAR and STANDING ARMY in the said PLANTATIONS, as shall be sufficient to enforce the EXECUTION of all such Acts of the BRITISH PARLIAMENT, as are already passed, or may hereafter be passed, relative to the said AMERICAN COLONIES.

To the INHABITANTS of BOSTON.

Friends and Brethren,

THE whole Artillery of the Malice of your Enemies is now leveled at you. The Colonies view it in this light and are acting accordingly. The Resolution to Enslave us all seems very determined and the System settled. The present Crisis is big with more Dangers and requires more Wisdom to meet it than any that has yet occurred. It becomes you therefore to conduct with more Firmness, than to be moved from the Purpose of sound Prudence, by the Petulance of Fools. Our Adversaries expect one or the other of two Consequences from the Measures pursued against you; either that you will be provoked to take some rash and precipitate Step, or that you will humble yourselves and kiss the Rod. Either conduct will gratify them. They are waiting for it. A wise Medium they fear; and they are already astonish'd to see that you pursue it. Little indeed you have to do, if any Thing, at present, but to bear up under your Misfortunes with Fortitude and Perseverance, and to convince the World that you can suffer long with Dignity, for the Preservation of the Liberties of your Country. Our Enemies, at a Distance, have full Expectation of your being totally deserted by the Colonies. You must by this Time be assured that they will certainly be disappointed. A general Congress draws near. Take no one Measure yet, least it should be hurtful to you and to us all. Had you made Payment for the Teas, it might have been construed by your Enemies an Acknowledgment of *Guilt*, or a mean Submission to the *unrighteous* Hand of Power. Your Friends also might have judg'd it *imprudent*; at least, it might have caused a *Division* among them, which is by all Means to be avoided. It cannot be too often repeated, that *Violence* and *Submission* would be equally fatal. *Give your Sister Colonies Time to think for you.* And constantly implore for them and for yourselves that Wisdom which is profitable to direct.

A COUNTRYMAN.

B O S T O N, July 11.

AS the Fourteenth Day of this Month is be observed in this Town as a Day of Fasting and earnest Prayer to Almighty God, that we may be relieved from the Distress under which we now labor; it is hoped that all serious Persons of all Denominations will join in a devout Observance of said Day, and that Heads of Families will, by their Example and Injunction upon their Children and Servants, endeavor that such a Fast is kept as the Lord has chosen; particularly it is hoped that none will be permitted to spend their Time in idle Diversions, more especially in resorting to the Place of Parade to see the Manœvres of the Soldiery, who certainly ought on that Day to be left without a single Spectator.

Messieurs Edes and Gill offer their Compliments to Mr. Treasurer Gray, and are fully sensible of the Regard he has for the Reputation of their Paper, manifested by his desiring them not to publish any Thing in his Favor; they think they shall have no Temptation to do any Thing contrary to his Wishes in that Respect.—The Difficulty in which the Treasurer is involved with Respect to the Credit he is to give to their Account of the Town of Worcester, is not worth remarking upon, as it is very indifferent to the Printers how they are estimated by Mr. Gray.

We hear the Acts for the *Impartial* Administration of Justice in the Province of Massachusetts Bay, and for the *better* regulating the Government of the said Province, are to take Place the first Day of August.

His Honor Governor Wanton, of Rhode-Island, has issued a Proclamation reccommending Thursday, the 14th Instant, as a Day of Fasting and Prayer, on Account of the dark Aspect of our public Affairs.

By several Vessels from Maryland and Virginia, we hear, that vast Quantities of Wheat and Flour are collecting in those Governments, for the Relief of the Poor in this distressed Town.

The news-papers from all quarters, in every British American colony, so far as we have yet received intelligence, are chiefly filled with accounts of meetings and resolutions of towns and counties, all to the same purpose—complaining of oppression, proposing a congress, a cessation of intercourse with Great-Britain, and a contribution for the relief of Boston Poor.

Copy of a Letter from Annapolis, (Maryland) to a Gentleman in Philadelphia, dated Friday, June 24, 1774.

"I have just time to inform you, that on Wednesday the meeting of Deputies from the Committees of the different counties of this province began here: the first and second days were spent in adjusting certain forms of doing business, and reading letters, &c. or rather business was delayed in expectation of hearing from your city. This day's post arriving, we immediately proceeded to express our sentiments of the situation of Boston, and the several acts passed relative to the government of their province, and then considered what would be the most effectual means to procure speedy relief to our suffering brethren of that town; many methods were proposed, which occasioned debates that lasted from 10 o'clock in the morning until 9 o'clock at night, when it was resolved, That a general non-importation from, and non-exportation to Great-Britain, should take place after a day to be agreed on at the general congress. Present 93 deputies.—As I was certain this intelligence will give pleasure to every real American, I have scratched off this scrawl, which goes by a servant, sent to overtake the post."

Since our last arrived in Town three Waggon Loads of Grain from the Towns of Groton, Pepperrell and Wrentham, for the Relief the industrious Poor of this town.

Friday last One Hundred and Five Sheep were received from our worthy Friends in Pomfret, in Connecticut, for the like charitable Purpose.——And we hear the Taverners on the Road were so kind as to refuse receiving any Payment for Entertainment or Forage.

The Tories give out that the Present of Sheep sent from the generous Town of Windham came only in consequence of Money sent from Boston to purchase them. *How weak, how false, how little, and how low!!*

The Hon. Committee of Correspondence for Connecticut, are to meet at New-London on Wednesday the 13th Inst, to agree upon some proper Measures to obtain a Redress of all American Grievances, and to choose a Committee to meet the Committees of the other Colonies in the general Congress to be holden at Philadelphia the first Day of September next.

Yesterday a Child was baptiz'd at the Rev. Dr. Eliot's Meeting by the Name of MOLINEUX

Extract of a Letter from London, April 19, 1774.

"Thirteen different Letters are sent to such Men as Administration thinks will accept of Presents and Favors, with Addresses for each Man to do his utmost to influence and cajole the ignorant, to deceive and mislead the wise—Money is sent to some one Printer in each Colony to be faithful to their Interest; use your best Endeavours to find them out and expose them; watch your News-Papers and be prudent, don't be rash in any Thing; be firm and steady."

A Letter from London, 12 May 1774.

IT will be very proper for you to inform the Inhabitants of all North America thro' the channel of the news paper, and request the Printers of every Colony to reprint the same, that it is a constant practice now with the Ministers here, to open all Letters from America that come through the channel of the Post Office, which are directed to those that they suspect of being friends to the injured and most oppressed Americans; therefore it is necessary to be cautious what letters are sent by the Packet or by any Captains who will not undertake to deliver them as directed with their own hands. If it will be of any public utility you may also inform America, that some public spirited American Merchants were very anxious and exerted themselves a good deal to get a Petition from the general body of Merchants to the House of Commons against the iniquitous and unjust Boston Port Bill. But it is no less strange than true, that this plan was totally defeated by the Boston Merchants alone, viz. Hayley and Hopkins, Champion & Dickson, Lane, Son and Fraser, and Harrison; refusing to join, or be at all concern'd in such a Petition. As these Merchants seemed in the first instance to be the most deeply concerned in point of private interest, (exclusive of Gratitude,) it was expected that some of them should take the lead; which every one of them refusing, no one else would venture on it, least those stiring *most*, who appear'd at present, *least* concern'd, should do the cause more *harm* than *good*; so a stop was put to the whole business here, and consequently in Bristol, Liverpool and the principle manufacturing Towns in England, where they expected such a step to be taken in London, and were ready to follow the example. After this, Champion and Dickson, Fraser, Hopkins and Harrison, waited privately on Lord North, to implore his Mercy, he told them, that Government was determined to proceed on their plan which was so settled, that the Merchants in England would hereafter get their Debts better paid, than they ever were before, with which they came back most perfectly satisfied. Had the above Merchants come forward, I do not believe one North American Merchant, from Nova-Scotia to Florida would have refused to join in the Petition; unless it had been Mr. John Blackburn a Merchant in the New York and Philadelphia Trade, and Mr. William Molleson (a Scotchman) in the Maryland Trade, who I am told has been very busy in traducing those Americans here, that have honestly borne their testimony against the iniquitous Bills by their Petitions. I know every thing written here to be Truth, therefore as such you may publish them.

Capt. Scott for this Place was expected to Sail from London in June.

N O R W I C H, July 7.

Last Monday Evening, Mr. Francis Green, an eminent Merchant of Boston, put up at a Tavern in Windham: As soon as the Inhabitants of that Town had Notice of his Arrival (and recollected that he was one of the insidious Crew who fabricated and subscribed the adulatory Address to strengthen the Hands of that parricidious Tool of Despotism, Thomas Hutchinson, Esq; late Governor of Massachusetts-Bay, previous to his Departure for England) they immediately assembled, and expressed great Uneasiness, that so daring an Enemy to the Liberties of his Country, should be entertained, or suffered to remain in their Town. A Committee was appointed, who intimated to Mr. Green, the Desire of the People, that he should forthwith leave the Town; but he pleaded Business, and remained there until Tuesday Forenoon, when the Threat of exalting him upon a Cart, operated so powerfully that he decamped with Precipitation.

On Tuesday Afternoon, Intelligence of the Proceedings of the People at Windham, were circulated in this Town; the same Evening the Friends of Liberty assembled on the PLAIN, and being certainly informed that Mr GREEN intended to be here next Morning, they agreed upon a proper Signal to be given the Moment he should make his Entry into Town, that they might wait on him and tender their Devoirs in Form.

On Wednesday Morning, at 7 o'Clock, Mr. Manning, *the Grave Digger*, announced the before-mentioned Gentleman's Arrival, by Ringing the Meeting-House Bell; a numerous and respectable Concourse of People instantly appeared upon the Plain, and appointed a Committee, who waited upon Mr. Green, and desired him to depart the Town in 15 Minutes, he appeared reluctant, and made the same Excuse that he did at Windham, but with much less Success, for a Horse and Cart was provided, so that he had no other Alternative, but to mount the Cart or his own Carriage; he chose the latter, and set out properly attended, with Drums beating, Horns blowing, &c.

A Subscription is now opened in this Town, for the Relief of such Poor in Boston, as may be distressed by the baneful Influence of the late Acts of the British Parliament: Two Hundred and Ninety-three Sheep, some Cash, and a Quantity of Wheat, Corn, &c. are already subscribed.

Messieurs EDES & GILL,

'TIS an old and just Observation, that Professions cost nothing; 'tis equally true, that when a Man parts with his Money in Support of any Cause, he evidences himself to be in earnest. I cannot but reverence my Fellow Countrymen, dispersed thro' this and the other Governments, for their liberal and unsollicited Contributions to support the Poor and suffering People of Boston, during the present Conflict. What amiable Charity? What glorious Magnanimity is here displayed? Shall such a Race of Patriots, shall such a Band of Friends be ever subdued? No, my persecuted Brethren of this Metropolis, you may rest assured that the Guardian God of New England, who holds the Hearts of his People in his Hands, has influenced your distant Brethren to this Benevolence; 'tis a glorious Pledge of that Harmony, that Unison of Sentiment and Action, which shall connect such a Band of Heroes, as to make a World combined against them to tremble. Cultivate this rich, this fruitful Blessing, an extensive Union,—when once 'tis effected, it will intimidate your Enemies, will animate your Friends, will convince them both that you must be invincible, and thus you will obtain a bloodless Victory.

G.

Messieurs EDES and GILL,

THE Card in Draper's Paper of Thursday last, is an Evidence of the great Value of your Paper. Complaints and Reflections from that old Lady, and all of her Complexion, result from a malignant Heart towards those who wish well to, and exert themselves for their Country; and therefore instead of depreciating, greatly enhance its Value. Tyrants and Oppressors of every Denomination, as well as those who have discover'd a Desire to advance their own little Interest, by favouring their horrid Designs, have often felt the seasonable and just Corrections that they have variously merited. No surprize then, that she should boil over in Invective against you and your Paper: But the same Versatility of Temper and Conduct which has always been the most striking Characteristic of her Life, when it may be convenient, may produce, in some Degree, the same Adulation towards you as has been most liberally conferr'd on One who I know said, in Times past, he could not put the least Confidence in her.

I shall only observe further, That I presume there was no Occasion for Concern lest you should say any Thing in Favor of her, as I can't conceive it possible, and have any Regard to Truth: Nor can you, I think, be desirous to hold up to the World one whom you must pity and despise, as being famous for the most infamous Abuse on Characters which she can only envy, but can never wound. *Your constant Reader and Friend.*

G. H.

Joseph Coolidge

INFORMS the Public, That he has IMPORTED in the Ship just arrived from London,

A fine Assortment of Guns, Trooping Pistols, Pocket ditto, Gun Locks, Swords, Violins, Fifes and Flutes, Stands of Cruetts, with Silver and Bone Tops, back Gammon Tables compleat; a Variety of Pocket Books for Gentlemen and Ladies; neat Gilt, Pinchbeck, Plated and black and common Shoe, Knee and Stock Buckles; Japan Trays, Waiters and Candlesticks; most sorts of Jewelry; Silver and Pinchbeck Watches, some as low as seven Dollars; Patent Watch Keys that shew the Day of the Month and Moons Age; Cutlery and Hard Ware, and a Variety of Toys and Trinkets, too many for an Advertisement: All which he will sell at the lowest reduced Prizes, at his Shop just above the Market, and directly opposite the new Auction-Room.

On WEDNESDAY 13th Inst.
At Ten in the Morning,
Will be Sold by PUBLIC VENDUE,
At RUSSELL's Auction-Room in Queen Street,

A Variety of English Goods as usual—and some House Furniture, among which are, a great Variety of China and Glass Ware—Also, a second-hand Chaise and Harness. J. RUSSELL, Auctioneer.

To be Sold cheap at Store No. 14, Long Wharff,

A few Tierces and Barrels MELASES, Casks of best Sort of Rice, and Barrels of Coffee.

Just Published, and to be Sold by Samuel Webb, *in Queen Street;*

A SERMON preached to the Ancient and Honorable ARTILLERY COMPANY in Boston, New-England, June 6th 1774. Being the Anniversary of their Election of Officers.

By JOHN LATHROP, A. M.
Pastor of the Second Church in Boston.

Subscribers are desired to send for their Books.

Province of the Massachusetts-Bay. } *To the Hon*ble. Samuel Dexter, *Esq; one of his Majesty's Justices of the Peace through the said Province.*

We the Subscribers, Proprietors of a Township, granted by the Great and General Court of the Province aforesaid, at their Session in February last, to *John Gardner*, and others, in Lieu of a Township, Number Six in the Line of Towns between *Connecticut* and *Merrimack Rivers*, lost by the late Settlement of *New-Hampshire*—request your Honour to call a Meeting of said Proprietors to be on Monday the 29th Day of *August* next, at the House of *Jonathan Wood*, Esq; Innholder in *Stow*, at Ten of the Clock in the Forenoon, then and there to choose a Moderator for said Meeting, also to choose a Proprietor's Clerk, Treasurer, and any other Proprietary Officer; to Grant such Sum or Sums of Money, as may be needful to discharge any Debts already due from said Proprietors, or to discharge any future Demands; to agree on some Method for calling Proprietors Meetings for the future. Also to agree on some Method for laying out said Township into Lots, and to do any other Thing proper for bringing forward the Settlement of said Township.

Stow, June 15, 1774.

John Whitcomb,
Jonathan Loring,
Henry Gardner,
Abner Cranson,
Micah Keys,
Daniel Hapgood,
Samuel Curtis.

Province of the Massachusetts-Bay.

(Seal.) *To* Henry Gardner, *of* Stow, *in the County of* Middlesex, *Esq; one of the principal Proprietors of the Township aforementioned,* Greeting.

In pursuance of the foregoing Appilcation and Request, you are hereby required to give Notice, in Time and Manner as the Law directs, to the Proprietors of the Township aforesaid, that they meet at the Time and Place, and for the Purposes expressed in the aforewritten Petition. Given under my Hand and Seal, this this sixth Day of July, Anno Domini, 1774, and in the fourteenth Year of his Majesty's Reign.

SAMUEL DEXTER, a Justice of the Peace through the Province of the Massachusetts-Bay.

Stow, July 6th 1774.

By Virtue of the above Warrant to me directed, The Proprietors above-mentioned, are required to meet at Time and Place above-mentioned, for the Purpose aforesaid.

HENRY GARDNER.

TO BE SOLD,
ON FRIDAY NEXT,
By *BENJAMIN CHURCH*,
At FOUR o'Clock in the Afternoon,

A General Assortment of European Articles, Linnens, Woollens, Checks, &c. &c. Some House Furniture, an 8-Day Clock, Mehogany Case of Draws, Watches, &c. &c.—At Four o Clock, P. M.—

The Sale of the House Goods, &c. belonging to the Estate of Experience Brewer, Widow, deceased, advertiz'd in our last to be sold on Tuesday the 12th Instant, is postponed for a short Time, due Notice of which will be given in this Paper.

New AUCTION-ROOM, Cornhill.

TO-MORROW at TEN o'Clock will be Sold by PUBLIC VENDUE, at GREENLEAF's Auction-Room,——

A Variety of Merchandize, amongst which are, a fine Assortment of Chinces and Callicoes, Copper-plate Furniture, printed Linnens, stamp'd Linen Handkerchiefs, border'd and check'd ditto, border'd Kenting ditto, fine Lawns, Catgut, Worsted & Thread Hose, Shalloons, Tammies, Russell Shoes, English Clogs, Sagathees, Velveretts, Broads Cloths, Forrest Cloths, Thicksetts, Manchester Checks, strip'd Hollands, Castor and Felt Hatts, a Parcel of Stone and Glass Ware, several Pair of rich Stone Shoe Buckles, &c. &c.

WILLIAM GREENLEAF, Auctioneer.

The Sale will begin at Ten o'Clock precisely.

Burials in the Town of BOSTON, since our last.
Five Whites. One Black.
Baptiz'd in the several Churches, Seven.

High Water at BOSTON, *for the present Week.*

Monday, 10 min. aft.	1	Friday, 5 min. after.	4
Tuesday, 56 min. aft.	1	Saturday, 50 min. aft.	5
Wednesday, 38 m. aft.	2	Lord's Day, 40 m. af.	6
Thursday, 20 min. aft.	3	D's First Q. 16 D. N. oo.	

CHoice Lisbon LEMMONS per Box. Lisbon, Madeira, Malaga, Vargin, Sherry, Shulsome WINE, per Quarter Cask.—Raisins per Cask, Citron per Box. Lisbon Oil per Cask. Dutch Brushes, Barcelona Handkerchiefs per Dozen, TO BE SOLD

By Archibald Cunningham,

At his Store in Ann-Street, Boston.

TO BE SOLD,

Several good Farms, with Dwelling-Houses, Barns, &c. thereon, pleasantly situated about 20 Miles from Boston, on a considerable Road.——The Payment may be made very easy.——Also several Rights of Land in a new Township. Enquire of Edes & Gill.

To be sold for Cash only,

A small Quantity of good dry Mehogany, fit for immediate Use: Inquire of Edes & Gill.

To be sold on very reasonable Terms,

The Hull of a double-deck'd Brigantine about 146 Tons Burthen, now launched in Taunton-River. Farther enquire of ARIEL SMITH, nearly opposite to the Head of Orange Tree-Lane, Boston, or Mr. JOB SMITH, at Taunton.

TO BE LETT,

A convenient Brick Tenement, near the Orange-Tree. Inquire of the Printers.

The Sloop JENNY, lying at the Long-Wharff at Salem, will sail in 10 Days, for Annapolis-Royal.——For Freight or Passage apply to GEORGE MITCHEL, on board said Sloop, or to his House on Winter's Wharff, Boston.

To be sold at Public Vendue, by Order of his Majesty's Justices of the Inferior Court, on the first Wednesday in August,

PART of the Real Estate of SAMUEL WELD, late of Roxbury, Joiner, deceas'd, viz. Half of a House, near the House known by the Name of the Greyhound Tavern, and 8 Acres of Land, near the Rev. Mr. Gordon's Meeting House. The Sale to be at said House on Wednesday the 3d of August, at Three o'Clock, P. M.

TO BE SOLD,

A large and convenient Dwelling House, situate on Spring Hill so called, in Portsmouth, in the Province of New Hampshire, near the Market, in the most principal Part of the Town for any Gentleman to carry on Trade, both by Sea & Land. Said House is almost New, and almost finished, with an excellent Cellar, and a back Yard, and a Garden, also a Warehouse and Stable, with many other Conveniences suitable for a Family. Inquire of the Printers.

IMPORTED in the last Ships from LONDON, and to be Sold by JOHN WHITE, near the Cornfield, Union Street.

AN Assortment of Goods, amongst which are ⅞, ⅝ and yard-wide Irish Linnen, Cotton and Linnen Check, newest fashioned Callicoes, Ribbons of all Sorts, Handkerchiefs of all sorts, Diaper Table Cloaths, Clouting Diaper, Russia Drabs, Nankeens, Women's Shoes and Clogs, silk Gloves and Mitts, Book Muslin, Cambricks and Lawns, Catgut, Patent and Spiders Net, Black, Bone and Blond Lace, White Blond and Thread ditto, Cheveaux de Frize, sprig'd and strip'd Silk Gauze, English and French Necklaces, Sarsnets and Sattins of all Colours, Cotton Hose.—A large Assortment of Looking Glasses, China, Glass and Earthern Ware, English Loaf Sugar, and a few fine Cheshire Cheeses.

A young Woman, with a good Breast of Milk would be glad to take a Child to Suckle.——Inquire of *Edes* and *Gill*.

CHARLESTOWN Stage No. 1. sets out with four good Horses for Salem, from Mr. WOART's Tavern every Morning at 8 o'Clock, and returns the same Day; it puts up at Mr. Goodhue's, in Salem. Any Gentlemen or Ladies who wants a Passage are desired to call at Admiral Vernon's, in King-street-Boston; or Mr. Woart's, in Charlestown, and leave their Names.—Also at the same Place, Stage No. 2, with four good Horses may be had to convey any Gentleman or Lady to any Part of this, or any other Province, or at so small a Distance as five or six Miles.

Any Gentlemen or Ladies who choose to go in either of the above Stages, will be accommodated in the best Manner, and the smallest Favour will be acknowledged,

By their humble Servant,

SAMUEL LORD.

Charlestown, June 22, 1774.

RAN away from the Subscriber on the Eighth of June Instant, at Night, a Negro Boy, about Seventeen Years of Age: Had on when he went off, a dark coloured cloth Jacket and Trowsers, and is branded on the Breast Delamote, very remarkable: said Fellow speaks tolerable good English, and some French. Whoever takes up said Fellow and Secures him in any of his Majesty's Goals, or Returns him to the Subscriber, shall have FIVE DOLLARS Reward, and all necessary Charges paid by ALLIN BROWN.

Providence, June 10, 1774.

To be Sold cheap for CASH.

A few Casks of good Sugars, West-India Rum, and a few Casks of Coffee.——Inquire at Cruft's Store, a little to the Northward of Hancock's Wharf, North-End.

GOODS at the *Sterling Cost.*

John Cunningham

HAS yet remaining a good Assortment of English and India GOODS, which he continues to sell at the Sterling Cost clear of Charges, at his Shop opposite to Mr. Gilbert Deblois's, near School-Street.

Choice Muscovado Sugars, Grenada Rum, Coffee, &c. &c. To be Sold by GABRIEL JOHONNOTT, at his Store South Side of Faneuil-Hall Market.

Doctor *Lagord*, Originally from France, practices Physick, Surgery and Midwifry, practised some Years at Braintree, but has lately removed to that Part of Cambridge called Menotomy, near the Meeting-House, at the Masons Arms Tavern, now kept by Benjamin Cooper from Boston; any Person who please to employ the said *Lagord* in any of the Branches, may speak with him at the above mentioned Place, where may be had good Entertainment for Gentlemen Travelers.—Near said Cooper's is the famous Menotomy Pond, where he keeps a neat Boat for Fishery.

A Young Woman with a good Breast of Milk, would go into a Family to Suckle a Child, or take it Home, as it may suit; her Character for Honesty is indisputable. Inquire of the Printers.

TO BE SOLD,

By Thomas Handasyd Peck,

At his Shop in Merchant's-Row, near the Golden Ball.

ALL Sorts of Linnen Linings suitable for Beaver, Beaveritt, Castor & Felt Hatts, black, blue and green Tabby Linings, Mohair Looping and Bands Silk ditto, Buttons and Loops newest Fashion, sundry Sorts of Chain and Shapes for Button Loops, Gold and Silver Buttons and Loops, white and yellow Triming for Childrens Hatts, white and yellow Bands & Buckles, Gold and Silver Chain, Brushes, Cards, Velures, Bowstrings, Luping-Needles, Nuts-skins, Camels Hair, Irons, Verdegrease, Capperas, Logwood, Beaver, Beaveritt, Castor and Felt Hatts, Childrens black turn-up Hatts, white ditto, also Strouds and Blankets suitable for the Indian Trade, Powder, Shot, and Russia Duck.

N. B. Cash given for Beaver, and all Sorts of Furs as usual.

To be sold upon reasonable Terms,

A HOUSE well situated, and well accommodated for a small Family, within 8 or 10 Miles of Boston. There is as much Land adjoining to the House as may be thought convenient. Enquire of Edes & Gill.

Halifax, Nova-Scotia, May 19, 1774.

TO BE SOLD at PUBLIC AUCTION,

On TUESDAY the Second Day of August next in the Town of Halifax, at the House of Mr. *John Rider*,

A VALUABLE Tract of Land or Township, commonly known by the Name of New-Jerusalem, or Port-Rosaway, on the Southern Shore of the Province of Nova-Scotia, containing One Hundred Thousand Acres of Land, granted by his Majesty to ALEXANDER MACNUTT, Esq; but lately the Property and Estate of BENJAMIN GERRISH, Esq; deceased, and contain several fine Harbours for Vessels or Ships of any Draught of Water and full of all Sorts of Fish, as Cod, Salmon, Mackrel, Herring, &c. &c. &c. extending about twelve Miles on the Sea Coast, well wooded and watered.

Conditions of Pay, viz. To pay 10 per cent. down in Cash, and the Remainder on executing the Deed of Sale for the same, which shall be within one Month after the Sale.

Also, a Lot of Land, an old House and Bake-House on the Beach, with a large Baking Oven, late in the Occupation of Mr. RICHARD JACOBS.

Also, a Lot of Land walled in with Stone, containing five Acres of Land more or less, lying on the Road to RICHARD JACOBS Farm.

Also, one Half of the Meeting-House Cellar.

Also, the late Dwelling-House of BENJAMIN GERRISH, Esq; deceased, with the front Yard and back Gardens and Out-Houses.

Also, a Wharf with four Stores thereon and a Coach-House and Stable.

Also, a Tract of Land, containing ten Thousand Acres, granted to BENJAMIN GERRISH, Esq; deceased, situate on the North Side of the Bason of Mines in the Province of Nova Scotia, comprehending the three Rivers commonly called and known by the Names of the Bass Rivers abounding with Shad, Salmon, Bass and other Kinds of Fish, and contains upwards of two Hundred Acres of Marsh Land, and was formerly a Settlement by the Accadeans. And also an Island called Moose-Island about one Mile distant, containing about one Hundred and Ninety Acres of rich Land. The aforesaid Bass Rivers are navigable for Vessels of 50 or 60 Tons and good Harbours.

Also, sixty one and half Acres of Dike Land in the Township of Horton on the Grand Pree.

Also, a Farm in the Township of Falmouth, now under good Improvement with a Dwelling-House and Barn and other Out-Houses, containing about Twelve Hundred and Fifty Acres of Land more or less, and all other Lands belonging to said Estate of BENJAMIN GERRISH, Esq;

N. B. In all the above Estates the Widow's Dower is to be excepted and treated for with her in Particulars for her Thirds during Life.

Conditions of Pay as aforesaid.

ALL Persons indebted for this Paper, whose Accounts have been above 12 Months standing, are requested to make immediate Payment.

KEYSER's

FAMOUS PILLS

So well known all over *Europe*, and in *this* and the *neighbouring Colonies*, for their superior Efficacy and peculiar Mildness, in perfectly eradicating every Degree of a certain Disease, without the least Trouble or Confinement.

The Public may be assured, that this excellent Medicine is beyond any Thing in all Foulness and Impurities of the Blood, having performed many astonishing Cures in Scorbutic Eruptions, Leprosies, White Swellings, Stiff Joints, Gout and Rheumatic Disorders, &c.

THESE PILLS ARE NOW SOLD BY

EDES and GILL,

(In Boxes of 7/6. L. M. each, *fresh imported*)

Who have in their Hands a Letter from the Widow KEYSER, and a Certificate from under her own Hand of the Genuineness of the above Pills; which any Person may have the Perusal of by applying to them at their Printing-Office in *Queen-Street*: Where may be had a Variety of Books, &c.

S & S Salisbury

Acquaint their Friends, they have just Imported in the last Ships from LONDON and BRISTOL,

A fresh Assortment of

—*Hard Ware GOODS*—

N. B. They have an Assortment of Nails in the Town of Marblehead, which they would be glad to dispose of, to be delivered there.

JOHN NOBLE,

(Post Rider from *Boston* to *Portsmouth*)

INFORMS the Public, That he has remov'd from Mr. Hubbard's at the Sign of Admiral Vernon, to Deacon Jones's at the Royal Exchange Tavern, in King-Street.

N. B. He arrives at Boston on Saturday Evenings and sets out for Portsmouth, early on Tuesday Mornings. Any Business and Packages delivered to him shall be executed with Care and Fidelity.

For LONDON,

The Ship DARTMOUTH,

JOS. ROTCH, Commander,

Will Sail in 20 Days from Dartmouth. For Passage apply to

FRANCIS ROTCH,

At his Store in King-Street,

Where is to be had,

A few Boxes choice Spermacæti Candles, a few Casks genuine Lisbon Wine, Barr Lead, and a Quantity of Brass Kettles.

TO BE SOLD,

A Farm with a Dwelling House, Barn & Shop thereon, lying in the Town of Braintree, North Precinct, situated on the Main Road to Plymouth, between the Meeting House and Brackett's Tavern, consisting of nine Acres of arrable Land, well Watered, five Acres of Fresh Meadow, and three or four Acres of Salt Marsh.——Any Person inclining to purchase the same may apply to Mr. John Mills, living on the Premises.

To be Sold for Want of Employ,

A Likely young Negro Man, who can shave and dress Hair, and is otherwise well qualified for a Gentleman's Servant. Inquire of Edes & Gill.

Frederick William Geyer

Acquaints his Friends and others, that he has removed from the Corner of Wings-Lane to the Store lately improved by Mr. Ward Nicholas Boylston, the door below Messi's Bethune and Prince, in King-Street,

BOSTON:

Where he continues selling English, India and Scotch Piece Goods, by Wholesale only, on the lowest Terms, for Cash or short Credit.

UMBRILLOES.

Umbrilloes of all sorts for Ladies & Gentlemen; made in the best Manner and to be sold by JOHN CUTLER, at the *Golden Cock*, in Marlborough-Street, Boston.

ALSO,

Umbrillo Sticks to sell uncovered, old Umbrilloes may be mended and covered at the same Place. All done at a low Rate.

Boston: Printed, by EDES & GILL, *in Queen-Street,* 1774.

H. Murdock
3/19/1919

THE
Boston- AND COUNTRY Gazette, JOURNAL.

No. 1005.

Containing the freshest Advices, Foreign and Domestic.

MONDAY, July 18, 1774.

Just Published, and Sold by EDES *and* GILL, *in Queen Street,* [*Price* 9d.]

The Nature and Effects of Drunkenness considered; with an Address to Tavern-Keepers, to Parents, and young People, relating to the Subject—In TWO DISCOURSES, delivered at Natick, the last Lord's Day in October, 1773.

By STEPHEN BADGER, A. M.
Pastor of the Christian Society there.

A L S O,

The Memoirs of the Life of the Rev. GEORGE WHITEFIELD, A. M,
Late Chaplain to the Countess of Huntingdon.

In which every circumstance worthy of notice, both in his private and public character is recorded. Faithfully selected from his original papers, journals and letters. Illustrated with a variety of interesting and entertaining Anecdotes, from the best authority.

To which is added, a particular account of his Death and Funeral; and Extracts from the Sermons which were Preached on that Occasion.

Compiled by the Rev. JOHN GILLIES, D. D.

Where likewise may be had, (Just Published,)

LIBERTY TRIUMPHANT; *or the downfall of* OPPRESSION.——Being a Characatura of the Destruction of the TEA at New-York.

This Day Published,

And Sold by JOHN KNEELAND, next to the Treasurer's Office in Milk-Street, Price Six Coppers.

EXTRACT of a SERMON, preached at the South Church in Boston, Nov. 27th, 1746. By the Rev. Mr. THOMAS PRINCE, occasioned by the surprizing Appearance of divine Providence for North-America, in the Destruction of the French Fleet and Army, sent to Chebucktah the preceeding Summer: And reprinted at this Time with a View to encourage and animate the People of GOD to put their Trust in Him, and to call upon his Name, under the severe and keen Distresses now taking Place in Boston and Charlestown, by the rigorous Execution of the Boston-PORT BILL.

Messieurs EDES and GILL,

THE eloquent Orators, who at a late Town-Meeting, employed all their Art to shew that the Non-Consumption Agreement would spread feuds and animosities through the Province, should have considered that most of themselves opened the Trenches of Civil Contention, in their base, *flattering* and (unless they are really the devotest Dupes of Despotism) *false* address to the late Governor Hutchinson; wherein they declare their *entire Satisfaction* with an Administration, unparalleled in the Annals of Massachusetts-Bay, since the Days of Sir Edmund Andros. I am informed that in a public Meeting of Billerica, a certain Justice whose extreme loyalty urged him to sign the Address to the *Promiser*, beg'd the Moderators Leave to offer something to his Fellow-Townsmen after the public Business was finished; and being obtained, he addressed the People, lamenting he had given them Umbrage, and begging to be again restored to their favour. A certain Gentleman answered him, by observing that conceiving the Justice's Motion to arise rather from a sense of the Inconveniences he suffered from his Neighbours with drawing their intercourse with him, than any Conviction he was under of having injured his Country, He proceeded to give a few Instances of what he knew to have happened to him; the first was respecting a Mower who has cut his Hay for several Years past; the Justice, he said, applied to this Person requesting him to come on such a Day, & begin his Mowing; the honest Man answered his Sythe would not cut Tory-Grass—another Neighbour's Oxen would not Plow Tory-Ground, and so on.——Nor much more comfortable is like to be the state of Mr. B-rtl-t, the noted Tea-Seller, of Haverhill, who in opposition to the Sense of the Town on their late Day of Fasting and Prayer, kept his Shop open the whole Day and took the eighth of a Dollar and one Copper for a Compensation of the irrecoverable Loss of the remaining Regard of his Fellow-Countrymen. It is said, however, this Hero begins to cry Peccavi, as well as the other.

HISTOR.

Mr. E. BURKE's SPEECH *at the last reading of the* Boston Port Bill.

I Trouble you, Sir, in the last stage of this Bill, because I would not appear petulent when my objections run to the whole of the Bill. I never knew any thing that has given me a more heart-felt sorrow than the present measure. This Bill is attempted to be hastened through the House in such a manner, that I can by no means assent to it; it is to be carried by force and threats into execution; and you have even refused to hear Mr. Bollan, their agent, declaring him to be no agent for Massachusetts-Bay, or properly authorised to present such petition; you have not now one left in England to be heard in behalf of the Colonies; the only obstruction that this Bill has had, has been owing to its *vis inertiæ*; but persons who oppose this Bill, are immediately put to the same kind of punishment in the public papers which offenders in America are. Look, Sir, into the publick papers, you will see Cinna, and a thousand other Roman names, throwing out their invectives, and tarring and feathering all those who dare oppose the Bill; I suppose I shall reap my share for such opposition; but, Sir, at all events I will enter my reasons and protest against this Bill, and will mount my *little palfrey*, and speak of the injustice which the Bill contains, with the greatest confidence. The grievance that is stated in the papers before you on the table, appear to be an universal resistance from all America, against any goods or merchandize that shall be loaded with taxes; [he desired that part of general Haldiman's letter declaring the resolution of the Americans not to submit to receive goods with duty upon them, be read; which was done] he said the whole meeting in the town of Boston consisted of six or seven hundred men of the first rank and opulent fortune in the place, that the proceedings were conducted with the utmost decency. He said, this was not a meeting of mean persons, but that the acts of resistance were all countenanced by universal consent. Observe, says he, that the disturbances are general; shew me one port in all America where the goods have been landed and vended; the distemper is general, but the punishment is local, by way of exchange. Whether it will be effectual or not, I do not know; but, Sir, let me paint to this House the impropriety of a measure like this; it is a remedy of the most uncertain operation; view but the consequence, and you will repent the measure; give orders at once to your Admirals to burn and destroy the town; that will be both *effectual, proper, & moderate*, and of a piece with the rest of your proceedings, *eventus tristis*. One town in proscription, the rest in rebellion, can never be a remedial measure for general disturbances. Have you considered, says he, whether you have troops and ships sufficient to enforce an universal proscription to the trade of the whole continent of America? If you have not, the attempt is childish, and the operation fruitless. Only, Sir, see the consequence of blocking up one port, for instance, that of Virginia Bay; which if you do, you will destroy the tobacco trade, and thereby bring, as it were, a certain ruin on your own merchants at Glasgow and Edinburgh. This bill has been thought a vigorous but not a rigorous punishment. It is my opinion that you might even punish the individuals who committed the violence, without involving the innocent; I should approve much of that; but, Sir, to take away the trade from the town of Boston, is surely a severe punishment. Would it not be a rigorous measure to take away the trade of the Thames, for instance, and direct the merchandize to be landed at Gravesend? I call this bill very unjust that is now to be adopted. Is it not fundamentally unjust to prevent the parties who have offended being heard in their defence? Justice, sir, is not to be measured by geographical lines nor distance. Every man, sir, is authorised to be a magistrate, to put a stop to disturbances which he perceives to be committed against his majesty's peace; but did you expect that the people who were not present at such disturbances, should be equally punished for not aiding and assisting in putting an end to those riots which they never saw or heard of? This, sir, says he, is surely a doctrine of devils, to require men to be present in every part of America wherever a riot happens; but this bill involves those who have never in the least been guilty; and then you again say, that the disturbances which did happen, ought to have been immediately put a stop to by the people of Boston, and that they were bound to preserve the good order of the town; but, sir, I have too much reverence for the image of God to conceive that the honourable gentleman (Mr. Welbore Ellis) does really and truly imbibe such doctrine. (He then read part of colonel Leslie's letter, No. 45, wherein the colonel said, that neither the governor nor the council, nor any of the Custom-House officers, have ever yet applied to me for any assistance; if they had, I could most certainly have put a stop to all their riot and violences, but not without some bloodshed, and firing upon their town, and killing many innocent people.) Why, sir, says he, did not the governor at once send for this assistance? Was it contrary to, or do you think he would have broken through his instructions if he had endeavoured, by such ways and means, to preserve the public peace, and prevent violences from being committed? The fault of this governor ought not to be the means of punishment for the innocent. You have found that there was no government there: why did not the governor exercise his authority? Why did not the ships execute their duty? What was the reason they did not act? Why is not Mr. Hancock, and the chief people who are known, punished, and not involve the innocent with the guilty in one universal calamity? You, surely, sir, cannot have power to take away the trade of a port, and call it privilege! Why was not your force that was present applied to quell the disturbances? How came they to be so feeble and inactive? How are you sure that the orders and frigates which you now send, will act better? I cannot think this, by any means, a prudent measure, to be blocking up one port after another; the consequence will be dreadful, and I am afraid destructive; you will draw a foreign force upon you, perhaps, at a time when you little suspect it; I will not say where that will end; I will be silent on that head, and go no further, but think of the consequence. Again, sir, in one of the clauses of the bill you proscribe the property of the people, to be governed and measured by the will of the crown. This is a ruinous and dangerous principle to adopt. There is an universal discontent throughout all America, from an internal bad government. There are but two ways to govern America, either to make it subservient to all your laws, or to let it govern itself by its own internal policy. I abhor the measure of taxation where it is only for a quarrel, and not for a revenue; a measure that is teazing and irritating without any good effect; but a revision of this question will one day or other come, wherein I hope to give my opinion. But this is the day that you wish to go to war with all America, in order to conciliate that country to this; and to say that America shall be obedient to all the laws of this country. I wish to see a new regulation and plan of a new legislation in that country, not founded on your laws and statutes here, but grounded upon the vital principles of English liberty.

L O N D O N.

April 27. Mr. Van has proposed an amendment to "The bill for the better regulation of the civil government of Massachusetts-Bay," which is to insert a clause for the more certain prevention of mischiefs for the future by taking from those rebellious people all implements of death whatever.

April 29. Commerce is a stronger Tie than Conquest. A brave People will be more useful Allies than either Subject or Slaves. India and America may one Day prove this Truth!

May 6. The bill for the better providing suitable quarters for Officers and Soldiers in his Majesty's service in North-America reported, with amendments, and ordered to be engrossed.

May 9. We hear that Lord Chatham means to attend in his place in the House of Peers, in order to deliver his sentiments respecting American affairs some day in the course of the present week.

Extract of a Letter from Vienna, dated April 17.

"It is universally reported here, that all the Courts of Europe, and the Pope at the head of them, are very seriously about to effect a total union between the three established churches; and that a Congress for that purpose will soon be appointed at Augsburg"

May 13. American quartering bill read a third time and ordered to be carried to the Lords by Sir Charles Whitworth.

The order of the day was read for the bill to regulate the future government, &c. to be read a third time; which being done, and the question put, Whether the bill should pass, another strong debate arose: the Duke of Richmond spoke first, and was answered by Lord Sandwich, Lord Lyttleton, Lord Shelburne, Lord Rochford, Lord Dartmouth, Lord Camden, Lord Mansfield, and the Marquis of Rockingham, which closed the debate.

The question was then put, and the House divided upon the question, That the bill do pass: contents with the proxies, 92; not contents with the proxies, 20.

Read a second time and committed the Bill for the more impartial Administration of Justice in the Province of Massachusetts-Bay

A regiment of foot, on the Irish establishment, has received orders to embark for North-America with all expedition.

Ordered, the Lords be summoned for this day on the second reading the Bill for the more impartial Administration of Justice in the Province of Massachusets-Bay.

Agreed to the report of the amendments made to the Bill for the more impartial Administration of Justice in the Province of the Massachusets-Bay.

Among other articles of our traffic to America, which there is the greatest reason to fear will be irrecoverably lost, is that of cordage, a great quantity of which were usually exported every year. A rope-maker at Deptford, who used formerly to have commissions annually for 4000. has not the last year sent 400l. The Dutch now supply almost all the colonies.

Lord North gave notice yesterday in the House of Commons that he would open the Budget on Wednesday next.

It was confidently reported this morning that yesterday evening an express arrived from Paris, with advice that the French King died on Tuesday night, at 10 o'clock, at Versailles, of the small-pox.

May 14. The Lords yesterday read a second time and committed the Bill for providing more commodious quarters for the troops in North America.

Extract of a Letter from the Hague, May 7.

"It was reported last week, but very much confirmed by the last mails, that a French camp of 40,000 men is ordered to be erected at Metz, and two others of 20,000 men each near Valenciennes.

"We are likewise informed, that a French army of 15,000 men have just been posted upon the coasts near Dunkirk.

P H I L A D E L P H I A, *June* 29.

Every Lover of his Country must exult in the Prospect of the Union of the Colonies.—"The proudest Minister of State" that England ever saw, we hope, (to borrow the emphatical Words of Dr. Smith's Speech in the State-House Yard) will, in a little while, be made to "TREMBLE."

P O R T S M O U T H, July 8.

We hear that Letters are sent to the respective Towns in this Province to appoint and empower Persons in each, to join in the choice of delegates for this government, to meet the general congress proposed.

To his Excellency Governor GAGE.

As a faithful Subject of *King George the Third*, and an Inhabitant of the Colony of the Massachusetts-Bay, I feel myself interested in all your Excellency's public Transactions; and I cannot believe you will deem me impertinent, if I freely express my Sentiments upon such Subjects of general Concern, as fall within the Compass of my Observation. If I can suggest any Thing that may be worthy of your Consideration, or in any small Degree conducive to the Welfare of my Country, I shall be truly happy.

It is the Part, Sir, of a prudent Man to avail himself not only of the Wisdom of those who have gone before him, and to pursue those Measures which have contributed to their Success, but also to profit by their Errors and Misconduct, and to avoid those Mistakes which occasioned their Disappointment and Disgrace.

So much has already been said concerning your Predecessors Mr. Bernard and Mr. Hutchinson, that I shall not take up your Time in giving my Thoughts concerning them, either as Men or Magistrates in general; but certain it is, that in the late Disputes between Great Britain & the Colonies, they both acted on very erroneous Principles; they laid it down as the Ground-work of their Proceedings, that a small Faction in the Town of BOSTON, occasioned all the Uneasiness that subsisted in America; it was therefore only necessary to quell these turbulent Spirits, and every Discontent would consequently cease. All their Letters to Administration which have come to public View, breathed this Sentiment, and his Majesty's Ministers seem to have adopted the same Opinion, and to have been actuated thereby in their Proceedings respecting this Country.——Troops were sent to Boston to keep the Inhabitants in Awe, and the General Assembly was ordered not to be held in Boston, lest the Members thereof should be influenced by the disaffected Inhabitants. You are, I doubt not, acquainted with the Success which attended these Measures; but however inadequate such Measures have hitherto been found, it does not appear that the true Cause of their want of Success is yet discovered by Administration, therefore upon the old Principle of subduing the Faction in Boston, an Act has lately passed for blocking up the Harbour of Boston, and a Fleet and Army have been ordered to support Government in Boston.

Boston, Sir, is not of so much Importance in the American Scale as is imagined. Every Part of the Province, every Part of the Continent, are justly incensed when they hear it asserted that they are led by the Town of Boston. They feel their own Strength—they know their own Motives of Conduct,—they are convinced that their Rights are invaded. It is from Nature, from the British Constitution and from the respective Charters of the Colonies, that they draw the Argument by which they defend their political Tenets; and altho' they compassionate the Distress of the Town of Boston, and do, and will afford them all the Relief they can; yet they never wou'd, even if it was to save that much-abused Town from being laid in Ashes, give up the Liberties of themselves and their Children. Armies may destroy the Inhabitants of Boston—Fleets may lay their Houses in Ruin, but this Slaughter and Desolation never will conquer the Yeomanry of America;—it may rouse Resentment, but never will force Submission. It is the worst Policy to injure the Sea Ports in America, they are the Links which connect Great-Britain and her Colonies. Embarrass them, and the Connection between Britain and America is weakened; destroy them, and the Connection between Britain and America is at an End.

Many false Reports will be made to your Excellency of the People over whom you preside. They will sometimes be represented to you as ready to break out into open Acts of Violence; at other Times you will be told they are so intimidated as to be willing to make the most abject Sacrifice of their Rights; both will be without Foundation. A constant Attention to the Temper of the People, (for want of which Mr. Bernard and Mr. Hutchinson were perpetually embarrassed) will put it in your Power by a just Representation of Affairs to do more for the Honor and Interest of Britain, and the Tranquility of the Colonies, than any one Person has ever yet done since the first Settlement of this Country.

I heartily pray that your Excellency may improve so glorious an Opportunity of distinguishing your Name in the List of American Governors.

I am, with due Respect to your Excellency,

A Freeholder in the County of Suffolk.

Messieurs EDES & GILL,

Please to insert the following and oblige

I. S. a Customer.

A *North Britain* extraordinary.

Addressed to all the People in *America*, particular in this Town and Province.

WHEN a man is led from principle to act contrary to my sentiments, or that of his country in general, I excuse him: but when I see a few, very few indeed compar'd with the body of the community, set themselves up in opposition to, and in direct violation of the constitution of this province, and that of the rights of all America, I look upon them unpardonable, because I know them to be actuated by dastardly, by selfish and pusilanimous motives. Some of those few are excuseable, since from the consideration of their miserable abilities, and wretched intellects, nothing else could be expected, than their becoming the dupes of more cunning and experienced sycophants. We rarely see a spirit of generosity warming the breasts and expanding the hearts of men, suddenly advanced from the dismal huts of Indigence and penury, to wanton in the cheerful apartments of affluence and plenty. Ingratitude is the vilest passion that can possess a man: it disgraces humanity and gives munificence the lie: but notwithstanding this, notorious instances have lately been exhibited of this execrable passion by men, who, from the favours of their fellow citizens now sit in the soft chair of abundance, who, otherwise would have continued immur'd in the hard lap of primæval nothingness. I say, nevertheless, such disgraceful men have set themselves up against the just claims is, *and laudable defence of, your natural and charter privileges. God be praised they are but few, and it is my sincere wish and Council, that every American, more especially every Bostonian and inhabitant of this Province, may keep the dependent foes at a distance, and for the future have no sort of connection or intercourse with them, or any on their account.*

AMERICANS!—*The Calamities that now involve the whole continent, particularly this devoted Town and Province, require a speedy and spirited opposition. The cure I conceive of, comprehends in it a thorough resistance. It is simply this,* TO STOP PURCHASING ANY BRITISH MANUFACTURES, *and thereby* keep your Money in your Pockets. Easy, *and at the same time* advantageous *is this proposal; and when at once it will be the saving of your Constitution, and enriching yourselves, I must not, indeed I cannot harbour the thought, of any of you refusing to comply with so reasonable and profitable a Condition. Where there are no* Purchasers, *there will be no* Venders. *England stands in more need of America's money, than this continent does of British manufactures: And six, nay four months stoppage of purchasing, will of consequence occasion a non-importation; in which case I am certain, even to a demonstration, of its operating in a total defeat of the present tyrannical and unrighteous administration; and that Great-Britain will be glad to accept of your Terms, and restore those Privileges that have been so forcibly, wickedly and unjustly ravished from you.*

My Brethren, "Stand fast in the liberties wherewith Christ hath made you free".

To the PRINTERS.

THE neutrality of the MILTONIANS *in this day of trial and distress, has been matter of much speculation. I shall not at present, assign the cause of their silence.*

But Messieurs Printers, *the Miltonians are roused: The late execrable* addresses *and the horrid* method *of obtaining them, has opened their eyes. The late act of parliament, they believe, was* planned *by a* tool, *they have been wont to idolize.*—Hutchinson *has effected "an abridgment of what are called English liberties,—and now the poor creature has enslaved his country, he has fled to his master for* refuge—there *to receive* not *a righteous reward,* but "to eat the bread of wickedness, and drink the wine of violence" and oppression.

Infatuated man! Your glass is almost run—you have almost filled up the measure of your wickedness. Then North *will not, cannot protect you—George the* Third, *with all his* fleets and armies *cannot secure your guilty soul from the arrest of death, nor with all his* mandates *bring it back from the* pit!

Go unnatural monster! Go carry your addresses to your King: But remember to tell him HOW you came by them—tell him conscious guilt preyed on your vitals, flushed on your hagard cheek, and made you tremble to think of seeing his face without letters of recommendation; but knowing you could not procure them honorably, tell him 'twas your own scheme, *to send forth in a private, cowardly manner, a number of servile* tools *to wheedle a few paltry signers,—no matter who—whether boys, servants, chimney-sweepers, or your own created justices—all will count, and* numbers *are chiefly aimed at.*

One of your sycophants, the notoriously infamous M-r-r-y, *has been dodging about our peaceful streets with a lying address in his hand, soliciting subscribers,—but* Hutchinson *and his* papistical Scotchmen, *are too well known among us. We detest and execrate them. 'Tis true the* pest *has seduced five or six;* some *of which he decoyed into a* barn, *and* one *of them was so* intoxicated, *that he could not write his name, however he made a W & M-rr y did the rest.* Another *is not more than one degree above an* ideot—*neither of which knew any thing that was in the paper. The horrid* lies *he told* some others *in order to make them sign, may be related another time.*

Further, He that hath ears to hear, *let him hear*—unparallelled impudence! Twice *he (M-rr-y) exhausted all his low cunning in trying to get good Deacon* Clap *to sign, but in vain: He resolves however to try again—The THIRD time he* assaults the Deacon on the high-way—*pulls out his ink and paper, and* insists *upon setting his* name to it—But the Deacon was firm. *The* Brass *goes on, Deacon I always thought you my friend till now—but I find you are not, for you won't sign this paper—come Deacon you had better sign, I assure you—you will not be sorry for it—if you can't see through it now,* no matter—*you may depend upon it you will bye and bye—it will all turn out right—you may rely upon what I tell you—come Deacon sign, you won't repent it, come don't be so scrupulous."* The Deacon continues firm. *"Well," says the* r-b-l, *"if you won't sign Deacon, come get up* behind *me and ride with me to my* house *and take a dinner."* There *the* beast *intended to have played another game. But the Deacon was* still proof *against his will*—and the Devil left him—and behold the guardian Angels of American liberty came and ministered unto the virtuous Deacon.

O Hutchinson! Hutchinson! Is this the way your tools *go about to get signers to your addresses!* O incorrigible! *Have you no feeling—is your conscience doubly seared—dare you, dare you show such addresses to your master*—addresses *so scandalously procured? Did you think* they *would convince the world that you were a good and righteous governor? No, you were not absurd enough: But, being determined, at all adventures, to ruin your country, you thought* they *would serve to breed intestine divisions—to set the towns through the province in a ferment—to set neighbour against neighbour—father against son, &c.*—and thus to make us an easier prey to our enemies. *Yes Dæmon! This was your main design, and we are sensible of it—many of your duped addressers are now convinced of it, and bitterly repent their stupidity—your wicked devices will therefore prove abortive. All parties see and* irresistibly feel *the necessity of a* firm UNION. *I dare answer for the firmness of* Milton; *tho' I hear Miller has told Governor Gage the greatest part of Milton are tories. Poor thing you will soon know the contrary—soon see you have forfeited the confidence of your* constituents *by* signing *an infamous address.*

MILTONIENSIS.

WANTS a Place, a Person who can take Care of Horses, drive a Coach, and would be very useful about a Gentleman's House. He can be recommended for Honesty, Sobriety and Diligence. Enquire at the Printers.

AT a Meeting of the Freeholders and other Inhabitants of the Town of Eastham, legally qualified and legally warned in publick Town Meeting assembled at the North Meeting House, on Tuesday 24th May 1774.

Deacon EDWARD KNOWLES, Moderator.

AFTER a long Debate the Town voted to chuse a Committee of three Men, viz. Messieurs Gideon Baty, Isaac Sparrow and Joseph Cole, to draft and make Report to the Town something to retrieve the injured Character of Col. Willard Knowles, then the Meeting adjourned for half an Hour to receive the Report of the Committee.

Met again according to Adjournment, and the Committee reported that there was a Disagreement amongst them, and the Town voted to add two more to the Committee, viz. Mess. Seth Knowles and Theophilus Hopkins, whom reported as followeth.

We the Subscribers recommend the following to be voted as the Opinion of this Town.

Voted, It is the Opinion of this Town, that the Concession that Col. Willard Knowles has made, viz.

That the Trading in the Tea cast ashore last Winter, in Clarks Brig, was not meant to militate with the public Liberties of this Country, as it was looked upon by him when he purchased it as a private Property; but if he had known it had been the Opinion of this Country for the Good of the Public to stop the Circulation of all dutiable Teas, he would not have traded or concerned therewith.

Wherefore we the Inhabitants of this Town, look upon Col. Knowles as a Friend to this Town and his Country; and we believe he would not willingly act any Thing that militates with the Liberties thereof.

And we hereby order the Town Clerk to obliterate and erase out of the Town's Books, all the calumniating Aspersions there recorded last Winter on his former Conduct: So that the said Colonel is now looked upon as a faithful Member of Society, notwithstanding the Suspicions and Aspersions that were heretofore published against him.

And the Town Clerk is desired to favour our Committee of Correspondence with the Proceedings of this Meeting, and they are hereby desired to publish to the World, in some of our public Papers at Boston, that the said Col. Knowles is in full Favour with this Town, and that we hope he may be received so abroad; for we are sure that all that passed was through Inadvertance or some Mistakes on both Parties.

Gideon Baty,
Seth Knowles, } Committee.
Theophilus Hopkins,

The above consented to by me, WILLARD KNOWLES.

Then a Vote was called, Whether the Town would receive the above as the Opinion of this Town, and the Vote passed by a great Majority in the Affirmative.

Attest, GIDEON BATY, Town-Clerk.

B O S T O N.

The Boston *Committee have received the following spirited Letter from the Committee of Correspondence of the respectable Town of* Glassenbury, *in the patriotic Colony of* Connecticut.

Glassenbury, in Connecticut, 23 June 1774.

GENTLEMEN,

WE cannot but heartily sympathize with you under the gloomy Prospects which at present are before you, upon Account of those oppressive Acts of Parliament which have lately been passed, respecting Boston in particular, and the Province of Massachusetts Bay in general. Especially when we consider that our Liberties and Privileges are so nearly and indissolubly connected with yours, that an Encroachment upon one, at least, destroys all the Security of the other. It seems the Parliament of Great Britain are determined to reduce America to a State of Vassalage, and, unless we all unite in the common Cause, they will undoubtedly accomplish their Design. We are much surprized to find so many of the Merchants in Boston courting Favor of the Tools of the Ministry, and heaping Encomiums on that Enemy to Liberty, that Traitor to his Country, and Abettor, if not Author, of all these Evils to America. However we hope the Spirit of Liberty is not entirely fled from Boston, but that you will yet hold out, and to the last resist and oppose those who are striving to enslave America. You may depend on us, and we believe all Connecticut, almost to a Man, to stand by you and assist you in the Defence of our invaluable Rights and Privileges, even to the sacrificing of our Lives and Fortunes in so good a Cause. You will see the Determinations and Resolves of this Town, which we have inclosed.—A Subscription is set on Foot for the Relief of the Poor in Boston, and what Money or Provisions shall be collected, we shall forward as soon as possible.—We are informed that your House of Representatives have appointed a Time for the Meeting of the general Congress, in which we hope all the Colonies will concur, and that a Non-Importation and Non-Exportation Agreement, will be immediately come into, which we doubt not will procure the desired Effect. And notwithstanding the gloomy Aspect of Things at present, we cannot but look forward, with fond Hopes and pleasing Expectations, to that glorious Æra, when America, in Spite of all the Efforts of her Enemies to the contrary, shall rise superior to all Opposition, overcome Oppression, be a Refuge for the Oppressed, a Nurse of Liberty, a Scourge to Tyranny, and the Envy of the World. Then (if you stand firm and unshaken amidst this Storm of Ministerial Vengeance) shall it be told to your everlasting Honor, that Boston stood foremost in the Cause of Liberty, when the greatest Power on Earth was striving to divest them of it; and by their noble Efforts, joined with the united Virtue of her Sister Colonies, they overcame, and thereby have transmitted to Posterity those invaluable Rights and Privileges, which their Fore-fathers purchased with their Blood. And now, Gentlemen, relying on your Steadiness and Firmness in the common Cause, we subscribe your most obedient humble Servants,

ELIZUR TALCOTT,	::	ISAAC MOSELEY,
WILLIAM WILLIAMS,	::	JOSIAH HALE,
EBEN'R PLUMMER,	::	Committee.

CHARLES-TOWN, South-Carolina, June 20.

Letters from the Southern Parts of North-Carolina assure us, that the Inhabitants there will go as far in Defence of American Liberty as can be expected—and recommend, if a Congress should be deemed the first step necessary to be taken, that Subscriptions, or rather Collections, be set on Foot throughout the Continent, to raise and remit a Sum of Money to the Community in Boston, for the Relief of the most Distressed of our *suffering Brethren* here, who must stand in equal Need of such Assistance, as if their Town had been destroyed by Fire.—And we have the Pleasure to learn, that the Inhabitants of this Province, generally, seem ready to contribute their Mite, as soon as proper Persons are named to receive what their benevolent Hearts shall induce them to offer.

NORWICH, *July* 14.

Yesterday the Committee of Correspondence for the Connecticut met in New-London agreable to Appointment, and in Pursuance of an Act of the House of Representatives, at their last Session, they then and there nominated the Hon. *Eliphalet Dyer*, the Hon. *William Samuel Johnson, Erastus Wolcot, Silas Deane*, and *Richard Law*, Esq'rs; and authorized and impowered, either three of them, to meet the General Congress, of the Commissioners or Committees of the Sister Colonies, at Philadelphia, on the first Day of September next, or at such other Times and Place as may be agreed on, to consult Measures for the best Good and Happiness of English America.——Which Appointment being noticed to the Commander of the Battery and the Commanders of the Ships in the Harbour, they fired a general Salute, and the Evening was concluded with social Joy and decent Mirth.

BOSTON, July 18.

Thursday last was observed as a Day of Fasting and Prayer in this and the Province of New-Hampshire, on the present alarming Situation of our public Affairs.

It is with the greatest Pleasure, we can inform the Publick, that the Hon. JOHN HANCOCK, Esq; has so far recovered his Health, as to be able to walk abroad; and in the Course of the past Week, has twice honored this Office with his Presence. He likewise attended divine Service Yesterday.

Twenty Gentlemen of South-Carolina, have presented the industrious Poor of this devoted Town with 205 Tierces of Rice, which arrived at Salem last Monday—for which their grateful Thanks are acknowledged.

A Committee of Thirteen Gentlemen are appointed in Charlestown, South-Carolina, "to receive Donations for the Relief of our distressed Brethren in this Town, now suffering for the common Cause of all America, under the most cruel, arbitrary and tyrannical Act of the British Parliament, for the shutting up of this Port."

Extract of a Letter from a Gentleman in Charlestown, South-Carolina, dated June 30, 1774.

"*The Inhabitants of Boston are cruelly treated—The People here pitty and feel greatly for them Subscriptions are open, and large Donations are made every Day for their Relief. A Sloop sailed Yesterday for Salem, with 205 Barrels of Rice, besides a considerable Sum in Specie, and it is expected they will be able to collect the Value of 1000 Barrels of Rice. A Gentleman of this Province now in England, wrote to his Correspondent here to give not less than £.50 Sterling, but if he thought it proper, to give as far as £.500.*" [A Cordial this, for the industrious Poor!]

Friday last a Number of public-spirited Gentlemen at Marblehead, raised a Subscription for 207 Quintals of Cod Fish, about 50 Jarrs of Oyl, and £.40 Lawful in Specie, for the Use of the industrious Poor of this Town, at this critical Conjuncture of our public Affairs, which is to be forward To Morrow, if the Weather permits.

This is now the 48th Day since the Siege of Boston began; and notwithstanding our accumulating Distresses, the Inhabitants continue to exhibit that calm Firmness and Unanimity, which astonishes our Enemies——Notwithstanding a Report industriously propagated, that a Number of Persons in the Confidence of their Fellow-Citizens were to be apprehended and sent Home for Trial or we know not what, no one of them has left his Ground;—if any unfair Practices should hereafter take Place, this Province and Continent have it in their Power to do themselves Justice. The little Tribe of Addressers, Protestors, &c. are still restless, in order to push themselves into View, but it will not be wondered at by our Brethren in the other Colonies, when they consider how long Boston has been the Head-Quarters of Ministerial Corruption, and what Engines have been set at work to debauch the necessitous and mislead the vain and unwary.——A few Justices of the County of Worcester and Plymouth stand foremost in the Rank of Prostitutes, and the latter have stupidly aimed at paying at Compliment to the G———r in their late Address, by a gross Abuse offered our Clergy; strangely imagining that the Ministers of this Province might be treated with less Delicacy and Deference than the Clergy of Canada.——

—The Inhabitants of this Town are greatly supported under the Weight of Ministerial Vengeance, by the kind sympathy and generous donations of our Brethren and Friends, through the Province and Continent; it indeed seems as if their Prophecy would soon be verified in Boston's becoming the Granary of North-America, may the behavior of its Inhabitants continue to deserve their Praise and Bounty. A whole Continent is now awake and active, one Spirit actuates the whole, and all unite in Prayers to the Supreme Disposer of Events, that the Liberties of America may yet be preserved. Last Thursday was a Solemn Day in this Town; the Shops and Streets empty, and the Churches full—may the Day be followed with true Repentance and Amendment of Life, and all the Ills we suffer now, like scatter'd Clouds shall pass away.

Mr. Job Wheelwright has ordered his Name out of the List of Protestors against the solemn League and Covenant.

The 30th ult. the Rev. Mr. Hezekiah Taylor was ordained Pastor of the Church at New-Fane, in the Province of New-York.

A Spirit of Falshood and Perversion hath ever characterized our public Enemies. THIS SPIRIT is now busy in various Parts of the Province. Hence in one Place it is propagated, that the Donations of our *sympathizing* BRETHREN are so numerous and valuable, that BOSTON will grow rich from the Charities of their public Friends; and threfore they represent Boston as no Object of Charity. In another Place, it is given out, that the Sons of Liberty in order to make a Show of *Assistance* from their Conntrymen, *send Money* into the Country to purchase pretended free Gifts. And this last Report is made by Men who in the next Breath will tell you, that the SONS OF LIBERTY are the Scum of the Earth, the Dregs of the People, and *Poor to a Proverb*.

Another Lie circulated with Industry is, that these Charities are given in Order to keep us from *imploring* an opening of our Port, that as soon as OUR NEIGHBOURS have got all our Trade well secured, they will *desert* Boston and *leave it a Sacrifice*.

Another Falshood is, that these Donations *sound big*, but are *really trifling Matters*.

Such Shifts are our Enemies put to.

A Correspondent now travelling in the Country, gives us the above Intelligence, and assures us, that ALL OUR COUNTRYMEN *are rousing themselves*. They are not now to be deceived as formerly:—they know the Tools & Understrappers of our inveterate Foes—*and mark them*.

Extract of a Letter from London, May 14, 1774.

"Opinions here are various concerning the Reception the Port-Bill will meet with at Boston; no one can advise what is best to be done in the Case. I have sent you the News-Papers for the last Week, by which you may see what the Ministry are now about. It is tho't the Bills will all pass, but we are not certain, for Lord North begins to repent of his evil Actions, by Reason of a Conference which he has lately had with Mr. ——— who has behaved extreamly well in this Affair, and has done all which lay in his Power for the Bostonians: The People here in general are in Favor of the Bostonians, and say they have been greatly imposed upon; you will see by the Papers that the King of France is very ill of the Small-Pox, but it is reported as absolute Fact to Day, that he is really dead, and that he died last Sunday. Provided it is true, it is thought we shall have a War with France very soon, which I wish may be the Case, as I think that would be the only Thing to settle the Difference with America."

We hear that the Prime Minister and his Zany long J. and short Bob, have very much exhausted themselves the Week past, by close Attendance.—It is sometime since they issued their secret Orders to their Understrappers of the Peace to play their Pop Guns upon the Protestant Clergy.

We are well informed that the greatest Part of the Province of New Hampshire, have come in to the Non-Consumption Agreement.

By Accounts from the North & South, East and West of this Province—the Non Consumption Agreement is come into with scarce a dissentient in many Towns.

Large Orders for Fall Goods, have been countermanded, occasioned by the Non Consumptive Agreements.

Extract of a letter, dated Philadelphia, July —, 1774.

"We daily receive dismal accounts from the back parts of this and the neighbouring provinces.—The Indians seem determined to go to war; many white people, consisting of whole families, have already been scalped. Thousands are leaving their habitations in the new settlements.

"People here are not backward in saying, that Lord North is at the bottom of all this; for you must know the Indians were first provoked by some murders committed among them by one Col. Cressop, who, it is said, was encouraged in his direful proceedings by a certain great man in power, who is one of Lord North's correspondents, I mean G. D--more of V—g—a".

W hear a Vessel is arrived at Plymouth, in a short Passage from St. Ubes; the Master of which informs that Advice was receiv'd there of the Death of the French King and also of the King of Prussia:—And that a French Fleet had sailed from Brest to assist the Turks against the Russians. Whether this be true or not Time will soon discover.

We hear that the tradesmen and farmers of the city and county of Philadelphia, are determined to enter into an association, to purchase no more British goods ('till the late acts of parliament are repealed) if the voice of the proposed congress should be in favour of a non-importation agreement.

Petersham, 15th July 1774.

YESTERDAY was kept here as a Day of Fasting and Prayer by a great Number of respectable Inhabitants; the Reverend Mr. Aaron Whitney not inclining to keep that Day, Mr. Samuel Dennis delivered two Discourses from the following Words, in the 4th Chap. of the Book of Esther and 16 Ver. *Go, gather together all the Jews that are present in Shushan, and fast ye for me, and neither eat nor drink for three Days, Night or Day: I also and my Maidens will fast likewise, and so will I go in unto the King, which is not according to Law; and if I perish, I perish.*——The whole was extremely well adapted, and acknowledged by the Audience to surpass any Thing they had ever heard deliver'd in the Town on the Occasion.

THE Inhabitants of this Town are reminded that the May Meeting stands adjourn'd to To-Morrow, at Nine o'Clock in the Forenoon, at Faneuil-Hall.——It is hoped there will be general and punctual Attendance, as the Grant of Monies, Salaries, &c. are then to be made——The Meeting relative to the Boston Port-Bill is adjourned to said Day, Ten o'Clock A. M. when it is expected the Committee on Ways and Means for employing the Poor, will make Report.

Susanna Renken,

INFORMS her Customers and others, That she has removed from Fore-street, to a little above the Hay-Market, where she has for Sale, a Variety of

English and India GOODS,

Groceries of all Sorts, West-India & New-England Rum

TO BE SOLD.

ON THURSDAY NEXT,

By *BENJAMIN CHURCH*,

At FOUR o'Clock in the Afternoon,

A General assortment of European Articles, Linnens, Woollens, Checks, &c. &c. Some House Furniture, an 8-Day Clock, Mehogany Case of Draws, Watches, &c. &c.—At Four o Clock, P. M—

WHEREAS I did suddenly and inadvertently sign an Address to the late Governor Hutchinson with some others, (Justices of the Peace) of Middlesex, being in great Haste, and not so well considering every Part thereof, nor the dangerous Consequences of said Address, am very sorry for it: And as it hath offended my Christian Brethren and Neighbours, I do hereby desire their Forgiveness, and a Restoration to their Friendship.

Billerica, July the 13, 1774. THOMAS KIDDER.

TO BE SOLD,

A House known by the Name

of CONCERT HALL. Enquire of *William Turner*, who has a great Collection of MUSIC which he will sell at the Sterling Cost without Charges, viz.

The Periodical Overturnes to No 36, Two Setts of Back's do. One Sett Shirindl's 1st Opera. Two Setts Able's 1st and 7th Opera, Handal's 65 Overtures, Ferrari's Quarters, Lord Kelly's and Stamitz's do. Barbandt's Simponies, Lord Kelly's Overtures, Humphries, Stanley's, Avison's, Corelli's Albertie's, Geminiani's, Heass's & Felton's Concertos, Campionis, Trios, Fisher's Overtures, Barthelemon's do. 1 Sett Back's Songs, and 4 Violins.

N. B. Said *Turner* continues to teach Cotillons at the above-mentioned Hall, Fencing also.

Thomas Turner

Begs Leave to inform the Public,

That he has opened a School opposite the Rev. Dr. COOPER's Meeting-House, where he teaches Dancing in the politest Manner, and doubts not of giving Satisfaction to Gentlemen or Ladies, who would choose to recommend their Children to him, to acquire so eligible an Accomplishment. Likewise the useful Art of Fencing, agreeable to the best Rules establish'd for that Purpose.

N. B. Due Care shall be taken that the greatest Decency and good Manners be observ'd by his Scholars.

Benjamin Goldthwait

Would inform his Friends, kind Customers and others, That he has just receiv'd by Capt Loring from London a small Invoice of GOODS, *suitable to the present Season, viz.*

Exceeding neat figur'd Jeanes, Thread ditto, plain, coloured and white ditto; Also, very neat Silk Jeans, fine white Irish Tick for Waistcoats and Breeches, white corded Dimothy, Silk knit Patterns, striped Damaskus, with sundry other Articles.——The above being a Consignment, will be Sold very low.

☞ *The Taylor's Business is carried on as usual at his Shop just above Concert-Hall, in all its various Branches, in the genteelest Manner, and with the utmost Dispatch.*

Embroidery in Gold, Silver and Twist, is done in the best Manner at said Shop.

TAKEN up by me the Subscriber in Pomfret, the 20th of May last, a brown Mare, about 14 Hands high, 14 or 15 Years old, Paces and Trots, is bad to catch, bad to get on, but very good after mounted. Said Mare has a Number of white Spots on her Back, a small white Streak across her Nose, occasioned by an Halter, one hind Foot white. The Owner may have her, by applying to me the Subscriber, and paying the Charges. ISRAEL PUTNAM.

New AUCTION-ROOM, Cornhill.

On WEDNESDAY NEXT, at TEN o'Clock, Will be Sold by PUBLIC VENDUE, At GREENLEAF's Auction Room,

A Variety of English Goods as usual—

And at Twelve o'Clock will be Sold a very good Saddle Horse. WILLIAM GREENLEAF, Auctioneer.

The Sale will begin at Ten o'Clock precisely.

At GOULD's *Auction Office*, In Back-Street,

On TUESDAY next,

At TEN in the Morning,

Will be Sold by PUBLIC VENDUE,

A Variety of English and Hard Ware GOODS,

Also some House Furniture.

R. GOULD, Auctioneer.

Just Published, and to be Sold by Samuel Webb, *in Queen-Street;*

A SERMON preached to the Ancient and Honorable ARTILLERY-COMPANY in Boston, New-England, June 6th 1774. Being the Anniversary of their Election of Officers.

By JOHN LATHROP, A. M.

Pastor of the Second Church in Boston.

Subscribers are desired to send for their Books.

Burials in the Town of BOSTON, since our last.

Ten Whites. One Black.

Baptiz'd in the several Churches, Five.

High Water at BOSTON, for the present Week.

Monday, 20 min. aft.	6	Friday, 19 min. after	10
Tuesday, 10 min. aft.	7	Saturday, 25 min. aft.	11
Wednesday, 9 m. aft.	8	Lord's-Day, 38 m. af.	12
Thursday, 8 min. aft.	9	*Full* ☉ 23 *Day* 3 *Morn.*	

From the MORNING POST, &c.

TO LORD NORTH.

My Lord,

'TIS but seldom I trouble your Lordship or the public with my sentiments touching parliamentary affairs, my profession leads me to the pursuit of a different study, and my attention is never engaged in a political broil, in which those of my profession are not deeply concerned; and be assured, my Lord, that nothing less than the certainty of that once honorable profession sinking into contempt, and bringing on it the curses of the injured innocent, and the detestation of all men, could have induced me to take up my pen. I revere the name, and have studied the duty of a soldier from my infancy; and when that duty was confined to the legal protection and defence of the state, and the laws of the realm, it was a pleasure as well as an honour to wear a *cockade*; and suffer me to remind your Lordship, that in the old King's days, a *soldier* had a friend in every house: the sad reverse, now alas! only brings to mind that we once were happy.

It is only within the circle of a few years past that the army, my Lord, could with any degree of propriety be deservedly branded with the epithets of *military executioners*,—that firebrand of cruelty, that very sperm and essence of Scottish tyranny, Lieutenant General M——, began the bloody tragedy, by massacreing the people, and clipping the ears of the civil magistrates in Canada, about the year 1761; since which the succession of a brutal and corrupt administration have, with equal violence to the known laws of God and society, made streams of innocent blood flow in the streets of our capitals, both at home and abroad, to the disgrace of human nature, and the total dishonor and infamy of the army.

The time is now coming, and we hope is near at hand when that blood unjustly and wantonly spilt in Great Britain, and in America, will from the earth call aloud for vengeance, the perpetrators brought to condign punishment, and the land, as well as the name of Soldier, be freed from the curse.

Your expedition to Boston goes on rapidly, my Lord, and you carry your measures in parliament with as much ease, and with as high a hand, as if the whole power of legislation and taxation were vested in your bosom solely. But softly, my Lord, are you sure these measures will take on the west side the Atlantic? And have you considered well and reconciled yourself to the consequences if they should not? Perhaps your Lordship depends upon the circumstance of the people of Boston acting in open and avowed rebellion to justify every part of your conduct:—there, my Lord, you will find yourself fatally mistaken. The inhabitants of that town, and indeed of the whole province, are too great politicians to be ever drove into a measure of that nature, they have disputed every inch of ground with you, upon the principles of the British constitution, and the express letter of their charter. You have fairly lost the field, and now you are preparing to attack them upon new ground—by condemning them unheard, and stripping them of every right and privilege at one stroke. How earnestly does your Lordship strive to make that brave and hardy race of men desperate, and to force them into that rebellion the enemies of the state so much wish for: and how stupidly insensible and regardless of the consequences, which you must know can be nothing less than inevitable ruin and bankruptcy on the trading part of this kingdom.

What a happy Æra for the court of Versailles, who have long wished for a favourable moment to regain their possessions in the western world; but be that as it may, it is well worth your Lordship's while to reflect how contemptible you must appear in the opinion of every thinking and judicious man, when it is made known that those very measures you have fostered, and are now palming upon the House of Parliament, were planned and formed in Boston by those enemies to mankind, Hutchinson, Flucker, Oliver, Sewall, Trobridge, Paxton, and Rugles, and delivered into your hands ready cut & dried, by Sir Francis Bernard.

These facts (which are known to but few people) I shall take occasion to elucidate in my next, and will conclude this letter with the invocation of the poet;

If, ye powers divine!
Ye mark the movements of this nether world,
And bring them to account,
Crush! crush! these vipers,
Who, singled out by a community to guard their rights,
Shall, for a grasp of filthy ore, or paltry office,
Betray them to the foe.

A SOLDIER.

ALL Persons indebted for this Paper, whose Accounts have been above 12 Months standing, are requested to make immediate Payment.

Joseph Coolidge

INFORMS the Public, That he has IMPORTED in the Ships just arrived from London,

A fine Assortment of Guns, Trooping Pistols, Pocket ditto, Gun Locks, Swords, Violins, Fifes and Flutes, Stands of Cruetts, with Silver and Bone Tops, Back Gammon Tables compleat; a Variety of Pocket Books for Gentlemen and Ladies; neat Gilt, Pinchbeck, Plated and black and common Shoe, Knee and Stock Buckles; Japan Trays, Waiters and Candlesticks; most sorts of Jewelry; Silver and Pinchbeck Watches, some as low as seven Dollars; Patent Watch Keys that shew the Day of the Month and Moons Age; Cutlery and Hard Ware, and a Variety of Toys and Trinkets, too many for an Advertisement: All which he will sell at the lowest reduced Prizes, at his Shop just above the Market, and directly opposite the new Auction-Room.

To be Sold cheap at Store No. 14, Long Wharff,

A few Tierces and Barrels MELASES, Casks of best Sort of Rice, and Barrels of Coffee.

CREAM WARE.

Two Crates of elegant Cream Pencil Ware, one Crate of Gally Pots, several Bags Spikes, Deck and Sheathing Nails of different sizes, six Barrels of Durham Mustard in quarter Pound Bottles, a few Boxes 18 Inch Tip'd Pipes, one Case of Hats from Beaver to Felts, with a few Pipes of quarter Casks of Fyal Wines, to be Sold cheap, By

William Hoskins.

WANTED,

A Negro Man from 18 to 30 Years of Age, that will steal, lie and get Drunk. Any Person having such an one to dispose of, may hear of a Purchaser by applying to the Printers hereof.

Province of the Massachusetts-Bay. } *To the Hon*ble. Samuel Dexter, *Esq; one of his Majesty's Justices of the Peace through the said Province.*

We the Subscribers, Proprietors of a Township, granted by the Great and General Court of the Province aforesaid, at their Session in February last, to *John Gardner*, and others, in Lieu of a Township, Number Six in the Line of Towns between *Connecticut* and *Merrimack Rivers*, lost by the late Settlement of *New-Hampshire*—request your Honour to call a Meeting of said Proprietors to be on Monday the 29th Day of *August* next, at the House of *Jonathan Wood*, Esq; Innholder in *Stow*, at Ten of the Clock in the Forenoon, then and there to choose a Moderator for said Meeting, also to choose a Proprietor's Clerk, Treasurer, and any other Proprietary Officer; to Grant such Sum or Sums of Money, as may be needful to discharge any Debts already due from said Proprietors, or to discharge any future Demands; to agree on some Method for calling Proprietors Meetings for the future. Also to agree on some Method for laying out said Township into Lots, and to do any other Thing proper for bringing forward the Settlement of said Township.

Stow, June 15, 1774.

John Whitcomb,
Jonathan Loring,
Henry Gardner,
Abner Cranson,
Micah Keys,
Daniel Hapgood,
Samuel Curtis.

Province of the Massachusetts-Bay.

(Seal.) *To* Henry Gardner, *of* Stow, *in the County of Middlesex, Esq; one of the principal Proprietors of the Township aforementioned,* Greeting.

In pursuance of the foregoing Application and Request, you are hereby required to give Notice, in Time and Manner as the Law directs, to the Proprietors of the Township aforesaid, that they meet at the Time and Place, and for the Purposes expressed in the aforewritten Petition. Given under my Hand and Seal, this sixth Day of July, Anno Domini, 1774, and in the fourteenth Year of his Majesty's Reign.

SAMUEL DEXTER, a Justice of the Peace through the Province of the Massachusetts-Bay.

Stow, July 6th 1774.

By Virtue of the above Warrant to me directed, The Proprietors above mentioned, are required to meet at Time and Place above-mentioned, for the Purpose aforesaid.

HENRY GARDNER.

CHoice Lisbon LEMMONS per Box.

Lisbon, Madeira, Malaga, Virgin, Sherry, Shullowe WINE, per Quarter Cask.—Raisins per Cask, Citron per Box. Lisbon Oil per Cask, Dutch Brushes, Barcelona Handkerchiefs per Dozen, TO BE SOLD

By Archibald Cunningham,

At his Store in Ann-Street, Boston.

TO BE SOLD,

Several good Farms, with Dwelling-Houses, Barns, &c. thereon, pleasantly situated about 20 Miles from Boston, on a considerable Road.——The Payment may be made very easy.——Also several Rights of Land in a new Township. Enquire of Edes & Gill.

To be sold for Cash only,

A small Quantity of good dry Mehogany, fit for immediate Use; Inquire of Edes & Gill.

KEYSER's

FAMOUS PILLS

So well known all over *Europe*, and in *this* and the *neighbouring Colonies*, for their superior Efficacy and peculiar Mildness, in perfectly eradicating every Degree of a certain Disease, without the least Trouble or Confinement.

The Public may be assured, that this excellent Medicine is beyond any Thing in all Foulness and Impurities of the Blood, having performed many astonishing Cures in Scorbutic Eruptions, Leprosies, White Swellings, Stiff Joints, Gout and Rheumatic Disorders, &c.

THESE PILLS ARE NOW SOLD BY

EDES and GILL,

(In Boxes of 7/6. L. M. each, *fresh imported*) Who have in their Hands a Letter from the Widow KEYSER, and a Certificate from under her own Hand of the Genuineness of the above Pills; which any Person may have the Perusal of by applying to them at their Printing-Office in *Queen-Street*: Where may be had a Variety of Books, &c

To be sold on very reasonable Terms,

The Hull of a double-deck'd Brigantine about 146 Tons Burthen, now launched in Taunton-River. Farther enquire of ABIEL SMITH, nearly opposite to the Head of Orange Tree-Lane, Boston, or Mr. JOB SMITH, at Taunton.

TO BE LETT,

A convenient Brick Tenement, near the Orange-Tree. Inquire of the Printers.

The Sloop JENNY, lying at the Long-Wharff at Salem, will sail in 10 Days, for Annapolis-Royal.——For Freight or Passage apply to GEORGE MITCHEL, on board said Sloop, or to his House on Winter's Wharff, Boston.

To be Sold at Public Vendue, by Order of his Majesty's Justices of the Inferior Court, on the first Wednesday in August,

PART of the Real Estate of SAMUEL WELD, late of Roxbury, Joiner, deceas'd, viz. Half of a House, near the House known by the Name of the Greyhound Tavern, and 8 Acres of Land, near the Rev. Mr. Gordon's Meeting House. The Sale to be at said House on Wednesday the 3d of August, at Three o'Clock, P. M.

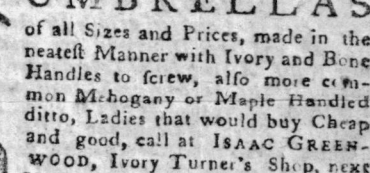

UMBRELLAS of all Sizes and Prices, made in the neatest Manner with Ivory and Bone Handles to screw, also more common Mehogany or Maple Handled ditto, Ladies that would buy Cheap and good, call at ISAAC GREENWOOD, Ivory Turner's Shop, next Shop to Dr. CLARKS, North-End, Boston; where you may have your old Umbrella sticks mended and covered, your Ivory and bone stick Fans mended, Gentlemen may have India Canes, neat Ivory and Bone, headed, Hickery Stick, Ivory or Bone, handled, Chaise Whips, Hidrometers for proving Spirits, German Flutes, ditto Tiped with Ivory Fife, Billiard Balls, and many other Articles. Such Gentlemen as are Building may have their Banisters and Posts, Pillers for Frunticepieces and Porticoes, Balls and Flower Pots, or any other Ornaments, turned or twisted in the neatest Manner with Fidelity and Dispatch at the above Shop, all Favours from those that have and shall Imploy duly acknowledged, by their humble Servant,

ISAAC GREENWOOD.

TO BE SOLD,

A large and convenient Dwelling House, situate on Spring Hill so called, in Portsmouth, in the Province of New Hampshire, near the Market, in the most principal Part of the Town for any Gentleman to carry on Trade, both by Sea & Land. Said House is almost New, and almost finished, with an excellent Cellar, and a back Yard, and a Garden, also a Warehouse and Stable, with many other Conveniences suitable for a Family. Inquire of the Printers.

IMPORTED in the last Ships from LONDON, and to be Sold by JOHN WHITE, near the Cornfield, Union Street.

AN Assortment of Goods, amongst which are 7/8, 3/4, and yard-wide Irish Linnen, Cotton and Linnen Check, newest fashioned Callicoes, Ribbons of all Sorts, Handkerchiefs of all sorts, Diaper Table Cloaths, Clouting Diaper, Russia Diabs, Nankeens, Women's Shoes and Clogs, silk Gloves and Mitts, Book Muslin, Cambricks and Lawns, Catgut, Patent and Spiders Net, Black, Bone and Blond Lace, White Blond and Thread ditto, Cheveaux de Frize, sprig'd and strip'd Silk Gauze, English and French Necklaces, Sarsnets and Sattins of all Colours, Cotton Hose.—A large Assortment of Looking Glasses, China, Glass and Earthern Ware, English Loaf Sugar, and a few fine Cheshire Cheeses.

A young Woman, with a good Breast of Milk would be glad to take a Child to Suckle.——Inquire of *Edes and Gill.*

Boston: Printed, by EDES & GILL, *in Queen-Street*, 1774.

THE
Boston-Gazette, AND COUNTRY JOURNAL.

No. 1006

Containing the freshest Advices, Foreign and Domestic.

MONDAY, July 25, 1774.

At a Meeting of Sixty Gentlemen, Deputies of the several Towns in the County of Berkshire, *appointed to consult and advise what was necessary and prudent to be done by the Inhabitants of this County in the present alarming Situation of our public Affairs, met at* Stockbridge July 6, 1774.

JOHN ASHLEY, Esq; unanimously chosen Chairman.

Mr. Theodore Sedgwick chosen Clerk.

Mr. Williams, Mr. Sedgwick, Mr. Curtis, Mr. Brown and Mr. Hopkins, being appointed, reported the following Resolves, viz.

1st RESOLVED, That King GEORGE the Third is our rightful King, and that we will bear true Allegiance to him

2. *Resolved*, That the Inhabitants of his Majesty's Colonies in America, are justly intitled to all the Rights and Liberties that the Inhabitants of Great-Britain are intitled to, which Rights and Liberties have been particularly confirmed to the Inhabitants of this Province by Charter.

3. *Resolved*, That it is one of the grand Rights and Liberties of said Inhabitants of Great-Britain, that they cannot constitutionally be deprived of their Property, but by their own Consent.

4. *Resolved*, That the late Act of the British Parliament for *giving* and *granting* to his *Majesty* a *Duty* upon all Teas, imported from Great-Britain into America, which Duty by said Act is made payable here, for the Purpose of raising a Revenue, was made without the Consent of the Inhabitants of America; whereby their Property is taken from them without their Consent; and therefore ought to be opposed in all legal and prudent Ways.

5. *Resolved*, That it is an undoubted Right of the Inhabitants of said Colonies in all Actions to be tried by their Peers of the Vicinity; and therefore that all those Acts of the British Parliament, that any way respect the collecting the Duties aforesaid, whereby the *Trial by Jury* is taken away, or whereby the ancient *Trial by Jury* is in any Way altered, are unconstitutional and oppressive.

6. *Resolved*, That wherever any Franchises and Liberties are granted to a Corporation or Body Politic, those Franchises and Liberties cannot legally be taken from such Corporations and Bodies Politic, but by their Consent or by Forfeiture: That the Inhabitants of this Province have many great and invaluable Franchises and Liberties granted to them by Charter; which Franchises and Liberties have not been forfeited or resigned by said Inhabitants: That by the late Acts of the British Parliament, some of the most valuable of those Franchises and Liberties of the said Inhabitants are taken from them without even the Form of a Trial. Therefore,

7. *Resolved*, That it is the indispensible Duty of every Person who would preserve to himself and Posterity, the inestimable Blessings of Liberty, by all constitutional Ways and Means in his Power, to endeavour to avert the much dreaded Consequences of these arbitrary and oppressive Acts; and that for that Purpose, it is prudent for the Inhabitants of the said Colonies to enter into an Agreement not to purchase or consume the Manufactures of Great-Britain, under such Limitations and Exceptions as shall be agreed upon; and that such a Non-Consumption Agreement is neither unwarrantable, hostile, traiterous nor contrary to our Allegiance due to the King; but tends to promote the Peace, good Order, and Safety of the Community.

Which said Report being maturely considered, it was put to Vote, Paragraph by Paragraph, and each and every Paragraph thereof is unanimously accepted.

A Committee being appointed to make Draught of the Form of a Solemn League and Covenant, to be recommended to be Signed by the Inhabitants of this County, to prevent the Consumption of the Merchandize of Great-Britain; the following Draught is reported, viz.

Whereas the Parliament of Great-Britain, have of late undertaken to give and grant away our Money, without our Knowledge or Consent; and in Order to compel us to a servile Submission to the above Measures, have proceeded to block up the Harbour of Boston; also have or are about to vacate the Charter, and repeal certain Laws of this Province heretofore enacted by the General Court, *and confirmed by the* King *and his* Predecessors: *Therefore as a Mean to obtain a speedy Redress of the aforesaid Grievances, we do hereby solemnly and in good Faith* Covenant *and* Engage *with each other,*

1. That we will not import, purchase or consume, or suffer any Person by, for or under us, to import, purchase or consume, in any Manner whatever, any Goods, Wares or Merchandize, which shall arrive in America from Great-Britain, from and after the First Day of October One Thousand seven Hundred and seventy-four, or such other Time as shall hereafter be agreed upon by the American Congress, nor any Goods, which shall be ordered from thence after this Day, untill our Charter and constitutional Rights shall be restored or untill it shall be determined by the Major Part of our Brethren in this and the neighbouring Colonies, that a Non-Importation and Non-Consumption Agreement will not have a Tendency to effect the desired End, or untill it shall be apparent that a Non-Importation or Non-Consumption Agreement will not be entered into by the Majority of this and the neighbouring Colonies, except such Articles as the said general Congress of North America shall agree to import, purchase and consume.

2. We do further Covenant and Agree that we will observe the most strict Obedience to all constitutional Laws and Authority, and will at all Times exert ourselves to the utmost, for the Discouragement of all Licenciousness, and suppressing all Mobs and Riots.

3. We will exert ourselves as far as in us lies, in promoting Love, Peace and Unanimity among each other; and for that End we engage to avoid all unnecessary Law-Suits whatever.

4. As a strict and proper Adherence to this present Agreement will (if not seasonably provided against) involve us in many Difficulties and Inconveniencies; we do promise and agree, that we will take the most prudent Care for the raising and preserving Sheep, for the manufacturing all such Clothes as shall be most useful and necessary; for the raising of Flax and manufacturing Linens. Further, that we will by every prudent Method endeavour to guard against all those Inconveniencies which may otherwise arise, from the foregoing Agreement.

5. That if any Person shall refuse to sign this or a similar Covenant, or after having signed it, shall not adhere to the real Intent and Meaning thereof, he or they shall be treated by us, with all that Neglect they justly deserve.

6. That if this or a similar Covenant shall (after the First Day of August next) be offered to any Trader or Shop-keeper in this County, and he or they shall refuse to sign the same, for the Space of forty-eight Hours, that we will not from thenceforth purchase any Articles of British Manufactures from him or them, untill such Time as he or they shall sign this or a similar Covenant.

Witness our Hands, this Day of July, Anno Domini, 1774.

Which being several Times distinctly read, it was put Paragraph by Paragraph, and accepted.

This Congress, in Deference to the Resolves of the late House of Representatives, in Imitation of the pious Example of the Rev. the Pastors of the Associated Churches in the Town of Boston, and from a Sense of their Dependance on *God* for every Mercy, do earnestly recommend to all Denominations of Christians in this County, to set apart and observe Thursday the Fourteenth Day of July Current, as a Day of public Fasting and Prayer, to implore the Divine Assistance, that he would in Mercy interpose and avert all those Evils with which we are threatened.

And each and every Member of this Congress are enjoined to inform the several Ministers of the several religious Assemblies to which they belong hereof.

Voted, That the several Members of this Congress do recommend to the Charity of the Inhabitants of the several Towns and Places to which they belong, the distressed Circumstances of the poor of the Towns of Boston and Charlestown, and that whatever shall be collected for them be remitted in Fat Cattle in the next Fall, by such Ways & Means as shall be hereafter agreed upon.

Voted unanimously, That Thanks be given to Col. Ashley, for his constant Attendance, Uprightness and Impartiality as Chairman.

Voted, That the Clerk be enjoined to make a fair Copy of the Proceedings of this Meeting, and transmit the same to the Committee of Correspondence of the Town of Boston.

Voted to Dissolve this Meeting; and it is Dissolved accordingly.

The foregoing is a true Copy.

Attest THEODORE SEDGWICK, Clerk.

N. B. The Proceedings aforesaid were preceded by an animated Prayer, made by the Rev'd Mr. West.

BOSTON, July 21.

We hear from Cambridge that yesterday the Degrees were conferred on the Candidates by a general Diploma; of which the following is an exemplification, *viz.*

SENATUS Academiæ Cantabrigiensis in Nova Anglia, omnibus in Christo fidelibus ad quos præsentes literæ pervenerint, salutem in Domino sempiternam.

Notum facimus, quod Nos (consentientibus Honorandis admodum ac Reverendis Academiæ nostræ Inspectoribus) per præsentes admittimus

Dominos

Daniel Adams	Thomam Loring
Josephum Allen	Benjamin Lovell
Jonathan Allen	Nathan Morey
Fisher Ames	Benjamin Muzzy
Edvardum Barnard	Brinley Silvester Oliver
Franciscum Borland	Daniel Parker
Johannem Bradford	Benjamin Putnam
Jabez Chickering	Jacobum Putnam
Johannem Clarke	Johannem Rice
Josephum Crocker	Thomam Rindge Rogers
Isaiam Doane	Jacobum Sheaffe
Ricardum-Rosewell Eliot	Josiam Smith
Josephum Emerson	Mosem Taft
Samuel Emery	Johannem Thaxter
Abel F sk	Nathaniel Thomas
Gulielmum Fogg	Benjamin Thurston
Timotheum Dwight	Onesiphorum Tilestone
Gulielmum Gallison	Johannem Tucker
Asahel Goodenow	Jahacobum Welsh
Josephum Hall	Laban Wheaton
Josephum Haven	Bela Whipple
Gulielmum Hobart	Thomam Rice Willard
Gulielmum Jennison	Timotheum Trumball
Samuel Jennison	
Robertum Junkins	Jacobum Ivers

Antedictæ Academiæ Alumnos, ad Primum Gradum in Artibus.

Dominos etiam Abiel Smith, admissum ad Baccalaureatum, Anno 1764,
Ephraim Wales, Anno 1768.
Thomam Kast, Anno 1769.
et Johannem Winthrop, Anno 1770.

Samuel-Hirst Sparhawk	Josephum Avery
Jacobum Bowdoin	Johannem Frothingham
Andream Bradford	Michael Joy
Samuel Paine	David Osgood
Gulielmum Vassall	Johannem Warren
Samuel Phillips	Crocker Sampson
Daniel Murray	Samuel Nye
Daniel Rogers	Gulielmum Scott
Josephum Emerson	Abraham Watson
Johannem Alford Mason	Thomam Edwards
David Parsons	Perez Morton
Walter Hastings	Jonathan Norwood
Jahacobum Bacon	Melzar Turner Oakman
Mosem Hale	Israel Keith
David Toppan	Nathaniel Dickinson
Samuel Plummer	Johannem Noyes
Johannem White	Gad Stebbins
Josephum Pearse Palmer	Mosem Everett
Gulielmum Cheever	Mosem Adams
Greenleaf Dole	Samuel Wheeler
Zedekiam Sangar	Benjamin Curtis
Isaac Bangs	Jonathan French
Johannem Tracy	Gulielmum Scales
Josuam Dodge	Benjamin Hasey
Daniel Tyler	

Alumnos quoque Academiæ antedictæ ad Secundum Gradum in Artibus, dantes et concedentes iis omnia insignia, jura, privilegia, dignitates ac honores ad Gradus suos spectantia.

In cujus rei testimonium, communi hujusce Universitatis Sigillo Literis hisce appenso, Chirographa apposuimus, Die vicesimo Julii, Anno Salutis Millesimo septingentesimo septuagesimo quarto.

LOCUS SIGILLI.

NATHANAEL APPLETON,
JOHANNES WINTHROP,
ANDREAS ELIOT,
SAMUEL COOPER,
JOHANNES WADSWORTH, } Socii.

JOHANNES HANCOCK, Thesaurarius.

RESOLUTIONS

UNANIMOUSLY *entered into by the Inhabitants of* SOUTH CAROLINA, *at a* GENERAL MEETING, *held at* CHARLES-TOWN *in the said Colony, on* Wednesday, Thursday *and* Friday *the 6th, 7th and 8th Days of* July 1774.

Resolved, THAT his Majesty's Subjects in North-America owe the same Allegiauce to the Crown of Great-Britain, that is due from His Subjects born in Great-Britain.

Resolved, That His Majesty's Subjects in America are intitled to all the inherent Rights and Liberties of his natural-born Subjects within the Kingdom of Great-Britain.

Resolved, That it is repugnant to the Rights of the People, that any Taxes should be imposed on them, unless with their own Consent, given personally, or by their Representatives.

Resolved, That it is a fundamental Right which his Majesty's Liege Subjects are intitled unto, That no Man should suffer in his Person or Property without a fair Trial, and Judgment given, by his Peers, or by the Law of the Land.

Resolved, That all Trials of Treason, Misprision of Treason, or for any Felony or Crime whatever, committed and done in his Majesty's Colony, by any Person or Persons residing therein, ought of Right to be had and conducted in and before His Majesty's Courts held within the said Colony, according to the fixed and known Course of Proceeding, and that the Seizing any Person or Persons residing in this Colony, suspected of any Crime whatever committed therein, and sending such Person or Persons to Places beyond the Sea to be tried, is oppressive and illegal, and highly derogatory to the Rights of British Subjects; as thereby the inestimable Privilege of being tried by a Jury from the Vicinage, as well as the Benefit of summoning and procuring Witnesses on such Trial, will be taken away from the Party accused.

Resolved, That the Statute made in the 35th Year of Henry VIII. Chap. 2, entitled, "an Act for the Trial of Treasons committed out of the King's Dominions" does not extend, and cannot, but by an arbitrary & cruel Construction be construed to extend, to Treasons, Misprisions of Treasons, or Concealment of Treasons committed in any of his Majesty's American Colonies, where there is sufficient Provision, by the Law of the Land, for the impartial Trial of all such Persons as are charged with, and for the due Punishment of, those Offences.

Resolved, That the late Act for shutting up the Port of Boston, and the two Bills relative to Boston, which, by the last Accounts from Great-Britain, had been brought into Parliament, there read and committed, are of the most alarming Nature to all his Majesty's Subjects in America—are calculated to deprive many Thousand Americans of their Rights, Properties and Privileges, in a most cruel, oppressive and unconstitutional Manner—are most dangerous Precedents, and, tho' levelled immediately at the People of Boston, very manifestly and glaringly shew, if the Inhabitants of that Town are INTIMIDATED INTO A MEAN SUBMISSION TO SAID ACTS, that the like are designed for all the Colonies; when not even the Shadow of Liberty to his Person, or of Security to his Property, will be left to any of his Majesty's Subjects residing on the American Continent.

Resolved therefore, That not only the Dictates of Humanity, but the soundest Principles of true Policy and Self-Preservation, make it absolutely necessary, for the Inhabitants of all the Colonies in America to assist and support the People of Boston, by all lawful Ways in their Power; and especially, to leave no justifiable Means untried to procure a Repeal of those Acts immediately relative to them, and also of all others affecting the constitutional Rights and Liberties of America in general. As the best Means to effect this most desirable End,

Resolved, That Henry Middleton, John Rutledge, Christopher Gadsden, Thomas Lynch and Edward Rutledge, Esqrs. be and they are hereby nominated and appointed Deputies, on the Part and Behalf of this Colony, to meet the Deputies of the several Colonies of North-America, in general Congress, the first Monday in September next, at Philadelphia, or at any other Time or Place that may be generally agreed on; there to consider the Act lately passed, and Bills depending in Parliament, with Regard to the Port of Boston and Province of Massachusetts-Bay, which Act and Bills, in the Precedent and Consequences, affect the whole Continent—also the Grievances under which America labours by Reason of the several Acts of Parliament that impose Taxes or Duties for raising a Revenue, and lay unnecessary Restraints and Burdens on Trade—and of the Statutes, parliamentary Acts and Royal Instructions which make an invidious Distinction between His Majesty's Subjects in Great-Britain and in America—with full Power and Authority, in behalf of us and our Constituents, to concert, agree to, and effectually prosecute such legal Measures (by which we, for ourselves and them, most solemnly engage to abide) as in the Opinion of the said Deputies, and of the Deputies so to be assembled, shall be most likely to obtain a Repeal of the said Acts, and a Redress of those Grievances.

Resolved, That we will agree to pay the Expence of such Gentlemen as may be fixed upon to be sent upon this Business.

Resolved, That while the oppressive Acts relative to Boston are enforced, we will chearfully, from Time to Time, contribute towards the Relief of such poor Persons there, whose unfortunate Circumstances, occasioned by the Operation of those Acts, may be thought to stand in Need of most Assistance.

Resolved, That we will, by all Means in our Power, endeavour to preserve Harmony and Union amongst all the Colonies.

Resolved, That a Committee of Ninety-nine Persons be now appointed, to act as a General Committee, to correspond with the Committees of the other Colonies, and do all Matters & Things necessary to carry these Resolutions into Execution; and that any Twenty one of them met together may proceed on Business—their Power to continue till the next General Meeting.—And in Case of the Death, Departure from the Province, or Refusal to act of any or either of them, the Parish or District for which such Person dying, removing, or refusing to act, was chosen, shall fill up the Vacancy.

The COMMITTEE were then accordingly chosen.

NEW-YORK, July 18.

Wednesday Night last our Committee of Correspondence met, and drew up a Set of Resolves on the present alarming Occasion, which were printed in Hand Bills, and sent about the Town the next Morning, for the Approbation of the Inhabitants thereof; who are to assemble at the Coffee-House To-Morrow at 12 o'Clock, either to approve or disapprove of the same. At the same Time the People are to testify their Approbation of the five Gentlemen nominated by the Committee to attend as Delagates at the general Congress, viz. Mr. Duane, Mr. Philip Livingston, Mr. John Alsop, Mr. Isaac Low, and Mr. John Jay.

NEWPORT, *July* 18.

Many parts of the Country are raising subscriptions for the humane and generous purpose of supporting the poor of Boston; and there would have been a subscription vigorously put forward in this town, last week, had it not been for the supplies which were sent from other parts, on which account it was thought best to omit it till the next session of our Assembly, when 'tis not doubted they will do something handsome, it being absolutely more necessary to assist the inhabitants of that town in this last struggle for American liberty, than if it had been laid in ashes.

Yesterday arrived here the brig Caty, Capt. James Frost, in nine Weeks from London.

The most authentic accounts by Capt. Frost are, That the people in England are as anxious to hear the reception the infamous PORT-BILL *met with, as if their lives depended on the event; that many imagined the appearance of the troops and ships would strike such a panic into the Bostonians, that they would immediately submit, and pay for the tea; that others were afraid the southern colonies would absolutely refuse to support them, and that they must give up; but that universally, except court sycophants, ministerial tools and hungry dependants, they wished, devoutly wished, the colonies to unite, and stand firm, otherwise liberty would be banished the face of the earth, or at least be no where found but in wilds and desarts! That the tradesmen began to be very fearful of our stopping trade, a considerable number of whom would have embarked with Capt. Frost, but that he could not bring them; and that it was generally thought, if the Colonies stood out, as became free-born Americans, that curse to the nation, L—d N—h, would soon be in danger of losing his head, the people being almost ripe for any thing.*

PORTSMOUTH, July 22.

On Wednesday last arrived here the Ship Dartmouth, Capt. Giddings from London, but brings nothing later than we have already had.

On the same Day arrived the Sloop Molly, Capt. Odiorne, in 7 Days from Halifax, being the same Vessel that carried the TEA from this Place: The Captain assures us that he safely landed that disagreeable Commodity there, though much against the Minds of the Inhabitants, who are determined not purchase it. TEA is sold there at Half a Dollar per Pound.

UNITED WE STAND—DIVIDED WE FALL.

BOSTON, July 25.

Extract of a Letter from Alexandria, (Virginia,) to a Gentleman in Town, dated July 6, 1774.

"The following Supscription for the Benefit and Relief of those, (the industrious Poor of the Town of Boston,) who by the late cruel Act of Parliament, are deprived of their daily Labour and Bread, to prevent the Inhabitants sinking under the Oppression or Migrating, to keep up that manly Spirit that has made them dear to every American, through the Envy of an arbitrary Parliament, is from the County of Fairfax, in this Colony, viz. £.273 in Specie, (equal to Lawful,) 38 Barrels of Flour, and 150 Bushels of Wheat.——This Subscription being but few Days on Foot, we have not had an Opportunity to present it to the Country in general; a larger Sum will be given.—Mr. Henly Yesterday returned from Dumfrise, after consulting the Committee of Prince-William County, in which a Subscription is going on generously; this Day he sets out to consult the Committees of Loudoun and Frederick Counties, in each of which, a Spirit, becoming generous and free-born Sons of Liberty, are in the like Manner testified: Indeed all Virginia and Maryland are contributing for the Relief of Boston.——The Subscription is to be laid out in Corn and Flour, to be shipped and consigned to the Hon. James Bowdoin & John Hancock, Esqrs; Mr. Samuel Adams, Isaac Smith, Esq; and the Gentlemen Committee of Correspondence in Boston, to be distributed in such Manner as they shall think most proper, among the Persons reduced to Want and Indigence by Means of the cruel and unjust Act of Parliament. We are in Expectation of our Schooner Nassau every Day, shall load her with a Cargo to be presented as by the inclosed Paper.—Our Association was put off, as the People from the Country could not attend, being in the Midst of Harvest and bad Weather, they would have lost much Grain.—But be assured Virginia and Maryland are determined to unite with the Colonies.—Firmness and Intrepidity is their Character."

Extract of a Letter from a Gentleman of the first Character and Fortune in Charlestown, South-Carolina, to his Friend at Boston, dated 12 July, 1774.

"Your Situation at this Time is truly *hazardous* and *trying*, but *you will not fail for want of Support, because* ALL BRITISH AMERICA ARE YOUR FRIENDS. For GOD's Sake BE FIRM and *discreet* at this Time. The good People of this Colony have sent you one Sloop-Load of Rice, and *we shall send you more.*——I should suppose that a Non Im-and-Non-Exportation would bring us Relief.—I think this seems to be the Sense of almost all the Colonies.——And such a Measure would place America in such a consequential Point of View, as would astonish all Europe. I think we have the Cards in our our Hands; but if we do not play them with Caution, we shall be juggled out of the Game.

"OUR *Fears* are *about you, that you may despond,* AND GIVE UP; for I am sorry to see *you have* SO MANY ADDERS *in your own Bosom, who may sting you to Death.*—Pity it is, that Hutchinson should have gone Home with so many Names to ADDRESSES: *It will do you no good,* BUT MUCH HURT, I fear.

"At this Time of imminent Danger, POLITICKS should be the Theme of the Day, and our Dreams at Night should be of the Situation of our Country. However bad it is, *if* BOSTON DOES BUT PERSEVERE, *and be prudent,* HER SISTERS and NEIGHBOURS *will work out her Salvation, without recourse to* ARMS.——UNANIMITY must be THE GREAT LEADING STARR."

I am, &c.

Extract of a Letter from a Gentlemen in Rhode-Island, to his Friend in this Town, dated July 22, 1774.

"Two Vessels from Charlestown, South-Carolina, arrived here last Night; they have subscribed 2000 Tierces of Rice for your Town;—two Vessels were loading for Boston with some of the Rice when the last Advices came away."

Thursday last the Delegates from the several Towns in the Province of New Hampshire met at Exeter, when they made Choice of Col. Nathaniel Folsom of Exeter, and Major John Sullavin of Durham, to represent that Province at the general Congress.

By a very late Letter, we are informed that the People of New-York have unanimously Voted that the Resolves proposed to them were destitute of vigour, sense and integrity—that they have chosen a Committee of fifteen Persons to draw up new Resolves, and that Messi'rs McDougal and Lispenard two unexceptionable Friends of Liberty were added to the Delegates.

A Correspondent says, It is expected that the CONGRESS will recommend to the People of this Continent to enter into an Engagement not to purchase any Goods of the English East India Company, or their Factors, until the Company hath made *Compensation* to Boston, and other Towns on the Continent, which have suffered in Consequence of said Company's *basely* sending their *detested Tea* to America.

Mr. PELATIAH WEBSTER of Philadelphia has given Orders to his Correspondent here to pay into the Hands of the Treasurer of the Committee for receiving Donations, *Ten Pounds* Lawful Money, for the Use of the industrious Poor who are now suffering in Consequence of the Boston Port Bill.

Last Week the Corporation of Harvard College made Choice of the Rev. Dr. SAMUEL LANGDON of Portsmouth as President of that Society.

Last Saturday Night departed this Life, Mr. Johnson Jackson, Aged 63 Years,—His Funeral is To-Morrow at 5 o'Clock Afternoon, where his Friends & Acquaintaace are desired to attend.

DIED.] Mr. Elisha Eaton, Housewright.

On the 15th Instant, at New-York, John Aspinwall, Esq; a noted Merchant of that Place, Æt. 69.

——— On the 17th Instant, at his Seat in Lancaster, MICHAEL TROLLETT, Esq; Æt. 61.

[*The Address to Governor* GAGE, *we are obliged to omit this Week for want of Room.*]

Messieurs EDES & GILL,

IT is confidently said that a Number of Monied Men, such as I—c W——w and among the Rest the pious Dr. P——n, have combined together to furnish Monies to let on Interest to Persons in the Country on express Condition of their giving their Votes and Interest at Elections for such Persons as shall be recommended to them; and the famous Col. J-n s of W st-n is to be the Manager of this new Scheme of Corruption. We have now stood a Nine Years Siege of Bullying and endeavouring to gain old Birds with the Chaff of Smiles and Commissions; but finding Men in all Ages and Countries pretty nearly alike, Philip has at last recurred to the *potent Argument* which has convinced nearly all Mankind, that Tyranny is the best Kind of Civil Government. I sincerely hope, my dear Fellow-Countrymen, that there will be *one People* at least, found too wise and virtuous to be the Gudgeons of such an infernal Conspiracy of Traitors to the Constitution of this yet happy Country; and spurn their fatal Hook let them bait it in what Manner they please. Is not this consonant with the Advice received in Captain Loring, that *Money* was now concluded upon as the sole Means to be depended on to answer the Ends of Administration? And does not this account for the pious Hutchinson's Rejection of the Bill against Bribery and Corruption? Col. Jones, it is remembered, was as much concerned lest this Bill should produce Perjuries and other bad Consequences, as certain Gentlemen are that the Non-Consumption Agreement will have those dreadful Effects.

What an obstinate, what a silly Cabal of State Sharpers are we plagued with! Eternally striving to impose Cheats on men a Thousand Times more knowing than themselves. *In vain*, says Solomon, *is a Net spread in the Sight of any Bird.* But these Wiseacres dig Pits in the Sight of all Men, and when they find they cannot draw People into one, they in a like open Manner dig, and strive to force them into another.

PRÆDICUS.

PHILADELPHIA, July 11.

Extract of a Letter from Winchester, in Virginia, to a Gentleman in this City, dated June 21st, 1774.

"We are here inlisting all the Men that can be got to go against the Indians; there are some Companies gone out and more will go this Week, they are promised by Government 50s. a Month; we are informed that upwards of 2000 men are gone against them from the Upper Counties. We expect a very hot Indian War."

NEW-YORK, July 14.

By Capt. Barber, who left Lisbon the 30th of May, we have a certain account of the death of King Louis the XVth of FRANCE; the Ambassador of that kingdom having acquainted his Majesty of Portugal, in form, of this very important and truly interesting event.

The demise of the gentle, human, and universally beloved King of France, is like to produce an extensive variety of consequences, affecting the political systems of every nation in Europe. The administration of the affairs of the new Monarch, Louis 16th, who was born August 23, 1754, and married May 16, 1770, to a sister of the Emperor of Germany, will probably fall again into the Duke of Choiseuil's hands (a much abler speculist than his Grace of Aguillon; this last mentioned Nobleman was brought into the direction of the late King's business, through the influence of Madame Barre, whose dominion at Versailles is now at an end) in which case the Courts of France & Spain will probably join in the execution of an enterprize concerted ever since the commencement of the last peace, for during the negociation of it, the injunction of Madame de Pompadour, a former favourite of Louis 15, was, "Labour, my "dear Choiseuil, to make peace on the most rea-"sonable conditions that may be; after which "prepare for war."—Amongst the many other effects produced from the departure of this pacific King, the inhabitants of America may, without presumption, hope for such an alteration in the present affairs as will remove all complaints, and conciliate the affections of every soul upon this powerful continent, whose force when heartily joined in the cause of Great Britain, against her enemies, howsoever powerful, may eminently contribute to conquer the Spaniards and the Gauls, and to perpetuate to the Mother Country, the rank of sole Arbitress of the Universe.

BOSTON, July 25.

A Correspondent from an inland Part of the Country informs us, that he has fallen upon the following short and comprehensive Model of an Agreement, which bids fair to give universal Satisfaction.

WE the Subscribers Inhabitants of the Town of———, do sincerely and truly covenant and agree to and with each other, that we will not for ourselves or any for or under us purchase or consume any Goods, Wares or Manufactures which shall be imported from Great-Britain after the 31st of August 1774, until the Congress of Deputies from the several Colonies shall determine what Articles (if any) to except, and that we will thereafter respecting the Use and Consumption of such British Articles as may not be excepted religiously abide by the Determinations of said Congress.

ONE GUINEA REWARD.

WHEREAS on or about the 14th Instant, some evil-minded Person or Persons entered the North Battery in this Town, and took the Halliards from the Flag Staff—Whoever will discover the Thief or Thieves so that he or they may be brought to Justice, shall be paid the above Reward. NAT. BARBER, Capt.

Boston, July 21, 1774.

FIVE DOLLARS REWARD.

WHEREAS last Wednesday Night the Accompting-House of the Subscriber was broke open, and sundry Things stole, viz, 1 blue Surtuit Coat with Blue Buttons, 1 Thickset ditto without Lining, 1 small Looking Glass, one Beaver Hat, 1 50s. Piece, 2 Dollars and and about 20s. O. T. in Coppers, and sundry other Things. Whoever will give Information, so that the Person who stole them may be brought to Justice, shall have Five Dollars Reward. JOHN NEWELL.

Boston, July 23, 1774.

FOR LONDON,

The Brigantine BETSEY, about 120 Tons burthen, JAMES WISHART Master,

WILL sail from Plymouth with all convenient speed, having the greatest Part of her Cargo on board and engag'd:—For Freight or Passage apply to the Master on board, or at Mr. Solomon Davis's Store in Boston. ——Who has for Sale——

Choice Port and Teneriffe WINE.

WANTED in a small Family,

A Maid that can be well recommended.

Inquire of the Printers.

TO BE SOLD.

The Lease of a Farm in Lancaster,

(lately belonging to Michael Trollett, *Esq; deceased) for the Term of ten Years and nine Months from the 10th of* July *instant, together with all the Crop upon the Ground, and Hay in the Barn, with or without the Stock, and Farming Utensils belonging thereto. The Farm consists of 58 Acres of Mowing, Pasturing and Tillage, and 8 Acres of Wood Land, with Liberty to cut what Wood may be necessary for Firing. The House has lately been thoroughly repair'd, paper'd and painted. it has two Rooms on a Floor of more than 20 Feet each, a very large Kitchen and Dairy Room, a large Barn, with good Stable and Coach House, and Convenience for a large Stock of horn'd Cattle, a Corn House and two Poultry Houses, in a large Poultry Yard well fenc'd, a large Garden handsomely laid out and well stor'd with a Variety of the best Fruit Trees, and newly fenc'd: it is in every Part in thorough good Repair, and suitable for any Gentleman who may incline to retire to an agreeable Neighbourhood, and most pleasing Situation; it stands upon an Eminence, and commands the View of an extensive Interval, terminated by a Hill of Woods. Any Person inclining to purchase the Premisses, may apply to* RICHARD LECHMERE *of* Boston, *who has Power to dispose of the same.*

N. B. *There is also a large Shop belonging to it suitable for any Sort of Business.*

CHEAP GOODS.

There is now Selling off, by Wholesale and Retail, at BICKER's Auction Room near the Market, Boston. Most kinds of English, India and Scotch GOODS, Among which are many Articles suitable for the Fall Trade. (6 w.)

PUBLIC VENDUE.

THIS and TO-MORROW Evening,

At BICKER's Auction-Room,

Near the Market, BOSTON.

Where will be Sold a great Variety of GOODS, Among which are

Twenty Pieces Irish Linnens, Cotton Checks, Calicoes, Patches, Painted Linnens, Broad Cloths, Serges, Men's and Women's Cotton and Thread Hose, Handkerchiefs, sundry sorts Hard-Ware, several Feather Beds, 2 Fowling Pieces, 3 Desks, 3 Silver Watches, second-hand Wearing Apparel, &c. &c. &c.

M. BICKER, Auctioneer.

The Sale will begin This & To-morrow Evening 8 Clock.

WHEREAS publick Notice has been given to the Proprietors of a Township lying on both Sides Little-Amarasgoggin River, in the County of Cumberland, in the late Province of Maine, granted by the Great and General Court on the 11th Day of June, A. D. 1771, to Capt. Joshua Fuller, and others, of the Taxes that have been granted on their Rights in said Township; several of which Proprietors are delinquent in the Payment of said Taxes: They are therefore hereby Notified that unless they Pay said Taxes to DAVID SANGER, of Watertown, Collector and Treasurer for said Proprietors, by One o'Clock in the Afternoon of the 31st Day of August next, their respective Rights will be Sold (as the Law directs) for the Payment of their Taxes and Incidental Charges: The Sale to begin at 2 o'Clock in said Afternoon, at the Dwelling House of Mr. ISAAC GLEASON, Innholder in Waltham, and continued (if need be) by Adjournment till the whole be Sold.

June 30, 1774. ALEX. SHEPARD, JOSIAH BROWN, JOSIAH BISCO, } Committee for Sale.

Choice Cheshire Cheese,

to be Sold by ELIZABETH PERKINS in King-Street.

TO BE SOLD or LET,

By Thomas Robinson,

A Brewery and two Malt Houses in NEWPORT, capable of manufactoring 6000 Bushels of Barley, with every Conveniency, as Cellars, &c. for carrying on the Business of Brewing; a great Plenty of the best of Barley is raised in this Colony, from whence the Brewery may be supply'd cheaper than in any Colony in America. An English Brewer who comes well recommended may also be hired to conduct the Brewing and Malting. Any Person that inclines to purchase, may by giving good Security have one or more Years to pay the Money: For further Information apply to PHILIP DUMARESQ in Boston, or THOMAS ROBINSON in Newport, Rhode-Island.

All Persons who have any Demands on the Estate of Captain *Barnabas Binney*, deceased, late of Boston, are desired to bring in their Accounts immediately to his Son *Barnabas Binney*, Sole Executor: And all Persons indebted to said Estate, are desired to make Payment to the same as soon as possible.

LAST Tuesday Afternoon was stolen out of the House of the Subscriber, a Silver Watch, China Face, crack'd a-cross the same and inside the Case a Print representing Curiosity, with a stript Lutestring Ribbon for a String, a white Stone Seal on the same, with an Anchor engraved thereon, Maker's Name Rob. Rich, London, No. 2971. Whoever shall apprehend the Thief or Thieves, and return the Watch to the Subscriber, shall have Three Dollars Reward.

Malden, July 21, 1774. ELISHA STORY.

ALL Persons Indebted to, or that have any Demands on the Estate of Mr. EDWARD SPRAGUE, late of Boston, Housewright, deceased, are desired to bring in their Accounts to Martha Sprague, Administratrix on said Estate, in Order for Settlement.

Four Dollars Reward.

RANAWAY from his Master MARK HUNKING of Barrington, in New Hampshire, a Negro Servant named CÆSAR:—Had on when he went away, a striped homespun lappel'd Waistcoat, a Tow Shirt, black Serge Breeches, grey Jacket, a pair of Breeches and Jacket of a black and Hemlock dye, striped Tow Trowsers, black and white Yarn Stockings. He is a strait Limb'd Fellow about 5 Feet nine Inches high, very white Teeth, smiling Countenance; was bro't up to Farming Work.—Whoever shall take up said Runaway, and secure him so that his Master may have him again, shall have Four Dollars Reward, and all necessary Charges paid by MARK HUNKING.

N. B. All Masters of Vessels and others are forbid carrying him off, as they would avoid the penalty of the Law. *Barrington, July 12, 1774.*

A Young Woman with a good Breast of Milk, that can be well recommended, would be glad to go into a Gentleman's Family to suckle. Inquire of Edes and Gill.

TO BE SOLD,

ON THURSDAY NEXT,

By *BENJAMIN CHURCH*,

At FOUR o'Clock in the Afternoon,

A General Assortment of European Articles, Linnens, Woollens, Checks, &c. &c. Some House Furniture, an 8-Day Clock, Mehogany Case of Draws, Watches, &c. &c.—At Four o Clock, P. M—

TO BE SOLD,

The House known by the Name of CONCERT HALL. Enquire of *William Turner*, who has a great Collection of MUSIC which he will sell at the Sterling Cost without Charges, viz.

The Periodical Overturnes to No. 36, Two Setts of Bach's do. One Sett Schwindls 1st Opera. Two Setts Able's 1st and 7th Opera, Handel's 65 Overtures, Ferrari's Quartetts, Lord Kelly's and Stamitz's do. Barbandi's Sinfonias, Lord Kelly's Overtures, Humphries, Stanley's, Avison's, Corelli's Albertie's, Geminiani's, Heass's & Felton's Concertos, Campionis, Trios, Fisher's Overtures, Barthelemon's do. 1 Sett Bach's Songs, and 4 Violins.

N. B. Said *Turner* continues to teach Cotillons at the above-mentioned Hall, Fencing also.

New AUCTION-ROOM, Cornhill.

On WEDNESDAY NEXT, at TEN o'Clock, Will be Sold by PUBLIC VENDUE, At GREENLEAF's Auction-Room,

A large Assortment of English Goods as usual—Also some House Furniture.

WM. GREENLEAF, Auctioneer.

The Sale will begin at Ten o'Clock precisely.

Burials in the Town of BOSTON, since our last.

Four Whites. NO Black.

Baptiz'd in the several Churches, Fourteen.

High Water at BOSTON, for the present Week.

Monday, 36 min. aft. 1	Friday, 31 min. after	4
Tuesday, 23 min. aft. 2	Saturday, 20 min. aft.	5
Wednesday, 12 m. aft. 3	Lord's-Day, 5 m. af.	6
Thursday, 50 min. aft. 3	D's last Qr. 30 D. 2 M.	

Messieurs EDES & GILL,

Please to insert the following.

A Serious Call from the Town of Boston, to the Massachusetts, and all the other Colonies in North-America, to join with them in setting apart some Time for extraordinary Prayer, at this alarming Crisis of our public Affairs, when threatened to be deprived of every Thing that is dear and valuable.

The Time determined upon to meet at the Throne of Grace as above proposed, is from seven to eight o'Clock every Lord's-Day Morning, and to continue 'till all the Grievances that we justly complain of are removed.

It is seasonable, and necessary, and what God himself hath directed to, to call upon him in the Day of Trouble; and he has encouraged us to do it, by promising Success. Moreover, this has been done by the People of God in all Ages of the Church, and they never failed of Success, when it has been accompanied with a universal Repentance, and turning to God, which is what we would earnestly recommend and urge.

Our present Embarrasments are well known, and to whom should we look but to God, through Jesus Christ? Vain is the Help of Man. The Name of the Lord is a strong Tower, whereinto the Righteous run, and are safe. And he is able to turn the Counsel of every Ahithophel into Foolishness, and to do exceeding abundantly above all that we are able to ask, or Think. Through God we may do valiantly, and tread them under that rise up against us. And should not one City go to another City, and say, Let us go speedily to pray before the Lord? What more adviseable? And what can be more agreeable to all serious People, who are now trembling for the Ark of God?

Our Rights and Privileges which we derive from God, and Nature, and our most excellent Constitution, are in the utmost Danger, and unless God should appear for us and lend his Help, deplorable will our Case be, and that of Posterity. The Glory would depart from us, and a Train of Evils would follow, the remote Prospect of which is enough to make a Person of any Thought at all to shudder. Dark Days we have seen, but none so dark as the present. It is a very melancholy, distressing Time. But who knows what God may do in Answer to Prayer? Who knows but we may yet see good Days, according to the Days wherein we have seen Evil? If he should pour out his Spirit upon us as a Spirit of Supplication, Humiliation, Reformation, Conviction, Conversion and Sanctification, we should have no Reason to doubt but he would return, and visit this Vine which his own Right Hand hath planted. Former Experience of remarkable Deliverances, are enough to satisfy us of Success, and to put us upon the agreeable and necessary Duty now urged upon all, more especially those that have an Interest at the Throne of Grace.

To mention Instances of the Success of Prayer upon sacred Record, would be almost endless, and altogether needless, as we trust there is a Bible in every House, and that it is daily look'd into.—All that we would mention further here, is, by Way of serious Quere; Whether a Neglect of Prayer at such a Time as this, would not be an unpardonable Neglect? And a Non-Compliance with the above Proposal, a sad Evidence that God designs us for Ruin? The whole Province, and all the Colonies being connected with us.

And altho' our particular Errand at the Throne of Grace is the Removal of our Grievances, and the Restoration of Peace to the Mother Country and Colonies; yet we should not be unmindful of the rising Generation, That the Offspring of our Christian Heroes may never be the Plague of the Church and Country, but a Seed to serve the Lord; that so the Religion of Jesus may be handed down in its Purity, from one Generation to another, till Time shall be no more.

N. B. The Time to begin the propos'd Exercise, is the next Lord's Day Morning after the Receipt of this Proposal; and from thence to be continued, either in the Family or Closet, 'till our Sorrow is turned into Joy.

P. S. The Printers in the other Colonies are desired to publish the above in their Papers.

Benjamin Goldthwait

Would inform his Friends, kind Customers and others, That he has just receiv'd by Capt Loring from London a small Invoice of GOODS, *suitable to the present Season, viz.*

Exceeding neat figur'd Jeanes, Thread ditto, plain, coloured and white ditto; Also, very neat Silk Jeans, fine white Irish Tick for Waistcoats and Breeches, white corded Dimothy, Silk knit Patterns, striped Damaskus, with sundry other Articles.——The above being a Consignment, will be Sold very low.

☞ *The Taylor's Business is carried on as usual at his Shop just above Concert-Hall, in all its various Branches, in the genteelest Manner, and with the utmost Dispatch.*

Embroidery in Gold, Silver and Twist, is done in the best Manner at said Shop.

Just Published, and Sold by EDES *and* GILL, *in Queen-Street,* [*Price* 9d.]

The Nature and Effects of Drunkenness considered;

with an Address to Tavern-Keepers, to Parents, and young People, relating to the Subject.—In TWO DISCOURSES, delivered at Natick, the last Lord's Day in October, 1773.

By STEPHEN BADGER, A. M.

Pastor of the Christian Society there.

A L S O,

The Memoirs of the Life of the Rev. GEORGE WHITEFIELD, A. M,

Late Chaplain to the Countess of Huntingdon.

In which every circumstance worthy of notice, both in his private and public character is recorded. Faithfully selected from his original papers, journals and letters. Illustrated with a variety of interesting and entertaining Anecdotes, from the best authority.

To which is added, a particular account of his Death and Funeral; and Extracts from the Sermons which were Preached on that Occasion.

Compiled by the Rev. JOHN GILLIES, D. D.

Where likewise may be had, (*Just Published,*)

LIBERTY TRIUMPHANT; *or the downfall of* OPPRESSION.——Being a Characatura of the Destruction of the TEA at New-York.

KEYSER's FAMOUS PILLS

So well known all over *Europe*, and in *this* and the *neighbouring Colonies*, for their superior Efficacy and peculiar Mildness, in perfectly eradicating every Degree of a certain Disease, without the least Trouble or Confinement.

The Public may be assured, that this excellent Medicine is beyond any Thing in all Foulness and Impurities of the Blood, having performed many astonishing Cures in Scorbutic Eruptions, Leprosies, White Swellings, Stiff Joints, Gout and Rheumatic Disorders, &c.

THESE PILLS ARE NOW SOLD BY

EDES and GILL,

(In Boxes of 7/6. L. M. each, *fresh imported*)

Who have in their Hands a Letter from the Widow KEYSER, and a Certificate from under her own Hand of the Genuineness of the above Pills; which any Person may have the Perusal of by applying to them at their Printing-Office in *Queen-Street*: Where may be had a Variety of Books, &c.

Joseph Coolidge

INFORMS the Public, That he has IMPORTED in the Ships just arrived from London,

A fine Assortment of Guns, Trooping Pistols, Pocket ditto, Gun Locks, Swords, Violins, Fifes and Flutes, Stands of Cruetts, with Silver and Bone Tops, Back Gammon Tables compleat; a Variety of Pocket Books for Gentlemen and Ladies; neat Gilt, Pinchbeck, Plated and black and common Shoe, Knee and Stock Buckles; Japan Trays, Waiters and Candlesticks; most sorts of Jewelry; Silver and Pinchbeck Watches, some as low as seven Dollars; Patent Watch Keys that shew the Day of the Month and Moons Age; Cutlery and Hard Ware, and a Variety of Toys and Trinkets, too many for an Advertisement: All which he will sell at the lowest reduced Prizes, at his Shop just above the Market, and directly opposite the new Auction-Room.

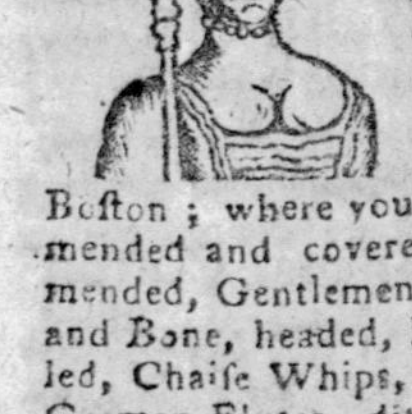

UMBRELLAS

of all Sizes and Prices, made in the neatest Manner with Ivory and Bone Handles to screw, also more common Mahogany or Maple Handled ditto, Ladies that would buy Cheap and good, call at ISAAC GREENWOOD, Ivory Turner's Shop, next Shop to Dr. CLARKS, North-End, Boston; where you may have your old Umbrella sticks mended and covered, your Ivory and bone stick Fans mended, Gentlemen may have India Canes, neat Ivory and Bone, headed, Hickery Stick, Ivory or Bone, handled, Chaise Whips, Hidremeters for proving Spirits, German Flutes, ditto Tiped with Ivory Fife, Billiard Balls, and many other Articles. Such Gentlemen as are Building may have their Banisters and Posts, Pillers for Fronticepieces and Porticoes, Balls and Flower Pots, or any other Ornaments, turned or twisted in the neatest Manner with Fidelity and Dispatch at the above Shop, all Favours from those that have and shall Imploy duly acknowledged, by their humble Servant,

ISAAC GREENWOOD.

This Day Published,

And Sold by JOHN KNEELAND, next to the Treasurer's Office in Milk-Street. Price Six Coppers.

EXTRACT of a SERMON, preached at the South Church in Boston, Nov. 27th, 1746. By the Rev. Mr. THOMAS PRINCE, occasioned by the surprizing Appearance of divine Providence for North-America, in the Destruction of the French Fleet and Army, sent to Chebucktah the preceeding Summer: And reprinted at this Time with a View to encourage and animate the People of GOD to put their Trust in Him, and to call upon his Name, under the severe and keen Distresses now taking Place in Boston and Charlestown, by the rigorous Execution of the Boston-PORT BILL.

Thomas Turner

Begs Leave to inform the Public,

That he has opened a School opposite the Rev. Dr. COOPER's Meeting-House, where he teaches Dancing in the politest Manner, and doubts not of giving Satisfaction to Gentlemen or Ladies, who would choose to recommend their Children to him, to acquire so eligible an Accomplishment. Likewise the useful Art of Fencing, agreeable to the best Rules establish'd for that Purpose.

N. B. Due Care shall be taken that the greatest Decency and good Manners be observ'd by his Scholars.

Susanna Renken,

INFORMS her Customers and others, That she has removed from Fore-street, to a little above the Hay-Market, where she has for Sale, a Variety of

English and India GOODS,

Groceries of all Sorts, West-India & New-England Rum.

WANTS a Place, a Person who can take Care of Horses, drive a Coach, and would be very useful about a Gentleman's House. He can be recommended for Honesty, Sobriety and Diligence. Enquire at the Printers.

TAKEN up by me the Subscriber in Pomfret, the 20th of May last, a brown Mare, about 14 Hands high, 14 or 15 Years old, Paces and Trots, is bad to catch, bad to get on, but very good after mounted. Said Mare has a Number of white Spots on her Back, a small white Streak across her Nose, occasioned by an Halter, one hind Foot white. The Owner may have her, by applying to me the Subscriber, and paying the Charges. ISRAEL PUTNAM.

CREAM WARE.

Two Crates of elegant Cream Pencil Ware, one Crate of Gally Pots, several Bags Spikes, Deck and Sheathing Nails of different sizes, six Barrels of Durham Mustard in quarter Pound Bottles, a few Boxes 18 Inch Tip'd Pipes, one Case & Hats from Beaver to Felts, with a few Pipes of quarter Casks of Fyal Wines, to be Sold cheap, By

William Hoskins.

To be Sold cheap at Store No. 14, Long Wharff.

A few Tierces and Barrels MELASES, Casks of best Sort of Rice, and Barrels of Coffee.

W A N T E D,

A Negro Man from 18 to 30 Years of Age, that will steal, lie and get Drunk. Any Person having such an one to dispose of, may hear of a Purchaser by applying to the Printers hereof.

Province of the Massachusetts-Bay. } *To the Hon*ble. Samuel Dexter, *Esq; one of his Majesty's Justices of the Peace through the said Province.*

We the Subscribers, Proprietors of a Township, granted by the Great and General Court of the Province aforesaid, at their Session in February last, to *John Gardner*, and others, in Lieu of a Township, Number Six in the Line of Towns between *Connecticut* and *Merrimack Rivers*, lost by the late Settlement of *New-Hampshire*—request your Honour to call a Meeting of said Proprietors to be on Monday the 29th Day of *August* next, at the House of *Jonathan Wood*, Esq; Innholder in *Stow*, at Ten of the Clock in the Forenoon, then and there to choose a Moderator for said Meeting, also to choose a Proprietor's Clerk, Treasurer, and any other Proprietary Officer; to Grant such Sum or Sums of Money, as may be needful to discharge any Debts already due from said Proprietors, or to discharge any future Demands; to agree on some Method for calling Proprietors Meetings for the future Also to agree on some Method for laying out said Township into Lots, and to do any other Thing proper for bringing forward the Settlement of said Township.

Stow, June 15, 1774.

John Whitcomb,
Jonathan Loring,
Henry Gardner,
Abner Cranson,
Micah Keys,
Daniel Hapgood,
Samuel Curtis.

Province of the Massachusetts-Bay.

(Seal.) *To* Henry Gardner, *of* Stow, *in the County of* Middlesex, *Esq; one of the principal Proprietors of the Township aforementioned,* Greeting.

In pursuance of the foregoing Appilcation and Request, you are hereby required to give Notice, in Time and Manner as the Law directs, to the Proprietors of the Township aforesaid, that they meet at the Time and Place, and for the Purposes expressed in the aforewritten Petition. Given under my Hand and Seal, this this sixth Day of July, Anno Domini, 1774, and in the fourteenth Year of his Majesty's Reign.

SAMUEL DEXTER, a Justice of the Peace through the Province of the Massachusetts-Bay.

Stow, July 6th, 1774.

By Virtue of the above Warrant to me directed, The Proprietors above mentioned, are required to meet at Time and Place above-mentioned, for the Purpose aforesaid.

HENRY GARDNER.

Boston: Printed by EDES & GILL, *in Queen-Street,* 1774.

No. 1007.

THE Boston- Gazette, AND COUNTRY JOURNAL.

Containing the freshest Advices, Foreign and Domestic.

MONDAY, August 1, 1774.

THIS DAY PUBLISHED,
(Price 9d.)
And sold by EDES *and* GILL, *in Queen-Stret.*

CONSIDERATIONS ON THE MEASURES CARRYING ON WITH RESPECT TO THE BRITISH COLONIES IN NORTH-AMERICA.

There is neither King or Sovereign Lord on Earth, who has beyond his own Domain power to lay one Farthing on his Subjects without the grant and consent of those, who pay it; unless he does it by tyranny and violence.

Phillippe de Commines, Ch. 108.

THIS is a most masterly performance, written since the framing the several Acts against BOSTON and AMERICA, and the best calculated to convince the Ministry, the people of England, and all the world, of the absurdity and wickedness of the late acts, and ruinous consequences, to England at least, that would certainly attend their being carried into execution.

Our last accounts, say, this pamphlet has had a wonderful effect in removing the prejudices and convincing the people of England.

To the PRINTERS,

You are desired to publish the following Address to the Citizens of New-York, *on the present* critical *Situation of Affairs, lately published in that City.* *Your's,* A. B.

To the CITIZENS *of* New-York.

WERE I neither a Philadelphian, a New-Yorker, a Bostonian nor even a native of this continent, as a friend to the rights of mankind, I should interest myself in the fate of America. America must at present be considered as the principal, or indeed the only remaining seat of liberty.—In Corsica, Sweden, Poland, she has been borne down by the direct hand of violence; and in our parent country, she is sapp'd by corruption to so dangerous a degree, that she totters from the foundation, and unless propp'd by the virtue and spirit of her colonies, she must inevitably fall to the ground. A regular plan has been formed by the present court, for the introduction of arbitrary power;—this is no declamation, and did the size of this paper admit of it, I could prove the truth of the assertion by numberless instances: The privileges, and indeed natural rights of the subject, have been invaded in every part of the empire, one while by open force, another by cabal and the arts of corruption.—Even the islands of Minorca, Jersey, Guernsey, have not been protected by their insignificance, from the scourge of tyranny.—Great-Britain and Ireland have been drained almost of the last farthing, not for any national purposes, but to increase the influence of the crown, in creating new placemen, pensioners, and of course enemies to the public welfare, and liberty.

General warrants, violation of the rights of election, the disfranchisement of the proprietors of the East-India stock, murders committed, murderers pardoned, encouraged, rewarded, and the other overtacts (of treason, I may say) which the ministry have been guilty of against law, magna charta, and the English constitution, are so notorious, that it is almost impertinent to mention th[illegible]; but there are other indications, or rather evidences of the temper and views of the court, which ought not to be passed over in silence, and which must convince the subjects that they are to expect nothing but from their own virtue and firmness.——

Every writer in support of boundless prerogative, every jacobite historian, (the Humes, Gurthries and Smollet's) has been caressed, placed or pensioned: Attacks have been made under the auspicies of the court, not only on the revolution, and the principal promoters of the revolution, but a scheme has been laid, and to the utmost of their power carried into execution, to proscribe virtue itself, by subverting the reputation of her brightest models.—They argue thus; *if we can spread the persuasion, that public virtue never did exist in a human breast, that patriotism has been in all ages only a mask for designing men; we shall gain the following point, we shall render mankind totally indifferent who are in office, who are not; whether a Pitt or a Bute—what maxims we rule by, what maxims we repudiate, whether we profess those of an Alfred, or a Stuart, will be a matter of indifference to the public, if we can once convince them, that their interests ever have been, and ever will be equally out of the question.—When we have thus destroyed all political confidence, we have reason to flatter ourselves that the people will not be such fools as to think of opposition or resistance, but without giving themselves any unnecessary trouble, submit to the yoke we are preparing for them.* To accomplish these pious purposes, some fit instrument was to be sought and found, some man of a sufficiently corrupt heart, to qualify him for the task. This instrument was found in a certain Sir John Dalrymple, (who in the administration of Lord Rockingham had been turned out of an important office in Scotland, for manifest corrupt practices.—He was detached into France, and recommended by Lord Mansfield, and another very great personage, to the famous Duke D'Aiguillon; he, who had trampled on the few remaining laws of France, and exterminated their virtuous Parliaments.—The Duke D'Aiguillon, with the candour (as this Dalrymple tells us) inseparable from every minister of a great King, catches the idea of our court, (and as might be expected from so natural an ally) patronizes the project, and consigns to their agent, the key of the *depote des affaires etrangeres.**—Here he sets himself to work, to rummage, to garble, to defalcate, to forge,—for without straining inferences, it is almost certain that he did forge—at length he triumphantly sallies forth, with the testimonies, as he hopes to persuade us, of the non-existence of human virtue, with proofs that her brightest patterns were knaves and hypocrites. It would be easy (tho' here might be thought tedious) to overturn the whole foundation, or at least defeat the intended effects of this abominable production;—but I cannot help remarking, that were the proofs of Sydney and Russel's being traytors irrefregable, he who should produce them, would be held in abhorrence by every friend to humanity.

It is necessary that some models of human virtue should be held up to our imitation: He who would remove from our sight these few models which history has left to us, would check every noble ardour of the soul, as it would then appear madness to attempt attaining what is incompatible with our nature. It may now perhaps be asked, what can be the intention (in an address to the citizens of New York) of so long a preamble on the conduct and spirit of the court, in matters which do not particularly relate to America. I will explain to you my intention; it is to convince you, that when a spirit so hostile to general liberty prevails, in those who have the power at home, you have only to hope for redress of grievances from the united virtue and firmness of the colonies; that the idea of proceeding by petition and remonstrance, is the most ridiculous idea that ever entered into weak heads. Can you seriously think your petitions would have any effect at this instant, when the confidence and temerity of the ministry are mounted to so much higher a pitch than we have hitherto seen them? Can you seriously think that your petitions would operate more strongly on so firmly a fixed minister, backed by a vast majority in parliament, than the petitions of the city of London, and the principal counties of England, with the first men of property and character, and a considerable number of the members at their head did on a minister less firmly seated, a minister, not only less firmly seated, but perhaps a much less bold and determined foe to liberty, than the present.—It is no calumny, it is no exaggeration to say, that Lord North is a determined foe to liberty.—He is so by inheritance; descended from one of the most forward and active instruments of tyranny under Charles the second; every speech, every action of his life, demonstrates him to be the genuine offspring.—On the brave Corsicans he never bestowed a gentler Epithet than rebels and traitors.—The mention of American liberties, the supposition that they had any liberties, always threw him into a frenzy of rage,—foaming at the mouth, and with eyes starting from their sockets, He has denounced, or rather vomitted forth eternal war against you & your posterity.—He has had the arrogance, the madness to declare, in the open senate, that he never would receive, never hear any petitions from America, until he had her at his feet.

When it is considered that this avowed foe, and persecutor of America; this furious fanatick in despotism, is now become the omnipotent minister, I must repeat, that the idea of redressing grievances by petition and remonstrance, is the most contemptible idea, that ever entered into weak heads. It is indeed so very contemptible, that we cannot suppose those who adopt it are in earnest;—it is impossible not to suspect them of sinister designs.—They must mean, under the cloak of coolness and moderation, to check the vigour, so absolutely requisite at this juncture, and to prevent the only possible means of redress; they must mean to recommend themselves to the future favour of your oppressors.—They perhaps already devour in their minds, contracts, salaries, and pensions, for which, (if the ministry succeed) funds will be immediately established out of the fruits of your honest labour and industry.—They must be conscious that all the force and troops they can employ, will not effect their purposes, unless the corruption of your own members powerfully co-operates.—Upon the whole, considering the critical situation of affairs, the impending ruin over our heads, I cannot help being a good deal surprised and somewhat shocked, at the conduct of this city—Is this a time to amuse yourselves with narrow local politicks and disputes? Is this a time, when the dearest interests of yourselves, of posterity, and of mankind are at stake, (for the cause of liberty is the cause of mankind?) Is this a time I say, to indulge your little prejudices, jealouses, and personal piques? For shame citizens, discard all such disgraceful sentiments; assume a more noble character; save yourselves from the infamy which threatens you; let not the common ruin be laid to your charge. For my own part, I neither pretend to approve nor to condemn the measure which the committee hath lately thought proper to censure.——But this I will pretend to say, that the publishing the censure, may have most pernicious consequences; it may, by propagating the opinion of divisions starting up in this leading capital, repress the ardour of your own counties of the other colonies, discourage your friends at home, and give fresh vigour to your enemies; and (the haste with which the publishing this censure was pressed with the professed intention of transmitting it by the packet) gives, I must confess, a very suspicious air to its authors.—the design could not be good. It has already furnished matter of triumph to the enemies of liberty. One man in particular (he is indeed an official man, not a native of this country, and remarkable for his alacrity in political wickedness) sings *te deum* I am told, in all companies on this occasion, considering the victory as insured to his idol despotism.—There are now some farther consequences to be apprehended from the present conduct of this city, which perhaps have not occurred to you, and which therefore I shall beg leave to offer to your consideration.—Is it not to be apprehended that the Bostonians, when they turn their eyes and address their prayers to you, as a leading people of America, for succour in their distress; and when instead of the vigour and noble spirit they had reason to expect from your former exertions, they see nothing but backwardness, frivolous delays, and (as to them it will appear) total dearth of spirit; is it not to be apprehended, that having no prospect of relief, they may grow desperate? And that their despair, in conjunction with the corruption of individuals among themselves, (for you may be assured that General Gage has unlimit-ed

(Turn to the last Page.)

* *Office of records of foreign affairs.*

To the PUBLIC.

BEING informed by the Printers that I—c W——w, Esq; and Dr. P——n, have complained of their being unjustly treated in the Piece signed PRÆDICUS in the last Number of this Paper relative to the said Gentlemen's being Members of a certain Combination who 'tis said determine to let Monies to such Electors only as will vote for Courtiers. I thereupon applied to the Person who was next to the first reporter, and was informed by him that I—c W——w was only mentioned as a monied Man in that Interest, but was not affirmed to be in the Combination, ——but he still affirms that such a Combination was declared to him by a Gentleman of good Credit, from whom he expects an authentic List of the Members of this pious Institution, who were declared to the said first Reporter without Reserve.

PRÆDICUS.

Dr. P——n's Friend who applied to the Printer denies his having any Hand in so villainous a Project as the above.

PHILADELPHIA, *July* 21.

We hear that the Assembly of this province which are now met, have resolved themselves into a grand Committee, and have appointed tomorrow at 10 o'clock, for the consideration of sundry letters from the Committees of our sister colonies, relative to American grievances; at which time, we are likewise informed, our provincial Committee, who are also sitting here, will have leave to attend the debates.

Last Friday afternoon, agreeable to invitation from the Committee of this city, Delegates from the several county Committees, viz. Bucks, Chester, Lancaster, York, Cumberland, Bedford, Berks, Northampton & Northumberland, met the Committee for this city and county, and we hear they have been engaged in preparing a set of General Resolves, declaratory of the sense of this province, on the present state of British America, and the peculiar sufferings of our Brethren in Boston, and the Massachusetts Bay. We are assured that there is great unanimity in their councils and determinations, and that a happy presage may be formed of a general concurrence and support, in such measures as shall be found necessary to preserve and secure the rights and liberties of the inhabitants of this country.—The Resolves not being quite finished, we are obliged to postpone the publication of them to our next. We are informed, that a more full and ample declaration of our present grievances, and a suggestion of the mode of redress, so as to relieve the distressed Bostonians, ease the minds of the other colonists, and draw some just and equitable line between the mother country and the colonies, is under the consideration of this respectable meeting, and will be conveyed to the Hon. House of Representatives, as the advice or instructions of a number of their constituents, on this important occasion: which will also, in due time, be communicated to the public.

Capt. Osborne from Ferrol, which he left on the 6th ult. confirms the account of the Death of *LOUIS* XV. King of France; and adds, that the Duc de Choiseul, and his Party, were come into favour with the young King, and that Madam Barre, the late King's Mistress, the Duc de Aguillon, the late prime Minister, and all that Party, were banished the Court.

On Friday last arrived at Newcastle the Ship Peace and Plenty, Capt. M'Kenzie, with 400 passengers from Belfast.

NEW-YORK, *July* 25.

Thursday last three Transports arrived here from Boston; they are now taking in Ordnance, and a Proportion of Military Stores, among which are 500 Barrels of Gun Powder; and we hear the Royal Welch Fuzileers, now here, are to embark this Week on board the said Transports, with a Detachment of the Train of Artillery, and to sail directly for Boston.

"*From a Rascal in Office of Exports and Imports in Boston, (one Murray) to his Friend, D. Ar. M'Neil in Carolina.*

Our Sons of Liberty, as you'll see by the Papers, have at length procured for themselves a smart Dose of Correction, but they make Faces and take it with a bad Grace, which will not make the Operation the gentler. Will your Colony and others of the same Stamp, take warning by our Discipline? If they do not, they will certainly come in for their Share, now John Bull is roused.

The late Feats here have had one good Effect, to put Government in mind of some, who dared to show themselves in support of it, among others, your humble Servant is like to come in for a small Acknowledgment—about 150l. per Annum, in Office of Inspector of Exports and Imports, lately held by Thomas Erving, Esq; who is appointed Receiver General for your Province—the good of this Office to me is, that it can be executed without taking me quite from my beloved Amusement, this Farm."

Letters from London, as late as May 14th, mention a great Change in the Sentiments of the People, respecting the Guilt of the Bostonians, in destroying the Tea. The Representations of that Circumstance were so unfair, and so industriously propagated among all ranks of people, that a general Rage possessed the Body of the Nation against us. A worthy Writer has lately published a Pamphlet, setting Things in a true Light, which has had amazing Success.

Saturday last we received Advice from Albany, of the Death of that truly great and good Man, Sir WILLIAM JOHNSON, Bart. at his Seat at Johnson Hall, on Monday the 11th Instant.

BOSTON, August 1.

MORE than sixty days have expired, since Boston, by a late Edict of the British Parliament, has been besieged by a British Fleet and Army, and its trade annihilated: The inhabitants now receive that insult and damage, which was never experienced in the hottest wars we have been engaged in with France and Spain, and their allies, the Savages of the American woods:—The particulars of the siege, and the manœuvres of our enemies, may in future be told by some able historian. Suffice it at present to inform the world, that tho' wood and provisions have been allowed us by said Port-Act, the introduction of these articles has been attended with such loss of time and unnecessary charges as greatly to raise the price of fuel upon the poor inhabitants: No wood can be brought from the rivers and bays included in our harbour, upon which we depended for a considerable part of our supply: No goods of any kind are suffered to be waterborne within a circle of sixty miles: No timber, boards, shingles, bricks, lime, sand, &c. &c. are to be transported from one wharf to another; and so even the tradesmen, not immediately dependent upon shipping are thrown out of business. No barrels of liquors, bread, flour, &c. are suffered to be brought a few rods in our row boats, or across our shortest ferries; and even the vessels on the stocks, which have for some time past been ready for launching, cannot be put into the water, without their being exposed to a threatned seizure. Neither is the dry'd table fish and oil, the charity of our Marblehead friends, nor rice, the generous present of the Carolinians, nor even house-sand, to be brought us by water, but must be encumbered with the great charge of about 30 miles: We are also cut off from the advantage and profit of supplying as usual an extent of seacoast on the north and south of more than 100 leagues, even with British merchandize.—And when any of these hardships and distresses are mentioned to those insolents in office, the Commissioners and their understrappers, we are told, it was the design of the act, and that it is not their intent to lessen these difficulties:——This is the treatment meted out by a British minister to a Town and Province, by whose exertions in a late war, the strong Fortress of Louisbourgh was taken, which purchased the Peace of Europe and delivered Britons from their terrible apprehensions of an invasion by French flatbottomed Boats. What further cruelties we are to suffer we know not; but whether America, or even this single town is in this way to be brought to the feet of Lord North, with the full surrender of their inestimable rights and liberties, time only can determine.——

By Capt. Lovett lately arrived at Portsmouth from Antigua, we learn, that the Merchants and Planters were in great Consternation there on reading the Proposals of the Colonies for suspending their Supplies of Lumber and Provisions; which they agree must be ruinous to them; and in Consequence they have appropriated a third of their Cane-Plantations for the culture of Indian Corn, Yams, Potatoes, &c. for the maintenance of their Slaves, in Case the suspension does take Place. It is further said, Antigua has sent home a Remonstrance on that head, and prayed Great-Britain, either to open the Port of Boston, and let them have Provisions as usual, or furnish them with the absolute Necessaries of Life, themselves; otherwise, say they, their Sugar Planting must speedily come to an End, as they can neither support their Slaves, nor ship the Sugars home for want of Casks. Notwithstanding the Distress in which they foresee they must be involved by our discontinuance of Trade with them, they generously commended us for the Resolutions, acknowledging that in our Circumstances any Measure we can lay hold on for Relief from the Chains imposing upon us is fully justifiable. An instance of their Generosity and Patriotism Capt. Lovett had the Pleasure of witnessing. That old troubler of Boston, Capt. Bruce, was railing against this Town in a large Company at a principal Tavern at Dinner while he was there; and after he had expatiated largely on the Abuse he had suffered for bringing his blessed Cargo of Tea, (though by the way the old Catiff was used more tenderly than any Ship Master concerned in that rascally Jobb) and hoped the next Freight he brought them would be Soldiers; a Gentleman stept calmly up to him, and asked him whether he had not for many Years got his Bread from the People against whom he was now so bitterly inveighing? And being answered in the affirmative, he caught Bruce by the Nose and led him out of the Company, requiring him to keep his distance, as a dirty Ingrate, unworthy of any Gentleman's Company or Countenance. The Company present on this agreed for the future not to afford him an Ounce of Freight on any Terms.——A fine Circle truly Captain Bruce! You ought indeed to be noticed by his Lordship; for 'tis great odds if you are not as Stiff as Obstinate, as wrong Headed a Miscreant as ever listed under his Banner.

Extract of a letter from a gentleman in St. Eustatia to his friend in Boston, dated the 4th of July past.

"I am extremely concerned at the measures pursuing by Great Britain against the Colonies: for poor Boston in particular! It could never be meant that she would be the sole butt of their —— I will call no harsh names. The rest of the Colonies were in full perspective—Gradual in execution was the most probable means of gaining and establishing a precedent. The Capital subdued to obedience would have been sufficient, to every purpose. By obedience I mean obedience to the extraordinary new mandates; and I can assure you that but few who know the interest of the English Caribee Islands but must, and do approve the measures adopted by the town of Boston. It cannot be conceived by you on the Continent, what a confusion the suspension of supplies to the Islands would occasion. Insurrections among the negroes must be the inevitable consequence. Hunger is and ever will be a means to appease its gnawings. The Islands formerly raised Negroe provisions, such as yams, potatoes and indian-corn nearly sufficient for each plantation, and had from North-America the remainder. But the grounds so appropriated, have of late years been constantly improved in canes as more profitable; and the food bro't from the Colonies being not only cheaper, but more solid and agreeable in taste; the withdraw of it from the slaves now accustomed to it, would be sufficient to breed a mutiny throughout the Estates. The property of many of these Estates, improved by their agents, and stocked with, from 2 to 7 or 800 negroes, residing in many of the leading men in London, Bristol & other Capital Seaports, interest would render them your advocates rather than suffer such immense fortunes to run to ruin.

"In short a suspension of supplies would oblige the planters to discontinue the culture of canes, and it could by no means be speedily recovered. The islands cannot subsist for any time without provisions from the Continent; and few indeed of their inhabitants are there but already groan with apprehension, that the dreaded suspension may take place.

"I should conceive a second consideration would draw the attention of those Gentlemen to the common welfare, viz. the French King's death, and the measures that nation are taking in their Islands. It is not six months since several troops arrived in Martinico and Guadaloup, which are distributed in reinforcements to their garrisons. A continuance or renewal of this policy has very lately taken place. About eight days ago a Brig landed an hundred fresh troops at Port-Royal, and then proceeded to St. Domingo. The French say nine hundred more are on their passage for the same place in different vessels. Their artizans are all employed on fortresses adding and repairing; and many new batteries and redoubts are erecting in a private manner, even where no probable service by prevention to land, can be expected from them. In their gasconading way, they are very soon to conquer much of America as well as these Islands. War seems planing in Martinico, I hope no where else in this critical conjuncture. God only knows what would be the event. Their several preparations are unaccountable. I wish all matters were reconciled to be in readiness for what may happen."

At a legal Town-Meeting at Cambridge on Thursday last, a Committee was chosen to receive Donations for the Relief of their distressed Brethren in the Town of Boston.

A Cart-Load of new Pick-Axes was seen putting into a Store on the Long-Wharff last Saturday. *Quere,* What are we to apprehend from all these Warlike Preparations? Is a Fort to be erected in good earnest, and the Town to be awed into Submission by Cannons and Mortars? Forbid it Heaven! Rather let it become an Heap, and be rased to its Foundation, than one mean Concession be the Means of its Preservation!

We learn from Virginia and North-Carolina, that immense Quantities of Grain are subscrib'd for there, for the Benefit of the Poor of this devoted Town, which is to be forwarded hither as soon as their Crops are ripe.

Saturday last a Vessel arrived here with 1000 Bushels of Grain, as a Present for the distressed Poor of this Town, from our truly worthy Friends and Brethren of Weathersfield, in the Colony of Connecticut.

A Consignment of English GOODS,

Consisting of the following Articles, viz.

An Assortment of Hatt-Trimmings,

striped Damascus Bandanno and Barcelona Handkerchiefs, black Cravats, Knee-Garters, Coat-Bindings, Mohair and scarf Twist, death-head and metal Buttons, scarlet Gartering, steel-bow'd Spectacles, Needles and Purse Pins, Scotch Thread, a very neat silver-plated Coffee-Pot, silk Ferrets, worsted and silk Breeches Patterns, silk and thread Hose, striped Swanskins, Men and Boys Felt Hats, &c. &c.

To be Sold very low for Cash. Inquire of

William Palfrey.

FOUR DOLLARS REWARD.

RAN-away from her Master, Francis Shaw, a likely tall Negro Woman, known by the Name of Voilet Shaw, about 25 Years old; has a Blemish in one Eye, carried away with her a white Callico Riding Dress, a stript Callico Gown, a Claret coloured Poplin Gown, a stript blue and white Holland Gown, a Bengall Gown, and many other valuable Articles of Apparel.

Whoever apprehends her, and will return her to her Master in Boston, shall have four Dollars Reward and all necessary Charges paid. All Persons are cautioned against harbouring or carrying off said Negro Servant as they would avoid the Rigour of the Law.

BOSTON, *July* 29th, 1774.

To his Excellency Governor GAGE.

SIR,

THE very great Pains that are taken to make it believed both in this Country, and in Great-Britain, that no real Discontents prevail in the Colonies but such as are in the Town of Boston, or such as originated with or were fomented by some factious Persons there, convinces me of the great Hazard that is apprehended to the Cause of Oppression from a Discovery of the true State of Affairs in America. It has, upon the taking Place of some extraordinary Event, been in the Power of factious Men, by seizing the Passions for a Moment, to mislead the Multitude and drive them to commit such Extravagance as cool Reason can never justify; but, Sir, was it ever known that a few Men at one End of an extensive Continent shou'd be able to draw in Millions of equal Capacities and equal Advantages for obtaining Knowledge with themselves, to espouse their Cause and to continue so to do for Years together?—Unless there had been some real Cause of Complaint, wou'd it have been possible for Men divided in Interest and in religious Principles, as it were by Inspiration to have adopted the same Opinion at the same Time, though their local Distance rendered it impossible that there cou'd have been any Communication of Sentiments by which they might have been influenced?—and has not this been surprizingly the Case in the Disputes between Great-Britain and the Colonies? Have we not been astonished, not only at the Similarity of Arguments used by the Colonists, but also of the Measures pursued by them? have they blindly followed one another in Error, or have they calmly weighed and deliberated upon the State of publick Affairs, and with Caution resolved upon the Steps taken to obtain a Redress of their Grievances?——No one is at a Loss for an Answer to these Questions; but it is unnecessary to look back, it will be sufficient to take a View of the present State of the Colonies. See how unitedly they espouse the Cause of the oppressed Bostonians.—Attend to their Resolutions which all breathe the same Spirit—observe how generously they have contributed, and are still contributing to their Relief. They consider themselves as injured by every Hardship laid upon Boston; and whilst their compassionate Hearts melt at their Distresses, they venerate the Sufferers and almost envy them the Glory of suffering in the common Cause of virtuous Freedom.

Was not Lord North, Sir, very greatly mistaken, when he asserted that the People of America would not resent the Treatment given to Boston? Are the Colonies understood by the British Parliament? Do not the Measures pursued by them of late, discover such a want of Knowledge of the State, and Temper of the People, as would (if other Arguments were wanting) prove beyond a Possibility of Doubt, that it would be to the last Degree injurious to both Countries, for the British Parliament to exercise the Power of legislating for the Colonies.

The Bills for regulating the Government of this Colony, and for the Trial of Persons committing capital Offences here, may perhaps be thought capable of being carried into Execution. It may be apprehended that the other Colonies will not perceive that the same Stroke which destroys the Charter of this Colony, mortally wounds their Charters.——

It may be imagined that the Colonists will not discern that by an Alteration of their Charters, the Tenure of their Lands is also changed; and that the same Power which can essentially alter their Charters, can with equal Justice annihilate them; and that if their Charters are annihilated, time-serving Jurists will be of Opinion that their Lands thereby become the Property of the Crown, and that they may either be granted to other Persons, or to the present Possessors, upon such Terms as the Crown shall impose.—It may be believed, that none of our Land-Holders ever heard that when the old Charter of this Colony was said to be vacated in the Reign of King James II. the Government here insisted upon every Person's applying for new Grants of their Lands: And that large Fees were demanded for those Grants; and that such as did not comply, were threatened with the Loss of their Lands; and indeed had not the glorious Revolution taken Place, the Threat might have been executed.

You, Sir, know that the People bear these Things in their Minds, and that an Attempt to enforce such Acts would be like an Attempt to cut them intirely off from the Face of the Earth.

Your Excellency's Representations will have great Weight at the British Court. You may afford the King and his Ministers such Light with Respect to the Colonies, as may lead to Measures that will greatly promote the Welfare of both Countries; and there cannot be any Thing more noble, no Object can be more worthy of your Excellency's Ambition, than to be the Instrument of making the Reign of your Sovereign glorious, and of rendering his Subjects happy. I am,

With due Respect to your Excellency,

A Freeholder of the County of SUFFOLK.

(The Piece sign'd HAMPDEN *from our Correspondent in Rhode-Island, came to Hand too late for a Place in this Week's Paper, but shall be inserted in our next.)*

50 DOLLARS REWARD.

WHEREAS sundry Goods and Merchandize were taken and stolen out of the Store of the Subscriber in Boston, between the 20th Day of May and the 23d Day of July last, to the Amount of £.400 L. M. Part of which Goods and Merchandize were found in the Dwelling House or Store of Jonathan Brewer of Watertown, in the County of Middlesex, Trader. And whereas said Jonathan Brewer hath since made his Escape, and cannot be found. Whoever therefore will take up or apprehend the said Jonathan Brewer, so that he may be prosecuted according to Law for his said Offence, shall be paid the above Reward by me.——The said Brewer is a well-built Man, about 5 Feet and an half High, walks erect, and goes decently dress'd. Had on when he went away (as is supposed) a white Coat, and spotted Jacket and Breeches, his Hair is black and cut short, and he generally wears mixt-coloured Silk Stockings.

Boston, 1st August, 1774. FRED. WM. GEYER.

Fredk. Wm. Geyer & Abrm. Burgess,

BEG Leave to acquaint the Public, That they have entered into a Co-partnership, under the Firm of GEYER & BURGESS; and that they have on Hand a general Assortment of English, India and Scotch Piece Goods, which they are determined to sell on the lowest Terms, by Wholesale only, at their Store (the Door below Messrs. Bethune and Prince's) in King-Street, Boston.

Said GEYER requests all those indebted to him, or to the late Company of Frazier and Geyer, either on Bond, Note or Book, to make immediate Payment, otherwise they will be put in Suit. (6 weeks)

August 1, 1774.

20 Dollars Reward.

STOLEN out of the Store of the Subscriber, the Night of the 25th Instant, the following Goods, viz. A half Piece superfine blue Cloth, half Piece superfine garnet Cloth, two Bags Buttons, three Dozen Womens fine cotton Stockings, ten Dozen Spitalfield Handkerchiefs, one Piece Bandanno Handkerchiefs, three Bandanno Handkerchiefs, some Chocolate, Loaf-Sugar, a parcel Codlines, some Metal Buttons.

Whoever will give Intelligence of the above Goods, so that the Owner may have them again, shall be intitled to the above Reward. JOHN WINSLOW, jun.

TO BE SOLD *(Exceeding cheap)* BY

Joshua Blanchard, jun.

At his Store on Dock Square, BOSTON.

A Quantity of Bread, Superfine Flour, Philadelphia Barr Iron, a Quantity of excellent Bacon, and West-India Goods and Groceries of all kinds.

ABSENTED himself from his Master an Indented Servant, Named JAMES BAYLEY, about 17 Years of Age, five Feet five Inches high, flat Nose, large Mouth and Lips, short black Hair, Walks Lazy and heavy, and is very artful in making Keys to open and pick Locks; Stole and took with him when he went away a Buck coloured Ratteen Coat, a striped red and white Waistcoat, white Linnen Breeches, blue Yarn Stockings, a Pair of thin Pumps, a white Cotton Shirt, with Linnen Sleeves, one Tow Shirt, and a Beaver-hat Hat.——Whoever will take up said Run-away and secure him, and give Information to the Subscriber, so that he may have him again, shall have a handsome Reward and necessary Charges paid by JOHN BLACK.

Rutland District, July 25, 1774.

Daniel Bell,

At his Store near the East End of Faneuil-Hall, Has to sell,

A small Quantity of good Sugar, in Hogsheads or Barrels, very cheap for Cash.

TO BE SOLD,

ON THURSDAY EVENING NEXT,

By *BENJAMIN CHURCH,*

At his usual Place of Sale, To close an Invoice sent in for Sale, Consisting of,

WOOLENS, Linnens, Checks, Callicoes, Muslins, Handkerchiefs, Laces, Wool Cards, &c.&c.&c. Likewise sundry Articles of Houshold, as Desks, Tables, Feather Beds, Curtains, &c. an 8-Day Clock, Watches, &c. &c.——

All Persons indebted to, or that

have any Demands on the Estate of Mr. JOHN DE COSTA, late of Boston, Mason, deceas'd, are desired to come and settle the same with us the Subscribers, Executors.

Boston, July 29, 1774.

JOHN DECOSTA,
JONATHAN-ROUSE DECOSTA,
JOSEPH DECOSTA,
ELIZABETH DECOSTA,
JOSHUA DAVIS.

TO BE SOLD,

Two Chaise, with Harness compleat,

3 good Horses, Saddles, &c. Also a Variety of House Furniture, consisting of Mehogany Leather Bottom Chairs, round about ditto, one very neat Mehogany Hair Bottom Close-stool Chair, two easy ditto, a handsome Scrutoir, Mehogany Square Tables, Window Curtains, Bedding with Curtains, &c. Two Guns, and sundry other Articles. Enquire of JACOB WENDELL, near the King's Chapel, who has the Disposal of the same.

N. B. If the above Articles are not Sold by the 20th of August Instant, then to be Sold by publick Auction on said Day, at the House of Mr. Richard Surcomb, late of Boston, Baker, deceased, at New-Boston.

The Estate of Mr. *Benjamin Bagnall,*

late of *Boston,* Watch Maker, deceas'd, being rendered Insolvent, and 6 Months allowed the Creditors to bring in their Claims, and prove their Debts, the Commissioners appointed by the Hon. *Foster Hutchinson,* Esq; Judge of Probate for the County of *Suffolk,* to receive and examine said Claims, give Notice that they shall attend said Service at the British Coffee-House in King street, on the first Tuesday of *August,* and the five following Months from Six to Nine o'Clock, P. M.

Boston, July 28th, 1774.

WANTED,

A sober, honest Man, of good Character,

that can take Care of Horses and drive a Carriage. He must be well recommended. Inquire of the Printers.

TO BE SOLD,

A large & convenient Brick House,

fronting on the main Street in the Town of Providence, in the Colony of Rhode-Island; said House on the Front is three Stories high, has eight Rooms on each Floor, all finished, and in good Order; has, in the lower Story, four Shops for Sale of Goods; and has a good large Garden, and other Accommodations back of it; it might well accommodate several Families. The Owner would take the whole Pay for it in English or West-India Goods. For further Particulars, any Person inclining to purchase, may apply to JOHN FOSTER, Esq; in said Providence. (4w.)

A Young Woman with a good Breast of Milk, and can be well recommended, would be glad to go into a Gentleman's Family to suckle. Inquire of Edes and Gill.

WHEREAS publick Notice has been given to the Proprietors of a Township lying on both Sides Little-Amarasgoggin River, in the County of Cumberland, in the late Province of Maine, granted by the Great and General Court on the 11th Day of June, A. D. 1771, to Capt. Joshua Fuller, and others, of the Taxes that have been granted on their Rights in said Township; several of which Proprietors are delinquent in the Payment of said Taxes: They are therefore hereby Notified that unless they Pay said Taxes to DAVID SANGER, of Watertown, Collector and Treasurer for said Proprietors, by One o'Clock in the Afternoon of the 31st Day of August next, their respective Rights will be Sold (as the Law directs) for the Payment of their Taxes and Incidental Charges: The Sale to begin at 2 o'Clock in said Afternoon, at the Dwelling House of Mr. ISAAC GLEASON, Innholder in Waltham, and continued (if need be) by Adjournment till the whole be Sold.

June 30, 1774.

ALEX. SHEPARD,
JOSIAH BROWN,
JOSIAH BISCO, } Committee for Sale.

New AUCTION-ROOM, Cornhill.

TO MORROW MORNING, at TEN o'Clock, Will be Sold by PUBLIC VENDUE, At GREENLEAF'S Auction-Room,

A large Assortment of English Goods as usual—Among which are—a beautiful Assortment of Patches, Chints and Callicoes. Also two good Feather Beds. WM. GREENLEAF, Auctioneer.

The Sale will begin at Ten o'Clock precisely.

At GOULD's Auction-Office, In Back-Street,

On FRIDAY Next,

At Ten in the Morning, Will be Sold by PUBLIC VENDUE,

A Variety of English and Hard-Ware GOODS. *Also,* Some Houshold Furniture.

R. GOULD, Auctioneer.

For private Sale at said Office

BIBLES, Testaments, Psalm and Spelling Books, with a general Assortment of New Books, in History, Divinity, Novels, Plays, &c—Genuine Kippen Snuff, white Threads, Gauzes, one large and elegant Turkey Carpett, sundry Chaises, both New and Second-Hand.

CHEAP GOODS.

There is now Selling off, by Wholesale and Retail, at BICKER's Auction Room, near the Market, Boston.

Most kinds of English, India and Scotch GOODS, Among which are many Articles suitable for the Fall Trade. (6 w.)

Burials in the Town of BOSTON, since our last. Ten Whites. Two Black.

Baptiz'd in the several Churches, Twelve.

High Water at BOSTON, for the present Week.

Monday, 48 min. aft. 6	Friday, 4 min. after. 10
Tuesday, 40 min. aft. 7	Saturday, 50 min. aft. 10
Wednesday, 27 m. aft. 8	Lord's-Day, 30 m. af. 11
Thursday, 26 min. aft. 9	New D 7 D. 7 Morn.

ed credit on the treasury for the purposes of corruption) may drive them into the wish'd for fatal concession; the *general seal of American bondage —The admission of the right of taxing you without your own consent?* Is it not to be expected, that the instant they have divested themselves of the character of freemen and taken up that of slaves, they will become the favourite colony of the court? That it will then be discovered, that they have been misrepresented? That they had indeed for some time been deluded by a few factious demagogues, but that in fact they were a loyal, dutiful and affectionate people?——This will be the language affected by the General, and this will the ministry ostentatiously affect to believe.—When they have thus commuted the character of freemen for that of slaves will they not act the part natural to slaves? Be the ready instruments for reducing others to the same situation with themseves? And when a people so potent in numbers and other respects as New England, is thrown into the scale of the military, I am at a loss to know what means on this continent can be devised for resistance.

For my own part, O citizens of New-York, supposing myself a Bostonian, and that my country were reduced to the wretched situation I have described, through your dilatoriness, disaffection or want of virtue, I am afraid there is no measure (be it ever so tyrannical) my Lords and masters could dictate against you, which I should not from resentment, find a pleasure in puting into execution.—For instance should they think proper to revive in this particular province, the odious stamp act, (and such is the wantonness and insolence of tyranny, that they would probably choose it, in preference to any other mode of oppression, as a trophy of their victory) I should, I am afraid, with alacrity lend my hand to enforce it.—I am sensible that in hazarding these sentiments, I may give to many, a disadvantageous picture of my own disposition; it may be that I mistake myself, but as resentment operates so strongly on the human breast, even the best disposed, and as slavery so viciates the human heart, the apprehension is far from groundless.—This, at least, is certain, that should the people of Boston be enslaved, and have reason to impute their calamity in part, or principally to New York, there is no degree of animosity and hatred they could afterwards bear to New York, which would not in a great measure be justified; and it is equally certain, that the liberties of the betrayers would not long survive those which they had betrayed.

I must now, O citizens, intreat that you will attribute what I have offered, to the genuine motive; to an ardent zeal for the liberties of America, and the rights of mankind; that you will believe me at the same time most sincerely attached to the real interests of G. Britain; no man can have a higher reverence for the people of England than myself; I esteem them, in all respects the first people of the universe. But when our parent is thrown into a delirium, by the quackery of a murdering impostor, is it not the duty of her children to prevent her committing outrages, not only immediately destructive to themselves, but which must end in her own ruin? When her phrenzy is past, she will thank us for the pious restraint. There is one consideration which renders the present delusion of the people of England with respect to America, really wonderful; it is that the very same men should have been able to bring about this delusion, whom they themselves have ever held in contempt and abhorrence. The same men who within doors have violated, baffled, or eluded their most sacred laws, dissipated and refused to account for their treasures, treated with insult their petitions & remonstrances; and who have externally sacrificed their interests, annihilated their importance, and tarnished their glories?—That these men should have wrought upon them, is so preposterous and unnatural that the delusion cannot be of a long continuation, they must soon open their eyes; they will then thank Providence, that the sense and virtue of their colonies has saved them from the destruction into which their own infatuation would have plunged them—Such are the sentiments which I entertain, such are the principles I possess—and if you believe them sincere, they will be sufficient opologies for my addressing you in this extraordinary manner; and that they are sincere, I call to witness that eternal Being, who is the judge of the truth of all hearts. I shall now conclude with observing, that there are two roads presented to you; the one leading to security, freedom, happiness and honour; the other which terminates in wretchedness, slavery and infamy to you and your children's children—it is of the greatest concern, therefore, to be assured of the fidelity of your conductors. If they turn their eyes to the right or left, from the direct object of their charge, *the general welfare*, to little views of imagined self-interests, you and your posterity are lost. The more we reflect, the more we are struck with the importance of what you are now about to resolve, of the necessity there is of paying the most serious attention to the characters of those whom you shall appoint your Delegates.—If amongst those proposed for your election, there should be a man whom you think averse to schemes of non importation and even non exportation to the islands, if necessary——that is in fact a man whose mind has been so narrowed by commercial habits, that he would postpone the permanent security and freedom of the whole, to his own temporary personal advantages: Let him be rejected, as totally unworthy of so momentous, so dignified a trust—Is there a man who ever did, or you suppose ever will hold any office under a ministry odious as the present? Him reject, as destitute of all principle. But above all, is there a man who has upon the present occasion, been heard to propose or recommend petition and remonstrance as the properest mode of obtaining redress? Him reject with scorn and indignation—for if he is in earnest, his capacity must be miserably low indeed, and if he is not in earnest, he certainly means to betray *you*.

The most strenuous civil resistance is necessary to your salvation, unless you prefer a civil *war* a few months hence, to civil *resistance* now, or are determined to submit to absolute *slavery*. Let your choice of Delegates be proportioned to the importance of the occasion.—I do not think transcendent talents absolutely necessary; a common good understanding is sufficient, but unquestionable heartiness, zeal and fervor in the common cause, are indespensible—in short, let your choice correspond with what we are taught to expect from the other colonies, and not only the security, happiness and liberties of America will be fixed on a foundation which ages shall not shake, but you may re animate your parent country, by subverting a system of government which must otherwise speedily put an end to her existence.

ANGLUS AMERICANUS.

TO BE SOLD,

The Lease of a Farm in Lancaster,

(lately belonging to Michael Trellett, *Esq; deceased) for the Term of ten Years and nine Months from the 10th of* July *instant, together with all the Crop upon the Ground, and Hay in the Barn, with or without the Stock, and Farming Utensils belonging thereto. The Farm consists of 53 Acres of Mowing, Pasturing and Tillage, and 8 Acres of Wood Land, with Liberty to cut what Wood may be necessary for Firing. The House has lately been thoroughly repair'd, paper'd and painted, it has two Rooms on a Floor of more than 20 Feet each, a very large Kitchen and Dairy Room, a large Barn, with good Stable and Coach House, and Convenience for a large Stock of horn'd Cattle, a Corn House and two Poultry Houses, in a large Poultry Yard well fenc'd, a large Garden handsomely laid out and well stor'd with a Variety of the best Fruit Trees, and newly fenc'd: it is in every Part in thorough good Repair, and suitable for any Gentleman who may incline to retire to an agreeable Neighbourhood, and most pleasing Situation; it stands upon an Eminence and commands the View of an extensive Interval, terminated by a Hill of Woods. Any Person inclining to purchase the Premisses may apply to* RICHARD LECHMERE *of* Boston, *who has Power to dispose of the same.*

N. B. *There is also a large Shop belonging to it suitable for any Sort of Business.*

Choice Cheshire Cheese,

to be Sold by ELIZABETH PERKINS in King-Street.

TO BE SOLD or LET,

By Thomas Robinson,

A Brewery and two Malt Houses in NEWPORT, capable of manufactoring 6000 Bushels of Barley, with every Conveniency, as Cellars, &c. for carrying on the Business of Brewing; a great Plenty of the best of Barley is raised in this Colony, from whence the Brewery may be supply'd cheaper than in any Colony in America. An English Brewer who comes well recommended may also be hired to conduct the Brewing and Malting. Any Person that inclines to purchase, may by giving good Security have one or more Years to pay the Money: For further Information apply to PHILIP DUMARESQ in Boston, or THOMAS ROBINSON in Newport, Rhode-Island.

All Persons who have any De-

mands on the Estate of Captain *Barnabas Binney*, deceased, late of Boston, are desired to bring in their Accounts immediately to his Son *Barnabas Binney*, Sole Executor: And all Persons indebted to said Estate, are desired to make Payment to the same as soon as possible.

LAST Tuesday Afternoon was stolen out of the House of the Subscriber, a Silver Watch, China Face, crack'd across the same, and inside the Case a Print representing Curiosity, with a stript Lutestring Ribbon for a String, a white Stone Seal on the same, with an Anchor engraved thereon, Maker's Name Rob. Rich, London, No. 2971. Whoever shall apprehend the Thief or Thieves, and return the Watch to the Subscriber, shall have Three Dollars Reward.

Malden, July 22, 1774. ELISHA STORY.

For LONDON,

The Brigantine BETSEY, about 120 Tons burthen, JAMES WISHART Master,

WILL sail from Plymouth with all convenient speed, having the greatest Part of her Cargo on board and engag'd:—For Freight or Passage apply to the Master on board, or at Mr. Solomon Davis's Store in Boston. ———Who has for Sale———

Choice Port and Teneriffe WINE.

ONE GUINEA REWARD.

WHEREAS on or about the 14th Instant, some evil-minded Person or Persons entered the North Battery in this Town, and took the Halliards from the Flag Staff—Whoever will discover the Thief or Thieves so that he or they may be brought to Justice, shall be paid the above Reward. NAT. BARBER, Capt.

Boston, July 21, 1774.

FIVE DOLLARS REWARD.

WHEREAS last Wednesday Night the Accompting-House of the Subscriber was broke open, and sundry Things stole, viz, 1 blue Surtuit Coat with Blue Buttons, 1 Thickset ditto without Lining, 1 small Looking Glass, one Beaver Hat, 1 50s. Piece, 2 Dollars and and about 20s. O. T. in Coppers, and sundry other Things. Whoever will give Information, so that the Person who stole them may be brought to Justice, shall have Five Dollars Reward. JOHN NEWELL.

Boston, July 23, 1774.

ALL Persons Indebted to, or that have any Demands on the Estate of Mr. EDWARD SPRAGUE, late of Boston, Housewright, deceased, are desired to bring in their Accounts to Martha Sprague, Administratrix on said Estate, in Order for Settlement.

Four Dollars Reward.

RANAWAY from his Master MARK HUNKING of Barrington, in New Hampshire, a Negro Servant named CÆSAR:—Had on when he went away, a striped homespun lappel'd Waistcoat, a Tow Shirt, black Serge Breeches, grey Jacket, a pair of Breeches and Jacket of a black and Hemlock dye, striped Tow Trowsers, black and white Yarn Stockings. He is a strait Limb'd Fellow about 5 Feet nine Inches high, very white Teeth, smiling Countenance; was bro't up to Farming Work. —Whoever shall take up said Runaway, and secure him so that his Master may have him again, shall have Four Dollars Reward, and all necessary Charges paid by MARK HUNKING.

N. B. All Masters of Vessels and others are forbid carrying him off, as they would avoid the penalty of the Law. *Barrington, July* 22, 1774.

TO BE SOLD,

The House known by the Name

of CONCERT HALL. Enquire of *William Turner*, who has a great Collection of MUSIC which he will sell at the Sterling Cost without Charges, viz.

The Periodical Overtunes to No 36, Two Setts of Bach's do. One Sett Schwindls 1st Opera. Two Setts Able's 1st and 7th Opera, Handel's 65 Overtures, Ferrari's Quartetts, Lord Kelly's and Stamitz's do. Barbandi's Sinfonias, Lord Kelly's Overtures, Humphries, Stanley's, Avison's, Corelli's Albertie's, Geminiani's, Heas's & Felton's Concertos, Campionis, Trios, Fisher's Overtures, Barthelemon's do. 2 Sett Bach's Songs, and 4 Violins.

N. B. Said *Turner* continues to teach Cotillons at the above-mentioned Hall, Fencing also.

Thomas Turner

Begs Leave to inform the Public,

That he has opened a School opposite the Rev. Dr. COOPER's Meeting-House, where he teaches Dancing in the politest Manner, and doubts not of giving Satisfaction to Gentlemen or Ladies, who would choose to recommend their Children to him, to acquire so eligible an Accomplishment. Likewise the useful Art of Fencing, agreeable to the best Rules establish'd for that Purpose.

N. B. Due Care shall be taken that the greatest Decency and good Manners be observ'd by his Scholars.

Susanna Renken,

INFORMS her Customers and others, That she has removed from Fore-street, to a little above the Hay-Market, where she has for Sale, a Variety of

English and India GOODS,

Groceries of all Sorts, West-India & New-England Rum.

Benjamin Goldthwait

Would inform his Friends, kind Customers and others, That he has just receiv'd by Capt Loring from London a small Invoice of GOODS, *suitable to the present Season, viz. Exceeding neat figur'd Jeanes, Thread ditto, plain, coloured and white ditto; Also, very neat Silk Jeans, fine white Irish Tick for Waistcoats and Breeches, white corded Dimothy, Silk knit Patterns, striped Damoskus, with sundry other Articles.——The above being a Consignment, will be Sold very low.*

☞ *The Taylor's Business is carried on as usual at his Shop just above Concert-Hall, in all its various Branches, in the genteelest Manner, and with the utmost Dispatch.*

Embroidery in Gold, Silver and Twist, is done in the best Manner at said Shop.

Boston: Printed by EDES & GILL,
in Queen-Street, 1774.

THE Boston- AND COUNTRY Gazette, JOURNAL.

Containing the freshest Advices, Foreign and Domestic.

No. 1008.

MONDAY, August 8, 1774.

To the worthy Inhabitants of the Town of BOSTON.

MY DEAR BRETHREN,

THE manly Firmness with which you sustain every Kind of ministerial Abuse, Injury and Oppression, and support the glorious Cause of Liberty, reflects the highest Honor upon the Town. The few, very few amongst you, who have adopted the Principles of Slavery, serve like the Shade in a Picture to exhibit your Virtues in a more striking Point of Light: Unhappy Men, I sincerely pity them, that they should have so little Sense of the Dignity of human Nature, so little Sense of their Duty to God, as to wish to reduce rational Beings formed after his divine Image to a State of brutish or worse than brutish Servitude; that they should be so dead to all the Feelings of Humanity, publick Spirit and universal Benevolence, as to prefer the sordid Pleasure of being upper Slaves to foreign Tyrants, and under them tyrannizing over their Country, to the God-like Satisfaction of saving that Country. How wretchedly these Men mistake Happiness! All the Riches and Honor in the World cannot give any Pleasure in the least Degree equal to the sincere heart-felt Joy which the Patriot feels, in the Consciousness of having supported the Dignity, the Freedom & Happiness of his Country.

The Attempt made by these Men to annihilate your Committee of Correspondence, was very natural: The Robber does not wish to see our Property entirely secured. An Enemy about to invade a foreign Country, does not wish to see the Coasts well guarded and the Country universally alarmed. Upon the same Principles these Men wish the Dissolution of the Committee. They know that a Design was formed to rob the Americans of their Property; they hoped to share largely in the general Plunder; but they now see that by the Vigilance, Wisdom, and Fidelity of the several Committees of Correspondence, the People are universally apprized of their Danger, and will soon enter into such Measures for the common Security, as will infallibly blast all their unjust Expectations; and this is the true Source of all the Abuse thrown upon your Committee. But Oh, ye worthy few! Continue to treat all their Attempts with the Neglect which they deserve. Thus the generous Mastiff looks down with Pity and Contempt, upon the little noisy, impertinent Curs, which bark at him as he walks the Street. Your faithful Services have endeared you to the wise and good in every Colony. Continue your indefatigable Labours in the common Cause, and you will soon see the happy Success of them in the Salvation of your Country.

The Tools of Power and their Connections, I imagine, are daily persuading you, my Brethren, to submit to the Ministry. They *pretend* to pity your Distresses, and assure you that the only Way for you to get Relief is the making Compensation for the Tea, and submitting to the Revenue Acts. But did ever a Man preserve his Money, by delivering up his Purse to the Highwayman, who dared to demand it? Is it the Way to preserve Life to throw away our Arms and present our naked Bosoms to the Murderers Sword?

The Town of Boston has been resembled to Carthage, and threatned with the same Fate by a Member of Parliament: The Execution of the Sentence is already begun: It may not be amiss then, to turn to the History of that People. There had been too long and very bloody Wars between Rome and that City: The Romans were Victorious: But the Carthagenians, having in a few Years almost recovered their former State of Wealth and Power, the Romans looked upon them with a jealous Eye, and took every Opportunity (unless by an open War) to depress them. The Carthagenians dreading a War, and hoping by a proper Submission to conciliate the Roman Affection, sent Ambassadors to Rome with Orders to declare, that they entirely abandoned themselves and all they possessed to the Discretion of the Romans. The Senate of Rome in Return, granted them their Liberty; the Exercise of their own Laws, all their Territories and Possessions as private Persons or as a Republick, on Condition that in thirty Days they should send three Hundred Hostages to Lilybæum, and do what the Consuls should order them: This cruel Order was submitted to; the Hostages were immediately sent. They were the Flower and Hopes of the most noble Families of Carthage. Upon their Departure, nothing was heard but the most dismal Cries and Groans; the whole City was in Tears, and the Mothers of these devoted Youth tore their Hair and beat their Breasts in all the Agonies of Grief and Despair. They fastened their Arms round their lovely Offsprings, and could not be separated from them but by Force. This cruel Sacrifice, I should think, would have melted the Romans into Compassion; but it had no such Effect. Ambition and Tyranny are incapable of any humane or tender Feeling. The Deputies therefore attended the Roman Camp, and told the Consuls that they were come in the Name of the Senate of Carthage, to receive their Orders, which they were ready to obey in all Things. The Consul praised their good Disposition and ready Obedience, and ordered them to deliver up all their Arms. This fatal Order was complied with, and an infinite Number of Weapons of all kinds, and a fine Fleet of Ships accordingly delivered up. Would any Thing less than the entire Destruction of Carthage have satisfied the Romans. They would now have been perfectly content. They had wholly disarmed the Carthagenians and got all the noble Youth Hostages, as a Security for their quiet Submission. But all this did not satisfy them. The Consuls sternly told them, that the Senate of Rome had determined to destroy Carthage; that they must quit their City and remove to some other Part of their Territory, four Leagues from the Sea. This they refused to do. The Romans therefore attacked their City; which notwithstanding its defenceless State bravely sustained a most terrible Siege three whole Years. Had the Carthagenians preserved their Youth, the Navy and their Arms; had they united the neighbouring Nations against the common Oppressor, and immediately prepared for their Defence, they might perhaps have defeated the Romans & preserved their City entirely; or at least for many Years longer: But they by *imprudent Submissions* put themselves wholly in the Power of the Enemy; and the Consequences were, the miserable Death of several Hundred Thousand People, and the utter Destruction of their City! Take warning my dear Countrymen by this terrible Example.

What would the Minister have, if not the good of the Nation? You have invariably promoted it from the first Foundation of the Colony. In War you have bravely defended yourselves, and the neighbouring Colonies; you have taken a glorious Part in several foreign Expeditions; you have even by your Conquests given Peace to Europe; besides these important Advantages the Nation has received Millions by the Profits of your Commerce; every Thing more than a bare Subsistence which you could gather from all Quarters of the Globe being by you remitted to Great-Britain for her Manufactures. What would he have more? He tells you plainly that your Liberty, your Lives and Property must be *laid at his Feet*. But my Brethren, suffer every Thing, even the Horrors of civil War, sooner than make the vile Submission. Should you agree to pay for the Tea, something more would be demanded. Should that be complied with, something further would be still demanded. In short, nothing will satisfy him but destroying the Town or reducing it to a poor fishing Village. A Plan hath been formed and steadily pursued for changing the free Constitution of Britain into an absolute Monarchy. Luxury, Bribery and Corruption have given the Minister the absolute Command of England and Ireland. The only remaining Obstacle to his unlimited Power is the brave Resistance made by the Americans. *You* are amongst the first of those Sons of Freedom, who have bravely stemed the Torrent of Tyranny. You have penetrated and exposed the mischievous Designs of the Ministry. You have pointed out proper Measures to defeat those execrable Designs, and entered into those Measures with Spirit. This, and *not the Destruction of the Tea*, hath bro't down the Vengeance of the Ministry upon *you*. They have left you no Alternative; but to give up your Liberties and hold your Lives and Property as Slaves by their mere arbitrary Will and Pleasure, or nobly determine to maintain those just Rights and Priviliges, which, by the Laws of God and your Country, you are entitled to. You will never hesitate one Moment. I am sure, my generous Countrymen, *you* were born and nurtured in the Arms of Freedom. *You* were never yet conquered by any Power on Earth. *You* have vast and sure Resources. The Colonies now heartily united consider your Cause as their own. They will soon enter into spirited and effectual Measures for your Relief. A great Part of the People of England and Ireland will support you; and the Distress in which the Nation will soon be involved by the ill Conduct of the Minister, will soon compel him to change his Measures or sink under the Resentment of an injured People. Spurn therefore from your Presence and Councils forever, those who dare to propose the giving up our Liberties. Continue bravely to bear up under your present Distress. Persevere in the glorious Cause in which we are engaged. It is the Cause of our King, our Country, and of God himself. He conducted your Fathers to America, planted and preserved them in the Wilderness, that they might worship him in a Manner acceptable to him. You have always maintained the publick (and I hope private) Worship of God. You and almost all America, have lately addressed him in a most solemn Manner. He hath often delivered us when all human Help failed. Witness the Destruction of that French Fleet at Chebucta. He is the same gracious and all powerful Being. Let us my Brethren put our Trust in him; for in the Lord Jehovah is everlasting Strength. Let the Priests, the Ministers of the Lord weep between the Porch and the Altar; and let them (and all of us most devoutly) say, *Spare thy People, O Lord, and give not thine Heritage to Reproach*; and we may rely upon it that He will in due Time deliver us from all our Enemies, and continue us a great, a free and a happy People. I am,

My dear Brethren,
Your affectionate Countryman,
HAMPDEN.

Rhode Island, 21st July 1774.

THIS DAY PUBLISHED,
(Price 9d.)
And sold by EDES and GILL, in Queen-Street.

CONSIDERATIONS
ON THE
MEASURES CARRYING ON
WITH RESPECT TO THE
BRITISH COLONIES
IN
NORTH-AMERICA.

There is neither King or Sovereign Lord on Earth, who has beyond his own Demain power to lay one Farthing on his Subjects without the grant and consent of those, who pay it; unless he does it by tyranny and violence.
Phillippe de Commines, Ch. 108.

THIS is a most masterly performance, written since the framing the several Acts against BOSTON and AMERICA, and the best calculated to convince the Ministry, the people of England, and all the world, of the absurdity and wickedness of the late Acts, and ruinous consequences, to England at least, that would certainly attend their being carried into execution.

Our last accounts, say, this pamphlet has had a wonderful effect in removing the prejudices and convincing the people of England.

Daniel Bell,

At his Store near the East End of Faneuil-Hall, Has to sell,

A small Quantity of good Sugar, in Hogsheads or barrels, very cheap for Cash.

AT a general Meeting of the Freeholders and Inhabitants of the County of Fairfax, *on Monday the 18th Day of July 1774, at the Court-House in the Town of* Alexandria, GEORGE WASHINGTON, *Esq; Chairman, and* ROBERT HARRISON, *Gentleman, Clerk of the said Meeting.*

RESOLVED, That this colony and dominion of Virginia, can not be considered as a conquered country; and if it was, that the present inhabitants are the descendants not of the conquered, but of the conquerors; That the same was not settled at the national expence of England, but at the private expence of adventurers, our ancestors, by solemn compact with, and under the auspices and protection of the British crown, upon which we are in every respect as dependant, as the the people of Great-Britain, and in the same manner subject to all his Majesty's just, legal, and constitutional prerogatives.—That our ancestors when they left their native land, and settled in America, brought with them, even if the same had not been confirmed by Charters, the civil constitution and form of government of the country they came from; and were by the laws of nature and nations entitled to all its privileges, immunities, and advantages; which have descended to us their posterity, and ought of right, to be as fully enjoyed, as if we had still continued within the realm of England.

2. *Resolved*, That the most important and valuable part of the British constitution, upon which its very existence depends, is the fundamental principle of the people's being governed by no laws, to which they have not given their consent, by representatives freely chosen by themselves; who are affected by the laws they enact, equally with their constituents, to whom they are accountable, and whose burthens they share, in which consists the safety and happiness of the community: For if this part of the constitution was taken away, or materially altered, the government must degenerate either into an absolute and despotic monarchy, or a tyrannical aristocracy, and the freedom of the people be annihilated.

3. *Resolved* therefore, as the inhabitants of the American colonies are not, and from their situation, can not be represented in the British parliament, that the legislative power here, can of right be exercised only by our own provincial assemblies or parliaments, subject to the assent or negative of the British crown, to be declared within some proper limited time. But as it was tho't just and reasonable that the people of Great Britain shou'd reap advantages from the colonies adequate to the protection they afforded them, the British parliament have claimed and exercised the power of regulating our trade and commerce, so as to restrain our importing from foreign countries, such articles as they could furnish us with, of their own growth or manufacture, or exporting to foreign countries such articles and portions of our produce, as Great-Britain stood in need of, for her own consumption or manufacture, such a power directed with wisdom and moderation, seems necessary for the general good of that great body politick, of which we are a part; altho' in some degree repugnant to the principles of the constitution. Under this idea our ancestors submitted to it; the experience of more than a century, during the government of his Majesty's royal predecessors, hath proved its utility, and the reciprocal benefits flowing from it, produced mutual, uninterrupted harmony and good-will between the inhabitants of Great-Britain and her colonies; who during that long period, always considered themselves as one and the same people: and tho' such a power is capable of abuse, and in some instances hath been stretched beyond the original design and institution, yet to avoid strife and contention with our fellow subjects, and strongly impressed with the experience of mutual benefits, we always chearfully acquiesced in it, while the entire regulation of our internal policy, and giving and granting our own money, were preserved to our own provincial legislatures.

4. *Resolved*, That it is the duty of these colonies, on all emergencies, to contribute, in proportion to their abilities, situation and circumstances, to the necessary charge of supporting and defending the British empire, of which they are a part. That while we are treated upon an equal footing, with our fellow subjects, the motives of self-interest and preservation will be a sufficient obligation; as was evident thro' the course of the last war; and that no argument can be fairly applied to the British parliament's taxing us, upon a presumption that we should refuse a just, and reasonable contribution, but will equally operate, in justification, of the executive power's taxing the people of England, upon a supposition of their representatives refusing to grant the necessary supplies.

5. *Resolved*, That the claim lately assumed and exercised by the British parliament, of making such laws as they think fit, to govern the people of these colonies, & to extort from us our money without our consent, is not only diametrically contrary to the first principles of the constitution, and the original compacts by which we are dependant upon the British crown and government; but is totally incompatible with the privileges of a free people, and the natural rights of mankind; will render our own legislatures merely nominal and nugatory, and is calculated to reduce us from a state of freedom and happiness, to slavery and misery.

6. *Resolved*, That taxation and representation are in their nature inseperable; that the right of withholding, or giving and granting their own money, is the only effectual security to a free people, against the encroachments of despotism and tyranny; and that when ever they yield the one, they must quickly fall a prey to the other.

7. *Resolved*, That the powers over the people of America now claimed by the British house of commons, in whose election we have no share; on whose determinations we can have no influence; whose information must be always defective, and often false; who in many instances may have a separate, & in some an opposite interest to ours, and who are removed from those impressions of tenderness and compassion, arising from personal intercourse and connections, which soften the rigour of the most despotic governments, must, if continued, establish the most grievous and intollerable species of tyranny and oppression, that ever was inflicted upon mankind.

8. *Resolved*, That it is our greatest wish and inclination, as well as interest, forever to continue our connection with, and dependance upon the British government; but tho' we are its subjects, we will use every means, which Heaven hath given us, to prevent our becoming its slaves.

9. *Resolved*, That there is a premeditated design and system, formed and pursued by the British ministry, to introduce an arbitrary government into his Majesty's American dominions; to which end they are artfully prejudicing our Sovereign, and inflaming the minds of our fellow-subjects in Great-Britain; by propagating the most malevolent falsehoods; particularly, that there is an intention in the American colonies, to set up for independent states; endeavouring at the same time, by various acts of violence and oppression; by sudden and repeated dissolutions of our assemblies, whenever they presume to examine the illegality of ministerial mandates, or deliberate on the violated Rights of their constituents; and by breaking in upon the American Charters, to reduce us to a state of Desperation, and dissolve the original Compacts, by which our Ancestors bound themselves, and their posterity, to remain dependant upon the British crown: Which measures, unless effectually counteracted, will end in the ruin both of Great-Britain and her Colonies.

10. *Resolved*, That the several Acts of Parliament for raising a Revenue upon the people of America without their consent; the creating new and dangerous jurisdictions here; the taking away our trials by jury; the ordering persons upon criminal accusations, to be tried in another country, than that in which the fact is charged to have been committed; the Act inflicting ministerial —vengeance upon the town of Boston; and the two bills lately brought into Parliament, for abrogating the Charter of the Province of the Massachusetts-Bay, and for the protection and encouragement of murderers in the said province, are part of the above-mentioned iniquitous system. That the inhabitants of the town of Boston are now suffering in the common cause of all British America, and are justly entitled to its support and assistance; and that therefore a subscription ought immediately to be opened, and proper persons appointed, in every county in this Colony, to purchase provisions, and consign them to some gentlemen of character in Boston, to be distributed among the poorer sort of people there.

11. *Resolved*, That we will cordially join with our friends and brethren of this and the other Colonies, in such measures as shall be judged most effectual for procuring redress of our grievances; and that upon obtaining such redress, if the destruction of the Tea at Boston, be regarded as an invasion of private property, we shall be willing to contribute, towards paying the East India Company the value: But as we consider the said company as the tools and instruments of oppression, in the hands of government, and the cause of our present distress, it is the opinion of this meeting, that the people of these colonies should forbear all further dealings with them, by refusing to purchase any of their merchandize, until that peace, safety and good-order, which they have disturbed, be perfectly restored. And that all Tea now in this colony, or which shall be imported into it, shipped before the 1st of September next, should be deposited in some store-house, to be appointed by the respective Committees of each county, untill a sufficient sum of money be raised by subscription, to reimburse the owners the value, and then to be publickly burnt and destroyed; and if the same shall not be paid for & destroyed, as aforesaid, that it remain in the custody of the said Committes, at the risque of the owners, untill the act of parliament imposing a duty upon it, for raising a revenue in America, be repealed; and immediately afterwards, be delivered unto the several proprietors thereof, their agents or attornies.

12. *Resolved*, That nothing will so much contribute to defeat the pernicious designs of the common enemies of Great-Britain and her Colonies, as a firm union of the latter; who ought to regard every act of violence and oppression, inflicted upon any one of them, as aimed at all; and to effect this desirable purpose, that a Congress should be appointed, to consist of Deputies from all the Colonies, to concert a general and uniform plan for the defence and preservation of our common Rights, and concontinuing the connection and dependance of the said Colonies upon Great-Britain, under a just, lenient, permanent, and constitutional form of government.

13. *Resolved*, That our most sincere & cordial thanks be given to the patrons and friends of Liberty in Great-Britain, for their spirited and patriotic conduct, in support of our constitutional Rights and Privileges, and their generous efforts, to prevent the present distress and calamity of America.

14. *Resolved*, That every little jarring interest and dispute which has ever happened between these Colonies, should be buried in everlasting oblivion; that all manner of luxury and extravagance ought immediately to be laid aside, as totally inconsistent with the threatning and gloomy prospect before us; that it is the indispensable duty of all the gentlemen and men of fortune to set examples of temperance, fortitude, frugality and industry; and give every encouragement in their power, particularly by subscriptions and premiums, to the improvements of arts and manufactures; and we recommend it to such of the inhabitants who have large stocks of sheep, to sell to their neighbours at a moderate price, as the most certain means of speedily increasing our breed of sheep, and quantity of wool.

15. *Resolved*, That untill American grievances be redressed, by restoration of our just rights and privileges, no goods or merchandize whatsoever ought to be imported into this colony, which shall be shipped from G. Britain after the first Day of September next, except linnens not exceeding fifteen pence per yard, coarse woolen cloth not exceeding two shillings ster. per yard, nails, wire, and wire cards, needles & pins, paper, salt-petre, and medicines; which may be imported untill the first day of September 1776; and if any goods or merchandize, other than those here excepted, should be shipped from Great-Britain after the time aforesaid, to this colony, that the same immediately upon their arrival, should either be sent back again, by the owners, their agents or attornies, or stored and deposited in some warehouse, to be appointed by the Committees for each respective county, and there kept, at the risque and charge of the owners, to be delivered to them, when a free importation of goods hither shall again take place. And that the merchants and venders of goods and merchandize within this colony, ought not to take advantage of our present distress, but continue to sell the goods and merchandize which they now have, or which may be shipped to them before the 1st day of September next, at the same rate and prices they have been accustomed to do, within one year last past; and if any person shall sell such goods, on any other terms than above expressed, that no inhabitant of this Colony should at any time, forever thereafter, deal with him, his agent, factor or store keepers, for any commodity whatsoever.

16. *Resolved*, That it is the opinion of this meeting, that the merchants and venders of goods & merchandize within this Colony, should take an oath not to sell or dispose of any goods or merchandize whatsoever, which may be shipped from Great-Britain after the 1st day of September next, as aforesaid, except the articles before excepted, and that they will, upon receipt of such prohibitted goods, either send the same back again by the first opportunity, or deliver them to the Committees in the respective counties, to be deposited in some warehouse, at the risque and charge of the owners, until they, their agents or factors, shall be permitted to take them away by the said Committees: That the names of those who shall refuse to take such oath, be advertised by the respective Committees in the Counties wherein they reside; and to the end that the inhabitants of this Colony may know what merchants and venders of goods and merchandize shall have taken such oath, that the respective Committees should grant a certificate thereof to every such person who shall take the same.

17. *Resolved*, That it is the opinion of this meeting, that during our present difficulties and distress, no slaves ought to be imported into any of the British colonies on this continent; and we take this opportunity of declaring our most earnest wishes, to see an entire stop forever put to such a wicked, cruel, and unnatural trade.

18. *Resolved*, That no kind of lumber should be exported from this colony to the West-Indies, until America be restor'd to her constitutional rights and liberties, if the other colonies will accede to the like resolution; and that it be recommended to the general congress, to appoint as early a day as possible for stopping such exports.

19. *Resolved*, That it is the opinion of this meeting, if American grievances be not redressed, before the first day of November, one thousand seven hundred & seventy five, that all exports of produce, from the several colonies to great Britain should cease; and to carry the said resolution more effectually into execution, that we will not plant or cultivate any Tobacco, after the crop now growing; provided the same measure shall be adopted by the other colonies on this continent; as well those who have heretofore made Tobacco, as those who have not. And it is our opinion also, if the congress of deputies from the several colonies shall adopt the measure of non exportation to Great Britain, as the people will be thereby disabled from paying their debts, that no judgments should be rendered by the courts in the said colonies for any debt, after information of the said measures being determined upon.

20. *Resolved*, That it is the opinion of this meeting that a solemn covenant and association should be entered into, by the inhabitants of all the colonies upon oath, that they will not, after the times which shall be respectively agreed on, at the general congress, export any manner of lumber to the West-Indies nor any of their produce to Great Britain, or sell or dispose of the same, to any person who shall not have entered into the said covenant and association; and also that they will not import or receive, any goods or merchandize, which shall be shipped from Great Britain after the first day of September next, other than the before enumerated articles; nor buy or purchase any goods, except as before excepted, of any person whatsoever, who shall not have taken the oath herein before recommended to be taken by the merchants and venders of goods; nor buy or purchase any slaves hereafter imported into any part of this continent, until a free exportation and importation be again resolved on by the majority of the representatives or deputies, of the colonies; and that the respective committees of the counties in each colony, so soon as the covenant and association shall become general, publish by advertisements in their several counties, a list of the names of those, if any such there be, who will not accede thereto; that such traitors to their country may be publickly known and detested.

21. *Resolved*, That it is the opinion of this meeting, that this and the other associating colonies should break off all trade, intercourse and dealings with that colony, province or town, which shall decline or refuse to agree to the plan, which shall be adopted by the general congress.

22. *Resolved*, That should the town of Boston be forced to submit, to the late cruel and oppressive measures of government, that we shall not hold the same to be binding upon us, but will notwithstanding religiously maintain, and inviolably adhere to such measures, as shall be concerted by the general congress, for the preservation of our lives, liberties and fortunes.

23. *Resolved*, That it be recommended to the deputies of the general congress, to draw up and transmit an humble and dutiful petition and remonstrance to his Majesty, asserting with decent firmness, our just and constitutional rights and privileges; lamenting the fatal necessity of being compelled to enter into such measures as are disgusting to his Majesty and his parliament, or injurious to our fellow-subjects in Great-Britain; declaring in the strongest terms, our duty and affection to his Majesty's person, family and government, and our desire forever to continue our dependance upon Great-Britain; and most humbly conjuring and beseeching his Majesty not to reduce his faithful subjects of America to a state of desperation, and to reflect, that from our Sovereign, THERE CAN BE BUT ONE APPEAL. And it is the opinion of this meeting, that after such Petion and Romonstrance shall have been presented to his Majesty, the same should be printed in the public Papers, in all the principal towns in Great Britain.

24. *Resolved*, That George Washington, Esq; and Charles Broadwate, Gent. lately elected our Representatives to serve in the Assembly, attend the General Convention at Williamsburg on the 1st Day of August nex, and present these Resolves as the sense of the people of this county, upon the measures proper to be taken, in the present alarming & dangerous situation of America.

25. *Resolved*, That George Washington, Esq; John West, George Mason, William Ramsay, William Rumney, George Gilpen, Robert Hanson Harrison, John Carlyle, Robert Adams, John Dalton, Philip Alexander, James Kirk, William Brown, Charles Broadwater, William Payne, Martin Cockburn, Lee Massey, William Hartshorn, Thomas Triplett, Charles Alexander, Thos. Pollard, Townshend Dodge, junr. Edward Payne, Henry Gunnell and Thomas Lewis, be a Committee for this County; that they or a majority of them, on any emergency have power to call a general meeting, and to concert and adopt such measures as may be thought most necessary.

26. *Resolved*, That a Copy of these Proceedings be transmitted to the Printers at Williamsburg to be published.

A true Copy,

ROB. HARRISON, Clerk.

By Captain Candal, arrived at Philadelphia from Cadiz, and Captain Rolland, arrived at Salem from Falmouth, we have the following Advices, viz.

L O N D O N.

Westminster, May 20. This day his Majesty came to the the House of Peers, and being in his royal robes seated on the throne with the usual solemnity, Sir Francis Molineux, Gentleman Usher of the Black Rod, was sent with a message from his Majesty to the House of Commons, commanding their attendance in the House of Peers: The Commons being come thither accordingly, his Majesty was pleased to give his Royal assent to

An Act for better regulating the government of the province of the Massachusetts Bay, in New-England. And,

An Act for the impartial administration of justice in the Province of Massachusetts Bay, in New-England.

May 23. Many reports having been propagated with respect to the hostile intentions of the young King of France, we can with pleasure assure the public, that all the letters from Paris, hitherto received, declare he has given the strongest assurances to all the foreign Ministers who have condoled him upon the death of his grand-father, of persevering in the pacific system which prevails in Europe, and repeatedly expressed his wishes to accommodate matters between the Court of Petersburgh and the Porte.

Several families in Leeds, Yorkshire, (among which are butchers, joiners, &c.) are disposing of their effects in order to try their fortunes in the western world. There is scarce a week but some are setting off from that part of Yorkshire for the Plantations, finding it next to impossible, in the present lamentable state of trade, and the dearness of provisions, to provide in any sort for themselves and families. Some that have lately gone, and are now going, are persons of considerable property.

May 28. On Thursday came on, according to order, in the upper assembly, the third reading of the bill for providing quarters for the officers and troops in North-America. The bill was accordingly read a third time by the clerk; and upon the question being put, whether the bill should pass, Lord Chatham got up and spoke for upwards of an hour in a very nervous and very sensible manner. During the course of his speech, his Lordship highly condemned the refractory behaviour of the Americans, but at the same time disapproved of the measures taken by Administration, looking upon them as harsh, oppressive, and tyrannical. When he had concluded, Lord Suffolk spoke for a short time, and was answered by Lord Temple who closed the debate. The question was put, that this bill do now pass, and the House divided, contents 57, not contents 16.

The SENTIMENTS *of Messieurs* BARRE *and* FULLER, *on the* Last *of the* American Bills.

Colonel BARRE. I think it criminal to sit still upon the final decision of this question, as I cannot in any shape approve of this measure. I think the persons you employ to execute your laws, might have been protected in the execution of their duty, in a less exceptionable manner than the Bill proposes. Your army, in that country, has the casting voice; and it is dangerous to put any more power into their hands. Consider how long they will be content with 4d. per day; I am afraid not long. You have had one meeting already, you may soon have another; the people of America, will receive these regulations as edicts from an ARBITRARY GOVERNMENT. The heaviest offence they have been guilty of is, that they have resisted that law which bears such an arbitrary cast. I want to know if we, in this country, had not resisted such arbitrary laws in certain ancient times, whether we should have existed as a House of Commons here this day? I object much against the doctrine which I have heard laid down, that the particular exigency of the case countenanced the measure. I do not apprehend the Americans will abandon their priciples; for if they submit they are SLAVES: I therefore execrate the present measure in manner proposed.

Mr. FULLER. I will now take my leave of the whole plan and will give you my free opinion of it. You will commence your RUIN from this day, if you don't repeal that Tax which created all this disturbance; you will have no degree of confidence with the Americans; people won't trust you when your credit is gone: You may, I say, date your ruin from this day; and, I am sorry to say, that not only this House has fallen into that error, but that the people of this country approve of the measure. I find the people wish for the measures proposed in this Bill, as much as the majority here; it is not all owing to the JUNTO of a Ministry that these measures are taken, it is the people at large, whom I am sorry to say, are misled; they are in an error, but a short time will prove the evil tendency of this Bill. I think this Bill before us bears the least injury of any of the three; but if there ever was a nation running headlong to its ruin, it is this.

B O S T O N, August 8.

The Assembly of Pennsylvania have chosen the Hon. Joseph Galloway, *Speaker*; Samuel Rhoades, Thomas Mifflin, Charles Humphreys, John Morton, George Ross, and Edward Biddle, Esqrs; to attend the General Congress at Philadelphia the first of September next.

Another Supply of Three Hundred and Fifty Barrels of Rice, was ready to be shipped the 11th ult. at Charles-Town, South-Carolina, for the Use of the Sufferers in this Town, and may be soon expected.

Friday last arrived here the Scarborough Man of War Capt. ——— in 8 Weeks from London.—The Contents of the Budget bro't by him has not yet transpired.

The Cerberus Frigate lay ready, and was to sail for this Port also, as soon as she had received her Dispatches.

We hear that Thomas Oliver, Esq; of Cambridge, is appointed Lieutenant-Governor of this Province.

Saturday last arrived here the Transports from New-York with a Detachment of the Royal Artillery, and a Quantity of Ordnance, Stores, &c. together with the Royal Regiment of Welsh Fuzileers.

The same Day arrived here from Halifax, three Transports, with the 59th Regiment.

DIED] Last Evening, Mr. Joseph Jackson, his Funeral is to be on Wednesday next at five o'Clock, from his House in Back Street, at which Time his Friends and Acquaintance are requested to give their Attendance.

All Persons that have any Demands on the Estate of Mr. Johnson Jackson, *late of Boston, Distiller, deceased, are desired to send their Accounts to* Joseph Jackson, *at the South-End of Boston, sole Executor to the last Will and Testament of said deceas'd; and all Persons that are Indebted to said Estate are desired to make spedy Payment, as the Executor is determined the said Estate shall be Settled with all possible Expedition.*

To be sold by PUBLIC AUCTION,
On WEDNESDAY *the 10th Current,*
at Nine o'Clock in the Forenoon,
Part of the Houshold Furniture of Johnson Jackson, *deceased;—Consisting of Kitchen Furniture, as—*
Pewter, Brass, Copper, and Tin Ware, Feather Beds, Chairs, Looking Glasses, Tables, a very good 8-Day Clock, two Suits of Harrateen Curtains, a Chaise and riding Chair, sundry Pieces of Plate, &c.

The Sale to be at the late Dwelling-House of the deceased, at the South-End of Boston.

TO BE SOLD,
ON THURSDAY EVENING NEXT,
By *BENJAMIN CHURCH*,
At his usual Place of Sale,
To close an Invoice sent in for Sale,
Consisting of,

WOOLENS, Linnens, Checks, Callicoes, Muslins, Handkerchiefs, Laces, Wool Cards, &c.&c.&c. Likewise sundry Articles of Houshold, as Desks, Tables, Feather Beds, Curtains, &c. an 8-Day Clock, Watches, &c. &c.—

The Chaises, House Furniture, &c.

advertiz'd for Sale by JACOB WENDELL, in the last Page of this Paper, will be PUNCTUALLY Sold by PUBLICK AUCTION, on THURSDAY the 18th Day of this Instant August, at Three o'Clock, P. M.

N. B. The above Articles may be seen at the House of the late Mr. *Richard Surcomb*, Baker, the Day before the Sale. MOSES DESHON, Auctioneer.

WE the Subscribers being appointed Commissioners by the Hon. *John Cushing*, Esq; Judge of Probate for the County of Plymouth, to receive and examine the Claims of the several Creditors to the Estate of *Thomas Clapp*, late of Scituate, Esq; deceased, represented Insolvent, and six Months being allowed to receive said Claims. We do hereby Notify said Creditors, that we will attend upon said Business at the Dwelling-House of Mrs. *Esther Clapp*, in said Scituate, from Three to Seven of the Clock in the Afternoon, on the third Wednesdays of the six succeeding Months.

Scituate, July 29, 1774.

David Little, Junr.
Increase Clapp.

To be Sold for want of Employ only,
A likely Negro Boy, about 16 Years of Age.—He is strong, healthy, good-temper'd, sober and honest;—and, with a good Master would make a very faithful Servant. Inquire of Edes & Gill.

TO BE LETT, VERY CHEAP,
A good Shop towards the South-End:
Enquire of George Tet.

TO BE SOLD,

A Very handsome Phaeton, with Harness compleat, and a Driver's Seat to be used occasionally;

A Pair of young Bay Horses broke to the Carriage; And,

A fine riding Horse about 15 Hands high, half Blood, and about 6 Years old. Enquire of Edes & Gill.

CORNISH's *New England* Cod-Fish HOOKS, &c.

Abraham Cornish

Fish-Hook Maker from Exeter *in* ENGLAND,

ACQUAINTS his Friends and the Public, That he has removed from his Manufactory at the North End of BOSTON, to the Upper Part of CHARLESTOWN, where he continues to make all Sorts of FISH HOOKS, warranted of the best Quality;—being made of the best Wire only, better shap'd to take Fish, and each Hook prov'd before put up, (which is not done in England.) From several Years Experience, they have been found much superior to any imported, and are universally approv'd; for which Reasons, he flatters himself, that all concerned in the Fishery, will favour him with their Custom, as they will thereby promote their own private Interest, and render this Country an essential Service, by establishing a Manufacture necessary to its Prosperity.——For the better accommodating those who may purchase his Hooks, they are Sold by Messrs. LEE & JONES, near the Swing-Bridge in Boston, who will always keep by them a sufficient Quantity to supply the American Fishery.—Said LEE & JONES, have for Sale, a few Hogsheads of Jamaica and Barbados Rum, genuine Kippen's and Rapee Snuff, a Variety of Looking Glasses, a Quantity of Lynn Shoes, a few Cases of blue and white China Cups and Saucers, Corks, Gold and Silver Laces, a Variety of Stone, Glass and Cream-coloured Ware, Silver and Pinchbec Watches, a Variety of Silks, Laces and Muslins, Tambour Muslin Aprons and Ruffles; and a general Assortment of Piece Goods.

ALSO, Nails of all Sorts to be delivered at Marblehead.

To the Worshipful *Jeremiah Powell*, Esq; one of his Majesty's Justices of the Peace throughout the Province of the *Massachusetts-Bay*.

We the Subscribers Proprietors of a Tract of Land about twenty Miles square, lying and bordering upon *Piscataqua* River, in the County of *York*, late in the Province of *Main*, which descended to us from *Francis Small*, late of *Truro*, in the County of *Barnstable*, in the said Province of the *Massachusetts-Bay* deceas'd, who purchased the same from one Capt. *Sandy*, an Indian Sagamore, being desirous of embodying ourselves as a Propriety & acting as such agreeable to the Law in such Case made and provided. Do hereby humbly request that your Worship would order a Meeting of said Proprietors to be held at the House of Mr. *Moses Shattuck* of *Falmouth*, in the County of *Cumberland*, Innholder, on the eighteenth Day of *September* next, at two of the Clock in the Afternoon, to act on the following Articles, *viz.* 1st. To choose a Moderator. 2dly. To choose a Proprietor's Clerk. 3dly. To choose a Committee to transact such prudential Affairs of said Proprietors as they may commit. 4thly. To vote what Money may be thought necessary for defraying the Charges which my arise in promoting the Interest of said Propriety. 5thly. To agree on some Method for assessing and collecting the Monies, then or at any future Time voted by the said Proprietors. 6thly. To choose an Agent or Agents, to prosecute any Persons, who have, or may enter or trespass upon the said Land. And 7thly. To agree on some Method for calling Meetings in future.

Falmouth, July 6, 1774.

Samuel Freeman
Thomas Siminton
Mather Siminton
Elisha Small
Joshua Eldridge
Jacob Waterhouse
Pelatiah Fernald.

Province of the MASSACHUSETTS-BAY.

(L. S.) To Mr. SAMUEL FREEMAN of *Falmouth*, in the County of *Cumberland*, in said Province, one of the Proprietors, and Subscribers to the foregoing Petition, *Greeting*.

In pursuance of the aforegoing Application and Request, you are hereby required to give Notice (in Time and Manner as the Law directs) to the said Proprietors, that a Meeting of said Proprietors is to be holden at the Time and Place, and for the Purposes mentioned in the aforewritten Petition.

Given under my Hand and Seal, this 16th Day of July, *in the Fourteenth Year of his Majesty's Reign, Annoque Domini*, 1774.

JEREMIAH POWELL, a Justice of the Peace through the Province of the *Massachusetts-Bay*.

July 19, 1774.

By Virtue of the aforewritten Warrant to me directed, I do hereby notify and warn the aforesaid Proprietors to meet at the Time and Place, and for the Purposes expressed in the aforegoing Application.

SAMUEL FREEMAN.

Burials in the Town of BOSTON, since our last.
Two Whites. No Blacks.
Baptiz'd in the several Churches, Eighteen.

High Water at BOSTON, *for the present Week.*

Monday, 22 min. aft.	12	Friday, 0 min. after.	3
Tuesday, 0 min. aft.	1	Saturday, 42 min. aft.	3
Wednesday, 36 m. aft.	1	Lord's-Day, 27 m. af.	4
Thursday, 19 min. aft.	2	☽'s first Q. 14 D. 7 After.	

Messieurs EDES & GILL,

AN Address has lately been ordered to be transmitted to the late Governor Hutchinson, in the Name of the Justices of the Court of General Sessions of the Peace, and Inferior Court of Common Pleas for the County of Plimouth.

Certain it is, that the three Gentlemen who, at present, constitute the Court of Common Pleas within that County, gave their voice for it, and consequently it may with Propriety be stiled—An Address from the Court of Common Pleas.

Whether it may with equal Propriety be stiled an Address from the Court of General Sessions, we may be better able to judge, after mentioning some facts relative thereto.

A Motion was made in the Court of Sessions, for the Appointment of a Committee, to prepare an Address to Mr. Hutchinson. As a Motion for an Address from any of our Courts of Justice to a Governor, on his Removal from the Chair, was novel and unprecedented, it were to be wished the Gentleman who moved it had given some previous Notice of his Intention. This however was not done. The Motion was opposed by some Gentlemen then present, and would have been by others who would have tho't themselves in duty bound to have been present, if they had been advised of it—others were in doubt as to the propriety of it, it being unprecedented, and Mr. Hutchinson might, probably, be then arrived in Great-Britain. —A Majority however were in favor of the Motion, and a Committee was appointed for that purpose; but before they reported, so many of the Justices had withdrawn, (the Business of the Court being almost finished,) that there were only twelve present to consider it, of which number, six, besides the three Gentlemen of the Court of Common Pleas, were for accepting it.

Thus an Address, which when it appears here, will I believe, be thought very *adulatory*, an Address, expressive of an entire Approbation of that Gentleman's publick Conduct, has been transmitted across the Atlantic, in the Name of the Court of General Sessions of the Peace for the County of Plimouth, altho' not one third Part of the Gentlemen who constitute that Court, were present when it was considered.

A Consignment of English GOODS,

Consisting of the following Articles, viz.

An Assortment of Hatt-Trimmings, striped Damascus Bandanno and Barcelona Handkerchiefs, black Cravats, Knee-Garters, Coat-Binding, Mohair and scarf Twist, death-head and metal Buttons, scarlet Gartering, steel-bow'd Spectacles, Needles and Purse Pins, Scotch Thread, a very neat silver-plated Coffee-Pot, silk Ferrets, worsted and silk Breeches Patterns, silk and thread Hose, striped Swanskins, Men and Boys Felt Hats, &c. &c.

To be Sold very low for Cash. Inquire of

William Palfrey.

TO BE SOLD,

A large & convenient Brick House,

fronting on the main Street in the Town of Providence, in the Colony of Rhode-Island; said House on the Front is three Stories high, has eight Rooms on each Floor, all finished, and in good Order; has, in the lower Story, four Shops for Sale of Goods; and has a good large Garden, and other Accommodations back of it; it might well accommodate several Families. The Owner would take the whole Pay for it in English or West-India Goods. For further Particulars, any Person inclining to purchase, may apply to JOHN FOSTER, Esq; in said Providence. (4w.)

W A N T E D,

A sober, honest Man, of good Character, that can take Care of Horses and drive a Carriage. He must be well recommended. Inquire of the Printers.

The Estate of Mr. *Benjamin Bagnall*, late of *Boston*, Watch Maker, deceas'd, being rendered Insolvent, and 6 Months allowed the Creditors to bring in their Claims, and prove their Debts, the Commissioners appointed by the Hon. *Foster Hutchinson*, Esq; Judge of Probate for the County of *Suffolk*, to receive and examine said Claims, give Notice that they shall attend said Service at the British Coffee-House in King street, on the first Tuesday of *August*, and the five following Months from Six to Nine o'Clock, P. M.

Boston, July 28th, 1774.

T O B E S O L D,

Two Chaise, with Harness com-

pleat, 3 good Horses, Saddles, &c. Also a Variety of House Furniture, consisting of Mehogany Leather Bottom Chairs, round-about ditto, one very neat Mehogany Hair Bottom Close-stool Chair, two easy ditto, a handsome Scrutoir, Mehogany Square Tables, Window Curtains, Bedding with Curtains, &c. Two Guns, and sundry other Articles. Enquire of JACOB WENDELL, near the King's Chapel, who has the Disposal of the same.

N. B. If the above Articles are not Sold by the 20th of August Instant, then to be Sold by publick Auction on said Day, at the House of Mr. Richard Surcomb, late of Boston, Baker, deceased, at New-Boston.

---

50 DOLLARS REWARD.

WHEREAS sundry Goods and Merchandize were taken and stolen out of the Store of the Subscriber in Boston, between the 20th Day of May and the 23d Day of July last, to the amount of £.400 L. M. Part of which Goods and Merchandize were found in the Dwelling House or Store of Jonathan Brewer of Watertown, in the County of Middlesex, Trader. And whereas said Jonathan Brewer hath since made his Escape, and cannot be found. Whoever therefore will take up or apprehend the said Jonathan Brewer, so that he may be prosecuted according to Law for his said Offence, shall be paid the above Reward by me.——The said Brewer is a well-built Man, about 5 Feet and an half High, walks erect, and goes decently dressed. Had on when he went away (as is supposed) a white Coat, and spotted Jacket and Breeches, his Hair is black and cut short, and he generally wears mixt-coloured Silk Stockings.

Boston, 1st August, 1774. FRED. WM GEYER.

Fredk. Wm. Geyer & Abrm. Burgess,

BEG Leave to acquaint the Public, That they have entered into a Co-partnership, under the Firm of GEYER & BURGESS; and that they have on Hand a general Assortment of English, India and Scotch Piece Goods, which they are determined to sell on the lowest Terms, by Wholesale only, at their Store (the Door below Messi's. Bethune and Prince's) in King-Street, Boston.

Said GEYER requests all those indebted to him, or to the late Company of Frazier and Geyer, either on Bond, Note or Book, to make immediate Payment, otherwise they will be put in Suit. (6 weeks)

August 1, 1774.

---

20 Dollars Reward.

STOLEN out of the Store of the Subscriber, the Night of the 25th Instant, the following Goods, viz. A half Piece superfine blue Cloth, half Piece superfine garnet Cloth, two Bags Buttons, three Dozen Womens fine cotton Stockings, ten Dozen Spitalfield Handkerchiefs, one Piece Bandanno Handkerchiefs, three Bandanno Handkerchiefs, some Chocolate, Loaf-Sugar, a parcel Codlines, some Metal Buttons.

Whoever will give Intelligence of the above Goods, so that the Owner may have them again shall be intitled to the above Reward. JOHN WINSLOW, jun.

T O B E S O L D (*Exceeding cheap*) B Y

Joshua Blanchard, jun.

At his Store on Dock Square, BOSTON.

A Quantity of Bread, Superfine Flour, Philadelphia Barr-Iron, a Quantity of excellent Bacon, and West-India Goods and Groceries of all kinds.

All Persons indebted to, or that

have any Demands on the Estate of Mr. JOHN DE COSTA, late of Boston, Mass, deceas'd, are desired to come and settle the same with us the Subscribers, Executors.

Boston, July 29, 1774.

ISAAC DECOSTA,
JONATHAN-ROUSE DECOSTA.
JOSEPH DECOSTA,
ELIZABETH DECOSTA,
JOSHUA DAVIS.

ABSENTED himself from his Master an Indented Servant, Named JAMES BAYLEY, about 27 Years of Age, five Feet five Inches high, flat Nose, large Mouth and Lips, short black Hair, Walks Lazy and heavy, and is very artful in making Keys to open and pick Locks; Stole and took with him when he went away a Brick coloured Ratteen Coat, a striped red and white Waistcoat, white Linnen Breeches, blue Yarn Stockings, a Pair of thin Pumps, a white Cotton Shirt, with Linnen Sleeves, one Tow Shirt, and a Beaver-nit Hat.——Whoever will take up said Run-away and secure him, and give Information to the Subscriber, so that he may have him again, shall have a handsome Reward and necessary Charges paid by JOHN BLACK.

Rutland District, *July* 25, 1774.

Choice Cheshire Cheese,

to be Sold by ELIZABETH PERKINS in King-Street.

WHEREAS publick Notice has been given to the Proprietors of a Township lying on both Sides Little-Amarascoggin River, in the County of Cumberland, in the late Province of Maine, granted by the Great and General Court on the 25th Day of June, A. D. 1771, to Capt. Joshua Fuller, and others, of the Taxes that have been granted on their Rights in said Township a several of which Proprietors are delinquent in the Payment of said Taxes: They are therefore hereby Notified that unless they Pay said Taxes to DAVID SANGER, of Watertown, Collector and Treasurer for said Proprietors, by One o'Clock in the Afternoon of the 31st Day of August next, their respective Rights will be Sold (as the Law directs) for the Payment of their Taxes and Incidental Charges: The Sale to begin at 2 o'Clock in said Afternoon, at the Dwelling House of Mr. ISAAC GLEASON, Innholder in Waltham, and continued (if need be) by Adjournment till the whole be Sold.

June 30, 1774.

ALEX. SHEPARD,
JOSIAH BROWN,
JOSIAH BISCO,
} Committee for Sale.

ALL Persons Indebted to, or that have any Demands on the Estate of Mr. EDWARD SPRAGUE, late of Boston, Housewright, deceased, are desired to bring in their Accounts to Martha Sprague, Administratrix on said Estate, in Order for Settlement.

T O B E S O L D or L E T,

By Thomas Robinson,

A Brewery and two Malt Houses in NEWPORT, capable of manufactoring 6000 Bushels of Barley, with every Conveniency, as Cellars, &c. for carrying on the Business of Brewing; a great Plenty of the best of Barley is raised in this Colony, from whence the Brewery may be supply'd cheaper than in any Colony in America. An English Brewer who comes well recommended may also be hired to conduct the Brewing and Malting. Any Person that inclines to purchase, may by giving good Security have one or more Years to pay the Money: For further Information apply to PHILIP DUMARESQ in Boston, or THOMAS ROBINSON in Newport, Rhode Island.

TO BE SOLD,

The Lease of a Farm in Lancaster,

(lately belonging to Michael Trollett, Esq; deceased) for the Term of ten Years and nine Months from the 10th of July instant, together with all the Crop upon the Ground, and Hay in the Barn, with or without the Stock, and Farming Utensils belonging thereto. The Farm consists of 58 Acres of Mowing, Pasturing and Tillage, and 8 Acres of Wood Land, with Liberty to cut what Wood may be necessary for Firing. The House has lately been thoroughly repair'd, paper'd and painted it has two Rooms on a Floor of more than 20 Feet each, a very large Kitchen and Dairy Room a large Barn, with good Stable and Coach House, and Conveniences for a large Stock of horn'd Cattle, a Corn House and two Poultry Houses, in a large Poultry Yard well fenc'd, a large Garden handsomely laid out and well stor'd with a Variety of the best Fruit Trees, and newly fenc'd: it is in every Part in thorough good Repair, and suitable for any Gentleman who may incline to retire to an agreeable Neighbourhood, and most pleasing Situation; it stands upon an Eminence, and commands the View of an extensive Interval, terminated by a Hill of Woods. Any Person inclining to purchase the Premisses may apply to RICHARD LECHMERE *of* Boston, *who has Power to dispose of the same.*

N. B. *There is also a large Shop belonging to it suitable for any Sort of Business.*

All Persons who have any De-

mands on the Estate of Captain *Barnabas Binney*, deceased, late of Boston, are desired to bring in their Accounts immediately to his Son *Barnabas Binney*, Sole Executor: And all Persons indebted to said Estate, are desired to make Payment to the same as soon as possible.

LAST Tuesday Afternoon was stolen out of the House of the Subscriber, a Silver Watch, China Face, crack'd across the same, and inside the Case a Print representing Curiosity, with a stript Lutestring Ribbon for a String, a white Stone Seal on the same, with an Anchor engraved thereon, Maker's Name Rob. Rich, London, No. 2971. Whoever shall apprehend the Thief or Thieves, and return the Watch to the Subscriber, shall have Three Dollars Reward.

Malden, July 21, 1774. ELISHA STORY.

FOR L O N D O N,

The Brigantine BETSEY, about 120 Tons burthen, JAMES WISHART Master,

WILL sail from Plymouth with all convenient speed, having the greatest Part of her Cargo on board and engag'd:—For Freight or Passage apply to the Master on board, or at Mr. Solomon Davis's Store in Boston. ———Who has for Sale———

Choice Port and Teneriffe WINE.

ONE GUINEA REWARD.

WHEREAS on or about the 14th Instant, some evil minded Person or Persons entered the North Battery in this Town, and took the Halliards from the Flag Staff—Whoever will discover the Thief or Thieves so that he or they may be brought to Justice, shall be paid the above Reward. NAT. BARBER, Capt.

Boston, July 21, 1774.

F I V E D O L L A R S R E W A R D.

WHEREAS last Wednesday Night the Accompting-House of the Subscriber was broke open, and sundry Things stole, viz. 1 blue Surtuit Coat with Blue Buttons, 1 Thickset ditto without Lining, 1 small Looking Glass, one Beaver Hat, 1 50s. Piece, 2 Dollars and and about 20s. O. T. in Coppers, and sundry other Things. Whoever will give Information, so that the Person who stole them may be brought to Justice, shall have Five Dollars Reward. JOHN NEWELL.

Boston, July 23, 1774.

Four Dollars Reward.

RANAWAY from his Master MARK HUNKING of Barrington, in New Hampshire, a Negro Servant named CÆSAR:—Had on when he went away, a striped homespun lappel'd Waistcoat, a Tow Shirt, black Serge Breeches, grey Jacket, a pair of Breeches and Jacket of a black and Hemlock dye, striped Tow Trowsers, black and white Yarn Stockings. He is a strait Limb'd Fellow about 5 Feet nine Inches high, very white Teeth, smiling Countenance; was bro't up to Farming Work. —Whoever shall take up said Runaway, and secure him so that his Master may have him again, shall have Four Dollars Reward, and all necessary Charges paid by MARK HUNKING.

N. B. All Masters of Vessels and others are forbid carrying him off, as they would avoid the penalty of the Law. *Barrington, July* 12, 1774.

Boston: Printed, by EDES & GILL,
in Queen-Street, 1774.

THE
Boston-Gazette, AND COUNTRY JOURNAL.

No. 1009.

Containing the freshest Advices, Foreign and Domestic.

MONDAY, *August* 15, 1774.

Some further particulars relating to the proceedings at Charlestown, South Carolina, on the 6th, 7th and 8th of July, at the appointment of Delegates to represent and act for that Colony at the General Congress from all the British Colonies in America, to be held in Philadelphia in September next.

CHARLES-TOWN, South-Carolina, July 11.

IN consequence of the advertisements lately published by the general committee, and other proper means used to obtain the sense of the whole colony on the present alarming state of American affairs; on Wednesday last, the 6th instant, the largest body of the most respectable inhabitants that had ever been seen together upon any public occasion here, or perhaps any where in America, (for Gentlemen of the greatest property and character, animated with an ardent zeal to relieve their suffering brethren, and to preserve their own freedom and the birthrights of their posterity, notwithstanding the extreme inconvenience of the season, from even the remotest parts of the country, attended) met at the Exchange in this town, in order to "consider of the papers, "letters, and resolutions that had been transmitted to the said committee from the northern colonies; and also of the steps necessary to be pursued in union with the inhabitants of our sister colonies on this continent, to avert the dangers impending over American liberties in general, by the late hostile act of parliament against Boston, and other arbitrary measures of the British Ministry,"—and, after choosing the Hon. Col. Powel (who had presided at all the former general meetings) for their Chairman, and the same Secretary as had hitherto served, *continued* in solemn deliberation upon these important matters, on that and the two succeeding days, during which the following resolves were unanimously entered into.— [*For the Resolutions, see this Gazette of the 25th ultimo.*]

July 8. It was further unanimously resolved, that copies of all the foregoing resolutions be transmitted to every colony on this continent, from Canada to West-Florida, accompanied with a letter to each respectively, signed by the Chairman, inviting them to unite with us; and that, as Capt. Hunt had voluntarily detained his vessel for some days, on purpose to carry an account of the transactions of the present meeting to New-York, copies of the whole should be delivered to him, together with the thanks of the meeting, which he received accordingly. The thanks of the meeting were also given to Col. Powel, the Hon. Rawlins Lowndes, and the Secretary, after which the general meeting was dissolved.

Upon the 9th resolve, (for naming 5 deputies,) three several questions were put, viz. 1st, Whether the appointment of Deputies was a necessary measure. 2d, Whether they should be invested with the full powers therein expressed. 3dly, Whether the number of Deputies should be five? All which passing unanimously in the affirmative, it was proposed and agreed to unanimously, that the Deputies should be chosen by ballot, and that every free white person residing in the province, should be entitled to a vote? that the poll should be open'd at two o'clock and closed at six. A balloting box was accordingly provided; the votes were received, and at midnight, in presence of several hundred spectators, the election was declared, in favor of the gentlemen whose names are inserted in the resolution.——And that Lord North may not be misinformed in the case, as he has been in most others, by being told, that this was the meeting of a rabble, and the election of a mob, we shall take the liberty here to subjoin a list of the members of our present honorable Commons House of Assembly; all of whom voted except five, who were by sickness or accident prevented from attending. [*Here followed the names of the Commons House of Assembly.*] Besides these, there were at least as many gentlemen, who had been representatives of the people in former assemblies, who voted on this occasion.

In the course of the debates during these important transactions (for every point underwent the fullest discussion) the greatest unanimity appeared; each one considered his neighbour as a free born American, and overlooked all distinctions. As in the deluge of old, the wolf and the lamb swam together, so the sense of our common danger extinguished all private considerations. The set of advocates for the present misguided administration, whose chains had often been heard to clatter in private companies, were all struck dumb, and kept aloof from the public debates. The colony was ready to go into resolutions of non importation, and non exportation if it had been found absolutely necessary; but it was tho't most proper to invest our deputies with absolute power, to agree with the other members of a Congress in any measures; that so they might take place from one end of this extensive continent to the other, on one and the same day: And several of the principal merchants made a public declaration, in behalf of the rest, that, in order to quiet the minds of the people, they were ready and willing to enter into any agreement, not only to desist importing British or East India goods, wines and slaves, but also to countermand all orders already sent, till the event of the Congress should be known; which declaration was received with a loud and general plaudit.—Rejoice ye friends of freedom in GEORGIA! and hasten to do likewise. Be comforted ye oppressed Bostonians! and exult ye northern votaries of liberty! that the sacred rays of freedom, which used to beam from you on us, are now reverberated, with double efficacy, back upon yourselves, from your weaker sister CAROLINA, who stands foremost in a resolution to sacrifice her All in your defence. And tremble ye minions of slavery!—a blow will soon be struck, if you urge us to that extremity, which will convince you, that one soul animates three millions of brave Americans, tho' extended over a long tract of two thousand miles. Ye vainly thought we were a Rope of Sand; but you will find, unless we are put on the same footing with Englishmen, before nine months, millions of people, who depend on America for their daily bread, will curse you with their dying groans.

Three of the present deputies appointed to represent this colony, in a General Congress, to be soon held at the northward, viz. *Christopher Gadsden, Thomas Lynch*, and *John Rutledge*, Esqrs; were our Deputies at the former Congress.

Friday Evening, the new General Committee met, and chose Col. Charles Pinckney, (one of the representatives for the Parish of St. Philip, Charles-Town) for their Chairman, and Peter Timothy, for their Secretary. The said Committee also met this day, when they agreed to have stated meetings, and to sit again on Wednesday the 20th instant, at 6 o'clock in the evening, at the house of Mr. Charles Ramage, and on every other Wednesday after, at the same hour and place.

Copies of the resolutions of the late General Meetings, accompanied with a circular letter, have already been dispatched to every colony on this continent, from Canada to Georgia inclusive.

Three hundred and fifty more barrels of rice are now ready to be shipped, as soon as a proper vessel can be procured to carry it, for the relief of the poor sufferers in Boston.

From the *ESSEX GAZETTE*.

To the G——r.

May it please your Excellency,

YOUR Proclamation of the 29th ult. which you thought fit to issue—"In Tenderness to the Inhabitants of this Province; and to the End, that none, who may hereafter engage in such dangerous Combinations, may plead in Excuse of their Conduct, *that they were ignorant of the Crime*, in which they were involving themselves;" I have carefully perused again and again; and if it were Fact, that the Non-Importation and Non-Consumption Agreements, which the several Towns in this Province are coming into with so great Celerity and Chearfulness, were *unlawful*, and their subscribing the same, an *unwarrantable hostile and traiterous Combination—contrary to their Allegiance due to the King—and destructive of the lawful Authority of the British Parliament, and of the Peace, good Order and Safety of the Community—of high Criminality and dangerous Consequences to themselves*,* all must acknowledge, in this Case, that you have acted the Part of a very tender, benevolent and faithful G——r, in cautioning, &c. the People against entering into such Agreements; but I beg Leave to acquaint your Ex——y, that I am not yet convinced, that these Agreements of Non-importation and Non-Consumption referred to, are unlawful and criminal in any Degree, or in the least contrary to our Allegiance to the King; and I perswade myself, that if your Ex——y, or any other Person, that is a Friend to the British Constitution of Government, English Liberty, the venerable Rules of Justice, the sacred Faith of the King, &c. will condescend cooly to consider the following Facts, the same will and must be of my Opinion, viz.

It is Fact, that our Forefathers, who first came into New-England, fled hither from the Oppression and Persecution of the tyrannic Stuart-Race.

It is Fact, that when they arrived here, they found this Land inhabited by divers Nations of aboriginal Natives, who were the Proprietors & Lords of the Country.

It is Fact, that they purchased both the Soil and the Dominion or Sovereignty of the Country of the Natives, and were at the sole Cost (without any Help from the Crown or Mother-State,) in their Settlement here, and Defence of their purchased Country and Jurisdiction in all the Indian Wars of long Continuance.

It is Fact, that the several Colonies were incorporated into particular distinct States, and became distinct Branches of the British Empire by a sacred Compact betwixt the King of Great Britain and the several Colonies expressed in their respective Charters; in which the King engages his Faith to protect us in the Enjoyment of all the Privileges of his good Subjects inhabiting in Great-Britain, and we engage our Allegiance to him as our rightful Sovereign.

It is Fact, that it is a Privilege of the Inhabitants of Great-Britain to tax themselves for the Support of Government, and to be exempt from all Taxation to be imposed on them, by any other State or Persons whatsoever, without their own Consent. And it is Fact, that the same Privilege is engaged to the Colonists by the King in his sacred Compacts.

It is Fact, that in an Empire, consisting of divers distinct States united to one political Head by a distinct Compact between the said Head & each State; each State must have its particular *Magna Charta* Constitution, or essential Form; from whence it follows as true in Fact, (1.) That all these several States are Sister-States and Fellow-Subjects of the same Monarch equally, though one may be called the Mother State for something merely circumstantial. (2.) That the Mother-State, (so called) has no more Right or Authority to give and grant the Money belonging to any one of the Colony-States, for the Purpose of raising a Revenue to his Majesty without their Consent, than the Colony-States have to give and grant the Money of the Mother-State without her Consent. (3.) That if the Mother-State claims Authority over the Colony States to tax them at Pleasure, without their Consent, the Mother-State does in Effect say, that the Colony-States are not her Fellow-Subjects, but her *Slaves*; to say that we are Subjects of the Subjects of the King, would be a Solecism; but to claim Authority to tax us without our Consent, is to claim more than the King claims of his Subjects; Tyrants claim such Authority over their Slaves. (4.) That if *the King violates his sacred Faith* to, and Compact with any one State of his Empire, *he discharges the same from their Allegiance to him, dismembers them from the Empire and reduces them to a State of Nature*, SO THAT, IN THIS CASE, HE CEASES TO BE THEIR KING, AND HIS GOVERNOR SET OVER SUCH A COLONY AS HIS REPRESENTATIVE, CEASES TO HAVE ANY LAWFUL AUTHORITY TO GOVERN THAT PEOPLE; AND THE PEOPLE ARE AT LIBERTY TO INCORPORATE THEMSELVES INTO AN INDEPENDENT STATE, AND TO APPLY TO WHAT POTENTATE OR STATES THEY PLEASE FOR PROTECTION, AND NO STATE IN THAT EMPIRE HAS ANY LAWFUL AUTHORITY TO INTERRUPT THEM IN IT.

It is Fact, that the British House of Commons, by an Act granting certain Duties in the British Colonies and Plantations for the express Purpose of raising a Revenue to his Majesty, have given & granted our Money without our Consent: And it is Fact, that they claim Authority to tax the Colonies in all Cases whatsoever, and has not his Majesty given his Assent to these Acts? And can this be reconciled with his keeping his sacred Faith inviolate?

It is Fact, that the East-India Company's Teas sent to Boston, in Consequence of another Act of the British Parliament to support the extorted Revenue, would have returned to the Owners without being destroyed here, as well as what was sent to the other Colonies, if Governor Hutchinson and the Consignees had been as prudent and patriotic as the Governors and Consignees in the other Colonies.—

(*See last Page for the Remainder*,)

---

* "*Fully implying, if not expressly denouncing the "the Destruction of all, that refuse to subscribe those unlawful Combinations, tending directly to Sedition, civil "War and Rebellion" &c, as is most falsely asserted by the Worcester Faction!*

By the Mercury Packet, Capt. DILLON, *who arrived at New-York, in 8 Weeks from Falmouth, we have the following Advices.*

The following "Act for the better providing suitable Quarters for Officers and Soldiers in his Majesty's Service in North-America," *has passed both Houses of Parliament and received the Royal Assent.*

WHEREAS Doubts have been entertained, whether Troops can be quartered otherwise than in Barracks, in case Barracks have been provided sufficient for the quartering of all the Officers and Soldiers within any Town, Township, City, District or Place, within his Majesty's Dominions in *North-America*: And whereas it may frequently happen, from the Situation of such Barracks, that, if Troops should be quartered therein, they would not be stationed where their Presence may be necessary and required: Be it therefore enacted by the King's most Excellent Majesty, by and with the Advice and Consent of the Lords Spiritual and Temporal, and Commons, in this present Parliament assembled, and by the Authority of the same, That, in such Cases, it shall and may be lawful for the Persons who now are, or may be hereafter, authorised by Law, in any of the Provinces within his Majesty's Dominions in *North America*, and they are hereby respectively authorised, impowered, and directed, on the Requisition of the Officer who, for the Time being, has the Command of his Majesty's Forces in *North-America*, to cause any Officers or Soldiers in his Majesty's Service to be quartered and billetted in such Manner as is now directed by Law, where no Barracks are provided by the Colonies.

And be it further enacted by the Authority aforesaid, That if it shall happen at any Time that any Officers or Soldiers in his Majesty's Service shall remain within any of the said Colonies without Quarters, for the Space of Twenty-four Hours after such Quarters shall have been demanded, it shall and may be lawful for the Governor of the Province to order and direct such and so many uninhabited Houses, Out houses, Barns, or other Buildings, as he shall think necessary to be taken, (making a reasonable allowance for the same,) and make fit for the Reception of such Officers and Soldiers, and to put and quarter such Officers and Soldiers therein, for such Time as he shall think proper.

And be it further enacted by the Authority aforesaid, That this Act, and every Thing herein contained, shall continue and be in Force, in all his Majesty's Dominions in *North-America*, until the Twenty-fourth Day of *March*, One thousand seven hundred and seventy-six.

LONDON, *May* 24. A gentleman who arrived from Paris says, that when he left that City, which was on Wednesday last, it was asserted as a fact that Madam Barre lay in a convent at the point of death; and it was generally believed there, that something had been given her to put an end to her existence. He further declared, that it was generally believed at Paris, that a war would break out between England and France in less than eight months, especially if the Duke de Nivernois and Choiseul should be at the head of affairs.

May 31. During the late debates on American measures in the Upper Assembly, a noble Duke, remarkably distinguished for his popularity, in the course of his speech, said, "that if the Americans were thus to be treated, he could not help wishing them success in their resistance. Upon which Lord Mansfield got up, and after apologizing for expressions spoken in heat of argument, said, he was very sure the noble Duke would correct himself. His Grace soon after rose, but instead of correcting himself repeated his expression, and formally appealed to the Bench of Bishops, whether it did not well become a Christian to wish relief to all those who were heavy laden.

Letters from Dantzic mention, that the Magistrates of that city had received intelligence of the King of Prussia's being in such a way that it was past the power of medicine to relieve him; but that they had used every precaution to keep it a secret, for fear of the exultations of the populace.

June 1. The report which had been asserted in the papers of Mr. Frazer's being refused to land as English Consul at Algiers, is now said to be without foundation, and that no such advices have been received.

Monday letters were received in town from Falmouth, which mention the arrival of the Hon. William Tryon, Esq; Governor of New-York, in the Mercury packet boat. He has obtained leave of his Majesty to come over, on his own private affairs.

In the House of Commons yesterday, Mr. Baker presented a Petition from Thomas and William Penn, owners of great Part of the Province of Philadelphia, setting forth, That by a bill depending in that House, for the better securing the Civil Government of Quebec, they were apprehensive their Property in the province of Philadelphia would be greatly injured, and therefore praying that the said Bill might not pass into a Law, untill they had been heard by themselves, or Council, against the Bill.

NEWPORT, August 8.

We are assured that Capt. William Bull, in a sloop from this place, but last from the West-Indies, is arrived at Wilmington, N. Carolina, and that the inhabitants of that place have bought his vessel, and are loading her with provisions for the support of the town of Boston; which ought to be supported at the expence of the last mite, and even the last drop of blood in North-America, for their noble stand against the oppression and tyranny of a miserably corrupt, debauched and almost bankrupt administration, devoid of sense, humanity, and every principle superior to that of mere brutes; an administration, compared with whom a common highway robber, is almost a saint.

At a general meeting of the committees of the several counties of this province of New-Jersey, held at New-Brunswick, July 21, 22 and 23, they came into a number of sensible, spirited resolves; appointed Messrs. James Kinsey, William Livingston, John De Hart, Stephen Crane, and Richard Smith, delegates to attend the general congress; strongly recommended a non-importation and non-consumption agreement; and engaged to set on foot collections or subscriptions in their respective counties, for the sufferers of the town of Boston.

NEWBURY-PORT, August 10.

At a Town meeting held Wednesday last, this Town Voted Two hundred Pounds Lawful Money, as a Donation for the industrious poor, who are suffering a political persecution in the Town of Boston.

SALEM, August 9, 1774.

The following is a List of the Gentlemen appointed, by his Majesty, Counsellers of this Province, agreeable to a late Act of Parliament, but in direct Violation of our Charter; viz.

Thomas Oliver, Esq; (Lieut. Governor.	Joseph Green, Esq;
	James Boutineau, Esq;
Thomas Flucker, Esq;	Andrew Oliver, Esq;
Peter Oliver, Esq;	Josiah Edson, Esq;
Foster Hutchinson, Esq;	Richard Leechmere, Esq;
Tho. Hutchinson, Esq;	Joshua Loring, Esq;
Harrison Gray, Esq;	John Worthington, Esq;
Samuel Danforth, Esq;	Timothy Paine, Esq;
John Erving, sen. Esq;	William Pepperrell, Esq;
James Russell, Esq;	Jeremiah Powell, Esq;
Timothy Ruggles, Esq;	Jonathan Simpson, Esq;
Joseph Lee, Esq;	John Murray, Esq;
Isaac Winslow, Esq;	Daniel Leonard, Esq;
Israel Williams, Esq;	Thomas Palmer, Esq;
George Watson, Esq;	Isaac Royal, Esq;
Nat. Ray Thomas, Esq;	Robert Hooper, Esq;
Tim. Woodbridge, Esq;	Abijah Willard, Esq;
William Vassall, Esq;	John Erving, jun. Esq;
William Brown, Esq;	

Province of *Massachusetts Bay*, } *Salem, August* 8 1774.

HIS Majesty having been pleased to appoint the Hon. *Thomas Oliver*, Esq; to be Lieutenant Governor of this Province; his Honor's Commission was accordingly this Day published in the Council Chamber, and the several Oaths administred to him, by his Excellency the Governor. After which the following Gentlemen took the Oaths necessary to qualify themselves for a Seat in Council, being appointed by Mandamus from his Majesty.

Hon. *Thomas Oliver*, Esq; Lieut. Governor.

Thomas Flucker, Esq;	William Brown, Esq;
Foster Hutchinson, Esq;	James Boutineau, Esq;
Harrison Gray, Esq;	Joshua Loring, Esq;
Joseph Lee, Esq;	William Pepperrell, Esq;
Isaac Winslow, Esq;	John Erving, jun. Esq;

BOSTON, August 15.

Wednesday Morning the Hon. Thomas Cushing, Esq; Mr. Samuel Adams, John Adams and Robert-Treat Paine, Esqrs; the Delegates appointed by the Hon. Commons House of Assembly, for this Province, to attend the General Congress to be holden at Philadelphia, some Time next Month, sat out from hence, attended by a Number of Gentlemen, who accompanied them to Watertown, where they were met by many others, who provided an elegant Entertainment for them; after Dinner they proceeded on their Journey, intending to reach Southborough that Evening.

Some Days before the Departure of the Committee for the Congress, Mr. BOWDOIN sent them a Letter acquainting them, That he had had Hopes of proceeding with them to the Congress, but Mrs. BOWDOIN's ill State of Health, occasioned by a long continued Slow Fever, necessitated him to lay aside all Thoughts of it.

The Delagates from New Hampshire passed through this Town the next Day, on their Way to Philadelphia.

Last Wednesday Night, about 11 o'Clock, a Fire broke out in a large Brick Dwelling-House in Fish-Street, near the Old North-Meeting, occupied by Mr. Zachariah Morton, Baker, Mr. Murphy, and a Number of others: The Fire had got to such an Heighth, and raged so furiously, before the unhappy Tenants were apprized of it, that several of them with much difficulty, were obliged to escape out of the Chamber Windows, naked, and some much burnt.—Five others perished in the Flames, viz. Mrs. Ruth Murphy, Wife of Mr. Nicholas Murphy, Mariner, who it is said was far gone with Child; Ruth and Catherine Murphy, her Children; Mrs. Elly Flinn, Wife to Mr. Flinn, now in the Alms-House, and Mrs. Hannah Whittemore, Widow.—The Bodies were taken out of the Ruins next Day, burnt in a very shocking Manner.—The House was soon consumed with most of the Furniture; but it being a very calm Night, and a plentiful Supply of Water, together with the Dexterity of the Inhabitants in the Management of the Engines, &c. the Fire was under Providence, prevented spreading any further.

A Jury of Inquest was summoned on the Bodies, who brought in a Verdict, That said Persons being in a Dwelling-House which accidentally took Fire, and they not having it in their Power to escape, were suffocated and burned, and by that Means came to their Deaths.

We are told that Earl Percy generously offered the Service of a Number of Soldiery, who could be confided in, if the Inhabitants thought proper; but the Regulations observed in this Town, in Time of Fire, rendered their Assistance unnecessary.

We hear that his Excellency Governor Gage desired the Attendance of the Selectmen of this Town at the Province-House on Saturday last; when he informed them of that Clause in the late Act of Parliament, forbidding Town-Meetings, without special Leave of the Governor, and gave the same to them to read; which being done, his Excellency told them he was ready on Application to give Liberty for a Town's Meeting, if he should judge it expedient; and being told, that the Provincial Law had been the Rule of their Conduct in these Matters, He said he was determined to carry the Acts of Parliament into Execution, and they must be answerable for any bad Consequences.

Saturday last 376 Sheep were received from our sympathising Brethren of Lebanon, in the Colony of Connecticut, as a Donation for the Benefit of the industrious Poor in this distressed Town.

Extract of a Letter from a principal Manufacturer in England, to a House in this Town.

"I understand no Goods can be ship'd you from London, as your Port is shut by the late cruel Proceedings of Government, which I hope they'l soon repent of. Your Goods, and a Quantity more made and finish'd for your Markets, are now laying in my Warehouses, until our wise and gracious Governors shall think proper to unshackle Trade with you, which I hope will be soon, or the Consequence must be very disagreeable and distressing to Thousands."

Extract of a Letter from a Gentleman of eminence in London, to his Friend in this Town.

"The late Proceedings relative to the faithful Province of Massachusetts, and the Town of Boston, give general Dissatisfaction, and make many very uneasy, who sincerely wish you the Wisdom and Fortitude your disagreeable Situation requires: Oh for an Increase of the stern Virtue of the noble Ancestors of the present Race of New-England Men, whose Fortitude dar'd every Thing rather than submit to Slavery. I send you this per the Packet, the Barbarity of the Times not admitting the usual Conveyances."

Extract of a Letter from one of the first and best of Men in a distant Colony, to his Friend at Boston.

"You and your worthy fellow-sufferers would receive a glimpse of Joy amidst your distresses to know, with what sympathy the Inhabitants of this Province consider your case. What *never* happened before, has happened now. The COUNTRY PEOPLE have so exact a knowledge of fact and of the consequences attending a surrender of the points now in question, that they are, *if possible*, more zealous than the CITIZENS who lay in the direct line of information. Doubt not, that *every thing bears a most favorable aspect.*

"May God Almighty bless you, and my beloved Brethren in Boston and Massachusetts-Bay. My heart is full. The time will come, I hope, when I may congratulate them on a more stable security of their liberty, than they ever yet have enjoyed.

"Our COUNTRY PEOPLE appear to me to be very firm. They look to the *last extremity with spirit*. It is right they should—if they will submit their resentment to the guidance of Reason."

The Antigua-Mercury of July 2d, says,—— "By an order of the French Court, every tenth acre of land, occupied by the planters in the Islands of Martinico and Guadalupe, is to be applied to rearing provisions, cattle, &c.

We are credibly informed that a deputy sheriff in the County of Bristol said that for a single Joannes he would drive down all the Easton addressers to Gen. Gage and shew them to him in person, having a single writ or execution against every individual man of them.

JULY 18 1774—Departed this Life at *Concord*, Captain JONATHAN HEYWOOD, in the 57th Year of his Age; a Son of the *pious* and much respected Deacon *Heywood* of the same Place, long since deceased.——He was a kind *Husband*, a tender *Father*, a generous and sincere *Friend*—He was careful to maintain the Worship of GOD in his *Family*, and discovered, *even to the last*, an Attachment to the Religion which he profess'd—He was one of those noble *Heroes* who steadily opposed the Steps that were taken in that Place to overthrow the *Order* of the *Churches* in this Land, and was taken away before the Cause was finally and meanly given up.——The Words of the Evangelical Prophet are abundantly verified—*The Righteous is taken away from the Evil to come.* Isaiah lvii. 1.—May Heaven support the *Widow*, and the *Fatherless Children.*

AN EXTRAORDINARY INSTANCE OF GRATITUDE.

Messieurs EDES & GILL,

IN your Paper of 11th of July, we are informed of the generous Intention of the Town of Cambridge to contribute towards the Relief of their distress'd Brethren in the Town of Boston; and that they had chosen a Committee to receive the Donations that might be made for that Purpose. This Act was conformable to the general Disposition of the worthy Inhabitants of that respectable Town. *But it was opposed!* By whom? you will ask. I answer, by that Pattern of Justice, *Gratitude* and publick Spirit, John Dennie, Esq; one of Mr. Hutchinson's favorite Justices; who lately having suffered by Fire, had such a Sum collected for him (one single, no Way remarkably deserving Individual) in the Town of Boston, that if the whole Town of Cambridge will return half as much to the Hundreds suffering here, it will be accounted much more than we can reasonably expect from them.

Gratiam referendam non habito respectu ad pretii magnitudinem, sed ad ingenium et voluntatem conferentis.

DIOTOGENES PYTHAGORAS.

Two Laws, says Seneca, bind Givers and Receivers, the first to forget instantly their having bestowed; the latter, *never to forget* their having received.

A CONTRIBUTOR.

BARLEY.

A Quantity is wanted to be delivered at Beverly or Salem, for which the Cash will be paid on Delivery. Enquire at Store No. 20, on the Long Wharff, Boston; where may be had, Coffee in Barrels, old red Port Wine in Quarter Casks; choice new Flour and Pease in Barrels; a small Consignment of Hosiery and Gloves; all which will be disposed of on the lowest Terms for Cash.

THE Subscriber finding that he could get no Satisfaction in a legal Way, takes the Freedom to acquaint the Pub- lick with the Treatment that he met with at the Boston- Neck Guard, by the Officer of the Guard, Lieut. William Cochran of the 23d Regiment. And he does it the rather on Account of the many Insults, Abuses and Wrongs, that he understands have been daily offered to others.

On the 12th of this Instant, driving his Waggon out of Town, which was not loaded with any contraband Goods, he was, contrary to all Law, stop'd and detain'd by the a- foresaid Officer, near two Hours with his Waggon putting him under Guard, using him with rough and very indecent Language, and not suffering him to go out to give any Thing to his Cattle! some of the Soldiers at the some Time taking a Keg of Rum out of his Cart, which he was oblig'd to consent to their doing after they had propos'd it, to prevent greater Abuse and Wrong, &c. And when set at Liberty by the Officer of the Guard, demanding Satisfaction for this cruel Treatment, all the Satisfaction that he could get, was, That if he did not go about his Business, he would put him under Guard again. Attest.

JONAS WILDER, of Lancaster.

Boston, August 13, 1774.

New-York, July 27, 1774.

Fifty Pounds Reward.

WHEREAS on the 19th of June last past a certain JOSEPH THORP was entrusted at New-York with a considerable sum of money in Half Johannes, of nine penny weight, to be delivered by him at Quebec, and as he has not yet made his appearance there, with other suspicious circumstances, it is apprehended he is gone off with the money. He is a native of England, about 35 Years of Age, six feet high, swarthy complexion, very dark keen eyes, with pimples in his face, and pitted with the small pox, of a slender make, stoops as he walks, talks rather slow, with some small impediment in his speech, wears a wig and is very fond of smoaking. He lived some some time in Boston, from whence he remov- ed to Quebec, assuming the character of a merchant in both places; he was also once in trade in New-Castle, Virginia, and has a brother settled there. He went on board Captain John F. Pruym, for Albany, and landed at Pougheipsciglh, from whence he hired a waggon to carry him to New-Haven—He took with him a blue casamir and dark brown suit of cloaths.

Whoever secures the said JOSEPH THORP in any of his Majesty's goals on this continent, shall be entitled to ten per cent. on the sum recovered, and the above re- ward of Fifty Pounds when convicted. Apply to Curson and Seton of New-York, Joseph Wharton, jun. of Phi- ladelphia, Robert Christie, of Biltimore, James Gibson and Co. Virginia, John Bondfield of Quebec, or Mela- tiah Bourne of Boston. It is requested of those who may have seen this Joseph Thorp, since the 19th of June last past, or know any Thing of the Rout he has taken, that they convey the most early Intelligence thoreof to any of the above persons, which will be gratefully ac- knowledged.

All Masters of Vessels are forewarned from taking him off the Continent.

TO BE SOLD,

A Tract of Land at a Place called

Deer-Island, in Penobscot Bay, containing Six or Seven Hundred Acres, with a Dwelling-House, Corn-Mill, Saw-Mill and a Wharff thereon, the Estate of Capt. Nathaniel Kent, late of Gloucester, deceased. For Par- ticulars, enquire of Sarah Kent, Executor of said Estate.

Glocester, 11th August 1774.

Next Thursday Evening,

TO BE SOLD,

By BENJAMIN CHURCH,

At his usual Place of Sale,

CLOTH Camblets—Calamancoes—Calicoes—Lin- nens—Checks—Muslins—Hard Ware, as Case Knives and Forks—Penknives—Shoe Buckles—Buttons —House Furniture, viz. Feather Beds, Tables, Desks, an 8 Day Clock, Watches, &c. &c.

N. B. A good Chaise and Harness.

THURSDAY EVENING.

All Persons who have any De-

mands on the Estate of Benjamin Chamberlain Bunker, late of Charlestown, Innholder, deceased, are desired to bring in their Accounts immediately to Hannah Bunker, Widow, sole Executrix to said Estate: And all Persons indebted to said Estate, are desired to make Payment to said Administratrix, as soon as possible, in Order for a speedy Settlement of said Estate.

New AUCTION-ROOM, Cornhill.

TO MORROW MORNING, at TEN o'Clock, Will be Sold by PUBLIC VENDUE, At GREENLEAF'S Auction-Room,

A Variety of Goods as usual, two

good Feather Beds. W. GREENLEAF, Auctioneer.

The Sale will begin at Ten o'Clock precisely.

NOTICE is again given, That the Commissioners appointed by the Hon. Foster Hutchinson, Esq; Judge of Probate for the County of Suffolk, to examine the Claims to the Estate of Capt. SAMUEL SNOW, late of Boston, deceased, represented Insolvent, will con- tinue to attend that Service at the British Coffee House, the second Tuesday in the three next ensuing Months, being the three last Months allowed for that Purpose, from 6 to 8 o'Clock in the Evening; that no Person may plead their not having suitable Notice of it.

BOSTON, Aug. 13, 1774. JOB PRINCE. JOHN CARNES.

And all Persons that are indebted to said Estate, or that have Accounts not settled, together with all Freigh- ters, are desired to come and settle the same with John Carnes, at the South-End, Attorney to Sarah Snow, Administrator to said Estate.

Messrs. EDES & GILL. Boston, Aug. 12.

THE CHARTER of this Province has of late been grossly mutilated by the Hand of POWER, without the least Form of LAW; nor would it be much surpriz- ing if the same Power, in the Career of its present In- toxication, should imperiously proceed to stab the most vital Part of it, by declaring our lower House of Assem- bly totally inconvenient, or wanting essential Re-form: more especially, as such an Aim of Assassination stands fair to find SECONDS among ourselves, in this Day, when some of the very Sons of the Massachusetts' dare impi- ously stand forth SWORN ENEMIES to its ancient Con- stitution.

The inclosed Extracts of a Letter from London, may serve to elucidate the ungenerous Principles now prevail- ing among those who expect us to look up to them, as the hereditary Moulders of our Rights and Privileges: And your Publication of them may confirm the spirited Colonists in a vigorous Claim and Support of those Forms of Government in whose Erection they have had a Voice, and which they have experienced to be good.

Your's, J. L.

"GENTLEMEN, Inner-Temple, March 19 1774.

"I have presented the Papers you have done me the Honor of transmitting to me, concerning your desire of having an House of Assembly in the Province of Quebec to my Lord Dartmouth, and have waited upon his Lord- ship at his Levee since I did so; but his Lordship has not informed me of the Sentiments of himself, or any o- ther of his Majesty's Ministers of State concerning your Request; so that I cannot yet transmit to you any In- formation upon that subject. But I conjecture that his Majesty's Servants are of Opinion that the State of the Province is not yet quite ripe for the Establishment of an Assembly, and that they rather incline for the present to supply the want of one by establishing a Legislative Council, nominated by the King, with sufficient Powers to do the necessary Business of the Province, 'till the more natural and constitutional Measure of a General Assem- bly shall appear to them more practicable.——In order to facilitate the Attainment of your Wishes, I here beg Leave to hint to you, that I believe it would greatly con- tribute to that End, if you would previously declare that you conceive the British Parliament to have a compleat Legislative Authority over the Province of Quebec, and that such Authority will continue after the Establishment of an Assembly; and that you and the other Petitioners are willing that every Member of such future Assembly should be required to recognize the said supreme Autho- rity in every Article whatsoever, both of Legislation and Taxation, in the plainest and strongest Terms, before he is permitted to take his Seat. Such a previous Declara- tion would greatly tend to remove the Prejudices now subsisting in the Minds of many People in England a- gainst the Erection of new Houses of Assembly in Ame- rica.——I know nothing that would contribute more to your obtaining an Assembly, than your making a De- claration of this Kind. I hope soon to wait on Lord Dartmouth again, and to hear from his Lordship the King's Answer to your Petition; and when I have re- ceived it, I will transmit it to you without Delay.

I remain, &c.

To the Committee of the Petitioners for an Assembly in the Province of Quebec."

To be sold on very reasonable Terms,

The Hull of a double-deck'd Brigantine

about 146 Tons Burthen, now launched in Taunton- River. Farther enquire of ABIEL SMITH, nearly opposite to the Head of Orange-Tree Lane, Boston, or Mr. JOB SMITH, at Taunton.

For private Sale,

At the New-Auction-Room South Side of the Town-House,

A very great Variety of House and

other Furniture.—The Particulars in our next.

WHEREAS the Committee for managing the Pru- dentials of the Proprietors of New Boston, in New-Hampshire, have received a Request from Ten of the said Proprietors to call a Meeting of said Proprietors for the following Purposes, viz.—To chuse a Proprie- tor's Clerk, the former Clerk being dead.—To chuse a Committee to defend or carry on any Law-Suits that is or may be bro't against them, or to sue any Person or Persons that may be Trespassers on any of their Lands in said Town.—And as two of the Standing Committee are dead, to chuse two in their Room; or to chuse a new standing Committee, as the said Proprietors shall think proper.—And to know if the said Proprietors will direct the said Committee to sell any of their undivided Land.

The said Proprietors are hereby notified to meet at the House of Thomas Harwood's, in Dunstable, on Tuesday the 13th Day of September, 1774, at Ten o'Clock in the Forenoon.

The Proprietors of Silvester Town,

lying on Androsgoggin-River, in the County of Cum- berland, are hereby again notified that said Proprietors, at their Meeting legally held by Adjournment, on the 7th Day of October, 1772, voted a Tax of 30s. on a Right, to be paid to Mr. Charles Turner, Proprietor's Treasurer, on or before the 15th Day of March, 1773, and on the 10th Day of May 1774, voted a further Tax of 20s. on a Right, to be paid to the Treasurer afore- said, on or before the 10th Day of September, 1774: And whereas many of the said Proprietors are delin- quent in paying the former of said Taxes;—therefore unless said Taxes shall be paid to the Treasurer afore- said, on or before the 25th Day of October, 1774; so much of said delinquent Proprietors Lands will be sold at public Sale on said Day, as shall be sufficient to pay said Taxes, and all necessary Charge, at the House of Mr. Daniel Baker, Innholder in Pembroke, at Three o'Clock, P. M. Said Vendue to be adjourned if Occa- sion require.

Per Order of the Committee,

WILLIAM TURNER, Propr's Clerk.

Scituate, August 6, 1774.

WHEREAS the Chaise House of the Subscriber was broke open last Saturday-Night, and stole a Russet-breasted Saddle, Housing half worn, with a Cut in the Seat, ript in the Breast; also a Curb Bridle, with double Reins. Whoever shall apprehend the Thief, and return the Saddle, shall have Two Dollars Reward.

Malden, August 10, 1774. ELIAKIM WILLIS.

To be sold by PUBLIC AUCTION, On THURSDAY the 18th Current, at Three o'Clock in the Afternoon,

Two Chaise, with Harness com-

pleat, 3 good Horses, Saddles, &c. Also a Variety of House Furniture, consisting of Mehogany Leather Bot- tom Chairs, round-about ditto, one very neat Mehogany Hair Bottom Close-stool Chair, two easy ditto, a hand- some Scrutoir, Mehogany Square Tables, Window Cur- tains, Bedding with Curtains, &c. Two Guns, and sun- dry other Articles. Enquire of JACOB WENDELL, near the King's Chapel, who has the Disposal of the same.

N. B. The above Articles may be seen at the House of the late Mr. Richard Surcomb, Baker, the Day before the Sale. MOSES DESHON, Auctioneer.

Daniel Bell,

At his Store near the East End of Faneuil-Hall, Has to sell,

A small Quantity of good Sugar, in

Hogsheads or Barrels, very cheap for Cash.

TO BE SOLD,

A Very handsome Phaeton, with Harness compleat, and a Driver's Seat to be used occasionally;

A Pair of young Bay Horses broke to the Carriage; And,

A fine riding Horse about 15 Hands high, half Blood, and about 6 Years old. Enquire of Edes & Gill.

Province of the Massachusetts Bay. } To the Hon. Samuel Dexter, Esq; one of his Majesty's Justices of the Peace through the said Province.

We the Subscribers, Proprietors of a

Township, granted by the Great and General Court of the Province aforesaid, at their Session in February last, to John Gardner, and others, in Lieu of a Township, Number Six in the Line of Towns between Connecticut and Merrimack Rivers, lost by the late Settlement of New-Hampshire—requests your Honor to call a Meet- ing of said Proprietors to be on Monday the 29th Day of August next, at the House of Jonathan Wood, Esq; Innholder in Stow, at Ten of the Clock in the Fore- noon, then and there to choose a Moderator for said Meeting, also to choose a Proprietor's Clerk, Treasurer, and any other Proprietary Officer; to Grant such Sum or Sums of Money, as may be needful to discharge any Debts already due from said Proprietors, or to discharge any future Demands; to agree on some Method for calling Proprietors Meetings for the future. Also to agree on some Method for laying out said Township into Lots, and to do any other Thing proper for bring- ing forward the Settlement of said Township.

John Whitcomb,
Jonathan Loring,
Henry Gardner,
Abner Cranson,
Micah Keys,
Daniel Hapgood,
Samuel Curtis.

Stow, June 25, 1774.

Province of the Massachusetts-Bay.

SEAL

To Henry Gardner, of Stow,

in the County of Middlesex, Esq; one of the principal Proprietors of the Township aforementioned, GREETING,

In pursuance of the foregoing Application

and Request, you are hereby required to give Notice, in Time & Manner as the Law Directs, to the Proprietors of the Township aforesaid, that they meet at the Time and Place, and for the Purpose expressed in the afore- written Petition. Given under my Hand and Seal, this sixth Day of July, Anno Domini, 1774, and in the Fourteenth Year of his Majesty's Reign.

SAMUEL DEXTER, a Justice of the Peace through the Province of the Massachusetts-Bay.

Stow, July 6th, 1774.

By Virtue of the above Warrant to me directed, The Proprietors above-mentioned, are required to meet at Time and Place above-mentioned, for the Purpose aforesaid. HENRY GARDNER.

Custom-House, Port of Salem and Marblehead, August 8.

Entred In, Decker & Clapp from Barbados. Williams and Waters from St. Nichola. Laha from Halifax. Adams from St. Lucia. Bates & Hatch from Canso. Freeman and Thompson from Quebec. Stevens from Guadaloup. Rolland from Falmouth. Burroughs from New Haven. Furbeck from Jamaica.

Outward Bound. Boyd for Newfoundland. Cook for Philadelphia. Atkins for Quebec. Sanders and Adams for West-Indies.

Burials in the Town of BOSTON, since our last.

Sixteen Whites. One Black.

Baptiz'd in the several Churches, Seven.

High Water at BOSTON, for the present Week.

Monday, 18 min. aft. 5	Friday, 4 min. after, 9
Tuesday, 16 min. aft. 6	Saturday, 4 min. aft. 10
Wednesday, 12 m. aft. 7	Lord's-Day, 58 m. af. 10
Thursday, 10 min. aft. 8	D's first Qr. 14 D 7 Aft.

Colonies.—That the Town of Boston did what they could to procure the Return of it to the Owners, and that it has never been made to appear, that so much as one of the Inhabitants of Boston had a Hand in destroying it! And yet

It is Fact, that the Town of Boston, as the Capital of the Province, has been accused, judged and condemned unheard to suffer a very cruel Punishment by the British Parliament, for the Destruction of those Teas, without the least Trial according to the Rules of Justice in all civilized Nations, whether Protestant, Papal or Pagan!!! It is Fact, Sir, that the Port and Harbour of Boston is now blocked up by Ships of War! That regular Troops are erecting Batteries against the Town upon the Common! By whose Order? The British Parliament? And did not our King give his Assent to this Bill? *And what is all this short of a formal waging and levying War against this Province?* It is not a protecting of us in the Enjoyment of the Privileges of his Subjects in Great-Britain!

It is Fact, Sir, that we have all along been as loyal Subjects to his Britannic Majesty as any he has in his vast Empire—That we like the British Constitution of Government well;—That what we have been striving for is only the Enjoyment of our Charter Privileges—That we sorely lament the Infractions made upon our Charter Privileges, and that we deprecate a being totally and finally broken off from the British Empire.

It is Fact, Sir, that the Colonies and this Province in particular, have all along done their Quota towards the Support and Defence of the British Empire, not only in a Time of War by supplying the Fleets and Armies with Men, but at all Times by our Trade and Commerce, which, it seems, the Mother State of late have looked upon as nothing: Therefore as their Ships and Troops have beleaguered the Capital of this Province in a hostile Appearance, as though they had in *a formal Manner declared War against this State*, IT IS HIGHLY NECESSARY that we should put a Stop to all Trade and Commerce with the Mother-State and with all among ourselves, that shall import from Great-Britain, as inimical to their Country, till the Mother-State shall withdraw their hostile Measures and acknowledge us to be a Sister-State, intitled to the Enjoyment of the same Privileges which they claim as Englishmen, or untill his Britannic Majesty shall be pleased to restore to us all our Charter-Privileges, which, we have never done any Thing, as a People, to forfeit the Enjoyment of.

It is Fact, Sir, that we have not so much as a distant Thought, considered as a People, to submit to the pretended Authority or Claims of the Mother-State to tax the Colonies without our Consent: We know that we are contending for the Rights of Men, of Englishmen and of Christians. And though you did not see fit to appoint a Day of Fasting in Compliance with the united Request of both Houses of the General Assembly, that Ministers and People throughout the Province might on the same Day humble themselves before God for our Sins and Provocations against Heaven, and implore the Almighty Ruler of the World to heal the wide Breach in the British Empire; yet we are determined, in secret, in private and public in our separate Congregations for the Worship of God, to be addressing the Throne of that Supreme Being, by whom Kings Reign, and Princes dedecree Justice, who is higher than the highest, and does regard, when there is "the Oppression of the Poor, and violent perverting of Justice and Judgment in a Province"—who in a singular Manner planted, defended and increased our Fathers, in this Land; and has rebuked Kings for the Sake of his praying People;—and we have not the least Doubt, our Cause being so righteous, but He will arise for our Deliverance, after he has sufficiently corrected and humbled us for our Sins against Heaven.

I beg Leave to conclude with the Words of a Jewish Politician upon divine Record, viz. "And now I say "unto you, refrain from these Men and let them alone; "for if this Counsel or this Work be of Men, it will "come to nought; but if it be of God, ye cannot o-"verthrow it, &c." Acts v. 39 40.

VOX VOCIFERANTIS IN EREMO.*

July 8, 1774.

* The Voice of one crying in the Wilderness.

HALIFAX (NOVA SCOTIA,) July 9, 1774.

Messieurs EDES & GILL,

The Friends to the Cause of Liberty in this Town request the immediate publication of the following in your Gazette.——

ON Thursday the 7th Instant, arrived here the Sloop Molly, Capt Odiorn, Master, from Piscataqua, having on board 27 Chests Bohea Tea, which was Consigned to Edward Parry, of that Place, the Property of the East-India Company; and by said Parry ship'd and Consign'd to G. H. Monk, Clerk of the Supreme Court here, to be by him disposed of to the Inhabitants of this Province, which Consignment, the said Monk most readily accepted, and with the Aid and Assistance of J. C. of this Town, Truckman, secured the said 27 Chests Bohea Tea in a Store belonging to Robert Campbell, who as readily hired his Store for that Purpose, in opposition to several principal Merchants, who had prior Applications for their Stores, and had nobly refused.

Notwithstanding however that the said odious Weed has been here imported and landed in this Town, to the Grief and Distress of many of the Inhabitants thereof, and which was suffered only through utter Inability to prevent it. It is the absolute and declared Determination of a great Number of the most respectable and popular Merchants, Traders & Inhabitants of this Town, on any Account whatever, not only, not to purchase any of the said Tea themselves, but forever to refrain from all and every kind and degree of Dealing & Commerce with any Person or Persons whatever, who may be base enough to prefer their private Interest to the public Welfare, and the liberty of the present, and succeeding Generations, by purchasing any of the said detestable Tea. It would have been an unspeakable Pleasure afforded to the Friends of the present glorious Struggle for Liberty in this Town to have borne their public Testimony in the Face of the World, but the Abridgment of that great priviledge, Town Meetings, utterly prevents; however, the worthy and spirited Sons of Liberty through the Continent of America, who have many glorious Advantages which we earnestly long for, will 'tis hoped accept the comparatively feeble Efforts of their true Friends in this Town, to regain our primitive and rightful Liberties, as British Subjects, which we behold with great Concern, most shamefully invaded and trampled on by our Fellow Subjects in Old England.

And we sincerely wish our American Brethren Success in their glorious Struggles to preserve their Rights and Liberties, and to hand them down to Posterity undiminished.

Messieurs PRINTERS,

Please to insert the following in your next, and you'll oblige your constant Readers.

WHEREAS E——r B——sh *of late moved into the N. W. Precinct of C-mb—e, and is the only one that has sign'd, to our Surprize and Detestation, the Letter of Recommendation of Governor Hutchinson, for his late Administration of Government, which, we think, very erroneous and detrimental to the Province.—We desire therefore, that he, without a humble Recantation for what he has done, would forthwith remove out of said Precinct for Fear the Infection should spread any further*

SONS OF LIBERTY.

The foregoing would have been inserted some Weeks past, but being mislaid, prevented its Publication 'till this Time.

TO BE LETT, VERY CHEAP,

A good Shop towards the South-End:

Enquire of George Trott.

All Persons that have any Demands

on the Estate of Mr. Johnson Jackson, *late of Boston, Distiller, deceased, are desired to send their Accounts to* Joseph Jackson, *at the South-End of Boston, sole Executor to the last Will and Testament of said deceas'd; and all Persons that are Indebted to said Estate are desired to make speedy Payment, as the Executor is determined the said Estate shall be Settled with all possible Expedition.*

WE the Subscribers being appointed Commissioners by the Hon. *John Cushing*, Esq; Judge of Probate for the County of Plymouth, to receive and examine the Claims of the several Creditors to the Estate of *Thomas Clapp*, late of Scituate, Esq; deceased, represented Insolvent, and six Months being allowed to receive said Claims. We do hereby Notify said Creditors, that we will attend upon said Business at the Dwelling-House of Mrs. *Esther Clapp*, in said Scituate, from Three to Seven of the Clock in the Afternoon, on the third Wednesdays of the six succeeding Months.

Scituate, July 29, 1774. *David Little*, Junr. *Increase Clapp.*

To be Sold for want of Employ only,

A likely Negro Boy, about 16 Years

of Age.—He is strong, healthy, good-temper'd, sober and honest;—and, with a good Master would make a very faithful Servant. Inquire of Edes & Gill.

CORNISH's *New England* Cod-Fish HOOKS, &c.

Abraham Cornish

Fish-Hook Maker from Exeter *in* ENGLAND,

ACQUAINTS his Friends and the Public, That he has removed from his Manufactory at the North End of BOSTON, to the Upper Part of CHARLESTOWN, where he continues to make all Sorts of FISH HOOKS, warranted of the best Quality;—being made of the best Wire only, better shap'd to take Fish, and each Hook prov'd before put up, (which is not done in England.) From several Years Experience, they have been found much superior to any imported, and are universally approv'd; for which Reasons, he flatters himself, that all concerned in the Fishery, will favour him with their Custom, as they will thereby promote their own private Interest, and render this Country an essential Service, by establishing a Manufacture necessary to its Prosperity.——For the better accommodating those who may purchase his Hooks, they are Sold by Messirs. LEE & JONES, near the Swing-Bridge in Boston, who will always keep by them a sufficient Quantity to supply the American Fishery.—Said LEE & JONES, have for Sale, a few Hogsheads of Jamaica and Barbados Rum, genuine Kippen's and Rapee Snuff, a Variety of Looking Glasses, a Quantity of Lynn Shoes, a few Cases of blue and white China Cups and Saucers, Corks, Gold and Silver Laces, a Variety of Stone, Glass and Cream-coloured Ware, Silver and Pinchbec Watches, a Variety of Silks, Laces and Muslins, Tambour Muslin Aprons and Ruffles; and a general Assortment of Piece Goods.

ALSO, Nails of all Sorts to be delivered at Marblehead.

WANTED,

A sober, honest Man, of good Character,

that can take Care of Horses and drive a Carriage. He must be well recommended. Inquire of the Printers.

The Estate of Mr. *Benjamin Bagnall*,

late of *Boston*, Watch Maker, deceas'd, being rendered Insolvent, and 6 Months allowed the Creditors to bring in their Claims, and prove their Debts, the Commissioners appointed by the Hon. *Foster Hutchinson*, Esq; Judge of Probate for the County of *Suffolk*, to receive and examine said Claims, give Notice that they shall attend said Service at the British Coffee-House in King street, on the first Tuesday of *August*, and the five following Months from Six to Nine o'Clock, P. M.

Boston, July 28th, 1774.

A Young Woman with a good Breast of Milk, and can be well recommended, would be glad to go into a Gentleman's Family to suckle. Inquire of Edes and Gill.

A Consignment of English GOODS,

Consisting of the following Articles, viz.

An Assortment of Hatt-Trimmings,

striped Damascus Bandanno and Barcelona Handkerchiefs, black Cravats, Knee-Garters, Coat-Bindings, Mohair and scarf Twist, death head and metal Buttons, scarlet Gartering, steel-bow'd Spectacles, Needles and Purse Pins, Scotch Thread, a very neat silver-plated Coffee-Pot, silk Ferrets, worsted and silk Breeches Patterns, silk and thread Hose, striped Swanskins, Men and Boys Felt Hats, &c. &c.

To be Sold very low for Cash. Inquire of

William Palfrey.

TO BE SOLD,

A large & convenient Brick House,

fronting on the main Street in the Town of Providence, in the Colony of Rhode-Island; said House on the Front is three Stories high, has eight Rooms on each Floor, all finished, and in good Order; has, in the lower Story, four Shops for Sale of Goods; and has a good large Garden, and other Accommodations back of it; it might well accommodate several Families. The Owner would take the whole Pay for it in English or West-India Goods. For further Particulars, any Person inclining to purchase, may apply to JOHN FOSTER, Esq; in said Providence. (4w.)

---

50 *DOLLARS REWARD.*

WHEREAS sundry Goods and Merchandize were taken and stolen out of the Store of the Subscriber in Boston, between the 20th Day of May and the 23d Day of July last, to the Amount of £.400 L. M. Part of which Goods and Merchandize were found in the Dwelling House or Store of Jonathan Brewer of Watertown, in the County of Middlesex, Trader. And whereas said Jonathan Brewer hath since made his Escape, and cannot be found. Whoever therefore will take up or apprehend the said Jonathan Brewer, so that he may be prosecuted according to Law for his said Offence, shall be paid the above Reward by me.——The said Brewer is a well-built Man, about 5 Feet and an half High, walks erect, and goes decently dress'd. Had on when he went away (as is supposed) a white Coat, and spotted Jacket and Breeches, his Hair is black and cut short, and he generally wears mix'-coloured Silk Stockings.

Boston, 1st August, 1774. FRED. WM. GEYER.

Fred[k]. W[m]. Geyer & Abr[m]. Burgess,

BEG Leave to acquaint the Public, That they have entered into a Co-partnership, under the Firm of GEYER & BURGESS; and that they have on Hand a general Assortment of English, India and Scotch Piece Goods, which they are determined to sell on the lowest Terms, by Wholesale only, at their Store (the Door below Messirs. Bethune and Prince's) in King-Street, Boston.

Said GEYER requests all those indebted to him, or to the late Company of Frazier and Geyer, either on Bond, Note or Book, to make immediate Payment, otherwise they will be put in Suit. (6 weeks)

August 1, 1774.

---

20 Dollars Reward.

STOLEN out of the Store of the Subscriber, the Night of the 25th Instant, the following Goods, viz. A half Piece superfine blue Cloth, half Piece superfine garnet Cloth, two Bags Buttons, three Dozen Womens fine cotton Stockings, ten Dozen Spitalsfield Handkerchiefs, one Piece Bandanno Handkerchiefs, three Bandanno Handkerchiefs, some Chocolate, Loaf-Sugar, a parcel Codlines, some Metal Buttons.

Whoever will give Intelligence of the above Goods, so that the Owner may have them again, shall be intitled to the above Reward. JOHN WINSLOW, jun.

TO BE SOLD (*Exceeding cheap*) BY

Joshua Blanchard, jun.

At his Store on Dock-Square, BOSTON.

A Quantity of Bread, Superfine Flour,

Philadelphia Bar-Iron, a Quantity of excellent Bacon, and West-India Goods and Groceries of all kinds.

All Persons indebted to, or that

have any Demands on the Estate of Mr. JOHN DE COSTA, late of Boston, Mason, deceas'd, are desired to come and settle the same with us the Subscribers, Executors.

ISAAC DECOSTA,
JONATHAN-ROUSE DECOSTA.
JOSEPH DECOSTA,
ELIZABETH DECOSTA,
JOSHUA DAVIS.

Boston, July 29, 1774.

ABSENTED himself from his Master an Indented Servant, Named JAMES BAYLEY, about 17 Years of Age, five Feet five Inches high, flat Nose, large Mouth and Lips, short black Hair, Walks Lazy and heavy, and is very artful in making Keys to open and pick Locks; Stole and took with him when he went away a Brick coloured Ratteen Coat, a striped red and white Waistcoat, white Linnen Breeches, blue Yarn Stockings, a Pair of thin Pumps, a white Cotton Shirt, with Linnen Sleeves, one Tow Shirt, and a Beaver-tit Hat.——Whoever will take up said Run-away and secure him, and give Information to the Subscriber, so that he may have him again, shall have a handsome Reward and necessary Charges paid by JOHN BLACK.

Rutland District, *July* 25, 1774.

Boston: Printed, by EDES & GILL,
in Queen-Street, 1774.

THE Boston- AND COUNTRY Gazette, JOURNAL.

No. 1010.

Containing the freshest Advices, Foreign and Domestic.

MONDAY, August 22, 1774.

By a Vessel arrived at Philadelphia from Lisbon, we have the following advices, viz.

HOUSE of LORDS. PROTEST.
Die Mercurij, 18° Maij, 1774.

THE order of the day being read for the 2d reading of the bill, intituled, "an Act for the impartial Administration of Justice in the Cases of Persons questioned for any Acts done by them in the Execution of the Law; or for the Suppression of Riots and Tumults in the Province of the Massachuset's Bay, in New-England;" and for the Lords to be summoned;
The said bill was accordingly read a 3d time.
Moved, That the bill do pass,
Which being objected to,
After a long debate,
The question was put, whether this bill shall pass? It was resolved in the affirmative.

Contents —— 43
Not contents —— 12

Dissentient,

1st, BECAUSE no evidence whatsoever has been laid before the House, tending to prove, that persons acting in support of public authority, and indicted for murder, cannot receive a fair trial within the province, which is the object of this bill. On the contrary, it has appeared, that an officer of the army, charged with murder, has there received a fair and equitable trial, and been acquitted. This fact has happened even since the commencement of the present unhappy dissentions.

2dly, Because, after the proscription of the port of Boston, the disfranchisement of the colony of the Massachusett's Bay, and in the variety of provisions which have been made in this session for new modelling the whole polity and judicature of that province, this bill is an humiliating confession of the weakness and inefficacy of all the proceedings of Parliament. By supposing that it may be impracticable, by any means that the public wisdom could devise, to obtain a fair trial there for any who act under government, the House is made virtually to acknowledge the British government to be universally odious to the whole province. By supposing the case, that such trial may be equally impracticable in every other province of America, parliament does in effect admit that its authority is, or probably may, become hateful to all the colonies. This, we apprehend, is to publish to the world, in terms the most emphatical, the little confidence the supreme legislature reposes in the affection of so large and important a part of the British empire. If parliament believed that any considerable number of the people in the colonies were willing to act in support of British government, it is evident that we might safely trust the persons so acting to their fellow colonists for a fair trial for acts done in consequence of such support. The bill, therefore, amounts to a declaration that the House knows no means of retaining the colonies in due obedience, but by an army rendered independent of the ordinary course of law in the place where they are employed.

3dly, Because we think that a military force, sufficient for governing upon this plan, cannot be maintained without the inevitable ruin of the nation.

Lastly, Because this bill seems to be one of the many experiments towards an introduction of essential innovations into the government of this empire. The virtual indemnity provided by this bill for those who shall be indicted for murders committed under colour of office, can answer no other purpose. We consider that to be an indemnity which renders trial, and consequently punishment impracticable. And it is impracticable when the very Governor, under whose authority acts of violence may be committed, is impowered to send the instruments of that violence to three thousand miles distance from the scene of their offence, the reach of their prosecutor, and the local evidence which may tend to their conviction. The authority given by this bill to compel the transportation from America to Great Britain, of any number of witnesses at the pleasure of the parties prosecuting and prosecuted, without any regard to their age, sex, health, circumstances, business or duties, seems to us so extravagant in its principle, and so impracticable in its execution, as to confirm us further in our opinion of the spirit which animates the whole system of the present American regulations.

RICHMOND, PORTLAND,
FITZWILLIAM, CRAVEN,
PONSONBY, LEINSTER,
ROCKINGHAM, MANCHESTER.

LONDON, June 1.

The following are the heads of Lord Chatham's speech in the House of Lords on Friday last on the third reading of the bill for the quartering of the soldiers in North America.

HE began, by taking a very extensive and philosophical view of the first settlements in America, which, he said, had they been planted by any other kingdom than ours, the inhabitants would probably have carried with them the chains of slavery, and a spirit of despotism; but as they were, they ought to be remembered as great instances to instruct the world to what a stretch of liberty mankind will naturally attain when they are left to the free exercise of themselves. He then condemned several parts of the late conduct of the Americans, particularly that of the Bostonians respecting the tea, which he said was contrary to all the laws of policy, civilization and humanity; but though he thus, in the candour of opinion, and on an important question, when every thing should be laid open and impartially examined into, condemned some part of the American conduct, he must reprobate the whole of government's acts relative to taxation; that this was his former opinion, and that he would maintain it till death, That this country had no right under Heaven, to tax America; that it was contrary to all the principles of justice and civil policy, and that neither the exigencies of the state, the growth of power, nor even the acquiescence of the taxes, could justify it upon any occasion whatever. He concluded by going into the conduct of the Rockingham party, which he severely reprehended.

He spoke for an hour and ten minutes, seemed no way impaired in his voice, strength, or oratorial abilities, and was listened to with profound attention.

The advocates for the present administration have industriously circulated a report, that when the Sheriffs of London waited on Lord Chatham, he told them, the present measures against America were exceedingly proper, and the minister would have deserved to loose his head, if he had not acted exactly as he has done; this is precisely the reverse of the truth. That great man declared, that it was to the last degree unprecedented and unjust to punish men without being heard. That the Americans had been always ready to grant supplies when constitutionally required; which he himself had fully experienced. That this country could not exist without her American commerce, which was an ample retribution for our protection. He added, that he was perfectly persuaded that America would never think of refusing obedience to parliament, as long as we abstained from so gross an act of oppression and injustice, as forcing our hands into their purses.

A correspondent observes, that the North American charters, like other literary lumber, will soon be declared no tangible substances.

General Gage, 'tis said, has the most extensive Commission that ever any Governor or Commander was invested with; but from the known humanity of that gentleman, there is no reason to fear that he will make any farther use of it than what duty and justice prompt him to.

By advices from Corsica, it appears that a plot had been formed to cut off all the French in that island, on Ascension Day, which probably would have taken place, but that it was discovered by a young girl, a native of Corsica, anxious for the preservation of her lover, a Frenchman.

Died, a few days since, at Backway, near Cambridge, Philip Billes, Esq: possessed of a considerable fortune, which he had left to two gentlemen, no relations, on condition of seeing him buried under Liberty Tree at Boston, in New England.

Extract of a Letter from a Gentleman of Distinction, dated LONDON, June 1, 1774.

SIR,

IN the absence of ——— I received your favor addressed to him of March 31st per ———, and also your very worthy friend Mr. ———'s letter of April 4, addressed to the same person, thro' the hands of ———, of which you will be so good as to inform him, and at the same time show him this which cannot be an answer to either, as the present plan of ministerial policy is to open letters directed to any friend of liberty, and secrete them if they will answer their wicked purposes.—This goes per the ———, and will be only a short account of facts, on which you are to form your own measures, since I cannot per this conveyance, venture to give any advice, even if it were necessary, but your own good sense and discernment, with the knowledge you have of the temper of America, will direct you infinitely better than it is in my power to do.—The Boston Port Bill, that for taking away every privilege granted your Province by Charter, and the MURTHER BILL, or that which holds out impunity to the soldiers, for massacring all the inhabitants in Massachusetts-Bay, you must receive before this gets to hand.—They require no comment, *as they are the most open and explicit* DECLARATION OF WAR, *that can be made against your province.* In the first instance, that is, against the Boston Port Bill there would have been a full petition from the merchants and traders in London, had it not been from all the Boston merchants, except Mr. Bromfield of your province, refusing absolutely to take the lead, or any part in such petition.—This obstructed any opposition without doors, except from the few North-Americans then in London who did their duty by petitioning against all the Bills in their several stages.—Within doors the first Bill particularly, was smuggled through both houses as fast as possible, with the doors close lock'd and all but members excluded, whenever American business was on the carpet, besides, three writers were hired by the treasury during the whole time and for some weeks previous, to fill all the public papers with virulent abuse against you and the grossest falsehood, in order to inflame the minds of the people that the wicked and treasonable designs (which the ministry meant to make the several branches of the legislature, screen them from the just punishment for, by passing the several above mentioned bills,) might not be observed till it was too late to prevent the mischief. You have not a friend, nor indeed is there one friend even to the liberties of this country in the whole administration; lord ——— notwithstanding his fawning and deceitful expressions to the Americans, is in the cabinet, so determin'd and violent an enemy to you as any in this country. Lord Chatham, Camden & Shelburne entertain the same sentiments respecting America that they formerly did, and what may appear strange, is, nevertheless true, we have made lord ——— a convert to American justice.—The sentiments of the Rockingham party are express'd in their protest against the last bills, which has been sent you.—But the great misfortune to this country as well as America, is, that the Rockingham and Chatham people have no confidence in, or connection with each other, and till they firmly unite there will be no chance of the present ministry being shaken or any other that may be appointed, even if they were all coblers or shoeblacks, for indeed the leaders of the present set are all ——— Adventurers and a worse set cannot be pick'd out of the whole kingdom. The highest and lowest ranks of people in this country are so totally debauched and dissipated that no good can be expected from them, all the virtue and old English spirit that is left among us, is in the middling rank, where you have many friends, and it is to that rank you are to apply, by affectionate memorials and representations to increase your friends & strengthen your interest here; but after all, America must work her own salvation, and the most certain, safe and effectual mode of doing it, is clearly pointed out by our wise ministers, in blocking up the port of Boston—Be calm and determin'd.—This country must feel before they will compel the ministers to do you justice. Six months ago I should have prefer'd your moderate plan of demands, but now 'tis too late, the rubicon is pass'd by, our minister's and Mr. ———'s plan must be pursued, or you must be slaves. I speak my mind with perfect submission to your superior judgment. A bill has been sent from the Lords to the Commons, for regulating the government of Quebec. The bounds of this province are fix'd thus, "All the said territories, islands and countries heretofore " part of the province of Canada in North-America ex- " tending southward to the banks of the river Ohio, west- " ward to the banks of Mississippe, and northward to the " southern boundary of the territory granted to the " merchants adventurers of England trading to Hudson's- " Bay." The bill is perpetual, the ROMAN CATHOLIC is *the only established religion*, with licence in the crown if it pleases, to *tolerate the protestant religion*. The English laws are expressly excluded, except in criminal cases, and the Canadian or French laws are substituted in their stead; the legislature is to consist of the Governor and Council of 17 or 23 members, all appointed during pleasure, and paid by the king.—This bill has been twice read and committed in the lower house, to-morrow it is to be before a committee of the whole house, and I have no doubt will pass into a law as it now stands, tho' council are to be heard and witnesses examined on the part of the British merchants against the use of the French laws; and on the part of Mr. Penn, one of the proprietors of Pennsylvania, against the bounds, as they include a considerable part of his province. You shall have the act by Capt. Scott, in about ten days. The object of this bill is too evident to be doubted; *in the first place to* CUT OFF ALL THE LIBERTIES OF THE REST OF AMERICA, by the means of Quebec, and then by a *coupdemain*, after the example of Sweden, which is infinitely approv'd at our court, *to take away the liberties of this country.* The other day Lord North brought into the house some resolutions which were agreed to be form'd into a bill, to lay a duty of 1s. per gallon on all rum imported into Quebec, from the North-American colonies and foreign colonies, 6d. per gallon on all molasses, from the same place, 6d. per gallon on British spirits, and rum imported immediately from the British West-India Islands, and 3d. per gallon on all molasses from the British West-Indies. He did not leave us to doubt his intentions, because he told them; which were, *to oppress the North-American colonies,* and encourage the trade of Quebec immediately with the West-Indies, and *also to* SET THE NORTH-AMERICAN AND WEST-INDIA IN- TERES AT VARIANCE, *according to the Machiavellian doctrine*, divide & impera.

You will hear again soon from your most obedient, humble servant, and friend,

Last Saturday Evening arrived in this Town Mr. —— Abbot *Express from the worthy & patriotic* Elbridge Gerry, *Esq; late Member for* Marblehead, *to the Committee of Correspondence in* Boston, *with the following Letter and Advices.*

Marblehead, Aug. 20, 1774.

Gentlemen,

CAPTAIN Calley arrived here from Falmouth this Morning, having left the same the 10th of July. I have procured all the Papers which he brought, and think them of too much Consequence to be detained from the Metropolis any Time. I heartily congratulate you on the Dawn of *Reason* appearing in the East, and hope we shall again see *it* in Britain at its meridian Height, and every corrupted Prostitute now in Government as effectually stigmatized by the People, as was wicked Cain under the peculiar Displeasure of his Maker.

When Capt. Calley arrived at Falmouth, America was so unpopular, that the Place was disagreeable to him, there were however Friends to America, but they chose to be silent; a few Days after his Arrival, the Post arrived with Advices of the Quebec Bill, and the Petition of London relative to it, which so incensed the People that they declared for America, and imprecated every Anathema upon it, if it should submit to the late Acts of Parliament. You will find the Sense of G. Britain by the Papers and the highest Tories here change their Notes, declaring since Calley's Arrival, "they will take up Arms if Attempts are made to enforce the Acts", but no Dependence is placed in Men who are looking for a safe Retreat to the *strongest* and not *honest* Side.

L O N D O N, June 22.

This day, his Majesty went to the House of Peers, and gave the royal assent to the several bills which were ready.

After which his Majesty was pleased to make the following most gracious speech to both Houses.

My Lords, and Gentlemen,

"I HAVE observed, with the utmost satisfaction, the many eminent proofs you have given of your zealous and prudent attention to the public service, during the course of this very interesting session of Parliament.

The necessity of providing some effectual remedy for the great and manifold mischiefs, both public and private, arising from the impaired state of the gold coin, induced me, at the opening of the session, to recommend that important object to your consideration: In the several measures you have taken for the redress of those evils, you have sufficiently manifested, as well your regard to the general credit and commercial interests of the kingdom, as to the immediate ease and accommodation of my people.

The very peculiar circumstances of embarrassment in which the province of Quebec was involved, had rendered the proper adjustment, & regulation of the government thereof, a matter of no small difficulty. The bill which you prepared for that purpose, and to which I have now given my assent, is founded on the clearest principles of justice and humanity; and will, I doubt not, have the best effects in quieting the minds, and promoting the happiness of my Canadian subjects.

I have long seen with concern, a dangerous spirit of resistance to my government, and to the execution of the laws, prevailing in the province of Massachusett's Bay, in New-England. It proceeded, at length, to such an extremity, as to render your immediate interposition indispensibly necessary; and you have accordingly, made provision as well for the suppression of the present disorders, as for the prevention of the like in future. The temper, and firmness, with which you have conducted yourselves in this important business, and the general concurrence with which the resolution of maintaining the authority of the laws, in every part of my dominions, hath been adopted, and supported, cannot fail of giving the greatest weight to the measures which have been the result of your deliberations. Nothing that depends on me shall be wanting to render them effectual. It is my most anxious desire to see my deluded subjects, in that part of the world, returning to a sense of their duty, acquiescing in that just subordination to the authority, and maintaining that due regard to the commercial interests of this country, which must ever be inseperably connected with their own real prosperity and advantage.

Nothing material has happened since your meeting, with respect to the war between Russia and the Porte; and it is with pleasure I can inform you, that the very friendly assurances which I continue to receive from the neighbouring Powers, give me the strongest reason to believe, that they have the same good dispositions as myself, to preserve the tranquility of the rest of Europe.

Gentlemen of the House of Commons,

I thank you for the supplies which you have so cheerfully given; and I see, with great satisfaction, that notwithstanding the ample grants you have made for the several establishments, and the compensation which has been so properly provided for the holders of the deficient gold coin, you have been able to make a further progress in the reduction of the national debt.

My Lords and Gentlemen,

I have nothing to recommend to you, but that you would carry into your respective counties, the same affectionate attachment to my person and government, and the same zeal for the maintenance of the public welfare, which have distinguished all your proceedings in this session of Parliament."

His Majesty's Speech being ended, the Lord Chancellor, having received directions from his Majesty, says,

My Lords and Gentlemen,

"IT is his Majesty's royal will and pleasure that this Parliament be prorogued to Thursday the fourth day of August next, to be then here holden; and this Parliament is accordingly prorogued to Thursday the fourth day of August next."

Some of the Populace behaved very rudely when his Majesty was passing from St. James's to the House of Peers, by hissing, groaning, and crying out, "No Popery, No French Government."

June 13. The Lord President of the Council and Lord North were sent for early Yesterday Morning to Kew where they were some Time closetted with his Majesty; said to have been on Account of some very important dispatches received the preceeding Night from Berlin.

It is said the last Ship from Philadelphia brings the worst cold Tea the Ministry ever tasted.

The following is a skech of a popular Nobleman's Speech on American Affairs:

"MY LORDS, *Want of health has hitherto prevented me from giving my sentiments on the several bills which have come under your consideration with respect to America; I hope I may therefore be indulged in the opportunity of travelling out of the line of the present matter of the day. I shall endeavour to speak with tenderness and caution; I know your Lordships can't bear much; I will be, if possible, void of offence.—Was I in Boston I would say they were wrong, to destroy the property of the India Company; I say here, you have been the original aggressors; a Law is past which may seal my lips; but were I to speak what I think, and what I know to be constitutional, I would tell you—you have in weakness written a dead letter—you have set up an image which you dare not own, and which the people of America laugh at; I would tell you, you have no right to touch the pocket, much less the life, of a fellow subject in America; he submits himself to the necessity of your laws relative to trade, and the regulation of a national Commerce, because he sees the necessity; he agrees to buy the Wool, employ the Weaver, and to be measured by the Taylor you recommend; but when he has put on his clothes, he says they are his own; he says, you shall not have his coat, because he is no longer sure of his waistcoat and breeches.*

"*My Lords, you have lived upon the support and industry of America these forty years; you have the great materials of commerce not only cheaper from America than you used to have them from other countries, but you pay for those materials with wrought goods, which over-balances the account, and draws from them every shilling they have. This is the great, the solid, the supporting, the salutary contribution which America pays, and which saves this venerable fabrick from falling into the dust. They will either laugh at, or resent your present measures with equal success: if they have coolness they will make you sensible of what you loose; if they have recourse to arms, you must be the first, perhaps the only sufferers; you must be undone; they may work out their salvation; I am an old man in public business, my advice arises from experience; it may be worth something; recall your scanty forces from the wretched employment of murder; they are neither able or willing to execute your commands; be friends with America for your own interest and your own safety; you will want her affection when her sword is turned against you; a few ragged Highlanders obliged you to call upon a Royal General, and a body of disciplined troops, to save this country; half a milion of brave and desperate men nursed to arms must eventually prevail. I have one word for that Rev. Bench. I want to know how they reconcile it to the true principles of Christianity, to spill the blood of America like water.*" [*Quere.* How similar this to the Account of L—d C——m's Speech given the Public by that vigilant Collector of authentic Particulars, Mrs. MARGARET DRAPER, vid Mass. Gazette, Aug. 11.]

June 20. By a Vessel that sailed from New-York May 14th, information had been received, that an account of the Boston Port-bill had just arrived there; that the country was extremely inflamed at that severe act; that a Meeting was to be held the next day; and that a non-importation association, it was imagined, would be unanimously agreed to by all the Colonies.—A measure that cannot fail distressing, to the last degree, the unhappy manufacturers of this country.

Our Custom-house laws will, it is said, undergo a revision, in order to receive certain amendments essential to our commercial convenience.

It is reported, that some of the ablest in the Ministry were against bringing on the business of the Quebec bill at that time, as it will throw a great weight in the popular scale at the next general election, and will cost many of the present majority their seats in parliament.

Betts are five to four at the West end of the town, that the Bostonian and Quebec Bills turn out the Ministry before Michaelmas day next; and five to one, war or no war, that they are *outed* before the first of January 1775.

Yesterday the Lord Mayor, Alderman Crosby, Lewes, and Plomer, the Recorder, upwards of 150 of the Common Council, and City Officers, went in procession from Guildhall to St. James's (Alderman Sawbridge joined them in the way) in order to present an address and petition to his Majesty, previous to going to the House, relative to the bill for the government of Quebec. They arrived at St. James's a quarter before one. A little before two the Lord Chamberlain waited on the Lord Mayor with a message from the King, which he had committed in writing, in order to prevent any mistake; it was read, and the purport was, that as the prayer of the petition was relative to a bill that had passed both Houses of Parliament, he could give no answer; the Lord Mayor immediately sent the Remembrancer to present his duty to the King, and inform his Majesty, that they waited to present their Address agreeable to his Majesty's order, which in a little time was complied with; and it was read by the Recorder.——After the Petition was read, an answer was given, said to be in purport as follows: That as the business on which they came was before Parliament, his Majesty could say nothing farther to the petition.

June 25. It may be depended upon, that a Great Personage has signified his displeasure by letter, on the D— of G———r's dividing against the Canada bill.

Hints of restoration, if asked for, have been made to Dr. Franklin, but declined.

June 27. The Quebec act is the only statute which has been passed these two hundred years to establish Popery and arbitrary Power in the British dominions.

Orders were sent off to Ireland in the course of last week for four more regiments to hold themselves in readiness to embark for Boston on the first notice.

By the most authentic accounts from Boston we learn, that the method the Bostonians mean to defeat the late acts passed by the British legislature, is not by absolute resistance, but by a deep laid system of combination with the other colonies to break off all commercial intercourse with their mother country.

Capt. Chubb, arrived at Bristol, on the 11th May, took up a Boat, having on board Capt. Andrew Greave, of the Sloop Jenny, belonging to Falmouth, New-England, with his crew, 6 in number, whose vessel was cast away as they were going into Tobago.

June 28. The Quebec bill, says a correspondent, is only a well concerted scheme to give a check to the rest of our colonies, and to keep them in awe——a difference in religion, laws, and dependency, will keep up a strong animosity; and there is no doubt but every encouragement that can possibly be afforded to these licensed slaves, these children of Popery supported by a Protestant Court, will be given, in order to subdue these head-strong Colonists who pretend to be governed by English laws.

Since the Parliament broke up, orders have been sent to all the manufacturing counties to postpone the completion of the commissions which were executing for American exportation.

June 30. The most intelligent merchants in the Boston trade are of opinion that if the port of Boston is shut up six months, the trade will be irrecoverable, and there is no suffering the act to take place under a three months exclusion from trade; so that they have a most ticklish part to act.

We are assured that the naval preparations at the different seaports have been ordered to be expedited ever since the arrival of the intelligence from Boston.

Yesterday afternoon arrived off Dover, the Minerva, Callahan, from Boston for London, and with him Governer Hutchinson and Family, who immediately set off for town, and arrived here this morning.

July 2. When the Jew bill passed, there was but one dissentient Bishop; when popery was lately established by an act of Parliament there was not even one.

DIED.] Yesterday Morning, at Holland House, the Right Hon. Henry Fox, Lord Holland, Baron of Foxley, in Wilts, Clerk of the Pells in Ireland for life, and also for the lives of his two sons. His Lordship is succeeded in title and estate by his eldest son, Stephen Fox, Esq; now Lord Holland, which vacates his seat in Parliament for the city of Salisbury.———Wednesday last, in the afternoon, at his house at Little Ealing, Zachary Pearce, D. D. Lord Bishop of Rochester, aged 84.

It said that the names of those who voted for the Quebec bill are circulated in almost every city and borough in England and Scotland; and the next general election will determine whether the Pope or the voice of the people is to chuse a British Parliament.

July 5. They who know the City of Boston well, know that the Merchants who signed the Address to Governor Hutchinson, consisted of 124 Gentlemen, and they who are acquainted with the Town well know that the far greater Part of the Gentlemen of Property are in that List. [*Every Body knows* (the Addressers excepted) *that this is an infamous Lie.*]

July 6. We are confidently assured the Parliament will be dissolved very soon after the prorogation of it.

The designs of the Ministry can be no longer a secret; they have already in fact, though not in form, declared war against the North Americans; for in the duties proposed to be laid on all rums imported into Quebec, they have put the French, Danish, and Dutch, on a level with those from America, six-pence per gallon being the duty intended for each.

Since the accession of the present French King to the throne of that kingdom, there have been several messengers sent from hence to Lord Stormont at Versailles. It seems as if there was a necessity of temporising greatly; and it will be well if his Lordship suffers no great perplexity from such a variety of instructions and orders.

Upon the King's giving his royal assent to the obnoxious Quebec bill, and thereby breaking his coronation oath, led me to enquire the framers and advisers of it; when it was said the Scotch were the first that framed and advised it. Our resentment then ought to fall upon them, who, not content with having every place of profit both in and out of the kingdom, are, *weazel-like*, sapping, undermining and subverting this once happy constitution. Is there an Ambassador scarce abroad but is Scotch, a Governor or Consul but what are Scotch? Look at home, you will see them in the most lucrative employs, and the navy and army filled with them. Is there a command in the navy given but a Scotchman has it; the same likewise in the army? All this is not to be wondered at: If the Thane and Jefferies issue their mandate to the respective First Lords of the Treasury and Admiralty, the Secretary at War, &c. it must be complied with, for they hold *their places* upon no other tenure. Therefore, until the Thane and the Jefferies have lost all confidence of their master's ear, the Scotch will ever be promoted in preference to the English. So prone to tyranny and absolute power are the Scotch, that *even* the Dey of Algiers would not suffer the Consul Frazer to land there for fear of being deposed by him.

N E W - Y O R K, August 15.

We hear that two of the Delegates to attend the Congress at Philadelphia the first of next Month, are arrived there from Charlestown, South-Carolina.

The Assembly of the Lower Counties upon Delaware, have appointed Cæsar Rodney, Thomas M'Kean, and George Read, Esquires, their Deputies at the Congress.

Saturday Morning last the Sloop Phœnix, Capt. Dickinson, arrived here in 13 Days from Charles-Town, in South-Carolina, and has brought 376 Barrels of Rice, to be sold in this Place, and the neat Proceeds thereof to be remitted to Boston; being a Present from the People of Carolina to the Sufferers in the Province of the Massachusetts-Bay.

Collections are now making in the different Wards of this City for the like laudable Purpose; and the Committee of this Place have sent Circular Letters to all the Counties in our Government to accelerate Measures of a similar Kind.

WILMINGTON, (North-Carolina) July 20.

On Thursday last, a subscription was begun for supplying the Inhabitants of the town of Boston with a quantity of provisions, thereby to administer to the relief of the poor of that place, who, by the entire stagnation of trade occasioned by the infamous Port bill, are now deprived of the means of obtaining a subsistence by their daily labour; when in a very short time, a considerable sum was subscribed by several of the Inhabitants of Cape Fear for that charitable purpose. Parker Quince, Esq; of Brunswick, has upon this occasion, offered a vessel to convey the provisions with out a farthing expence to the subscribers, and Captain Budd & his Sailors have agreed to navigate her to Salem gratis.

BOSTON, August 22.

We hear that at a Meeting of the CADET COMPANY last Week, a Letter was laid before them from Mr. Secretary Flucker to Col. Hancock, acquainting him that the Governor had no further Occasion for him as Commander of that Corps. Upon which the Company voted a Committee to wait on his Excellency with a Message, informing him, that in Consequence of his extraordinary Dismission of their first Officer, they had judged proper to return the Standard, which as Commander in Chief he had presented the Company on his taking the Chair, and to acquaint him they no longer considered themselves as the Governor's independent Company of Cadets. We expect to be able in our next Paper to gratify the Public with the Particulars of this Affair.

Amidst all our Calamities this Town has had the satisfaction to be visited by two of the greatest Military Characters of the present Age, viz. CHARLES LEE, Esq; formerly an Officer in the British Service, and since the Reduction of the French Settlements on this Continent, being still fond of improving his Talents in that Way, he went to Poland, served the King several Years in Quality of Aid du Camp, and had a General's Staff conferred upon him, by that great, that virtuous and unfortunate Prince : The other Hero is the Renowned Col. PUTNAM, so well known throughout North-America that no Words are necessary to inform the Public any farther concerning him, than that his Generosity led him to Boston, to Cherish his oppressed Brethren and Support them by every Means in his Power ; a fine drove of Sheep was one Article of Comfort he was commissioned to present us with.

General Lee set off for the Southern Colonies last Wednesday Afternoon.——Colonel Putnam returns to Pomfret in Connecticut this Day.

Extract of a Letter from Newport, Rhode Island, Aug. 19.

"Capt. Budd, in a Sloop from Wilmington, North-Carolina, arrived here last Tuesday, with a Load of Provisions for the Poor of the Town of Boston ; the Captain being sick is the Reason why she has not sailed again for Salem. The Tories in this Town, and some other Parts of the Colony, are endeavouring to prevent any Grant being made by our Assembly, and we are to have a Town-Meeting this Day to instruct the Deputies to vote for a Grant for the Town of Boston. Our present Assembly, last Session, promised they would assist the Town of Boston; and as this Assembly can never exist again, after next Week, if they don't do something, they will sink themselves into the lowest degree of Contempt."

By a Gentleman just arrived from Barbadoes, we are informed that the inhabitants of that place approve of the conduct of the Bostonians in asserting their liberties, and commend us for our resolution to suspend trade with them, and are determined to turn their cane ground into provision ground, and acknowledge it would be best for us to stop all exports and imports to and from the West Indies——that Antigua had remonstrated home against the acts as unjust, and there was a strong talk of doing the same at Barbados.

Last Monday Week when the Hon. ISAAC ROYALL, Esq; was informed by the Governor, that he was appointed by his Majesty's Mandamus, to be one of the Majesty's new Council, he, as a worthy Patriot, absolutely declined accepting a Seat at the new appointed Board.

Tuesday last the following Gentlemen took the Oaths requisite to qualify them for their Seat at the Council Board, viz.

Samuel Danforth, Esq;   Timothy Paine, Esq;
Peter Oliver, Esq;   Abijah Willard, Esq;
Richard Lechmere, Esq;   Thomas Hutchinson, jun. Esq;
Jonathan Simpson, Esq;   John Murray, Esq;
Josiah Edson, Esq;   Daniel Leonard, Esq;
Nathaniel Ray Thomas, Esq;   George Watson, Esq;
Timothy Ruggles, Esq;

Departed this Life the 20th Instant, Mr. WILLIAM MAXWELL, aged 61. His Funeral is to be To-Morrow Afternoon, at 5 o'Clock, from his House in King-Street, where his Friends and Acquaintance are requested to give their Attendance.

Died last Monday Evening at Concord, Thomas Whiting, Esq; of that Place, aged 58.

TO BE SOLD
By JOHN BAKER,
in Back-Street,

About 400 Quintals of good Merchantable and Jamaica Fish, either by large or small Quantities.

ALL Persons indebted to the Estate of Capt. William Wingfield, late of Boston, Merchant deceased, are desired to make immediate Payment to Edward Procter, Sole Executor of his last Will :——And all those who have any Demands on said Estate, are desired forthwith to bring them in to said Executor, in Order to a speedy Settlement. Boston, Aug. 20. 1774.

All Persons who have any Demands on the Estate of John Englesby, *late of Boston, Mariner, deceased, are desired to bring in their Accounts to* Cuthbert Englesby, *of said Boston, Administrator to said Estate : And all who are indebted to said Estate are desired to make immediate Payment to said Administrator.*

James Henderson

ACQUAINTS his Customers and others, That he has to sale a compleat Assortment of *English, India,* and *Scotch* GOODS, suitable to all Seasons, which he will sell by Wholesale and Retail, cheap for Cash, at his Shop in Ann-Street, BOSTON.——Amongst which is——

A beautiful Assortment of Brocaded SILKS, Ducapes, strip'd, plain and changeable Lutestrings, Sattins and Modes of all widths, a fine Assortment of the newest Fashion Ribbons, to be sold very low, plain strip'd and flower'd Muslins, &c. &c. &c.

TO BE SOLD,
By Capt. *Jeduthen Baldwin, of Brookfield,*

And may be entered upon immediately ;

A FARM in Shutsbury, containing about 137 Acres of choice Land, 40 Acres of it is the best of Land for Plowing. There is about 50 Acres that will make the best of Mowing, all well Watered. There is a low House with a Cellar under the whole neatly Stoned, the Chimney is set on an Arch. There is three Rooms with Fire Places, besides a Bed-Room. There is a pretty young Orchard that made a few Barrels of Cyder last Year. There is about eight Acres of the said Place planted with Corn, and sow'd with Grain this Year, and five Acres more cleared to be sow'd this Fall with Rye and other Seeds. There is a few Loads of Hay cut there this Year, and Pasturing for a few Cattle. The Whole may be had now for about £.1200 Old Tenor.

A GREAT PENNYWORTH !

Also to be Sold——About 130 or 150 Acres of choice Land for Pasturing, on Coy's-Hill, in Brookfield, that is well fenced, and divided into several Pastures, well into Grass.

FOR LONDON,
The Brigantine KATY, 100 Tons Burthen,
JOHN DAVIS, Master,

WILL sail from Plymouth with all convenient Speed, having the greatest Part of her Cargo on Board and engag'd :——For Freight or Passage apply to the Master on Board, or at Mr. Solomon Davis's Store in Boston.

WHEREAS Jonathan Fales of Walpole, in the County of Suffolk, a Non Compos Mentis, did on the Fifteenth Day of June last, leave his House and Family in said Walpole, and has not been Home since. The said Fales is a large fat Man about 5 Feet 10 Inches high. Had on when he went away, a brown Home-made Coat, without a Jacket, stript Linnen Breeches and a grey Pair of Stockings. If any Person will be so kind to a distressed Woman as to bring him home (without abusing him) or give Information that he may be found they shall be honorably rewarded, by me the Subscriber. ELIZABETH FALES.

Walpole, the 19th of August, 1774.

TO BE SOLD OR LETT,

A large handsome Double House, pleasantly situated in Medford, together with one Acre of Land, with a Garden and Barn thereon, about a Quarter of a Mile West from the Meeting-House. Enquire of Samuel Reaves, living near the Premises.

Next Thursday Evening,
TO BE SOLD,
By BENJAMIN CHURCH,
At his usual Place of Sale,

CLOTH Camblets——Calamancoes——Calicoes——Linnens——Check——Muslins——Hard Ware, as Case Knives and Forks——Pen knives——Shoe Buckles——Buttons——House Furniture, viz. Feather Beds, Tables, Desks, an 8-Day Clock, Watches, &c. &c.

N. B. A good Chaise and Harness.

THURSDAY EVENING.

BOSTON, August 15. 1774.

STOLEN out of the Pasture of the Subscriber last Night, or this Morning, a light brown Horse, about 14 Hands high, black Tail and Mane, except a small white Lock in the Mane, near the Withers, has a little Blemish in his off Eye, is rather short of his Bigness, Paces chiefly, answers to the Name of Bonne ; he is about 13 or 14 Years old.——The suspected Thief is a short thick Fellow, wears a reddish coloured Coat, a Bob Wig, is bow-legged, sometimes calls himself a Dutchman and at others a Carolinian. Whoever shall bring the Horse to me, shall have FOUR DOLLARS Reward, and TEN DOLLARS for the Thief on Conviction, and all necessary Charges paid by
JOSEPH BRADFORD.

THIS DAY,

At THREE o'Clock will be sold by Public VENDUE, at Mr. Jackson's Store in King-Street,

A Quantity of Brown, China, Stone, and Earthen WARE. R. GOULD, Auctioneer.

At GOULD's *Auction Office,* In Back-Street,
On FRIDAY Next,
At Ten in the Morning,
Will be Sold by PUBLIC VENDUE,

A Variety of Houshold Furniture,
ALSO, Some ENGLISH GOODS.
R. GOULD, Auctioneer.

For PRIVATE SALE, at said Office,

A few handsome Needle Worked Aprons, one exceeding neat Chaise fit for any Gentleman, a small Invoice of Patent Medicines warranted fresh and genuine.

THIS DAY PUBLISHED,
THE FOURTH EDITION,
(Price 9d.)
And sold by EDES and GILL, in Queen Street,

CONSIDERATIONS
ON THE
MEASURES CARRYING ON
WITH RESPECT TO THE
BRITISH COLONIES
IN
NORTH-AMERICA.

There is neither King or Sovereign Lord on Earth, who has beyond his own Domain power to lay one Farthing on his Subjects without the grant and consent of those, who pay it; unless he does it by tyranny and violence.

Phillippe de Commines, Ch. 108.

THIS is a most masterly performance, written since the framing the several Acts against BOSTON and AMERICA, and the best calculated to convince the Ministry, the people of England, and all the world, of the absurdity and wickedness of the late acts, and ruinous consequences, to England at least, that would certainly attend their being carried into execution.

Our last accounts say, this pamphlet has had a wonderful effect in removing the prejudices and convincing the people of England.

TO BE LETT,

A Neat genteel Brick Tenement in Cambridge Street, near the Orange-Tree.
Enquire of Edes & Gill.

TO BE SOLD

A Right of Land containing about 500 Acres, in a Township granted by the Great and General Court, of the Province of Massachusetts-Bay, to Samuel Livermore, Esq; and others, lying on both sides of Androscoggin River, adjoining Sylvester Township, in the County of Cumberland. Inquire of the Printers.

For private Sale,

At the New-Auction-Room South Side of the Town-House, viz. Houshold Furniture, Consisting of PARLOUR, Chamber, and Kitchen Furniture, such as Looking Glasses, Tables, Chairs and Book-Cases, Desks, Pewter, Brass, Copper, Iron and Tin Ware of all sorts, a genteel 8-Day Clock, Gold, Silver and Pinchbeck Watches, a Barometer, a Number of Iron Weights, (Quarters, half Quarters and 7 Pounds,) Plate, viz. a genteel Silver Nearm, Tankard, Cassing-dishes, Porringers, Salts, Pepper Boxes, Sugar Tongs, strainer, Silver Hilted Swords ; new and second-hand Guns and Bayonets, Beaver and Gold Lac'd Hatts, Silver and Bone Handle Knives and Forks ; ENGLISH GOODS, viz. Irish Linnens, Broad Cloths, Forrest ditto, white Flannel, purple, olive and black Cotton Velvets, Chintz, Callicoes, Shaloons, Callamancoes, Tammies, Stuffs, Durants of all Colours, Silk, Cotton, Thread & Worsted Hose, Capuchin Silks of all Colours, Sarsnets of all Colours, Silk Gauzes, Lawns, Dimothy's, black Sattin and Chip Hatts, printed Table Cloths, Breeches Pieces, Pound Threads, white and clouded Riding Hatts, Mens black Bags, handsome Ribbons, a handsome Garter, Ducapes, Bodices, Pound Silks, white and black Silk Gloves and Mitts, Cafe Wax Work ; Women's Wearing Apparel, viz. Dark Tabby Gown and Apron, Brocade, blue Lutestring, Negligee, Sattin Quilts, a Lutestring Sack, Damask and Diaper Table Linnens, Pillow Cases, Cotton and Linnen Sheets, white Counterpins, a handsome Camp Bedstead and Curtains compleat, Men's Second-hand Wearing Apparel, and a Variety of other Articles.——

Also, Damascenes and Tobines, choice Indigo and Pepper, by the Hundred or Dozen, Claret WINE per Cask, Groce or Dozen.

N. B. At said Auction Room constant Attendance is given to receive all Kinds of Goods for private and public Sale.

NOTICE is again given, That the Commissioners appointed by the Hon. Foster Hutchinson, Esq; Judge of Probate for the County of Suffolk, to examine the Claims to the Estate of Capt. SAMUEL SNOW, late of Boston, deceased, represented Insolvent, will continue to attend that Service at the British Coffee House, the second Tuesday in the three next ensuing Months, being the three last Months allowed for that Purpose, from 6 to 9 o'Clock in the Evening ; that no Person may plead their not having suitable Notice of it.

BOSTON, Aug. 13. 1774.   JOB PRINCE.
                           JOHN CARNES.

And all Persons that are indebted to said Estate, or that have Accounts not settled, together with all Freighters, are desired to come and settle the same with John Carnes, at the South-End, Attorney to Sarah Snow, Administratrix to said Estate.

All Persons who have any Demands on the Estate of Benjamin Chamberlain Bunker, *late of Charlestown, Innholder, deceased, are desired to bring in their Accounts immediately to* Hannah Bunker, Widow, *sole Executrix to said Estate : And all Persons indebted to said Estate, are desired to make Payment to said Administratrix as soon as possible, in Order for a speedy Settlement of said Estate.*

Burials in the Town of BOSTON, since our last.
Six Whites.   No Blacks.
Baptiz'd in the several Churches, Five.

High Water at BOSTON for the present Week.
Monday, 50 min. aft. 11   Friday 23 min. after. 3
Tuesday, 48 min. aft. 12   Saturday, 10 min. aft. 4
Wednesday 45 m. aft. 1   Lord's Day, 55 m af. 4
Thursday, 30 min. aft. 2   Full ☾ Yesterday 10 M.

AT a Meeting of the Town of Plimouth, *aſſembled and held at the Court-Houſe in* Plimouth, *on Monday the Fifteenth Day of* Auguſt, Anno Domini, 1774. *by Virtue of a Warrant from the Selectmen of ſaid Town, dated the 28th Day of* July *laſt.*

AT ſaid Meeting, *VOTED*, That whereas a certain Publication in the Maſſachuſetts Gazette, of July the 14th laſt, purporting to be the cordial Congratulations of the Juſtices of the Courts of General Seſſions of the Peace, and Inferiour Court of Common Pleas, for the County of Plimouth, to his Excellency *Thomas Gage*, Eſq; on his Appointment to the high Office of firſt Magiſtrate of this Province, &c. contains injurious Reflections on, and illiberal Inſinuations concerning the Body of the Clergy, and the Committees of Correſpondents, in the ſeveral Towns in this Province, as if the ſaid Committees had aſſumed a Title, and Buſineſs, without the Appointment of their ſeveral Towns, and had been encouraged and ſupported by the Clergy in an unjuſtifiable Influence on the People. We the Inhabitants of the Town of Plimouth, the Capital & Shire Town of ſaid County, conceive it our Duty to bear our Teſtimony againſt ſaid Publication, its Aiders and Abettors. And therefore,

VOTE and *RESOLVE*, 1. That we ourſelves, and we conceive by far the greater Part of the County, have a great Reſpect for the Clergy in this Province, and the Conduct of a Majority of them, relative to the political Circumſtances of the Country.

2. That the Committee of Correſpondence of this Town, and we conceive thoſe of the other Towns, where they ſubſiſt, are regularly appointed by their ſeveral Towns, for very valuable Purpoſes, and have anſwered the Expectations of their Conſtituents, and are therefore intitled to Countenance and Reſpect from all Men, and Bodies of Men.

3. That the ſolemn Leagues and Covenants, entering into, appear to us, calculated to increaſe the Honour and Dignity of our Sovereign, to promote the true Intereſt of our parent Country, and to reſtore the Harmony of Society.

A true Copy, Atteſt.

EPHRAIM SPOONER, Town-Clerk.

TO BE SOLD,

A Tract of Land at a Place called

Deer Iſland, in *Penobſcot Bay*, containing Six or Seven Hundred Acres, with a Dwelling-Houſe, Corn-Mill, Saw Mill and a Wharff thereon, the Eſtate of Capt. *Nathaniel Kent*, late of *Glouceſter*, deceaſed. For Particulars, enquire of *Sarah Kent*, Executor of ſaid Eſtate.

Gloceſter, 11th Auguſt 1774.

To be ſold on very reaſonable Terms,

The Hull of a double-deck'd Brigantine

about 146 Tons Burthen, now launched in Taunton-River. Farther enquire of ABIEL SMITH, nearly oppoſite to the Head of Orange-Tree Lane, Boſton, or Mr. JOB SMITH, at Taunton.

WHEREAS the Committee for managing the Prudentials of the Proprietors of New Boſton, in New-Hampſhire, have received a Requeſt from Ten of the ſaid Proprietors to call a Meeting of ſaid Proprietors for the following Purpoſes, viz.—To chuſe a Proprietor's Clerk, the former Clerk being dead.—To chuſe a Committee to defend or carry on any Law-Suits that is or may be bro't againſt them, or to ſue any Perſon or Perſons that may be Treſpaſſers on any of their Lands in ſaid Town.—And as two of the Standing Committee are dead, to chuſe two in their Room; or to chuſe a new ſtanding Committee, as the ſaid Proprietors ſhall think proper.—And to know if the ſaid Proprietors will direct the ſaid Committee to ſell any of their undivided Land.

The ſaid Proprietors are hereby notified to meet at the Houſe of Thomas Harwood's, in Dunſtable, on Tueſday the 13th Day of September, 1774, at Ten o'Clock in the Forenoon.

The Proprietors of *Silveſter* Town,

lying on Androſgoggin-River, in the County of Cumberland, are hereby again notified that ſaid Proprietors, at their Meeting legally held by Adjournment, on the 7th Day of October, 1772, voted a Tax of 30s. on a Right, to be paid to Mr. Charles Turner, Proprietor's Treaſurer, on or before the 15th Day of March, 1773, and on the 20th Day of May 1774, voted a further Tax of 20s. on a Right, to be paid to the Treaſurer aforeſaid, on or before the 10th Day of September, 1774: And whereas many of the ſaid Proprietors are delinquent in paying the former of ſaid Taxes;—therefore unleſs ſaid Taxes ſhall be paid to the Treaſurer aforeſaid, on or before the 25th Day of October, 1774; ſo much of ſaid delinquent Proprietors Lands will be ſold at public Sale on ſaid Day, as ſhall be ſufficient to pay ſaid Taxes, and all neceſſary Charge, at the Houſe of Mr. Daniel Baker, Innholder in Pembroke, at Three o'Clock, P. M. Said Vendue to be adjourned if Occaſion require.

Per Order of the Committee,

WILLIAM TURNER, *Propr's Clerk.*

Scituate, Auguſt 6, 1774.

WHEREAS the Chaiſe Houſe of the Subſcriber was broke open laſt Saturday-Night, and ſtole a Ruſſet-breaſted Saddle, Houſing half worn, with a Cut in the Seat, ript in the Breaſt; alſo a Curb Bridle, with double Reins. Whoever ſhall apprehend the Thief, and return the Saddle, ſhall have Two Dollars Reward.

Malden, Auguſt 20, 1774. ELIAKIM WILLIS.

New-York, July 27, 1774.

Fifty Pounds Reward.

WHEREAS on the 19th of June laſt paſt a certain JOSEPH THORP as entruſted at New-York with a conſiderable ſum of money in Half Johannes, of nine penny weight, to be delivered by him at Quebec, and as he has not yet made his appearance there, with other ſuſpicious circumſtances, it is apprehended he is gone off with the money. He is a native of England, about 35 Years of Age, ſix feet high, ſwarthy complexion, very dark keen eyes, with pimples in his face, and pitted with the ſmall pox, of a ſlender make, ſtoops as he walks, talks rather ſlow, with ſome ſmall impediment in his ſpeech, wears a wig and is very fond of ſmoaking. He lived ſome ſome time in Boſton, from whence he removed to Quebec, aſſuming the character of a merchant in both places; he was alſo once in trade in New-Caſtle, Virginia, and has a brother ſettled there. He went on board Captain John F. Pruym, for Albany, and landed at Pougheipſcigh, from whence he hired a waggon to carry him to New-Haven—He took with him a blue calamir and dark brown ſuit of cloaths.

Whoever ſecures the ſaid JOSEPH THORP in any of his Majeſty's goals on this continent, ſhall be entitled to ten per cent. on the ſum recovered, and the above reward of Fifty Pounds when convicted. Apply to Curſon and Seton of New-York, Joſeph Wharton, jun. of Philadelphia, Robert Chriſtie, of Baltimore, James Gibſon and Co. Virginia, John Bondfield of Quebec, or Melatiah Bourne of Boſton. It is requeſted of thoſe who may have ſeen this Joſeph Thorp, ſince the 19th of June laſt paſt, or know any Thing of the Rout he has taken, that they convey the moſt early Intelligence thereof to any of the above perſons, which will be gratefully acknowledged.

All Maſters of Veſſels are forewarned from taking him off the Continent.

To the Worſhipful *Jeremiah Powell*,

Eſq; one of his Majeſty's Juſtices of the Peace throughout the Province of the *Maſſachuſetts Bay.*

We the Subſcribers Proprietors

of a Tract of Land about twenty Miles ſquare, lying and bordering upon *Piſcataqua*-River, in the County of *York*, late in the Province of *Main*, which deſcended to us from *Francis Small*, late of *Truro*, in the County of *Barnſtable*, in the ſaid Province of the *Maſſachuſetts-Bay* deceas'd, who purchaſed the ſame from one Capt. *Sandy*, an Indian Sagamore, being deſirous of embodying ourſelves as a Propriety & acting as ſuch agreeable to the Law in ſuch Caſe made and provided. Do hereby humbly requeſt that your Worſhip would order a Meeting of ſaid Proprietors to be held at the Houſe of Mr. *Moſes Shattuck* of *Falmouth*, in the County of *Cumberland*, Innholder, on the eighteenth Day of *September* next, at two of the Clock in the Afternoon, to act on the following Articles, *viz.* 1ſt. To chooſe a Moderator. 2dly. To chooſe a Proprietor's Clerk. 3dly. To chooſe a Committee to tranſact ſuch prudential Affairs of ſaid Proprietors as they may commit. 4thly. To vote what Money may be thought neceſſary for defraying the Charges which my ariſe in promoting the Intereſt of ſaid Propriety. 5thly. To agree on ſome Method for aſſeſſing and collecting the Monies, then or at any future Time voted by the ſaid Proprietors. 6thly. To chooſe an Agent or Agents, to proſecute any Perſons, who have, or may enter or treſpaſs upon the ſaid Land. And 7thly. To agree on ſome Method for calling Meetings in future.

Falmouth, July 6, 1774.

Samuel Freeman	*Eliſha Small*
Thomas Siminton	*Joſhua Eldridge*
Mather Siminton	*Jacob Waterhouſe*
	Pelatiah Fernald.

Province of the MASSACHUSETTS-BAY.

{ L. S. } To Mr. SAMUEL FREEMAN of *Falmouth*, in the County of *Cumberland*, in ſaid Province, one of the Proprietors, and Subſcribers to the foregoing Petition, *Greeting*

In purſuance of the aforeging Application and Requeſt, you are hereby required to give Notice (in Time and Manner as the Law directs) to the ſaid Proprietors, that a Meeting of ſaid Proprietors is to be holden at the Time and Place, and for the Purpoſes mentioned in the aforewritten Petition.

Given under my Hand and Seal, this 16th Day of July, *in the Fourteenth Year of his Majeſty's Reign, Annoque Domini, 1774.*

JEREMIAH POWELL, a Juſtice of the Peace through the Province of the *Maſſachuſetts-Bay.*

July 19. 1774.

By Virtue of the aforewritten Warrant to me directed, I do hereby notify and warn the aforeſaid Proprietors to meet at the Time and Place, and for the Purpoſes expreſſed in the aforegoing Application.

SAMUEL FREEMAN.

Daniel Bell,

At his Store near the Eaſt End of Faneuil-Hall, Has to ſell,

A ſmall Quantity of good Sugar, in Hogſheads or Barrels, very cheap for Caſh.

TO BE SOLD,

A Very handſome Phaeton, with Harneſs compleat, and a Driver's Seat to be uſed occaſionally;

A Pair of young Bay Horſes broke to the Carriage; And,

A fine riding Horſe about 15 Hands high, half-Blood, and about 6 Years old. Enquire of Edes & Gill.

BARLEY.

A Quantity is wanted to be delivered at Beverly or Salem, for which the Caſh will be paid on Delivery. Enquire at Store No. 20, on the Long Wharff, Boſton; where may be had, Coffee in Barrels, old red Port Wine in Quarter Caſks; choice new Flour and Peaſe in Barrels; a ſmall Conſignment of Hoſiery and Gloves; all which will be diſpoſed of on the loweſt Terms for Caſh.

TO BE LETT, VERY CHEAP,

A good Shop towards the South-End:

Enquire of George Trott.

All Perſons that have any Demands on the Eſtate of Mr. Johnſon Jackſon, *late of Boſton, Diſtiller, deceaſed, are deſired to ſend their Accounts to* Joſeph Jackſon, *at the South-End of Boſton, ſole Executor to the laſt Will and Teſtament of ſaid deceas'd; and all Perſons that are Indebted to ſaid Eſtate are deſired to make ſpedy Payment, as the Executor is determined the ſaid Eſtate ſhall be Settled with all poſſible Expedition.*

WE the Subſcribers being appointed Commiſſioners by the Hon. *John Cuſhing*, Eſq; Judge of Probate for the County of Plymouth, to receive and examine the Claims of the ſeveral Creditors to the Eſtate of *Thomas Clapp*, late of Scituate, Eſq; deceaſed, repreſented Inſolvent, and ſix Months being allowed to receive ſaid Claims. We do hereby Notify ſaid Creditors, that we will attend upon ſaid Buſineſs at the Dwelling-Houſe of Mrs. *Eſther Clapp*, in ſaid Scituate, from Three to Seven of the Clock in the Afternoon, on the third Wedneſdays of the ſix ſucceeding Months.

Scituate, July 29. 1774.

David Little, Junr.
Increaſe Clapp.

To be Sold for want of Employ only,

A likely Negro Boy, about 16 Years

of Age.—He is ſtrong, healthy, good-temper'd, ſober and honeſt;—and, with a good Maſter would make a very faithful Servant. Inquire of Edes & Gill.

Fredk. Wm. Geyer & Abrm. Burgeſs,

BEG Leave to acquaint the Public, That they have entered into a Co-partnerſhip, under the Firm of GEYER & BURGESS; and that they have on Hand a general Aſſortment of Engliſh, India and Scotch Piece Goods, which they are determined to ſell on the loweſt Terms, by Wholeſale only, at their Store (the Door below Meſſirs. Bethune and Prince's) in King-Street, Boſton.

Said GEYER requeſts all thoſe indebted to him, or to the late Company of Frazier and Geyer, either on Bond, Note or Book, to make immediate Payment, otherwiſe they will be put in Suit. (6 weeks.)

Auguſt 1, 1774.

CORNISH's *New-England* Cod-Fiſh HOOKS, &c.

Abraham Corniſh

Fiſh-Hook Maker from Exeter *in* ENGLAND,

ACQUAINTS his Friends and the Public, That he has removed from his Manufactory at the North End of BOSTON, to the Upper Part of CHARLESTOWN, where he continues to make all Sorts of FISH HOOKS, warranted of the beſt Quality;—being made of the beſt Wire only, better ſhap'd to take Fiſh, and each Hook prov'd before put up, (which is not done in England.) From ſeveral Years Experience, they have been found much ſuperior to any imported, and are univerſally approv'd; for which Reaſons, he flatters himſelf, that all concerned in the Fiſhery, will favour him with their Cuſtom, as they will thereby promote their own private Intereſt, and render this Country an eſſential Service, by eſtabliſhing a Manufacture neceſſary to its Proſperity.——For the better accommodating thoſe who may purchaſe his Hooks, they are Sold by Meſſirs. LEE & JONES, near the Swing-Bridge in Boſton, who will always keep by them a ſufficient Quantity to ſupply the American Fiſhery.—Said LEE & JONES, have for Sale, a few Hogſheads of Jamaica and Barbados Rum, genuine Kippen's and Rapee Snuff, a Variety of Looking Glaſſes, a Quantity of Lynn Shoes, a few Caſes of blue and white China Cups and Saucers, Corks, Gold and Silver Laces, a Variety of Stone, Glaſs and Cream-coloured Ware, Silver and Pinchbec Watches, a Variety of Silks, Laces and Muſlins, Tambour Muſlin Aprons and Ruffles; and a general Aſſortment of Piece Goods.

ALSO, Nails of all Sorts to be delivered at Marblehead.

W A N T E D,

A ſober, honeſt Man, of good Character, that can take Care of Horſes and drive a Carriage. He muſt be well recommended. Inquire of the Printers.

TO BE SOLD,

A large & convenient Brick Houſe,

fronting on the main Street in the Town of Providence, in the Colony of Rhode Iſland; ſaid Houſe on the Front is three Stories high, has eight Rooms on each Floor, all finiſhed, and in good Order; has, in the lower Story, four Shops for Sale of Goods; and has a good large Garden, and other Accommodations back of it; it might well accommodate ſeveral Families. The Owner would take the whole Pay for it in Engliſh or Weſt-India Goods. For further Particulars, any Perſon inclining to purchaſe, may apply to JOHN FOSTER, Eſq; in ſaid Providence. (4w.)

Boſton: Printed, by EDES & GILL,
in Queen-Street, 1774.

THE Boston-Gazette, AND COUNTRY JOURNAL.

Containing the freshest Advices, Foreign and Domestic.

No. 1011.

MONDAY, August 29, 1774.

Messieurs Edes & Gill,

THE late Dismission of Col. Hancock from the Command of the Cadets, with the Dissolution of that Corps consequent thereon, having occasioned much Speculation, and many imperfect Accounts; in Order to prevent further Misrepresentations you are desir'd to insert the following, which may be depended on.

Your humble Servant,
DUNCAN INGRAHAM, Junr. Clerk.
By Order of the Company.

AT a regular Meeting on Monday Evening 15th August 1774, Col. HANCOCK laid before the Company the following Letter, which he had receiv'd from Mr. Secretary FLUCKER, viz.

Salem, August 1st, 1774.

SIR,

I AM directed by his Excellency the Captain General to acquaint you, that he has no further Service for you, as Captain of the Governor's Company of Cadets, and you are hereby dismiss'd from that Command. I am, Sir,

Your most obedient Servant,
THOS. FLUCKER, Sec'y.

The Colonel after taking a polite and affectionate Leave retir'd. The Company then chose a Chairman and Clerk, and, after mature Deliberation, the Company voted *Nem. Con.* to return his Excellency the Standard with the following Message, by a Committee of three.

Boston, August 15th, 1774.

To his Excellency THOMAS GAGE, Esq;
Captain General and Commander in Chief of his Majesty's Province of the Massachusetts-Bay.

May it please your Excellency,

IT having been this Day communicated to us in a regular Meeting, that your Excellency has thought fit to displace the Honorable JOHN HANCOCK Esq; from his Command as Captain of the Cadet Company, they take the earliest Opportunity to express their extreme Regret at this Removal of their first Officer; and considering the Distinction with which they have hitherto been favour'd in the Choice and Continuation of their Officers, they look upon this Dismission as disbanding the Corps.—— They have therefore judged proper to return your Excellency the Standard you presented to the Company upon your taking the Chair of Government, and at the same Time, take the Liberty to inform your Excellency that from the Day of the Removal of Colonel HANCOCK from his Command, they no longer consider themselves as the Governor's independant Company of Cadets.

DUNCAN INGRAHAM, Junr. Clerk,
per Order of the Company.

The Committee accordingly waited on the Governor the next Day at Salem, and deliver'd the Message with the Standard, and receiv'd from his Excellency this verbal Answer, viz.

GENTLEMEN,

COLONEL Hancock has used me Ill, and has not treated me with that Respect that is due to the Governor of the Province; therefore I dismiss'd him!—I will not be treated Ill by Colonel Hancock, nor any other Man in the Province.— Had I known your Intentions, I would have disbanded you before.

Gentlemen, I accept the Standard.
Attest. GABRIEL JOHONNOT, Chairman
(of the Committee.)

The Company also voted that a Committee of Eleven, wait on Colonel Hancock with the following Address.

To the Honorable JOHN HANCOCK, Esq;

SIR,

THE Governor having thought fit to dismiss you from your Command as Colonel of the Cadet Company; We the Subscribers, who were Members of that Body, beg Leave to wait on you, with our sincerest Acknowledgments for your Conduct; and to assure you that we entertain a most grateful Sense of the many Instances of your spirited, generous, and noble Exertions, for the Honor of the Corps.

We leave to the Gratitude of your Country in general, to pay their disinterested Tribute of Applause to your extensive public Merits. 'Tis in the View of an Officer only, we would now consider you, at no Loss in that Character, for the amplest Field of Eulogium. It is principally owing to you Sir, that the Company acquir'd such Reputation, as to continue an Object worthy of your Patronage and Command; nor can we suppress the Emotions of Regret which we sensibly feel, at thus parting with an Officer, who whilst in Command, so eminently supported the Honor of the Company; and who on all Occasions of public Appearance, conducted with that Spirit, and Military Knowledge, as at once to reflect Honor on himself, and give Distinction to the Corps.

At a Period, when the "Post of Honor is a private Station," it cannot be thought strange, that a Gentleman of your distinguished Character, should meet with every Discouragement from Men in Power.

We will no longer detain you, Sir, than by an Assurance that it is the fervent Wish of our Hearts, that your Health may be speedily and perfectly restored; that you may long live to support the superior Character you have hitherto maintain'd; and that our Country may never want so illustrious a Citizen, to animate and conduct the Cause of VIRTUE and of FREEDOM.

Boston, August 18, 1774.

The above Address, signed by fifty-two Members, was accordingly presented; and the Committee received the following Answer, viz.

GENTLEMEN,

THE very respectful Notice you are pleased to take of my Dismission from the Command of the Company of Cadets, cannot fail to excite my warmest Gratitude.

The Pleasure which I ever felt in being at the Head of so respectable a Corps, was greatly augmented by a Recollection that my Appointment to that Command, was in Consequence of YOUR free Choice and unanimous Request.—The honorable Testimony which you have given of my Conduct in that Department, will always afford me the sincerest Pleasure.

I am ever ready to appear in a public Station, when the Honor or the Interest of the Community calls me; but shall always prefer Retirement in a private Station to being a Tool in the Hand of Power to oppress my Countrymen.—The only Regret I feel upon this Event is, my being obliged to take my Leave of you, Gentlemen, in my Military Capacity; but I shall ever hold you near to my Heart as Friends and Fellow Citizens: And if it should ever be in my Power to promote the Interest of the Individuals who composed the Corps, I shall gladly embrace the Opportunity.

I feel myself interested to encourage Military Knowledge in America, and in this Province and Town in particular; and am happy in believing that the Company of Cadets have, by their Example, and the deserved Reputation which they have acquir'd greatly contributed to rouse the martial Spirit of my Countrymen, and to raise in them an Emulation to excell in the noble and too often necessary Art of War.

Your benevolent Wishes for the Recovery of my Health, demand the most grateful Return.—— Nothing in this Life can make me more desirous of a Restoration to Health, than that I may in some Measure merit the Esteem of my Country; and as far as is possible, justify the favourable Sentiments which you are pleased to entertain of me.

I am with great Respect and Esteem,
Gentlemen,
Your most obliged and obedient,
humble Servant,
Boston, Aug. 22, 1774. JOHN HANCOCK.

☞ Any Observations on the above are unnecessary—The Public are left to make their own Reflections.

BOSTON, August 29.

Extract of a Letter from Dartmouth, dated August 20th, 1774.

"THE more I think upon, the more confirmed I am in the opinion, that every official act of our civil officers after the first day of July last, is a concession to the pretended authority of Parliament to make laws binding, &c. for from and after the said first of July, our civil officers hold and execute their commissions at the will and pleasure of the Governor, (which they did not, by our Charter) and the authority which he has to continue or remove them, is given to him by the act of Parliament. This is also evident by the proviso in said act, which continues all such officers in commission till death, or removal by the Governor, (the other avoidance may be or construed to mean a reserved power, as well as a resignation) and I don't see how any one can execute a commission without supposing and acknowledging the authority to be good, which continues such commission in being, and if the Governor has power to appoint and remove, those who gave him that power, have, at least, had it to give, and besides, that they should hold their commissions under parliamentary authority, appears to be one chief design of parliament in passing the act, for after vacating the existence of the Council, they constitute a new one, with all the powers and privileges of the former, except in this very point of constituting civil officers, intending thereby that all officers which originated by any powers in the council, should thenceforth cease and determine; and in fact they must, upon the destruction of the power which gave them existence, unless some new power upholds them in being, which parliamentary view and design is evident by the said proviso, for if said act does not, in the nature and spirit of it, annihilate both the origin and operation of those commissions, then that provision, for continuing them in being, notwithstanding said act, and during the governor's pleasure is null, void, futile and ridiculous, because they would have remained so without such provision, and if that proviso is of any validity and significancy at all, then those officers hold their commissions by virtue of it, or in other words, by virtue of parliamentary authority granted to the governor, therefore which way soever the argument be considered, the conclusion will follow, that those officers hold their commissions by the authority of parliament expressed in said act. Thus it seems we paid obedience to an act of parliament before we knew such an act was passed; who then can pretend that we are a disobedient people. That those officers hold their commissions by virtue of the Governor's proclamation, does not appear to me to be the case, for the efficacy of that proclamation depended upon the concurring powers, vested in the council with respect to any new appointments, and even with respect to the continuance of the old ones; therefore destroying the powers of the council, destroys the efficacy and operation of the proclamation, which depended upon those powers; and those further orders therein mentioned, are given by the act of parliament. If my opinion is erroneous, you must impute it to more zeal than knowledge. That the judges of the superior court thus hold their commissions, I suppose to be indisputable; therefore those who have any matter cognizable by said court, ought not by any means to appear while they sit, nor even before the inferior court; for then the sheriff will have no occasion to return jurors, nor can the courts execute their commissions. Some people here, are so much of my opinion, that they are determined not to sue for their dues; some yet think otherwise. This is a point of so much importance, that I think it ought soon to be settled. The opinion of your Committee will go far towards settling of it. We are collecting the sentiments of the Committees around us.—Another point appears to me of like consequence, (viz) Whether to chuse Representatives or not, in case warrants should be issued for the choice of them before next May. I think we cannot in such case chuse them, without complying with the act of parliament, and thereby acknowledging their Right to make laws obligatory on us. But I fear I trespass upon your patience, and so conclude,——"

(See Supplement.)

Messieurs EDES & GILL,

Please to publish the following State of the Merits and Services of the Province of the Massachusetts-Bay, their Exertions and Expences in the common Cause, drawn up by a Committee of both Houses of Assembly, of which the late Governor HUTCHINSON *was Chairman, and transmitted to* JASPER MAUDUIT, *Esq; Agent for the Province, in a Letter dated the* 17*th* Decr. 1764.

Brief State of the Merits and Services of the Province of Massachusetts-Bay, *their Exertions and Expences in the common Cause.*

ONE great Reason alledged for imposing Taxes upon the Colonies, ungranted by their own Representatives, by the mere Authority of Parliament, being this; that they ought to contribute to defray the Charges of a War undertaken for their Defence, to which those who alledge this Reason suppose they have never yet sufficiently contributed. The Province of the Massachusetts-Bay deem it proper briefly to set forth their own Merits and Services, their Exertions and Expences in the common Cause, from their first Incorporation to the present Time.

1620. In the Year 1620, the Colony of New-Plymouth, now merged and included in the present Province of the Massachusetts-Bay, was begun to be planted by Governor Bradford and others, a very small but vigorous Number. These by their Prudence and Vigilance supported themselves in a wild Desert, surrounded by Indians, without any Assistance from the Crown of Great-Britain.

1629. In the Year 1629, the old Colony of the Massachusetts Bay was begun to be planted, the Adventurers having before obtained from King Charles the First, an ample Charter, on the Faith whereof they made those Beginnings in Colonizing, which have increased to this very Day, though the said Charter hath long since been lost to them.

It appears from the earliest Records of this Colony, that their first Cares were to train the Inhabitants to Arms, to build Fortifications on their Sea-Coast, to provide for Alarms in any appearing Danger; and before the Year 1636, they had built a Fort in Boston, one in Charlestown, one in Salem, besides lesser Fortifications on the inland side.

Whoever should read these old Records can hardly help pitying a feeble Number separated by an immense Ocean from the Capital of their Government, surrounded by Savages of whose good Will they had no Assurance, conflicting with Hunger, Cold, Nakedness, and every other Hardship of a Desert, in these first Attempts to extend the Empire of Great Britain.

Yet feeble as they then were, their Efforts were not confined to the Defence of their Home Possessions; their Views even then were enlarged to the Conquest of the Territories possessed by other European Nations, which they deemed to belong to the Crown of Great-Britain: Wherefore

1635. In the Year 1635, Edwd. Winslow, Esq; of the Colony of New-Plymouth preferr'd, on behalf all the Plantations in New-England, an humble Address to the Lords Commissioners of the Plantations, setting forth, "That his Majesty's Territories were encroached upon by the French and Dutch, praying that his Majesty would either procure Peace with those foreign States, or else to give special Warrant to the Petitioners, and the English Colonies to right themselves against all foreign Enemies.

This Petition was very favourably received by their Lordships; especially as Mr. Winslow offered on the Behalf of the Colonies to be at all Charges if they might be furnished with Authority from his Majesty. Mr. Winslow was therefore divers Times directed to attend their Lordships on this Subject. Had this been granted, perhaps the Causes of the last War had never subsisted. But alas! the last Time Mr. Winslow was heard upon it, Archbishop Laud was at the Board. He having heard that Winslow was puritannically affected, fell into Interrogations about Winslow's Conduct in America. Winslow was too honest to conceal his Puritan Principles, so the Archbishop prevailed with the Lords "by vehement Importunity" to consent to Winslow's Commitment; and he was accordingly committed to the Fleet Prison, where he lay seventeen Weeks. Thus ended his Agency.

1637. There being only fourteen Towns in the Colony, they raised One hundred and sixty Men against the Pequots, a numerous and warlike People dwelling out of the Massachusetts Territory, but formidable by their Neighbourhood. This Force, joined with that of the other Infant Colonies, entirely extirpated that fierce People.

1643. In the Year 1643 the Massachusetts and the other Colonies, to wit, Plymouth, Connecticut, and New-Haven, entered into an Union, and were to support each other in all future Wars in a just Proportion to the Number of Males in each Colony; which Union subsisted till the Time the first Charter was vacated. To this it was much if not entirely, owing, that the feeble settlements of Connecticut and New Haven were not overrun and conquer'd by their Dutch Neighbours, who claimed all their Lands.

1645. In 1645 the united Colonies raised Three hundred Men, whereof One hundred and ninety by the Massachusetts, to attack the Narragansetts, another warlike Indian Nation. But these Indians were affrighted at these Preparations, and made their Submission and Peace on the Terms proposed by the English.

1664. The Colony on the Requisition of King Charles 2d. raised Two hundred Men for the Reduction of Manhadoes (now New York) then in the Dutch Power: But that Country yielding to the Naval Force sent from England, the Men aforesaid never Marched.

1675 to 1686 } This Colony was near all this Time, with very short Intermission, engaged in Wars with the Indians whereof Philip was Sachem, with the Narragansetts, and with the River-Indians so called, and with the Eastern Indians excited and stirred up by the French: which together threatned no less than the total Extirpation of the English here. In the Course of these Wars many Towns on the Eastern and Western Frontiers were destroyed, the Inhabitants killed or captivated, their Houses burned and Substance consumed. Yet in all this Time the Colony asked no assistance from the Crown, but bore the heavy Load themselves. For which they were even reproved by the Earl of Anglesey in a Letter to Governor Leverett——His Lordship thought they could never be equal to such Wars themselves, and that it was their Duty to have applied to his Majesty for help. Nevertheless they received none; they survived all these Terrors to be a second and third Time a Theatre of like tragical Events.

In this Period, in the general shipwreck of Charters in the arbitrary Reign of Charles the 2d there was a Judgment against that of the Massachusetts-Bay. This loyal Province was the only one, which was not restored by the Revolution to all they lost.

1690. The Massachusetts Colony raised Eight hundred Men for the Reduction of Nova Scotia, commanded by Sir William Phips. By these it was reduced, and remained subject to the English untill the Peace of Ryswick, when King William gave it up to the French.

The same Year they raised about Two thousand Men for the Reduction of Canada; and a Fleet of between thirty and forty sail.—Though this last Attempt was unsuccessful, it does not appear to be ill planned. Charlevoix the French Historian speaks very disrespectfully of Sir William, yet says, "It is certain that if Count Frontenac (the French Governor) had happened "to have arrived three Days after Phips's approach, he would have found Phips in Possession of his Capital when he arrived there himself; and that if the English Fleet had not been "much detained by contrary Winds, or had had "better Pilots, Quebec would have been taken "before it would have been known at Montreal "that it was besieged."

Charlevoix, vol. 3d, Page 110.

However it was a great Exertion in the Colony to raise such a Force, and the great Loss of their Men, not indeed by the Enemy, but by Pestilential Sicknesses, &c. was to a young county irreparable—During all the Rest of that War, untill the Peace of Riswick, the Colony had its Hands quite full. The French had no better Card to play than to induce the Indians by religious Motives and temporal Rewards, to plunder and massacre our People. We were therefore obliged to build and maintain many Forts, and keep great Numbers of Soldiers in Pay. And though the Province was greatly harrassed and scourged by the French and Indians, had many Towns desolated, and the Inhabitants killed and captivated, yet they finally kept Possession of all the Territory granted them.

The Peace of Riswick was short and disturbed, the Indians had made Peace, but were always faithless. Having therefore their spiritual Fathers to excite and quicken their natural Barbarity, they kept the Province in a perpetual Alarm, even before the War was declared between the two Crowns.

1701 to 1713 } But as soon as the War was declared in Europe, all Restraint was taken off from these Savages, and the Province experienced the like Cruelties from them as before, had many of their Towns destroyed, their Inhabitants massacred and captivated, and were kept in perpetual Alarm from their Incursions and Hostilities.

Yet even in this War their Home-Distresses hindered not their meditating Conquests for the British Crown.

They made at their own Expence one Expedition against Port-Royal, which failed. They raised also the greater Number of the Land Forces which were commanded by General Nicholson in 1710, by which Nova-Scotia was reduced to the British Obedience, to which it hath ever since remained subject.——The late Queen in 1709, signified her Desire to the Colonies of an Attack upon Canada, with which this Province very readily concurred, raised all the Men desired. And tho' the Ministry did not think fit to pursue the Affair at that Time, this Province was nearly at the same Expence, as if they had gone on.—Afterwards in the memorable Expedition under Hill, this poor Province exhausted and impoverished as it was, bore its full Share in the Burthen and in the Loss of that fatal Affair.

It ought not to be forgotten, that in this Period, notwithstanding their Hands were so full at Home, they gave Assistance even to the distant Parts of the British Dominions. At the Desire of the Colony of Jamaica, they sent there two Companies of Foot, commanded by Col. Walton, and Capt. Larimore, who arrived safe at Jamaica, served there two Years, and very few of the Soldiers returned to their native Country.

1714 to 1744 } We pass over with slight mention the Indian Wars from the Peace of Utrecht to the War proclaimed in 1744. In this Period the Province was at a great Expence and Cost, were obliged to maintain many Forts, frequently suffered greatly from the Indians Murders and Depredations. It shall suffice to mention, that tho' in many Respects we were unfortunate, yet the Province defended finally its whole Territory, and particularly that Part of it from Sagadahock to St. Croix Rivers; and the Enemy were at last obliged to sue for Peace in good Earnest, to take it on English Terms, and (to do them Justice) they kept it 'till the next French War was proclaimed.

In this Period, War being declared with Spain, in 1740, a Number of Troops were to be raised in America, for his Majesty's Service, with which this Province most readily complied, raised more than was required, or than Officers and Arms were sent for; and of the Number that actually embarked for that Service, scare One in Fifty ever returned.

1744. The Declaration of War with France arrived here, while the General Court was sitting. They made immediate Provision for raising Forces for Annapolis, which arrived in good Season.—Divers Times after this Nova-Scotia attacked by the French, was relieved by Forces sent hence: So that Possession was always kept of it for the Crown of G. Britain, during that improsperous War.

1745. In the latter End of the Year 1744 and beginning of the Year 1745, was formed by the Massachusetts Bay and the other New England Governments that memorable Expedition against Louisbourg, which reduced that American Dunkirk, and furnished the English Ministry at the Treaty of Aix la Chapelle with an equivalent to balance the rapid Conquests and Acquisitions of the French in Flanders. Of how much Importance this was in the Opinion of the French, appeared from their demanding two Hostages of the first Nobility in England, as Pledges of its Restitution.

It is true the Charge of this Expedition was repaid by the Nation in 1748; yet that ought not to lessen the Merits of the New England Attempt. For,

1. They began it when they had no Promise, and very little Prospect of being so reimbursed.

2. If it had not succeeded, and they had not been so reimbursed, it must have involved them in the greatest Distress. This they saw; yet cheerfully run so great a Risque for the public Service.

3. It would have cost the Crown more than double the Sum paid the New-England Governments, to have sent an Armament from Great Britain for the Reduction of the same Place. And the Success would not have been so likely as formed from New-England.

Let it be further considered, what an heavy Loss the Province met with there, which never was, and indeed cannot be made up. That is in the Flower of their Youth, wasted and destroyed by Camp Fevers and other Sicknesses, and the Hardships and Distresses of the Siege.

1746. The Expedition intended by the Crown this Year proved abortive; and the Forces destined for that Purpose were afterwards countermanded. The Readiness of the Province to raise the Men required appeared; they actually raised them, and kept them on Foot 'till the Fall.

The short Interval of Peace that followed the Peace of Aix la-Chapelle, was continually interrupted by the French making new Incroachments, building new Forts, and surrounding the English Colonies on all Sides. So that in

1754, The Province judged it necessary to raise 800 Men to march them to the Eastward, to build a Fort, which they called Fort-Halifax, at Sixty Miles Distance from the Mouth of Sagadahock or Kennebec River, in the Indian Rout from Canada. The Cost of this Expedition was thirteen Thousand seven Hundred and eighty two Pounds fou

Shillings and three Pence, Proclamation Money, and the building and supplying that Fort was six Thousand five Hundred and sixty seven Pounds eighteen Shillings and one Penny.

1755. This Province, with the other New-England Governments and New York, formed an Expedition against Crown-Point. Then it was that the memorable Battle was fought near Lake-George, in which the French General Dieskau was taken Prisoner, and the French totally routed. The Cost of this Expedition to the Province was one Hundred and four Thousand and fifty-two Pounds sixteen Shillings and eleven Pence. In the same Year, by Forces chiefly raised in the Massachusetts, tho' paid by the Crown, Fort Beausejour was taken, and the French Inhabitants of Nova-Scotia were removed and distributed among the English Colonies. This was a most wise Step, but it was a Source of great Expence to this Province, who for some Time supported at a common Expence those sent here; and after they had resided here some Years, parcelled them out among the several Towns in the Province. And they have been, and still remain an heavy Bill of Charge to this Province.

1756. The next Year War being declared, the Province hoped to finish the Work begun the last Year, and raised a mighty Armament which was intended against Crown Point: but upon the Arrival of Lord Loudon from England, his Lordship thought proper that the Forces should not proceed. The Cost to the Province this Year was ninety seven Thousand five Hundred and eighty two Pounds one Shilling and eight Pence.

1757. This Year Lord Loudon intending only to act on the defensive on the Continent did not demand the same Number of Soldiers as the last year. The Number demanded was raised. The Expence of these Men to the Province was sixty six Thousand two Hundred and one Pounds nineteen Shillings and two Pence. This Year Fort William-Henry was taken by the French. The Alarm given by that occasioned a March of the Militia of the Province towards the Frontiers, which it was expected in the Insolence of Success the French would have attacked. The Cost of this March was twelve Thousand nine Hundred and eighty Pounds fifteen Shillings and two Pence.

1758. Letters from the Rt. Hon. Mr. Secretary Pitt were received the Beginning of this Year: whence the Province hoped for a vigorous Campaign, and therefore straining their utmost Ability raised seven Thousand Men for the service. The Cost of this Year was one Hundred and forty Thousand two Hundred Pounds.

1759, 1760, 1761, 1762, } The Province in all these Years raised the full Number assigned them, and by garrisoning Louisbourg and Nova-Scotia in some of these Years, they gave Opportunity to the regular Forces to retain Canada. The whole Cost of their Expeditions from 1755 to 1762, both inclusive, was nine Hundred and forty three Thousand eight Hundred and thirty nine Pounds twelve Shillings and nine Pence.

The Cost of Scouting Companies sent into the Indian Country from 1755 to 1760, both inclusive, was twenty seven Thousand four Hundred and ninety six Pounds and seven Pence.

Two armed Vessels built and maintained for the Protection of their Trade cost thirty four Thousand seven Hundred and ninety five Pounds fourteen Shillings and six Pence.

These Expences together make one Million thirty nine thousand three Hundred and ninety Pounds five Shillings and four Pence.

It is to be observed here that these Sums being much greater than could be raised on the People each Year, the Province was annually obliged to take up large Sums on Interest, and some Years to anticipate and mortgage the standing Revenues of the Government for Security to the Lenders.

The Province do not forget: They remember and acknowledge with great Gratitude the Sums bestowed on them by the Nation in the course of the last War—Without these it would have been absolutely impossible for them to have proceeded in their Levies above one or two Years. But notwithstanding these they were at the conclusion of the War, and still are very much in debt. And it will take them many Years, with all the Resources in their Power, even though their Trade was allowed to continue on the Foot it was at the Conclusion of the War to clear their Debts.

In the above Sums the Cost of many Forts and Garrisons on their Frontiers are not included. Neither can any Estimate be made of the Cost to Individuals by the Demand of personal Service. For the Numbers raised in all these Years together being equal to the whole Militia, it hath come to the Turn of every enlisted Soldier in the whole Militia to serve once. And they who could not serve in Person, which were much the greater Number, were obliged to hire others at a great Premium in their Room. And they who could not be impressed, yet that the Burthen might not lie too heavy on the others, very often advanced largely to encourage the Levies. Even now the Province having Indians on their Frontiers are obliged to keep up Garrisons for the Defence of their Infant Settlements, though the Indians profess to be at Peace and we cannot charge them with any inimical Intentions.

The Expence of supporting Castle William in Time of Peace is (communibus Annis) eighteen Hundred Pounds a Year; in Time of War at least one third more, exclusive of the Augmentations and Repairs.

Upon the whole, this Country, granted by the King of Great-Britain to his Subjects, included also in Grants made by the French King to his Subjects, was at a very critical Time settled by the Subjects of the former, who also fairly purchased the Indian Claim.

From small Beginnings, through innumerable Toils, Hardships and Sufferings, a rude Desert is become a well-peopled and fruitful Plantation. From its first Infancy to its present Age of Puberty, the Colony with no Expence to the Crown hath defended the Territory granted to it; and thereby hath mightily extended the British Empire, and immensely encreased the British Commerce: It hath ever been ready to afford its utmost Help when the King's Service called, hath actually made divers valuable Conquests for the Crown, and by its great Exertions and Expences in the late War has impoverished and enfeebled itself, so as it will not in many Years recover the athletic State it was in at the Beginning of the late French War.

It is not intended by any thing here said to derogate from the Merits of the other Colonies: most of them have had their Share in these great Conquests; and without the joint and united Vigour of so many, so much could never have been accomplish'd. Nor do the Massachusetts desire to be distinguish'd from the other Colonies by any new Grants and Immunities. Neither are they seeking any further Rewards. They desire only that the Privileges their Ancestors purchased so dearly, and they have never forfeited, may be continued to them. Being conscious to themselves of entire Loyalty to his most excellent Majesty, and dutiful Respects to the Parent State, they trust the Wisdom and Justice of the Nation will allow them the Possession of all the Rights, Privileges and Immunities, which the Subjects of Great-Britain do and ought to enjoy.

An Act of Parliament

For making more effectual Provision for the Government of the Province of QUEBEC, *in NORTH-AMERICA.*

WHEREAS His Majesty, by His Royal Proclamation, bearing Date the Seventh Day of *October*, in the Third Year of his Reign, thought fit to declare the Provisions which had been made in respect to certain Countries, Territories, and Islands in *America*, ceded to his Majesty by the definitive Treaty of Peace, concluded at *Paris* on the Tenth Day of *February*, One thousand Seven hundred and Sixty-three:

And Whereas, by the Arrangements made by the said Royal Proclamation, a very large Part of the Territory of *Canada*, within which there were several Colonies and Settlements of the Subjects of *France*, who claimed to remain therein under the Faith of the said Treaty, was left, without any Provision being made for the Administration of Civil Government therein, and other Parts of the said Country, where sedentary Fisheries had been established and carried on by the Subjects of *France*, Inhabitants of the said Province of *Canada*, under Grants and Concessions from the Government thereof, were annexed to the Government of *Newfoundland*, and thereby subjected to Regulations inconsistent with the Nature of such Fisheries:

May it therefore please your Most Excellent MAJESTY, That it may be Enacted; *And be it Enacted* by the KING's most Excellent Majesty, by and with the Advice and Consent of the Lords Spiritual and Temporal, and Commons, in this present Parliament assembled, and by the Authority of the same, That all the said Territories, Islands, and Countries, heretofore Part of the Province of *Canada*, in *North America*, extending southward to the Banks of the River *Ohio*, westward to the Banks of *Missisippi*, and nothward to the southern Boundary of the Territory granted to the Merchants Adventures of *England* trading to *Hudson's Bay*, and which said Territories, Islands, and Countries, are not within the Limits of some other *British* Colony, as allowed and confirmed by the Crown, or which have, since the Tenth of *February*, One thousand Seven hundred and Sixty-three, been made Part of the Government of *Newfoundland*, be, and they are hereby, during His Majesty's Pleasure, annexed to, and made Part and Parcel of the Province of *Quebec*, as created and established by the said Royal Proclamation of the Seventh of *October*, One thousand Seven hundred and Sixty-three.

And whereas the Provisions made by the said Proclamation, in respect to the Civil Government of the said Province of *Quebec*, and the Powers and Authorities given to the Governor and other Civil Officers of the said Province, by the Grants and Commissions issued in Consequence thereof, have been found, upon Experience, to be inapplicale to the State and Circumstances of the said Province, the Inhabitants whereof amounting, at the Conquest, to above One hundred thousand Persons, professing the Religion of the Church of *Rome*, and enjoying an established Form of Constitution, and System of Laws, by which their Persons and Property had been protected, governed, and ordered, for a long Series of Years, from the First Establishment of the said Province of *Canada*; *Be it therefore further Enacted* by the Authority aforesaid, That the said Proclamation, so far as the same relates to the said Province of *Quebec*, and the Commission under the Authority whereof the Government of the said Province is at present administered, and all and every the Ordinance and Ordinances made by the Governor and Council of *Quebec* for the Time being, relative to the Civil Government and Administration of Justice in the said Province, and all Commissions to Judges and other Officers thereof, be, and the same are hereby revoked, annulled, and made void, from and after the First Day of *May*, One thousand Seven hundred and Seventy-five.

And for the more perfect Security and Ease of the Minds of the inhabitants of the said Province, *It is hereby Declared* That His Majesty's Subjects professing the Religion of the Church of *Rome*, of and in the said Province of *Quebec*, as the same is described in and by the said Proclamation and Commissions and also of all the Territories, Part of the Province of *Canada*, at the Time of the Conquest thereof, which are hereby annexed, during His Majesty's Pleasure, to the said Government of *Quebec*, may have, hold and enjoy the free Exercise of the Religion of the Church of *Rome*, subject to the King's Supremacy as is declared and established by an Act made in the First Year of the Reign of Queen *Elizabeth*, over all the Dominions and Countries which then did, or thereafter should belong to the Imperial Crown of this Realm; and that the Clergy of the said Church may hold, receive, and enjoy their accustomed Dues and Rights, with respect to such Persons only as shall profess the said Religion.

Provided Nevertheless, That nothing herein contained shall extend, or be construed to extend, to the disabling His Majesty, His Heirs or Successors, from making such Provision for the Encouragement of the Protestant Religion, and for the Maintenance and Support of a Protestant Clergy within the said Province, as he or they shall, from Time to Time, think necessary and expedient.

And be it further Enacted by the Authority aforesaid, That all His Majesty's *Canadian* Subjects within the Province of *Quebec*, the Religious Orders and Communities only excepted, may also hold and enjoy their Property and Possessions, together with all Customs and Usages relative thereto and all other their Civil Rights, in as large, ample, and beneficial Manner, as if the said Proclamation, Commissions, Ordinances, and other Acts and Instruments, had not been made, and as may consist with their Allegiance to His Majesty, and Subjection to the Crown and Parliament of *Great-Britain*; and that, in all Matters of Controversy relative to Property and Civil Rights, Resort shall be had to the Laws of *Canada*, for the Decision of the same; and all Causes that shall hereafter be instituted in any of the Courts of Justice, to be appointed within and for the said Province by His Majesty, His Heirs and Successors shall, with respect to such Property and Rights, be determined by the Judges of the same, agreeably to the said Laws and Customs of *Canada*, and the several Ordinances that shall, from Time to Time, be passed in the said Province by the Governor, Lieutenant-Governor, or Commander in Chief for the Time being, by and with the Advice and Consent of the Legislative Council of the same, to be appointed in Manner herein-after mentioned.

Provided always, That it shall and may be lawful to and for every Person, that is Owner of any Lands, Goods, or Credits in the said Province, and that has a Right to alienate the said Lands, Goods, or Credits, in his or her Life-time, by Deed of Sale, Gift, or otherwise, to devise or bequeath the same, at his or her Death, by his or her last Will and Testament; any Law, Usage, or Custom heretofore, or now prevailing in the Province, to the contrary hereof in any-wise notwithstanding.

Provided also, That nothing in this Act contained shall extend, or be construed to extend, to any Lands that have been granted by His Majesty, or shall hereafter be granted by His Majesty, His Heirs and Successors, to be holden in free and common Soccage.

And whereas the Certainty and Lenity of the Criminal Law of *England*, and the Benefits and Advantages resulting from the Use of it, have been sensibly felt by the Inhabitants, from an Experience of more than Nine Years, during which it has been uniformly administered; *Be it therefore further Enacted* by the Authority aforesaid, That the same shall continue to be administered, and shall be observed as Law, in the Province of *Quebec*, as well in the Description and Quality of the Offence, as in the Method of Prosecution and Trial, and the Punishments and Forfeitures thereby inflicted, to the Exclusion of every other Rule of Criminal Law, or Mode of Proceeding thereon, which did or might prevail in the said Province before the Year of our Lord One thousand Seven hundred and Sixty-four; any Thing in this Act to the contrary thereof in any Respect notwithstanding; subject nevertheless to such Alterations and Amendments, as the Governor, Lieutenant Governor, or Commander in Chief for the Time being, by and with the Advice and Consent of the Legislative Council of said Province, hereafter to be appointed, shall, from Time to Time, cause to be made therein, in Manner herein-after directed.

And whereas it may be necessary to ordain many Regulations, for the future Welfare and good Government of the Province of *Quebec*, the Occasions of which cannot now be foreseen, nor without much Delay and Inconvenience be provided for, without intrusting that Authority for a certain Time, and under proper Restrictions, to Persons resident there:

And whereas it is at present inexpedient to call an Assembly; *Be it therefore Enacted* by the Authority aforesaid, That it shall and may be lawful for His Majesty, His Heirs and Successors, by Warrant under His or their Signet, or Sign Manual, and with the Advice of the Privy Council, to constitute and appoint a Council for the Affairs of the Province of *Quebec*, to consist of such Persons resident there, not exceeding Twenty-three, nor less than Seventeen, as His Majesty, His Heirs and Successors, shall be pleased to appoint; and, upon the Death, Removal, or Absence of any of the Members of the said Council, in like Manner to constitute and appoint such and so many other Person or Persons as shall be necessary to supply the Vacancy or Vacancies; which Council, so appointed, and nominated, or the major Part thereof, shall have full Power and Authority to make Ordinances for the Peace, Welfare, and good Government of the said Province, with the Consent of His Majesty's Governor, or in his Absence of the Lieutenant Governor, or Commander in Chief for the Time being.

Provided always, That nothing in this Act contained, shall extend to authorise or impower the said Legislative Council to lay any Taxes or Duties within the said Province.

Provided also, and be it Enacted by the Authority aforesaid, That every Ordinance so to be made shall, within Six Months, be transmitted by the Governor, or, in his Absence, by the Lieutenant Governor or Commander in Chief for the Time being, and laid before His Majesty, for His Royal Approbation; and if His Majesty shall think fit to disallow thereof, the same shall cease and be void from the Time that His Majesty's Order in Council thereupon shall be promulgated at *Quebec*.

Provided also, That no Ordinance touching Religion, or by which any Punishment may be inflicted greater than Fine or Imprisonment for Three Months, shall be of any Force or Effect, until the same shall have received His Majesty's Approbation.

Provided also, That no Ordinance shall be passed, at any Meeting of the Council, except between the First Day of *January* and the First Day of *May*, unless upon some urgent Occasion, in which Case, every Member thereof resident at *Quebec*, or within Fifty Miles thereof, shall be personally summoned by the Governor, or, in his Absence, by the Lieutenant Governor or Commander in Chief for the Time being, to attend the same.

And be it further Enacted by the Authority aforesaid, That nothing herein contained shall extend, or be construed to extend, to prevent or hinder His Majesty, His Heirs and Successors, by His or their Letters Patent, under the Great Seal of *Great Britain*, from erecting, constituting, and appointing, such Courts of Criminal, Civil, and Ecclesiastical Jurisdiction, within and for the said Province of *Quebec*, and appointing, from Time to Time the Judges and Officers thereof, as His Majesty, His Heirs and Successors, shall think necessary and proper, for the Circumstances of the said Province.

ALL Perſons indebted for this Paper, whoſe Accounts have been above 12 Months ſtanding, are requeſted to make immediate Payment.

THIS DA PUBLISHED,
THE FOURTH EDITION,
(Price 9d.)
And ſold by EDES *and* GILL, *in Queen-Stret.*

CONSIDERATIONS
ON THE
MEASURES CARRYING ON
WITH RESPECT TO THE
BRITISH COLONIES
IN
NORTH-AMERICA.

There is neither King or Sovereign Lord on Earth, who has beyond his own Domain power to lay one Farthing on his Subjects without the grant and conſent of thoſe, who pay it; unleſs he does it by tyranny and violence.

Phillippe de Commines, Ch. 103.

THIS is a moſt maſterly performance, written ſince the framing the ſeveral Acts againſt BOSTON and AMERICA, and the beſt calculated to convince the Miniſtry, the people of England, and all the world, of the abſurdity and wickedneſs of the late acts, and ruinous conſequences, to England at leaſt, that would certainly attend their being carried into execution.

Our laſt accounts, ſay, this pamphlet has had a wonderful effect in removing the prejudices and convincing the pe ple of England.

The above Pamphlet, which ſells in London at 1ſ. 6d. Sterling, is ſold here at 9d. Lawful, which is but juſt Three Farthings more than one Third of the Price of the London Edition.

TO BE LETT,

A Neat genteel Brick Tenement in Cambridge Street, near the Orange-Tree.
Enquire of Edes & Gill.

TO BE SOLD

A Right of Land containing about 500 Acres, in a Townſhip granted by the Great and General Court, of the Province of Maſſachuſetts-Bay, to Samuel Livermore, Eſq; and others, lying on both ſides of Androſcogging-River, adjoining Sylveſter Townſhip, in the County of Cumberland. Inquire of the Printers.

James Henderſon

ACQUAINTS his Cuſtomers and others, That he has for Sale a compleat Aſſortment of

Engliſh, India, and *Scotch* GOODS,

ſuitable to all Seaſons, which he will ſell by Wholeſale and Retail, cheap for Caſh, at his Shop in Ann-Street, BOSTON. ——Amongſt which is——

A beautiful Aſſortment of Brocaded SILKS, Ducapes, ſtrip'd, plain and changeable Luteſtrings, Sattins and Modes of all widths, a fine Aſſortment of the neweſt faſhion Ribbons, to be ſold very low, plain ſtrip'd and flower'd Muſlins, &c. &c. &c.

TO BE SOLD,

By Capt. *Jeduthen Baldwin*, of *Brookſield*,

And may be entered upon immediately;

A FARM in Shutesbury, containing about 137 Acres of choice Land, 40 Acres of it is the beſt of Land for Plowing. There is about 50 Acres that will make the beſt of Mowing, all well Watered. There is a low Houſe with a Cellar under the whole neatly Stoned, the Chimney is ſet on an Arch. There is three Rooms with Fire Places, beſides a Bed-Room. There is a pretty young Orchard that made a few Barrels of Cyder laſt Year. There is about eight Acres of the ſaid Place planted with Corn, and ſow'd with Grain this Year, and five Acres more cleared to be ſow'd this Fall with Rye and other Seeds. There is a few Loads of Hay cut there this Year, and Paſturing for a few Cattle. The Whole may be had now for about £.1200 Old Tenor.

A GREAT PENNYWORTH!

Alſo to be Sold—About 130 or 150 Acres of choice Land for Paſturing, on Coy's-Hill, in Brookfield, that is well fenced, and divided into ſeveral Paſtures, well into Graſs.

TO BE SOLD

By JOHN BAKER,

in Back-Street,

About 400 Quintals of good Merchantable and Jamaica Fiſh, either by large or ſmall Quantities.

ALL Perſons indebted to the Eſtate of Capt. William Wingfield, late of Boſton, Merchant deceaſed, are deſired to make immediate Payment to Edward Procter, Sole Executor of his laſt Will:—And all thoſe who have any Demands on ſaid Eſtate, are deſired forthwith to bring them in to ſaid Executor, in Order to a ſpeedy Settlement. Boſton, Aug. 20, 1774.

All Perſons who have any Demands on the Eſtate of John Engleſby, *late of* Boſton, *Marriner, deceaſed, are deſired to bring in their Accounts to* Cuthbert Engleſby, *of ſaid* Boſton, *Adminiſtrator to ſaid Eſtate: And all who are indebted to ſaid Eſtate are deſired to make immediate Payment to ſaid Adminiſtrator.*

FOR LONDON,

The Brigantine KATY, 100 Tons Burthen,
JOHN DAVIS, Maſter,

WILL ſail from Plymouth with all convenient Speed, having the greateſt Part of her Cargo on Board and engag'd:—For Freight or Paſſage apply to the Maſter on Board, or at Mr. Solomon Davis's Store in Boſton.

WHEREAS Jonathan Fales *of Walpole, in the County of Suffolk, a Non Compos Mentis, did on the Fifteenth Day of June laſt, leave his Houſe and Family in ſaid Walpole, and has not been Home ſince. The ſaid Fales is a large fat Man, about 5 Feet 10 Inches high. Had on when he went away, a brown Home-made Coat, without a Jacket, ſtript Linnen Breeches, and a grey Pair of Stockings. If any Perſon will be ſo kind to a diſtreſs'd Woman as to bring him home (without abuſing him) or give Information that he may be found, they ſhall be honorably rewarded, by me the Subſcriber.* ELIZABETH FALES.

Walpole, the 19th of Auguſt, 1774.

TO BE SOLD OR LETT,

A large handſome Double House,

pleaſantly ſituated in Medford, together with one Acre of Land, with a Garden and Barn thereon, about a Quarter of a Mile Weſt from the Meeting-Houſe. Enquire of Samuel Reeves, living near the Premiſes.

BOSTON, Auguſt 15, 1774.

STOLEN out of the Paſture of the Subſcriber laſt Night, or this Morning, a light brown Horſe, about 14 Hands high, black Tail and Mane, except a ſmall white Lock in the Mane, near the Wethers, has a little Blemiſh in his off Eye, is rather ſhort of his Bigneſs, Paces chiefly, anſwers to the Name of Bonne; he is about 13 or 14 Years old.——The ſuſpected Thief is a ſhort thick Fellow, wears a reddiſh coloured Coat, a Bob Wig, and is bow-leged, ſometimes calls himſelf a Dutchman and at others a Carolinian. Whoever ſhall bring the Horſe to me, ſhall have FOUR DOLLARS Reward, and TEN DOLLARS for the Thief on Conviction, and all neceſſary Charges paid by

JOSEPH BRADFORD.

For private Sale,

At the New-Auction-Room South Side of the Town-Houſe, *viz.* Houſhold Furniture, Conſiſting of

PARLOUR, Chamber, and Kitchen Furniture, ſuch as Looking Glaſſes, Tables, Chairs and Book-Caſes, Deſks, Pewter, Braſs, Copper, Iron and Tin Ware of all ſorts, a genteel 8-Day Clock, Gold, Silver and Pinchbeck Watches, a Barometer, a Number of Iron Weights, (Quarters, half Quarters and 7 Pounds,) Plate, viz. a genteel ſilver Nearn, Tankard, Chaffindiſhes, Porringers, Salts, Pepper Boxes, Sugar Tongs, Strainer, Silver Hilted Swords; new and ſecond-hand Guns and Bayonets, Beaver and Gold Lac'd Hatts, Silver and Bone Handle Knives and Forks; ENGLISH GOODS, viz. Iriſh Linnens, Broad Cloths, Forreſt ditto, white Flannel, purple, olive and black Cotton Velvetts, Chintz, Callicoes, Shalloons, Callamancoes, Tammies, Stuffs, Durants of all Colours, Silk, Cotton, Thread & Worſted Hoſe, Capuchin Silks of all Colours, Sarſnets of all Colours, Silk Gauzes, Lawns, Dimothy's, black Sattin and Chip Hatts, printed Table Cloths, Breeches Pieces, Pound Threads, white and colour'd Riding Hatts, Mens black Bags, handſome Ribbons, a handſome Guiter, Ducapes, Brolioes, Pound Silks, white and black Silk Gloves and Mitts, Caſe Wax Work; Women's Wearing Apparel, viz. Dark Tabby Gown and Apron, Brocade, blue Luteſtring, Negligee, Sattin Quilts, a Luteſtring Sack, Damaſk and Diaper Table Linnens, Pillow Caſes, Cotton and Linnen Sheets, white Counterpins, a handſome Camp Bedſtead and Curtains compleat, Men's Second-hand Wearing Apparrel, and a Variety of other Articles.—

Alſo, Damaſkcuſes and Tobines, choice Indigo and Pepper, by the Hundred or Dozen, Claret WINE per Caſk, Groce or Dozen.

N. B. *At ſaid Auction Room conſtant Attendance is given to receive all Kinds of Goods for private and public Sale.*

NOTICE is again given, That the Commiſſioners appointed by the Hon. Foſter Hutchinſon, Eſq; Judge of Probate for the County of Suffolk, to examine the Claims to the Eſtate of Capt. SAMUEL SNOW, late of Boſton, deceaſed, repreſented Inſolvent, will continue to attend that Service at the Britiſh Coffee Houſe, the ſecond Tueſday in the three next enſuing Months, being the three laſt Months allowed for that Purpoſe, from 6 to 9 o'Clock in the Evening; that no Perſon may plead their not having ſuitable Notice of it.

BOSTON, Aug. 13, 1774. JOB PRINCE,
JOHN CARNES.

And all Perſons that are indebted to ſaid Eſtate, or that have Accounts not ſettled, together with all Freighters, are deſired to come and ſettle the ſame with John Carnes, at the South-End, Attorney to Sarah Snow, Adminiſtratrix to ſaid Eſtate.

All Perſons who have any Demands on the Eſtate of Benjamin Chamberlain Bunker, *late of* Charleſtown, *Innholder, deceaſed, are deſired to bring in their Accounts immediately to* Hannah Bunker, *Widow, ſole Executrix to ſaid Eſtate: And all Perſons indebted to ſaid Eſtate, are deſired to make Payment to ſaid Adminiſtratrix, as ſoon as poſſible, in Order for a ſpeedy Settlement of ſaid Eſtate.*

To be ſold on very reaſonable Terms,

The Hull of a double-deck'd Brigantine

about 146 Tons Burthen, now launched in Taunton-River. Farther enquire of ABIEL SMITH, nearly oppoſite to the Head of Orange-Tree Lane, Boſton, or Mr. JOB SMITH, at Taunton.

TO BE SOLD,

A Tract of Land at a Place called

Deer-Iſland, in *Penobſcot-Bay,* containing Six or Seven Hundred Acres, with a Dwelling-Houſe, Corn-Mill, Saw-Mill and a Wharff thereon, the Eſtate of Capt. *Nathaniel Kent,* late of *Glouceſter,* deceaſed. For Particulars, enquire of *Sarah Kent,* Executor of ſaid Eſtate.

Glouceſter, 11th Auguſt 1774.

WHEREAS the Committee for managing the Prudentials of the Proprietors of New Boſton, in New-Hampſhire, have received a Requeſt from Ten of the ſaid Proprietors to call a Meeting of ſaid Proprietors for the following Purpoſes, viz.—To chuſe a Proprietor's Clerk, the former Clerk being dead.—To chuſe a Committee to defend or carry on any Law-Suits that is or may be bro't againſt them, or to ſue any Perſon or Perſons that may be Treſpaſſers on any of their Lands in ſaid Town.—And as two of the Standing Committee are dead, to chuſe two in their Room; or to chuſe a new ſtanding Committee, as the ſaid Proprietors ſhall think proper.—And to know if the ſaid Proprietors will direct the ſaid Committee to ſell any of their undivided Land.

The ſaid Proprietors are hereby notified to meet at the Houſe of Thomas Harwood's, in Dunſtable, on Tueſday the 13th Day of September, 1774, at Ten o'Clock in the Forenoon.

The Proprietors of *Silveſter* Town,

lying on Androſgoggin-River, in the County of Cumberland, are hereby again notified that ſaid Proprietors, at their Meeting legally held by Adjournment, on the 7th Day of October, 1772, voted a Tax of 30s. on a Right, to be paid to Mr. Charles Turner, Proprietor's Treaſurer, on or before the 15th Day of March, 1773, and on the 10th Day of May 1774, voted a further Tax of 20s. on a Right, to be paid to the Treaſurer aforeſaid, on or before the 10th Day of September, 1774: And whereas many of the ſaid Proprietors are delinquent in paying the former of ſaid Taxes;—therefore unleſs ſaid Taxes ſhall be paid to the Treaſurer aforeſaid, on or before the 25th Day of October, 1774; ſo much of ſaid delinquent Proprietors Lands will be ſold at public Sale on ſaid Day, as ſhall be ſufficient to pay ſaid Taxes, and all neceſſary Charge, at the Houſe of Mr. Daniel Baker, Innholder in Pembroke, at Three o'Clock, P. M. Said Vendue to be adjourned if Occaſion require. *Per Order of the Committee,*

WILLIAM TURNER, *Propr's Clerk.*

Scituate, Auguſt 6, 1774.

WHEREAS the Chaiſe Houſe of the Subſcriber was broke open laſt Saturday-Night, and ſtole a Ruſſet-breaſted Saddle, Houſing half worn, with a Cut in the Seat, ript in the Breaſt; alſo a Curb Bridle, with double Reins. Whoever ſhall apprehend the Thief, and return the Saddle, ſhall have Two Dollars Reward.

Malden, Auguſt 10, 1774. ELIAKIM WILLIS.

New-York, July 27, 1774.

Fifty Pounds Reward.

WHEREAS on the 19th of June laſt paſt a certain JOSEPH THORP as entruſted at New-York with a conſiderable ſum of money in Half Johannes, of nine penny weight, to be delivered by him at Quebec, and as he has not yet made his appearance there, with other ſuſpicious circumſtances, it is apprehended he is gone off with the money. He is a native of England, about 35 Years of Age, ſix feet high, ſwarthy complexion, very dark keen eyes, with pimples in his face, and pitted with the ſmall pox, of a ſlender make, ſtoops as he walks, talks rather ſlow, with ſome ſmall impediment in his ſpeech, wears a wig and is very fond of ſmoaking. He lived ſome ſome time in Boſton, from whence he removed to Quebec, aſſuming the character of a merchant in both places; he was alſo once in trade in New-Caſtle, Virginia, and has a brother ſettled there. He went on board Captain John F. Pruym, for Albany, and landed at Pougheipſcigh, from whence he hired a waggon to carry him to New-Haven.—He took with him a blue calamir and dark brown ſuit of cloaths.

Whoever ſecures the ſaid JOSEPH THORP in any of his Majeſty's goals on this continent, ſhall be entitled to ten per cent. on the ſum recovered, and the above reward of Fifty Pounds when convicted. Apply to Curſon and Seton of New-York, Joseph Wharton, jun. of Philadelphia, Robert Chriſtie, of Baltimore, James Gibſon and Co. Virginia, John Bondfield of Quebec, or Melatiah Bourne of Boſton. It is requeſted of thoſe who may have ſeen this Joſeph Thorp, ſince the 19th of June laſt paſt, or know any Thing of the Rout he has taken, that they convey the moſt early Intelligence thereof to any of the above perſons, which will be gratefully acknowledged.

All Maſters of Veſſels are forewarned from taking him off the Continent.

Fred^k. W^m. Geyer & Abr^m. Burgeſs,

BEG Leave to acquaint the Public, That they have entered into a Co-partnerſhip, under the Firm of GEYER & BURGESS; and that they have on Hand a general Aſſortment of Engliſh, India and Scotch Piece Goods, which they are determined to ſell on the loweſt Terms, by Wholeſale only, at their Store (the Door below Meſſrs. Bethune and Prince's) in King Street, Boſton.

Said GEYER requeſts all thoſe indebted to him, or to the late Company of Frazier and Geyer, either on Bond, Note or Book, to make immediate Payment, otherwiſe they will be put in Suit. (6 weeks.)

Auguſt 1, 1774.

Boſton: Printed, by EDES & GILL,
in Queen-Street, 1774.

SUPPLEMENT to the *Boston*-Gazette, &c. of (No. 1011.)

MONDAY, August 29, 1774.

The following is the Continuation of the Address to the Inhabitants of the Massachusetts-Bay, begun in last Thursday's Spy, but handed in too late for the Paper; and is inserted here on Account of the great Importance of its timely Appearance.

AND as if this degradation of a material branch of your legislature were not sufficient to reduce you to the most abject state of vassallage, this same uncontrolled commander has every branch of the executive power absolutely in his own hands, and can nominate and appoint judges, commissioners of oyer and terminer, sheriffs, provosts, marshals, justices of the peace, &c. *without advice of council*, and displace them at pleasure, in direct opposition to the express words of the charter, and the usage of every state that pretends the least regard for the old Saxon forms. So that in direct violation of solemn charters, and every idea of a free government, you have Lords temporal at least, imposed upon you, not authorized by the choice of your Representatives more than inheriting their high stations from the virtue, honor and eminence of their ancestors; you have judges, not as at the beginning, sage, learned, impartial gentlemen, who had nothing but duty to GOD and their *country*, to influence their decisions, but creatures whose whole political existence depends on the breath of a minister, as despotic on the present plan in this province, as the Grand Vizir is in Damascus. What have you to expect from this combination of avowed enemies to our former happy constitution of civil government? Can you bear to have them trample it under foot? Can you suffer your indignation to slumber while you read of their taking solemn oaths to destroy you? Are not those twenty-six who have accepted of this odious delegation, *sworn enemies* to your peace and happiness? Are they not monsters of iniquity, born for a curse to their country, a reproach to the age they live in; a scandal to the land which has produced such determined *traitors* to its liberties, such usurpers of so important a deparment in its Goverment!!! Where are the laws against the highest crimes commissable in civil society? Do they, and shall they sleep eternally? Shall every villain for the smallest fee of office, venture on the fatal alteration of his country's established rules and orders, and be safe in so doing? Has not Goldthwait, the clerk of your courts, in direct violation of the oaths of office, in direct opposition to the laws and immemorial usages of the Province, issued his warrants for a return of freeholders from whom jurors are to be packed by the sheriff, according to the new mode of government? Do any of them hesitate to wound the Constitution in any article which falls within their particular department? Where then is safety to be expected for yourselves or posterity, but in your determination, at all events, to put an end to this system of usurpation, corruption, perjury and tyranny? If you suffer one step to take place and be established, another will succeed, and an everlasting farewell may soon be taken of all your dear-bought Rights, Liberties and Immunities. Should you not therefore, in the most public and solemn manner, forbid every clerk of a court, sheriff, constable, judge, or *usurping* councellor, at their utmost peril, to act, or be aiding, or any wise instrumental in putting those fatal ordinances into execution; and see that your warning is duly regarded. You have the power and the right. You have more, you have God on your side, who has made it your duty next to his own immediate adoration, to reverence and maintain the laws and constitution of your country. From the performance of this duty, nothing can excuse you, but your absolute incapacity to perform it. I trust none of you has either will or occasion to plead such an excuse. Your cause is just, your remedy plain and effectual, being pointed out in your charter, the only legal rule of your civil conduct, let Lord North & his partizans preach what they please. The great *Law of Nature* dictates, and your charter directs you to "put in warlike posture the inhabitants of this province or territory, and to lead and conduct them and with them to expulse, repel, resist and pursue by force of arms";—— "And also to kill, slay and destroy, and conquer by all fitting ways, enterprizes and means whatsoever, *all and every such person and persons* as shall at any time hereafter attempt or enterprize the *destruction invasion, detriment or annoyance* of the said province or territory." I by no means advise the taking up of arms rashly, lightly or inconsiderately. I would have it done for no other end than the defence of our Lives, Liberties and Estates. Acts of a foreign legislature are made, and armed troops sent to enforce them, which openly strikes at all these; and will any man say such a violent invasion, when it proceeds to the detriment, annoyance and destruction of the People, should not be opposed? The man who arms himself in defence of his Life, Liberty, Fortune, Laws and Constitution of his Country, can never be accounted a Rebel by any but a Banditti of villains, whose praise would be infamy, whose censure would be praise.

MASSACHUSETTENSIS.

INSTRUCTIONS for the Deputies appointed to meet in General Congress on the Part of the Colony of Virginia.

THE unhappy Disputes between Great-Britain and her American Colonies, which began about the third Year of the Reign of his present Majesty, and since continually increasing, have proceeded to lengths so dangerous and alarming as to excite just apprehensions in the minds of his Majesty's faithful subjects of this colony, that they are in danger of being deprived of their natural, ancient, constitutional and chartered Rights, have compell'd them to take the same into their most serious consideration; and, being deprived of their usual and accustomed mode of making known their Grievances, have appointed us their Representatives to consider what is proper to be done in this dangerous crisis of American affairs. It being our opinion that the united wisdom of North-America should be collected in a General Congress of all the Colonies, we have appointed the Hon. Peyton Randolph, *Esq;* Richard Henry Lee, George Washington, Patrick Henry, Richard Bland, Benjamin Harrison *and* Edmund Pendleton, *Esquires, Deputies to represent this Colony in the said Congress, to be held at* Philadelphia *on the first Monday in* September *next.*

And that they may be the better inform'd of our sentiments touching the conduct we wish them to observe on this important occasion, we desire that they will express, in the first place, our faith and true allegiance to his Majesty King George the Third, our lawful and rightful Sovereign; and that we are determin'd with our lives and fortunes, to support him in the legal exercise of all his just Rights and Prerogatives. And however misrepresented, we sincerely approve of a constitutional connection with Great-Britain, and wish most ardently a Return of that intercourse of affection and commercial connection that formerly united both countries, which can only be effected by a removal of those causes of discontent which have of late unhappily divided us.

It cannot admit of a doubt but that British subjects in America are entitled to the same Rights and Privileges as their fellow subjects possess in Britain; and therefore, that the power assumed by the British parliament to bind America by their statutes, in all cases whatsoever, is unconstitutional, and the source of these unhappy differences.

The end of government would be defeated by the British parliament exercising a power over the lives, the property, and the liberty of the American subject; who are not, and, from their local circumstances, cannot, be there represented. Of this nature we consider the several acts of parliament for raising a revenue in America, for extending the jurisdiction of the courts of Admiralty, for seizing American subjects and transporting them to Britain to be tried for crimes committed in America, and the several late oppressive acts respecting the town of Boston *and province of the* Massachusetts Bay.

The original constitution of the American colonies possessing their assemblies with the sole right of directing their internal polity, it is absolutely destructive of the end of their institution that their legislatures should be suspended, or prevented, by hasty dissolutions, from exercising their legislative powers.

Wanting the protection of Britain, we have long acquiesced in their acts of navigation restrictive of our commerce, which we consider as an ample recompence for such protection; but as those acts derive their efficacy from that foundation alone, we have reason to expect they will be restrain'd so as to produce the reasonable purposes of Britain, and not injurious to us.

To obtain redress of these grievances, without which the people of America can neither be safe, free nor happy, they are willing to undergo the great inconvenience that will be derived to them from stopping all imports whatever from Great-Britain after the first day of November *next; and also cease exporting any commodity whatever to the same place after the 10th day of* August 1775. *The earnest desire we have to make as quick and full payment as possible of our debts to Great Britain, and to avoid the heavy injury that would arise to this country from an earlier adoption of the non-exportation plan, after the people have already applied so much of their labour to the perfecting the present crop, by which means they have been prevented from pursuing other methods of clothing, and supporting their families, have rendered it necessary to restrain you in this article of non-exportation; but it is our desire that you cordially co-operate with our sister colonies in general Congress, in such other just and proper methods as they, or the majority, shall deem necessary for the accomplishment of these valuable ends.*

The Proclamation issued by General Gage, in the government of the province of the Massachusetts-Bay, *declaring it Treason for the inhabitants of that province to assemble themselves to consider of their grievances and form associations for their common conduct on the occasion, and requiring the civil magistrate and officers to apprehend all such persons to be tried for their supposed offences; is the most alarming process that ever appeared in a British government; that the said General Gage hath thereby assumed and taken upon himself powers denied by the constitution to our legal Sovereign; that he not having condescended to disclose by what authority he exercises such extensive and unheard of powers, we are at a loss to determine whether he intends to justify himself as the Representative of the King, or as the commander in chief of his Majesty's forces in North-America. If he considers himself as acting in the character of his Majesty's Representative, we would remind him that the statute of 25th Edward 3d, has expressed and defined all treasonable offences; and that the legislature of Great-Britain hath declared that no offence shall be construed to be treason, but such as is pointed out by that statute; and that this was done to take out of the hands of tyrannical Kings, and of weak and wicked ministers, that deadly weapon, which constructive treason had furnished them with, and which had drawn the blood of the best and honestest men in the kingdom; and that the King of Great-Britain hath no right by his proclamation to subject his people to imprisonment, pains and penalties.*

That if the said General Gage conceives he is empowered to act in this Manner, as the commander in chief of his Majesty's forces in America, this illegal and odious proclamation must be considered as a plain and full declaration that this despotic viceroy will be bound by no law, nor regard the constitutional rights of his Majesty's subjects, whenever they interfere with the plan he has formed for oppressing the good people of the Massachusetts-Bay; and therefore, that the executing, or attempting to execute such proclamation, will justify resistance and reprisal.

To his Excellency Governor GAGE.

SIR,

YOU have yet the power of saving yourself from infamy—do not loose the few moments which providence favors you with—stop before you plunge into that gulph where hope never comes and where you must be forever under the dominion of despair—instantly call in the aid of the Constitutional Council of the Province—request them to use the power and influence they have with the people, to quiet their disturbed minds until redress can be had of their grievances from Great-Britain—sooth the just indignation of the people by mild and gentle advice and most explicit promises to use all means in your power to restore their rights which have been unjustly ravished from them.—Let this be your part and it may be the salvation of the British Empire.—I am unknown to you and my advice may be despised, you will however remember that this advice has been given you and that it will appear in Judgment against you, shou'd any fatal consequences follow your refusal to comply with it.—I have now a few words to say to the Gentlemen who have, under color of a mandamus from the King, taken the Oaths as Councellors for this Province.

Gentlemen, it is your duty as Christians, subjects of the king of Great-Britain, and inhabitants of this Province instantly to resign your offices and publickly to acknowledge your error and beg pardon of your Countrymen—without doing this immediately, you may justly expect that all intercourse between you and your fellow subjects will be forever cut off——No one will buy or improve your houses or your lands——your fields will be left untilled, and your estates real and personal be of no value to you or your posterity——A proverbial ignominy will be perpetually entailed on your names and families, and you will be accountable to God and your own Consciences for all the evils which your wicked ambition may occasion——Remember the things that belong to your peace before they are everlastingly hidden from your eyes.

MICAIAH.

Messieurs EDES & GILL,

Please to insert the following in your next.

WHEREAS I am informed that I am hardly censured by a number of persons in this town as a lewd woman, on my pardoning one Corporal M'Kenny, *of his Majesty's 5th regiment of foot, who assaulted me in my privy and used me in a ridiculous manner; but making my address to Earl* Persey, *he immediately ordered him to be confined, tried and sentenced by* Courtmartial, *to be reduced to the ranks and receive* one hundred lashes, *as you may see in the copy of his trial and sentence which I requested of the Colonel for my own satisfaction, as well as others, least the virtuous part of my sex might probably imagine I laid no punishment upon him, but believe my friends (if any I have) that I did not show so much lenity because I admired him, surely I had more reason to abhor than admire. I should be glad to know the persons, or at least they would make themselves known to me, either by way of letter or by publishing in your next, what reason they have for so wrongfully censuring me, as they have in this affair; I can say with truth, I did what I did out of a good end, little thinking but what I should be commended instead of being ridiculed; on the Earls word and honor, I forgave the prisoner, that he the prisoner should never molest me nor mine, nor approach my dwelling, if he did he should be inflicted with treble times the punishment now laid on him. If I had been a lewd woman I should perhaps laid ten times the punishment on him to make me appear virtuous to the eyes of the world.*

I am your humble servant, S. M.

Proceedings of a Regimental COURTMARTIAL *held in His Majesty's 5th Regiment of Foot, by Order of the Commanding Officer,* August 6, 1774.

Capt. *William Battier*, President.

Lieut. *John Jackson*, Ens. *John Ballaguire*,	Members.	Lieut. *R. Croker*, Ens. *W Nunwick*,

THE Court proceeded to the Tryal of Corporal *McKenny*, of Capt. *Downes's* Company, confined by the Commanding Officer, for abusing and Ill-treating a Town's Woman, *Sarah Muncrief*, informs the Court that on Tuesday the 2d Inst. about the Hour of Twelve in the Forenoon, the Prisoner came to her House to inquire for one *Delbrenton*, and on being told she was not in the House, that then the Prisoner inquired for *Kate Derby*, on which he was told that she might be within, but did not live in that Part of the House, on which the Prisoner went away; in a few Minutes after the Deponent went to a Necessary-House and shut the Door after her, on which some Person came and opened the Door, which proved to be the Prisoner, who rushed in and took the Deponent by the Arms and put her on her Back, on which she called out Murder several Times, and immediately the Prisoner took her by the Throat with one Hand and with the other he took up her Petticoats, and that he pressed, in which Time *Kate Derby* came to her Relief and put the Prisoner off, and then said you are an impertinent Dog, and that she would have him punished, on which he drew his Bayonet and she made her Escape into the House, on which he attempted to follow her, but that *Katey Derby* held him which prevented him.

Corporal *McKenny* being put on his Defence, says that he did take hold of a Woman in the Necessary-House, but can't say whether this is the Woman; and further says that on her desiring him to take off her that he did.

The Court are of Opinion that the Prisoner is Guilty of the Crime, and of a Breach of the 3d Article and 20th Section of the Articles of War, and do Sentence him to be reduced to the Ranks, and receive *One Hundred Lashes* in the usual Manner, by the Drummers of the Regiment.

WM. BATTIER, Capt. and President.

A true Copy, BEN. BAKER, Adjutant 5th Foot.

SALEM, August 16, 1774.

On the 20th of this Instant printed Notifications were posted up in this Town, desiring the Merchants, Freeholders, and other Inhabitants, to meet at the Town-house chamber last Wednesday at Nine o'Clock in the Morning, to appoint Deputies to meet at Ipswich on the 6th of September next, with the Deputies of the other Towns in the County, to consider of, and determine on such Measures as the late Acts of Parliament and our other Grievances render necessary and expedient. These Notifications purported, that it was the Desire of the Committee of Correspondence that the Inhabitants should thus assemble.—On Wednesday Morning at Eight o' Clock the Governor sent a Request to the Committee, that they would meet him at Nine o'Clock, telling them he had something of Importance to communicate to them.— They waited upon him accordingly, and were asked by him if they avowed those Notifications? Being answered that it was known they were posted by Order of the Committee, he then desired them to disperse the Inhabitants, who being assembled by them they must abide all the Consequences. It was answered, that the Inhabitants being met together would do what they thought fit, and that the Committee could not oblige them to disperse. His Excellency declared it was an unlawful, seditious meeting; it was replied, neither the Committee nor the Inhabitants supposed the Meeting was contrary even to the Act of Parliament, much less to the Laws of the Province. The Governor recurred, I am not going to enter into a Conversation on the Matter; I came to execute the Laws, not to dispute them, and I am determined to execute them. If the People do not disperse, the Sheriff will go first; if he is disobeyed, and needs Support, I will Support him. This he uttered, with much Vehemence of Voice and Gesture.——————— The Governor had ordered Troops to be in Readiness: They prepared accordingly as if for Battle, left their Encampment, and marched to the Entrance of the Town, there halted and loaded, and then about Eighty advanced within an Eighth of a Mile from the Town-House: But before this Movement of the Troops was known to the Inhabitants, and while the Committee were in Conference with the Governor, the whole Business of the Meeting was transacted, being merely to chuse Delegates for the County Meeting. After the Meeting was over, News came that the Troops were on the March; but they were now ordered to return to the Camp.—Yesterday Peter Frye, Esq; (by express Orders from the Governor, as he declared to the Committee) issued a Warrant for arresting the Committee of Correspondence, for unlawfully and seditiously causing the People to assemble by that Notification, without Leave from the Governor, in open Contempt of the Laws, against the Peace, and the Statute in that Case made and provided. Two of the Committee who were first arrested recogniz'd, each in One Hundred Pounds, without Sureties, to appear at the next Superior Court at Salem, to answer to the above-mentioned Charge. The rest of the Committee, who were arrested some Time after, have refused to recognize.

Previous to the Town-Meeting, the Governor issued a Proclamation "prohibiting all Persons from attending said Meeting, as they will be chargeable with all the ill Consequences that may follow theron, and answer the same at their Peril."

BOSTON, August 29.

We hear from Salem, that last Week the Hon. ANDREW OLIVER, Esq; waited upon his Excellency the Governor with a Resignation of his Seat at the Council Board.

In our next we shall endeavor to give our Readers a particular Account of the Proceeding of the People with some of the Mandamus Gentry, viz. Willard, Paine, Murry, Ruggles, Leonard and Edson, not having Room for it this Week.

A Correspondent says, the Province will never rest while one Man who has accepted any Office under the Sanction of the new Acts of Parliament is possessed of any one Post of Power or Profit in the Country, and untill every one of them by great Penitence obtain Forgiveness, or leave America,———— and untill all your Addressors to Hutchinson have by humbling themselves regained the good Will of the Country, and the City of Boston in particular——or else are removed off from the Continent.

A PROPOSAL *from different Parts of the Country— It is proposed that an Estimate should be formed by indifferent People of the Value of all the Real Estates in Boston, that so if the Estates in should be sunk in their Value by the Port Bill's continuing to be inforced, or should otherwise be ruined by the Rage of our common Enemies, the Country might be able to form a Judgment of the Retribution that should be made to the Sufferers.——This does Honor to the public Virtue of our Country.*

A fire broke out at Salem on Wednesday Morning, about two o'Clock, which consumed four or five Shops, occupied by Coopers, a Blacksmith, &c. together with a large Warehouse, belonging to Capt. George Dodge, containing a Quantity of Molasses, about 500 Bushels of Corn, &c. a great Part of which were destroyed. Three valuable Distill Houses, besides other large Buildings, were in eminent Danger; but by the Vigilance of the Inhabitants, with a full Supply of Water, they were happily preserved.

Wednesday arrived at Marblehead, Capt. Perkins from Baltimore, with 3000 Bushels of Indian Corn, 20 Barrels of Rye Meal, and 21 Barrels of Bread, sent by the Inhabitants of that Place for the Benefit of the Poor of Boston; together with 1000 Bushels of Corn from Annapolis, sent in the same Vessel, and for the same benevolent Purpose.

Extract of a Letter from a principal Town in one of the Southern Colonies.

"THE Province of the Massachusetts Bay, and the Town of Boston, (in our Opinion) are intitled to the most grateful Thanks of all English America, for the very important Part they have acted in the first Settlement of this Country; and for their noble and costly Exertions, and the copious Effusion of their Blood, in its Defence against her innumerable Indian and French Enemies. The King and Nation of G. Britain are also indebted to you for the great Hand you have had in enlarging the Dominions of the one, and greatly encreasing the beneficial Commerce of the other. And neither the one nor the other of those Services could ever have been effected, but by the Influence of that very Spirit of Liberty, at which the British Administration seem so enrag'd, and are so determined to crush. You have borne your Burdens and struggled without their Aid, with the Instruments of Culture in one Hand, and the Weapons of War in the other, for necessary Defence, while laboring for daily Bread, and subduing the rugged Soil. Your Toils and your Perils would have been absolutely insupportable, but for the all chearing influence of the Heaven born Maid, that Spirit and Thirst of religious and civil Liberty, which inspired you and our fathers with divine Enthusiasm to attempt, (and blessed be the Lord who enabled them) to accomplish the Wonders which our Eyes behold.

You had the most cogent Reasons to believe that a Nation renowned thro'out the World for its strong and inviolable Attachment to, and manly Struggles in Defence of Liberty; would never suffer that inestimable Jewel, for which they themselves have shed Rivers of Blood, to be wrested from you by the hand of Violence; and more especially as it would lay a sure Foundation for the Destruction of their own remaining Privileges; and for the vast Diminution or total Loss of their immensely beneficial American Commerce.

"Strange also that a King, possessed of any just and humane Sentiments, should be so regardless of the Merits and Rights of his Americans, and the Interest and Welfare of his British Subjects, as to attempt to rend out of the Hands of the former, all the Fruits of their unparalleled Sufferings and Hardships, for the Pleasure of ruling over the Bodies of Slaves, instead of reigning in the Hearts of Freemen, most willing to be his loyal Subjects forever, according to the Constitution of his Crown and Kingdom, and even at the immense Hazard of obtaining by Force at most, far less, than what the Crown and Kingdom might continue to receive by our free Consent.

"But such is the astonishing Infatuation of the Times, that the Lust of Tyranny is revived, and risen high in Great-Britain; and Liberty is to be hunted from the Globe, and quit the Dwellings of Men. A more finished and perfect Definition and Picture of Despotism cannot be drawn by the Skill of Man, than is portray'd in the famous declaratory Bill or Act of the British Parliament, passed a few Years since. Nor can that be carried into more compleat and perfect Execution (save in Extent of its Operation only) than by that Prodigy of Oppression and Injustice, the Boston-Port Bill, and by two other Acts destroying the ancient Charter and Constitutional Rights of your Colony.

"Well might the short sighted Minister think, the Blows were so sudden and severe; he had done the worst and that unless Blood and dismal Carnage prevented, he had effectually subjugated you, and that the rest would fall an easy Prey. But he was totally ignorant of your, and the Virtue, Spirit and Knowledge of America, while he confidently believed, that you would lie down and kiss his Feet; and that the rest would patiently see you in that humble Posture, and deem you solely aimed at, and justly punished for suffering the Destruction of private Property in your Harbour, and some paltry Wretches to be dressed in Tar and Feathers.

"But America sees with other Eyes, and perfectly knows that you are only designed for the first Victim in the Hecatomb of Sacrifice to be offered to the God of Oppression, and will not therefore willingly suffer you to bleed at the Shrine of his Brazen Altar, untill we all bleed and die together." — —.

The July Packet arrived at New-York last Monday after the Paper was printed off—We do not learn the Packet has bro't any News later than what we inserted in our last.—No New-York Paper receiv'd by the last Mail.

The Delegates from this Province and New-Hampshire arrived at New-York last Saturday Se'nnight.

Letters from Philadelphia say, that city only has raised FOUR THOUSAND pounds, that currency, for the support of Boston; and that every other town in Pennsylvania government are doing in proportion.

Next Thursday Evening,

TO BE SOLD,

By *BENJAMIN CHURCH,*

At his usual Place of Sale,

CLOTH Camblets—Calamancoes—Calicoes—Linnens—Checks—Muslins—Hard Ware, as Case Knives and Forks—Penknives—Shoe Buckles—Buttons—House Furniture, viz. Feather Beds, Tables, Desks, an 8-Day Clock, Watches, &c. &c.

N. B. A good Chaise and Harness.

THURSDAY EVENING.

New AUCTION-ROOM, Cornhill.

TO MORROW MORNING, at TEN o'Clock,

Will be Sold by PUBLIC VENDUE,

At GREENLEAF's Auction-Room,

A great Variety of Womens Wearing Apparel, belonging to a Lady in a distant Province, and never worn in this Town, amongst them are,—Twelve rich Sacks and Petticoats, many of them almost new, a Number of other Gowns of fine Muslin Chints, &c. Sundry Sattin Cloaks, Shades, Silk Aprons, Russel Petticoats, Callico, Linnen, Dimothy and Flannel ditto, Bonnets and Hatts, Gauze, Catgut, Silk, Kenting and Muslin Handkerchiefs, double-Lawn Dresden-work'd and other Ruffles, Linnen, Muslin and Gauze Aprons, a Variety of Caps with rich Laces, Cotton and silk Hose, silk and worsted Shoes, Ermine Muffs and Tippets and furr'd Border, Silk Stomachers, Ribbons, and a Quantity of Wearing Linnen, a Man's Scarlet Jacket trim'd with Gold Lace. Also a Variety of English Goods as usual—A Bag of ungin'd Cotton Wool, and two good Feather Beds, one Cask Snuff, and some Money Scales.

W. GREENLEAF, Auctioneer.

The Sale will begin To-Morrow Morning Ten o'Clock.

Thomas Walley,

Begs Leave to inform his Friends

and Customers, that he is Removed from his Store on Dock-Square, to the first Store in BUTLER's-ROW, lately Improved by Mr. *Samuel Allene Otis*, being the opposite Corner to Mr. *Thomas Handasyde Peck*, Hatter, where he continues to sell all Sorts of Groceries as usual, by Wholesale and Retail, at the lowest Rates, and his Customers, may depend they shall be as well used, as at any Store in Boston.

N. B. A Quantity of choice Raisins in good Order, Teneriffe Wine by the Pipe, Hogshead or Quarter Cask, very best Lisbon and M. Malaga, by the Quarter Cask, also race and ground Ginger,—at said Store.

BUTLER's-ROW, No. 1.

All Persons that have any Demands on the Estate of Mr. JOSEPH JACKSON, late of Boston, Truckman, deceased, are desired to bring in their several Demands to ABIGAIL JACKSON, sole Executrix to said Estate.—And those who are indebted to said Estate, are requested to settle and pay the same to said Executrix immediately.

TO BE SOLD at the Royal Exchange Tavern in King-Street, Boston.

At PUBLIC VENDUE,

On Wednesday the Fourteenth Day of September next, at Ten o'Clock in the Forenoon,

The following Lots of Land, viz.

Lot marked F, 2. in the first Range of Lots, containing about six Thousand Acres (exclusive of Settlers Lots interspersed) being near one Mile wide and fifteen Miles long, and fronting on *Kennebeck*-River, on the West-side of it, about ten Miles above Fort Halifax: to be divided and Sold in two Parts.

Lot marked B. D. 1. in the second range of Lots, about six Miles above *Norridgwalk*, on the West Side of *Kinnebeck* River, and fronting thereon, containing about seven Thousand Acres, exclusive of Settlers Lots interspersed, being one Mile wide, and 15 Miles long.

Lot marked C. A. 1. in the third range of Lots, near the Falls of *Cariotonka*, about twelves Miles above *Norridgwalk*, on the West Side of *Kennebeck* River, and fronting thereon, containing about 7000 Acres, exclusive of Settlers Lots interspersed, being one Mile wide, and fifteen Miles long.

Lot No. 20, called a Ten Mile back Lot, on the West Side of Kennebec-River, containing about 4800 Acres.

Three Lots of Land, viz. Lot No. 22, on the East Side of *Kennebec*-River, about 300 Poles above *Fort-Western*, No 86, on the East Side of said River, about 9 Miles and 120 Poles above *Fort-Western*, and also Lot No. 20, on the West Side of said River, about one Mile and 230 Poles above *Fort-Western*, containing 400 Acres each.

Also all the Islands in Cobbiseconte Pond, and all the Islands in *Kennebeck*-River, above *Fort-Halifax*. The Pay will be made easy to the Purchasers.

For further Particulars, enquire of *Henry Alline*, jun. at his Office in King-Street, *Boston*. *June* 10, 1774.

Boston, Aug. 26, 1774. HAVING observed a Paragraph in the Spy of Thursday last, intimating that I had been rigorously treated in bringing a Load of Sand to this Town.—This may Certify, That it is utterly a Mistake; that I was kindly indulged in my Request for Permission to bring up that Article.

ROBT. FAIRSERVICE.

RAN-away from his Master, on the 25th Instant, a Negro Fellow named CATO, about 20 Years of Age, about 5 Feet 8 Inches high, a thick well set Fellow. Had on when he went away, a thin Homespun Coat, a Woollen Shirt, and Tow Trowsers.—Whoever shall take up said Runaway, and convey him to his Master in Salem, shall have TWO DOLLARS Reward, and all necessary Charges paid by me.

DANIEL MALLOON.

All Masters of Vessels and others, are hereby cautioned against concealing, harbouring or entertaining said Runaway, on Penalty of the Law.

SALEM, August 29. 1774.

Five Dollars Reward.

STOLEN out of the Stable of the Subscriber in Ipswich, on the 25th of August a dark Bay Horse, about 10 Years of Age, Trotts and Paces, has a black Main and Tail, is very tender Mouthed, likewise a Saddle and Bridle, the Makers Name Sharwin, the Saddle is lined with white Flannel, and has a main Pillion for a Portmanteau.—Whoever shall secure said Horse, Saddle and Bridle, so that the Owner may have him again, and secure the Thief, so that he be bro't to Justice, shall have the above Reward, and four Dollars for the Horse only.

Ipswich, Aug. 26. 1774. JACOB TREADWELL,

TO-MORROW MORNING,

At Ten in the Morning,

Will be Sold by PUBLIC VENDUE,

All the Houshold Furniture of Mrs. EDWARDS, deceas'd, at her House in Quaker Lane,

——Consisting of——

MAhogany and Walnut Leather Bottom'd Chairs Chamber and Common ditto, one Mahogany Desk, Mahogany and other Tables, one Easy Chair, &c.

Burials in the Town of BOSTON, since our last.

Nine Whites. No Blacks.

Baptiz'd in the several Churches, Sixteen.

High Water at BOSTON, *for the present Week.*

Monday, 42 min. aft.	5	Friday, 56 min. after.	8
Tuesday, 33 min. aft.	6	Saturday, 42 min. aft.	9
Wednesday, 21 m. aft.	7	Lord's Day, 26 m. af.	10
Thursday, 9 min. aft.	8	☽'s Last Quarter Yeste.	

THE

Boston-

AND

COUNTRY

Gazette,

JOURNAL.

No. 1012

Containing the freshest Advices, Foreign and Domestic.

MONDAY, September 5, 1774.

AT a Meeting of the Committees of Correspondence from a Majority of the Towns in the County of *Worcester*, convened at *Worcester*, on Tuesday the 9th Day of August 1774, and continued by Adjournment, the following Votes were passed.

1. *Resolved*, That we bear all true allegiance to his Majesty King George 3d, and that we will to the utmost of our power, defend his Person, Crown and Dignity, and at the same time we disclaim any Jurisdiction in the Commons of Great Britain over his Majesty's Subjects in America.

2. *Resolved*, That the Charter of this Province is the Basis of our Allegiance to his Majesty, wherein, on his part, the royal Faith is plighted to protect & defend us his American Subjects, in the free & full Enjoyment of each and every Right & Liberty enjoyed by his Subjects in Great Britain; his American Subjects likewise bear him true Alegiance.

3. *Resolved*, That we have within ourselves, the exclusive Right of originating each and every Law respecting ourselves, and ought to be on an equal Footing with his Majesty's Subjects in Great Britain.

4. *Resolved*, That an attempt to vacate said Charter by either Party, without the Consent of the other, has a Tendency to dissolve the Union between Great Britain and this Province, to destroy the Allegiance we owe to the King, and to set aside the sacred Obligations he is under to his Subjects here.

3. *Resolved*, That the Right lately assumed by the Parliament of Great Britain over this Province, wherein they claim a disposal of our Lives and Properties, and to alter and disannul our Charter without our consent, is a great and high-handed Claim of arbitrary Power.

6. *Resolved*, That as Parliament have not only adopted the aforementioned principle, but have actually put it into Practice by taxing the Americans, and most cruelly blocking up the Harbour of Boston, in order to force this Province to a Submission to such Power, and have farther proceeded to pass several Acts to change our free Constitution in such manner, which, if effected, will render our Lives and Properties wholly insecure. Therefore,

7. *Resolved*, That it is the indisputable Duty of every American, and more especially of this Province, to unite in every virtuous Opposition that can be devised, in order to save ourselves and Posterity from inevitable Ruin: And in the first Place we greatly approve of the Agreement entered and entering into thro' this and the neighbouring Provinces, for the Non-Consumption of British Goods. This, we apprehend, will have a tendency to convince our Brethren in Britain, that more is to be gained in the way of Justice, from our Friendship and Affection, than by Extortion and arbitrary Power. We apprehend that the Ballance of our Trade with Britain has been greatly in their favor; that we can do much better without it than they can; and that the increase of such Trade heretofore, was greatly occasioned by the regard and affection borne by the Americans to their Brethren in Britain. Such an Agreement, if strictly adhered to, will greatly prevent Extravagance, save our Money, encourage our own Manufactures, and reform our Manners.

8. *Resolved*, That those Justices of the Court of General Sessions and Common Pleas for this County, who in a late Address to his Excellency Governor Gage aspersed the good People of this County, have thereby discovered that they were destitute of that tender regard which we might justly expect in our present distressed Situation.

VOTED, That we most earnestly recommend it to the several Towns in this County (and if it should not be thought too arrogant) to every Town in the Province, to meet and adopt some wise, prudent, and spirited Measures, in order to prevent the Execution of these most alarming Acts of Parliament, respecting our Constitution.

The above Resolves were passed without one dissentient.

Voted, That this Meeting be adjourned to the last Tuesday in August Instant, at 10 o'Clock, A. M.

By Order of the Committee of Correspondence, met in Convention, SAM. BAKER.

Attest. *Wm. Henshaw*, Clerk.

From the Public Advertiser, London, *May* 10. 1774.

WHEN I read the Fable of the old Woman who killed her Hen to get all the golden Eggs at once, I thought it the most unmeaning of all Æsop's, as neither my Master nor my Father could make out a Case for me to which I could apply it cleaverly; but our present Conduct towards the North Americans is exactly the Thing, and convinces me that there are Statesmen infinitely more foolish than the old Woman; for could she have brought her Hen to Life again she never would have attempted a second Experiment. We have it in our Power to restore Life and Vigour to our American Trade, but instead of so doing, we seem determined not only to destroy it effectually, but to make those industrious People our Enemies, or at least to put the Nation to an immense Expence in supporting an Army and Navy from which we can derive no other Consequence than impoverishing them to our own Ruin; for as to the Pretext of ascertaining their Dependence on Great Britain, no Man in his Senses can seriously make Use of it, as the Americans never attempted to deny it, though they refused to be taxed by us. Every thinking Englishman must feel how inexpedient it would be for us that they were to be taxed otherwise than by themselves in their Assemblies. Let not Lord North, however, be blamed for pushing the Plan of Despotism laid down for him. The Primum Mobile has been silly enough to recommend a Plan which he's too short-sighted to foresee the fatal Consequences, and his Successors, under his Direction, must carry it on, or give Way to others who will, or even do worse if possible. It was upon the same Principle that the great Pitt adopted continental Measures, though so much against his own Judgment.

Just Published, and Sold by EDES *and* GILL, *in Queen-Street*, [*Price* 9d.]

The Memoirs of the Life of the Rev.

GEORGE WHITEFIELD, A. M,

Late Chaplain to the Countess of Huntingdon.

Compiled by the Rev. JOHN GILLIES, D. D.

Messieurs EDES & GILL,

Arthur Young, *Esq;* of Hertfordshire *in Old England (an Author well known and esteem'd at Home, tho' but little read in this Country) in the Year* 1768, *made a Six Months Tour through the North of England, which was published the succeeding Year in four Volumes Octavo—a second Edition was printed in* 1771. *The following Quotations from this last Edition Vol.* 3d *p.* 187—194 *inserted in your Paper, will oblige many other Readers, besides your humble Servant*,

Aug. 26, 1774 AN INDEPENDENT WHIG.

"THE *Manchester* Manufactures are divided into four Branches; the Fustian, the Check, the Hat, the Worsted small Wares.

All these are divided into numerous Branches, of distinct and separate Work—in that of Fustian are thirteen.—— These Branches of Manufacture work both for Exportation and Home Consumption: Many low priced Goods they make for *North-America*, and many fine ones for the *West-Indies*. The whole Business was exceeding brisk during the War, and very bad after the Peace; but now are pretty good again, tho' not equal to what they were during the War. All the Revolutions of late in the *North-American* Affairs, are felt severely in this Branch. It was never known in it, that poor People applied for Work and could not get it, except in the Stagnation caused by the Stamp-Act.

The Check Branch like the Fustian Works both for Exportation and Home consumption, but *vastly more* for the former than the latter. During the War the demand was extremely brisk; very dull upon the peace, but lately has arisen greatly, tho' not equal to the war; and the interceptions caus'd by the convulsion in *America*, very severely felt by every Workman in this Branch: none ever offer'd for Work but they at once had it, except upon the Regulation of the Cutting off their Trade with the *Spaniards* and the *Stamp Act*.— The last Advices received from *America* have had a similar effect, for many Hands were paid off in consequence of them.—The number of Spinners employ'd in and out of *Manchester* is immense; they reckon thirty Thousand Souls in that Town; and fifty Thousand Manufacturers employed *out* of it.—— *America* takes THREE-FOURTHS of all the Manufactures of MANCHESTER."

ST. CROIX, JULY 9.

On the 3d of June, about five o'Clock in the morning, some small shocks of an Earthquake were felt at an Indian village, about six leagues from Guatimala, and very near the coast of the South Sea, but did then no damage except alarming the inhabitants. The shocks continued with trifling intermissions, 'till five o'clock in the evening, when the effects of nature began to break forth in all their terrors; lightning and thunder were incessant, attended with a heavier rain than was ever known there; the sea rose in such a convulsive manner, that it overflowed the highest banks, and at the same time the land was so agitated by the earthquake, that the village was solely destroyed in a short time, and not a trace of it left. The major part of the inhabitants, on the first appearances of the tempest, had fled towards the city of Guatimala, but found no shelter there, that unhappy place being involved in more misery than where they fled from. The two famous mountains near that place were in a state of the greatest eruption: The one which emits a liquid fire and amazing large stones, threw out its most enraged force, on the devoted city; the other, which, in a like manner issues out water, deluged the land about, and was full fraught with destruction. The violent shocks of the earthquake, the lightning, thunder, and rain made one dreadful scene of confusion not to be paralleled. This war of nature commenced in its full force about eight o'clock in the evening, and continued raging 'till the night of the 7th day, in which time the university, the public courts of justice, the cathedral, the parochial churches, all the public edifices, were destroyed, either by the earthquake, by the fire and stones from the mountains or by the impetuosity of the river which rose above its banks, and bore every thing before it with the greatest violence. Chasms of a great extent were made in the earth, and many whole houses, with numbers of the miserable inhabitants fell in and were seen no more. But how can the anguish of the unhappy sufferers be described? The acts of devotion which their tortur'd fears prompted them to use were all in vain; their priests swallowed up, struck dead, or otherwise destroyed in the very moment of administring absolution. Many appalled by the scene, stood fixed, and received the inevitable death that awaited; those who escaped from the city were encircled with dangers and death, the fields afforded no shelter, the earth was convulsed, as with pain, and the volcanos and rocks with which that country abounds, were raging with fire, and throwing out stones of a most prodigious size.

"On the night of the 7th, about the hour of ten, the mountain raged excessively, the earth shook with great violence, and the thunder encreased; this lasted about 5 minutes, when the whole city of Guatimala was destroyed, was swallowed in a wide casm, a rent in nature, and the fiery earth spread over in a manner which soon obscured it from sight.— The elements now as gratified with their prey, calmed most surprizingly: by the noon of the next day every thing was again calm and serene, but the face of the earth was altered, the city was gone, the burning mountain shook in its base, and other rocks sunk with their tops on the earth; the river was parted in many places, and formed into standing pools of a bitter, smoaky water, and the fine vale was covered with large stones, and the lava (cooled) which had issued from the mountains. The numbers of people lost are not yet, nor possibly ever will be, really ascertained, as those who may have escaped have not yet been heard of, except the President of the audience, the Bishop of the place, and about 170 others, who have providentially escaped to Trinidad, or Sonsonate, about 30 leagues from Guatimala, and about 200 who have arrived here.

"This event may be considered as one of the most dreadful that ever happened: in its beginning, continuance, and consequences equally dreadful & tremendous. The vicious lives of the inhabitants of that fated city, and in fact of many other cities of Spanish America, would justify an opinion that the Creator of all things did not suffer such a punishment to fall in vain."

Messieurs EDES & GILL,

It would be received as a Favour from you to give the following a Place in your next, as every Thing of a public Nature is at this Time subject to Misrepresentation.

On Saturday the 27th of August 1774, upwards of a Thousand respectable Inhabitants of a Number of Towns in the County of *Worcester*, thought proper in a very decent and orderly Manner to wait on John Murray, Esq; of Rutland, in Order to converse with him upon his new and unconstitutional Appointment and Acceptance as a Councellor: But said Assembly after being conven'd found themselves under a great Disappointment, by being satisfied that on the preceeding Evening he was apprized of the laudable Intensions of the People, and conscious at the same Time of the Atrociousness of his Crime, did on said Evening abscond from his Dwelling, and fled to the City of Refuge for Protection. The People so assembled being disappointed concluded to retire after voting to leave the following with his Family, to be transmitted to him for his Consideration.

Rutland, August 27, 1774.

To John Murray, *Esq;*

SIR,

AS you have proved yourself to be an open Enemy to this Province, by your late Conduct in general, and in particular in accepting of the late Appointment as an unconstitutional Counsellor; in Consequence whereof, a large Number of Men from several Towns are assembled, who are fully determined to prevent your holding said Office as Counsellor, at the Risque of our Lives and Fortunes; and not finding you at Home, think proper to propose to your serious Consideration the following viz.

That you make an immediate Resignation of your Office, as a Counsellor.

Your Compliance as above, published in each of the Boston News-Prints by the Tenth Day of September next, will save the People of this County the Trouble of waiting on you immediately afterwards.

In the Name and Behalf of the whole Assembly now present. WILLARD MOORE,

(*Chairman of a Committee chosen for the Purposes abovesaid.*

BOSTON, September 5.

Last Tuesday Evening was Married, by the Rev'd. Dr. COOPER, Mr. THOMAS MELVILL, to Miss PRISCILLA SCOLLAY, Daughter of JOHN SCOLLAY, Esq; an agreeable and accomplish'd young Lady.

On Monday last died at Dunstable, Mr. JOSEPH TYLER, of this Town, Merchant.

BOSTON, September 5.

The following is a true Copy of a Letter, said to be wrote by General Brattle, to the Commander in Chief, (and pick'd up in this Town last Week,) viz.

Cambridge, August 27, 1774.

MR. Brattle presents his Duty to Gov. Gage. He apprehends it his Duty to acquaint his Excellency from Time to Time with every Thing he hears and knows to be true and is of Importance in these troublesome Times, which is the Apology Mr. Brattle makes for troubling the General with this Letter.

Capt. Minot of Concord, a very worthy Man, this Minute informed Mr. Brattle that there had been repeatedly made pressing Applications to him to warn his Company to meet at one Minute's Warning, equipt with Arms and Ammunition, according to Law, he had constantly denied them, adding, if he did not gratify them he should be constrained to quit his Farms and Town; Mr. Brattle told him he had better do that than lose his Life and be hanged for a Rebel, he observed that many Captains had done it, though not in the Regiment to which he belonged, which was and is under Col. Elisha Jones, but in a neighbouring Regiment.

Mr. Brattle begs Leave humbly to quere, Whether it would not be best that there should not be one Commission Officer of the Militia in the Province.

This Morning the Select Men of Medford, came and received their Town Stock of Powder, which was in the Arsenal on Quarry-Hill, so that there is now therein, the King's Powder only, which shall remain there as a sacred Depositum till ordered out by the Capt. General.

To his Excellency General Gage, &c. &c. &c.

‡† *General BRATTLE's Address to the Public respecting the foregoing Letter, we are oblig'd to omit this Week, only for want of Room.*

CAPTAIN Minot of Concord, the Gentleman whom Brigadier Brattle had a conference with relative to his mustering the company under his command, declares, That on the 29th day of August past, he had occasion to wait on General Brattle to pay him some interest money for a person living at New-Ipswich, in New-Hampshire, which was the only errand capt. Minot had to general Brattle.

After that business was over, general Brattle asked capt. Minot his opinion, whether the people would let the court sit at Concord. He replied he believed they would if they went on in the old way. Mr. Brattle said they had stopt one court going on in the old way; and if they stopt this court, it would be said that the people would have no court either in the new or old way.

Captain Minot then asked general Brattle whether he thought it adviseable for him to call his company together? General Brattle answered by no means. Captain Minot then told the general he had had several applications made to him to call his company together equipt according to law. The general then asked, had any other companies met in that manner? Captain Minot answered not in their regiment, but he believed they had in others. Then brigadier Brattle replied, he thought it by no means adviseable, as it would be deem'd rebellion.

Captain Minot then told general Brattle that nineteen in twenty in the compass of his observation were of opinion that the late acts intended to change the constitution of this government, were made with design to enslave this people, and said that if any of the inhabitants were slain by the soldiery, the country would come down, and that he must accompany them, or be in danger of losing his life and farm; subjoining that he thought it the duty of every man to take & encourage every prudent and moderate measure that could be devised for the relief of his country.

Captain Minot further declares, that when he went to general Brattle's he had no intent to enter into any political discourse whatever, nor ask his opinion on any matter relative to his assembling his company, or any thing else, saving paying the interest for his neighbour as aforesaid.

From this state of the case captain Minot flatters himself that no judicious person will receive a disadvantageous representation of his conduct in this matter, without recurring to some better evidence for the impeachment of his veracity than general Brattle's billet to Governor Gage. His ambition has ever been to stand fair with his fellow-countrymen. For which end he makes, signs and publishes this declaration.

JONAS MINOT.

Suffolk, ss. *Boston, September 3, 1774.*

THE above-named Jonas Minot, personally appearing, maketh Oath to the Truth of the foregoing Deposition by him subscribed. Before me,

EDM. QUINCY, J. Pacis.

ON Wednesday last, the new Divan (consisting of the wretched Fugitives with whom the just Indignation of their respective Townsmen by a well-deserved Expulsion, have filled this capital) usurped the Seats round the Council Board in Boston. Their Deliberations have not hitherto transpired: And with equal Secrecy, on Thursday morning half after four, about 260 troops embarked on board 13 boats at the long-wharff, and proceeded up Mistic river to Temple's farm, where they landed, and went to the powder house on quarry-hill in Charlestown bounds, whence they have taken 250 half barrels of powder, the whole store there, and carried it to the castle.

A detachment from this corps went to Cambridge, and brought off two field pieces, which, had lately been sent there for col. Brattle's regiment. The preparation for this scandalous expedition, caused much speculation, as some who were near the Governor gave out that he had sworn the committee of Salem should recognize or be imprisoned; nay some said put on board the Scarborough and sent to England forthwith. The committee of Boston sent off an express after 10 on Wednesday evening to advise their brethren of Salem of what they apprehended was coming against them, who received their message with great politeness, and returned an answer purporting their readiness to receive any attack they might be exposed to for acting in pursuance to the laws and interest of their country as became men and christians.

From these several hostile appearances the county of Middlesex took the alarm, and on Thursday evening began to collect in large bodies with their arms, provisions and ammunition, determining by some means to give a check to a power which so openly threatened their destruction, and in such a clandestine manner robbed them of the means of their defence. And on Friday morning some thousands of them had advanced to Cambridge armed only with sticks, as they had left their fire arms, &c. at some distance behind them. Some indeed had collected on Thursday evening and surrounded the attorney-general's house, who is also judge of admiralty on the new plan for Nova-Scotia; and being provoked by the firing of a Gun from a window, they broke some glass, but did no more mischief. The company however concerned in this were mostly boys and negroes who soon dispersed.

On perceiving the concourse on Friday morning, the committee of Cambridge sent express to Charlestown, who communicated the intelligence to Boston, and their respective committees proceeded to Cambridge without delay. When the first of the Boston committee came up they found some thousands of people assembled round the court-house steps, and judge Danforth standing upon them, speaking to the body, declaring in substance, that having now arrived at a very advanced age, and spent the greater part in the service of the public, it was a great mortification to him to find a step lately taken by him so disagreeable to his country in which he conscienciously had meaned to serve them, but finding their general sense against his holding a seat at the council board on the new establishment, he assured them that he had resigned said office, and would never henceforth accept or act in any office inconsistent with the charter rights of his country; and in confirmation of said declaration, he delivered the following certificate drawn up by himself and signed with his own hand, viz.

ALTHO' *I have this Day made an open Declaration to a great Concourse of People who Assembled at Cambridge, that I had resign'd my Seat at the Council Board, yet for the further Satisfaction of all, I do hereby declare under my Hand, that such resignation has actually been made, and that it is my full purpose not to be any way concern'd as a Member of the Council, at any Time hereafter.*

Sept. 2d, 1774 S DANFORTH.

A true Copy,

Attest. N. CUDWORTH, Cl.

Judge Lee was also on the court-house steps, and delivered his mind to the body in terms similar to those used by Judge Danforth, and delivered the following declaration also drawn up and signed by him, viz.

Cambridge 2d Sept. 1774.

AS *great Numbers of the Inhabitants of the County are come into this Town, since my Satisfying those who were met, not only by Declaration, but by reading to them what I wrote to the Governor at my Resignation, and being desirous to give the whole County and Province full Satisfaction in this Matter, I hereby declare my Resignation of a Seat in the new constituted Council, and my Determination to give no further Attendance.*

A true Copy, JOS. LEE.
Test. NATH. CUDWORTH, Cl.

Upon this a Vote was called for to see if the body was satisfied with the declarations and resignations abovesaid, and passed in the affirmative, nem. con.

It was then moved to know whether that body would signify their abhorrence of mobs, riots and the destruction of private property, and passed in the affirmative, nem. con.

Col. Phips the high sheriff of the county then came before the committee of the body and complained that he had been hardly spoken of for the part he had acted in delivering the powder in Charlestown magazine to the soldiery; which, the committee candidly considered and reported to the body that it was their opinion the high sheriff was excuseable as he had acted in conformity to his order from the commander in chief. Col. Phips also delivered the following declaration by him subscribed, viz.

Colonel PHIPS's Answer to the Hon.ble Body now in Meeting upon the Common, viz.

THAT *I will not execute any Precept that shall be sent me under the new Acts of Parliament for the altering the Constitution of the Province of the Massachusetts Bay, and that I will recall all the Venires that I have sent out under the new Establishment.*

Cambridge, Sept. 2d, 1774. DAVID PHIPS.
A true Copy, Test. NATH. CUDWORTH, Cl.

Which was accepted as satisfactory.

About 8 o'clock his honor Lieut. Governor Oliver set off from Cambridge to Boston, and informed Governor Gage of the true state of matters, and the business of the people; ————— ————— which, as his honor told the Admiral, were not a mad mob, but the freeholders of the county, promising to return in two hours & confer further with them on his own circumstance as president of the council. On mr. Oliver's return he came to the committee and signified what he had delivered to the body in the morning, viz. that as the commissions of Lieut. Governor and president of the council, seem'd tack'd together, he should undoubtedly incur his majesty's displeasure if he resign'd the latter, and pretended to hold the former; and no body appeared to have any objection to his enjoying the place he held constitutionally, he begged he might not be pressed to incur that displeasure at the instance of a single county, while any other councellor held on the new establishment. Assuring them however, that in case the mind of the whole province collected in congress or otherwise appeared for his resignation, he would by no means act in opposition to it. This seemed satisfactory to the committee, and they were preparing to deliver it to the body, when commissioner Hallowell came through the town on his way to Boston. The sight of that obnoxious person so inflamed the people that in a few minutes above 160 horsemen were drawn up and proceeding in pursuit of him on the full gallop. Capt. Gardner of Cambridge first began a parley with one of the foremost, which caused them to halt till he delivered his mind very fully in dissuasion of the pursuit, and was seconded by mr. Deavens of Charlestown and Dr. Young of Boston. They generally observed that the object of the Body's attention that day seemed to be the resignation of unconstitutional councellors, and that it might introduce confusion into the proceedings of the day if any thing else was brought upon the carpet till that important business was finished; and in a little time the gentlemen dismounted their horses and returned to the body.

But Mr. Hallowell did not entirely escape, as one gentleman of a small stature pushed on before the general body & followed Hallowell, who made the best of his way till he got into Roxbury, where mr. ———— overtook and stopped him in his chaise. Hallowell snapped his pistols at him, but could not disengage himself from him till he quitted the chaise and mounted his servant's horse, on which he drove into Boston with all the speed he could make; till the horse failing within the gate, he ran on foot to the camp, thro' which he spread consternation, telling them he was pursued by some thousands, who would be in town at his heels and destroy all friends of government before them.

A gentleman in Boston observing the motion in the camp, and concluding they were on the point of marching to Cambridge, from both ends of the town communicated the alarm to Dr. Roberts then at Charlestown ferry, who having a very fleet horse brought the news in a few minutes to the committee, then at dinner. The intelligence was instantly diffused, and the people whose arms were nearest sent persons to bring them; while horsemen were dispatched both ways to gain more certain advice of the true state of the soldiery. A greater fervor and Resolution probably never appeared among any troops. The dispatches soon returning, and assuring the body that the soldiers still remained, and were likely to remain in their camp, they resumed their business with spirit, and resolved to leave no unconstitutional officer within their reach in possession of his place. On this the committee assembled again, and drew up the paper of which the following is a copy, and at the head of the body delivered it to Lieut. Governor Oliver to sign, with which he complied, after obtaining their consent to add the latter clause implying the force by which he was compelled to do it. Mr. Mason, clerk of the county of Middlesex, also engaged in his office to do no one thing in obedience to the new acts of parliament impairing our charter,

Cambridge, Sept. 2, 1774.

I THOMAS OLIVER being appointed by his Majesty to a Seat at the Council Board, upon and in Conformity to the late Act of Parliament, entitled, An Act for the better Regulation of the Province of Massachusetts Bay, which being a manifest Infringement of the Charter Rights and Privileges of this People; I do hereby in conformity to the Commands of the Body of this County now convened, most solemnly renounce and resign my Seat at said unconstitutional Board, and hereby firmly Promise and Engage, as a Man of Honor and a Christian, that I never will hereafter upon any Terms whatsoever accept a Seat at said Board on the present novel and oppressive Plan of Government.

My House at Cambridge being surrounded by about four Thousand People, in Compliance with their Commands I sign my Name.

THOMAS OLIVER.

Messrs. EDES and GILL, *Printers.*

Please to insert the following in your next Monday's Paper, and you'll oblige your humble Servant,

THAD^s. MASON.

OBSERVING in the public News Papers, printed Yesterday, the Declaration and Acknowledgment of Ezekiel Goldthwait, Esq; and Mr. Ezekiel Price, joint Clerks of the Court of General Sessions of the Peace in the County of Suffolk, of their Error in signing and sending out Warrants to the Constables of the respective Towns in said County, for their returning Lists of Persons, in their Town, qualified to serve as Jurors, as required by a late Act of Parliament.

I think it my Duty to the Public in general and to the County of Middlesex in particular;

First, To lay before them some Circumstances I was under at the Time of the said Act's taking Place; I had been, for some Time, and then was, labouring under Indisposition of Body and much confined, occasioned by a dislocated Shoulder, and the Act aforesaid arriving but a very few Days before the Time for sending out the Warrants aforesaid; I had not Opportunity of advising with those, who certainly had more knowledge of the Law and the Operations thereof, than I ever pretended to have; nor was I apprized at the Meeting of the Clerks, mentioned in Mr. Goldthwait's Declaration; but finding that the Clerks of two or three Counties had, and, as I was informed, others had also, issued such Warrants, and apprehending that the Clerks of all the Counties would also do it: I at that Time, thought it my Duty (tho' erroneously) in an Official Way, to issue Warrants, which I did and delivered them to the Sheriff of the County to disperse: Altho' at that Time I was sorry I was obliged to do it.

Thro' the Favour of my very good Friends in the County of Middlesex, I have now been Clerk of their Courts for thirty-eight Years; in all which Time it has been constantly my Ambition, and Endeavour to be punctual, faithful and diligent in that Office: And I don't know, that in all that Time, I have given Occasion to any one Person to tax me with any wilful or careless Omission of my Duty in that Trust. And,

Secondly, Publickly to acknowledge my Error (in Judgment) and Rashness in issuing such Warrants, without duly considering and weighing the Consequences attending it; For which I heartily ask Pardon of all my Countrymen, and particularly of the County of Middlesex, which, I assure them, I do with much higher Pleasure and Satisfaction, than signing the unconstitutional Warrants aforesaid: And hope (on Consideration of of the perplexed trying Situation of Affairs) to obtain that Candor and Charity "which covereth" (even) "a Multitude of Errors and Faults."

And as to my political Sentiments, I can appeal to all my Friends and Acquaintance (some of whom are of the most considerable Characters in the Province) that ever since the Origin of the Stamp Act (which first plann'd the Slavery of the Americans) I have been steady, uniform and persevering in Opposition to all the Attempts the British Parliament have made to subjugate the Colonies to the most abject, cruel and oppressive Slavery: And utterly abjure, abhor and detest the severe, unconstitutional, oppressive and cruel Acts passed in their late Session relative to this Province.

And rather than conform myself to them, or any Part of them, I will resign my Office, (tho' the sole Support of myself, in my advanced Age and a large Family depends thereon) and rely on the Charity of my (too much oppressed out) charitable Fellow-Sufferers.

Charlestown, Sept. 2, 1774. THADDEUS MASON.

The Gentlemen from Boston, Charlestown and Cambridge having provided some refreshment for their greatly fatigued brethren, they chearfully accepted it, took leave and departed in high good humour and well satisfied.

Sturbridge, Aug. 25, 1774.

WHEREAS I ABIJAH WILLARD of Lancaster, have been appointed by Mandamus a Counsellor for this Province, and have without due Consideration taken the Oath, do now freely and solemnly declare that I am heartily sorry that I have taken the said Oath, and do hereby solemnly and in good Faith Promise and Engage that I will not sit nor act in the said Council, nor in any other that shall be appointed in such Manner and Form; but that I will as much in me lies, maintain the Charter Rights and Liberties of this Province, and do hereby ask forgiveness of all the honest, worthy Gentlemen that I have offended by taking the abovesaid Oath, and desire this may be inserted in the public Prints.

Witness my Hand, ABIJAH WILLARD.

To my worthy Town and Countrymen.

Gentlemen,

AS I have given you great Offence by signing an Adress to Governor Hutchinson (upon his leaving the Province) and as it always gives Pain to offend or disoblige even a single Neighbour; this has been much increased as the Public are so much concerned in it: And had I conceived that the generality of the People so much disliked an Address to Mr. Hutchinson, it should not have had my Name to it, as I always place the Friendship and good-will of my Fellow-Men in the first Class of this World's Enjoyments. I am very sorry I ever signed it, and hope the Publick will freely forgive,

Gentlemen, Your humble Servant,

Charlestown, Sept. 3, 1774. *JOHN WHITE.*

Sudbury, August 31st, 1774.

WHEREAS my inadvertently signing an Address with a Number of others the Justices of the County of Middlesex, to the late Governor of this Province, T. Hutchinson, Esq; has given occasion of Offence to the Country in general, and this Town in particular; I hereby publickly acknowledge that I am very sorry for signing the same; and that I will not for the future do any Thing to hurt the Liberties or Privileges of my Country:—And whereas there was a Report to my Disadvantage, that I had spoke to one Arnold of Marlboro' for a Number of Chains and other Utensils for the Use of the Troops, I hereby inform the Public that I have made it appear to the Satisfaction of the People that said Report was groundless. WM. BALDWIN.

AS it is publickly reported that the Powder which was taken out of the Powder-House at Charlestown last Thursday Morning is a consolidated Body, and of no Consequence—I think it my Duty, (as I have for a Number of Years had the Care of it as to sunning and turning it,) to declare, that it appeared to me to be as good and free from Dampness, or any Damage, as any could be. The last Time I sunned it, was last June.

WM. GAMAGE.

William Angier, Stephen Palmer, James Read, Samuel Gamage, the Names of those who assisted the last Time it was aired, are ready to testify to the abovewritten. *Cambridge, September 3, 1774.*

Tis said an article deliberated upon by the Divan last Wednesday was the disarming of the town of Boston, and as much of the province as might be, to which sundry new councellors advised. Was this also for the good of your country, Gentlemen!

Governor Gage has at length laid his hand on private property, so far as to deny one cask of powder to be delivered out of the powder house on any condition whatever.

On Saturday afternoon 4 large field pieces were dragged by the soldiery, and placed at the only avenue by land to this city.

Same Afternoon the Lively Frigate of 20 Guns came to her Moorings in the Ferry way between Boston and Charlestown.

Same Evening the Military Watch consisting of 16 or 17 Men who patrol between Winisimit and Charlestown Ferries, laid hold on two Women to abuse them; but on their crying out let them go again. ——*Insult upon Insult.*——

"We are able to assure the Public from good Authority, that Isaac Winslow, Esq; one of the lately appointed Counsellors, waited on Governor Gage last Monday, when he made an absolute and full Resignation of his Place at the Board; since which he has not appeared in Council, but given the strongest Assurances that he never will act in that Station: Several of the most respectable Gentlemen, who have appeared foremost in the Cause of their Country's Liberties have paid their Compliments to him on account of his Resignation."

We also have it from good Authority, that last Saturday Afternoon the Honorable Mr. Treasurer Gray, likewise resigned his Seat at the Council Board.

Extract of a letter from a Gentleman at *Wilmington, North-Carolina,* to his Friend in *Boston,* dated August 2d, 1774.

"*As to public Matters I shall likewise please you, when I inform you that a patriotic Spirit possesses every Bosom, which all Ranks of Persons seem emulous to express by Actions as well as by words; even those few from whom another Conduct was expected, have surprised the World by a Zeal for the Service of our suffering Brethren in Boston, and a Liberality in contributing to their Relief, which, till this Occasion gave them an Opportunity of displaying, scarce any body supposed them capable of.—A Subscription having been set on foot for the Support of the Bostonians (suffering nobly in the common Cause of America) a very few Days, from a few Individuals, produced as much as loaded the Vessel by which this Letter comes. And by this Time, I have no doubt, enough is collected to load another. Nor is this all; for there is apparent in almost every Individual a proper Sense of the injury done to the Colonies, in the Tendency of those oppressive Acts of Parliament, and a determined Spirit of Opposition and Resentment worthy of a Human Bosom, in the Great Cause of Liberty.*

"*A numerous and respectable Meeting of the Six Counties in the District of Wilmington has been had, and they have without one dissenting Voice, Resolved upon pursuing every legal and rightful Measure, to aid and assist their Sister Colony of the Massachusetts-Bay to the utmost of their Power, and have sent Expresses to every County in the Province, strictly recommending a Subscription in each of them for the same Purpose. A general Meeting of all the Members of Assembly is to be had in a few Days at Johnson Court-House, to elect Delegates to attend the General Congress on Philadelphia, the first Monday in September.*"

Extract of another Letter from *Wilmington,* dated August 3.

"*No sooner was a Subscription put about for the Relief of our suffering Brethren in Boston, than in a few Days I am told Two Thousand Pounds our Currency was raised, and it is expected something very considerable will be contributed at Newbern and Edenton for the same noble Purpose, as Subscriptions are set on foot in every County in the Province. You will receive this by Mr. Parker Quince who generously made an Offer of his Vessel to carry a Load of Provisions to Boston, Freight Free, and what redounds to the Honour of the Tars, the Master and Mariners navigate her without receiving one Farthing Wages (tru'y patriotick!) It is supposed L——d N——h will hang himself in his Rope of Sand.*"

We are told that 20 out of the 36 new appointed Councellors, (exclusive of Mr. Palmer, who is absent from the Province, and Mr. Woodbridge, who died before the Mandamus's were received) have either refused to take the Oath, or have since resigned their Seats at that unconstitutional Board.

Last Thursday Evening in several different Fire Societies, were suspended Capt. John Gore, Mr. Henry Leddel, Mr. Edward Cox, Mr. James Asbby, Mr. Wm. Burton, Mr. Wm. McAlpine and Mr. Wilson, for signing an Address to the late *infamous* Gov. Hutchinson.

Yesterday the Canso came as far up Gallows Bay as she could find Water, with intent to command the Neck.

To the PUBLIC.

BEING informed that a Report has prevailed in the distant parts of this County, and in many other Parts of the Province, that at a late Town-Meeting held in Cambridge I openly declared that Judge Trowbridge with some other Gentlemen, Inhabitants of this Town, were concerned in framing and drafting one or more of the late Acts of Parliament relating to this Province—that I *knew* it—that the Act or Acts were wrote in my Office, and (as one of my Informants expressed himself) that they urged me to *sign* the Act or Acts together with them, but that I utterly refused to do it. That I added, notwithstanding my most intimate connexion with, and relation to Judge Trowbridge, conceiving this Matter of great Importance to my Country, I cou'd not in Conscience refrain from making this public Declaration of it—I think is my Duty, as speedily as may be, in the most publick Manner to declare that I never made any such Declaration, or one of a similar Import in Town-Meeting; and for the Truth of this I appeal to all my Townsmen who were present at the Meeting, and heard what I there said; which was upon a Subject *totally* different from that of the above supposed Declaration. And I further say that I never did make any such Declaration, or one of a similar Import, in any other Place: And that I know not of any Person being, nor do I *believe,* or *suspect* that Judge Trowbridge was, directly or indirectly concerned in framing or drafting the said Acts of Parliament or either of them—that I never *saw* either of the said Acts before they were published here, and that the above Report is, *in every Particular thereof,* false and groundless. FRA. DANA.

Cambridee, September 3, 1774.

THE PROCEEDINGS *of the whole County of Middlesex, held at* Concord *the 30th & 31st ult. will be in our next.*

EBENEZER BRADISH's *Deelaration came too late for this Day's Paper.*

BRANDY & GENEVA.

A few Pipes Old Brandy and Geneva by the Case To be SOLD by

CHARLES MILLER

At his Store in King-Street.

To be SOLD and Enter'd upon directly,

The Distill House and Land with the Stills, Worms and other usual necessaries belonging to the Distill House, belonging to the Estate of Mr. JOHNSON JACKSON, deceas'd, situate at the South End of Boston. Inquire of JOSEPH JACKSON at the South End, Executor to said Estate.

Also, A few Hogsheads of New-England Rum, and some Spirits of different Sorts.

MUSICAL CLOCKS.

To be Sold Musical Clocks that go by Springs, also Musical Clocks that go by Weights, and play a different Tune each Day in the Week, on Sunday's a Psalm Tune. Inquire of BENJA. WILLARD Clock & Watch Maker in Roxbury Street near Boston: Where all sorts of Clocks are made in the newest Form, and Warranted to go without Variation, and many without Cleaning. Also Clock Cases are made at the same Place, in various Forms and in the best Manner, and Cheaper than can be purchas'd in London. Also Convey'd with Clocks to any Part of the Country.

All the Branches of this Business is likewise carried on at his Shop at Grafton.

TO BE SOLD,

By *BENJAMIN CHURCH,*

Next Thursday Evening,

A Variety of valuable Furniture—as Tables—Chairs—Glasses—Feather Beds—Bedsteads a Mehogany Desk—Pewter—Brass, &c.—Sundry European Articles—Linnens, Woollens, Silks—Cutlery and Brazery Ware, &c. &c.—A new Sukey compleat—a good Chaise—Watches, &c. &c.

New AUCTION-ROOM, Cornhill

TO MORROW MORNING, at TEN o'Clock, Will be Sold by PUBLIC VENDUE, At GREENLEAF's Auction-Room,

A Variety of English Goods as usual.

Wm. GREENLEAF, Auctioneer.

The Sale will begin at TEN o'Clock precisely.

Burials in the Town of BOSTON, since our last.

Eight Whites. No Blacks.

Baptiz'd in the several Churches, Nine.

High Water at BOSTON, *for the present Week.*

Monday, 15 min. aft. 11 | Friday, 20 min. after. 2
Tuesday, 52 min. aft. 11 | Saturday, 10 min. aft. 3
Wednesday, 40 m. aft. 12 | Lord's-Day 57 m. af. 3
Thursday, 30 min. aft. 1 | New D 5 Day 9 After

HOUSE of LORDS, May 23.

Summary of Wednesday's Debate on third reading of the bill for securing the military from a trial in America for murders committed in support of Government.

THE business was opened by Lord Buckinghamshire, who confessed this to be the most exceptionable of the American measures, but tho't it was excused by necessity.

He was answered by Lord Shelburne, who spoke with great ability, spirit, and knowledge of the subject.

The Lords Denbeigh, Sandwich, and the Chancellor, were the chief supporters of the bill. The Duke of Manchester spoke with that grace of manner and elegance which so peculiarly distinguish him.

The Marquis of Rockingham spoke late in the debate. His speech lasted near three quarters of an hour; never was more attention given to a speaker on any occasion. He spoke with all the weight and authority of an able statesman, and all the feeling of a patriot, deeply concerned for the interest of his country. He entered fully into the civil policy which had originally given rise to the disturbances in America, and in consequence produced bills and regulations so ill calculated to allay them. He took post upon the measure of his own Administration, the repeal of the stamp-act, on which he argued with great force. He insisted that repeal to be no more than a return to the antient policy of Great Britain, from which the tax had been a deviation. He then stated the new taxes laid on after his removal from office, as originating from no plan of policy whatever, but merely as the result of a pique and passion; that they were in effect confess'd to be so, because they were afterwards repealed for the greater part, as being laid by the avowal of Administra ion itself, in contradiction to all the principles of commerce.

That the tea duty, equally uncommercial and *unproductive*, was left as a pepper corn, merely for the sake of a contest with America, as the Ministry had likewise avowed. He censured very severely the doctrine of taxing for the sole purpose of exercising an invidious right, and that taxes ought to be for the real purpose of supporting government, and not purely to irritate and stir up dangerous questions. That the stamp act was a great object, and might have produced in time considerable revenues; but to risque the whole trade of England, and the affections of the Americans, in a quarrel with the colonies, for peppercorns, he thought a very unwise proceeding.

After this he entered into the particulars of the bill, and, among other things, in answer to the difficulties asserted to be laid on ocersffi, without such protection, as was given by this bill, he said that he thought the condition of men of honour and sensibility to be far worse under this bill; for that no acquittal could be honorable, where the prosecutor had not the usual means of securing a fair trial. He concluded by a very emphatical recommendation of temper, as necessary in all things, but particularly in measures of this nature, and in subjects of so much delicacy; his own remarkable calmness and steadiness of mind gave additional force to this part of his speech.

The Duke of Richmond spoke last in the debate, and with his usual spirit, pointed his answer chiefly from what fell from the Chancellor & Lord Shelburne; he concluded by recommending to the perusal of the House, a pamphlet, called Considerations on the Measures carrying on against America. [*which pamphlet may be had of the printers of this Gazette,*] and the Bishop of St. Asaph's Sermon, preached 1773, before the society for propagating the gospel, as containing the soundest doctrines and the best policy.

LONDON, June 23.

The Park, Whitehall, and other parts of Parliament Street, were thronged with multitudes of people in dress and appearance much above the common level. As the King passed they gave him a most cordial salute of *groans* and *hisses*; the universal cry was, "No popery! No French laws! No protestant popish King! The Duke of Gloucester for ever!" His Majesty was observed several times to change colour, but whether from a consciousness that he was suffering in a *religious* cause, or whether from the supreme delight he felt at passing an act so universally *odious* to the *factious* citizens, he *bronzed* it out with a tolerable share of *firmness*. When he had executed the *Romish business*, by passing the Quebec bill, the people, on his return grew exceedingly clamorous; they groaned most hideously until the stage coach arrived opposite Mr. Churchill's house, in Parliament street, when (Mr. Wilkes being at the window) a loud *huzza* ensued; the King bowed, but the people, too honest to deceive his Majesty, instantly shouted, "*Wilkes for ever!*" The state coach had no sooner entered the Park, than the multitude who had accompanied it to the Parliament House being joined by a prodigious concourse of people, the hisses, groans, and cry of "No popery! No French laws! The Protestant Duke of Gloucester!" became incessant. The King once leaning his head towards the coach window, which was beset with numbers, a fellow, with great jocularity, called out, "God bless your Majesty's head, but damn *Lord Bute's!*" his Majesty reddened, but soon collected his *firmness*, shewed as much contempt for the rabble as James II, when he took water to *escape* their fury (and being safely embarked) let a f—t to shew how much he despised them. A fellow returning through the park with the sword of state on his shoulder, the case which contained it being shaped exactly like a *crucifix*, some of the mob insisted upon seeing the contents; the fellow stopped and opened the case, but when they perceived it contained only a very harmless sword they went away, saying, "they really thought it was a present from the court of Rome of a *popish crucifix*, for the use of the *protestant King of England!*"

NEW-YORK, August 25.

We hear that last Monday morning as two of the Gentlemen appointed by the committee to collect for our suffereing brethren in Boston, set out upon that business, the first Gentleman they called upon was Mr. D—e, who generously presented them with ten pounds in cash, and the best pipe of Brandy in his distillery, valued at twenty-eight pounds; observing, at the same time, that the generosity of the Virginians & Carolinians &c. was great and honorable with respect to food, but he thought such glorious sufferers for the common good ought to drink as well as eat.

SALEM, August 30, 1774.

The following Gentlemen are chosen Delegates for the several Towns undermentioned, to represent them at the County Meeting, which are all we have been able as yet to collect.

For *Salem*, Hon. Richard Derby, Esq; Mr. John Pickering, jun. Mr. Jonathan Ropes, Capt. Timothy Pickering, Capt. Jonathan Gardner, jun. and Capt. Richard Manning.

For *Newbury-Port*, Tristram Dalton, Esq; Mr. Jonathan Jackson, Capt. Jonathan Greenleaf, Mr. Stephen Cross, and Mr. John Bromfield.

For *Marblehead*, Jeremiah Lee & Azor Orne, Esq'rs. and Messrs. Elbridge Gerry, Joshua Orne and William Dolliber.

For *Lynn*, Dr. John Flagg, Mr. John Mansfield and Deacon Daniel Mansfield.

For *Beverly*, Capt. Benjamin Lovet, Messrs. Samuel Goodridge and Joseph Wood.

For *Manchester*, Colonel John Lee and Dr. Joseph Whipple.

Messieurs EDES and GILL,

Please to insert the following, and you will gratify your humble Servant—quæ est quod est.

ABout ten Days since, there came a villainous Pedlar to a Store in Leominster, who, upon Examination, was found to have a Quantity of the destructive & detestable Weed Tea—which he asserted he had bro't with him in a late Foreign Voyage, and pretended he was carrying it Home to his dear Wife; but it seems he had not the greatest Regard and Affection for her, by his giving her Poison.—However he offer'd his Tea for sale, thinking the Store keeper to be an Enemy to his Country, but, to his great Sorrow, he soon found it was not so, for by this Time the Shop was well stor'd with true Whigs, (a most respectable Assortment,) who, it seems, were privately invited there by the Store-keeper; at first sight, struck a horrid damp on the Tea-Merchant; and perhaps caus'd as violent an agitation in his knees, as ever was in those of Belshazzer; so that he cry'd for Quarter, begging they wou'd not cloath him in the modern Dress, the Weather being excessively hot. The Whigs granted his Petition, but repeatedly exhorted him to reform, and be no longer an Enemy to himself and Country;—and finally they made him three very friendly Proposals, which were as follows, that he shou'd either immediately burn that Tea, at his own Cost, or at theirs, or have it taken by Force and consum'd:—The former of which he very readily agreed to, by burning the Tea.—He then departed heartily thanking them for their Kindness and Benevolence toward him.

But Lenity cannot, must not be exercis'd toward these Enemies much longer;—it is to be fear'd the direful Period is at Hand, when the Sons of Liberty will be bound in Duty, both to God and themselves, to hang, drown, or otherwise demolish these execrable Villains from the Face of the Earth, that Posterity may enjoy a peaceful and happy Land, preserv'd from utter Ruin, by the noble Efforts of Freedom's Sons.—Oh! That the refulgent Rays of Liberty might penetrate the transparent Skulls of those abandon'd Few, who are ever plotting their Country's Ruin.

RUTH.

ADVERTISEMENT.

South-Meeting-House, in Eastham }
22d of August, 1774. }

RAN AWAY, this Day, from Town-Meeting. He had clandestinely taken from the Constable the Warrant for calling a Meeting to raise Money for the Support of the Gospel in this Place He carried the Warrant with him. The People therefore were oblig'd to return Home without effecting this necessary Business. 'Tis probable he is in Hopes to get some in every Town to join with him, and by some such Craft, to prevent the preaching of the Gospel for the future throughout this Province. M j-r P. and S. Kn-l-s are his confederates. S. D. a Selectman went off with him, they were seen to travel Westward. It is conjectured C-l-n-l K. and J. D. Esq; are also in the Plot. The Clerk is a Man of more than middling Stature, & appears (upon strict Examination) to be a determined Foe to American Liberty. Had on when he went off, a Callico Banyan. 'Tis likely he may have, in one of his Pockets an Ink-Pot, and in the other, a Petition to his E——y for calling a Town Meeting. Whoever will secure said Clerk from doing any further Mischief, or bring him to be a Friend to American Liberty, shall have *Two Shillings* Reward, and necessary Charges paid by

ONE HUNDRED and TWELVE.

N. B. All Towns are hereby cautioned, to keep Books of Record out of his Reach, lest he daub them wih his Ink Mop, as he hath done the Records of Eastham, from which Records he hath given off 3 Copies of the Proceedings of one particular Meeting, and neither of them agree with each other, yet they are signed after this Manner Attest,

GIDEON BATY, *Town-Clerk.*

THIS DAY PUBLISHED,
THE FOURTH EDITION,
(Price 9d.)
And sold by EDES *and* GILL, *in Queen-Street.*

CONSIDERATIONS
ON THE
MEASURES CARRYING ON
WITH RESPECT TO THE
BRITISH COLONIES
IN
NORTH-AMERICA.

There is neither King or Sovereign Lord on Earth, who has beyond his own Domain power to lay one Farthing on his Subjects without the grant and consent of those, who pay it; unless he does it by tyranny and violence.

Phillippe de Commines, Ch. 108.

THIS is a most masterly performance, written since the framing the several Acts against BOSTON and AMERICA, and the best calculated to convince the Ministry, the people of England, and all the world, of the absurdity and wickedness of the late acts, and ruinous consequences, to England at least, that would certainly attend their being carried into execution.

Our last accounts, say, this pamphlet has had a wonderful effect in removing the prejudices and convincing the people of England.

The above Pamphlet, which sells in London at 1s. 6d. Sterling, is sold here at 9d. Lawful, which is but just Three Farthings more than one Third of the Price of the London Edition.

SIXTY DOLLARS REWARD.

WHEREAS it was this Day discovered that the Powder-House in Wrentham, within about five Weeks last past, was broken open by some ill-minded Person or Persons, and from thence was stolen six Half Barrels of Powder, with about thirteen Hundred Flints, and some Lead, the Quantity not yet known. Whoever shall make Discovery of said Person or Persons concerned in the abovesaid Theft, so as they may be brought to Justice, shall have the above Reward paid by me.

By Order of the Selectmen of the Town of Wrentham.

JOHN MESSENGER, *Town-Clerk.*

Wrentham, August 29, 1774.

Abraham Hunt
HAS FOR SALE,
At his Celler under the Old Brick Meeting-House,
The best old Sterling Madeira, by the Pipe, Quarter Cask or Dozen; also Port Wine by the Dozen, and choice VINEGAR for Pickles.

TO LET,
Two very convenient Tenements in Governor's Alley, near the Province House, one of them has a good Shop a joining.
Inquire of the Printers.

A Wet Nurse with a good young Breast of Milk, wants a Place in a Gentleman's Family.
Inquire of Edes and Gill.

Boston: Printed, by EDES & GILL,
in Queen-Street, 1774.

SUPPLEMENT to the *Boston*-Gazette, &c. of (No. 1012.)

MONDAY, *September* 5, 1774.

Messieurs PRINTERS,

Please to insert the following in your next paper, and you will oblige your most humble servant, E. G.

IN the Supplement to the last Monday's Gazette, a writer under the signature of Massachusettensis, after calling me by name, plainly intimates *that I have wounded the constitution of my country in my department of clerk of the sessions.* This cruel insinuation not only tends to render me odious to the world of mankind, but exhibiting me to my countrymen as their enemy, at this time of public calamity, must render me singularly hateful. To one conscious of deserving a very different character, such treatment must be a very severe trial, as it must affect every man of sentiment and feeling.—Soon after the arrival of an act of Parliament, entitled an act for better regulating the government of the province of the Massachusetts-Bay, in North-America, two or three clerks of the court of sessions, of different counties, happening to meet; naturally fell into conversation upon the subject of their duty in consequence of the requirements of that act. On this sudden meeting, and short consultation, finding ourselves directed by that law, we supposed ourselves bound in duty to issue warrants for the return of jurors, in the manner thereby required. Upon this sudden opinion it was, that twenty warrants were issued to the constables of the several towns in the county of Suffolk, agreeable to the directions of the same act; ten of which were signed by me, and the remaining ten by Mr. Ezekiel Price, joint clerk with me. At the time I signed, I did not suppose any one town in the county would take the least notice of such warrant, and with pleasure I find upon enquiry, that my expectations have been answered.

The science of the law hath never been my professed study, tho' the mere mechanical business of a clerk's office hath been my employ for many years. As therefore it has not been my study *to know* any more than *to determine* what is *the law of the land*, my erroneous sentiments (which I am now fully convinced they were) upon that act will be readily pardoned by the candid and humane. I can say for myself, and I believe for my brethren, that it was an error of judgment only, which every good man will chearfully forgive. And I now publickly declare that it was not for the least inclination I had to comply with this, or any other of the acts of Parliament lately passed, relative to North-America, that I signed said ten warrants, for I detest said acts as much as any man on the continent, they being in my opinion, unconstitutional, severe, and oppressive to every person who dwells upon it. These are my sentiments and I am extremely sorry that I ever signed one of said warrants, or any other paper that has given the least umbrage to the community. And I do also declare, that if I am ever required to do any business in my office, in conformity to said act of Pailament, I shall refuse it, altho' by such refusal I may loose my place.

The public are now left to determine upon the *justice* and *generosity* of *singling* me out from the rest of my brethren, as if I alone had fallen into this error. Surely it is not a time to exasperate our fellow citizens without sufficient cause, when the public grievances and great calamities of the day, call for the union of all good men. As no man therefore more deeply feels for the present afflictions of this town and country, or would more sincerely engage in every laudable method for their abatement or removal, I cannot suppose myself altogether unworthy, and therefore hope to receive the continued friendship and approbation of my fellow citizens and countrymen. EZEKIEL GOLDTHWAIT.

Boston, August 30, 1774.

Messieurs PRINTERS,

Please to insert the following,

To my respectable Fellow Citizens and Countrymen.

HAVING never read the act of parliament, intitled an act for the better regulating the government of the province of Massachusetts-Bay, I was ignorant of the command therein to the Clerks of the Courts of Sessions, to issue precepts to the several Constables respecting Jurors, until Ezekiel Goldthwait, Esq; joint Clerk with me of said Court, delivered me printed forms of said precepts, which he and some other Clerks of said Court upon consulting together, had agreed to issue; after Mr. Goldthwait had signed the precept for Boston and nine other towns in the county, I signed the remainder;—but as soon as I had time to consider and reflect on the matter, I was convinced of my error and misconduct, and deeply affected with it————Through my whole life it has been my constant endeavour in every department to gain the friendship and esteem of my fellow citizens, which I have always valued beyond the most lucrative post in the power of man to bestow, and their displeasure at any part of my conduct will ever give me sensible pain. The late unconstitutional, cruel and oppressive acts of parliament, I detest and abhor as much as any man in the Colonies, and rather than conform to any part of them, I will resign my office, if the consequence should be that I beg my bread; I would therefore intreat that I may still be happy in the continuance of your esteem and friendship. EZEKIEL PRICE.

Messieurs PRINTERS,

THE freemen who were returned to serve as Grand Jurors at the Superior Court for this term, made their appearance in the Court-House yesterday; and before a numerous assembly, (Peter Oliver, Edmund Trowbridge, Foster Hutchinson, William Cushing and William Brown Esquires sitting on the bench as judges,) they all to the number of twenty two declined acting as Jurors for reasons which they had previously drawn up in writing and signed, and appointed to be read there by their Chairman, but the above said Judges refusing to hear the same openly read, desired to have the reading of it to themselves, which being complied with, the Jurymen withdrew from the Court-House to the Exchange tavern, where they unanimously voted that in order to justify their refusal to the world, their aforementioned reasons should be printed in the public papers.———I send you a copy for that purpose, and am your humble servant. A JURYMAN.

"BOSTON, *August* 30th, 1774.

"COUNTY OF SUFFOLK.

"WE who are returned by the several towns in this county, to serve as Grand Jurors at the Superior Court for this present term, being actuated by a zealous regard for peace and good order, and a sincere desire to promote Justice, righteousness and good government, as being essential to the happiness of the community; would now most gladly proceed to the discharge of the important duty required in that department, could we perswade ourselves that by doing thus, it would tend to our own reputation, or promote the welfare of our country: But when we consider the dangerous inroads that have been made upon our civil constitution, the violent attempts now making to alter and annul the most essential parts of our Charter, granted by the most solemn faith of Kings, and repeatedly recognized by British Kings and parliaments; while we see the open and avowed design of establishing the most compleat system of depotism in this province, and thereby reducing the free born inhabitants thereof to the most abject state of slavery and bondage; we feel ourselves necessarily constrained to decline being impannelled, for reasons that we are ready to offer to the Court if permitted, which are as follows.

"First. Because Peter Oliver, Esq; who sits as Chief Judge of this Court, has been charged with high crimes and misdemeanors, by the late hon. House of Representatives, the grand inquest of this province; of which crimes he has never been legally acquitted, but has been declared by that House to be unqualified to act as Judge of this Court.

"Secondly. Because by a late act of the British parliament, for altering the constitution of this province, the continuance of the present Judges of this Court, as well as the appointment of others, from the first day of July last, is made to depend solely on the King's pleasure, vastly different from the tenure of the British Judges; and as we apprehend they now hold their places, only in consequence of that act, all the judicial proceedings of the Court, will be taken as concessions to the validity of the same, to which we dare not consent.

"Thirdly. Because three of the Judges, being the major part of the Court, namely the said Peter Oliver, Esq; Foster Hutchinson, Esq; and William Brown, Esq; by taking the oath of Councellors, under authority of the aforesaid act, are (as we are informed) sworn to carry into execution, all the late grievous acts of the British parliament, among the last of which is one, made ostensibly for the impartial administration of justice in this province, but as we fear, really for the impunity of such persons, as shall under pretext of executing those acts, murder any of the inhabitants thereof, which acts appear to us to be utterly repugnant to every idea of justice and common humanity, and are justly complained of throughout America, as highly injurious and oppressive to the good people of this province, and manifestly destructive of their natural, as well as constitutional rights.

"Fourthly. Because we believe in our consciences that our acting in concert with a Court so constituted and under such circumstances, would be so far betraying the just and sacred rights of our native land, which were not the gift of Kings, but were purchased solely with the toil, the blood and treasure of our worthy and revered ancestors, and which we look upon ourselves under the most sacred and inviolable obligations to maintain, and to transmit whole and entire to our posterity.

"Therefore we the subscribers unanimously decline serving as Grand Jurors at this Court.

"Ebenezer Hancock,	Boston,
Peter Boyer,	ditto,
Joseph Hall,	ditto,
Thomas Crafts, jun.	ditto,
James Ivers,	ditto,
Paul Revere,	ditto,
Robert Williams,	Roxbury,
William Thompson,	Brookline,
Abraham Wheeler,	Dorchester,
Joseph Jones,	Milton,
Nathaniel Belcher,	Braintree,
Samuel Hobart,	Hingham,
Joseph Poole,	Weymouth,
William Bullard,	Dedham,
Jonathan Day,	Needham,
Abijah Upham,	Stoughton,
Moses Richardson,	Medway,
Henry Plymton,	Medfield,
Lemuel Kalloc,	Wrentham,
Joseph Willet,	Walpole,
Thomas Pratt,	Chelsea,
Nicholas Book,	Bellingham."

B O S T O N. September 5.

Last Tuesday being the day the Superior Court was to be holden here, the Chief Justice, Peter Oliver, Esq; and the other Justices of said Court, together with a number of gentlemen of the bar, attended by the High and Deputy Sheriffs walked in procession from the state-house to the court-house, in Queen-street. When the Court were seated and the usual proclamations made, a list of the names of the gentlemen returned to serve as Grand Jurors, was presented to them, and the Court appointed Mr. Ebenezer Hancock, Foreman, but he refusing to be sworn, and the question being put to them all, severally, whether they would take the oath, they one and all refused; and being asked whether they had any reasons to offer for their thus refusing; they answered they had, and that they were committed to writing; the Court requested to see them, but the Jurors refused giving the Court the original paper unless they were first permitted to read it in Court, or after reading the Court would promise to return it to them again.

The Petit Jurors were then called for, and a list of their names being handed to the Court they appointed Mr. Bartholomew Kneeland, Foreman, of the first jury, and Mr. Nathan Frazer of the second. Mr. Kneeland had the oath proposed to him, which he declined taking and being asked for what reasons, referred to a paper which he said was drawn up with their unanimous consent, and begged leave to read to the Court. The Court refused to hear the paper read, and the oath was proposed to each Juror in order, and declined as by the Foreman. Their reasons being demanded. they generally referred to the paper, till it came to turn of Mr. Thomas Chase, who beged leave to read the paper then in his hand; but was told by the Chief Justice that he might give his own reasons without reading the paper; to which he agreed, and said that one of his reasons was that Peter Oliver, Esq; Chief Justice of that Court, stood impeached by the late hon. House of Representatives of this province, in their own name, and in the name of this province, of divers high crimes and misdemeanors.---Being asked by the Chief Justice if he gave that as a reason for his refusing to be sworn, he answered 'yes, that is one reason.' The Court then called upon another of the Petit Jurors to be sworn, but he refused, and referred to the paper for his reasons, as aforesaid. The Chief Justice then desired the Court might peruse the paper, which should be returned to the Jurors again; which was agreed to, read and returned. The Court then proposed the same condition to the Grand Jury, which was complied with, and the contents delivered, which are inserted in this day's paper, see the the piece signed ' A JURYMAN.'

The reasons of the Petit Jurors were as follows.

"BOSTON, *August* 30, 1774.

"SUFFOLK, ss.

"*To the Honourable the Justices of the Superiour Court of Judicature, Court of Assize, &c.*

"MAY IT PLEASE YOUR HONOURS,

"WE the subscribers, returned by this county to serve as Petit Jurors this term, beg leave to acquaint your Honours, that as the hon. Peter Oliver, Esq; stands impeached by the late hon. House of Commons of this province, in their own name, and in the name of the people of this province, of high crimes and misdemeanors; which impeachment, with the reasons therefor, as they are public, would be needless for us to repeat.

"We would also beg leave to acquaint your Honours, that as by a late act of the British parliament, the continuance of the Judges of the Superior Court, is since the first of July last, made to depend upon said act, which it is apprehended places their dependance entirely upon the crown, and which is esteemed a great infringement of the charter rights of this province.

"Taking the above premises into our most serious consideration, we beg leave to acquaint your Honours, that we cannot in our consciences, from a sense of that duty we owe to our country, to ourselves, and to posterity, act against the united voice of this people:——Therefore beg your Honours will excuse us when we say, we decline serving as Petit Jurors for this Court. (Signed)

"Josiah Waters,	Elisha Cushing,
Samuel Ridgeway,	Ignatius Orcutt,
Nathan Frazier,	Elijah Monk,
Robert Wire,	Henry Stone,
Bartholomew Kneeland,	William Draper,
Thomas Chase,	Jonathan Parker,
John Cunningham,	Ebenezer Kingsbury,
Joseph Brewer,	Samuel Payson,
Jacob Sharp,	Joseph Morse,
Timothy Tilestone,	Ralph Day,
Samuel Sprague,	Nathaniel Lewis,
Ebenezer Swift,	Eliakim Cook,
Eliphalet Sawer,	Joseph Lovell,
Thomas White,	Elias Thayer,
Thomas Nash,	Theodore Mann,
Nath'l Holbrook, jun.	James Blake."
Elijah Jening,	

After the Court had read the papers, the Clerk of the Court, by order of the Chief Justice, asked them seriatim, if they would be sworn, and every one refused. The Court said they would consider of their reasons, and the Juries withdrew. The Court then adjourned to ten o'clock next day, when they met exclusive of Mr. Oliver, and to the inexpressible grief of their fellow citizens, went on to such business as is usually transacted, without Juries.

A Town-Meeting was held by adjournment at Faneuil-Hall, Tuesday last, and after liberty was voted for the laying out a Brick-Yard for the employment of the poor, the meeting was adjourned to Tuesday fortnight, in order to receive the report of a committee relative to filling up part of the town-dock.

Town meetings, and county meetings, are now held and calling in all parts of the province, a provincial congress is like to be soon appointed.

On Monday last the freeholders and other inhabitants of Roxbury, held a meeting, in that town, and chose their delegates for a county meeting. At this meeting we are informed Isaac Winslow, Esq; made it known, that he should resign his office as counsellor.

The spirit of the people, was never known to be so great since the first settlement of the colonies, as it is at this time. People in the country for hundreds of miles, are prepared and determine to "DIE or be FREE."

Extract of a letter from Leicester, August, 1774.

"Yesterday Mr. Paine, of Worcester, was visited by near 3000 people; notice was given of the intended visit the day before, from one town to another, though the warning was so short, the above number collected and most of them entered the town before 7 o'clock in the morning; they all marched into the town in order and drew up on the common, and behaved admirably well; they chose a committee of 2 or 3 men from each company to wait upon Mr. Paine and demand a resignation of his office as counseller; that committee being large they chose from among themselves a sub-committee, who went to his house, where he agreed to resign that office, and drew up an acknowlegment, mentioning his obligation to the county for favours done him, his sorrow for taking the oath, and promise that he never would act in that office contrary to the charter; after which he came with the committee to the common, where the people were drawed up in two bodies, making a lane between them, through which the committee and he passed and read divers times as they passed along, the said acknowledgment; they then returned in a peaceable manner to their own homes, except about five hundred who repaired to Rutland to demand the like promise from Col. Murray; when they arrived there, they were joined by about one thousand more from towns above, proceeding as they did at Worcester in chusing a committee, who went to the house, and being admitted, enquired for Col. Murray; his sons informed them he was not at home, but set off for Boston the preceeding evening; the committee made report to the company, which did not give satisfaction, they insisted upon searching the house, which was thoroughly done, as also the barns, out houses and stables, after which the committee wrote a letter to Col. Murray, informing him that unless he resigned his office by the tenth of September next, and published such resignation in the Boston News-papers, he would be waited upon again in his return home.

The people in this country seem determined to oppose all officers holding commissions otherwise than our Charter directs, and will to the last extremity oppose these unconstitutional acts, and prevent their being executed in this county.———I heard there was a number marching to Hardwick, to visit the Brigadier the same day they went to Worcester and Rutland; but hearing he was not at home they dispersed."

ALL Persons indebted for this Paper, whose Accounts have been above 12 Months standing, are requested to make immediate Payment.

Whereas the Proprietors of the Township of Land lying on both sides *Androscoggin-River*, in the County of Cumberland, granted June 11th 1771, to *Samuel Livermore*, Esq; and others, at their Meeting on February 24th 1773, voted and granted a Tax of *Twenty-four Shillings* Lawful Money, on each Right, to be paid *Leonard Williams* Esq; their Treasurer, on or before the first Day of October then next ensuing, and again on November 3d, 1773, voted and granted a further Tax of *Forty Eight Shillings*, on each Right, to be paid their Treasurer, as follows, viz. the one half thereof, on or before the next Meeting of said Proprietors, which was on March 16th 1774, and the other half on or before the first Instant; said Taxes having been made and published as the Law directs. Notwithstanding which the Owners of the Rights granted on the Rights of

Capt. *Samuel Googen*,	*Nathaniel Whitmore*,
Capt. *John Hazzeltime*,	*John Maddock*,
Ens. *Thomas Harrington*,	*Benjamin Corey*, and
Eliphalet Lyon,	*David Knapp*.

Are delinquent in paying said Taxes, amounting to £. 3 12s. on each Right. Public Notice is hereby given that the whole of said Rights, and so much of all the others, as are delinquent in paying either, or part of either Tax, will be sold at PUBLIC VENDUE, at the House of *Micajah Gleason*, Innholder in Framingham, on Wednesday the 12th Day of October next, if not prevented by payment of said Taxes, before said Time: The Sale to begin at Nine o'Clock, A. M. and continued by Adjournment (if need be) till the whole be sold, or so much as is sufficient to pay said Taxes.

Waltham, August 10, 1774. — *Leonard Williams*, *Elijah Livermore*, *Elisha Harrington*. } Assessors and Committee for sale of Delinquents Rights.

The Proprietors aforesaid, are hereby notified, to meet at the House of *Micajah Gleason*, aforesaid, on said 12th Day of October next, at nine o'Clock, A. M. To chuse a Moderator for said Meeting.

To agree on some Method to record the Bounds of the Lots.

To confirm their former Votes and Proceedings, or any, or either of them, (if need be.)

To hear the Report of their Committee, appointed to agree with some Person or Persons to build a Saw-Mill and Grist Mill on said Propriety, and give them further Directions in said Affair.

To grant Money to encourage some Person or Persons, to build said Mills, and to encourage the Ten first Settlers in said Township, according to their Vote at their last Meeting, and to clear Roads, & build Bridges, and for whatever else they shall think proper.

To clear Roads and build Bridges, and finally to pass any Vote or Votes, relating to any or either of the foregoing Articles, or any other that shall be thought conducive to the Interest of said Propriety.

Waltham, Aug. 10th 1774. — *Leonard Williams*, *Elijah Livermore*, *Elisha Harrington*. } Committee for calling Meetings.

TO BE SOLD at the Royal Exchange Tavern in King-Street, Boston.

At PUBLIC VENDUE,

On Wednesday the Fourteenth Day of September next, at Ten o'Clock in the Forenoon, *The following Lots of Land, viz.*

Lot marked F, 2. in the first Range of Lots, containing about six Thousand Acres (exclusive of Settlers Lots interspersed) being near one Mile wide and fifteen Miles long, and fronting on *Kennebeck* River, on the West-side of it, about ten Miles above FortHalifax: to be divided and Sold in two Parts.

Lot marked B. D. 1. in the second range of Lots, about six Miles above *Norridgwalk*, on the West Side of *Kennebeck* River, and fronting thereon, containing about seven Thousand Acres, exclusive of Settlers Lots interspersed, being one Mile wide, and 15 Miles long.

Lot marked C. A. 1. in the third range of Lots, near the Falls of *Cariotonka*, about twelve Miles above *Norridgwalk*, on the West Side of *Kennebeck-River*, and fronting thereon, containing about 7000 Acres, exclusive of Settlers Lots interspersed, being one Mile wide, and fifteen Miles long.

Lot No. 20, called a Ten Mile back Lot, on the West Side of Kennebec-River, containing about 4800 Acres.

Three Lots of Land, viz. Lot No. 32, on the East Side of *Kennebec*-River, about 300 Poles above *Fort-Western*, No. 86, on the East Side of said River, about 9 Miles and 120 Poles above *Fort-Western*, and also Lot No. 20, on the West Side of said River, about one Mile and 230 Poles above *Fort-Western*, containing 400 Acres each.

Also all the Islands in Cobbiseconte Pond, and all the Islands in *Kennebeck*-River, above *Fort-Halifax*. The Pay will be made easy to the Purchasers.

For further Particulars, enquire of *Henry Alline*, jun. at his Office in King-Street, *Boston*. *June 10, 1774.*

Boston, Aug. 26, 1774. HAVING observed a Paragraph in the Spy of Thursday last, intimating that I had been rigorously treated in bringing a Load of Sand to this Town.—This may Certify, That it is utterly a Mistake; that I was kindly indulged in my Request for Permission to bring up that Article.

ROBT. FAIRSERVICE.

Thomas Walley,

Begs Leave to inform his Friends

and Customers, that he is Removed from his Store on Dock-Square, to the first Store in BUTLER'S ROW, lately Improved by Mr. *Samuel Allene Otis*, being the opposite Corner to Mr. *Thomas Handasyde Peck*, Hatter, where he continues to sell all Sorts of Groceries as usual, by Wholesale and Retail, at the lowest Rates, and his Customers, may depend they shall be as well used, as at any Store in Boston.

N. B. A Quantity of choice Raisins in good Order, Teneriff Wine by the Pipe, Hogshead or Quarter Cask, very best Lisbon and M. Malaga, by the Quarter Cask, also race and ground Ginger,—at said Store.

BUTLER's-ROW, No. 1.

All Persons that have any Demands on the Estate of Mr. JOSEPH JACKSON, late of Boston, Truckman, deceased, are desired to bring in their several Demands to ABIGAIL JACKSON, sole Executrix to said Estate.—And those who are indebted to said Estate, are requested to settle and pay the same to said Executrix immediately.

RAN-away from his Master, on the 25th Instant, a Negro Fellow named CATO, about 20 Years of Age, about 5 Feet 8 Inches high, a thick well-set Fellow. Had on when he went away, a thin Homespun Coat, a Woollen Shirt, and Tow Trowsers.—Whoever shall take up said Runaway, and convey him to his Master in Salem, shall have TWO DOLLARS Reward, and all necessary Charges paid by me.

DANIEL MALLOON.

All Masters of Vessels and others, are hereby cautioned against concealing, harbouring or entertaining said Runaway, on Penalty of the Law.

SALEM, August 29, 1774.

Five Dollars Reward.

STOLEN out of the Stable of the Subscriber in Ipswich, on the 25th of August a dark Bay Horse, about 10 Years of Age, Trotts and Paces, has a black Main and Tail, is very tender Mouthed, likewise a Saddle and Bridle, the Makers Name Sharwin, the Saddle is lined with white Flannel, and has a main Pillion, for a Portmanteau.—Whoever shall secure said Horse, Saddle and Bridle, so that the Owner may have him again, and secure the Thief, so that he be bro't to Justice, shall have the above Reward, and four Dollars for the Horse only.

Ipswich, Aug. 26, 1774. JACOB TREADWELL.

TO BE SOLD

A Right of Land containing about 500 Acres, in a Township granted by the Great and General Court, of the Province of Massachusetts-Bay, to Samuel Livermore, Esq; and others, lying on both sides of Androscogging River, adjoining Sylvester Township, in the County of Cumberland. Inquire of the Printers.

James Henderson

ACQUAINTS his Customers and others, That he has for Sale a compleat Assortment of

English, *India*, and *Scotch* GOODS,

suitable to all Seasons, which he will sell by Wholesale and Retail, cheap for Cash, at his Shop in Ann-Street, BOSTON.———Amongst which is———

A beautiful Assortment of Brocaded SILKS, Ducapes, strip'd, plain and changeable Lutestrings, Sattins and Modes of all widths, a fine Assortment of the newest fashion Ribbons, to be sold very low, plain strip'd and flower'd Muslins, &c. &c. &c.

TO BE SOLD,

By Capt. *Jeduthen Baldwin*, of *Brookfield*,

And may be entered upon immediately;

A FARM in Shutesbury, containing about 137 Acres of choice Land, 40 Acres of it is the best of Land for Plowing. There is about 50 Acres that will make the best of Mowing, all well Watered. There is a low House with a Cellar under the whole neatly Stoned, the Chimney is set on an Arch. There is three Rooms with Fire Places, besides a Bed-Room. There is a pretty young Orchard that made a few Barrels of Cyder last Year. There is about eight Acres of the said Place planted with Corn, and sow'd with Grain this Year, and five Acres more cleared to be sow'd this Fall with Rye and other Seeds. There is a few Loads of Hay cut there this Year, and Pasturing for a few Cattle. The Whole may be had now for about £.1200 Old Tenor.

A GREAT PENNYWORTH!

Also to be Sold—About 130 or 150 Acres of choice Land for Pasturing, on Coy's-Hill, in Brookfield, that is well fenced, and divided into several Pastures, well into Grass.

TO BE SOLD

By JOHN BAKER,

in Back-Street,

About 400 Quintals of good Merchantable and Jamaica Fish, either by large or small Quantities.

ALL Persons indebted to the Estate of Capt. William Winpfield, late of Boston, Merchant deceased, are desired to make immediate Payment to Edward Procter, Sole Executor of his last Will:—And all those who have any Demands on said Estate, are desired forthwith to bring them in to said Executor, in Order to a speedy Settlement.

Boston, Aug. 20, 1774.

FOR LONDON,

The Brigantine KATY, 100 Tons Burthen, JOHN DAVIS, Master,

WILL sail from Plymouth with all convenient Speed, having the greatest Part of her Cargo on Board and engag'd:—For Freight or Passage apply to the Master on Board, or at Mr. Solomon Davis's Store in Boston.

TO BE LETT,

A Neat genteel Brick Tenement in Cambridge Street, near the Orange Tree.

Enquire of Edes & Gill.

All Persons who have any Demands on the Estate of John Englesby, late of Boston, Marriner, deceased, are desired to bring in their Accounts to Cuthbert Englesby, of said Boston, Administrator to said Estate: And all who are indebted to said Estate are desired to make immediate Payment to said Administrator.

WHEREAS Jonathan Fales of Walpole, in the County of Suffolk, a Non Compos Mentis, did on the Fifteenth Day of June last, leave his House and Family in said Walpole, and has not been Home since. The said Fales is a large fat Man, about 5 Feet 10 Inches high. Had on when he went away, a brown Home-made Coat, without a Jacket, stript Linnen Breeches, and a grey Pair of Stockings. If any Person will be so kind to a distress'd Woman as to bring him home (without abusing him) or give Information that he may be found, they shall be honorably rewarded, by me the Subscriber. ELIZABETH FALES.

Walpole, the 19th of August, 1774.

TO BE SOLD OR LETT,

A large handsome Double House,

pleasantly situated in Medford, together with one Acre of Land, with a Garden and Barn thereon, about a Quarter of a Mile West from the Meeting-House. Enquire of Samuel Reeves, living near the Premises.

BOSTON, August 15, 1774.

STOLEN out of the Pasture of the Subscriber last Night, or this Morning, a light brown Horse, about 14 Hands high, black Tail and Mane, except a small white Lock in the Mane, near the Wethers, has a little Blemish in his off Eye, is rather short of his Bigness, Paces chiefly, answers to the Name of Bonne; he is about 13 or 14 Years old.——The suspected Thief is a short thick Fellow, wears a reddish-coloured Coat, a Bob Wig, and is bow-leged, sometimes calls himself a Dutchman and at others a Carolinian. Whoever shall bring the Horse to me, shall have FOUR DOLLARS Reward, and TEN DOLLARS for the Thief on Conviction, and all necessary Charges paid by

JOSEPH BRADFORD.

For private Sale,

At the New-Auction-Room South Side of the Town House, *viz.* Houshold Furniture, Consisting of

PARLOUR, Chamber, and Kitchen Furniture, such as Looking Glasses, Tables, Chairs and Book-Cases, Desks, Pewter, Brass, Copper, Iron and Tin Ware of all sorts, a genteel 8-Day Clock, Gold, Silver and Pinchbeck Watches, a Barometer, a Number of Iron Weights, (Quarters, half Quarters and 7 Pounds,) Plate, viz. a genteel silver Nearn, Tankard, Chaffindishes, Porringers, Salts, Pepper Boxes, Sugar Tongs, Strainer, Silver Hilted Swords; new and second-hand Guns and Bayonets, Beaver and Gold Lac'd Hatts, Silver and Bone Handle Knives and Forks; ENGLISH GOODS, viz. Irish Linnens, Broad Cloths, Forrest ditto, white Flannel, purple, olive and black Cotton Velvetts, Chintz, Callicoes, Shalloons, Callamancoes, Tammies, Stuffs, Durants of all Colours, Silk, Cotton, Thread & Worsted Hose, Capuchin Silks of all Colours, Sarsnets of all Colours, Silk Gauzes, Lawns, Dimothy's, black Sattin and Chip Hatts, printed Table Cloths, Breeches Pieces, Pound Threads, white and colour'd Riding Hatts, Mens black Bags, handsome Ribbons, a handsome Guiter, Ducapes, Broliges, Pound Silks, white and black Silk Gloves and Mitts, Case Wax Work; Women's Wearing Apparel, viz. Dark Tabby Gown and Apron, Brocade, blue Lutestring, Negligee, Sattin Quilts, a Lutestring Sack, Damask and Diaper Table Linnens, Pillow Cases, Cotton and Linnen Sheets, white Counterpins, a handsome Camp Bedstead and Curtains compleat, Men's Second-hand Wearing Apparel, and a Variety of other Articles.—

Also, Damaskcuses and Tobines, choice Indigo and Pepper, by the Hundred or Dozen, Claret WINE per Cask, Groce or Dozen.

N. B. *At said Auction Room constant Attendance is given to receive all Kinds of Goods for private and public Sale.*

NOTICE is again given, That the Commissioners appointed by the Hon. Foster Hutchinson, Esq; Judge of Probate for the County of Suffolk, to examine the Claims to the Estate of Capt. SAMUEL SNOW, late of Boston, deceased, represented Insolvent, will continue to attend that Service at the British Coffee House, the second Tuesday in the three next ensuing Months, being the three last Months allowed for that Purpose, from 6 to 9 o'Clock in the Evening; that no Person may plead their not having sufficient Notice of it.

BOSTON, Aug. 13, 1774. JOB PRINCE, JOHN CARNES.

And all Persons that are indebted to said Estate, or that have Accounts not settled, together with all Freighters, are desired to come and settle the same with John Carnes, at the South-End, Attorney to Sarah Snow, Administratrix to said Estate.

Boston: Printed, by EDES & GILL *in Queen-Street*, 1774.

No. 1013.

THE Boston-Gazette, AND COUNTRY JOURNAL.

Containing the freshest Advices, Foreign and Domestic.

MONDAY, September 12, 1774.

To the PUBLIC.

Boston, September 2, 1774.

I THINK it but Justice to myself to give an Account of my Conduct, for which I am blamed; and to obviate some Mistakes which are believed. His Excellency Governor Gage wrote me in the Words following: "*Sir, as I am informed there are several Military Stores in your Charge, at Cambridge; I beg the Favour of you to send me a Return of them, as soon as convenient, specifying the different Sorts of each.* T. Gage. *To Major General Brattle.*"—Which Order I obeyed; the like I did to Governors Pownal, Bernard and Hutchinson: In doing of which, every Soldier will say, I did but my Duty. But it is affirmed, I advised the Governor to remove the Powder; this I positively deny, because it is absolutely false.—it never so much as entered into my Mind or Thought. After I had made my Return, I never heard one Word about the Affair till the Night before last, when Sheriff Phipps came to my House, with the Governor's Order to deliver him the Powder and Guns; the Keys of the Powder-House I then delivered him and wrote to Mr. Mason, who had the Care of the Guns under me, to deliver them, which I suppose he did; both I imagine were taken, but where transported I know not. I wrote to the Governor what is contained in the Hand-Bill lately printed? I did not write the Governor the Grounds and Reasons of the Quere therein contained; but I will now mention them: They proceeded from a real Regard both to the Commission Officers and to the Province: First to the Commission Officers; I thought and still think it was best for them; many of whom I thought would be unwilling to issue their Warrants, and if they did not, I apprehended they might meet with some Difficulty; and those that did, I was not convinced so great Good would result therefrom as if another Method was taken: Secondly, I thought, and still think, it would be much better for the Province; for supposing there was not one Commission Officer for the present in it, what Damage could the Province sustain? It may be answered, Commission Officers are supposed to be the most understanding in Military Affairs; I grant it: But supposing their Commissions were vacated, supposing the respective Companies in the Province were disposed and determined to do any one Matter or Thing, which they imagined to be for its Safety; and proper Persons were to be employed to lead them, &c. doth their not having Commissions in the least unfit them from being employed in the particular Services they may be chosen to execute; and in this Way cannot any One conceive that some bad Consequences might be possibly prevented. Is it not easy to conceive, that the Commission Officers, leading their respective Companies, might in the Eyes of the Judicious be looked upon more blameable in doing such and such Things, than they would be if they were not Military Officers, and did not act under Commission? Might not the Difference with respect to the Province be looked upon very great both at home and here. It was suggested that General Gage demanded the Towns Stocks of Powder; this certainly he did not, the above Order speaks for itself. As I would not have delivered the Provincial Powder to any one but to his Excellency or Order, so the Towns Stocks I would have delivered to none but to the Selectmen or their Order. Upon the whole, the Threatnings I have met with, my Banishment from my own Home, the Place of my Nativity, my House being searched, though I am informed it was without Damage, and the Sense of the People, touching my Conduct, &c. cannot but be grievous, yet this Grief is much lessened by the Pleasure arising in my Mind, from a Consciousness that I am a Friend to my Country; and, in the above Instances, that I really acted according to my best Judgment for its true Interest. I am extremely sorry for what has taken Place; I hope I may be forgiven, and desire it of all that are offended, since I acted from an honest, friendly Principle, though it might be a mistaken one.

W. BRATTLE

Mr. BRADISH's *Declaration.*

WHEREAS I have signed an Address to Governor Hutchinson, which I now find is disagreeable to my Countrymen, and now am convinced was improper and imprudent, and am sincerely sorry for it; and I am now willing to make this public Recantation:

And I do now publickly declare, that I have not at any Time taken any Commission under the late Acts of Parliament for altering the Form of Government in the Province of the Massachusetts Bay; and that I will not at any Time hereafter, accept of any; and that I will not act in any Shape under the aforesaid Acts. And I also declare, that I will see this Declaration printed in the public News Paper.—And that I will do all in my Power for the Good of the Province.

EBEN'r BRADISH, jun.

ON Saturday last a Number of Persons assembled at Cambridge N. W. Precinct, to the Amount of about One Hundred, and out of that Body they chose seven Men as a Committee to wait upon Antill Gallop, who is a Deputy-Sheriff for the County of Middlesex. When the Committee came, they asked him, Whether he ever dispersed any Precepts for choosing Jurymen according to the late Act of Parliament? He answered in the Affirmative.—Then they went on to demand of him a Declaration that he never would execute any Precept that should hereafter come to him under this new Regulation.——

He drew up as followeth, *viz.*

THAT I, as Deputy Sheriff under Col. Phips, will not execute any Precept that shall be sent me under the new Act of Parliament, for the altering the Constitution of the Province of the Massachusetts Bay; and that I will not take the Commission under any Sheriff that is unconstitutionally appointed.—And that I will take Care to have this Declaration published in the News-Paper.

Cambridge, Sept. 3 1774. ANTILL GALLOP.

Messieurs EDES & GILL,

Please to insert the following Confession made by Mr. Elisha Harrington *of Weston, Deputy Sheriff for the County of Middlesex; which Confession he* subscribed, *and publickly read in the Presence of a large Concourse of People from the neighbouring Towns (as follows) and you will oblige your constant Readers.*

Weston, August 31st, 1774.

WHEREAS I have operated in the new System of Laws, by distributing Veniries to the Constables of the several Towns in the County of Middlesex in the Province of the Massachusetts-Bay in New-England, requiring them to return the Names of such Persons as are qualified to serve as Jurors at the several Courts in said County, agreeable to the late Act of Parliament, which is a Grievance to all Well wishers to their Country, it being contrary to the Charter of said Province, granted by King William and Queen Mary; all which Conduct I do acknowledge, and am heartily sorry for it. And I do promise and engage to collect said Veniries, if they can be had, and return them from whence they came, within two Days from the Date above. And I do further engage, that I will not for the future officiate in any Office contrary to the aforesaid Charter. And this Confession of mine, I do consent should be published in Messieurs Edes and Gill's Paper.

HALIFAX, September 2.

Extract of a Letter from a Gentleman at Winsor, (Nova-Scotia) to a Gentleman in this Town, dated August 22, 1774.

"Such a Spirit of Liberty breathes even here at Windsor, (and I hope will through the other Townships) that a Chest of that infamous Tea, the Property of the East-India Company, which has been privately convey'd from your Town, in Order to be sent to Cornwallis, was, with the greatest Difficulty, convey'd into Mr. George Deschamp's Store; not a Person being found to assist in doing the same, untill Mr. Burbridge and Mr. Isaac Deschamps assisted with their own Hands. Had it not been immediately sent by Water to Cornwallis, it would have shared the Fate of the Boston Tea. The Trucks which brought it to this Place, tho' deposited in Mr. Deschamps Yard, was taken out on Saturday Night and totally demolished, being cut to Pieces. The above may be depended on as Fact."

BOSTON, September 12.

Extract of a Letter from East-Haddam, *in* Connecticut, *dated* August 4, 1774.

—"This Colony has a Sympathy for Boston, under her present Sufferings.—A Subscription Paper is opened in this Town; and I believe in a Month's Time, we shall send you a small Drove of Sheep."

NEW-YORK, *August* 29 1774.

PROPOSALS for Printing by SUBSCRIPTION,

THE Works of the much admired FLAVIUS JOSEPHUS, in four Volumes, large Octavo, at the moderate Price of One Dollar and one Quarter of a Dollar each Volume, neatly Bound and Letter'd, equal to the London Edition sold at Eight Dollars.

This Work is printed on a good Paper, and in a clear and large elegant Type—No Money is expected but on Delivery of each Volume. As soon as each Volume is finished, Notice will be given in the Public Papers.——The first and second Volumes are near finished already; the third and fourth Volumes will soon be put in the Press, and dispatched with all Speed.

I need not expatiate on the Character of this elegant Writer and profound Historian, as his Reputation is so universally known among all Gentlemen conversant in the Literary World, and so greatly approved of by all who have had the perusing of his Works, that they rely more upon the Veracity of his Writings, than all the Greek and Latin Historians put together.

I am the Public's humble Servant,

JOHN MCGIBBONS.

SUBSCRIPTIONS are taken in by EDES & GILL.

By the Ship Julius Cæsar, Captain Tate, arrived at Salem last Tuesday in seven Weeks from London, we have Prints to the 15th of July, from which we have taken the following Advices, viz.

LONDON, *June* 15.

IT was yesterday currently reported at St. James's, that the B[illegible] Bishops will make a Protest against the Quebec Bill.

A person arrived from the West-Indies, and who was lately at the Havannah, says, the land forces of the Spaniards posted at that place, amount to upwards of 13,000 men, besides a well manned fleet stationed there, ready to act on the shortest notice,

It is a fundamental principle of the English Constitution that whenever any territories are added to, and become a part of, the dominions of the Crown, the people of such territories shall enjoy the Laws and Liberties of Englishmen. The free Constitution of England abhors all ideas of Slavery, and does not admit that the people inhabiting any part of its dominions should be under Arbitrary Power, and be Slaves, instead of Subjects, of the Crown; but the Bill now in Parliament, for the Government of Quebec, contradicts the Principles of our Constitution, puts all the people under the despotic Laws of France. and establishes POPERY and TYRANNY. The Bill is, indeed, High Treason against the Constitution of England; and if the Minister be not IMPEACHED for avowing the principles of it, and supporting it, there can be no spirit or virtue in the nation.

It is amazing, that a Bill should be brought into Parliament for establishing Popery and Tyranny, under the reign of a Prince of the House of Hanover, to whom the people of England gave the Crown, for the very purpose of preserving them from Popery and arbitrary power! but by such Bill, as well as by many other late transactions, it plainly appears, that the friends of the abdicated Family now hold the reins of power, and seem to be preparing for ANOTHER RESTORATION.

June 23. Yesterday the concourse of people who followed his Majesty to and from the House of Peers, kept continually roaring out, D--n him, there goes the Pope.

They write from Boston, in New England, that some French and Spanish Agents were lately committed to the Town Gaol, for inveigling ship carpenters, caulkers, &c. to go to the Havannah, on promise of great encouragement.

The French King has given the most satisfactory assurances to the States General, that the losses which their subjects sustained in the late reign shall be amply made up.

Southampton, July 1. We are assured, that the Active frigate, which arrived at Portsmouth some time ago from Boston, brought orders to several Merchants in Bristol for goods to a considerable amount; the principal people of the place being sincerely disposed to continue on an amicable footing with Great-Britain, and using their utmost endeavors to keep the factious rabble in order. Four of the Ringleaders, it is said, are ordered to England in irons. There is great reason to believe, therefore, that the trade will again flourish in that quarter of the world. *A Fib!*

July 11. The contemptible state of the factious people at Boston may be easily discovered by the several Addresses to Governor Hutchinson on his departure from America. These Addresses are signed by about two hundred of the principal Merchants of the Town of Boston, and the most respectable Gentleman at the Bar, whilst the Protest of the Faction against the Addresses is issued forth to the Public, unsupported even by a single name, and is, in fact, the PROTEST OF NOBODY against most of the men of property in the place.

[*To the intelligent and wise, it was very obvious what were the Motives of pushing the Addresses to Governor Hutchinson:—The ostensible Pretences were to screen him from censure in England, and usher him into Royal Favor; but every wise Man knew, that it was to wound the* COMMON CAUSE *of American Liberty. The Event verifies this Truth.——Let those Addressers therefore confess frankly the Imposition upon them, or be content to be hated—pursued—and punished in this Life—and after a shameful End (which GOD grant them!) to be loaded with the Curses of their Children, and all Posterity.*]

July 12. Private letters from Cadiz mention, that the Dey of Algiers had declared war against the English.

July 15. We hear it is settled to keep eight regiments of foot constantly in America.

Orders are issued from the War-Office, for all the officers and men belonging to the garrisons in Minorca, who are absent upon furlow, to repair to their corps immediately.

Letters from Lisbon, dated the 18th of June, 1774. mention, that within a fortnight upwards of forty sail of ships from America, all laden with Corn, had arrived there, which they were in hopes would greatly lower the markets.

The Coronation of the King and Queen of France, it is said, is fixed to be on his birth day, which is September the Fourteenth,

To Governor GAGE.

I Have address'd you under various signatures, such as a Freeholder of the County of Suffolk—Fabius—and Micaiah. I have from motives which I think truly honorable given you the best advice in my power, and I am very certain that you might have profited by them had you not been made to believe that the writer was an enemy to you and to Great-Britain. I assure you I am a real friend to Great-Britain, and I have no enmity to you, nor do I envy you the honor of being captain general of the province, or commander in chief of the King's troops in America; I rather pity your situation, especially when I consider that the false reports propagated concerning this country in England were the cause of your undertaking a business which if you had well understood you never wou'd have engaged in. And when I reflect that upon your arrival you cou'd not avoid falling into an intimacy with many persons who never did and never can know the true state of this country—persons with whom every wise and honest man avoids entering into any free conversation upon publick affairs. But you may yet deserve the thanks of every well-wisher to Britain and America by a prudent manly conduct. Impossibilities are not expected from you. Had you thirty thousand of the best troops in Europe it wou'd be impossible for them *as enemies* to march thirty miles from this town into the country, and be assured that every thing which has an hostile appearance in you or the troops under your command, instead of intimidating the people, awakes their martial ardor. I advise you to withdraw your field pieces from Boston neck, and to return the ships which now lay in Charles's river and at the southern part of the town to their usual stations,—to treat the inhabitants of Boston as friends and fellow subjects—to consider the yeomanry of the country as a sensible brave body of men, not to suffer any who are near you to speak of them as a body of ignorant thoughtless men, nosed by a few designing factious leaders.———Not to suffer their free spirits to be insulted by the stupid vauntings of those who boast of being able to march unmolested in military triumph from one end of the continent to the other with five thousand British troops, when probably the poor Gascon is not able to march from one end to the other of the little closet which resounds with his boastings.—And suffer me once more to tell you, that you will act very wisely in calling in the old constitutional Council of the Province to support and advise you.—Consider of this matter—determine with judgment. Be assured your compliance with, or refusal of, this advice, will be carefully weighed in Great Britain; and you must believe that it cannot be unknown there, that you received this Advice at a time when you might have availed yourself of it.

A Freeholder of the County of SUFFOLK.

PHILADELPHIA, AUGUST 31.

Last Week Col. Nathaniel Folsom, and Major John Sullivan, Delegates from New-Hampshire, arrived here.

On Monday Evening the Hon. Thomas Cushing, Esq; Samuel Adams, John Adams, and Robert Treat Paine, Esquires, Delegates from Boston, arrived in this City.

The Gentlemen Delegates from Connecticut are expected in Town this Evening.

As are those from Virginia and Maryland on Friday.

NEWPORT, September 5.

Yesterday an express arrived at Providence from Plainfield, to inquire into the account of the Powder's being stolen by Gage's orders, informing that there were near ten thousand men in arms, in that Part of the country, ready to march to Boston, if needed.

About ten o'clock last night an express arrived in this town, for commissions for a number of military officers in the western parts of this colony, and informs that Col. Putnam had marched from Connecticut, for Cambridge, with 1500 men, and that Col. Saltonstall was to march this day with another body, and that all the country were prodigiously enraged, they having been informed that a party of soldiers had marched to Framingham, to seize the powder of that town, and had killed 6 of the inhabitants outright.

Subscriptions are now raising in this town, for the poor, and suffering, inhabitants of the town of Boston; and in several other towns in this colony, concerning which we hope to give a good account in a short time.

BOSTON, September 12.

Wednesday General Gage, accompanied by Ld. Percy, the Admiral, and other Officers, critically surveyed the Mill-Creek, which divides the Town.

Lieutenant Governor Oliver has removed his Family and Goods from Cambridge to this Town.

Last Week Jonathan Simpson, Esq; resigned his Seat at the Council Board.

The counter part of General Brattle thinks it convenient for him this week to deny his resignation; therefore the Hon. Harrison Gray, Esq; may still be looked upon a Member of his Majesty's *Mandamus* Council for this Province, till another change of times.

All that compose the new Council, who have not resigned their Seats, at the Council Board, are in Town.

Monday sailed the Scarborough Man of War with dispatches for England.

Monday Morning came to Town from North-Yarmouth, the Hon. JEREMIAH POWELL, Esq; who the same Forenoon waited upon his Excellency the Governor and declined accepting a Seat at the Council Board by Mandamus.

By Letters from Connecticut, and by several credible Gentlemen arrived from thence, we are informed that there were not less than 40,000 Men, in Motion, and under Arms on their Way to Boston, on Saturday, Sunday and Monday last, having heard a false Report that the Troops had Fired upon the People, and Killed several of the Inhabitants: Twelve Hundred arrived at Hartford from Farmington, and other places forty Miles beyond Hartford, Yesterday Week, on their Way to this Place, so rapidly did the News fly. But being informed by expresses that it was a false report, they returned home declaring themselves ready at a minute's warning to arm again, and fight for their country, and distressed Brethren of Boston.

We hear that near 6000 Men assembled at Worcester, on Monday and Tuesday last, who prevented the Inferior Court from sitting there.

In several Towns towards Connecticut, the Meeting Houses were shut up Yesterday-se'nnight and the People all under Arms.

We hear from the County of Plymouth, that last Wednesday upwards of 2000 of the substantial Yeomanry, collected from the several Towns of Plymouth, Hanover and Pembroke, repaired to the House of Nathaniel Ray Thomas of Marshfield, one of the new Council; but he having had some previous Intimation of the intended Visit of the People, he thought it unsafe to remain even in Marshfield, and accordingly fled the night before with all Speed to the city of Refuge.

A Correspondent informs us, that "on Saturday last about 300 Men waited upon Col. Elisha Jones, at Weston, and made his Mightiness walk through their Ranks with his Hat off, and express his Sorrow for past Offences, and promise not to be Guilty of the like for the future."

Last Monday the Selectmen of this Town waited on his Excellency Governor Gage, to acquaint him that the Inhabitants were much alarmed to find that he had ordered the breaking up the Ground near the Fortification, on the Neck, and requested of his Excellency that he would explain to them his design in that extraordinary Movement, that they might thereby have it in their Power to quiet the Minds of the People.

When his Excellency replied to the following purpose, "That he had no intention of stopping up the Avenue to the Town, or of obstructing the Inhabitants, or any of the Country People coming in or going out of the Town as usual—That he had taken his Measures, and that he was to protect his Majesty's Subjects, and his Majesty's Troops in this Town, and that he had no intention of any thing hostile against the Inhabitants.

And on Friday last the Select Men again waited on his Excellency, with the following Address, viz.

May it please your Excellency,

THE Selectmen of Boston at the earnest desire of a number of Gentlemen of the Town and Country, again wait on your Excellency to acquaint you, that since our late Application the apprehensions of the People not only of this but of the neighbouring Towns are greatly increased, by observing the design of erecting a Fortress at the Entrance of the Town; and of reducing this Metropolis in other respects to the state of a Garrison—this with complaints lately made, of abuse from some of the Guards posted in that Quarter in assaulting and forceably detaining several Persons, who were peaceably passing in and out of the Town, may discourage the Market People from coming in with their Provisions as usual, & oblige the Inhabitants to abandon the Town.——This Event we greatly deprecate as it will produce Miseries which may hurry the Province into Acts of Desperation.

We should therefore think ourselves happy if we could satisfy the People that your Excellency would suspend your present Design and not add to the Distresses of the Inhabitants occasioned by the Port Bill, that of Garrisoning the Town.

JOHN SCOLLAY, Chairman of the Selectmen.

To which his Excellency was pleased to return the following Answer.

GENTLEMEN,

WHEN you lately applied to me respecting my ordering some Cannon to be placed at the Entrance of this Town, which you term the erecting a Fortress; I so fully expressed my Sentiments, that I thought you was satisfied the People had nothing to fear from that Measure, as no use would be made thereof, unless their hostile Proceedings should make it necessary, but as you have this day acquainted me, that their Fears are rather increased, I have tho't Proper to assure you, that I have no Intention to prevent the free Egress, and Regress of any Person to and from the Town, or of reducing it to the state of a Garrison, neither shall I suffer any under my Command to injure the Person or Property of any of his Majesty's Subjects. But as it is my Duty, so it shall be my Endeavor to preserve the Peace, and promote the happiness of every Individual; and I earnestly recommend to you, and every Inhabitant, to cultivate the same Spirit—And heartily wish they may live quietly and happily in the Town.

Boston Sept. 9th, 1774. THOS. GAGE.

To the Gentlemen Selectmen of the Town of Boston.

The RESOLVES *of the Delegates of the County of SUFFOLK are come to Hand, but too lengthy for this Day's Paper.*

The Proceedings of the Essex *County Convention, just come to Hand, are so lengthy that we are obliged to give the Public the 7th Resolve only this Week, as that Resolve appears to us of singular Importance to the whole Province at this Juncture.*

That it is the Opinion of this Body of Delegates, that a Provincial Congress is absolutely necessary in our present unhappy Situation; and that as Writs are now issued for the Election of Representatives for a General Assembly, to be held at SALEM on the fifth Day of October next, the Representatives so Elected will properly form such Provincial Congress. And it is further our Opinion, that these Representatives should be instructed by their several Towns to Resolve themselves into a Provincial Congress accordingly; if when assembled they shall deem it necessary or expedient; in Order to consult and determine on such Measures as they judge will tend to promote the true interest of his Majesty, and the peace, welfare and prosperity of the province.

The Town of Marblehead have agreed that their Regiment of Militia shall turn out four Times in a Week, with Arms and Ammunition according to Law, in order to perfect themselves in the Military Art.

We hear the Town of Ipswich have voted to present the Town of Boston with one Hundred Pounds Lawful Money, for the Use of their Poor.

A number of the Poor of this Town are now employed about making Bricks at the new Yard, belonging to the Town, on the Neck.

Wednesday sailed the Transports from this Harbour, in order, as it is said, to fetch Troops from Philadelphia and Quebec.

Since our last 4 24-Pounders and 8 9-Pounders have been transported from Castle-William to this Town, and are now placed at the Fortification.

Last Friday Morning, just at Eight o'Clock, one Valentine Ducket, who deserted from the 59th Regiment about two Years since, and was apprehended about three Weeks ago in this Town, was shot for the Crime in the Rear of the Camp at the Bottom of the Common.

Saturday last the 59th Regiment arrived in Town from Salem, and are now encamped on Boston-Neck.

On Tuesday the 30th of August, the Day the County Court was to set at Springfield, a great Concourse of People, judg'd about 3000, assembled at the Court-House in that Place, and appointed a Committee to wait on the Court and request their Appearance amongst the People, which they immediately complied with; when they very willingly signed the following Engagement, viz.

WE the Subscribers, do severally promise, and solemnly engage to all People now assembled at Springfield, in the County of Hampshire, on the 30th Day of August 1774, that we never will take, hold, execute, or exercise, any Commission, Office or Employment whatsoever, under, or by Virtue of, or in any Manner derived from any Authority pretended or attempted to be given by a late Act of Parliament, entitled, "An Act for the better regulating the Government of the Province of the Massachusetts-Bay in New England."

Israel Williams, Oliver Partridge, Timothy Dwight, Thomas Williams, John Worthington, Joseph Hawley, William Williams, Simeon Strong, Moses Bliss, Jona. Ashley, Elisha Porter, William Billings, John Phelps, Solomon Stoddard, Justus Ely, Caleb Strong, Samuel Fowler, Jonathan Bliss.

After the above was delivered to the People in Writing, they all dispersed.

Salem, Friday, Sept. 9, 1774. *Jeremiah Lee,* Esq; *Dr. Samuel Holten, and Mr. Elbridge Gerry, waited on the Hon. William Browne, Esq; at Boston, with the 5th Resolve of the Delegates of this County, and received the following Answer, viz.*

GENTLEMEN,

I Cannot consent to defeat his Majesty's Intentions and disappoint his Expectations by abandoning a Post to which he has been graciously pleased to appoint me;—an Appointment made without my Solicitation or Privity, and accepted by me from a sense of Duty to the King, and the Hopes of serving my Country. I wish therefore to give him no Cause to suspect my Fidelity, and I assure you I will do nothing without a due Regard to their true Interest. "As a Judge, and in every other Capacity" I intend to act with Honor and Integrity, and to exert my best Abilities; and be assured that neither Persuasions shall allure me, nor shall Menaces compel me to any Thing derogatory to the Character of a Councellor of his Majesty's Province of the Massachusetts-Bay.

Boston, Sept. 9 1774. WM. BROWNE.

To *Jer. Lee,* Esq; *Dr. Sam. Holten,* & Mr. *Elbridge Gerry.*

Mr. FRYE's *frank and generous* Declaration.

IN Consequence of an express Order from Governor Gage I issued a Warrant, grounding it upon the late Act of Parliament for altering the Constitution of this Province, against seven Gentlemen, Members of the Committee of Correspondence in Salem, for causing the Inhabitants of the Town to assemble for the Purpose of chusing Delegates for the County Meeting held at Ipswich; in Consequence thereof two of them were arrested and gave Bond to appear at the next Superior Court to be held at Salem to answer for their so doing: These two Bonds I have this Day freely, of my own Accord, delivered up to the Persons who gave them, and have recalled the Warrant. Further I declare that I will not accept of any Commission under the said Act of Parliament, nor do any Thing either in my publick or private Capacity to carry it into Execution: And therefore hope to be restored to that Friendship & Regard with my Fellow-Citizens and Countrymen which I heretofore enjoyed.

P. FRYE.

Salem Sept. 8. 1774.

BOSTON.

SALEM, September 9. *Last Tuesday arrived here the Ship Julius Cæsar, Charles Fea, Master, from London, having on board Thirty Chests and three half Chests of Tea, the Property of one Montgomery of London, consigned to Messrs Smith and Atkinson, Merchants in Boston, who were equally surprized and offended at the Consignment, it being intirely unknown to them before the Ship's Arrival; and they solemnly declare, that Mr. Montgomery, previous to this Consignment, never had any Intercourse or commercial Correspondence with either of them. As soon as the Committee of Correspondence here had made Discovery of the Tea, the Master sent an Express to Smith and Atkinson; and the next Morning Mr. Smith came to Town, and frankly declared that the Tea should not be landed, nor any Duty paid on it here if he could possibly prevent its being done. On Tuesday & Wednesday Nights the Committee set Guards in the Ship. On Thursday Messrs. Smith and Atkinson procured a Vessel to take the Tea on board and carry it to Halifax. That Night also a Guard was set. And this Morning, at Day-light the Tea was taken out, and put on board the Vessel procured to receive it, in Presence of the Guard; who having taken the Marks and Numbers of the Chest, found them to agree with the Bill of Laden and the Cocket. By Seven o'Clock the Vessel, with the Tea on board got under Sail and before Ten was out of the Harbour with a fair Wind.*

Messrs. Smith and Atkinson in the whole Affair conducted like Men of Honour, and entirely to the Satisfaction of the Committee, having used their utmost endeavours to dispose of the Tea in a Manner the least exceptionable.

Friday Night last died, in the 81st Year of his Age, Mr. Joseph Lasinby, Keeper of the Work House in this Town. His Remains are to be interr'd from Mr. Ebenezer Brown's in Middle-Street, To-Morrow Afternoon, at Half after 4 o'Clock, when his Friends and Acquaintance are desired to attend.

Concord, September 3 1774.

I The Subscriber being sensible of the great Uneasiness that has arisen relating to my signing in Favour of the late Governor Hutchinson, for which I am heartily sorry, for I did it in haste; and I solemnly declare, that I detest those unconstitutional Acts, and would not take any Post of Honor or Profit under the same.

As witness my Hand, CHARLES PRESCOTT.

Concord, September 3, 1774.

THIS may certify all whom it may concern, That I the Subscriber promise, that whereas I have from the High Sheriff receiv'd several Venires, some of which I have delivered out—will take back what I have delivered out, and return the whole back to the High Sheriff; and do hereby promise not to act as a Deputy Sheriff, or any other Station under this new Mode of Government. As witness my hand, DANIEL HEALD.

N. B. *I will return the said Veniries within ten Days from the Date hereof, if they can be procured, and make return to some one of the Committee that shall be chosen to receive the same.*

Test. John Meriam,
Fra Faulkner,
James Parks.

Messi'rs PRINTERS,

Please to insert the following in your next Paper.

WHEREAS I the Subscriber have by signing an Address (with some others) to the late Governor, offended and incurred the Displeasure of many of my good Friends and Countrymen, the Loss of whose Favour I greatly regret: In consequence of which Conduct of mine, a considerable Number of my Countrymen visited me at my House on Friday Evening the 2d Instant, and manifested to me their Uneasiness at my so doing—Upon which I told them, that as my signing said Address was so disagreable and offensive, I was sorry that I had done it; that I never did it with the least design of injuring the Liberties of the People, or of affronting any Person. ——I was then asked, whether I had not given it as my opinion, that the Parliament of Great-Britain had just Right to impose what Taxes they pleased on the Colonies? I answered, that I never had, and that I detested the Sentiment. ——Having answered all the Questions and Objections and delivered them what I said in Writing, they declared themselves satisfied, and said they thought what I had done would give universal Satisfaction. Upon which they withdrew in a very peaceable orderly Manner, after having, in a very friendly manner, bid me Good-night.——In Justice to the Persons who visited me I must say their Treatment of me was very civil and inoffensive. But being informed that it is reported by some, that I have since reflected on the Company, I hereby declare that there is no Truth in the Assertion, and that I have never spoke but with respect of the said Company. And as I heartily wish for a speedy Redress of our Grievances, so I also wish to see the full Restoration of that brotherly Love and good Fellowship which is so necessary to the rendering Life comfortable.

E. POND.

AS no Man has the Good of Society and his Country at Heart more than I have, so none desire to merit the just Esteem and Good-Will of their Fellow-Men more than I do: But unhappily I have in some Measure forfeited their Regard in acting in the Capacity of my Office as a Deputy-Sheriff in the County of Suffolk, by dispersing certain Letters, wherein I understood was contained Writs of Venire Facias, for the Return of Jurors, as required by the late Act of Parliament, directed to the Constables of several Towns in said County, tending to put the Laws of this new and unconstitutional Plan in Execution; and altho' at that Time I had no intent to assist in forcing said Act, yet since it has given general Disatisfaction, I confess I am sorry that ever I meddled with so disagreeable a Service, and for the future, am determined not to act any Thing contrary to the old established Laws of my Country; and as I hope all good Men will receive me into their favour and esteem so I always have been ready when called upon, in a rational Way, to give every Man Satisfaction,

Braintree, Sept. 10th, 1774. JNO. VINTON.

We hear that a Mast-Ship arrived at Portsmouth last Thursday, (tho' the Hampshire Gazette makes no mention of it,) with 30 Chests of that accursed Herb TEA, consign'd to Mr. Edward Parry, of that Place; and that the People there had taken it under their Care, and determined to re-ship it for Halifax or elsewhere.

Died the 6th Instant, Mrs. Susanna Griggs, aged 69, Relict of the late Mr. Jacob Griggs, of this Town.

To the PUBLIC.

WHEREAS I the Subscriber, by inadvertently signing an Address to the late Governor Hutchinson, on his Departure from this Province to Great-Britain, have incurred general Displeasure, tho' at the Time of signing said Address I had no sinister Views, (especially by weakning any Link in the golden Chain of Liberty) and as the Friendship and Esteem of my fellow Men lies near my Heart, would hereby assure the Public, that I am truly sorry for the Occasion of their Displeasure, and shall in future demonstrate how ready I am (if call'd to it) to defend the Liberties and Privileges of my Country, both sacred and civil, and shall therefore hope for their Forgiveness, and a perfect Restoration to their Friendship.

JOHN FOWLE.

Marblehead, September 10, 1774.

Cambridge, September 9th, 1774.

THESE may Certify the Public, That I had not the Assistance of Mr. *Ebenezer Bradish* of *Cambridge*, in Removing the Powder from Quarry-Hill in any Manner whatever.

D. PHIPS.

And whereas it has been reported to my Disadvantage, that my Horses were assisting in removing the two borrowed Cannon, from Cambridge to Boston, from whence they came; it is true one of them was, but when I let the Horses I let them to go in Chaise, and did not think it was for the Purpose of removing the Cannon, if I had, they should not have gone about any such Business, which has proved so disagreeable to my Countrymen.—And what Col. Phips has certified as above, with this my Declaration, I hope will be satisfactory to the Publick.

EBENEZER BRADISH.

Weston, September 3 1774.

I Elisha Jones, *Esq; do declare and say, I never have taken any Commission under the new Mode of Government set up by the late Acts of Parliament; and I promise that I never will take any Commission, nor act under the late Acts of Parliament. I also agree that the above may be put into the public News-Papers.*

In Witness whereof I have set my Hand,

ELISHA JONES.

I also declare that I did not recommend Governor Hutchinson. ELISHA JONES.

WE the Subscribers being sensible that we were too hasty in signing that Paper that was signed by a Number of the Inhabitants of the Town of Easton, relating to the Difficulties subsisting in this Province, and do hereby make a publick Recantation of the same, acknowledging that it was done without due Consideration.

Easton, September 1, 1774.

Ebenezer Phillips,
Samuel Stone,
James Stacey,
Nathaniel Woodcock,
David Stone.

Daniel Bell

Would Inform his kind Friends and Customers, that he has Removed to the Store lately occupied by Messrs. Thomas and Elisha Hutchinson, directly opposite the East-End of Faneuil-Hall; where he has to sell, an Assortment of West-India Goods, upon the lowest terms for Cash, as usual.

Also a Quantity of good white Beans to be disposed of very Cheap, and a few Barrels of Pitch.

John Hunt,

Begs Leave to acquaint his Customers and others, that he has entered into a Co-partnership with JOSEPH SHERBURNE, jun. under the Firm of

Hunt and *Sherburne*,

And that they have for Sale, a large and compleat Assortment of *London*, *Sheffield*, *Birmingham* & *Bristol* Hard Wares, consisting of too many Articles to be enumerated; which they are determined to sell by Wholesale and Retail, at the very lowest Rates, at their Shop next Door Northward of the Sign of the Heart & Crown, Cornhill, BOSTON.

N.B. A parcel of Hatters Trimmings very Cheap.

TO BE LETT,

A very convenient Tenement, situated near the Market. Inquire of Edes and Gill.

A very likely Female Negro Child to be given away. Inquire of Edes and Gill.

RAN away from the Subscriber, at Manchester, Yesterday; two Negroes, viz. CHESTER, alias TITUS, about 30 Years of Age 5 Feet 9 Inches high, well Limb'd, a stammering Speech, and one or more of his Toes partly lost by Frost. Had on when he went away, and carried with him, a brown colour'd all Wool Coat, light colour'd BroadCloth ditto, trim'd with Green, two striped Jackets, blue Breeches and a Pair of Trowsers.—CÆSAR, a slim Boy about 17 Years of Age. Carried with him a light colour'd BroadClothCoat, trimm'd with Green, Leather Breeches, two under Jackets, one Callico, the other whitish Broad Cloth with Metal Buttons, a Pair of Trowsers &c.

Whoever shall take up said Run-aways or either of them, and return them to their Master at Manchester, or Secure them in any of his Majesty's Goals, and give notice thereof shall have four Dollars Reward for each Negro, and all necessary Charges paid by JOHN LEE.

Manchester, Septem. 8, 1774.

N B. All Masters of Vessels and others are cautioned against Harbouring or Carrying off said Servants on Penalty of the Law.

The Remainder of the Shop Goods,

and House Furniture, belonging to the Estate of Mr. WILLIAM WINGFIELD, deceas'd, are now selling off at a very low Rate, at said Deceased's House, near the Conduit. There is also to be Sold, an honest Negro Woman.

TO-MORROW Morning, IX o'Clock

Will be Sold by PUBLIC VENDUE, at the House of the late Widow *Tate's*, at the Head of *Gray's* Wharf,

All the Houshold Furniture of

the late John Tate, of Boston, Mariner, consisting of, Sundry Pieces of Plate, Feather Beds and Bedding, Looking Glasses, Mehogany Desks, Tables, Chairs and other Furniture. BENJA. CHURCH, Auctioneer.

To-Morrow Morning, NINE o'Clock.

TO BE SOLD,

By *BENJAMIN CHURCH*,

At his usual Place of Sale,

Next Thursday Evening,

A Variety of valuable Furniture—as Tables—Chairs—Glasses—Feather Beds—Bedsteads a Mehogany Desk—Pewter—Brass, &c.—Sundry European Articles—Linnens, Wollens, Silks—Cutlery and Brazery Ware, &c. &c.—A new Sulkey compleat—a good Chaise—Watches, &c. &c.

New AUCTION-ROOM, Cornhill.

TO MORROW MORNING, at TEN o'Clock,

Will be Sold by PUBLIC VENDUE,

At GREENLEAF's Auction-Room,

A great Variety of Goods—consisting of—

Broad Cloths, Kerseys, Shalloons,

Grograms, Callamanco's, Poplins, Missionetts, Durants, Plushes, Sattens, Modes, Sarsnetts, Taffaty's, Checks, Silk Mitts & Handkerchiefs, Ribbons, Callico's, Chints, a Variety of Men's and Women's Apparel, among which are many valuable Garments, never Worn in this Province. Wm. GREENLEAF, Auctioneer.

The Sale will begin at TEN o'Clock precisely.

On THURSDAY next,

At TEN o'Clock,

Will be Sold by PUBLIC VENDUE,

At the New Auction-Room South Side of the Town House,

House Furniture belonging to a Lady leaving the Province, viz.

Handsome Mehogany Leather Bottom Chairs, black Walnut Plush and Straw Bottom ditto, Round-about ditto, Mehogany Dining, Spring & Chamber Tables, Looking Glasses, Glass Pictures, Feather Beds and Bedsteds, a full Suit of Crimson Marine Curtains, Glass Lanthorn, a handsome case of Wax Work, a variety of Kitchen Furniture, such as Pewter, Brass, Copper, Iron and Tin Ware; also a variety of China, Glass, Delph and Stone Ware, Shop Scales & Weights, Men and Women's Wearing Apparel, and a variety of other Articles. AND. OLIVER, Auctioneer.

Wednesday next—at TEN o'Clock.

N. B. At said Auction-Room constant Attendance is given to receive all kind of Goods for Public and Private Sale.

TO-MORROW, at ONE o'Clock,

Will be Sold by PUBLICK VENDUE, at the New-Auction-Room South Side of the Town-House.

A good Pair of Curricle Horses—

ANDREW OLIVER, Auctioneer.

MONDAY, 12th September 1774.

At GOULD's *Auction Office*, In Back-Street,

To-Morrow, at Ten o'Clock,

Will be Sold by Public Vendue,

All Kinds of House-Furniture, belonging to a Gentleman, deceased, Wearing Apparel, a sett of Saddler's Tools, a Quantity of very good Indigo, and a few Barrels of Coffee.——At One o'Clock precisely, will be put up, a very handsome Chaise almost new, with Harnessing compleat. R. GOULD, Auctioneer.

For PRIVATE SALE, at said Office.

Brocaded Shoes, Hard Ware Goods, Lawns, Gauzes, Kippens Snuff, and a general Assortment of Books, &c. Also a Schooner about 40 Tons, well found, which can be cleared out.

New AUCTION-ROOM, Dock-Square,

On WEDNESDAY next,

At TEN in the Morning,

Will be Sold by PUBLIC VENDUE,

At HUNTER's Auction-Room,

(Lately improved as a Store by Mr. Thomas Walley)

A large Assortment of English GOODS,

——*Amongst which are*,——

Irish Linnens, Callicoes, Chints, printed Linnens, Muslins, strip'd, flower'd and plain Lawns, Lawn Aprons, Stampt and Check'd Linnen Handkerchiefs, Ribbons, India Taffatys, Ginghams, Bed Ticks, Men's and Women's Worsted Hose, Breeches Patterns, Cambleteens, Tammys, Shalloons, Silk Mitts, Felt Hatts, &c. Wm. HUNTER, Auctioneer.

Wednesday Morning the Sale to begin at Ten o'Clock.

Burials in the Town of BOSTON, since our last.

Ten Whites. No Blacks.

Baptiz'd in the several Churches, Twelve

High Water at BOSTON, *for the present Week.*

Monday, 40 min. aft.	4	Friday, 14 min. after.	8
Tuesday, 30 min. aft.	5	Saturday, 4 min. aft.	9
Wednesday, 28 m. aft.	6	Lord's-Day 57 m. af.	9
Thursday, 24 min. aft.	7	D's FrstQ. 13 Day 1 M.	

William Breck,

Begs Leave to inform his Friends and Cuſtomers,

THAT he has removed from his Shop at the *Golden-Key*, in Ann-Street, to a Shop near the Hay-Market, next Door to Dr. *Daniel Scott's*, at the Sign of the *Leopard*, South-End of BOSTON.

Where he continues to Sell.

A General Aſſortment of Hard Ware Goods, together with a full Aſſortment of Tin Ware, at the loweſt Prices for Caſh.

Whereas the Great and General Court

or Aſſembly of this Province, at their Seſſion begun and held at Boſton on the Sixth Day of January 1773, by an Act then paſſed intitled, "An Act to make Proviſion for the aſſeſſing the Monies "upon the Lands of the Proprietors in the Townſhip of Aſhfield, "in the County of Hampſhire, which are due from the ſaid Pro-"prietors to defrey the Charges hereafter mentioned, and to pro-"vide a Method for the collecting and levying the ſame," appointed us the Subſcribers a Committee to aſcertain and determine what was then due to the Rev. Mr. Jacob Sherwin, Miniſter of ſaid Aſhfield, for and towards his Settlement in the Miniſtry there by Virtue of his Contract with the Proprietors; alſo what was due and unpaid towards the building of the Meeting-Houſe there and the Charges and Expences incurred in and about the ſame; and certain other Charges mentioned in the ſaid Act, and to aſſeſs ſuch Sums as we ſhould judge due, on the Lands already laid out in the ſaid Townſhip, (the publick Rights excepted) ſuch Proportion as ſhould appear to us not to have been already paid; and alſo to aſcertain what might be due to the ſaid Mr. Sherwin for his Salary, agreable to his Contract with the Proprietors, ſince his Settlement, to the Time the ſaid Act was made, and to aſſeſs ſuch Sum on the Lands of the Proprietors already laid out, (the public Rights and the Lands of the Baptiſts in the ſaid Town excepted) each Lot its due and equal Proportion according to its nominal Quantity, and in Caſe any of the Proprietors ſhould neglect to pay ſuch Sums as he ſhould be aſſeſſed to the Collector for the Space of Ninety Days, Notice of ſuch Aſſeſſment, having been given by ſaid Committee, in manner as is provided by a Law of this Province, made in the ſecond year of his preſent Majeſty's Reign, intitled, "An Act to ſubject the unimproved "Lands within this Province to be ſold for the payment of Taxes "aſſeſſed on them by Order of the General Court and Votes and "Agreements of the Proprietors thereof, and to enable Proprie-"tors of new Plantations to levy Province and County Taxes "laid on them," then and in ſuch Caſe the ſaid Committee or the major part of them may make ſale of ſo much of ſuch delinquent Proprietors Land there, as ſhall be neceſſary for the payment of ſuch Sums and reaſonable Charges ariſing thereon, in ſuch manner as in and by the laſt mentioned Act is provided for the payment of ſuch Taxes and Charges. And by an Act made and paſſed by the ſaid Great and General Court holden at Boſton in February, 1774, in Addition to the Act firſt above mentioned, the ſaid Committee were further impowered to determine what Sums were due to divers Perſons, and on divers Conſiderations mentioned in the ſaid Additional Act, and to aſſeſs the ſame agreable to the Directions given in the ſaid Act, and alſo to levy the Monies ſo aſſeſſed in the ſame way and manner as in and by the ſaid firſt mentioned Act, it is provided and directed we ſhould levy the Monies we were impowered by that Act to aſſeſs: And whereas we have made, and duly poſted the ſeveral Aſſeſſments we were authorized & impowered by the aforeſaid Acts to make, and the Proprietors or Owners of the ſeveral Lots contained in the following Liſts refuſe or neglect to pay the Sums aſſeſſed or their Lands, which are annexed to the reſpective Numbers—

viz—Houſe Lots.		Second Diviſion.		Third Diviſion.	
No. 4.	£.2 5 5 3	No. 2	£.4 10 11 3	No. 8.	£.4 10 11 3
5.	2 5 5 3	3.	7 1 3	10.	9 6 4 3
6.	12 1 2	8.	4 13 2 1.	11.	5 4 11 3
10.	3 11 1	10.	7 3 3	12.	2 5 5 2
11.	10 11 3½	11.	4 10 11 3	13.	8 6
12.	10 0	12.	4 10 11 3	14.	4 10 11 3
17.	10 11 3	13.	4 10 11 3	15.	4 10 11 3
20.	10 0 3	15.	4 10 11 3	22.	4 10 11 3
21.	18 6 2	6.	4 10 11 3	24.	9 6 4 3
22.	4 2	17.	4 10 11 3	25.	4 10 11 3
26.	4 4 7 3	21.	7 8 8 1	26.	9 17 1 1
27.	10 11	22.	1 7 1	27.	4 11 3
28.	1 5 10 3	23.	5 19 9 1	30.	3 7 2
29.	2 5 5 3	25.	4 10 11 3	31.	4 10 11 3
30.	2 5 5 3	26.	1 0 0	32.	9 6 4 3
31.	3 1 2	31.	4 10 11 3	33.	4 10 11 3
32.	2 5 5 3	34.	9 6 4 3	34.	14 11 3
35.	3 7 1	37.	4 10 11 3	37.	4 10 11 3
39.	2 5 5 3	38.	6 18 8 1	38.	2 5 6
40.	2 5 5 3	41.	4 10 3	40.	4 10 11 3
41.	2 5 5 3	45.	9 6 4 3	43.	5 10 11 3
42.	7 5 3	46.	4 10 11 3	44.	4 2 8
45.	15 6	50.	5 9 2	45.	5 8 2 3
46.	2 5 5 3	52.	1 14 11	48.	4 10 11 3
52.	2 5 5 3	53.	7 8 3/5	49.	1 5 0
59.	2 5 5 3	54.	4 10 11 3	50.	4 10 11 3
62.	10 0	55.	14 0	56.	4 10 11 3
		56.	4 10 11 3	57.	4 10 11 3
Mill Lot.	2 5 6 1	57.	4 10 11 3	58.	4 10 11 3
		59.	4 11 3	59.	4 10 11 3
		60.	4 10 11 3	61.	4 10 11 3
		62.	4 10 11 3	63.	4 10 11 3
		63.	9 5 10 1		

The Owners of the ſeveral Lots aforeſaid are hereby notified that ſo much of their reſpective Lots aboveſaid will be ſold at Public Vendue, to be opened on the 28th Day of December next, at the Dwelling-Houſe of Samuel Belding, in Aſhfield aforeſaid, at 10 o'Clock in the Forenoon, and continued from Day to Day, if there be Occaſion, as ſhall be neceſſary to pay the Sums annexed to the ſaid Numbers reſpectively as aboveſaid, and the reaſonable Charges, unleſs the ſame be paid to one of us, or to Lieut. Obadiah Dickinſon of Hatfield, Proprietors Treaſurer, before that Day.

August 25th, 1774.

JED'H FOSTER,
WM. WILLIAMS, } Committee.
THO'S DENNEY,

TO BE SOLD,

A genteel new finiſh'd HOUSE and

STORE, accommodated with a pretty Piece of Land, good Well of Water, COOPER'S SHOP, &c. extreemly well ſituated in the Center of the Town, about 30 Miles from Boſton, long noted, and much eſteem'd as one of the beſt Spots in the Province for a Trader: it has the privilege of a *Licence*—Alſo the POTASH WORKS in ſaid Town, with all the Utenſels fit to go immediately to Work: The whole to be Sold reaſonably, and on the moſt eaſy Terms, as a quarter of the Value paid at the delivery, or ſoon after, would anſwer the end of the Seller.

For further Particulars, inquire of the Printers hereof.

Good OLD Tallow CANDLES

Made laſt Winter.

Sperma-Ceti and *Bayberry-Wax* Candles.

ALSO,

Refin'd Sperma Ceti Oil, by the Caſk, or in ſmaller Quantities. *Tallow* and *Cotton Wick*. The *beſt* of *Hogs Fatt*, by the Barrel or leſs. Sold by

JOHN LANGDON,

In *Fleet Street*, near the *Old North* Meeting Houſe.

TO BE SOLD.

WANT of Health and a Deſire to lead a retired Life, induces the Subſcriber to offer for Sale on reaſonable Terms a good Farm, ſituate in Pomfret, in the Colony of Connecticut, lying on Quinabaugh River, adjoining the Road leading from Boſton to Hartford, containing one hundred and ſeventy Acres of Land, conveniently accommodated with Ploughing, Mowing, Paſture and Wood-Land; a good Orchard, with two Dwelling Houſes, a Barn, a Malt Houſe, a Fulling Mill, and Clothier's Shop, with three Iron Screw Preſſes, a Smith's Shop with two Trip-Hammers, a Mill to grind Scythes, alſo two Griſt Mills, which may be warranted to grind more than two hundred Buſhels in twelve Hours, with Water to carry them conſtantly in the drieſt Seaſon.

The above Works are moſtly new, and in good Repair, and largely ſupplied with Cuſtom; being a good Seat for all Kinds of Buſineſs. Whoever inclines to purchaſe may know the Terms by applying to Benjamin Cargill, the Owner, living on the Premiſes.

Pomfret, Aug. 30, 1774. BENJAMIN CARGILL.

N. B. *The ſaid Cargill wants to hire immediately one or two good ſmart Hands, to work at the Clothiers Buſineſs, for which good Wages will be given; ſuch as can only ſhear well will anſwer. A well recommended Maltſter is alſo wanted.*

WHEREAS on the 20th Day of October, A. D. 1761, The Proprietors of the Town of Stockbridge, formerly in the Province of New-Hampſhire, at a legal Meeting then held, Voted, That a Tax or Aſſeſſment of Three Hundred and Sixty Dollars, be raiſed and aſſeſſed on the Original Proprietors of ſaid Town, to defrey the neceſſary Charges of the ſaid Town. And whereas each Proprietor's Share of ſaid Tax is Five Dollars, as mentioned in the Liſt committed to me as Collector of the ſaid Town. And whereas ſundry of ſaid Proprietors have to this Day omitted paying me their Proportion of ſaid Tax, altho' they have been legally notified and warned ſo to do many Years ago—Whoſe Names with the Sums due from each of them are as follows, viz. Joſhua Henſhaw, Eſq; five Dollars; Jeremiah Green, Eſq; five Dollars; John Cunnable, five Dollars; Andrew Belcher, Eſq; five Dollars; Joſhua Orne, five Dollars: James Friend, five Dollars; Daniel Warner, five Dollars; James Nevin, five Dollars; Geo. Wentworth, five Dollars; John Sherburn, five Dollars; Henry Dering, five Dollars; John Winthrop, Eſq; five Dollars; Edward Wigglesworth, five Dollars; Rev. Nathaniel Appleton, five Dollars; Joſhua Wentworth, five Dollars; Samuel Wentworth, Eſq; five Dollars; Samuel Warner, five Dollars; Nathaniel Warner, five Dollars; his Excellency Thomas Hutchinſon, Eſq; five Dollars; Hon. Jacob Wendell, Eſq; five Dollars; Benning Wentworth, Eſq; late Governor, ten Dollars.

Theſe are to Notify and Warn the Delinquent Proprietors afore-named and all other Perſons concerned, that unleſs they Pay me the ſeveral Sums aforeſaid raiſed as a Tax on their ſeveral Rights on or before the twenty fourth Day of September inſtant, That ſo much of their Original Rights in the ſaid Town of Stockbridge, will be Sold by me at Public Auction, at the Houſe of Henry Wiſe, Innholder in Ipſwich, in the Province of Maſſachuſetts-Bay, on the 26th Day of September currant, at 3 o'Clock, Afternoon, to defrey ſaid Taxes.

Wm. DODGE, Collector.

Ipſwich, Septem. 1ſt, 1774.

WHEREAS on the 20th Day of October, A. D. 1761, the Proprietors of the Town of Bernard, formerly in the Province of New-Hampſhire, at a legal Meeting then held, Voted that a Tax or Aſſeſſment of Three Hundred and forty-five Dollars be raiſed and aſſeſſed on the Original Proprietors of ſaid Town, to defrey the neceſſary Charges of the ſaid Town. And whereas each Proprietor's Share of ſaid Tax is five Dollars, as mentioned in the Liſt committed to me as Collector of the ſaid Town. And whereas ſundry of ſaid Proprietors have to this Day omitted paying me their Proportion of ſaid Tax, altho' they have been legally notified and warned ſo to do many Years ago, whoſe Names with the Sums due from each of them are as follows, viz. Richard Champney, five Dollars; Daniel Warner, Eſq; five Dollars; Jonathan Lovewell, Eſq; five Dollars; Samuel Sherburn, Eſq; five Dollars; George Jaffrey, Eſq; five Dollars; Rev. Anthony Wibird, five Dollars; Eliſha Story, five Dollars; Thales Greenwood, five Dollars; John Wendell, five Dollars; James McDonaugh, five Dollars; Hunting Wentworth, Eſq; five Dollars; Joſeph Newmarch, five Dollars; Richard Emory, five Dollars; Samuel Wentworth, Eſq; five Dollars; Benning Wentworth, Eſq; late Governor, ten Dollars.

THESE are therefore to notify and warn the delinquent Proprietors afore-named, and all other Perſons concerned, that unleſs they pay me their ſeveral Sums aforeſaid, raiſed as a Tax on their ſeveral Rights, on or before the 24th Day of September Inſtant, that ſo much of their Original Rights in the ſaid Town of Bernard, will be ſold by me, at public Vendue, at the Houſe of Henry Wiſe, Innholder in Ipſwich, in the Province of Maſſachuſetts-Bay, on the 26th Day of September Current, at Three o'Clock Afternoon, to defrey ſaid Taxes.

Ipſwich, Sept. 1, 1774. WM. DODGE, Collector.

A Wet Nurſe with a good young Breaſt of Milk, wants a Place in a Gentleman's Family. Inquire of Edes and Gill.

All Perſons that have any Demands on

the Eſtate of Mr. JOSEPH JACKSON, late of Boſton, Truckman, deceaſed, are deſired to bring in their ſeveral Demands to ABIGAIL JACKSON, ſole Executrix to ſaid Eſtate—And thoſe who are indebted to ſaid Eſtate, are requeſted to ſettle and pay the ſame to ſaid Executrix immediately.

Boſton Aug. 26, 1774. HAVING obſerved a Paragraph in the Spy of Thurſday laſt, intimating that I had been rigorouſly treated in bringing a Load of Sand to this Town.—This may Certify, That it is utterly a Miſtake; that I was kindly indulged in my Requeſt for Permiſſion to bring up that Article.

ROBT. FAIRSERVICE.

Whereas the Proprietors of the

Townſhip of Land lying on both ſides *Androſcoggin-River*, in the County of Cumberland, granted June 11th 1771, to *Samuel Livermore*, Eſq; and others, at their Meeting on February 24th 1773, voted and granted a Tax of *Twenty-four Shillings* Lawful Money, on each Right, to be paid *Leonard Williams*, Eſq; their Treaſurer, on or before the firſt Day of October then next enſuing, and again on November 3d, 1773, voted and granted a further Tax of *Forty Eight Shillings*, on each Right, to be paid their Treaſurer, as follows, viz. the one half thereof, on or before the next Meeting of ſaid Proprietors, which was on March 16th 1774, and the other half on or before the firſt Inſtant; ſaid Taxes having been made and publiſhed as the Law directs. Notwithſtanding which the Owners of the Rights granted on the Rights of

Capt. *Samuel Googen*, *Nathaniel Whitmore*,
Capt. *John Hazzeltime*, *John Maddock*,
Ens. *Thomas Harrington*, *Benjamin Corey*, and
Eliphalet Lyon, *David Knapp*.

Are delinquent in paying ſaid Taxes, amounting to £.3 12*s.* on each Right. Public Notice is hereby given that the whole of ſaid Rights, and ſo much of all the others, as are delinquent in paying either, or part of either Tax, will be Sold at PUBLIC VENDUE, at the Houſe of *Micajah Gleaſon*, Innholder in Framingham, on Wedneſday the 12th Day of October next, if not prevented by payment of ſaid Taxes, before ſaid Time: The Sale to begin at Nine o'Clock, A. M. and continued by Adjournment (if need be) till the whole be Sold, or ſo much as is ſufficient to pay ſaid Taxes.

Waltham, Auguſt 10, 1774.

Leonard Williams, *Elijah Livermore*, *Eliſha Harrington.* } Aſſeſſors and Committee for ſale of Delinquents Rights.

The Proprietors aforeſaid, are

hereby notified, to meet at the Houſe of *Micajah Gleaſon*, aforeſaid, on ſaid 12th Day of October next, at nine o'Clock, A. M. To chuſe a Moderator for ſaid Meeting.

To agree on ſome Method to record the Bounds of the Lots.

To confirm their former Votes and Proceedings, or any, or either of them, (if need be.)

To hear the Report of their Committee, appointed to agree with ſome Perſon or Perſons to build a Saw-Mill and Griſt Mill on ſaid Propriety, and give them further Directions in ſaid Affair.

To grant Money to encourage ſome Perſon or Perſons, to build ſaid Mills, and to encourage the Ten firſt Settlers in ſaid Townſhip, according to their Vote at their laſt Meeting, and to clear Roads, & build Bridges, and for whatever elſe they ſhall think proper.

To clear Roads and build Bridges, and finally to paſs any Vote or Votes, relating to any or either of the foregoing Articles, or any other that ſhall be thought conducive to the Intereſt of ſaid Propriety.

Waltham, Aug. 10th 1774.

Leonard Wiliams, *Elijah Livlrmore*, *Eliſha Harrington.* } Committee for calling Meetings.

TO BE SOLD at the Royal Exchange

Tavern in King-Street, Boſton.

At PUBLIC VENDUE,

On Wedneſday the Fourteenth Day of September next, at Ten o'Clock in the Forenoon,

The following Lots of Land, viz.

Lot marked F, 2. in the firſt

Range of Lots, containing about ſix Thouſand Acres (excluſive of Settlers Lots interſperſed) being near one Mile wide and fifteen Miles long, and fronting on *Kennebeck* River, on the Weſt ſide of it, about ten Miles above Fort Halifax: to be divided and Sold in two Parts.

Lot marked B. D. 1. in the ſecond range of Lots, about ſix Miles above *Norridgwalk*, on the Weſt Side of *Kennebeck* River, and fronting thereon, containing about ſeven Thouſand Acres, excluſive of Settlers Lots interſperſed, being one Mile wide, and 15 Miles long.

Lot marked C. A. 1. in the third range of Lots, near the Falls of *Cariotonka*, about twelves Miles above *Norridgwalk*, on the Weſt Side of *Kennebeck*-River, and fronting thereon, containing about 7000 Acres, excluſive of Settlers Lots interſperſed, being one Mile wide, and fifteen Miles long.

Lot No. 20, called a Ten Mile back Lot, on the Weſt Side of Kennebec-River, containing about 4800 Acres.

Three Lots of Land, viz. Lot No. 32, on the Eaſt Side of *Kennebec*-River, about 300 Poles above *Fort-Weſtern*, No 86, on the Eaſt Side of ſaid River, about 9 Miles and 120 Poles above *Fort-Weſtern*, and alſo Lot No. 20, on the Weſt Side of ſaid River, about one Mile & 130 Poles above *Fort-Weſtern*, containing 400 Acres each.

Alſo all the Iſlands in Cobbiſeconte Pond, and all the Iſlands in *Kennebeck*-River, above *Fort-Halifax*. The Pay will be made eaſy to the Purchaſers.

For further Particulars, enquire of *Henry Allint.* jun. at his Office in King-Street, *Boſton.* *June 10, 1774.*

Boſton: Printed, by EDES & GILL,

SUPPLEMENT to the *Boston-Gazette*, &c. of (N° 1013.)

MONDAY, September 12, 1774.

AT a Meeting of the following Gentlemen, being Committees from every Town and District in the County of Middlesex, and Province of Massachusetts-Bay, held at Concord, in said County, on the 30th and 31st Days of August 1774, to consult upon Measures proper to be taken at the present very important Day, viz.

Capt. Thomas Gardner
Capt. Sam. Whittemore
Mr. Abraham Watson
Mr. Samuel Thatcher
Capt. Eliphalet Robbins
Capt. Ephraim Frost
Mr. Joseph Wellington
Mr. Nath. Sparhawk
Capt. Isaac Foster
Mr. Peter Edes
Mr. William Wyer
David Cheever, Esq;
Mr. Richard Deavens
Mr. John Frothingham
Mr. John Codman
Dr. Isaac Foster
Mr. Samuel White
Mr. Josiah Capen
Mr. David Beamus
Mr. David Sanger
Mr. Elijah Bond
Mr. Ephraim Wood, jun.
Mr. John Flint
Mr. Nathan Merriam
Mr. William Clark
Mr. Joshua Hammond
Capt. Jonas Stone
Mr. Edward Durant
Capt. Samuel Wyman
Mr. Robert Douglas
Dr. Samuel Blodget
Mr. Loammi Baldwin
Capt. Ezekiel How
Mr. John Maynard
Mr. Phinehas Gleason
Mr. Sarson Belcher
Mr. Thomas Plympton
Mr. Hezekiah Maynard
Dr. Samuel Curtis
Mr. Alpheus Wood
Mr. Edward Barnes
Mr. William Boyd
Mr. Ebenezer Bridge, jun.
Mr. Joshua Abbot
Capt. Ralph Hill
Mr. William Thompson
Dr. Timothy Danforth
Capt. Josiah Bowers
Mr. Solomon Pollard
Capt. Thad. Bowman
Mr. Jonas Stone
Mr. Joseph Loring
Mr. Benjamin Brown
Joseph Haven, Esq;
Capt. Josiah Stone
Mr. William Brown
Mr. David Haven
Mr. Ebenezer Marshall
Mr. Jon. Williams Austin
Mr. Simeon Spaulding
Mr. Samuel Stevens, jun.
Mr. Benjamin Walker
Capt. Francis Harris
Mr. Asa Holden
Mr. Obadiah Sartwell
Mr. Benjamin Brown
Mr. Jonathan Flint
Mr. Joseph Parker
Capt. John Dexter
Capt. Ebenezer Harnden
mr. Thomas Hill
mr. Samuel Sprague
mr. James Kettell
mr. Benjamin Pierce
mr Thomas Rand

Mr Josiah Smith
mr Joshua Symonds
mr Eben. Brooks, jun.
Captain Josiah Hartwell
mr Oliver Hoar
mr Daniel Rogers, jun
mr Samuel Park
Capt Thomas Mellen
Capt Roger Dench
mr Jacob Gibbs
Capt Jonathan Minot
mr John Abbot
Dr Asaph Fletcher
mr Nathaniel Boynton
mr Zacheus Wright
Capt Richard Sangar
mr Benjamin Fassett
mr Samuel Bullard
Capt William Coolidge
mr Jonathan Hammond
mr Samuel Harrington
mr Jacob Bigelow
Capt Abijah Brown
mr Jonathan Stow
Capt Daniel Taylor
mr James Hosley
mr James Locke
Henry Gardner, Esq;
mr John Marble
Dr Charles Whitman
Capt Phinehas Taylor
mr Joseph Bryant
mr James Hay
mr Edward Buckman
James Prescott, Esq;
Oliver Prescott, Esq;
Capt Josiah Sartwell
Capt Benjamin Jaquith
mr Timothy Walker
mr Edward Kendell
mr William Boden
mr Thomas Upham
mr Abel Perry
mr Hezekiah Broad
mr Peter Colburn
mr Ephraim Colburn
mr Stephen Davis
John Read, Esq;
mr Joseph Hartwell
mr John Moore
Capt John Webber
mr Daniel Mellen
mr Aaron Phipps
mr Joshua Hemenway
mr Francis Faulkner
mr John Heywood
mr Ephraim Hapgood
Capt William Prescott
mr Henry Woods
mr William Green
mr Nehemiah Hobart
mr Charles Withrell
Capt Edmund Bancroft
mr Josiah Fisk
mr Samuel Farrar
Capt Abijah Pierce
Capt Eleazer Brooks
Capt Joseph Butterfield
mr Joseph Danforth
mr Lemuel Perham
mr Jonathan Brown
mr Aaron Beard
mr David Bayley
mr Ebenezer Stone
mr Jonathan Locke

The Honorable JAMES PRESCOT, Esq; Chosen Chairman.

After having read the late Act of the British Parliament, entitled "An Act for the better regulating the Government of the Province of Massachusetts Bay in New-England," and debated thereon;

Voted, That a Committee be appointed to take into Consideration the said Act, and report to this Meeting.

Voted, That Mr. *Jonathan Williams Austin* of *Chelmsford*, Captain *Thomas Gardner* of *Cambridge*, Doctor *Isaac Foster* of *Charlestown*, Capt. *Josiah Stone* of *Framingham*, Mr. *Richard Deavens* of *Charlestown*, Doctor *Oliver Prescot* of *Groton*, *Henry Gardner*, Esq; of *Stow*, Mr. *William Brown* of *Framingham*, and Mr. *Ebenezer Bridge*, jun. of *Billerica*, be the Committee.

Who reported as follows.

IT is evident to every attentive Mind, that this Province is in a very dangerous and alarming Situation. We are obliged to say, however painful it may be to us, that the Question now is, Whether by a Submission to some late Acts of the Parliament of Great-Britain, we are contented to be the most abject Slaves, and entail that Slavery on Posterity after us, or by a manly, joint and virtuous Opposition assert & support our Freedom.

There is a Mode of Conduct, which in our very critical Circumstances, we wou'd wish to adopt a Conduct, on the one Hand, never tamely submissive to Tyranny and Oppression, on the other, never degenerating into Rage, Passion and Confusion. This is a Spirit, which, we revere as we find it exhibited in former Ages, and will command Applause to latest Posterity.

The late Acts of Parliament pervade the whole System of Jurisprudence, by which Means, we think, the Fountains of Justice are fatally corrupted. Our Defence must therefore be *immediate* in Proportion to the Suddenness of the Attack, and *vigorous* in Proportion to the Danger.

We must NOW exert ourselves, or all those Efforts, which for ten Years past, have brightened the Annals of this Country, will be totally frustrated. LIFE & DEATH, or what is more, FREEDOM & SLAVERY are in a peculiar Sense now before us, and the Choice and Success, under God, depend greatly upon ourselves. We are therefore bound, as struggling not only for ourselves, but future Generations, to express our Sentiments in the following Resolves; Sentiments, which, we think, are founded in Truth and Justice, and therefore Sentiments we are determined to abide by.

RESOLVED, That as true and loyal Subjects of our gracious Sovereign, George the Third, King of Great-Britain, &c. We by no Means intend to withdraw our Allegiance from him; but, while permitted the free Exercise of our natural and Charter Rights, are resolved to expend Life and Treasure in his Service.

Resolved, That when our Ancestors emigrated from Great-Britain, Charters and solemn Stipulations expressed the Conditions, and what particular Rights they yielded; what each Party had to do and perform, and which each of the contracting Parties were equally bound by.

Resolved, That we know of no Instance, in which this Province has transgressed the Rules on their Part, or any Ways forfeited their natural and Charter Rights to any Power on Earth.

Resolved, That the Parliament of Great-Britain have exercised a Power contrary to the above-mentioned Charter, by passing Acts, which hold up their absolute Supremacy over the Colonists; by another Act blocking up the Port of Boston; and by two late Acts, the one entitled—An Act for better regulating the Government of the Province of Massachusetts Bay, the other entituled, an Act for the more impartial Administration of Justice in said Province; & by enforcing all these iniquitous Acts with a large armed Force to dragoon & enslave us.

Resolved, That the late Act of Parliament, entitled an Act for the better Regulating the Government of the Province of the Mass. Bay in N. England, expressly acknowledges the Authority of the Charter, granted by their Majesties King William and Queen Mary to said Province; and that the only Reasons, suggested in the Preamble to said Act, which is intended to deprive us of the Privileges confirmed to us by said Charter, are the Inexpediency of continuing those Privileges, and a Charge of their having been forfeited, to which Charge the Province has had no Opportunity of answering.

Resolved, That a Debtor may as justly refuse to pay his Debts, because it is inexpedient for him, as the Parliament of Great-Britain deprive us of our Charter-Privileges; because it is inexpedient to a corrupt Administration for us to enjoy them.

Resolved, That in all free States there must be an Equilibrium in the Legislative Body, without which constitutional Check, they cannot be said to be a free People.

Resolved, That the late Act, which ordains a Council to be appointed by his Majesty, his Heirs and Successors, from Time, to Time, by Warrant under his or their Signet or Sign Manual, and which ordains that the said Counsellors shall hold their Offices respectively for and during the Pleasure of his Majesty, his Heirs and Successors, effectually alters the constitutional Equilibrium, renders the Council absolute Tools and Creatures, and entirely destroys the Importance of the Representative Body.

Resolved, That no State can long exist free and happy, where the Course of Justice is obstructed, and that when Trials by Juries, which are the grand Bulwarks of Life and Property, are destroyed or weakened, a People falls immediately under arbitrary Power.

Resolved, That the late Act which gives the Governor of this Province a Power of appointing Judges of the Superior and Inferior Courts, Commissioners of Oyer and Terminer, the Attorney-General, Provosts, Marshalls, and Justices of the Peace, and to remove all of them (the Judges of the Superior Court excepted) without Consent of Council, entirely subverts a free Administration of Justice, as the fatal Experience of Mankind, in all Ages, has testified, that there is no greater Species of Corruption, than when judicial and executive Officers depend, for their Existence and Support, on a Power independent of the People.

Resolved, That by ordaining Jurors to be summoned by the Sheriff only, which Sheriff is to be appointed by the Governor without Consent of Council, that Security which results from a Trial by our Peers is rendered altogether precarious, and is not only an evident Infraction upon our Charter, but a Subversion of our common Rights as Englishmen.

Resolved, That every People have an absolute Right of meeting together to consult upon common Grievances, and to Petition, remonstrate and use every legal Method for their Removal.

Resolved, That the Act which prohibits these Constitutional Meetings cuts away the Scaffolding of English Freedom, and reduces us to a most abject State of Vassallage and Slavery.

Resolved, That it is our Opinion, these late Acts if quietly submitted to, will annihilate the last Vestiges of Liberty in this Province, and therefore we must be justified, by God and the World, in never submitting to them.

Resolved, That it is the Opinion of this Body, that the present Act, respecting the Government of the Province of Massachusetts-Bay, is an *artful, deep-laid* Plan of Oppression and Despotism, that it requires great Skill and Wisdom to counteract it. This Wisdom we have endeavoured to collect from the united Sentiments of the County;—And although we are grieved that we are obliged to mention any Thing that may be attended with such very important Consequences, as may now ensue, yet a Sense of our Duty as Men, as Freemen, as Christian Freemen, united in the firmest Bonds, obliges us to resolve, that every Civil Officer now in Commission in this Province, and acting in Conformity to the late Act of Parliament, is not an Officer agreeable to our Charter, therefore unconstitutional, and ought to be opposed, in the Manner hereafter recommended.

Resolved, That we will obey all such Civil Officers, now in Commission, whose Commissions were issued before the first Day of July 1774, and support them in the Execution of their Offices according to the manner usual before the late Attempt to alter the Constitution of this Province; nay, even although the Governor should attempt to revoke their Commissions. But that if any of said Officers shall accept a Commission under the present Plan of arbitrary Government, or in any way or manner whatever, assist the Governor or Administration in the Assault now making on our Rights and Liberties, we will consider them as having forfeited their Commissions, and yield them no Obedience.

Resolved, That whereas the Hon. Samuel Danforth, and Joseph Lee, Esqs; two of the Judges of the Inferior Court of Common Pleas, for this County have accepted Commissions, under the new Act, by being sworn Members of his Majesty's Council appointed by said Act: We therefore look upon them utterly incapable of holding any Office whatever. And whereas a Venire, on the late Act of Parliament, has issued from the Court of Sessions, signed by the Clerk, We think they come under a preceeding Resolve, of acting in Conformity to the new Act of Parliament. We therefore Resolve that, a Submission to Courts thus acting and under these Disqualifications, is a Submission to the Act itself, and of Consequence, as we are resolved never to submit one Iota to the Act, we will not submit to Courts thus constituted and thus acting in Conformity to said Act.

Resolved, That as, in Consequence of the former Resolve, all Business at the Inferior Court of

Common Pleas and Court of General Sessions of the Peace next to be holden at Concord, must cease; to prevent the many Inconveniences that may arise therefrom. We Resolve that all Actions, Writs, Suits, &c. brought to said Court, ought to remain in the same Condition, as at present, (unless settled by Consent of Parties) 'till we know the Result of a Provincial and Continental Congress. And we Resolve, that no Plaintiff, in any Cause, Action or Writ aforesaid, ought to enter said Action in said Court thus declared to be unconstitutional. And we Resolve, if the Court shall sit in Defiance to the Voice of the County, and default Actions and issue Executions accordingly, no Officer ought to serve such Process. And we are also determined to support all Constables, Jurors and other Officers, who from these constitutional Principles shall refuse Obedience to Courts which we have resolved are founded on the Destruction of our Charter.

Resolved, That it is the Opinion of this Body of Delegates, that a Provincial Congress is absolutely necessary, in our present unhappy Situation.

These are Sentiments, which we are obliged to express, as these Acts are intended *immediately* to take Place. We must *now* either oppose them, or tamely give up all we have been struggling for. It is this that has forced us so soon on these very important Resolves. However we do it with humble Deference to the Provincial and Continental Congress, by whose Resolutions we are determined to abide; to whom, and the World, we cheerfully appeal for the Uprightness of our Conduct.

On the whole, these are "great and profound Questions." We are grieved to find ourselves reduced to the Necessity of entering into the Discussion of them. But we deprecate a State of Slavery.——Our Fathers left a fair Inheritance to us, purchased by a Waste of Blood and Treasure. This we are resolved to transmit equally fair to our Children after us. No Danger shall affright, no Difficulties intimidate us. And if in support of our Rights we are called to encounter even Death, we are yet undaunted, sensible that HE can never die too soon, who lays down his Life in support of the Laws and Liberties of his Country.

Which Report being maturely deliberated,

Voted, That the Sense of the whole Body respecting the same, be collected by Yeas and Nays; which being done, there were 146 Yeas & 4 Nays.

Voted, That it be recommended to the several Towns and Districts in this County, that each appoint one or more Delegates to attend a Provincial Meeting to be holden at Concord on the second Tuesday of October next.

Voted, That a fair Copy of the Proceedings of this meeting be made out and forwarded to the grand continental Congress, and also to the Town Clerk of each Town in this County.

Voted, That the Thanks of this meeting be given to the Hon. JAMES PRESCOT, Esq; for his faithful Services as Chairman.

Voted, That this Meeting be Dissolved, and it was accordingly Dissolved. A true Copy,

Attest. EBENEZER BRIDGE, Clerk.

AT a Meeting of the Committees of Correspondence from each and every Town and District in the County of Worcester, convened at the Court House in said Worcester by Adjournment on Tuesday and Wednesday the 30th and 31st of August 1774. At which were present 130 Members, together with a Number of Gentlemen from several Towns, the following Resolutions were passed.

WHEREAS the Charter of this Province, as well as Laws enacted by Virtue of the same, and confirmed by royal assent, have been by the Parliament of Great-Britain, without the least colour of Right or Justice declared in part null and void; and in conformity to an Act of said Parliament, Persons are appointed to fill certain offices of Government in ways and under influences wholly unknown before in this Province, incompatible with its Charter, and forming a compleat System of Tyranny; and whereas no power on Earth hath a right without the consent of this Province to alter the minutest tittle of its Charter, or abrogate any Act whatever made in pursuance of it, and confirmed by the Royal assent, or constitute Officers of Government in ways not directed by Charter; and as we are assured that some Officers of the executive Courts in this County have Officially conducted in compliance with, and in conformity to the late Acts of Parliament altering our free Constitution: And as the sitting of said Courts may have a tendency to affect the Good People of this County in such manner as may insensibly lead them to submit to the Chains of Slavery formed by our Enemies.

1st. Therefore Resolved That it is the indispensible duty of the Inhabitants of this County by the best ways and means, to prevent the setting of the respective Courts under such Regulations as are set forth in a late act of Parliament, intitled an act for Regulating the civil Government of the Massachusetts-Bay.

2dly. Resolved That in order to prevent the execution of the late Act of Parliament respecting the Courts, that it be recommended to the Inhabitants of this County to attend in Person the next Inferiour Court of Common Pleas and General Sessions to be holden at Worcester in and for said County, on the sixth Day of September next.

3dly. Resolved, That it be recommended to the several Towns, that they chuse proper, and a sufficient number of Officers, to regulate the movements of each Town, and prevent any disorder which may otherwise happen; and that it be enjoined on the Inhabitants of each respective Town, that they adhere strictly to the orders and directions of such Officers.

4thly. And whereas the Courts of Justice will necessarily be impeded by the Opposition to the said Acts of Parliament, therefore Resolved, that it be recommended to the Inhabitants of this Province in general, and County in particular, that they depute Persons to represent them in one general provincial Convention to be convened at——on the second Tuesday of October next, to devise proper ways and means to reassume our original mode of Government, whereby the most dignified Servants were (as they ever ought to be) dependant on the People for their Existence as such; or some other as may appear to them best calculated to regain and secure our violated Rights. The justness of our complaints and modes of Redress, we submit to the determination of our Sister Colonies, being, in our Opinion, the only just Tribunal we can appeal to on Earth.

5thly. Resolved, That it be recommended, that such Innholders and Retailers who shall be approbated by the Select-Men in their respective Towns, to continue and exercise their respective Functions, provided they strictly adhere to the Law of this Province respecting Innholders and Retailers.

6thly. Resolved, That it be recommended to the several Towns, that they indemnify their Constables for neglecting to return Lists of Persons qualified to serve as Jurors.

7thly. Resolved, That as the ordinary course of Justice will be stayed in consequence of the late arbitrary and oppressive Acts of the British Parliament, we would earnestly recommend it to every Inhabitant of this County to pay his just Debts so soon as possible, without any disputes or Litigations.

8thly. Resolved, that the dark and gloomy aspect of our public affairs have thrown this Province into great Convulsions, and the minds of the People greatly agitated with the near views of impending Ruin; we earnestly recommend it to every one, and we engage ourselves, to use our utmost Influence in suppressing all riotous and disorderly proceedings in our respective Towns.

Voted, That it be recommended to the several Towns to pay no regard to the late Acts of Parliament respecting calling Town Meetings, but proceed in the usual Manner; and also that they pay no Submission to said Acts in any Respect.

By order of the Committees of Correspondence in Convention. *William Young*, Chairman.

Copy examined

Attest. *William Henshaw*, Clerk.

BRANDY & GENEVA.

A few Pipes Old Brandy and Geneva by the Case To be SOLD by

CHARLES MILLER

At his Store in King-Street.

To be SOLD and Enter'd upon directly,

The Distill House and Land with the Stills, Worms and other usual necessaries belonging to the Distill House, belonging to the Estate of Mr. JOHNSON JACKSON, deceas'd, situate at the South End of Boston. Inquire of JOSEPH JACKSON at the South End, Executor to said Estate.

Also, A few Hogsheads of New-England Rum, and some Spirits of different Sorts.

MUSICAL CLOCKS.

To be Sold Musical Clocks that go by Springs, also Musical Clocks that go by Weights, and play a different Tune each Day in the Week, on Sunday's a Psalm Tune. Inquire of BENJA. WILLARD Clock & Watch Maker in Roxbury Street near Boston. Where all sorts of Clocks are made in the newest Form, and Warranted to go without Variation, and many without Cleaning. Also Clock Cases are made at the same Place, in various Forms and in the best Manner, and Cheaper than can be purchas'd in London. Also Convey'd with Clocks to any Part of the Country.

All the Branches of this Business is likewise carried on at his Shop at Grafton.

TO LET,

Two very convenient Tenements in Governor's Alley, near the Province House, one of them has a good Shop adjoining.

Inquire of the Printers.

SIXTY DOLLARS REWARD.

WHEREAS it was this Day discovered that the Powder-House in Wrentham, within about five Weeks last past, was broken open by some ill-minded Person or Persons, and from thence was stolen six Half Barrels of Powder, with about thirteen Hundred Flints, and some Lead, the Quantity not yet known. Whoever shall make Discovery of said Person or Persons concerned in the abovesaid Theft, so as they may be brought to Justice, shall have the above Reward paid by me.

By Order of the Selectmen of the Town of Wrentham.

JOHN MESSENGER, *Town-Clerk.*

Wrentham, August 29. 1774.

Abraham Hunt

HAS FOR SALE,

At his Celler under the Old Brick Meeting-House,

The best old Sterling Madeira, by the Pipe, Quarter Cask or Dozen; also Port Wine by the Dozen, and choice VINEGAR for Pickles.

A Wet Nurse with a good young Breast of Milk, wants a Place in a Gentleman's Family, Inquire of Edes and Gill.

TO BE SOLD

Thomas Walley,

Begs Leave to inform his Friends and Customers, that he is Removed from his Store on Dock-Square, to the first Store in BUTLER's-ROW, lately Improved by *Mr. Samuel Allene Otis*, being the opposite Corner to Mr. *Thomas Handasyde Peck*, Hatter, where he continues to sell all Sorts of Groceries as usual, by Wholesale and Retail, at the lowest Rates, and his Customers, may depend they shall be as well used, as at any Store in Boston.

N. B. A Quantity of choice Raisins in good Order, Teneriffe Wine by the Pipe, Hogshead or Quarter Cask, very best Lisbon and M. Malaga, by the Quarter Cask, also race and ground Ginger,—at said Store.

BUTLER's-ROW, No. 1.

Five Dollars Reward.

STOLEN out of the Stable of the Subscriber in Ipswich, on the 25th of August a dark Bay Horse, about 10 Years of Age, Trotts and Paces, has a black Main and Tail, is very tender Mouthed, likewise a Saddle and Bridle, the Makers Name Sharwin, the Saddle is lined with white Flannel, and has a main Pillion, for a Portmanteau.—Whoever shall secure said Horse, Saddle and Bridle, so that the Owner may have him again, and secure the Thief, so that he be bro't to Justice, shall have the above Reward, and four Dollars for the Horse only.

Ipswich, Aug. 26, 1774. JACOB TREADWELL.

RAN away from his Master, on the 25th Instant, a Negro Fellow named CATO, about 20 Years of Age, about 5 Feet 8 Inches high, a thick well set Fellow. Had on when he went away, a thin Homespun Coat, a Woollen Shirt, and Tow Trowsers.—Whoever shall take up said Runaway, and convey him to his Master in Salem, shall have TWO DOLLARS Reward, and all necessary Charges paid by me.

DANIEL MALLOON.

All Masters of Vessels and others, are hereby cautioned against concealing, harbouring or entertaining said Runaway, on Penalty of the Law.

SALEM, August 29, 1774.

THIS DAY PUBLISHED,

THE FOURTH EDITION,

(*Price 9d.*)

And sold by EDES *and* GILL, *in Queen-Street.*

CONSIDERATIONS ON THE MEASURES CARRYING ON WITH RESPECT TO THE BRITISH COLONIES IN NORTH-AMERICA.

There is neither King or Sovereign Lord on Earth, who has beyond his own Domain power to lay one Farthing on his Subjects without the grant and consent of those, who pay it; unless he does it by tyranny and violence.

Phillippe de Commines, Ch. 108.

THIS is a most masterly performance, written since the framing the several Acts against BOSTON and AMERICA, and the best calculated to convince the Ministry, the people of England, and all the world, of the absurdity and wickedness of the late acts, and ruinous consequences, to England at least, that would certainly attend their being carried into execution.

Our last accounts, say, this pamphlet has had a wonderful effect in removing the prejudices and convincing the people of England.

The above Pamphlet, which sells in London at 1s. 6d. Sterling, is sold here at 9d. Lawful, which is but just Three Farthings more than one Third of the Price of the London Edition.

Boston: Printed, by EDES & GILL, *in Queen-Street*, 1774.

H. Murdock 3/19/1919

THE
Boston-Gazette,
AND
COUNTRY JOURNAL.

No. 1914.

Containing the freshest Advices, Foreign and Domestic.

MONDAY, September 19, 1774.

At a Meeting of the Delegates

of every Town and District in the County of *Suffolk*, on Tuesday the Sixth of *September*, at the House of Mr. *Richard Woodward* of *Dedham*, and by Adjournment at the House of Mr. *Daniel Vose* of *Milton*, on Friday the Ninth Instant, Mr. JOSEPH PALMER, being chosen Moderator, and WILLIAM THOMPSON, Esq; Clerk, a Committee was chosen to bring in a Report to the Convention, and the following being several Times read and put Paragraph by Paragraph, was UNANIMOUSLY voted, *Viz.*

WHEREAS *the Power, but not the Justice; the Vengeance, but not the Wisdom of Great-Britain, which of old persecuted, scourged and exiled our fugitive Parents from their native Shores, now pursues us their guiltless Children with unrelenting Severity—And whereas this then savage and uncultivated Desart was purchased by the Toil and Treasure or acquired by the Valor and Blood of those our venerable Progenitors, who bequeathed to us the dear-bought Inheritance, who consigned it to our Care and Protection; the most sacred Obligations are upon us to transmit the glorious Purchase, unfettered by Power, unclogg'd with Shackles, to our innocent and beloved Offspring. On the Fortitude—on the Wisdom and on the Exertions of this important Day, is suspended the Fate of this New World, and of unborn Millions.——If a boundless Extent of Continent, swarming with Millions, will tamely submit to live, move and have their Being at the arbitrary Will of a licentious Minister, they basely yield to voluntary Slavery, and future Generations shall load their Memories with unceasing Execrations.—On the other Hand, if we arrest the Hand which would ransack our Pockets, if we disarm the Parricide who points the Dagger to our Bosoms, if we nobly defeat that fatal Edict which proclaims a* Power to frame Laws for us in all Cases whatsoever, *thereby entailing the endless and numberless Curses of Slavery upon Us, our Heirs and their Heirs for ever; if we successfully resist that unparallelled Usurpation of unconstitutional Power, whereby our Capital is robbed of the Means of Life, whereby the Streets of Boston are thronged with military Executioners, whereby our Coasts are lined, and Harbours crowded with Ships of War, whereby the Charter of the Colony, that sacred Barrier against the Encroachments of Tyranny, is mutilated, and in effect annihilated; whereby a murderous Law is framed to shelter Villains from the Hand of Justice; whereby that unalienable and inestimable Inheritance, which we derived from Nature, the Constitution of Britain, which was covenanted to us in the Charter of the Province, is totally wrecked, annulled and vacated;—Posterity will acknowledge that Virtue which preserved them free and happy; and while we enjoy the Rewards and Blessings of the Faithful, the Torrent of Panegyrick will roll down our Reputations to that latest Period, when the Streams of Time shall be absorbed in the Abyss of Eternity.*

Therefore, WE HAVE RESOLVED, AND DO RESOLVE,

1. That whereas his Majesty GEORGE the Third is the rightful Successor to the Throne of Great-Britain, and justly entitled to the Allegiance of the British Realm, and agreeable to *Compact*, of the English Colonies in America.—Therefore we the Heirs and Successors of the first Planters of this Colony, do chearfully acknowledge the said GEORGE the Third to be our rightful Sovereign, and that said Covenant is the Tenure and Claim on which are founded our Allegiance and Submission.

2. That it is an indispensable Duty which we owe to GOD, our Country, Ourselves and Posterity, by all lawful Ways and Means in our Power, to maintain, defend and preserve those civil and religious Rights and Liberties for which many of our Fathers fought—bled——and died; and to hand them down entire to future Generations.

3. That the late Acts of the British Parliament for blocking up the Harbour of Boston, and for altering the established Form of Government in this Colony; and for screening the most flagitious Violaters of the Laws of the Province from a legal Trial, are gross Infractions of those Rights to which we are justly entitled by the Laws of Nature, the British Constitution, and the Charter of the Province.

4. That no Obedience is due from this Province to either or any Part of the Acts abovementioned; but that they be rejected as the Attempts of a wicked Administration to enslave America.

5. That so long as the Justices of our Superior Courts of Judicature, Court of Assize, and General Goal Delivery, and Inferior Courts of Common Pleas in this County, are appointed, or hold their Places by any other Tenure than that which the Charter and the Laws of the Province direct; they must be considered as under undue Influence, and are therefore unconstitutional Officers, and as such no Regard ought to be paid to them by the People of this County.

6. That if the Justices of the Superior Court of Judicature, Court of Assize, &c. Justices of the Court of Common Pleas, or of the General Sessions of the Peace, shall sit and act during their present disqualified State, this County will support and bear harmless all Sheriffs and their Deputies, Constables, Jurors and other Officers, who shall refuse to carry into Execution the Orders of said Courts: And as far as is possible to prevent the Inconveniencies that must attend the Suspension of the Courts of Justice, we do earnestly recommend it to all Creditors to exercise all reasonable and generous Forbearance to their Debtors, and to all Debtors to discharge their just Debts with all possible Speed, and if any Disputes concerning Debts or Trespasses shou'd arise, which cannot be setled by the Parties, we recommend it to them to submit all such Causes to Arbitration; and if the Parties or either of them shall refuse so to do, they ought to be considered as co-operating with the Enemies of this Country.

7. That it be recommended to the Collectors of Taxes, Constables and all other Officers who have publick Monies in their Hands, to retain the same, and not to make any Payment thereof to the Province or County Treasurers, untill the Civil Government of the Province is placed upon a constitutional Foundation, or untill it shall otherwise be ordered by the proposed Provincial Congress.

8. That the Persons who have accepted Seats at the Council Board by Virtue of a Mandamus from the King, in Conformity to the late Act of the British Parliament, entitled, "An Act for regulating the Government of the Massachusetts-Bay," have acted in direct Violation of the Duty they owe to their Country, and have thereby given great and just Offence to this People. Therefore,

Resolved, That this County do recommend it to all Persons who have so highly offended by accepting said Department, and have not already publickly resigned their Seats at the Council Board, to make publick Resignations of their Places at said Board, on or before the TWENTIETH Day of this Instant *September*; and that all Persons neglecting so to do shall from and after said Day be considered by this County as obstinate and incorrigible Enemies to this Colony.

9. That the Fortifications begun and now carrying on upon Boston Neck are justly alarming to this County, and give us Reason to apprehend some hostile Intention against that Town, more especially as the Commander in Chief has in a very extraordinary Manner removed the Powder from the Magazine at Charlestown, and has also forbidden the Keeper of the Magazine at Boston to deliver out to the Owners the Powder which they had lodged in said Magazine.

10. That the late Act of Parliament for establishing the Roman Catholic Religion, and the French Laws in that extensive Country now called Canada, is dangerous in an extreme Degree to the Protestant Religion, and to the civil Rights and Liberties of all America; and therefore as Men and Protestant Christians we are indispensibly obliged to take all proper Measures for *our* Security.

11. That whereas our Enemies have flattered themselves that they shall make an easy Prey of this numerous, brave and hardy People, from an Apprehension that they are unacquainted with military Discipline, We therefore for the Honor, Defence and Security of this County and Province advise, as it has been recommended to take away all Commissions from the Officers of the Militia, that those who now hold Commissions or such other Persons be elected in each Town as Officers in the Militia as shall be judged of sufficient Capacity for that Purpose, and who have evidenced themselves the inflexible Friends to the Rights of the People, and that the Inhabitants of those Towns and Districts who are qualified do use their utmost Diligence to acquaint themselves with the Art of War as soon as possible, and do for that Purpose appear under Arms at least once every Week.

12. That during the present hostile Appearances on the Part of Great-Britain, notwithstanding the many Insults and Oppressions which we most sensibly resent; yet nevertheless from our Affection to his Majesty which we have at all Times evidenced; we are determined to act merely upon the Defensive, so long as such Conduct may be vindicated by Reason and the Principles of Self-preservation, but no longer.

13. That as we understand it has been in Contemplation to apprehend sundry Persons of this County who have rendered themselves conspicuous in contending for the violated Rights and Liberties of their Countrymen, we do recommend, that, shou'd such an audacious Measure be put in practice, to seize and keep in safe Custody every Servant of the present tyrannical and unconstitutional Government throughout the County and Province, untill the Persons so apprehended be liberated from the Hands of our Adversaries, and restored safe and uninjured to their respective Friends and Families.

14. That untill our Rights are fully restored to us, we will to the utmost of our Power (and recommend the same to the other Counties) withhold all commercial Intercourse with Great-Britain Ireland and the West-Indies, and abstain from the Consumption of British Merchandize and Manufactures, and especially of East-India Teas and Piece Goods, with such Additions, Alterations and Exceptions only as the *Grand Congress* of the Colonies may agree to.

15. That under our present Circumstances it is incumbent on us to encourage Arts and Manufactures amongst us by all Means in our Power, and that *Joseph Palmer*, Esq; of *Braintree*, Mr. *Ebenezer Dorr* of *Roxbury*, Mr. *James Boies* and Mr. *Edward Preston* of *Milton*, and Mr. *Nathaniel Guild* of *Walpole*, be and hereby are appointed a Committee to consider of the best Ways and Means to promote and establish the same, and report to this Convention as soon as may be.

16. That the Exigences of our public Affairs demand that a provincial Congress be called, to concert such Measures as may be adopted and vigorously executed by the whole People; and we do recommend it to the several Towns in this County, to chuse Members for such a Provincial Congress, to be holden at Concord on the second Tuesday of October next ensuing.

17. That this County confiding in the Wisdom and Integrity of the Continental Congress now sitting at Philadelphia, will pay all due Respect and Submission to such Measures as may be recommended by them to the Colonies, for the Restoration and Establishment of our just Rights, civil and religious, and for renewing that Harmony and Union between Great-Britain and the Colonies, so earnestly wished for by all good Men.

18. *Whereas the universal Uneasiness which prevails among all Orders of Men, arising from the wicked and oppressive Measures of the present Administration, may influence some unthinking Persons to commit Outrage upon private Property:*—We would heartily recommend to all Persons of this Community, not to engage in any Routs, Riots or licentious Attacks upon the Properties of any Person whatsoever, as being subversive of all Order and Government; but by a steady, manly, uniform and persevering Opposition, to convince our Enemies that in a Contest so important, in a Cause so solemn, our Conduct shall be such as to merit the Approbation of the Wise, and the Admiration of the brave and free of every Age and of every Country.

19. That

19. That should our Enemies, by any sudden Manœuvres, render it necessary for us to ask the Aid and Assistance of our Brethren in the Country, some one of the Committee of Correspondence, or a Selectman of such Town, or the Town adjoining, where such Hostilities shall commence, or shall be expected to commence, shall dispatch Couriers with written Messages to the Selectmen or Committees of Correspondence of the several Towns in the Vicinity, with a written Account of such Matter, who shall dispatch others to Committees or Selectmen more remote, 'till proper and sufficient Assistance be obtained; and that the Expence of said Couriers be defrayed by the County, untill it shall be otherwise ordered by the Provincial Congress.

Attest. WILLIAM THOMPSON, *Clerk.*

At a Meeting of the Delegates of the several Towns in the County of Suffolk, held at Milton on Friday last, it was Voted, *That Joseph Warren, Esq; Dr. Benjamin Church, Mr. Joseph Palmer, Col. Ebenezer Thayer, Capt. Lemuel Robinson, William Holden, Esq; Capt. John Homans, Capt. William Heath, Col. William Taylor, Dr. Samuel Gardner, Isaac Gardner, Esq; Capt. Benjamin White, Capt. Thomas Aspinwall, Nathaniel Sumner, Esq; and Mr. Richard Woodward, be a Committee to wait on his Excellency the Governor with the following Address, which they accordingly presented.*

To his Excellency THOMAS GAGE, Esq; Captain General and Commander in Chief, of His Majesty's Province of Massachusetts-Bay.

May it please your Excellency,

THE County of Suffolk being greatly, and in their Opinion justly alarmed, at the formidable Appearances of Hostility, now threatning his Majesty's good Subjects of this County, and more particularly of the Town of Boston, the loyal and faithful Capital of this Province, beg Leave to address your Excellency, and to represent that the Apprehensions of the People are more especially increased, by the dangerous Design now carrying into Execution, of repairing and mantling the Fortification at the South Entrance of the Town of Boston, which when compleated, may at any Time be improved to aggravate the Miseries of that already impoverished and distressed City; by intercepting the wonted and necessary Intercourse between the Town and Country, and compel the wretched Inhabitants to the most ignominious State of Humiliation & Vassalage, by depriving them of the necessary Supplies of Provisions, for which they are chiefly dependant on that Communication.

We have been informed that your Excellency, in consequence of the Application of the Selectmen of Boston, has indeed disavowed any Intention to injure the Town in your present Manœuvres, and expressed your Purpose to be for the Security of the Troops, and his Majesty's Subjects in the Town. We are at a loss to guess, may it please your Excellency, from whence your want of Confidence in the loyal and orderly People of this County could originate; a Measure so formidable carried into Execution, from a preconceived tho' causeless Jealousy, of the insecurity of his Majesty's Troops and Subjects in the Town, deeply wounds the Loyalty, and is an additional Injury to the faithful Subjects of this County, and affords a strong Motive for this Application: We therefore intreat your Excellency to desist from your Design, assuring your Excellency, that the People of this County are by no means disposed to injure his Majesty's Troops; they think themselves aggrieved and oppressed by the late Acts of Parliament, and are resolved by Divine Assistance, never to submit to them; but have no Inclination to commence a War with his Majesty's Troops—and beg leave to observe to your Excellency, that the Ferment now excited in the Minds of the People, is occasioned by some late Transactions; by seizing the Powder in the Arsenel at Charlestown; by withholding the Powder lodged in the Magazine of the Town of Boston, from the legal Proprietors; insulting, beating and abusing Passengers to and from the Town, by the Soldiery, in which they have been encouraged by some of their Officers; putting the People in fear, and menacing them in their nightly Patrol in the neighbouring Town, and more particularly by the Fortifying the sole Avenue by Land to the Town of Boston.

In Duty therefore to his Majesty and to your Excellency, and for the Restoration of Order and Security to this County—we the Delegates from the several Towns in this County, being commissioned for this Purpose, beg your Excellency's Attention to this our humble and faithful Address, assuring you that Nothing less than an immediate Removal of the Ordnance, and restoring the Entrance into that Town, to it's former State, and an effectual Stop of all Insults and Abuses in future, can place the Inhabitants of this County, in that State of Peace and Tranquility, in which every free Subject ought to live.

By Order of the Committee,

Boston, Sept. 10, 1774. JOSEPH WARREN, Chairman.

The GOVERNOR's Answer.

GENTLEMEN,

I Hoped the Assurances I gave the Selectmen of Boston on the Subject you now Address me, had been satisfactory to every Body. I cannot possibly intercept the Intercourse between the Town and the Country; it is my Duty and Intent to encourage it; and it is as much inconsistent with my Duty and Intent, to form the strange Scheme you are pleased to suggest of reducing the Inhabitants to a State of Humiliation and Vassalage, by stopping their Supplies; nor have I made it easier to effect this, than what Nature has made it. You mention the Soldiers insulting, beating and abusing Passengers as a common Thing; an Instance perhaps may be given of the bad Behaviour of some disorderly Soldiers; but I must appeal to the Inhabitants of both Town and Country, for their general good Behaviour, from their first Arrival to this Time.

I would ask what Occasion there is for such Numbers going armed in and out of the Town, and through the Country in an hostile Manner? or why were the Guns removed privately in the Night, from the Battery at Charlestown?

The refusing Submission to the late Act of Parliament, I find general through-out the Province; and I shall lay the same before his Majesty.

Boston, Sept 12, 1774. THO'S GAGE.

Upon receiving the above Answer of his Excellency, the Committee met together, and having carefully perused the same, were unanimously of Opinion, That his Excellency's Answer could not be deemed satisfactory to the County.—And further, That his Excellency in his Reply had been pleased to propose several Questions, which, if unanswered by the Committee, would leave on the Minds of Persons not fully acquainted with the State of Facts, some very disagreeable Impressions concerning the Conduct and Behaviour of the People in this County and Province. And the following Address was unanimously voted to be presented to his Excellency.

May it please your Excellency,

THE Answer you have been pleased to favour us with to the Address this Day presented to you, gives us Satisfaction so far as it relates to your own Intentions; and we thank your Excellency for the Declaration which you have made, that it is your Duty and Interest to encourage an Intercourse between Town and Country; and we intreat your Indulgence while we modestly reply to the Questions proposed in your Answer. Your Excellency is too well acquainted with the human Heart not to be sensible that it is natural for the People to be soured by Oppression, and jealous for their personal Security, when their Exertions for the Preservation of their Rights are construed into Treason and Rebellion. Our Liberties are invaded by Acts of the British Parliament, Troops are sent to enforce those Acts. They are now erecting Fortifications at the Entrance of the Town of Boston, upon the compleating those, the Inhabitants of the Town of Boston will be in the Power of a Soldiery who must implicitly obey the Orders of an Administration who have hitherto evidenced no singular Regard to the Liberties of America. The Town is already greatly impoverished and distress'd by the Operation of the barbarous Port-Bill. Your Excellency, we are persuaded, from Principles of Humanity, would refuse to be an Actor in the tragical Scene that must ensue upon shutting up the Avenues to the Town, and reducing the Inhabitants by Distress and Famine, to a disgraceful and slavish Submission; but that cruel Work may possibly be reserved for a Successor, disposed and instructed thereto. Daily Supplies of Provisions are necessary for the Subsistence of the Inhabitants of the Town. The Country disgusted and jealous at the formidable Operations now carrying on, survey with Horror, a Plan concerted—whereby the Inhabitants of the Town of Boston may be imprisoned and starved at the Will of a Military Commander. They kindly invite them to abandon the Town, and earnestly solicit them to share the homely Banquet of Peace in the Country. Should their Refusal involve them in Miseries hitherto unheard of, and hardly conceiv'd of, the Country must stand acquitted, and will not hold their Liberties so loosely as to sacrifice them to the Obstinacy of their Brethren in Boston.

Your Excellency has been pleased to order the Powder from the Magazine in Charlestown, to forbid the Delivery of the Powder in the Magazine of Boston to the legal Proprietors, to seize the Cannon at Cambridge, and bring a formidable Number from Castle William, which are now placed at the Entrance of the Town of Boston. And have likewise, in Addition to the Troops now here, been pleased to send for Reinforcements to Quebec and other Parts of the Continent. These things, Sir, together with the Disposition of the Ships of War, we humbly think sufficiently justify the Proceedings for which your Excellency seems to be at a Loss to account.

Your Excellency has suggested that Nature has made it easy to cut off the Communication between Town and Country. Our only Request is, that the Entrance into the Town may remain as Nature has formed it.

If Security to his Majesty's Troops is the only Design in the late Manœuvre, we beg leave to assure your Excellency that the most certain, and by far the most honorable Method of making them secure and safe, will be to give the People of the Province the strongest Proof that no Design is forming against their Liberties. And we again solicit your Excellency with that Earnestness which becomes us on this important Occasion to desist from every Thing which has a Tendency to alarm them, and particularly from Fortifying the Entrance into the Town of Boston.

We rely on your Excellency's Wisdom and Candor, that, in your proposed Representation to our common Sovereign, you will Endeavour to redeem us from the Distresses which we apprehend were occasion'd by the grossest Misinformation, and that you will assure his Majesty that no wish of Independency, no adverse Sentiments or Designs towards his Majesty or his Troops now here, actuate his good Subjects in this Colony, but that their sole Intention is to preserve pure and inviolate those Rights to which, as Men, and English Americans, they are justly intitled and which have been guaranteed to them by his Majesty's Royal Predecessors.

By Order of the Committee,

Boston, Sept. 12, 1774. JOSEPH WARREN, *Chairman.*

A Copy of the above was delivered to Mr. Secretary Flucker by the Chairman, with a Desire that he would as soon as was convenient, present it to the Governor, and request his Excellency to appoint a Time for receiving it in Form. The Secretary informed the Chairman the ensuing Day, that he had seen the Governor, and had given him the Copy of the Address, but that he declined receiving it in Form. The Chairman mentioned to him the Importance of the Business, declaring his Belief that the Troops were not in any Danger; and that no Persons has, so far as he had been informed, taken any Steps which indicated any hostile Intention, untill the seizing and carrying off the Powder from the Magazine in the County of Middlesex; and that if any ill Consequences should arise that should affect the Interest of Great-Britain, the most candid and judicious both in Europe and America, would consider the Author of the Ferment now raised in the Minds of the People, as accountable for whatever Consequences might follow from it. He therefore desired the Secretary once more to make Application to his Excellency, and to state the Affair to him in that serious Manner which the Case seemed to require.———The Secretary accordingly made a second Application to the Governor, but received for Answer, That he had given all the Satisfaction in his Power, and he could not see that any further Argumentation upon the Subject would be to any good Purpose. Upon this, the Committee were again convened, and it was unanimously Resolved, that they had executed the Commission entrusted to them by the County, to the utmost of their Ability—And after voting that the Reply to his Excellency's Answer should be inserted in the public Papers as soon as possible, they adjourned without Day. It is observable, that every Vote passed by the Delegates of the County, and by the Committee appointed to wait on the Governor, was unanimous.

CONCORD, 13th September, 1774.

AT a Meeting of a great Number of the Freeholders and others, Inhabitants of the County of Middlesex, assembled upon the Common in said Town; proceeded to the Choice of a Committee from each Town there present; which Committee being met, *Voted,*

It as their Opinion, That the Court of General Sessions of the Peace, ought not to be opened, or to set at present.——*And also Voted,*

That a Sub-Committee of Five, wait on the Justices of said Court, and inform them of the above Vote.—— Said Committee being chose accordingly, waited on the aforesaid Justices with said Vote—which to their very great Credit they readily complied with; and for the Satisfaction of the People then present, signed to the following Declaration, viz.

Concord, 13th September 1774.

WHEREAS there is a Meeting of a great Number of the Freeholders and others, Inhabitants of the County of Middlesex, now assembled upon the Common in said Town, have by their Committee in Consequence of the Desire of the Justices of the Court of General Sessions of the Peace in and for the County of Middlesex, whose Names are hereto subscribed, being all the Justices now present, informing us of a Vote of the said Committee, *viz.*

That it is their Opinion that the Court of General Sessions of the Peace ought not to be open'd or to sit at present.

We therefore, in Agreement with said Committee, publickly declare, that it is not expedient for his Majesty's Justices of the said Court to open or hold the same, least it should be construed that we act in Consequence of the late unconstitutional Act of Parliament, intitled An Act for better regulating the Government of the Massachusetts-Bay, for the Satisfaction of the People, we thus publickly promise, that we will not open, nor in any Way proceed to the Business of said Court. In witness whereof we sign our Names.

Thad. Mason, Joseph Haven, Josiah Johnson, William Stickney, Henry Gardner, Abraham Fuller, Jonas Dix, Daniel Bliss, Samuel Bancroft. *(A true Copy.)*

While the Sub-Committee were compromising that Matter, two Deputy-Sheriffs were had before the Committee, for posting the following Proclamation upon the Court-House Door, and daring publickly to read the same, viz. *Cambridge, September the 9th, 1774.*

PUBLIC Notice is hereby given, That His Majesty's Inferior Court of Common Pleas, for the County of Middlesex, which was to have been holden at Concord, in said County, on the second Tuesday in this Month, is now adjourn'd by Order of the Justices of said Court to the third Tuesday in October next, then to be held at the Court-House in said Concord, at Ten of the Clock in the Morning; all Persons concern'd are to govern themselves accordingly.

DAVID PHIPS, Sherriff.

For which Offence, said Sheriffs made the following Acknowledgment, and were dismiss'd, viz.

WHEREAS we, Antill Gallop, *a late Deputy Sheriff, and* William How, *also a late Deputy Sheriff and Cryer in the Court, both of the County of Middlesex, have received a Proclamation from the honorable* Samuel Danforth, Joseph Lee, *and* James Russell, *Esq'rs; late Justices of the Inferior Court of Common Pleas for the County aforesaid, for the Purpose of Adjourning said Court at* Concord, *which was to have been held this Day.*

We do hereby acknowledge, that we did inadvertently, and without Consideration, in Obedience to the said Justices, and not thinking ourselves as acting under the new Plan of Government, proceed to read said Proclamation at the Court-House Door, in Opposition to the Voice of the County; for which we are heartily sorry, and do promise not to make any Return on said Proclamation; and further that we promise and engage, that we will not in any Ways be aiding or assisting in bringing on the unconstitutional Plan of Government. Witness our Hands,

Concord, 13th Sept. 1774. Antill Gallop, Wm. How.

N. B. *I further declare that I will resign my Commission of Deputy Sheriff, after I've compleated all the Business that I have now in my Hands, and that I will not undertake any further Business in said Office.*

(A true Copy.) Antill Gallop.

Upon which the Body Voted the same to be satisfactory; and adjourned said Meeting to the Third Tuesday in October next, agreeable to the Proclamation for adjourning the Inferior Court of Common Pleas.

Concord, 13th September 1774.

WHEREAS I Daniel Heald, a Deputy Sheriff of this County, did last Monday inadvertently set up a Proclamation on the Court-House Door, for the Adjournment of the Court to be held there this Day. And finding that in so doing I have acted directly contrary to the Sense of the Body of People convened this Day, I do hereby acknowledge myself sincerely sorry for my Conduct, and do solemnly promise that for the future I will carefully avoid acting contrary to the Minds of this Body with Respect to any unconstitutional Acts of Parliament. *(A true Copy.)* DANIEL HEALD.

A young Man that can be well Recommended, would let himself, being used to tending a Grist Mill and Saw Mill. Inquire of the Printers.

Convention in Concord Sept. 1774.

NEW-YORK, September 12.

The Inhabitants of Georgia have published a Set of Resolves upon the present disordered State of the Colonies, similar to those of many of the other Provinces; but Non-Importation Measures are not mentioned; nor have they chosen Deputies to meet at the Congress.

A Letter from Philadelphia of the 8th Instant, says, "The Congress opened last Monday, when the Hon. Peyton Randolph, Esq; was chosen Chairman, and Mr. Charles Thompson, Secretary: There is a Guard kept at the Door of the House (Carpenter's Hall) in which they meet, & the Result of those Meetings are confined so close among themselves, that scarce the least Syllable of their Proceedings reach the Ears of the expecting Publick: The worthy Farmer, together with Thomas Willing, Esq; are both, by the united Voice of the respective Body of Delegates, called in, to give their Assistance, to the great Satisfaction and Pleasure of the People.

NORWICH, September 15.

A Correspondent begs Leave to propose to the Consideration of the Public, since the grand American Controversy grows and daily appears more and more serious, whether it is not expedient, very important and necessary, for the Colonies forthwith to raise an Army of Observation, and send it near the expected Scene of Action, and let them be increased from Time to Time as our Enemies increase, and kept in constant Exercise and Discipline.—A Preparation & Readiness for the defensive or offensive Operations, may, and often has, prevented the Necessity of Execution; but if that Necessity does take Place, as there is great Probability it will; should we not, in such a Case, be in an infinitely better Situation, than to have our scattered Forces, (though almost innumerable) to collect from all Parts of the Continent, after our Antagonists are well fortified, their Numbers full, and have struck some important and fatal Blow.

By a Gentleman who left Philadelphia on Wednesday the 7th Instant, we learn, that no Part of the Proceedings of the Grand Congress had transpired, except their Determination on the Mode of voting, which was, that each Colony should have one Voice.

PORTSMOUTH, Sept. 16.

Thursday last arrived here Captain Norman in the Fox Mast-Ship, with 30 Chests of TEA, consigned to Edward Parry, Esq; who refused the Consignment; upon the People's being acquainted with this repeated Insult (of the East India Company) to the Colonies, they were greatly alarmed, and had almost absolutely determined to oblige the Ship to return to London, with the Tea only, but through the polite Behavior of the Captain, who was ready to submit to any Thing the People thought proper upon the Occasion, he was permitted to send the Tea to Halifax, and it was put on Board Capt. Fernald, who sailed for Halifax with it last Sunday. In future no such Indulgence will be allowed to the Enemies of America. Quere, Whether the Duty has not been paid?

BOSTON, September 19.

Last Monday Capt. JONATHAN GREENLEAF, was unanimously chosen to represent the Town of Newbury-Port in General Court.

Mr. John Pickering, jun. and Mr. Jonathan Ropes, were the same Day unanimously chosen to represent the Town of Salem.

Mr. Jabez Fisher is unanimously chosen to represent the Town of Wrenthem.

Last Tuesday the Inhabitants of this Town met at Faneuil Hall, by adjournment of the May Meeting, in expectation of receiving the Reports of several Committees, who not being ready to Report, the Meeting was further Adjourned to the last Tuesday in October next.

Last Week the Cannon at the Batteries back of Governor's Island were removed by Order of the General.

Wednesday last the Rev. Mr. David Osgood, was Ordained a Pastor of the Church at Medford.

Same Day was held in this Town the annual Convention of the Episcopal Clergy.

Same Night all the Cannon in the North Battery, were spiked up, it is said to be done by about 100 Men, (who came in Boats) from the Men of War in the Harbour. *Another* SECRET *Expedition.*

The Tea lately arrived in the Mary and Jane, Capt. Chapman, at Norfolk in Virginia, is to be returned in the same ship, by orders of the owners, in consequence of their having been waited on by the committee of that town.

Friday last a Gentleman remark'd, that he thought it very hard to publish such a Piece in the Spy against the Treasurer. A By-Stander ask'd why? Because says the Gentleman, *every Word of it is true.*

Our last advices from Virginia inform us that Lord Dunmore, at the head of near 3000 men, was marching against the indians who by some means, or other, have been troublesome in that quarter.

We have received from Worcester the recantation of John Chandler, Esq; and forty two others, of the protestors, against the proceedings of that town, which gave such just cause of offence to the public; as also the acknowledgement of six Justices of that county, for having aspersed the people in an address to General Gage.—Want of room prevents their being inserted in this paper.

MARRIED.] *Mr. William Phillips, jun. to Miss Meriam Mason.*

[A MILITARY COUNTRYMAN in our next.]

(Advertisements omitted, will be in our next.)

TO LET,

Two very convenient Tenements in Governor's Alley, near the Province House, one of them has a good Shop adjoining.

Inquire of the Printers.

Messieurs EDES and GILL,

IT is hoped, if there should be an Election of Representatives, that no Town will *inadvertently* choose any one of the Gentlemen that compose the *constitutional* Council of this Province. They ought to be present when the Assembly convenes, and crowd off the *Usurpers.* We acknowledge those who were Counsellors at the last Session, and have not since *abdicated*, by joining with the *Traitors* to our Constitution, as His Majesty's Council, *and we acknowledge no other.* Don't let us by choosing Counsellors for Representatives in Effect say, they have lost their former Character. Let them be ever so worthy of a Choice, we are not to consider them as eligible at present. They are still the second Branch of the Legislature, and never the less so for the late *arbitrary Act of Parliament*, and *the Mandamus of the King* in Consequence of it.

NOVANG.

September 6, 1774.

THE Inhabitants of the Town of Littleton being assembled at the Meeting-House in said Town; First voted and chose Mr. Robert Harris Moderator of said Meeting.

2. Chose Captain Jonathan Reed, Mr. Robert Harris and Mr. Aaron Jewett, a Committee of Correspondence for Littleton.

3. Voted that the present Committee should go to Groton, to meet the Committees of the several Towns in the Neighbourhood on Friday next, agreeable to the Desire of said Committees.

4. Voted, That the Proceedings of this Meeting be published in the publick News-Papers.

A true Copy of the Proceedings,

Attest. OLIVER HOAR, Town-Clerk.

To the PRINTERS. *Lancaster, Sept. 9, 1774.*

LIVING at a Distance, it was some Time before I see Lieutenant Cockran's pompous Answer to the Facts I published the Week before relative to the Treatment I met with from him, and the Soldiers upon the Neck Guard with him; and although I thought at first that it was not worth while to Answer him, I have since thought otherwise, and if he desires it he shall have my Oath affixed to my Assertions, and a Number of Evidences produced.—His Representation is foreign from the Truth in almost if not every particular. I was stopt and detain'd near two Hours with my Team, bunch'd and drag'd into the Guard House, put under the care of Three Soldiers with their Guns and Bayonets, and told to go out at my peril. A Keg of Rum was taken out of my Waggon, and would have been I imagine drink'd had it not been for the Serjeant of the Guard. But they insisted notwithstanding upon my giving them a Pistereen, which for the sake of Peace I did.—And as for the indecent Language, it was as I represented, which I am ready to make Oath to, as I am to all that is above written and that I before publish'd.—But I shall take no more Notice of his Scribbling in future, and suspend the Matter till I can get Satisfaction for my Abuses in a Legal Way, and I hope, the Time is near when I shall have Opportunity to do it, with many Others who have been abused in like Manner.

JONAS WYMAN.

To be Sold by Public Vendue, on FRIDAY the Fourteenth Day of October next, at Twelve o'Clock, A. M. by Order of the Superior Court,

THE Real Estate of WILLIAM STERLING, deceased, consisting of a Front End of a Dwelling-House, situated at the North End of Boston, near Winisimet Ferry. JACOB COOPER, Auctioneer.

To be Sold by JONATHAN DAVIS, at Bull's Wharff, the following West India Goods, viz. Choice St. Vincent & Barbados Rum, Jamaica Spirits, Jamaica Sugars, Rase Ginger, Cotton Wool, Indigo of the best Quality, and Turk's Island Salt. Said DAVIS also has to sell eight Thousand Pipe Staves which are at Salem; the Terms of Sale of which may be known by inquiring of Mr. Haskell Darby of Salem, or Jonathan Davis of Boston.

TO BE SOLD,

By Richard Cranch,

Near the Mill-Bridge, BOSTON,

A very Elegant SPINNET, (Harris's make)—Also, an Assortment of WATCHES.

All Persons indebted to, or that have any Demands on the Estate of Capt. Thomas Cordis, late of Concord, Mariner, deceas'd, are desired to bring in their Accounts to Mrs. Elizabeth Cordis, or Capt. Elnathan Jones, of said Concord, Administrators on said Estate, in Order for Settlement.

WANTED,

A capable Lad, as an Apprentice in the English Goods Way. Enquire of Edes & Gill.

TO BE SOLD,

By *BENJAMIN CHURCH*,

At his usual Place of Sale,

Next Thursday Evening,

SUNDRY European Articles, consisting of Cloths—Calamancoes—Irish Linnens—Cotton Checks—Sheeting—Velvets—Muslins—Handkerchiefs—Cutlery and Braziery Ware—Sundry Articles of House Furniture—Wearing Apparrel—Chaise & Harness, Watches, &c. &c.

New AUCTION-ROOM, Cornhill

TO MORROW MORNING, at TEN o'Clock,

Will be Sold by PUBLIC VENDUE,

At GREENLEAF's Auction-Room,

A Variety of English Goods as usual, and some House Furniture.

WM. GREENLEAF, Auctioneer.

The Sale will begin at Ten o'Clock.

At the GOLDEN-KEY,

In Ann-Street, near the Draw-Bridge,

(The Shop lately improved by Mr. *William Greck*,)

Are to be Sold by Wholesale and Retail,

COTTON WOOL,

Loaf and brown Sugars,	Rice
Green Coffee,	West India Rum
Chocolate,	Brandy,
Flour,	Ginger,
Mustard,	Crown and Bar Soap,
Piemento, and all other Spices,	Starch,
	Hair Powder,
Raisins,	Indigo, and

A small Assortment of Crockery Ware, &c. &c. for a very moderate Profit, by

John Fenno.

TO-MORROW,

At Ten o'Clock in the Morning,

Will be sold by PUBLIC VENDUE,

All the Houshold Furniture of Mr. COLBORN BARRELL, (who embarks for England in a short Time) at his House directly opposite the North Grammer School, consisting of,

MAHOGONY dining, tea, card, writing and corner Tables, Looking-Glasses, very large and elegant, one Mahogony Chest upon Chests of Draws, Mahogony Hair-bottom'd Chairs, Leather-bottom'd chamber and common ditto, one easy Chair, wilton & common floor and stair Carpets of different Sizes, steel, Prince's metal, brass and common Hand Irons, one exceeding good 8-day spring Clock, China and Glass Ware, four posts, common and camp Bedsteds, Feather Beds and Beding, bed and window Curtains, different Sorts, Pictures, one Mahogony Bureau, brass and copper Scales and Weights, one Lady's riding Saddle, one Kitchen Jack, brass Kettles, Fish ditto, with all other Sorts of Kitchen Furniture, &c. &c. R. GOULD, Auctioneer.

The Furniture may be viewed the Day before the Sale.

N. B. All Persons that have any Demands on said Barrel, are desired to call upon him for a Settlement.

Province of the MASSACHUSETTS BAY.

Cumberland, ss.

Notice is hereby given to the Delinquent Proprietors of the Town of New-Glocester, in said County, That unless they pay the several Sums hereafter affixed to each Delinquent Right respectively, together with incidental Charges, to Mr. Isaac Parsons, of said New-Glocester, before the 6th Day of December next they may expect that so much of each of such Delinquent Right in said Town will be sold at Public Vendue, at the House of Mr. Isaac Parsons abovesaid, on the aforesaid Sixth Day of December, as will be sufficient to discharge their several Arrearages, with the Charges as aforesaid. The Sale to begin at Ten of the Clock in the Forenoon, and to continue from Time to Time, until the whole is Sold.

The Rights that are delinquent, are as followt, viz.

Rights.	£.	s.	d.	Rights.	£.	s.	d.
No. 1	4	13	10	No. 38	4	12	0
4	4	5	9	39	32	15	1
7	10	4	4	42	4	5	9
10	4	0	0	45	5	5	11
13	13	4	6	46	5	5	11
16	5	3	4	52	4	5	9
20	16	16	10	54	3	12	9
22	4	18	4	56	7	19	7
24	9	19	7	58	10	4	4
26	4	5	9	61	11	4	8
31	9	0	6	63	3	3	4

New-Glocester, Sept. 1, 1774

SIMON NOYES,
EBENEZER MASON,
ISAAC PARSONS, } Committee and Assessors.

WHEREAS on the 20th Day of October, A. D. 1761, the Proprietors of the Town of Bernard, formerly in the Province of New-Hampshire, at a legal Meeting then held, Voted that a Tax or Assessment of Three Hundred and forty-five Dollars be raised and assessed on the Original Proprietors of said Town, to defrey the necessary Charges of the said Town. And whereas each Proprietor's Share of said Tax is five Dollars, as mentioned in the List committed to me as Collector of the said Town. And whereas sundry of said Proprietors have to this Day omitted paying me their Proportion of said Tax, altho' they have been legally notified and warned so to do many Years ago, whose Names with the Sums due from each of them are as follows, viz. Richard Champney, five Dollars; Daniel Warner, Esq; five Dollars; Jonathan Lovewell, Esq; five Dollars; Samuel Sherburn, Esq; five Dollars; George Jaffrey, Esq; five Dollars; Rev. Anthony Wibird, five Dollars; Elisha Story, five Dollars; Thales Greenwood, five Dollars; John Wendell, five Dollars; James McDonaugh, five Dollars; Hunting Wentworth, Esq; five Dollars; Joseph Newmarch, five Dollars; Richard Emory, five Dollars; Samuel Wentworth, Esq; five Dollars; Benning Wentworth, Esq; late Governor, ten Dollars.

THESE are therefore to notify and warn the delinquent Propproprietors afore-named, and all other Persons concerned, that unless they pay me their several Sums aforesaid, raised as a Tax on their several Rights, on or before the 24th Day of September Instant, that so much of their Original Rights in the said Town of Bernard, will be sold by me, at public Vendue, at the House of Henry Wise, Innholder in Ipswich, in the Province of Massachusetts-Bay, on the 26th Day of September Current, at Three o'Clock Afternoon, to defrey said Taxes.

Ipswich, Sept. 1, 1774. WM. DODGE, Collector.

Burials in the Town of BOSTON, since our last.

Twelve Whites. No Blacks.

Baptiz'd in the several Churches, Eight.

High Water at BOSTON, *for the present Week.*

Monday, 45 min. aft. 10	Friday, 10 min. after. 2
Tuesday, 33 min. aft. 11	Saturday, 59 min. aft. 2
Wednesday, 28 m. aft. 12	Lord's Day 46 m. af. 3
Thursday, 20 min. aft. 1	Full ● 19 Day 9 Aftn.

At a Meeting of the Delegates from every Town in the County of Essex in the Province of Massachusetts-Bay, held at Ipswich in said County on the 6th and 7th Days of September, 1774.

Present 68 Delegates.

Voted, JEREMIAH LEE, Esq; Chairman.

SEVERAL Papers relative to the Situation of our public Affairs, and the alteration of our Constitution and Laws intended by the late Act of Parliament for regulating the Government of this Province, as also the said Act, being read; after Consultation and Debate had thereon, a Committee of nine Persons were appointed to consider and Report on the same. The Committee reported a Number of Resolves, which they thought necessary to be entered into by the County at this Time: Which Resolves, after being read several Times, debated on and amended, were unanimously accepted, the Delegates, one by one, declaring their Assent.

The Report is as follows:

The Delegates appointed by the several Towns in this County to meet together at this alarming Crisis, to consider and determine on such Measures, as shall appear to be Expedient for the County to adopt: deeply impressed with a Sense of the importance of this Delegation, of the Abilities and Qualifications necessary for conducting our public Affairs with Wisdom and Prudence, but with the Firmness and Resolution becoming Freemen: With the Respect and Deference due to the Sentiments of our Brethren in the other Counties of the Province, with Submission to the future Determinations of a Provincial Assembly, and the Decisions of the grand American Congress,—do, in the Name of the County, make the following Resolves, viz.

1st. *That the several Acts of Parliament, which infringe the just Rights of the Colonies, and of this Province in Particular, being Subjects of Deliberation before the Continental Congress, renders it Expedient for this County, to suspend their Determinations respecting them; except so far as their immediate Operation requires immediate Opposition. That the Act of Parliament, entitled "An Act for the better regulating the Government of the Province of the Massachusett-Bay in New-England," being a most dangerous Infraction of our Constitutional & Charter Rights, and tending to a total Subversion of the Government of the Province, and Destruction of our Liberties; and having been with uncommon Zeal, with Arbitrary Exertions, and Military Violence, attempted to be carried into Execution; and this Zeal, these Exertions, and this Violence, still continuing:—From the sacred Regard, the inviolable Attachment we owe to those Rights, which are essential to, and distinguish us as Englishmen and Freemen; and from a tender Concern for the Peace of this County, we are bound to pursue all reasonable Measures, by which any Attempts to enforce an immediate Obedience to that Act, may be defeated.*

2d. *That the Judges, Justices and other Civil Officers in this County appointed agreeably to the Charter and the Laws of the Province, are the only Civil Officers in the County, whom we may lawfully obey: That no Authority whatever can remove these Officers, except that which is constituted pursuant to the Charter and those Laws: That it is the Duty of these Officers to continue in the Execution of their respective Trusts, as if the aforementioned Act of Parliament had never been made: And that while they thus continue, untainted by any Official Conduct, in conformity to that Act, we will vigorously Support them therein, to the utmost of our Power, indemnify them in their Persons and Property, and to their Lawful Doings yield a ready Obedience.*

3d. *That all Civil Officers in the Province, as well as private Persons, who shall dare to Conduct in conformity to the aforementioned Act, for violating the Charter and Constitution of the Province, are, and will be considered by this County as its unnatural and malignant Enemies; and, in the Opinion of this Body, such Men, while they persist in such Conduct, and so contribute to involve the Colonies in all the Horrors of a Civil War, are unfit for Civil Society; their Lands ought not to be til'ed by the Labour of an American, nor their Families supplied with his Cloathing or Food.*

4th. [*This 4th Resolve, which respected* Peter Frye, *Esq; is omitted by the Direction of the Delegates of* Salem, Marblehead *and* Danvers, *they supposing his frank and generous Declaration, inserted in this Paper, would give full Satisfaction to the County, and render a Publication of this Resolve superfluous and improper.*]

5th, *That a Committee be raised to wait on the Hon William Browne, Esq; of Salem, and acquaint him, that with Grief this County has viewed his exertions for carrying into execution Acts of Parliament calculated to enslave and ruin his native Land; that while the County would continue the Respect for several Years paid him, it firmly Resolves to detach from every future Connection all such as shall persist in supporting, or any ways countenancing the late arbitrary Edicts of Parliament; that the Delegates in the Name of the County request him to excuse them from the painful necessity of considering and treating him as an Enemy to his Country, and therefore that he would resign his Office as Counsellor on the late Establishment, and decline as a Judge (and in every other Capacity) to execute the late Acts of Parliament, and all others deemed by the Province unconstitutional and Oppressive.* [Mr. Browne's Answer to the Committee, who waited on him with this Resolve, was published in our last Monday's Gazette.]

6th. *That, in the Opinion of this Body, all Town-Meetings in this County ought to be called agreeably to the Laws of the Province, and the ancient Usage of the County.*

7th. *That it is the Opinion of this Body of Delegates, that a Provincial Congress is absolutely necessary in our present unhappy Situation; and that as Writs are now issued for the Election of Representatives for a General Assembly, to be held at* SALEM *on the fifth Day of October next, the Representatives so elected, will properly form such Provincial Congress. And it is further our Opinion, that these Representatives should be instructed by their several Towns to Resolve themselves into a Provincial Congress accordingly; if when assembled they shall deem it Necessary or Expedient; in order to consult and determine on such Measures as they judge will tend to promote the true Interest of his Majesty, and the Peace, Welfare & Prosperity of the Province.*

8th. *Deeply affected with a Sense of the Miseries and Calamities now impending over the Colonies, and this Province in Particular, we are compelled to form these Resolutions; which (as we apprehend) being founded in Justice and Necessity, on the Principles of our natural, essential and unalienable Rights, we are determined to abide by. At the same Time we frankly and with Sincerity declare, that we still hold ourselves Subjects of His Majesty King* GEORGE *the Third—as such will bear him true Allegiance, and are ready with our Lives and Fortunes, to support and defend his Person, Crown and Dignity, and his constitutional Authority over us. But by the Horrors of Slavery—by the Dignity and Happiness attending virtuous Freedom, we are constrained to declare, that we hold our Liberties too dear to be sported with, and are therefore most seriously determined to defend them. This, in the present Dispute, we conceive may be effected by peaceable Measures: But, though above all Things (Slavery excepted) we deprecate the Evils of a Civil-War—though we are deeply anxious to restore and preserve a Harmony with our Brethren in Great-Britain; yet, if the Despotism and Violence of our Enemies should finally reduce us to the sad Necessity, we, undaunted, are ready to appeal to the last Resort of States; and will in Support of our Rights encounter even Death, "Sensible that he can never die too soon, who lays down his Life in Support of the Laws and Liberties of his Country."*

Voted, *That a Committee be chosen to notify the Members of this Body, to assemble again when they shall think it Necessary; and that the Members from Salem and Marblehead, be this Committee; and that they or the major Part of them be, and they are hereby impowered to issue Notifications accordingly.*

A true Copy,

JOHN PICKERING, jun. Clerk.

Whereas the Great and General Court

or Assembly of this Province, at their Session begun and held at Boston on the Sixth Day of January 1773, by an Act then passed intitled, "An Act to make Provision for the assessing the Monies "upon the Lands of the Proprietors in the Township of Ashfield, "in the County of Hampshire, which are due from the said Pro-"prietors to defrey the Charges hereafter mentioned, and to pro-"vide a Method for the collecting and levying the same," appointed us the Subscribers a Committee to ascertain and determine what was then due to the Rev. Mr. Jacob Sherwin, Minister of said Ashfield, for and towards his Settlement in the Ministry there by Virtue of his Contract with the Proprietors; also what was due and unpaid towards the building of the Meeting-House there and the Charges and Expences incurred in and about the same; and certain other Charges mentioned in the said Act, and to assess such Sums as we should judge due, on the Lands already laid out in the said Township, (the publick Rights excepted) such Proportion as should appear to us not to have been already paid; and also to ascertain what might be due to the said Mr. Sherwin for his Salary, agreable to his Contract with the Proprietors, since his Settlement, to the Time the said Act was made, and to assess such Sum on the Lands of the Proprietors already laid out, (the public Rights and the Lands of the Baptists in the said Town excepted) each Lot its due and equal Proportion according to its nominal Quantity, and in Case any of the Proprietors should neglect to pay such Sums as he should be assessed to the Collector for the Space of Ninety Days, Notice of such Assessment, having been given by said Committee, in manner as is provided by a Law of this Province, made in the second year of his present Majesty's Reign, intitled, "An Act to subject the unimproved "Lands within this Province to be sold for the payment of Taxes "assessed on them by Order of the General Court and Votes and "Agreements of the Proprietors thereof, and to enable Proprie-"tors of new Plantations to levy Province and County Taxes "laid on them," then and in such Case the said Committee or the major part of them may make sale of so much of such delinquent Proprietors Land there, as shall be necessary for the payment of such Sums and reasonable Charges arising thereon, in such manner as in and by the last mentioned Act is provided for the payment of such Taxes and Charges. And by an Act made and passed by the said Great and General Court holden at Boston in February, 1774, in Addition to the Act first above mentioned, the said Committee were further impowered to determine what Sums were due to divers Persons, and on divers Considerations mentioned in the said Additional Act, and to assess the same agreable to the Directions given in the said Act, and also to levy the Monies so assessed in the same way and manner as in and by the said first mentioned Act, it is provided and directed we should levy the Monies we were impowered by that Act to assess: And whereas we have made, and duly posted the several Assessments we were authorized & impowered by the aforesaid Acts to make, and the Proprietors or Owners of the several Lots contained in the following Lists refuse or neglect to pay the Sums assessed or their Lands, which are annexed to the respective Numbers—viz—

House Lots.					Second Division.					Third Division.				
No. 4.	£.2	5	5	3	No. 2.	£.4	10	11	3	No. 8.	£.4	10	11	3
5.	2	5	5	3	3.		7	1	3	10.	9	6	4	3
6.		12	1	2	8.	4	13	2	1	11.	5	4	11	3
10.		3	11	1	10.		7	3	3	12.	2	5	5	2
11.		10	11	3½	11.	4	10	11	3	13.		8	6	
12.		10	0		12.	4	10	11	3	14.	4	10	11	3
17.		10	11	3	13.	4	10	11	3	15.	4	10	11	3
20.		10	0	3	15.	4	10	11	3	22.	4	10	11	3
21.		18	6	2	16.	4	10	11	3	24.	9	6	4	3
22.		4	2		17.	4	10	11	3	25.	4	10	11	3
26.	4	4	7	3	21.	7	8	8	1	26.	9	17	1	1
27.		10	11		22.	1		7	1	27.	4		11	2
28.	1	5	10	3	23.	5	19	9	1	30.		3	7	3
29.	2	5	5	3	25.	4	10	11	3	31.	4	10	11	3
30.	2	5	5	3	26.	1	0	0		32.	9	6	4	3
31.		3	1	2	31.	4	10	11	3	33.	4	10	11	3
32.	2	5	5	3	34.	9	6	4	3	34.		14	11	3
35.		3	7	1	37.	4	10	11	3	37.	4	10	11	3
39.	2	5	5	3	38.	6	18	8	1	38.	2	5	6	
40.	2	5	5	3	41.		4	10	3	40.	4	10	11	3
41.	2	5	5	3	45.	9	6	4	3	43.	5	10	11	3
42.		7	5	3	46.	4	10	11	3	44.	4	2	8	
45.		15	6		50.		5	9	2	45.	5	8	2	3
46.	2	5	5	3	52.	1	14	11		48.	4	10	11	3
52.	2	5	5	3	53.		7	8	$\frac{3}{5}$	49.	1	5	0	
59.	2	5	5	3	54.	4	10	11	3	50.	4	10	11	3
62.		10	0		55.		14	0		56.	4	10	11	3
					56.	4	10	11	3	57.	4	10	11	3
Mill Lot.	2	5	6	1	57.	4	10	11	3	58.	4	10	11	3
					59.	4		11	3	59.	4	10	11	3
					60.	4	10	11	3	61.	4	10	11	3
					62.	4	10	11	3	63.	4	10	11	3
					63.	9	5	10	1					

The Owners of the several Lots aforesaid are hereby notified that so much of their respective Lots abovesaid will be sold at Public Vendue, to be opened on the 28th Day of December next, at the Dwelling-House of Samuel Belding, in Ashfield aforesaid, at 10 o'Clock in the Forenoon, and continued from Day to Day, if there be Occasion, as shall be necessary to pay the Sums annexed to the said Numbers respectively as abovesaid, and the reasonable Charges, unless the same be paid to one of us, or to Lieut. Obadiah Dickinson of Hatfield, Proprietors Treasurer, before that Day.

August 25th, 1774.

JED'H FOSTER,
WM. WILLIAMS, } Committee.
THO'S DENNEY,

John Hunt,

Begs Leave to acquaint his Customers and others, that he has entered into a Co-partnership with JOSEPH SHERBURNE, jun. under the Firm of

Hunt and *Sherburne*,

And that they have for Sale, a large and compleat Assortment of *London*, *Sheffield*, *Birmingham* & *Bristol* Hard Wares, consisting of too many Articles to be enumerated; which they are determined to sell by Wholesale and Retail, at the very lowest Rates, at their Shop next Door Northward of the Sign of the Heart & Crown, Cornhill, BOSTON.

N.B. A parcel of Hatters Trimmings very Cheap.

WHEREAS on the 20th Day of October, A. D. 1761, The Proprietors of the Town of Stockbridge, formerly in the Province of New-Hampshire, at a legal Meeting then held, Voted, That a Tax or Assessment of Three Hundred and Sixty Dollars, be raised and assessed on the Original Proprietors of said Town, to defrey the necessary Charges of the said Town. And whereas each Proprietor's Share of said Tax is Five Dollars, as mentioned in the List committed to me as Collector of the said Town. And whereas sundry of said Proprietors have to this Day omitted paying me their Proportion of said Tax, altho' they have been legally notified and warned so to do many Years ago—Whose Names with the Sums due from each of them are as follows, viz. Joshua Henshaw, Esq; five Dollars; Jeremiah Green, Esq; five Dollars; John Cunnable, five Dollars; Andrew Belcher, Esq; five Dollars; Joshua Orne, five Dollars: James Friend, five Dollars; Daniel Warner, five Dollars; James Nevin, five Dollars; Geo. Wentworth, five Dollars; John Sherburn, five Dollars; Henry Dering, five Dollars; John Winthrop, Esq; five Dollars; Edward Wigglesworth, five Dollars; Rev. Nathaniel Appleton, five Dollars; Joshua Wentworth, five Dollars; Samuel Wentworth, Esq; five Dollars; Samuel Warner, five Dollars; Nathaniel Warner, five Dollars; his Excellency Thomas Hutchinson, Esq; five Dollars; Hon. Jacob Wendell, Esq; five Dollars; Benning Wentworth, Esq; late Governor, ten Dollars.

These are to Notify and Warn the Delinquent Proprietors afore-named and all other Persons concerned, that unless they Pay me the several Sums aforesaid raised as a Tax on their several Rights on or before the twenty fourth Day of September instant, That so much of their Original Rights in the said Town of Stockbridge, will be Sold by me at Public Auction, at the House of Henry Wise, Innholder in Ipswich, in the Province of Massachusetts-Bay, on the 26th Day of September currant, at 3 o'Clock, Afternoon, to defrey said Taxes.

Wm. DODGE, Collector.

Ipswich, Septem. 1st, 1774.

Whereas the Proprietors of the

Township of Land lying on both sides *Androscogging-River*, in the County of Cumberland, granted June 11th 1771, to *Samuel Livermore*, Esq; and others, at their Meeting on February 24th 1773, voted and granted a Tax of *Twenty-four Shillings* Lawful Money, on each Right, to be paid *Leonard Williams*, Esq; their Treasurer, on or before the first Day of October then next ensuing, and again on November 3d, 1773, voted and granted a further Tax of *Forty Eight Shillings*, on each Right, to be paid their Treasurer, as follows, viz. the one half thereof, on or before the next Meeting of said Proprietors, which was on March 16th 1774, and the other half on or before the first Instant; said Taxes having been made and published as the Law directs. Notwithstanding which the Owners of the Rights granted on the Rights of

Capt. *Samuel Googen*, *Nathaniel Whitmore*,
Capt. *John Hazzeltime*, *John Maddock*,
Ens. *Thomas Harrington*, *Benjamin Corey*, and
Eliphalet Lyon, *David Knapp*.

Are delinquent in paying said Taxes, amounting to £.3 12s. on each Right. Public Notice is hereby given that the whole of said Rights, and so much of all the others, as are delinquent in paying either, or part of either Tax, will be Sold at PUBLIC VENDUE, at the House of *Micajah Gleason*, Innholder in Framingham, on Wednesday the 12th Day of October next, if not prevented by payment of said Taxes, before said Time: The Sale to begin at Nine o'Clock, A. M. and continued by Adjournment (if need be) till the whole be Sold, or so much as is sufficient to pay said Taxes.

Waltham, August 10, 1774.

Leonard Williams,
Elijah Livermore, } Assessors and Committe for sale of Delinquents Rights.
Elisha Harrington.

The Proprietors aforesaid, are

hereby notified, to meet at the House of *Micajah Gleason*, aforesaid, on said 12th Day of October next, at nine o'Clock, A. M. To chuse a Moderator for said Meeting.

To agree on some Method to record the Bounds of the Lots.

To confirm their former Votes and Proceedings, or any, or either of them, (if need be.)

To hear the Report of their Committee, appointed to agree with some Person or Persons to build a Saw-Mill and Grist Mill on said Propriety, and give them further Directions in said Affair.

To grant Money to encourage some Person or Persons, to build said Mills, and to encourage the Ten first Settlers in said Township, according to their Vote at their last Meeting, and to clear Roads, & build Bridges, and for whatever else they shall think proper.

To clear Roads and build Bridges, and finally to pass any Vote or Votes, relating to any or either of the foregoing Articles, or any other that shall be thought conducive to the Interest of said Propriety.

Waltham, Aug. 10th 1774.

Leonard Williams,
Elijah Livlrmore, } Committee for calling Meetings.
Elisha Harrington.

Boston: Printed, by EDES & GILL,

No. 1015

THE
Boston-Gazette,
AND
COUNTRY JOURNAL.

Containing the freshest Advices, Foreign and Domestic.

MONDAY, September 26, 1774.

Tuesday Evening Captain Scott, arrived at Salem from London, after a Passage of 7 Weeks, by whom we have received several Papers, but they contain few Articles of News; the following are the most Material.

GENOA, *June 29.*

A REPORT prevails, that his Catholic Majesty hath forbidden the entry of the Russian ships into his ports.

Lisbon, July 14. The Ship named Quintos, from Rio de Janeiro, cast anchor in this port the 4th. She has on board about 6 millions of Cruzades, [15 millions of Livres.] one third of which is on the King's account, the two others on account of the Merchants.

Paris, July 4. The King has actually recalled the Count de Broglio from his Exile, and has granted him permission to return to Court.

LONDON.

July 2. It is said that the names of those who voted for the Quebec bill are circulated in almost every city and borough in England and Scotland and the next general election will determine whether the Pope or the voice of the people is to choose a British Parliament.

Extract of a letter from Bury St. Edmunds, July. 5.

"The signing the Quebec bill has given great spirits to the Roman Catholics of this county; they now begin to triumph, and do not scruple to declare, that in a few years they shall have the same privileges allowed them here as the Roman Catholics have at Quebec. We have at this time four mass houses, which are open every day; one in the Southgate street, one in the Northgate street, one in the Westgate-street, and one in the Risbygate-street; they draw a number of people after them, especially the lower sort, whom they obtain by presents, &c."

July 6. Marshall Romanzow having received a reinforcement of 10,000 regular troops, and 30,000 recruits, caused the greatest part of his army to pass the Danube, between the 20th and 22d of last month.

July 15. This day a Cabinet Council was held at St. James's upon affairs of importance, but no part of the subject matter has yet transpired.

July 18. Some pasquinades of a serious and treasonable nature have been stuck up publickly at the palace of St. James's.——No public notice hath been taken of such libels.

The King's flying escort is encreased, and the soldiers ride with their swords in hand.

The people of America are still unanimous to abide by the exportation and importation resolutions.

July 21. Candidates are very busy in the country engaging the interest of the Freeholders: Some of them (Court Candidates it is very natural to suppose) go among the poor Electors and purchase a Chicken or a Duck, and give five or ten Guineas for it; *but this is Generosity, not Bribery.*

It is now much whispered that the Premier says, he will get a *good* new Parliament together, and then retire from the bustle & fatigue of office; but the people of England before he makes his Exit, would no doubt be glad to know whether the word *good* is to be taken in the *ministerial* or *true* Acceptation.

It is remarked by a Correspondent, as a very whimsical Circumstance, that many Thousands make themselves unhappy about the Religion of the Canadians, who have no Religion of their own.

July 22. The Court has given Orders to General Gage to make certain Proposals on the Opening of the Provincial Assembly at Salem, the Motive of which shall be to engage the Assembly to pass an Act for granting an Indemnification for the Tea destroyed.

Admiral Knowles, who had entered into the Service of Russia, has asked and obtained his Dismission. This Officer is returning to England, but he is to retain the Half of his Appointment.

Subjects, like Lovers, says a Correspondant, see nothing but perfection in a new Sovereign; but acquaintance teaches them that Women and Kings are almost universally the same.

Yesterday Evening was privately baptized at Gloucester house, the new-born Daughter of their Royal Highnesses the Duke and Duchess of Gloucester, by the Name of Caroline Augusta Maria. The Sponsors were, their Royal Highnesses the Duchess of Gloucester, the Hereditary Princess of Brunswick, and the Prince of Brunswick.

The Court of Berlin, it is said, has declared against receiving any more Memorials concerning the disputes with Dantzick.

Yesterday Morning at 8 o'clock died, after a lingering illness, at Holland House, near Kensington, the Right Hon. Caroline, Lady Holland, Lady of the late Lord Holland.

We import Corn from America, and our People export themselves to that Country: We have more Provisions then, and a smaller Consumption. Our Country yields its full Crops, yet Provisions rather encrease in Price. These Things are fact, but they correspond not well together.

It is now said, that a noble Lord has so ably and so happily pleaded in the Behalf of a certain Set of disobedient Subjects, that the Cause will very soon be removed, in order that the Effect may cease.

THE Committee (consisting of the following Members, namely,

Mr. Samuel Adams,	Mr. John White,
John Rowe, Esq;	Mr. Gibbins Sharpe,
Thomas Boylston, Esq;	Capt. William Mackey,
William Phillips, Esq;	Mr. Thomas Greenough,
Doct. Joseph Warren,	Capt. Samuel Partidge,
John Adams, Esq;	Benjamin Austin, Esq;
Josiah Quincy, jun. Esq;	Mr. Jonathan Mason,
Hon. Thomas Cushing, Esq;	Mr. John Brown,
Mr. Henderson Inckes,	Mr. James Richardson,
Mr. William Molineaux,	Mr. Thomas Crafts, jun.
Mr. Nathaniel Appleton,	Mr. Henry Hill,
Capt. Fortesque Vernon,	Mr. Joshua Henshaw, jun.
Capt. Edward Procter,	Mr. David Jeffries,)

appointed by the Town of Boston to receive Donations for the charitable purpose of relieving and employing the Poor, suffering by means of the Act of Parliament, commonly called the Boston Port-Bill, would gratefully acknowledge the receipt of many generous Collections made in several of our sympathising sister Colonies, as well as charitable Donations from many Towns in this Province, and private Friends to this cruelly oppressed and patient People.

The Committee consider themselves at all times answerable to their Constituents, and as peculiarly accountable to their munificent Benefactors, who ought ever to have all reasonable satisfaction touching the disposition of their Charities.

The Trust reposed in the Committee is important, and its discharge extremely arduous. And when the powers and dispositions of those who trouble us are properly considered, so far from receiving support and aid in the relief of this distressed Town, it must be obvious that many unnecessary difficulties and embarrassments would be thrown in the way. Many are the public Works (to which large grants and subscriptions would chearfully be made by Persons who would be peculiarly benefitted thereby) such as the building of a Bridge over Charles-River, and another over to Dorchester Neck, the erecting of Hospitals and other large and much wanted public Edifices, which might be carried on to the immediate and great relief of the Poor, if the Province was now blessed with a constitutional and patriotic Legislature existing within it. Miserable is the state of that Community who have the *Forms* but not the *Powers* of good Government:---but much more miserable are they who have *neither*. Whoever therefore fully considers the difficulties of every sort with which the Committee have to engage, will view all their actions with an eye of charity and candor, and will be far from hastily giving credit to the malicious whispers and slanderous sarcasms of our public enemies. Surely better evidence than this ought to be given, before Americans should entertain jealousies, and doubt the integrity, of distant Brethren.

In order for the regular conduct of business, for the satisfaction of candid enquirers, as well as the silencing slanderous reports, the Committee very early opened a compleat set of books, which have been kept in the most regular manner. In them are entered all the Donations as they are received, and from whom; together with a fair record of all matters which come before the Committee and their proceedings thereupon. These books are open every day for the inspection of all persons.

The Committee, having set several days, and by themselves and their Sub-Committees, had various consultations, notified the Inhabitants, that they should attend every afternoon for ten days (Lord's-day excepted) for all classes of People suffering by the Port-Bill, to lay their circumstances before the Committee, that the distressed might (if possible) be employed in their several occupations. Accordingly, great numbers of various classes applied, especially Mechanicks and Laborers: Of the latter the circumstances of much the greater part called for immediate relief.

In this exigency, several plans were proposed, but they all required time to be further considered and better digested, before they could be carried into practice. The only proposal, therefore, which could be carried into execution with the speed necessary to give bread and employ to the most indigent laborers, was the repair and pavement of some of our public streets. This, therefore, it was thought most eligible to adopt. Accordingly it was proposed to the Selectmen of the Town (who are surveyors of the streets) that if they would engage in repairing those parts of the Town which most wanted it, that the Committee of Donations &c. would contribute towards the payment of the laborers out of the donations made for employing the Poor. The Selectmen acceding to this eligible way of giving *immediate* employ and sustenance to necessitous laborers, numbers of our most indigent inhabitants were by this plan kept from the dangers of idleness and enabled to earn bread for their present support.

Immediate relief being thus afforded to the indigent, the next consideration of the Committee was for a method to employ the Poor and pay them out of the donations in such a manner, as that returns might be made into the common stock, which might serve for their future employ and maintenance. The best plan of this sort, in the opinion of the Committee, was the erecting a Brick-yard on part of the Town's land well adapted for such a purpose. Accordingly application was forthwith made and leave obtained from the Town for the laying out such a Yard on the Neck, and the making of Bricks therein now employs upwards of an hundred Poor every day. These Bricks, when burnt, the Committee intend to sell at the best price they can obtain, and the money arising from the sale will be again improved in some way the most likely to keep the Poor from the distresses of hunger and the temptations of idleness.

The Committee have agreed to build a house for sale, as soon as materials can be collected (which however is extremely difficult, considering the tenor and mode of putting in execution the Boston Port-Act) and several vessels will be set up as soon as the Common Stock shall be sufficient for the work.

In order to make the employment of the Poor as universal as possible, the Committee have purchased Wool, Flax and Cotton, to be distributed to Spinners and Knitters in the Town, and Looms are erecting for weaving Baizes, Cotton and Linen.

The Committee also distribute Leather to the Shoemakers and take their manufactures in pay, and with them also pay daily laborers.

The Committee are in expectation of nail-rods and other raw materials, with which they hope to employ the Blacksmiths and some other Tradesmen, in the severities of the Winter.

The Committee have given the above account of their doings for the satisfaction of the Public, and flatter themselves it will meet with the approbation of the generous Benefactors to this grievously oppressed and suffering People. The Committee attend every day upon the business of their appointment; almost the whole of their time is taken up in the discharge of their trust. They have no motive to encourage them in their labors, but the hopes of doing good in this day of their Country's trial and calamity. They shall consider themselves as happy if they answer the end of their appointment.—That they may attain this end, they ask the advice of the wise and good, and shall ever consider the counsel of friends to the common cause as deserving their thanks and most mature consideration.

The Committee take this opportunity to inform the World, and especially their munificent Benefactors, that the House of Representatives at their last session having recommended to the Province to make Collections for the Poor of Boston and Charlestown, suffering by occasion of the before-mentioned Act, the Town of Boston early passed a vote that Seven per Cent. of all Donations transmitted to this Town should be delivered to our Brethren of Charlestown, who are mutually supposed injured in that proportion by the Boston Port-Act.

The Regular Overseers of the Poor of this Town still continue their usual care and supply of the Town-Poor, while this Committee confine (as much as possible) their attention and relief to such as are reduced to severe sufferings by the measures of the present Administration of Britain and the grievous mode of carrying those measures into execution.

PROVIDENCE, *September 17.*

"At two o'clock in the morning, on Tuesday last, an express arrived in this town from East-Greenwich, in the county of Kent, with advice that a mob was raised, consisting of some hundreds of people, who threatened, and were hourly expected to come to destroy said Town of East-Greenwich, in order to shew their resentment of the injury which they said had been offered to Stephen Arnold, of Warwick, Esq; one of the Justices of the Inferior Court of Common Pleas in that County, who had been charged with industriously propagating principles unfriendly to American Liberty, and had been hung in Effigy by some of the people at East Greenwich. This intelligence was immediately communicated to his Honor the Deputy-Governor, who ordered the Sheriff, with the companies of Cadets & Light-Infantry of this town, and others of the Militia, to arm themselves, and proceed immediately to East-Greenwich, to assist the Sheriff of that County in dispersing said mob. The companies of Militia accordingly armed, marched immediately, and arrived there by 9 o'clock the same morning, where a Committee was appointed and sent to the mob, about two miles distant from the town, to warn them of the bad consequences of their unlawful proceedings, and to demand some of the principal persons among them, to come immediately into town, and settle the affair; whereupon the said Stephen Arnold, Esq; and some others, came from the mob, and met the Militia, and a great number of people, convened at the Court-house, where, after being made acquainted with their resolute determination, he signed the following Declaration and Confession:

WHEREAS I the Subscriber have lately in the Town received great indignity, by being hung in Effigy by some evil minded Persons to me unknown; and from many Reports which have been circulated in the County, I was led to think my Person and Family unsafe; and being actuated by the Motives of Fear and Resentment, without maturely considering the Consequences, have been concerned by associating with divers People of this County, with Intention of repairing to this Town, and making a Declaration of that Right, which as a Subject I apprehend I was entitled to: And whereas the said Assembly was unlawful, which hath occasioned much Fear and Distress to the Inhabitants of this Town in particular, and many others in general; for all which I do hereby express my hearty Sorrow, and wish to obtain the favorable Opinion of this public Assembly, especially as I am a Friend to the Liberty of my Country, and disapprove those Measures which have been calculated to tax America without her Consent.

East-Greenwich, Sept. 13. STEPHEN ARNOLD.

SALEM, September 20.

Letters from a Gentleman in Philadelphia, to his Friends in this Place, dated the 2d Inst. say,—"The whole Attention and Conversation is wrapped up in the Congress, and every Mouth wishing them Success—they are greatly respected, as Men of Wisdom, from whom the People ardently expect the Salvation of America. Every one prays for their Success,—the Canada Bill serves greatly to cement them to our Welfare, and the Unanimity expected in their Councils almost assures them of it. What Measures will be adopted is as yet very uncertain; some think non-exportation and non-importation to West-Indies and Great-Britain, others only to Great-Britain: But by what I can gather, it will be only with Great-Britain for the present, and the West-Indies conditionally, at some future Meeting of the Congress, if they find the first ineffectual. Government has not in this Place one who dares appear its Advocate. The Members from Virginia were just now received with Ringing of Bells, and other Marks of a most hearty Welcome. Upon the whole, every Thing bears a most promising Appearance for the future Welfare of America."

BOSTON, September 26.

By Mr. PAUL REVERE, *who returned Expreſs from Philadelphia laſt Friday Evening, we have the following important Intelligence.*

PHILADELPHIA, *September* 17, 1774.

SIR,

WE received your Favor of the 11th Inſtant, together with the Reſolutions of the County of Suffolk, and communicated the ſame to the Congreſs: In Conſequence of which, they paſſed the ſeveral Reſolutions which will be delivered you by Mr. Revere, together with a Letter from the Preſident. They highly applaud the wiſe, temperate and ſpirited Conduct of our People, in their Oppoſition to the late Act for altering our Conſtitution. Theſe Reſolves will, we truſt, ſupport and comfort our Friends, and confound our Enemies. In Behalf of myſelf and Brethren,

I am with Reſpect,
Your moſt humble Servant,
THOMAS CUSHING.

JOSEPH WARREN, Eſq;

Philadelphia, 17th Sept. 1774.

SIR,

YOUR Letter of the 11th Inſtant, directed "To the Honorable *Thomas Cuſhing*, Eſq; and the other Gentlemen of the Congreſs, Members for Maſſachuſetts-Bay," together with the Reſolutions entered into by the Delegates of the ſeveral Towns in the County of Suffolk, and their Addreſs to his Excellency Governor Gage were communicated to the Congreſs, whereupon the Congreſs came into the following unanimous Reſolves, which by their Order I tranſmit to you to be communicated to the Committee of Correſpondence for the Town of Boſton.

I am, Sir,
your moſt obedient Servant,
PEYTON RANDOLPH.

JOSEPH WARREN, Eſq;

IN CONGRESS, *Saturday September* 17, 1774.

A LETTER from Dr *JoſephWarren*, & ſundry Reſolutions entered into by the County of *Suffolk*, on Tueſday the 6th of this Inſtant, and an Addreſs from the Delegates of the ſaid County to his Excellency Governor GAGE, dated the 9th Inſtant, were read. Whereupon,

RESOLVED *unanimouſly*, That this Aſſembly deeply feels the ſuffering of their Countrymen in the Maſſachuſetts Bay, under the Operation of the late unjuſt, cruel and oppreſſive Acts of the Britiſh Parliament.—That they moſt thoroughly approve the Wiſdom and Fortitude with which Oppoſition to theſe wicked Miniſterial Meaſures has hitherto been conducted, and they earneſtly recommend to their Brethren a perſeverance in the ſame firm and temperate Conduct, as expreſſed in the Reſolutions determined upon at a Meeting of the Delegates for the County of Suffolk, on Tueſday the ſixth inſtant; truſting that the Effect of the united Efforts of North-America in their behalf, will carry ſuch Conviction to the Britiſh Nation, of the unwiſe, unjuſt and ruinous Policy of the preſent Adminiſtration, as quickly to introduce better Men and wiſer Meaſures.

RESOLVED *unanimouſly*, That Contributions from all the Colonies for ſupplying the Neceſſities and alleviating the Diſtreſſes of our Brethren at Boſton, ought to be continued in ſuch Manner and ſo long as their Occaſions may require.

A true Extract from the Minutes.
CHARLES THOMPSON, Sec^y.

Delegates who attend the Congreſs.

From *NEW-HAMPSHIRE*.
Major John Sullivan, Col. Nathaniel Folſom.

From *MASSACHUSETTS-BAY*.
Hon. Thomas Cuſhing, Eſq; Mr. Samuel Adams, John Adams and Robert Treat Paine, Eſq'rs.

From *RHODE-ISLAND*.
Hon. Stephen Hopkins, Eſq; Hon. Samuel Ward, Eſq;

From *CONNECTICUT*.
Hon. Eliphalet Dyer, Silas Deane, and Hon. Roger Sherman, Eſq'rs;

From *NEW-YORK*.
James Duane, John Jay, Philip Livingſton, Iſaac Low, Col. William Floyd, and Henry Weſner, Eſq'rs.

From *NEW-JERSEY*.
James Kinſey, William Livingſton, John D'Hart, Stephen Crane, and Richard Smith, Eſq'rs;

From *PENNSYLVANIA*.
Hon. Joſeph Galloway, Samuel Rhoads, Thomas Mifflin, Charles Humphreys, John Morton, Edward Biddle, and George Roſs, Eſq'rs.

From *New-Caſtle*, *Kent* and *Suſſex* Government.
Cæſar Rodney, Thomas M'Kean, and George Read, Eſq'rs.

From *MARYLAND*.
Matthew Tilgman, Thomas Johnſon, junr. Robert Goldſborough, William Paca, and Samuel Chaſe, Eſq'rs.

From *VIRGINIA*.
Hon. Peyton Randolph, Richard Henry Lee, George Waſhington, Patrick Henry, Richard Bland, Benjamin Harriſon, and Edmund Pendleton, Eſq'rs;

From *NORTH-CAROLINA*.
William Hooper, and Joſeph Hewes, Eſq'rs.

From *SOUTH-CAROLINA*.
Hon. Henry Middleton, John Rutledge, Thomas Lynch, Chriſtopher Gadſden, and Edward Rutledge, Eſq'rs

---

Meſſieurs PRINTERS, *Sept.* 24. 1774.

AS I have been informed that the Conduct of ſome few Perſons of the Epiſcopal Denomination, in maintaining Principles inconſiſtent with the Rights and Liberties of Mankind, has given Offence to ſome of the zealous Friends of this Country, I think myſelf obliged to publiſh the following Extract of a Letter, dated September 9, 1774, which I received from my worthy and patriotic Friend, Mr. *Samuel Adams*, a Member of the Congreſs now ſitting in Philadelphia, by which it appears that, however injudicious ſome Individuals may have been, the Gentlemen of the Eſtabliſhed Church of England are Men of the moſt juſt and liberal Sentiments, and are high in the Eſteem of the moſt ſenſible and reſolute Defenders of the Rights of the People of this Continent.——And I earneſtly requeſt my Countrymen to avoid every Thing which our Enemies may make uſe of to prejudice our Epiſcopal Brethren againſt us, by repreſenting us as diſpoſed to diſturb them in the free exerciſe of their religious Privileges, to which we know they have the moſt undoubted Claim; and which from a real Regard to the Honor and Intereſt of my Country, and the Rights of Mankind; I hope they will enjoy unmoleſted as long as the Name of America is known in the World. J. WARREN.

"After ſettling the Mode of voting, which is by giving each Colony an equal Voice, it was agreed to open the Buſineſs with Prayer. As many of our *warmeſt Friends* are *Members of the Church of England*, thought it prudent as well on that as on ſome other Accounts to move that the Service ſhould be performed by a Clergyman of that Denomination. Accordingly the Leſſons of the Day and Prayer were read by the Reverend Mr. DUCHÉ, who afterwards made a moſt excellent extemporary Prayer, by which he diſcovered himſelf to be a Gentleman of Senſe and Piety, and a warm Advocate for the religious and civil Rights of America."

PHILADELPHIA, *September* 19.

On Friday laſt the Honorable Delegates, now met in General Congreſs, were elegantly entertained by the Gentlemen of this City. Having met at the City Tavern about 3 o'Clock, they were conducted from thence to the State Houſe, by the Managers of the Entertainment, where they were received by a very large Company compoſed of the Clergy, ſuch genteel Strangers as happened to be in Town, and a Number of reſpectable Citizens, making in the whole near 500—After Dinner the following Toaſts were drank, accompanied by Muſick and a diſcharge of Cannon.

1 The KING.
2 The QUEEN.
3 The Duke of Glouceſter.
4 The Prince of Wales and Royal Family.
5 Perpetual Union to the Colonies.
6 May the Colonies faithfully execute what the Congreſs ſhall wiſely Reſolve.
7 The much injured Town of Boſton and Province of Maſſachuſetts-Bay.
8 May Great-Britain be Juſt, and America free.
9 No unconſtitutional Standing Armies.
10 May the Cloud which hangs over Great-Britain and the Colonies, burſt ONLY on the Heads of the preſent Miniſtry.
11 May every American hand down to Poſterity pure and untainted the Liberty he has derived from his Anceſtors.
12 May no Man enjoy Freedom, who has not Spirit to defend it.
13 May the perſecuted Genius of Liberty find a laſting aſylum in America.
14 May Britiſh Swords never be drawn in Defence of Tyranny.
15 The Arts and Manufactures of America.
16 Confuſion to the Authors of the Canada Bill.
17 The Liberty of the Preſs.
18 A happy Reconciliation between Great-Britain and her Colonies, on a conſtitutional Ground.
19 The virtuous Few in both Houſes of Parliament.
20 The City of London.
21 Lord Chatham.
22 Lord Cambden.
23 Biſhop of St. Aſaph.
24 Duke of Richmond.
25 Sir George Saville.
26 Mr. Burke.
27 General Conway.
28 Mr. Dunning.
29 Mr. Sawbridge.
30 Dr. Franklin.
31 Mr. Dulany.
32 Mr. Hancock.

The acclamations with which ſeveral of them were received, not only teſtified the ſenſe of the honor confer'd by ſuch worthy Gueſts, but the fulleſt confidence in their Wiſdom and Integrity, and a firm Reſolution to adopt and ſupport ſuch Meaſures as they ſhall direct for the public good at this alarming Criſis.

NEW-YORK *Sept.* 15.

On Friday laſt, Numbers of the following Card were diſtributed about this City.

A CARD.

New-York, September 9th, 1774.

THE thanks of the public are preſented to thoſe worthy citizens, who have, to their immortal honour, nobly refuſed to let their veſſels for the baſe purpoſe of tranſporting troops, ammunition, &c. to oppreſs the brave defenders of American liberty, who are already ſuffering in the common cauſe.—Such patriotic conduct merits applauſe, as much as a contrary one would the contempt and indignation of every generous mind.

Yeſterday Evening Numbers of the following Hand Bills were diſtributed about this City:

TO THE PUBLIC.

AS the Merchants of this city have ſo nobly refuſed letting their veſſels to the tools of government for the baſe purpoſe of tranſporting troops and military ſtores to Boſton; *for enforcing the cruel and arbitrary edicts of a corrupt miniſtry, on that virtuous people now ſuffering in the glorious cauſe of American freedom; it is therefore hoped that no pilot will be found ſo loſt to all ſenſe of duty to his country, as to aſſiſt in that deteſtable work. Mr. Francis Poſt inadvertently engaged to make ſome cheſts for the tranſportation of arms; and Mr. Jonathan Hampton, in like manner, undertook to contract with houſe carpenters, for the purpoſe (as is ſuppoſed) of building barracks at Boſton; but when their fellow-citizens repreſented to them the tendency of their conduct, they immediately declined the abominable ſervice. After theſe laudable examples of the merchants, and tradeſmen of this city, there is no doubt but their patriotic conduct will be followed by all their fellow citizens. But, notwithſtanding ſhould any ſordid miſcreant be found amongſt us, who will aid the enemies of this country to ſubvert her liberties, he muſt not be ſurpriſed if that vengeance overtakes him, which is the reward juſtly due to parricides.*

THE FREE CITIZENS.

New-York, Sept. 14, 1774.

BOSTON, September 26.

Wedneſday laſt the Freeholders and other Inhabitants of Boſton, met at Faneuil-Hall, for the Choice of Repreſentatives, to ſerve in the Great and General Court to be conven'd at Salem the 5th of next Month, when the following Gentlemen were choſen, viz.

The Hon. THOMAS CUSHING, Eſq;
Mr. SAMUEL ADAMS,
Hon. JOHN HANCOCK, Eſq; and
WILLIAM PHILLIPS, Eſq;

Laſt Friday the Town made Choice of
Dr. *Joſeph Warren*,
Dr. *Benjamin Church*, and,
Mr. *Nathaniel Appleton*,
to ſerve as Delegates in the Provincial Congreſs, to be held at Concord on the ſecond Tueſday of October next, in Addition to the four Repreſentatives of this Town—and the following Inſtructions for our Repreſentatives were Voted, *viz.*

GENTLEMEN,

AS we have now choſen you to repreſent us in the Great and General Court to be holden at Salem, on Wedneſday the fifth Day of October next enſuing. We do hereby Inſtruct you, that in all your Doings as Members of the Houſe of Repreſentatives, you adhere firmly to the Charter of this Province granted by their Majeſties K. William & Q. Mary; and that you do no Act which can poſſibly be conſtrued into an Acknowledgment of the Validity of the Act of the Britiſh Parliament for altering the Government of Maſſachuſetts-Bay; more eſpecially, that you acknowledge the Hon. Board of Counſellors elected by the General Court at their Seſſion in May laſt, as the only rightful and conſtitutional Council of this Province. And as we have Reaſon to believe that a conſcientious Diſcharge of your Duty will produce your Diſſolution as an Houſe of Repreſentatives, We do hereby impower and inſtruct you to join with the Members who may be ſent from this and the other Towns in the Province, and to meet with them at a Time to be agreed on, in a general Provincial Congreſs, to act upon ſuch Matters as may come before you in ſuch a Manner as ſhall appear to you moſt conducive to the true Intereſt of this Town and Province, and moſt likely to preſerve the Liberties of all America.

At a Meeting of the Selectmen and Committee of Correſpondence, September 24, 1774.

OUR Friends in the neighbouring Towns and the Country in general, having expreſs'd their Uneaſineſs leſt the Workmen in this Town by aſſiſting the Army in building Barracks ſhould give Occaſion of Umbrage to their Friends who dwell more remote, whether in this or the neighbouring Colonies, particularly to our Brethren of New-York, who have nobly rejected the Application of the Barrack Maſter for Mechanicks and other Aſſiſtants from that Place;—Therefore having debated this Matter, in compliance with the Application of our Friends in the Country,—It is the Opinion of this joint Committee that ſhould the Mechanicks or other Inhabitants of this Town, aſſiſt the Troops by furniſhing them with Artificers, Labourers, or Materials of any kind to build Barracks or other Places of Accommodation for the Troops, they will probably incur the Diſpleaſure of their Brethren, who may withold their Contributions for the Relief of the Town, and deem them as Enemies to the Rights and Liberties of America, by furniſhing the Troops with Conveniences for their Reſidence and Accommodation in this Town.

FELLOW COUNTRYMEN and CITIZENS,

THE greatest *Hero* of the present age tells us that "*The entire prosperity of every state rests upon the discipline of its army.*" Convinced of the truth of this, I have in a series of *Publications* for *years* past been striving to animate you to cultivate the *art of war*; in one of those publications I told you that if you "imagined that this country had *done* with *war*, I was of opinion that as yet it had not seen more than the *buds of it*," and howsoever mistaken you might then think I was in this particular, perhaps you now begin to think a little more seriously that I was not altogether so.—And when war and rumours of war, and the prospect of having your garments rolled in blood sounds daily more piercing in your *ears*; shall I be thought impertinent if I again attempt to turn your attention to this *important object*, and truly important it is, for on the art of war (as I have repeatedly told you) your *temporal salvation under Heaven depends*."——This art is divided into two parts, the *sublime* and *common detail*, the latter being *mechanical* may be soon learnt, a few weeks will fit the *soldier* for the service—but the former requires the closest and continued application and practice, and seldom appears *conspicuous* but when *displayed by a genius*. However my countrymen, let not this observation discourage you, the God of nature has formed you perhaps equal to any people on earth, both as to *courage*, *strength* and *genius*, you abound with *rough diamonds*, nothing more is wanting than that they be *polished*.—To assist you in this, permit me to recite part of a former publication (for altho' this subject should be exhausted, which however is *not* the *case*, yet were it so *its importance* would make a repetition *seasonable*) describing part of the character and some of the ideas of a great officer.

"This master workman sees the whole service in one comprehensive view; he sees what number of troops will be *necessary* for the *campaign*—what men are most suitable for the service—he sees the recruits new raised—drilled to *discipline*—formed into *companies* and *battallions*—the encampment or encampments formed—what *magazines* will be necessary and where they ought to be erected—what provisions will be necessary and how they must be furnished—what ordinance and implements will be needfull, which he will determine by the situation and strength of the country—in what manner his baggage and provisions are to be conveyed from place to place, whether by *land* or *water*, all of which is provided for.—In marching into an enemies country he sees what disposition is necessary—what camps will be the most *secure* and will make every possible advantage of *rivers*, *ponds*, *morasses* and *woods*, and take the precautions necessary for security—what troops will be needful to cover the *magazines*, *convoys* for *detachments*, &c.—when he decamps considers where his greatest danger on the march will be, whether in *front* or *rear*, on *right* or *left*, and orders accordingly—how intelligence of the enemies situation and numbers must be obtained. Having with the *glance of the eye* seen the *field of battle*, he makes his dispositions accordingly, taking care to *dispose* of each corps in such a manner as not to *obstruct* or *endanger* but to *support* each other,—if the attack be obstinate he sees how it must be *supported*—if he happens to be victorious, how he must *improve* his advantage—if he is defeated how he must *secure* his retreat, if he has a *river* in his rear he will in *time secure* a safe passage if possible by erecting *batteries* on the *opposite side* and improving every *defile* that he can possess himself of in the rear," and the like, which are a few of the many *objects* that engage the attention of a *commander*.——And now my dear *countrymen*, and you in particular, whom providence has entrusted with *a military genius*,—arise, for this work belongeth to *you*.—He who gave you this *talent* expects that you improve it for the good of your *generation*—and does it not grow daily, more and more, *apparent* that you *ought* to be *up* and *doing*;—on your exertions is suspended the fate of this *new world*, and of *unborn millions*.——Clear I am that providence has put it in the *power* of the people of *America*, (with a common blessing) if *united*, to do *themselves justice*.——Should any say that I am aiming at *independance*, God forbid, my earnest wish, my *constant endeavor* has *been* and still *is*, to *cultivate* and *establish union* and *harmony* between *Great-Britain* and the *Colonies* on the *footing* of *constitutional* and *equal liberty*, so long as the *sun* and *moon* shall *endure*—I wish no more than to be *a free subject*—I never will be *a slave*, unless compelled to be so after the most *vigorous efforts*.—This my *renowned countrymen* I take to be your sentiments, (a few, *a very few Issachars excepted*—) stand fast therefore in the liberty wherewith the *Supreme Being* hath made you *free*.—You are to use all lawful endeavors to preserve your own *lives*, *liberties* and *properties*—and when you view the great warlike preparations which are carrying on at this time in the *Metropolis* and on the *Avenue* leading to it, (*which it is certain is not against a common enemy*) I am not at all surprised that you are *alarmed*.—However, my dear Countrymen, let me intreat you by your conduct to convince the *world*, that you are *deficient* neither in *fortitude* or *policy*.—The vast *hostile preparations* which are now making will *justify* you before *God* and *men*, in preparing for your *own defence*.—*Withold your hands from violence*, but be not *allured* from your watch and *duty* by *soft answers*.—He who is a master of the art of war knows how to dissemble, and when to act the *lyon*, the *fox*, or the *lamb*, as will best serve his *circumstances* or *designs*, ever therefore keep in mind the following approved *military maxims*, viz. *That the safetest way to treat with an enemy is sword in hand—and that distrust is the mother of security.* (But here I cannot but pause and drop a tear at the thought that those who are brethren, should be jealous of each other, and should be preparing for war as if common enemies. O Britain! Britain! Britain! thou who stilest thyself the mother country, are these hostile preparations the kind soothings of a tender mother? You have been told that your children are refractory, but will a wise mother chastise her children, will she unrelentingly pursue them to death, at the motion of an unrelenting nurse, who instead of carefully nourishing the children and concealing their little follies, and cheering the parent with accounts of their good behaviour, is seeking the destruction of both, perhaps either to gratify her own will, or please and serve another, whose interest she has more at heart than that of her mistress.)

Nature and *convenience* has formed your country for defence—*believe me* it may be defended almost inch by inch, your whole country has *breast works already erected against small arms*—every *stone wall* and *logg fence* is a *breast work*—*fascine batteries* may be any where erected with *ease* and *expedition*—your *workmen* are second to none on earth.—Consult well the chapter of *ambuscade*, *surprize* and *stratagem*—a few months will make *many thousands* of your *numerous militia* equal to any of those called *regular troops* in *discipline*—may God more abundantly endow you with *wisdom*, *skill* and *fortitude*, and may you do valiantly for God and the *cities* of your God—and should it be the fate of any of you to lose your lives in defence of your *country* and *its liberties*,—should you be forced to it, remember that *posterity* will reap the *fruits* of your *sufferings* (as you do of those your worthy ancestors, many of whom watered the ground on which you tread with their *blood*!) will rise up and call you blessed.

Adieu, A MILITARY COUNTRYMAN.

BOSTON, September 26.

The following Letter dated September 12, *from one of the best Characters in a distant Part of the Province, to his Friend in* Boston, *merits the Attention of the Public.*

Dear Sir,

I Imagine that by this time you are made in a good degree acquainted with the general commotion that has been lately caused by the mistaken report that the army was come out of Boston and murthering the people in the country, and taking from them their ammunition—the movements in Connecticut have been great, still greater in this province—thousands of men have muster'd, arm'd, travelled some on horseback, some on foot, twenty, thirty and forty miles.—I apprehend that such mistakes and the alarms occasioned by them will be likely by and by to harden the people so that there will be great danger of their not moving at all, or not in season when there shall be real necessity of it——It appears to me, Sir, therefore absolutely necessary that there should be a number of vigilant, judicious, trusty and faithful men appointed in Boston, another set of like men in Roxbury, another in Charlestown, and perhaps in other places, whose Names shall be published to the Country, whose particular duty and business it shall be to determine where the aid and assistance of the country shall be called for, and that the call and demand be always in writing under the hands of such committee or some of them, and that they signify for what time the people should come prepared to stay, if the occasion will permit so much writing; something of this sort I humbly conceive, may be proper for the present to prevent groundless alarms, and that the people below, in case of emergencies, may have timely and necessary relief. But it seems to me most clear, that there is immediate necessity of a Provincial Congress or Convention, to settle more matters than I can now enumerate, as well the above. *I am, &c.*

Extract of a Letter from Philadelphia, Sept. 19 1774.

"The Resolves of the County of Suffolk were read in Congress with applause. The inclosed Resolutions were unanimously passed, which give you a *faint* Idea of the Spirit of that August Body.——AMERICA will make a point of supporting Boston to the UTMOST."

Extract of a Letter from Philadelphia, Sept. 18

"The Contempt and Abhorrence in which *Addressors*, *Protestors*, and *sworn Councellors* are held here, are ineffable."

Extract of another Letter from Philadelphia, Sept. 18.

"I send the Votes of Yesterday, which is the only thing the Members of the Congress are at Liberty to mention, even to the People out of Doors here.—THE CONGRESS will support BOSTON and the Massachusetts, or PERISH WITH THEM. But they wish that Blood may be spared, if possible, and all Ruptures with the Troops avoided."

Capt. William Wyer of the Brig Polley arrived at Cape Ann on Saturday last, from Tetuan, on the Coast of Barbary, in 47 Days, informs that the Alarm Frigate arrived from Smyrna at Gibraltar a few Days before he sailed, with Advices that the Russians and Turks had a Battle near the Danube, in which the latter was defeated with the loss of 60 000 Men, which Battle it was generally suggested would settle the present Russian and Turkish Wars. In latt. 41 N. long. 50 W. he spoke the Brig Dolphin, John Reynolds, Master, from Philadelphia, bound for London, out 14 Days, all Well.

In Capt. Scott is come, a BELL for the Reverend Doctor COOPER's Meeting-House, which weighs 2700 said to be the largest on this Continent, and is the generous Present of the Hon. JOHN HANCOCK, Esq; to that Society.

☞ Mr. *Brown*'s Relation of the Treatment he met with at a late Court Martial, we are oblig'd to postpone this Week for want of Room.

DIED.] Yesterday Morning, Mrs. *Sarah Sharrad*, aged 63. Her Funeral is to be attended from the House of Mr. Stephen Harris, Baker, on Wednesday next.——Miss *Rebecca Fitch*, aged 19, Daughter of Mr. Timothy Fitch, of this Town, Merchant.

Died at Faulkland's-Island, Mr. Edward Langdon, Son of Mr. John Langdon, of this Town.

On WEDNESDAY next,
At TEN in the Morning,
Will be Sold by PUBLIC VENDUE,
At RUSSELL's Auction-Room,
In Queen-Street,
A Variety of House Furniture,
—*Amongst which are*,—
A Mahogany Desk and BookCase, one Walnut ditto, Chest of Draws, Tables, Chairs, Looking Glasses, one eight Day Clock, Feather Beds, Bedsteads and Bedding, Mattresses, two Field Bedsteads with Curtains, a variety of Kitchen Furniture, &c. &c.
J. RUSSELL, Auctioneer.
Wednesday next—Ten o'Clock.

Writing and Arithmetic
To be taught in Evenings.
The School to be open'd 1st Monday in October next, at the Writing School House in Queen-Street, and to be continued for the Season.
Where due Care will be taken for Instruction in its various Branches as usual, and it is hoped will meet with a like Acceptance, which shall be the Aim of the Subscriber, an Assistant in one of the public Schools.
Sept. 19. WILLIAM DALL, Jun.

An Evening SCHOOL
WILL be opened on Monday October 31, at the South Writing School, where WRITING and ARITHMETIC is taught in the most concise and methodical Manner.——*Attendance at the usual Hours.* *Sept.* 22.

Caleb Call, of *Charlestown*, Baker,
ACQUAINTS his Friends and Customers, that he will supply them with his White Bisket, at the usual Price, either at *Salem* or *Marblehead*, upon their Writing to him, or applying to Messrs. *Hooper* and *Whittemore*, Coopers, on *Elany's* Wharfe in *Salem*.

NARRAGANSET-CHEESE.
A Quantity that is extraordinary good, (very like) to Cheshire, to be sold at the Store of PENUEL BOWEN, opposite to the Golden-Ball.

SWEET FLOUR.
To be Sold by HABIJAH SAVAGE, at his Store No. 16 on the Long Wharf,
A few Barrels of Choice Flour, old Jamaica Spirits, West India Rum, Brandy, best Jamaica Sugar, Indigo, Molasses, Rice, Case Bottles, Cases with 12 or 15 Bottles, Cocoa, Peas, Calavances, white Beans, Corn and a Cask of Currants, cheap.

The Commissioners appointed by the Hon. Foster Hutchinson, Esq; Judge of Probate, &c. for the County of Suffolk, to receive and examine the Claims of the several Creditors to the Estate of Mr. Isaac Cazneau, late of Boston, Sadler, deceas'd, represented Insolvent.——Give Notice that they shall attend said Service at the British-Coffee-House in King-Street, on the second Thursday in the six following Months, from Six to Nine o'Clock, P. M.

Boston, Sept. 15th, 1774.

Burials in the Town of BOSTON, since our last.
Fifteen Whites. Four Blacks.
Baptiz'd in the several Churches, Nineteen.

High Water at BOSTON, for the present Week.

Monday, 35 min. aft.	4	Friday, 55 min. after	7
Tuesday, 24 min. aft.	5	Saturday, 40 min. af.	8
Wednesday 14 m. aft.	6	Lord's Day 25 m. af.	9
Thursday, 5 min. aft.	7	D' Last Q. 27 Day 2 Aft.	

THIS DAY PUBLISHED,
And sold by the Printers hereof; Price 9d.
CONSIDERATION on the Measures carrying on with respect to the British Colonies in North-America.

All Persons indebted to, or that have any Demands on the Estate of Capt. Thomas Cordis, late of Concord, Mariner, deceas'd, are desired to bring in their Accounts to Mrs. Elizabeth Cordis, or Capt. Elnathan Jones, of said Concord, Administrators on said Estate, in Order for Settlement.

To be Sold by Public Vendue, on FRIDAY the Fourteenth Day of October next, at Twelve o'Clock, A. M. by Order of the Superior Court,

THE Real Estate of WILLIAM STERLING, deceased, consisting of a Front End of a Dwelling-House, situated at the North End of Boston, near Winisimet Ferry. JACOB COOPER, Auctioneer.

To be Sold by JONATHAN DAVIS, at Bull's Wharff, the following West-India Goods, viz. Choice St. Vincent & Barbados Rum, Jamaica Spirits, Jamaica Sugars, Race Ginger, Cotton Wool, Indigo of the best Quality, and Turk's Island Salt. Said DAVIS also has to sell eight Thousand Pipe Staves which are at Salem; the Terms of Sale of which may be known by inquiring of Mr. Haskell Darby of Salem, or Jonathan Davis of Boston.

Whereas the Great and General Court or Assembly of this Province, at their Session begun and held at Boston on the Sixth day of January 1773, by an Act then passed, intitled, "An Act to make Provision for the assessing the Monies upon the Lands of the Proprietors in the Township of Ashfield, in the County of Hampshire, which are due from the said Proprietors to defrey the Charges hereafter mentioned, and to provide a Method for the collecting and levying the same," appointed us the Subscribers a Committee to ascertain and determine what was then due to the Rev. Mr. Jacob Sherwin, Minister of said Ashfield, for and towards his Settlement in the Ministry there by Virtue of his Contract with the Proprietors; also what was due and unpaid towards the building of the Meeting-House there and the Charges and Expences incurred in and about the same; and certain other Charges mentioned in the said Act, and to assess such Sums as we should judge due, on the Lands already laid out in the said Township, (the publick Rights excepted) such Proportion as should appear to us not to have been already paid; and also to ascertain what might be due to the said Mr. Sherwin for his Salary, agreable to his Contract with the Proprietors, since his Settlement, to the Time the said Act was made, and to assess such Sums on the Lands of the Proprietors already laid out, (the public Rights and the Lands of the Baptists in the said Town excepted) each Lot its due and equal Proportion according to its nominal Quantity, and in Case any of the Proprietors should neglect to pay such Sums as he should be assessed to the Collector for the Space of Ninety Days, Notice of such Assessment having been given by said Committee, in manner as is provided by a Law of this Province, made in the second year of his present Majesty's Reign, intitled, "An Act to subject the unimproved Lands within this Province to be sold for the payment of Taxes assessed on them by Order of the General Court and Votes and Agreements of the Proprietors thereof, and to enable Proprietors of new Plantations to levy Province and County Taxes upon them," then and in such Case the said Committee or the major part of them may make Sale of so much of such delinquent Proprietors Land there, as shall be necessary for the payment of such Sums and reasonable Charges arising thereon, in such manner as in and by the last mentioned Act is provided for. And by an Act made and passed by the said Great and General Court holden at Boston in February, 1774, in Addition to the Act first above mentioned, the said Committee were further impowered to determine what Sums were due to divers Persons, and on divers Considerations mentioned in the said Additional Act, and to assess the same agreable to the Directions given in the said Act, and also to levy the Monies so assessed in the same way and manner as in and by the said first mentioned Act, it is provided and directed we should levy the Monies we were impowered by that Act to assess: And whereas we have made, and duly posted the several Assessments we were authorized & impowered by the aforesaid Acts to make, and the Proprietors or Owners of the several Lots contained in the following Lists refuse or neglect to pay the Sums assessed on their Lands, which are annexed to the respective Numbers, or their Lands, viz.—

House Lots.				Second Division.				Third Division.			
No. 4	£.2	5	5	No. 2	£.4	10	11	No. 8	£.4	10	11
5.	2	5	5	3.		7	13	10.	9	6	4
6.		12	1	8.	4	13	2	11.	4	11	3
10.	3	11	1	10.		7	3	12.	4	5	2
11.		10	11½	11.	4	10	11	13.		8	6
12.	10			12.	4	10	11	14.	4	10	11
16.	10	11	3	13.	4	10	11	15.	4	10	11
17.	10	11		14.	4	10	11	22.	4	10	11
20.	18	6	2	16.	4	10	11	24.	9	6	4
21.	4	2		17.	4	10	11	25.	4	10	11
22.		4	2	21.	4	7	3	26.	9	17	1
26.	4	4	7	22.	1	7	1	27.	4	10	11
27.		10	11	23.	5	19	9	30.		3	7
28.	1	5	10	25.	4	10	11	31.	9	6	4
29.	2	5	5	26.		10		32.	9	6	4
30.	2	5	3	31.	4	10	11	33.	4	10	11
32.	2	5	5	34.	9	6	4	34.	14	11	3
33.	2	5	3	37.	4	10	11	37.	8	2	6
35.		3	7	38.	10	8	1				
39.	2	5	5	41.	4	10	11	40.	4	10	11
40.	2	5	5	42.	4	10	11	43.	4	10	11
41.	2	5	3	43.	4	10	11	44.	4	2	1
42.		7	5	45.	6	5	9	45.	4	10	11
45.		15		52.	14	11	1	49.	1	5	0
46.	2	5	5	53.		7	8	50.	4	10	11
52.	2	5	5	54.	4	10	11	56.	4	10	11
59.	10	0	0	55.		14	0	57.	4	10	11
				56.	4	10	11	58.	4	10	11
Mill Lot. 2	5	6	1	57.	4	10	11	59.	4	10	11
				59.	4	11	3	60.	4	10	11
				62.	4	10	11	63.	4	10	11

The Owners of the several Lots aforesaid are hereby notified that so much of their respective Lots aforesaid will be sold at Public Vendue, to be opened on the 28th Day of December next, at the Dwelling-House of Samuel Belding, in Ashfield aforesaid, at 10 o'Clock in the Forenoon, and continued from Day to Day, if there be Occasion, as shall be necessary to pay the Sums annexed to the said Numbers respectively as abovesaid, and the reasonable Charges, unless the same be paid to one of us, or to Lieut. Obadiah Dickinson of Hatfield, Proprietors Treasurer, before that Day. JED'H FOSTER, WM. WILLIAMS, Committee. THO'S DENNEY,
August 25th, 1774.

At the GOLDEN-KEY,
In Ann-Street, near the Draw-Bridge, (The Shop lately improved by Mr. William Breck,) Are to be Sold by Wholesale and Retail,

COTTON WOOL,

Loaf and brown Sugars, Rice
Green Coffee, West India Rum
Chocolate, Brandy,
Flour, Ginger,
Mustard, Crown and Bar Soap,
Pimento, and all Starch,
other Spices, Hair Powder,
Raisins, Indigo, and

A small Assortment of Crockery Ware, &c. &c. for a very moderate Profit, by

John Fenno.

Daniel Bell

Would Inform his kind Friends and Customers, that he has Removed to the Store lately occupied by Messrs. Thomas and Elisha Hutchinson, directly opposite the East End of Faneuil-Hall; where he has to sell, an Assortment of West-India Goods, upon the lowest terms for Cash, as usual.

Also a Quantity of good white Beans to be disposed of very Cheap, and a few Barrels of Pitch.

Good OLD Tallow CANDLES
Made last Winter.
Sperma-Ceti and Bayberry-Wax Candles.
ALSO,
Refin'd Sperma-Ceti Oil, by the Cask, or in smaller Quantities. Tallow and Cotton Wick. The best of Hogs Fatt, by the Barrel or less. Sold by

JOHN LANGDON,

In Fleet Street, near the Old North Meeting-House.

TO BE SOLD,

A genteel new finish'd HOUSE and STORE, accommodated with a pretty Piece of Land, good Well of Water, COOPER's SHOP, &c. extremely well situated in the Center of the Town, about 30 Miles from Boston, long noted, and much esteem'd as one of the best Spots in the Province for a Trader: it has the privilege of a Licence—Also the POTASH WORKS in said Town, with all the Utensils fit to go immediately to Work: The whole to be Sold reasonably, and on the most easy Terms, as a quarter of the Value paid at the delivery, or soon after, would answer the end of the Seller.

For further Particulars, inquire of the Printers hereof.

A Wet Nurse with a good young Breast of Milk, wants a Place in a Gentleman's Family. Inquire of Edes and Gill.

TO BE SOLD.

WANT of Health and a Desire to lead a retired Life, induces the Subscriber to offer for Sale on reasonable Terms a good Farm, situate in Pomfret, in the Colony of Connecticut, lying on Quinabough River, adjoining the Road leading from Boston to Hartford, containing one hundred and seventy Acres of Land, conveniently accommodated with Ploughing, Mowing, Pasture and Wood-Land; a good Orchard; with two Dwelling Houses, a Barn, a Malt House, a Fulling Mill, and Clothier's Shop, with three Iron Screw Presses, a Smith's Shop with two Trip-Hammers, a Mill to grind Scythes, also two Grist Mills, which may be warranted to grind more than two hundred Bushels in twelve Hours, with Water to carry them constantly in the driest Season.

The above Works are mostly new, and in good Repair, and largely supplied with Custom; being a good Seat for all Kinds of Business. Whoever inclines to purchase may know the Terms by applying to Benjamin Cargill, the Owner, living on the Premises.
BENJAMIN CARGILL.
Pomfret, Aug. 30, 1774.

N. B. The said Cargill wants to hire immediately one or two good smart Hands, to work at the Clothiers Business, for which good Wages will be given; such as can only shear well will answer. A well recommended Maltster is also wanted.

RAN away from the Subscriber, at Manchester, Yesterday; two Negroes, viz. CHESTER, alias TITUS, about 30 Years of Age 5 Feet 9 Inches high, well Limb'd, a stammering Speech, and one or more of his Toes partly lost by Frost. Had on when he went away, and carried with him, a brown colour'd all Wool Coat, light colour'd BroadCloth ditto, trim'd with Green, two striped Jackets, blue Breeches and a Pair of Trowsers.

CÆSAR, a slim Boy about 17 Years of Age. Carried with him a light colour'd BroadCloth Coat, trimm'd with Green, Leather Breeches, two under Jackets, one Callico, the other whitish Broad Cloth with Metal Buttons, a Pair of Trowsers &c.

Whoever shall take up said Run-aways or either of them, and return them to their Master at Manchester, or Secure them in any of his Majesty's Goals, and give notice thereof shall have four Dollars Reward for each Negro, and all necessary Charges paid by JOHN LEE.
Manchester, Septem. 8, 1774.

N. B. All Masters of Vessels and others are cautioned against Harbouring or Carrying off said Servants on Penalty of the Law.

TO BE LETT,

A very convenient Tenement, situated near the Market. Inquire of Edes and Gill.

A very likely Female Negro Child to be given away. Inquire of Edes and Gill.

TO BE SOLD,
By Richard Cranch,
Near the Mill-Bridge, BOSTON,
A very Elegant SPINNET, (Harris's make)—Also, an Assortment of WATCHES.

Province of the MASSACHUSETTS BAY.
Cumberland, ss.

Notice is hereby given to the Delinquent Proprietors of the Town of New-Gloucester, in said County, That unless they pay the several Sums hereafter affixed to each Delinquent Right respectively, together with incidental Charges, to Mr. Isaac Parsons, of said New-Gloucester, before the 6th Day of December next, they may expect that so much of each of such Delinquent Right in said Town will be sold at Public Vendue, at the House of Mr. Isaac Parsons aforesaid, on the aforesaid Sixth Day of December, as will be sufficient to discharge their several Arrearages, with the Charges as aforesaid. The Sale to begin at Ten of the Clock in the Forenoon, and to continue from Time to Time, until the whole is Sold.

The Rights that are delinquent, are as follows, viz.

Rights.	£.	s.	d.	Rights.	£.	s.	d.
No. 2	4	13	10	No. 38	4	12	0
4	4	5	9	39	12	15	1
7	10	4	4	42	4	5	9
10	4	0	0	45	5	5	11
13	13	4	6	46	5	5	11
16	4	5	9	52	4	5	9
20	16	16	10	54	3	12	9
22	4	18	4	56	7	19	7
24	9	19	7	58	10	4	4
26	4	5	9	61	11	4	8
31	9	0	6	63	3	3	1

SIMON NOYES, Committee
EBENEZER MASON, and
ISAAC PARSONS, Assessors.
New-Gloucester, Sept. 1, 1774.

WHEREAS on the 20th Day of October, A. D. 1761, the Proprietors of the Town of Bernard, formerly in the Province of New-Hampshire at a legal Meeting then held, Voted that a Tax or Assessment of Three Hundred and forty-five Dollars be raised and assessed on the Original Proprietors of said Town, to defrey the necessary Charges of the said Town. And whereas each Proprietor's Share of said Tax is five Dollars, as mentioned in the List committed to me as Collector of the said Town. And whereas sundry of said Proprietors have to this Day omitted paying me their Proportion of said Tax, altho' they have been legally notified and warned so to do many Years ago, whose Names with the Sums due from each of them are as follows, viz. Richard Champney, five Dollars; Daniel Warner, Esq; five Dollars; Jonathan Lovewell, Esq; five Dollars; Samuel Sherburn, Esq; five Dollars; George Jeffrey, Esq; five Dollars; Rev. Anthony Wibird, five Dollars; Elisha Story, five Dollars; Thales Greenwood, five Dollars; John Wendell, five Dollars; James McDonaugh, five Dollars; Hunting Wentworth, Esq; five Dollars; Joseph Nevmarch, five Dollars; Richard Emory, five Dollars; Samuel Wentworth, Esq; five Dollars; Benning Wentworth, Esq; late Governor, ten Dollars.

THESE are therefore to notify and warn the delinquent Proprietors afore-named, and all other Persons concerned, that unless they pay me their several Sums aforesaid, raised as a Tax on their several Rights, on or before the 24th Day of September Instant, that so much of their Original Rights in the said Town of Bernard, will be sold by me, at public Vendue, at the House of Henry Wise, Innholder in Ipswich, in the Province of Massachusetts-Bay, on the 26th Day of September Current, at Three o'Clock Afternoon, to defrey said Taxes.
Ipswich, Sept. 1, 1774. WM. DODGE, Collector.

WHEREAS on the 20th Day of October, A. D. 1761, The Proprietors of the Town of Stockbridge, formerly in the Province of New-Hampshire, at a legal Meeting then held, Voted, That a Tax or Assessment of Three Hundred and Sixty Dollars, be raised and assessed on the Original Proprietors of said Town, to defrey the necessary Charges of the said Town. And whereas each Proprietor's Share of said Tax is Five Dollars, as mentioned in the List committed to me as Collector of the said Town. And whereas sundry of said Proprietors have to this Day omitted paying me their Proportion of said Tax, altho' they have been legally notified and warned so to do many Years ago; Whose Names with the Sums due from each of them are as follows, viz. Joshua Henshaw, Esq; five Dollars; Jeremiah Green, Esq; five Dollars; John Cunnable, five Dollars; Andrew Belcher, Esq; five Dollars; Joshua Orne, five Dollars; James Friend, five Dollars; Daniel Warner, five Dollars; James Nevin, five Dollars; Geo. Wentworth, five Dollars; John Sherburn, five Dollars; Henry Dering, five Dollars; John Winthrop, Esq; five Dollars; Edward Wigglesworth, five Dollars; Rev. Nathaniel Appleton, five Dollars; Joshua Wentworth, five Dollars; Samuel Wentworth, Esq; five Dollars; Samuel Warner, five Dollars; Nathaniel Warner, five Dollars; his Excellency Thomas Hutchinson, Esq; five Dollars; Hon. Jacob Wendell, Esq; five Dollars; Benning Wentworth, Esq; late Governor, ten Dollars.

These are to Notify and Warn the Delinquent Proprietors afore-named and all other Persons concerned, that unless they Pay me the several Sums aforesaid raised as a Tax on their several Rights on or before the twenty fourth Day of September instant, That so much of their Original Rights in the said Town of Stockbridge, will be Sold by me at Public Auction, at the House of Henry Wise, Innholder in Ipswich, in the Province of Massachusetts-Bay, on the 26th Day of September currant, at 3 o'Clock, Afternoon, to defrey said Taxes.
Ipswich, Septem. 1st, 1774.
Wm. DODGE, Collector.

Boston: Printed, by EDES & GILL.

No. 1016

THE

Boston-Gazette, AND COUNTRY JOURNAL.

Containing the freshest Advices, Foreign and Domestic.

MONDAY, October 3, 1774.

Instructions of the Town of *Malden*.

To Capt. EBENEZER HARNDEN.

SIR.

THE Trust devolved by your Fellow Citizens upon you at this Time is the greatest and most important which you could at *any* Time receive, our All now lies at Stake, and if the Machinations of the Enemies to our Public Happiness should succeed, we may bid adieu to the flattering Prospects we have hitherto indulged of enjoying ourselves and transmitting to our posterity those Rights and Liberties which our illustrious Ancestors purchased at the greatest Expence and which they transmitted to us a fair, an ample inheritance.

The Subversion of the Charter of this Province and the Usurpation of Seats round the Council Board by a number of Men whose Ambition and Avarice (we are constrained to say) have induced them to betray their Country and stain their own Names with indelible Infamy, demand our most watchful Attention at this Day; it is upon these Heads, Sir, that we now particularly instruct you, and we give it you in most solemn charge, as you would not act a part Abhorrent to your Constituents, as you would not bring upon yourself the Execrations of Millions, that you in no sense nor manner whatever acknowledge these Men as Councellors of this Province, that you do not give them the smallest degree of Countenance, but that you treat them with that Contempt, Indignation and Abhorrence which their unparallelled Perfidy most justly deserves; we do not, we are perswaded, feel or express an undue Resentment at these unhappy creatures, but to see Men acting such a Part as they have acted towards their native Country, calls for the highest Indignation of every virtuous, of every generous Breast.

We also instruct you, if it shall be agreeable to the Sentiments of your respected fellow Senators (in whose Wisdom and Integrity we have the fullest Confidence) that you desire the Members of the Constitutional Council of this Province to meet together, and in that Capacity proceed to such Acts of Advice and Authority as they may deem meet, to which we promise to yield the same Regard as though the hand of Power had not driven them from their Seats, or the mean the contemptible Wretches we but now mentioned had not usurped them.

We need not inform you of our firm, our deliberate Resolution rather to risque our Lives and Fortunes than to submit to those unrighteous Acts of the British Parliament which pretend to Regulate the Government of this Province, nor need we instruct you, in your Legislative Capacity to make the most vigorous Opposition to them; had we not had full confidence in you that you detested these Acts of Power and Injustice we should never have chosen you to represent us in the General Assembly.

The People in this Province are a free and a brave People, and *we* with them, are determined, in the strength of our God, that we will, in spite of open force and private Treachery, Live and Die as becomes the Descendents of such Ancestors as ours, who sacrificed their All that they and their Posterity might be *free*.

The above is a true Copy of instructions Voted by the Town of *Malden*, to be given to their Representative, at a legal Town Meeting by Adjournment, Sept. 23d, 1774.

Attest. NATNL JENKINS, Town Clerk.

Messieurs EDES and GILL,

As a Specimen of the impartial administration of justice, which may be expected, if ever the new plan of government should take place — Please to insert the following in your next, which will oblige your most humble servant, ENOCH BROWN.

Boston-Neck, Sept. 24, 1774.

ON Saturday the 17th instant, about 3 o'clock, P. M. as I was passing through my store I was alarm'd by the noise of six or seven soldiers, who I observed greatly obstructed business with customers from the country.—I requested them to leave the store immediately, which had been repeatedly urg'd before my coming; at the same time, one of the soldiers having called for rum, the drawer ask'd him what he had to receive it in, he replied he would drink it, when I immediately took it, and returned it to the drawer, saying I will have no rum drank in the store; upon which a soldier said, you are a damn'd saucy fellow, and walk'd out with the rest, and stopping at the door, he not only insulted me with the most abusive language, but attempted to strike me with a large club, which was prevented by one of his companions, he then swore he would fight me—I told him he was a dirty scoundrel, and that I would have better satisfaction than I could take myself, and ran immediately towards the camp followed by the soldiers, when he who had insulted me, threw away his club, and coming near the camp endeavoured to get out of my sight—I call'd for an officer, but saw none in or near the street above a serjeant, and observing the fellow continuing his course towards town, I still kept before him, and was entertain'd the whole way with the agreeable epithets of *damn'd rogue, damn'd thief, damn'd rebellious rascal*, and that I was at the head of the rebels, and would be hang'd —when I arrived at the guard-house, I complain'd to an officer, who refer'd me to Col. Maddison, I then returned home, after having by accident heard the name of the soldier, whom they call'd Hamilton, and who happened unfortunately to be unknown to all of whom I enquired.

On the Monday morning following, I waited on Col. Maddison, who received me with great politeness, sent for a captain, and also for the soldier, who was then under guard, as the Col. inform'd me, for getting drunk. When Hamilton appeared, and I had declared he was the person who had abus'd me, the Col. remanded him to confinement, and sent to a court-martial then sitting, to suspend his trial, as there was another crime to be added to his charge, and I was desired to attend the next morning at 10 o'clock with my evidence; I attended accordingly, with Mr. Nathaniel Barber, jun. and Mr. Shattuck, and after waiting about three hours, we were admitted—Col. Maddison was not present at the court—when I was desired to relate what I had to offer by way of complaint against the prisoner, I endeavoured to divest myself of all prejudice, and to relate the affair with a strict regard to the truth, which I am positive I did; my relation was received with proper attention, and wrote down as I gave it. I then declared to their honours, (for so I at first address'd them, tho' soon convinc'd of my error) that I had no pique against the prisoner, neither was I prejudiced against the soldiers in general, and was sorry for the occasion of the present complaint, but that the prisoner had abused me so grosly, without the least provocation, that justice to the public as well as myself, oblig'd me to prosecute the affair. My evidence was then called upon, who confirm'd what I had said, when the prisoner was put upon his defence, who declared that I had abused him shamefully, that I threw rum on him, that I collar'd him, push'd or kick'd him out of the store, and repeatedly damn'd him and all his colour, all which is most notoriously false, as can be fully and amply proved, notwithstanding which two other soldiers who were present confirm'd it with additions; upon which one of the court, as I suppos'd, (for I knew none of their HONOURS names) arose, and desired to be heard in behalf of the prisoner, he observ'd that if the prisoner had inadvertently called the complainant a rebel, it was nevertheless his true character, for that he avowed those principles, and had acknowledg'd his being with the rioters at Cambridge, who were about to commit the very last act of rebellion by firing upon his Majesty's troops; and further added, that the people were using all means in their power, to have the soldiery punished, by getting them drunk, enticing them to desert, &c. These with many very unjust and bitter invectives against the Province in general, were the substance of the plea *in behalf of the prisoner*. I told the court that I did not come to answer for the conduct of others. The advocate for the prisoner, then ask'd me if I did not remember speaking with two officers the evening following the meeting of the people at Cambridge, I answer'd, that I well remembered it; to which he replied, that the affair was not done with, and that his Excellency had been made acquainted with it.—I told him, I was not conscious of having said any thing that concerned his Excellency, or which I could not answer. The affair to which he alluded was as follows.

On the evening of the day on which a large number of people assembled at Cambridge, being at supper, some of my people came in and inform'd me that a party of soldiers had gone towards Roxbury, I went immediately out into the street, when I heard a drum and fife playing in Roxbury, at the same time observing two officers near my house, I went up to them, and address'd them as follows.—Gentlemen, I suppose you have sent the soldiers to Roxbury, in consequence of hearing a fife and drum, yes, answered they; I then assured them there were only two lads who were practising to improve; no, no, they are beating a challenge, by God! said one—I again assured them they were only boys, who I imagin'd had no such design, or any intention to affront the gentlemen of the army—ay, ay, that's a stale story says one, boys, ha! there has been a riot in the country to day, they were boys too were they? No, answered I—they were men, AND BEHAVED LIKE MEN, of which you would have been convinced had you been present as I was—why did they not came to Boston, he ask'd? they expected you at Cambridge I replied, oh! they did! did they? and you was there with them was you? very well—we shall acquaint the General of this, and further said, they would go back immediately and send over a stronger party.—Well, gentlemen, said I, if you are determined to acquaint the General, you may want my name, which is Brown, and I live on the Neck; soon after this, the stronger party came over, and by this time the other party had returned from Roxbury with the boy's fife. The parties meeting directly opposite my house, I heard one ask, have you got the drum? no, answered another.—But to return to the court-martial. The officer who spoke as before related, ask'd Mr. Barber whether there was not a man in town called Major Barber—yes sir, replied Mr. Barber and he is my father.——The officer then said, that Major Barber was declared rebel, and told the son that he was doubtless tainted with the same principles, and therefore unworthy to be admitted an evidence against a soldier; to which Mr. Barber replied that his father was an honest man, but be that as it might, he thought it extremely hard to be censur'd for his father's conduct? A very honest man indeed! return'd the officer, and he a very loyal subject I suppose, pointing to me—this was spoke with a sneer, and occasion'd a general laugh!—by this time two officers came to the door of the tent and said, that hearing of the trial they thought it their duty to acquaint the court that the complainant was inimical to government, that he had avow'd such principles, and had acknowledg'd himself concern'd in the late riotous and rebellious proceedings at Cambridge—upon which one of the officers who had not spoke before, said he thought I ought to be confin'd, and the General inform'd that such a man was in the camp—no says another, the general knows the story and his name; well, answer'd I, and I live on the neck? yes, replied another and you'll be hang'd by the neck before long; and turning to the prisoner, ask'd him if he really call'd the complainant a rebel? who answer'd he believ'd he did? you call'd him right, return'd the officer—and when you call an hundred of them rebels, you give ninety-nine of them their true character.—The officer who wrote down the several declarations and whom I suppos'd to be chairman or president, then very severely reprimanded or rather insulted and vilified me, in terms which I cannot particularly recollect, and therefore wave the relation, after which the officer who first spoke in behalf of the prisoner, told me if I wanted farther satisfaction I might fight the prisoner, and he wou'd lay five guineas that he shou'd lick me;—I replied, I hope sir, you don't think I put myself upon a level with a *common soldier*? I hope not, says he, the soldier is a much better man than you are, he is a gentleman by profession.——Thus ended this truly respectable and august court, which I thought bore some resemblance to that court held in Great-Britain, where Governor HUTCHINSON was tried, and so clearly, fairly, and honourably acquitted.

Messieurs PRINTERS,—In confirmation of the foregoing, please also to insert the following Deposition; which will oblige many of your customers, as well as the subscribers.

WE the subscribers being present at the trial of James Hamilton, *by a court-martial held by the officers of the 4th regiment, in the Common, the 20th inst. do declare that the foregoing relation published by* Mr. Enoch Brown, *respecting the conduct of said court, is the truth; and farther add, that the president or chairman, while reprimanding* Mr. Brown, *said, how dare you—you rascal! who art a rebel—have the impudence to come here to complain of a soldier, and bring for evidence the son of a declared rebel.*

Signed by WILLIAM SHATTUCK,
NATH'L BARBER, jun.

Suffolk *ss.* Boston *Sept.* 27, 1774.

THEN the within named Mess. *William Shattuck*, and *Nathaniel Barber*, jun. made solemn oath to the truth of this declaration subscribed by them. Before me,

BELCHER NOYES, Justice ò Peace.

JOSIAH QUINCY, Jun'r.

Having resigned his Business into the Hands of Mr. PEREZ MORTON, and embarked for London, desires all his Clients who want to know the state of their Affairs, to call on said Morton for Information:—All Persons who are indebted to said Quincy, *on Account*, are desired to make Payment to said Morton, and any who may have Damands on said Quincy, are requested to apply to the same Gentleman for their Discharge.—Those Persons who owe the said Quincy, on Bond or Note, are hereby notified to make their Payments to WILLIAM PHILLIPS, Esq; Attorney to JOSIAH QUINCY, jun.

TO BE SOLD Cheap

At *Benjamin Goldthwait*'s Shop,

just above Concert-Hall, Boston.

Superfine Scarlet and white Broad-Cloths, superfine Garnett ditto, white & Buff Casimeers, figur'd Velvets, Corduroy of all colours, silk and worsted Breeches Patterns of all colours, &c. &c.

The Taylor's Business as usual, is carried on in the best Manner at said Shop.

☞ At his Cellar near said Shop is to be sold choice ORANGE JUICE, by the Cask or smaller Quantity.

AT a Convention of Committees for the County of Worcester, *held by Adjournment at the Court-House in said* Worcester, *on the 29th of* August, *and continued by Adjournments to the 21st of* September, *the following* Votes *and* Resolves *passed, viz.*

VOTED, That if there be an Invasion or Danger of an Invasion in any Town in this County, that then such Town shall by their Committee of Correspondence, or some other proper Persons, send Letters by Post immediately to the Committees of the adjoining Towns, who shall send to other Committees in the Towns adjoining them, that they all come properly armed and accoutred to protect and defend the Place invaded.

Voted, That it be recommended to the Military Officers in this County, that they resign their Offices to their respective Colonels.

Voted, That the Field Officers in this County resign their Offices, and publish such Resignation in all the Boston News-Papers.

Voted, That it be recommended to the several Towns in this County, to chuse proper and a sufficient Number of Military Officers for each of their Towns.

Voted, To accept the Report of the Committee respecting the civil Officers of this County, which is as follows.

Whereas the late Act of Parliament, intitled, An Act for the better regulating his Majesty's Government of the Massachusetts Bay, *is evidently designed to prevent any Civil Officers from holding their Places by Virtue of the Charter thereof; and as it is necessary to have Officers till further Provision may be made:* Therefore,

Resolved, That the Justices of the Peace for this County, who were in said Office the last Day of *June* past, except *Timothy Ruggles*, *John Murray* and *James Putnam*, Esq'rs; be hereby desired to act in said Office as single Justices, except in judicial Proceedings merely civil—Also, that the Judge of Probate, Sheriff and Coroners, who were in said Offices on the last Day of *June* past, exercise their respective Offices, till the rising of the Provincial Congress proposed to sit at *Concord* on the second Tuesday of *October* next, notwithstanding any pretended Supercedias that may be sent them or any of them, or any Proclamation designed to prevent them from holding and exercising their said Offices: And we hereby also recommend to the People of this County, that they consider and treat them as being in their said Offices, and support and defend them in the Execution thereof according to the Laws of this Province.

Voted, As the Opinion of this Body, that the Sheriff do not adjourn the Superior Court appointed by Law to be held this Day, and that he retain such as are or may be committed as Criminals in his Custody until they have a Trial.

Resolved, That as the ordinary Courts of Justice will be stayed in Consequence of the late arbitrary and oppressive Acts of the British Parliament, We would earnestly recommend it to every Inhabitant of this County, to pay his just Debts as soon as possible, without any Disputes or Litigations—"And if any Disputes concerning Debts or Trespasses should arise, which cannot be settled by "the Parties, we recommend it to them to submit "all such Causes to Arbitration, and if the Parties "or either of them shall refuse so to do, they "ought to be consider'd as co-operating with the "Enemies of this Country.

Voted, To accept the Report of the Committee relative to the instructing the Representatives for this County, which is as follows,

That it be recommended to the several Towns and Districts, that they instruct their Representatives who may be chosen to meet at *Salem* in *October* next, absolutely to refuse to be sworn by any Officer or Officers but such as are or may be appointed according to the Constitution, or to act as one Branch of the Legislature, in Concert with any other, except such as are or may be appointed according to the Charter of this Province; and that they refuse to give their Attendance at *Boston* while the Town is invested with Troops and Ships of War, and should there be any Thing to prevent their acting with such a Governor and Council as is expresly set forth in the Charter, that then they immediately repair to the Town of *Concord*, and there join in a Provincial Congress with such other Members as are or may be chosen for that Purpose, to act and determine on such Measures as they shall judge proper, to extricate this Colony out of their present unhappy Circumstances.

Voted, That it be recommended to the several Towns and Districts in this County, that they provide themselves immediately with one or more Field-Pieces, mounted and fitted for Use; and also a sufficient Quantity of Ammunition for the same; and that the Officers appoint a suitable Number of Men out of their respective Companies to manage said Field-Pieces.

Whereas the People of this County are under solemn Obligations not to purchase any Goods that shall be imported from Great-Britain after the last Day of August, 1774, which they determine most sacredly to adhere to, until our many Grievances be redressed. Therefore,

Voted, That it be recommended, and we do earnestly recommend it to the Committees of Correspondence or Selectmen in the several Sea Port Towns in this Province, to appoint, or cause to be appointed, Committees to inspect the Imports that have or shall be made since the last Day of August aforesaid, and publish all such in the Boston News-Papers, with the Names of the Importers, that so we may carefully avoid all such in our Dealings for the future.

Voted, To chuse a standing Committee for the County, to correspond with the Committees of Correspondence for the several Counties, and elsewhere, as they shall think proper: Also to prepare Matters proper to lay before this Body at their several Meetings, to give the earliest Intelligence to the several Committees in this County, of any new Attack upon the Liberties of this People, and call a County Convention at any Time, as Occasion may require.——Therefore, *Voted*, That the Committees of Correspondence for the Towns of Worcester and Leicester, be a Committee for the Purposes aforesaid; and that Messirs. Thomas Denny, Joseph Henshaw and Joshua Bigelow be added to the above Committee.

Voted, To take Notice of Mr. Sheriff Chandler, for carrying an Address to Governor Gage.

Voted, That a Committee wait on the Sheriff, and require his Attendance before this Body for presenting (with others the Justices of the County of Worcester) the Address to Governor Gage.

Voted, That the following Declaration, signed by the Sheriff, should be accepted.

Whereas the Convention of Committees have expressed their Uneasiness to the Sheriff of this County, now present before the Convention, for presenting with others, an Address to Governor Gage, which he frankly declares was precipitately done by him; that he is sorry for it, and disclaims an Intention to do any Thing against the Minds of the Inhabitants of this County; and had he known it would have given Offence, he would not have presented said Address. GARDNER CHANDLER.

As the several Regiments in this County are large and inconvenient, by the Increase of its Inhabitants since the first Settlement of said Regiments. Therefore, *Voted*, That they be divided into seven distinct Regiments, in the following manner, viz.

1st. Worcester, Leicester, Holden, Spencer, Paxton.

2d. Sutton, Oxford, Sturbridge, Charlton, Dudley.

3d. Lancaster, Bolton, Harvard, Lunenburg, Leominster, Fitchburg, Ashburnham, Westminster.

4th. Brookfield, Western, Braintree, Hardwick and Oakham.

5. Rutland, Hutchinson, Petersham, Athol, Templeton, Winchendon, Royalston, Hubbard's-Town and Princeton.

6th. Southborough, Westborough, Northborough, Shrewsbury and Grafton.

7th. Mendon, Uxbridge, Northbridge, Upton and Douglass.

Voted, That it be recommended to the several Towns in this County, to chuse proper, and a sufficient Number of Military Officers for each of their Towns; and that the Captains, Lieutenants and Ensigns in each Regiment, who are chosen by the People, do convene on or before the Tenth Day of October next, at some convenient Place in each Regiment, and choose their Field Officers, to command the Militia, until they be constitutionally appointed; and that it be recommended to the Officers in each Town in this County, to inlist one Third of the Men in their respective Towns, between Sixteen and Sixty Years of Age, to be at a Minute's Warning; and that it be recommended to each Town in this County, to chuse a sufficient Number of Men as a Committee to supply and support those Troops that shall move upon any Emergency.

Voted, That this Meeting be adjourned to the first Tuesday in December next.

Attest. Wm. HENSHAW, Clerk.

Evening School.

THIS Evening *JOHN GRIFFITH*'s School in Hanover Street will be opened, to teach Writing and Arithmetic, from 6 to 8 o'Clock, where those who incline to be taught may apply.

STOLEN out of a Pasture in Charlestown, about Four Miles from the Ferry, on Monday Night last, a light Red Mare, Four Years old, with a white Spot on her Nose, her Fore Mane long, her other Mane hanging the off side, her Feet lighter Colour than her Body, Fourteen Hands and half high. Whoever shall take up said Mare, and return her to the Owner, shall have FOUR DOLLARS Reward, or TEN DOLLARS for the Thief and Horse, and all necessary Charges paid, by

Charlestown, Sept. 27, 1774. STEPHEN GODDARD.

N. B. The following Bill, supposed to be drop'd by the Thief, was taken up in the Pasture from whence the Mare was stolen, viz. Breakfast, 3s. 6. Punch, 1s. Porter, 2s. 3. Wine, 15s. 6. Dinner, 4. Horses 1s. 6d. Total, £ 1. 7s. 9d.

William Bant

BEGS Leave to inform his Friends, Customers and others, That he has to sell by Wholesale and Retail at his Store fronting Dock-Square, Boston——A general Assortment of *English* and *India*

GOODS,

Suitable for the approaching Season: *(the whole of which was imported before the 31st of August last.)* Among his GOODS is a prime Choice of superfine Scarlet, Pompadore, white, green, pea green, sea green, barry, black, blue, brown and cloth colour'd BROAD CLOTHS; midling and low priz'd Ditto, with Shalloons and Trimmings to match the Cloths: ALSO of SILKS, viz.—Padusoys, Ducapes, Mantuas, Lutestrings, English and India Damasks, *a Piece of fine white Lutestring*, single and double Sattins, black, white and crimson figur'd Sattin, black, blue, green and white half yard Persians, ell-wide Persians, half-ell and ell-wide Alamodes, Brolios, black, blue and crimson thick Corduroys for Men's Waistcoats; and a Variety of other Articles that are commonly in Use at this Season of the Year.

☞ The above mentioned GOODS will be disposed of at the very lowest Rates, as said Bant is extremely desirous of exchanging all or any of them, for an Article, which is more convenient for him, in these troublesome Times, viz. CASH.

Providence STAGE COACH,

Kept by ANDREW COMSTOCK & SAMUEL BARTER.

WHO beg Leave to inform the Public, That they have removed from the White Horse Tavern to Mr. Jolley Allen's, a few Doors South of the Governor's, in Marlborough Street; where the greatest Care will be taken of all Bundles, Letters, &c. with which they may be entrusted:—They keep several Setts of the best Horses on purpose for this Business, and will engage to carry Passengers with the greatest Expedition, at the cheapest Rate.

FOUR DOLLARS REWARD.

RAN-AWAY from the Subscriber on the 22d of September, at Night, a Negro Man Servant, by the Name of CATO, about Five Feet and Eight Inches high, very thick Lips, speaks broken, and Walks as if he was lame in his Heels. Had on when he went away, a Cloth colour'd Coat, with Pewter Buttons, old Leather Breeches, a Tow Shirt, old Shoes with Silver plate Buckles, wore a Cap, and shoves round his Neck, and very high on his Forehead: Carried away with him a Callico Banyan, fine Linen Shirt, Check Linen Trowsers, grey Wigg, also carries or Wears a Felt Hatt with a Silver Lace on it, had a Violin and carries it in a green Bays Bag. Whosoever will return the Runaway to his Master in Winchenden, sha'l have the above Reward and all necessary Charges paid by LEVI NICHOL.

Winchenden, Sept. 23d, 1774.

EIGHT DOLLARS REWARD.

STOLEN out of the Tan House of the Subscriber, on Friday Evening last, a Quantity of SOLE LEATHER. Whoever will secure the Thief or Thieves, so that he or they shall be confined in any of his Majesty's Goals, shall be paid the above Reward by me

Charlestown, Oct. 3d. JAMES TRUMBALL.

ALL Persons having any Demand on the Estate of Mr. *John Ruggles*, late of Boston, Housewright, deceas'd, are desired to bring in their Accounts—And all Persons indebted to said Estate are desired to make payment to *Hannah Ruggles*, Administratrix, or to *Samuel Ruggles*, jun'r, her Attorney.

At GOULD's Auction-Office in Back-Street,

Will be Sold by PUBLIC VENDUE,

TO-MORROW

At Ten o'Clock in the Morning,

A Variety of Houshold Furniture,—Consisting of LOOKING GLASSES, Tables, Chairs, Chests of Draws, Feather Beds and Bedsteads, Desks, Kitchen Furniture, &c. Also, Wearing Apparel, and sundry Sorts of English Goods.

N. B. At one o'Clock will be put up two Second-Hand Chaises, with Harnessing compleat.

New AUCTION ROOM, Dock Square;

On WEDNESDAY next,

At TEN in the Morning,

Will be Sold by PUBLIC VENDUE.

At HUNTER's Auction-Room,

(Lately improved as a Store by Mr. Thomas Walley)

A large Assortment of English GOODS,

Amongst which are,

3-4, 7-8 and yard wide Irish Linnens, Callicoes, Check, stampt Kenting and Linnen Handkerchiefs, a variety of flower'd, strip'd and plain Lawns, Ribbons, Taffaties, Sattins, Modes, Broad Cloths, Kerseys, Duffils, Blankets, Velverets, Breeches Patterns, Worsted Hose, Sewing Silks, Twist and Metal Buttons, sundry sorts of Hard Ware Goods, and a Quantity of Moose Skin Breeches, Men's Shoes, &c. &c.

WM. HUNTER, Auctioneer.

Also, Chairs, Tables, Desks, Feather Beds, Brass Kettles, and sundry sorts of Kitchen Furniture.

Wednesday Morning the Sale to begin at 10 o'Clock.

Writing and Arithmetic

To be taught in Evenings.

The School to be open'd 1st Monday in October next, at the Writing School House in Queen-Street, and to be continued for the Season.

Where due Care will be taken for Instruction in its various Branches as usual, and it is hoped will meet with a like Acceptance, which shall be the Aim of the Subscriber, an Assistant in one of the public Schools.

Sept. 19. WILLIAM DALL, Jun.

PHILADELPHIA, *September* 21.

An Order to purchase 800 Pieces of Blankets is received from Gen. Gage, by a Gentleman in this city. It is hoped every Merchant will follow the example of the worthy Gentleman who was first applied to, who refused to sell any blankets, for the use of an army sent against his country.

NEW-YORK, September 26.

Saturday last the Remainder of the Transports came up from Boston; as did also Capt. Marshall in the Ship Hill, from Ireland, but last from Newcastle on Deleware.

The Norwich Paper, in Connecticut, of September 13, furnishes us with the following Paragraph.

A Correspondent begs Leave to propose to the Consideration of the Public, since the grand American Controversy grows and daily appears more and more serious, whether it is not expedient, very important and necessary, for the Colonies forthwith to raise an Army of Observation, and send it near the expected Scene of Action, and let them be increased from Time to Time as our Enemies increase, and kept in constant Exercise and Discipline.—A Preparation and Readiness for the defensive or offensive Operations, may, and often has, prevented the Necessity of Execution; but if Necessity does take Place, as there is great Probability it will; should we not, in such a Case, be in an infinitely better Situation, than to have our scattered Forces, (though almost innumerable) to collect from all Parts of the continent, after our Antagonists are well fortified, their Numbers full, and have struck some important and fatal blow.

NEWPOT, September 21.

Chamberlain and Mitchelson, from the Massachusetts-Bay, arrived at New-Haven the night before Commencement; but it being soon known that they were some of the gang of addressors, they were obliged to put off early next morning.

Jared Ingersol, judge of the court of admiralty at Philadelphia, has been obliged to decamp from Connecticut, his native place, on account of his abominable tory principles.

Capt. Kilburn, arrived at Newport from Virginia, informs that, a few days before he sailed, a vessel arrived there from England with intelligence to the 13th of August, one article of which was, that the popular rage ran so high in London, on account of the late measures, that the king had been seized in his carriage by the people who would have dragged him out, had not his guards interposed and rescued him.——*No French laws! No Popery!* Is the general cry in England: So that we hope soon to hear of the *downfall* of the Pope and the Whore of Babylon, after which the world may expect some peace.

PORTSMOUTH, (New Hampshire) Sept. 22.

We hear from Old-York, that on Friday last, a Quantity of TEA arrived there, said to be from Liverpool; upon which the Town assembled, and chose a Committee to take and secure it, 'till further Discovery could be made, and it was put into a Store of Capt. Groro's; and the Evening following a Number of Pickwacket Indians came into Town and broke open said Store, and carried it off; which has not been heard of since. The Quantity of Tea was said to be about 150 wt. and belong'd to Capt James Donnel and the Master.

NEWBURY PORT, September 28.

The Inferior Court of Common Pleas is now sitting in this Town, upon the old constitutional form of government; and the people of all ranks seem determined to make the minds of the Court easy, and defend them from insults, if any should be offered: The Resolves of a County Congress has all the good effect on the minds of the people that any legislative acts could have; the utmost care and circumspection is taken by the Committee of Safety, chosen by the town to keep every matter in its proper channel.

SALEM, Sept. 27, 1774.

On Saturday last came to this town, one Nutting of Cambridge, in order to engage carpenters to assist in building barracks for the troops at Boston; but those of that occupation here being informed that it would be disagreeable to their worthy, oppressed brethren in that town, as well as to the country in general, nobly refused having any thing to do in so disgraceful a service; and the poor —— very prudently decamped the following morning.

30. This Morning Capt. Howes, in a Brig, arrived here from Quebec, with Eleven Hundred Bushels of Wheat, for the Use of the Poor of the Town of Boston.

Another Vessel is soon to sail from that Place with a large Quantity of Grain, for the same charitable Purpose.

BOSTON, October 3.

The following was receiv'd by the Committee of Correspondence, by the last Post.

PHILADELPHIA.

In CONGRESS, *Thursday Sept.* 22, 1774.

RESOLVED,

THAT the Congress request the Merchants and others, in the several Colonies, not to send to Great Britain any Orders for Goods, and to direct the execution of all Orders already sent, to be delayed or suspended, untill the sense of the Congress, on the means to be taken for the preservation of the Liberties of *America* is made public.

An Extract from the Minutes,

CHARLES THOMSON, *Sec.*

Wednesday last his Excellency the Governor was pleased to issue a Proclamation to "excuse and discharge all such Persons as have been or may be elected and deputed Representatives, from giving their Attendance," on Account of "the extraordinary Resolves which have been passed in many of the Counties, the Instructions given by the Town of Boston, and some other Towns, to their Representatives, and the present disorder'd and unhappy State of the Province."

"We have the Pleasure to assure the Public, That at the earnest request of a Number of the wisest and best Friends to American Liberties (in this and other Colonies) JOSIAH QUINCY, jun. Esq; sailed for England last Wednelday Morning, on board Capt. Lyde.—Mr. Quincy's Acquaintance with the other Colonies, and his perfect Knowledge of the State of the Province, renders him capable of doing eminent Service to his Country; and his firm Attachment to the Rights of Mankind, give us good Reason to hope, that he will employ his Opportunities and Talents to the mutual and lasting Welfare of the Old and New World."

Extract of a Letter from New-York, Sept. 25, 1774.

"By Letters in the last Ship at Philadelphia from London, mention is made of a Letter from Governor Franklin, dated the 21st of May, advising the Ministry to send more Men of War to batter down the capital Towns, which would bring them to Submission. A Gentleman at Philadelphia has received a Letter from Dr. Franklin, where he says, he never knew what Pain was, untill he saw his Son's Letter to the Ministry. The Inhabitants have sent for the Governor to go to Philadelphia to clear the Matter up; but the Letter from his Father confirms it to be too true. This Matter makes much Stir at Philadelphia."

Extract of a Letter from Worcester, Sept. 27, 1774.

"Yesterday we had a Meeting of all the Male Inhabitants of this Town, from the Age of 16 to 70, who formed themselves into Companies, and proceeded to the Choice of Officers; those who held their Commissions under Hutchinson, (except a few) having resigned them.—One third Part of the Inhabitants were appointed to be in Readiness to march at a Minute's Warning to whatever Place their Assistance may be wanting.

"On Friday next there will be a Meeting of the County Committee, in Order to remonstrate to General Gage, respecting his Fortifications at the only Entrance by Land into our much esteemed Capital."

Extract of a Letter from London, July 30, 1774.

"Do not be surprized if you should hear that other Bills, worse if possible than those you have heard of, should pass next Sessions of Parliament, as I am told there are some for dividing and seperating the Provinces, taking away the Charters of some, and abolishing the Government of others and joining them to others."

James Murray, Esq; is appointed Inspector of Imports and Exports, and Register of Shipping in North America, in the Room of *Thomas Irving,* Esquire, preferr'd.

This may inform the Public, That one ——— Caldwell, was met at New-Liverpool on his Way to Halifax, with a design (as was reported) to buy Tea and carry the same to Plymouth for sale.

Joseph Scott, Esq; Ironmonger, in Union-Street, Addressor and Protestor, has given his countrymen great uneasiness, and they express the greatest dissatisfaction at his conduct, he having either *sold* or *lent* to the troops, near five hundred pounds sterling worth of cannon, cannon balls, and other implements of war, hundreds of people were about his house last Wednesday and in the evening, but by the vigilance of a number of credible gentlemen of this town, no damage was done to his person or property.

Last Week a Quantity of Tea was destroyed at Plymouth, having been smuggled in there from Halifax.

Wednesday last the Rev. Mr MOSES EVERETT was Ordained to the pastoral Care of the Church in Dorchester

Sept. 10th Died at Tisbury, in the 74th Year of his Age, *Nathaniel Hancock,* Esq; who had formerly been for many Years Pastor of the Church of Christ in that Town.

A MILITARY COUNTRYMAN, in our next. Also the *Resolves* of the Town of *Fairfield,* in the Colony of *Connecticut.*

To the PUBLIC.

AMIDST the various Enjoyments of human Life, none affords me greater Satisfaction, than the Society and Esteem of my fellow Men, which I find I have in a great Measure lost, by signing an Address to the late Governor Hutchinson: And had I the least Suspicion that the said Address would have given such general Discontent, it should not have had my Name to it. I am heartily sorry, for the Offence it has occasioned, and I do hereby renounce said Address in all Respects, and beg the Forgiveness of the Public, and to be reinstated in their Favor, assuring them that none shall be foremost in the Defence of the Liberties and Privileges of their Country, both civil and religious, than their humble Servant,

Marblehead, Sept. 4, JOHN WEBB.

On FRIDAY next, between One & Two o'Clook, will be sold by Public Vendue, at the Bunch of Grapes Tavern in King Street,

Two Pipes of Choice *Madeira* Wine,

Samples to be seen at the Place of Sale, and at the New Auction-Room South Side the Town-House, the Day before the Sale. Andrew Oliver Auctioneer.

A Vessel is arrived at Rhode-Island from London, which she left the middle of August; but we have not as yet received any publick Prints or other Intelligence by her.

Our worthy brethren in the country may be assured, that some of the most intelligent, affable and civil of the troops, now quartered in this capital, daily make excursions into our country towns, *in disguise,* where they mix with *all sorts* of people, prompting the talkative to tell *all they know,* and the weak and immoral to tell *much more.* Now, as secrecy is the characteristic of our enemies, so openness and frankness, is peculiar to our honest husbandmen: When *the former,* therefore, are SPIES in the last, *the latter* ought to be *reserved,* and UPON THEIR GUARD. *A word to* THE WISE.

An old warrior in the country, has constructed a machine for fighting, which he says, for a close attack, is much superior to a bayonet, or any other instrument ever yet in use. The art of war is the universal study, all are animated with the highest ardour for liberty, and, "*O save my country, heaven!* is the universal prayer.

A correspondent informs us, "that in travelling three hundred miles in New-England, he has not seen one person who gave the least countenance to the late tyrannical measures of parliament; but on the contrary, the people in every part of the country are prepared to meet the last efforts of tyranny, and are determined to spend all their treasure and their blood in defence of their rights."

DIED] At Providence, Mr. Rebecca Snow, Consort of the Rev. Mr. Joseph Snow, aged 48.

Caleb Blanchard

in Union-Street,

Has on Hand, a large Assortment of Goods suitable for the Season, which he will sell at the very lowest Rates for ready Money.

Just Imported, by

Geyer and Burgess,

in the Ship London, Capt. Calef, from London,

A general Assortment of English and India Piece Goods, which they will sell on the most reasonable Terms by Wholesale only, at their Store in King-Street, Boston.

They would also acquaint their Customers and others, who carry their Goods by Water, that they have taken a Store at Salem, near the Town-House, where they may be supply'd with equal Variety, and on the same Terms as at Boston.

An Evening School

Will be opened on Monday next, by JOHN DRUITT, at his School in Hanover Street, near Concert-Hall, where Reading, Writing, and Arithmetic will be taught after the most approved Method—NAVIGATION and BOOK-KEEPING on moderate Terms; in Compliance with the Times no Entrance will be requir'd.——His Hours of Attendance will be from 6 till 9 o'Clock, (P. M.)

☞ To the LADIES,

He begs Leave to acquaint those who wou'dn't choose to attend a School, or that the Inclemency of the approaching Season might hinder, that he will wait on them at their Places of Abode, at any Hour from 8 to 11 in the Forenoon, or from 2 'till 4 in the Afternoon.

Mrs. DRUITT has lower'd her Terms for plain Sewing to *Eight Pence* Law. Money per Week, (her other Works as usual) and hopes to convince those who are pleas'd to try, that there is as much to be learn'd in Winter as in Summer.

STOP THIEF!

ABSCONDED from the Subscriber on the 3d Day of August last, a Negro Man, called TOM, had on a Pair of black Plush Breeches, a light colour'd ragged Jacket, Lame in both his Feet: Said Negro return'd the last Night broke open his Master's Stable, Stole from thence a valuable Chesnut-colour'd Horse, with a small white Spot on his Forehead, Paces and Trots light, and took a Saddle (with a white Houser) and Bridle; he has with him a counterfeit Pass.

Whoever will take up said Thief and Horse, shall have FOUR DOLLARS, and all necessary Charges paid, by SIMEON POLLEY.

Boston, Sept. 28, 1774.

NARRAGANSET-CHEESE.

A Quantity that is extraordinary good, (very like) to Cheshire, to be sold at the Store of PENUEL BOWEN, opposite to the Golden-Ball.

An Evening SCHOOL

WILL be opened on Monday October 3d, at the South Writing School, where WRITING and ARITHMETIC is taught in the most concise and methodical Manner.—— *Attendance at the usual Hours.* *Sept* 22.

Caleb Call, of *Charlestown,* Baker,

ACQUAINTS his Friends and Customers, that he will supply them with his White Bisket, at the usual Price, either at *Salem* or *Marblehead,* upon their Writing to him, or applying to Messrs. *Hooper* and *Whittemore,* Coopers, on *Elany's* Wharfe in *Salem.*

Burials in the Town of BOSTON, since our last.

Seventeen Whites. One Black.

Baptiz'd in the several Churches, Eleven.

High Water at BOSTON, *for the present Week.*

Monday, 10 min. aft. 10	Friday, 0 min. after 1
Tuesday, 50 min. aft. 10	Saturday, 44 min. aft. 1
Wednesday, 31 m. aft. 11	Lord's-Day 36 m. af. 2
Thursday, 12 min. aft. 12	D's New 5 Day 10 Morn.

At a Meeting of the Freeholders and other Inhabitants of the Town of Rochester, the 13th inst. to consult upon, and determine what Measures to take with Nathaniel Ruggles and Samuel Sprague, Esqrs; who for several Years past, have appeared inimical to their Country, by strenuously opposing and censuring every Method taken by the People to obtain a Redress of their political Grievances; after chusing a Moderator, the Town made Choice of a Committee to wait upon the above-named Gentlemen, and desire their Attendance at the Meeting, which they complied with, and signed the following Confession and Declaration, viz.

WE the Subscribers have given great umbrage and uneasiness to our fellow-townsmen, by counteracting, both in our publick and private conduct, the measures which have been adopted by them and the country in general, in order to obtain a repeal of the late unconstitutional acts of the British Parliament, with regard to the American Colonies; we do now express our sorrow for what we have done in that regard, and ask forgiveness of our fellow-townsmen and countrymen; and promise that we will not for the future, do or say any thing to promote, justify or encourage said acts of Parliament, but on the contrary, will do all in our power to discountenance and discourage them. And we do now freely declare it as our opinion, that the late acts of Parliament imposing taxes on America, are unconstitutional, being directly contrary to our charter, and particularly the act for blocking up the port of Boston, and that for regulating the government of this Province, we look upon to be altogether arbitrary, unjust and cruel, and do declare our abhorrence and detestation of them; and also of the act commonly called the Canada or Quebec Bill, establishing popery and French government in one of the American Colonies, which in a short time may spread over the whole continent, to the destruction of the civil and religious rights of all America. And whereas we were concerned in an address lately presented to Thomas Hutchinson, Esq; late governor of this Province, by a number of the justices of the county of Plymouth, in which address we approv'd of and applauded the person of said Hutchinson, at which our fellow-townsmen are much griev'd and offended, we acknowledge we were wrong in what we did in regard to said address, and do now rescind and retract what we then did.

And we also declare, that if we, or either of us, are required to do any business in our office in conformity to the abovesaid acts of Parliament, we will refuse it, although by such refusal we lose our places.

Nathaniel Ruggles,
Samuel Sprague.

Enoch Hammond, Esq; of the same Town and County, being suspected by some of the people of being faulty with regard to said address, was called upon by the Town to confess it, or declare his innocence, upon which he wrote and signed as follows, viz.

The address to governor Hutchinson, abovementioned, I did not encourage, but abhor'd and publickly oppos'd it.

Enoch Hammond.

The Commissioners appointed

by the Hon. Foster Hutchinson, Esq; Judge of Probate, &c. for the County of Suffolk, to receive and examine the Claims of the several Creditors to the Estate of Mr. Isaac Cazneau, late of Boston, Sadler, deceas'd, represented Insolvent.——Give Notice that they shall attend said Service at the British-Coffee-House in King-Street, on the second Thursday in the six following Months, from Six to Nine o'Clock, P. M.

Boston, Sept. 15th, 1774.

SWEET FLOUR.

To be Sold by HABIJAH SAVAGE, at his Store No. 16 on the Long Wharf,

A few Barrels of Choice Flour, old Jamaica Spirits, West-India Rum, Brandy, best Jamaica Sugar, Indigo, Molasses, Rice, Case Bottles, Cases with 12 or 15 Bottles, Cocoa, Peas, Calavances, white Beans, Corn and a Cask of Currants, cheap.

Notice is hereby given to the Delinquent Proprietors of the Town of New-Glocester, in said County, That unless they pay the several Sums hereafter affixed to each Delinquent Right respectively, together with incidental Charges, to Mr Isaac Parsons, of said New-Glocester, before the 6th Day of December next, they may expect that so much of each of such Delinquent Right in said Town will be sold at Public Vendue, at the House of Mr. Isaac Parsons abovesaid, on the aforesaid Sixth Day of December, as will be sufficient to discharge their several Arrearages, with the Charges as aforesaid. The Sale to begin at Ten of the Clock in the Forenoon, and to continue from Time to Time, until the whole is Sold.

The Rights that are delinquent, are as follows, viz.

Rights.	£.	s.	d.	Rights.	£.	s.	d.
No. 1	4	13	10	No. 38	4	12	0
4	4	5	9	39	12	15	1
7	10	4	4	42	4	5	9
10	4	0	0	45	5	5	11
13	13	4	6	46	5	5	11
16	5	3	4	52	4	5	9
20	16	16	10	54	3	12	9
22	4	18	4	56	7	19	7
24	9	19	7	58	10	4	4
26	4	5	9	61	11	4	8
31	9	0	6	63	3	3	1

New-Glocester, Sept. 1, 1774.

SIMON NOYES,
EBENEZER MASON,
ISAAC PARSONS, } Committee and Assessors.

BRANDY & GENEVA.

A few Pipes Old Brandy and Geneva by the Case To be SOLD by

CHARLES MILLER

At his Store in King Street.

To be Sold by Public Vendue, on FRIDAY the Fourteenth Day of October Inst. at Twelve o'Clock, A. M. by Order of the Superior Court,

THE Real Estate of WILLIAM STERLING, deceased, consisting of a Front End of a Dwelling-House, situated at the North End of Boston, near Winisimet-Ferry.

JACOB COOPER, Auctioneer.

TO BE SOLD,

By Richard Cranch,

Near the Mill-Bridge, BOSTON,

A very Elegant SPINNET, (Harris's make)—Also, an Assortment of WATCHES.

At the GOLDEN-KEY,

In Ann-Street, near the Draw-Bridge,
(The Shop lately improved by Mr. *William Breck*,)
Are to be Sold by Wholesale and Retail,

COTTON WOOL,

Loaf and brown Sugars,	Rice
Green Coffee,	West India Rum
Chocolate,	Brandy,
Flour,	Ginger,
Mustard,	Crown and Bar Soap,
Piemento, and all other Spices,	Starch,
	Hair Powder,
Raisins,	Indigo, and

A small Assortment of Crockery Ware, &c. &c. for a very moderate Profit, by

John Fenno.

Daniel Bell

Would Inform his kind Friends and Customers, that he has Removed to the Store lately occupied by Messrs. Thomas and Elisha Hutchinson, directly opposite the East-End of Faneuil-Hall; where he has to sell, an Assortment of West-India Goods, upon the lowest terms for Cash, as usual.

Also a Quantity of good white Beans to be disposed of very Cheap, and a few Barrels of Pitch.

To be Sold by JONATHAN DAVIS,

at Bull's Wharff, the following West-India Goods, viz. Choice St. Vincent & Barbados Rum, Jamaica Spirits, Jamaica Sugars, Rase Ginger, Cotton Wool, Indigo of the best Quality, and Turk's Island Salt. Said DAVIS also has to sell eight Thousand Pipe Staves which are at Salem; the Terms of Sale of which may be known by inquiring of Mr. Haskell Darby of Salem, or Jonathan Davis of Boston.

All Persons indebted to, or that have any Demands on the Estate of Capt. Thomas Cordis, late of Concord, Mariner, deceas'd, are desired to bring in their Accounts to Mrs. Elizabeth Cordis, or Capt. Elnathan Jones, of said Concord, Administrators on said Estate, in Order for Settlement.

Good OLD Tallow CANDLES

Made last Winter.

Sperma-Ceti and *Bayberry-Wax* Candles.

ALSO,

Refin'd Sperma Ceti Oil, by the Cask, or in smaller Quantities. *Tallow* and *Cotton Wick.* The *best of Hogs-Fatt*, by the Barrel or less. Sold by

JOHN LANGDON,

In *Fleet Street*, near the *Old North* Meeting House.

TO BE SOLD,

A genteel new finish'd HOUSE and STORE, accommodated with a pretty Piece of Land, good Well of Water, COOPER'S SHOP, &c. extreemly well situated in the Center of the Town, about 30 Miles from Boston, long noted, and much esteem'd as one of the best Spots in the Province for a Trader: it has the privilege of a *Licence.*—Also the POTASH WORKS in said Town, with all the Utensels fit to go immediately to Work: The whole to be Sold reasonably, and on the most easy Terms, as a quarter of the Value paid at the delivery, or soon after, would answer the end of the Seller.

For further Particulars, inquire of the Printers hereof.

A Wet Nurse with a good young Breast of Milk, wants a Place in a Gentleman's Family.

Inquire of Edes and Gill.

TO BE LETT,

A very convenient Tenement, situated near the Market. Inquire of Edes and Gill.

TO LET,

Two very convenient Tenements in Governor's Alley, near the Province House, one of them has a good Shop adjoining.

Inquire of the Printers.

A young Man that can be well Recommended, would let himself, being used to tending a Grist Mill and Saw Mill. Inquire of the Printers.

A very likely Female Negro Child to be given away. Inquire of Edes and Gill.

Thomas Walley,

Begs Leave to inform his Friends and Customers, that he is Removed from his Store on Dock-Square, to the first Store in BUTLER's-ROW, lately Improved by Mr. *Samuel Allene Otis*, being the opposite Corner to Mr. *Thomas Handasyde Peck*, Hatter, where he continues to sell all Sorts of Groceries as usual, by Wholesale and Retail, at the lowest Rates, and his Customers, may depend they shall be as well used, as at any Store in Boston.

N. B. A Quantity of choice Raisins in good Order, Teneriffe Wine by the Pipe, Hogshead or Quarter Cask, very best Lisbon and M. Malaga, by the Quarter Cask, also race and ground Ginger,—at said Store.

BUTLER's-ROW, No. 1.

John Hunt,

Begs Leave to acquaint his Customers and others, that he has entered into a Co-partnership with JOSEPH SHERBURNE, jun. under the Firm of

Hunt and *Sherburne*,

And that they have for Sale, a large and compleat Assortment of *London*, *Sheffield*, *Birmingham* & *Bristol* Hard Wares, consisting of too many Articles to be enumerated; which they are determined to sell by Wholesale and Retail, at the very lowest Rates, at their Shop next Door Northward of the Sign of the Heart & Crown, Cornhill, BOSTON.

N.B. A parcel of Hatters Trimmings very Cheap.

TO BE SOLD.

WANT of Health and a Desire to lead a retired Life, induces the Subscriber to offer for Sale on reasonable Terms a good Farm, situate in Pomfret, in the Colony of Connecticut, lying on Quinabough River, adjoining the Road leading from Boston to Hartford, containing one hundred and seventy Acres of Land, conveniently accommodated with Ploughing, Mowing, Pasture and Wood-Land; a good Orchard, with two Dwelling Houses, a Barn, a Malt House, a Fulling Mill, and Clothier's Shop, with three Iron Screw Presses, a Smith's Shop with two Trip-Hammers, a Mill to grind Scythes, also two Grist Mills, which may be warranted to grind more than two hundred Bushels in twelve Hours, with Water to carry them constantly in the driest Season.

The above Works are mostly new, and in good Repair, and largely supplied with Custom; being a good Seat for all Kinds of Business. Whoever inclines to purchase may know the Terms by applying to Benjamin Cargill, the Owner, living on the Premises.

Pomfret, Aug 30, 1774. BENJAMIN CARGILL.

N. B. *The said Cargill wants to hire immediately one or two good smart Hands, to work at the Clothiers Business, for which good Wages will be given; such as can only shear well will answer. A well recommended Maltster is also wanted.*

Abraham Hunt

HAS FOR SALE,

At his Celler under the Old Brick Meeting-House,

The best old Sterling Madeira, by the Pipe, Quarter Cask or Dozen; also Port Wine by the Dozen, and choice VINEGAR for Pickles.

To be SOLD and Enter'd upon directly,

The Distill House and Land with the Stills, Worms and other usual necessaries belonging to the Distill House, belonging to the Estate of Mr. JOHNSON JACKSON, deceas'd, situate at the South End of Boston. Inquire of JOSEPH JACKSON at the South End, Executor to said Estate.

Also, A few Hogsheads of New-England Rum, and some Spirits of different Sorts.

MUSICAL CLOCKS.

To be Sold Musical Clocks that go by Springs, also Musical Clocks that go by Weights, and play a different Tune each Day in the Week, on Sunday's a Psalm Tune. Inquire of BENJA. WILLARD Clock & Watch Maker in Roxbury Street near Boston. Where all sorts of Clocks are made in the newest Form, and Warranted to go without Variation, and many without Cleaning. Also Clock Cases are made at the same Place, in various Forms and in the best Manner, and Cheaper than can be purchas'd in London. Also Convey'd with Clocks to any Part of the Country.

All the Branches of this Business is likewise carried on at his Shop at Grafton.

SIXTY DOLLARS REWARD.

WHEREAS it was this Day discovered that the Powder-House in Wrentham, within about five Weeks last past, was broken open by some ill-minded Person or Persons, and from thence was stolen six Half Barrels of Powder, with about thirteen Hundred Flints, and some Lead, the Quantity not yet known. Whoever shall make Discovery of said Person or Persons concerned in the abovesaid Theft, so as they may be brought to Justice, shall have the above Reward paid by me.

By Order of the Selectmen of the Town of Wrentham.

JOHN MESSENGER, *Town-Clerk.*

Wrentham, August 29, 1774.

Boston: Printed, by EDES & GILL.

THE

Boston-Gazette,

AND

COUNTRY JOURNAL.

No. 1017.

Containing the freshest Advices, Foreign and Domestic.

MONDAY, October 10, 1774.

FELLOW COUNTRYMEN and CITIZENS.

IN my last, I hinted a few things for the consideration of your *military genius's*; considering them as the *main spring* of motion in all *military operations*, for as the great *Xenophon* tells us, "*an army without officers, is like a body without a soul.*"—Having attempted to assist you in the winding up of this *spring*, permit me now to turn your attention to the body that is to be moved by it, and offer a few hints respecting the common detail or *mechanical* part of the *art of war*, it is here supposed that the number of men their age and condition has been determined, that they are now enlisted (the same rule serves for your common militia companies) and are to be drilled to discipline (as to their arms accoutrements or uniforms I shall not at this time mention them) here the first *object* is to make them *strictly attentive*,—to stand *strait* and *firm* upon their *legs*, and in every other *position* agreeable to the *directions* in the *plan* of *discipline* which they are to *practice* in a *soldier-like* manner—which is to be adjusted before any motions of the *manual* exercise are attempted.—But here methinks I hear some enquiring what exercise is best since some *companies* practice upon one plan, and some upon another—some prefering the *manual exercise ordered by his Majesty in* 1764, whilst others give the preference to the *Norfolk plan of discipline*—my own opinion is, that an exercise might be *compiled* from the *two*—*preferable* to either,—but taking them seperate must give my voice in favor of the *former* as being the most *graceful and soldier like*—whilst the latter appears calculated for those who are not quite so *adroit* as *soldiers should be*—However the *knowledge* of *either* will fit men for the service—but it must be remembered that *all* the *companies* which *belong to*, or *are intended* to compose *one regiment*, must practice the *same exercise*—But this matter being determined by the *commander in chief*, or agreed upon by the *chief officers* of each *regiment*, the *drill officers* will proceed to instruct the men (here it is presumed that each officer *well knows* his duty, *otherwise* he will be *a blind leader* of the blind) and carefully show them how to perform *every* motion *precisely*, for unless errors are corrected when committed a *corps* may be practising *seven years* and never be *perfected*—they should therefore be taught a motion over and *over again*, and *cautioned* (if it be a motion which they do not *readily* apprehend) *before* the word of command be given *how to perform it*.—The *proficiency* which a *soldier* will soon make when *properly* instructed is truly surprising—But the *cardinal* point is to teach them how to use their *legs*, (which a *great military genius* tells us is of more importance than the use of their arms) and to *prime* and *load* with *agility*—and *fire* with *precision*; the greatest attention therefore must be given to this, and so soon as the men are taught how to handle their *arms properly*, the greatest part of their time should be spent in the practice of it, and the *various modes* of *firing*;—whether *standing*, *advancing*, *retreating*, defending *parapets*, *streets*, *bridges* or *defiles*, made as *familiar* to them as *possible*.—As to the *maneuvres*, if the men are properly taught the *steps*, can *march, wheel and face regularly*, *a fruitful genius* will put them upon performing an infinity of *evolutions* both *elegant* and *useful*—however for your first practice, permit me to *recommend* those *manœuvres* at present performed by the *army*, which are *chiefly* annexed to the *manual exercise ordered by his majesty in* 1764, (which may be had of Mess'rs Fleets printers in Boston) and are *vastly* preferable to those contained in the *Norfolk plan of discipline*. I shall at this *time* mention but one thing more, which is to *recommend the frequent* breaking and forming the *company* or *battalion*, or *dispersing* and *rallying*, it is very easily performed—the distance from the *colours*, or *centre*, the *wing*—the *rank*—the *right* and *left hand* men are what they are to *guide* themselves by, and if attended to, a *company* or *regiment* altho' entirely broken may almost *instantly* form in their *proper* order; great advantage *hath* and may *again accrue*, from *suddenly dispersing* and *rallying*. But after all that has been, or can be said upon this *subject*, the most *effectual* method to have your *militia formidable*, is to establish it *similar* or *nearly similar* to that in *Great-Britain*.—A certain part of your present numerous *militia* (between a certain age) must be formed into *companies* of about *fifty men* each, *nine* of those *companies* into a *battalion*, and being properly *armed* and *accoutered*, the several *companies & battalions* must be *officered*, with *gentlemen* of a *truly military turn*, which should be the *principle* if not *sole* qualification for *commissions*, your *militia* will then soon make a *fine figure*, and in order to *facilitate* the matter, two or three *provincial adjutants* of *sufficient ability*, should be appointed, whose business it should be *constantly* to repair from *company* to *company*, and from one *battalion* to *another* (giving notice to the officers of each, when and where to attend) carefully instructing the *commission* and *non-commission officers*, in every part of their duty respecting the service; this would establish a uniformity of discipline throughout the *whole*, and most admirably aid and assist the *officers* who it must be *supposed*, in many places, will stand in need of *instruction* and *advice*.—The expence attending this would be *inconsiderable*, and ways and means might be devised to defrey it; your *militia* in such case would be at all times *ready to take the field*—be a safeguard to their country and a *terror* to its *enemies*—But this is a subject so copious that I cannot at this time enter minutely into it. When I have leisure I have more to offer—at present adieu,

A MILITARY COUNTRYMAN.

P. S. In my last, in the paragraph, for "your *workmen* are second to none on earth" read your *marksmen* are second &c.

From the *NEW-LONDON* Paper of Sept. 23.

WINDHAM, Sept. 5, 1774.

WHoever set on foot the alarm from Boston, whether friend or enemy, we cannot but think it will prove signally serviceable to the liberties of our country; as it will inspirit our brethren, in all parts to hold themselves in readiness, against any future attacks; encourage our friends in that distress'd capital; dissuade our enemies from the practice of unprovoked hostilities, and convince them, that North-Americans have too much virtue and firmness, to yield up their liberty, that sacred inheritance from God and nature; to the will of any despot or the caprices of ministerial avarice and ambition.

On the receipt of the alarming news here, which was supposed undoubtedly to be authentic, the most tumultuous and opposite passions seemed to take possession of every breast; on the one hand *pity*, for the cruel fate of Boston and her murdered sons, on the other *rage* and *determined vengeance*, on their murderers.—Couriers were immediately dispatched to every quarter, with most surprizing expedition——To arms! to arms! was the universal cry——Instantly nothing was seen, on all sides, but men, of all ages and characters, cleansing and burnishing their arms, furnishing themselves with provisions and warlike stores, & preparing for an immediate march; gentlemen of rank and fortune, exhorting and encouraging others, by their advice and example, and the very women lending their helping hands, with the utmost readiness and assiduity, to expedite the march; which began in a few hours from the receipt of the intelligence, and was performed with the utmost decency and order; each man was mounted on a good horse, well equipt with military accoutrements, ammunition, provisions, &c. a few only excepted, who could not procure horses, snatched up their muskets and sat out on foot. The roads were all crowded with armed men, marching for Boston with the greatest rapidity, but without noise or tumult. No frantic mirth or empty boasting, or irregularity of any kind, disgraced their march; but silent firmness and invincible intrepidity were portrayed in every face. Every company pushed forward with such expedition, that, 'tis believed, in forty-eight hours from first receiving the news, succours would have arrived at Boston, from the distance of one hundred miles. By the most moderate computation, in the colony of Connecticut alone, there were not less than twenty thousand men, compleatly armed, actually on their march for Boston, with full speed, until counter intelligence was received on the road.

The junction of this body with the whole force of Massachusetts-Bay, Rhode-Island, &c. which, doubtless, would have been effected in less than two days, had the alarm been real, would have formed a more numerous, and considering the motive for which they took arms, viz. *pro aris & focis*, a more formidable army than ever appeared in America, and perhaps even in Europe itself, in the present age. The number, at a low computation, would have exceeded one hundred thousand men. This number, tho' surprising, no one will think exaggerated, who is well acquainted with the interior parts of the New-England colonies; and what had been the consequence, had the intelligence proved true, on which this grand movement was made, requires not the penetration of a Newton to discern.

Now therefore judge, ye mercenary tools of a despotic ministry; reflect, ye infamous minions of American tyranny; what had been your fate, had you felt but one hundredth part of the weight of the just resentment of this innumerable host? Thank your kind stars, that the intelligence on which these men were called to arms, proved to be premature. Had not this been the case; had these sons of freedom continued their route to Boston, and there, as they justly might, have made reprisals; who, think ye would have fell the first sacrifice to the *manes* of those slaughtered sons of liberty? Ye unrighteous senators, who have sworn to oppress, to enslave your country! Ye unconstitutional judges, who would make traffic of the properties, the liberties, the lives and even the very souls of your countrymen! Ye servile, cowardly addressers of H———n, that wicked parricide, that monster of a man, that butcher of the human race, on whose accursed head descend the united anathemas of all the American world, your little devoted tribe excepted—*you* have reason to tremble—even the sight of this innumerable company of your injured, betrayed, incensed fellowmen, would have froze your hearts with terror: and, if you are not now dead to reflection and remorse, the present horrors of your guilty consciences must, in some measure, anticipate your fate.—The uplifted arm of vengeance, would have fallen light on the soldiery, in comparison of what you might justly have expected. You would have fallen the first sacrifice. You who have been nourished on the paps, and fostered in the arms, of America, our common mother, who owe all your little importance to her indulgent smiles, who, when she was basely attacked, were the first to aim the deadly poignard at her bosom—you would certainly, you would justly, have fallen, the first victims to their righteous resentment—then must your lot have been forever fixed, in the land of darkness and despair, where, with unavailing tears and unpitied cries, you would never, to the remotest ages, make an adequate atonement for your infamous parricide. The whole tribe of you would have been extirpated from the face of God's earth, and your names buried in eternal oblivion or mentioned but with hissing and reproach;——take warning therefore from this, and instantly make your peace with God, and with your country; lull not yourselves into a fatal security, because the sword of justice is now returned into its sheath; for although New-England will never be the aggressor, yet, at what time, the blood of her innocent loyal sons shall be copiously shed, by the wanton hand of despotism, then shall the awful genius of America rouse from his slumber, and hurl inevitable destruction on the devoted heads of those, once her children, who doted to be traitors to her righteous cause, and on all who imbrue their hands in her innocent blood.

HARMONIUS & ARISTOGITON.

Nathan Frazier

BEGS leave to inform the Public, that in consequence of the Boston Port-Bill, and with a view of accommodating those of his Customers to whom it may be most convenient to have their Supplies conveyed by Water, he has opened a Store in Salem, (the one lately Improved by Mr. John Johnson, and next Door to Mr. John Gool's) where he has for Sale an Assortment of Goods suitable for the Season.——Said FRAZIER still continues his Business at his Store in *Boston* as usual; His Customers may be supplied at either of said Stores, Wholesale and Retail, on the most reasonable Terms for ready Money.—He will give his Personal Attendance, for the present at his *Salem* Store.

Colony of RHODE-ISLAND *&c.*

WHEREAS John Wiley of Providence, in the County of Providence, in the Colony aforesaid, Merchant, preferred a Petition unto the General Assembly of the said Colony, representing that he is an insolvent Debtor, and praying that he may be admitted to the Benefit of an Act passed in June A. D. 1756, entitled, "An Act for the Relief of Insolvent Debtors." Whereupon the General Assembly referred the said Petition, and ordered that the Creditors of the said John Wiley should be notified by an Advertisement to be inserted in the Newport Mercury, the Providence Gazette, and in one of the Boston News-Papers, to appear at the next Session to answer the same:—I do therefore hereby notify the Creditors of the said John Wiley to appear (if they shall think fit) at the General Assembly to be holden at Providence, in and for the said Colony, on the last Wednesday in October next, then and there to shew Cause, (if any they have) why the said Petition should not be granted. HENRY WARD, Sec'y.

NEWHALL and HICHBORN,

BEG leave to acquaint their Customers and others, in this and the neighbouring Parts, that they Propose carrying on the Cooper's Business in all its Branches, at Salem; and have opened a Shop for that Purpose, near the Distill-House of Mr. JONATHAN ROPES, in Salem.

N. B. As they also carry on the same business in Boston as usual, one of them may always be found in each Place.

BOSTON, October 10.

WEDNESDAY last the Members chosen in Consequence of Governor GAGE's late Writs for calling a General Assembly, met at the Court House in Salem pursuant to the Precepts; and after waiting a Day without being admitted to the usual Oaths, which should have been administred by the Governor or other constitutional Officers; and having chosen the Honorable JOHN HANCOCK, Esq; to be their Chairman, and BENJAMIN LINCOLN, Esq; Clerk, they proceeded to Business, and passed the following Resolves.

Province of the MASSACHUSETTS-BAY.

In the Court House at Salem, October 7, 1774.

WHEREAS *his Excellency* Thomas Gage, *Esq; did issue Writs bearing Date the First of September last, for the Election of Members to serve as Representatives in a Great and General Court, which he did "think fit and appoint" to be convened and holden the 5th Day of October Instant, at the Court House in this Place: And whereas a Majority of Members duly Elected in Consequence of said Writ, did attend at said Court-House the Time appointed, there to be qualified according to Charter for taking Seats and acting as Representatives in said Great and General Court; but were not met by the Governor, or other constitutional Officer or Officers by him appointed for administring the usual Oaths, and qualifying them thereto. And whereas a Proclamation bearing Date the 28th of September last, and published in sundry News Papers, with the Signature of his Excellency, contains many Reflections on this Province, as being in a tumultuous and disorderly State; and appears to have been considered by his Excellency as a constitutional Discharge of all such Persons as have been elected in Consequence of his Excellency's said Writ. ——The Members aforesaid so attending, having considered the Measures which his Excellency has been pleased to take by his said Proclamation, and finding them to be unconstitutional, unjust, and disrespectful to the Province, think it their Duty to pass the following Resolves.*

Therefore, *RESOLVED* as the Opinion of said Members,

1. That by the Royal Charter of the Province, the Governor for the Time being, is expresly oblig'd to convene "upon every last Wednesday in the Month of May, every Year for ever, and at such other *Times* as he shall *think fit and appoint*, a Great and General Court." And therefore that, as his Excellency *had thought fit, and by his Writ appointed* a Great and General Court to be convened on the Fifth Day of October Instant, his Conduct in preventing the same is against the express Words, as well as true Sense and Meaning of the Charter, and unconstitutional; more especially as by Charter his Excellency's Power "to adjourn, prorogue and dissolve all Great and General Courts," doth not take Place after said Courts shall be appointed, until they have first "met and convened."

2d. That the Constitutional Government of the Inhabitants of this Province being by a considerable Military Force at this Time attempted to be surperceded and annulled, and the People under the most alarming and just Apprehensions of Slavery, having in their laudable Endeavours to preserve themselves therefrom, discovered upon all Occasions the greatest Aversion to Disorder and Tumult; it must be evident to all attending to his Excellency's said Proclamation, that his Representations of the Province, as being in a tumultuous and disordered State, are Reflections the Inhabitants have by no Means merited; and therefore that they are highly injurious & unkind.

3dly. That as the pretended Cause of his Excellency's Proclamation for discharging the Members elected by the Province in pursuance of his Writs, has for a considerable Time existed, his Excellency's Conduct in choosing to issue said Proclamation (had it been in other Respects unexceptionable) but a few Days before the Court was to have been convened, and thereby unavoidably putting to unnecessary Expence and Trouble a great Majority of Members from the Extremities of the Province, is a Measure by no Means consistent with the Dignity of the Province; and therefore it ought to be considered as a disrespectful Treatment of the Province, and as an Oposition to that Reconciliation between Great-Britain and the Colonies so ardently wished for by all the Friends of both.

4thly. That some of the Causes assigned as aforesaid for this unconstitutional and wanton Prevention of the General Court, have in all good Governments been considered among the greatest Reasons for convening a Parliament or Assembly, and therefore the Proclamation is considered as a further Proof, not only of his Excellency's Disaffection towards the Province, but of the Necessity of its most vigorous and immediate Exertions for preserving the Freedom and Constitution thereof.

Upon a Motion made and seconded, *Voted*, That the Members aforesaid, do now Resolve themselves into a Provincial Congress, to be joined by such other Persons as have been or shall be chosen for that Purpose, to take into Consideration the dangerous and alarming Situation of public Affairs in this Province, and to consult and determine on such Measures as they shall judge will tend to promote the true Interest of his Majesty in the Peace, Welfare and Prosperity of the Province.

Copy Attest. BENJ^a. LINCOLN, *Clerk.*

A Provincial CONGRESS being thus formed, and having chosen the Hon. JOHN HANCOCK, Esq; Chairman, and BENJ^a. LINCOLN, Esq; Clerk, they Adjourned to the Court-House in *Concord*, there to meet on TUESDAY the Eleventh Day of *October* Instant, at Ten o'Clock in the Forenoon.

[We hear that the Number of Representatives from the several Towns, which met at *Salem* last Week, consisted of 90.]

AT a Meeting of the Delagates of every Town in the County of Plymouth, *in the Province of* Massachusetts-Bay, *held at* Plimpton *in said County, on Monday the 26th, and by Adjournment at the County House in* Plymouth, *on Tuesday the 27th Day of* Sept. 1774. *viz.*

FLYMOUTH. Hon. James Warren, Esq; Mr. John Torrey, Capt. Theophilus Cotton, William Watson, Esq; Mr. Thomas Lothrop.

SCITUATE Nathan Cushing, Esq; John Cushing, jun. Esq; Capt. Israel Vinal, jun. Mr. Barnabas Little, Mr. William Turner, Capt. Joseph Tolman.

WAREHAM. Mr. Ebenezer Briggs, Mr. Barnabas Bates.

MARSHFIELD. Capt. Anthony Thomas, Capt. William Thomas.

ABINGTON. Dr. David Jones, Capt. Woodbridge Brown, Mr. William Reed, jun.

BRIDGEWATER. Capt. Edward Mitchell, Mr. Nathaniel Reynolds, Mr. Nathan Mitchell, Mr. Thomas Hooper.

KINGSTON John Thomas, Esq; Capt. John Gray, Mr. William Drew.

HANOVER. Capt. Joseph Cushing, Mr. Joseph Ramsdel, Mr. Joshua Simmons, Capt. Robert Eels, Dr. Lemuel Cushing.

PEMPROKE. Capt. John Turner, Dr. Jeremiah Hall, Mr. Seth Briggs, Capt Edward Thomas, Capt. Elijah Cushing.

DUXBOROUGH. Capt Wait Wadsworth, Mr. Geo. Partridge, Mr. Peleg Wadsworth.

HALLIFAX Mr. Barnabas Thomson, Mr. Moses Inglee, Mr. Ebenezer Thomas.

MIDDLEBOROUGH. Capt. Ebenezer Sprout, Mr. John Miller, Mr. Ebenezer Wood, Mr. Benjamin Tucker, Mr. Nathaniel Foster.

ROCHESTER. Capt. Ebenezer White, Mr. Nathaniel Hammond, Mr. Nathan Nye.

PLIMTON. Mr. William Ripley, Mr. Samuel Lucas, Mr. Seth Cushing.

VOTED, The Hon. JAMES WARREN, Esq; Chairman.

A COMMITTEE of Nine, viz. *James Warren*, Esq; *Nathan Cushing*, Esq; Captain *Joseph Cushing*, *John Thomas*, Esq; Dr. *Jones*, Mr. *John Torry*, Mr. *Thomas Lothrop*, Mr. *George Partridge* and Dr. *Jeremiah Hall*, were chosen to bring in at the Adjournment a Report to this body, and the following being several times read, and put Paragraph by Paragraph, was unanimously Voted, viz.

WHEREAS the British Administration, instead of cultivating that harmony and affection, which have so long subsisted, to the great mutual advantage of both Britain and the Colonies, have for a series of years, without provocation, without justice or good policy, in breach of faith, the laws of gratitude, the natural connections and commercial interests of both countries, been attacking with persevering and unrelenting injustice the Rights of the Colonists; and have added from one time to another, insults to oppressions, till both have become (more especially in this colony) intolerable, and every person who has the feelings of a man, and any sense of the rights of mankind, and the value of our happy constitution, finds it now necessary to exert himself, to the utmost of his power, to preserve them. We who are returned from the several towns in the county of *Plymouth*, and now met on the ground, first trod by our venerable ancestors, and at the place, providence directed them to, as an asylum from the persecuting rage and oppression, of their contemporaries in Britain; feeling the same spirit, and actuated in defence of our rights, by the same principles, which animated them in acquiring and transmitting them to us, and succeeding posterity, in a manner which ever distinguish the heroism and virtue of their characters, DO RESOLVE.

1. That the inhabitants of the American colonies, are intitled to all the natural rights of mankind, and are by right subject to the controul of no power on earth, but by their own consent.

2. That the inhabitants of this province have no other political connection with, or dependance on Britain, than what was originally by our ancestors, for themselves and posterity stipulated with the King, and in the form of a grant from him express'd in the Charter.

3. That the interposition of any other power on earth in our affairs, and more especially in attempts to tax or even legislate for us. And that of the King himself, in any other manner than is express'd and provided for, in the original compact, is an infraction of our natural and constitutional Rights.

4. That the people of this province have at all times been loyal and dutiful subjects to the King of Great-Britain, have observed all the conditions of their original compact, borne great affection to his other subjects, in all parts of his dominions, and are ready, at all times, to render him that allegiance, which his protection of our Rights intitle him to, and to sacrifice our lives and fortunes in defence of his person and constitutional government.

5. That the Parliament of Great-Britain has not only assumed, but exercised with unexampled severity, a power over these colonies, to legislate for, and tax them, without their own consent, and by several acts passed in the late session of parliament, for blocking up the port of Boston, the better regulating the government of the province of the Massachusetts Bay, the screening the most flagitious violaters of the laws of the province from a legal tryal, and the establishing the Roman Catholick religion in that extensive country called Canada, has shewn their determination to deprive us of both our civil and religious Rights.

6. That it is a duty every man and body of men, owes to posterity, as well as to God and their country, to oppose with all their power the execution of said acts, and that we strongly recommend it to the inhabitants of the province never to submit to them in any instance whatever.

7. That the provision made in one of said acts for the appointment of a council and of civil officers, in this province, and the tenure of their several offices, together with the manner of returning jurors, at once destroys every idea of free legislation, and an impartial administration of justice, and breaks down that inestimable barrier of liberty, and security of life and property, a trial by our peers, by rendering the whole of them a set of ministerial tools and hirelings.

8. That those persons, who have accepted seats at the council board, by mandamus from the King, in conformity to a late act of the British parliament, have violated the fundamental rights of the society they belonged to, have traiterously attempted to destroy the constitution of their country, which they were bound by the laws of God and man to defend; and have by their persevering obstinacy, against the entreaties of their fellow-countrymen, exposed themselves to their just resentment and indignation.

9. That the judges, justices, sheriffs and other civil officers in the province, who were appointed to their several offices agreeable to the charter and laws of the same, and refuse to act in conformity to the acts of parliament, or to assist administration in the execution of them, are the only proper persons who are entitled to the obedience of the people; and that we will aid and support them in the execution of their offices, in the manner usual, before the attempt to alter the constitution of the province, and indemnify their persons and property; and that no legal authority can remove them from their respective offices, except that which is constituted pursuant to the charter, and the laws of this province.

10. That all officers and private persons, who shall presume to conform to, or by any means aid and assist the execution of the late acts of parliament, do by such conduct forfeit that protection and friendship good men in society are entitled to, are and ought to be considered and treated as our inveterate enemies, as men lost to every sense of virtue, and the obligations due to God and man.

11. That every people have a right to meet together when they please, to consult upon their grievances, and the proper methods to be taken for their removal; and that any act which prohibits such meeting, strikes at the foundation of freedom, and will reduce to slavery and misery such as submit to it.

12. That the present exigencies of our public affairs, renders it absolutely necessary that there be a Provincial Congress; and we do recommend it to the several Towns in this county to intrust their Representatives to form themselves into such a Congress, agreeable to the seventh Resolve of the Delegates for the county of Essex for the purposes there mentioned.

13. That our enemies may be disappointed, and we be the better enabled to make that last appeal which the laws of God and nature will justify—We recommend it to the people of this county, to apply themselves with all diligence, and in the most effectual manner, to learn military discipline, and to equip themselves *immediately* with arms and ammunition according to law.

14. That whereas the present circumstances of the Province are such, that if the public monies now raised should be paid into the public treasuries, they may be misapplied, perhaps to purposes detrimental to the interest of the people—We therefore recommend to the collectors of taxes, sheriffs and other officers in this county, to retain the same in their hands, and not to make any payment thereof to the province treasurer, until the civil government of the province is placed upon a constitutional foundation, or until it shall otherwise be ordered by the proposed Provincial Congress; and that they be indemnified in their persons and property for so doing.

15. That the fortifications erected on Boston neck, the seizing the powder in the magazine at Charlestown, the prohibiting the keeper of the magazine at Boston to deliver out powder which is private property, and many other instances of the conduct of the army and commander in chief, are justly alarming, and give us the strongest reasons to apprehend hostile intentions against the town of Boston in particular, and the province in general.

16. That if any persons who have distinguished themselves by virtuously contending for the violated rights and liberties of this country, should be seized in order to be transported to England, or in any way subjected to the tyrannical power of administration now prevailing—We do recommend that the good people of this county immediately make reprisals, by seizing and keeping in safe custody, every servant of the present tyrannical government, and all such as are known to have favoured and abetted their measures, and detain them till our friends are restored safe and uninjured to their respective families.

17. That it is highly proper and necessary for the Towns to continue to meet and transact their affairs as usual, and we recommend to the Selectmen of the several Towns in this County, to issue their Warrants for calling Town Meetings agreeable to the Laws of the Province, and former Usages, and to the Constables to warn the same, whenever their Circumstances require it, and to the People in the County to support each other in the exercise of a Privilege and a Right by long experience found

so beneficial to their interest and happiness.

18. That it is justifiable in, and proper for, the People at such a time as this, to prevent any Courts sitting and proceeding to business, or any Officer of any Court executing his office, who shall refuse when requested to make and sign a full and ample declaration, expressing their abhorrence of the late innovations attempted in our Constitution, and that they do not now, nor will at any time hereafter, hold their commissions in any other way than what is prescribed by the Charter and well known Constitution of this Province, and that they will not in any way countenance, aid or support the execution of the late acts of Parliament.

19. That the circumstances of the country require and make it necessary that we should (until our Rights are fully restored) withhold all commercial intercourse with Great-Britain and Ireland, and refrain from the consumption of British Manufactures and Merchandize, especially East-India Teas, and other Goods, subject to such additions, alterations and exceptions only, as the *Grand Congress* of the Colonies may agree to.

20. We recommend to the several Towns in this County, to make provision for, and to order the payment of their several Representatives out of their Town-Treasuries, in order to do justice to them, and at the same time defeat one of the machinations of our enemies.

21. That those Justices of the Courts of General Sessions of the Peace and Common Pleas for this County, who at the last Term, in the name of the whole, addressed his Excellency Governor GAGE, have therein, wantonly, without reason and without provocation, aspersed the Clergy, the Committees of Correspondence, and other good People of this County, and thereby shewn that they have no tender feelings for the distresses of their Country, and can rejoice at their calamities.

22. That this County should entertain a high sense of gratitude for the benevolent alacrity and readiness shewn by our Brethren in the other Colonies to aid and support this Province under our present distresses, and to come to our relief, whenever the blood-thirsty malice of our enemies shall make it necessary.

23. That Edward Winslow, jun. one of the two clerks of the Court of General Sessions of the Peace, and Court of Common Pleas, for this County, has, by refusing this Body a copy of an Address made at the last Term in this County, to *Thomas Hutchinson*, Esq; betrayed the Trust reposed in him, and by refusing his Attendance when requested, treated the Body of this County with insult and contempt, and by that means rendered himself unworthy to serve the County in said office.

24. That it be earnestly recommended to the Inhabitants of this County, that they carefully avoid all Riots, Routs, Tumults and Disturbances, under our present distressed Circumstances, and that they maintain all that Peace and good Order that the Nature of our present Situation will admit. *A true Copy.*

THOMAS LOTHROP, Clerk.

Mess. EDES and GILL,

As the Provincial Congress is to meet To-Morrow and sit at Concord, on Business of the greatest Importance that ever came before an Assembly, since the Massachusetts was a Government: And as at least one principal Town has (I hear) instructed its Delegates to endeavour that the Councellors appointed by Mandamus, those detested YET LIVING MISCREANTS, *who have solemnly taken the Oath of God to act in an Office, subversive of, and as appears, with intent to destroy the Constitution of this their Native Land! be Impeached and Tryed for High Treason against the State. You are requested to insert in your next Paper the following Opinion of that Great and Good Man, Lord* SOMERS, *his Judgment of whole Kingdoms, viz.*

"Major hæreditas venit unicuique nostrum a "jure et legibus quam a parentibus." 2 Inst. 56.

"The *first and highest Treason* is that which is "committed *against the Constitution.*" Lord Sommers's Judgment of whole Kingdoms, p. 8.—"Est autem "*injuria* omne quod non *jure* fit." Fleta, l. 2, c. 1. And, on the other hand, "they neither are, nor can be "Traitors, who endeavour to preserve and maintain the "Constitution; but they are the Traitors, who design "and pursue the subversion of it; they are the Rebels, "that go about to overthrow the Government of their "Country; whereas such as seek to support and defend "it are the *truly loyal persons*, and do act conformable to "the ties and obligations of fealty." Lord Sommers, p. 9.—Agreeable to this doctrine was the answer of Dr. Sharp, archbishop of York, when the question was put to him, "How a person, who had sworn Allegiance "to King James, could, with a good conscience, take "the same oath to King William?" To which he replied, "That the laws of the land are the only rule of "our conscience in this matter, and we are no further "bound to pay obedience to governors, nor to any other "governors than the Laws enjoin. *If*, therefore, K. W. "in the eye of the Law, be our King, we must in conscience pay obedience to him as such. I take this" (says he) "for a certain truth, that, *as the Law makes* "*the King*, so the same *Law* extends, or limits, or *transfers*, our obedience and allegiance; and all Oaths imposed by the Law oblige the conscience no further "than the Law meant they should oblige. Only this "is always to be remembered, that whatever Obedience "the Laws of the land require of us, it is to be understood with this proviso, that it be not contradictory to "the Laws of God. But in that case we must obey "passively, though we cannot obey actively: and with "this tacit condition I do suppose all oaths of fidelity in "the world are given and taken." Life of Abp. Sharp, part 3d, page 24 25, and 26. MS. wrote by his Son, for the use of his Grandchildren.

SALEM, October 7.

Yesterday Morning about Three o'Clock a most terrible Fire broke out here which began in a Store belonging to, and by the Dwelling-House of Peter Frye, Esq; in King-Street, which raged to a Degree never before known in this Town or County, whereby nine Dwelling Houses, and a Number of Stores and Shops, besides the Rev. Dr. Whittaker's Meeting House were consumed.

PHILADELPHIA, September 28.

We are assured that General Carlton, Governor of Quebec, is sailed from England, and has Orders to raise 30,000 Canadians, who are to act under the Mandates of Lord North, who we are told, has *sworn*, that *he will lay the Americans at his Feet.*

BOSTON, October 10.

Extract of a Letter from Philadelphia, Sept. 30, 1774.

"The Congress have determined upon a Non-exportation Agreement, to take Place next September, in Case the obnoxious Acts are not repealed before that Time."

The Postscript of another Letter from that Place informs us, "That at Newcastle, 400 Miles from Boston, 1000 Men were in Arms in 100 Hours from the Date of Col. Putnam's Letter, and on the Account thereof."

Last Friday Morning Morning died Mr. Samuel Ruggles, aged 67 Years, a noted Housewright of this Town. His Funeral will be this Afternoon, at 5 o'Clock, when his Friends and Acquaintance are desir'd to attend.

Died last Thursday at Princeton, greatly lamented, Miss Nabby Tailer, of this Town.

Died at Charlestown, Mrs. Mary Rogers, Wife to Mr. Jacob Rogers, late a Lieutenant of his Majesty's Navy. Her Funeral is to be this Afternoon at 4 o'Clock, from their House in Charlestown; when the attendance of their Friends is requested.

Messi'rs EDES & GILL. *By inserting the following two Weeks in your Paper, will much oblige*

Your humble Servant, RICHARD HINKLEY.

SOME Time since I sign'd an Address to Governor Hutchinson on his leaving this Province, which I acknowledge was done through Inadvertency, not thinking of the many bad Consequences which might arise therefrom. I hereby desire the Publick to forgive me for that one Act of Impudence, and promise never to do any Thing of the like Nature again, but assure them I will do all in my Power to help the common Cause, which we are all so deeply concerned in.

THE Bishop of St. Asaph's excellent SPEECH, intended to have been spoken on the Bill for altering the Constitution of this Government, will be Published To-Morrow in a Pamphlet, and to be sold by the Printers.——It was sold in England for ONE SHILLING STERLING, but the Price here is no more than *Six Coppers.* We set it at this low Price in order that it may be universally purchased and read: It is (at the particular Desire of many Gentlemen) printed in a Pamphlet, rather than News-Papers, that the Contents of so truly valuable a Performance may be more effectually preserved for the Perusal of future Generations.

William Blair Townsend,

At the Three Doves,

In Marlborough-Street, Boston;

Hereby advertizes his Customers and ohters, That he is now selling off his Shop Goods for *Cash*, by Wholesale and Retail, at the low Rate of Eleven for One, on the true Sterling Cost; (being as low as they can be imported) consisting chiefly of Woollens, and well suited for the approaching Winter Season; *and which they may depend were imported, before the oppressive acts on this Town and Province were laid*; and may therefore be safely transported *by Land*, and Sold in any Town of said Province, without any Breach on the solemn League and Covenant our worthy Friends in the Country have justly entered into, in Defence of themselves and their Posterity.

N. B. Those that incline to purchase, are desired to apply speedily; as said TOWNSEND is determined to remove into a clear Air in the Country, *very soon.*

☞ *Imported before August last,*

And now for Sale, at the Shop of

Duncan Ingraham, Jun.

In Union-Street, *BOSTON*,

An Assortment of English, India and Scotch Goods, at a very moderate Profit, Wholesale and Retail. O. 10 6 w.

N. B. Wanted at said Shop 300 Yards Check Woollen ⅞ Wide, for which English or West-India Goods will be given in Payment.

TO BE SOLD,

Ten or Twelve Thousand seasoned Pine BOARDS. Inquire of the Printers.

LANDED from on Board Capt. DIAMOND's Schooner, on Monday last, on WHEELWRIGHT's Wharf, in Boston, a Trunk directed to THOMAS FLUCKER, Esq; on a Card nail'd thereon, No. 2, & contained a Quantity of Linnen, sundry Suits of Apparel, and some small Articles—Whoever can Inform the Printers where said Trunk may be found shall be well rewarded.

For LONDON.

THE Mast-Ship FOX, ZACHARIAH NORMAN, *Commander, having good Accommodations and Conveniences for a few genteel Passengers: Will sail from Portsmouth in New-Hampshire, about the 20th of this Month;—apply to Edward Parry, or Capt. Norman, at Portsmouth.*

October 3, 1774.

JUST PUBLISHED, and to be Sold at GREENLEAF's Printing-Office in Hanover Street,

[Embellished with an elegant Engraving]

NUMBER VIII, of

The Royal American Magazine.

TO BE SOLD,

Five Barrels of BEEF, in good Order, on reasonable Terms, if apply'd for immediately. Enquire of *Thomas Clarke*, near the Rev. Mr. *Adams's* Meeting-House in *Roxbury.*

TWO DOLLARS REWARD.

STRAYED or Stolen out of the Pasture of MARY TUFTS, in Medford, a large dark bay Horse, about 11 Years old, 15 Hands high, his Mane cut on the right side, a Star in his Forehead, White by his Nose, Trots and Paces, carries his Head low. Whoever will bring said Horse to me the Subscriber, shall have the above Reward, and all necessary Charges paid by

MARY TUFTS.

TO BE SOLD

10,000 Acres of very fine Land, in the Island of St. JOHN's, being half of one of the best Townships in it, About 500 Acres of which are clear'd and mostly arable Land. 'Tis situated on a Navigable River, 25 Miles above Charlotte Town, the Seat of Government, with which it has Communication both by River and a good Cart Road. There are some Families from Nantucket settled upon it. The Townships adjoining are well settled, and the Island in general in a Prosperous way. Captain *Holland*, who survey'd the Island, reports this Township to the Board of Trade, by whose Order he survey'd it, in the following Words, viz. "*Clear'd Lands* 1000 *Acres, Houses* 30, *pretty well situated for Fishing and Tillage, or Pasture, inferior to none upon the Island; there is also Plenty of Game and Fish.*"

Also, to be sold by the same Person,

10,000 Acres of choice good Land on the River St. John's in the Bay of Fundy, all settled agreeable to the Terms required by Government, which secures it forever from Forfeiture. For further Particulars enquire of Mr. *Warden*, Merchant, at his Store on Green's Wharf, or of the Printers hereof.

This is to Notify the Proprietors of Pearsontown, in the County of Cumberland, that at a legal Meeting of said Proprietors, held at Falmouth in said County, on the 31st Day of March last, a tax of fifteen shillings was assess'd on each right for the support of the Minister and other necessary charges, for bringing forward the settlement of said township, and to pay said tax or assessment (as well as former arrearages of taxes due on their several rights heretofore granted by said proprietors, and legally advertiz'd) to Ephraim Jones of said Falmouth, treasurer of said proprietors, or to the subscribers the proprietors committee, on or before the 9th day of January next, otherwise their several lots and rights there, will be sold at Public Vendue at the House of Mr. Moses Shattuck, Innholder, in said Falmouth, on the said 9th day of January next for the payment of said taxes as the Law directs: The said sale to begin at ten of the clock in the forenoon.

Falmouth, Sept. 6, 1774. Enoch Freeman, Moses Pearson, Ste. Longfellow } Propriet's Com'tee.

STOLEN out of a Pasture at Roxbury on Thursday Night the 6th Instant, a brown Mare about 14 Hands high, she has a Star in her Forehead, one of her Fetter-Lock Joints of her hind Feet white, her Main hangs on the near Side, and a Feather on the other Side of her Neck, she is uncommonly square built and Trots strong and bold, she has a lofty Carriage and carries a high Tail. Whoever apprehends the Thief so that he may be brought to Justice, and returns the Mare to Mr. Joseph Morton at Boston, at the sign of the white Horse, South-End, shall have THIRTY DOLLARS *Reward, and if the Mare alone Fifteen Dollars, and all necessary Charges paid. by me the Subscriber,*

Boston, Oct. 10, 1774. *JOSEPH MORTON.*

TAKEN up by me the Subscriber, on the 25th ulto. a Sorrel Horse. The Owner may have him again, proving his Property and paying the Charges, by applying to Seth Clark, of Medfield.

Stop Thief!

WHEREAS the Shop of the Subscriber was last Night broke open, and robbed of Twelve Beaver and Six Beaverett HATTS.—This is to promise a Reward of TEN DOLLARS, to any Person who shall discover the Thief or Thieves, so that he or they may be convicted thereof, and the HATTS recovered, and in Proportion for any Part of them.

JAMES CODNER.

Boston, Tuesday Morning, October 4, 1774

New AUCTION-ROOM, Cornhill

TO MORROW MORNING, at TEN o'Clock,

Will be sold by PUBLIC VENDUE,

At GREENLEAF's Auction Room,

A Variety of English Goods as usual.

On WEDNESDAY next,

At TEN in the Morning,

Will be Sold by PUBLIC VENDUE,

At HUNTER's Auction-Room,

(Lately improved as a Store by Mr. Thomas Walley)

A large Assortment of ENGLISH GOODS as usual.

WM. HUNTER, Auctioneer.

Also, Two Casks of Kippen's Snuff

Wednesday Morning the Sale to begin at 10 o'Clock.

Burials in the Town of BOSTON, since our last.

Seventeen Whites. NO Black.

Baptiz'd in the several Churches, Five.

High Water at BOSTON, *for the present Week.*

Monday, 28 min. aft.	3	Friday, 8 min. after.	7
Tuesday, 22 min. aft.	4	Saturday, 58 min. aft.	7
Wednesday, 19 m. aft.	5	Lord's Day 46 m. af.	8
Thursday, 12 min. aft.	6	☽'s First Q. 12 Day 7 M.	

(Advertisments omitted, will be in our next.)

11. 12. Will. 3. 4. Par. 3.

"THAT if any Papist, or Person making Professions of the Popish Religion, shall be convict of keeping School, or taking upon themselves the Education or Government, *or boarding of Youth*, in any Place within this Realm, *or the Dominions thereunto belonging*, they shall be adjudged to PERPETUAL IMPRISONMENT." ——Good Law: If this shall be the Punishment only for boarding Youth, or keeping School, &c. Pray what shall we think of those Right Reverend Fathers in God, those precious Saints of the Earth, who have established the Roman Catholic Religion at Quebec; for we may reasonably suppose that the Parliament were mainly guided in Matters of Religion, more especially by Christ's Vicegerants, by that truly pious——venerable and learned Set of Men:——Good God! Are such the truly, pious, venerable and learned? Who then are the impious, profane and ignorant! O England!!! Where are you? What are you about? IN GOD's NAME, I CALL UPON YOU. Will you not rise in the Cause of your God? I shudder——I leave you in the Hands of that Almighty Being who cannot be deceived, and who will not be mocked; who is able to espouse and fully to vindicate his own Cause.——Surely they who are not for us, are against us——who profess the Religion of the meek and lowly Jesus? These dreadful Right Reverend Fathers in God—who have established (if I may be allowed the Expression) the Religion *of the fallen Angels*, by Act of Parliament, or that Religion which is at Antipodes with the true and holy Religion of Jesus? Why the same Set of Right Rev. Creatures——Surely God's Patience is lengthened out even to Long-Suffering!

Oh England! Have you forgot the glorious Revolution which set the Ancestors of our present King (who glories in being born a Briton) upon the Throne? Remember that what is begun at Quebec, must and will end in *London*, UNLESS——it is well known to a Set of Men (who arrogantly assume to themselves the Stile and Title of *Lords Spiritual*, which by the Way I look upon as bordering upon Profanity; as also that of *our most Gracious Sovereign*; for God is my most gracious Sovereign and none but he; George the Third is my Earthly King, and that by Compact, nor do I owe him Allegiance longer than he affords me his Protection.) I say it is well known to these Reverend Gentry, that I could easily adduce many, many more Authorities, and which look them fuller in the Face, but at present for their sakes I forbear, and hope I shall not be oblig'd to rally again.—The English Bishops go to bed with me at Night and rise with me in the Morning, I am constrained to give them all the Credit due to such a notorious set of Beings—they have indeed in one respect literally conformed to St. Paul's Charge to Timothy, *i. e.* they have been instant *out of Season* or as it is understood by some unseasonably, as in the Case of Quebec: I would just ask these Holy Ghost Men whether they in Conscience think, that were the Apostle Paul, permitted to come amongst some of them on Christmas Eve say, when they may be suppos'd to be as full of the Spirit as at almost any time; whether he would confirm their rectilineal descent from him and the rest of the holy Apostles?—I cannot say but that I have some Scruples—much may be said on that Head—I judge not in that Matter, but chearfully leave that and them to him who Judgeth right; and among other Things for the establishing (mainly thro' their Instrumentality) the Romish Religion at Quebec, Anno 1774.——I must say for my self, I never thought that these Absolvers were descended as they contend for, though I have heard some shrewd Arguments that there was even more than a bare probability that they might possibly have descended from some one Individual of them full as Notorious as was even St. Paul himself, and that before his Conversion,—but as I understand that, that will be made one of the disputable Questions the ensuing Commencement, shall wave it for the present, after all am apt to think it will remain problematical at least, as there are so many large Chasms to fill up, however what they cannot prove directly, they may according to some modern Doctrine affirm by a seeming necessary Consequence or Implication.

J. TILLOTSON.

THIS DAY PUBLISHED,

And sold by the Printers hereof; Price 9d.

CONSIDERATION on the Measures carrying on with respect to the British Colonies in North-America.

JOSIAH QUINCY, Jun'r.

Having resigned his Business into the Hands of Mr. PEREZ MORTON, and embarked for London, desires all his Clients who want to know the state of their Affairs, to call on said Morton for Information:—All Persons who are indebted to said Quincy, *on Account*, are desired to make Payment to said Morton, and any who may have Damands on said Quincy, are requested to apply to the same Gentleman for their Discharge.—Those Persons who owe the said Quincy, on Bond or Note, are hereby notified to make their Payments to WILLIAM PHILLIPS, Esq; Attorney to JOSIAH QUINCY, jun.

Caleb Blanchard

in Union-Street,

Has on Hand, a large Assortment of Goods suitable for the Season, which he will sell at the very lowest Rates for ready Money.

TO BE SOLD Cheap

At *Benjamin Goldthwait's* Shop,

just above Concert-Hall, Boston.

Superfine Scarlet and white Broad-Cloths, superfine Garnett ditto, white & Buff Casimeers, figur'd Velvets, Corduroy of all colours, silk and worsted Breeches Patterns of all colours, &c. &c.

The Taylor's Business as usual, is carried on in the best Manner at said Shop.

☞ At his Cellar near said Shop is to be sold choice ORANGE JUICE, by the Cask or smaller Quantity.

Evening School.

THIS Evening *JOHN GRIFFITH*'s School in Hanover Street will be opened, to teach Writing and Arithmetic, from 6 to 8 o'Clock, where those who incline to be taught may apply.

William Bant

BEGS Leave to inform his Friends, Customers and others, That he has to sell by Wholesale and Retail at his Store fronting Dock-Square, Boston——

A general Assortment of *English* and *India*

GOODS,

Suitable for the approaching Season: (*the whole of which was imported before the 31st of August last.*) Among his GOODS is a prime Choice of superfine

Scarlet, Pompadore, white, green, pea green, sea green, barry, black, blue, brown and cloth colour'd BROAD CLOTHS; midling and low priz'd Ditto, with Shalloons and Trimmings to match the Cloths: ALSO of SILKS, viz.—Padusoys, Ducapes, Mantuas, Lutestrings, English and India Damasks, *a Piece of fine white Lutestring*, single and double Sattins, black, white and crimson figur'd Sattin, black, blue, green and white half yard Persians, ell-wide Persians, half ell and ell-wide Alamodes, Brolios, black, blue and crimson thick Corduroys for Men's Waistcoats; and a Variety of other Articles that are commonly in Use at this Season of the Year.

☞ The above mentioned GOODS will be disposed of at the very lowest Rates, as said Bant is extremely desirous of exchanging all or any of them, for an Article, which is more convenient for him, in these troublesome Times, viz. CASH.

Just Imported, by

Geyer and Burgess,

In the Ship London, Capt. Calef, from London,

A general Assortment of English and India Piece Goods, which they will sell on the most reasonable Terms by Wholesale only, at their Store in King-Street, Boston.

They would also acquaint their Customers and others, who carry their Goods by Water, that they have taken a Store at Salem, near the Town-House, where they may be supply'd with equal Variety, and on the same Terms as at Boston.

An Evening School

Will be opened on Monday next, by JOHN DRUITT, at his School in Hanover Street, near Concert-Hall, where Reading, Writing, and Arithmetic will be taught after the most approved Method—NAVIGATION and BOOK KEEPING on moderate Terms; in Compliance with the Times no Entrance will be requir'd.——His Hours of Attendance will be from 6 till 9 o'Clock, (P. M.)

☞ To the LADIES,

He begs Leave to acquaint those who wou'dn't choose to attend a School, or that the Inclemency of the approaching Season might hinder, that he will wait on them at their Places of Abode, at any Hour from 8 to 11 in the Forenoon, or from 2 'till 4 in the Afternoon.

Mrs. DRUITT has lower'd her Terms for plain Sewing to *Eight Pence* Law. Money per Week, (her other Works as usual) and hopes to convince those who are pleas'd to try, that there is as much to be learn'd in Winter as in Summer.

ALL Persons having any Demand on the Estate of Mr. *John Ruggles*, late of Boston, Housewright, deceas'd, are desired to bring in their Accounts—And all Persons indebted to said Estate are desired to make payment to *Hannah Ruggles*, Administratrix, or to *Samuel Ruggles*, jun'r. her Attorney.

Providence STAGE COACH,

Kept by ANDREW COMSTOCK & SAMUEL BARTER.

WHO beg Leave to inform the Public, That they have removed from the White Horse Tavern to Mr. Jolley Allen's, a few Doors South of the Governor's, in Marlborough Street; where the greatest Care will be taken of all Bundles, Letters, &c. with which they may be entrusted:—They keep several Setts of the best Horses on purpose for this Business, and will engage to carry Passengers with the greatest Expedition, at the cheapest Rate.

EIGHT DOLLARS REWARD.

STOLEN out of the Tan House of the Subscriber, on Friday Evening last, a Quantity of SOLE LEATHER. Whoever will secure the Thief or Thieves, so that he or they shall be confined in any of his Majesty's Goals, shall be paid the above Reward by me

Charlestown, Oct. 3d. JAMES TRUMBALL.

FOUR DOLLARS REWARD.

RAN-AWAY from the Subscriber on the 22d of September, at Night, a Negro Man Servant, by the Name of CATO, about Five Feet and Eight Inches high, very thick Lips, speaks broken, and Walks as if he was lame in his Heels. Had on when he went away, a Cloth colour'd Coat, with Pewter Buttons, old Leather Breeches, a Tow Shirt, old Shoes with Silver plate Buckles, wore a Cap, and shoves round his Neck, and very high on his Forehead: Carried away with him a Callico Banyan, fine Linen Shirt, Check Linen Trowsers, grey Wigg, also carries or Wears a Felt Hatt with a Silver Lace on it, had a Violin and carries it in a green Bays Bag. Whosoever will return the Runaway to his Master in Winchenden, shall have the above Reward and all necessary Charges paid by LEVI NICHOL.

Winchenden, Sept. 23d, 1774.

STOP THIEF!

ABSCONDED from the Subscriber on the 3d Day of August last, a Negro Man, called TOM, had on a Pair of black Plush Breeches, a light coloured ragged Jacket, Lame in both his Feet: Said Negro return'd the last Night broke open his Master's Stable, stole from thence a valuable Chesnut-colour'd Horse, with a small white Spot on his Forehead, Paces and Trots light, and took a Saddle (with a white Housen) and Bridle; he has with him a counterfeit Pass.

Whoever will take up said Thief and Horse, shall have FOUR DOLLARS, and all necessary Charges paid, by SIMEON POLLEY.

Boston, Sept. 28, 1774.

COLONY OF RHODE-ISLAND.

WHEREAS ELEAZER TREVETT, jun'r. of Newport, in the County of Newport, Marriner, preferred a Petition unto the General Assembly, representing that he is an Insolvent Debtor, and praying that he may be admitted to the Benefit of an Act pass'd in June, A. D. 1756, entitled "An Act for the Relief of Insolvent Debtors," Whereupon the General Assembly referred the said Petition to the next Sessions and Ordered that in the mean Time his Creditors should be Notified by an Advertisement to be inserted in the Newport Mercury, the Providence Gazette, and in one of the Boston News Papers, to appear then and answer the same: I do therefore hereby Notify the Creditors of the said ELEAZER TREVETT, jun'r. to appear if they shall think fit at the General Assembly to be holden at Providence, in and for the said Colony, on the last Wednesday in October next, then and there to shew Cause if any they have, why the said Petition should not be granted.

HENRY WARD, Secr'y.

STOLEN out of a Pasture in Charlestown, about Four Miles from the Ferry, on Monday Night last, a light Red Mare, Four Years old, with a white Spot on her Nose, her Fore Mane long, her other Mane hanging the off Side, her Feet lighter Colour than her Body, Fourteen Hands and half high. Whoever shall take up said Mare, and return her to the Owner, shall have FOUR DOLLARS Reward, or TEN DOLLARS for the Thief and Horse, and all necessary Charges paid, by

Charlestown, Sept. 27, 1774. STEPHEN GODDARD.

N. B. The following Bill, supposed to be drop'd by the Thief, was taken up in the Pasture from whence the Mare was stolen, viz. Breakfast, 3s. 6. Punch, 1s. Porter, 2s. 3. Wine, 15s. 6. Dinner, 4s. Horses 1s. 6d. Total, £ 1. 7s. 9d.

Caleb Call, of Charlestown, Baker,

ACQUAINTS his Friends and Customers, that he will supply them with his White Bisket, at the usual Price, either at *Salem* or *Marblehead*, upon their Writing to him, or applying to Messrs. *Hooper* and *Whittemore*, Coopers, on *Blany's* Wharfe in *Salem*.

Writing and Arithmetic

To be taught in Evenings.

The School to be open'd 1st Monday in October next, at the Writing School House in Queen-Street, and to be continued for the Season.

Where due Care will be taken for Instruction in its various Branches as usual, and it is hoped will meet with a like Acceptance, which shall be the Aim of the Subscriber, an Assistant in one of the public Schools.

Sept. 19. WILLIAM DALL, Jun.

An Evening SCHOOL

WILL be opened on Monday October 3d, at the South Writing School, where WRITING and ARITHMETIC is taught in the most concise and methodical Manner.—— *Attendance at the usual Hours.* *Sept. 22.*

NARRAGANSET-CHEESE.

A Quantity that is extraordinary good, (very like) to Cheshire, to be sold at the Store of PENUEL BOWEN, opposite to the Golden-Ball.

BRANDY & GENEVA.

A few Pipes Old Brandy and Geneva by the Case To be SOLD by

CHARLES MILLER

At his Store in King-Street.

SWEET FLOUR.

To be Sold by HABIJAH SAVAGE, at his Store No. 16 on the Long Wharf,

A few Barrels of Choice Flour, old Jamaica Spirits, West India Rum, Brandy, best Jamaica Sugar, Indigo, Molasses, Rice, Case Bottles, Cases with 12 or 15 Bottles, Cocoa, Peas, Calavances, white Beans, Corn and a Cask of Currants, cheap.

The Commissioners appointed

by the Hon. Foster Hutchinson, Esq; Judge of Probate, &c. for the County of Suffolk, to receive and examine the Claims of the several Creditors to the Estate of Mr. Isaac Cazneau, late of Boston, Sadler, deceas'd, represented Insolvent.——Give Notice that they shall attend said Service at the British-Coffee-House in King-Street, on the second Thursday in the six following Months, from Six to Nine o'Clock, P. M.

Boston, Sept. 15th, 1774.

Boston: Printed, by EDES & GILL, *in Queen-Street*, 1774.

No. 1018.

THE Boston- Gazette, AND COUNTRY JOURNAL.

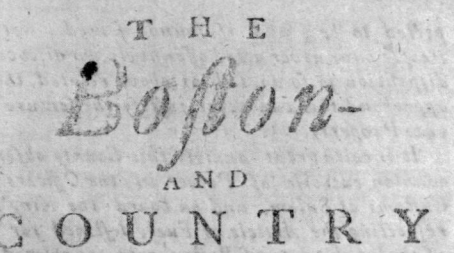

Containing the freshest Advices, Foreign and Domestic.

MONDAY, October 17, 1774.

Monday last Capt. Calahan, *arrived at Salem in 7 Weeks from London, by whom we have the following Advices.*

VIENNA, August 3.

THIS Day at Noon a Courier arrived here with the News of Peace between Russia and the Porte having been concluded on the 17th of July, at the Head Quarters at Buyak Canarochi, and signed, on the Part of their respective Sovereigns, by Marshal Count Romanzow, and Achmed Effendi, Chiaga to the Grand Vizir. (*London Gazette.*)

LONDON,

Aug. 8. *A Correspondent says, the solemn League and Covenant entered into by the Bostonians, is little better than quarrelling with their* Bread and Butter; *for, when they agree to withhold all commercial Intercourse with Great-Britain, they in Effect say, we will not for the future eat or drink, and, as long as we live, we will go naked; they cannot be ignorant, however they may boast, that every Article of Life has been procured by them from England or other Nations; their Port being blocked up, will prevent their smuggling, and they may be sure a strict Watch will be kept by the government at Boston to prevent any Intercourse between that People and other Nations, so that the Natives will have nothing to swallow but the Covenant, and nothing to cover them but the Paper which contains the Form, unless their proud Stomachs come down, and the stubborn Child will take its Bread and Butter from Mamma. It is to be wished too, the naughty covenanting Child is not making a Rod for its own Breech; if the Bostonians find a Precedent for a solemn League and Covenant in the last Century, they must recollect it was during the Time of a Civil War, and would have been considered and punished as Treason, had the Law and Constitution of this Country been at that Time in full Vigour. Our Correspondent has admired, he says, the Spirit of Freedom which has hitherto appeared in the Conduct of the Americans; but he sees with Concern this open Declaration of War with the People of England; they held before by Charter, which they may now change for a Tenure by Treaty; they can now remonstrate as chartered Subjects; they must then sue under the Right of Conquest.*

August 10. *Orders have been given for a further considerable Body of Troops to be held in Readiness for Embarkation to North-America.*

Aug. 11. *Some Accounts of a very alarming Nature are said to have been received by the Ministry concerning the Conduct of the Americans.*

It is privately whispered that within these few Days some very disagreeable Things have passed between our Ministers and the Dutch Ambassador, concerning some late Transactions in America, which have hitherto been concealed from the public Eye.

Several Transport Ships are contracted for on Government Account, to carry more Forces to America.

We hear it is under Consideration to raise a Regiment in the Province of Canada, to be called the Royal Canadians, which are to be officered chiefly by Natives of that Province.

Upon a very moderate Computation it appears, that 60,000 Men are slaughtered every Campaign while the War continues between the Turks and Russians.

Aug. 13. *An Express was sent off 3 Weeks ago to Canada to arm the Militia of that Country with all convenient Speed. The Reason of this Order may be easily guesed at--- to have a Body of Forces in Readiness to assist the Operations of General Gage, in reducing the Malecontents of the Provinces.*

A Correspondent says, that among all the caballing of the Righteous of Boston, and elsewhere in the Massachusetts, &c. nothing appears in their Resolutions in regard to the Payment of the Tea they plundered and destroyed; hence he observes may be known, what an admirable Assembly of Knaves and Trators have been lately grouped together on some late patriotic Occasions.

The same Correspondent adds, that the Patriots may make themselves easy in regard to the naked Poles on Temple Bar, which they have made such a Rout about lately.--- as in all Probability they will be soon decorated with some of the patriotic Noddles of the Boston Saints.

The People of America are unanimous in their Resolutions never to submit to Taxation; and Government is now strangely embarrassed how to withdraw, with any Degree of Credit, their Necks from these now impolitic Steel Traps.

Aug. 15. Letters in Town from Boston bring Accounts, that all Hopes of Accommodation with the Mother Country are over. If any Hopes had remained, General Gage would only have prorogued, and not dissolved their Assembly. The Consequences are evident; their Non-Importation Scheme will likely become general over all America; so that blocking up the Port of Boston, instead of being a Punishment on the Americans, will in fact, annihilate our Export Trade to America, and fall heavy on the British Merchants and Manufacturers.

Aug. 16 *A Gentleman lately arrived from Quebec assures us, that when he was there the Protestants were obliged to exercise their Religion in secret for fear of the Resentment of the Roman Catholics. What then can we expect will be the Fate of the poor Protestants under the late famous Quebec Bill, which we are told, "is founded on the clearest Principles of Justice and Humanity?"*

It is reported that Governor HUTCHINSON will have a Pension for Life on the Irish Establishment.

Aug. 17. *A Correspondent recommends the Framers of the Quebec Bill, to bring in another Bill, for the Establishment of the Protestant Religion also in Canada, that his Majesty's Subjects of both Persuasions may be on a Level.*

August 18. Tuesday the Right Hon. the Earl of Bute arrived at his House in South-Audley-Street from his Seat at Luton-Hoo, in Bedfordshire.

The Right Hon. Lord Camden is greatly indisposed at his Seat at Camden Place, in Kent, and is attended by Dr. Batty and other Physicians.

If we quarrel with the Americans, says a Correspondent, Emigration will be a more melancholy Affair than it has yet been considered, as every Person lost to England will be one gained to the Colonists; and what will this, with the usual Inerease, amount to in Half a Century?

The Warsaw Gazette, of July 27, gives the following Account of the Terms of the Peace concluded between Russia and the Porte on the 17th ult. Russia is to have 20'000'000 Loewen-dollars, as a Compensation for the Expence of the War; she is also to have free Navigation on the Black Sea, and the Independency of the Crimea is to be allowed. According to that Gazette, the Peace was signed between Prince Repnin and Reis Effendi. Thus at last an End is put to a War, in which it is thought not less than three or four hundred thousand Men have been carried off; and of which neither Side will have much to boast.—As the Turks give no Detail of their Military Transactions, and the Russians only such a one as is suited to the Meridian of their own People, and calculated for certain Purposes, no regular Account of their Losses is to be expected, until some future Manstein, among their foreign Officers, shall get free from the Shackles of Power, and give an Account of Things as they really were.

The Peace between the Turks and Russians will, of course, cause the Russian Fleet to return home; but as it will be too late in the Season for them to get to Cronstadt, it is to be hoped if their Ships are suffered to enter any of our Ports to winter, Care will be taken that no Infection may be communicated, as there have been many Reports that they have had infectious Diseases on board their Fleet in the Mediterranean.

'Tis certainly true, that the Settlements on the Continent of America have been made at the Expence of much Blood and Treasure to the Mother Country; and that, Parent-like, she has used every Means in her Power to promote the Trade of her American Children, though they have not (on many Occasions) made the most dutiful Returns. The Smuggling they have practised; and the insolent Behaviour they have made use of to the Officers sent thither, are very high insults to the Mother Country, and Forbearance so long the real Cause of the open and avowed ill Treatment of her at this Time. Had the Stamp Act been proceeded on, and carried into Execution, they would not have dared to have made Tea-pots of their Harbours, and given their finny Inhabitants an East-Indian Decoction. We have only to blame our own Weakness; for, like an over-fond Parent, we have spoiled our Children, and now wonder why they are so rude, though we ourselves were the Cause of it.

The Powers of Europe behave complaisantly to each other for Fear of a War. The same Passions, says a Correspondent, govern the Man and the Child. We dread the Rod from a Consciousness of having deserved it.

We hear that a certain triple-crowned old Lady, who now rules a City, which formerly ruled the World, has wrote a Letter of Thanks to Somebody, for a late ACT of Indulgence to her dear Children to the Westward of the Atlantic Ocean.

Yesterday some dispatches arrived at Lord Dartmouth's office with some dispatches from his Excellency Sir Basil Keith, governor of Jamaica.

Three men of war of the line are now under sailing orders, as a reinforcement to the squadron on the Mediterranean station, in consequence of some dispatches received from the Governor of Gibralter.

We are informed, that one House in this City only, remits over to Holland, half yearly, 60,000l. for the Interest of Money which the Dutch have in our Public Funds.

They write from Paris, that it was daily expected there to hear of the Disgrace of two very celebrated and popular Noblemen in that City in consequence of some secret Transactions which have been carried on since the late King's Death, and are just come to Light.

TO be Sold by the Subscriber, a FARM lying in the Heart of the Town of Rochester, in the County of Plymouth, containing about 100 Acres, with a large Dwelling House, Barn and Corn-House on the same, well fenced, a good Orchard, a good Well of Water &c. exceeding for Tillage, and a large Proportion of Fresh Meadow and Pasture Ground, very convenient for a Trader or Tradesman. It is the Tenement the late Rev. Mr. Timothy Ruggles owned at his Decease. The Premises may be purchased very cheap for Cash or short Credit. TIMOTHY RUGGLES.

October 10, 1774.

To be Sold to the highest Bidder, by Virtue of an Order of the Superior Court;

A Part of the Real Estate of Caleb Dana, late of Cambridge, in the County of Middlesex, Esq; deceased, for the Payment of his Debts, and the Charges of Sale, viz.

Several Lots of Land lying in the Town of *Royalston*, in the County of *Worcester*, containing in the Whole, 1500 Acres. The Sale to be at the House of Mr. JACOB EASTY, Innholder, in said *Royalston*, on Thursday the 24th Day of November next, at Nine o'Clock in the Forenoon. GEO. DANA, Executor.

Ashburnham, October 13th, 1774.

WHEREAS I *Samuel Wilder*, having this day been called before a considerable and respectable body of Gentlemen, who this day met for to examine into my conduct: I hereby (for myself) acknowledge that my conduct in many respects with regard to public affairs, in this distress for liberty—has been very blameable—altho' I think the charge alledg'd against me in some circumstances goes beyond what I'm guilty of—Yet I acknowledge myself to blame in many respects, and do hereby ask the forgiveness of this body of Gentlemen, and hereby acknowledge the kind and generous conduct of these Gentlemen with me, and do hereby promise that I will for the future do all that lyes in my power to prevent all and every act of Parliament tending to deprive us of our natural Charter Rights. I do hereby promise that after the reading and acknowledging this Instrument I will not in any way make any sport or complaint of the treatment I have met with this day, and I further promise that I will pursue all laudable measures for obtaining and preserving our Charter Rights: And I pray Gentlemen that I may be restor'd into your favourable opinion and brotherly friendship.

SAMl. WILDER.

I willingly consent to have this publish'd. } *Ashburnham, Sept. 13, 1774.*

N. B. The foregoing is (Verbatim) a true Copy of the Confessions of the above named Gentleman, who was put into Office by Mr. Hutchinson, the late Governor of this Province, and by the stile and sense of said Confessions, we may judge of the Qualifications by him thought necessary to intitle him to a Commission.

Samuel Abbot

Informs his Customers and others,

That he is now selling off his Goods (all which were imported before the 1st of *August* last) extreme cheap for cash, at his Store the head of *Green's* Wharf, nigh the Market.

He once more requests all Persons who are indebted to him, and to the late Co-partnership of *Samuel Abbot* and Company, to make immediate Payment.

LEE & JONES,

At their Store near the Swing-Bridge, have for Sale

A general Assortment of Piece Goods

suitible for the present Season,

A beautiful Variety of Brocades, figur'd & strip'd Lutestrings, Taffaties & Gorgoreens, black Armozeens and Padusoys, flower'd Sattins of all Colours for Ladies Cloaths, a few best Ermine Muffs and Tippets.—— Gold and Silver Laces, Silver Watches, Looking Glasses, Paper-Hangings, Corks, a few Cases of blue and white China Cups and Saucers, Liverpool and Glass Ware.

West India RUM by the Hogshead,

Cornish's New-England FISH-HOOKS.

*** Also *Nails of all Sorts* to be deliver'd at *Marblehead.*

TO BE SOLD,

Ten or Twelve Thousand seasoned Pine BOARDS. Inquire of the Printers.

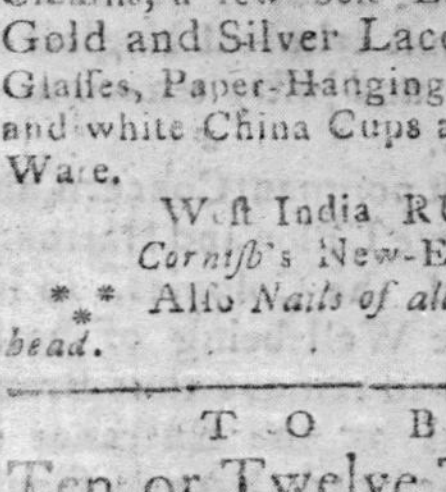

For LONDON.

THE Mast-Ship FOX, ZACHARIAH NORMAN, *Commander, having good Accommodations and Conveniences for a few genteel Passengers: Will sail from Portsmouth in New-Hampshire, about the 20th of this Month;—apply to Edward Parry, or Capt. Norman, at Portsmouth.* October 3. 1774.

TWO DOLLARS REWARD.

STRAYED or Stolen out of the Pasture of MARY TUFTS, in Medford, a large dark bay Horse, about 11 Years old, 15 Hands high, his Mane cut on the right side, a Star in his Forehead, White by his Nose, Trots and Paces, carries his Head low. Whoever will bring said Horse to me the Subscriber, shall have the above Reward, and all necessary Charges paid by

MARY TUFTS.

BOSTON, October 17.

On TUESDAY the 11th Instant the PROVINCIAL CONGRESS met at *Concord*, when the Hon. JOHN HANCOCK, Esq; was chosen President, and BENJAMIN LINCOLN, Esq; Secretary.

FRIDAY last the following Message was presented to his Excellency the Governor, *viz*.

In Provincial Congress, Thursday, Octo. 13. 1774.

ORDERED, That Col. *Lee*, Hon. Col. *Ward*, Col. *Orne*, Capt. *Gardner*, *Henry Gardner*, Esq; Mr. *Devins*, Mr. *Gorham*, Capt. *Browne*, Col. *Pomeroy*, Hon. Col. *Prescot*, Col. *Thayer*, Mr. *Williams*, Capt. *Heath*, Capt. *Upham*, Mr. *Barns*, Capt. *Doolittle*, Mr. *Lothrop*, Major *Thompson*, Mr. *Palmer*, Mr. *Pickering* and Capt. *Thompson*, be a Committee to wait on his Excellency with the following Message.

JOHN HANCOCK, *President*.

May it please your Excellency,

THE Delegates from the several Towns in the Province of the Massachusetts-Bay, having convened in General Congress, beg leave to address your Excellency: The distressed and miserable State of the Province, occasioned by the intolerable Grievances and Oppressions to which this People are subjected, and the Danger and Destruction to which they are exposed, of which your Excellency must be sensible, and the want of a General Assembly have rendered it indispensably necessary to collect the Wisdom of the Province by their Delegates in this Congress, to concert some adequate Remedy for preventing impending Ruin, and providing for the public Safety.

It is with the utmost Concern we see your hostile Preparations which have spread such an Alarm throughout this Province and the whole Continent, as threatens to involve us in all the Confusion and Horrors of a Civil War; and while we contemplate an Event so deeply to be regretted by every good Man, it must occasion the Surprize and Astonishment of all Mankind, that such Measures are pursued against a People whose Love of Order, Attachment to Britain, and Loyalty to their Prince, have ever been exemplary.

Your Excellency must be sensible that the sole End of Government is the Protection and Security of the People; whenever therefore that Power which was originally instituted to effect these important and valuable Purposes, is employed to harrass, distress or enslave the People, in this Case it becomes a Curse rather than a Blessing. The most painful Apprehensions are excited in our Minds by the Measures now pursuing, the vigorous Execution of the Port-Bill with improved Severity, must eventually reduce the Capital and its numerous Dependancies to a State of Poverty and Ruin: The Acts for altering the Charter and the Administration of Justice in the Colony, are manifestly designed to abridge this People of their Rights, and to licence Murders; and if carried into Execution, will reduce them to a State of Slavery: The Number of Troops in the Capital encreasing by daily Accessions drawn from the whole Continent, together with the formidable and hostile Preparations which you are now making on Boston Neck, in our Opinion greatly endanger the Lives, Liberties and Properties, not only of our Brethren in the Town of Boston, but of this Province in general. Permit us to ask your Excellency! Whether an inattentive and unconcerned Acquiescence to such alarming, such menacing Measures, would not evidence a State of Insanity; or whether the delaying to take every possible Precaution for the Security of the Province, would not be the most criminal Neglect in a People heretofore rigidly and justly tenacious of their Constitutional Rights.

Penetrated with the most poignant Concern, and ardently solicitous to preserve Union and Harmony between Great-Britain and the Colonies, so indispensably necessary to the Well-being of both, we entreat your Excellency to remove that Brand of Contention, the Fortress at the Entrance of Boston: We are much concerned that you should have been induced to construct it, and thereby causelesly excite such a Spirit of Resentment and Indignation as now generally prevails. We assure you, Sir! that the good People of this Colony never have had the least Intention to do any Injury to his Majesty's Troops; but on the contrary most earnestly desire that every Obstacle to treating them as Fellow-Subjects may be immediately removed; and are constrained to tell your Excellency, that the Minds of the People will never be relieved till those hostile Works are demolished: And we request you, as you regard his Majesty's Honor and Interest, the Dignity and Happiness of the Empire, and the Peace and Welfare of this Province, that you immediately desist from the Fortress now constructing at the South Entrance into the Town of Boston, and restore the Pass to its natural State.

In Provincial Congress at Concord, Oct. 14. 1774.

RESOLVED, That the several Constables and Collectors of Taxes throughout the Province, who have or shall have any Monies in their Hands collected on Province Assessments, be advised not to pay the same or any Part thereof to the Hon. *Harrison Gray*, Esq; but that such Constables and Collectors, as also such Constables and Collectors as have or shall have any County Monies in their Hands, take and observe such Orders and Directions touching the same, as shall be given them by the several Towns and Districts by whom they were chosen. And that the Sheriffs and Deputy Sheriffs of the several Counties in the Province, who have in their Hands any Province Monies, be also advised not to pay the same to the said *Harrison Gray*, Esq; but that they retain the same in their Hands respectively, until the further Advice of a Provincial Congress or Order from a constitutional Assembly of this Province. And that the present Assessors of the several Towns and Districts in the Province be advised to proceed to make Assessments of the Tax granted by the Great and General Court of the Province at their last *May* Session, and that such Assessments be duly paid by the Persons assessed to such Person or Persons as shall be ordered by the said Towns and Districts respectively. And the Congress strongly recommend the Payment of the Tax accordingly.

A true Extract from the Minutes,

BENJAMIN LINCOLN, Secr.

[There were above 260 Members present at the Provincial Congress when the foregoing Message passed, with only one Dissentient.]

The Provincial Congress adjourn'd from Concord on Friday last, to this Day, to meet at Cambridge.

Friday last the following ADDRESS from the County of Worcester, was presented to His Excellency the Governor, *viz*.

To his Excellency THOMAS GAGE, Esq; Governor of his Majesty's Province of the *Massachusetts-Bay*, and Commander in Chief of the King's Forces in *North-America*.

May it please your Excellency,

THE People of the County of Worcester being earnestly sollicitous for the Peace and Welfare of the Province in general, cannot view the Measures now pursuing by your Excellency but with encreasing Jealousy, as they apprehend there has not, nor does at present exist, any just Occasion for the formidable hostile Preparations making on the Neck, leading to our distressed Capital.

It is a Matter of such Notoriety that your Excellency must be sensible, there was not the least Opposition made to obstruct the Introduction of the King's Troops at their first landing, nor have the People since that Time discovered any Intention to disturb them, till your Excellency was pleased to order the Seizure of the Powder in the Arsenal at Charlestown, in a private Manner which occasioned the Report that a Skirmish had happened between a Party of the King's Troops and the People at Cambridge, in which several of the latter fell, this caused the People to arm and march from divers Parts of the Country; but no sooner was that Report proved false, than they returned peaceably to their respective Homes.

The Inhabitants of the Province in general, and Town of Boston, have ever given Cause for those cruel and arbitrary Acts, for blockading their Harbour and subverting the Charter by altering the Civil Government of the Province, which however, this People are determined by the Divine Favour, never to submit to, but with their Lives, notwithstanding they are aggrieved at the King's Displeasure against them, through the Instigation of traiterous and designing Men.

This County finds it difficult to comprehend the Motives for the present hostile Parade, unless it be in Consequence of some preconcerted Plan to subject the already greatly distressed Town of Boston to mean Compliances or Military Contributions. They are equally at a Loss to account for your Excellency's Conduct towards the County of Suffolk, as in your Answer to their Address, remonstrating against fortifying the only Avenue to the Town, which by that Means may in some future Time be improved to cut off the Communication between Town and Country, and thereby reduce the miserable Inhabitants to the greatest Straits. Your Excellency is pleased in Answer to observe that you had not made it easier to effect this, than what Nature has made it; if so, the Country cannot conceive, why this Expence and Damage of the Town to no Purpose: Your Excellency is likewise pleased to take Notice of the general good Behaviour of the Soldiers, but at the same Time pass over that Part, complaining of the Detention of private Property, and proceed to answer by Way of Quere, to which you would not permit a Reply. This County are constrained to observe, they apprehend the People justifiable in providing for their own Defence, while they understood there was no passing the Neck without Examination, the Cannon at the North-Battery spiked up, and many Places searched, where Arms and Ammunition were suspected to be; and if found, seized; yet as the People have never acted offensively, nor discovered any disposition so to do, till as above related, the County apprehend this can never justify the seizure of private Property.

It is with great anxiety the County observes the wanton exercise of Power in the Officers of the Customs at Salem, and on board the King's Ships respecting the Article of Fuel, destined for the Use of the Inhabitants of Boston, who are obliged to have it with the additional Charge of landing and relanding at Salem, before it can proceed; when your Excellency must be sensible the Act, which is the professed Rule of Conduct expresly excepts Fuel and Victuals which may be brought to Boston by taking on board one or more Officers at Salem (who at the aforesaid Charge) while that destined for the Troops proceeds direct, free from the same. There are many other Things which bear extremely hard on the Inhabitants, while they are prohibited from transporting the smallest Articles from one Part of the Town to another, water born, without Danger of a Seizure or to get Hay, Cattle, &c. from any of the Islands, notwithstanding there is no other way of Transportation.

Your Excellency, we apprehend, must have been greatly misinformed of the Character of this People, to suppose such Severities tend either to a Submission to the Acts, or Reconciliation with the Troops; and the County are sorry to find the Execution of the Acts attempted with an higher hand than was intended, unless the Acts themselves should be thought too lenient.

Bringing into the Town a Number of Cannon from Castle-William, sending for a further Reinforcement of Troops, with other concurring Circumstances, strongly indicating some dangerous Design, has justly excited in the Minds of the People Apprehensions of the most alarming Nature, and the Authors must be held accountable for all the Blood and Carnage made in Consequence thereof. Therefore this County, in Duty to God, their Country, themselves and Posterity, do remonstrate to, and earnestly desire your Excellency, as you regard the Service of the King and the Peace and Welfare of the Province, to desist from any further hostile Preparations, and give the People Assurances thereof, by levelling the Intrenchments and dismantling the Fortifications, which will have a Tendency to satisfy their Doubts, and restore that Confidence so essential to their Quiet and his Majesty's Service.

By Order of the Convention of Committees for the County of WORCESTER.

HIS EXCELLENCY'S Answer.

Gentlemen,

I HAVE repeatedly given the strongest Assurances that I intended nothing hostile against the Town or Country, and therefore desire you to ease the Minds of the People against any Reports that may have been industriously spread amongst them to the contrary; my Wish is to preserve Peace and Tranquility.

With Respect to the Execution of the Port-Bill, it is a Matter belonging to other Departments; and if any Thing is done not warranted by said Act, the Law is open for Redress.

THO's. GAGE.

The following Extract of a Letter from the Rev. Mr. Peters of Hebron, in Connecticut, was read last Thursday in the Provincial Congress at Concord.

Dear Mother, Boston, Sept. 28, 1774.

I AM yet well and doing Business for my intended Rout; I hear that a Mob was gathered for me the Day after I left Hebron, what they have done I cannot yet find out. As Jonathan will be obliged to attend at New Haven when the Assembly sits, I desire him to let Mr. Jarvis, Andrews, Hubbard, &c. collect all Facts touching Mobs and Insults offered the Clergy of our Church or her Ministers, likewise to send me a Copy of the Clergy's Petition to Governor Trumbul, and what he said in Answer. If Jonathan is hurt or my House hurt or Damage done, let that be transmitted me within 14 Days, or after that send those Accounts to the Care of Mr. Rice Williams a Woolen Draper in London. I am in high spirits —I should be happy if my Friends and Relations at Hebron were provided for at these bad Times, when Things are growing worse. Six Regiments are coming over from England and sundry Men of War; so soon as they come, hanging-work will go on, and Destruction will attend first the Sea-Port Towns, the Lintel sprinkled on the side Post will preserve the faithful. I wish Hannah to take some Papers which she and I laid away and bring them to me, she knows where they be, or burn them if this Letter appears to be opened before it is opened by you. Mr. Bebee and Mr. Daniel Jones, Mr. Warner and Griffith of Millington, must draw up a Narrative of their Sufferings, and such Words as Col. Spencer &c. have spoke by way of Encouragement to Mobs, and let Dr. Bebee send the same to me, to the Care of Mr. Thomas Brown, Merchant in Boston.

[Further Accounts of said Peters in our next.]

GRENADA, August 24.

Yesterday came on before Alexander Middleton, Esq; Judge Surrogate of the Court of Vice-Admiralty, the examination of Henry Lenard, Charles Ingersol and Thomas Sawyer, concerning an act of piracy committed on board the sloop Hannah, belonging to Mr. Oliver Bowen, of Savannah in Georgia, merchant.

It appeared by the examinations, that on the first day of June last, the said sloop sailed from Cape Anne for Demarara, with a cargo of lumber, under the command of Captain William Barber, having on board Samuel Hendley, Son of Mr. Henry Hendley living at Wheeler's Point, in Boston, as Mate, the said Henry Lenard, Charle Ingersol, and Thomas Sawyer as mariners, and Samuel Brown as Cook.

That on the 23d of the said month of June, about 4 o'clock in the afternoon, in latitude 29, as the Mate was upon the stern, striking at a dolphin Brown threw him overboard, and upon the Captain's hearing the cry of murder, he came upon deck, and finding the mate overboard threw out a plank for his assistance, and in doing so was thrown overboard also by the said Brown.

That Lenard attempted to put the helm down and put out the boat for the assistance of the Captain and mate, but was prevented from doing either by Brown and Sawyer, who brought up a case bottle of rum, drank to each other, and seemed well pleased with what they had done, and notwithstanding the cries and intreaties of the Captain and Mate, would not put about the vessel, or give them any assistance.

Some days after this, they filled up new articles, for the vessel, Brown assuming the name of the owner, Sawyer that of the Captain, and Ingersoll that of the Mate, and proceeded on their voyage to this island, where they passed by those names untill this horrid affair was discovered, and we are informed, that what gave rise to the discovery was comparing the signing of the receipt for the sloop and cargo, which had been sold to Bartlet, Campbell and Bartlet, with the signing of the register.

PHILADELPHIA, October 5.

Although we may have Blankets enough to keep us warm for this winter, yet, in all probability, we may want next, if a Non-Importation should take place, and we be drained of what few there is in this place; therefore, the venders of BLANKETS are desired to be cautious to whom they sell, as the order for that article is renewed to a Gentleman in this city, from General Gage, for the use of his soldiery, who are at the siege of Boston.

We are informed from good authority that the King sent a message to the Bishop of London the day after he refused to vote for the Popish Quebec bill, discharging him from all future services at the Privy-Council.

NEW-YORK October 13.

This Morning Maj. Gen. Haldimand will embark on board the Countess of Darlington transport, attended by Major of Brigade Moncrieffe, Capt. Gamble, Assistant Quarter-master-General, Capt. Brehm, Aid du Camp, and Capt. Hutchinson; with General Haldiman will also embark Col. Prescott of the Royal Fuzileers, a company of Royal Artillery, with a large Quantity of Ordnance Stores for Castle William. The companies of the Royal Regiment of Ireland, under the command of Capt. Shee, and the 47th Regiment commanded by Maj. Cairncross, were embarked on board the Empress of Russia, and other Transports for the Port of Boston.

The following is the Order in which his Majesty's Troops are to be quartered at Boston, provided the intended barracks should not be compleated before the Winter sets in:

The King's own Reg. At the Still-House, New-Boston.
The 5th Regiment. From Liberty Tree to the Neck.
The Royal Welsh, and 38th Regiment. Near Fort-Hill.
The 43d Regiment. Near the Market.
The 64th Regiment. To remain at the Castle.
The Royals of Ireland, the 10th, 47th, and 52d Regiments, are on their Arrival to be Quartered in Town.

We hear that 5000 French Regulars have been lately landed at the Island of Hispaniola from Old France.

Nothing has, since our last, transpired from the General Congress at Philadelphia. Mr. Paul Revere, who pass'd through this City about nine days ago express from Boston to the Delegates, waits for the result of their determinations upon the important business which occasioned his Journey.

The vessel in which Dr. Benjamin Franklin had taken his passage for Philadelphia, is arrived at that place with letters intimating, that when he was on the point of departure, the Earl of Chatham sent for him, and after a long conference convinced him of the necessity of his deferring his embarkation until after the next session of parliament, in which that Nobleman, aided with his intelligence of the proceedings of the Colonies intends to make the most vigorous efforts in favour of this country.

BOSTON, October 17.

UPWARDS of five Months have expired since this devoted Town has experienced all the horrors of the Port-Bill, and as if these were not sufficient to satiate the malice of our enemies, Severities which that Act, vengeful as it is, did not know of, have been grafted upon it. Many instances might be mentioned, suffice it to say, that a Scow with boards and old iron has been seized in a Mill Pond, and libelled in an Admiralty Court; a Boat owned by one Stewart, with sand for our floors, has been taken in the harbour and the sand thrown into the sea without the form of a trial; as was a Lighter load of Hay coming up from Braintree: the produce of Islands near the Town have not been suffer'd to be taken off; and a Float carrying Sheep to feed on one of those Islands, has been obliged to carry them back again: Bread, Meal, and other Provisions were not suffered to pass a little ferry to Charlestown, and their Ferry-Boats have been taken and detained for daring to attempt a passage after 9 o'clock at night: Our numerous Poor are suffering by the Rise of Wood, Butter, Cheese, and other Provisions, not permitted to be brought up as usual from the little Rivers and Bays in our Harbour, and when our Tyrants have been expostulated with for these illegal Proceedings, they have insultingly reply'd, that, agreeable to the Act of Parliament, it was to distress us: and this their Intention has been so effectually accomplished, that it may be affirmed, without exaggeration, the loss this Town has sustained within only one Month of our Blockade, exceeds the whole Amount of those generous Donations received from our sympathizing Friends thro' the Continent. Added to all this, our Town is surrounded with Ships of War; and it is said the Fleet at Newfoundland are to winter in this harbour: formidable Fortifications are erected and others erecting at the only Avenue to the Town: Chains and Chevaux de Frise already provided to stop up the Entrance at pleasure: Four Regiments encamped upon the Common, with a large Train of Artillery and Matrosses; one Regiment on Fort-Hill, one on the new Fortifications on the Neck, and another Regiment at Castle-William; three Companies just arrived in the Rose Man of War from Newfoundland, Transports dispatched some time past to New York for two Regiments from thence and the Jersies, and to Quebec for two Regiments from that Quarter; military Stores and Implements of all kinds are collecting in this Town, which has now the Appearance of a Garrison. Reports are propagated here, and the English Papers announce that six more Regiments are coming from Europe. What may be the Intention of all this, and what ought to be the Conduct of this and the other Provinces upon so alarming an occasion, we shall not pretend to say. This Capital is a Spectacle to them and to the whole World, a striking Example of what is to be expected from the uncontroulable Power claimed by a British Parliament over these Colonies that have not a single Representative in it; but under all these sufferings and terrors Boston has not as yet renounced the great and common cause for which it suffers.———

At a Legal Town Meeting held at Portsmouth on Monday last, it was voted that £. 200 be paid by the Select Men to the Committee in Boston, for the Use of the suffering Poor in this Town.

Extract of a Letter from a Merchant in England, to his Friend in this Town.

"With pleasure I observe your accounts of the purposes and hopes of your town, and heartily wish all the sister colonies may join therein, as the most effectual as well as easiest and peaceable manner of bringing administration to a sense of their ill proceedings.

"Alarming as your treatment is, which gives great displeasure to all true friends of liberty, the late bill for the government of Quebec is more so, as there is no room left to wonder if in the next sessions of Parliament an attempt is made to introduce the same laws and religion throughout the British Empire, and there is but little doubt of our right reverend Lord Bishops concurrence, as not one of 'em oppos'd the late extraordinary steps; but there is one above them, who I hope will frustrate all the evil purposes that may be plotted against his church and people, wishing you a speedy restoration to liberty, as well as myself and friends every where; I remain, &c."

Extract of another Letter from a Merchant in the West of England, to his Friend in this Town.

"I think every honest Briton must applaud the noble stand making on your side the atlantic for liberty, and wish unity and stability amongst all the colonies, as a necessary pre-requisite to the expectance of success."

Extract of another Letter from a principal Manufacturer in London, to his Friend in this Town.

"I want to know if any friend hath sign'd the Covenant lately started at Boston: We are all alarm'd here, some for fear they shall have no more trade to America, and others for fear the Americans will give way, and at length submit and become so fetter'd and shackled as never more to get freed.—Some think as your Gov. hath issued out his proclamation against signing the Covenant, so he or others will issue out a proclamation against having a Congress, & no such meeting will ever be had.—Some think the Quebec bill will alarm the Americans more generally than shuting up the Boston port; we are anxious for the arrival of every ship, and disappointed when it comes, because we don't hear more. I am no politician but a lover of liberty, civil and religious, and warm in sentiment for the Americans to preserve their valuable rights and privileges, but whether this can be done, or which way it's not in my power to tell: If you cou'd be unanimous throughout the whole provinces, as one man, you might do any thing; but unless this is the case, I fear your resolves &c. will fail.

Last Thursday Morning departed this Life, greatly lamented, WILLIAM WHITE, Esq; Aged 58, who was one of the Overseers of the Poor of this Town for several Years. His Remains will be interr'd this Afternoon at 4 Clock at which Time his Friends and Acquaintance are desir'd to attend.

Died last Saturday Morning of an Apoplexy, Mrs. *Hannah Colman*, Relict of the late *Benjamin Colman*, Merchant. Her Funeral is to be To-Morrow Afternoon at 4 o'Clock, from the North End, where her Friends and Relations are desired to attend.

Died. Mr. Robert Balls, a noted Pilot, and Keeper of Boston Light-House.

Mr. William Greenleaf, Hatter, upwards of 80.

Whereas a Report has been spread in the Town of Boston, *and other places, That a considerable Number of People in this Town, had enter'd into a Combination to disturb and barrass the Rev. Mr.* Winslow, *and others, Members of the Church of* England, *with a view to oblige them to leave the Town; and no Evidence appearing to support the Charge, Therefore unanimously Voted, That said Report is Malicious, False and Injurious, and calculated to defame this Town; and that we protest against all such Combinations as subversive of good Government, We being as ready to allow the same Right of private Judgment to others which we claim for ourselves.*

A true Copy from the Town Records,

Attest. ELISHA NILES, *Town-Clerk.*

Braintree, October 6, 1774.

LOST this Morning about Eight o'Clock, between the Stores of Enoch Brown on the Neck, and Mr. Daniel Brown's of Roxbury, a dark blue and white Handkerchief, with Four Pounds Lawful Money in Silver mostly Change, tied in one Corner. Any Person that finds said Handkerchief, are desired to convey it to either of the said Stores, and they shall be generously Rewarded.

Saturday, October 15, 1774.

STEARN's Almanack for 1775, will be Published To-Morrow, and Sold by *Edes & Gill* and *T. & J. Fleet.*

To be Sold by T. and J. FLEET, in Cornhill, [*Price, only Five Coppers.*]

An Address to Protestant Dissenters of all Denominations, on the approaching Election of Members of Parliament, with respect to the State of PUBLIC LIBERTY in general, and of AMERICAN AFFAIRS in particular.——

[*This excellent Pamphlet was received by the last Vessel from London, and is well worthy the Perusal of every North-American, & Friend of the British Constitution.*]

Cyrus Baldwin,

HEREBY informs his Customers and others, that he has to Sell at his Shop in Cornhill, near the Town-House in BOSTON,

A general Assortment of English, India and Scotch Goods, imported before the 31st of last August, which he is determined to Sell at the usual Advance he Sold at before the Northern Blockade, consisting of Superfine, Midling and Low priz'd Broad Cloths, Kerseys, Serges, Beaver Coatings, Scotch Carpets and Carpetting, Plaids, Hair Plushes and Cotton Velvets, Muffs and Tippets, very neat Silk ditto, Choice Firkin Butter, Indigo and Snuff, with too many other Articles to be here enumerated.

He earnestly requests all those who are Indebted to him to make speedy Payment.

N. B. Said Baldwin *is neither Addresser, Protester, nor Roman Catholick.*

For LONDON,

THE Ship *Julias Cæsar*, (CHARLES FEA, Commander,) being a prime Sailer, and having excellent Accommodations for Passengers; will certainly Sail on or before the first of November next, having one Half of her Cargo engaged.—For Freight or Passage, apply to the Master on Board said Ship, lying at the Long-Wharf in Salem, or to Messieurs SMITH and ATKINSON, at their Store in King-Street. Oct. 6, 1774.

To be Sold for Cash only,

A small Quantity of good dry MEHOGANY, BOARDS and PLANK, fit for immediate Use. Enquire of Edes & Gill.

TO BE LETT,

A convenient Dwelling-House in Hanover-Street, opposite Mr. Benja. Andrew's; Three Rooms upon a Floor, Wood House and Barn, a good Pump and Rain Water Cistern.——Inquire of William Fowle, living in said House; Where may be had a few Firkins of Choice Nova-Scotia Butter and a small Quantity of Spring Beaver.

WANTED, a good HORSE, that will go well in a Chaise, and Trots light in a Saddle. Inquire of the Printers, or of Thomas Hudson.

All Persons having any Demand on the Estate of Mr. *John Soren*, late of Boston, Baker, deceas'd, are desir'd to bring in their Accounts; and all Persons indebted to said Estate, are desired to make Payment to *Ann Soren*, Administratrix.

WANTED,

To improve for a Business of public Utility, a large convenient Room in the South Part of the Town.——Further particulars may be known by Inquiring of the Printers.

New AUCTION-ROOM, Cornhill
TO MORROW MORNING, at TEN o'Clock,
Will be sold by PUBLIC VENDUE,
At GREENLEAF's Auction Room,
A Variety of English GOODS,—amongst which are Duffils, Bath Coatings, Broad Cloths, Forrest Cloths, Kerseys, Plains, Shalloons, Callimancoes, Tammys, &c.
Sale begins 10 o'Clock. *Wm. Greenleaf*, Auct'r.

At GOULD's Auction-Office in Back-Street,
On FRIDAY next, at 10 o'Clock in the Morning,
Will be Sold by PUBLIC VENDUE,
A general Assortment of English and Hard Ware Goods. R. GOULD, Auctioneer.

A great Variety of English and Scotch GOODS, are now selling off by Wholesale and Retail, (at an uncommon low Rate,)
At *BICKER*'s Auction-Room,
near the Market,
A grand assortment of Cambleteens and Cotton and Linnen Checks.

On FRIDAY next,
At TEN in the Morning,
Will be Sold by PUBLIC VENDUE,
At HUNTER's Auction-Room,
(Lately improved as a Store by Mr. Thomas Walley)
A large Assortment of ENGLISH GOODS taken by Execution.——The Particulars in the next Thursday's Papers. WM. HUNTER, Auctioneer.

Burials in the Town of BOSTON, since our last.
Fifteen Whites. NO Blacks.
Baptiz'd in the several Churches, Eight.

High Water at BOSTON, for the present Week.

Monday, 34 min. aft. 9	Friday, 59 min. after. 12
Tuesday, 22 min. aft. 10	Saturday, 46 min. aft. 1
Wednesday, 10 m. aft. 11	Lord's Day 33 m. af. 2
Thursday, 8 min. aft. 12	Full ● 19 Day 9 Morn.

(Advertisements omitted, will be in our next.)

William Blair Townsend,

At the Three Doves,
In Marlborough-Street, Boston;

Hereby advertizes his Customers and others, That he is now selling off his Shop Goods for *Cash*, by Wholesale and Retail, at the low Rate of Eleven for One, on the true Sterling Cost; (being as low as they can be imported) consisting chiefly of Woollens, and well suited for the approaching Winter Season; *and which they may depend were imported, before the oppressive acts on this Town and Province were laid*; and may therefore be safely transported *by Land*, and Sold in any Town of said Province, without any Breach on the solemn League and Covenant our worthy Friends in the Country have justly entered into, in Defence of themselves and their Posterity.

N. B. Those that incline to purchase, are desired to apply speedily; as said TOWNSEND is determined to remove into a clear Air in the Country, *very soon*.

TAKEN up by me the Subscriber, on the 25th ult. a Sorrel Horse. The Owner may have him again, proving his Property and paying the Charges, by applying to Seth Clark, of Medfield.

Stop Thief!

WHEREAS the Shop of the Subscriber was last Night broke open, and robbed of Twelve Beaver and Six Beaverett HATTS.—This is to promise a Reward of TEN DOLLARS, to any Person who shall discover the Thief or Thieves, so that he or they may be convicted thereof, and the HATTS recovered, and in Proportion for any Part of them.

JAMES CODNER.

Boston, Tuesday Morning, October 4, 1774.

T O B E S O L D

10,000 Acres of very fine Land, in the

Island of St. JOHN's, being half of one of the best Townships in it, About 500 Acres of which are clear'd and mostly arable Land. 'Tis situated on a Navigable River, 25 Miles above Charlotte Town, the Seat of Government, with which it has Communication both by River and a good Cart Road. There are some Families from Nantucket settled upon it. The Townships adjoining are well settled, and the Island in general in a Prosperous way. Captain *Holland*, who survey'd the Island, reports this Township to the Board of Trade, by whose Order he survey'd it, in the following Words, viz. "*Clear'd Lands 1000 Acres, Houses 30, pretty well situated for Fishing and Tillage, or Pasture, inferior to none upon the Island; there is also Plenty of Game and Fish.*"

Also, to be sold by the same Person,

10,000 Acres of choice good Land on the River St. John's in the Bay of Fundy, all settled agreeable to the Terms required by Government, which secures it forever from Forfeiture. For further Particulars enquire of Mr. *Warden*, Merchant, at his Store on Green's Wharf, or of the Printers hereof.

This is to Notify the Proprietors of

Pearsontown, in the County of Cumberland, that at a legal Meeting of said Proprietors, held at Falmouth in said County, on the 31st Day of March last, a tax of fifteen shillings was assess'd on each right for the support of the Minister and other necessary charges, for bringing forward the settlement of said township, and to pay said tax or assessment (as well as former arrearages of taxes due on their several rights heretofore granted by said proprietors, and legally advertiz'd) to Ephraim Jones of said Falmouth, treasurer of said proprietors, or to the subscribers the proprietors committee, on or before the 9th day of January next, otherwise their several lots and rights there, will be sold at Public Vendue at the House of Mr. Moses Shattuck, Innholder, in said Falmouth, on the said 9th day of January next for the payment of said taxes as the Law directs: The said sale to begin at ten of the clock in the forenoon.

Falmouth, Sept. 6, 1774. Enoch Freeman, Moses Pearson, Ste. Longfellow } Propriet's Com'tee.

STOLEN out of a Pasture at Roxbury on Thursday Night the 6th Instant, a brown Mare about 14 Hands high, she has a Star in her Forehead, one of her Fetter-Lock Joints of her hind Feet white, her Main hangs on the near Side, and a Feather on the other Side of her Neck, she is uncommonly square built and Trots strong and bold, she has a lofty Carriage and carries a high Tail. Whoever apprehends the Thief so that he may be brought to Justice, and returns the Mare to Mr. Joseph Morton at Boston, at the sign of the white Horse, South-End, shall have THIRTY DOLLARS *Reward, and if the Mare alone Fifteen Dollars, and all necessary Charges paid, by me the Subscriber,*

Boston, Oct. 10, 1774. *JOSEPH MORTON.*

Colony of RHODE-ISLAND, *&c.*

WHEREAS John Wiley of Providence, in the County of Providence, in the Colony aforesaid, Merchant, preferred a Petition unto the General Assembly of the said Colony, representing that he is an insolvent Debtor, and praying that he may be admitted to the Benefit of an Act passed in June A. D. 1756, entitled, "An Act for the Relief of Insolvent Debtors." Whereupon the General Assembly referred the said Petition, and ordered that the Creditors of the said John Wiley should be notified by an Advertisement to be inserted in the Newport Mercury, the Providence Gazette, and in one of the Boston News-Papers, to appear at the next Session to answer the same:—I do therefore hereby notify the Creditors of the said John Wiley to appear (if they shall think fit) at the General Assembly to be holden at Providence, in and for the said Colony, on the last Wednesday in October next, then and there to shew Cause, (if any they have) why the said Petition should not be granted.

HENRY WARD, Secr'y.

Nathan Frazier

BEGS leave to inform the Public, that in consequence of the Boston Port-Bill, and with a view of accommodating those of his Customers to whom it may be most convenient to have their Supplies conveyed by Water, he has opened a Store in Salem, (the one lately Improved by Mr. John Johnson, and next Door to Mr. John Gool's) where he has for Sale an Assortment of Goods suitable for the Season.——Said FRAZIER still continues his Business at his Store in *Boston* as usual: His Customers may be supplied at either of said Stores, Wholesale and Retail, on the most reasonable Terms for ready Money.—He will give his Personal Attendance, for the present at his *Salem* Store.

NEWHALL and HICHBORN,

BEG leave to acquaint their Customers and others, in this and the neighbouring Parts, that they Propose carrying on the Cooper's Business in all its Branches, at Salem; and have opened a Shop for that Purpose, near the Distill-House of Mr. JONATHAN ROPES, in Salem.

N. B. As they also carry on the same business in Boston as usual, one of them may always be found in each Place.

JOSIAH QUINCY, Jun'r.

Having resigned his Business into the Hands of Mr. PEREZ MORTON, and embarked for London, desires all his Clients who want to know the state of their Affairs, to call on said Morton for Information:—All Persons who are indebted to said Quincy, *on Account*, are desired to make Payment to said Morton, and any who may have Damands on said Quincy, are requested to apply to the same Gentleman for their Discharge.—Those Persons who owe the said Quincy, on Bond or Note, are hereby notified to make their Payments to WILLIAM PHILLIPS, Esq; Attorney to JOSIAH QUINCY, jun.

Caleb Blanchard

in Union-Street,

Has on Hand, a large Assortment of Goods suitable for the Season, which he will sell at the very lowest Rates for ready Money.

Just Imported, by

Geyer and Burgess,

in the Ship London, Capt. Calef, from London,

A general Assortment of English and India Piece Goods, which they will sell on the most reasonable Terms by Wholesale only, at their Store in King-Street, Boston.

They would also acquaint their Customers and others, who carry their Goods by Water, that they have taken a Store at Salem, near the Town-House, where they may be supply'd with equal Variety, and on the same Terms as at Boston.

T O B E S O L D Cheap

At *Benjamin Goldthwait*'s Shop,

just above Concert-Hall, Boston.

Superfine Scarlet and white Broad-Cloths, superfine Garnett ditto, white & Buff Casimeers, figur'd Velvets, Corduroy of all colours, silk and worsted Breeches Patterns of all colours, &c. &c.

The Taylor's Business as usual, is carried on in the best Manner at said Shop.

☞ At his Cellar near said Shop is to be sold choice ORANGE JUICE, by the Cask or smaller Quantity.

An Evening School

Will be opened on Monday next, by JOHN DRUITT, at his School in Hanover Street, near Concert-Hall, where Reading, Writing, and Arithmetic will be taught after the most approved Method—NAVIGATION and BOOK KEEPING on moderate Terms; in Compliance with the Times no Entrance will be requir'd.——His Hours of Attendance will be from 6 till 9 o'Clock, (P. M.)

☞ To the LADIES,

He begs Leave to acquaint those who wou'dn't choose to attend a School, or that the Inclemency of the approaching Season might hinder, that he will wait on them at their Places of Abode, at any Hour from 8 to 11 in the Forenoon, or from 2 'till 4 in the Afternoon.

Mrs. DRUITT has lower'd her Terms for plain Sewing to *Eight Pence* Law. Money per Week, (her other Works as usual) and hopes to convince those who are pleas'd to try, that there is as much to be learn'd in Winter as in Summer.

ALL Persons having any Demand on the Estate of Mr. *John Ruggles*, late of Boston, Housewright, deceas'd, are desired to bring in their Accounts—And all Persons indebted to said Estate are desired to make payment to *Hannah Ruggles*, Administratrix, or to *Samuel Ruggles*, jun'r. her Attorney.

Providence STAGE COACH,

Kept by ANDREW COMSTOCK & SAMUEL BARTER.

WHO beg Leave to inform the Public, That they have removed from the White Horse Tavern to Mr. Jolley Allen's, a few Doors South of the Governor's, in Marlborough Street; where the greatest Care will be taken of all Bundles, Letters, &c. with which they may be entrusted:—They keep several Setts of the best Horses on purpose for this Business, and will engage to carry Passengers with the greatest Expedition, at the cheapest Rate.

William Bant

BEGS Leave to inform his Friends, Customers and others, That he has to sell by Wholesale and Retail at his Store fronting Dock-square, Boston——

A general Assortment of *English* and *India*

G O O D S,

Suitable for the approaching Season: (*the whole of which was imported before the 31st of August last.*) Among his GOODS is a prime Choice of superfine

Scarlet, Pompadore, white, green, pea green, sea green, barry, black, blue, brown and cloth colour'd BROAD CLOTHS; middling and low priz'd Ditto, with Shalloons and Trimmings to match the Cloths: ALSO of SILKS, viz.—Padusoys, Ducapes, Mantuas, Lutestrings, English and India Damasks, *a Piece of fine white Lutestring*, single and double Sattins, black, white and crimson figur'd Sattin, black, blue green and white half yard Persians, ell-wide Persians, half ell and ell-wide Alamodes, Brolios, black, blue and crimson thick Corduroys for Men's Waistcoats; and a Variety of other Articles that are commonly in Use at this Season of the Year.

☞ The above mentioned GOODS will be disposed of at the very lowest Rates, as said Bant is extremely desirous of exchanging all or any of them, for an Article, which is more convenient for him, in these troublesome Times, viz. C A S H.

EIGHT DOLLARS REWARD.

STOLEN out of the Tan House of the Subscriber, on Friday Evening last, a Quantity of SOLE LEATHER. Whoever will secure the Thief or Thieves, so that he or they shall be confined in any of his Majesty's Goals, shall be paid the above Reward by me

Charlestown, Oct. 3d. JAMES TRUMBALL.

FOUR DOLLARS REWARD.

RAN AWAY from the Subscriber on the 22d of September, at Night, a Negro Man Servant, by the Name of CATO, about Five Feet and Eight Inches high, very thick Lips, speaks broken, and Walks as if he was lame in his Heels. Had on when he went away, a Cloth colour'd Coat, with Pewter Buttons, old Leather Breeches, a Tow Shirt, old Shoes with Silver plate Buckles, wore a Cap, and shoves round his Neck, and very high on his Forehead: Carried away with him a Callico Banyan, fine Linen Shirt, Check Linen Trowsers, grey Wigg, also carries or Wears a Felt Hatt with a Silver Lace on it, had a Violin and carries it in a green Bays Bag. Whosoever will return the Runaway to his Master in Winchenden, shall have the above Reward and all necessary Charges paid by LEVI NICHOL.

Winchenden, Sept. 23d, 1774.

STOP THIEF!

ABSCONDED from the Subscriber on the 3d Day of August last, a Negro Man, called TOM, had on a Pair of black Plush Breeches, a light colour'd ragged Jacket, Lame in both his Feet: Said Negro return'd the last Night broke open his Master's Stable, Stole from thence a valuable Chesnut-colour'd Horse, with a small white Spot on his Forehead, Paces and Trots light, and took a Saddle (with a white Housen) and Bridle; he has with him a counterfeit Pass.

Whoever will take up said Thief and Horse, shall have FOUR DOLLARS, and all necessary Charges paid, by SIMEON POLLEY.

Boston, Sept. 28, 1774.

COLONY OF RHODE-ISLAND.

WHEREAS ELEAZER TREVETT, jun'r. of Newport, in the County of Newport, Mariner, preferred a Petition unto the General Assembly, representing that he is an Insolvent Debtor, and praying that he may be admitted to the Benefit of an Act passed in June, A. D. 1756, entitled "An Act for the Relief of Insolvent Debtors," Whereupon the General Assembly referred the said Petition to the next Sessions and Ordered that in the mean Time his Creditors should be Notified by an Advertisement to be inserted in the Newport Mercury, the Providence Gazette, and in one of the Boston News Papers, to appear then and answer the same: I do therefore hereby Notify the Creditors of the said ELEAZER TREVETT, jun'r. to appear if they shall think fit at the General Assembly to be holden at Providence, in and for the said Colony, on the last Wednesday in October next, then and there to shew Cause if any they have, why the said Petition should not be granted.

HENRY WARD, Secr'y.

STOLEN out of a Pasture in Charlestown, about Four Miles from the Ferry, on Monday Night last, a light Red Mare, Four Years old, with a white Spot on her Nose, her Fore Mane long, her other Mane hanging the off Side, her Feet lighter Colour than her Body, Fourteen Hands and half high. Whoever shall take up said Mare, and return her to the Owner, shall have FOUR DOLLARS Reward, or TEN DOLLARS for the Thief and Horse, and all necessary Charges paid, by

Charlestown, Sept. 27, 1774. STEPHEN GODDARD.

N. B. The following Bill, supposed to be drop'd by the Thief, was taken up in the Pasture from whence the Mare was stolen, viz. Breakfast, 3s. 6. Punch, 1s. Porter, 2s. 3. Wine, 15s. 6. Dinner, 4s. Horses 1s. 6d. Total, £ 1. 7s. 9d.

Caleb Call, of Charlestown, Baker,

ACQUAINTS his Friends and Customers, that he will supply them with his White Bisket, at the usual Price, either at *Salem* or *Marblehead*, upon their Writing to him, or applying to Messrs. *Hooper* and *Whittemore*, Coopers, on *Blany's* Wharfe in *Salem*.

Boston: Printed, by EDES & GILL,
in Queen-Street, 1774.

THE
Boston-Gazette,
AND
COUNTRY JOURNAL.

No. 1019.

Containing the freshest Advices, Foreign and Domestic.

MONDAY, October 24, 1774.

The following Lucubration is said to be the Genius of a certain well known J—n M—n, *employ'd by the Ministry for Scribbling against the Colonies, and this Province in particular.*

LONDON, August 6.

SUBSTANCE *of several* LETTERS *from* BOSTON, *dated in* June *and the Beginning of* July, *received by the* Captain man of war.

"Boston is at present the scene of politics. The Faction in that town has lately suffered greatly by desertion; and the moderate and good part of the inhabitants have acquired new life and vigour from the measures of Parliament, and from the temperate, yet firm Administration of Governor Gage. On the meeting of the General Court, at Salem, early in June, the Governor informed them it was expected they would vote compensation for the loss sustained by the India Company; of this the Assembly took no notice: To keep their transactions and debates from transpiring, they kept their doors locked, and no other part of their determinations has been published, but their choice of five Deputies to attend a General Convention of the Colonies proposed to be held at Philadelphia. This Convention is conjectured to have been formed by Dr. Franklin, as it is intended the several Deputies are to assemble in the town where his interest is strongest; and as Mr. Dickenson, of Philadelphia, the Propagator of Sedition in the Colonies, has again drawn his grey-goose quill to support the drooping spirits of Faction, and is again buoying up the Colonies, by retailing his own nonsense, along with the so often refuted and exploded absurdities and reveries of the Lords Camden and Chatham—factious absurdities, of which both those Lords have been long ashamed. If this proposed Convention should ever meet, it will be productive of no other effect than a few insignificant Resolutions about fantastical ideal Rights, which the very Deputies, who will vote and sign them, know perfectly well neither they, nor their Constituents, are intitled to; nay, they will not assemble together with any real confidence in each other, the former duplicity of the people of Boston having infused into all the other Colonies a suspicion and distrust, which the most solemn asseverations of the professing Saints never will be able to obliterate. On a former occasion, when the other Colonies proposed a Convention, and appointed Deputies, the Town of Boston refused to agree, giving for a reason, that there were not six people in their Town whom they could trust. Such a true and unguarded confession was very properly retorted upon them by the Merchants of New York, who justly observed, that they could not expect the other Colonies would enter into any association with men who were so distrustful of one another, and who owned there were not six honest men among them.—Now the Faction at Boston are so lowered, that they are forced to have recourse to a Convention—a measure which they five years ago unanimously rejected. This new mode of proceeding will end in the same ridiculous manner as their late projects, for erecting new Post-Offices, and starving the West India Planters. The Bostonians assured us, that both these plans met with the unanimous concurrence of all the Colonies on the Continent; but no person who had authentic information gave any credit to them, and they were in the right, for no sooner did we hear of these seditious projects than they vanished like a dream. The Convention is not designed by the other Colonies as any thing serious; it was only proposed by the Merchants of New-York as a put off to the very modest request of the Boston Rebels to shut up the Harbour of New-York, because Parliament had blockaded the Harbour of Boston. The New-York Committee, which consists of fifty-one of the most capital Merchants, was chosen on purpose to counteract their own seditious rabble, and the measures of the Traitors of Boston: And the New-York Deputies will most probably advise the Bostonians, at their Congress, to pay for the Tea which they wantonly and unjustly destroyed, Mr. Low and the New York Committee having already given the Bostonians the same good advice.—With respect to the Massachusetts Assembly, which met the 7th of June, they were soon dissolved by the Governor, for their refractory, unconstitutional conduct, in laying taxes on the people, without the consent of his Majesty's Representative, in order to support their rebellion. Before their dissolution they sent a message to Governor Gage, in which they highly reflected on the conduct of their former Governors, Sir Francis Bernard and Mr. Hutchinson; but the Governor would not hear, to an end, their abusive message, telling them that both those Gentlemen, after being heard by the Privy Council had been honourably acquitted of all the Charges against them, and their conduct had received his Majesty's approbation; therefore their message was not only an insult to the Privy Council, but to his Majesty. They also refused to admit the Secretary into their House with a message from the Governor: They were dissolved by a Proclamation read on the Stairs leading to their House, several of their Members and many other people being present."——

GRAND AMERICAN CONGRESS.

PHILADELPHIA, 1774.

In CONGRESS, *Saturday October 8th*, 1774.

RESOLVED, That the Congress approve of the Opposition by the Inhabitants of the Massachusetts Bay, to the Execution of the late Acts of Parliament, and if the same should be attempted to be carried into Execution by Force, all America, in such Case, ought to support them in their Opposition.

In Congress, Monday October 10.

Resolved unanimously, That it is the Opinion of this Body, that the Removal of the People of Boston into the Country, would be not only extremely difficult in the Execution, but so important in its Consequences, as to require the utmost Deliberation, before it is adopted; but in Case the Provincial Meeting of that Colony shall judge it absolutely necessary, it is the Opinion of the Congress, that all America ought to contribute towards Recompensing them for the Injury, they may thereby sustain, and it will be recommended accordingly.

In Congress, October 10.

Resolved, That every Person or Persons whatsoever, who shall take, accept or act, under any Commission, or Authority, in any wise derived from the Act of Parliament, passed last Session, changing the Form of Government, and violating the Charter of the Province of Massachusetts-Bay, ought to be held in Detestation and Abhorrence by all good Men, and considered as the wicked Tools of that Despotism, which is preparing to destroy those Rights which God, Nature and Compact have given to America.

In Congress, Tuesday October 11.

As the Congress has given General GAGE, an Assurance of the peaceable Disposition of the People of Boston,

Resolved unanimously, That they be advised still to conduct themselves peaceably towards his Excellency General GAGE, and his Majesty's Troops, now stationed in the Town of Boston, as far as can possibly be consistent with their immediate Safety, and the Security of the Town, avoiding and Discountenancing every Violation of his Majesty's Property, or any Insult on his Troops; and that they peaceably and firmly persevere in the Line they are now conducting themselves, on the Defensive.

In Congress, October 11, 1774.

Resolved, That the Congress recommend to the Inhabitants of the Colony of Massachusetts-Bay, to submit to a Suspension of the Administration of Justice, where it cannot be procured in a legal and peaceable Manner, under the Rules of the present Charter, and Laws of the Colony founded thereon, until the Effect of their Application for a Repeal of the Act by which their Charter Rights are infringed, is known.

BOSTON, October 24.

Monday last his Excellency gave the following Answer to the Address of the Provincial Congress, viz.

To Col. *Lee*, Hon. *Col. Ward*, Col. *Orne*, Capt. *Gardner*, *Henry Gardner*, Esq; Mr. *Devens*, Mr. *Gorham*, Capt. *Browne*, Col. *Pomeroy*, Hon. Col. *Prescott*, Col. *Thayer*, Mr. *Williams*, Capt. *Heath*, Captain *Upham*, Mr. *Barns*, Captain *Doolittle*, Mr. *Lothrop*, Major *Thompson*, Mr. *Palmer*, Mr. *Pickering*, and Captain *Thompson*, said to be ordered in Provincial Congress, Thursday October 13th, 1774, a Committee to wait on his Excellency with a Message.

GENTLEMEN,

THE previous Menaces daily thrown out and the unusual, warlike Preparations, throughout the Country, made it an act of Duty in me to pursue the Measures I have taken in constructing what you call a Fortress, which unless annoyed, will annoy Nobody.—It is surely highly exasperating, as well as ungenerous even to hint that the Lives, Liberties, or Properties of any Persons except avowed Enemies are in danger from Britons; Britain can never harbour the black Design of wantonly destroying or enslaving any People on Earth; and notwithstanding the Enmity shewn the King's Troops, by withholding from them almost every Necessary for their Preservation, they have not as yet discovered the Resentment which might justly be expected to arise from such hostile Treatment.

No Person can be more solicitous than myself, to preserve Union and Harmony between Great-Britain and her Colonies, and I ardently wish to contribute to the Completion of a Work so salutary to both Countries: But an open and avowed Disobedience to all her Authority, is only bidding Defiance to the Mother Country, and gives little Hopes of bringing a spirited Nation to that favourable Disposition, which a more decent and dutiful Conduct might effect.

Whilst you complain of Acts of Parliament that make Alterations in your Charter, and put you in some Degree on the same Footing with many other Provinces, you will not forget that by your present assembling, you are yourselves subverting that Charter, and now acting in direct Violation of your own Constitution. It is my Duty therefore, however irregular your Application is, to warn you of the Rock you are upon, and to require you to desist from such illegal and unconstitutional Proceedings.

THO. GAGE.

Tuesday last about noon-day, one Samuel Dyer, a sailor, lately arrived from London, who appears disordered in his senses, snapped a pistol at Major Montasour, and then drew a hanger from the side of Col. Cleveland, with which he wounded him in the neck, happily not mortal: he was apprehended at Cambridge, and is now in Boston goal. This man says, he was sent to England this summer in a man of war, in Irons, on suspicion of enticing men to desert from the troops here, but discharged by order of administration.

A correspondent desires to be informed, whether Lord North has really got the French and Spanish Ministry to sign a *solemn League and Covenant*, not to attack any part of North-America, as their knowledge of this whole continent, being stript almost bare of British troops, to assist in carrying on the siege of Boston, might otherwise encourage them to such an attempt.

Last Saturday sev'nnight, a pail or tub was taken up at the North part of the town, which contained, upon examining the contents, the entire skin of a woman (except the face part) that seemed, by some circumstances, to have been but lately fleed from the body:—Various are the conjectures upon this very uncommon discovery, which perhaps time will unfold.

TO THE PRINTERS.

Please to insert the following in your next, for the Benefit of the Public.

THE Town of MARLBOROUGH having entered into a Covenant for a Non-Consumption of British Goods in it, *viz.* "That after this or a similar Covenant has been offer'd to any Person, and they refuse to sign it, or produce the Oath therein specified to the same Purpose; we will publish their Names to the World."

Agreeable to a Vote of the said Town, we do publish the following Persons as refusers to sign said Covenant, or produce the Oath. *viz*

JONATHAN LORING, TIMOTHY BAKER,
ABNER SHERMAN, JOHN BRIGHAM,
HENRY BRIGHAM.

By Order, and in behalf of the Committee of Correspondence. HEZEKIAH MAYNARD, Chairman.

Marlborough, October 10, 1774.

JUST PUBLISHED,

And to sold by T. & J. Fleet, *in Cornhill, and by* Edes & Gill *in Queen-Street*, Boston.

The North American's

ALMANACK

Being the Gentleman and Ladies Diary for the Year of our Lord Christ 1775.

Being the third after Bissextile or Leap Year.

Containing, the Lunations, Eclipses of the Luminaries, Sun and Moon's rising and setting, Moon's Place, Time of High-Water at Boston, both Morning and Evening, the rising, southing and setting of the seven Stars, Clock Equations, Interest Tables, the Weight and Value of Coins as they pass in New-England; Spring Tides; Judgment of the Weather; Feasts and Fasts of the Church of England; Friends Meetings, with an Explanation of the same; the Settings of the Courts in the four New-England Governments; Publick Roads, with the intermediate Miles and Stages to put up at; Chronological Tables, containing all the Kings and Queens Names that have reigned in England since it was first so called, with an Account of the Time that each King and Queen reigned; Physical Receipts, shewing proper Methods of Cure for the Asthma, Burns, Consumptions, Coughs, Cholic, Head-Ach, Gout, Scurvy, Fever, Jaundice, Rheumatism and Tooth-Ach; a Recipe for Thriving; how to prevent Anger, &c. The Difference of High-Water at several Places on the Continent; the Cause of the Rain-Bow; Explanation of the Names of the twelve Calender Months; Directions relating to the purchasing of Land, &c. Some of the Evils that attend Gaming; with other Things very instructive and entertaining.——

By SAMUEL STEARNS,

Student in Physick and Astronomy.

Mess. Edes and Gill,

By inserting the following, taken from a Book, entitled, "A System of Camp Discipline," &c. *you will oblige a constant Reader.* A. B.

"*Massacre of* Glenco.

January, 1692. *Argyle's* Regiment went to that Country, supposed to take up those who refused to take the Oaths, *&c.*

Glenco met them, and asked if they came as Friends? All the Officers gave their Parole they came as such, and would not hurt him or any of his Friends; on which he gave them a welcome Reception, and entertain'd them as Friends in the most hospitable Manner, 15 Days. The very last Day, Captain *C—p—ll*, the Commanding Officer, played with *Glenco* at Cards till past 7 at Night, when he received the following Letter from Major *Duncanson*.

SIR,

YOU are hereby ordered to fall on the Rebels, the *M'Donalds* of *Glenco*, and put all to the Sword under 70. You are to have special Care that the old Fox and his Cubs do not escape: Secure the Avenues that no one gets off. This you are to put in Execution at 5 in the Morning precisely. By that time, or soon after, I'll endeavour to be with you with a stronger Party; if I am not with you by 5. you are not to stay for me, but to fall on; this is by the King's special Command, for the Good and Safety of the Country, that these Miscreants be cut off, Root and Branch. See that this be put in Execution without Feud or Favour, or you must expect to be treated as not true to the King and Government, nor a Man fit to bear the King's Commission, *&c.*

R. Duncanson. 11 *Feb.* 1692.

Another Order was sent to Major *Duncanson*, from Col. *James Hamilton*, to the same Purport. After the Receipt of these Orders, the Soldiers were billetted 2, 3, or 5 in each House, according to the Number of Persons in each Family, and all kindly received. About 5 they began, and murdered 38 in a few Minutes, among whom were *Glenco* and *M'Donald* of *Achintricken*, with Col. *Hill's* Protection in his Pocket. Among the many Cruelties committed on this Occasion, it is said a Boy about 8, seeing his Parents weltering in their Blood, run to Captain *Ca——ll*, grasping him about his Legs, crying for Mercy, and offering to be his Servant for Life; the Captain was inclined to save him, but one *Drummond* struck him instantly dead. Many Circumstances of this unparallelled Butchery are shocking, and almost incredible. *Glenco* was shot through the Head, as he was giving Orders for the Entertainment of his Murderers, and undressing for Bed, and immediately expired in his Lady's Arms; with which Fright she died the next Day. This horrid Massacre was perpetrated when the poor Souls were asleep. By the Hand of Providence this Night proved very boisterous, which retarded the Arrival of a Party of 400 Soldiers, who were to fall on the other End of the *Glen*, at the same Hour. There were about 200 People butchered in this Manner by these Savages, who could in cool Blood execute such cruel Orders in their native Country. The Parliament took Cognizance of it, but the Orders were produced, signed, and counter-signed by the King; and that Enquiry only forced *Hamilton*, *&c.* to abscond."

Copy of a Letter from the Rev'd Samuel Peters, *to the Rev'd Dr.* Auchmuty *of New-York.*

Rev. Sir, *Boston, October* 1, 1774.

THE riots and mobs that have attended me and my house set on by the Go—— of Connecticut, have compelled me to take up my abode here; and the clergy of Connecticut, must fall a sacrifice with the several churches, very soon, to the rage of the puritan mobility, if the old serpent that dragon, is not bound.—Yesterday I waited on his Excellency, the admiral, &c. Dr. Caner, Mr. Trothbeck, Dr. Boyles, &c. I am soon to sail for England. I shall stand in need of your letters, and the letters of the clergy of New-York. Direct to Mr. Rice Williams, Woollen Draper, in London, where I shall put up at: Judge Auchmuty, will do all that is reasonable for their neighbouring charter, necessity calls for such friendship, as the head is sick and heart faint, and spiritual iniquity rides in high places, halberts, pistols and swords, see the proclamation I sent you by my nephew, on their pious sabbath day, the 4th of last month, when the preachers and magistrates left the pulpits, &c. for the gun and drum, and set off for Boston, cursing the King and Lord North, general Gage, the bishops and their cursed curates, and the church of England; and for my telling the church people not to take up arms, &c. it being high treason, &c. The sons of liberty have almost killed one of my church, tarred & feather'd two, abused others, and on the 6th day destroyed my windows, and rent my cloaths, even my gown, &c. Crying out down with the church, the rage of popery, &c. Their rebellion is obvious, and treason is common, and robbery is their daily devotion. The bounds of New York may directly extend to Connecticut river, Boston meet them, and New Hampshire take the province of Main, Rhode Island be swallowed up as Dathan. Pray loose no time, nor fear worse times than attend,

Rev. Sir,

Your very humble Servant,

SAMUEL PETERS.

To Dr. Auchmuty, New-York.

N. B. I wrote the clergy of Connecticut, the letters may be intercepted, pray acquaint Mr. Dibble, &c.

L O N D O N, *August* 6.

☞ To censure the measures of Administration respecting AMERICA, is not an easy task, without having recourse to epithets too harsh for a paper. To say that they are "UNJUST, CRUEL, TYRANNIC, and INEFFECTUAL," is to say no more than what the Americans feel, and Englishmen can demonstrate. They are unjust to an extreme, because they violate the Colony Charters, and thus, instead of supporting Government, they DISSOLVE it; for the respective Charters of the different Colonies are the only foundations of that SOCIAL COMPACT whereby allegiance and protection are mutually promised, and mutually expected on the part of Great Britain and America; take away or ANNIHILATE this social compact, on what can the claim to sovereignty be founded? And where is the difference between a total annihilation, or a partial invasion? The Colonists accepted their Charters on the plighted faith of Government; their promise of allegiance pre supposed a conditional obligation on the part of Government; it pre-supposed that their Charters should be maintained INVIOLATE. If it be urged, "that the power which granted might "take away at pleasure," I deny the position as a matter of RIGHT, for the superiority of power does not constitute a RIGHT. The Americans, by soliciting the protection of Great-Britain clearly acknowledge mutual compact ratified by both parties, on this only do they found the sovereignty of Great-Britain in point of RIGHT. The mutual compacts to the solemn ratification of which both parties have assented, are the several CHARTERS of the different Colonies; these Charters are so many COVENANTS, the stipulated conditions of which are presumed to be equally binding on the GRANTOR and the GRANTEE. It is totally immaterial which of the parties first violates the condition of the instruments; when violated, the compact is to all intents and purposes DISSOLVED, and that which should be binding on both ceases from thenceforward to be binding on either. The single question then to be decided is, "whether (admitting the existance of such a "social compact) it was not FIRST broken on the "part of GREAT-BRITAIN?" For if the violation came from the protecting power, what would have been barely unjust in the Americans was doubly so in Great Britain; the superiority of power is an aggravation of the offence; the abuse of authority is more shameless when the means of supporting that authority are more effectual. In the matter of TAXATION then I will venture to affirm, Great Britain FIRST violated the social compact subsisting between her and America. We have no more right to tax the Americans, unless through the medium of their REPRESENTATIVES, than we have to tax the IRISH, but through the medium of THEIR Representatives. The IRISH HOUSE OF COMMONS, and the AMERICAN HOUSE OF REPRESENTATIVES are, to the inhabitants of the respective countries, exactly upon an equal footing. Would the IRISH complain of being taxed by the English WITHOUT the consent of their own Representatives? Would they call the very attempt UNCONSTITUTIONAL? Would they remonstrate against, and RESIST such attempt by every legal mode? Would they not deem it an infringment on their liberties? Would they be satisfied, because a Lord Lieutenant (like another TRAITEROUS HUTCHINSON) recommended an "abridgment of Irish Liberties?" These questions will apply exactly to the Americans; the cases are precisely similar; the answers to the one solve the difficulties of both; if then the TAXATION MEASURES of Great-Britain were UNJUST in the first instance, the Ministers of this country, not the Patriots of America, are to blame for each resulting evil; nor have the subsequent measures of the present SAGE at the helm been only as UNJUST as those of his predecessors; he has exceeded them as much in the CRUELTY as tyranny of his proceedings. The BOSTON PORT BILL is a BLOODY EDICT that would shock the feelings of a sanguinary SEJANUS; it spares neither innocence, age, sex, nor condition; —it involves an whole people in one common ruin;—it lays waste private property, reduces the wealthy to beggary, and deprives the industrious of BREAD;—it seems intentionally framed to subjugate a Province by STARVING ITS INHABITANTS, unless relieved by the neighbouring Colonies. The Bostonians must be reduced to absolute FAMINE—Children, with locks distorted, in the agonies of hunger, may grasp their parent's knees, and call impetuous for food—the aged may droop, the young be reduced to ghastly spectres for want of common sustenance! these are evils the bill for shutting up the Port of Boston MAY produce; and if they happen not, their prevention will be owing, not to the humanity of the Minister, for he is callous to such paltry feelings, but to the generosity of the other Colonies. What man who feels within his breast a glow of pity can refuse it vent, even with a sympathetic TEAR (that tell-tale herald of commiseration) should pace it down his cheeks? Who can forego a curse of execration on the Minister whose savage measures MAY produce such woes? Is this the rectitude of the CABINET COURIER? Where is the EQUITY of which he so much boasts? Where that CANDOR about which he cants like any preaching cobler? We know by what balance we ought to weigh his deserts; we know, lumpish as he is, that if thrown into the scale of MERIT, he will kick the beam, and be found "lighter than vanity itself." There is but one way of properly adjusting his WEIGHT, and that would be quite a PHILOSOPHICAL EXPERIMENT: the specific gravity of his carcase should be determined by SUSPENSION: in that condition, for about half an hour, he should be left, an HANGING SPECTACLE, between earth and air, on which good men might gaze—the bad might take example.

Messieurs Edes & Gill,

Bridgwater, October 10, 1774.

P*ASSING* a *Road in this Town the other Day, I observed at a Distance forward the Appearance of a Person hanging by the Neck on a Gallows about* 15 *Feet high; upon advancing, I perceived a considerable Discolouration of his Face, which I suppose was owing to a Stagnation of the Blood, and should have remained ignorant of his Person, had I not discovered an Inscription over his Head, in large Capitals, thus, COL. E—S—N. I found he had hung there some Time; and was inform'd, that being a Traitor to his Country, there was no one, (not even his dearly beloved Lieutenant Colonel,) who would vouchsafe the Kindness to cut him down, so that he would in all Probability be soon reduced to a Skeleton.—This ignominious Fate its thought will soon be the Portion of several others of the same Club, and be a solemn Warning to every one who seek to be aggrandiz'd upon their Country's Ruin.* Your's, Observator.

This Day is Published,

By John Dickenson, Esq;

A true Friend to the Liberties of America,

An E S S A Y

ON THE

Constitutional Power of Great Britain

OVER

The Colonies of America:

With the Resolves of the Committee for the Province of Pennsylvania, and their Instructions to their Representatives in Assembly.

(*Sold by* Edes *and* Gill, *Price* 2s. Lawful Money.)

JOSEPH PEIRCE,

Hereby informs his good Customers, and others, That he has Removed to a new Shop, making the Corner northerly of the Old-Brick Meeting-House, and fronting the West End of the Town House, in Boston; where he has for Sale, a very large Assortment of English and other GOODS: He hopes for a Continuance of their Favors, which he will endeavor to merit by serving them on the *best* Terms.

L O S T.

An old Sea-Chest, (supposed to be taken out of Captain Mason's Store on the Long Wharff in Salem,) broad at the Bottom, painted blue but much wore off. If it has any Mark, it's J. M. Should it be opened, it contains Weston's Stenography, some Books of Physick, and some of Divinity, and considerable Writings, and both Men and Womens Cloth. Whoever shall give Information of the said Chest to the Rev. Dr. Whittaker in Salem, or the Rev. Samuel Stillman in Boston, so that the Subscriber may have it, they shall be well rewarded, and all reasonable Charges paid by

JOHN MARTIN.

All Persons having any Demands on the Estate of Mr. *Samuel Ruggles*, late of Boston, Housewright, deceased, are desired to bring in their Accounts and receive their Dues.——And all Persons indebted to said Estate are desired to make Payment to

Samuel Ruggles, Administrator.

L O N D O N,

Aug. 8. We hear a duty is to be laid next session on HEMP raised in America, and the revenue to be given in pensions to BUTE, MANSFIELD, NORTH, HUTCHINSON, and GAGE. *This the Americans might agree to pay one year, on assurance of the Pensioners becoming Knights of the Halter.*

There is no doubt but Hutchinson's situation is very critical, Sir Walter Raleigh lost his life on American business, but he was a warrior, a scholar, and an honest man. Few such men have been beheaded, and was there now a man so wise, it would be impolitic to kill him in his Saturnian age of lead.

The soldiers are so caressed in America, that they desert daily. "Who would fardels bear" that could have land for nothing, peace, plenty, and a fine country?

The Ministry are now so sick of this American business, that they want the people of Boston to accept the duty on tea (to save their blushes) and then they will immediately repeal it. If the people of America are such yankee doodles to be taken in such a trap, they do not deserve the liberty they struggle for. No! let them who made the diabolical act withdraw it. Ye Ministers, do you not know it is glorious to repent!

The timid hares about court (and indeed there are many) begin to shrink, and even talk that Governor Hutchinson led them into all these errors by his letters. If he has erred (say they) is it fit we should suffer? let him suffer for his errors; men should be cautious how they act in the affairs of two nations!

Lord North begins to skulk; he feels the ribband gall his neck; he talks of *haltering* it to a rope, and wishes it about a certain Governor's neck.

PHILADELPHIA, October 12.

We have authority to assure the public, that the reports which have been circulated respecting a neighbouring Governor, having wrote to the Ministry, recommending certain hostile measures against America, are without any just foundation.

Extract of a Letter from London, dated August 6, 1774.

"Our News-Papers are replete with alarming Resolutions and Associations on your side the water, which does not a little affect our Ministry,—It is an unlocked for event.— The talk is, that these worthy men will make the late Governor *Hutchinson the Scape Goat*, if no other resource is to be found."

NEW-YORK October 17.

A Writer in one of the English Papers says, It is confidently asserted, that some secret Proposals have been made to Government by the Inhabitants of Boston, of such a Nature that it is imagined all differences will soon be happily conciliated.

NEWPORT, October 17.

Last Thursday evening, 9 minutes past 7 o'clock, mean time, we had a pretty sensible shock of an earthquake; and some think they felt a fainter one between 11 and 12 at night.

Last Friday Capt. Baron, and on Saturday Capt. John Thurston, arrived here from Lisbon: Capt. Thurston, who came away the 4th of September, says they had an account that the negotiating of peace between the Russians and Turks was broke off, and that they were preparing for a vigorous prosecution of the war.

BOSTON, October 24.

In Provincial Congress, October 21, 1774.

WHEREAS sundry Persons now in Boston, having as Mandamus Counsellors or in other Capacities, accepted or acted under Commissions or Authority derived from the Act of Parliament passed last Session, for changing the Form of Government and violating the Charter of this Province; and by such disgraceful, such detestable Conduct, having counteracted not only the Sense of this Province, but of the united American Colonies in Grand Congress expressed: Therefore,

RESOLVED, That the Persons aforesaid, who shall not give Satisfaction to this injured Province and Continent within Ten Days from the Publication of this Resolve, by causing to be published in all the Boston News-Papers Acknowledgments of their former Misconduct, and Renunciations of the Commissions and Authority mentioned, ought to be considered as infamous Betrayers of their Country. And that a Committee of Congress be ordered to cause their Names to be published repeatedly, that the Inhabitants of this Province, by having them entered on the Records of each Town as *Rebels against the State*, may send them down to Posterity with the Infamy they deserve; and that other Parts of America may have an Opportunity of stigmatizing them in such Ways as shall effectually answer a similar Purpose.

Resolved, That it is hereby recommended to the good People of this Province, so far to forgive such of the obnoxious Persons aforesaid, who shall have given the Satisfaction required in the preceeding Resolve, as not to molest them for their past Misconduct. *A true Extract from the Minutes,*

BENJAMIN LINCOLN, Sec'ry.

In Provincial Congress, Octo. 21, 1774.

WHEREAS the unnecessary and extravagant Consumption of East-India Teas in Time past has much contributed to the political Destruction of this Province, and as Tea has been the Mean by which a corrupt Administration have attempted to tax, enslave and ruin us: Therefore,

RESOLVED, That this Congress do earnestly recommend to the People of this Province an Abhorrence and Detestation of all Kinds of East-India Teas, as the baneful Vehicle of a corrupt and venal Administration, for the Purpose of introducing Despotism and Slavery into this once happy Country; and that every Individual in this Province ought totally to disuse the same; and it is also recommended that every Town and District appoint a Committee to post up in some public Place the Names of all such in their respective Towns and Districts, who shall sell or consume so extravagant and unnecessary an Article of Luxury.

A true Extract from the Minutes.

BENJAMIN LINCOLN, Sec'y.

In Provincial Congress at Cambridge, Oct. 22d, 1774.

FROM a Consideration of the Continuance of the Gospel among us, and the Smiles of Divine Providence upon us with regard to the Seasons of the Year, and the general Health which has been enjoyed; and in particular, from a consideration of the Union which so remarkably prevails not only in this Province, but thro' the Continent, at this alarming Crisis.

It is *RESOLVED*, as the Sense of this Congress, That it is highly proper that a Day of PUBLIC THANKSGIVING should be observed throughout this Province; and it is accordingly recommended to the several religious Assemblies in the Province, that *Thursday the fifteenth Day of December* next, be observed as a Day of THANKSGIVING, to render Thanks to Almighty GOD for all the Blessings we enjoy. At the same Time, we think it incumbent on this People to humble themselves before God on account of their Sins, for which he hath been pleased in his righteous Judgment to suffer so great a Calamity to befal us, as the present Controversy between Great Britain and the Colonies; as also to implore the Divine Blessing upon us, that by the assistance of his Grace we may be enabled to reform whatever is amiss among us, that so God may be pleased to continue to us the Blessings we enjoy, and remove the Tokens of his Displeasure, by causing Harmony and Union to be restored between Great-Britain and these Colonies, that we may again rejoice in the Smiles of our Sovereign and the possession of those Privileges which have been transmitted to us, and have the hopeful prospect that they shall be handed down intire to Posterity, under the Protestant Succession in the illustrious House of Hanover.

By Order of the Provincial Congress,
JOHN HANCOCK, President.

On Saturday Morning last, after three Days Illness, departed this Life, Mr. WILLIAM MOLINEAUX, *in the 58th Year of his Age, a noted Merchant of this Town.—But what rendered this Gentleman more eminently conspicuous was, his inflexible Attachment to the Liberties of America—At this Crisis, when to evidence a Desire to serve or relieve their distressed, and oppressed Country, is denominated Folly, by the mercenary or timorous Worldling, 'tis not to be wondered that Mr.* MOLINEAUX, *who was unappalled at Danger, and inaccessible to Bribe or Corruption, should become obnoxious to the Minion and Sycophant, for his ebullient Zeal in so noble a Cause.—His Time and his Labour were with unremitted Ardor applied to the public Service: That Boston should become the Victim of Brutal Oppressors, was to him insupportable: He could not suppress his Resentment on seeing the Sons of Riot and Rapine thus prey on her desolated Bosom: 'Twas his Pride to confront the Power and Malice of his Country's Foes; 'twas his constant Wish and unremitted Effort to defeat them.—It may with Truth be said of this Friend of Mankind, that he died a Martyr to the Interests of America. His Watchfulness, Labours, Distresses and Exertions to promote the general Interest, produced an Inflamation in his Bowels: The Disease was rapid and poignant; but in the severest Pangs, he rose superior to Complaint; he felt no Distresses but for the Public.*

O SAVE MY COUNTRY HEAVEN! he said, and died. His Remains are to be interred at Four o'Clock this Afternoon, when his Friends and Acquaintance are desired to give their Attendance.

We are informed that ARNOLD WELLS, Esq; Owner of the Vessel which brought a Present of Wheat from our Brethren of Quebec, has generously declined taking any Thing as Freight for the same.

A Drove of Sheep from our Brethren of Scituate in the Colony of Rhode-Island for our suffering Poor, were receiv'd last Saturday Morning.

Capt. Brown arrived at Salem with a generous donation from our worthy sympathising brethren of the county of Monmouth, in New-Jersey, consisting of twelve hundred bushels of Rye, and fifty barrels of Rye Flour.

Capt. Boyd is arrived at Salem in a schooner from Hartford, in Connecticut, and has brought about nine hundred bushels of grain for the poor of this town.

Last Week the Rev. Dr. Langdon, of Portsmouth, was installed president of Harvard-College in Cambridge; he having accepted the invitation of the corporation to discharge the duties of that important office.

We hear from Grafton, that on the 19th of this Month, the Rev. Mr. Daniel Grosvenor, was Ordained to the Pastoral Care of the Church and People in that Place.—The Rev. Mr. Putnam began with Prayer, the Rev. Mr. Grosvenor of Scituate preached a Sermon suitable to the Occasion, from Genesis 45th Chap. 24th Ver. "See that ye fall not out of the Way"; the Rev. Mr. Fish prayed before the Charge, the Rev. Mr. Hall gave the Charge, the Rev. Mr. Whitney prayed after the Charge, the Rev. Mr. Frost gave the Right Hand.

Yesterday the Troops from New York arrived here.

We hear from Ashford, in Connecticut, that on Thursday evening last, there was a shock of an earthquake at that place, which lasted about two minutes; the noise commonly attending this Phænomenon was heard some time before the shock was felt.

We hear from EASTON, that on Thursday the 13th Instant, 53 of the amiable Daughters of Liberty met at the House of the Rev. Mr. Campbell, about One o'Clock in the Afternoon, and presented Mrs. Campbell with Two Hundred and Eighty Skeins of Cotton, Linnen, Worsted, Woolen and Tow Yarn, likewise some pieces of Cloth, Stockings, &c. then they all Walked in Order by Procession to the Meeting-House, where a Sermon was Preached suitable to the Occasion by their Rev. Pastor; and after Divine Service, they return'd in the same orderly Procession to the Rev. Mr. Campbell's House, where they pleasantly regail'd themselves with Cakes, Cheese and Wine, and then they seasonably retir'd to their respective Families—the whole was Conducted with the greatest Decency and good Order. Every Countenance indicated a Noble Spirit for Liberty and the promotion of our own Manufactures.

On WEDESDAY next, 26th Instant,
At TEN o'Clock in the Morning,
Will be sold by PUBLIC VENDUE,
At RUSSELL's Auction-Room, in Queen-Street,
A Variety of HARD-WARE, belonging to the Estate of a Gentleman lately deceas'd, *viz*

BRASS Kettles, Skillets, Warming Pans, Frying-Pans, Saws, Chizzles, Locks, Hinges, Gimblets, Aul-Blades, Cod-Hooks, pewter Basons and Porringers, Iron-Potts, Dish Kittles, Baking-Pans, Skillets.

Also, a Variety of House-Furniture, a Folio Bible, with Humphry's Annotations, adorn'd with Cutts.

An Assortment of Glass in Boxes, &c. &c.

J. RUSSELL, Auctioneer.

Duncan Ingraham, Jun.

Has now for Sale, a Parcel of well-bought GOODS, which he will sell on very advantageous Terms (for the Purchaser) at his Shop in Union-Street, Boston; among his Goods are the following, which he will sell uncommonly low for Cash, viz.

Colour'd Silk Hose various Prices,
Outsize white ditto,
A Variety of Silk Mitts and Gloves,
2 Cases Silver-handled Knives and Forks,
Blue and white India China—Cups and Saucers,
Pint and half Pint Bowles,
Table Cloths from 35*s*. O. T. to £.11 5*s*. very nice,
Black and colour'd figur'd Sattins,
Black and colour'd Capuchin Silks.

A Quantity of SHINGLES to be Sold cheap. Inquire of Edes and Gill.

TO BE SOLD, for CASH,
Some very genteel Houshold Furniture, if apply'd for this Week, by a Gentleman going out of Town; for Particulars enquire of Edes & Gill.

TO BE LET,
A convenient Shop on the North Side of the Town-House, a very suitable Place for Business.
Inquire of Edes & Gill.

WANTED to purchase, for a particular Use, a large Quantity of the stript Ground or Wall-Squarrel Skins. Whoever will procure and bring to *Thomas Courtney*, Taylor, facing the South Door of the Town House, Boston; He will take all that comes to hand, untill such Time as an Advertisement to the contrary is out in the Paper.

FIFTEEN DOLLARS REWARD.

RAN-AWAY from me the Subscriber on Thursday the Twentieth of October Instant, a Negro Man named CÆSAR, about 26 Years Old, five Feet four Inches high: had on when he went away, a Green Ratteen Coat, Red Everlasting Jacket, White Linnen Breeches, Blue Yarn Stockings, he has a Mark or Scar over one of his Eyes, the little Finger of his left Hand is a little crooked by the Cut of a Sickle; it is suspected that some one assisted him by changing Cloaths or gave him a pass: Whoever will take up said Negro and return him to me, or confine him to any of his Majesty's Goals, so that he may be return'd to me, shall have the above Reward and all necessary Charges paid by

SIMEON HAZELTINE.

Hardwick, October 21, 1774.

New AUCTION-ROOM, Cornhill
TO MORROW MORNING, at TEN o'Clock,
Will be sold by PUBLIC VENDUE,
At GREENLEAF's Auction Room,
A Variety of English GOODS, as usual.
Sale begins 10 o'Clock. *Wm. Greenleaf*, Auct'r.

New AUCTION-ROOM, Dock Square,
On FRIDAY next,
At TEN in the Morning,
Will be Sold by PUBLIC VENDUE,
At HUNTER's Auction-Room,
(Lately improved as a Store by Mr. Thomas Walley)
A great Variety of ENGLISH GOODS.
—The Particulars in the next Thursday's Papers.—
WM. HUNTER, Auctioneer.

Burials in the Town of BOSTON, since our last.
Seven Whites. Four Blacks.
Baptiz'd in the several Churches, Twelve.

High Water at BOSTON, for the present Week.

Monday, 20 min. aft.	3	Friday, 33 min. after.	6
Tuesday, 11 min. aft.	4	Saturday, 12 min. aft.	7
Wednesday, 1 m. aft.	5	Lord's Day, 4 m. af.	8
Thursday, 52 min. aft.	5	☾'s last Q. 27	[illegible]

THIS DAY PUBLISHED,

And sold by the Printers hereof; Price 9d.

CONSIDERATION on the Measures carrying on with respect to the British Colonies in North-America.

ALSO,

THE Bishop of St. Asaph's excellent SPEECH, intended to have been spoken on the Bill for altering the Constitution of this Government. ——This Pamphlet was sold in England for ONE SHILLING STERLING, but the Price here is no more than *Six Coppers*. We set it at this low Price in order that it may be universally purchased and read: It is (at the particular Desire of many Gentlemen) printed in a Pamphlet, rather than News-Papers, that the Contents of so truly valuable a Performance may be more effectually preserved for the Perusal of future Generations.

To be Sold by T. and J. FLEET, in Cornhill, [*Price, only Five Coppers.*]

An Address to Protestant Dissenters of all Denominations, on the approaching Election of Members of Parliament, with respect to the State of PUBLIC LIBERTY in general, and of AMERICAN AFFAIRS in particular.——

[*This excellent Pamphlet was received by the last Vessel from London, and is well worthy the Perusal of every North-American, & Friend of the British Constitution.*]

Samuel Abbot

Informs his Customers and others, That he is now selling off his Goods (all which were imported before the 1st of *August* last) extreme cheap for cash, at his Store the head of *Green's* Wharf, nigh the Market.

He once more requests all Persons who are indebted to him, and to the late Co-partnership of *Samuel Abbot* and Company, to make immediate Payment.

LEE & JONES,

At their Store near the Swing-Bridge, have for Sale

A general Assortment of Piece Goods suitable for the present Season,

A beautiful Variety of Brocades, figur'd & strip'd Lutestrings, Taffaties & Gorgoreens, black Armozeens and Padusoys, flower'd Sattins of all Colours for Ladies Cloaths, a few best Ermine Muffs and Tippets.—— Gold and Silver Laces, Silver Watches, Looking Glasses, Paper-Hangings, Corks, a few Cases of blue and white China Cups and Saucers, Liverpool and Glass Ware.

West-India RUM by the Hogshead, *Cornish's* New-England FISH-HOOKS.

*** *Also Nails of all Sorts to be deliver'd at Marblehead.*

Cyrus Baldwin,

HEREBY informs his Customers and others, that he has to Sell at his Shop in Cornhill, near the Town-House in BOSTON,

A general Assortment of English, India and Scotch Goods, imported before the 31st of last August, which he is determined to Sell at the usual Advance he Sold at before the Northern Blockade, consisting of Superfine, Midling and Low priz'd Broad Cloths, Kerseys, Serges, Beaver Coatings, Scotch Carpets and Carpetting, Plaids, Hair Plushes and Cotton Velvets, Muffs and Tippets, very neat Silk ditto, Choice Firkin Butter, Indigo and Snuff, with too many other Articles to be here enumerated.

He earnestly requests all those who are Indebted to him to make speedy Payment.

N. B. Said Baldwin is neither Addresser, Protester, nor Roman Catholick.

For LONDON,

THE Ship *Julias Cæsar*, (CHARLES FEA, Commander,) being a prime Sailer, and having excellent Accommodations for Passengers; will certainly Sail on or before the first of November next, having one Half of her Cargo engaged.—For Freight or Passage, apply to the Master on Board said Ship, lying at the Long-Wharf in Salem, or to Messieurs SMITH and ATKINSON, at their Store in King-Street. Oct. 6, 1774.

To be Sold for Cash only,

A small Quantity of good dry MEHOGANY, BOARDS and PLANK, fit for immediate Use. Enquire of Edes & Gill.

All Persons having any Demand on the Estate of Mr. *John Soren*, late of Boston, Baker, deceas'd, are desir'd to bring in their Accounts; and all Persons indebted to said Estate, are desired to make Payment to *Ann Soren*, Administratrix.

WANTED,

To improve for a Business of public Utility, a large convenient Room in the South Part of the Town.——Further particulars may be known by Inquiring of the Printers.

WANTED, a good HORSE, that will go well in a Chaise, and Trots light in a Saddle. Inquire of the Printers, or of Thomas Hudson

LOST this Morning about Eight o'Clock, between the Stores of Enoch Brown on the Neck, and Mr. Daniel Brown's of Roxbury, a dark blue and white Handkerchief, with Four Pounds Lawful Money in Silver mostly Change, tied in one Corner. Any Person that finds said Handkerchief, are desired to convey it to either of the said Stores, and they shall be generously Rewarded. Saturday, October 15, 1774.

TO BE LETT,

A convenient Dwelling-House in Hanover-Street, opposite Mr. Benj. Andrew's; Three Rooms upon a Floor, Wood House and Barn, a good Pump and Rain Water Cistern.——Inquire of William Fowle, living in said House; Where may be had a few Firkins of Choice Nova-Scotia Butter and a small Quantity of Spring Beaver.

To be Sold to the highest Bidder, by Virtue of an Order of the Superior Court;

A Part of the Real Estate of Caleb Dana, late of Cambridge, in the County of Middlesex, Esq; deceased, for the Payment of his Debts, and the Charges of Sale, viz.

Several Lots of Land lying in the Town of *Royalston*, in the County of *Worcester*, containing in the Whole, 1500 Acres. The Sale to be at the House of Mr. JACOB EASTY, Innholder, in said *Royalston*, on Thursday the 24th Day of November next, at Nine o'Clock in the Forenoon. GLO. DANA, Executor.

Ashburnham, October 13th, 1774.

☞ *Imported before August last,* And now for Sale, at the Shop of

Duncan Ingraham, Jun.

In Union-Street, BOSTON,

An Assortment of English, India and Scotch Goods, at a very moderate Profit, Wholesale and Retail. O. 10. 6w.

N. B. Wanted at said Shop 300 Yards Check Woollen ⅞ Wide, for which English or West-India Goods will be given in Payment.

TO be Sold by the Subscriber, a FARM lying in the Heart of the Town of Rochester, in the County of Plymouth, containing about 200 Acres, with a large Dwelling House, Barn and Corn-House on the same, well fenced, a good Orchard, a good Well of Water, &c. exceeding fit for Tillage, and a large Proportion of Fresh Meadow and Pasture Ground, very convenient for a Trader or Tradesman. It is the Tenement the late Rev. Mr. Timothy Ruggles owned at his Decease. The Premises may be purchased very cheap for Cash or short Credit. TIMOTHY RUGGLES.

October 10, 1774.

TO BE SOLD,

Five Barrels of BEEF, in good Order, on reasonable Terms, if apply'd for immediately. Enquire of *Thomas Clarke*, near the Rev. Mr. *Adams's* Meeting-House in *Roxbury*.

Nathan Frazier

BEGS leave to inform the Public, that in consequence of the Boston Port-Bill, and with a view of accommodating those of his Customers to whom it may be most convenient to have their Supplies conveyed by Water, he has opened a Store in Salem, (the one lately Improved by Mr. John Johnson, and next Door to Mr. John Gool's) where he has for Sale an Assortment of Goods suitable for the Season.——Said FRAZIER still continues his Business at his Store in *Boston* as usual: His Customers may be supplied at either of said Stores, Wholesale and Retail, on the most reasonable Terms for ready Money.—He will give his Personal Attendance, for the present at his *Salem* Store.

TWO DOLLARS REWARD.

STRAYED or Stolen out of the Pasture of MARY TUFTS, in Medford, a large dark bay Horse, about 11 Years old, 15 Hands high, his Mane cut on the right side, a Star in his Forehead, White by his Nose, Trots and Paces, carries his Head low. Whoever will bring said Horse to me the Subscriber, shall have the above Reward, and all necessary Charges paid by MARY TUFTS.

For LONDON.

THE Mast-Ship FOX, ZACHARIAH NORMAN, *Commander, having good Accommodations and Conveniences for a few genteel Passengers: Will sail from Portsmouth in New-Hampshire, about the 20th of this Month;—apply to Edward Parry, or Capt. Norman, at Portsmouth.* *October 3, 1774.*

TO BE SOLD,

Ten or Twelve Thousand seasoned Pine BOARDS. Inquire of the Printers.

NEWHALL and HICHBORN,

BEG leave to acquaint their Customers and others, in this and the neighbouring Parts, that they Propose carrying on the Cooper's Business in all its Branches, at Salem; and have opened a Shop for that Purpose, near the Distill-House of Mr. JONATHAN ROPES, in Salem.

N. B. As they also carry on the same business in Boston as usual, one of them may always be found in each Place.

TAKEN up by me the Subscriber, on the 25th ult. a Sorrel Horse. The Owner may have him again, proving his Property and paying the Charges, by applying to Seth Clark, of Medfield.

Caleb Call, of Charlestown, Baker,

ACQUAINTS his Friends and Customers, that he will supply them with his White Bisket, at the usual Price, either at *Salem* or *Marblehead*, upon their Writing to him, or applying to Messrs. *Hooper* and *Whittemore*, Coopers, on *Blany's* Wharfe in *Salem*.

William Blair Townsend,

At the Three Doves, In Marlborough-Street, Boston;

Hereby advertizes his Customers and others, That he is now selling off his Shop Goods for *Cash*, by Wholesale and Retail, at the low Rate of Eleven for One, on the true Sterling Cost; (being as low as they can be imported) consisting chiefly of Woollens, and well suited for the approaching Winter Season; *and which they may depend were imported, before the oppressive acts on this Town and Province were laid*; and may therefore be safely transported by *Land*, and Sold in any Town of said Province, without any Breach on the solemn League and Covenant our worthy Friends in the Country have justly entered into, in Defence of themselves and their Posterity.

N. B. Those that incline to purchase, are desired to apply speedily; as said TOWNSEND is determined to remove into a clear Air in the Country, *very soon*.

Stop Thief!

WHEREAS the Shop of the Subscriber was last Night broke open, and robbed of Twelve Beaver and Six Beaverett HATTS.—This is to promise a Reward of TEN DOLLARS, to any Person who shall discover the Thief or Thieves, so that he or they may be convicted thereof, and the HATTS recovered, and in Proportion for any Part of them. JAMES CODNER.

Boston, Tuesday Morning, October 4, 1774.

TO BE SOLD

10,000 Acres of very fine Land, in the Island of St. JOHN's, being half of one of the best Townships in it. About 500 Acres of which are clear'd and mostly arable Land. 'Tis situated on a Navigable River, 25 Miles above Charlotte Town, the Seat of Government, with which it has Communication both by River and a good Cart Road. There are some Families from Nantucket settled upon it. The Townships adjoining are well settled, and the Island in general in a Prosperous way. Captain *Holland*, who survey'd the Island, reports this Township to the Board of Trade, by whose Order he survey'd it, in the following Words, viz. "*Clear'd Lands 1000 Acres, Houses 30, pretty well situated for Fishing and Tillage, or Pasture, inferior to none upon the Island; there is also Plenty of Game and Fish.*"

Also, to be sold by the same Person, 10,000 Acres of choice good Land on the River St. John's in the Bay of Fundy, all settled agreeable to the Terms required by Government, which secures it forever from Forfeiture. For further Particulars enquire of Mr. *Warden*, Merchant, at his Store on Green's Wharf, or of the Printers hereof.

This is to Notify the Proprietors of Pearsontown, in the County of Cumberland, that at a legal Meeting of said Proprietors, held at Falmouth in said County, on the 31st Day of March last, a tax of fifteen shillings was assess'd on each right for the support of the Minister and other necessary charges, for bringing forward the settlement of said township, and to pay said tax or assessment (as well as former arrearages of taxes due on their several rights heretofore granted by said proprietors, and legally advertiz'd) to Ephraim Jones of said Falmouth, treasurer of said proprietors, or to the subscribers the proprietors committee, on or before the 9th day of January next, otherwise their several lots and rights there, will be sold at Public Vendue at the House of Mr. Moses Shattuck, Innholder, in said Falmouth, on the said 9th day of January next for the payment of said taxes as the Law directs: The said sale to begin at ten of the clock in the forenoon.

Falmouth, Sept. 6, 1774. Enoch Freeman, Moses Pearson, Ste. Longfellow } Propriet's Com'tee.

Colony of RHODE-ISLAND, *&c.*

WHEREAS John Wiley of Providence, in the County of Providence, in the Colony aforesaid, Merchant, preferred a Petition unto the General Assembly of the said Colony, representing that he is an insolvent Debtor, and praying that he may be admitted to the Benefit of an Act passed in June A. D. 1756, entitled, "An Act for the Relief of Insolvent Debtors." Whereupon the General Assembly referred the said Petition, and ordered that the Creditors of the said John Wiley should be notified by an Advertisement to be inserted in the Newport Mercury, the Providence Gazette, and in one of the Boston News-Papers, to appear at the next Session to answer the same:—I do therefore hereby notify the Creditors of the said John Wiley to appear (if they shall think fit) at the General Assembly to be holden at Providence, in and for the said Colony, on the last Wednesday in October next, then and there to shew Cause, (if any they have) why the said Petition should not granted. HENRY WARD, Secr'y.

STOLEN out of a Pasture at Roxbury on Thursday Night the 6th Instant, a brown Mare about 14 Hands high, she has a Star in her Forehead, one of her Fetter-Lock Joints of her hind Feet white, her Main hangs on the near Side, and a Feather on the other Side of her Neck, she is uncommonly square built and Trots strong and bold, she has a lofty Carriage and carries a high Tail. Whoever apprehends the Thief so that he may be brought to Justice, and returns the Mare to Mr. Joseph Morton at Boston, at the sign of the white Horse, South-End, shall have THIRTY DOLLARS *Reward, and if the Mare alone Fifteen Dollars, and all necessary Charges paid, by me the Subscriber,*

Boston, Oct. 10, 1774. JOSEPH MORTON.

Boston: Printed, by EDES & GILL, *in Queen-Street,* 1774.

No. 1020.

THE Boston-Gazette, AND COUNTRY JOURNAL.

Containing the freshest Advices, Foreign and Domestic.

MONDAY, October 31, 1774.

Last Monday arrived at Salem, the Ship Friendship, Captain Tyler, in 44 Days from Bristol, by whom we have the following FRESH ADVICES, viz.

WARSAW, *August 3.*

A Russian officer is arrived here as Courier from General Romanzow, with the important news of peace between Russia and the Porte being concluded to the great advantage of the former. This most glorious peace, ever concluded by the Russians, was signed the 21st of July at Kout Chouce Kninardzi, near Silistria, by Prince Repnin, and the Turkish Plenipotentiaries, Nissangi Resni, Archmet Effendi, & Ibrahim Miconib Reis Effendi; and afterwards ratified by the Field-Marshal Count Romanzow, and the Grand Vizir. The treaty contains 28 articles, but the following most material ones are all that are at present known.

1. *The absolute independence of the Crimea, and that their Chans shall for the future have no further duties to render the Grand Signior than such as are due to him as the supreme Calif of the Mahometan religion.*

2. *Russia shall have a free navigation and trade in the Black Sea, and in all the harbours, rivers, and ports of the Turkish empire.*

3. *The fortresses of Asoph, Jenekale, Kertisch & Kinburn, with their districts, and a tract of land between the rivers Bog and Dnieper, shall belong to Russia.*

4. *Russia shall have the liberty of building new fortresses, and repairing the old ones, as they shall think fit.*

5. *The Porte shall always give the reigning Sovereign of Russia the title of Padischah, that is, Emperor of All the Russias.*

6. *Russia returns all her conquests, stipulating certain prerogatives and privileges for the Inhabitants of the provinces and islands restored, which puts them in security. And*

7. *The Porte engages to pay Russia a large sum of money, not less than 48 millions, nor more than 70 millions of Piasters, to defray the expences that empire has been at during the war, & to give them all the artillery they have in their army.*

The deplorable situation to which the Grand Vizir was reduced by the wise manœuvres of the Field-Marshal Count Romanzow, was the cause of this great event. The Marshal having first sent about 50,000 of his own men over the Danube, passed it himself without any obstacle from the Grand Vizir. He then kept Silistria in awe with a corps under Major General Lloyd, (an Englishman) and Ruzug, with another division, under General Soltikow, who at the same time cut off the communication between the Grand Vizir, together with the grand Turkish army, and their magazines; and intercepted all their provisions. He placed General Kamenski in an advanced position, to stop any succours that might come to their relief. An Ottoman corps, with 500 waggons from Adrianople, escorted by 28,000 men, was coming for that purpose, but was beaten by General Kameski and all the waggons taken; an account of which being brought to the Turkish camp, the Grand Vizir found his army ready to mutiny for want of provision, and that he could not give battle in that position without manifestly exposing himself to a defeat; therefore after attempting to no purpose, the renewal of negociations, and the recommending of a congress, was obliged, on the 21st of July, to sign the conditions which the Russians imposed, and which are nearly the same as they required at the congresses of Boczani and Bucharest, in 1772 and 1773.

By the modern Universal Table of Coins, a piastre is valued at 3s. 7d. At that rate, if the Turks are to pay the Russians only 40 millions of piastres, that will make a sum of near 7 million sterl. The articles do not mention when the money is to be paid; but probably it will be by instalments,

Paris, August 15. *Some letters from Madrid mention, that differences have arisen between that Court and Portugal regarding the limits of Paraguay and Brasil, and some frauds which have been committed there, and these differences went so far as that the Spaniards, with the loss of 100 men, have taken a Portuguese fort.*

LONDON, August 13.

It is said that Sir George Howard will very soon be appointed Governor to one of the principal Colonies in North-America.

Yesterday arrived a Mail from New-York, which brings a long detail of the proceedings of a numerous meeting of the inhabitants of that city, in which they have taken the resolution of sending deputies to a general Congress of the Colonies to be held at Philadelphia, to agree to a Non-importation from Great Britain, until the act for blocking up the port of Boston be repealed.

Aug. 18. *Letters from Charlestown, South Carolina, dated the 5th of July, mention that their resolutions are the same as in the other Colonies to support the Bostonians. They have already sent a cargo of 264 barrels of rice to Salem, for the support of the poor necessitous inhabitants at Boston.*

Some alarming accounts are said to be received express from Boston, which have thrown the Ministry into very great confusion, as it was a circumstance they were not at all guarded against. The particulars have not as yet transpired; but the substance is, that numbers of the soldiery, partly from inclination, & partly from offers of lands and settlements from the natives, have gone over to the popular side.

It is said that a battalion of the guards will have orders to hold themselves in readiness to embark for Boston on the shortest notice.

A private letter from Boston, by the last mail mentions, that the inhabitants of Boston will not permit any naval officer to come on shore with his sword on.

Aug. 20. *It is plain by the Quebec bill, that the Protestant religion is not so much as tolerated now in Canada; it is left to future consideration, and it is believed to a very late day; as the French ministers, and their flocks of Protestants, to the number of some thousands, are flying away to our adjacent colonies, from persecution, and perhaps torture.*

It is said, and we hope with truth, that a public subscription will be soon opened in this Metropolis for the distressed inhabitants of Boston, now suffering in the common cause of liberty, & grievously oppressed by the hand of power.

Orders were on Thursday sent off from the War-office to Ireland, to discharge the transports which were taken up at Cork and Kinsale on government account, a stop being put to the embarkation of troops from that Kingdom.

Aug. 23. *A private letter from Boston assures us, that upwards of 300 of the troops are deserted from those that are encamped on the Common, who have met with the greatest encouragement from the Traders in the interior parts of the country, where they are now settled; and it is added, that others are deserting every day.*

If a petition and remonstrance should be agreed on by all the provinces in America, as most persons think will be the case, it is expected to arrive against the meeting of the Parliament, and will probably take as much time in discussing as the acts that have given cause to it, took in framing & passing.

August 25. We hear that the last Resolution in the Cabinet relative to the Bostonians was as follows—To use conciliating Measures *for the present*---call the Parliament together early in this Winter, and *prevail* upon them to pass an Act empowering a Committee of 12 (of whom G. Gage is to be President) to forfeit the Lands and Properties of all those *refractory* Spirits who sign Conventions, or any other way disturb the public Tranquility.——This immediate Attack upon private Property, with a Power of devolving it on others, is thought the most direct Scheme of bringing them to Obedience.

There is a Bustle among the Great not usual at this Time of the Year; most People think concerning the State of Affairs in America; but others assert the Continent of Europe affords matter which takes up no small share of their Attention.

It is asserted that two American Governors (from whose Honor and Veracity great Expectations are formed) are ordered Home, in order that the Ministry may have certain Demonstration of the real Disposition of our Colonists.

It appears by Intelligence communicated in Letters brought by the Bridgewater, that the Spanish Governor of the Manillas has sent a peremptory Message to Mr. Harbord, Governor of the English East-India Company's new Settlement at Balambanca, that if he does not immediately, on receipt of that notice, retire with all the English, who are with him on that Island, he shall according to the Instructions of his Court, send a sufficient Force to bring away, and destroy all such Works and Fortifications as shall have been erected.— It is presumed that Mr. Harbord will not conform to this Requisition, & that in all probability the Spaniard will carry his Threats into Execution; in which case the whole of this Transaction will extremely resemble what happened at Falkland's Island; the Court of Spain having, previous to the Establishment of this Settlement, made the strongest Remonstrances to our Ministry against that Measure, which occasioned a delay of carrying the Design into Execution for a considerable Time. It may easily be concluded, that this Intelligence adds greatly to the embarrassment of Administration here, who had before a sufficient Load of perplexing Affairs on their Hands.

Aug. 27. *The Americans pretend, that they are about to enter into non-importation agreements. But it is an incontestible truth, that they have at this instant given orders for five times more goods than the English chuse to trust them with. Their view is, first to get as far in debt as they can; and then, pretending that they cannot pay, unless their demands are complied with, to raise a murmur among the English merchants and manufacturers. In the next place, when they have imported vast quantities, and filled their own warehouses, they will be forming* patriotic *associations not to import:—A ready way to enrich themselves, by not paying for what they buy, and raising the price of what they sell.*

The affairs of America will soon wear a better aspect, the Court being determined to withdraw their pretensions against them.

Fourteen sail of transports, from 200 to 500 tons burthern are ordered to be taken up at different ports for government service.

Aug. 29. *We hear express orders have been sent over to the Commander in Chief to prevent the American Congress at every event. But other accounts say the deliberations of the American General Congress are impatiently waited for, and with more attention, by France and Spain, than even those of the British Parliament have been for some years past. They have already their Agents and Spies in the Colonies.*

The most sincere, as well as solemn engagements, we are informed, have, within these few days, been entered into by the Kings of Great-Britain and France, for the cultivating the utmost friendship possible between the two crowns during their lives. But it is feared that no engagements will prevent a Frenchman from pursuing his interest.

Extract of a Letter from the Hague, August 26.

"It is reported here that War is declared between Spain and Portugal, and that in Consequence of a former Treaty the Court of Madrid has demanded of Versailles a Corps of 50,000 Men. If this News is confirmed, England must assist Portugal, her old Friend and Ally.

"A Treaty is reported to be on foot between the Courts of Turin and Versailles, by virtue of which his Most Christian Majesty is to cede Corsica to the King of Sardinia, reserving, however, the Privilege of free Entrance for all French Ships into the different Ports of the Island, and an uninterrupted Trade. This Treaty is said to be far advanced, and even that the formal cession of Corsica will be made before Christmas next; but we must wait further Confirmation of this Account before it can be intirely credited, particularly as Nothing is yet talked of, as an equivalent from Sardinia to France for the cession."

A report prevails that a certain assembly in America (Boston) lately offered their allegiance to the young King of France, on condition of his taking them under his protection, which he, much to his honor, refused, giving them for answer, that he had dissatisfied subjects enough already.

Aug. 30. It is said that Tuesday the 15th of November, is the Day fixed for the meeting of Parliament.

Aug. 31. Yesterday upwards of 700 Letters from Philadelphia and different Parts of America, were delivered at the Post-Office.

A few days ago Lord Mansfield set out for Paris —This step seems extraordinary. But the friends of the Ministry say, that Lord Stormont keeping only low company at Paris, has occasioned the French Court to treat him very coldly, and that Lord Mansfield is gone to instruct him better.—May be so —But a message, which the Emperor caused his ambassador here to deliver a few days ago, seems to put a different complexion upon it. The Ambassador demanded an audience, at which, it is said, he expressed himself to this effect: "If the King of Great-Britain avowed the language lately held by his Electoral Minister, he must expect the Emperor to oppose him in every step he took in the Empire." It was asked to have this message in writing; but the Ambassador did not chuse to comply with that request.

Sept. 1. Yesterday morning early an Express was received at St. James's, from Paris, which was thought to be of such importanco that it was sent of immediately to Kew.

The seeming shew of a dispute between the Courts of Lisbon and Madrid is looked on merely as a rumour to amuse the other powers of Europe, while some specious measures are transacting, which they wish to keep secret.

A subscription is about to be opened for the relief of the Bostonians. The Lord Mayor, Mr. George Healy, and several other principal Merchants and Gentlemen have intimated their intentions to become liberal subscribers.

It is remarkable that the Inhabitants of Massachusets Bay were the only Colony who refused to give up their Charter when it was revoked by the arbitrary James the Second; the banishment of that Prince rescued them from the punishment which, to his shame, he would have inflicted upon them for their principles of liberty.

It is reported that a certain great man, who has been often courted of late to undertake a share in the administration of government, has insisted on an immediate repeal of the Boston Port-Bill, before he will enter into any negociation whatever.

We are informed from Cadiz, that open hostilities are absolutely commenced between Spain and Portugal in the Old World, as well as in the New, & that two ships of each nation have had an engagement in sight of that port, which ended to the disadvantage of the Portuguese, who drew off much damaged from the action.

Sep. 2. It is said the Parliament will meet pursuant to their last adjournment, and sit a few weeks on account of American Affairs.

A Report prevails that a certain American Assembly had made offers of allegiance to the young King of France, who not only rejected them, but entered into a solemn Engagement with the King of England mutually to defend and support each other during life.

Very vigorous measures are now taking by administration, to enforce their resolutions against the Americans; and it is said that some of the principal gentlemen who distinguished themselves in America, in defence of their charter rights, are to be brought over, in order for an enquiry to be made into their conduct.

Government in many Boroughs is said to have conciliated measures, and have settled it with opposition to bring in one Member, rather than have the expence of a contested Election.

It is reported that orders are sent to Ireland for some of the regiments there to be got in readiness for immediate embarkation.

According to the complexion of things in the country, it is now believed, that opposition will have a very strong and formidable majority.

BARNSTABLE, October 10, 1774.

Meſſieurs EDES & GILL,

Pleaſe to publiſh the following in your next Paper, and you'll oblige a Number of your Friends & Cuſtomers.

ON Tueſday the 27th ultimo, the time for the Court of General Seſſions of the Peace and Inferior Court of Common Pleas for this County to ſit, a great number of people from this, and the neighbouring counties of Plymouth and Briſtol, being aſſembled before the court-houſe door in this town; after chuſing a Moderator, Voted and Reſolved, That it was inexpedient for ſaid Courts to ſit, under the preſent ſituation of our publick affairs, until the opinion of the Continental or of a Provincial Congreſs could be known; and therefore choſe a committee, viz. Dr. Nathaniel Freeman and Mr. Stephen Nye, of Sandwich, Capt. Daniel Crocker of Barnſtable, Capt. Noah Fearing of Wareham, and Dr. John Pitcher of Rochester, to preſent the following addreſs to the Juſtices of ſaid Court, being then convened at the Houſe of Mr. Crocker, Innholder in this Town.

To the honorable Juſtices of his Majeſty's Inferior Court of Common Pleas, and Court of General Seſſions of the Peace, for the County of Barnſtable.

May it pleaſe your Honours,

THE Inhabitants of this province, being greatly alarmed at the late unconſtitutional acts of the Britiſh Parliament, conſidering them as calculated to eſtabliſh tyranny and oppreſſion inſtead of the once happy conſtitution of this province; in conſequence of which many reſpectable counties in the ſame, have prevented the ſitting of the inferior courts, as well as ſuperior; we judge, not from an apprehenſion, merely, that they were not *conſtitutional*; but, from a ſuppoſition, that there might be appeals from *them* to the *ſuperior court*, the chief juſtice of which receiving his ſupport from the crown, independent of the grants of the people, cannot fail to have an unhappy biaſs in favour of ſaid unconſtitutional acts; and two others, of the ſuperior judges, having ſworn to carry the ſame acts into execution; and judging, that by proceeding upon appeals from a court friendly to the conſtitution, and zealous for their country's cauſe, to the ſaid *ſuperior court*, we might in *this way*, if no other, open a door for the ſaid chief juſtice and his aſſiſtants to execute their commiſſions on the plan of the ſaid oppreſſive act.

Wherefore a great number of the inhabitants of the county of Barnſtable, being now convened, with many others from the ſeveral counties in Old Plymouth colony, taking into ſerious conſideration the neceſſity of uſing every precaution to prevent the operation of ſaid acts, and believing the following one neceſſary, do humbly requeſt your honours to deſiſt from all buſineſs in ſaid courts, and from holding any ſeſſions thereof, till the minds of the Continental, or of a Provincial Congreſs, be obtained.— And that your Honours would aſſure this body, that you will not, in any manner, aſſiſt in carrying ſaid unconſtitutional acts into execution, hold any commiſſion in conſequence [illegible] the new eſtabliſhment, or in any manner conform thereto; but that you will uſe your utmoſt endeavours to prevent the ſame from taking Place.

	N. Freeman,	A Committee choſen
	S. Nye,	by the Body of the
	D. Crocker,	People to preſent
Barnſtable, Sept.	*N. Fearing,*	this Addreſs to your
27, 1774.	*J. Pitcher,*	Hon'rs in their name

The addreſs being preſented accordingly, the Juſtices after taking the ſame into conſideration, returned the following anſwer, viz.

To *Nathaniel Freeman, John Pitcher, Stephen Nye,* and *Noah Fearing*, a committee, as they ſay, choſen by the body of the people, to preſent an addreſs, this 27th of September, 1774, to the honorable Juſtices of his Majeſty's Inferior Court of Common Pleas, and Court of General Seſſions of the Peace—Said Addreſs being preſented to the Juſtices of ſaid County, or at leaſt as many as are preſent: The ſaid Juſtices in anſwer thereto, ſay,

THAT they are as much concerned at the late unconſtitutional acts of the Britiſh parliament, as the body of the people are; but apprehend, that the People's embodying this day, to hinder ſaid Court's ſitting, as uſual, will not help the matter; eſpecially as ſaid court was about to ſit in the ſame conſtitutional way as we have always done ever ſince we have been a county; and had ſaid court been ſuffer'd to have been open'd they would have proceeded in the ſame regular manner as uſual. And as to appeals ſhould there be any, they will be to the next Superior Court of Judicature, &c. and they can't poſſibly be tried, till we have a conſtitutional one—And we are ſorry that we are interrupted, for unleſs we can proceed to open ſaid courts and adjourn, we can be in no capacity to proceed when we hear the opinion of the general congreſs, or a provincial one; and as to the aſſurance, you requeſt that we would not aſſiſt in carrying ſaid unconſtitutional act into execution, you may be fully aſſured, that there is not one of the ſaid juſtices, that incline to do it, or to hold any commiſſion in conſequence thereof; and ſhall do all that is in our power in a *conſtitutional way*, to prevent ſaid act from taking place——Therefore, we the ſaid juſtices, expreſs our utmoſt concern that the ſaid courts of juſtice, in this, or any other county, ſhould be turned out of their ordinary, or conſtitutional courſe, by the people of this province, until the minds of the continential or a provincial congreſs can be fully known, as we can by no means, apprehend that any ill conſequences can attend the ſetting of ſaid court, until this month expires.

James Otis, Thomas Smith, Edward Bacon, David Gorham, Solomon Otis, Kenelm Winſlow, Joſeph Otis, Iſaac Hinckley, Nymphas Marſton, David Thatcher, Daniel Davis, Melatiah Bourn, Shearjaſhub Bourn.

The anſwer being communicated to the people, after taking the ſame into conſideration and thoroughly deliberating thereon, two of the Juſtices of ſaid court having ſign'd an addreſs to the late governor Hutchinſon, upon his departure from the province; one of them an old *Reſcinder*, *two*, voters againſt the General Congreſs, *one or more* aiding and aſſiſting in vending the Eaſt India company's Tea laſt winter, another concern'd in endeavouring to procure a mob to deſtroy private property, on purpoſe, as is apprehended, to bring an odium on the friends of liberty; theſe conſiderations with others, evinced the neceſſity of ſome better aſſurance, that they would hold no commiſſions in conſequence of ſaid acts, than barely ſaying they did not *incline to do it.* And conſidering, that if cauſes were tried by the Inferior Court, appealed and *then*, no final iſſue, till we have a conſtitutional Superior court, it might be attended with more difficulty, coſt and damages to the parties, than to ſuſpend any proceſs at all, till ſuch court can be had; as in caſe of proceſs and appeal, the plaintiff muſt not only lay out of his principal, but of an additional bill of coſts, —Beſides in caſe of final iſſue, it might be only making work for unconſtitutional ſheriffs; theſe apprehenſions, added to the great indignation of the people, towards ſome tools of miniſterial corruption and oppreſſion, who never can give ſatisfaction, while in office, induced them to reſolve and vote, that notwithſtanding what the court had offered, they ſtill thought it inexpedient for them to ſet, and that their anſwer ſhould be immediately returned them, as being by no means ſatisfactory in any particular. A committee of the body accordingly returned it, and informed the Juſtices, that the people deſired to know whether they determined to ſet or not, as a court; the Juſtices then told the Committee they ſhould not.— A committee then waited on them, by order of the people, and deſired them to ſign a ſolemn declaration, that they would not accept of any commiſſion, in conſequence of the late acts of the Britiſh parliament, or do any buſineſs, in their reſpective offices, in conformity thereto; they alſo waited on the high ſheriff, to deſire the ſame of him; and on David Gorham and Shearjaſhub Bourn, Eſqrs; to acquaint them of the reſentment and juſt indignation of the people towards them, for addreſſing the late infamous governor Hutchinſon, upon his departure from this province, whereby they uſed their endeavours to ſupport, encourage and applaud, a *known Traitor*, and *inveterate Enemy*, to the country.———That ſaid addreſs was, in the apprehenſion of the people, no leſs falſe and deſigning, than flattering and fulſome, and diſcovered the unparallelled vanity, inſolence and audacity of the addreſſors, in daring, openly, to contradict the united expreſs'd ſentiments of both houſes of the General Court, as well as of all America; by which conduct, they have forfeited the eſteem of the public, and enliſted under the banners of ſaid Hutchinſon, as enemies to the cauſe of liberty; for which they ought immediately to make ſatisfaction to the offended public.

The Juſtices and Sheriff ſigned the reſpective *declarations*, and the Addreſſors the reſpective *confeſſions*, encloſed herewith, [*which we are obliged to omit this Week.*] which were voted ſatisfactory.

The body of people then voted and reſolved, That the Military officers holding commiſſions under a Captain-General, at the head of forces raiſed againſt the Rights and Properties, and conſequently the Lives of the inhabitants of this country, and who is conſtantly making hoſtile preparations againſt it, muſt themſelves be conſidered as enemies to the country likewiſe, unleſs they immediately reſign their commiſſions: And therefore a committee was choſen to apply to, and acquaint them herewith, and to deſire them to reſign accordingly; and alſo to apply to the deputy-ſheriffs for them to ſign a declaration, reſpecting ſaid oppreſſive acts, ſuitable to their office.

The body of the people alſo voted to addreſs the honorable James Otis, Eſq; of this Town, as one of the conſtitutional Councellors of the Province, and pray his Honor's Attendance at the General Court, to be holden at Salem on the 5th Day of October next—The whole body accordingly marched in proceſſion to him, and preſented him the following Addreſs, viz.

To the Honorable JAMES OTIS, Eſq;

May it pleaſe your Honour,

THE body of people aſſembled from the ſeveral counties of Barnſtable, Plymouth and Briſtol, on the 28th day of Sept. 1774, at or near the court houſe in Barnſtable, beg leave to addreſs your honour, as one of his majeſty's conſtitutional council of this province; and to aſſure you that we entertain a very high and grateful ſenſe of that *integrity*, and of thoſe *abilities*, which have long diſtinguiſhed you, as in every important truſt repoſed in you by the public, ſo eſpecially in the capacity we now conſider you.

And whereas his excellency, the governor of this Province, hath iſſued writs for electing a new houſe of repreſentatives, to meet at Salem, on the 5th day of October next, and notwithſtanding a number of councellors have been appointed by mandamus from his majeſty, in conſequence of a late act of the Britiſh parliament; but preſuming the repreſentatives of this people yet determined to be free, never will, or ought, to conſent to do any buſineſs with them, and as we look upon the council choſe laſt May by the great and general court according to charter to be the only conſtitutional council of this province; we do therefore, pray your honour, that you would attend the great and general court at Salem the next ſeſſions, in ſaid capacity; and, that you would continue thoſe endeavours to obtain a redreſs of the grievances ſo juſtly complained of by the people, which have long diſtinguiſhed you as an able defender of our conſtitution and liberties: And now wiſhing your Honor the ſupport of Heaven in your advanced age, that you may much longer remain a bleſſing to this province, and enjoy the happineſs of ſeeing thoſe Rights reſtored, which have been moſt injuriouſly wreſted from us, we beg leave to ſubſcribe ourſelves, your Honor's moſt obedient humble Servants,

	Nath'l. Freeman,	
	Stephen Nye,	A Committee
Barnſtable, Sept.	*Joſ. Haskel, 3d.*	in Behalf of the
28, 1774	*Noah Fearing,*	People.
	John Pitcher.	

To the above Addreſs, Colonel OTIS was pleaſed to return the following Anſwer, viz.

GENTLEMEN,

YOUR very complaiſant Addreſs to me as a conſtitutional Councellor of this Province, deſiring me to attend my Duty at Salem on the 5th of October, the Time when the General Court is to ſet, I am oblig'd to you for; and for putting me in Mind of my Duty; and I am determined to attend at Salem at that Time, in Caſe my Health permits. I am,

Your very humble Servant, JAMES OTIS.

Barnſtable, September 28, 1774.

The people expreſs'd their high eſteem of that honourable Gentleman, their grateful ſenſe of his paſt ſervices, their ſanguine expectation of his future exertions, and hearty approbation of his obliging anſwer to their addreſs, by giving him three cheers, and then march'd back in proceſſion to the court-houſe.

The people voted and reſolved, that as the town of Boſton was now ſuffering in a common cauſe, they would uſe their endeavours to relieve them, by encouraging and procuring donations for their ſupport—that they would immediately provide themſelves with arms and ammunition, and hold themſelves in readineſs to aſſiſt, in defending the town of Boſton, and the rights and liberties of this country, which they never would give up, but with their lives and fortunes—that they would not import any more goods from Great Britain, or purchaſe any imported by others, after that time, till the port of Boſton be opened, and the late oppreſſive acts repealed—that they would uſe their endeavours to ſuppreſs common pedlars, &c. And that this body have not met together in a riotous, wanton or diſorderly manner, with a deſign of injuring the perſon or property of any body, nor paſſed the above votes and reſolutions in oppoſition to good government, or diſloyalty to our ſovereign; but from a painful neceſſity of exerting ourſelves, in a ſerious, ſteady and determined manner, to prevent the total extirpation of liberty, juſtice and religion from our land. And we do expreſs our abhorrence and deteſtation of all riotous and diſorderly proceedings, our determination to uſe our utmoſt endeavours to keep the peace, to prevent and ſuppreſs all mobs, riots and tumults, and to procure a due ſubmiſſion to the laws of the land.

Information being made to the people, that the towns of Barnſtable, Yarmouth and Eaſtham, (whoſe late repreſentatives voted againſt the grand continential congreſs,) in their late election, had left out thoſe perſons, and choſen others to repreſent their reſpective towns, whoſe attachment to the cauſe of their Country was too well known not to excite joy on ſuch a happy change, the people teſtified their hearty approbation thereof by three cheers. And after finiſhing their buſineſs with the utmoſt decency and good order, the people diſperſed to their reſpective homes.

NEW HAVEN, October 21.

Colony of Connecticut, October 20, 1774.

In the Houſe of Repreſentatives,

Reſolved unanimouſly,

THAT Contributions from all the Towns in this Colony for ſupplying the Neceſſities, and alleviating the Diſtreſſes of our Brethren at Boſton, ought to be continued, in ſuch Manner and ſo long as their Occaſions may require.

Teſt. RICH'D LAW, Clerk.

At an adjourned Town Meeting held in this Town, laſt Tueſday, a Number of Perſons were appointed to receive Subſcriptions for the relief of the neceſſitous Inhabitants of the Town of Boſton.

For LONDON,

The Ship JOHN WILKES, JAMES HALL, Commander, Will certainly ſail from Newport, Rhode-Iſland, on or before the 10th of November at fartheſt:—For Paſſage apply to FRANCIS ROTCH, at his Store at Bedford in Dartmouth, or the Maſter on board.

Bedford, (in Dartmouth) October 27, 1774.

JUST RE-PRINTED, (*Price 8d. L. M.*)

And to be ſold by *Z. Fowle*, near Charleſtown-Ferry, *S. Whiting*, in Marſhall's-Lane, and *E. Steel*, Boſton.

A faithful Teſtimony to *New-England*,

By the following celebrated Authors, viz.

I. Mr. *Jonathan Mitchell*, extracted from an Inſtrument of his, dated December 31, 1662.

II. Mr. *John Higginſon*, ſtated in a Sermon to the General Court, May 27, 1663.

III. Hon. *William Stoughton*, Eſq; in a Sermon preached by him, in the Audience of the General-Court, April 1663.

IV. The Teſtimony finiſhed by Dr. *Increaſe Mather*, who ſays, I do now with my dying Hand ſign my concurrence to the above.——This Book is really worth peruſal, it exhibits a recognition of our Father's pious Errand in this Wilderneſs.

Taken by EXECUTION

And to be Sold To-Morrow Morning at Ten o'Clock, By PUBLIC VENDUE,

At *Gould*'s Auction-Office,

In Back-Street,

A valuable Aſſortment of ENGLISH GOODS,

—Amongſt which are,—

BAIZES, Duffils, Kerſeys, Ratteens, Broad Cloths, Coatings, Serges, Shalloons, Worſted Hoſe, Breeches Patterns, Camblets, Cambleteens, ſtriped Hollands, Dowlaſs, Sattins, figur'd and plain Modes, India and Engliſh Taffatys, Cravatts, figur'd and plain Gauzes, Catguts, Paris Nets, Laces, Calicoes, Printed & Check'd Linnen Handkerchiefs, figur'd and plain Lawns, Ladies Pocket Books, a variety of Brazery and Cutlary Ware, with a great Variety of other Articles, alſo a quantity of good Cheeſe, Dutch Looking Glaſſes, Two Feather Beds, Chairs, Tables, &c. &c.

At One o'Clock preciſely will be put up a ſecond-hand Chaiſe with Harneſſing compleat.

R. GOULD, Auctioneer.

New AUCTION-ROOM, Dock-Square.

On WEDNESDAY next,

At TEN in the Morning,

Will be Sold by PUBLIC VENDUE,

At HUNTER's Auction-Room,

(Lately improved as a Store by Mr. Thomas Waller)

A great Variety of ENGLISH GOODS, as uſual.

WM. HUNTER, Auctioneer.

ALSO, Some Houſe Furniture, and a Quantity of new Tin Ware, and Tinſmith's Tools.

CAMBRIDGE.

In Provincial Congress, October 26. 1774.

WHEREAS *in Consequence of the present unhappy Disputes between Great-Britain and the Colonies, a formidable Body of Troops with warlike Preparations of every Sort are already arrived at, and others destined for the Metropolis of this Province; and the expressed Design of their being sent is to execute Acts of the British Parliament, utterly subversive of the Constitution of the Province: And whereas his Excellency General Gage has attempted by his Troops to disperse the Inhabitants of Salem, whilst assembled to consult Measures for preserving their Freedom; and to subjugate the Province to arbitrary Government;—And proceeding to still more unjustifiable and alarming Lengths has Fortified against the Country the Capital of the Province, and thus greatly endangered the Lives, Liberties and Properties of its oppressed Citizens;—invaded private property by unlawfully seizing and retaining large Quantities of Ammunition in the Arsenal at Boston and sundry Pieces of Ordnance in the same Town—committed to the Custody of his Troops the Arms, Ammunition, Ordnance and Warlike Stores of all Sorts, provided at the Public Expence for the Use of the Province, and by all possible Means endeavoured to place the Province entirely in a defenceless State—at the same Time having neglected and altogether Disregarded Assurances from this Congress, of the pacific Dispositions of the Inhabitants of the Province, and Intreaties that he would cease from Measures which tended to prevent a Restoration of Harmony between Great-Britain and the Colonies:*

Wherefore it is the Opinion of this Congress—that notwithstanding nothing but Slavery ought more to be deprecated than Hostilities with Great-Britain—notwithstanding the Province has not the most distant Design of attacking, annoying or molesting his Majesty's Troops aforesaid, but on the other Hand will consider and treat every Attempt of the Kind as well as all Measures tending to prevent a Reconciliation between Britain and the Colonies as the highest Degree of Enmity to the Province——Nevertheless there is great Reason from the Considerations aforesaid, to be apprehensive of the most fatal Consequences; and that the Province may be in some Degree provided against the same, and under full Persuasion that the Measures expressed in the following Resolves are perfectly consistent with such Resolves of the Continental Congress as have been communicated to us,

It is *Resolved*, and hereby Recommended to the several Companies of Militia in this Province, who have not already chosen and appointed Officers, that they meet forthwith, and elect Officers to Command their respective Companies; and that the Officers so chosen assemble as soon as may be; and where the said Officers shall judge the Limits of the present Regiments too extensive, that they divide them, and settle and determine their Limits, and proceed to elect Field Officers to Command the respective Regiments so formed; and that the Field-Officers so elected, forthwith endeavour to enlist one Quarter at the least of the Number of the respective Companies, and form them into Companies of fifty Privates at the least, who shall equip and hold themselves in Readiness to march at the shortest Notice; and that each and every Company so formed, choose a Captain and two Lieutenants to command them on any necessary and emergent Service: And that the said Captain and Subalterns so elected, form the said Companies into Battalions, to consist of nine Companies each; and that the Captains and Subalterns of each Battalion so formed proceed to elect Field Officers to command the same. And this Congress doth most earnestly recommend that all the aforesaid Elections be proceeded in and made with due Deliberation and generous Regard to the public Service.

Also *Resolved*, That as the Security of the Lives, Liberties and Properties of the Inhabitants of this Province depends under Providence on their Knowledge and Skill in the Art Military, and in their being properly and effectually armed and equipt, if any of said Inhabitants are not provided with Arms and Ammunition according to Law, they immediately provide themselves therewith; and that they use their utmost Diligence to perfect themselves in Military Skill; and that if any Town or District within the Province is not provided with the full Town Stock of Arms and Ammunition according to Law, the Selectmen of such Town or District take effectual Care without Delay to provide the same.

A true Extract from the Minutes,
BENJAMIN LINCOLN, Secy.
[*The foregoing passed almost Unanimously.*]

In Provincial Congress, October 28, 1774.

WHEREAS this Province have not as yet received from the Continental Congress such explicit Directions, respecting Non-Importation and Non-Consumption Agreements as are expected: And whereas the greatest Part of the Inhabitants of this Colony have lately entered into Non-Importation & Non-Consumption Agreements, the good Effects of which are very conspicuous.—

Therefore, *RESOLVED*, That this Congress approve of the said Agreements, and earnestly recommend to all the Inhabitants of this Colony strictly to conform to the same, untill the further Sense of the Continental or this Provincial Congress is made Public. And further, this Congress highly applaud the Conduct of those Patriotic Merchants who have generously refrained from Importing British Goods since the Commencement of the Cruel Boston Port Bill; at the same Time reflect with Pain on the Conduct of those, who have sordidly preferred their private Interest to the Salvation of their suffering Country, by continuing to Import as usual; and Recommend it to the Inhabitants of the Province, that they discourage the Conduct of said Importers by refusing to Purchase any Article whatever of them.

A true Extract from the Minutes,
BENJAMIN LINCOLN, Secy.

In Provincial Congress, October 28, 1774.

IT has been recommended by the Congress, That whereas the Monies heretofore granted and ordered to be assessed by the General Court of this Province, and not paid into the Province Treasury, the same should not be paid to the Hon. Harrison Gray, Esq; for Reasons most obvious.

Therefore, *Resolved*, That Henry Gardner, Esq; of Stow, be and hereby is appointed Receiver-General, untill the further Order of this or some other Congress, or House of Representatives of this Province; whose Business it shall be to receive all such Monies as shall be offered to be paid into his Hands, to the Use of the Province, by the several Constables, Collectors or other Persons, by Order of the several Towns or Districts, and to give his Receipt for the same.—And it is hereby recommended to the several Towns and Districts within this Province, that they immediately call Town and District Meetings, and give Directions to all Constables, Collectors and other Persons, who may have any Part of the Province Tax of such Town or District in their respective Hands or Possessions, in Consequence of any late Order and Directions of any Town or District; that he or they immediately pay the same to the said Henry Gardner, Esq; for the Purpose aforesaid. And it is also recommended, that the several Towns and Districts in said Directions, signify & expresly engage to such Constable, Collector or other Person, as shall have their said Monies in their Hands, that their paying the same to Henry Gardner, Esq; aforesaid, and producing his Receipt therefor, shall ever hereafter operate as an effectual Discharge to such Person for the same. And it is hereby recommended, That the like Order be observed respecting the Tax ordered by the Great and General Court at their last May Session. And it is further recommended to all Sheriffs, Deputy Sheriffs and Coroners, who may have in their Hands any Monies belonging to the Province, that they immediately pay the same to the said Receiver General, taking his Receipt therefor. And the said Henry Gardner, Esq; the Receiver General shall be accountable to this or some other Congress or House of Representatives of this Province.

And to the End that all the Monies heretofore assessed in Pursuance of any former Grants and Orders of the Great and General Court or Assembly of this Province, and hitherto uncollected by the several Constables and Collectors to whom the several Lists of Assessments thereof were commited, may be effectually levied and collected; and also to the End that all the Monies granted and ordered to be assessed by the General Court at their Sessions in May last, which have been assessed, or which may be assessed, be also speedily and punctually collected; it is earnestly recommended by this Body to the several Constables and Collectors respectively, who have such Assessments in their Hands, or to whom any Assessments yet to be made may be committed by the Assessors of any Town or District, that, in levying and collecting the respective Part or Proportion of the total of such Assessment, therein set down to the several Persons named therein, they should act and proceed in the same Way and Manner as is expressed and prescribed in the Form of a Warrant given and contained in one Act or Law of this Province, intitled "An Act prescribing the Form of a Warrant for collecting of Town Assessments," &c. And it is also hereby strongly recommended to all the Inhabitants of the several Towns and Districts in this Province, that they without fail do afford to their respective Constables and Collectors, all that Aid and Assistance which shall be necessary to enable them in that Manner to levy the Contents of such Assessments; and that they do oblige and compel the said Constables and Collectors to comply with and execute the Directions of this Resolve, in as much as the present most alarming Situation and Circumstances of this Province do make it absolutely necessary for the Safety thereof.

A true Extract from the Minutes,
BENJAMIN LINCOLN, Sec'ry.

In Provincial Congress, October 29, 1774

RESOLVED, That it be recommended to the Inhabitants of this Province, that in Order to their perfecting themselves in the Military Art, they proceed in the Method ordered by his Majesty in the Year 1764; it being in the Opinion of this Congress, the best calculated for Appearance and Defence.

A true Extract from the Minutes,
BENJAMIN LINCOLN, Sec'ry.
[The Congress then Adjourn'd to the 23d of next Month.]

BOSTON, *October* 31.

We are just informed that the Continental Congress have agreed upon a Petition to the King, an Address to the Inhabitants of North-America, one to the Inhabitants of Canada, and another to the Inhabitants of Britain; as also upon a Non-Importation, a Non-Exportation & a Non Consumption-Agreement; but the Particulars have not transpired——It was expected the Members from this Province would leave Philadelphia the 26th Inst.

Tuesday last the Town met according to Adjournment, and having finished the Business before them, adjourn'd 'till To-Morrow, when 'tis desired there would be a general Attendance.

It was currently said, and generally believed in Bristol, the Day before Captain Tyler sailed, that a War would very shortly commence between Spain & Portugal.

We find no mention made in the public Prints of any more Troops being ordered to America.

It was said an Embargo was laid in Ireland on all salt Provisions going to the Spanish and French West Indies.—And that the Duke de Choiseul was established as Prime Minister in France.

Last Week the Captains Coffin and Hood arrived at Salem from London, but no later Intelligence is receiv'd by them than what is inserted in the first Page.

Last Friday several Transports arrived here with Troops from Quebeck.

MARRIED.] Capt. John Foster Williams to Miss Hannah Homer.

On Wednesday last died at Charlestown after a tedious Illness, Mrs. MARY FOSTER, Relict of the late RICHARD FOSTER, Esq; Mrs. FOSTER was a Person of a truly Christian Disposition, and peculiarly solicitous to discharge the several Duties of Life *without Partiality and without Hypocrisy*;—very discrete, humane and charitable; calm and unmoved at the various and inevitable Events of Providence, and griev'd only at the Sufferings of the Meek and Innocent, *the Wickedness of the Wicked, and the Evils of Sin.* the Loss of such a Christian, such a Mother, such a Relative, Neighbour and Friend, will deeply affect the virtuous and good. She descended from Ancestors of the first Characters in the Province, whom she hath honour'd in the Conduct of her Life; and the Voice of all remind us that,

"*The sweet Remembrance of the Just,*
"*Shall flourish when they sleep in Dust.*"

Died.] Mrs. *Hannah Billings*, Aged 37, Consort of Mr. *Richard Billings*, jun. Her Funeral is to be attended To-Morrow Afternoon, when her Friends and Acquaintance are requested to attend.

WHEREAS I the Subscriber signed an Address to the late Governor Hutchinson—I wish the Devil had had said Address before I had seen it.
Marblehead, October 24 1774. J. FOWLE.

WHEREAS I the Subscriber signed an Address to the late Governor Hutchinson—I wish the Devil had had said Address before I had seen it.
Marblehead, October 24, 1774 JOHN PRENTICE.

ANY Person proving Property in a Cable and two Anchors taken up in the River St. Lawrence, may have have them by applying to the Printers and paying Salvage.

Taken up last Week a Canoe almost new. The Owner by applying to the Printers may have her again, paying Charges.

THIS DAY PUBLISHED,
NUMBER VIII. of
The Royal American Magazine;
OR, UNIVERSAL
Repository of Instruction and Amusement,
For SEPTEMBER 1774.

New-Castle Coals

Just Imported at 12 Dollars per Chaldron; Coffee in Tierces at 10*d*. per lb. good red Port Wine in Quarter Casks at £.8.——A few Dozen of Philadelphia Porter, the first ever exported from that Place, and little, if any Thing, inferior to the London Porter, at 11*s*. 4*d*. per Dozen, to be sold at Minot's T, adjoining the Long-Wharff. Enquire at said T of Lewis Grant, or at Store No. 20 on the Long Wharff. 31 *Octo.* 1774.

Burials in the Town of BOSTON, since our last.
Sixteen Whites. No Blacks.
Baptiz'd in the several Churches, Seven.

High Water at BOSTON, for the present Week.

Monday, 48 min. aft.	8	Friday, 6 min. after.	12
Tuesday, 26 min. aft.	9	Saturday 40 min. aft.	12
Wednesday, 14 m. aft.	10	Lord's Day, 26 m. aft.	1
Thursday, 7 min. aft.	11	New Moon 3 Day 10 Aft.	

The second Meeting of the Delegates for the County of Plymouth.

PLYMOUTH, *October* 11, 1774. THE Delegates for the County of Plymouth, met at the Court-House according to Adjournment on Tuesday the 4th of October Instant, being the Day on which the Courts of Common Pleas and General Sessions of the Peace were to set, a Committee was appointed to wait on the Justices with a Copy of the 18th Resolve, and request their Compliance therewith, upon which they sent the following Declaration, which after some Debate was voted satisfactory, & agreeable to the Spirit of the 18th Resolve.

" WE the Subscribers Justices of the Court of General Sessions of the Peace and Court of Common Pleas for the County of Plymouth, Do hereby express and declare our Abhorrence and Detestation, of the late Innovations, attempted in our Constitution, by sundry late Acts of Parliament; and that we do not now, nor will, at any Time hereafter, hold or exercise our Commissions in any other Way than what is prescribed by our Charter and well-known Constitution; and that we will not in any Way countenance, aid or support the Execution of the late Acts of Parliament for altering the Charter and Government of this Province.

" Thomas Foster, Gamaliel Bradford, Thomas Mayhew, Edward Winslow, Joseph Josselyn, Daniel Johnson, Briggs Alden, John Cushing, Jun. Nathan Cushing, John Cotton, William Sever, Abijah White, Gideon Bradford, John Thomas, Nathaniel Clap, Pelham Winslow, Josiah Cushing, Nathan Howard,——

Notwithstanding which Declaration, in Consequence of several Messages from the Justices of the Court of General Sessions of the Peace, and Court of Common Pleas for this County — Voted that as Matters are circumstanced, we think it inexpedient for the Courts to set at present, or make any Adjournment; and at the same Time, that such of the said Justices as have been concerned in making the Addresses to Governor Gage and the late Governor Hutchinson, do make full and ample Reparation (so far as is in their Power) for the Aspersions cast, and Injury done their Country by those Means; and that nothing short of the Error and Fault of their Conduct, in these Respects, (expressed in Writing and signed by them) can make such Reparation, and give Satisfaction to the People, which Vote being made known to the Justices, they returned the following Answer.

" The Justices of the Courts of General Sessions of the Peace and Inferior Court of Common Pleas now met at Plymouth, for the County of Plymouth, taking into Consideration the great Uneasiness the County in general is in, on Account of the late Oppressive Acts of Parliament, and agreable to the Request of a Committee, from the Body of the People, and the Advice of the County Congress now Assembled in Plymouth, Do hereby declare, that we will not open, set, act or do, or adjourn either of said Courts, 'till the Determination of the Continential Congress is known."

By Order of the Justices of the Courts of Common Pleas, and General Sessions of the Peace.

EDWARD WINSLOW, Clerk.

Plymouth, October 4 1774.

Great Pains were taken at the first Meeting to obtain the Copy of an Address passed at the last Sessions of the Courts, &c. and several Committees were chosen to apply to Edward Winslow, Esq; and Son, joint Clerks, for that Purpose; the latter contemptuously left the Office, and upon application being made to him, refused to attend the Convention; but the former (personally appearing) declared in the most solemn Manner (as he had before done to the Committees) that the Address was not inserted in the Records, and that after the most diligent search, he could not find the Original, the same Answer being given on the Adjournment, viz: that it was not to be found, the following Vote was carried to the Justices who address'd the Governors, (together with the 21st Resolve, which has been already Published)

" Notwithstanding the many fruitless Attempts made by this Convention, to obtain a Copy of an Address of the Justices of the Courts of Common Pleas and General Sessions of the Peace for the County of Plymouth, to our late Governor Hutchinson, yet having sufficient evidence that said Address contains a full Justification of his Administration when Governor of this Province, as being friendly to its Constitution and Rights, therefore Resolved that the Authors of said Address, have shewn a Disregard to Truth, as well as to the Liberties and Happiness of their Country, and have thereby shewn their Acquiescence, in that well known Principle of said Hutchinson, viz. the Necessity of an Abridgment of what are called English Liberties. After which a recantation was brought, signed by all the Justices present, who Addressed the Governors, and is as follows.

" *WHEREAS we the Subscribers at the last Court of General Sessions of the Peace and Court of Common Pleas held at Plymouth, &c. on the first Tuesday of July last, Voted Addresses to Governor Gage and Governor Hutchinson, WE do now solemnly declare that what induced us so to do, was the Hopes by Means of their Influence and Assistance, we might get rid of the oppressive Acts of Parliament lately made, since which we are fully convinced that we were mistaken, and guilty of an Error in Judgment; and are heartily sorry that we were any Ways aiding or assisting therein; and humbly ask the Forgiveness of Town County and Province, that we may be reinstated to their Esteem and Favour, and hereby promise that we will not do any Thing to enforce the late unconstitutional Acts of Parliament; and wherein we have given Offence to the Clergy and Committees of Correspondence, we do hereby ask their Forgiveness.*

" Thomas Foster, Gamaliel Bradford, Joseph Josselyn, Briggs Alden, Abijah White, Edward Winslow, Pelham Winslow, Gideon Bradford."

After voting Thanks to the Chairman for his good Services, this Convention was adjourned to the First Tuesday of November next. *A true Copy,*

THOMAS LOTHROP, Clerk.

JOSEPH PEIRCE,

Hereby informs his good Customers, and others, That he has Removed to a new Shop, making the Corner northerly of the Old-Brick Meeting-House, and fronting the West End of the Town House, in BOSTON; where he has for Sale, a very large Assortment of English and other GOODS: He hopes for a Continuance of their Favors, which he will endeavor to merit by serving them on the *best* Terms.

Duncan Ingraham, Jun.

Has now for Sale, a Parcel of well-bought GOODS, which he will sell on very advantageons Terms (for the Purchaser) at his Shop in Union-Street, Boston; among his Goods are the following, which he will sell uncommonly low for Cash, viz.

Colour'd Silk Hose various Prices,
Outsize white ditto,
A Variety of Silk Mitts and Glover,
2 Cases Silver-handled Knives and Forks,
Blue and white India China—Cups and Saucers,
Pint and half Pint Bowles,
Table Cloths from 35*s*. O. T. to £.11 5*s*. very nice,
Black and colour'd figur'd Sattins,
Black and colour'd Capuchin Silks.

All Persons having any Demands

on the Estate of Mr. *Samuel Ruggles*, late of Boston, Housewright, deceased, are desired to bring in their Accounts and receive their Dues.——And all Persons indebted to said Estate are desired to make Payment to

SAMUEL RUGGLES, Administrator.

A Quantity of SHINGLES to be

Sold cheap. Inquire of Edes and Gill.

TO BE SOLD, for CASH,

Some very genteel Houshold Furniture,

if apply'd for this Week, by a Gentleman going out of Town; for Particulars enquire of Edes & Gill.

TO BE LET,

A convenient Shop on the North Side

of the Town-House, a very suitable Place for Business. Inquire of Edes & Gill.

WANTED to purchase, for a particular Use, a large Quantity of the stript Ground or Wall-Squarrel Skins. Whoever will procure and bring to *Thomas Courtney*, Taylor, facing the South Door of the Town House, Boston: He will take all that comes to hand, untill such Time as an Advertisment to the contrary is put in the Paper.

L O S T.

An old Sea-Chest, (supposed to be

taken out of Captain Mason's Store on the Long Wharff in Salem,) broad at the Bottom, painted blue but much wore off. If it has any Mark, it's J. M. Should it be opened, it contains Weston's Stenography, some Books of Physick, and some of Divinity, and considerable Writings, and both Men and Womens Cloths. Whoever shall give Information of the said Chest to the Rev. Dr. Whittaker in Salem, or the Rev. Samuel Stillman in Boston, so that the Subscriber may have it, they shall be well rewarded, and all reasonable Charges paid by

JOHN MARTIN.

FIFTEEN DOLLARS REWARD.

RAN-AWAY from me the Subscriber on Thursday the Twentieth of October Instant, a Negro Man named CÆSAR, about 26 Years Old, five Feet four Inches high: had on when he went away, a Green Ratteen Coat, Red Everlasting Jacket, White Linnen Breeches, Blue Yarn Stockings, he has a Mark or Scar over one of his Eyes, the little Finger of his left Hand is a little crooked by the Cut of a Sickle; it is suspected that some one assisted him by changing Cloaths or gave him a pass: Whoever will take up said Negro and return him to me, or confine him to any of his Majesty's Goals, so that he may be return'd to me, shall have the above Reward and all necessary Charges paid by

SIMEON HAZELTINE.

Hardwick, October 21, 1774.

TO BE LETT,

A convenient Dwelling-House in Hanover-

Street, opposite Mr. Benja. Andrew's; Three Rooms upon a Floor, Wood House and Barn, a good Pump and Rain Water Cistern.——Inquire of William Fowle, living in said House; Where may be had a few Firkins of Choice Nova-Scotia Butter and a small Quantity of Spring Beaver.

To be Sold to the highest Bidder, by Virtue of an Order of the Superior Court;

A Part of the Real Estate of Caleb Dana, late of Cambridge, in the County of Middlesex, Esq; deceased, for the Payment of his Debts, and the Charges of Sale, viz.

Several Lots of Land lying in the Town of *Royalston*, in the County of *Worcester*, containing in the Whole, 1500 Acres. The Sale to be at the House of Mr. JACOB EASTY, Innholder, in said *Royalston*, on Thursday the 24th Day of November next, at Nine o'Clock in the Forenoon.

GEO. DANA, Executor.

Ashburnham, October 13th, 1774.

TO BE SOLD,

Five Barrels of BEEF, in good Order,

on reasonable Terms, if apply'd for immediately. Enquire of *Thomas Clarke*, near the Rev. Mr. *Adams's* Meeting-House in *Roxbury*.

To be Sold by T. and J. FLEET, in Cornhill,

[*Price, only Five Coppers.*]

An Address to Protestant Dissenters of all

Denominations, on the approaching Election of Members of Parliament, with respect to the State of PUBLIC LIBERTY in general, and of AMERICAN AFFAIRS in particular.——

[*This excellent Pamphlet was received by the last Vessel from* London, *and is well worthy the Perusal of every* North-American, *& Friend of the British Constitution.*]

Samuel Abbot

Informs his Customers and others,

That he is now selling off his Goods (all which were imported before the 1st of *August* last) extreme cheap for cash, at his Store the head of *Green's* Wharf, nigh the Market.

He once more requests all Persons who are indebted to him, and to the late Co-partnership of *Samuel Abbot* and Company, to make immediate Payment.

LEE & JONES,

At their Store near the Swing-Bridge, have for Sale

A general Assortment of Piece Goods suitable for the present Season,

A beautiful Variety of Brocades, figur'd & strip'd Lutestrings, Taffaties & Gorgoreens, black Armozeens and Padusoys, flower'd Sattins of all Colours for Ladies Cloaths, a few best Ermine Muffs and Tippets.——Gold and Silver Laces, Silver Watches, Looking Glasses, Paper-Hangings, Corks, a few Cases of blue and white China Cups and Saucers, Liverpool and Glass Ware.

West-India RUM by the Hogshead,
Cornish's New-England FISH-HOOKS.

*** Also *Nails of all Sorts* to be deliver'd at *Marblehead.*

Cyrus Baldwin,

HEREBY informs his Customers and others, that he has to Sell at his Shop in Cornhill, near the Town-House in BOSTON.

A general Assortment of English, India and Scotch Goods, imported before the 31st of last August, which he is determined to Sell at the usual Advance he Sold at before the Northern Blockade, consisting of Superfine, Midling and Low priz'd Broad Cloths, Kerseys, Serges, Beaver Coatings, Scotch Carpets and Carpetting, Plaids, Hair Plushes and Cotton Velvets, Muffs and Tippets, very neat Silk ditto, Choice Firkin Butter, Indigo and Snuff, with too many other Articles to be here enumerated.

He earnestly requests all those who are Indebted to him to make speedy Payment.

N. B. Said Baldwin *is neither Addresser, Protester, nor Roman Catholick.*

For L O N D O N,

THE Ship *Julias Cæsar*, (CHARLES FEA, Commander,) being a prime Sailer, and having excellent Accommodations for Passengers; will certainly Sail on or before the first of November next, having one Half of her Cargo engaged.—For Freight or Passage, apply to the Master on Board said Ship, lying at the Long-Wharf in Salem, or to Messieurs SMITH and ATKINSON, at their Store in King-Street. Oct. 6, 1774.

To be Sold for Cash only,

A small Quantity of good dry

MEHOGANY, BOARDS and PLANK, fit for immediate Use. Enquire of Edes & Gill.

All Persons having any Demand on the

Estate of Mr. *John Soren*, late of Boston, Baker, deceas'd, are desir'd to bring in their Accounts; and all Persons indebted to said Estate, are desired to make Payment to *Ann Soren*, Administratrix.

W A N T E D,

To improve for a Business of public

Utility, a large convenient Room in the South Part of the Town.——Further particulars may be known by Inquiring of the Printers.

WANTED, a good HORSE, that will go well in a Chaise, and Trots light in a Saddle. Inquire of the Printers, or of Thomas Hudson

LOST this Morning about Eight o'Clock, between the Stores of Enoch Brown on the Neck, and Mr. Daniel Brown's of Roxbury, a dark blue and white Handkerchief, with Four Pounds Lawful Money in Silver mostly Change, tied in one Corner. Any Person that finds said Handkerchief, are desired to convey it to either of the said Stores, and they shall be generously Rewarded. Saturday, October 15, 1774.

TO be Sold by the Subscriber, a FARM lying in the Heart of the Town of Rochester, in the County of Plymouth, containing about 100 Acres, with a large Dwelling-House, Barn and Corn-House on the same, well fenced, a good Orchard, a good Well of Water, &c. exceeding for Tillage, and a large Proportion of Fresh Meadow and Pasture Ground, very convenient for a Trader or Tradesman. It is the Tenement the late Rev. Mr. Timothy Ruggles owned at his Decease. The Premises may be purchased very cheap for Cash or short Credit.

TIMOTHY RUGGLES.

October 10, 1774.

Boston: Printed, by EDES & GILL, *in Queen-Street*, 1774.

No. 1021.

THE Boſton-Gazette, AND COUNTRY JOURNAL.

Containing the freſheſt Advices, *Foreign and Domeſtic.*

MONDAY, *November* 7, 1774.

Extract from the Votes and Proceedings of the American Continental Congreſt.

ASSOCIATION, &c.

WE his Majeſty's moſt loyal Subjects, the Delegates of the ſeveral Colonies of New-Hampſhire, Maſſachuſetts Bay, Rhode-Iſland, Connecticut, New York, New Jerſey, Pennſylvania, the Three Lower Counties of Newcaſtle, Kent, and Suſſex, on Delaware, Maryland, Virginia, North-Carolina, and South-Carolina, deputed to repreſent them in a continental Congreſs, held in the city of Philadelphia, on the fifth day of September, 1774, avowing our allegiance to his Majeſty, our affection and regard for our fellow-ſubjects in Great-Britain and elſewhere, affected with the deepeſt anxiety, and moſt alarming apprehenſions at thoſe Grievances and diſtreſſes, with which his Majeſty's American ſubjects are oppreſſed, and having taken under our moſt ſerious deliberation, the ſtate of the whole continent, find, that the preſent unhappy ſituation of our affairs, is occaſioned by a ruinous ſyſtem of colony-adminiſtration adopted by the Britiſh Miniſtry about the year 1763, evidently calculated for enſlaving theſe Colonies, and, with them, the Britiſh Empire. In proſecution of which ſyſtem, various Acts of Parliament have been paſſed for raiſing a Revenne in America, for depriving the American ſubjects, in many inſtances, of the conſtitutional trial by jury, expoſing their lives to danger, by directing a new and illegal trial beyond the ſeas, for crimes alledged to have been committed in America; And in proſecution of the ſame ſyſtem, ſeveral late, cruel, and oppreſſive Acts have been paſſed reſpecting the town of Boſton and the Maſſachuſetts-Bay, and alſo an Act for extending the province of Quebec, ſo as to border on the weſtern frontiers of theſe Colonies, eſtabliſhing an arbitrary government therein, and diſcouraging the ſettlement of Britiſh ſubjects in that wide-extended country; thus by the influence of civil principles and ancient prejudices to diſpoſe the inhabitants to act with hoſtility againſt the free Proteſtant Colonies, whenever a wicked Miniſtry ſhall chuſe ſo to direct them.

To obtain redreſs of theſe grievances, which threaten deſtruction to the lives, liberty, and property of his Majeſty's ſubjects in North-America, we are of opinion, that a non-importation, non-conſumption, and non-exportation agreement, faithfully adhered to, will prove the moſt ſpeedy, effectual, and peaceable meaſure:—And therefore we do, for ourſelves, and the inhabitants of the ſeveral Colonies, whom we repreſent, firmly agree and aſſociate under the ſacred ties of virtue, honor, and love of our country, as follows:

Firſt. That from and after the firſt day of December next, we will not import into Britiſh America, from Great-Britain or Ireland, any goods, wares or merchandize whatſoever, or from any other place any ſuch goods, wares or merchandize, as ſhall have been exported from Great-Britain or Ireland; nor will we, after that day, import any Eaſt India tea from any part of the world; nor any molaſſes, ſyrrups, paneles, coffee, or piemento, from the Britiſh plantations, or from Dominica; nor wines from Madeira, or the Weſtern Iſlands; nor foreign Indigo.

Second. That we will neither import, nor purchaſe any ſlave imported after the 1ſt day of December next, after which time, we will wholly diſcontinue the ſlave-trade, and will neither be concerned in it ourſelves, nor will we hire our veſſels, nor ſell our commodities or manufactures to thoſe who are concerned in it.

Third. As a non-conſumption agreement, ſtrictly adhered to, will be an effectual ſecurity for the obſervation of the non-importation, we, as above, ſolemnly agree and aſſociate, that, from this day, we will not purchaſe or uſe any tea imported on account of the Eaſt-India company, or any on which a duty hath been or ſhall be paid; and from and after the 1ſt day of March next, we will not purchaſe or uſe any Eaſt-India tea whatever, nor will we, nor ſhall any perſon for or under us, purchaſe or uſe any of thoſe goods, wares, or merchandize, we have agreed not to import, which we ſhall know, or have cauſe to ſuſpect, were imported after the firſt day of December, except ſuch as come under the rules and directions of the tenth article hereafter mentioned.

Fourth. The earneſt deſire we have, not to injure our fellow-ſubjects in Great-Britain, Ireland, or the Weſt-Indies, induces us to ſuſpend a non-exportation until the tenth day of September, 1775; at which time if the ſaid Acts and parts of Acts of the Britiſh parliament, herein after mentioned, are not repealed, we will not, directly or indirectly, export any merchandize or commodity whatſoever, to Great Britain, Ireland or the Weſt-Indies, except Rice to Europe.

Fifth. Such as are merchants, and uſe the Britiſh and Iriſh Trade, will give orders, as ſoon as poſſible, to their factors, agents and correſpondents, in Great-Britain and Ireland, not to ſhip any goods to them on any pretence whatſoever, as they cannot be received in America; and if any merchant reſiding in Great-Britain or Ireland, ſhall directly or indirectly ſhip any goods, wares or merchandize, for America, in order to break the ſaid non importation agreement, or in any manner contravene the ſame, on ſuch unworthy conduct being well atteſted, it ought to be made public; and, on the ſame being ſo done, we will not from thenceforth have any commercial connexion with ſuch merchant.

Sixth. That ſuch as are owners of veſſels will give poſitive orders to their captains, or maſters, not to receive on board their veſſels any goods prohibited by the ſaid non-importation agreement, on pain of immediate diſmiſſion from their ſervice.

Seventh. We will uſe our utmoſt endeavours to improve the breed of ſheep, and increaſe their numbers to the greateſt extent, and to that end, we will kill them as ſparingly as may be, eſpecially thoſe of the moſt profitable kind; nor will we export any to the Weſt-Indies, or elſewhere; and thoſe of us who are or may become overſtocked with, or can conveniently ſpare any ſheep, will diſpoſe of them to our neighbours, eſpecially to the poorer ſort, on moderate terms.

Eight. That we will in our ſeveral ſtations encourage frugality, œconomy, and induſtry; and promote agriculture, arts, and the manufactures of this country, eſpecially that of wool; and will diſcountenance and diſcourage, every ſpecies of extravagance and diſſipation, eſpecially all horſe-racing, and all kinds of gaming, cock fighting, exhibitions of ſhews, plays, and other expenſive diverſions and entertainments. And on the death of any relation or friend, none of us, or any of our families, will go into any further mourning-dreſs, than a black crape or ribbon on the arm or hat for Gentlemen, and a black ribbon and necklace for Ladies, and we will diſcontinue the giving of gloves and ſcarfs at funerals.

Ninth. That ſuch as are venders of goods or merchandize, will not take advantage of the ſcarcity of goods that may be occaſioned by this aſſociation, but will ſell the ſame at the rates we have been reſpectively accuſtomed to do, for twelve months laſt paſt.—And if any vender of goods or merchandize, ſhall ſell any ſuch goods on higher terms, or ſhall in any manner, or by any device whatſoever, violate or depart from this agreement, no perſon ought, nor will any of us deal with any ſuch perſon, or his or her factor or agent, at any time thereafter, for any commodity whatever.

Tenth. In caſe any merchant, trader, or other perſons ſhall import any goods or merchandize after the firſt day of February next, the ſame ought forthwith at the election of the owner, to be either re-ſhipped or delivered up to the committee of the county, or town wherein they ſhall be imported, to be ſtored at the riſque of the importer, until the non-importation agreement ſhall ceaſe, or be ſold under the direction of the committee aforeſaid; and in the laſt mentioned caſe, the owner or owners of ſuch goods, ſhall be reimburſed (out of the ſales) the firſt coſt and charges, the profit if any, to be applied towards relieving and employing ſuch poor inhabitants of the town of Boſton, as are immediate ſufferers by the Boſton Port-Bill; and a particular account of all goods ſo returned, ſtored, or ſold, to be inſerted in the public papers; and if any goods or merchandizes ſhall be imported after the ſaid firſt day of February, the ſame ought forthwith to be ſent back again, without breaking any of the packages thereof.

Eleventh. That a committee be choſen in every county, city, and town, by thoſe who are qualified to vote for Repreſentatives in the Legiſlature, whoſe buſineſs it ſhall be attentively to obſerve the conduct of all perſons touching this aſſociation; and when it ſhall be made to appear to the ſatisfaction of a majority of any ſuch committee, that any perſon within the limits of their appointment has violated this aſſociation, that ſuch majority do forthwith cauſe the truth of the caſe to be publiſhed in the Gazette, to the end that all ſuch foes to the rights of Britiſh America may be publicly known, and univerſally contemned as the enemies of American liberty; and thenceforth we reſpectively will break off all dealings with him or her.

Twelfth. That the committee of correſpondence in the reſpective colonies do frequently inſpect the entries of their cuſtom-houſes, and inform each other from time to time of the true ſtate thereof, and of every other material circumſtance that may occur relative to this aſſociation.

Thirteenth. That all manufactures of this country be ſold at reaſonable prices, ſo that no undue advantage be taken of a future ſcarcity of goods.

Fourteenth. And we do further agree and reſolve, that we will have no trade, commerce, dealings or intercourſe whatſoever, with any colony or province, in North-America, which ſhall not accede to, or which ſhall hereafter violate this aſſociation, but will hold them as unworthy of the rights of freedom, and as inimical to the liberties of their country.

And we do ſolemnly bind ourſelves and our conſtituents, under the ties aforeſaid, to adhere to this aſſociation until ſuch parts of the ſeveral Acts of parliament paſſed ſince the cloſe of the laſt war, as impoſe or continue duties on Tea, Wine, Molaſſes, Syrups, Paneles, Coffee, Sugar, Piemento, Indigo, Foreign Paper, Glaſs, and Painters Colours, imported into America, and extend the Powers of the Admiralty courts beyond their ancient limits, deprive the American Subject of trial by jury, authorize the Judge's certificate to indemnify the proſecutor from damages, that he might otherwiſe be liable to from a trial by his peers, require oppreſſive ſecurity from a claimant of ſhips or goods ſeized, before he ſhall be allowed to defend his property, are repealed.—And until that part of the Act of the 12. G. 3. chap. 24, entitled, "An Act for the better ſecuring his Majeſty's dock yards, magazines, ſhips, ammunition, and ſtores," by which, any perſons charged with committing any of the offences therein deſcribed, in America, may be tried in any ſhire or county within the realm, is repealed—And until the four Acts paſſed in the laſt ſeſſion of Parliament, *viz.* That for ſtopping the port and blocking up the harbour of Boſton—That for altering the charter and government of the Maſſachuſetts Bay—And that which is entitled "An Act for the better adminiſtration of juſtice, &c.——And that "For extending the limits of Quebec, &c. are repealed. And we recommend it to the provincial conventions, and to the committees in the reſpective Colonies, to eſtabliſh ſuch further regulations as they may think proper, for carrying into execution this Aſſociation.

The foregoing Aſſociation being determined upon by the CONGRESS, was ordered to be ſubſcribed by the ſeveral Members thereof; and thereupon we have hereunto ſet our reſpective names accordingly.

In Congreſs, Philadelphia, October 20, 1774.

Signed,

PEYTON RANDOLPH, *Preſident.*

For New-Hampſhire. *John Sullivan, Nathaniel Folſom.*

Maſſachuſetts-Bay. *Thomas Cuſhing, Samuel Adams, John Adams, Robert Treat Paine.*

Rhode-Iſland. *Stephen Hopkins, Samuel Ward*

Connecticut. *Eliphalet Dyer, Roger Sherman, Silas Deane.*

New-York. *Iſaac Low, John Alſop, John Jay, James Duane, William Floyd, Henry Wiſener, S. Boerum.*

New Jersey. *James Kinsey, William Livingston, Stephen Crane, Richard Smith.*

Pennsylvania. *Joseph Galloway, John Dickinson, Charles Humphreys, Thomas Mifflin, Edward Biddle, John Morton, George Ross.*

New-Castle, &c. *Cæsar Rodney, Thomas M' Keane, George Read.*

Maryland. *Matthew Tilghman, Thomas Johnson, William Paca, Samuel Chase.*

Virginia. *Richard Henry Lee, George Washington, P. Henry, jun. Richard Bland, Benjamin Harrison, Edmund Pendleton.*

North-Carolina. *William Hooper, Joseph Hewes, R. Caswell.*

South-Carolina. *Henry Middleton, Thomas Lynch, Christopher Gadsden, John Rutledge, Edward Rutledge.*

[The foregoing ASSOCIATION is copied exactly from the Newport Edition—But we find by the New-York Gazette the following Omission in the Tenth Article, which the Reader is desired to correct.

Tenth. In Case any Merchant, Tader, or other Persons, shall import any Goods or Merchandize, *after the first Day of December, and before the first Day of February next,* the same ought forthwith at the election of the owner, &c.]

The Address of the Grand Congress, to the Inhabitants of the British Colonies) concludes as follows,

"At this unhappy period, we have been authorized and directed to meet and consult together for the welfare of our common country. We accepted the important trust with diffidence, but have endeavoured to discharge it with integrity. Tho' the state of these colonies would certainly justify other measures than we have advised; yet weighty reasons determined us to prefer those which we have adopted. In the first place, it appeared to us a conduct becoming the character these colonies have ever sustained, to perform, even in the midst of the unnatural distresses and imminent dangers that surround them, every act of loyalty; and therefore, we were induced to offer once more to his Majesty, the petitions of his faithful and oppressed subjects in America. Secondly, regarding with the tender affection, which we know to be so universal among our countrymen, the people of the kingdom from which we derive our original, we could not forbear to regulate our steps by an expectation of receiving full conviction, that the colonists are equally dear to them. Between these provinces and that body subsists the social band, which we ardently wish *may never* be dissolved, and which *cannot* be dissolved, until their minds shall become *indisputably hostile*, or their *inattention* shall permit those who are thus hostile, to persist in prosecuting with the powers of the realm the destructive measures already operating against the colonists; and in either case shall reduce the latter to such a situation, that they shall be compelled to renounce every regard, but that of self-preservation. Notwithstanding the vehemence with which affairs have been impelled, they have not yet reached that fatal point. We do not incline to accelerate their motion, already alarmingly rapid; we have chosen a method of opposition, that does not preclude a hearty reconciliation with our fellow-citizens on the other side the Atlantic. We deeply deplore the urgent necessity that presses us to an immediate interruption of commerce, that may prove injurious to them. We trust they will acquit us of any unkind intentions towards them, by reflecting that we subject ourselves to similar inconveniences; that we are driven by the hands of violence into unexperienced, and unexpected public convulsions, and that we are contending for freedom, so often contended for by our ancestors.

The people of England will soon have an opportunity of declaring their sentiments concerning our cause. In their piety, generosity and good sense, we repose high confidence; and cannot, upon a review of past events, be persuaded, that *they*, the defenders of true religion, and the asserters of the rights of mankind, will take part against their affectionate protestant brethren in the colonies, in favour of *our open* and *their own secret* secret enemies; whose intrigues, for several years past, have been wholly exercised in sapping the foundations of civil and religious liberty.

Another reason, that engaged us to prefer the commercial mode of opposition, arose from an assurance, that this mode will prove efficatious, if it be persisted in with fidelity and virtue; and that your conduct will be influenced by those laudable principles, cannot be questioned. Your own salvation and that of your posterity now depends upon yourselves. You have already shown that you entertain a proper sense of the blessings you are striving to retain. Against the temporary inconveniences you may suffer from a stoppage of trade, you will weigh in the opposite balance, the endless miseries you and your descendants must endure from an established arbitrary power. You will not forget the honour of your country, that must from your behaviour take its title in the estimation of the world, to glory, or to shame; and you will, with the deepest attention, reflect, that if the peaceable mode of opposition recommended by us, be broken and rendered ineffectual, as your cruel and haughty ministerial enemies, from a contemptuous opinion of your firmness, insolently predict will be the case, you must inevitably be reduced to choose, either a more dangerous contest, or a final, ruinous, and infamous submission.

Motives thus cogent; arising from the emergency of your unhappy condition, must excite your utmost diligence and zeal, to give all possible energy to the pacific measures calculated for your relief: but we think ourselves bound in duty to observe to you, that the scheme agitated against these colonies, have been so conducted, as to render it prudent, that you should extend your views to the most unhappy events and be in all respects prepared for every contingency. Above all things we earnestly entreat you, with devotion of spirit, penitence of heart, and amendment of life, to humble yourselves and implore the favour of Almighty God. And we fervently beseech his divine goodness, to take you into his gracious protection.

By the Harriott *Packet, Capt* Lee, *who is arrived at New York from Falmouth, we have the following Advices to the 10th of September, viz.*

LONDON, August 22.

Sept. 6. A compact is lately sign'd between our Court and that of the three Northern Powers; by which, in case of a continental War, they have stipulated to furnish Great Britain between them with 60 000 men, so that there will be no necessity to send a man out of England.

A letter from Edingburg says, accounts are received in town of a revolution in Russia; the Empress is said to be dethroned and imprisoned, and the Grand Duke placed in her stead.

Advice is said to be received, that three Spanish men of war had sunk a Portuguese frigate off the Canary islands and all on board perished.

By a letter from Lisbon to a gentlemen at Westminster, we learn that a squadron of 7 Spanish men of war of the line and 2 frigates, have been cruizing off that port for some time past.

On Saturday orders were sent to Portsmouth and Plimouth, for the guardships to be mann'd to their full compliment, both sailors and marines.

It is not settled when the Parliament is to meet, but a Council will be held the latter end of this week, when it is expected a Proclamation will be issued for calling them together early in November.

Sept. 8. The following, it is said, is the foundation of the dispute between the courts of Madrid & Lisbon, when the late disturbance happened in Spanish America, about two years ago, a great many of the principal inhabitants of Chiloe, after been driven from their native settlements, crossed the river Plata, and took shelter in the Portuguese settlement of St. Salvador, where tho' their persons were suffered to be free, they were stripp'd of all their effects. About a twelve month after, a general pacification being concluded between the Indians and Spaniards, these Chiefs went back to their own country, and complained of the usage they received of the Portuguese, which the court of Madrid is now contending. It appears that St. Salvador, and all the lands as far as Cape Thomas, did originally belong to the Spaniards.

On Monday a messenger was sent with dispatches to the commissioners of Portsmouth and Plymouth with orders for fitting out six ships of the line.

Sept. 10. Yesterday a messenger was sent off to Lord Mansfield at Paris; and another with some to Lord Grantham at Madrid.

An Evening Paper says, "We are assured from good authority, that Gen. Charlton is gone over to his government of Quebec, with positive orders to embody 30,000 Roman Catholick Canadians immediately as a militia, who are to be under the same military law as regular troops.

A letter from Madrid, of Aug. 19th, says, "It is really amazing to behold the assiduity and diligence with which the Spaniards are making their great preparations both by land and sea, which fully proves their intentions of carrying on the war they are going to engage in with the utmost spirit. Recruits are raising in every province and General O'Reilly has just marched with a large body of horse and foot to form a camp near the frontiers of Portugal; and in a few days a manifesto of war will be published."

PHILADELPHIA, October 19.

A correspondent observes, that an old ingenious mechanic having taken under his serious consideration the many audacious insults given by the soldiery, to the good people of the town of Boston—fired with the love of liberty and the preservation of his countrymen, he set himself to work, and has compleated an engine that will throw five hundred gallons of melted brimstone, in the space of one minnte, to the distance of one hundred and twenty yards. It is judged by every person skilled in mechanism, who has seen this uncommonly curious constructed machine perform, that it will do more execution, in one hour, than any twelve pieces of the best cannon planted on Boston-Neck,—This most extraordinary *physical* implement of war, it is said, will speedily be sent to our brave suffering brethren in the town of Boston; and which, if it doth not entirely remove General Gage's *horn-work*, will, it is probable, effectually stop a certain infectious disease, by curing the scabby *ministerial gang* of their *itching disorder*.

NEW-YORK, October 27.

Extract of a Letter from London, dated September 3 1774.

"The tools of administration, are at present more than usually calm; a calm that perhaps may be only a prelude to a storm; they are anxiously waiting a result of the Congress, and judging of the Americans, by themselves, were so sanguine in their expectations that the terror of their armaments would frighten you into submission to their edict, that they cannot yet erase the idea, but still expect you to beg mercy, cap in hand. An express was sent to General Amherst, who had a private conference, but the result is not known. It is said that it was proposed to him to go with 1.00 Hanoverians to America, or the 3d regiment of the guards, &c. and that Sir William Draper is appointed a Governor and is going with troops (it is supposed) to New-York. Mansfield is gone to France, many think, to concert measures with the French court against America, or to bring in the Pretender. It is whisper'd that the friends at court will themselves invite him, and lay the blame on the Americans;—a similar conduct has been pursued with regard to the Indies, and with some of your colony disputes about patents and boundaries.

"Many of your friends here are horribly afraid that some of the baits laid by the ministry to enslave you will succeed. It is said many of your leading men will be tempted by lucrative places, as agents or contractors for government, in the purchase of wheat and other necessary articles; which, beside raising domestic enemies (the most dangerous of any among yourselves, (will answer the double purpose of reducing you to poverty (in the midst of plenty) and then to slavery. Besides, it is proposed to lay many tempting advantages in the way of those who join in the scheme, from which all other are to be excluded; in short, your virtue will be tried to the utmost, by those whose long practice and experience in all the arts of corruption, will be but two likely to ensure them success, and will make it necessary to exert your utmost vigilance to guard against deception, and especially that you be not betrayed by those in whom you may confide among yourselves.

Your committee disputes have been published in all the papers, over and over, and have been disadvantageous to your cause. Lord Chatham and all your friends, are anxiously concerned at your critical situation; but your unanimity, and the spirit and propriety of your resolutions, rejoiced the hearts of every friend to constitutional freedom, and has done the highest honour to America. Maintain your firmness and unanimity, and depend upon Heaven for success; hope nothing from the people here—but if you persevere—we shall soon join you by thousands; more and more daily espouse your cause, and I believe it will shortly be as much ours as yours. It will not be worth while to send here any deputies from the Congress,—they would only be insulted and treated with contempt; but at home they may do all the business effectually. I expect 1500 respectable people of considerable property, will shortly remove to reside in America, but the Ministry, in order to discourage emigration, are endeavouring to make living there as uneasy as it is here, &c.

Extract of a letter from London, dated August 27, 1774.

MY DEAR FRIEND,

"I add these few lines to assure you, that the Ministry have extended the influence of the Treasury, to America.—People have been consulted here, to know who are the fittest objects of bribery, and most powerful to create divisions among you.—Warrants have been granted to the Secretary of State, for America, expressly for *secret services*.——What can it be for but to corrupt and divide?

P. S. Publish the above instantly, 'tis true and ought to be known."

Extract of a Letter from a Gentleman in London to his Correspondent in New-York.

"Something has been done, or intended to be done by Administration to divide the principal Merchants of New-York—I do not know precisely the sum to be given, but you may risque your Life upon it, that the the Treasury has been open to some of the leading Men among you,—the Minister has taken great pains to learn who are best worth his Purchase,—you must Guess who are his Objects, by the Actions and Conduct of the Slaves he has made,—watch them attentively and you will find them out——They are the first Class with Respect to Family and Fortune; be therefore on your Guard, and trust only in the Spirit of the People at large."

The embarrassments occasioned to administration, by the refractory behaviour of the King of Spain, who is on the point of denouncing war against Portugal, and of quarrelling with the English nation, will be greatly increased on the arrival of the Scarborough man of War, which sailed from Boston the 5th of September, with his Excellency General Gage's dispatches, presently after the memorable alarm, which for a few days occasioned great agitations in the eastern provinces.

Mr. Thomas Charles Williams, who arrived here yesterday in the ship Samson, Capt. Coupar, from London, is extremely uneasy at a report being spread, that he shipped the Tea lately destroyed at Annapolis in Maryland, as mentioned in this day's paper. He assures the public the said report is groundless, and intreats they will suspend their opinion upon that matter a few days, when he hopes to give them the fullest proofs of his innocence.

October 31. Letters from London say, "A War with Spain is daily expected, the British Minister at the Spanish Court having informed his Catholic Majesty, that in Case he attacked the Portuguese, an English Fleet would immediately pay a Visit to the Port of Cadiz."

BOSTON, *November* 7.

The Grand Continental Congress, which met at Philadelphia the 5th of September last, broke up on Wednesday the 26th of October; the Delegates from this Province, are expected to arrive in Town on Wednesday next.——The Proceedings of this Congress, containing Extracts from their Votes and Proceedings, viz. the Bill of Rights, a List of Grievances, the Association, an Address to the People of Great-Britain, and a Memorial to the Inhabitants of the British American Colonies, will soon be published.

MARRIED] *James Urquhart*, Esq; a Captain in the 14th Regiment, to Miss *Hannah Flucker*, Daughter of the Hon. *Thomas Flucker*, Esq; Secretary of this Province.

(For the Letter to General Gage from the Grand Congress—the Address to him from the Provincial Congress—and the Destruction of the Tea at Maryland, see last Page.)

Extract of a Letter from a Gentleman in London to his Friend in Boston, dated Sept. 1, 1774.

"--I have been a Tour upwards of 1500 Miles—I do assure you in my whole Travels I have found two out of three in Favour of Boston, and the People in general seem to be much pleas'd that you make such a steady Stand; the People on this Side the Water ever expected you would have submitted immediately; the Ministry are much disappointed, and by what I can gather they much repent of what has been done. I have heard it's a Plan of ——, and was determined to gain the Point. I tell them that they may break the Necks of the Bostonians, but they never will bend them; nothing but a steady Stand will bring Matters to rights. I shan't embark any Goods until I find Matters are settled to the Satisfaction of this Country and America. The Friends of America increases daily. I am in hopes a Subscription will be set on Foot for Boston. I urge it very strongly."

Extract of a Letter from a Gentleman of the Law in London, to a Correspondent in this Town.

I AM greatly concerned for the late attempts that have been made on this side the water against the *natural rights* of the English American Subjects, and of the people of your Town in particular: But I have some Satisfaction however, in finding (upon the most careful Examination of the best Authorities) that the new Acts are totally *null and void* in themselves, from their defects in the fundamental Principles of Law: And I now employ all the Time that I can spare (which is indeed but very little) in preparing a Tract concerning the *Eternal Law which limits Legislature*; wherein I trust I shall prove my assertion.

[*This Pamphlet is now printed, and may be had of the Printers hereof.*

The People of Boston I hope will continue most strictly to maintain their *loyalty* and *constitutional allegiance to the British Crown*, at the same time that they assert their natural liberty. I hope also that they will most carefully avoid every act of violence on their part, howsoever they may think themselves obliged to prepare for a legal defence of their Rights.——Rights did I say!—No People have *any right* or just title to *Liberty*, who tolerate among them the slavery and oppression either of strangers or of white servants; for slavery has ever been providentially the just punishment of such *tyranny!* Let the American subjects therefore "put away *the accursed thing* from among them" (if they hope for the divine blessing) that they, themselves, may have a just and clear title to *natural liberty*; because the first principle of *eternal law* (next to the love of God) is "to do as we would be done by."——

On Friday Evening last, in pursuing a Person who had been guilty of breaking the Peace in Charlestown, a Barrel and Bag of Tea were stumbled on, which were immediately carried to the Training-Field, and committed to the Flames; after they were consumed, (and the Boys which a Bonfire commonly draws, dispersed,) it was suggested there was more in the same Place; a Search was made, and enough found to fill a large Hogshead, which was conveyed to a Place called the Green, before Cape-Breton Tavern, and a Quantity of Faggots being laid round it, they were set on Fire, and the whole consumed. Every Thing was conducted with such Stillness and Order, that many People knew nothing of it untill the next Morning. It is supposed the Quantity consumed was between 4 & 500 Weight.

N. B. We learn that a Gentleman belonging to Newbury Port, was very active in the Demolition of the above Tea.

I send you here a little Book,
for you to look upon;
That you may see your Father's Face,
Now he is dead and gone.

"I Must own, Sir, I can see but one Reason for raising at this present Juncture, this additional Number of Troops, and that is to strengthen the Hands of the Minister against the next Elections by giving him the Power of disposing of *Commissions* to the *Sons*, Brothers, Nephews, Cousins, and Friends of such as have Interest in Boroughs into some of which perhaps, Troops may be sent to procure the free Election of their Members, in Imitation of the late Czarina sending her Troops into Poland to secure the free Election of a King.

"But still there is one Thing more fatal than all I have yet named that *must be* the Consequence of so great a Body of Troops being kept on Foot in *England*, and *will be the finishing Stroke to all our Liberties*. For as the Towns in *England* will not be able much longer to contain Quarters for them, most of those who keep public Houses being near ruined by Soldier's billeted on them; so *on Pretence of the Necessity of it*, Barracks will be built for quartering them, which will be as so many Fortresses WITH STRONG GARRISONS IN THEM, erected in all Parts of *England*, WHICH CAN TEND TO NOTHING, but by Degrees to subdue and enslave the Kingdom.

"But if ever this Scheme should be attempted, it will be incumbent on every *Englishman* to endeavour to prevent it by *all* Methods, and as it would be *the last Stand* that could be ever made for our Liberties, rather than suffer it to be put in Execution, IT WOULD BE OUR DUTY TO DRAW OUR SWORDS, AND NEVER PUT THEM UP, till *our Liberties were secured*, and the *Authors of our intended slavery brought to condign Punishment*.——I hope I shall be forgiven if during the Debates I shall take the Liberty of speaking again; for *I am determined to fight Inch by Inch*, every Proposition that tends, as I think this does, to the enslaving my Country."

Lord Viscount GAGE *(Father of his Excellency General* GAGE*) his Speech in 1739. Parlia. Deb. book 11. p. 388. See Moral. on standing Armies.*

Mess. EDES and GILL,

Please to insert the following in your next.

MANY able pens have shewn the inconvenience and danger arising to communities from standing armies in time of peace; the absolute dependance of both officers & soldiers on the Prince under whom they serve, of the subalterns and soldiers on their superiors gives such weight to the commander in chief as can not be balanced by the disinterested honesty, wealth or influence of the best men in any community. Nay however *undesigning* the Prince, however humane and prudent the commander of such forces, the following facts will demonstrate the danger of stationing large bodies of them in populous places. One Daniel Wiswal after having been legally warned out of Charlestown, removed to Boston with his Family, and on the 4th of May 1774 (before any Troops arrived here) at the solicitation of the Selectmen of Boston, grounded on his keeping an infamous house, and not being an inhabitant of said town, a warrant was granted by Esq; for removing him and his family to the place from whence they came, this warrant was committed to Mr. Jonathan Bennet a constable of Boston, who repeatedly requested Wiswal to remove without subjecting himself to the disgrace of being carried out which he as often promised, relying upon which promises Bennet delayed executing his warrant until Wiswal's growing enormities, supplying the guard at the ferry with liquor, by which they were often kept all night intoxicated, insulting, wounding and endangering the lives of peaceable passengers, his wife's openly entertaining notorious prostitutes, thereby encouraging & inciting youth to those vices it is apt enough of itself to indulge in, induced the Selectmen to order their immediate removal; accordingly on the first inst. Mr. Bennet went to their house with proper assistance, and being told that Wiswal was in the camp informed his wife that he should remove as many of the family as he could find; after many frivolous excuses she pretended to send a boy for a ridinghood (but in reality to inform her husband of what was transacting), for the constable growing impatient she pulled her ridinghood out of a drawer, and with her child and an apprentice went with him to Charlestown, where while she was delivering to the constable of Charlestown her husband attended by a Serjeant and six Privates, appeared at the Door, Wiswall asking if his Wife was there, she reply'd, yes Deary, and escaping from the Constables, got among the Soldiers, who were immediately ordered to Prime and Load; the Serjeant then addressing himself to the people and advising them to take it patiently carried her off in triumph; the occasion of this extraordinary military manœuvre was this, as soon as Wiswall heard of his wife's situation, he apply'd to Lieut. Col. Walcot of the 5th regiment, informing him that his house had been beset by a mob, and his wife and child taken out of it, for no other reason than because he had made a few pair of shoes for the soldiers, upon which Col. Walcot rather hastily ordered the above party for their relief, thus by the villainous misrepresentation of an obscure person, and the credulity and suddeness of Col. Walcot many valuable lives might have been lost, had not the constables prudently prefer'd an application to the General for redress, to the calling in that assistance the posse comitatus were ready to afford them.——————

Upon laying the matter before General Gage the next Day he expressed his disapprobation of the steps taken by the military, and desired the Selectmen to continue their exertions in suppressing disorderly houses; Col. Walcot also expressed his sorrow for the step he had so imprudently taken, with an assurance that he would carefully avoid every thing of the kind in future; the Woman was peaceably conveyed to Charlestown, and from thence to Cambridge.

On Monday last died of a consumptive Disorder; and on Thursday was decently interr'd, Mr. JOHN BOX, aged 75 Years, who for upwards of 40 Years was an eminent Ropemaker in this Town; he was a Man of a fair unblemish'd Character, strictly just in his Dealings; a constant Attender of divine Worship; several Years (in Turn) a Warden at King's Chaple and one of the Vestry, an Assistant and promoter to the rebuilding that Church; he was no medler in Politicks, yet a Well-Wisher to the Public Welfare, he loved Order and condemned too great a stretch of Power; much Esteemed by his worthy Acquaintance and by the Public in general, he was a tender and affectionate Husband and Parent.——The ancient and honorable Society of Free Masons, conducted his Body to the Burial-Place, in Token of a tender Regard, to their worthy deceas'd Brother.——He has left a Wife and several Children of Adult Age to mourn the Loss of a Husband and Parent.

Leicester, October 24, 1774.—On Monday last departed this Life, greatly lamented, Mrs. *Elizabeth Henshaw*, the pious and amiable Consort of *Daniel Henshaw*, Esq; of this Town. Her Life a Blessing, and her End Peace. Her Remains were decently interr'd on Thursday last.

This is to notify the Public, That

the Charlestown Stage-Coach, No. 1, which heretofore set off from Mr. Woart's Tavern in Charlestown, at 8 o' Clock, for Salem, will, for the future, set off at 9 o'Clock every Day in the Week, Sunday excepted, and another from Mr. Goodhue's in Salem, return to Charlestown.

Robert Wyer, Sailmaker,

HEREBY informs his Customers and others, That he is removed his Loft from the Head of Rowe's Wharff, to the new Loft lately built on Halliwell's Ship-Yard, where they may depend on being served with Fidelity and Dispatch, as usual.

N. B. Said Wyer would take a Boy as an Apprentice, that can be well recommended.

The Copartnership of *Brown* and

Shattuck will be mutually Dissolved the 14th Instant.—Those who have any Demands on said Company, are desired to send in their Accounts; and those indebted, are requested to make immediate Payment.

All Persons having Demands on the

Estate of *Joseph* and *Joseph Wheeler*, jun. of Boston, deceas'd, and those who are Indebted to said Estate, are desired to bring in their Accounts to John Lucas, Administrator in Order to Settlement.

Town and Country Store,

At the Head of Dock-Square.

WARD & FENNO

SELL West-India, and a great Variety of other Goods, CHEAP ENOUGH.

A few Tubs very good BUTTER

to be Sold by JOSIAH WATERS and SON, in Ann-Street.

To be Sold or Lett, and may be entered upon immediately.

A House and about Four Acres of

Land in Dorchester, about four Miles from Boston) with every Accommodation suitable for a Gentleman. Enquire of JOHN VASSALL.

JOHN GRAHAM,

HAS just Imported a large Quantity of Old Jamaica Spirits of the best kind, and will be Sold by the Hogshead, Barrel or less Quantity if required, Coffee and Chocolate, &c.

The above will be Sold at reasonable Rates for Cash, at his Store on Wendel's Wharf, near the South Battery Fort-Hill.

To be Sold at the Royal Exchange Tavern in King-Street, Boston.

At Publick Vendue,

On THURSDAY the First Day of *December* next, at Eleven o'Clock in the Forenoon.

The following Lots of Land, viz.

Lot No. 20, called a 10 Mile back Lot, on the West side of Kennebeck-River, containing about 4800 Acres.

Lot marked F. 2. in the first Range of Lots, containing about 6000 Acres (exclusive of Settlers Lots interspersed) being near one Mile wide, and fifteen Miles long, and fronting on Kennebeck-River, on the West side of it, about ten Miles above Fort-Halifax, to be divided and sold in two Parts.

A Lot to the Northward of ditto, and fronting on little Norridgwalk-River, about 3200 Acres.

Lot marked B D. 1. in the second Range of Lots, about six Miles above Norridgwalk, on the West side of Kennebeck-River, and fronting thereon, containing about 7000 Acres, (exclusive of Settlers Lots interspersed) being 1 Mile wide, and 15 Miles long.

Lot marked C. A 1. in the third Range of Lots, near the Falls of Coriontonka, about 12 Miles above Norridgwalk, on the West side of Kennebeck-River, and fronting thereon, containing about 7000 Acres, (exclusive of Settlers Lots interspersed) being 1 Mile wide and 15 Miles long.

Three Lots of Land, viz. Lot No. 32, on the East side of Kennebeck-River, about a Mile above Fort-Western—No. 86, on the East side of said River, about 9 Miles above Fort-Western: and Lot No. 20, on the West side of said River, about 1 Mile and ½ above Fort-Western, containing 400 Acres each.

Also all the Islands in Cobbisseconte Pond, and all the Islands in Kennebeck-River above Fort-Halifax.

For further Particulars enquire of HENRY ALLINE, jun. at his Office in King-Street, Boston.

Boston, November 2d, 1774.

Burials in the Town of BOSTON, since our last.

Fifteen Whites. Three Blacks.

Baptiz'd in the several Churches, Fourteen.

High Water at BOSTON, *for the present Week.*

Monday, 25 min. aft. 2	Friday, 8 min. after. 6
Tuesday, 23 min. aft. 3	Saturday, 56 min. aft. 7
Wednesday, 19 m. aft. 4	Lord's Day, 39 m. af. 8
Thursday, 15 min. aft. 5	Moon's First Qr. 10 Day,

The following is a Copy of the Letter from the Grand American Congress to General Gage, viz.

SIR, PHILADELPHIA, *October* 10, 1774.

THE inhabitants of Boston have informed us, the representatives of his Majesty's faithful subjects in all the colonies from Nova-Scotia to Georgia, that, the fortifications erecting within that town, the frequent invasions of private property, and the repeated insults they receive from the soldiery, have given them great reason to suspect a plan is formed very destructive to them, and tending to overthrow the liberties of America.

Your Excellency cannot be a stranger to the sentiments of America, with respect to the acts of parliament, under the execution of which those unhappy people are oppressed, the approbation universally expressed of their conduct, and the determined resolution of the colonies, for the preservation of their common rights, to unite in their opposition to those acts. In consequence of those sentiments, they have appointed us the guardians of their rights and liberties; and we are under the deepest concern, that whilst we are pursuing every dutiful and peaceable measure, to procure a cordial and effectual reconciliation between Great-Britain and the colonies, your Excellency should proceed in a manner that bears so hostile an appearance, and which even those oppressive acts do not warrant.

We intreat your Excellency to consider, what a tendency this conduct must have to irritate and force a people, however well disposed to peaceable measures, into hostilities, which may prevent the endeavours of this Congress to restore a good understanding with the parent state, and may involve us in the horrors of a civil war.

In order therefore, to quiet the minds and remove the reasonable jealousies of the people, that they may not be driven to a state of desperation, being fully persuaded of their peaceable disposition towards the King's troops could they be assured of their own safety, we hope, Sir, you will discontinue the fortifications in and about Boston, prevent any further invasions of private property, restrain the irregularities of the soldiers, and give orders that the communication between the town and the country, may be open, unmolested and free.

Signed by order and in behalf of the General Congress.

To his Excellency Thomas Gage, Esq; P. R. President.

In Provincial Congress, October 29, 1774.

Ordered, That Captain Heath, Captain White, Captain Gardner, Mr. Cheever, and Mr. Devens, be a Committee, to wait upon his Excellency with the following Message. JOHN HANCOCK, Pres.

May it please your Excellency,

THE province having been repeatedly alarmed at your Excellency's unusual and warlike preparations since your arrival into it, and having by this Congress expressed a reasonable expectation, that you would desist from, and demolish your fortifications on Boston-neck; it must afford matter of astonishment, not only to the province, but the whole continent, that you should treat our importunate applications with manifest insensibility and disregard. The Congress are possessed of a writing with your signature, which purports itself to be a message to this body, although addressed to sundry gentlemen by name, who officiating as our committee presented an address to your Excellency. We are surprised at your saying that "what we call a fortress, unless annoyed, will annoy nobody," when from your acquaintance with the constitution of Britain, and of the province, over which you have been by his Majesty commissioned to preside, you must know that barely keeping a standing army in the province, in time of peace, without consent of the Representatives, is against law, and must be considered as a great grievance to the subjects; a grievance which this people could not with due regard to their freedom endure, was there not reason to hope that his Majestty, upon being undeceived, would order redress! Is it not astonishing then, Sir, that you should have ventured to assert, that a fortress, by whatever name your Excellency is pleased to call it, which put it in the power of the standing army, which you command, to cut off communication between the country and the capital of this province, to imprison the many thousand inhabitants of the town of Boston, to insult and destroy them upon the least, or even without any provocation, and which is evidently a continual annoyance to that oppressed community, "unless annoyed will annoy nobody?"

A retrospect of your Excellency's conduct since your late residence in this province, we conclude will convince you of that truth, the meer hinting of which you tell us is highly exasperating as well as ungenerous. We presume your Excellency will not deny, that you have exerted yourself to execute the acts, made to subvert the constitution of the province. Although your Excellency's connections with a ministry inimical to the province, and your being surrounded with men of the worst political principles, preclude a prospect of your fully exercising toward this province, your wonted benevolence and humanity; yet, Sir, we pray you to indulge your social virtues so far as to consider the necessary feelings of this people under the hand of oppression. Have not invasions of private property by your Excellency been *repeatedly* made at Boston? Have not the inhabitants of Salem, whilst peaceably assembled, for concerting measures to preserve their freedom, and unprepared to defend themselves, been in imminent danger from your troops? Have you not by removing the ammunition of the province, and by all other means in your power endeavoured to put it in a state utterly defenceless? Have you not expressly declared, that resentment might be justly expected "from your troops, merely in consequence of a refusal of some inhabitants of the province to supply them with property undeniably their own? Surely these are questions founded on incontestible facts, which we think must prove that while the avowed enemies of Great-Britain and the colonies, are protected by your Excellency, the lives, liberties and properties of the inhabitants of the province, who are real friends to the British constitution, are greatly endangered, whilst under the controul of your standing army.

It must be matter of grief to every true Briton that the honor of British troops is sullied by the infamous errand on which they are sent to America; and whilst in the unjust cause in which you are engaged, menaces will never produce submission from the people of this province. Your Excellency as well as the army, can only preserve your honour by refusing to submit to the most disgraceful prostitution of subserving plans so injurious to this people, so notoriously iniquitous and cruel.---Your Excellency professes to be solicitous for preserving union and harmony between Great Britain and the colonies, and we sincerely hope that you will distinguish yourself, by exertions for this purpose; for should you be an instrument of involving in a civil war this oppressed and injured land, it must forever deprive you of that tranquility, which finally bids adieu to those, whose hands have been polluted with innocent blood. ---Your Excellency reminds us of the spirit of the British nation; we partake, we rejoice in her honours, and especially revere her for her great national virtues: We hope she will never veil her glory, or hazard success by exerting that spirit in support of tyranny.

Your Excellency's strange misconception of facts, is not less conspicuous in the close of your message, than in many other parts of it. You have suggested that the conduct of the province for supporting the constitution, is an instance of its violation—to declare the truth relative to this matter, must be a full vindication of our conduct therein: The powers placed in your Excellency for the good of the province to convene, adjourn, prorogue, and dissolve the General Court have been perverted to ruin and enslave the province,—while our constituents, the loyal subjects of his Majesty have been compelled for the laudable purposes of preserving the constitution, and therein their freedom, to obtain the wisdom of the province, in a way which is not only justifiable by reason, but under the present exigencies of the state, directed by the principles of the constitution itself; warranted by the most approved precedent and example, and sanctified by the British nation at the revolution, upon the strength and validity of which precedent, the whole British constitution now stands; his present Majesty wears his crown, and all subordinate officers hold their places; and although we are willing to put the most favourable construction on the warning you have been pleased to give us of the "rock on which we are," we beg leave to inform you, that our constituents do not expect that in the execution of that important trust, which they have reposed in us, we should be wholly guided by your advice, and we trust, Sir, that we shall not fail in our duty to our country, and loyalty to our King, or in a proper respect to your Excellency.

ANNAPOLIS, *(Maryland) October* 20.

THE brig Peggy Stewart, Captain Jackson, from London, having on board 17 packages, containing 2320 lb. of that detestable weed tea, arrived here on Friday last. The tea was consigned to Thomas Charles Williams & Company, merchants in this city. Those of the committee for Anne Arundel county who were in town, hearing of the arrival of said vessel, met in the afternoon, and were informed the said vessel, had been entered in the forenoon of that day, *and the duty on the tea paid to the Collector, by Mr. Anthony Stewart, one of the Owners of said brig.*—Four only of the Committee being present, it was thought adviseable to call a Meeting of the People.—Notice was thereupon immediately given.—Many of the inhabitants, together with a number of gentlemen from Anne-Arundel, Baltimore, and other counties, who were attending the provincial court, met, and having called before them the Importers and the Captain of the ship, together with the Deputy Collector—the question was moved and seconded, whether the tea should be landed in America or not? And the question being put, was unanimously determined in the negative. A committee of twelve persons was thereupon appointed to attend landing the other goods on board said vessel, and to prevent landing the tea. After which the meeting adjourned to Wednesday the 19th, at a 11 o'clock. At which time the members of the committee, and other the inhabitants of the county, were requested to attend at this place. In consequence of this adjournment, a great number of very respectable gentlemen from Anne-Arundle, Baltimore, and Prince George's counties met here, and amongst others, 8 of the committee for Anne-Arundel county. Those of the committee proceeded to examine into the affair, calling before them Messrs. James and Joseph Williams, and Anthony Stewart, and also took into consideration, an offer made by said Williams's and Stewart, to destroy the tea, and make such concessions as might be satisfactory to the committee and the people assembled. The committee were of opinion, if the tea was destroyed by the voluntary act of the owners, and proper concessions made, that nothing further ought to be required. This their opinion being reported to the assembly, was not satisfactory to all present. Mr. Stewart then voluntarily offered to burn the vessel and the tea in her, and that proper acknowledgments should be made and published in the Maryland Gazette. Those acknowledgments were accordingly made, and are as follows.

"We James Williams, Joseph Williams, and Anthony Stewart, do severally acknowledge, that we have committed a most daring insult, and act of the most pernicious tendency to the liberties of America; we the said Williams's in *importing the tea*, and said Stewart *in paying the duty thereon*, and thereby deservedly incurred the displeasure of the people now convened, and all others interested in the preservation of the constitutional rights and liberties of North America, do ask pardon for the same; and we solemnly declare, for the future, that we never will infringe any resolution formed by the people for the salvation of their rights, nor will we do any act that may be injurious to the liberties of the people: and to shew our desire of living in amity with the friends to America, we do request this meeting, or as many as may choose to attend, to be present at any place where the people shall appoint, & we will there commit to the flames, or otherwise destroy, as the people may choose, the detestable article which has been the cause of this our misconduct."

ANTHONY STEWART,
JOSEPH WILLIAMS,
JAMES WILLIAMS.

After which Mr. Stewart, and Messrs. James & Joseph Williams, owners of the tea, went on board said vessel with her sails and colours flying, and voluntarily set fire to the tea, and in a few hours, the whole, together with the vessel, was consumed in the presence of a great number of spectators. *Annapolis, Oct.* 18th, 1774.

The committee for Anne-Arundel county received information from Baltimore, that a considerable quantity of tea was expected on board the Generous Friends, Captain Nairne: The ship arrived on Saturday evening the 15th inst. and on examination, it did not appear by the cockets, or entry at the collector's office, that any tea had been on board. It appeared by a letter to Mr. Hodgkin, that six chests of tea had been shipped, and that Captain Nairne refused to sail from London until the tea was re-landed, for which conduct Captain Nairne had the thanks of the committee.

By Order, JOHN DUCKET, Clk. Com.

New-Castle Coals

Just Imported at 12 Dollars per Chaldron; Coffee in Tierces at 10*d.* per lb. good red Port Wine in Quarter Casks at £.8.——A few Dozen of Philadelphia Porter, the first ever exported from that Place, and little, if any Thing, inferior to the London Porter, at 11*s.* 4*d.* per Dozen, to be sold at Minot's T, adjoining the Long-Wharff. Enquire at said T of Lewis Grant, or at Store No. 20 on the Long Wharff. 31 *Octo.* 1774.

ANY Person proving Property in a Cable and two Anchors taken up in the River St. Lawrence, may have have them by applying to the Printers and paying Salvage.

Taken up last Week a Canoe

almost new. The Owner by applying to the Printers may have her again, paying Charges.

JUST RE-PRINTED, *(Price 8d. L. M.)*
And to be sold by *Z. Fowle*, near Charlestown Ferry, *S. Whiting*, in Marshall's-Lane, and *E. Steel*, Boston.

A faithful Testimony to *New-England*,

By the following celebrated Authors, viz.

I. Mr. *Jonathan Mitchell*, extracted from an Instrument of his, dated December 31, 1662.

II. Mr. *John Higginson*, stated in a Sermon to the General Court, May 27, 1663.

III. Hon. *William Stoughton*, Esq; in a Sermon preached by him, in the Audience of the General-Court, April 1663.

IV. The Testimony finished by Dr. *Increase Mather*, who says, I do now with my dying Hand sign my concurrence to the above.——This Book is really worth perusal, it exhibits a recognition of our Father's pious Errand in this Wilderness.

For LONDON,

The Ship JOHN WILKES, JAMES HALL, Commander, Will certainly sail from Newport, Rhode-Island, on or before the 10th of November at farthest:—For Passage apply to FRANCIS ROTCH, at his Store at Bedford in Dartmouth, or the Master on board.

Bedford, (in Dartmouth) October 27, 1774.

JOSEPH PEIRCE,

Hereby informs his good Customers,

and others, That he has Removed to a new Shop, making the Corner northerly of the Old-Brick Meeting-House, and fronting the West End of the Town House, in BOSTON; where he has for Sale, a very large Assortment of English and other GOODS: He hopes for a Continuance of their Favors, which he will endeavor to merit by serving them on the *best* Terms.

Duncan Ingraham, Jun.

Has now for Sale, a Parcel of well-

bought GOODS, which he will sell on very advantageons Terms (for the Purchaser) at his Shop in Union-Street, Boston; among his Goods are the following, which he will sell uncommonly low for Cash, viz.

Colour'd Silk Hose various Prices,
Outsize white ditto,
A Variety of Silk Mitts and Gloves,
2 Cases Silver-handled Knives and Forks,
Blue and white India China—Cups and Saucers,
Pint and half Pint Bowles,
Table Cloths from 35*s* O. T. to £.11 5*s.* very nice,
Black and colour'd figur'd Sattins,
Black and colour'd Capuchin Silks.

All Persons having any Demands

on the Estate of Mr. *Samuel Ruggles*, late of Boston, Housewright, deceased, are desired to bring in their Accounts and receive their Dues.——And all Persons indebted to said Estate are desired to make Payment to

SAMUEL RUGGLES, Administrator.

A Quantity of SHINGLES to be

Sold cheap Inquire of Edes and Gill.

TO BE SOLD, for CASH,

Some very genteel Houshold Furni-

ture, if apply'd for this Week, by a Gentleman going out of Town; for Particulars enquire of Edes & Gill.

TO BE LET,

A convenient Shop on the North Side

of the Town-House, a very suitable Place for Business.

Inquire of Edes & Gill.

WANTED to purchase, for a particular Use, a large Quantity of the stript Ground or Wall-Squarrel skins. Whoever will procure and bring to *Thomas Courtney*, Taylor, facing the South Door of the Town House, Boston: He will take all that comes to hand, untill such Time as an Advertisement to the contrary is put in the Paper.

L O S T.

An old Sea-Chest, (supposed to be

taken out of Captain Mason's Store on the Long Wharff in Salem,) broad at the Bottom, painted blue but much wore off. If it has any Mark, it's J. M. Should it be opened, it contains Weston's Stenography, some Books of Physick, and some of Divinity, and considerable Writings, and both Men and Womens Cloths. Whoever shall give Information of the said Chest to the Rev. Dr. Whittaker in Salem, or the Rev. Samuel Stillman in Boston, so that the Subscriber may have it, they shall be well rewarded, and all reasonable Charges paid by

JOHN MARTIN.

FIFTEEN DOLLARS REWARD.

RAN-AWAY from me the Subscriber on Thursday the Twentieth of October Instant, a Negro Man named CÆSAR, about 26 Years Old, five Feet four Inches high: had on when he went away, a Green Ratteen Coat, Red Everlasting Jacket, White Linnen Breeches, Blue Yarn Stockings, he has a Mark or Scar over one of his Eyes, the little Finger of his left Hand is a little crooked by the Cut of a Sickle; it is suspected that some one assisted him by changing Cloaths or gave him a pass: Whoever will take up said Negro and return him to me, or confine him to any of his Majesty's Goals, so that he may be return'd to me, shall have the above Reward and all necessary Charges paid by

SIMEON HAZELTINE.

Hardwick, October 21, 1774.

Boston: Printed, by EDES & GILL.
in Queen-Street, 1774.

THE

Boston-Gazette, AND COUNTRY JOURNAL.

No. 1022

Containing the freshest Advices, Foreign and Domestic.

MONDAY, November 14, 1774.

From the NEW-LONDON GAZETTE.

Mr. GRREN,

As my letter to Captain Cleveland, written in consequence of the late alarm, has circulated far and wide, and made unfavourable impressions on the minds of some, 'tis desired that you and the several printers in the other colonies upon the continent, would give the following piece a place in your papers, and you will oblige Your humble Servant,

ISRAEL PUTNAM.

Pomfret, 3d October, 1774.

IN Mr. Gaine's New-York Gazette of the 12th of September, I am called upon to set the affair of my writing a letter to Capt. Cleveland, in a true light; which was written in consequence of intelligence brought me by Capt. Keyes on the 3d of September last. Being then at home about my lawful business, said Keyes came to my house about 11 o'Clock, A. M. and informed me that an express came from Boston to Oxford, who set out from thence on the preceeding evening, and brought the alarming tidings contained in my letter herein inserted. The true state of the case, as I have since learned is as follows. ——— Wilcot, Esq; of Oxford, hearing the news, posted his son off towards Boston, to learn the certainty of the report; and when he came to Grafton, about 35 miles from Boston, he heard a further confirmation of it, and returned immediately back to Oxford; when the said Wilcot, (his father) sent him to Dudley, to Carter's tavern, where one Mr. Clarke of that town, a trader, happened to be, and he came to his father Capt. Clarke, of Woodstock, who came to said Keys; and on his coming to me with the strongest assurances of the truth and reality of said report, I wrote the following letter to Capt. Aaron Cleveland, of Canterbury. "Mr. "Keyes this moment brought us the news that the men "of war and troops, began to fire upon the people last "night at sun set at Boston, when a post was immedi-"ately sent off to inform the country. He informs that "the artillery played all night—that the people were "universally rallying from Boston as far as here, and "desire all the assistance possible. This first commence-"ment of hostilities was occasioned by the country's be-"ing robbed of their powder, from Boston as far as "Framingham; and when found out, the persons who "went to take the perpetrator of the horrid deed, (who "had fled to the camp) were immediately fired upon—"six of our number were killed the first shot, and a num-"ber wounded; and beg you will rally all the forces "you can, and be upon the march immediately for the "relief of Boston and the people that way.

ISRAEL PUTNAM."

The title of *Lieut. Col. of the Connecticut forces*, I did not assume in my said letter, it being inserted in the New-York paper by the printer's own capricious whim, or to gratify some of his votaries. The above letter is as nearly conformable to the original as I can recollect, not having a copy of it. By comparing which with that inserted in said Gaine's paper, the reader will perceive they somewhat differ; whether the difference arises from a wrong copy sent forward by Capt. Cleveland, or from some other cause, I am not able to determine.—I hope the reader will make proper allowance for incorrectness, when he considers, that it was written in great haste, and the author aimed at nothing but plain matters of fact, as they were delivered to him, not expecting said letter would have been transported through the continent, subject to the critical inspection of the learned in every town.

The writer in Mr. Gaine's paper of Sept. 19th, who stiles himself *A New-York Freeholder*, introduces his piece with a rhetorical picture of the horrors of a civil war; which though I agree with him that it brings a train of evils along with it; yet when driven to a state of desperation, by the oppressive hand of tyranny, and the lawless violence of arbitrary power, what people on earth would not be justified, in the eye of right reason and common sense, for resistance, even to the shedding of blood, if the preservation of their liberties demanded it? After having said sufficient to alarm the fears of all those who have a pusillanimity of soul, or rather an infamous desire of screening their Jacobitic principles under the masque of a dread of consequences, he ushers in this paragraph with a sneer, "Col. Putnam's famous letter (forwarded by special messengers to New York and Philadelphia) and the consequences it produced, are very recent and fresh in our memories."—Then after reciting some parts of my letter, he proceeds——"The evident confusion of ideas in this letter, betrays the state of the poor Colonel's mind, whilst writing it, and shews he did not possess that calm fortitude which is so necessary to insure success in military enterprises." Paying all due deference to this author's learning, and his undoubted acquaintance with the rules of grammar and criticism, I would beg leave to ask him, whether he does not betray a total want of the feelings of humanity, if he supposes in the midst of confusion, when the passions are agitated with a real belief of thousands of their fellow-countrymen being slain, and the inhabitants of a whole city just upon the eve of being made a sacrifice, by the rapine and fury of a merciless soldiery, and their city laid in ashes by the fire of ships of war, he or any one else could sit down under the possession of a calmness of soul becoming a Roman senator, and attend to all the rules of composition, in writing a letter, to make a representation of plain matters of facts, under the hieroglyphical similitude of tropes and figures? He goes on to cast a censure upon the New-England colonies, saying that the above-mentioned report "has eventually made evident, past all doubt, that many in the New-England colonies are disposed and ripe for the most violent measures;" This is as gross a falshood as the Boston alarm, and discovers the evident disposition of the author to cast an odium upon the patriotic sons of New-England, whose arms are emblazoned with humanity; who wish to gain a redress of their grievances by the most pacific and gentle means: but rather than submit to slavery, are determined to drench their swords in blood, and die gloriously, or live free?—Under whose banners, possibly this Jesuitical pretender to friendship for the liberties of America and the British constitution, may be glad to take sanctuary, when the virtuous inhabitants of the colony, into which he fled from the Scotch rebellion, may find him out, and pass that act of outlawry against him, which every jacobitic hypocrite deserves.

Now, I submit it to the determination of every candid unprejudiced reader, whether my conduct in writing the aforementioned letter, merits the imputation of imprudence asserted by said writer; or whether they would have had me tamely sit down, and been a spectator of the inhuman sacrifice of my friends and fellow-countrymen, or (in other words) Nero like, have set down and fiddled, while I really supposed Boston was in flames, or exerted myself for their relief? And pray, in what easier way could I have proceeded than in writing to one of the militia captains; (whom I desired to forward the intelligence to the adjacent towns) when I really believed the story to be true? Which having done, I immediately mounted my horse, and made the best of my way to Boston, having only four gentlemen to accompany me. Having proceeded as far as Douglass, which is about thirty miles from my house, I met Capt. Hill of that town, with his company who had been down within about thirty miles of Boston, and had just returned; he informed me that the alarm was false, and that the forces of Worcester and Sutton, were upon their return.

I then turned my course homewards, without loss of time, and reached my house Sunday morning about sunrising, taking care to acquaint the people on the road, that they need not proceed any further. Immediately on my return, I sent an express to Capt. Cleveland, letting him know what intelligence I had heard, and desiring him to give the like information to the adjoining towns southward.

I believe the alarm was first occasioned by Mr. Benjamin Hollowell, who going into Boston, in a great fright, informed the army that he had killed one man and wounded another, while they were pursuing him from Cambridge, and that the country were all in arms, marching into Boston; which threw the military into great consternation; and they were quickly paraded and put into the most convenient posture of defence; in which situation they remained till next day. In the midst of this hurry and confusion, I believe a post was dispatched into the country, but by whom, or to answer what purpose, I cannot tell; but what took place in consequence of it is evident.—Gen. Gage's apprehension of danger, was so great, that he speedily began to fortify the entrance of the town, to prevent a surprise from the enemy without.§

From what has been said, I believe it will sufficiently appear, that I was not the first inventor of this alarm. And I am told from good authority, that the people were in motion in the northwest part of the Massachusetts government, even to the distance of one hundred miles from Boston, who were alarmed by an express sent thither (by the same Wilcot abovementioned) before the news reached me; which I think is enough to silence the ill-natured aspersions of every cavilling *Tory*, against my conduct, and make them, dog like, draw in their tails, and lop their ears, and skulk into some obscure hole or kennel, to hide themselves from the contempt of the world; having evidently discovered their attempt to stir up a spirit of animosity and disunion among the good people of the colonies, which I pray God may prove abortive.

ISRAEL PUTNAM.

To the INHABITANTS of the PROVINCE of QUEBEC.

Friends and Fellow-Subjects,

WE, the DELEGATES of the Colonies of New-Hampshire, Massachusetts-Bay, Rhode-Island and Providence Plantations, Connecticut, New-York, New-Jersey, Pennsylvania, the counties of Newcastle, Kent and Sussex on Delaware, Maryland, Virginia, North Carolina, and South-Carolina, deputed by the Inhabitants of the said colonies, to represent them in a General Congress at Philadelphia, in the province of Pennsylvania, to consult together concerning the best methods to obtain redress of our afflicting grievances, having accordingly assembled, and taken into our most serious consideration the state of public affairs on this continent, have thought proper to address your province, as a member therein deeply interested.

When the fortune of war, after a gallant and glorious resistance, had incorporated you with the body of English subjects, we rejoiced in the truly valuable addition, both on our own and your account; expecting, as courage and generosity are naturally united, our brave enemies would become our hearty friends, and that the Divine Being would bless to you the dispensations of his over-ruling providence, by securing to you and your latest posterity the inestimable advantages of a free English constitution of government, which it is the privilege of all English subjects to enjoy.

These hopes were confirmed by the King's proclamation, issued in the year 1763, plighting the public faith for your full enjoyment of those advantages.

Little did we imagine that any succeeding ministers would so audaciously and cruelly abuse the royal authority, as to withhold from you the fruition of the irrevocable rights, to which you were thus justly entitled.

But since we have lived to see the unexpected time, when ministers of this flagitious temper have dared to violate the most sacred compacts and obligations, and as you educated under another form of government, have artfully been kept from discovering the unspeakable worth of that form you are now undoubtedly entitled to, we esteem it our duty, for the weighty reasons herein after mentioned, to explain to you some of its most important branches.

"In every human society," says the celebrated Marquis Beccaria, "there is an effort continually tending to confer on one part the height of power and happiness, and to reduce the other to the extreme of weakness and misery. The intent of good laws is to oppose this effort, and to diffuse their influence universally and equally.

Rulers stimulated by this pernicious "effort," and subjects, animated by the just "intent of opposing good laws against it," have occasioned that vast variety of events, that fill the histories of so many nations. All these histories demonstrate the truth of this simple position, that to live by the will of one man, or set of men, is the production of misery to all men.

On the solid foundation of this principle, Englishmen reared up the fabrick of their constitution with such a strength, as for ages to defy time, tyranny, treachery, internal and foreign wars: and as an illustrious author ‡ of your nation, hereafter mentioned, observes, "They gave the people of their colonies the form of their own government, and this government carrying prosperity along with it, they have grown great nations in the forests they were sent to inhabit."

In this form the first grand right is, that of the people having a share in their own government, by their representatives, chosen by themselves, and in consequence of being ruled by laws which they themselves approve, not by edicts of men over whom they have no controul. This is a bulwark surrounding and defending their property, which by their honest cares and labours they have acquired, so that no portions of it can legally be taken from them, but with their own full and free consent, when they in their judgment deem it just and necessary to give them for public services, and precisely direct the easiest, cheapest, and most equal methods, in which they shall be collected.

The influence of this right extends still farther. If money is wanted by rulers, who have in any manner oppressed the people, they may retain it, until their grievances are redressed; and thus peaceably procure relief, without trusting to despised petitions, or disturbing the public tranquility.

The next great right is that of trial by jury. This provides, that neither life, liberty nor property can be taken from the possessor, until twelve of his unexceptionable countrymen and peers, of his vicinage, who from that neighbourhood may reasonably be supposed to be acquainted with his character, and the characters of the witnesses, upon a fair trial, and full enquiry, face to face, in open court, before as many of the people as choose to

‡ *Montesquieu.*

attend, shall pass their sentence upon oath against him; a sentence that cannot injure him, without injuring their own reputation, and probably their interest also; as the question may turn on points that, in some degree, concern the general welfare; and if it does not, their verdict may form a precedent, that on a similar trial of their own, may militate against them.

Another right relates merely to the liberty of the person. If a subject is seized and imprisoned, though by order of government, he may, by virtue of this right, immediately obtain a writ, termed a Habeas Corpus, from a judge, whose sworn duty it is to grant it, and thereupon procure any illegal restraint to be quickly enquired into and redressed.

A fourth right is, that of holding lands by the tenure of easy rents, and not by rigorous and oppressive services, frequently forcing the possessors from their families and their business, to perform what ought to be done, in all well regulated states, by men hired for the purpose.

The last right we shall mention, regards the freedom of the press. The importance of this consists, besides the advancement of truth, science and morality, and arts in general, in its diffusion of liberal sentiments on the administration of government, its ready communication of thoughts between subjects, and its consequential promotion of union among them, whereby oppressive officers are ashamed or intimidated into more honorable and just modes of conducting affairs.

These are the invaluable rights that form a considerable part of our mild system of government; that, sending its equitable energy thro' all ranks and classes of men, defends the poor from the rich, the weak from the powerful, the industrious from the rapacious, the peaceable from the violent, the tenants from the lords, & all from their superiors.

These are the rights, without which a people cannot be free and happy, and under the protecting and encouraging influence of which, these colonies have hitherto so amazingly flourished and encreased. These are the rights a profligate ministry are now striving, by force of arms, to ravish from us, and which we are, with one mind, resolved never to resign but with our lives.

These are the rights you are entitled to, and ought at this moment in perfection to exercise. And what is offered to you by the late act of Parliament in their place? Liberty of conscience in your religion? No. God gave it to you; and the temporal powers with which you have been and are connected, firmly stipulated for your enjoyment of it. It laws divine and human, could secure it against the despotic caprices of wicked men, it was secured before. Are the French laws in civil cases restored? It seems so. But observe the cautious kindness of the ministers who pretend to be your benefactors. The words of the statute are, that those "laws shall be the rule, until they shall be varied or altered by any ordinances of the Governor and Council." Is the "certainty and lenity of the criminal law of England, and its benefits and advantages," commended in the said statute, and said to "have been sensibly felt by you," secured to you and your descendants? No. They are too subject to arbitrary "alterations" by the Governor and Council; and a power is expresly reserved of appointing "such courts of criminal, civil and ecclesiastical jurisdiction, as shall be tho't proper." Such is the precarious tenure of mere will, by which you hold your lives and religion.

The Crown and its Ministers are impowered, as far as they could be by Parliament, to establish even the *Inquisition* itself among you. Have you an assembly composed of worthy men, elected by yourselves, and in whom you can confide to make laws for you, to watch over your welfare, and to direct in what quantity, and in what manner, your money shall be taken from you? No. The power of making laws for you is lodged in the Governor and Council, all of them dependant upon, and removeable at the *pleasure* of a Minister.—Besides, another late statute, made without your consent, has subjected you to the impositions of *Excise*, the horror of all free states; they wresting your property from you by the most odious of taxes, and laying open to insolent tax-gatherers, houses the scenes of domestic peace and comfort, and called the castles of English subjects in the books of their laws. And in the very act for altering your government, and intended to flatter you, you are not authorized to "assess, levy or apply any *rates & taxes*, but for the inferior purposes of *making roads*, and erecting and repairing *public buildings*, or for other *local conveniencies, within your respective towns and districts.*" Why this degrading distinction? Ought not the property honestly acquired by *Canadians* to be held as sacred as that of *Englishmen*? Have not Canadians sense enough to attend to any other public affairs, than gathering stones from one place and piling them up in another? Unhappy people! who are not only injured but insulted. Nay more!—With such a superlative contempt of your understanding and spirit has an insolent Ministry presumed to think of you, our respectable fellow subjects, according to the information we have received, as firmly to persuade themselves that your gratitude, for the injuries and insults they have recently offered to you, will engage you to take up arms, and render yourselves the ridicule and detestation of the world, by becoming tools, in their hands, to assist them in taking that freedom from *us*, which they have treacherously denied to *you*; the unavoidable consequence of which attempt, if successful, would be the extinction of all hopes of you or your posterity being ever restored to freedom: For idiotcy itself cannot believe, that, when their drudgery is performed, they will treat you with less cruelty than they have us, who are of the same blood with themselves.

What would your countryman, the immortal *Montesquieu*, have said to such a plan of domination, as has been framed for you? Hear his words, with an intenseness thought suited to the importance of the subject.— "In a free state, every man who is supposed a free agent, *ought to be concerned in his own government*: Therefore the *legislative* should reside in the whole body of the *people*, or their *representatives*."—"The political liberty of the subject is *a tranquility of mind*, arising from the opinion each person has of his *safety*. In order to have this liberty, it is requisite the government be so constituted, as that one man need not be *afraid* of another. When the power of *making* laws, and the power of *executing* them, are *united* in the same person, or in the same body of Magistrates, *there can be no liberty*; because apprehensions may arise, lest the same *Monarch* or *Senate* should *enact* tyrannical laws, to *execute* them in a tyrannical manner."

"The power of *judging* should be exercised by persons taken from the *body of the people*, at certain times of the year, and pursuant to a form & manner prescribed by law. *There is no liberty*, if the power of *judging* be not *separated* from the *legislative* and *executive* powers."

"Military men belong to a profession, which *may be* useful, but *is often* dangerous."—The enjoyment of liberty, and even its support and preservation consists in every man's being allowed to speak his thoughts, and lay open his sentiments.

Apply these decisive maxims, sanctified by the authority of a name which all Europe reveres, to your own state. You have a Governor, it may be urged, vested with the *executive* powers, or the powers of *administration*. In him, and in your Council, is lodged the power of *making laws*. You have *Judges*, who are to *decide* every cause affecting your lives, liberty or property. Here is, indeed, an appearance of the several powers being *separated* and *distributed* into *different* hands, for checks one upon another, the only effectual mode ever invented by the wit of men, to promote their freedom & prosperity. But scorning to be illuded by a tinsel'd outside, and exerting the natural sagacity of Frenchmen, *examine* the specious device, and you will find it, to use an expression of holy writ, "a painted sepulchre," for burying your lives, liberty and property.

Your *Judges*, and your *Legislative Council*, as it is called, are *dependant* on your *Governor*, and *he* is *dependant* on the servant of the Crown in Great-Britain. The *legislative, executive* and *judging* powers are *all* moved by the nods of a Minister. Privileges and immunities last no longer than his smiles. When he frowns, their feeble forms dissolve. Such a treacherous ingenuity has been exerted in drawing up the code lately offered you, that every sentence, beginning with a benevolent pretension, concludes with a destructive power; and the substance of the whole, divested of its smooth words, is—that the Crown and its Minister shall be as absolute throughout your extended province, as the despots of Asia or Africa. What can protect your property from taxing edicts, and the rapacity of necessitous and cruel masters? your persons from Letters de Cachet, goals, dungeons, and oppressive services? your lives & general liberty from arbitrary and unfeeling rulers? We defy you, casting your view upon every side, to discover a single circumstance, promising from any quarter the faintest hope of liberty to you or your posterity, but from an entire adoption into the union of these Colonies.

What advice would the truly great man before mentioned, that advocate of freedom and humanity, give you, was he now living, and knew that we, your numerous and powerful neighbours, animated by a just love of our invaded rights, and united by the indissoluble bands of affection and interest, called upon you, by every obligation of regard for yourselves and your children, as we now do, to join us in our righteous contest, to make common cause with us therein, and take a noble chance of emerging from a humiliating subjection under Government, Intendants, and Military Tyrants, into the firm rank and condition of English freemen, whose custom it is, derived from their ancestors, to make those tremble, who dare to think of making them miserable?"

Would not this be the purport of his address? "Seize the opportunity presented to you by Providence itself. You have been conquered into liberty, if you act as you ought. This work is not of man. You are a small people, compared to those who with open arms invite you into a fellowship. A moment's reflection should convince you, which will be the most for your interest and happiness, to have all the rest of North-America your unalterable friends, or your inveterate enemies. The injuries of Boston have rouzed and associated every colony, from Nova Scotia to Georgia. Your province is the only link wanting to compleat the bright and strong chain of union. Nature has joined your country to theirs. Do you join your political interests. For their own sakes, they never will desert or betray you. Be assured that the happiness of a people inevitably depends on their liberty, and their spirit to assert it. The value and extent of the advantages tendered to you are immense. Heaven grant you may not discover them to be blessings after they have bid you an eternal adieu."

We are too well acquainted with the liberality of sentiment distinguishing your nation, to imagine, that difference of religion will prejudice you against a hearty amity with us. You know, that the transcendant nature of freedom elevates those, who unite in her cause, above all such low minded infirmities. The Swiss Cantons furnish a memorable proof of this truth. Their union is composed of Catholic and Protestant states, living in the utmost concord and peace with one another, and thereby enabled, ever since they bravely vindicated their freedom, to defy and defeat every tyrant that has invaded them.

Should there be any among you, as there generally are in all societies, who prefer the favours of ministers, and their own interests, to the welfare of their country, the temper of such selfish persons will render them incredibly active in opposing all publick-spirited measures, from an expectation of being well-rewarded for their sordid industry, by their superiors; but we doubt not you will be upon your guard against such men and not sacrifice the liberty and happiness of the whole Canadian people and their posterity, to gratify the avarice and ambition of individuals.

We do not ask you, by this address, to commence acts of hostility against the government of our common Sovereign. We only invite you to consult your own glory and welfare, and not to suffer yourselves to be inveigled or intimidated by infamous ministers so far, as to become the instruments of their cruelty and despotism; but to unite with us in one social compact, formed on the generous principles of equal liberty, and cemented by such an exchange of beneficial and endearing offices as to render it perpetual. In order to complete this highly desireable union, we submit it to your consideration, whether it may not be expedient for you to meet together in your several towns and districts, and elect deputies, who afterwards meeting in a provincial congress, may chuse delegates, to represent your province in the continental Congress to be held at Philadelphia on the tenth day of May, 1775.

In this present Congress, beginning on the 5th of the last month, and continued to this day, it has been, with universal pleasure, and an unanimous vote, resolved, That we should consider the violation of your rights, by the act for altering the government of your province, as a violation of our own, and that you should be invited to accede to our confederation, which has no other objects than the perfect security of the natural and civil rights of all the constituent members, according to their respective circumstances, and the preservation of a happy and lasting connection with Great Britain, on the salutary and constitutional principles herein before mentioned. For effecting these purposes, we have addressed an humble and loyal petition to his Majesty, praying relief of our grievances; and have associated to stop all importations from Great Britain and Ireland, after the first day of December, and all exportations to those kingdoms and the West Indies, after the 10th day of next September, unless the said grievances are redressed.

That Almighty God may incline your minds to approve our equitable and necessary measures, to add yourselves to us, to put your fate, whenever you suffer injuries which you are determined to oppose, not on the small influence of your single province, but on the consolidated powers of North-America, and may grant to our joint exertions an event as happy as our cause is just is the fervent prayer of us, your sincere and affectionate friends and fellow-subjects.

By Order of the Congress,
HENRY MIDDLETON, *President.*
October 26, 1774.

HALIFAX, October 25.

We are informed by a Gentleman of undoubted veracity lately arrived from Quebec—that the principal Merchants of that City had received a Letter from the General Congress; inviting them to subscribe to the Measures adopted by the southern Colonies, but that the Letter was burnt in the presence of them all save two New-England people, who had been for sometime past collecting Provision for their distress'd Brethren at Boston; which Collection amounted to 25 bushels of Wheat, but when they applied for a Ship to carry the same to Boston they were refused from all quarters, nor could they for love or money have one for that purpose, so steady are these loyal and happy people to the interest and welfare of Government.

[In full Demonstration that this is a most infernal Falsehood, by ministerial Tools, Pensioners, &c. calculated for the Meridian of the North, and more particularly for the Isle of BUTE; Lately has arrived here 1040 Bushels of Wheat from the worthy Inhabitants of Canada. Moreover there is certain Intelligence from thence by a Vessel arrived at Salem on Friday last, that the Canadians, French as well as British, are much dissatisfied with all the Revenue Acts for North-America; as also with what is called the Quebec Bill, thinking it too great a Sacrifice when entitled to a Toleration by a Treaty on Conquest. It is asserted that Town-Meetings are held on these Affairs from Mont Real to Quebec, and reported that they have chosen Delegates for the Continental Congress in May next, and are preparing Petitions and Remonstrances for the Repeal of the Quebec Bill.]

PHILADELPHIA, November 2.

We hear that his Excellency General Gage, commander in chief of his Majesty's forces in North America & Governor of Boston, has received instructions from the Ministry in case of necessity, to withdraw any number of his Majesty's troops he shall think necessary from the Regiments stationed in the West-India islands to his assistance; and that notice of the same has also been received by the different Governors in the said islands.

NORWICH, Nov. 10.

On Friday last the General Assembly of this Colony ended their Fall Sessions at New-Haven,—We hear they have constituted a Regiment of Militia in every Town of this Colony.—The Field Officers nominated to command the Norwich Regiment are Capt. Jedediah Huntington, Col. Capt. —— Abbot, Lieut. Col. and Capt. Zebdiel Rogers, Major.

BOSTON, *November 14.*

Last Wednesday evening arrived in town, the Hon. Thomas Cushing, Esq, Mr. Samuel Adams, and John Adams, Esq; Delegates from this province, to the late GRAND AMERICAN CONGRESS. The people testified their joy at their safe arrival, by ringing of the bells, &c.

Robert-Treat Paine, Esq; the other Delegate for this Province, took Passage at New York and arrived at Rhode-Island last Week; since which, we hear, he has returned Home safe.

The Delagates for New Hampshire, arrived at Portsmouth, from Philadelphia, on Tuesday last, and were joyfully received by the inhabitants.

The following is sent to the Press as an Extract of a Letter of a late Date from a Gentleman in London to his Friend in a Neighboring Colony.

"SINCE I sent off my last Intelligence, I have seen one of the principal Men in this Kingdom, who was much alarmed at Governor Hutchinson's being addressed by the People of Boston, which, at first, he could not understand, as they, and all America, had, with one Voice, exclaimed against his Administration.—This, he could not then account for; but said that there were some fresh Hopes at Court of America's Submission to all the new Acts; as your Enemies were triumphing on Account of their being likely to succeed.—He said that the Quebec Bill was big with the most dreadful Consequences to the Colonies; the Papists being set up as a Scourge to them, and that if they did submit, all was lost!—It would be the Destruction of the English Nation!—He expected that America would be involved in Blood, &c. now the Roman Catholicks were authorised to execute the Ministerial Vengeance on the Colonies.—Some think G—r T— has advised this Scheme, before he set out, whilst others think him a good Man: But be that as it may, he is an Englishman, bred at Court—a Soldier in the Guards—and is a Friend to the present Measures.—He recommended M. W—, who has given the Ministry Encouragement to think that New-York will not join Boston; and that he will do his best to prevent it, for which, he was to have been Lieut. Governor: but it was advised not to supercede G. Colden, whose Age and Experience gave him the Preference. However he is offered a genteel Post, if he can effect a Disunion; as much depends on that, in order to keep Peace here."

"It is earnestly wished that you may not suffer yourselves to be deluded and imposed upon by the low Cunning of a few Men that have not Honesty enough to withstand the vile Offers of the Ministry, who have bought off the Parliament with the People's Money, and let the Soldiery over them."

"Mr. K— has the Offer of a Present to keep New-York in good Order—Some Overtures are to be sent to Albany, in order to silence the Dutch in those Parts, &c.—This looks as if they intended to Conquer you by Art rather than by Force, but there is no Dependance."

"All is now Hurry and Confusion again, many blaming the present Measures, and expecting that Lord North will lose his Place; nay, some go so far as to lay Wagers that he will lose his Head."

"The Middlesex Address to Hutchinson was altogether a smuggled Affair, and by no Means the Voice of the City. It was known but to very few, and this few of no Note or Influence, the principal People being gone to their Estates in the Country and knew Nothing of it.—But it is intended to be sent privately to Boston to alarm and deceive them."

"Governor Hutchinson is every Day with Lord Dartmouth, and, it is said, declares that Taxation will not do in America *now*."

"Your only Resource is in not sending for any more Goods 'till your Grievances are redressed; and this you have in your Power."

Last Thursday an Inquisition was taken on the Body of Richard Cuitt, and the Jurors returned the following Verdict, viz. "That the said Cuitt was a Mariner on board the Thomas and Richard Transport Ship, commanded by Cuthbert Park, laying at Hancock's Wharf, and did on this 10th Day of November, between the Hours of 7 and 8 of the Clock in the Morning, cut thro' his Windpipe with a Razor, and then and there voluntarily and feloniously as a Felon of himself, did kill and murder himself, against the Peace of our Sovereign Lord the King, his Crown and Dignity."—The Remains of this unhappy Person were immediately buried in the Manner and Form, as by the Law prescribed.

A PROCLAMATION.

SINCE an Assembly most unlawful,
At Cambridge met in Congress awful,
October last, did then presume,
The Powers of Government t'assume;
And slighting British Administration,
Dar'd rashly seek their own Salvation;
By ordering every sturdy Farmer,
To be prepar'd with proper Armour.
('Tis what indeed the Law requires,
But different quite from our Desires.)
Nay further daring, ousted those,
Who for their Suppleness were chose,
All Martial Matters to adjust,
And bid chuse Men whom they could trust:
Which Step our deep-laid Scheme 'tis fear'd,
Will make a Business devilish hard;
And also doubting ancient Gray,
Order'd their Constables to pay,
Whate'er they to the Province owe,
To honest Gardiner of Stow.
By which the Man by Law appointed
Of fingering Cash is disappointed,
And we ourselves do them Impeach
For placing it beyond our reach,
By venturing to recommend
To those who on their Faith depend,
In common Cause to exert their Powers,
Preferring their Advice to ours;
All which Proceedings plainly tend
To render futile the great End
Of present venal Administration,
I therefore issue Proclamation
That Sheriffs, Constables, Collectors,
Dispise the Men who I call Hectors,
Even although their Country deem
Them worthy of her best Esteem,
Forbidding all to pay attention
To said Provincial Convention,
Exhorting Perjury to hate all,
Except in Kings a Sin most fatal,
That they to me may be more stable
I promise them as soon as able
The Congress, Gardiner, and so forth,
I'll make Submit to good Lord North.

The most ancient and benevolent Order of the Friendly Brothers of St. *Patrick*.

THE principal Knot of the 47th Regiment, is to meet on Thursday next, the 17th Instant, at Col. *Ingersol's* Tavern.

Dinner to be on the Table at Four o'Clock.

By Order of the President,
JHFCSPK, 47th Rt.

Such continued regular Friendly Brothers as chuse to visit the Knot, are requested to leave their Names at the Bar before Wednesday Evening.

The Co-Partnership of *Box* and *Austin*, being dissolved by the Death of Mr. *Box*, This is to desire all Persons who have any Demands on said Company, to bring in and settle their Accounts with the surviving Partner, *Benjamin Austin*. And all those who are indebted to the late Company, are requested to make immediate Payment.

N. B. The Business of Ropemaking is still carried on by said *Austin*.

English Grammar,

WHOEVER considers the Inconveniencies to which young Persons must be subject through Life, where a proper Acquaintance with Letters, and Language is wanting; and the great Advantages which must arise to those who are designed to act any considerable Part in Life, from a thorough Knowledge of the Use of Letters, and Propriety of Language, especially of that, which they have by far the most Occasion to use,

Must, undoubtedly, be sensible, that the Study of English Grammar, or the Art of Reading, Speaking and Writing the English Language with strict Propriety, and Elegance, is well worthy the Attention of Youth, as a material Part of their Education.

Such Parents, or Guardians, as are disposed to have their Children instructed in this important Branch, (or rather Foundation) of Science, may be faithfully served for that Purpose, at the English Grammar School, in Milk-Street——by

WILLIAM PAYNE.

☞ LADIES who chuse to be instructed at Home, may be waited on with the utmost Complaisance, and strictest Attention, as often as the Nature of the Business requires, and at such Hours as shall be most convenient.

Writing and Arithmetic will be taught to such as desire it, and Letter-Writing in Form.

He will receive the Commands of such as shall please to favour him therewith, at his School in Milk-Street, or at his Lodgings at Mr. *Benjamin Gray's* in King-Street.

On WEDESDY the 30th Instant,
At TEN o'Clock in the Morning,
Will be sold by PUBLIC VENDUE,
At RUSSELL's Auction-Room, in Queen-Street,
A large Collection of New and Old BOOKS——Printed Catalogues may be had, Gratis, the Monday preceeding the Sale, of
J. RUSSELL, Auctioneer.

ALL Persons indebted to the Estate of WILLIAM WHITE, Esq; late of Boston, deceased, are desired to pay the same to PHILLIPS WHITE of South-Hampton, in the Province of New-Hampshire, Executor of the last Will and Testament of the said WILLIAM WHITE; and those to whom said Estate is indebted are desired to send in their Demands to said Executor.

For the Convenience of many concerned, he purposes to be at Boston from the Sixth Day of December next—Ten Days; from the First Day of February—six Days; and from the Twentieth Day of March—Six Days.

Enquire for the said WHITE, at the Shop of Mrs. *Margarett Phillips*, in Cornhill.

To be sold Part of the Estate of the abovesaid WILLIAM WHITE, at Public Vendue, to the highest Bidder, on Thursday the Eighth Day of December next, viz. The House where the said Deceased lately dwelt, pleasantly situated at the North End of *Boston*, with Brick Store, Stable, Wood-House, &c. Three beautiful Gardens adjoining, &c. &c. and a small Piece of Land near Charlestown-Ferry.—Also a small Dwelling-House in Hull-Street; and a large Store in Queen-Street.——The Vendue to be at last-mentioned Store, at Ten o'Clock in the Forenoon of said Day.—The Conditions of Sale to be seen at the Time and Place of Sale.

N. B. The Premises may be viewed on Tuesday and Wednesday preceeding the Day of Sale.

All Persons that are indebted to the Estate of Mr. JOHN BOX, Sen'r, late of Boston, deceased, are requested to discharge the same; and all those who have Demands upon the Deceased's Estate, are desired to produce their Claims to

Boston, 14th Nov. 1774. *Lydia Box*, *John Box*, *W. Hoskins*. } Executors.

Daniel Silsby,

Has to sell by Wholesale and Retail, at his Store, opposite South-Side *Faneuil-Hall*,

SUGARS Loaf and Brown, Coffee, Chocolate, Rice, Starch, Indigo, Ginger, Allspice, Pepper, Nutmegs, and other Spices; Marseilles and Lisbon OIL, Jamaica Spirit, West-India and New-England Rum, Brandy, Malaga Wine, Crown Soap, 15 & 18 Inch Pipes, Redwood, Logwood, Raisin, and Currants.

ALSO, CHEESE, a very considerable Quantity of *Firkin Butter*, &c.

All of which he will sell as cheap as can be bought at any Store in Boston.

Just arrived, and to be Sold by
WARD & FENNO,
At their Store, at the Head of Dock-Square,
COTTON WOOL per Bag, and Limes per Cask.—Good Connecticut Cheese, Firkin Butter, West India Goods, Spices, &c.

N. B. Goods sold on Commissions at the above Store.

Wanted in a small Family, a Man Servant, who can be well recommended.
Enquire of Edes and Gill.

New AUCTION-ROOM, Cornhill
TO MORROW MORNING, at TEN o'Clock,
Will be sold by PUBLIC VENDUE,
At GREENLEAF's Auction Room,
A Variety of English GOODS, as usual.
Sale begins 10 o'Clock. *Wm. Greenleaf, Auct'r.*

At Gould's Auction-Office,

In Back-Street,
On FRIDAY next,
At TEN in the Morning,
Will be Sold by PUBLIC VENDUE,
A Variety of English GOODS, and Houshold Furniture. R. GOULD, Auctioneer.

N. B. At said Office may be had at private Sale, 8-Day Clocks, of various Prices.

One Turkey Carpet, one Pyramid with Glasses compleat.

Country Traders & others

(Who purchase with Cash,)

MAY have an Opportunity greatly to their Advantage, by speedily applying at BICKER's Auction Room, near the Market, Boston.——Where is sent for Sale—A fine Parcel of middling and low-priced Broad Cloths, of the most fashionable Colours, which will be sold at too low a Rate.

N. B. A great Variety of other Goods, at private Sale, as cheap as usual.

Burials in the Town of BOSTON, since our last.
Thirteen Whites. No Blacks.
Baptiz'd in the several Churches, Six.

High Water at BOSTON, for the present Week.

Monday, 22 min. aft. 8	Friday, 28 min. after. 11
Tuesday, 10 min. aft. 9	Saturday, 26 min. aft. 12
Wednesday, 50 m. aft. 9	Lord's Day, 20 m. af. 1
Thursday, 38 min. aft. 10	Full Moon 18 Day Morn

WHEREAS the Great and General Court or Assembly of this Province, at their Session begun and held the 27th Day of May, 1772, granted a Tax of Two Pence per Acre for one Year next to come; and one Penny per Acre for a second Year next to come, on all the Lands in the District of Hubbardston, in the County of Worcester. And whereas the first and second Years Taxes have been duly assessed and posted, as is by Law directed, and some Proprietors or Owners of said Lands have neglected or refused to pay their Tax; the General Court in said Act did empower the Assessors of said Taxes to sell so much of the Delinquent Proprietors Lands as shall be necessary to pay and satisfy such Taxes, and other necessary intervening Charges. The Owners of the following Lands are delinquent in paying their Taxes, (viz.) The first Year's Tax.

House-Lots.		Pay.			Great Farms.		Pay.		
No. Acres.		£	s.	d.	No. Acres.		£	s.	d.
3	50	0	8	4	1	481	4	2	0
8	76	0	12	8	2	104	0	17	4
14	100	0	16	8	3	120	1	0	0
20	112½	0	18	9	4	50	0	8	4
26	14	0	2	4	5	30	0	5	0
35	7½	0	1	3	11	200	1	13	4
37	135	1	2	6	12	210	1	15	0
38	135	1	2	6	13	28	0	4	8
42	120	1	0	0	15	200	1	13	4
43	120	1	0	0	18	320	2	13	4
44	70	0	11	8	20	319	2	13	2
45	66	0	11	0	22	128	1	1	4
53	23	0	3	10	24	295	2	9	2
55	120	1	0	0	25	241	2	2	0
56	109½	0	18	3	28	172	1	8	8
58	81	0	13	6	31	137	1	2	10
59	102½	0	17	1	32	117	0	19	7
62	100	0	16	8	33	346	2	17	8
63	100	0	16	8	Letter Lots.				
64	100	0	16	8	B.	77	0	12	10
					D.	60½	0	10	1
					L.	70	0	11	8
					O.	90	0	15	0

Notice is hereby given to the abovesaid Delinquents, that so much of their Lands will be sold at a public Vendue, (as to pay their Taxes and other necessary intervening Charges) at the House of Mr. John Ames, Innholder in Hubbardston, on Tuesday the 7th Day of March next, at Ten o'Clock in the Forenoon, and to be continued from Day to Day, by Adjournment, till the Third Day, if not sold before, unless said Taxes and Charges be paid to the Assessors before said Sale.

Hubbardston, Nov. 4, 1774. John Wood, } Assessors.
Joseph Grimes,

The Second Year's Tax.

House-Lots.		Pay.			Great-Farms.		Pay.		
No. Acres.		£	s.	d.	No. Acres.		£	s.	d.
2	50	0	4	2	1	481	2	0	1
3	50	0	4	2	2	295	1	4	7
4	60	0	5	0	3	481	2	0	1
5	100	0	8	4	4	435	1	16	3
6	70	0	5	10	5	4	0	0	4
8	76	0	6	4	9	340	1	8	4
11	135	0	11	3	10	508	2	2	4
13	112	0	9	4	11	200	0	16	8
14	100	0	8	4	12	474	1	19	6
15	100	0	8	4	13	474	1	19	6
17	100	0	8	4	14	474	1	19	6
20	112	0	9	4	15	275	1	2	11
26	14	0	1	2	16	240	1	0	0
28	121	0	10	4	17	212	0	17	8
31	100	0	8	4	18	530	2	4	2
32	100	0	8	4	20	319	1	6	7
33	60	0	5	0	21	458	1	18	2
34	112	0	9	4	22	128	0	10	8
36	121	0	10	1	24	295	1	4	7
37	135	0	11	3	25	241	1	0	1
38	135	0	11	3	26	486	2	0	6
39	8	0	0	8	27	356	1	9	8
40	120	0	10	0	28	472	1	19	4
42	120	0	10	0	29	540	2	5	0
43	120	0	10	0	30	550	2	5	10
44	120	0	10	0	31	340	1	8	4
45	116	0	9	8	32	470	1	19	2
46	120	0	10	0	33	476	1	19	8
48	135	0	11	3	Letter Lots.				
50	100	0	8	4	B.	77	0	6	5
51	109	0	9	1	C.	57	0	4	9
52	110	0	9	2	E.	76	0	6	4
53	23	0	1	11	F.	60	0	5	0
54	111	0	9	3	G.	53½	0	4	6
55	120	0	10	0	H.	66	0	5	6
56	109	0	9	1	K.	57	0	4	9
57	135	0	11	3	L.	70	0	5	10
58	144	0	12	0	O.	90	0	7	6
59	102	0	8	6					
60	100	0	8	4					
62	100	0	8	4					
63	100	0	8	4					
64	100	0	8	4					
65	100	0	8	4					
66	100	0	8	4					
67	100	0	8	4					
68	100	0	8	4					

Notice is hereby given to the abovesaid Delinquents, that so much of their Lands will be sold at a public Vendue, (as to pay their Taxes and other necessary intervening Charges) at the House of Mr. John Ames, Innholder in Hubbardston, on Tuesday the 14th Day of March next, at Ten o'Clock in the Forenoon, and to be continued from Day to Day, by Adjournment, till the Third Day, if not sold before, unless said Taxes and Charges be paid to the Assessors before said Sale.

Hubbardston, Nov. 4, 1774. John Wood, } Assessors.
Joseph Grimes,

This is to notify the Public, That the Charlestown Stage-Coach, No. 1, which heretofore set off from Mr. Woart's Tavern in Charlestown at 8 o'Clock, for Salem, will, for the future, set off at 9 o'Clock every Day in the Week, Sunday excepted, and another from Mr. Goodhue's in Salem, return to Charlestown.

Imported in Capt. Robson, from London, & to be sold by
Peter Hughes,
At his Store in King-Street,

English, Russia and Ravens Duck, Tickienburgs, Oznabrigs, Broad Cloths, Duffils, Beaver Coatings, Cod and Mackrel Lines and Hooks, Sail, Sein and Whipping Twine, 4d. 6d. 8d. and 10d Nails, Sheathing and Drawing ditto, 6 by 8, 7 by 9 & 8 by 10 Glass, Pepper, Gun Powder in Half and Quarter Barrels, 10, 15, 18 and 21 Inch Pipes, single, double and refined Loaf Sugar, Florence Oil, Split Peas, Buntins, Shot, Spices, Durham Mustard, also a few Casks of Burton and Yorkshire Ale.

Boston, Nov. 7th, 1774.

To be Sold at Public Vendue on Wednesday the 30th Day of November, at One o'Clock, P.M. at the House of Capt. Ephraim Jackson, Innholder at Newton.

A FARM containing 100 Acres of choice good Land, lying in said Newton, now in the Occupation of Mr. Samuel Woodward, with a Dwelling House and two Barns standing thereon.——The Privileges of said Farm may be seen any Day by applying to Samuel Woodward on said Farm.

WHEREAS the Proprietors of Sudbury-Canada, (so called) being a Township granted to Josiah Richardson, Esq; and others, in the County of Cumberland, at a legal Meeting by Adjournment on the 17th Day of August, A.D. 1773, granted a Tax of Twenty Shillings, L.M. on each single Right. Also the said Proprietors at a legal Meeting by Adjournment on the 7th Day of December A.D. 1773, granted another Tax of Forty Shillings L.M. on each single Right to defray the Charges of clearing a Road to the said Township and other necessary Charges: Also the said Proprietors at a legal Meeting by Adjournment on the 6th Day of April A.D. 1774, granted another Tax of Twenty Shillings L.M. on each single Right, publick Rights excepted, to defray the Charges of building Mills in said Township: And altho' the said Taxes have been published according to Law, and Payment requested, nevertheless several of the said Proprietors are delinquent in the Payment of the said Taxes: Publick Notice is therefore hereby given to said Delinquents, that unless their Taxes are paid to Cornelius Wood of Sudbury, Treasurer, or to us the Subscribers, by Ten o'Clock in the Morning of the 13th Day of December next, their Rights will be sold as the Law directs, for the Payment of their Taxes and Charges arising by the Sale, and the Sale to begin at Eleven o'Clock in said Morning, at the Dwelling-House of Isaac Gleason, Innholder in Waltham, and continued by Adjournment (if need be) till the whole be sold.

Cornelius Wood, } Proprietors
Elijah Bent,   } Committee.
Josiah Stone.

Robert Wyer, Sailmaker,
HEREBY informs his Customers and others, That he is removed his Loft from the Head of Rowe's Wharff, to the new Loft lately built on Hallowell's Ship-Yard, where they may depend on being served with Fidelity and Dispatch, as usual.
N.B. Said Wyer would take a Boy as an Apprentice, that can be well recommended.

The Copartnership of Brown and Shattuck will be mutually Dissolved the 14th Instant.——Those who have any Demands on said Company, are desired to send in their Accounts; and those indebted, are requested to make immediate Payment.

All Persons having Demands on the Estate of Joseph and Joseph Wheeler, jun. of Boston, deceas'd, and those who are Indebted to said Estate, are desired to bring in their Accounts to John Lucas, Administrator in Order to Settlement.

Town and Country Store,
At the Head of Dock-Square.
WARD & FENNO
SELL West-India, and a great Variety of other Goods, CHEAP ENOUGH.

A few Tubs very good BUTTER to be Sold by JOSIAH WATERS and SON, in Ann-Street.

To be Sold or Lett, and may be entered upon immediately.
A House and about Four Acres of Land in Dorchester, about four Miles from Boston) with every Accommodation suitable for a Gentleman. Enquire of JOHN VASSALL.

JOHN GRAHAM,
HAS just Imported a large Quantity of Old Jamaica Spirits of the best kind, and will be Sold by the Hogshead, Barrel or lesser Quantity if required, Coffee and Chocolate, &c.
The above will be Sold at reasonable Rates for Cash, at his Store on Wendel's Wharf, near the South Battery Fort-Hill.

New-Castle Coals
Just Imported at 12 Dollars per Chaldron; Coffee in Tierces at 10d. per lb. good red Port Wine in Quarter Casks at £.8.—A few Dozen of Philadelphia Porter, the first ever exported from that Place, and little, if any Thing, inferior to the London Porter, at 11s. 4d. per Dozen, to be sold at Minot's T, adjoining the Long-Wharff. Enquire at said T of Lewis Grant, or at Store No. 20 on the Long Wharff. 31 Octo. 1774.

AT a Meeting of the Inhabitants of the Town of Fairfield, legally warned and held on the 20th Day of September, A.D. 1774, for the express Purpose of considering the distressed State of the Town of Boston and providing them some Relief, the following Resolves were unanimously passed and ordered to be made publick.

THIS Meeting taking into Consideration the distressed and perplexed State of the Province of Massachusetts-Bay, and more especially the Town of Boston, who are groaning under Tyranny and cruel Oppression, and viewing the secret Machinations and wicked Attempts of arbitrary Ministers and a corrupt Parliament to bring us into Bondage, think ourselves bound in Duty to ourselves, our Country and Posterity, to publish our Sentiments of these Things.

And as the good People of this and the neighbouring Colonies in America have ever testified their Loyalty to the King on every Occasion, we think it unnecessary to make any further Declaration on that Head, only that we shall ever return our Affection to the King and consider ourselves his Subjects, and be willing to assist him in support of his just Prerogative and against all his Enemies, so long as he continues to reign over us according to the Constitution; which is the Foundation on which he Himself stands as our King.

And we firmly persuade ourselves, that whenever any single Person or Body of Men attempt an Invasion of the Rights and Privileges of others, Opposition and Resistance are justifiable, and even indispensible.

And as we are fully convinced that the late Act of Parliament made for the Purpose of raising a Revenue in America, and other Acts curtailing the Charter Rights of the Province of Massachusetts-Bay and shutting up the Port of Boston, and the alarming Quebec Bill, cannot be justified upon constitutional Principles, but are a very high-handed and dangerous Attempt to destroy our Peace and Security and reduce us to a State of Slavery: We are determined, in conjunction with our distressed Fellow-Subjects in this and the neighbouring Colonies, to exert ourselves in every prudent, peaceable and manly way, becoming Christians and those who have a just Sense of constitutional Liberty, to defend ourselves and our Brethren in the full and quiet Possession and Enjoyment of our Rights and Privileges. And we sympathize with our afflicted Brethren of the Massachusetts, and Boston especially, under their present Load of Oppression: We consider them as suffering for us as well as themselves; we wish them all needed Wisdom and Fortitude, and will cheerfully lend our Aid and Assistance to comfort and support them in their manly and glorious Struggle for Liberty.

We have great Dependance on the Wisdom of that respectable Body of Patriots who are now at Philadelphia from the several Colonies on the Continent, to consult the Interest of the Mother-Country and America, to restore Peace and Liberty among us, and bring about a Reconciliation. And we feel ourselves disposed to wait the Result of their Councils and Deliberations, and to acquiesce in such Measures as shall be adopted by them; unless a sudden Emergency should call for our Exertion.

Test. NATHAN BULKELEY, Town-Clerk.

To be Sold at the Royal Exchange Tavern in King-Street, Boston.
At Publick Vendue,
On THURSDAY the First Day of December next, at Eleven o'Clock in the Forenoon.
The following Lots of Land, viz.

Lot No. 20, called a 10 Mile back Lot, on the West side of Kennebeck-River, containing about 4800 Acres.

Lot marked F. 2. in the first Range of Lots, containing about 6000 Acres (exclusive of Settlers Lots interspersed) being near one Mile wide, and fifteen Miles long, and fronting on Kennebeck-River, on the West side of it, about ten Miles above Fort-Halifax, to be divided and sold in two Parts.

A Lot to the Northward of ditto, and fronting on little Norridgwalk-River, about 3200 Acres.

Lot marked B D. 1. in the second Range of Lots, about six Miles above Norridgwa'k, on the West side of Kennebeck-River, and fronting thereon, containing about 7000 Acres, (exclusive of Settlers Lots interspersed) being 1 Mile wide, and 15 Miles long.

Lot marked C. A 1. in the third Range of Lots, near the Falls of Coriontonka, about 12 Miles above Norridgwalk, on the West side of Kennebeck-River, and fronting thereon, containing about 7000 Acres, (exclusive of Settlers Lots interspersed) being 1 Mile wide and 15 Miles long.

Three Lots of Land, viz. Lot No. 32, on the East side of Kennebeck-River, about a Mile above Fort-Western—No. 36, on the East side of said River, about 9 Miles above Fort-Western: and Lot No. 20, on the West side of said River, about 1 Mile and ½ above Fort-Western, containing 400 Acres each.

Also all the Islands in Cobbiseconte Pond, and all the Islands in Kennebeck-River above Fort-Halifax.

For further Particulars enquire of HENRY ALLINE, jun. at his Office in King-Street, Boston.

Boston, November 2d, 1774.

For LONDON,
The Ship JOHN WILKES, JAMES HALL Commander, Will certainly sail from Newport, Rhode-Island, on or before the 10th of November at farthest:—For Passage apply to FRANCIS ROTCH, at his Store at Bedford in Dartmouth, or the Master on board.

Bedford, (in Dartmouth) October 27, 1774.

ANY Person proving Property in a Cable and two Anchors taken up in the River St. Lawrence, may have them by applying to the Printers and paying Salvage.

Taken up last Week a Canoe almost new. The Owner by applying to the Printers may have her again, paying Charges.

A Wet Nurse, with a good Breast of Milk, would take a Child to suckle. Inquire of the Printers.

Boston: Printed by EDES & GILL, in Queen-Street, 1774.

No. 1023

THE
Boston-Gazette, AND COUNTRY JOURNAL.

Containing the freshest Advices, Foreign and Domestic.

MONDAY, November 21, 1774.

Fresh Advices from London.

From the LONDON GAZETTE, October 1, 1774.

By the KING.

A PROCLAMATION

For Dissolving the present Parliament, and Declaring the Calling of another.

GEORGE R.

WHEREAS We have thought fit, by and with the Advice of our Privy Council, to Dissolve this present Parliament, which now stands prorogued to Tuesday the Fifteenth Day of November next: We do, for that End, publish this Our Royal Proclamation; and do hereby Dissolve the said Parliament accordingly. And the Lords Spiritual and Temporal, and the Knights, Citizens, and Burgesses, and the Commissioners for Shires and Burghs, of the House of Commons, are discharged from their Meeting, and Attendance, on Tuesday the said Fifteenth Day of November next. And We being desirous and resolved, as soon as may be, to meet Our People, and to have their Advice in Parliament, do hereby make known to all Our loving Subjects, Our Royal Will and Pleasure to call a new Parliament: And do hereby further declare, That, with the Advice of Our Privy Council, We have, this Day, given Order to Our Chancellor of Great Britain, to issue Our Writs, in due Form, for Calling a New Parliament; which Writs are to bear Teste on Saturday the first Day of October next, and to be returnable on Tuesday the Twenty-Ninth Day of November following.

Given at Our Court at St. James's, the Thirteenth Day of September, One Thousand Seven Hundred and Seventy Four, in the Fourteenth Year of Our Reign.

LONDON, October 1.

THE sudden Dissolution of Parliament has given rise to a great variety of conjectures, among which are the following: That it is principally occasioned by the present critical situation of affairs in North America, which renders the advice of a new Parliament necessary. Others more confidentally assert, that the many spirited Resolutions entered into by the several Candidates for seats in the new Parliament, hastened the dissolution of the old, as the Ministry did not know to what lengths such proceedings might be carried, and what trouble such spirited exertions in favor of the patriotic party might cause them.——Some say the accounts lately received from the Courts of Sweden, Vienna, France and Spain, have been of so perplexing a nature, that a new Parliament was become absolutely necessary, to advise and assist his Majesty in the present alarming state of affairs.

It is now expected that a general change of the Ministry will take place before the meeting of Parliament.

It is said some advices of the most important nature were received on Tuesday from America.

A letter from Philadelphia, of August 4th, gives the following account. viz. "In the colony of Massachusets Bay, about eight weeks ago, the militia was mustered, which consisted of 119,600 effective men, belonging to that Colony only, all trained and disciplined as well as the best troops in Great Britain. They were exercised a few days ago at the place were the regulars are encamped; the commanding Officer of whom ordered them to disperse, or that he would bring his troops against them. This occasion'd some words, and the Colonel of the militia told the commanding Officer of the King's troops, that if he would bring double the number of regulars into the field, he with his men would decide the fate of America with him; however, matters being amicably settled, the Colonel of the militia desired the Officer of the regulars to exercise his men, when the militia fired nine times in a minute by companies, to the surprize of all present."

General Gage hath absolute orders from the Court to prevent the meetings of the Congress, and to seize all such people as attempt to assemble.

A report prevails, that General Gage is killed, and that two regiments of his troops had revolted.

It was yesterday reported, that advice had been received of there having been some commotions at Boston, and that a great number of the army have deserted, and that some mischief had been done.

LONDON, September 27.

YEsterday the Lord Mayor, the two Sheriffs, Aldermen Wilkes and Sawbridge, and a number of the Freeholders of Middlesex, met at the Mile-End Assembly room, in order to nominate proper persons to represent the said county in the ensuing Parliament. The first business was to determine on the different articles that the candidates to be put in nomination should subscribe, which were to the following purport: That, if chosen, they should endeavor to obtain a bill for the shortening the duration of Parliaments; a bill for the exclusion of Placemen and Pensioners; a bill for the more equal representation of the People; and a bill to repeal the four late acts respecting the Americans.

The Sheriffs asked the Freeholders if they were willing their Candidates should be bound to the aforesaid articles; when about six persons held up their hands against the question. This being decided in the affirmative, John Wilkes, Esq; was nominated as a Candidate, and all hands held up for him, except five or six. The Sheriffs next put up Serjeant Glynn, who had every hand held up in his favour. Upon Mr. Sawbridge's motion the two Candidates were jointly put up, which was received with the greatest applause. Lastly the Sheriffs enquired if any other Gentleman was to be proposed as a Candidate; whereupon one Gentleman was mentioned, but no person seconded the motion.

The nomination being thus concluded, Mr. Wilkes assured the Freeholders he was ready to bind himself by the terms they proposed, as he agreed to every one of them. He thanked the Freeholders for that farther mark of their approbation, and begged leave to assure them every part of his conduct should be uniformly such as he hoped would continue that confidence, as he was determined through life to pursue the same great end. This speech was received with applause.

The following is a copy of the engagement signed by John Wilkes and John Glynn, Esqrs.

We [John Wilkes and John Glynn] *do solemnly promise and engage ourselves to our constituents, if we have the honour of being chosen the Representatives in Parliament of the county of Middlesex, that we will endeavor to the utmost of our power to restore and defend the excellent form of government modelled and established at the Revolution, and to promote acts of legislature, for shortning the duration of Parliaments, for excluding placemen and pensioners from the House of Commons, for a more fair and equal representation of the people, for vindicating the injured rights of the freeholders of this county, and the whole body of electors of this united kingdom, and an act for the repeal of the four late acts respecting America, the Quebec act, establishing popery, and the system of French Canadian laws in that extensive province, the Boston port act, the act for altering the charter of the province of Massachusetts-Bay, and the act for the trial in Europe of persons accused of criminal offences in America, being fully persuaded that the passing of such acts will be of the utmost importance for the security of our excellent constitution, and the restoration of the rights & liberties of our fellow subjects in America.*

John Wilkes, John Glynn."

It is to be hoped that the electors in every county, city and town in Great Britain, will insist upon the like engagement from those they chuse.

Oct. 1. At the close of the poll for Lord Mayor this day, the number was as follows:

Lord Mayor,	—	605
Alderman Wilkes,	—	602
Sir J. Esdale,	—	588
Alderman Kennet,	—	566

Orders, it is said, are dispatched to the commander in chief in North America, to cause any six of the Deputies to the Congress to be intercepted on their way, and by that means to frustrate the intention, by not permitting it to be general.

'Tis to hoped that the people at the next general election will have an eye to those who have promoted the passing of several unpopular and unconstitutional bills: the promoters of the Quebec bill ought not to be forgotten, who have denied English subjects a trial by Jury, and encouraged the infamous practice of *Lettres de Cachet*, by refusing to grant the liberty of the *Habeus Corpus* act to persons confined by an act of power. And lastly, these ought to be had in everlasting remembrance, who endeavored to destroy the freedom of election, by rendering of no effect the votes of the electors of the county of Middlesex.

It is now generally known that Lord Mansfield's visit to the French court is entirely a political one. Some particular matters were entrusted to him, which could not be committed to the care of any other person.

Sept. 29. No more troops will be sent from Ireland to America, but from Great Britain. This regulation has been occasioned by the great desertion of the Irish regiments under General Gage.

We hear administration intends to be before-hand with the Patriots, by bringing in a bill next session of Parliament to make a final settlement of American affairs, if the Colonies furnish them with any pretence to save their honour.

It is assured that government is much deceived in the conduct of the Americans; their cool, deliberate and prudent measures, having confounded their foes, and gained them many friends.

This being Michaelmas-day the Right Hon. the Lord Mayor, attended by the Aldermen, Sheriffs, Recorder, and other city Officers, met at Guildhall, where the two Sheriffs mounted the Hustings, and proceeded to the election of a Lord Mayor. The several Aldermen below having been seperately put up, the Lord Mayor was then nominated, when the show of hands appeared in favor of his Lordship and Mr. Alderman Wilkes; but a poll was demanded in behalf of Sir James Esdaile, and Mr. Alderman Kennett, which began immediately.

Sept. 10. It is said, that the desertion amongst the troops at Boston daily encreases. Private advices from America mention, that more than 300 of the soldiers have quitted their respective regiments. The sagacity of General Gage has been exerted to prevent this alarming evil, but hitherto the General's stratagems have all proved ineffectual; the men who are placed as centinels to hinder others from deserting, are themselves the very men who take the most sudden flight; and if this defection amongst the troops has happened at the commencement of the siege, nothing short of a total desertion is to be expected before the conclusion of the campaign.

Sept. 13. There are said to be at least upwards of 15 000 soldiers cantoned along the coast of Spain from Barchelona to Alicant, which are continually increasing, stretching towards the French boundaries, but with what view, in the present appearance of things is hard to determine.

Sept. 14. A letter from Amsterdam says, "Your disputes with America have so alarmed this country, that it is with difficulty we can get some bills discounted, even at large premiums."

Summonses, we are assured, are issued for a grand Privy Council, to be held on Tuesday next at the Cockpit, Whitehall, on the affairs of America. Governor HUTCHINSON will then, we are informed, be sworn in one of his Majesty's Privy Council.

It was on Thursday strongly reported that a disagreement had happened among some officers of state, relating to the affairs of America, and that several resignations were expected to be the consequence. Some of the members are said to be advocates for lenitive measures, while others as strongly insist on the necessity of *enforceing* obedience.

A scheme is in agitation for establishing a company of artillery in North-America, who are to be independant of the detachments sent from England.

Thursday night a Messenger was sent off from St. James's with dispatches to Lord Mansfield and Lord Stormont, at Paris; likewise he was charged with dispatches for the Court of Turin; and for Mr. Strange his Majesty's Resident at Venice.

A great number of journeymen Clothiers from Wiltshire and Gloucestershire, are going over to New-York, to be employed in the woolen manufactories in that province.

Saturday a Jew underwent a severe discipline on board a West-India ship in the river (for cheating one of the Sailors, by selling him a ring and a pair of buckles of adulterated base metal, for gold and silver) in the following manner: They first stripp'd him entirely, then tarred him all over from head to foot, after which they stuck him full of Feathers, and then carried the poor son of Levi on shore, where he was hunted by men, women and children, to his habitation, which was near two miles.

Wednesday morning early a duel was fought in Lamb's Conduit-fields, behind the Foundling-hospital, between two Brothers, on account of a well-known Woman of pleasure, in which the eldest was so desperately wounded, that he was obliged to be carried off by the seconds.

Sept. 11. A stop is ordered to be immediately put to the exportation of brass and iron ordnance, from any of the ports of this kingdom, except on government account.

Copy of a Letter from Governor Hutchinson *to the Earl of* Dartmouth, *dated* Boston, March 9th; 1774.

My Lord,

SINCE the date of No. 41, the chief business of the house and of the council has been to bring about by some means or other, the removal of the chief justice, and for this purpose they have turned and tortured the charter to such a degree as to frame a constitution quite different from what was ever intended. The articles of impeachment will leave a lasting stain upon the character of the government. Finding that every attempt to compel me to a compliance with, or connivance at their unwarrantable measures was ineffectual, and having some intimations that the indecency with which both the king and the parliament had been treated by them, would oblige me put an end to their sitting; the council and the house each prepared a long message, both of them rude and abusive to me, the former explaining the constitution of the governor and council in so strange a manner, and by such futile arguments and inconclusive reasoning, that they have greatly dishonored themselves with all the judicious and candid part of the world under whose observation they may fall, and the latter coming but little short of it. There will not be time to copy them before the post goes out. I will have the whole proceedings respecting the chief justice copied, and send them by the next opportunity under the province seal. After persisting in a measure so affrontive to his Majesty, I could not have justified the omission of a proper resentment, which I expressed in a short message, and this morning ordered a prorogation, great part of their business being unfinished. Sunday the 6th Inst. a vessel arrived from London, having on board about 30 chests of tea on account of several traders in tea; the next day the vessel was hauled to the wharf where the vessels lay which had the East-India company's tea, and in the evening a sufficient number of persons disguised like Indians went on board and destroyed the tea in a short time, and the next morning the vessel was hauled to the long wharf, where vessels from London generally unload, to take out the rest of her goods. The owners of the tea are very silent, and I think if they could find out who were the immediate actors, they would not venture at present to bring any action in the law against them. If they had attempted to land it, it is probable they would have shared in the fate of the consignees of the company's teas, neither of which have been able to return to the town since they were first banished.

I am, &c. THOs. HUTCHINSON.

LONDON, *September* 13.

The following is said to be an authentic Copy of a Letter very recently received from a General Officer some Time since sent to America, in a very important and critical Situation, by a Noble Lord in a very high Office:

(COPY.)

"My Lord,

"IT is with the most poignant regret that I find myself greatly necessiated to demand a total exemption from all those restrictions, which are laid upon me by the private orders, and a fuller scope to exert more immediate powers, as the only means left me to form any hopes of effecting the great and arduous task I have undertaken. I have, my Lord, long known the people I have now to deal with; and am well assured, they are in the extent bitter enemies to all conciliatory measures, where they think the entrance upon them may throw an odium on their unanimity, or put their public spirit to the least doubt. I had the honour to deliver my sentiments and opinion to your Lordship, before my embarkation, on these people and their prejudices, which, to my great astonishment, I now find most obstinately rooted; and every day brings me new fears, that I shall be reduced to the cruel necessity of doing my duty to my Country and my Royal Master, in a way that will, I am certain, be as painful to your Lordship as to myself, and which I have most studiously endeavoured to avoid. According to the express commands of my most gracious Master, which I had the honour to receive from him before my departure, I entered on the most lenient measures at first, and acted with circumspection and secrecy, as my arrival added fuel to the flame of the party, as it was universally propagated and believed that I came to act more in my military capacity than my civil. I found the means, my Lord, to gain the secrets of the party, and endeavoured, by every means, to convince some of the leaders, that I came more as a mediator than to enforce. I gave them to know, that the most soothing measures would be used if they would deserve them; that the King desired nothing more ardently than the affection of his American subjects, and a good understanding with his Colonies, but that it was firmly resolved to gain an honourable & just reparation for the insults offered, and the great disobedience to his M----'s government and authority; and this reparation must be gained; this return to obedience must be established by means the most coercive and severe; but such is their fatal obstinacy, that every effort for conciliation was refused. As the military force was indeed feared, the cunning and policy of these people immediately suggested the means of debauching the soldiers from their duty, in which they had too great success, before I could have the power of exerting my authority in stopping a defection, which a short time would have rendered very general. I have, my Lord, offered such terms to these deluded men, as are infinitely more lenient than they deserve, and which, should they refuse accepting, I am determined to make some very severe examples, which I am very certain will prove the ultimate resource I shall reap any benefit from, respecting the intent I am to accomplish. I must assure your Lordship, that I shall have occasion for a considerable reinforcement of troops, on whose duty and obedience dependance can be placed; and the more immediate the supply, the more effectual service it will render me. Your Lordship's judgment will point out the most proper, but I could wish that . . .

. . . .

may be preferred, as my intimate knowledge with them leaves no doubt of their affection to the service. I have pleasure, however, of affirming to your Lordship, that a considerable number of the most respectable people here are well affected to his Majesty, and have very much distinguished themselves in opposition to the most extravagant schemes of the party, which is indeed a most violent and large majority. I have, my Lord, to the utmost extent of my power, executed those private matters given to me in charge by your Lordship, and by their success am still more confirmed in your Lordship's profound political researches, and extensive knowledge of mankind in general. I need not use arguments to assure your Lordship, that I am most firmly attached to an honorable discharge of my commission, or that I have the honour to be,

My LORD,

Your Lordship's, in all sincerity,

———"

[*If this should appear to be a Letter written by General G—e, it is the most extraordinary of the Kind that has yet been made publick, and requires very particular Attention.*]

Sept. 14. *It is generally thought that the m——y will find it necessary to get the Boston Port-bill repealed the next session of p——t, if at least they hope for any success at the ensuing general election.*

BOSTON, *November* 21.

Extract of a Letter from Philadelphia, Nov. 9.

"*A Letter inserted in our Gazette from General G—e to Lord North, was taken from the London Chronicle of the* 13*th of September, published by Strahan*, one of the King's Printers.——*It is damn'd here as* authentic."

At a Meeting of the Inhabitants of this Town by adjournment, November 7th, the Committee appointed for that Purpose, made the following Report, which was accepted by the Town.

"WHEREAS sundry Regiments of his Majesty's Troops are contrary to Law, and to the great annoyance and detriment of his Majesty's good Subjects of this Province, now stationed in the Town of Boston, in a Time of profound Peace, for the avowed Purposes of carrying into execution sundry Acts of the British Parliament, tending to enslave the People, and to subvert the Constitution of the Province, which it is our Duty to Protest against on all Occasions; yet, nevertheless, we, the Inhabitants of the Town of Boston, in Town-Meeting legally assembled, taking into serious Consideration, the distressed Circumstances of this Metropolis, and being anxious still to use our best Endeavours to preserve that Decency and Order for which the Town has ever been remarkable, relying on the justice of our Cause, and considering the united Endeavours of the Colonies, the Wisdom of the Continential Congress, the Justice and Clemency of our Sovereign, and the Smiles of Divine Providence, that our Grievances will shortly be redressed, and our unalineable and precious Rights, Liberties and Privileges be restored and secured to us upon a just and permanent basis. Therefore we recommend,

'That as his Excellency the Governor has assured the Town, that he will do all in his Power to secure the Peace and good Order of the Town;

'That the Town on their Part will exert their best Endeavours to effect the same desirable Purpose; and to this End would augment the Town Watch, and it is recommended to the Selectmen of the Town, that they increase the Watch to the number of twelve Men in each Watch-House, for the security and safety of the Inhabitants, and that they be directed to patrole the Streets of the Town for the whole Night the ensuing Season.

'And it is earnestly desired that his Majesty's Justices of the Peace, and other Peace Officers would exert their Authority for the observance of the Laws, and preservation of Peace and Order, and that when they hear of any Disturbance, they would not wait for a Complaint, but call on the Inhabitants, who will at all Times be ready in assisting to disperse such Persons, or in bringing Offenders of what Rank or Order soever to Justice.

'As in our present situation it is incumbent upon us particularly to attend to the Peace and good Order of the Town, it is therefore earnestly recommended to the Inhabitants to do all in their Power to prevent and suppress any Quarrels or Disturbances. And it is seriously recommended to all Masters of Families that they restrain their Children and Servants from going abroad after Nine o'Clock in the Evening, unless on necessary Business.

'And it is further recommended to the Selectmen of the Town to injoin upon all Retailers and Taverners of the Town, that they strictly conform to the Laws of the Province, relating to disorderly Persons."

Attest. W. COOPER, Town-Clerk.

The following Extract from a Law of this Province, for the suppressing of Drunkenness, &c. is printed by Order of the Select-Men, that no one when prosecuted, for the Breach of said Laws, may plead Ignorance as an Excuse.

"*BE it therefore Enacted by the Lieutenant-Governor, Council and Representatives in General Court Assembled, and by the Authority of the same, that from and after the Publication hereof, every Person and Persons now Licensed or that shall hereafter obtain Licence to Retail Wine and Strong Liquors to be spent out of Doors, and not otherwise, who shall be convicted of entertaining or suffering any Person or Persons to sit drinking or tipling in their Houses, Cellars, Backsides or within any of the Dependencies of such Houses, or of selling any other Sort of Drink than what they have Licence for, shall incur and suffer the like Penalties and Forfeitures as may by Law be inflicted upon Persons selling without Licence, to be recovered and employed in Manner as by the said Law is directed.*"

The following donations has been received during the course of the week past, for the relief of the poor, suffering by means of the Port-Bill, viz. From Chestertown and Candy Parish, in the province of New-Hampshire, 3l. and 84 sheep.—From Concord, on Pennecook River, New-Hampshire, 30 Bushel of Peas.—From Rehoboth 14l.—From Rehoboth and East-Greenwich, 112 Sheep.—From Tiverton, 72 Sheep.—From Glassenbury, 160 Bushels of Grain.—From Southington, 150 Bushels of Grain.——From Weathersfield, 73 Bushels of Grain.—From Middletown, 1080 Bushels of Grain.——From Mr. Samuel Moody, School-Master, at Newbury-Falls, 5 Guineas.

The Town of Marblehead, at a full Meeting on Monday the 7th Instant, unanimously made Choice of a large Committee for executing the Plans of the Continential and Provincial Congresses. It likewise appointed a Day for choosing Militia Officers, and a Committee for each Company to give personal Warning to all on the Alarm List for the Purpose mentioned. Directions were given by the Town to the Clerk, for entering on the Records such Persons as should by the Province be considered and published as "*Rebels against the State*"; and to the Constables and Collectors to pay to Henry Gardner, Esq; Monies which they then had, or in future might have in their Hands, belonging to the Province; the Advertisements of the late Treasurer Gray being treated with the Contempt due to one on the *Rebel List*. A Company and Train of Artillery will, by private Subscription, be likewise provided in said Town for Defence of American Freedom.——Surely the Colonies are in Earnest for preserving their Liberties, and a general Attention to the Art Military will in a short Time render them secure, notwithstanding the Designs of oppressive Tyranny.——May Military Discipline, then, immediately take Place throughout America.

We hear that the Connecticut Delegates, upon their Return, made Report to the General Assembly, then sitting, who unanimously approved of the Proceedings of the Congress and sent Orders into the different Towns for a strict Compliance therewith.

We hear from Malden, that on the first Instant the Commission Officers of that Town resigned their Commissions at the Head of the Company, and were unanimously elected to the same Offices they sustained before.

It is said, the Pennsylvania Assembly is summoned to meet, in Consequence of a Letter from the Right Hon. Lord Dartmouth, to his Honor Governor Penn; in which it is desired that the Members would state the Grievances of the People, in order to their being laid before the King. We are told that his Lordship has written Letters of the same Purport to the other Governors in America.

Last Tuesday the Troops quitted their Encampments on the Common and Fort-Hill, and are now in Barracks at different Parts of the Town.

Captain Joseph Deane, in a Ship from Surrinam, bound into Salem, was cast away on Monday Morning, last Week, at the East End of Martha's Vineyard; the Vessel with a Cargo of 300 Hogsheads of Molasses, entirely lost.

Last Wednesday Morning departed this Life, (in Consequence of the Wounds he lately received by being thrown out of a Carriage,) THOMAS GRAY, Esq; Merchant, aged 53.—His Remains were decently interr'd last Friday Afternoon.

Messieurs EDES & GILL,

GENTLEMEN, *Quebec, 24 October,* 1774.

AT the Request of the Gentlemen of a Committee from Montreal, I send you the inclosed, with an Assurance that it is a true Translation from the French Original; and beg that you'll insert it in your useful Paper, that the Sentiments of a very (if not the most) considerable Number of our Canadian Brethren and Fellow-Subjects in this Province may appear in a just Light to our Brethren in the Province of the Massachusetts. I am, &c. — —

"INSTRUCTIONS to the English Gentlemen of the Committee at Montreal, from the Canadian FARMERS, &c. translated into English, viz.

"*WE the Canadian Farmers and others, being greatly alarmed at a late Act of Parliament, which re-establishes the ancient Laws of this Country, the bad Effects of which we too severely felt during the French Government; and being entirely satisfied under the English Laws as administered in this Province, beg Leave to acquaint the Gentlemen of the Committee for Montreal, that any legal Steps they shall take for the Repeal of the said Act, will be approved of by us; and we sincerely hope and pray, that they will use all Means in their Power for the same, by petitioning his Majesty, and representing to the Merchants of London the flourishing State of the Trade and Agriculture of this Province since the Conquest thereof, which we attribute to that Freedom which every one has enjoyed under the English Laws —And we hereby declare, that we never had any Hand in a certain Petition, said to be sent to his Majesty, in the Name, and in Behalf of all the Canadians, for obtaining said Act; nor have we, nor any Part of the Country where we reside, been in any wise consulted thereupon. Therefore we verily believe, the said Petition was contrived and obtained in a clandestine and fraudulent Manner, by a few artful designing Men, in Order to get themselves into Posts of Profit and Honor.*"

PHILADELPHIA, November 9.

In the course of the last week two very respectable [persons] in this city, upon the death of near relations, exhibited a laudable example of public virtue to their fellow-citizens, by strictly complying with the association of the General Congress as to mourning dress on the melancholy occasion.

NEW-YORK, Nov. 10.

By a vessel arrived from England at Philadelphia, we have an account of the ship Lady Gage's safe arrival, her letters were delivered on the 13th of September.

An account has been received by way of Canada, that Captain Lord, commanding a detachment of his Majesty's Royal Regiment of Ireland, at the Cascaskies, in the Illionois country, with three of his men were fired upon, killed and scalped by the Indians; the particulars we have not been able as yet to procure.

An Estimate of the number of souls in the following Provinces, made in Congress, 1774.
In Massachusetts, 400,000. New-Hampshire, 150,000. Rhode-Island, 59,678. Connecticut, 192,000. New-York, 250,000. New-Jersey, 130,000. Pensylvania, including the Lower Counties, 350,000. Maryland, 320,000. Virginia, 650,000. North-Carolina, 300,000. South-Carolina, 225,000.—Total 3,026,678.

On Monday last a discovery being made, that 18 Sheep were on board a Sloop in the harbour, bound for the West-Indies, a number of Citizens waited on the Captain, and informed him that the exportation of sheep was contrary to a resolution of the Continental Congress, and thereupon obtained his promise that they should be re-landed, and not carried out of the harbour. The people were satisfied & patiently waited till evening, when a report prevailing that the vessel was to sail that night; about two hundred inhabitants assembled on the wharf, appointed and sent four persons to wait on the Committee of Correspondence, and request their advice concerning the measures proper to be taken. By their advice the Merchant to whom the vessel came consigned, was sent for, and desired to cause the sheep to be landed and delivered to one of the Committee, appointed on this occasion, by the people, which person gave his promise to return the sheep as soon as the vessel had sailed. Accordingly the sheep were landed, delivered, and soon after the vessel was sailed, returned to the Proprietor; on which the people being well satisfied, peaceably dispersed.

Sir John Johnson, Knight and Baronet, is appointed Major General of the Militia, both Horse and Foot, in the Northen District of this Province, vice his Father, the worthy Sir William Johnson, deceased.

Extract of a Letter dated the 9th of October, 1774. from a Gentleman in Montreal, to his Friend in New-York.

"I must beg leave to trouble you to get the inclosed printed in Mr. Holt's Paper, as soon as possible, and send me an Account of the Charge, which shall be paid (together with the Postage of this Letter)—The Paper contains the Resolves of all the English Inhabitants of Montreal, at a full Meeting, where they shewed their Abhorrence of the Quebec Act, which establishes the French Laws in this Province, and puts the Lives and Properties of every Person in it, in the Power of the Governor; who, when the Act takes Place, will have a much greater Power than a Spanish Vice Roy. The Canadians in general are greatly alarmed at being put under their former Laws, of which they had long severely felt the bad Effects—tho' the French Noblesse and Gentry, indeed, are very well pleased with the new Act, which restores the old, as they expect to lord it over the industrious Farmer and Trader, and live upon their Spoils, as they did before the Conquest. These Latter, tho' greatly dissatisfied and alarmed at this Act, dare not complain for fear of the Displeasure of their Priests, who rule and govern this whole Country as they please; however, all the English in the Province (except a few Tools and Dependents of the Governor) are unanimous, and determined to struggle hard to obtain a Repeal of this abominable Act; which, if continued, would greatly hurt the Trade of New York, and the other Colonies joining on us. It has been said that some Canadian Regiments would be raised & sent against you; but depend on it, none will go willingly, except their Officers; and for the others it will require a Regiment of Soldiers, to a Regiment of Canadians, to make them go; besides they cannot without ruining the Country spare 2000 Men out of it.

"You may acquaint the Printer with all the foregoing Particulars, that he may be able to undeceive the Publick, and contradict, what has been said relating to this Matter, in Mr. Gaine's Paper, &c."

AT a General Meeting of the English Inhabitants of the Town of Montreal, to consult on the most proper and best Method to represent to his Majesty and the Parliament, a true State of this Province, by acquainting them of the Share we have of the Trade, the landed Property we possess, the miserable State we found this Province in, and the flourishing State we have brought it to; the Recompence we are to receive by a late Act of Parliament is, to be deprived of those valuable Parts of our Constitution, the Trial by Jury, and the Habeas Corpus Act, and subjected to Laws made by a Legislative Council, composed of People entirely dependent on the Governor, and agreable to the despotic Laws of France.—And that, if such an Act takes Place, as we shall have no Security for our Property nor Religion (the Roman Catholic Religion being, by said Act, the established Religion of the Country) we must be reduced to the unhappy Necessity of living as Slaves, or abandoning the Country, and a great Part of our Property; and the Province must return to its former miserable Situation.—There was the greatest Unanimity amongst the English, when the following Gentlemen, viz.

Thomas Walker, Esq; | Mr. John Blake,
Isaac Todd, Esq; | Mr. Alex. Paterson,
Mr. James Price, | Mr. John Porteus,

were chosen a Committee, to repair to Quebec, to act in Conjunction with the English there, on this alarming Occasion. They likewise entered into a very generous Subscription for the Expence that might attend their obtaining Relief.

NEW-HAVEN, November 8.

There were Sheep on board three Vessels in this Port, cleared for Exportation; but all have been brought on Shore again, by the Owners and Masters Orders, not one being allowed to be carried away.

NEW-LONDON, November 11.

The Committee of Correspondence for the Town of New-London, hereby notify all concerned, That they think it their Duty to inforce the Observance of the 7th Article of the Association against the Exportation of SHEEP, recommended by the General Congress; until another Committee is appointed for that Purpose: And all Vessels sailing from this Port will be strictly inspected, that a due Observance may be paid to every Article of said Association, in such Manner as by the Congress is directed.

NEWPORT, November 14.

We hear the Pope has given Lord North an invitation to go to Rome: his Holiness having a mind to reward his good services done the Catholic faith, by conferring on him some dignified office in the Romish church; his Holiness declaring his Lordship the only Christian minister who has been at the head of affairs in Great-Britain, since the revolution; and tis said his Holiness is in great hopes of bringing about another revolution in that island, to re-establish Popery, and bring G—— the third to kiss his Holiness's great toe, and humbly acknowledge his supremacy throughout Christendom.

The Rose man of war, lately arrived here, and haled into winter quarters, is now preparing to sail again, and tis said she is bound to New-London: But some think she is ordered home, with very afflicting news to Lord North, viz. That the Canadians will not join Gen. Gage in the ministerial plan of enslaving or massacreing their Protestant Neighbours.

SALEM, November 15.

At a Meeting of the People (both of the Alarm and Training Band) of the first Company in Danvers, being Part of the first Regiment in the County of Essex, held at said Danvers, the 9th of November, 1774, for the Purpose of chusing Officers for said Company, in Observance of the Recommendation of the Provincial Congress.

Voted, Dr. Samuel Holten, Chairman for said Meeting.
Voted, Mr. Samuel Flint, Captain.
Voted, Mr. Daniel Putnam, 1st Lieutenant.
Voted, Mr. Joseph Putnam, jun. 2d Lieutenant.
Voted, Mr. Asa Prince, Ensign.

Attest, ASA PUTNAM, Clerk of said Meeting.

BOSTON, November 21.

Extract of a Letter from a Gentleman of Eminence in London, to a Gentleman in Boston, dated Sept. 3, 1774.

"The Coolness, Temper and Firmness of the American Proceedings; the Unanimity of all the Colonies, in the same Sentiments of their Rights, and of the Injustice offered to Boston; and the Patience with which those Injuries are at present borne, *without the least Appearance of Submission*; have a good deal surprized and disappointed our Enemies, and the Tone of publick Conversation, which has been violently against us, begins evidently to turn; so that I make no doubt that before the Meeting of Parliament it will be as general in our Favour. All who know well the State of Things here, agree, that if the NON-CONSUMPTION Agreement should become general, and be firmly adhered to, this Ministry must be ruined, and our Friends succeed them—You will see a stronger Opposition in our Favour at the next Meeting of Parliament than appear'd in the last—But we must depend chiefly upon ourselves."

Some of the latest Letters from London say, There is a good Prospect of a happy Change of Members of Parliament, at the ensuing Election—that Hutchinson meets with the thorough Contempt of the wisest among the Nobility—That the People in general began to be convinced that he and others have abused the Nation by false Representations of the Colonies, and this Province and Town in particular; and that our Grievances will be redressed.——Other Letters advise us, that the Lesson of Administration to us is, to prepare for a further Struggle, and be in Readiness for the *extreme Event*.——A Lesson which true Wisdom dictates to a People threatened as we are, to learn without the least Delay.

We are informed, that among other capital Grievances sent from the Continental Congress to be laid before the Throne, the Appointment of the Commander in Chief of his Majesty's Forces in North-America, to the Government of a Colony, is mentioned (and very justly) as one.

A Gentleman in a Southern Colony in a Letter to his Friend in this Town, mentions the Death of Mr. MOLINEAUX, and Col. DENNY, with great Regret. "I trust in God, says he, that the Labours of those HEROES have left such Impressions as will never be eras'd from the Minds of Thousands; and that whilst dead their Examples will be eloquent."

Extract of a Letter from Newfoundland, October 9.

"On the first instant, a letter was delivered from General Gage's Secretary to our Governor, after being arrived 24 hours, which shews it was not express; however, as all great men are full of expectations, he thought it might be a feather in his cap, and ordered the ship Rose to sail on four hours notice for Boston (although under sailing orders for England) with the Commandant and Officers, and about 100 men, to assist in intimidating the poor Bostonians.

Yesterday Morning departed this Life, Capt. Jonathan Clark, Ætat 82.—The Funeral to be on Tuesday at four o'Clock, P. M. when his Friends and Acquaintance are desired to attend.

Died at Danvers Mr. THOMAS NELSON, in the 104th Year of his Age. He was born at Norwich, in England, June 1671, in the Reign of King Charles the II. At the Revolution he was an Apprentice to a Weaver in that City when he inlisted as a Soldier under King William, to go over to Ireland, to drive out James II: He served also in Queen Ann's Wars; was a Sailor in the Fleet under Sir Cloudsley Shovel, at the Siege and taking of Barcelona, and was in the Expedition to Canada, 1711, at which Time he settled at Danvers, and till within this Year or two, was able to walk Miles. He had but one Eye, and his Hair white like the driven Snow, but retained his Reason, and walked remarkably erect.——"At length the weary Wheels of Life stood still."

To the PUBLIC.

WHEREAS a Letter from London, dated May 12, 1774, was published in this Gazette on Monday July 11. last, severely reflecting upon several eminent Merchants in London, which has given great Umbrage to some.——In Consequence of a particular Application, in Justice to ourselves, to those Gentlemen, and to the Public, we do hereby declare, that the said Letter came to us from Britain, only with this Signature, viz. "The American Spy in London." We have not the least Knowledge of the Author. EDES & GILL.

TO BE SOLD

About 150 Hogsheads of St. Martin's SALT. ALSO,

A Sloop about 84 Tons Burthen, fitted for the Sea. Inquire of the Printers.

William Turner

Begs Leave to inform his Friends, He proposes to open a School on Tuesday Evening next, at Concert-Hall, to teach the polite Dances call'd Cotillons, and assures those Gentlemen who propose being his Pupils, he will attend two Evenings in the Week, viz. Tuesday and Friday.

N. B. Musick and Fencing taught likewise.

WANTED,

About £. 1200 Sterling Cash, for which good Real Security will be given. Enquire of Edes and Gill.

TO BE SOLD for CASH,

White Flint Glass Ware per Box, viz.
Common sorted Cruets & Salts, } 2s. to the Dozen, at
Ditto   Tumblers,   } 4s. 6d. Sterling
Ditto   Wine Glasses,   } per Dozen.
Ditto Mustard-Pots, 2s. to the Doz. at 6/6d. per Doz.
Per the Crate, Apothecaries green Glass Vials sorted at 10s. Sterling per Groce.
Per the Crate, Green Half Pint Dram Bottles, 144 to the Groce, at 10/6d. Sterl. per Groce.
Brass Kettles, at 16½ Sterling per lb.
Broad Cloths and Worsted Hair Plush, blue, green and scarlet, at the Sterling Cost.
Enquire of Edes & Gill.

Made and sold by *Isaac White*,

near the Hay-Market, South-End,
Good Dip'd Tallow-Candles, at 5s. O. T. per Box.
Likewise, Good Mould Tallow and Bayberry-Wax Candles—Also Tallow per Barrel—Good Hard & Soft SOAP.

A Wet Nurse with a good young Breast of Milk, would take a Child to Suckle. Inquire of Edes and Gill.

ALL Persons indebted to the Estate of WILLIAM WHITE, Esq; late of Boston, deceased, are desired to pay the same to PHILLIPS WHITE of South-Hampton, in the Province of New-Hampshire, Executor of the last Will and Testament of the said WILLIAM WHITE; and those to whom said Estate is indebted are desired to send in their Demands to said Executor.

For the Convenience of many concerned, he purposes to be at Boston from the Sixth Day of December next—Ten Days; from the First Day of February—six Days; and from the Twentieth Day of March—Six Days.

Enquire for the said WHITE, at the Shop of Mrs. Margarett Phillips, in Cornhill.

To be sold Part of the Estate of the aforesaid WILLIAM WHITE, at Public Vendue, to the highest Bidder, on Thursday the Eighth Day of December next, viz. The House where the said Deceased lately dwelt, pleasantly situated at the North End of Boston, with Brick Store, Stable, Wood-House, &c. Three beautiful Gardens adjoining, &c. &c. and a small Piece of Land near Charlestown-Ferry—Also a small Dwelling-House in Hull-Street; and a large Store in Queen-Street.—The Vendue to be at last-mentioned Store, at Ten o'Clock in the Forenoon of said Day.—The Conditions of Sale to be seen at the Time and Place of Sale.

N. B. The Premises may be viewed on Tuesday and Wednesday preceeding the Day of Sale.

At Gould's Auction-Office,

In Back-Street,

On FRIDAY next,

At TEN in the Morning,

Will be Sold by PUBLIC VENDUE,

A Variety of English GOODS, and Household Furniture. R. GOULD, Auctioneer.

Country Traders & others

(Who purchase with Cash,)

MAY have an Opportunity greatly to their Advantage, by speedily applying at BICKER's Auction Room, near the Market, Boston.—Where is sent for Sale—A fine Parcel of middling and low-priced Broad Cloths, of the most fashionable Colours, which will be sold at too low a Rate.

N. B. A great Variety of other Goods, at private Sale, as cheap as usual.

Burials in the Town of BOSTON, since our last.
Eighteen Whites.   No Blacks.
Baptiz'd in the several Churches, Five.

High Water at BOSTON, for the present Week.
Monday,   12 min. aft. 2 | Friday,   11 min. after. 5
Tuesday,   0 min. aft. 3 | Saturday, 53 min. aft. 5
Wednesday, 42 min. aft. 3 | Lord's-Day, 34 min. af. 6
Thursday, 28 min. aft. 4 | D'sLastQ. 26 Day 6M.

English Grammar,

WHOEVER considers the Inconveniencies to which young Persons must be subject through Life, where a proper Acquaintance with Letters, and Language is wanting; and the great Advantages which must arise to those who are designed to act any considerable Part in Life, from a thorough Knowledge of the Use of Letters, and Propriety of Language, especially of that, which they have by far the most Occasion to use,

Must, undoubtedly, be sensible, that the Study of English Grammar, or the Art of Reading, Speaking and Writing the English Language with strict Propriety, and Elegance, is well worthy the Attention of Youth, as a material Part of their Education.

Such Parents, or Guardians, as are disposed to have their Children instructed in this important Branch, (or rather Foundation) of Science, may be faithfully served for that Purpose, at the English Grammar School, in Milk-Street——by

WILLIAM PAYNE.

☞ LADIES who chuse to be instructed at Home, may be waited on with the utmost Complaisance, and strictest Attention, as often as the Nature of the Business requires, and at such Hours as shall be most convenient.

Writing and Arithmetic will be taught to such as desire it, and Letter-Writing in Form.

He will receive the Commands of such as shall please to favour him therewith, at his School in Milk-Street, or at his Lodgings at Mr. *Benjamin Gray's* in King-Street.

The Co-Partnership of *Box* and *Austin*,

being dissolved by the Death of Mr. *Box*, This is to desire all Persons who have any Demands on said Company, to bring in and settle their Accounts with the surviving Partner, *Benjamin Austin*. And all those who are indebted to the late Company, are requested to make immediate Payment.

N. B. The Business of Ropemaking is still carried on by said *Austin*.

All Persons that are indebted to

the Estate of Mr. JOHN BOX, Sen'r, late of Boston, deceased, are requested to discharge the same; and all those who have Demands upon the Deceased's Estate, are desired to produce their Claims to

Lydia Box,
John Box, } Executors.
W. Hoskins,

Boston, 14th Nov. 1774.

Daniel Silsby,

Has to sell by Wholesale and Retail, at his Store, opposite South-Side Faneuil-Hall,

SUGARS Loaf and Brown, Coffee, Chocolate, Rice, Starch, Indigo, Ginger, Allspice, Pepper, Nutmegs, and the Spices; Marseilles and Lisbon OIL, Jamaica Spirit, West-India and New-England Rum, Brandy, Malaga Wine, Crown Soap, 15 & 18 Inch Pipes, Red-wood, Logwood, Raisins, and Currants.

CHEESE, a very considerable Quantity of the best Sorts, &c.

All which he will sell as cheap as can be bought at any Store in Boston.

Just received, and to be Sold by

WARD & FENNO,

At their Store, at the Head of Dock-Square,

COTTON WOOL per Bag, and Limes per Cask.— Good Connecticut Cheese, Firkin Butter, West-India Goods, Spices, &c.

N. B. Goods sold on Commissions at the above Store.

To be Sold at the Royal Exchange
Tavern in King-Street, Boston.

At Publick Vendue,

On THURSDAY the First Day of *December* next, at Eleven o'Clock in the Forenoon.

The following Lots of Land, viz.

Lot No. 20, called a 10 Mile back Lot, on the West side of Kennebeck-River, containing about 4800 Acres.

Lot marked F. 2. in the first Range of Lots, containing about 6000 Acres (exclusive of Settlers Lots interspersed) being near one Mile wide, and fifteen Miles long, and fronting on Kennebeck-River, on the West side of it, about ten Miles above Fort Halifax, to be divided and sold in two Parts.

A Lot to the Northward of ditto, and fronting on little Norridgewalk-River, about 3200 Acres.

Lot marked B D. 1. in the second Range of Lots, about six Miles above Norridgwalk, on the West side of Kennebeck-River, and fronting thereon, containing about 7000 Acres, (exclusive of Settlers Lots interspersed) being 1 Mile wide, and 15 Miles long.

Lot marked C. A. 1. in the third Range of Lots, near the Falls of Cariontonka, about 12 Miles above Norridgwalk, on the West side of Kennebeck-River, and fronting thereon, containing about 7000 Acres, (exclusive of Settlers Lots interspersed) being 1 Mile wide, and 15 Miles long.

Three Lots of Land, viz. Lot No. 32, on the East side of Kennebeck-River, about a Mile above Fort-Western—No. 86, on the East side of said River, about 9 Miles above Fort-Western; and Lot No. 20, on the West side of said River, about 1 Mile and ½ above Fort-Western, containing 400 Acres each.

Also all the Islands in Cobbisseconte Pond, and all the Islands in Kennebeck-River above Fort-Halifax.

For further Particulars enquire of HENRY ALLINE, jun. at his Office in King-Street, Boston.

Boston, November 2d, 1774.

This is to notify the Public, That

the Charlestown Stage Coach, No. 1, which heretofore set off from Mr. Wyart's Tavern in Charlestown at 8 o'Clock, for so em, will, for the future, set off at 9 o'Clock every Day in the Week, Sunday excepted, and another from Mr. Goodhue's in Salem, return to Charlestown.

WHEREAS the Great and General Court or Assembly of this Province, at their Session begun and held the 27th Day of May, 1772, granted a Tax of Two Pence per Acre for one Year next to come; and one Penny per Acre for a second Year next to come, on all the Lands in the District of Hubbardston, in the County of Worcester. And whereas the first and second Years Taxes have been duly assessed and posted, as is by Law directed; and some Proprietors or Owners of said Lands have neglected or refused to pay their Tax; the General Court in said Act did empower the Assessors of said Taxes to sell so much of the Delinquent Proprietors Lands as shall be necessary to pay and satisfy such Taxes, and other necessary intervening Charges. The Owners of the following Lands are delinquent in paying their Taxes, (viz.) The first Year's Tax.

House-Lots.		Pay.			Great Farms.		Pay.		
No.	Acres.	£.	s.	d.	No.	Acres.	£.	s.	d.
3	50	0	8	4	1	481	4	2	0
8	76	0	12	8	2	104	0	17	4
14	100	0	16	8	3	120	1	0	0
20	112½	0	18	9	4	50	0	8	4
24	14	0	2	4	5	30	0	5	0
35	7¼	0	1	3	11	200	1	13	4
37	135	1	2	6	12	210	1	15	0
38	135	1	2	6	13	28	0	4	8
42	120	1	0	0	15	200	1	13	4
43	120	1	0	0	18	320	2	13	4
44	70	0	11	8	20	319	2	13	2
45	66	0	11	0	22	128	1	1	4
53	23	0	3	10	24	295	2	9	2
55	120	1	0	0	25	241	2	0	2
56	109½	0	18	3	28	172	1	8	8
58	81	0	13	6	31	137	1	2	10
59	102½	0	17	1	32	117	0	19	7
62	100	0	16	8	33	346	2	17	8
63	100	0	16	8		Letter Lots.			
64	100	0	16	8	B.	77	0	12	10
					D.	60½	0	10	1
					L.	70	0	11	8
					O.	90	0	15	0

Notice is hereby given to the abovesaid Delinquents that so much of their Lands will be sold at a public Vendue, (as to pay their Taxes and other necessary intervening Charges) at the House of Mr. John Ames, Innholder in Hubbardston, on Tuesday the 7th Day of March next, at Ten o'Clock in the Forenoon, and to be continued from Day to Day, by Adjournment, till the Third Day, if not sold before, unless said Taxes and Charges be paid to the Assessors before said Sale.

Hubbardston, Nov. 4, 1774.

John Wood, } Assessors.
Joseph Grimes,

The Second Year's Tax.

House-Lots.		Pay.			Great Farms.		Pay.		
No.	Acres.	£.	s.	d.	No.	Acres.	£.	s.	d.
2	50	0	4	2	1	481	2	0	1
3	50	0	4	2	2	295	1	4	7
4	60	0	5	0	3	481	2	0	1
5	100	0	8	4	4	435	1	16	3
6	100	0	8	4	7	4	0	0	2
8	76	0	6	4	9	340	1	8	4
11	135	0	11	3	10	508	2	2	4
13	112	0	9	4	11	200	0	16	8
14	100	0	8	4	12	474	1	19	6
15	100	0	8	4	13	474	1	19	6
17	100	0	8	4	14	474	1	19	6
20	112	0	9	4	15	275	1	2	11
26	14	0	1	2	16	240	1	0	0
28	121	0	10	1	17	212	0	17	8
31	100	0	8	4	18	530	2	4	2
32	100	0	8	4	20	319	1	6	7
33	60	0	5	0	21	458	1	18	2
34	150	0	12	6	22	128	0	10	8
36	151	0	10	1	24	295	1	4	7
37	135	0	11	3	25	241	1	0	1
38	135	0	11	3	26	486	2	0	6
39	100	0	8	4	27	356	1	9	8
42	120	0	10	0	28	472	1	19	4
43	120	0	10	0	29	540	2	5	0
44	120	0	10	0	30	550	2	5	10
45	116	0	9	8	31	340	1	8	4
46	120	0	10	0	32	470	1	19	2
48	135	0	11	3	33	476	1	19	8
50	100	0	8	4		Letter Lots.			
51	109	0	9	1					
52	110	0	9	2	B.	77	0	6	5
53	23	0	1	11	C.	57	0	4	9
54	111	0	9	3	E.	76	0	6	4
55	100	0	8	4	D.	60	0	5	0
56	109	0	9	1	G.	53½	0	4	5
57	135	0	11	3	H.	66	0	5	6
58	144	0	12	0	K.	57	0	4	9
59	102	0	8	6	L.	70	0	5	10
60	100	0	8	4	O.	90	0	7	6
62	100	0	8	4					
63	100	0	8	4					
64	100	0	8	4					
65	100	0	8	4					
66	100	0	8	4					
67	100	0	8	4					
68	100	0	8	4					

Notice is hereby given to the abovesaid Delinquents, that so much of their Lands will be sold at a public Vendue, (as to pay their Taxes and other necessary intervening Charges) at the House of Mr. John Ames, Innholder in Hubbardston, on Tuesday the 14th Day of March next, at Ten o'Clock in the Forenoon, and to be continued from Day to Day, by Adjournment, till the Third Day, if not sold before, unless said Taxes and Charges be paid to the Assessors before said Sale.

Hubbardston, Nov. 4, 1774.

John Wood, } Assessors.
Joseph Grimes,

Imported in Capt. Robson, from London, and to be sold by

Peter Hughes,

At his Store in King-Street,

ENGLISH, Russia and Ravens Duck, Tickenburgs, Oznabrigs, Broad Cloths, Duffils, Beaver Coatings, Cod and Mackrel Lines and Hooks, Sail, Sein and Whipping Twine, 4d. 6d. 8d. and 10d Nails, Sheathing and Drawing ditto, 6 by 8, 7 by 9, & 8 by 10 Glass, Pepper, Gun Powder in Half and Quarter Barrels, 10, 15, 18 and 21 Inch Pipes, single, double and refined Loaf Sugar, Florence Oil, Split Peas, Bunting, Shot, Spices, Durham Mustard, also a few Casks of Burton and Yorkshire Ale.

Boston, Nov. 7th, 1774.

To be Sold at Public Vendue on Wednesday the 30th Day of November, at One o'Clock, P. M. at the House of Capt. *Ephraim Jackson*, Innholder at Newton.

A FARM containing 100 Acres of choice good Land, lying in said Newton, now in the Occupation of Mr. *Samuel Woodward*, with a Dwelling House and two Barns standing thereon.—— The Privileges of said Farm may be seen any Day by applying to *Samuel Woodward* on said Farm.

WHEREAS the Proprietors of Sudbury-Canada, (so called) being a Township granted to Josiah Richardson, Esq; and others, in the County of Cumberland, at a legal Meeting by Adjournment on the 17th Day of August, A. D. 1773, granted a Tax of Twenty Shillings, L. M. on each single Right. Also the said Proprietors at a legal Meeting by Adjournment on the 7th Day of December A. D. 1773, granted another Tax of Forty Shillings L. M. on each single Right to defray the Charges of clearing a Road to the said Township and other necessary Charges: Also the said Proprietors at a legal Meeting by Adjournment on the 6th Day of April A. D. 1774, granted another Tax of Twenty Shillings L. M. on each single Right, publick Rights excepted, to defray the Charges of building Mills in said Township: And altho' the said Taxes have been duly published according to Law, and Payment requested, nevertheless several of the said Proprietors are delinquent in the Payment of the said Taxes: Publick Notice is therefore hereby given to said Delinquents, that unless their Taxes are paid to Cornelius Wood of Sudbury, Treasurer, or to us the Subscribers, by Ten o'Clock in the Morning of the 13th Day of December next, their Rights will be sold as the Law directs, for the Payment of their Taxes and Charges arising by the Sale, and the Sale to begin at Eleven o'Clock in said Morning, at the Dwelling-House of Isaac Gleasons, Innholder in Waltham, and continued by Adjournment (if need be) till the whole be sold.

Cornelius Wood,
Elijah Bent, } Proprietors
Josiah Stone. } Committee.

The Partnership of Wyer and

Larkin being Dissolved;

Robert Wyer, Sailmaker,

HEREBY informs his Customers and others, That he is removed his Loft from the Head of Rowe's Wharff, to the new Loft lately built on Hallowell's Ship-Yard, where they may depend on being served with Fidelity and Dispatch, as usual.

N. B. Said Wyer would take a Boy as an Apprentice, that can be well recommended.

The Copartnership of *Brown* and

Shattuck will be mutually Dissolved the 14th Instant.— Those who have any Demands on said Company, are desired to send in their Accounts; and those indebted, are requested to make immediate Payment.

All Persons having Demands on the

Estate of *Joseph* and *Joseph Wheeler*, jun. of Boston, deceas'd, and those who are Indebted to said Estate, are desired to bring in their Accounts to John Lucas, Administrator in Order to Settlement.

Town and Country Store,

At the Head of Dock-Square.

WARD & FENNO

SELL West-India, and a great Variety of other Goods, CHEAP ENOUGH.

A few Tubs very good BUTTER

to be Sold by JOSIAH WATERS and SON, in Ann-Street.

To be Sold or Lett, and may be entered upon immediately.

A House and about Four Acres of Land in Dorchester, about four Miles from Boston) with every Accommodation suitable for a Gentleman. Enquire of JOHN VASSALL.

JOHN GRAHAM,

HAS just Imported a large Quantity of Old Jamaica Spirits of the best kind, and will be Sold by the Hogshead, Barrel or less Quantity if required, Coffee and Chocolate, &c.

The above will be Sold at reasonable Rates for Cash, at his Store on Wendel's Wharf, near the South Battery, Fort-Hill.

Boston: Printed, by EDES & GILL, in Queen-Street, 1774.

THE *Boston*-GAZETTE, AND COUNTRY JOURNAL.

No. 1024.

Containing the freshest Advices, Foreign and Domestic.

MONDAY, November 28, 1774.

AT a Meeting of Committees from the several Towns in the County of BARNSTABLE, *met and convened at the Court-House in said County, on Wednesday the 16th Day of November, A. D. 1774.*

Hon. JAMES OTIS, Esq; being chosen Moderator, and

Col. JOSEPH OTIS, Clerk.

AFTER taking into serious Consideration the distress'd and difficult situation of our public Affairs, arising from the repeated unjust Attempts of an arbitrary Administration, to deprive us of our civil Rights and Liberties, and to subject our Lives and Properties to the Will and Controul of the British Parliament; in direct violation of the most solemn Compact between the King and the Inhabitants of this Province, as well as of the British Constitution itself; which cruel Attempts have appeared in various Instances; but more especially in the several Acts passed in the last Session of the British Parliament, respecting the Massachusetts-Bay and Quebec, which are too well known to need a repetition of their Titles. We do therefore think it a Duty incumbent on us to bear our public Testimony against them, and to join in the general Endeavours of this Country to prevent the total extinction of Civil and Religious Liberty. We do therefore RESOLVE,

1st. That we recognize King *GEORGE* the Third, of Great-Britain as our rightful Sovereign.

2d. That we apprehend, the Parliament of Great-Britain have no right to dispose of our Properties, alter our Constitution, or make Laws binding upon us, without our Consent.

3d. That the Acts of Parliament referred to as above, are, in our apprehension, not only Unconstitutional, but a most unparalled Instance of Injustice, Cruelty and Oppression, which ought never to be submitted to.

4th. That we do hereby approve of, acquiesce in, and solemly engage to Conform to the Resolves and Recommendations of the Continental and Provincial Congress, so far as we have been acquainted with their Proceedings; esteeming them the most prudent Method of opposing said Acts, and the most likely Means of obtaining a Redress of our Grievances. And therefore,

5th. We do recommend it to the Inhabitants of this County, to subscribe the Association, agreed upon by the Continental Congress, with the following Addition, viz. "We the Subscribers do solemnly agree and promise, that we will observe and conform to the above Association, and do hereby make it our own particular Act and Covenant, and do further engage, that from and after the Date hereof, we will not Buy, Sell, Transport or Drink or suffer our Families to Buy, Sell, Transport or Drink any kind of India Tea, whether Imported on Account of the East-India Company, or any other, or from any Part of the World till we obtain as ample Redress of our Grievances, as is specified in the said Association, as witness our Hands this Seventh Day of November, A. D. 1774," and that each Member of this Congress do immediately Sign said Association with said Addition: And that we Recommend it to every Town in the County, who have not already chosen, to choose Committees, to see that the Inhabitants of their respective Towns Sign as above; and to inspect and inquire if any Person act contrary to said Association and Addition, and in case they do, or any refuse to Sign said Association, &c. to Publish their Names to the World.

6th. That we will ourselves, and do earnestly Recommend it to the Inhabitants of this County, to use their utmost Endeavours to suppress all Mobs, Riots and Breaches of the Peace.

7th. That in Order to keep Peace and good Regulation in the County, and that the Lives, Liberties and Properties of the People may be safe, we do Recommend it to the several Justices of the Peace in the County, who were in Office before the last Day of June past, to Act in their said Offices, in their single Capacity, except in Judicial Proceedings merely civil: and that they exert themselves, agreeable to the Laws of the Province relative to the suppression of Vice, Immorality, Breaches of the Peace and all high-handed Offences; and to use their Endeavours to prevent Mobs, Riots, Routs and unlawful Assemblies; and to preserve the Peace of the County: and we Recommend it to the Sheriffs to retain such Persons as are or shall be Committed, as Criminals, in his Custody, until they have a Trial, any Supersedeas or Proclamation to the contrary notwithstanding; at least, until the Minds of the Provincial Congress be expressed, respecting this Matter; and we do hereby recommend it to the Inhabitants of this County, to aid and assist the Justices and Sheriff in the execution of their Offices as above.

8th. That a Committee of this County be chosen by this Congress, to Correspond with the Committees of the other Counties in this Province, as Occasion may require;

Col. *Nathaniel Freeman*, Col. *Joseph Otis*,
Mr. *Thomas Paine*, *Daniel Davis*, Esq; and
Mr. *Job Crocker*, were unanimously chosen.

9th. That it be recommended to every Town in this County who have not chosen Committees of Correspondence, to choose them; and likewise, for every Town in the County to send Members to the Provincial Congress.

10th. That it be recommended to the several Towns in this County to call Meetings and vote their Approbation of, and hearty Concurrence with, the Resolves and Recommendations of the Continental, Provincial, and this County Congress.

11th. That it be recommended to the several Towns of this County to raise Subscriptions for the Relief of our suffering Brethren in Boston.

12th. That it be recommended to the Inhabitants of the County to use their Endeavours to suppress common Pedlars of Scotch, English and India Goods; and that the several Inhabitants in the County be desired, in the name of this Congress, to refuse Entertainment to them; and that the Clerk hereof serve the Innholders with a Copy of this Resolve.

13th. That it be recommended to the several Military Companies in the East Regiment in this County, who have not yet chosen their Officers, to choose them, assoon as may be, agreeable to the Resolves and Recommendations of the Provincial Congress: And we do Recommend it to the several Military Officers, who are, or may be chosen in the County, to require all, who are liable by Law of the Province, to attend Military Exercises and Obey their Officers; and that the Officers see that all in both Lists be provided with Arms and Ammunition according to Law: And in case any refuse to Obey their Military Officers, we recommend it to the Inhabitants of the County, to assist them in *enforcing* Obedience to their Orders, agreeable to the Law of this Province.

14th. That a Committee be chosen to consider further of our public Grievances, and of the State of this County, and report at the adjournment of this Meeting.

The Hon. *James Otis*, Esq; Col. *Joseph Otis*,
Col. *N. Freeman*, Capt. *Joseph Doane*,
Mr. *Thomas Payne*, *Daniel Davis*, Esq; and
Capt. *Jonathan Howes*, were accordingly chosen.

15th. VOTED, That the County's Committee of Correspondence be desired to procure printed Copies of the Proceedings of this Congress, and the above mentioned Association, and that they transmit Two Setts to each Town in the County, to be directed to their respective Committees of Correspondence.

The Congress then, after each Member had sign'd the said Association with said Addition, and voted their Thanks to the Moderator, Clerk, and Col. Freeman, for their good Services, adjourn'd to the second Tuesday in January next. *A true Copy*,

JOSEPH OTIS, Clerk.

AT a meeting of the Blacksmiths of the *County of Worcester*, convened at Worcester on the 8th Day of September last, and continued by adjournment to the 8th Day of November, 1774, the following resolutions were come into, viz.

WHEREAS at a meeting of the Delegates from the counties of Worcester, Middlesex and Essex, with the committee of correspondence of the town of Boston in behalf of the county of Suffolk, holden at Boston the 26th Day of August 1774, it was resolved—That all such officers or private persons as have given sufficient proof of their enmity to the people and constitution of this country, should be held in contempt, and that those who are connected with them ought to seperate from them; labourers to shun their vineyards, merchants, husbandmen and others to withhold their commerce and supplies.

IN compliance therefore to a resolution of so respectable a body as aforesaid, so reasonable in its contents, and so necessary at this distressing day of trial—We the subscribers being deeply impressed with a sense of our duty to our country, paternal affection for our children and unborn millions, as also for our personal rights and liberties, solemnly covenant, agree and engage to and with each other, that from and after the first day of December 1774, we will not, according to the best of our knowledge, any or either of us, nor any person by our direction, order or approbation, for or under any or either of us, do or perform, any Blacksmith's work or business of any kind whatever for any person or persons whom we esteem enemies to this country, commonly known by the name of tories, viz. all counsellors in this province appointed by mandamus who have not publickly resigned said office, also every person who addressed governor Hutchinson at his departure from this province, who have not publickly recanted, also every officer exercising authority by virtue of any commission they hold tending to carry any of the late oppressive acts of parliament into execution in America; and in particular we will not do any work for Tim. Ruggles of Hardwick, John Murray of Rutland, and James Putnam of Worcester, Esq'rs; nor for any person or persons cultivating, tilling, improving, dressing, hireing or occupying any of their lands or tenements.—Also we agree to refuse our work of every kind as aforesaid to all and every person or persons who shall not have signed the non-consumption agreement, or have entered into a similar contract or engagement, or that shall not strictly conform to the association or covenant agreed upon and signed by the *Continental Congress* lately convened at Philadelphia.

We further agree that we will not do any work for any mechanick, tradesman, labourer or others, that shall work for, or in any ways, or by any means whatever, aid, assist, or promote the business, or pecuniary advantage, pleasures, or profits of any the said enemies to this country.

Resolved, That all lawful ways and means ought to be adopted by the whole body of the people of this province, to discountenance all our inveterate political enemies in manner as aforesaid.—Therefore we earnestly recommend it to all denominations of artificers that they call meetings of their respective craftsmen in their several counties as soon as may be, and enter into associations and agreements for said purposes, and that all husbandmen, labourers, &c. do the like: And that whoever shall be guilty of any breach of any or either of the articles or agreements, be held by us in contempt as enemies to our common rights.

ROSS WYMAN, Chairman.

John Campbell,	*Nathaniel Heywood*,	*Henry Gaschet*,
Isaac Gleason,	*Eben. Wellington*,	*Eleazer Upham*,
Jonah How,	*Adam Walker*,	*Daniel Phillips*,
Mark Heard,	*Levi Gaschet*,	*Asa Waite*,
Moses Harrington,	*John Pollard*,	*James Ames*,
M. Brooks,	*Samuel Gould*,	*Thomas Mann*,
Thomas Farnsworth,	*Thadeus Pollard*,	*Jonathan Force*.
Samuel Sawyer, jr.	*John Abbot*,	*Phinehas Haskell*,
Job Spafford,	*Henry Gale*,	*Sampson Wetherell*,
Eben. Wellington, jr.	*Ebenezer Belknap*,	*Jonathan Waite*,
Samuel Stearns,	*Henry Rice*,	*Phinehas Gleason*,
Samuel Jones,	*Abraham Gale*,	*John Beeton*.
Joseph Fletcher,	*Noah Brooks*,	*Zadock Putnam*.
Seth Heywood,	*Seth Washburn*,	

Attest, TIMOTHY BIGELOW, Clerk.

NORWICH, November 1.

Last Evening Joseph Atwood, a notorious Thief, was brought from the Landing and committed to the Goal in this Town: This artful Freebooter, had, on the preceeding Evening secreted himself in a Store of Mr. Joseph Howland, and after it was shut up, began to Rummage; he visited the Till from which he extracted 50s. L. M. being all the Cash there deposited; he afterwards inspected the Goods, and supplied himself with Necessaries to the amount of 18l. Having gratified his Rapacity, he thought proper to retreat; but in the Lofts of the Store, which is very large there are Scuttles, through which Casks, &c. are hoisted and lowered; these being accidentally left open, in stumbled our hapless Hero, and descended in an instant, from the upper Loft to the Floor of the Cellar, the Distance between which is about 30 Feet, there prostrate, with his Head lacerated, his Shoulder dislocated, and in a State of utter Insensibility, remained for a considerable Time, the identical nocturnal Adventurer, who in the Fall preceeding this, was exalted to the Top of the Gallows, in Boston when Levi Ames was executed: However, he recovered and escaped, with his Booty, out of a Window; but was next Morning apprehended, conducted to the Place of Flagelation and had ten Stripes, properly administered: During the Performance of that Operation one of his Friends, then present, burst into an immoderate fit of Laughter; but he had much better have repressed his Resibility on that Occasion, for the suffering Culprit provoked at his unseasonable Mirth impeached him of stealing four dress'd Skins from Mr. Chenea, and advised the Officers to search the Fellow's Chest, which Request they complied with, found the Leather and secured the Thief.—We hear that Atwood, when upon Examination, and since his commitment, has confessed that he has been privy to several Villainies, in concert with a Gang of Banditti who are hovering about this Town.

WHEREAS I, Joseph Lee, of Concord, Physician, on the Evening of the 1st ult. did rashly and without Consideration, make a private and precipitate journey from Concord to Cambridge, to inform judge Lee, that the Country was assembling to come down (and on no other business) that he & others concern'd might prepare themselves for the Event, and with an avowed Intention to deceive the People; by which the Parties assembling might have been exposed to the brutal Rage of the Soldiery, who had timely Notice to have way-laid the Roads and fired on them while unarmed and Defenceless in the dark.

By which imprudent Conduct, I might have prevented the salutary Designs of my Countrymen, whose innocent intentions were only to request certain Gentlemen, sworn into Office on the new system of Government, to resign their Offices, in order to prevent the Operation of that (so much detested) Act of the British Parliament for regulating the Civil Government of the Massachusetts Bay: By all which I have justly drawn upon me the displeasure of my Country.

When I cooly reflect on my own imprudence, it fills my Mind with the deepest Anxiety.

I deprecate the resentment of my injured Country, humbly confess my Errors, and implore the Forgiveness of a generous and free People. Solemnly declaring that for the future, never to convey any intelligence to any of the Court Party neither directly nor indirectly, by which the designs of the People may be frustrated in opposing the barbarous Policy, of an arbitrary, wicked and corrupt Administration.

JOSEPH LEE.

Concord, Sept. 19th, 1774.

By Order of the Committee, Wm. BURROWS, *Clerk*.

Since our last Captain Folgier arrived at Salem from London, and has bro't Prints to the 28th of September, from which we have extracted the following Articles of Intelligence.

LONDON, Sept. 14.

Extract of a private letter from the Hague, September 9.

"The war which was expected in Europe ever since the year 1770, but hitherto prevented by the pusilanimity of a certain Ministry, who would rather suffer the grossest affronts than venture to enter into any dispute, was expected to break out immediately after the disease of the late French King.—The expectation answered so far, that a great change immediately took place among the French Ministry, when all those who were known to be inclined to be pacific were looked upon as traitors to their country, and have been exiled and banished the court; but all those who were known to be inclined to war, have been preferred and called into office. In this situation of the French cabinet, joined in their interest with that of Spain, the expected war should have broke out some months ago; but the true reason and policy of that hesitation is the following:—The British Ministry had, ever since the present reign, a desire to enslave the colonies of America, and to render the King despotic in these vast and extensive provinces; but this plan could not have been carried into execution, because it was contrary to the interest of France and Spain, both which courts always rather wished to see the prerogative power of a British King limited as much as possible. Whether it was a secret article of the peace settled between the beligerent powers, in the year 1763, or whether it was settled and effected in the latter end of the late reign in France, by a corrupted French Ministry, that France shall not intermeddle in the disputes between Great-Britain and her colonies, is unknown; tho' so much is sure, that the British Ministry had a solemn promise from the leaders of the French cabinet not to interfere in these affairs. As soon as that solemn promise was given to the British Ministry, they began to operate, and to lay the affair before the Parliament, being sure to carry every motion by a majority. Scarce was the above deep laid plan of the Ministry begun to be carried into execution, but the French King died, and an utter change happened among the Ministry there, to the greatest disappointment of the British Ministry. A declaration, however, was immediately made by the young French King, engaging to observe the same friendship with his neighbours as his illustrious predecessor did; and in the mean time, ordered to bring both his land and sea forces in the best situation, to be in readiness at a moment's notice, for no other reason but to watch very anxiously the resolutions of the General Assemblies of America.

"As soon as the disputes between Great-Britain and her Colonies shall come to blows, France and Spain will immediately take the advantage of it, and attack Great-Britain with power and vigour. This intention of the French and Spaniards is foreseen by the British Court, who continually send instructions to their Ambassadors to enquire for the reason of the preparations of war, which are carried on with so much assiduity in France and Spain; but the answer these Ambassadors generally receive is very indifferent.—In this manner France and Spain are watching the result of the British Americans, and how this quarrel will end; and the British Ministry, on the other hand, are keeping backwards from executing their plan in America, till they know how matters will be settled at the Courts of France and Spain.

Sept. 19. The Ministry are perplexed to the last degree relative to what ultimate part they shall take concerning America; every dispatch they receive at present from that quarter of the world, affording rather a fresh choice of difficulties, than any encouragement to get rid of them. In this dilemma, the medium of a patched-up, servile policy is adopted, which is to secure, at all events, the continuance of a French peace (no matter how much national honour is sacrificed for the purpose) and then try the *full force of the bayonet* beyond the Atlantic. What a wretched situation then is this country reduced to? forced to bear insults from its *avowed enemies*, for the purpose of trampling on the *lives*, *liberties*, and *properties*, of its *own subjects*.

The patriots in both kingdoms are collecting their utmost force, in order to perform some new political manoeuvres the ensuing winter. It is generally expected it will be to use the old proverb, "*A warm sessions*, and the Minister very hard driven," as it is very well known that more than one or two acts which have been done in the present parliament, will be moved most strenuously to be repealed. Should Lord North not be able to stand against this united force, his power will be at an end, and there will be new Minister to meet the new Parliament; and perhaps this may be productive of more changes in administration, particularly in the chairs of both Houses.

Sept. 24 Some advices have been received from General Gage within these few days, which are kept very secret; but it is reported, that some of the persons concerned in promoting the meetings of the people are taken into custody, and put on board one of his Majesty's ships of war, in order to be sent to England.

In the late Queen Ann's reign, when Lord Corunbury was Governor of New-York, a committee was appointed by the general assembly of that province to examine into the grievances of their constitution. This committee paying due attention to the prerogatives of the crown, and the liberty of the subject, proceeded to draw up several noble and spirited resolves, which were approved by the assembly then sitting; who thereupon exhibited a complaint to her Majesty, against Lord Corunbury's haughty and oppressive government. To which the Queen returned this truly gracious answer; "I have heard the cries of my injured subjects, nor will I countenance my nearest relation in oppressing my people." Though Lord Corunbury was her cousin she divested him of his commission, and put Lord Lovelace in his place —— *If his present Majesty had judged as wisely, we should have had no American disturbances.*

Sept. 26. Letters from Candiz say, that three Portugueze vessels had been brought into that port by the Spaniards; but it was thought they would not be condemned without orders from Madrid.

Extract of a Letter from the Hague, Sept. 16.

"The States have frequent councils of late, and are making preparations for war, though with as little noise as possible. The Spanish ministers have frequent conferences; and these two powers seem to be upon the most friendly footing. If you do not settle matters soon with your colonies, you may expect a division of the British territories will be attempted. Your ministry are heartily despised here, and our politicians say, that this is the most favourable opportunity for your enemies to come to blows with you."

CHARLES-TOWN, *October* 25.

By Capt. Richard Grinnel, in the sloop Maria, who arrived here the 7th instant, in 37 days, from the Island Delos, on the coast of Africa, we have the following account, "That Capt. Daniel Darby, in a brig belonging to New-York, had made several attempts to sail from the coast, but meeting with misfortunes was obliged to put back. In the last attempt, he got about 30 leagues out at sea, when his slaves rose, and in the engagement killed his chief mate, and before they could conquer the slaves, they were obliged to kill a nnmber of them, which made him put back again, and after he had arrived at the island Delos, his people all left him. Capt. Gideon, in a brig belonging to Liverpool, had arrived on the coast, and went into the river Pungeos, in order to slave off, and had not been there but a few days before he was cut off by the natives.

PHILADELPHIA, Nov. 15.

We are informed, that a few Days ago Jesse Hand, Esq; of Cape May, came to this City with a genteel Sum of Money, generously subscribed by the People of that Place, to be laid out for the use of the Poor of Boston.

On the 10th of October there was an engagement between the Virginians and Indians, at the great Kanhawa,—Col. Andrew Lewis, had the command of about 1400 Virginians, was attacked by about 900 Indians, on his way to the Shawanese town.——The engagement began an hour after sunrise, and lasted till late in the afternoon; when the Indians fled, the Virginians found and scalped 20 Indians, and they suppose many more were killed.

LIST of killed and wounded Virginians.

Killed.		Wounded.	
Colonel	Charles Lewis,	Captains	W. Fleming, since
Major	John Field,		J. Dickenson, (dead.
Captain	John Murray,		Thomas Blueford,
	Robert M'Clenachan,		John Stidman,
	Samuel Wilson,	Lieuts.	——Goodman,
	James Ward,		——Robeson,
Lieut.	Hugh Allen,		——Lard,
Ensigns	——Candiff,		——Vannes,
	——Baker,		79 Privates.
	44 privates.		

Extract of a Letter from a Gentleman in Alexandria, Virginia, to his Friend in this City, dated Nov. 7.

"I have no news excepting that the Virginians and the Indians have had a battle the 10th of last month, on the Great Kanhawa, in which the Virginians had 150 killed & wounded. There were found on the field only 19 Indians, among which were 5 different nations. —This news came to town the night before last."

Immediately after the action an express was sent to Lord Dunmore, who, we are informed, with 1000 men is gone to attack the principal Shawanese town.

NEW-YORK, *November* 17.

Extract of a Letter dated at Quebec October 30.

"A Committee is arrived here from the English Inhabitants in Montreal, who have met a Committee of the Inhabitants of this Place, and are drawing up a Petition to his Majesty, against the Act of Parliament for regulating the Government of this Province, and hope they will meet with Success."

NEW-YORK, November 21.

A Letter from Philadelphia of Nov. 17 1774, says, Yesterday came to Town a Man from Pittsburgh, and says Lord Dunmore has had a Meeting with the Indians and made Peace, demanding nothing more than the restoring of any white Persons they have among them, and such Horses as they stole from the Frontiers."

Capt. Hunt, from Charlestown in South-Carolina, informs us, That the Ship Britannia, Capt. Ball, arrived there from London a few Days before he sailed, and that a Passenger who came into the Vessel had in a clandestine Manner got on board 8 Chests of Tea, which the Capt. on his Arrival made kown to the Committee, who soon caused the Gentleman to order his India Commodity to be thrown into the Ssa; that Capt. Moore arrived there from Philadelphia the 4th of Nov. with the Delegates from the Congress, who were received by their Fellow Citizens with the ringing of Bells, &c. and that on the 5th of November the Inhabitants of Charlestown gave up most of the Tea they had in their Houses to be burnt in one general Bonfire.

TO THE PUBLIC.

I Purpose for my own satisfaction and to gratify the curious, to make daily observations of the temperament of the weather, as to heat and cold, as shewn by Farenheit's Thermometer; and at the end of every month for several months, and perhaps a whole year together, to publish in the news paper, the medium *of the several heights of the mercury, taken at sunrise, noon and sunset; the observations to begin the first day of December next.----And would hereby propose to such Gentlemen as are owners of Farenheit's Thermometer, in different parts of this, or the neighbouring colonies to make & publish the like observations monthly, in the public papers; by such a method may be easily known the different degrees of cold or heat in different parts of the colony or continent, a thing which has never yet been done. And the several printers are desired to insert the above in their respective papers the first opportunity.*

I am the public's most obedient Servant,

NEH. STRONG.

P. S. I shall always keep the Thermometer exposed to the open air, free from the influence of the heat of any fires, or rays of the sun.

Yale-College, (Connecticut,) *November* 14, 1774.

NEWPORT, November 21.

The Committees of Correspondence in the sea-port towns, in Connecticut, are very active in preventing the exportation of sheep, agreeable to the 7th article of the association of the Congress; having already stopped several parcels.

The General Assembly of Connecticut, have chosen Eliphalet Dyer, Roger Sherman, Silas Deane, Titus Hosmer, & Jonathan Sturgis, Elqrs; to be their Delegates at the next Continental Congress, the 10th of May.

Warrents are issued for convening the General Assembly of this colony, at Providence, on Monday the 5th of December.

BOSTON, November 28.

BY the last Vessel from England we have it from undoubted Authority that the Members of both Houses who are Friends to America, have frequently Communications, for the Purpose of dropping their private Misunderstandings, and uniting in the public Cause, which at present needs their joint Assistance, since a Breach with America, hazarded by the late harsh Measures, may be ruinous to the general Welfare of the British Empire, and notwithstanding it has been industriously represented that Lord Chatham has deserted our Cause, it may be certainly depended upon by the Public, that the contrary is the Truth, and that his Sentiments are such as America could wish.

In the violent Storm on Monday Night last, considerable Damage was done to Wharves, and to the Shipping in this Harbour; two or three of the Transports, had their Sterns beat in, and otherwise much hurt: Several other Vessels lost their Top-Masts, &c. A small Vessel in the Government Service, lying at a Wharf, was sunk. Tops of many Chimneys thrown down, and other Damage done at different Parts of the Town.

The Day before the above Storm, Capt. Ackworth, bound from Newfoundlnd for Salem, arrived at Cape-Ann, from whence we hear he sent his Letters and a Number of Bills to this Place, and sailed a few Hours before the Storm for Newbury-Port, but the Storm increased to such a Degree, that his Vessel was cast away, which, with the Gargo, Himself, Mate, some Passengers, &c. were lost. Only two Hands we hear were saved.

Several Vessels were drove ashore at Newbury-Port, and others laying at the Wharves, greatly damaged.—We fear of hearing further Damage.

Wednesday last the Provincial Congress met at Cambridge, opened their second Sessions accarding to adjournment.—Nothing has as yet transpired.

Since the Proceedings of the Continential Congress have been made public, there have been several Funerals of Persons of considerable Note in this Town, whose Relations omitted the usual Practice of giving Gloves, conformable to that wise and prudent Measure recommended by the worthy Members of said Congress, whose noble Resolutions, under God, we trust will be the Salvation of America.

We hear that there was a Meeting in the Town of Roxbury, the last Week, for the Choice of Military Officers for the first Parish, when the Rev. Mr. Adams, opened the Meeting with a Prayer, after which he was chosen Moderator; they then proceeded to the choice of Officers for one Company, as follows, viz.

Capt. Joseph Heath,	Captain.
Mr. John Greaton,	Lieutenant,
Mr. Joshua Felton,	Ensign.

And at another Meeting since, in said Parish, they made choice of the following Officers, for another Company, viz.

Mr. Aaron Davis,	Captain.
Mr. Robert Pierpoint,	Lieutenant.
Mr. Nathaniel Felton,	Ensign, And,
Capt. Joseph Williams,	Serjeant.

Agreeable to the Advice of the respectable Provincial Congress, the Training-Band Company in Lynn, North Parish, being a Part of the first Regiment in the County of Essex, formerly commanded by William Browne, Esq; politically deceased of a pestilent and mortal Disorder, and now buried in the ignominious Ruins at Boston; met on Monday the 15th Instant, and after choosing Deacon Nathaniel Bancroft for their Chairman, elected Mr. Joseph Gowen, Captain; Mr. Nathaniel Shearman, 1st Lieutenant, and Mr. John Perkins, Ensign.

At a Meeting of the Inhabitants of Anne-Arundel County, and the City of Annapolis, last Wednesday, a Committee of 44 Persons was chosen for that County and City, to carry into Execution the Association agreed on by the American Congress.

The Inhabitants of the City of Philadelphia, agreeable to the Resolves of the General Congress, have appointed a Committee of 61 Gentlemen, to co-operate with the other Committees that are, or may be chosen on this Continent.

We hear the Re-ve-rend *Samuel Peters* of Hebron, whose Intentions were published in his jargon Epistles in the Connecticut Courant, No. 512, not being able to procure a Passage to London on board any Vessel bound to that Place from Boston, went to Salem for that Purpose, where, meeting with a like Disappointment, he immediately return'd by Way of Dartmouth-College, to Hebron, where it is said he keeps himself concealed, to avoid the Tokens of Resentment which he has justly *merited* from the good People of that Colony: But it is hoped his *insignificance* will protect him from any Injury either in Person or Estate.

DONATIONS received since our last.

From the County of Litchfield (in Connecticut) 19*l* 3*s* 0*d*. and 51 Head Cattle.

From Colchester, 94 Sheep and 5 Cattle.

From Fairfield, 750 Bushels Grain.

Nov. 26. Of Mr. Sylvanus How of Petersham, Eleven Quarters of Mutton, 123*lb*. Weight.

The Proceedings of York County Congress being so lengthy, and coming to Hand so late, we are oblig'd to Postpone them this Week. Their 7th Resolve is as follows, viz.

7. Whereas there have been several Sums of Money raised by the General Assembly of this Province, and committed to the Constables to collect, and pay the same unto Harrison Gray, Esq; Treasurer of the Province, and it evidently appearing by the late Conduct of said Treasurer, that he is not of a sound Mind, whereby there is Danger of hispaying the Monies belonging to the Province to other Purposes than that for which it was raised; therefore this Congress recommend to the Inhabitants of each Town in this County to secure the Monies that is or may be collected by said Constables, in such Manner as that they may command the same, until the said Harrison Gray, Esq; hath his Reason restored to him; or some other Treasurer be constitutionally chosen.

Died last Night at Roxbury, after a short Illness, Mr. INCREASE SUMNER, aged 62.——His Funeral is to be on Wednesday next, when his Friends are requested to attend.

Died at Watertown, the Rev. Mr. SETH STORER, aged 73.

☞ *AS the Appearance of the Small-Pox in this Town has given rise to various Reports; the Public are hereby informed, that last Monday Night the Selectmen were acquainted by a Surgeon of the Army, that five Children in a House occupied by a Soldier of the 59th Regiment were seized with that Disorder, all of whom were sent early the next Morning to the Hospital at New-Boston, as was a Soldier of the same Regiment the Day following.—These are the only Persons in Town who have the Infection, and are all in a fair Way of Recovery —— Upon a strict Enquiry made thro' the Regiments by Order of the Governor, no one has been found among them that appears to have even the Symptoms of that Distemper,— the Rumour that some Soldiers or their Children were to be innoculated, is without Foundation; such a Measure having been forbid on Pain of his Excellency's highest Displeasure. It is supposed this Disease was taken from a Child brought from New-York in one of the Transports, which died a Fortnight ago. And the Public may be assured that the greatest Care has been taken to prevent a Communication of the Infection.*

By Order of the Selectmen,
WILLIAM COOPER, *Town-Clerk.*

JUST PUBLISHED and to be sold by the Printers hereof,

THE
FIRST BOOK
OF THE
AMERICAN
CHRONICLES
OF THE
TIMES.

Choice RAISINS by the Cask, CURRANTS, and all sorts of SPICES, to be sold at

Thomas Walley's

Store, Butler's-Row, No. I. ALSO,

Old Jamaica and common West-India RUM, Teneriffe Wine by the Pipe, Hogshead or Quarter Cask. Also, genuine Lisbon Wine, excellent Dumb Fish, Citron, Figs, Bolting Cloths, Dutch Looking-Glasses. All sorts of Groceries as usual. All at at the lowest Prices for Cash.

N. B. A Quantity of Mustard Seed, and Snuff Bottles, to be sold very cheap.

CANDLES.

Dipp'd Tallow CANDLES per Box, at 5*s.* Old Tenor per lb.

Mould Tallow,
Pure Myrtle Wax, } Candles.
Sperma-Ceti

ALSO, TALLOW by the Barrell, Spermaceti OIL for Lamps, and HOG's-FAT, sold by JOHN LANGDON, in Fleet-Street, at the Head of the Hon. JOHN HANCOCK, Esq's; Wharf.

All Persons indebted to or having any Demands upon the Estate of THOMAS GRAY, Esq; deceased, are desired to settle the same with

Boston, Nov. 26, 1774. WILLIAM GRAY, ELLIS GRAY, EDWARD GRAY. } Executors.

All Persons having Demands on the Estate of Jonathan Clark, late of Boston, Merchant deceased, and those who are Indebted to said Estate are desired to bring in their Accounts to Ezekiel Lewis, Administrator on said Estate in Order to Settlement.

☞ *A House and a valuable Spot of Land situate in Long Lane, belonging to said Estate, to be sold, enquire of said Administrator.* Boston, Nov. 28, 1774.

IF the Person who on the 11th of this Instant took a small Pocket Volume of the Bible, beginning with the Prophet Isaiah, being Part of a Sett neatly bound with blue Morocco Leather, gilt and mark'd 2 on the Back (out of the House in Queen-Street, lately occupied by John Adams, Esq;) will return it to the Place it was taken from, or to the Printers hereof, no Questions shall be ask'd; if not, as the Person is known, he may expect to be expos'd.

Taken up in Medford River on Tuesday the 22d Instant, a small Moses Boat, 11 Feet Keel. The Owner may have her again paying Charges. Inquire of Edes and Gill.

On Wednesday next, (being 30th Inst.)
At TEN o'Clock in the Morning,
Will be sold by PUBLIC VENDUE,
At RUSSELL's Auction-Room, in Queen-Street,
A very large Collection of new and old BOOKS, in Law, Divinity, History, &c.
Printed Catalogues may be had of
J. RUSSEL, Auctioneer.

On FRIDAY next,
At TEN in the Morning,
Will be Sold by PUBLIC VENDUE,
At the House of the late Capt. JONATHAN CLARKE,
In Long-Lane,
All the House Furniture of the said deceased,
—Amongst which are,—
Tables, Chairs, Looking Glasses, Feather Beds, Bedsteads and Bedding, a good Eight Day Clock, Glass and China Ware, Kitchen Furniture, &c.
J. RUSSELL, Auctioneer.

N. B. The Furniture may be viewed the Day before the Sale. Friday next X o'Clock.

PUBLIC AUCTION,
TO BE SOLD,
By *BENJAMIN CHURCH,*
At his usual Place of Sale,
On *Thursday Evening Next,*
To begin at Six o'Clock,
A great Variety of valuable articles, viz.

Broad Cloths—Serges—Forrest Cloths —Duffils—Camblets—Calamancoes—Cotton Checks—Linnens—Sheeting Holland—Linnen and Barcelona Handkerchiefs—Cutlary—Case Knives and Forks, &c. Sundry Articles of Houshold—Tables—Chairs, Feather Beds, &c. Wearing Apparel new and second hand.

N. B. The Goods to be view'd the Day of Sale. Thursday Evening next.

New Auction-Room, *Cornhill.*
To-Morrow Morning at Ten o'Clock,
Will be Sold, by PUBLIC VENDUE,
At GREENLEAF's Auction-Room,
A Great Variety of GOODS (belonging to a Gentleman leaving the Province) amongst which are,

Broad Cloths, Duffils, Plains, Fearnoughts, Shalloons, Durants, Tammies, Plain and Corded Poplins, Allopeens, Worsted Stuffs, Corded and Figured Dimothy, Stamp'd and Checked Handkerchiefs, Worsted Hose, Manchester Bed Ticks, Castor and Felt Hatts, &c.

Sale begins 10 o'Clock. *Wm. Greenleaf,* Auct'r.

This day was published,
And to be sold either by the Thousand, Hundred, Groce, Dozen, or Single,
[*Embellished with two plates, one representing an Antient Astrologer, the other a* FEMALE SOLDIER.]

THOMAS's
NEW-ENGLAND
ALMANACK,
OR THE
Massachusetts Calendar,
For the Year of our Lord Christ, 1775.
Being the Third after Bissextile or Leap-Year.

From the Creation of the World, according to the best of Prophane History,	5724
But by the Account of Holy Scriptures,	5737
Julian Period,	6488
From Noah's Flood,	4069
From the Destruction of Sodom,	3677
From the building of Rome,	2926
From the building of London,	2882
From the Destruction of Troy,	657
Higaria, or the Flight of Mahomet,	1184
New-England first planted,	166
Planting the Massachusetts-Bay,	147
Building of Boston the Capital of N. E.	145
Founding of Harvard College,	136
Of King George the IIId's. Reign,	15

CONTAINING,

Eclipses. Names of the Twelve Signs, and the Parts they govern. Names of the Planets and Aspects. Vulgar Notes. Friends Yearly Meetings. Sun's rising and setting. Full and Change of the Moon. Moon's rising and setting. Moon's Place. Time of High Water. Festivals of the Church of England, and other remarkable Days. Judgment of the Weather. Time of the Superior and Inferior Courts setting in the four Governments of New-England. Select Maxims. Observations on each Month in the Year. A Fragment of antient Poetry, collected in the Highlands of Scotland, and translated from the Gallic or Erse Language. The Athenian Orator, a Fable, in Verse. The Difference between To-Day and To-Morrow. ALSO,

The LIFE and ADVENTURES of
A FEMALE SOLDIER.
To the whole is added,
The ASSOCIATION of the Grand AMERICAN CONGRESS, which is absolutely necessary for every American to be acquainted with.
(*Price only Six Coppers single.*)

Very great Allowances are made to those who buy to sell again.
Printed and sold by ISAIAH THOMAS, at his Printing-Office, near the MILL-BRIDGE.

WANTED,
About £.1200 Sterling Cash, for which good Real Security will be given. Enquire of Edes and Gill.

TO BE SOLD BY
Newell and Hichborn,
At SALEM,
A few Barrels and Half Barrels New PORK.

All Persons who are indebted to the Estate of the late Mr. William Molineux, deceased: Also all Persons who had Demands on, or were indebted to him as Attorney to others, are desired to make them known, and to pay their respective Dues to the Subscriber, who is fully empowered to adjust and receive the same.

THOMAS APTHORP.

Gould's Auction-Office,
In Back-Street,
On Tuesday 6th of December next,
At TEN o'Clock in the Morning,
At which Time will begin to be Sold by Public Vendue.

A very large and valuable Assortment of English Goods, together with a great variety of Braziery and Cutlary Ware, the Property of a Gentleman deceased. R. GOULD, Auctioneer.

N. B. The Sale will be continued by Adjournment till the whole is sold.

Gilbert Deblois,

Informs his Customers that he has for Sale at his Shop opposite the Bottom of School-Street,

A very large and compleat Assortment of GOODS,
Suitable for the Season,
very cheap for CASH,
Among which are,

8/4, 9/4, 10/4, 11/4, Bed Blankets, Rugs, &c.
Scarlet, blue, white, buff, & other colour'd Broad Cloths,
Blue, scarlet and green Whitneys,
Bath Beavers, Coatings, Lambskins, &c.
White mill'd Flannels and Baizes, Ironing-Cloths,
Wide and narrow Baizes of all Colours and Prices,
A fine Assortment of Womens new fashioned Stuffs,
Choice Cambleteens at 9d Sterl. per Yard,
All Colours and Prices for Camblets or Riding-Hoods,
A great Variety of Silks, for the Ladies,
A compleat Assortment of Hosiery, & mill'd Gloves, some of which suitable for the Gentlemen of the Army & Navy,
Irish Linnens, of all Wedths and Prices,
Cheap Carpets and Carpeting; Calicoes,
China Ware, Loaf-Sugar, Spices, &c.
Looking-Glasses,—Scales,—Kippen's Snuff,
Firkin Butter at 6d Sterl. per Pound,
Gold and Silver Laces, &c. &c. *Fifes,* Violins,
French Horns, &c. Swords and Pistols,
German Steel, Barr Lead, Nails,
With almost every other Article of GOODS, Imported to America, from Great-Britain, Scotland and Ireland,
La Composition pour Nettoyer silver Lace, Embroidery and any sort plain and wrought plate.

Boston, Novem. 23, 1774.

TO BE SOLD
About 150 Hogsheads of *St. Martin's* SALT. ALSO,
A Sloop about 84 Tons Burthen, fitted for the Sea. Inquire of the Printers.

William Turner

Begs Leave to inform his Friends, He proposes to open a School on Tuesday Evening next, at Concert-Hall, to teach the polite Dances call'd Cotillons, and assures those Gentlemen who propose being his Pupils, he will attend two Evenings in the Week, viz. Tuesday and Friday.

N. B. Musick and Fencing taught likewise.

Country Traders & others
(Who purchase with Cash,)

MAY have an Opportunity greatly to their Advantage, by speedily applying at BICKER's Auction Room, near the Market, Boston.——Where is sent for Sale—A fine Parcel of middling and low-priced Broad Cloths, of the most fashionable Colours, which will be sold at too low a Rate.

N. B. A great Variety of other Goods, at private Sale, as cheap as usual.

Port of SALEM *and* MARBLEHEAD.
INWARD ENTRIES,

Forrester, Falmouth: Sheppard, London: Mackay and Rider, Gaudaloup: Dennis, Barbados and Turks-Island: Jones, Cadiz: Low, New-London: Ingersoll, Newfoundland: Gail, Dominica: Emerton, St. Eustatia & Turks-Island.

OUTWARD BOUND.

Willson, New-Haven: Downes, Mississippi: Southward and Dean, Jamaica: Hatch, North-Carolina: Foster, Virginia: Symonds, Maryland: Snow, West-Indies: Cox and Archer, South-Carolina.

Burials in the Town of BOSTON, since our last.
Thirteen Whites. Two Blacks.
Baptiz'd in the several Churches, Sixteen.

High Water at BOSTON, *for the present Week.*

Monday, 22 min. aft. 7	Friday, 33 min. after. 10
Tuesday, 11 min. aft. 8	Saturday, 26 min. aft. 11
Wednesday, 50 m. aft. 8	Lord's-Day, 14 m. af. 12
Thursday, 38 min. aft. 9	New D 3 Day 9 Morn.

Made and sold by *Isaac White*,

near the Hay-Market, South-End,

Good Dip'd Tallow-Candles, at 5s. O. T. per Box.

Likewise, Good Mould Tallow and Bayberry-Wax Candles—Also Tallow per Barrel—Good Hard & Soft SOAP.

TO BE SOLD for CASH,

White Flint Glass Ware per Box, *viz.*

Common sorted Crewets & Salts, Ditto Tumblers, Ditto Wine Glasses, } 25 to the Dozen, at 4s. 6d. Sterling per Dozen.

Ditto Mustard-Pots, 25 to the Doz. at 6/6d. per Doz.

Per the Crate, Apothecaries green Glass Vials sorted at 10s. Sterling per Groce.

Per the Crate, Green Half Pint Dram Bottles, 144 to the Groce, at 10/6d. Sterl. per Groce.

Brass Kettles, at 16½ Serling per lb.

Broad Cloths and Worsted Hair Plush, blue, green and scarlet, at the Sterling Cost.

Enquire of Edes & Gill.

A Wet Nurse with a good young Breast

of Milk, would take a Child to Suckle. Inquire of Edes and Gill.

To be Sold at Public Vendue on Wednesday the 30th Day of November, at One o'Clock, P. M. at the House of Capt. *Ephraim Jackson*, Innholder at Newton.

A FARM containing 100 Acres of choice good Land, lying in said Newton, now in the Occupation of Mr. *Samuel Woodward*, with a Dwelling House and two Barns standing thereon.—— The Privileges of said Farm may be seen any Day by applying to *Samuel Woodward* on said Farm.

Just arrived, and to be Sold by

W A R D & F E N N O,

At their Store, at the Head of Dock-Square,

COTTON WOOL per Bag, and Limes per Cask.—Good Connecticut Cheese, Firkin Butter, West India Goods, Spices, &c.

N. B. Goods sold on Commissions at the above Store.

ALL Persons indebted to the Estate of WILLIAM WHITE, Esq; late of Boston, deceased, are desired to pay the same to PHILLIPS WHITE of South-Hampton, in the Province of New-Hampshire, Executor of the last Will and Testament of the said WILLIAM WHITE; and those to whom said Estate is indebted are desired to send in their Demands to said Executor.

For the Convenience of many concerned, he purposes to be at Boston from the Sixth Day of December next—Ten Days; from the First Day of February—six Days; and from the Twentieth Day of March—Six Days.

Enquire for the said WHITE, at the Shop of Mrs. *Margarett Phillips*, in Cornhill.

To be sold Part of the Estate of the abovesaid WILLIAM WHITE, at Public Vendue, to the highest Bidder, on Thursday the Eighth Day of December next, viz. The House where the said Deceased lately dwelt, pleasantly situated at the North End of *Boston*, with Brick Store, Stable, Wood-House, &c. Three beautiful Gardens adjoining, &c. &c. and a small Piece of Land near Charlestown-Ferry.—Also a small Dwelling-House in Hull-Street; and a large Store in Queen-Street.——The Vendue to be at last-mentioned Store, at Ten o'Clock in the Forenoon of said Day.—The Conditions of Sale to be seen at the Time and Place of Sale.

N. B. The Premises may be viewed on Tuesday and Wednesday preceeding the Day of Sale.

To be Sold at the Royal Exchange Tavern in King-Street, Boston.

At Publick Vendue,

On THURSDAY the First Day of *December* next, at Eleven o'Clock in the Forenoon.

The following Lots of Land, viz.

Lot No. 20, called a 10 Mile back Lot, on the West side of Kennebeck-River, containing about 4800 Acres.

Lot marked F. 2. in the first Range of Lots, containing about 6000 Acres (exclusive of Settlers Lots interspersed) being near one Mile wide, and fifteen Miles long, and fronting on Kennebeck-River, on the West side of it, about ten Miles above Fort-Halifax, to be divided and sold in two Parts.

A Lot to the Northward of ditto, and fronting on little Norridgwalk-River, about 3200 Acres.

Lot marked B D. 1. in the second Range of Lots, about six Miles above Norridgwalk, on the West side of Kennebeck-River, and fronting thereon, containing about 7000 Acres, (exclusive of Settlers Lots interspersed) being 1 Mile wide, and 15 Miles long.

Lot marked C. A 1. in the third Range of Lots, near the Falls of Coriontonka, about 12 Miles above Norridgwalk, on the West side of Kennebeck-River, and fronting thereon, containing about 7000 Acres, (exclusive of Settlers Lots interspersed) being 1 Mile wide and 15 Miles long.

Three Lots of Land, viz. Lot No. 32, on the East side of Kennebeck-River, about a Mile above Fort-Western—No. 86, on the East side of said River, about 9 Miles above Fort-Western: and Lot No. 20, on the West side of said River, about 1 Mile and ½ above Fort-Western, containing 400 Acres each.

Also all the Islands in Cobbisecont Pond, and all the Islands in Kennebeck-River above Fort-Halifax.

For further Particulars enquire of HENRY ALLINE, jun. at his Office in King-Street, Boston.

Boston, November 2d, 1774.

This is to notify the Public, That

the Charlestown Stage-Coach, No. 1, which heretofore set off from Mr. Woart's Tavern in Charlestown at 8 o'Clock, for Salem, will, for the future, set off at 9 o'Clock every Day in the Week, Sunday excepted, and another from Mr. Goodhue's in Salem, return to Charlestown.

WHEREAS the Great and General Court or Assembly of this Province, at their Session begun and held the 27th Day of May, 1772, granted a Tax of Two Pence per Acre for one Year next to come; and one Penny per Acre for a second Year next to come, on all the Lands in the District of Hubbardston, in the County of Worcester. And whereas the first and second Years Taxes have been duly assessed and posted, as is by Law directed, and some Proprietors or Owners of said Lands have neglected or refused to pay their Tax; the General Court in said Act did empower the Assessors of said Taxes to sell so much of the Delinquent Proprietors Lands as shall be necessary to pay and satisfy such Taxes, and other necessary intervening Charges. The Owners of the following Lands are delinquent in paying their Taxes, (viz.) The first Year's Tax.

House-Lots.

No.	Acres.	Pay. £.	s.	d.
3	50	0	8	4
8	76	0	12	8
14	100	0	16	8
20	112½	0	18	9
26	14	0	2	4
35	7½	0	1	3
37	135	1	2	6
38	135	1	2	6
42	120	1	0	0
43	120	1	0	0
44	70	0	11	8
45	66	0	11	0
53	23	0	3	10
55	120	1	0	0
56	109½	0	18	3
58	81	0	13	6
59	102½	0	17	1
62	100	0	16	8
63	100	0	16	8
64	100	0	16	8

Great-Farms.

No.	Acres.	Pay. £.	s.	d.
1	481	4	2	0
2	104	0	17	4
3	120	1	0	0
4	50	0	8	4
5	30	0	5	0
11	200	1	13	4
12	210	1	15	0
13	28	0	4	8
15	200	1	13	4
18	320	2	13	4
20	319	2	13	2
22	128	1	1	4
24	295	2	9	2
25	241	2	2	0
28	172	1	8	8
[illegible]	137	1	2	10
32	117	0	19	7
33	346	2	17	8
Letter Lots.				
B.	77	0	12	10
D	60½	0	10	1
L.	70	0	11	8
O.	90	0	15	0

Notice is hereby given to the abovesaid Delinquents that so much of their Lands will be sold at a public Vendue. (as to pay their Taxes and other necessary intervening Charges) at the House of Mr. John Ames, Innholder in Hubbardston, on Tuesday the 7th Day of March next, at Ten o'Clock in the Forenoon, and to be continued from Day to Day, by Adjournment, till the Third Day, if not sold before, unless said Taxes and Charges be paid to the Assessors before said Sale.

Hubbardston, Nov. 4, 1774.

John Wood, *Joseph Grimes,* } Assessors.

The Second Year's Tax.

House-Lots.

No.	Acres.	Pay. £.	s.	d.
2	50	0	4	2
3	50	0	4	2
4	60	0	5	0
5	100	0	8	4
6	100	0	8	4
8	76	0	6	4
11	135	0	11	3
13	112	0	9	4
14	100	0	8	4
15	100	0	8	4
17	100	0	8	4
20	112	0	9	4
26	14	0	1	2
28	121	0	10	4
31	100	0	8	4
32	100	0	8	4
33	60	0	5	0
34	112	0	9	4
36	121	0	10	1
37	135	0	11	3
38	135	0	11	3
39	8	0	0	8
40	120	0	10	0
42	120	0	10	0
43	120	0	10	0
44	120	0	10	0
45	116	0	9	8
46	120	0	10	0
48	135	0	11	3
50	100	0	8	4
51	109	0	9	1
52	110	0	9	2
53	23	0	1	11
54	111	0	9	3
55	120	0	10	0
56	109	0	9	1
57	135	0	11	3
58	144	0	12	0
59	102	0	8	6
60	100	0	8	4
62	100	0	8	4
63	100	0	8	4
64	100	0	8	4
65	100	0	8	4
66	100	0	8	4
67	100	0	8	4
68	100	0	8	4

Great-Farms.

No.	Acres.	Pay. £.	s.	d.
1	481	2	0	1
2	295	1	4	7
3	481	2	0	1
4	435	1	16	3
5	4	0	0	4
9	340	1	8	4
10	508	2	2	4
11	200	0	16	8
12	474	1	19	6
13	474	1	19	6
14	474	1	19	6
15	275	1	2	11
16	240	1	0	0
17	212	0	17	8
18	530	2	4	2
20	319	1	6	7
21	458	1	18	2
22	128	0	10	8
24	295	1	4	7
25	241	1	0	1
26	486	2	0	6
27	356	1	9	8
28	472	1	19	4
29	540	2	5	0
30	550	2	5	10
31	340	1	8	4
32	470	1	19	2
33	476	1	19	8
Letter Lots.				
B.	77	0	6	5
C.	57	0	4	9
E.	76	0	6	4
D	60	0	5	0
G	53½	0	4	6
H.	66	0	5	6
K.	57	0	4	9
L.	70	0	5	10
O.	90	0	7	6

Notice is hereby given to the abovesaid Delinquents, that so much of their Lands will be sold at a public Vendue, (as to pay their Taxes and other necessary intervening Charges) at the House of Mr. John Ames, Innholder in Hubbardston, on Tuesday the 14th Day of March next, at Ten o'Clock in the Forenoon, and to be continued from Day to Day, by Adjournment, till the Third Day, if not sold before, unless said Taxes and Charges be paid to the Assessors before said Sale.

Hubbardston, Nov. 4, 1774.

John Wood, *Joseph Grimes,* } Assessors.

Imported in Capt. Robson, from London, and to be sold by

Peter Hughes,

At his Store in King-Street,

English, Russia and Ravens Duck,

Tickienburgs, Oznabrigs, Broad Cloths, Duffils, Beaver Coatings, Cod and Mackrel Lines and Hooks, Sail, Sein and Whipping Twine, 4d, 6d, 8d, and 10d Nails, Sheathing and Drawing ditto, 6 by 8, 7 by 9, & 8 by 10 Glass, Pepper, Gun Powder in Half and Quarter Barrels, 10, 15, 18 and 21 Inch Pipes, single, double and refined Loaf Sugar, Florence Oil, Split Peas, Buntins, Shot, Spices, Durham Mustard, also a few Casks of Burton and Yorkshire Ale.

Daniel Silsby,

Has to sell by Wholesale and Retail, at his Store, opposite South-Side *Faneuil-Hall*,

SUGARS Loaf and Brown, Coffee, Chocolate, Rice, Starch, Indigo, Ginger, Allspice, Pepper, Nutmegs, and other Spices; Marseilles and Lisbon OIL, Jamaica Spirit, West-India and New-England Rum, Brandy, Malaga Wine, Crown Soap, 15 & 18 Inch Pipes, Redwood, Logwood, Raisin, and Currants.

ALSO, CHEESE, a very considerable Quantity of *Firkin Butter*, &c.

All of which he will sell as cheap as can be bought at any Store in Boston.

The Co-Partnership of *Box* and *Austin*,

being dissolved by the Death of Mr. *Box*, This is to desire all Persons who have any Demands on said Company, to bring in and settle their Accounts with the surviving Partner, *Benjamin Austin*. And all those who are indebted to the late Company, are requested to make immediate Payment.

N. B. The Business of Ropemaking is still carried on by said *Austin*.

All Persons that are indebted to

the Estate of Mr. JOHN BOX, Sen'r, late of Boston, deceased, are requested to discharge the same; and all those who have Demands upon the Deceased's Estate, are desired to produce their Claims to

Boston, 14th Nov. 1774. *Lydia Box,* *John Box,* *W. Hoskins.* } *Executors.*

English Grammar,

WHOEVER considers the Inconveniencies to which young Persons must be subject through Life, where a proper Acquaintance with Letters, and Language is wanting; and the great Advantages which must arise to those who are designed to act any considerable Part in Life, from a thorough Knowledge of the Use of Letters, and Propriety of Language, especially of that, which they have by far the most Occasion to use,

Must, undoubtedly, be sensible, that the Study of English Grammar, or the Art of Reading, Speaking and Writing the English Language with strict Propriety, and Elegance, is well worthy the Attention of Youth, as a material Part of their Education.

Such Parents, or Guardians, as are disposed to have their Children instructed in this important Branch, (or rather Foundation) of Science, may be faithfully served for that Purpose, at the English Grammar School, in Milk-Street——by

WILLIAM PAYNE.

☞ LADIES who chuse to be instructed at Home, may be waited on with the utmost Complaisance, and strictest Attention, as often as the Nature of the Business requires, and at such Hours as shall be most convenient.

Writing and Arithmetic will be taught to such as desire it, and Letter-Writing in Form.

He will receive the Commands of such as shall please to favour him therewith, at his School in Milk-Street, or at his Lodgings at Mr. *Benjamin Gray's* in King-Street.

WHEREAS the Proprietors of Sudbury-Canada, (so called) being a Township granted to Josiah Richardson, Esq; and others, in the County of Cumberland, at a legal Meeting by Adjournment on the 17th Day of August, A. D. 1773, granted a Tax of Twenty Shillings, L. M. on each single Right. Also the said Proprietors at a legal Meeting by Adjournment on the 7th Day of December A. D. 1773, granted another Tax of Forty Shillings L. M. on each single Right to defray the Charges of clearing a Road to the said Township and other necessary Charges: Also the said Proprietors at a legal Meeting by Adjournment on the 6th Day of April A. D. 1774, granted another Tax of Twenty Shillings L. M. on each single Right, publick Rights excepted, to defray the Charges of building Mills in said Township: And altho' the said Taxes have been published according to Law, and Payment requested, nevertheless several of the said Proprieters are delinquent in the Payment of the said Taxes: Publick Notice is therefore hereby given to said Delinquents, that unless their Taxes are paid to Cornelius Wood of Sudbury, Treasurer, or to us the Subscribers, by Ten o'Clock in the Morning of the 13th Day of December next, their Rights will be sold as the Law directs, for the Payment of their Taxes and Charges arising by the Sale, and the Sale to begin at Eleven o'Clock in said Morning, at the Dwelling-House of Isasc Gleasons, Innholder in Waltham, and continued by Adjournment (if need be) till the whole be sold.

Cornelius Wood, *Elijah Bent,* *Josiah Stone.* } Proprietors Committee.

Boston: Printed, by EDES & GILL. *in Queen-Street,* 1774.

No. 1025.

THE Boston-Gazette, AND COUNTRY JOURNAL.

Containing the freshest Advices, Foreign and Domestic.

MONDAY, December 5, 1774.

Proceedings of York County Congress.

WE his Majesty's loyal Subjects the Delegates of the several Towns of the County of YORK, deputed to meet in County Congress, held at WELLS the Sixteenth Day of November, 1774, truly professing ourselves liege Subjects of His Majesty King GEORGE the Third, and sincere Friends to all our fellow Subjects in Britain and the Colonies: for the necessary defence of our Liberties and Privileges, come into the following Resolutions.

1. *Resolved*, That his Majesty's Subjects in the Province of the Massachusett's-Bay, as well as in the other English American Colonies, have full Right and Authority to Tax themselves, and grant their own Monies, by their several General Assemblies, for all such Purposes, and in such Manner as they shall see fit; and that no other State, Prince or Parliament whatever hath, or under the present Constitution of said Colonies can have, right or authority, to grant the money of said subjects, or tax them in any other manner whatever: And therefore that the several acts of the British parliament, made for the express purpose and design, not only of raising a revenue to his Majesty, by Duties to be paid on goods landed in said Colonies, but establishing a precedent for further illegal taxation of the people therein, are unconstitutional, unjust and oppressive, and never ought to have force in the Colonies; and all subsequent acts made to enforce the same, more especially that for blocking the port of Boston, are hostile, cruel and arbitrary.

2. *Resolved*, That all civil officers within this county, duly appointed by virtue of, and pursuant to, the charter of William and Mary, ought to use and exercise the several powers and authorities to their respective offices belonging, agreeable to the laws of the province of the Massachusett's-Bay, in the same way and manner, in every respect, intent and purpose, as tho' the said acts had never been passed: And that all persons ought to aid, assist and countenance them therein. And particularly that the *Venires* for Jurors for the several courts of Justice in this County, ought to be issued as heretofore has been used and accustomed, agreeable to the laws of the province aforesaid; and that due obedience ought to be paid thereto: And that a spirit of peace, friendship and harmony may subsist and be cultivated among the inhabitants of said County, the said Congress do recommend to them, that they produce no suit against each other, unless on some urgent necessity.

3. *Resolved*, That this Congress recommend to every individual in this County, in their several stations, to use their utmost endeavours to promote peace and good order. It is also recommended to the several Towns, forthwith to meet and chuse a committee, whose business it shall be to see that the Association of the Continental Congress enter'd into in behalf of their Constituents, be strictly observed and kept; and if any person or persons shall violate the same, said Committee are advised to post their names in the several public houses of entertainment in the county; and also publish a state of facts in the several public news-papers, to the end, all persons may withdraw from him, her or them, all commercial intercourse and connection whatsoever. And that no Riots, Disorders or Tumults may take place in said County, which in their nature and tendency are as well subversive of all civil government, as destructive to the very end and design of the present struggle for Liberty, (and the present plan proposed and recommended by the Continental Congress for our deliverance) the said Congress do recommend to the Inhabitants thereof, that they do not with violence damage or injure the person or property of any one, that shall either break thro' said association, or do any other matter or thing against the liberties of the country, but shall immediately give information to the Committee of the Town where the offence is committed, that such persons may be treated as aforesaid.

4. Whereas the late Sir WILLIAM PEPPERRELL, Baronet, deceased, (well known, honoured and respected in Great Britain and America for his eminent services) in his life-time did honestly acquire a large and extensive Real Estate in this County, and gave the highest evidence, not only of his being a sincere friend to the rights of men in general, but having a paternal love to this County in particular. And whereas the said Sir William by his last Will and Testament made his Grandson the present Sir William Pepperrell, Esq; Residuary Legatee and possessor of the greatest part of said Estate, and the said William Pepperrell, Esq; hath with purpose to carry into Force and Execution Acts of the British Parliament made with apparent design to Enslave the free and loyal People of this Continent, did accept, and now holds a Seat at the pretended Board of Councellors in this Province, as well in direct repeal of the Charter thereof, as against the solemn Compact of Kings, and the Inherent Rights of the People: It is therefore Resolved, that the said William Pepperrell, Esq; hath thereby justly forfeited the Confidence and Friendship of all true Friends to American Liberty, and with other pretended Councellors now holding their Seats in like Manner, ought to be detested by all good Men: And it is hereby recommended to the good People of this County, that as soon as the present Leases made to any of them by said Pepperrell are expired, they immediately withdraw all Connection, Commerce and Dealings from him—and that they take no further lease or conveyance of his Farms, Mills or Appurtenances thereto belonging, (*where the said Pepperrell is sole receiver and appropriator of the rents and profits thereof*) until he shall resign his said Seat pretendedly acquired by Mandamus: And if any Person shall remain or become Tenant on such Estate to said Pepperrell after the expiration of their present lease; we recommend to the good People of this County not only to withdraw all connection and commercial intercourse with them, but to treat them in manner provided by the *third* Resolve of this Congress.

5. And that the *Association* aforesaid be not violated, it is recommended that the Law of this Province respecting Hawkers, Pedlars, and Petty-Chapmen, be duly put in Execution, and if any Taverner or Innholder shall knowingly entertain them, or permit and suffer any Vendue or Sale of Goods in their respective Houses by any such Person, said Taverner or Innholder be taken due Notice of by the Select-Men, and that it be advised that the Select-Men do not approve or recommend any such Taverner or Innholder as a suitable person to renew his or her Licence; and it is also recommended to the People of this County, not to trade with Pedlars, Hawkers, or Petty-Chapmen.

6. To ease the Minds of the good People of this County, this Congress do assure them, that on enquiry, We do not find that any Civil Officer or other Person therein, has made any attempt to put the Acts of Parliament aforesaid into Execution, and trust that none will attempt it.

7. Whereas there have been several sums of Money raised by the General Assembly of this Province, and committed to the Constables to collect, and pay the same unto *Harrison Gray*, Esq; Treasurer of this Province, and it evidently appearing by the late Conduct of said Treasurer that he is not of a sound Mind, whereby there is danger of paying the Monies belonging to the Province, to other Purposes than that for which it was raised; therefore this Congress recommend to the Inhabitants of each Town in this County to secure the Monies that is or may be collected by said Constables in such Manner as that they may command the same, until the said Harrison Gray, Esq; hath his Reason restored to him; or some other Treasurer be Constitutionally chosen.

8. Whereas the Delegates of the several Towns in the Province, while met at Cambridge to consult such Measures as might tend to put their Constituents in a posture of Defence, against the attack of Military Violence that might be offered, and while waiting the result of the Continental Congress, resolved on such Measures as they then tho't might put the Militia in a reputable and formidable footing; and it appearing that a cultivation of the Military Art, may have salutary Effects in the settlement of the present political Disputes:—We therefore recommend to the Militia of this County, that if the Provincial Congress when met again, as they soon will, do not alter the Plan by them proposed, the People of this County adopt the same.

9. *Resolved*, That the Thanks of this County be and hereby are given to the worthy and patriotic Members of the Continental Congress for their noble and faithful Exertions in the Cause of their Country, and are of Opinion, that the Rights of the American Colonies, are by them clearly and fully Stated, in their several Resolutions, and that the wise and prudent Plan by them projected, if carried into Execution, cannot fail to restore that Union and Harmony between Great-Britain and her Colonies, so ardently wished for by all good Men, and hope their Names will be handed with Honor to the latest Posterity.

The foregoing is a true Copy.

Attest, WILLIAM LEIGHTON, Clerk.

To WILLIAM PEPPERRELL, *Esq*;

WHILE your Brethren with whom you form an ignominious and unconstitutional Board, are attacked by the patriotic Pens of Freemen in each County, you cannot hope to set unnoticed amidst the mighty ruin you and they are hurling on this devoted Province; fully convinced not only of your error, but of your knowing and obstinately pursuing that error; we cannot but censure your criminal conduct.

As the County of York gave you that being which your late movements have rendered very exceptionable, you may not be surprized that the people of it should suppose you to deserve their particular notice: Your venerable and patriotic Grandsire by his honest industry accumulated in this County the most extensive estate that has perhaps by one Man in New-England been acquired; he not only acquired but enjoyed it with the smiles of his Sovereign, and thanks of his Country.——When the hour of his exit, filled with prayers and groans of his Country hastened, his laboring mind then wished a PEPPERRELL, not only to maintain his name but his character with his Countrymen.——You then was innocent, the guile of a courtier, and false splendor of unmerited title had not poisonously infested your tender mind——he bestowed his estate conditionally upon you, that you might inherit that with his name, honours and character.—You have the estate and name in possession; but the laurels he long wore in the richest verdure soon faded on your brow.—Instead of proving a friend to your country, you have assumed an office, as well against the charter rights of the people as every principle of benevolence, justice and humanity—Virtues that formed no inconsiderable part of your ancestor's character.

This County, by their Delegates met in Congress, seriously and dispassionately took your conduct under consideration, and resolved that your farms lay waste, your buildings become dunghills, and that none but the beasts of the field, reptiles of the earth, and owls of the desert inhabit those houses, which were lately the happy mansions of your Grandfather's tenants.—If you are not past it, pray reflect on the part you have acted—Can you suppose that Sir William would have given his estate to purchase chains of slavery for his countrymen?—or that he would not have rather given it to let his name rest in oblivion, than to have it supported thus ignominiously?——

While you are courting the tools of a vicious ministry, and selling your country to purchase the title of a Baronet, you may think these considerations below your notice; but the time will come, Sir, (if I augur right) when the character of your father shall cease to protect you, your estate be squandered, your purse, as it now bids fair for it, be exhausted; your country detest and despise you.—Then, Sir, enjoy the title of a Baronet, like a King without subjects—a North without treasuries—and a Cain without hope.

A YORKSHIREMAN.

Fresh Advices from London!

Brought by the Captains *Bruce* and *Shayler*, who arrived at Salem last Week.

LONDON, October 3.

THE Scarborough Man of War, Capt. Shad, from Boston is arrived at Portsmouth.

A Correspondent applauds Lord North upon dissolving the Parliament at this Juncture; the Affairs of America are brought to a Crisis; England must command, or strike to her Colonies, and that soon; the present Resolution is to command, which will furnish numberless Pretences to the popular Party, and at the Eve of a general Election might ruin the Minister before his Plan is completed; but when the new Parliament is met he will despise all popular Cries, and laugh at the feeble Rage of the Storm, when seven Years give him Plenty of Sea-Room.

Oct. 7. Yesterday afternoon, at 3 o'clock, the poll for Lord Mayor finally ended at Guildhall, when the numbers were,

For Mr. Wilkes	1957
The Lord Mayor	1923
Sir James Esdaile	1474
Mr. Alderman Kennet	1410

Oct. 10. On Sunday there was a large and respectable appearance of the Livery of London in common hall assembled, agreeable to public notices, for the purpose of receiving the return of the Court of Aldermen for Lord Mayor of this City for the year ensuing.

A little after twelve the Sheriffs came on the Hustings, and after the common Cryer had opened the Hall, the common Serjeant declared the state of the poll, and reported, that the Sheriffs were of opinion, that the election had fallen on John Wilkes, Esq and the Right Hon. the Lord Mayor.

The Sheriffs then returned to the Court of Aldermen, and about one o'clock they again returned, when the Recorder declared the election of the Court of Aldermen to have fallen on John Wilkes, Esq; which declaration was returned with repeated shouts of applause.

Mr. Wilkes then came forward, and was invested with the usual insignia of Office; after which he addressed the Common Hall as follows:

The SPEECH of the LORD MAYOR ELECT, JOHN WILKES, Esq; to the COMMON-HALL, October 8, 1774.

GENTLEMEN,

"PERMIT me to return you my most hearty Thanks for the greatest Honour a Subject can receive, the being called by the Voice of free Citizens to the Chief Magistracy of the Metropolis of the British Empire. The first Idea which must arise in a liberal mind, is, that the important & extensive Powers and Authority with which I am intrusted by you, are delegated to me only for your good, and the general benefit. You have enlarged my Powers of being useful to you, and constituted me the first Guardian of our common Rights and Franchises. Give me leave to assure you that so far from harbouring the impious tho't of invading your Liberties myself, I shall think it my Duty always, firmly and boldly to stand forth against the Enemies of public and legal Freedom. In this noble Cause I will most readily join you, and in all salutary Measures for the Preservation, or improvement, of the Constitution of our Country, and for the welfare of the Capital. I shall therefore most certainly call Common Halls and Common Councils on all important Occasions at your Requisition.

"*Gentlemen of the Livery*,

"As Chief Magistrate of the first City in the World, I promise you an upright and regular Administration of the public Justice, and I rely with Confidence on your favourable Acceptance of my sincere and zealous Endeavours in your service."

Octo. 7. Orders are sent from the War-Office to Ireland, for taking up immediately transports to carry two regiments of foot of that establishment over to America.

By advices from different Cities and Boroughs, very pleasant accounts are received of the industry used on both sides, to prevent bribery and corruption; bread, meat, wine and beer, are watched on both sides as if contraband goods; the agents employed by each Candidate are as keen as Custom-house Officers, and every man that eats or drinks seems to sculk like a smuggler. (*See last Page.*)

Laſt Saturday Evening the Scarborough Man of War, Capt. Barclay arrived here from England, with Diſpatches for his Excellency Governor Gage: Capt. Barclay left Plymouth the 24th of October, and has brought London Papers to the 18th, which having been favoured with, we have extracted the following Advices, viz.

Oct. 17. A Letter from Chatham, dated the 12th Inſtant, ſays, "a detachment of Marines, conſiſting of 150 men, excluſive of Officers, among whom is Major Pitcairn, is ordered to march from thence to Portſmouth, to be embarked in the Ships now fitting out at that Port for Boſton."

A letter from Rome, dated Sept. 22, mentions that his Holineſs the Pope, died there a few days before.

Oct. 18. By letters from Boſton of the 9th of of Auguſt, we are informed, that a detachment of 200 ſoldiers ſeized 315 barrels of gun-powder and 2 field pieces, upon Cambridge-iſland, about four miles from Boſton.

At the cloſe of the Poll this day, for the City of Weſtminſter, the number were as follow: Lord Percy, 4101; Lord Clinton, 3800; Lord Mountmorres, 2047; Lord Mahon, 1907; H. Cotes, Eſq; 104.

We are aſſured the accounts publiſhed in ſome of the papers, of their having been a diſturbance at Boſton, in which Lord Percy was killed, is totally void of foundation, and only calculated to alarm his friend; and abate the real zeal of the electors of Weſtminſter who have ſo nobly and generouſly ſhewn in his ſupport.

This day the Sheriffs will hold a Common Hall and declare Alderman Sawbridge, Hayley, Oliver and the Lord Mayor duly elected Members for this City, and return them accordingly.

We hear that Mr. Wilkes and Mr. Glynn will go to Brentford on Thurſday next, with the Lord Mayor from the Manſion Houſe, and that many Freeholders will accompany him.

The ſtate of the Poll laſt Saturday at Briſtol was as follows:

For Mr. Cruger 1160, Mr. Burke 903. Mr. Brickdale 690, and Lord Clare 79.

Colonel Barre is again choſen Member for Caine, in Wilts.

B O S T O N, December 5.

In Provincial CONGRESS, *Cambridge, December 1, 1774.*

WHEREAS by the rigorous Operation of the Boſton Port-Bill, *the Metropolis of this Province and the neighbouring Town of* Charleſtown, *have been brought into a moſt diſtreſſed State, many of the Inhabitants being deprived of the Means of procuring their Subſiſtance, and reduc'd to the cruel Alternative of quitting their Habitations; or of periſhing in them by Famine, if they had not been ſupported by the free and generous Contributions of our Siſter-Colonies, even from the remoteſt Parts of this Continent:*

RESOLVED, THAT the grateful Acknowledgments of this Congreſs be returned to the ſeveral Colonies, for having ſo deeply intereſted themſelves in Behalf of ſaid Towns under their preſent Sufferings in the common Cauſe: And that the Congreſs conſider theſe Donations, not merely as unexampled Acts of Benevolence to this Province in general, which has alſo greatly ſuffered, and of Charity to thoſe Towns in particular; but as convincing Proofs of the firm Attachment of all the Colonies to the glorious Cauſe of American Liberty, and of their fixed Determination to ſupport them in the noble Stand they are now making for the Liberties of themſelves and of all America.

Signed by Order of the Provincial Congreſs,

JOHN HANCOCK, *Preſident.*

Friday laſt the Provincial Congreſs made Choice of the Hon. JOHN HANCOCK, Eſq; the Hon. THOMAS CUSHING, Eſq; Mr. SAMUEL ADAMS, JOHN ADAMS, Eſq; and ROBERT-TREAT PAINE, Eſq; as Delegates to repreſent this Province at the Continental Congreſs, to be held at Philadelphia the 10th of May next.

By numerous Papers, printed on this Continent, we find that large Committees are appointed and appointing, throughout the Colonies, to ſee that the Regulations of the Congreſs are punctually complied with.

In the London papers for September is publiſhed the proceedings of the provincial Congreſs of New-Jerſey; the arrival of lieutenant Governor Oliver's commiſſion, and an account of the ſwearing in of twelve gentlemen as councellors, appointed by his Majeſty's mandamus; the appointment and departure of the gentlemen who were to repreſent this province in the grand American Congreſs; and an addreſs from the juſtices of the inferior court of common pleas for the county of Eſſex, &c.

By late accounts from England, brought by Capt. Shepard (excluſive of what was publiſhed in our paper before) we learn,—that aſſociations were forming in more than twenty counties there, to chuſe ſuch perſons only for members of Parliament as will ſupport the American cauſe:——The ſudden diſſolution of Parliament occaſioned a great ſhock to all ranks of People in England; and it was generally thought the new Parliament will be for redreſſing the American grievances.

Five thouſand people have embarked at Greenock ſince the month of March for America.

Captain Bruce left Graveſend the 11th of October, Capt. Brown was to ſail in 3 or 4 Days after him, and Capt. Fellows in about a Fortnight, for this Place. Four Sail of the Line were ordered the 6th of Oct. to be got ready with all ſpeed for Sea, and four Regiments, lay in readineſs at Ireland to embark, but for what Place was kept ſecret. That moſt of the Perſons of Note, and who are Friends to America, recommend by all Means, *Moderation* and *Calmneſs*, on our Parts, as the only Means, with dutiful and proper Petitions to the King and new Parliament; after which there is no doubt of obtaining Redreſs of any *real* Grievances we Labour under.

By the laſt Veſſels from London we learn that all the People of diſcernment are of opinion that if the American Congreſs ſhould reſolve on the Non Conſumption of the Manufactures of Britain the preſent Miniſtry muſt go out, and their late meaſures be all reverſed, that in ſhort ſuch a reſolution ſtrictly adhered to would in a peaceable and juſtifiable way do every thing for us that we can wiſh—it we at the ſame time avoided every thing that would give our Enemies an handle or advantage againſt us and that when the reſult of the Congreſs comes to be known, it is not doubted but an accommodation will take place and our undoubted rights will be acknowledged and eſtabliſhed.

We hear that the Electors of the Cities of London and Weſtminſter, the Borough of Southwark, the County of Middleſex and ſome other Places, have exacted of their Candidates Engagements under their Hands that they will among other Things endeavour a Repeal of the late Acts againſt America, and it is ſuppoſed the Example of the Metropolis will be followed in other Places, ſome late Pieces that have been publiſhed in England have had an extraordinary Effect, in altering the Sentiments of Multitudes with Regard to America.

Extract of a letter from Portſmouth, in England, dated October 4.

"Since the Scarborough man of war has arrived from Boſton, not one of the men have been ſuffered to come on ſhore, neither are their friends permitted to go on board. The ſhip is anchored at ſome diſtance from any other, and ſo careful are the officers to keep every thing ſecret, that when any proviſion is ſent on board they ſtand on the ſide of the ſhip to prevent any converſation paſſing between the people that carry it and the crew, from which it is conjectured that things are worſe at Boſton than government are willing the public ſhould be acquainted with. The men in the yards are ordered to work double tides, to get ſome ſhips ready for ſea as ſoon as poſſible: it is ſaid that they are to relieve the guardſhips, which are to come into dock to be cleared and victualled for a long voyage: By all the appearance here we are at the eve of a war."

Extract of a letter from London, dated October 4.

"The people here now ſeem to be heartily ſick of the meaſures that have been taken againſt your port and province, and I hear the miniſtry do not know which way to ſteer; they are loath to give up their tyrannical power, but they muſt if the colonies are ſtedfaſt. The news in your papers makes all the court party look blue. We do not yet know the contents of General Gage's expreſs. The friends of America increaſe faſt. Petitions are forming in all parts of the kingdom in favour of America. We are all impatient to know the reſult of the Congreſs. If the colonles are firm for one year, and neither import or export, it would eſtabliſh American freedom, for this country cannot ſupport itſelf without the colonies."

Yeſterday arrived at Salem, Capt. Brown from London.

Laſt Week was drove to Town by Mr. Silvanus Howe, of Peterſham, and ſold by Mr. John Robinſon of Dorcheſter, two Oxen, ſuppoſed to be the fatteſt and heavieſt that ever was raiſ'd in New-England; the Tallow weighing 464 lb. the amount of the whole 3237 lb.

Cambridge, November 29 1774.

At a Meeting of the Officers of the ſeveral Companies of Militia in the firſt Regiment in the County of Middleſex, for the Choice of Field-Officers: The following Gentlemen were Elected, viz.

Capt. THOMAS GARDNER,	*Colonel.*
Capt. WILLIAM BOND,	*Lieut. Colonel.*
Capt. WILLIAM CONANT,	*2d Lieut. Colonel.*
Capt. ABIJAH BROWN,	*Major.*
Capt. BENJAMIN HAMMOND,	*2d Major.*

Married, Mr. William Winter, aged 56, Notary Public, to Mrs. Abigail Oldham, aged 33.

THE late Grand Continental Congreſs at Philadelphia, among other of their Proceedings, prepared an Addreſs and Petition to his Majeſty (which will not be publiſhed till it is preſented to him) Copies of which Petition, &c. and of a Letter to the Colony Agents in London, were directed to be delivered to each of the provincial Aſſemblies, in America, to be by them tranſmitted to the ſaid Agents in London, who are deſired to requeſt the Aſſiſtance and Support of ſuch Noblemen and Gentlemen as were favourably diſpoſed towards the Britiſh American Colonies, in Order to get the ſaid Addreſs and Petition preſented, &c. and then cauſe it to be publiſhed. The following is a Copy of the Letter to the Agents:

Philadelphia, October 26, 1774.

Gentlemen,

WE give you the ſtrongeſt proof of our reliance on your zeal and attachment to the happineſs of America and the cauſe of liberty, when we commit the encloſed paper to your care.

We deſire you will deliver the petition into the hands of his Majeſty, and after it has been preſented, we wiſh it may be made public through the preſs, together with the liſt of grievances. And as we hope for great aſſiſtance from the ſpirit, virtue and juſtice of the nation, it is our earneſt deſire, that the moſt effectual care be taken, as early as poſſible to furniſh the trading cities and manufacturing towns, throughout the united kingdom, with our memorial to the people of Great-Britain.

We doubt not, but your good ſenſe and diſcernment will lead you to avail yourſelves of every aſſiſtance that may be derived from the advice and friendſhip of all great and good men, who may incline to aid the cauſe of liberty and mankind.

The gratitude of America, expreſſed in the encloſed vote of thanks, we deſire may be conveyed to the deſerving objects of it, in the manner that you think will be moſt acceptable to them.

It is propoſed that another Congreſs be held on the 10th of May next at this place; but in the mean time we beg the favour of you, Gentlemen, to tranſmit to the Speakers of the ſeveral Aſſemblies, the earlieſt information of the moſt authentic accounts you can collect, of all ſuch conduct and deſigns of the Miniſtry or Parliament, as it may concern America to know.

We are, with unfeigned eſteem and regard, Gentlemen, &c.

By order and in behalf of the Congreſs,

HENRY MIDDLETON, Preſident.

To Paul Wentworth, Eſq;

Doctor Benj. Franklin,	*Thomas Life, Eſq;*
William Bollan, Eſq;	*Edmund Burke, Eſq;*
Doctor Arthur Lee,	*Charles Garth, Eſq;*

The Congreſs alſo prepared a Letter to the People of the Colonies of St. John's, NovaScotia, Georgia, Eaſt and WeſtFlorida, who had not Deputies to repreſent them in the Congreſs. Of this Letter the following is a Copy:

Gentlemen, Philadelphia, Oct. 22, 1774.

THE preſent critical and truly alarming ſtate of American affairs, having been conſidered in a general Congreſs of Deputies from the Colonies of New-Hampſhire, Maſſachuſetts-Bay, Rhode Iſland and Providence Plantations, Connecticut, New-York, New-Jerſey, Pennſylvania, Newcaſtle, Kent and Suſſex, on Delaware; Maryland, Virginia, North Carolina, and South Carolina; with that attention and mature deliberation, which the important nature of the caſe demands; they have determined for themſelves, and the Colonies they repreſent, on the meaſures contained in the incloſed Papers; which meaſures they recommend to your Colony to be adopted, with all the earneſtneſs, that a well directed zeal for American liberty can prompt.

So rapidly violent and unjuſt has been the late conduct of the Britiſh adminiſtration againſt the Colonies, that either a baſe and ſlaviſh ſubmiſſion, under the loſs of their ancient, juſt and conſtitutional liberty, muſt quickly take place, or an adequate oppoſition be formed.

We pray God take you under his protection, and to preſerve the freedom of the whole Britiſh Empire.

By Order of the Congreſs,

HENRY MIDDLETON, Preſident.

Died in her 18th Year after a few Days Confinement, much lamented by all her Acquaintance, Miſs Sarah Cheever, Daughter to Abner Cheever, of Lynn, Eſq; her Character was ſpotleſs, & Life a ſtriking Inſtance of Piety.

We hear from Lynn, that Abner Cheever, Eſq; at a late Funeral of a near and very dear Relation, with juſt deference and ſubmiſſion, to a moſt excellent Reſolve of the Continental Congreſs wore not a ſingle Article of Mourning Apparal.—An Example worthy of imitation.

Donations receiv'd ſince our laſt.

MASSACHUSETTS-BAY.

Pittsfield, - - -	£.6 0 0
Mr. James Eaſton of ditto, -	0 12 0

40 Buſhels Rye from Chelmsford, ſome Time ſince, omitted by Miſtake.

CONNECTICUT.

Farmington, 204 Buſhels of Grain.
Chatham, 10 ſheep.
Mr. Aaron Cleveland, of Canterbury, 1 Fat Cow.

NEW-HAMPSHIRE.

Durham, 6 Fat Cattle, and -	2 2 0

New-Market, 4 Fat Cattle.
Statham, 3 Fat Cattle.

RHODE-ISLAND.

South Kingſtown, 105 Sheep.
Providence, 135 Sheep.

Meſſ. EDES and GILL,

I Have been informed that a certain Rope-maker in Marblehead, when deſired to ſubſcribe ſomething for the Relief of Perſons immediately ſuffering by the Execution of the Boſton Port-Bill, *refuſed to contribute any Thing to their Relief, and inſolently and barbarouſly declared that he would willingly ſubſcribe five hundred Halters for them.* If this is a Truth the Gentleman will do well to retract the infamous inhuman Declaration, as he has thereby given great Offence to ſome who are not uſed to put up with groſs Affronts.

Plymouth, November 29, 1774.

AT a Meeting of a large Number of the moſt reſpectable Inhabitants of this Town—it being ſuggeſted that Edward Winſlow, Eſq; who lately in a very inſulting and diſgraceful Manner deſerted from his Office, was about returning Home,

Voted, As the Opinion of this Body, that Edward Winſlow, jun. ought not, for the preſent, to be ſuffered to reſide in this Town.

Meſſieurs EDES & GILL,

THE Subſcriber begs Leave through the Channel of your Paper, to rectify a Miſtake made in the Liſt of Addreſſers—Thinks it a ſufficient Proof of his being entirely unacquainted with the Matter, when he aſſures the Public, that he was at Charleſtown-South Carolina, when the Addreſs was ſigned.

JOHN GRAY.

Messieurs P R I N T E R S.

Be pleased to insert in your next Paper, the following Extract of a letter from London, dated October 8, wrote by one of the first Character, especially for Knowledge, respecting the national Interest, as connected with that of the American Colonies, and you will oblige ninety-nine in an hundred of your readers.

Your's, &c. A. B.

"NEVER did I feel myself so anxious about publick affairs as at this moment. Our own interest is intimately connected with the perseverance of our American brethren in their opposition to the tyranny of our government. Should they continue firm, it will be scarcely possible that they should not succeed in preserving their Liberties; and the preservation of *their* Liberty ought to be an object of the last concern to all in this Country; for it is only among them we can hope to find it, after luxury, dissipation, a servile Parliament, and an overwhelming load of debts and taxes have completed its ruin here.——I cannot help believing that this will be the last struggle which America will have with us. If they are now steady and succeed, they will have no reason to fear any future attempts to enslave them. But if they now submit, they will be subdued forever, and the only nursery of freemen now in the world will be lost. May Heaven avert such a calamity!—I cannot indeed imagine a state of worse slavery than that in which the Colonies would be, were, they on this occasion to submit—to be not only subject to many hard restraints in acquiring their property, but to hold it, after being acquired, at the discretion of *our* rulers; to have no constitutions of government of their own, but to have their laws made and their governments modded by a legislature on the other side of the Atlantic, which cannot judge of their circumstances, in which they have no voice, and all whose acts are but little more than ecchoes to the will of the fool of the tyrant who happens to be minister in this country——What an abject condition would this be!——The present state of our Parliament is such that it is our own greatest calamity to be governed by it. How base would it be to wish the *Americans* involved in the same calamity? ——The mode of opposition which the Americans are likely to adopt must do them the greatest service, by checking luxury among them, and obliging them to save the money they now spend among us in purchasing superfluities. At the same time it must essentially injure us; for such are our present circumstances, that we hang upon the American trade; and the loss of it would sink the revenue, and soon bring on riots and insurrections, and a public bankruptcy. But I am not frightened by these consequences. The preservation of American liberty I think of unspeakably more importance than any temporary sufferings which can come upon us. I also consider our present state as so corrupt, and our excellent constitution of government as so entirely subverted by the unbounded influence of the Crown, that my only hopes arises from the prospect of a convulsion (dreadful while it lasts) which shall destroy artificial wealth and all the means of corruption, reduce us to poverty and simplicity, overturn the whole present system of policy, and be followed by the re-establishment of public liberty and virtue.

"I have been concerned to see in the *Pensylvania* instructions to their deputies a proposal that, previous to any other measures, a *memorial* or *remonstrance* should be presented to our government. The Colonies have, I think, already sufficiently try'd such methods as these. Our government, if consistent, would not receive any memorial from an assembly which they consider as illegal.—It is now too late for negociation, nor can it issue in any good to the American cause. Vigorous measures alone can be successful. And some think, that had the Americans fled immediately to the last resource, the quarrel might by this time have been almost decided; for the present ministry could not have found supplies for so horrid a service, and a change of men and of measures must have soon taken place.——

"The sentiments I have express'd, are those of the greatest part of my acquaintance, some of whom are persons of the first weight. I chuse to mention this, because I wish the Americans not to direct their resentment against all indiscriminately in this country. They may be assured, that they have a large body of friends here, who, from a sense of the rights of human nature, detest what has been done against them.——Perhaps the most provoking and mean of all the measures against them is the *Quebec* Bill, the plain design of which is to fix a body of Popish Slaves behind them, subject to the King's will, who may serve as a curb upon them.

"P.S. *The Scarborough, I find, is arrived from Boston, with accounts of a very interesting nature. Nothing that has happened at Boston since the 2d of September has yet transpired; and the government takes particular care to keep the accounts they have received of what passed on and after that day, a profound secret, by not suffering any of the crew to come ashore, or to hold any conversation with any visitants.—In the mean time, the parliament, which would have expired necessarily in the spring, has been suddenly dissolved; and the whole nation is now in a great ferment about electioneering. It is suspected that the design of Government, in this case, is to get a new Parliament returned as soon as possible, while the kingdom is in the dark, lest the news they have received, when known, should encrease the public clamour, and render it more difficult to get a Parliament they can influence. But we must soon know the whole truth.—Perhaps the sword has been drawn.—Indeed I cannot express how much I feel for you.*"——

POST-OFFICE, BOSTON Dec. 5. 1774.

THIS is to Inform the Public, that it's the Post Masters General's positive Orders that the Post-Riders leave this Office on Monday Mornings, precisely at 9 o'Clock, and proceed immediately out of Town with the Mail, of which all Persons concerned will please to take Notice.

The Treasurer for the County of Suffolk, gives Notice to all whom it may concern, that as he is obliged to leave the Town for a few Months, the Business of said County will be transacted by Mr. *Thomas Crafts*, jun. at his House near Liberty-Tree.

New Flour and Raisins.

John Kneeland,

At his Store the Head of Green's Wharff, opposite JOHN ROWE, Esq;——HAS FOR SALE——

A few Barrels new Philadelphia Flour, choice Raisins per Cask, Sugars, Coffee, Chocolate, West-India and New-England Rum, Brandy——Also, A few Pieces Ratteens, Coatings and Lambskins, to be sold very cheap.

Goods sold on low Commissions.

To-Morrow at Eleven o'Clock,

Will be sold by PUBLIC VENDUE, at Hickling's Wharff at New-Boston,

The Sloop Delight, 74 Tons burthen, with her Appurtenances, as she now lays at said Wharff.

☞ Inventory of her Stores, may be seen at the Place of Sale.

J. RUSSELL, Auctioneer.

New Auction-Room, *Cornhill.*

To-Morrow Morning at Ten o'Clock,

Will be Sold, by PUBLIC VENDUE,

At GREENLEAF's Auction-Room,

A very large Assortment of valuable Goods, (the Property of some Gentlemen leaving the Province,) consisting of,

BROAD Cloths, Forest Cloths, Plains, Cotton Velvets and Velverets, German Serges, Duffils, Carpeting, Shalloons, Tammies, Mens and Womens Hose of varisorts, Worsted Caps, a variety of Buttons, Poplins, Checks, Bed Ticks, Knives and Forks with Cases, Allapeens, several dozen Holland Shirts, silk Muffs, Castor & Felt Catts, &c. &c.

Wm. GREENLEAF, Auctioneer.

The Sale will begin at Ten o'Clock, and be continued in the Afternoon.

PUBLIC AUCTION,

TO BE SOLD.

By *BENJAMIN CHURCH,*

At his usual Place of Sale,

On *Thursday Next,*

At 3 o'Clock in the Afternoon

A large and valuable Assortment of EuropeanGoods, consisting of Woolens—Linnens—Silks, &c. Also some genteel and fashionable Articles of Household, viz. Mehogany Dining Tables—Side Boards—Beaureaus—Chest of Draws—a large Hall Glass Dressing ditto—Kitchen Furniture—to be seen the Day before the Sale—Feather Beds, &c. &c.—N. B. The Sale on Thursday next at 3 o'Clock, P. M.

New AUCTION-ROOM, Dock Square,

On TUESDAY next, at TEN o'Clock in the Morning,

Will be sold by PUBLIC VENDUE,

At HUNTER's Auction-Room,

A great Variety of ENGLISH GOODS,

——Amongst which are——

BROAD Cloths, Kerseys, Ratteens, Tammeys, Durants, Breeches Patterns, Worsted Hose and Mitts, Irish Linens, Checks, strip'd Hollands, Lawns, Cambricks, Ribbons, Drawboys, Velvets, Taffaties, Sattins, figur'd Modes, Silk Mitts, Sewing Silk, Silver Watches, &c. &c. WM. HUNTER, Auctioneer.

ALSO,—The damaged Linens which was advertized for last Friday's Sale, will be put up precisely at Twelve o'Clock. Wednesday the Sale begins at Ten o'Clock.

Taken up by *John Williams*, Tanner of Roxbury, on the 20th of November, a red and white COW, about 9 or 10 Years old. and on the 23d of said Month calved. Any Person owning said Cow, by applying to said *Williams*, may have her again by paying the Charges.

—Wanted in this Town—

An active, industrious, sober, honest, capable young Man, that has been brought up in a Retail Shop of English Goods, he must write a good Hand, quick at Figures and very obliging to the smallest Customers—Such a Person (and no other) may apply to the Printers for further Information.

Boston, December 5th, 1774.

James Bruce of Boston (at present in London) Mariner, maketh Oath, and saith, that he this Deponent has no Knowledge of, nor to the best of his Remembrance, was never in Company with a Captain Lovett, who is said by a Paragraph in the Boston Journal, dated 28 July, last, to have been in Company with this Deponent, at a Tavern in Antigua, and that the Contents of the Paragraph, there inserted (in order to hurt him this Deponent) is groundless and void of Truth, and that this Deponent never made use of any such Expressions there inserted, and further this Deponent saith, that he did not think or know at the Time he took the East Indie Company's Tea on Board the Ship Eleanor, that the same would have been either detrimental, or displeasing to the Town of Boston, otherwise himself and owners would not have suffered any of the said Tea to have been shipt on Board the said Ship Eleanor.

JAMES BRUCE.

Sworn before me at Shadwell, 16th Day of September,

JOHN SHERWOOD.

TO BE SOLD,

THE BRIG Benja and Salley, a good Vessel, Burthen about 140 Tuns, well Found, lying at Hutchinson's Wharf, Inquire of Capt. Edward Jarvi, near the New Brick Meeting House.

Choice RAISINS by the Cask, CURRANTS, and all sorts of SPICES, to be sold at

Thomas Walley's

Store, Butler's-Row, No. I. ALSO,

Old Jamaica and common West-India RUM, Teneriffe Wine by the Pipe, Hogshead or Quarter Cask. Also, genuine Lisbon Wine, excellent Dum Fish, Citron, Figs, Bolting Cloths, Dutch Looking-Glasses. All sorts of Groceries as usual. All at the lowest Prices for Cash.

N. B. A Quantity of Mustard Seed, and Snuff Bottles, to be sold very cheap.

All Persons having Demands on the Estate of Jonathan Clark, late of Boston, Merchant deceased, and those who are Indebted to said Estate are desired to bring in their Accounts to Ezekiel Lewis, Administrator on said Estate in Order to Settlement.

☞ *A House and a valuable Spot of Land situate in Long Lane, belonging to said Estate, to be sold enquire of said Administrator.* Boston, Nov. 28, 1774.

All Persons who are indebted to the Estate of the late Mr. William Molineux, deceased: Also all Persons who had Demands on, or were indebted to him as Attorney to others, are desired to make them known, and to pay their respective Dues to the Subscriber, who is fully empowered to adjust and receive the same.

THOMAS APTHORP.

All Persons indebted to or having any Demands upon the Estate of THOMAS GRAY, Esq; deceased, are desired to settle the same with

Boston, Nov. 26, 1774. WILLIAM GRAY, ELLIS GRAY, EDWARD GRAY. } Executors.

TO BE SOLD BY

Newell and Hichborn,

At SALEM,

A few Barrels and Half Barrels New PORK.

IF the Person who on the 11th of this Instant took a small Pocket Volume of the Bible, beginning with the Prophet Isaiah, being Part of a Sett neatly bound with blue Morroco Leather, gilt and mark'd 2 on the Back (out of the House in Queen-Street, lately occupied by John Adams, Esq;) will return it to the Place it was taken from, or to the Printers hereof, no Questions shall be ask'd; if not, as the Person is known, he may expect to be expos'd.

TO BE SOLD

About 150 Hogsheads of *St. Martin's* SALT. ALSO,

A Sloop about 84 Tons Burthen, fitted for the Sea. Inquire of the Printers.

Town and Country Shop keepers, Traders, and others are hereby Invited to

Gould's Auction-Office,

In Back-Street,

TO-MORROW Morning, at Ten o'Clock,

Will be Sold by PUBLIC VENDUE,

A very large and valuable Assortment of GOODS, (the Property of Mr. WILLIAM MOLLNEAUX, deceased) —— *Amongst which are* ——

BROAD-CLOTHS, Ratteens, Coatings, Plains, Sagathys, Cambletts, Everlastings, Men's and Women's Worsted Hose, Breeches Patterns, rich Cords, Allopeens, Cotton Caps, Velvet Shapes, figur'd Stuffs, Brocaded Shoes, Hatt Crapes, Tiffany, Laced and plain Hatts; a Quantity of Woolen and Linen Yarn, Wheels, and Reels, one Harpsichord, Beams, Scales and Weights, ; a Parcel of damaged Candles, Swivel Guns. Cohorns, Small Arms and Pistols; a great Variety of Metal Buttons, Table, Cuttoe & Peenknives, Microscopes, Hammers, Pinchers and Nippers of various sorts, Locks, Hinges, Chizzels, Goudges, Escutcheons, &c. Shoe and Knee Buckles, Bellowses, Box Irons, Weaver's Reeds, Snuff Boxes, Spurs, Candlesticks, Copper and Brass Boilers and Kettles, Stew and Sauce Pans, &c. &c. &c.

One Chaise and one Sulky, to be put up at 1 o'Clock

R. GOULD, Auctioneer.

Port of SALEM and MARBLEHEAD.

INWARD ENTRIES,

Bulloch and Bubier from Antigua; Foot and Frost, Gaspee; Folgier, London; Buffinton, Guadaloupe; Lovit, Granada; Lee, Martinico; Gerrish from St. Eustia; Cook and Rich, Canso; Eams, Newfoundland.

OUTWARD BOUND.

Badcock, Wallis, Leighton, Foster, Stone, Higginson and Groves, for Virginia; Landell, Furbeck, Symonds, Osborn and Cleaves, North-Carolina; Davis, Greely, Phelps, Obear and Snow, West-Indies.

Burials in the Town of BOSTON, since our last.

Fifteen Whites. No Blacks.

Baptiz'd in the several Churches, Eight.

High Water at BOSTON, for the present Week.

Monday, 8 min. aft.	1		Friday, 45 min. after.	4
Tuesday, 0 min. aft.	2		Saturday, 33 min. aft.	5
Wednesday, 56 m. aft.	2		Lord's Day, 18 m. af.	6
Thursday, 52 min. aft.	3		D's F. st Q. 10 Day, 1 M.	

Wednesday came on the Election for Members of Parliament for Guildford in Surrey, when Sir Fletcher Norton, and George Onslow, Esq; were chosen without opposition.

A correspondent assures us, that the utmost diligence is using at the Treasury and other public offices; for the safe return of those tried troops at St. Stephens, who understood when to say Aye or No, so exactly.

We are assured, that when the Scarborough man of war left Boston, the situation of that city was very critical, as well as the army. General Gage had offended the inhabitants by refusing for some days to admit some of the supplies from the other colonies: the next offence was took at his proclamation respecting the meetings of the select men. The militia have been exercised in their annual course; and both parties seeming to be apprehensive of the designs of the other, high words had arose; but it is said they proceeded no farther.

Besides the regular trained militia in New-England, all the planters sons and servants are taught to use the fowling piece from their youth, and generally fire single balls with great exactness at fowl or beast. A gentlemen well acquainted with that country is confident the four provinces can muster upwards of 12,000 of these marksmen in forty-eight hours.

Octo. 8. By authentick Letters received by the Scarborough Man of War, in 24 Days from Boston, an Account is brought, that the Massachusetts Province was in a very disordered and tumultuous State, more so than has ever yet been known, occasioned by the late Acts of Parliament respecting that province.

The latest private Letters and News-Papers received are to the 2d of September, which is the Season for the annual Muster of the Militia of that Country. Whether the General, from some Hints given him by Col. Brattle, or from the Jealous Fears so natural to one in his disagreeable Situation, was apprehensive of their doing something more than going through their common Exercise, is uncertain, but he thought proper to demand of Col. Brattle the Provincial Ammunition and Stores under his Care, which were delivered to the General, who then sent two Companies of his Soldiers up the River, by Night, and seized a large Magazine of Powder at the Town of Medford, in which there happened to be a private Property, as well as Provincial, to the latter of which, he, as Captain-General, had a Right. Upon hearing of this, the next Morning the Inhabitants of the neighbouring Towns, to the Amount of several Thousands, as the Letters say, assembled at Cambridge, mostly in Arms, with a Design to go to Boston, where the Powder had been carried and stored, to demand the same, and, if necessary, to attack the Troops; but upon the importunate Solicitations of the principal Gentlemen of the Town, they desisted, and, for that Time, contented themselves with going to the Houses of Mr. Sewall, the Attorney General, Mr. Phips, Colonel of the Provincial Horse, Mr. Hulton, a Commissioner of the Customs, Lieut. Governor Oliver, several of the new Council, and sundry other Crown Officers who they thought had shewn themselves unfriendly to the Province; some of these they obliged to resign, and to declare that they would no more Act under such arbitrary Laws: Others fled for their Lives, and were concealing themselves, from House to House, when these Letters came away, their own Houses being much damaged by the People, and it is said, some pulled down.

Upon opening the Courts at Term Time, the Juries throughout the Province unanimously refused to take the Oaths, or to act at all under their new Judges, and new Laws. The Clerks of the Courts have, in the News-Papers, declared their Sorrow for having issued the Warrants for summoning the said Juries according to the late Acts, and declare they will no more do so, let the Consequence be what it will; that they did not consider what they were about, and that if the People should forgive them, they could never forgive themselves.

The Governor's Company of Cadets, consisting wholly of Gentlemen of the Town, and who are mostly on the Side of Government, disbanded themselves, and returned to General Gage the Standard, which on his Arrival there, he, according to Custom, had presented them with. This was done upon the General's taking away Mr. Hancock's Commission, as Colonel of the Company. Governor Gage shewed himself to be much out of Temper when the Committee returned the Colours, alledging, that Colonel Hancock had used him ill.

Out of the 36 new Counsellors, only 13 had been prevailed with to take the Oaths, and of these five or six had resigned, some voluntarily, others through fear.

But what most irritated the People next to seizing their Arms and Ammunition, was the apprehending six Gentlemen, Select Men of the Town of Salem, who had assembled a Town Meeting, according to the old Custom, though contrary to the new Acts of Parliament, to chuse some publick Officers. Three of them were admitted to Bail, to stand Trial at the next Court, and three were sent to Goal, who on their Arrival, were by the Keeper refused Admittance, and remained under Arrest when the Scarborough sailed.

Yesterday morning his Majesty came to town by nine o'clock from Kew to Buckingham-House, where the Russian Ambassador was waiting his arrival.

A private letter from Hanover, by Yesterday's mail, has the following postscript: "It is reported here, that his Britannic Majesty intends to honor us with his presence, to take a tour thro' his German dominions, and to visit his Royal Sister, before the expiration of the present summer, or very early next spring. This report seems to gain ground, on account of the great preparations which are carrying on at the palace here; nay, several assert, that Baron Lichtenstein and Mr. Vangenheim have already received orders to set out for London, to attend his Majesty both on the voyage and journey."

On Tuesday evening, about seven o'clock, Lord North, on his return to Busby-park, was stopped at the end of Gunnersby-lane by a single highwayman; the postillion refusing to stop, the highwayman fired at him and wounded him, after which he robbed his Lordship of his watch and money

The report of several tons of gunpowder being taken from the Militia at Boston, tho' consisting of 10,000 men, is a ministerial puff of that magnitude, as most people think must be first blown up in the neighbourhood of St. James's.

It is said some disagreeable news is arrived from Boston. At Cambridge, about four miles from Boston, 8000 of the natives assembled before Brigadier Brattle's house and levelled it to the ground. Brattle belongs to the militia, and this outrage was occasion'd by sending word to General Gage that he was in possession of some powder, which the mob would seize if he did not come immediately, and take it into his custody. The same transaction happened at Salem, about twenty miles from Boston. It is also said, that upon Judge Oliver's attempting to sit at the Court-house, the mob pulled him from the bench, and that he was the next day obliged to be guarded by some of the military, while doing his duty as Judge.

Last Friday evening arrived at Spithead his Majesty's ship the Scarborough, Capt. Shad, express from Boston; she was only 24 days in her passage. She had dispatched her letters to town that were for Government a day or two before she arrived at Spithead; the contents of which it is imagined was the cause of the sudden dissolution of Parliament.

The dispatches received by the Scarborough man of war, though arrived five days from Boston, are of such a nature, as are not thought fit to be published. The answer from all the ministerial runners is, "that things are not mended;" from whence it is inferred, by those most conversant in Cabinet Etiquette, *"that things are much worse."*

Oct. 8. *A war, it is said, is inevitable in the North of Europe, designs of a most extraordinary nature being lately discovered to have been in agitation by the Courts of Vienna and Berlin.*

The Commerce, Ferguson, from Virginia, struck on Maidenhead Bank within Dublin Bar, and is since lost.

A Correspondent says he has been informed, by a Gentleman lately arrived from Philadelphia, that when Mr. John Malcomb, an Officer of the Customs at Boston, was leading, tarred and feathered, to the Gallows, with a Rope about his Neck, he was asked by one of the Mob whether he was not thirsty, which was natural to a Man expecting to be hanged. The unfortunate Officer of the Customs, as well as he could speak, answered yes; and immediately a large Bowl of strong Tea was put into his Hands, with Orders to drink the King's Health. Whether it was owing to Loyalty or Thirst is not meterial; poor Malcomb Half emptied the Bowl. He was then told he must mend his Draught, and drink the Queen's Health. Though he had done his utmost for the King, he found he must do something for the Queen; and having taken off Half the Remainder of the Bowl, he presented it back to the Persons from whom he had received it. Hold! hold! cries his Friend, you are not to forget the rest of the Royal Family; come, drink to the Prince of Wales. Replenish, replenish, cries the loyal American; and instantly poor Malcomb saw two Quarts more of what he was heartly sick of. Make Haste, cries another loyal American; you have nine more Healths to drink before you arrive at the Gallows, For God's Sake, Gentlemen, be merciful, I am ready to burst; if I drink a Drop more, I shall die. Suppose you do, cries one of the Mob you die in a good Cause, and it is as well to be drowned as hanged, and immediataly the drenching Horn was put to his Mouth, to the Health of the Bishop of Osnabrug; and, having gone through the other eight, he turned pale, shook his Head, and instantly filled the Bowl which he had just emptied. What, says the American, are you sick of the Royal Family? No, replies Malcomb, my Stomach nauseates the Tea; it rises at it like Poison. And yet, you Rascal, returns the American, your whole Fraternity at the Custom house would drench us with this Poison, and we are to have our Throats cut if it will not stay upon our Stomachs. The merciful Americans desisted, and the Procession was continued towards the Gallows.

NEW-YORK, Nov. 24.

To the PRINTER.

Yesterday was published by Mr. James Rivington, and sold to many people in town, a pamphlet, with the following false, arrogant, and impudent title, viz.

"Free thoughts on the proceedings of the continental congress held at Philadelphia, Sept. 5, 1774, wherein their errors are exhibited, their reasoning confuted, and the fatal tendency of their non-importation, non-exportation, and non-consumption measures, are laid open to the plainest understanding; and the only means pointed out for preserving our present happy constitution. In a letter to the farmers, and other inhabitants of North-America, in general; and to those of the province of New-York in particular. By a farmer—*hear me, for I will speak.*"

The same evening the above pamphlet was read in a company of 20 or 30 inhabitants of this city, who unanimously expressed the utmost abhorrence and detestation of the performance, as being one of the most treacherous, malicious, and wicked productions that has yet appeared, from the implacable enemies of the British colonies and nation.

The author has artfully endeavoured to deceive the ignorant and unwary, and sticks at no falshood to do it; but his reasoning is contemptible, and his conclusions absurd; which will be properly exposed as soon as time will permit—mean while it was with one consent concluded, to treat the pamphlet as it was thought the author deserved to be treated; and it was accordingly committed to the flames.

Since the above, we have just heard that another of the same pamphlets was treated in like manner in another company.—And some others burnt before Mr. Rivington's door. C. D.——

Two of the first mentioned company, by desire of the rest, came down to the Printer, to desire the above account might be published in this day's paper.

CANDLES.

Dipp'd Tallow CANDLES per Box,

at 5*s*. Old Tenor per lb.

Mould Tallow, *Pure* Myrtle Wax, Sperma-Ceti } Candles.

ALSO, TALLOW by the Barrell, Spermaceti OIL for Lamps, and HOG's-FAT, sold by JOHN LANGDON, in Fleet-Street, at the Head of the Hon. JOHN HANCOCK, Esq's; Wharf.

W A N T E D,

About £.1200 Sterling Cash, for which good Real security will be given. Enquire of Edes and Gill.

Gilbert Deblois,

Informs his Customers that he has for Sale at his Shop opposite the Bottom of School-Street,

A very large and compleat Assortment of GOODS,

Suitable for the Season,

very cheap for CASH,

Among which are,

$\frac{8}{4}$, $\frac{9}{4}$, $\frac{10}{4}$, $\frac{11}{4}$, Bed Blankets, Rugs, &c.

Scarlet, blue, white, buff, & other colour'd Broad Cloths,

Blue, scarlet and green Whitneys,

Bath Beavers, Coatings, Lambskins, &c.

White mill'd Flannels and Baizes, Ironing-Cloths,

Wide and narrow Baizes of all Colours and Prices,

A fine Assortment of Womens new fashioned Stuffs,

Choice Cambleteens at 9d Sterl. per Yard,

All Colours and Prices for Camblets or Riding-Hoods,

A great Variety of Silks, for the Ladies,

A compleat Assortment of Hosiery, & mill'd Gloves, some of which suitable for the Gentlemen of the Army & Navy,

Irish Linnens, of all Wedths and Prices,

Cheap Carpets and Carpeting; Calicoes,

China Ware, Loaf-Sugar, Spices, &c.

Looking Glasses,—Scates,—Kippen's Snuff,

Firkin Butter at 6d Sterl. per Pound,

Gold and Silver Laces, &c. &c. *Fifes*, Violins,

French Horns, &c. Swords and Pistols,

German Steel, Barr Lead, Nails,

With almost every other Article of GOODS, Imported to America, from Great-Britain, Scotland and Ireland,

La Composition pour Nettoyer silver Lace, Embroidery and any sort plain and wrought plate.

Boston, Novem. 23, 1774.

ALL Persons indebted to the Estate of WILLIAM WHITE, Esq; late of Boston, deceased, are desired to pay the same to PHILLIPS WHITE of South-Hampton, in the Province of New-Hampshire, Executor of the last Will and Testament of the said WILLIAM WHITE; and those to whom said Estate is indebted are desired to send in their Demands to said Executor.

For the Convenience of many concerned, he purposes to be at Boston from the Sixth Day of December next—Ten Days; from the First Day of February—six Days; and from the Twentieth Day of March—Six Days.

Enquire for the said WHITE, at the Shop of Mrs. *Margarett Phillips*, in Cornhill.

To be sold Part of the Estate of the abovesaid WILLIAM WHITE, at Public Vendue, to the highest Bidder, on Thursday the Eighth Day of December next, viz. The House where the said Deceased lately dwelt, pleasantly situated at the North End of *Boston*, with Brick Store, Stable, Wood-House, &c. Three beautiful Gardens adjoining, &c. &c. and a small Piece of Land near Charlestown-Ferry.—Also a small Dwelling-House in Hull-Street; and a large Store in Queen-Street.——The Vendue to be at last mentioned Store, at Ten o'Clock in the Forenoon of said Day.—The Conditions of Sale to be seen at the Time and Place of Sale.

N. B. The Premises may be viewed on Tuesday and Wednesday preceeding the Day of Sale.

Country Traders & others

(Who purchase with Cash,)

MAY have an Opportunity greatly to their Advantage, by speedily applying at BICKER's Auction Room, near the Market, Boston.——Where is sent for Sale—A fine Parcel of middling and low-priced Broad Cloths, of the most fashionable Colours, which will be sold at too low a Rate.

N. B. A great Variety of other Goods, at private Sale, as cheap as usual.

Made and sold by *Isaac White*,

near the Hay-Market, South-End,

Good Dip'd Tallow-Candles, at 5s. O. T. per Box.

Likewise, Good Mould Tallow and Bayberry-Wax Candles—Also Tallow per Barrel—Good Hard & Soft SOAP.

TO BE SOLD for CASH,

White Flint Glass Ware per Box, *viz.*

Common sorted Crewets & Salts,	}	25 to the Dozen, at
Ditto Tumblers,	}	4*s*. 6*d*. Sterling
Ditto Wine Glasses,	}	per Dozen.

Ditto Mustard-Pots, 25 to the Doz. at 6/6*d*. per Doz.

Per the Crate, Apothecaries green Glass Vials sorted at 10*s*. Sterling per Groce.

Per the Crate, Green Half Pint Dram Bottles, 144 to the Groce, at 10/6*d*. Sterl. per Groce.

Brass Kettles, at 16½ Serling per lb.

Broad Cloths and Worsted Hair Plush, blue, green and scarlet, at the Sterling Cost.

Enquire of Edes & Gill.

A Wet Nurse with a good young Breast of Milk, would take a Child to Suckle. Inquire of Edes and Gill.

Boston: Printed, by EDES & GILL. *in Queen-Street,* 1774.

THE Boston- AND COUNTRY Gazette, JOURNAL.

Containing the freshest Advices, Foreign and Domestic.

No. 1026.

MONDAY, December 12, 1774.

In PROVINCIAL CONGRESS.
Cambridge, December 5, 1774.
RESOLVED,

THAT the Proceedings of the American Continental Congress, held at Philadelphia on the Fifth of September last, and reported by the honourable Delegates from this Colony, have with the Deliberation due to their high Importance been considered by us, and the American Bill of Rights therein contained, appears to be formed with the greatest Ability and Judgment, to be founded on the immutable Laws of Nature and Reason, the Principles of the English Constitution, and respective Charters and Constitutions of the Colonies; and to be worthy of their most vigorous Support, as essentially necessary to Liberty—Likewise the ruinous and iniquitous Measures, which in Violation of these RIGHTS at present convulse and threaten Destruction to America, appear to be clearly pointed out, and judicious Plans adopted for defeating them.

RESOLVED, That the most grateful Acknowledgments are due to the truly honorable and patriotic Members of the Continental Congress, for their wise and able Exertions in the Cause of American Liberty: And this Congress in their own Names, and in Behalf of this Colony, do hereby with the utmost Sincerity express the same.

RESOLVED, That the Hon. JOHN HANCOCK, Hon. THOMAS CUSHING, Esqrs; Mr. SAMUEL ADAMS, JOHN ADAMS, and ROBERT-TREAT PAINE, Esqrs; or any three of them, be, and they hereby are, appointed and authorized to represent this Colony, on the Tenth of May next, or sooner if necessary, at the American Congress to be held at Philadelphia; with full Power with the Delegates from the other American Colonies, to concert, agree upon, direct and order such farther Measures, as shall to them appear to be best calculated for the Recovery and Establishment of American Rights and Liberties, and for the restoring Harmony between Great-Britain and the Colonies.

And whereas it is of the utmost Importance that the salutary Association of the Continental Congress be effectually executed; and the Plans of Foes to America defeated, who, *aided by tyrannical Power*, intend to import Goods, Wares and Merchandize prohibited by the Association, which may clandestinely be vended as Goods imported before the first of December Instant, by Assistance of such Merchants and Traders as to this Intent shall basely prostitute themselves; and it will be extremely difficult to distinguish between Goods imported before the said first of December, and such as after said Day shall, in Violation of the Association, be imported and secretly dispersed throughout the Colony;

And whereas it is expressly recommended by the Continental Congress " to the Provincial Conventions, and to the Committees in the respective Colonies, to establish such farther Regulations as they may think proper, for carrying into Execution their Association,"

RESOLVED, That from and after the Tenth Day of October next, it will be indispensably necessary that all Goods, Wares or Merchandize, directly or indirectly imported from Great-Britain or Ireland, Molasses, Syrups, Paneles, Coffee or Piemento, from the British Plantations or from Dominica; Wines from Madeira or the Western Islands, and foreign Indigo, should cease to be sold or purchased in this Colony, notwithstanding they shall have been imported before the first Day of December aforesaid; unless the Acts and Parts of Acts of Parliament (particularly enumerated in a Paragraph of the American Congress Association subsequent to the fourteenth Article) shall be then repealed. And it is hereby strongly recommended to the Inhabitants of the Towns and Districts in the Colony, that from and after the said Tenth of October, they cease to sell or purchase, and prevent from being exposed to Sale, within their respective Limits, any Goods, Wares, Merchandize, &c. above enumerated, which shall *at any Time* have been imported into America, whether before or after the first of December aforesaid; unless said Acts of Parliament shall be then repealed.

And it is likewise strongly recommended to the Committees of Inspection (which ought immediately to be chosen agreeably to the said Association by each Town and District in the Colony, not having already appointed such Committees) that they exert themselves in causing the Association as thereby directed, to be strictly executed. And that after the said Tenth Day of October (unless the Acts of Parliament aforesaid are repealed) they apply to all the Merchants and Traders in their respective Towns and Districts, and take a full Inventory of all the Goods, Wares and Merchandize aforesaid in their Possession, whether they shall have been Imported before or after the First of December aforesaid; requiring them to offer no more for Sale, until said Acts shall be repealed. And if any Merchant, Trader or others, shall refuse to have an Inventory taken, or shall offer for Sale after the said Tenth of October, any such Goods, Wares or Merchandize; it is expressly recommended to the Committees aforesaid, that they take the Goods into their Possession, to be Stored at the Risk of the proper Owners, until the Repeal of the Acts aforesaid, and Publish the Names of such refractory Merchants, Traders or Purchasers, that they may meet with the Merits of Enemies to their Country. And the Towns and Districts throughout the Province are also advised, that they by no Means fail vigorously to assist and support their Committees, in discharging this as well as the other Duties of their Offices, and to Cause this Resolution to be Executed by every Measure which they shall think necessary.

Signed by Order of the Provincial Congress,
JOHN HANCOCK, *President.*
A true Extract from the Minutes,
BENJAMIN LINCOLN, *Secretary.*

WILLIAMSBURG in Virginia, Nov. 10. This afternoon the whole body of merchants at present in this city, supposed to be between four and five hundred, waited upon the honorable PEYTON RANDOLPH, Esq; and the rest of the Delegates of this colony assembled at the capitol, and presented the following ADDRESS:

To the Honorable PEYTON RANDOLPH, Esq; Moderator, and the other DELEGATES of the People of Virginia, who assembled at the Capitol, in Williamsburg, on Wednesday the 9th of November 1774.
The Address of the MERCHANTS, TRADERS, and others, at a general Meeting in Williamsburg.

" GENTLEMEN,

" YOUR generous and voluntary interposition, at a time when we were under apprehensions that some measures would be adopted derogatory to the importance of the cause we wish to support with propriety, and contrary to the intention of the General Congress, and by your wisdom and prudence pointing out such methods of proceeding as have removed our fears, and given universal satisfaction, demands our most grateful acknowledgment.

Truly sensible of the necessity of preserving peace and harmony, not only between the different colonies, but also among all ranks and societies in each colony, and to show our readiness to concur in such prudent measures as are most likely to procure a redress of our grievances, we now present the association, voluntarily and generally signed; and as we, on our parts, resolve to adhere strictly thereto, we hope to be favoured with your advice and assistance on every future emergency."

To which they received the following ANSWER.

" GENTLEMEN,

" It gives us great satisfaction to find that our conduct has received the approbation of your respectable body, and you may be assured we shall on all occasions endeavour to move on the first principles of justice and the constitution. The delegates are very sensible of the great advantage this country will receive from your union with them, and they consider it as very meritorious that you, disregarding the influence of your commercial interest, have generously concurred with them in the great struggle for liberty. Such unanimity, we trust, will convince an inimical administration of the imprudence of their measures, and produce effects so salutary as to make us reflect with pleasure on the part we have taken in support of American freedom."

NEW LONDON, December, 2.

The Town of East Hampton on Long-Island, have laid a Tax upon the Town sufficient to raise One Hundred Pounds New York Currency, for the support of the industrious Poor in Boston. And.

A Subscription is also set on Foot in every Parish through the County of Suffolk, on Long Island, to raise Donations for the same laudable Purpose, a Committee appointed in each Parish to receive the same, and Instructions given to John Foster, Esq; of Southampton to collect such Grain, Flax, &c. as should be subscribed, and transport the same to Boston in the Month of March next.

THE Committees of Correspondence for the Towns of New London and Groton, being informed that Mr. *Philip Dumaresq*, Merchant of *Boston*, who was one of the Addressers to Gov. *Hutchinson*, arrived at New-London, last Evening, and put up at Mr. Thomas Allen's Innholder:—Thereupon we waited on said Mr. *Dumaresq*, at 9 o'Clock, A. M. and informed him that it would be disagreeable to the Inhabitants of the abovesaid Towns for him to continue long in said New-London:—and entered into a free Conversation with him relative to said Address. He assured us that he was sorry he ever signed it, and gave us the underwritten Declaration which was well approved of by said Committees.

New London, Nov. 29, 1774.

New London, November 29, 1774.

WHEREAS I signed an Address to Governor *Hutchinson*, in which I had no other View than the Welfare of *Great-Britain* and her Colonies, a Reconciliation between which I imagined would be forwarded thereby,—but being now sensible that it was an Error, am sorry that I signed it, and hope this sincere Declaration will reinstate me in the Favor of all true Friends to the Constitution of both Countries.

PH. DUMARESQ.

In Provincial Congress.

Cambridge, December 9, 1774.

RESOLVED,

THAT it is the clear Opinion of this Congress, that the first Article in the Association of the Continental Congress extends to all Goods, Wares and Merchandizes of the Growth, Production or Manufacture of any part of Europe, or any other part of the World, Imported from Great Britain or Ireland, in Case they have been Entred and Cleared in any Port of either of those Kingdoms, as fully as to Goods, Wares and Merchandizes of the Growth, Production & Manufactures of Great Britain or Ireland, and that the said first Article ought to be so construed by all concerned, and in that universal sense carried strictly into Execution.

Signed by Order of the Provincial Congress.

JOHN HANCOCK, President.

A true Extract from the Minutes,

BENJAMIN LINCOLN, Secretary.

In *Provincial Congress*, Cambridge, *Dec.* 10, 1774.

WHEREAS Attempts may be made by the inveterate Enemies of America to excite and raise Jealousies, if possible, among the Colonies, now happily united, relative to the Association of the Continental Congress, and as the Mode of selling Goods imported after the first Instant and before the first of February next, is not in the Tenth Article of the Association particularly pointed out, and some Doubts may arise relative to the same: Therefore,

Resolved, That it be and is hereby recommended to the Committees of Inspection in this Colony, that in carrying the Association aforesaid into Execution, they be careful to Conduct with the utmost Openess and Fairness; and particularly that in selling Goods imported from Great-Britain as above recited, they cause the same to be Advertized in the Boston and Salem News-Papers, at least ten Days before they shall be sold, and that they dispose of them to such Person or Persons as will give the highest Price.

Signed by Order of the Provincial Congress,

JOHN HANCOCK, President.

A true Extract from the Minutes.

BENJAMIN LINCOLN, Secretary.

In *Provincial Congress, Cambridge, Dec.* 10, 1774.

To the FREEHOLDERS *and other* INHABITANTS *of the Towns and Districts of* Massachusetts Bay.

FRIENDS and BRETHREN,

AT a Time when the good People of this Colony were deprived of their Laws, and the Administration of Justice, civil and criminal; when the cruel Oppressions brought on their Capital had stagnated almost all their Commerce; when a standing Army was illegally posted among us for the express Purpose of enforcing Submission to a System of Tyranny; and when the General Court was with the same Design prohibited to sit; we were chosen and empowered by you to assemble and consult upon Measures necessary for our common Safety and Defence.

With much Anxiety for the common Welfare, we have attended this Service; and upon the coolest Deliberation have adopted the Measures recommended to you.

We have still Confidence in the Wisdom, Justice and Goodness of our Sovereign, as well as the Integrity, Humanity and good Sense of the Nation: And if we had a reasonable Expectation that the Truth of Facts would be made known in England, we should entertain the most pleasing Hopes that the Measures concerted by the Colonies, jointly and severally, would procure a full Redress of our Grievances: But we are constrained in Justice to You, to Ourselves and Posterity, to say, that the incessant and unrelenting Malice of our Enemies, has bean so succesful as to fill the Court and Kingdom of Great Britain with Falshoods and Calumnies concerning us, and to excite the most bitter and groundless Prejudices against us; that the sudden Dissolution of Parliament, and the hasty Summons for a new Election, gives us Reason to apprehend that a Majority of the House of Commons will be again elected under the Influence of an arbitrary Ministry; and that the general Tenor of our Intelligence from Great-Britain, with the frequent Reinforcements of the Army and Navy at Boston, excites the strongest Jealousy that the System of Colony Administration, so unfriendly to the Protestant Religion, and destructive of American Liberty, is still to be pursued, and attempted with Force to be carried into Execution.

You are placed by Providence in the Post of Honor, because it is a Post of Danger—And while struggling for the noblest Objects, *the Liberties of your Country*, the *Happiness of Posterity*, and *Rights of human Nature*, the Eyes not only of North-America and the whole British Empire, but of all Europe, are upon you—Let us be therefore altogether solicious, that no disorderly Behaviour, nothing unbecoming our Characters as Americans, as Citizens, and Christians, be justly chargeable to us.

Whoever with a small Degree of Attention, contemplates the Commerce between Great Britain and America, will be convinced that a total Stoppage thereof will soon produce in Great-Britain such dangerous Effects, as cannot fail to convince the Ministry, Parliament and People, That it is their Interest and Duty to grant us Relief. Whoever considers the Number of brave Men inhabiting North-America will know, that a general Attention to Military Discipline, must so establish their Rights and Liberties, as under God, to render it impossible for an arbitrary Ministry of Britain to destroy them. These are Facts which our Enemies are apprised of, and if they will not be influenced by Principles of Justice, to alter their cruel Measures towards America, these ought to lead them thereto. They however hope to effect by Statagem what they may not obtain by Power, and are using Arts, by Assistance of base Scribblers, who undoubtedly receive their Bribes, and by many other Means, to raise Doubts & Divisions thro'out the Colonies, to defeat their iniquitous Designs. We think it necessary for each Town to be particularly careful strictly to execute the Plans of the Continental and Provincial Congresses; and while it censures its own Individuals, counteracting these Plans, that it be not deceived or diverted from its Duty by Rumours, should any take Place, to the Prejudice of other Communities. Your Provincial Congresses we have Reason to hope will HOLD UP the Towns, if any should be so lost as not to act their Parts, and none can doubt that the Coutinental Congresses will rectify Errors should any take Place in any Colony thro' the Subtilty of our Enemies—Surely no Arguments can be necessary to excite you to the most strict Adherance to the American Association, since the minutest Deviation in one Colony, especially in this, will probably be misrepresented in the others, to discourage their general Zeal and Perseverance, which however we assure ourselves cannot be effected.

Whilst the British Ministry are suffered with so high a Hand to tyrannize over America, no Part of it we presume can be negligent in guarding against the Ravages threatened by the Standing Army now in Boston; these Troops will undoubtedly be employed in Attempts to defeat the Association, which our Enemies cannot but fear will eventually defeat them; and so sanguinary are those our Enemies, as we have Reason to think, so thirsty for the Blood of this innocent People, who are only contending for their Rights, that we should be guilty of the most unpardonable Neglect, should we not apprize you of your Danger, which appears to us imminently great, and ought attentively to be guarded against. The Improvement of the Militia in general in the Art Military has been therefore thought necessary and strongly recommended by this Congress. We now think that particular Care should be taken by the Towns and Districts in this Colony, that each of the Minute Men not already provided therewith, should be immediately equipped with an effective Fire Arm, Bayonet, Pouch, Knapsack, Thirty Rounds of Cartridges and Ball, and that they be disciplined three Times a Week, and oftner as Opportunity may offer—To encourage these our worthy Countrymen to obtain the Skill of compleat Soldiers, We recommend it to the Towns and Districts forthwith to pay their own Minute Men a reasonable Consideration for their Services——And in Case of a general Muster, their farther Services must be recompenced by the Province—An Attention to discipline the Militia in general is however by no Means to be neglected.

With the utmost Chearfulness we assure you of our Determination to stand or fall with the Liberties of America; and while we humbly implore the sovereign Disposer of all Things, to whose divine Providence the Rights of his Creatures cannot be indifferent, to correct the Errors, and alter the Measures of an infatuated Ministry, We cannot doubt of his Support even in the extream Difficulties which we all may have to encounter. May all Means devised for our Safety by the general Congresses of America and Assemblies or Conventions of the Colonies be resolutely executed, and happily succeeded; and may this injured People be reinstated in the full Exercise of their Rights without the Evils and Devastations of a civil War.

Signed by Order of the Provincial Congress,

JOHN HANCOCK, *President.*

A true Extract from the Minutes,

BENJAMIN LINCOLN, *Secretary.*

In *Provincial Congress, Cambridge Dec.* 10, 1774.

INASMUCH as many States have been taught by fatal Experience, that Powers delegated by the People for long Periods have been abused to the endangering the Public Rights and Liberties: And this Congress having just Reason to suppose, that their Constituents, the good People of this Province, when they appointed their present Delegates, were not apprehensive that the Business necessary to be done would require their Attendance for any long Time,

Resolved, That the Adjournment of this Congress on the Twenty ninth Day of October last, was ordered and made from a due Consideration of the pressing Exigencies of the publick Affairs, and the evident Necessity of further Deliberation thereon.

And whereas for the Reason first mentioned it is not expedient that there should be a fruther Adjournment of this Congress; therefore Resolved, that after the Business necessary to be immediately dispatch'd shall be finished, the Congress be dissolved.

And this Congress being deeply impressed with a Sense of the increasing Dangers which threaten the Rights and Liberties of the People of this Province with total Ruin; our Adversaries being still indefatigable in their Attempts to carry into Execution their deep-laid Plans for that wicked Purpose: And considering the indispensable Necessity that an Assembly of the Province should be very frequently Sitting, to Consult and Devise Measures for their common Safety; Therefore

Resolved, That it be, and it is hereby earnestly recommended to the several Towns and Districts in this Province, that each of them do forthwith Elect and Depute as many Members as to them shall seem necessary and expedient, to Represent them in a Provincial Congress, to be held at Cambridge on the First Day of February next ensuing; to be chosen by such only as are Qualified by Law to Vote for Representatives in the General Assembly, and be continued by Adjournments, as they shall see Cause, untill the Tuesday next preceeding the last Wednesday in May next, and no longer; to Consult, Deliberate and Resolve upon such further Measures, as, under God, shall be effectual to save this People from impending Ruin, and to secure those inestimable Liberties, derived to us from our Ancestors, and which it is our Duty to preserve for Posterity.

And considering the great Uncertainty of the present Times, and that unexpected important Events may take place, from whence it may be absolutely necessary that the Delegates who may be Elected as above propos'd should meet sooner than the Day afore mentioned, it is recommended to the several Towns and Districts, that they Instruct and Authorize their said Delegates, to Assemble at Cambridge aforesaid, or any other place, upon Notice given them of the Necessity thereof, by the Delegates that may be chosen by the Towns of Charlestown, Cambridge, Brookline, Roxbury and Dorchester, or the Majority of them, in such Way as they shall judge proper. And it is further Recommended to the Delegates to be elected, that they Conform themselves to such Instructions.

Signed by Order of the Provincial Congress,

JOHN HANCOCK, President.

A true Extract from the Minutes.

BENJAMIN LINCOLN, Secretary.

[*The Association sent by Brigadier Ruggles, &c. to the Town of* Hardwick, *&c. together with his Son's Certificate thereof, and the Resolve of the Provincial Congress thereon, must be referr'd 'till our next.*]

B R I C K S.

FOUR HUNDRED THOUSAND BRICKS, Manufactured by the distressed, industrious Poor of the Town of Boston, assisted by the generous Donations of our benevolent and sympathizing Brethren of this and the other Colonies, and are to be sold for their farther Relief and Employment, by *Thomas Crafts*, jun. near Liberty-Tree.

JUST PUBLISHED,

[*Price* 1s. 4.]

And to be Sold by *John Kneeland*, Printer, in Milk-Street; *James Foster Condy*, Stationer, in Union-Street; and *Philip Freeman*, jun. near Liberty-Tree.

AN ORATION delivered on the

late public Commencement at Rhode-Island College in Providence, September 1774. Being a Plea for the Right of private Judgment in religious Matters; and for the Liberty of choosing our own Religion, corroborated by the well known Consequences of Priestly Power.

BY BARNABAS BINNEY, A. B.

PUBLIC AUCTION,

TO BE SOLD.

By *BENJAMIN CHURCH*,

At his usual Place of Sale,

TO-MORROW EVENING,

Broad-Cloths—plains—Bearskin——

Camblets—Stuffs—Irish Hollands—Checks—Bed Ticks—Handkerchiefs, &c. A Mahogany Case of Draws—Beareau—Desk—side Boards—Beds—Easy Chairs, and others, &c. &c.

TO-MORROW EVENING.

Salmon Twine.

JEREMIAH ALLEN has for Sale at his Shop in Ann-Street, a little North of the Draw Bridge——A Quantity of the best 3-Thread Salmon Twine. (6w.)

Joshua Blanchard,

AT the Old Shop and Wine Cellar on Dock-Square BOSTON, opposite Exchange,

yet continues to sell

W I N E S

of all Sorts as usual, and hath now on Sale a Parcel of fine old Serling Madeira from 3 Dollars to 8 Dollars per Dozen according to its Age and Quality; also by the Gallon or less Quantity, Fyal Wine at 25s. Old Tenor per Gallon, a better Sort on Maderia Lees at 30s. O. T.

West-India Proof genuine Rum.

Fine old Spirit, French and other Brandies.

Mr. BLANCHARD *thanks his Friends and the Publick for past Favours, and hopes in these hard Times their Continuance.*

He hath also to sell,

Cocoa, Loaf-Sugar, Raisins, Figgs, Currants, Spices, with a general Assortment of West-India Goods and Groceries, by Wholesale or Retail.

A Quantity of choice Honey,

All Persons who have any Demands on the Estate of Nathaniel Holmes, of Boston, deceased, are desired to bring in their Accounts to Rebecca Holmes, Executrix, for Adjustment: All those who are indebted to said Estate are desired to make immediate Payment to said Executrix.

William Fowle,

ACQUAINTS the Public, That he carries on the Sugar Baking Business, at the Sugar-House formerly Occupied by the late Nathaniel Holmes, deceased.

——Where he has ready for Sale——

Best double, single, and Lump Refin'd Loaf and brown SUGAR, MOLASSES, FLOUR and IRON, by Wholesale or Retail, cheap for Cash.

B O S T O N, December 12.

At a Meeting of the Freeholders and other Inhabitants of the Town of Boston, at Faneuil-Hall, on Wednesday the 7th Instant, by adjournment.

THE following Committee of 63 Persons were appointed to carry into Execution in the Town of *Boston*, the *Agreement* and *Association* of the late respectable CONTINENTAL CONGRESS.

Hon. Thomas Cushing, Esq; Hon. John Hancock, Esq; Mr. Samuel Adams, William Phillips, Esq; Col. Marshall, Mess. John Pitts, Oliver Wendell, and Samuel Austin, Benjamin Austin, Esq; Caleb Davis, Esqrs. Mess. William Davis and William Whitwell, Samuel Barrett and Jonathan Mason, Esqs; Capt. John Bradford, Mr. John Brown, Mr. William Powell, Major Boynton, Ezekiel Cheever, Esq; Captain Edward Proctor, Messrs. James Ivers, Ebenezer Hancock, William Greenleaf, Samuel Whitwell, Herman Brimmer, Martin Brimmer, and Peter Boyer, Dr. Benjamin Church, Dr. Joseph Warren, Joseph Greenleaf, Esq; Capt. Benjamin Waldo, Capt. John Pulling, Henry Bromfield, Esq; Mess. Paul Revere, John Winthrop and Samuel Pitts, Capt. Abiel Ruddock, Dr. Charles Jarvis, Thomas Chase, Major Nathaniel Barber, Capt. Fortesque Vernon, Capt. Job Prince, Capt. Hopkins, Mr. Moses Gill, Mr. Thomas Boylston, Capt. John Marston, Major Newman Greenough, Mess. Moses Grant, Ja. Foster Condy, Cyrus Baldwin, Bosinger Foster, Isaac Pierce, Enoch Brown, Joseph Eayres and Henry Bass, Capt. Samuel Patridge, Mr. Joshua Bracket, Jonathan Williams, Esq; Mr. Edward Davis, Capt. Eleazer Johnson, Mess. Elias Parkman and John Avery, Dr. Nathaniel Noyes.

Seven of whom are to be a Quorum.

At the above Meeting the following Gentlemen viz. Jonathan Williams, Esq; Moderator pro. tem. the Hon. James Otis, Esq; Dr. Benjamin Church, Dr. Joseph Warren, Mr. John Pitts, Joseph Greenleaf, Esq; and Mr. William Cooper, were appointed a Committee to draught a Vote of Thanks of the Town of Boston, expressive of their Gratitude for the benevolent Assistance which they have received from the other Colonies, during their present Calamities and particularly for the generous Recommendation of the respectable Continental Congress for further Support from their Colonies during their unhappy Struggle under the arbitrary and oppressive Measures of the present British Administration.

It is humbly recommended to the several Towns through this Province, as a Matter well worthy their Attention, that each Town publish and distribute as many of the Association Papers, as will serve every Master of a Family in each Town, who will then have his Duty plainly before him, and enable him to assist the several Committees that may be appointed for executing the noble Resolutions adopted by the Grand American Congress, for the Salvation of our Country. The Town of Weymouth have ordered a Number of these Papers to be published and every Man to be supplied therewith. This laudable Example it is to hoped, will be follow'd by every Town through this Province and Continent.

We learn from undoubted Authority, That Lord Dartmouth, Secretary of State, has wrote a circular Letter to the Governors upon this Continent, informing them, That his Majesty has thought fit, by his Order in Council, dated the 19th October 1774, to prohibit the Exportation from Great Britain, of Gun Powder or any Sort of Arms or Ammunition, and has signified to them his Majesty's Command, that they do take the most effectual Measures for arresting, detaining and securing any Gun Powder or any Sort of Arms or Ammunition, which may be attempted to be imported into the Province over which they respectively preside, unless the Masters of the Ship having such Military Stores on Board shall produce a Licence from his Majesty or the Privy Council for the Exportation of the same from some of the Ports of Great-Britain.

Our Brethren in the Country are cautioned to beware of false Brethren, as there are unfortunately such in almost every Town. Could we possibly conceive that such a Monster of Perfidy should inhabit any Town of this Province, as to become a Spy and base Betrayer of his Brethren, when they are struggling to redeem not only themselves, but the very Miscreant who abets the Conspiracy against them from the foul Fiend of Tyranny? I weep for the Degeneracy of my Countrymen! Reflect ye miserable Hirelings! on the necessary Consequences of your Apostacy at this distressing Juncture; and ye base Deserters of your Country's Cause, who are in League with the Enemies of America, who are preparing to revolt & cut the Throats of your Brethren, should the Hour of Hazard ever arrive; ye are known; our Abhorrence of your Conduct is enkindled, do not urge our Patience too far, the Hour of Vengeance comes louring on, the Hand of Desperation may urge a Stroke fatal to the Bosom that could harbour such infernal Designs: Ye Sons of Pet——m, W——r, W——n, &c. hear and forbear, and do no more so wickedly.

On Thursday last died here, Mrs. *Elizabeth Read*, aged 87. Her Funeral will be To-Morrow at Half after Three o'Clock, from the House of her Daughter, Mrs. Pierce in Sudbury-Street.—Her Friends and Acquaintance are desired to attend.

Saturday evening last departed this life after a short illness, Mr. William Hickling, a noted Distiller in this town, in the 71st year of his age; a man who in the long course of an effected life manifested all the virtues that dignify a private station.——His funeral will go from his late dwelling at West Boston on Wednesday, at half past three afternoon, where his friends and acquaintance are desired to attend.

Friday last died at Roxbury much lamented, Mr. BENJAMIN MAY, in the 67th Year of his Age; he was a truly respectable Member of Society—he was zealously attached to the Cause of his Country, and so deeply Concerned for it's Welfare, that perceiving his Strength was almost exhausted, he called his Friends round him about half an Hour before his Death, and earnestly requested them not to infringe the Resolutions taken for saving the Country, but in all Things relating to his Funeral, to adhere strictly to the Advice of the Continental Congress.

Donations receiv'd since our last.

NEW-HAMPSHIRE.

Londonderry, East & West Parishes, £. 45 11 10

MASSACHUSETTS-BAY.

North-Yarmouth, 35 Cords of Wood.

RHODE-ISLAND.

Newport, Cash. - - - - - 151 5 6

CONNECTICUT.

Waterbury, 52 Bushels Grain, and 3 Barrels Rye Flour.

PENSYLVANIA.

Philadelphia, 256 Barrels Flour.
105 Ship Stuff.

MARYLAND.

Talbot and Dorset Counties, 1641½ Bushels Grain.

The Public are hereby informed, that since our last Advertisement another Soldier of the 59th Regiment and a young Child, with the Small Pox, have been sent from the Barracks on Deane's Wharff to the Hospital at New-Boston; where due Care is taken to prevent a Communication of the Infection.

By Order of the Select-Men,

Boston, Dec. 11. WILLIAM COOPER, Town-Clerk.

General Post-Office, New-York 5th Dec. 1774.

The Deputy Post Masters General being desirous of faciliating Correspondence, have ordered that in Time to come there should be two Posts Weekly, for Canada, by way of Albany: Notice is hereby given, that from and after the 14th Day of December Instant, the Mails for Canada and Albany will be made up and dispatched from this Office on Wednesdays at 11 o'Clock in the Forenoon, and at 9 every Saturday Night. The Wednesdays Post will ride on the East Side of Hudson's River, and return to this Office with the Canada Mail on the Tuesday following, at 4 o'Clock in the Afternoon. The Saturday Night's Mail is to be conveyed to Albany, on the West Side of the River, and the Rider will return to this Office on the Saturday following at 12 o'Clock.

By Command of the Deputy Post Masters General.

RICH. N. COLDEN, D. Secr'y.

The most ancient and benevolent Order of the Friendly Brothers of St. *Patrick*.

THE principal Knot of the 47th Regiment, is to meet on Friday next, the 16th Instant, at the British Coffee-House.

Dinner to be on the Table at Three o'Clock.

By Order of the President,

J H F C S P K 47th Rt.

Such continued regular Friendly Brothers as chuse to visit the Knot, are requested to leave their Names at the Barr before Thursday Noon.

Stray'd away from me the Subscriber, in Newton, sometime in July last, a spotted or placked black and white Steer, two Years old. Whoever shall take up the said Steer, or give Information where he may be had, shall be handsomely rewarded by me, JOHN HEALY.

To be Sold by PUBLIC VENDUE,

On WEDNESDAY *the 22d Day of* March *next*,

At Eleven o'Clock Beforenoon, at the Royal-Exchange Tavern in King-Street, Boston, pursuant to a Vote of the Proprietors of the *Kennebeck*-*Purchase* from the late Colony of *New-Plymouth*, passed the Sixteenth Day of *November* last:

The following Tract of Land to be set up in undivided Twelfths, at 100l. L. M. for each Twelfth, being about 6000 Acres to a Twelfth.

A Tract of Land situated North-West from Fort-Halifax, and lying on each side of Little Norridgwalk River, and within 15 Miles of Kennebeck River, on the West side thereof, containing about 72000 Acres.

Provided nevertheless that if any Proprietor of the said Kennebeck Purchase shall chuse to retain his Share of the said Tract, and shall on or before Wednesday the 15th Day of March next, pay to Henry Alline, jun. Clerk of said Proprietors, his Proportion of 1200l. L. M. which is 100l. L. M. to one Twelfth, and so more or less, according to his Share or Interest in said Propriety, then such Share or Interest of the said Tract shall be reserved to him, but if Payment be not made on the said 15th Day of March next, then the whole of said Tract will be sold on said 22d Day of March next, without such Reservation. By Order of said Proprietors.

HENRY ALLINE, jun. Prop's Clerk.

Boston, December 10, 1774.

To-Morrow Morning at XI o'Clock,
Will be sold by Public Vendue, at Russell's Auction Room, Queen Street,

A few Casks of choice fresh Raisins.

J. RUSSELL, Auctioneer.

On WEDNESDAY next,
At ONE o'Clock, will be sold by Public Vendue, at the Bunch of Grapes, King-Street,

A few Half-Pipes Madeira WINE, one Cask and two Cases of Claret Wine.

J. RUSSELL, Auctioneer.

THE Brethren of the ancient and honorable Society of FREE and ACCEPTED MASONS are hereby notified; That the most Worshipful JOSEPH WARREN, Esq; Grand Master of Ancient, Free and Accepted Masons on the Continent of America, intends celebrating the Feast of St. John the Evangelist on Tuesday the 27th Instant, at Free Masons Hall, Boston, where the Brethren are required to attend the Festival.

By Order of the most Worshipful Grand Master,

W. HOSKINS, G. Secretary.

N.B. The Table will be furnished at 2 o'Clock, P.M. --Tickets to be had of Brothers Capt Caleb Hopkins, Andrew Newell, and William Hoskins.

Boston, Dec. 13, 1774.

T O B E S O L D *very cheap*,

The Schooner Hawk, about 65 Tons burthen, a Marblehead Fishing Vessel with a Sheath'd Bottom, good Sails and Rigging, lying at Mr. John Pulling's Wharff.——For Particulars inquire at

Archibald Cunningham's

Store in Ann-Street, near the Draw-Bridge.

——Where is to be sold——

Lisbon WINE per Cask,—Lisbon Oil per Cask,—Geneva per Case,—Raisins, Figs and Currants per Cask,—Firkin Butter,—Kippen's Snuff and Pig-Tail Tobacco,—Spices of all sorts,—Citron,—half Pint Dram Bottles per Crate or Groce,—Almonds,—choice Olives,—Capers,—Brown & Loaf Sugar,—Dutch Brushes in Setts or single,—Dutch Stone Ware per Crate or Dozen,—Corks,—Mason Glasses Engrav'd with the Arms,—best Durham Mustard in large and small Bottles,—Barcelona Handkerchiefs per Dozen.

TO BE SOLD, only for Want of Employ,

A likely, sprightly good-tempered Negro Boy, about 13 Years of Age. Inquire of Edes and Gill.

New Auction-Room, *Cornhill*.

To-Morrow Morning at Ten o'Clock,
Will be Sold, by PUBLIC VENDUE,
At GREENLEAF's Auction-Room,

A great Assortment of valuable Goods (part of which are Consignments from abroad, and the remainder belonging to some Gentlemen leaving the Province)

Consisting of,

SUperfine, midling and low priz'd broad cloths, mixt hunters, forest cloths, plains, kerseys, beaver coatings, crimson and black plushes, a few blankets, Wilton and Scotch carpeting, shalloons, water'd tammies, mens, womens and childrens worsted hose, black and cloth coloured breeches pieces, corded poplins, allopeens, surtout and coat buttons, a box of well assorted ribbons, in a lot, silk muffs, silver wire and cord, fine plain lawns, knives and forks with cases, a parcel of Holland shirts partly damaged, and many other articles, &c.

Wm. GREENLEAF, Auctioneer.

The Sale will begin at Ten o'Clock.

Gould's Auction-Office,

In Back-Street,
TO-MORROW Morning, at Ten o'Clock,
Will be sold by PUBLIC VENDUE,

A large and valuable Assortment of British and American Goods (the Property of Mr. WILLIAM MOLINEAUX, deceased)—*Amongst which are*,—

BRoad Cloths, Kerseys, Half-Thicks, Sagathees, Camblets, Everlastings, Men and Womens Worsted Hose, Breeches Patterns, worsted and silk Knee Garters, rich Cords, Allopeens, Bedtickings, Cotton Caps, check linnen and lawn Handkerchiefs, Hatts, Table Cuttoe and Penknives, Velvet Clogs, Stays, Snail and Gown Trimmings, Ribbons, Beams Scales and Weights, a Quantity of Linnen, Woolen and Carpeting Yarn, Box Irons, Knippers, Escutcheons, three large Coppers fit for Dying, Brewing, &c. Copper Pots, Boilers, Kettles and Sauce-Pans. Reels and Wheels, two 8 Day Clocks, Hot-Bed Glasses, a Quantity of old Iron, a Number of Iron-Bound Pipes, Puncheons, &c. plated and common Buckles, Dutch Pocket Glasses, one Lot of Pistols, &c.

Also, Feather Beds, Bedsteads, Curtains, Looking-Glasses, Bureaus, Tables, Chairs, &c.

R. GOULD, Auctioneer.

N. B. As this is the last Sale that will be kept at this Office this Season, and there being a large Assortment of Goods, which must absolutely be sold off—We would request our former kind Customers and others, to add to the many Favours already received, this of giving us their Attendance To-Morrow.

Burials in the Town of BOSTON, since our last.

Fifteen Whites. Two Blacks.

Baptiz'd in the several Churches, Six.

High Water at BOSTON, *for the present Week.*

Monday, 8 min. aft. 1	Friday, 46 min. after, 4
Tuesday, 0 min. aft. 2	Saturday, 33 min. aft. 5
Wednesday 56 m. aft. 2	Lord's Day, 18 m. af. 6
Thursday, 52 min. aft. 3	)'s First Q. 10 Day, M.

WILLIAMSBURG, (Virginia) November 10.

The Hon. Peyton Randolph, Esq; has received the following Letter from General GAGE, in answer to that wrote to him by the General Congress, on the 10th of Oct. last.

To the Hon. PEYTON RANDOLPH, Esq;

SIR, *Boston, Oct. 20, 1774.*

REPRESENTATIONS should be made with candour, and matters stated exactly as they stand. People would be led to believe, from your letter to me of the 10th inst. that works were raised against the town of Boston, private property invaded, the soldiers suffered to insult the inhabitants, & the communication between the town and country shut up and molested.

Nothing can be farther from the true situation of this place than the above stats. There is not a single gun pointed against the town, no man's property has been seized or hurt, except the king's, by the people's destroying straw, bricks, &c. bought for his service. No troops have given less cause for complaint, and greater care was never taken to prevent it; and such care and attention was never more necessary, from the insults and provocations daily given to both officers and soldiers. The communication between the town and country has been always free and unmolested, and is so still.

Two works of earth have been raised at some distance from the town, wide of the roads, and guns put in them. The remains of old works, going out of the town, have been strengthened, and guns placed there likewise. People will think differently, whether the hostile preparations throughout the country, and the menaces of blood and slaughter, made this necessary. But I am to do my duty.

It gives me pleasure that you are endeavouring at a cordial reconciliation with the mother country; which from what has transpired, I have despaired of. Nobody wishes better success to such measures than myself. I have endeavoured to be a mediator, if I could establish a foundation to work upon; and have strongly urged it to people here to pay for the tea, and send a proper memorial to the king, would be a good beginning on their side, and give their friends the opportunity they seek, to move in their support.

I do not believe that menaces and unfriendly proceedings will have the effect which many conceive. The spirit of the British nation was high when I left England, and such measures will not abate it. But I should hope that decency and moderation here would create the same disposition at home; and I ardently wish that the common enemies to both countries may see to their disappointment, that these disputes between the mother country and the colonies have terminated like the quarrels of lovers, and increased the affection which they ought to bear to each other.

I am, Sir,
Your most obedient humble servant,
THOMAS GAGE.

L O N D O N.

Sept. 10. The following authentic intelligence is a striking instance of the decay of our manufactories.—— Mess. Mauduit and Wright, for many years successively have bought in Wivelscomb, Semerset, between February and the end of June, three thousand pieces of the manufactory of that place, which were sent to North-America; but this season their number has not exceeded two hundred. When Mr. Mauduit or his partner visited the town, which was almost annually, the bells rang and there was a grand festival, but now the scene is sadly changed.

At a chapel at the west end of the town, the preacher in his prayer on Sunday last mentioned the Americans, praying that God would awaken them to a sense of religion, and that they might, after the example of their forefathers, who carried their lives in their hands, might be strengthened in supporting their privilege as men, and as free-born Britons, approving themselves the posterity of such who sought liberty to that wild desart, rather than submit to slavery at home.

Octo. 14. *By Accounts from Boston and New-York we are positively assured, that Things wear the worst aspect throughout the whole Continent of North-America; and that it is the decided Opinion of the most intelligent People there, that the Event of the present Disturbances will be either great Bloodshed, or a general Civil War from New-England to Georgia.*

The same Letters add, that all Business is totally at a stand, and that the Minds of nine tenths of the People seem to be intent much more on cultivating the Arts of War, than those of Peace.

The several marching Regiments on the British and Irish Establishments are ordered to be immediately recruited to their full compliment.

Octo. 15. *The Advices brought by the Scarborough Man of War are now no longer a secret; several private Letters being received since that Time, which give the same Information, and which is also confirmed by Letters bro't Yesterday by the Mail from New-York. By these Advices we find that Affairs with the Americans were then in the extreme of Confusion; the Sheriffs and other Officers of Justice have been made to sign a Declaration not to take Part in any way whatever in carrying the late Acts into Execution: The Lawyers are directed, by Notices fixed on their Doors, not to meet the Judges on Business upon Pain of Death; and the Parties summoned upon Juries have refused to take necessary Oaths; so that the Course of Justice was, in every respect, at a Stand. Add to these, an Officer of distinguished Character, who left England some time ago, not being able to get a Regiment, appears openly, and not only dissuades the Americans from any Obedience to the late Laws, but advises them to maintain their Rights by Force of Arms, offering, in that Case, to head them himself. It is but justice to the People in this Country to apprize them that their fellow Subjects in America, particularly in the Massachusetts Province, are in no less than a state of Rebellion. It has been found necessary, in Consequence of the above Advices, to order an addition to the Ships to be sent from Portsmouth and Plymouth to join the Admiral at Boston, and in which will be carried as many Land Forces as they can take in over and above their compliment.*

This day was published,
And to be sold either by the Thousand, Hundred, Groce, Dozen, or Single,
[*Embellished with two plates, one representing an* Antient Astrologer, *the other a* FEMALE SOLDIER.]

T H O M A S's NEW-ENGLAND ALMANACK, OR THE Massachusetts Calendar,

For the Year of our Lord Christ, 1775.
Being the Third after Bissextile or Leap-Year.

From the Creation of the World, according to the best of Prophane History,	5724
But by the Account of Holy Scriptures,	5737
Julian Period,	6488
From Noah's Flood,	4069
From the Destruction of Sodom,	3677
From the building of Rome,	2926
From the building of London,	2882
From the Destruction of Troy,	657
Higaria, or the Flight of Mahomet,	1184
New-England first planted,	166
Planting the Massachusetts-Bay,	147
Building of Boston the Capital of N. E.	145
Founding of Harvard College,	136
Of King George the IIId's. Reign,	15

C O N T A I N I N G,

Eclipses. Names of the Twelve Signs, and the Parts they govern. Names of the Planets and Aspects. Vulgar Notes. Friends Yearly Meetings. Sun's rising and setting. Full and Change of the Moon. Moon's rising and setting. Moon's Place. Time of High Water. Festivals of the Church of England, and other remarkable Days. Judgment of the Weather. Time of the Superior and Inferior Courts setting in the four Governments of New-England. Select Maxims. Observations on each Month in the Year. A Fragment of antient Poetry, collected in the Highlands of Scotland, and translated from the Gallic or Erse Language. The Athenian Orator, a Fable, in Verse. The Difference between To-Day and To-Morrow. Also,

The LIFE and ADVENTURES of
A FEMALE SOLDIER.
To the whole is added,
The ASSOCIATION of the Grand AMERICAN CONGRESS, which is absolutely necessary for every American to be acquainted with.

(Price only Six Coppers single.)

Very great Allowances are made to those who buy to sell again.
Printed and sold by ISAIAH THOMAS, at his Printing-Office, near the MILL-BRIDGE.

The Treasurer for the County of Suffolk, gives Notice to all whom it may concern, that as he is obliged to leave the Town for a few Months, the Business of said County will be transacted by Mr. *Thomas Crafts*, jun. at his House near Liberty-Tree.

New Flour and Raisins.

John Kneeland,

At his Store the Head of Greeo's Wharff, opposite JOHN ROWE, Esq;——HAS FOR SALE——
A few Barrels new Philadelphia Flour, choice Raisins per Cask, Sugars, Coffee, Chocolate, West-India and New-England Rum, Brandy——Also,
A few Pieces Ratteens, Coatings and Lambskins, to be sold very cheap.
Goods sold on low Commissions.

T O B E S O L D,

THE BRIG Benja. and Salley, a good Vessel Burthen about 140 Tuns, well Found, lying at Hutchinson's Wharf, Inquire of Capt. Edward Jarvis, near the New Brick Meeting House,

---

Taken up by *John Williams*, Tanner of Roxbury, on the 20th of November, a red and white COW, about 9 or 10 Years old, and on the 23d of said Month calved. Any Person owning said Cow, by applying to said *Williams*, may have her again by paying the Charges.

—Wanted in this Town—

An active, industrious, sober, honest, capable young Man, that has been brought up in a Retail Shop of English Goods, he must write a good Hand, quick at Figures and very obliging to the smallest Customers—Such a Person (and no other) may apply to the Printers for further Information.

Boston, December 5th, 1774.

James Bruce of Boston (at present in London) Mariner, maketh Oath, and saith, that he this Deponent has no Knowledge of, nor to the best of his Remembrance, was never in Company with a Captain Lovett, who is said by a Paragraph in the Boston Journal, dated 28 July, last, to have been in Company with this Deponent, at a Tavern in Antigua, and that the Contents of the Paragraph, there inserted (in order to hurt him this Deponent) is groundless and void of Truth, and that this Deponent never made use of any such Expressions there inserted, and further this Deponent saith, that he did not think or know at the Time he took the East India Company's Tea on Board the Ship Eleanor, that the same would have been either detrimental, or displeasing to the Town of Boston, otherwise himself and owners would not have suffered any of the said Tea to have been shipt on Board the said Ship Eleanor.

JAMES BRUCE.

Sworn before me at Shadwell, 16th Day of September,
JOHN SHERWOOD.

Choice RAISINS by the Cask CURRANTS, and all sorts of SPICES, to be sold a

Thomas Walley's

Store, Butler's-Row, No. I. ALSO,

Old Jamaica and common West-India RUM, Teneriffe Wine by the Pipe, Hogshead or Quarter Cask. Also, genuine Lisbon Wine, excellent Dumb Fish, Citron, Figs, Bolting Cloths, Dutch Looking-Glasses. All sorts of Groceries as usual. All at the lowest Prices for Cash.

N. B. A Quantity of Mustard Seed, and Snuff Bottles, to be sold very cheap.

T O B E S O L D B Y
Newell and Hichborn,
At S A L E M,
A few Barrels and Half Barrels New PORK.

T O B E S O L D
About 150 Hogsheads of *St. Martin's* S A L T. ALSO,
A Sloop about 84 Tons Burthen, fitted for the Sea. Inquire of the Printers.

C A N D L E S.

Dipp'd Tallow CANDLES per Box, at 5*s.* Old Tenor per lb.

Mould Tallow,
Pure Myrtle Wax, } Candles.
Sperma-Ceti

ALSO, TALLOW by the Barrell, Spermaceti OIL for Lamps, and HOG's-FAT, sold by JOHN LANGDON, in Fleet Street, at the Head of the Hon. JOHN HANCOCK, Esq's; Wharf.

Gilbert Deblois,

Informs his Customers that he has for Sale at his Shop opposite the Bottom of School-Street,
A very large and compleat Assortment of GOODS,
Suitable for the Season,
very cheap for CASH,
Among which are,
8/4, 9/4, 10/4, 11/4, Bed Blankets, Rugs, &c.
Scarlet, blue, white, buff, & other colour'd Broad Cloths,
Blue, scarlet and green Whitneys,
Bath Beavers, Coatings, Lambskins, &c.
White mill'd Flannels and Baizes, Ironing-Cloths,
Wide and narrow Baizes of all Colours and Prices,
A fine Assortment of Womens new fashioned Stuffs,
Choice Cambleteens at 9d Sterl. per Yard,
All Colours and Prices for Camblets or Riding-Hoods,
A great Variety of Silks, for the Ladies,
A compleat Assortment of Hosiery, & mill'd Gloves, some of which suitable for the Gentlemen of the Army & Navy,
Irish Linnens, of all Widths and Prices,
Cheap Carpets and Carpeting; Calicoes,
China Ware, Loaf-sugar, Spices, &c.
Looking-Glasses,—Scates,—Kippen's Snuff,
Firkin Butter at 6d Sterl. per Pound,
Gold and Silver Laces, &c. &c. *Fifes*, Violins,
French-Horns, &c. Swords and Pistols,
German Steel, Barr Lead, Nails,
With almost every other Article of GOODS, Imported to America, from Great-Britain, Scotland and Ireland,
A Composition for cleaning silver Lace, Embroidery and any sort plain and wrought plate.

Boston, Novem. 23, 1774.

All Persons indebted to or having any Demands upon the Estate of THOMAS GRAY, Esq; deceased, are desired to settle the same with

Boston, Nov. 26, 1774. WILLIAM GRAY, ELLIS GRAY, EDWARD GRAY. } Executors.

All Persons who are indebted to the Estate of the late Mr. William Molineux, deceased: Also all Persons who had Demands on, or were indebted to him as Attorney to others, are desired to make them known, and to pay their respective Dues to the Subscriber, who is fully empowered to adjust and receive the same.

THOMAS APTHORP.

All Persons having Demands on the Estate of Jonathan Clark, late of Boston, Merchant deceased, and those who are Indebted to said Estate are desired to bring in their Accounts to Ezekiel Lewis, Administrator on said Estate in Order to Settlement.

☞ *A House and a valuable Spot of Land situate in Long Lane, belonging to said Estate, to be sold enquire of said Administrator.* Boston, Nov. 28, 1774.

IF the Person who on the 12th of this Instant took a small Pocket Volume of the Bible, beginning with the Prophet Isaiah, being Part of a Sett neatly bound with blue Morroco Leather, gilt and mark'd 2 on the Back (out of the House in Queen-Street, lately occupied by John Adams, Esq;) will return it to the Place it was taken from, or to the Printers hereof, no Questions shall be ask'd; if not, as the Person is known, he may expect to be expos'd.

Boston: Printed, by EDES & GILL.
in Queen-Street, 1774.

THE Boston- AND COUNTRY Gazette, JOURNAL.

Containing the freshest Advices,   *Foreign and Domestic.*

No. 1027.

MONDAY, December 19, 1774.

In Provincial Congress, Cambridge Dec. 8th, 1774.

AS the Happiness of particular Families arises, in a great Degree, from their being more or less dependant upon others; and as the less occasion they have for any Article belonging to others, the more independent, and consequently, the happier they are: so, the Happiness of every Society of Men upon Earth, is to be estimated in a great Measure, upon their greater or less Dependance upon any other political Bodies; and from hence arises a forciable Argument, why every State ought to regulate their internal Policy, in such a manner as to furnish themselves, within their own Body, with every necessary Article for Subsistance and Defence: Otherwise their political Existance will depend upon others, who may take Advantage of such weakness, and reduce them to the lowest State of Vassallage and Slavery. For preventing so great an Evil, more to be dreaded than Death itself, it must be the Wisdom of this Colony, at all Times, more especially at this Time, when the Hand of Power is lashing us with the Scorpions of Despotism, to encourage Agriculture, Manufactures and Æconomy, so as to render this State as independent of every other State as the Nature of our Country will admit: from the Consideration thereof, and trusting that the Virtue of the People of this Colony is such, that the following Resolutions of this Congress, which must be productive of the greatest Good, will by them be effectually carried into Execution. And it is therefore RESOLVED,

1st. That we do recommend to the People the Improvement of their Breed of Sheep, and the greatest possible Increase of the same; and also the preferable Use of our own Woolen Manufactures; and to the Manufacturers, that they ask only reasonable Prices for their Goods; and especially a very careful sorting of the Wool, so that it may be Manufactured to the greatest Advantage, and as much as may be into the best Goods.

2d. We do also recommend to the People, the raising of Hemp and Flax: and as large Quantities of Flax Seed, more than may be wanted for Sowing, may be produced, we would also farther Recommend the Manufacturing the same into Oyl.

3d. We do likewise recommend the making of Nails; which we apprehend must meet with the strongest Encouragement from the Public, and be of lasting benefit both to the Manufacturer and the Public.

4th. The making of Steel, and the preferable Use of the same, we do also recommend to the Inhabitants of this Colony.

5th. We do in like Manner recommend the making Tin Plates, as an Article well worth the Attention of this People.

6th. As Fire Arms have been Manufactured in several Parts of this Colony, we do recommend the Use of such, in preference to any Imported: And we do recommend the making Gun Locks, and Furniture and other Locks, with other Articles in the Iron way.

7th. We do also earnestly recommend the making of Salt Petre, as an Article of vast Importance to be encouraged, as may be directed hereafter.

8th. That Gun Powder is also an Article of such Importance, that every Man among us who loves his Country, must with the Establishment of Manufactures for that Purpose, and, as there are the Ruins of several Powder Mills, and sundry Persons among us who are acquainted with that Business, We do heartily recommend its Encouragement, by repairing one or more of said Mills, or erecting others, and renewing said Business as soon as possible.

9th. That as several Paper Mills are now usefully employed, we do likewise recommend a preferable Use of our own Manufactures in this way; and a careful saving and collecting Rags, &c. and also that the Manufacturers give a generous Price for such Rags &c.

10th. That it will be the Interest, as well as the Duty of this Body, or of such as may succeed us, to make such effectual Provision for the farther manufacturing of the several Sorts of Glass, as that the same may be carried on to the mutual Benefit of the Undertaker and the Public, and firmly established in this Colony.

11th. That whereas Buttons of excellent Qualities and of various Sorts are manufactured among us, we do earnestly recommend the general Use of the same; so that the Manufactories may be extended to the Advantage of the People and Manufactures.

12th. That whereas Salt is an Article of vast Consumption within this Colony, and in its Fisheries, we do heartily recommend the making the same, in the several Ways wherein it is made in several Parts of Europe; especially in the Method used in that Part of France where they make Bay Salts.

13th. We do likewise recommend an encouragement of Horn Smiths in all their various Branches, as what will be of Public Utility.

14th. We do likewise recommend the establishment of one or more Manufactories for making Wool-Comber's Combs, as an Article necessary in our Woollen Manufactures.

15th. We do in like manner heartily recommend the preferable use of the Stocking and other Hosiery wove among ourselves, so as to enlarge the Manufactories thereof, in such a Manner as to encourage the Manufactures & serve the Country.

16th. As Madder is an Article of great Importance in the Dyer's Business, and which may be easily raised and cured among ourselves, we do therefore earnestly recommend the Raising and Curing the same.

17th. In order the more Effectually to carry these Resolutions into Effect, we do earnestly recommend, That a Society or Societies be established for the Purposes of Introducing and Establishing such Arts and Manufactures as may be useful to this People, and are not yet Introduced, and the more effectually Establishing such as we have already among us.

18th. We do recommend to the Inhabitants of this Province to make use of our own Manufactures, and those of our Sister Colonies, in preference to all other Manufactures.

Signed by Order of the Provincial Congress,
JOHN HANCOCK, President.
A true Extract from the Minutes.
BENJAMIN LINCOLN, Secretary.

In Provincial Congress, Cambridge, Dec. 9, 1774.

WHEREAS this Congress at their Session in October last, taking in Consideration the alarming State of this Colony, were, upon the most mature Deliberation, fully convinced, that to provide against the Danger to which it was then exposed, by a Standing Army illegally posted in Boston; and from Time to Time reinforced, for the purposes of subverting our ancient Constitution and the Liberties of all North-America; it was indispensably necessary that a considerable Sum of Money should be immediately laid out for the just Defence of this People: and whereas by a Resolve of the Congress bearing Date 28th said October, and published in the News Papers, it was among other Things earnestly recommended to the several Towns and Districts, that they would cause to be paid into the Hands of HENRY GARDNER, Esq; all the Province Monies due from them respectively, to supply the said pressing Exigencies of the Colony: And whereas the Danger which then threatned the Province, is still continued and daily-increasing: It is

RESOLVED, And hereby most earnestly recommended to all the Inhabitants of the Towns and Districts aforesaid, as they regard their own Safety and the Preservation of their inestimable Rights and Liberties, that they cause the Monies aforesaid, to be paid forthwith to the said HENRY GARDNER, Esq; who has given Bonds with sufficient Sureties to the Satisfaction of this Congress; and that they cause their respective proportions of the Tax granted by the General Court in June last, and all other the Province Monies due from them respectively, to be supplied in some Way that shall be more expeditious than the usual Mode of collecting the Taxes, in Order to prevent any Delay in providing against the iminent Danger above-mentioned—And the Members of the Congress are hereby desired to use their utmost Industry for having this Resolve speedily and punctually complied with; and the Sheriffs and Deputy Sheriffs of the several Counties to pay the Province Monies in their respective Hands as has been already recommended.

Signed by Order of the Provincial Congress,
JOHN HANCOCK, President.
A true Extract from the Minutes.
BENJAMIN LINCOLN, Secretary.

Mess. EDES and GILL,
Please to publish the following Extract from the Monthly Review for August last.

Observations on the Act of Parliament, commonly called the Boston Port-Bill; with Thoughts on Civil Society and Standing Armies. By Josiah Quincy, jun. Counsellor at Law in Boston. Boston, Printed. London, Re-Printed.

"ONE peculiar unlucky circumstance attending our American disputes, may be added to the rest, viz. That our fellow-subjects there are as well read in the nature and grounds of civil and religious liberty, as ourselves; as appears by many of their late publications, in which they oppose British pretensions on British principles; and this shrewd commentary on the Boston Port-Bill, will incline us to entertain a respectable opinion of their law pleaders. Where the cause is to be decided by pleading, it is not difficult to say what the issue would be; what it may be, according to the actual mode of prosecution is too disagreeable a prospect on either side to anticipate: the result must be waited with a painful anxiety by every true friend of liberty and of his country.

The incroachments of power are very naturally represented, but ably as this ingenious Barrister pleads the American cause, it is, it seems, in vain to urge it any more. Why reason is no longer the rule in political management, appears fully from what he says on a subject that intimately affects the whole empire, viz. that of a standing army! This was once an alarming object of senatorial complaint; but so it is, subjects complain till they are wearied, ministers sure of a tame majority, laugh at such ineffectual representations, outnumber the talkers, and thus, which is the most mortifying circumstance of all, employ the forms of the constitution to poison it.

A parent first cherishes and instructs his infant offspring, but the vigour of the one declining, perhaps the sooner for intemperance, while that of the other increases, their circumstances are at last inverted. Hence the parent grows indolent, careless and peevish; the young ones vigilant, prudent and assuming: Therefore among other remonstrances from the American shores, we are not to wonder at being reminded of an impending danger that we have too long forgot. Whether the remembrance may not come a day too late, and only to add to our sorrow, is a question well worth the attention of those who are qualified for the investigation, and empowered to act upon it.

☞ *A few of Mr. QUINCY'S Observations may be had of the Printers hereof.*

TO-MORROW, will be Published, and sold by EDES and GILL, in Queen-Street.
The MISERY and DUTY of an oppress'd and enslav'd People, represented in a

SERMON

Delivered at SALISBURY, July 14. 1774.
On a Day set apart for FASTING and PRAYER,
On Account of approaching public Calamities.
Published by Request.

By SAMUEL WEBSTER, A. M.
Pastor of a Church in SALISBURY.

NEHEMIAH IX. 36,——38.
Behold we are Servants this Day! And for the Land that thou gavest unto our Fathers, to eat the Fruit thereof, and the Good thereof, behold we are Servants in it! And it yieldeth much Increase unto the Kings which thou hast set over us, because of our Sins: Also they have Dominion over our Bodies and over our Cattle, at their Pleasure: And we are in great Distress! And because of all this, we make a sure Convenant, and write it, and our Princes, Levites & Priests seal unto it.

An Extract from a Pamphlet lately published in London, *entituled*, American Independence the Interest and Glory of Great-Britain. (*Dedicated to* Sir George Savile, *Baronet*,) *which came in the last Ship.*

"I Would not have the reader imagine, I mean to justify every tarring and feathering rioter at Boston, & all disorderly proceedings in America indiscriminately. Some of the people, I doubt not, may have been to blame; for the commonality of that country must have had a portion of wisdom and patience, which hath not at any time before been found in the world, had all their expressions of resentment for ill usage, been confined within the bounds of moderation. When governors become tyrants shall we wonder, that an injured and insulted people become riotous and unruly! Have ambitious and encroaching rulers ever yet thought of rendering *satisfaction*, or making *reparation*, for the cruellest injuries they have so constantly committed; and have they not always thought themselves wonderfully gracious and condescending, when they have merely *ceased to oppress*? but if a free people, finding their humble petitions, and most dutiful remonstrances scattered to the winds with contempt, being stung with a sense of accumulated wrongs, and feeling an indignation at being treated like slaves and villians, do but assault the meanest miscreant in the train of power; 'tis rebellions! felony! treason!—Gaols and gibbets, ball and bayonet, must here be the correctives. Is this human polity! Are these the proceedings of men, of fellow-creatures, of fellow-christians? When merely *ceasing to oppress*, is all the reparation required for a long train of injuries and insults; shall authority, with whom wisdom ought ever to reside, become deaf to that voice which called her into being, and think it meritorious to persist in doing wrong?

So universally have I heard the Bostonians condemned for destroying the *tea*, and the action pronounced illegal and rebellious, that I have taken some pains to examine all the particulars of that affair. Now, to my agreeable disappointment, and to the best of my judgment, instead of an act of rebellion, I find it one reflecting honour, and stamping the character of good subjects, on those who performed it; instead of being illegal, it appears to me to be warranted by the law of nature, the great origiaal of all human laws, when just. Those who would wish to think justly, and to speak honestly of this matter, will do well to examine for themselves. When they shall have so done, with care and candour, and admitting on my part, for the sake of taking no advantage in the argument, the Bostonian character to be as black as malignantly represented, I should be glad to propose to them this plain question: "What was possible for " the most wise and virtuous persons on earth, in " the place of the Bostonians, to have done, in " order to have performed their duty to the ut- " most, towards God and their country?"—To have shewn a passive obedience to an unjust act of parliament, in a case of such moment, and of so critical a nature, would have been treason to their country, and therefore not acceptable, I imagine, to God. I have introduced in various conversations, with sensible men, the same question I here propose, but never yet, I can aver with the strictest veracity, have I met with a solution of it, which did not confirm me in an opinion, that as wise and virtuous men, as good citizens, and true patriots, *they could not possibly have acted otherwise than as they did*. They had only this one alternative; they were driven to this dilemma by their magistrates, *either to suffer an insidious attempt against their sacred rights and liberties to take effect*, *or to destroy the hated instrument*. Having had *no other choice*, they must necessarily have either *done* this, or *suffered* that. Which ought to have been chosen by every brave and honest man, I leave the reader to determine. 'Tis visionary, even to childishness, to say, they might have permitted the tea to have been landed, and yet have defeated the tax, by unanimously refusing to have purchased it. The conductors of that noble action must have been patriots indeed, & most wonderfully wise, to have left their country, by going this way to work, at the discretion and mercy of the most ignorant and vicious of its inhabitants, to have relied upon the prudence and self denial of every tea-drinker in America! Besides that the wisdom of each well-meaning individual was not to be depended on for foreseeing all the ill-consequences of purchasing a pound of tea, nor their resolution in preventing them; I fear there might have been some traitors to the publick cause, some tools of government or the India Company, or some suspected persons at least, in whom to have confided, for not setting the example, and using all their cunning to seduce others, would not have argued any extraordinary degree of prudence. What teacher of morals or politics, ever was lunatic enough to build all his hopes of serving his country, on an expectation of bringing *every individual* of it to be of one mind, and as unanimously to act up to the same rigid prin iples of virtue? and which of us would care to risk the safety of the city of London from some dreadful calamity, on a confidence that every female, from the fine lady to the washerwoman, every man, from the minister of state down to the blackguard, might be prevailed upon totally to abstain from the use of tea, porter, or gin, *except the temptation was removed out of their way*.

To all my readers, except those unhappy ones, who have learned the fatal art of occasionally closing the mental eye, so as to admit just so much, and no more of the light of truth as their passions and prejudices will bear; I must needs think, it would be reflecting upon their understandings and their ingeniousness, to attempt any farther proof of my proposition, that the Bostonians did what was strictly consonant to right and justice in destroying the tea; but, in order to open the self closed, winking eyes of the prejudiced, I will propose one more comparison, which, I apprehend, will be admitted as a fair one, since it is agreed on all hands, except by the calm advancers of direct falshoods and lies, and the bold denyers of demonstration, that with regard to taxation, the colonists, as legitimate shoots from a parent stock of freedom, have at least an equal right to be their own taxmasters as the people of Ireland, which was a conquered, and every one knows, a very rebellious kingdom for many ages. Let then the reader only substitute Ireland and Dublin, for Massachusetts-Bay and Boston, and try the cause over again in his own mind. If he pleases, we will suppose, that instead of a duty on tea, we should attempt to touch the pockets of the Irish, by a duty on certain stamped papers, being publications of gross immoralities and blasphemies, tending to debauch the minds of the people, and fit them for slavery; and that an association of honest citizens of Dublin, more mindful of their duty to God and their County, than of obedience to an ordinance they held to be subversive of their liberties, should find this precious cargo, precisely in a similar situation with the tea at Boston; that the Lord Mayor, the magistrates, and revenue myrmidons, like the Boston governor and officers of customs, should all absolutely refuse their permission and clearances for its departure from the port, and the ship should be well imprisoned by surrounding batteries; then, what is to be done? what course is to be pursued? Shall those, who ought to be the guides & guardians of the city, admit these pernicious compositions within their walls; patiently behold them displayed in the shops, hawked about the streets, and dispersed through the country, with every art of invitation to those inclined to purchase? Is the city to be deluged with these impieties, and its manners, morals, and liberties undermined, rather than *an united company of merchants trading in mischief* should lose their property? a property not only detrimental in itself, but in this case made a venture, with a direct intention of betraying a brave and generous nation into obedience to a despotic ordinance, containing in it the seeds of a more complete tyranny, and used as the most tempting bait to lure the silly multitude into the political mouse trap; and therefore, on the principles of self preservation, and agreeable to the spirit of the law of nature and nations, subject to be destroyed, *if not removed upon fair warning*. Are the city guardians, I say, to observe all this, and content themselves all the while with a patriotic resolve, not to buy or to read a single paper, and with preaching to the unlistening people to follow their example? If this, in the enlightened and virtuous city of Dublin, would be an experiment, that even a driveller would hardly dream of making; how much less safe would it have been for the American patriots to have hazarded their all, on the universal good sense, on the piety and public spirit of the people, in the *stupid*, the *hypocritical*, the *impious*, the *ungrateful*, and *rebellious* town of Boston! What then, I once more ask, ought the patriots of Dublin or of Boston to have done? What! but with indignation to have cast the hated instrument of tyranny into the sea! whither its proprietors deserved also to have followed it headlong. Is it for this wise, brave, and generous action, that not only the actors of it, but the whole people of Boston, are now smarting under the heaviest vengeance of Great-Britain! of a people who have hitherto justly prided themselves in being the undaunted resisters of tyrants! Fie, boasters, fie! Britannia blushes for your degeneracy; she disowns ye for her sons. When a pawnbroker knowingly puts arms into the hands of a highwayman or ruffian, does any law insure to him payment for the same, at the hands of any one who, being assaulted, seized and destroyed them? Are not all deadly weapons, all snares, traps, and poisons, made use of in violation to the laws of civil society, for injuring any man in life, limb, or property, a *lawful spoil* to the injured party? When the miscreant, pick-pocket Jew, in the service of iniquity, was once driving a trade amongst the Westminster school-boys, with a parcel of TEA, out of the *green cannister* of the celebrated Mrs. *Phillips*, who, that had a spark of virtuous indignation, but applauded the *illegal proceedings* of the spirited master, when, disregarding the *laws of property*, he threw into the fire all of this *tea* he could lay his hands on; and, as little considering the penalties for an assault, horsed the vile factor, and scourged him to the quick?

I must therefore repeat, that the destroyers of the tea at Boston were, in my opinion, a band of virtuous patriots, whose names, when once made public, will doubtless be held in eternal veneration by their countrymen; and that the glorious *illegality* (if every statute, *whether just or unjust*, be properly comprehended in the word law) they atchieved, was an act of absolute moral and political *necessity*, and therefore exempt from even good laws; of singular wisdom, of strict justice, and remarkable temper and forbearance, considering their provocations, since it was done in *self defence*, with the greatest good order and decency, and unaccompanied with incivility to any one, or the smallest damage to any thing in the ships besides the treacherous tea. I must likewise repeat, that this tea, for the reasons I have given, and agreeable to the spirit of the law of nature and nations, was justly forfeited to the injured Americans; and that the East-India Company are not entitled to any satisfaction or payment for the same."

B O S T O N, December 19.

Thursday last was observed, agreable to the recommendation of the Provincial Congress, as a day of public Thanksgiving throughout this province.

On the late Thanksgiving-Day two or three weak and imbittered Persons, of the most insignificant and contemptible of all Sects, (who make Pretensions to Christianity) opened their Shops; five or six Soldiers passing one of them, made a full stop, and asked the deluded Owner whether he was not ashamed so to insult his Countrymen, and advised him to shut up his Shop and hide his Head, adding, that he was an Enemy to his Country.—As this was said by a Soldier, they may perhaps spare the cry of Persecution on the Occasion.

A Letter from Quebec, dated November 26, 1774, says, "That the Interpreter who has been sent to the Six Nations, to know if they will give their Assistance to the King's Troops against the Colonies (should there be Occasion for them) have given for Answer, That it is a Family Quarrel, and that they will by no Means interfere between the Parents and Children.—The Letter further adds, that they will also be very hard put to it to muster any Canadians for that Purpose.—May GOD preserve and defend you all."

By a Person lately arrived from Quebec, we learn further, that application had been made to the French Inhabitants of Canada to arm themselves against the Colonies; that they rejected the Proposal with Indignation, and declared that if any *one* Canadian should be deluded so far as to go against their Sister Colonies, they would send *ten* to their Relief.

[*What an Idea are we led to form of a British Administration;—by an Order of the Privy Council we are prohibited from procuring the Means of Defence, and at the same time the whole Influence of Government is exerted to stir up the Canadians and Savages to cut our Throats.—A Conduct not more base and inhumane than it is weak and impolitick.*]

We are told, that the military and naval expenditures at the town of Boston, since the blocking up the harbour, amounts to fifty thousand pounds sterling every three months.

We hear that a powerful fleet of the navy of Spain, with a well appointed army of land forces, are assembled at the Havanna, which occasions very serious apprehensions.

Capt. Samuel Wintworth of the Sloop Black Prince from Hispaniola bound for New-York, having lost her Sails, &c. is put into Plimouth to repair.

We learn from Rhode-Island that the People there view the political Manœuvrs of the British Ministry as foreboding the most vigorous Exertions of martial Force; and from this Apprehension the most effectual Methods have been and are adopting by their Legislative to defend themselves against any hostile Invasions of the Enemies to America.

We also learn that the People at Portsmouth, New Hampshire, and Towns adjacent, alarm'd with the same Apprehensions, have remov'd the Powder, a Number of Pieces Cannon and Small Arms, from the Fort at New Castle, to a Place of more Security.

Married.] Capt. Job Prince, jun. to Miss Elizabeth Cutler.—Mr. Joseph Adams, Physician, at Townsend, to Miss Lovy Lawrence, eldest Daughter of the Rev. Mr. Lawrence of Lincoln.

Wednesday Morning died, *Gabriel Maturine*, Esq; aged 44, Private Secretary to his Excellency General GAGE.

Yesterday died Mr Joshua Sroton Emmons, Tinman. His Funeral is to be To-Morrow.

Tuesday last died Mrs. Sarah Moorhead, aged 68, Relict of the late Rev. Mr. John Moorhead, deceas'd. Her Funeral is to be at 3 o'Clock this Afternoon, from her late Dwelling-House near Liberty-Tree.

Donations receiv'd since our last.

From MASSACHUSETTS-BAY.
Union Fire-Club at Salem, Cash, £. 40 0 0
Medfield, 22 Loads Wood,
21 Cheeses,
½ Barrel Pork.

NEW JERSEY.
From Joseph Ellis, Esq; Treasurer of the Committee of Correspondence of Gloucester-County in West-Jersey, by the Hands of the honorable Thomas Cushing, Esq; 534 Dollars.

VIRGINIA.
From Alexandria, 157 Barrels Flour.

Six Dollars from a Person unknown.

Last Wednesday, P. M. a Person in *Roxbury* sent to Town upwards of 400 *Cabbages*, to be distributed to the Poor by a Person whom he desired to attend that Service ; and they were accordingly all dealt out in about two Hours after they had been received.

The Publick are hereby informed that there are now but three People in the Hospital at New-Boston infected with the Small Pox, who will probably be dismissed from thence this Week ; that on Saturday Information was given that the Wife of Mr. Hill, Surgeon of the 59th Regiment and Three of their Children in a House in Hanover Street, near the Head of Cold-Land, as also Two Children of Lieut. Clarke's of said Regiment under the same Roof, have the Distemper, together with Three Children of Capt. Figs of the 59th Regiment, down a Yard opposite the White Horse, South End :— As it has been suggested that the above Children received the Infection by Innoculation, the Inhabitants may be assured, that such Measures will be pursued with the Delinquents, for the present and future Safety of the Town and Country, as the Laws of the Land require.
By Order of the Selectmen,
WILLIAM COOPER, *Town Clerk.*
Boston, Dec. 18, 1774.

TO BE SOLD,

Choice New-Castle Coals, on board the Big Dolphin, James Scott, Master, at the Long Wharff, or at William Dennie's Store in King-Street.

To be Sold, at Marblehead, a Quantity of Bottles in Hampers, some holding 9 Jills. Apply there to Major Gallison, or to William Dennie, at Boston.

Duncan Ingraham, jun.

WILL shortly embark for England.—Desires all those that are indebted to him, to make immediate Payment ; and all those to whom he is indebted, are desired to call and receive their respective Balances. (the)

TO BE SOLD,

A Piece of Land being a Wood Lot situate in the Town of Milton, containing Twenty six Acres and one Quarter of an Acre, belonging to the Estate of *Joseph Gooch,* Esq; late of Milton, deceased.
Any Person inclining to Purchase said Wood Lot, may apply to *William Gooch,* in King-Street, Boston, who is Attorney to *Thomas Hubbart*, sole Executor of said *Joseph Gooch*'s Will, who is fully Impowered by the Justices of the Superior Court to Sell the same and pass a Deed therefor.   Boston, Nov. 28, 1774.
N. B. All Persons are cautioned against Cutting or Carrying off any Wood or Timber from said Wood Lot, as they may depend on being Prosecuted with the utmost Severity of the Law.

PUBLIC AUCTION,
TO BE SOLD,
By BENJAMIN CHURCH,
At his usual Place of Sale,
On *Thursday* Next,

Broad-Cloths——Plains——Bearskin——
Cambiets——Stuffs——Irish Hollands——Checks——Bed Ticks
——Handkerchiefs, &c.——A Mahogany Case of Draws——Beareau——Desk——side Boards——Beds——Easy Chairs, and others——A Quantity of Buckram, House Furniture, &c.

Just Published (No. XI.)

The Royal American Magazine,

For November 1774, at Greenleaf's Printing-Office, near the Market, Boston.

At a Meeting of the Proprietors of COXHALL, (so called) in the County of York, conven'd at the Dwelling-House of Dr. Tyler Porter, Innholder in Wenham, on Monday the 31st Day of January, 1770. VOTED, That 12s. be and hereby is Granted and Ordered to be paid by the Proprietors on every Hundred Acre Right within said Tract of Land in proportion to their respective Interest therein, to be collected and paid to the Proprietor's Treasurer according to Law.—— And at a Legal Meeting of said Proprietors held by Adjournment, Feb. 1, 1774, at the House of Mrs. Susanna Stacy, Innholder in Ipswich : Also, Voted one other Tax of 12s. be and hereby is Granted and Ordered to be paid by the Proprietors of every Hundred Acre Right in said Tract of Land ; the above Taxes to be paid to Capt. Francis Goodhue, of Ipswich, their said Treasurer.
MICHAEL FARLEY, Prop's Clerk.
Ipswich, Dec. 16, 1774.
N. B. If the above Taxes are not paid to the aforesaid Treasurer by the last Tuesday of January next, the said Lands will be exposed to Sale at the House of the aforesaid Mrs. Susanna Stacy, Innholder in Ipswich, at 10 o'Clock in the Forenoon.
By Order of the Committee for Sale of Lands.
JOHN BAKER.

To be sold agreeable to the American CONGRESS ASSOCIATION, on Monday the 26th of December Instant, at public Auction, and at the House of Mr. Benjamin Burdick, in Marblehead,

SUCH a part of the Cargo of the Ship Champion, Capt. Nathaniel Fellows, arrived from London since the 1st day of December aforesaid, as has been already delivered to the Committee of Inspection of said Town. The Goods will be put up according to the Invoices, and sold to the highest Bidder.

Invoice, No. 1. Contains Russia Duck, Osnaburghs, Ticklinburgs, Ravens Duck, Baizes and Hemp, amounting to about 670l. sterling.
No. 2. Contains Hemp only, and amounts to about 130l. sterling.
No. 3. Contains Russia and Ravens Duck, Hemp and Ticklinburg, amounting to about 210l. sterling.
No. 4. Osnaburgs, R. mails, Steel Sconces, Irish Linnens, Checks, Womens Hose, Broom Heads, Tallow Brushes, Tar and Hearth ditto, White Lead, Boxes of Tin Plates, Shot, Sailers Caps, Mens Hats, Linings and Loops for ditto, stained Paper and Borders, Baizes, bound Books, Quills, Mariners Compasses, &c. &c. 290l. sterl.
No. 5. Contains 5-inch, and 4 and half inch Deck Nails, Sheathing, Drawing, 20d 10d 6d 4d & 3d Nails, Sail Needles, Pump, Clapper and Scupper Nails, Lead and Hemp, amount about 300l. sterling.
No. 6 Contains Irish Linnen, Pins, gilt Trunks Ticklinburg, Velvets, Sewing Silks, Twist, Bonnet Boards, Qualities, Skeleton Wire, Worsted, black and white Lace, brown Thread, Death head Buttons, Persians, Damasks and Lutestrings, &c. Sergedenims and Everlastings, Calicoes, Muslins, Nankeens, Dowlas, Russia Diaper, Italian Crapes, Chints, Silk Handkerchiefs, Patches, &c. amount about 710l. sterling.
No. 7. Containing sundry Medicinal Drugs, amount about 60l. sterling.

At the same Time and Place will be also Sold,

The whole Cargo of the Brigantine

POLLY, Capt. STEPHEN BLANEY, arrived from Falmouth, in Great Britain, since the first Day of December aforesaid.

Invoice No. 1. Containing 160 Boxes of Lemmons, 222 Casks of Raisins, 39 Quarter Casks of Wine, 30 Casks of Figs.
No. 2. Contains 32 Casks of Raisins.
No. 3. 30 Boxes of Lemmons, 16 Casks of Raisins, 2 Quarter Casks of Wine.
No. 4. 6 Casks Raisins, one Quarter Cask Wine.
No. 5. 10 Boxes of Lemmons, 16 Casks of Raisins, 8 Quarter Casks of Wine, 30 Casks of Figs.

N. B. Each Invoice will be put up at the Sterling Cost and Charges, and 1 per Cent Advance, and half per Cent for each Bidder. The Sale to begin at XI o'Clock, A. M.

The Committee of Inspection for the Town of PLYMOUTH, hereby give public Notice that there is to be sold at Plymouth, under their direction, (agreeable to the 10th Article of the Association of the American Continental Congress) on Monday the second Day of January next, at Ten o'Clock in the Forenoon,

One Hundred and Ten Quarter Casks

of Malaga WINE, fifty Boxes of LEMMONS, six hundred and ten Casks, and fifty Jarrs of RAISINS.— Imported in the Schooner Dove, Ebenezer Parker, Master, from Malaga, via Falmouth. Said Sale to be on board said Schooner.   JOHN TORREY, *Chairman.*
Plymouth, Decr 12, 1774.

The Committee of Inspection for the Town of Plimouth, hereby give Notice, That there are to be sold at the House of Mr. Howland, Innholder, at said Plimouth, on Tuesday the Third Day of January next, at Ten of the Clock in the Forenoon, under the Direction of said Committee (agreeable to the Tenth Article of the Association of the American Continental Congress) the following Articles imported in the Brig. *Esther,* Benjamin Smith, Master, from Liverpool, since the First Day of December Instant, viz.

Two Boxes Linnens, two Cases Woolens, one Barrel Hard ware, one Barrel Glass, one Case Velveret and Bindings, one Hogshead Checks and Fustians, one Cask bottled Ale, Twenty Crates Earthen Ware, 160 Tons Salt, 10 Chaldrons Coals. Also a small Quantity of Cheese and unpack'd Beer, and six Boxes of Irish Linnens. The Sale to continue 'till the whole is sold.
JOHN TORREY, *Chairman.*
Plimouth, December 12, 1774.

LAST Monday Night, between 11 and 12 o'Clock, some *well-bred Gentlemen* took the *Liberty* of breaking my Windows in a *most spirited Manner* : If any Person will be pleased to inform me of the Place of their Residence, (if they have any,) that I may make them a proper Acknowledgment for this *publick Mark of their Civility,* he shall be intitled to a Reward of Ten Dollars from his most humble Servant, JOHN TROUTBECK.

For the Benefit of the Underwriters,

WILL be Sold by Public Vendue, on Saturday next, at Ten in the Morning, on board the Schooner Rosenoble, now lying at a Wharff in Lynn,

1 Damaged Cable, and Part of an Anchor.

TO BE SOLD,

Two convenient Dwelling Houses, situated in King-Street, Boston : One opposite to the South Door of the Town House, at present in the Occupation of Mr. Thomas Courtney ; the other on the North Side of said Town House, improved by Mr. John Mand. Also a Brick Tenement, situated near the East End of Christ Church. For further Particulars, inquire of the Printers.   Dec. 19. 1774.

On Wednesday the 28th Instant,
At TEN o'Clock in the Morning,
Will be sold by Public Vendue, at Russell's Auction-Room, Queen Street,

A very large and valuable Collection

of genteel House-Furniture, belonging to a Gentleman who is out of the Province. Among which are, MOHOGANY Dining Tables, Tea Tables, Dressing Tables and Card Tables, Chest of Draws and Bureaus, hair-bottom, leather bottom & common Chairs, crimson worsted Harrateen Bed and Easy Chair, two blue and white Calico Beds, with Window Curtains, 4 Puffs and common Bedsteads, Sheets, Table Linnen and fine Blankets, Looking-Glasses, one 8 Day Clock, Carpets, Feather Beds, all Kinds of Kitchen Furniture, in Pewter, Brass, Copper, Iron and Tin, a great Variety of China, Glass, Stone and Delph Ware, a Chaise and Harness, and a Variety of Plate.   J. RUSSELL, *Auctioneer.*
The Sale will begin precisely at Ten.—Wednesday 28th.—

THIS DAY PUBLISHED,
[*Price Half-a-Pistareen.*]

And sold at John Boyle's Printing-Office, next Door to the *Three Doves* in Marlborough-Street.

The WONDER of WONDERS !

Or, the WONDERFUL APPEARANCE of an

Angel, Devil and Ghost,

To a GENTLEMAN in the Town of *Boston*, in the NIGHTS of the 14th, 15th, and 16th of *October* last : To whom in some Measure may be attributed the DISTRESSES that have of late fallen upon that unhappy METROPOLIS. Related to one of his NEIGHBOURS the Morning after the last Visitation, who wrote down the NARRATIVE from the GENTLEMAN's own Mouth ; and it is now made public at his Desire, as a solemn Warning to all those, who, for the sake of agrandizing themselves and their Families, would entail the most abject Wretchedness upon MILLIONS of their Fellow-Creatures.

Adorned with Four PLATES, viz. 1. The DEVIL.
2. An ANGEL, *with a Sword in one Hand, a pair of Scales in the other.* 3. BELZEBUB, *holding in his right hand a folio Book, and in his left a Halter.* 4. A GHOST, *having on a white Gown, his Hair much dishevelled.*

Left at a Shop in this Town, on Friday the 9th Instant, a Pocket-Book, containing valuable Articles ; among which was a Note of Hand given to Samuel and Stephen Salisbury, by Ephraim Harrington. The Owner may have the Pocket-Book again, paying the Charge of this Advertisement. Inquire of *Hopestill Foster,* near Dr. Byles's Meeting-House, South End of Boston.

Boston, December 16, 1774.
LOST between Liberty-Tree and the Town-House, last Tuesday Evening, a Silver Watch, with the Letters A. D. studded on the outside Case, Maker's Name *Thomas Blundell,* Dublin, No. 547. Had to it a Steel Chain, Brass Key, and a white Cornelian Seal set in Silver. Whoever will bring said Watch, &c. to Mr. John McLean, Watchmaker, in King Street, shall receive Three Dollars Reward.

N. B. If the above Watch should be offered in Pawn, or for Sale, it is requested it may be stopped, and the same Reward shall be given.

New Auction-Room, *Cornhill.*

To-Morrow Morning at Ten o'Clock,
Will be Sold, by PUBLIC VENDUE,
At GREENLEAF's Auction-Room,

A large and valuable Assortment of

English Goods.—Amongst which are—
SUperfine, middling and low pric'd Broad Cloths, Forrest Cloths, Kerseys, Plains, mixt Hunters, Fearnoughts, Blankets, black and crimson Plush, silk Velvet, Shalloons, water'd Tammies, Popplins, Allopeens, black and cloth colour'd Breeches Pieces, Mens and Childrens Worsted Hose, Silver Cord and Wire, and a Variety of other Articles.   Wm. GREENLEAF, *Auctioneer.*
The Sale will begin at Ten o'Clock.

NEW AUCTION-ROOM, Dock-Square,
On FRIDAY next, at TEN o'Clock in the Morning,
Will be sold by PUBLIC VENDUE,
At HUNTER's Auction-Room,

A great Variety of ENGLISH GOODS, as usual.   WM. HUNTER, *Auctioneer.*
(The Particulars in the Thursday's Papers.)

Gould's Auction-Office,
In Back-Street,
TO-MORROW Morning, at Ten o'Clock,
Will be Sold by PUBLIC VENDUE,
At the Province Manufactory-House,

All the Looms, Warping, Twisting and other Machines, Dying Presses, &c. belonging to the Estate of *William Molineaux,* deceased.
R. GOULD, *Auctioneer.*

Burials in the Town of BOSTON, since our last.
Seventeen Whites.   No Blacks.
Baptiz'd in the several Churches, Nine.
High Water at BOSTON, for the present Week.
Monday, 32 min. aft. 12 | Friday, 24 min. after 3
Tuesday, 26 min. aft. 1 | Saturday, 26 min. aft. 4
Wednesday, 19 m. aft. 2 | Lord's Day 9 m. af. 5
Thursday, 0 min. aft. 3 | D's LAST 25 Day Night

SALEM, *December 6.*

At a Town Meeting last Friday a Committee of 15 very respectable Inhabitants were chosen for carrying into Execution in this Town the Measures of the Congress.

BOSTON, December 19.

At a Meeting of the newly chosen Officers of the respective Companies, belonging to the Regiment, lately under the Command of the honorable Israel Williams, *Esq; Colonel, held at* Northampton, *in the County of* Hampshire, *on the 10th and 11th Days of* November *Instant.*

Lieutenant JOHN CHESTER WILLIAMS, Clerk.

Captain JONATHAN CLAP, Chairman.

VOTED, THAT considering the Numbers and Extent of said Regiment, as it now stands, that it is adviseable to divide the same; and that the same be and hereby is divided in the following Manner.

1st Regiment to consist of Northampton, Hatfield, Southampton, Williamsburg, Chesterfield, Worthington, Murrayfield, Norwich, Whately, Ashfield and No. 5.

2d Regiment to consist of Hadley, Sunderland, Leverett, Amherst, South-Hadley, Granby, Belcherstown, Pelham, Greenwich, Ware, New-Salem, Shutsbury and Ervinshire.

North Regiment, to consist of Deerfield, Montague, Northfield, Warwick, Bernardstown, Colrain, Greenfield, Shelburne, Conway, Charlemont, Murrayfield, and No. 7.

After which they unanimously made Choice of the Field Officers of the respective Regiments.

Voted, That all those who formerly held Commissions under his Excellency Thomas Hutchinson, as late Governor, be advised to make a Resignation of the same in Writing; and that the Clerk be desired to make a Draft for that Purpose.

The following being presented, Voted and accepted.

We the Subscribers, whose Names are hereunto affixed, do of our own free Will and Accord, freely, fully, and absolutely, resign, renounce & disclaim, any Power or Authority we have held, or might have, hold, use, possess, or enjoy, by Virtue of any Commission we have held under Thomas Hutchinson, Esq; late Governor of this Province. And that for the future, we will not exercise any Power or Authority by Virtue of the same. In Witness whereof, we have hereunto set our Hands this Tenth Day of November, Anno Domini, 1774.

Signed by,

Jonathan Clap, Josiah Chauncey, Israel Hubbard, Benjamin Ranney, Joseph Hooker, John Welle, Lemuel Pomeroy, John Nash, John Powers, jun. Wm. Brackinridge, Samuel Williams, Jonathan Osgood, Josiah Osgood, Samuel Bartlet, Benjamin Tupper, Daniel Gray Elisha Porter, Elijah Hunt, Abraham Cummings, Mat. Henry, Benjamin Phillips, John Chester Williams, David Wells, Ezra May, Joseph Lyman, Asahel Clap, John Field, Josiah White, Josiah Smith, Ruggles Woodbridge, Jonathan Bordwell, Joseph Cooke, Nahum Eager.

Voted, That the Norfolk Militia be the standing Exercise in these Regiments.

Voted, That the Proceedings of this Body be published.

After which the Meeting was dissolved.

Attest. JOHN CHESTER WILLIAMS, Clerk.

November 14, 1774.

The Town of Rehoboth being legally warned and assembled on the 21st ult. made Choice of Mr. Ephraim Storkweathers, Mr. Samuel Peck, Capt. Ebenezer Peck, Capt. Phillip Wheeler and Capt. Thomas Carpenter, a Committee for executing the Plans of the Continental Congress; and also gave Orders to the Constables and Collectors, to pay Henry Gardner of Stow, Esq; Monies which they then had or in future may have in their Hands, belonging to the Province, agreeable to a Resolve of the Provincial Congress, who have considered the late Treasurer Gray unworthy of any further Confidence, and an avowed Enemy to the Rights of America.

The Militia of the South Parish in Dedham met on Monday the 5th Instant, and made Choice of the following Gentlemen for their Officers, *viz.*

Lieutenant William Bullard, Captain,
Ensign John Morse, 1st Lieutenant,
Serjeant Nathaniel Lewis, 2d Lieutenant,
Serjeant Ebenezer Everett, jun. Ensign.

And such is the present Spirit for Military Discipline there, that the following may be depended on, *viz.*

A Company consisting upwards of Fifty, several of whom are above 70 Years of Age, met as above and are likewise determined to put themselves in such a Condition as to be in a State of Defence, and made Choice of *their* Officers as follows.

Nathaniel Sumner, Esq; Captain,
Deacon Ebenezer Everett, 1st Lieutenant,
Ensign John Dean, 2d ditto.
Major Eliphalet Fales, 1st Serjeant.
John Fairbank, 2d ditto.
Captain Nath. Dean, 3d ditto.
Ensign Seth Fuller, 4th ditto.
Deacon Moses Barker, Clerk.

We hear from Dorchester, that Timothy Tileston, lately took out of his Garden a Root of the Beet kind, which weighed Eighteen Pounds, supposed by many who saw it to be the largest ever seen in this Province.

BRICKS.

FOUR HUNDRED THOUSAND BRICKS, Manufactured by the distressed, industrious Poor of the Town of Boston, assisted by the generous Donations of our benevolent and sympathizing Brethren of this and the other Colonies, and are to be sold for their further Relief and Employment, by *Thomas Crafts*, jun. near Liberty-Tree.

General Post-Office, New-York, 5th Dec. 1774.

The Deputy Post Masters General being desirous of facilitating Correspondence, have ordered that in time to come there should be two Posts Weekly for Canada, by Way of Albany: Notice is hereby given, that from and after the 14th Day of December Instant, the Mails for Canada and Albany will be made up and dispatched from this Office on Wednesdays at 11 o'Clock in the Forenoon, and at 9 every Saturday Night. The Wednesdays Post will ride on the East Side of Hudson's River, and return to this Office with the Canada Mail on the Tuesday following, at 4 o'Clock in the Afternoon. The Saturday Night's Mail is to be conveyed to Albany, on the West Side of the River, and the Rider will return to this Office on the Saturday following at 12 o'Clock.

By Command of the Deputy Post Masters General.

RICH. N. COLDEN, D. Secr'y.

JUST PUBLISHED,

[*Price* 1s. 4.]

And to be Sold by *John Kneeland*, Printer, in Milk-Street; *James Foster Condy*, Stationer, in Union-Street; and *Philip Freeman*, jun. near Liberty-Tree.

AN ORATION delivered on the

late public Commencement at Rhode-Island College in Providence, September 1774. Being a Plea for the Right of private Judgment in religious Matters; and for the Liberty of choosing our own Religion, corroborated by the well known Consequences of Priestly Power.

BY BARNABAS BINNEY, A. B.

Salmon Twine.

JEREMIAH ALLEN has for Sale at his Shop in Ann-Street, a little North of the Draw Bridge —— A Quantity of the best 3-Thread Salmon Twine. (6w.)

THE Brethren of the ancient and honorable Society of FREE and ACCEPTED MASONS are hereby notified; That the most Worshipful JOSEPH WARREN, Esq; Grand Master of Ancient, Free and Accepted Masons on the Continent of America, intends celebrating the Feast of St. John the Evangelist on Tuesday the 27th Instant, at Free Masons Hall, Boston, where the Brethren are required to attend the Festival.

By Order of the most Worshipful Grand Master,

W. HOSKINS, G. Secretary.

N.B. The Table will be furnished at 2 o'Clock, P.M. --Tickets to be had of Brothers Capt Caleb Hopkins, Andrew Newell, and William Hoskins.

Boston, Dec. 13, 1774.

TO BE SOLD *very cheap*,

The Schooner Hawk, about 65 Tons burthen, a Marblehead Fishing Vessel with a Sheath'd Bottom, good Sails and Rigging, lying at Mr. John Pulling's Wharff. —— For Particulars inquire at

Archibald Cunningham's

Store in Ann-Street, near the Draw-Bridge.

—— Where is to be sold ——

Lisbon WINE per Cask, — Lisbon Oil per Cask, — Geneva per Case, — Raisins, Figs and Currants per Cask, — Firkin Butter, — Kippen's Snuff and Pig-Tail Tobacco, — Spices of all sorts, — Citron, — half Pint Dram Bottles per Crate or Groce, — Almonds, — choice Olives, — Capers, — Brown & Loaf Sugar, — Dutch Brushes in Setts or single, — Dutch Stone Ware per Crate or Dozen, — Corks, — Mason Glasses Engrav'd with the Arms, — best Durham Mustard in large and small Bottles, — Barcelona Handkerchiefs per Dozen.

TO BE SOLD, only for Want of Employ,

A likely, sprightly good-tempered

Negro Boy, about 13 Years of Age. Inquire of Edes and Gill.

Stray'd away from me the Sub-

scriber, in Newton, sometime in July last, a spotted or placked black and white Steer, two Years old. Whoever shall take up the said Steer, or give Information where he may be had, shall be handsomely rewarded by me,

JOHN HEALY.

To be Sold by PUBLIC VENDUE,

On WEDNESDAY *the 22d Day of* March *next*,

At Eleven o'Clock Beforenoon, at the Royal-Exchange Tavern in King-Street, Boston, pursuant to a Vote of the Proprietors of the *Kennebeck*-Purchase from the late Colony of *New-Plymouth*, passed the Sixteenth Day of *November* last:

The following Tract of Land to be set up in undivided Twelfths, at 100l. L. M. for each Twelfth, being about 6000 Acres to a Twelfth.

A Tract of Land situated North-West from Fort-Halifax, and lying on each side of Little Norridgwalk River, and within 15 Miles of Kennebeck River, on the West side thereof, containing about 72000 Acres.

Provided nevertheless that if any Proprietor of the said Kennebeck Purchase shall chuse to retain his Share of of the said Tract, and shall on or before Wednesday the 15th Day of March next, pay to Henry Alline, jun. Clerk of said Proprietors, his Proportion of 1200l. L. M. which is 100l. L. M. to one Twelfth, and so more or less, according to his Share or Interest in said Propriety, then such Share or Interest of the said Tract shall be reserved to him, but if Payment be not made on the said 15th Day of March next, then the whole of said Tract will be sold on said 22d Day of March next, without such Reservation. By Order of said Proprietors.

HENRY ALLINE, jun. Prop's Clerk.

Boston, December 10 1774.

Joshua Blanchard,

AT the Old Shop and Wine Cellar on Dock-Square BOSTON, opposite Exchange Lane,

yet continues to sell

WINES

of all Sorts as usual, and hath now on sale a Parcel of fine old Sterling Madeira from 3 Dollars to 8 Dollars per Dozen according to its Age and Quality; also by the Gallon or less Quantity, Fyal Wine at 25s. Old Tenor per Gallon, a better Sort on Maderia Lees at 30s. O. T.

West-India Proof genuine Rum.

Fine old Spirit, French and other Brandies.

Mr. BLANCHARD *thanks his Friends and the Publick for past Favours, and hopes in these hard Times their Continuance.*

He hath also to sell,

Cocoa, Loaf-Sugar, Raisins, Figgs, Currants, Spices, with a general Assortment of West-India Goods and Groceries, by Wholesale or Retail.

A Quantity of choice Honey.

All Persons who have any Demands

on the Estate of Nathaniel Holmes, of Boston, deceased, are desired to bring in their Accounts to Rebecca Holmes, Executrix, for Adjustment: All those who are indebted to said Estate are desired to make immediate Payment to said Executrix.

William Fowle,

ACQUAINTS the Public, That he carries on the Sugar-Baking Business, at the Sugar-House formerly Occupied by the late Nathaniel Holmes, deceased.

—— Where he has ready for Sale ——

Best double, single, and Lump Refin'd Loaf and brown SUGAR, MOLASSES, FLOUR and IRON, by Wholesale or Retail, cheap for Cash.

The Treasurer for the County of Suffolk,

gives Notice to all whom it may concern, that as he is obliged to leave the Town for a few Months, the Business of said County will be transacted by Mr. *Thomas Crafts*, jun. at his House near Liberty-Tree.

New Flour and Raisins.

John Kneeland,

At his Store the Head of Green's Wharff, opposite JOHN ROWE, Esq; —— HAS FOR SALE ——

A few Barrels new Philadelphia Flour, choice Raisins per Cask, Sugars, Coffee, Chocolate, West-India and New-England Rum, Brandy —— Also,

A few Pieces Ratteens, Coatings and Lambskins, to be sold very cheap.

Goods sold on low Commissions.

TO BE SOLD,

THE BRIG Benja. and Salley, a good Vessel Burthen about 140 Tuns, well Found, lying at Hutchinson's Wharf, Inquire of Capt. Edward Jarvis, near the New Brick Meeting House,

Taken up by *John Williams*, Tanner of Roxbury, on the 20th of November, a red and white COW, about 9 or 10 Years old. and on the 23d of said Month calved. Any Person owning said Cow, by applying to said *Williams*, may have her again by paying the Charges.

—Wanted in this Town—

An active, industrious, sober, honest, capable young Man, that has been brought up in a Retail Shop of English Goods, he must write a good Hand, quick at Figures and very obliging to the smallest Customers—Such a Person (and no other) may apply to the Printers for further Information.

Boston, December 5th, 1774.

James Bruce of Boston (at present in London) Mariner, maketh Oath, and saith, that he this Deponent has no Knowledge of, nor to the best of his Remembrance, was never in Company with a Captain Lovett, who is said by a Paragraph in the Boston Journal, dated 28 July, last, to have been in Company with this Deponent, at a Tavern in Antigua, and that the Contents of the Paragraph, there inserted (in order to hurt him this Deponent) is groundless and void of Truth, and that this Deponent never made use of any such Expressions there inserted, and further this Deponent saith, that he did not think or know at the Time he took the East India Company's Tea on Board the Ship Eleanor, that the same would have been either detrimental, or displeasing to the Town of Boston, otherwise himself and owners would not have suffered any of the said Tea to have been shipt on Board the said Ship Eleanor.

JAMES BRUCE.

Sworn before me at Shadwell, 16th Day of September,

JOHN SHERWOOD.

All Persons who are indebted to the Estate of the late Mr. William Molineux, deceased: Also all Persons who had Demands on, or were indebted to him as Attorney to others, are desired to make them known, and to pay their respective Dues to the Subscriber, who is fully empowered to adjust and receive the same.

THOMAS APTHORP

Boston: Printed, by EDES & GILL.
in Queen-Street, 1774.

THE Boston- AND COUNTRY Gazette, JOURNAL.

Containing the freshest Advices, Foreign and Domestic.

MONDAY, December 26, 1774.

THIS DAY PUBLISHED, and sold by EDES and GILL, in Queen-Street,
The MISERY and DUTY of an oppress'd and enslav'd People, represented in a
SERMON
Delivered at SALISBURY, July 14. 1774.
On a Day set apart for FASTING and PRAYER,
On account of approaching public Calamities.
Published by Request,
By SAMUEL WEBSTER, A. M.
Pastor of a Church in SALISBURY.
NEHEMIAH IX. 36,——38.
Behold we are Servants this Day! And for the Land that thou gavest unto our Fathers, to eat the Fruit thereof, and the Good thereof, behold we are Servants in it! And it yieldeth much Increase unto the Kings which thou hast set over us, because of our Sins: Also they have Dominion over our Bodies and over our Cattle, at their Pleasure: And we are in great Distress! And because of all this, we make a sure Covenant, and write it, and our Princes, Levites & Priests seal unto it.
☞ Subscribers are desired to call or send for their Books.

WILLIAMSBURG, (in Virginia) Nov. 24.

THE Inhabitants of York having been informed that the Virginia commanded by Howard Esten, had on board two half chests of tea shipped by John Norton, Esq; and sons, merchants in London, by order of Mess. Prentis and company, merchants in Williamsburg, assembled at 10 o'clock, this morning, and went on board the said ship, where they waited some time for the determination of the meeting of several members of the house of burgesses in Williamsburg, who had taken this matter under consideration. A messenger was then sent on shore to enquire for a letter from the meeting; but returning without one they immediately hoisted the tea out of the hold and threw it into the river, and then returned to the shore without doing damage to the ship or any other part of her cargo. On the Wednesday following the county committee met to consider of this matter; and after mature deliberation, came to the following resolutions:

Resolved, that we do highly approve of the conduct of the inhabitants of York, in destroying the tea on board the Virginia.

Resolved, that Mess. Prentis and company have incurred the displeasure of their countrymen, by not countermanding their orders for the tea, having had frequent opportunities to have done so; and that they ought to make proper concessions for such misconduct, or be made to feel the resentment of the public.

Resolved, that John Norton, Esq; of London must have known the determination of this colony with respect to tea, as the ship Virginia did not sail from thence till after the late assembly was dissolved, and the members of that assembly in behalf of the colony, immediately upon their dissolution, entered into a solemn negociation against that article.

Resolved therefore, to convince our enemies that we never will submit to any measure that may in the least endanger our liberties, which we are determined to defend at the risk of our lives, that the ship Virginia ought to clear out from hence in ballast, in eighteen days from this time.

Resolved, that Howard Esten, commander of the ship Virginia, acted imprudently in not remonstrating in stronger terms against the tea being put on board the ship, as he well knew it would be disagreeable to the inhabitants of this colony.

We submit to our countrymen whether every ship circumstanced as the Virginia was, ought not to share the same fate.

Signed by order of the committee,
WILLIAM RUSSEL, Clerk.

Gloucester county, November 7, 1774.

FROM certain information that the Virginia, captain Howard Esten, was arrived in York river with a quantity of tea on board, twenty-three members of the committee of Gloucester county, with a number of the inhabitants assembled at Gloucester-Town, to determine how the said tea should be disposed of.

Hearing that the members of the house of burgesses in Williamsburg, about eight o'clock this morning, had taken the matter under their consideration, we determined to wait the result of their deliberations. We accordingly waited till after twelve; but the determinations from Williamsburgh having not then come down, we repaired to the ship, in order to meet the committee of York, which we supposed to be a great number of those we discerned on board. On our arrival, we found that the tea had met with its deserved fate, for it had been committed to the waves. We then returned, and after mature deliberation came to the following resolutions:

Resolved, that John Norton, merchant in London, by sending over tea in his ship, has lent his little aid to the ministry for enslaving America, and been guilty of a daring insult upon the people of this colony, to whom he owes his ALL.

Resolved, that the ship Virginia, in which the detestable tea came, ought and shall return in twenty days from the date hereof.

Resolved, that no tobacco shall be shipped from this county on board the said ship, either to the owners or any other person whatsoever; and we do most earnestly recommend it to our countrymen to enter into the same resolution, in their respective counties.

Resolved, that the said Norton has forfeited all title to the confidence of this county, and that we will not in future consign tobacco, or any other commodity, to his house, until satisfactory concessions are made; and we recommend the same resolution to the rest of the colony.

Resolved, that John Prentis, who wrote for and to whom the tea was consigned, has justly incurred the censure of this country, and that he ought to be made a public example.

Resolved, that Howard Esten, commander of the Virginia, has acted imprudently, by which he has drawn on himself the displeasure of the people of this county.

Signed by order of the committee,
JASPER CLAYTON, Clerk.

Williamsburg, November 24, 1774.

IT gives me much concern to find that I have incurred the displeasure of the York and Gloucester committees, and thereby of the publick in general, for my omission in not countermanding the order which I sent to Mr. Norton for two half chests of tea; and do with truth declare, that I had not the least intention to give offence, nor did I mean an opposition to any measures for the public good. My countrymen, therefore, it is earnestly hoped, will readily forgive me for an act which may be interpreted so much to my discredit; and I again make this public declaration, that I had not the least design to act contrary to those principles which ought to govern every individual who has a just regard for the rights and liberties of America. JOHN PRENTIS.

WILLIAMSBURG, (Virginia) Dec. 1.

We have it from very good Authority, that his Excellency the Governor is on his Way to this Capital, having concluded a Peace with the several Tribes of Indians that have been at War with us, and taken Hostages of them for their faithful complying with the Terms of it, the principal of which are, that they shall totally abandon the Lands on this Side of the Ohio, (which River is to be the Boundary between them and the White People) and never more take up the Hatchet against the English. Thus, in little more than the Space of 5 Months, an End is put to a War which portended much Trouble and Mischief to the Inhabitants on the Frontiers, owing to the Zeal and good Conduct of the Officers and Commanders who went out in their Country's Defence, and the Bravery and Perseverance of all the Troops. Our Tributes of Praise are justly due to the gallant Men that fell, whose Deaths are a publick Loss, and irreparable so to their distressed Families and Friends; but their Names will be handed down to Posterity, with Honor.—The Army was broke up, and many of them had arrived at their respective Homes.

Extract of a Letter from a Gentleman in London, to his Correspondent in Williamsburg, Virginia.

"IF you submit to the last arbitrary and tyrannical acts of parliament, relative to Massachusetts-Bay and Quebec, there will not be a set of more abject slaves under Heaven than the North-Americans. You will be obliged to dig Tobacco, Iron, and whatever your good and virtuous Masters here want. The Marquis of Caermarthen, a Puppy just entered into the infernal Pack of Bloodhounds, said in the House of Commons, we sent such to those Colonies to labour for us, &c. And so sure as England now exists (it can not long, indeed, in its present State of Luxury, Debauchery, and Villainy) but I say, so long and so sure as it does exist in this State, if the Americans now submit, the Charters of all the other Colonies will be attacked, and treated as that of the Massachusetts-Bay has already been. This is determined I assure you. They were afraid to attack more than Boston at first, lest it might occasion a Union of the Colonies; but New-York, Pennsylvania, and South-Carolina, will be struck at, because they refused Entrance to the Tea; Connecticut, Rhode-Island, and all the old Provinces in America, impeached because their Charters are bad; and among the rest Virginia will be included, especially as you dared to go to prayers and fast. Remember this, and recollect, I pray, my dear, that I do not speak from Opinion, but from undoubted, uncontrovertible authority. The King will recommend it in his next speech to Parliament, finding his Colonies in North America are not properly governed, owing to the several Charters now subsisting in the said Colonies, &c. &c. &c. To prepare too for the more effectual Execution of this hellish Plan, Orders are sent to his Majesty's Catholic Province of Quebec immediately to raise and embody 4000 of his good and Catholic Subjects of Canada, to be formed into four Regiments, and to be commanded by Frenchmen; you may guess for what.—But lest you should not, I will tell you, that these good Subjects, and the Indians, are to be set to cut the Throats of the King's disaffected Subjects of the old Provinces, who sent at their own Expence 20 000 Men, last War, to make the Canadians subjects of the very virtuous and pious Prince George III. This is as true as holy Writ.

"I dare not tell you how I came by the knowledge of these schemes, as it would, were it discovered, prevent me from knowing and telling you more; but I hope it will rouse the people of North America to exert themselves, to convince the world that they will not wear the chains of 500 such traiterous and haughty tyrants. Better it is, far, to be subjected to any One that ever existed, who has, and can have, only his own vanity or caprice to satisfy, than to so numerous a body of needy, luxurious, mercenary rascals, who would even sell their king, could they find another to promise the addition of 100l. to the Chancellorship of Great-Britain, or 5l. to a gentleman usher. I cannot guess how, or by what means, you have been persuaded, in North-America, that you have any friends, really so from principle, in this country. It is true, some publickly declaim, and pretend to lament the situation of their brethren on the other side the atlantic; as they hope, being out of place, to climb up to preferment from espousing their quarrel. But, at the same time, I can venture to say, that there is not a person, male or female, resident in Great-Britain, and contributing to its taxes, from the Lord Chancellor to the shoeblack, who does not rejoice at this exertion of power; nor is there a manufacturer in England who does not say, trade will now revive, as our American subjects will be convinced we are no longer to be trifled with, and that they will now be properly punished, if they commit Riots, &c. as they will be bro't here and tried for their offences by a jury of englishmen, who will not be so complacent to them as the rascals in their own country were (who were all liable to be tried for treason & rebellion) with ten thousand speeches to the same effect. Now, lest you should call me a declaimer, and say I represented dangers without telling you how to avoid them, I will give you a specifick, which, if it fails to produce an immediate and effectual cure, I will acknowledge myself a quack in politicks and declare against any further practice in state disorders: It is a remedy easily administered, and can not, at least to sound constitutions, be unsalutable. Moreover, it is so cheap, and easily procured, that no person need advance sixpence, or——

out of his own house, to procure it, as it is only an agreement to stop all exports and imports.—Enter heartily, and with firmness, into such an association; and bind yourselves, even by an oath, not only to observe it individually, but to enforce it generally. If you do this, and these hellish acts are not sent back to the devil in less than eight months I will agree to be tarred and feathered, and hanged on Liberty-tree afterwards; but if you do not, I will venture to pronounce and declare, that for fifty years to come the people of North-America will be the most miserable of slaves. They will hold life and property only at the will and sufferance of their tyrannical and profligate oppressors. It must not, it cannot be so. Americans will be free; at least I hope so, especially as you have the means so much in your power. They are absolutely now in your hands, and you will justly merit every oppression & insult if you throw them away.

PHILADELPHIA, December 11.

Committee Chamber, Dec. 5th, 1774.

Moved and agreed,

THAT a Committee of Inspection and Observation be appointed to attend the execution of the first resolve of the Congress; and that this Committee (the President and Secretaries excepted) be divided for that business into six particular districts—the divisions as follow, viz. [*Here follow the names of the Committee.*]

Agreed, that it be recommended to the above Committee, that one person out of each district attend every day at ten o'clock at the London Coffee house, to inspect the arrival of all vessels, and to make every other necessary enquiry.

Ordered, That masters of vessels, pilots and others, be desired to give as early information as possible, at the London Coffee-house, of the arrival of all vessels at this port.

By Order of the Committee,

JACOB RUSH, *pro temp.* Secretary.

In ASSEMBLY.

December 10th, 1774. A. M.

THE House taking into consideration the report of the Committee appointed to attend the General Congress, and the papers therein referred to,

Resolved Unanimously, That this House approve the proceedings and resolves of the Congress; and do most seriously recommend to the good people of this province a strict attention to, and inviolable observation of the several matters and things contained in the Journal of the said Congress.

On Motion Ordered, That the above resolve be immediately made public.

Extract from the Journals,

CHARLES MOORE, *Clk of Assembly.*

NEW-YORK, December 15.

We hear that at a Meeting of the General Committee of this City and County, two Sub-Committees were appointed to superintend the Sales of two Cargoes of Goods arrived here since the first Day of December. And that it was the Opinion of the Committee, that all Goods, Wares and Merchandize, enumerated in the first Article of the Continental Congress, should be subject to the Regulations contained in the tenth Article.

Last Week several Parcels of Goods were sold here agreeable to the Association entered into by the Continental Congress.

Advices from all the colonies assure us of their unanimous concurrence in all the measures recommended by the General Congress.

By Letters from London, we learn, That there are more than one Hundred new Members in the present Parliament.

Last Week Captain Riker in a Schooner from Charles Town, arrived here with 103 Tierces of Rice, consigned to Philip Livingston and Charles M'Evers, Esq'rs; to be disposed of for the Support of the Poor of Boston, being Part of the generous Benefactions from the Province of South Carolina, for the Relief of the much injured and oppressed Inhabitants of that devoted Town.

The neat Proceeds of 375 Tierces of Rice (lately arrived here from Charles Town, in the Sloop Phenix, Capt. Dickenson) being also Part of the Benefactions from the same Place and for the same People) we hear amounted to 12,00l. and will be remitted in a few Days.

On Monday last, many Hand-bills having been seen about Town, advertising the intended Exhibition, that Evening, of two Puppet Shews, one in the Fields, the other at the Exchange; a considerable Number of respectable Citizens, duly sensible of the Importance of a strict Conformity to the Articles of the Association of the Grand General Congress, and of a sacred Regard to their Recommendations, had a Meeting on the above Advertisements, and deputed a Committee of their Body to inspect, and prevent the Exhibitions. The Committee found the Performers in the Exercise of their Vocation, before a considerable Number of Spectators, who all appeared in great Confusion on the Appearance of the Committee; and on being informed of their Business, and that such Meetings were contrary to the Recommendations of the Congress, offensive to the Inhabitants, and unsuitable to the present Situation of public Affairs, both the Companies precipitately dispersed, and the Managers promised that they would no more attempt any Thing of the Kind, without Leave of the Committee of Inspection.

We hear the letter of the General Congress, to the Inhabitants of Canada, had met with a very general & high approbation thro'out that country, where a translation of it had been published.

NEW-YORK, December 19.

His Majesty has been pleased to grant the Dignity of a Baronet of Great-Britain on William Pepperell, of Boston, in the Province of Massachusetts Bay, in America, Esq;

Mr. William Gage, second Son to General Gage, died in London about two Months ago.

Some Ships fitting out at the Port of Liverpool about 7 Weeks since, could not have Permission to take on board either Gunpowder, or any Kind of Guns, Swords, &c.

By a Gentleman who left Quebec about twenty Days ago, we learn, That the Reports we have had here of the Canadians and Indians being to be raised and sent to act against the People of Boston, &c. is entirely groundless; and that should a Thing of that Nature be proposed to the French, 'twould be rejected with Disdain.

The Suffolk County Resolves are published in the London Papers of the 29th of October, and has given some Uneasiness 'tis said to the Ministry.

NEW-HAVEN, December 14.

By a Gentleman lately from Canada, we are informed, "That *Mons. Partuise*, an Indian Interpreter, said to be lately sent by Governor *Carlton*, among the Six Nations, and other Indians, to know if they would join the king's troops against the American colonies, if required, was returned with the following answer, That they looked upon the dispute between Great Britain and the colonies, as a family quarrel between father and sons, (which they made no doubt would be amicably settled) and that it was contrary to their custom to interfere between parents and children; and that they were moreover apprehensive, in case they interfered, and the colonies got the better of the king's troops, they of course must fall a sacrifice to their resentment. He also informs us, that the priests and noblesse, employed to sound the French Canadians, have met with no better encouragement, they declaring that they look upon the other colonies as their brethren, and that they will by no means take up arms against them. And that it was generally imagined, by gentlemen best acquainted with the disposition of the Canadians, that it would be impossible to raise a single regiment in all Canada; and the farmers and tradesmen were preparing a petition to the court of Great Britain, begging that the French laws might not take place, but that the English laws might be continued, which they had found by experience to be much better, and with which they were extreamly well satisfied."

PORTSMOUTH, Dec. 23.

Mr. FRINTER,

AS the Affair of Removing the POWDER and some GUNS from the FORT, hath been Matter of some Speculation, I was determined to enquire and judge for myself: and find upon critical Examination, that the People of the Province of New-Hampshire are well known to have supported the Character of loyal Subjects of his MAJESTY. and have been distinguished for their Obedience to all Subordinate Officers, without carefully attending to the present Popular Patriotism of this Country. So far from pushing themselves into the *Front* in the present unhappy Disputes, they have been blamed for *falling too far in the Rear*.---But what will not the great Law of Nature, that Law of self-preservation, the Love of Life, and it's dear Connections, at Length effect? Alarmed with the Tendency of the Quebec Act, with Accounts that the *Canadians* and *Indians* (confirmed by some late Depredations committed by the latter upon the Frontiers of a neighbouring Government) were to be call'd fo th to enforce the late Acts of Parliament, so disagreeable to all the Colonies, long inured to defend themselves in the wide extended Frontiers of this Province, by their Valour, against the restless and cruel Savages of the Wilderness, without any other Aid, and while destitute of Arms necessary for such Defence, finding that his MAJESTY IN COUNCIL, not knowing their peculiar defenceless State, had been pleased to prohibit the Exportation of Powder, Arms and other warlike Stores to the Colonies without special Licence.-----Some of the good People of this Province, in the wonted honesty and Simplicity of their Hearts, imagined that nobody would have just Reason to complain of their too great Forwardness, if they seasonably removed some of the warlike Stores from the Fort nearer to their Frontiers, where the Fears of the Inhabitants were most excited, and where they had too great Reason to think such Stores would be soon wanted. Which they accordingly effected, without any great Tumult or Opposition; as it was not suspected that they had any d flo al or bad intenti ns. I give this simple Narrative of this Transaction, to prevent any Colourings or Exaggerations thereof that may be made by the Foes of America. A LOVER of ORDER.

TO be Sold by WILLIAM VERNON, a few Tierces good Shop SUGAR. Likewise a well-built Schooner about 90 Tons. For Particulars, enquire of said VERNON, at his House in Bennet-Street, North-End.

By the Mercury Packet, and several other Vessels arrived at the Southward, since our last, from Falmouth, Liverpool and Bristol, we have the following Advices, viz.

LONDON.

Oct. 15. A correspondent assures us, that notwithstanding the various causes *assigned* for the *sudden death* of the late Parliament that it died *rotten* of the *King's evil.*

Oct. 18. By authentic letters from Rome, we are assured the late pope was poisoned by the influence of the Jesuits, against which society he has distinguished himself in a very severe manner.

Many people censure the K— for the American business; he certainly does not act himself, but does implicitly as he is bid; but when Monarchs are so dictated to, and those councils prove detrimental to public good, does it not behove the people to enquire into the machinations of those, who are the conductors of such base matters?

One hundred thousand pounds, it is computed, will not defray the expences government, or the public, hath already been at, in their endeavour to subject the Americans, and yet they seem just where they were.

It is now determined to send a very considerable force, as well of ships as men, to Boston; and it is settled that General Gage is to enforce the Americans to obedience.

The marines under orders for Boston are to be disembarked there, and to act in conjunction with the land forces.

Oct. 20. This morning about 8 o'clock, a great number of freeholders of Middlesex, pursuant to advertisement, met John Wilkes and John Glynn, Esqrs, at the Mansion-house, from whence a cavalcade soon after set out for Brentford, with flags and French horns, and being nominated as fit persons to serve in the present Parliament, they were unanimously elected.

Oct. 22. An order of the council, dated the 19th inst. is published in this night's gazette, prohibiting the exportation of gun-powder and arms, from any part of the kingdom.

Lord Chatham still continues inflexible, notwithstanding, as it is said, he has within this month had offers to unite himself with administration, that few men in the kingdom would have withstood.

Wednesday Sir George Saville, and Mr. Lascelles were unanimously elected members for the county of York.

Also, Lord Algernon Percy, and Sir William Middleton, for Northumberland.

Lord Mansfield, we are informed, hath negociated the business he went on to the Court of France, in so compleat a manner, that we may expect to remain in tranquility with France some years; the French Monarch having assured his Lordship, that nothing is more distant from his thoughts, than breaking the peace with the Crown of G. Britain.

A report was yesterday current, that some bad news had arrived from America, which occasioned the holding a Cabinet-Council; it is added, that an express was dispatched from the Admiralty, for the ships now fitting out for Boston to sail with all possible dispatch.

The West-India Governors have received orders, we hear, to return home immediately, on account of repeated complaints of their inattention & inability.

Notwithstanding the ministerial accounts from America are kept a profound secret, the late embargo on gunpowder proves their fears respecting that country to be very great. Great quantities of nitre and salt-petre just shipped, are again disembarking in consequence of Saturday's Gazette.

Oct. 27. A letter received in town from an English Gentleman at Brest, says, that a French frigate and a snow lately sailed from that port for America, laden with firelocks, gunpowder, &c. It is added, that two experienced military Officers embarked on board the said frigate.

Oct. 29. Yesterday Mr. Remembrancer waited upon the Lord High Chancellor, and notified to his Lordship the election of Mr. Wilkes as Lord Mayor for the year ensuing, when Thursday next was appointed for the Lord Mayor elect being presented to the Chancellor.

Last night the following summons was sent to the several Aldermen:—"Your Worship is desired to be at Guildhall on Thursday next, at twelve o'clock in the forenoon, being the 3d of November, to accompany the Lord Mayor elect to the Lord Chancellor. His Lordship will be going from Guildhall, precisely at one, the Lord Chancellor having fixed for two o'clock.

Nov. 2. No poll for Members to represent Bristol, was ever known to continue so long as the present; it has held three weeks already, and it is imagined will not be yet finally closed for some days. The number of voters that have been made free is incredible, being near 2000, and a very considerable part of them even since the poll began.

Bristol, Nov. 1. State of the Poll this Day.

Cruger 3496.	Burke 2647.
Brickdale 2412.	Clare 276.

BOSTON, December 26.

Our brethren of New-Hampshire and Rhode-Island have signalized themselves in a manner that does them the greatest honour: And it is with pleasure we can add, that the Colony of Connecticut merit our highest regards for their present assiduity and vigilance in disciplining their militia, which consists of near 30 regiments,— Indeed the whole UNITED COLONIES are extreamly active and zealous in the common cause, all nobly exerting themselves for carrying into execution the measures agreed upon by the late continental congress, excepting a few disappointed, factious tories, some of whom are employed, *most infamously employed*, in villifying the most virtuous and amiable characters in America, and particularly in traducing the worthy members of the late continental assembly.

A Vessel loaded with upwards of 1000 Bushels of Corn, from Rappahannock in Virginia, for the suffering Poor of this Town, hath been blown off the Coast and is got to St. Eustatia, where the Cargo will be sold and the proceeds remitted to Boston.

Letters from London inform us, that the Empress of Russia, in consequence of the Advantages she has received from the Support afforded to her Operations by the Crown of Great-Britain in the late War against the Ottoman Empire, has granted to the Subjects of our most gracious Sovereign, a free Navigation in all the Seas of her Majesty's Realm, including those Rights secured to the Crown of Russia by the late glorious Peace concluded with the Turks.

On the 8th December Inst. Doctor JOHN TAYLOR of Lunenburgh, in Order for the Promotion of the *Military Art*, the Knowledge of which in these Times of Public Calamity seems indispensably necessary, *generously gave* to the Minute Company in that Town, 55 Military Books according to the Plan of Exercise ordered by his Majesty, Anno Domini, 1764; viz. One Book to *every* Officer and Soldier in said Company.——*A notable Instance of the Patriotic Spirit of the Donor.*

A Gentleman is arrived at Salem in a Vessel from Cape Nichola Mole, which he left the 17th November, just as he was coming away a Vessel arrived from the Island of Cuba, which she left only two Days before, the Master of which informed him that he was oblig'd to quit the Island in the greatest Hurry, and leave all his Cargo behind, there being so many Spanish Vessels cruizing to intercept all Provision Vessels bound to the Island of Jamaica, that it was hardly possible for any to escape; this may be depended on as a Fact, and all the French and Spaniards were employed Night and Day in repairing and building Fortifications with the greatest Expedition, and furnishing all their Garrisons with a large Stock of Provisions and Ammunition. During his Stay at the Mole, Transports were arriving daily with Troops and Provisions.

We hear that on Friday last a Soldier of the 64th Regiment was found froze to Death on Dorchester Neck.

Last Saturday Morning, one William Ferguson, a Soldier of the 10th Regiment, (lately arrived from Quebec,) aged 28, was shot at the Bottom of the Common in this Town, for Desertion.

Messieurs EDES & GILL,

I Can't forbear communicating thro' your Paper an Anecdote that gave me great Pleasure, and I doubt not will to most of your Readers. An aged Rev. Divine in a neighbouring Town, whose Praise is in all our Churches, attending a Funeral, before the Procession began, was presented with a Pair of Gloves, which he nobly refused, telling the Person who offer'd them, That the Continental Congress, in much Wisdom, and with great Consideration, had recommended many Rules of Frugality and Oeconomy as a Means of extricating us out of the State of Oppression we are now grievously suffering in, and he was determin'd to pay the strictest Regard to them himself; and the Disuse of Gloves at Funerals was one of them. Upon this, the Gloves which were spread on the Coffin for the Bearers were taken away. In this Instance we see what Effect the Advice and Example of our Spiritual Fathers may have, in promoting that patriotic Love of Liberty, which has from the earliest Days been the Characteristic of an American Divine, *and ought ever to be the predominant Principle in every Son and Daughter of* America.

Donations receiv'd since our last.

From MASSACHUSETTS-BAY.

North-Yarmouth, 8 Cords Wood.

Post Office, Boston, Dec. 26, 1774.

This is to inform the Public, That by Command of the Post Master General, the P—t will be dispatch'd from this Office, on Thursday next, at Nine o'Clock in the Morning; of which all concerned will please to take Notice.

TO LETT,

A House in Battery-MarchStreet, now occupied by Mr. PECK. Persons inclined to hire, may know the Terms by enquiring at said House.

Public Notice is hereby given,

That there is to be sold under the Direction of the Committee of Inspection for the Town of Plimouth (agreeable to the Tenth Article of the American Continental Association) a Cargo of Sea-Coal, about 140 Tons, and five Casks of Nails, imported in the Bri. Sea-Nymph, from Bristol, since the First of December Instant. The Sale to be at Plimouth, on board said Vessel, Monday the 2d Day of January next, at XI o'Clock Forenoon.

December 20 1774

TO BE SOLD

(Agreeable to the American Congress Association)

On FRIDAY the 6th of January next,

at PUBLIC AUCTION, at the House of Mr. Benjamin Burdick, *Innholder in Marblehead, The remaining Part of the Cargo of the Ship Champion, Capt.* Nathaniel Fellows, *as follows, viz.*

INVOICE 8, *a Sett of Rigging for a large Ship, consisting of Anchors, Cables, Iron Hearth, 51 Coyles Cordage, Blocks, Ship Chandlers Ware, &c.* Sterl. Cost about £ 430.

Invoice 9, Mustard and Spanish Brown

Cost about £. 6 0 0

Invoice 10, Cod Lines, Checks, Brass Chair Nails and Hemp. Sterl. Cost about £. 720.

Invoice 11, 4 Cask Porter in Bottles.

Cost unknown at present.

Invoice 12, 8 small Cask of Ink-Powder, and a few other Packages;—the Invoices of which have not yet been sent to the Committee of Inspection, but may be then seen, unless the Importers shall be so hardy as to refuse a Compliance with the Association.

AT

OTIS's Grocery Store,

Between Mr. Tho's. H. Peck's and the Vernon Corner,

GREEN COFFEE, per Bag or Dozen.

Spanish, French and Carolina INDIGO, per Dozen or single Pound.

SUGARS, per Hogshead or Barrel.

CHOCOLATE, per Box.

RAISINS.

A Quantity of dry'd ORANGE PEEL.

& REDWOOD,

Delivered at Marblehead, Providence or Boston.

ALSO,

West India GOODS and GROCERIES, *by Retail.*

Said OTIS dealing intirely for ready Money, *must sell cheap.*

Commission Business done as usual at said Store, with Punctuality and Attention.

ALSO,

A Parcel of excellent striped and checked Flannels.

N. B. Best Durham MUSTARD, in lb. ½ & ¼ lb. Bottles.

TO BE SOLD BY

Charles Miller,

At his Store in King-Street,

CHOICE Brandy in Pipes and Quarter Casks, Cases of Geneva, Cherry Rum, Cherry Brandy, Rasberry Brandy in Barrels, excellent Shrub in Barrels & Kegs, Loaf Sugar by Hogshead or single Loaf, superfine and common Philadelphia Flour, a few Bags Pepper, Raisins, Flour Mustard by large or small Quantities, &c. &c.

The above Articles will be Sold at a low Rate. As said MILLER intends soon to leave this Province for some Time, he requests those who are indebted to him to make immediate Payment; and those who have any Demands on him, to call & receive their respective Dues.

All Persons indebted to, or having any Demands upon the Estate of the Rev'd. Mr. SETH STORER, late of Watertown, deceased, are desired to settle the same with EBENEZER STORER, Executor.

Boston, December 26, 1774.

PUBLIC AUCTION,

TO BE SOLD,

By *BENJAMIN CHURCH,*

At his usual Place of Sale,

On *Thursday Next,*

Broad-Cloths—Plains—Bearskin—Camblets—Stuffs—Irish Hollands—Checks—Bed Ticks—Handkerchiefs, &c. A Mahogany Case of Draws—Beareau—Desk—side Boards—Beds—Easy Chairs, and others—A Quantity of Buckram, HouseFurniture, &c.

One Dollar Reward.

ANY Person that will give Information to the Printers of an old Negro Fellow named Cæsar, who went away some Time since, and is suppos'd to be strolling about in some of the neighbouring Towns, walks lame and talks much of being free, shall receive the above Reward. Had on when he went away a blue Jacket.

New Auction-Room, *Cornhill.*

To-Morrow Morning at Ten o'Clock,

Will be Sold, by PUBLIC VENDUE,

At GREENLEAF's Auction-Room,

A large and valuable Assortment of English Goods—*Amongst which are*—

VELVETS & Velverets, superfine Manchester Checks, Irish Linnens, Mens Buckrams, Oznabrigs, Silk Twist, Silk and Hair, Belladine Sewing Silks, fine Breeches Patterns, Shalloons, middling and low priced Broad Cloths, Mens Worsted Hose, fine Lawns, and sundry Houshold Furniture. Wm. GREENLEAF, Auctioneer.

N.B. A genteel Gold chas'd Watch suitable for a Lady.

The Sale will begin at Ten o'Clock.

THE Publick may be assured that the Small-Pox in this Town is now confined to two Families, viz. Capt. Figs, opposite the White Horse, and Lieut. Clarke's in Hanover Street; those who were Sick of that Disorder at Dr. Hill's and the Hospital being recovered; proper Care has been taken to cleanse Dr. Hill's House, and Guards are continued at those Places not yet clear of the Infection. No Inhabitant has hitherto taken the Distemper, and by the Care of his Excellency the Governor a Transport is provided for the reception of any Person belonging to the Army that should hereafter appear to have the Symptom of that Disorder.

By Order of the Selectmen,

WILLIAM COOPER, Town Clerk.

Boston, Decem 26, 1774.

On Wednesday the 28th Instant,

At TEN o'Clock in the Morning,

Will be sold by Public Vendue, at Russell's Auction-Room, Queen Street,

A very large and valuable Collection of genteel House-Furniture, belonging to a Gentleman who is out of the Province. *Among which are,*

MOHOGANY Dining Tables, Tea Tables, Dressing Tables and Card Tables, Chest of Draws and Bureaus, hair-bottom, leather bottom & common Chairs, crimson worsted Harrateen Bed and Easy Chair, two blue and white Callico Beds, with Window Curtains, 4 Posts and common Bedsteads, Sheets, Table Linnen and fine Blankets, Looking-Glasses, one 8 Day Clock, Carpets, Feather Beds, all Kinds of Kitchen Furniture, in Pewter, Brass, Copper, Iron and Tin, a great Variety of China, Glass, Stone and Delph Ware, a Chaise and Harness, and a Variety of Plate. J. RUSSELL, Auctioneer.

The Sale will begin precisely at Ten.—Wednesday 28th.—

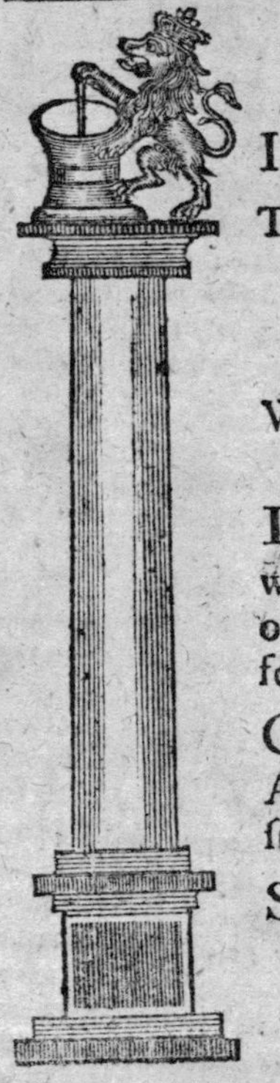

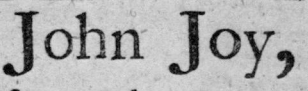

John Joy,

Informs the PUBLIC,

That he has removed to the Shop next Door North of Mr. GILBERT DEBLOIS's in Cornhill, BOSTON,

Where he has received a large and fresh Supply of

Druggs & Medicines,

which he will sell Wholesale or Retail, on the best Terms for Cash or Credit.

Country Practitioners, Apothecarys, &c. may be supply'd to great Advantage.

Surgeons Instruments, Groceries, and Dyers Stuffs, may be had cheap.

To be Sold by PUBLIC VENDUE,

On WEDNESDAY *the 22d Day of* March *next,*

At Eleven o'Clock Beforenoon, at the Royal-Exchange Tavern in King-Street, Boston, pursuant to a Vote of the Proprietors of the *Kennebeck*-Purchase from the late Colony of *New-Plymouth*, passed the Sixteenth Day of *November* last:

The following Tract of Land to be set up in undivided Twelfths, at 100l. L. M. for each Twelfth, being about 6000 Acres to a Twelfth.

A Tract of Land situated North-West from Fort-Halifax, and lying on each side of Little Norridgwalk River, and within 15 Miles of Kennebeck River, in the West side thereof, containing about 72000 Acres.

Provided nevertheless that if any Proprietor of the said Kennebeck Purchase shall chuse to retain his Share of of the said Tract, and shall on or before Wednesday the 15th Day of March next, pay to Henry Alline, jun. Clerk of said Proprietors, his Proportion of 1200l. L. M. which is 100l. L. M. to one Twelfth, and so more or less, according to his Share or Interest in said Propriety, then such Share or Interest of the said Tract shall be reserved to him, but if Payment be not made on the said 15th Day of March next, then the whole of said Tract will be sold on said 22d Day of March next, without such Reservation. By Order of said Proprietors.

HENRY ALLINE, jun. Prop's Clerk.

TO MORROW & WEDNESDAY Evenings,

Will be Sold by PUBLIC VENDUE,

At BICKER's Auction Room,

Near the Market, Boston:

A very large Assortment of English Goods,

——Among which are,——

Broad Cloths, Serges, Ratteens, Frizes, Halfthicks, Coatings, Kersey, Plains, Forest-Cloths, Irish Linnens, Checks, Camblets, Crapes, Worsted Hose, Worsted Mitts, Handkerchiefs of most kinds, several choice Feather Beds, Watches, &c.

Burials in the Town of BOSTON, since our last.

Twenty Whites. No Blacks.

Baptiz'd in the several Churches, Nine.

High Water at BOSTON, *for the present Week.*

Monday, 48 min. aft. 5	Friday, 10 min. after. 9
Tuesday, 30 min. aft. 6	Saturday, 6 min. aft. 10
Wednesday, 18 m. aft. 7	Lord's-Day, 53 m. af. 10
Thursday, 13 min. aft. 8	New Moon First Day.

Extract of a letter from a gentleman in Dublin, to his friend in Baltimore, 1774.

"I am sorry to hear, some with you speak so coolly of the Bostonians, I hoped there was not a colonist who would not with his fortune and life, defend that liberty and property, which a vile administration wishes, yearly wishes to destroy, an attention to traffick, will be of little value, while the means of protecting your wealth are neglected, suppose you possessed all the riches of Maryland, subject to the uncontrouled demands of a hungry rapacious ministry, can you say that such a precarious wealth, is to be counted only like the bee, you will be smoaked with Scotch brimstone, and robbed of the honey of your own earnings; sympathy is a poor tribute to those within reach of your relief, such an offering (if we can do no more) becomes us who are at this distance, but though Boston is far from our country, they are near, very near our hearts, and I am bold to say there is not one man in the kingdom (placemen and pensioners excepted) who would not succour them with his purse and person if possible. The important crisis of your country is ever uppermost in our thoughts, as the fate of liberty is suspended on your courage and unanimity; if you stand together as one man, the gates of hell cannot prevail against you: If you are crumbled into fractions you will be undone, you will be a disjointed prey to the more than savage beasts of despotism, and be left to bewail in sackcloth and ashes the false ideas of ballancing present profit——against future vassalage. A non-importation scheme firmly adhered to, would soon make Great-Britain sick of their most perfidious system, and would carry swarms of choice independent spirits into your hive, and though your traffic might languish for a time, and be barren for a season, yet like the fallowed ground it would yield a fruitful harvest, amply to recommend the loss of delay.—The prospect of liberty is one powerful inducement to emigration from this country. And as slavery advances here, your attraction grows stronger—but if the door of that asylum shall be shut against us, we will remain where we are, and not take the trouble of shifting the scene without changing the situation, (the present administration is a stink in the nostrials of all God's rational creation.) On our account then as well as your own, stand fast in the liberty wherewith your—ancestors have made you free, and suffer not yourselves to be entangled in ministerial bondage; where I one of you, which it is possible I soon shall, I should think the little power I possess, with my life into the bargain, well devoted to a cause, when the happiness of millions yet unborn, is so deeply involved."

THIS DAY PUBLISHED,

[Price *Half-a-Pistareen.*]

And sold at JOHN BOYLE's Printing-Office, next Door to the *Three Doves* in Marlborough-Street.

The WONDER of WONDERS!

Or, the WONDERFUL APPEARANCE of an

Angel, Devil and Ghost,

To a GENTLEMAN in the Town of *Boston*, in the NIGHTS of the 14th, 15th, and 16th of *October* last: To whom in some Measure may be attributed the DISTRESSES that have of late fallen upon that unhappy METROPOLIS. Related to one of his NEIGHBOURS the Morning after the last Visitation, who wrote down the NARRATIVE from the GENTLEMAN's own Mouth; and it is now made public at his Desire, as a solemn Warning to all those, who, for the sake of agrandizing themselves and their Families, would entail the most abject Wretchedness upon MILLIONS of their Fellow-Creatures.

Adorned with Four PLATES, viz. 1. The DEVIL. 2. An ANGEL, *with a Sword in one Hand, a pair of Scales in the other.* 3. BELZEBUB, *holding in his right hand a folio Book, and in his left a Halter.* 4. A GHOST, *having on a white Gown, his Hair much dishevelled.*—

TO BE SOLD,

Choice New-Castle Coals, on board the Brig Dolphin, James Scott, Master, at the Long Wharff, or at William Dennie's Store in King-Street.

To be Sold, at Marblehead, a Quantity of Bottles in Hampers, some holding 9 Jills. Apply there to Major Gallison, or to William Dennie, at Boston.

Duncan Ingraham, jun.

WILL shortly embark for England—Desires all those that are indebted to him, to make immediate Payment; and all those to whom he is indebted, are desired to call and receive their respective Balances. (tbc)

Left at a Shop in this Town, on Friday the 9th Instant, a Pocket-Book, containing valuable Articles; among which was a Note of Hand given to Samuel and Stephen Salisbury, by Ephraim Harrington. The Owner may have the Pocket-Book again, paying the Charge of this Advertisement. Inquire of *Hopestill Foster*, near Dr. Byles's Meeting-House, South End of Boston.

Boston, December 16, 1774.

LOST between Liberty-Tree and the Town-House, last Tuesday Evening, a Silver Watch, with the Letters A. D. studded on the outside Case, Maker's Name *Thomas Blundell*, Dublin, No. 547. Had to it a Steel Chain, Brass Key, and a white Cornelian Seal set in Silver. Whoever will bring said Watch, &c. to Mr. John McLean, Watchmaker, in King-Street, shall receive Three Dollars Reward.

N. B. If the above Watch should be offered in Pawn, or for Sale, it is requested it may be stopped, and the same Reward shall be given.

The Committee of Inspection for the Town of PLYMOUTH, hereby give public Notice that there is to be sold at Plymouth, under their direction, (agreeable to the 10th Article of the Association of the American Continental Congress) on Monday the second Day of January next, at Ten o'Clock in the Forenoon—

One Hundred and Ten Quarter Casks of Malaga WINE, fifty Boxes of LEMMONS, six hundred and ten Casks, and fifty Jarrs of RAISINS,—Imported in the Schooner Dove, Ebenezer Parker, Master, from Malaga, via Falmouth. Said Sale to be on board said Schooner. JOHN TORREY, Chairman.

Plymouth, Dec. 12, 1774.

The Committee of Inspection for the Town of Plimouth, hereby give Notice, That there are to be Sold at the House of Mr. Howland, Innholder, at said Plimouth, on Tuesday the Third Day of January next, at Ten of the Clock in the Forenoon, under the Direction of said Committee (agreeable to the Tenth Article of the Association of the American Continental Congress) the following Articles imported in the Brigt. Esther, Benjamin Smith, Master, from Liverpool, since the First Day of December Instant, viz.

Two Boxes Linnens, two Cases Woolens, one Barrel Hard Ware, one Barrel Glass, one Case Velveret and Bindings, one Hogshead Checks and Fustians, one Cask bottled Ale, Twenty Crates Earthen Ware, 160 Tons Salt, 30 Chaldrons Coals. Also a small Quantity of Cheese and unpack'd Beer, and six Boxes of Irish Linnens. The Sale to continue 'till the whole is sold.

JOHN TORREY, Chairman.

Plimouth, December 12, 1774.

LAST Monday Night, between 11 and 12 o'Clock, some *well-bred Gentlemen* took the *Liberty* of breaking my Windows in a *most spirited Manner*: If any Person will be pleased to inform me of the Place of their Residence, (if they have any,) that I may make them a proper Acknowledgment for this *publick Mark of their Civility*, he shall be intitled to a Reward of Ten Dollars from his most humble Servant, JOHN TROUTBECK.

TO BE SOLD,

Two convenient Dwelling Houses, situated in King-Street, Boston: One opposite to the South Door of the Town House, at present in the Occupation of Mr. Thomas Courtney; the other on the North Side of said Town House, improved by Mr. John Maud. Also a Brick Tenement, situated near the East End of Christ Church. For further Particulars, inquire of the Printers. Dec. 29 1774.

TO BE SOLD,

A Piece of Land being a Wood Lot situate in the Town of Milton, containing Twenty six Acres and one Quarter of an Acre, belonging to the Estate of *Joseph Gooch*, Esq; late of Milton, deceased.

Any Person inclining to Purchase said Wood Lot, may apply to *William Gooch*, in King-Street, Boston, who is Attorney to *Thomas Hubbart*, sole Executor of said *Joseph Gooch*'s Will, who is fully Impowered by the Justices of the Superior Court to Sell the same and pass a Deed therefor. *Boston, Nov. 28, 1774.*

N. B. All Persons are cautioned against Cutting or Carrying off any Wood or Timber from said Wood Lot, as they may depend on being Prosecuted with the utmost Severity of the Law.

At a Meeting of the Proprietors of COXHALL, (so called) in the Conty of York, conven'd at the Dwelling-House of Dr. Tyler Porter, Innholder in Wenham, on Mondey the 31st Day of January, 1770. VOTED, That 12*s.* be and hereby is Granted and Ordered to be paid by the Proprietors on every Hundred Acre Right within said Tract of Land in proportion to their respective Interest therein, to be collected and paid to the Proprietor's Treasurer according to Law.--- And at a Legal Meeting of said Proprietors held by Adjournment, Feb. 1, 1774, at the House of Mrs. Susanna Stacy, Innholder In Ipswich: Also, Voted one other Tax of 12*s.* be and hereby is Granted and Ordered to be paid by the Proprietors of every Hundred Acre Right in said Tract of Land; the above Taxes to be paid to Capt. Francis Goodhue, of Ipswich, their said Treasurer.

MICHAEL FARLEY, Prop's Clerk.

Ipswich, Dec. 16, 1774.

N. B. If the above Taxes are not paid to the aforesaid Treasurer by the last Tuesday of January next, the said Lands will be exposed to sale at the House of the aforesaid Mrs. Susanna Stacy, Innholder iu Ipswich, at 10 o'Clock in the Forenoon.

By Order of the Committee for Sale of Lands.

JOHN BAKER.

JUST PUBLISHED,

[*Price* 1s. 4.]

And to be Sold by *John Kneeland*, Printer, in Milk-Street; *James Foster Condy*, Stationer, in Union-Street; and *Philip Freeman*, jun. near Liberty-Tree.

AN ORATION delivered on the late public Commencement at Rhode-Island College in Providence, September 1774. Being a Plea for the Right of private Judgment in religious Matters; and for the Liberty of choosing our own Religion, corroborated by the well known Consequences of Priestly Power.

BY BARNABAS BINNEY, A. B.

BRICKS.

FOUR HUNDRED THOUSAND BRICKS, Manufactured by the distressed, industrious Poor of the Town of Boston, assisted by the generous Donations of our benevolent and sympathizing Brethren of this and the other Colonies, and are to be sold for their further Relief and Employment, by *Thomas Crafts*, jun. near Liberty-Tree.

Geralen Post-Office, New-York, 5th Dec. 1774.

The Deputy Post Masters General being desirous of facilitating Correspondence, have ordered that in Time to come there should be two Posts Weekly, for Canada, by way of Albany: Notice is hereby given, that from and after the 14th Day of December Instant, the Mails for Canada and Albany will be made up and dispatched from this Office on Wednesdays at 11 o'Clock in the Forenoon, and at 9 every Saturday Night. The Wednesdays Post will ride on the East Side of Hudson's River, and return to this Office with the Canada Mail on the Tuesday following, at 4 o'Clock in the Afternoon. The Saturday Night's Mail is to be conveyed to Albany, on the West Side of the River, and the Rider will return to this Office on the Saturday following at 12 o'Clock.

By Command of the Deputy Post Masters General.

RICH. N. COLDEN, D. Secr'y.

Salmon Twine.

JEREMIAH ALLEN has for Sale at his Shop in Ann-Street, a little North of the Draw Bridge—— A Quantity of the best 3-Thread Salmon Twine. (6w.)

THE Brethren of the ancient and honorable Society of FREE and ACCEPTED MASONS are hereby notified; That the most Worshipful JOSEPH WARREN, Esq; Grand Master of Ancient, Free and Accepted Masons on the Continent of America, intends celebrating the Feast of St. John the Evangelist on Tuesday the 27th Instant, at Free Masons Hall, Boston, where the Brethren are required to attend the Festival.

By Order of the most Worshipful Grand Master,

W. HOSKINR, G. Secretary.

N.B. The Table will be furnished at 2 o'Clock, P.M. ---Tickets to be had of Brothers Capt Caleb Hopkins, Andrew Newell, and William Hoskins.

Boston, Dec. 13, 1774.

Joshua Blanchard,

AT the Old Shop and Wine Cellar on Dock-Square BOSTON, opposite Exchange Lane,

yet continues to sell

WINES

of all Sorts as usual, and hath now on Sale a Parcel of fine old Serling Madeira from 3 Dollars to 8 Dollars per Dozen according to its Age and Quality; also by the Gallon or less Quantity, Fyal Wine at 25s. Old Tenor per Gallon, a better Sort on Maderia Lees at 30s. O. T.

West-India Proof genuine Rum.

Fine old Spirit, French and other Brandies.

Mr. BLANCHARD *thanks his Friends and the Publick for past Favours, and hopes in these* hard *Times their Continuance.*

He hath also to sell,

Cocoa, Loaf-Sugar, Raisins, Figgs, Currants, Spices, with a general Assortment of West-India Goods and Groceries, by Wholesale or Retail.

A Quantity of choice Honey.

TO BE SOLD *very cheap*,

The Schooner Hawk, about 65 Tons burthen, a Marblehead Fishing Vessel with a Sheath'd Bottom, good Sails and Rigging, lying at Mr. John Puling's Wharff.——For Particulars inquire at

Archibald Cunningham's

Store in Ann-Street, near the Draw-Bridge.

——Where is to be sold——

Lisbon WINE per Cask,—Lisbon Oil per Cask,—Geneva per Case,—Raisins, Figs and Currants per Cask,—Firkin Butter,—Kippen's Snuff and Pig-Tail Tobacco,—Spices of all sorts,—Citron,—half Pint Dram Bottles per Crate or Groce,—Almonds,—choice Olives,—Capers,—Brown & Loaf Sugar,—Dutch Brushes in Setts or single,—Dutch Stone Ware per Crate or Dozen,—Corks,—Mason Glasses Engrav'd with the Arms,—best Durham Mustard in large and small Bottles,—Barcelona Handkerchiefs per Dozen.

All Persons who have any Demands on the Estate of Nathaniel Holmes, of Boston, deceased, are desired to bring in their Accounts to Rebecca Holmes, Executrix, for Adjustment: All those who are indebted to said Estate are desired to make immediate Payment to said Executrix.

William Fowle,

ACQUAINTS the Public, That he carries on the Sugar-Baking Business, at the Sugar-House formerly Occupied by the late Nathaniel Holmes, deceased.

——Where he has ready for Sale——

Best double, single, and Lump Refin'd Loaf and brown SUGAR, MOLASSES, FLOUR and IRON, by Wholesale or Retail, cheap for Cash.

TO BE SOLD, only for Want of Employ,

A likely, sprightly good-tempered Negro Boy, about 13 Yeass of Age. Inquire of Edes and Gill.

Stray'd away from me the Subscriber, in Newton, sometime in July last, a spotted or placked black and white Steer, two Years old. Whoever shall take up the said Steer, or give Information where he may be had, shall be handsomely rewarded by me JOHN HEALY.

Boston: Printed, by EDES & GILL.

in Queen-Street, 1774.

All pages are reproduced from original newspapers in the collection of The American Antiquarian Society, Worcester, Massachusetts, except for the following, which are from the collection in the Massachusetts Historical Society, Boston, Massachusetts:

Jan. 3, pp. 2, 3, 4	July 4, pp. 1, 2	Sept. 26, pp. 2, 3
Jan. 24, pp. 1, 2, 3, 4	July 11, pp. 1, 2, 3, 4	Oct. 3, p. 2
Feb. 28, p. 2	August 1, pp. 1, 2, 3, 4	Oct. 10, pp. 1, 2, 3
March 28, pp. 3, 4	August 15, pp. 1, 2	Oct. 17, pp. 1, 4
April 18, pp. 1, 2, 3, 4	August 22, pp. 3, 4	Oct. 24, pp. 1, 2, 4
May 2, supplements 1, 2	August 29, pp. 2, 4, supplements 1, 2	Oct. 31, pp. 1, 2
May 9, pp. 1, 4	Sept. 5, pp. 1, 2, 3, 4, supplements 1, 2	Nov. 7, p. 1
May 16, p. 2		Nov. 21, pp. 2, 3, 4
May 23, pp. 1, 4	Sept. 12, supplement 2	Dec. 5, pp. 1, 3
June 6, pp. 2, 3	Sept. 19, p. 4	Dec. 19, pp. 1, 2
June 13, p. 2		Dec. 26, p. 1
June 20, pp. 1, 2		

THE BOSTON GAZETTE: 1774
has been printed in an edition of nineteen hundred and fifty copies by The Meriden Gravure Company, Meriden, Connecticut and The Godine Press, Brookline, Massachusetts. Through the special efforts of Harold Hugo, original copies of THE BOSTON GAZETTE *were obtained from the American Antiquarian Society, Worcester, Massachusetts and the Massachusetts Historical Society, Boston, and used in this facsimile edition. The book, designed at The Godine Press, is printed in Monotype Van Dijck set by Mackenzie and Harris, San Francisco and printed on Almanac Text, specially made by the Monadnock Mills and supplied by the Pratt Paper Company of Boston. This is Copy Number:* 1916